1995 -75ᵀᴴ Year in the NFL Edition

PACKER LEGENDS IN FACTS

Your Most Accurate Source of
Stats ● Rosters ● Team History
and
All Team Photos
of

The
Green Bay Packers
1919 ● 1995

by
Eric Goska

TECH/DATA
PUBLICATIONS
A DIVISION OF LITH-O-LUX CORPORATION

Front Cover

> *"Appointment with Destiny"*

The cover photo was chosen with an eye toward a third straight postseason meeting of the Packers and Cowboys. Packers veterans and newcomers alike know such a clash is the final stop on Green Bays' road to the Super Bowl in 1996.

Photo Credit — Vernon Biever Photo

Back Cover

Photo Credits
Lambeau Field — Courtesy of The Green Bay Packers
Green Bay Press-Gazette

ISBN: 0-937816-37-X U.S. $29.95

First Edition .... **August, 1992**
Second Printing of First Edition .... **November, 1992**
NEW Revised 75th Anniversary Edition .... **August, 1993**
NEW Revised 75th NFL Anniversary Edition . **August, 1995**
Second Printing of 75th NFL Edition .... **December 1995**

PROUDLY PUBLISHED IN THE UNITED STATES OF AMERICA
by

TECH/DATA PUBLICATIONS
A Division of Lith-O-Lux Corporation
Mailing Address: P. O. Box 396
Germantown, Wisconsin 53022
414/251-7027   Fax: 414/251-5478

Printed in the U. S. A.

Dedication

To my mother and father,

Barbara and Ronald Goska,

who taught me patience, perseverence,

and positive thinking . . . .

three ingredients without which

this book could never have been written.

FOREWORD

If you had told me three years ago that there would be a third edition of this book, I would not have believed you. At the same time, had you told me that heading into the 1995 NFL season, the Packers would be coming off of three straight winning seasons, I would have chuckled.

But, you know, both are true. You hold in your hands the latest updated, expanded account of the Packers team from its inception in 1919 to 1995. As you read this, you're probably getting goosebumps in anticipation of a third straight playoff appearance by the Green and Gold. It's a great time to be a Packer fan.

I'd like to thank the tens of thousands who've purchased and enjoyed the first two editions. I appreciate your support and interest. If not for you, this dream of mine would have died with the first edition. But instead, because of you, it lives on. Thank you.

If you would like to write to me with comments or questions, I'll try to respond as time allows.

My address is: 1575 Cass Street
                    Green Bay, Wisconsin 54302

Eric Goska

Green Bay Press-Gazette photo

Ron Wolf, Don Hutson and Mike Holmgren display a replica of Hutson's jersey number 14 at the July 1994 dedication of the new, state-of-the-art Don Hutson indoor Packer Practice Facility in Green Bay.

Vernon Biever Photo

TABLE OF CONTENTS

The Regular Season
The teams, 1921-94

Annual Individual Leaders

Top Single-Game Performances

All-Time Lists

The Record Book

The Postseason
The Playoff Games

All-Time Leaders

The Record Book

The Off-Season

ACKNOWLEDGEMENTS

There are a great many individuals who, without their assistance and guidance, this book would not have been possible. First and foremost are Lee Remmel, executive director of public relations for the Green Bay Packers and the late Shirley Leonard, who was the team's public relations secretary for many years. Lee and Shirley allowed me to spend day upon day in their offices going through old programs, score sheets, media guides, and a variety of other documents which proved invaluable. They never turned me away when I pestered them for places, names, and dates and for that I am grateful.

Art Daley, former sports editor of the *Green Bay Press-Gazette* and former publisher and editorial director of the *Green Bay Packer Yearbook* provided many pieces of the puzzle. Art put me on to the idea of a Packers "encyclopedia." In the 1970s he began work on his own version. When I came to him, he offered team photos, rosters, players' jersey numbers and other necessities. I thank him for his help.

The many excellent photos in this work came from a variety of sources. The bulk are from the *Green Bay Press-Gazette*. Photo editor John Robb graciously sold and developed many of the action pictures from 1941-94 at a cost which did not bankrupt. He, Sandee Gerbers and Joan Gutheridge spent many hours in the darkroom and I truly appreciate their efforts.

Vernon Biever, longtime Packers photographer, provided some playoff pictures including the infamous shot of Bart Starr's game-winning quarterback sneak in the "Ice Bowl". That particular photograph was taken by his son John.

Lee Lefebvre helped with some early photographs including actions shots taken by his father in 1937 and 1938. Tom Pigeon allowed me to use photos from his vast collection, including a couple of rare color pictures from a 1940 Packers-Eagles contest. AP/Wide World and UPI/Bettmann in New York helped with early championship game photographs.

Green Bay Press-Gazette photo

59 straight: In 1992, Sterling Sharpe broke the Packers record for most consecutive games with at least one reception. Above, referee Howard Roe and teammate Brett Favre congratulate Sharpe after he surpassed James Lofton's record with a catch against the Steelers in Green Bay.

Bob McGinn, now with the *Milwaukee Journal Sentinel*, opened his files to me and suggested edits. I gained valuable information from his work and from his advice. Kevin Isaacson, former sports editor of the *Press-Gazette*, read my manuscript and offered suggestions.

Finally, I wish to thank my publisher, Pat Canter, of Tech Data publications. His efforts and those of Pete Prime of Oconomowoc helped make this dream come true. Thank you.

Acknowledgements . . . continued

Many others contributed. If I have left anyone out, I regret the oversight.

Mr. Don Langenkamp
Mrs. Lois Lawniczak
Mrs. Dorothy Wittig
Mr. Steven P. Gietschier, The Sporting News
Mr. John Bostrom, Chicago Bears
Mr. Scott Berchtold, Green Bay Packers
Mr. Chuck Giordana, Green Bay Packers Hall of
    Fame
Mr. Keith Newton, Indianapolis Colts
Mr. Mike Taylor, Los Angeles Raiders
Mr. Ed Croke, New York Giants
Mr. Jim Gallagher, Philadelphia Eagles
Mr. Bob Rose, Phoenix Cardinals
Mr. Dan Edwards, Pittsburgh Steelers
Mr. Jerry Walker, San Francisco 49ers
Mr. John C. Konoza, Washington Redskins
The Atlanta Falcons
The Cleveland Browns
The Detroit Lions
The Minnesota Vikings
The New England Patriots
The New York Jets
Mr. Solon S. Barnett, Jr.
Mr. John R. Biolo
Mr. Tony Canadeo
Mr. Lon Evans
Mr. Bob Kercher
Mr. Darrell R. Lester
Mr. George McInerney
Mr. Bernard J. Scherer
Mr. Seymour Siwoff, Elias Sports Bureau
Mr. Steve Hirdt, Elias Sports Bureau
Mr. Chris Thorn, Elias Sports Bureau
Ms. Nancy J. Pierce, NFL Alumni
Mr. Joe Horrigan, NFL Hall of Fame
Ms. Leslie Hammond, NFL Promotions
Mr. Jim Heffernan, NFL Director of Public Relations
Mr. Paul Spinelli, NFL Properties
Ms. Carol O'Brien, University of Minnesota
Mr. John (Spinarkle) Eisenreich
Mr. Brian (Boo) O'Connor

and my "Sweety" Ann. F. Walsh (soon to be Goska)

The Sport Information Offices of:

Auburn University
Baylor University
Bucknell University
Catholic University
Duke University
Florida University
Fresno State University
Georgetown University
Indiana University
Kalamazoo University
Lincoln University
Memphis State University

Notre Dame University
Rice University
St. Mary's University (CA)
Southern Methodist University
Texas Christian University
Texas A&M University
University of Alabama
University of California-Los Angeles
University of Cincinnati
Univerity of Iowa
University of Miami-Ohio
University of Michigan
University of Minnesota-Duluth
University of Missouri
University of Nebraska
University of New Mexico
University of San Francisco
University of Southern California
University of Utah
University of Washington
Washington & Jefferson

Green Bay Press-Gazette photo

Paul Hornung (5) takes on Myron Pottios (66) of the Rams in a 1966 game.

Lynn Dickey

Green Bay Press-Gazette photo

Paul Coffman

Green Bay Press-Gazette photo

EXPLANATION OF ABBREVIATIONS

GB = Green Bay
OPP = opponents
Att. = attendance
Att = attempts
Yds = yards
Avg = average per attempt
LG = longest gain
TD = touchdown
No = number
Com = completions
In = number of passes had intercepted
YL = yards lost attempting to pass
Tk/Yds = number of times sacked and yards lost
Rate = player's passer rating
In20 = number of punts inside opponents' 20-yard line
TB = number of punts in end zone for a touchback
HB = number of punts had blocked
FC = number of fair catches
TDr = touchdowns rushing
TDp = touchdowns receiving
TDrt = touchdowns on returns and recoveries
PAT = points after touchdown
FG = field goals
S = safeties
TP = total points

Fum = number of fumbles committed
Ow = number of own fumbles recovered
Op = number of opponents' fumbles recovered
Tot = number of total fumbles recovered
W = wins
L = losses
T = ties
Pct = team's winning percentage
PF = points a team scored (points for)
PA = points a team gave up (points against)
Pos = position
Ht = height
Wt = weight
DOB = date of birth
G = number of games played
Rnd = round
Rush = number of yards rushing
Rec = number of yards receiving
P-rt = number of yards on punt returns
K-rt = number of yards on kickoff returns
Int = number of yards on interception returns
Fum = number of yards on recovered fumbles
Tot = total yards gained
100 = number of 100-yard games

THE TOWN TEAMS

This autumn, thousands of young men will strap on uniforms, travel to nearby fields and spend a few hours tossing, kicking and catching an oblong object known as a football. The scene, on a smaller scale, will be nothing new to Green Bay, where the city has supported football for nearly a century.

The first recorded semi-pro football game in Green Bay took place on October 1, 1896. Marinette defeated the locals 24-0. From that point on, with the exception of 1916, Green Bay fielded a town team every year through the end of World War I.

In 1917, a group of "all-stars" from the city defeated the Badgers of Marinette 27-0. Nate Abrams played end. Playing right halfback for Green Bay was one Earl Louis (Curly) Lambeau.

The following year, on September 15, a team called the "Skidoos" beat De Pere 13-0. Nate Abrams again held down an end spot, while a Lambeau manned the right half back slot. (Whether that was Curly is unknown). The following week, many of the same players defeated Marinette 42-0 using the name "Whales." Lambeau was not among them.

Talent was scarce that year. A war raged overseas. A meeting was held on October 9, 1918 in the editorial room of the *Green Bay Press-Gazette*. Football, it was decided upon, would continue. With Nate Abrams as captain, the city team played on through the end of November.

Two events occurred in 1919 that signaled the birth of the Packers. First, Curly Lambeau, and not Nate Abrams, was named captain of the squad on August 14, 1919. And second, the city team was sponsored by the Indian Packing Company leading directly to the nickname "Packers."

1919

Standing (L-R): Nichols, Powers, Coffeen, M. Zoll, Martin, Sauber, Martell, Leaper, Ladrow, Desjardins, C. Zoll, Muldoon, Rosenow, Petcka, George Whitney Calhoun. **Center:** Lambeau.
Sitting (L-R): Abrams, Gavin, McLean, Bero.

1920

Front Row (L-R): M. Zoll, Leaper, C. Zoll, Martell, McLean, Abrams, Medley. **Second Row (L-R):** Tebo, Petcka, Gavin, Wheeler, Lambeau, Ladrow, Wagner, Dalton, Jonet.
Back Row (L-R): Delloye, Powers, Dwyer, Klaus, Nichols, Rosenow, Wilson, Sauber, Murphy.

Results

Date	GB		OPP
9/14	53	Menominee	0
9/21	61	Marinette	0
9/28	54	New London	0
10/5	87	Sheboygan	0
10/12	76	Racine	6
10/19	33	Ishpeming	0
10/26	85	Oshkosh	0
11/2	53	Milwaukee A.C.	0
11/9	46	Chicago A.C.	0
11/16	17	Stambaugh	0
11/23	0	Beloit	6
	565		12

The following played with the Packers in 1919.

Abrams, Nate
Bero, Henry (Tubby)
Bradlee
Coffeen, Jim
Desjardin, Jim
Dwyer, Dutch
Dwyer, Riggie
Gallagher, Jen
Gavin, Fritz
Ladrow, Wally
Lambeau, Curly
Leaper, Wes
Martell, Herm
Martin, Al
McLean, Ray
Muldoon, Andy
Nichols
Petcka, Al
Powers, Sam
Rosenow, Gus
Sauber, Charlie
Wheeler, Lyle (Cowboy)
Wilson, Milt
Zoll, Martin
Zoll, Carl

Results

Date	GB		OPP
9/26	3	Chicago	3
10/3	56	Kaukauna	0
10/10	3	Stambaugh	0
10/17	25	Marinette	0
10/24	62	De Pere	0
10/31	7	Beloit	0
11/7	9	Milwaukee	0
11/14	3	Beloit	14
11/21	19	Menominee	7
11/25	14	Stambaugh	0
11/28	26	Milwaukee A.C.	0
	227		24

The following played with the Packers in 1920.

Abrams, Nate
Bero, Henry (Tubby)
Buck, Howard (Cub)
Dalton
Dwyer, Dutch
Gallagher, Jen
Gavin, Fritz
Klaus, Fee
Ladrow, Wally
Lambeau, Curly
Leaper, Wes
Malis
Martell, Herm
McLean, Ray
Medley
Murphy
Nichols
Petcka, Al
Powers, Sam
Rosenow, Gus
Sauber, Charlie
Smith
Wagner, Buff
Wheeler, Lyle (Cowboy)
Wilson, Milt
Zoll, Martin
Zoll, Carl

SEVENTY-FIVE SEASONS

of
PROFESSIONAL
FOOTBALL
1921 - 1995

Malcolm Snyder (67) is flanked by Atlanta's Don Hansen (58) and George Kunz (75) in rain-soaked Milwaukee County Stadium on October 22, 1972.

Football ... Green Bay..... Throw in the word professional and the story of the Packers begins in the fall of 1921. From the 1890's, the city had supported a variety of football teams. In 1919, the Indian Packing Company sponsored a team and Earl Louis (Curly) Lambeau was elected captain. George Whitney Calhoun, sports editor of the *Green Bay Press-Gazette*, handled the publicity. The team, referred to as the "Packers", raced unbeaten through all-comers, outscoring opponents 565-6, until a final 6-0 loss to Beloit ended the season. A year later in 1920, the Indian Packing Company sold out to the Acme Packing Corporation. Acme took up the sponsorship and the Green Bay Acme Packers rolled to a 9-1-1 record.

That year, 1920, saw the birth of the American Professional Football Association (APFA). Lambeau and the Acme Packers missed a chance to join the league that year. In 1921, the league reorganized itself. On August 27, John and Emmett Clair of the Acme Packing Corporation were granted a franchise.

Green Bay engaged a quartet of semi-pro teams before opening its league schedule. On September 25, the Packers knocked off the Chicago Boosters 13-0. The team then gained wins over Rockford 49-0, Chicago-Hamburg 40-0 and Beloit 7-0.

On October 23, 1921 at Hagemeister Park on the city's east side, the Packers played what is considered their first professional game. Their opponent on that historic Sunday hailed from Minnesota. The Marines, as they were known, quickly took a 6-0 lead. Green Bay struggled, unable to score through three-and-a-half quarters. Finally, with less than five minutes remaining, the Packers put together a drive that reached the Marines' four-yard line. From there, Art Schmael scored and with Howard (Cub) Buck holding, Lambeau delivered the kick that provided the margin of victory in Green Bay's first league win.

Following that initial victory, Green Bay posted two more wins against a tie and two losses. One of the setbacks laid the groundwork for one of the longest and greatest rivalries in professional football.

On November 27, the Packers invaded Cubs Park in Chicago to face the 6-1 Chicago Staleys. Green Bay stumbled 20-0 in that final game of the year. The Packers fell behind 14-0 but the Staleys weren't satisfied. George Halas hauled in a touchdown pass from Chick Harley to cap off that first meeting between the Packers and Staleys, who, a year later, became known as the Bears.

Stiller photo

(L-R): Herm Martell, Ray Lambeau, Jim Cook, Nate Abrams, Bill (Gus) DuMoe, Lyle (Cowboy) Wheeler, Buff Wagner, Frank Coughlin, Norm Barry, Joseph Carey, Richard (Jab) Murray, Curly Lambeau, Dave Hayes, Howard (Cub) Buck, Art Schmael, Milt Wilson, Wally Ladrow, Grover Malone, Fee Klaus, Lynn (Tubby) Howard, Sammy Powers, Ray McLean, unknown, Emmett Clair.

TEAM STATISTICS

Regular Season   3-2-1

Date	GB		OPP
10/23	7	Minneapolis Marines	6
10/30	3	Rock Island Independents	13
11/6	43	Evansville Crimson Giants	6
11/13	14	Hammond Pros	7
11/20	3	at Chicago Cardinals	3
11/27	0	at Chicago Staleys	20

Score By Periods

	1	2	3	4	Total
Packers	24	15	14	17	70
Opponents	13	14	7	21	55

1921

INDIVIDUAL STATISTICS

Touchdown Passes

	No
Lambeau	1
Packers	**1**
Opponents	2

Scoring

	TDr	TDp	TDrt	PAT	FG	S	TP
Lambeau	2	0	0	7	3	0	28
DuMoe	0	1	1	0	0	0	12
Schmael	2	0	0	0	0	0	12
Abrams	0	0	1	0	0	0	6
N. Barry	1	0	0	0	0	0	6
L. Howard	1	0	0	0	0	0	6
Packers	**6**	**1**	**2**	**7**	**3**	**0**	**70**
Opponents	5	2	1	4	1	0	55

NFL STANDINGS

	W	L	T	Pct
Chicago Staleys	9	1	1	.900
Buffalo All-Americans	9	1	2	.900
Akron Pros	8	3	1	.727
Canton Bulldogs	5	2	3	.714
Rock Island Independents	4	2	1	.667
Evansville Crimson Giants	3	2	0	.600
Green Bay Packers	**3**	**2**	**1**	**.600**
Dayton Triangles	4	4	1	.500
Chicago Cardinals	3	3	2	.500
Rochester Jeffersons	2	3	0	.400
Cleveland Indians	3	5	0	.375
Washington Senators	1	2	0	.333
Cincinnati Celts	1	3	0	.250
Hammond Pros	1	3	1	.250
Minneapolis Marines	1	3	1	.250
Detroit Heralds	1	5	1	.167
Columbus Panhandles	1	8	0	.111
Tonawanda Kardex	0	1	0	.000
Muncie Flyers	0	2	0	.000
Louisville Brecks	0	2	0	.000
New York Giants	0	2	0	.000

ROSTER

Name	Pos	Ht	Wt	College
Abrams, Nate	E	5-7	160	No college
Barry, Norm	B	5-9	170	Notre Dame
Buck, Howard (Cub)	T	6-3	250	Wisconsin
Carey, Joseph	G	6-0	185	No college
Cook, Jim	G	6-2	245	Wisconsin
Coughlin, Frank	T	6-2	215	Notre Dame
DuMoe, Bill (Gus)	E	5-11	165	Notre Dame
Hayes, Dave	E	5-11	165	Notre Dame
Howard, Lynn (Tubby)	B	5-11	210	Indiana
Keefe, Emmett	G	6-1	210	Notre Dame
Klaus, Fee	C	6-1	180	No college
Kliebhan, Roger	B	6-0	210	UW-Milwaukee
Ladrow, Wally	B	6-0	185	No college
Lambeau, Earl (Curly)	B	6-0	190	Notre Dame
Malone, Grover	B	5-10	195	Notre Dame
Martel, Herman	E	6-0	160	No college
McLean, Ray (Toody)	B	5-9	165	No college
Murray, Richard (Jab)	T	6-3	250	Marquette
Powers, Sammy	G	6-0	150	Northern Michigan
Schmaehl, Art	B	5-10	165	No college
Smith, Warren	C	6-1	215	Carleton
Wagner, Buff	B	5-9	165	Northern Michigan
Wheeler, Lyle (Cowboy)	E	6-0	190	Ripon
Wilson, Milt	G	6-1	201	UW-Oshkosh
Zoll, Martin	G	5-11	188	No college

The following also played with the Packers in non-league games.

Name	Pos	Ht	Wt	College
Douglas, George	C	6-2	200	Marquette
Elliott, Burton	B	6-0	185	Marquette
Gavin, Fritz	E	6-0	195	Marquette
Glick, Eddie	B	5-11	165	Marquette
Lande, Cliff	E	5-11	180	Carroll
Leaper, Wes	E	6-1	190	Wisconsin
Oakes, Bill	T	6-3	220	Haskell
Rosenow, Gus	B	6-0	185	Ripon
Sullivan, Walter	G	6-0	195	Beloit
Zoll, Carl	G	5-11	240	No college

For a while, beginning in late January when the league expelled the Packers from its ranks, it appeared as though Green Bay might have seen the last of professional football. Curly Lambeau's team had used a number of college players in a game in 1921. At the winter AFPA meeting, John Clair surrendered the franchise.

Lambeau took advantage of the situation and applied for the franchise. He heard no word from the league regarding his application until June when he was required to reapply for it. He did and on June 24, 1922, the league gave Lambeau the right to field a team and compete in what then had become the National Football League.

The team's troubles were far from over, however. The money raised for the season eventually ran out. A rainy season kept attendance low. In order to protect its interests, the team bought rain insurance and expected to collect after a particularly soggy game with Columbus on November 5. Unfortunately, the amount of rainfall came up three one hundredths of an inch short of the necessary amount for a payoff.

The financially troubled team continued to play but suffered another blow when it had to cancel a lucrative Thanksgiving Day meeting with the Bears after George Halas demanded a $4,000 guarantee to come to Green Bay. A non-league game with Duluth was substituted, but rain led management to question whether or not to play it. Lambeau and George Calhoun approached A.B. Turnbull, business manager of the *Green Bay Press-Gazette*, who told them to go ahead and play the game – he would advance them enough money to meet the guarantee. In addition, Turnbull promised to rally support in the community, targeting area merchants in particular, for contributions. Turnbull's intervention allowed the team to finish out the year.

Three key players were added to the club in 1922: Francis (Jug) Earpe, Howard (Whitey) Woodin, and Charlie Mathys. Earpe, a sturdy guard from Monmouth, played 11 years with the team while Woodin, a tackle from Marquette, lasted a decade. Mathys was a hometown product who had played at West High School. He played for five seasons at quarterback and led the team in touchdown passes with seven in 1925.

Three opening losses followed by a pair of ties kept the Packers from any hopes of a championship. On November 5, the team finally recorded a win when Howard (Cub) Buck kicked a field goal to beat Columbus 3-0. The Packers defeated Minneapolis 14-6 and then struggled to a 3-3 tie with Racine. In week nine, Lambeau ran for a pair of touchdowns as Green Bay toppled Milwaukee 13-0. A final, 14-0 victory at Racine left the Packers with a 4-3-3 record, good only for a seventh-place tie with the Dayton Triangles.

Stiller Photo

TOP ROW: (L-R) Lynn (Tubby) Howard, Francis (Jug) Earpe, Howard (Whitey) Woodin, Dave Hayes.
MIDDLE ROW: (L-R) Curly Lambeau, Howard (Cub) Buck, Lyle (Cowboy) Wheeler, Milton (Moose) Gardner, Charlie Mathys.
BOTTOM ROW: (L-R) Walter Niemann, Dewey Lyle, Tommy Mills, Richard (Jab) Murray.

TEAM STATISTICS

Regular Season 4-3-3

Date	GB		OPP
10/1	14	at Rock Island Independents	19
10/8	6	Racine Legion	10
10/15	3	at Chicago Cardinals	16
10/22	0	at Milwaukee Badgers	0
10/29	0	Rock Island Independents	0
11/5	3	Columbus Panhandles	0
11/12	14	Minneapolis Marines	6
11/19	3	at Racine Legion	3
11/26	13	Milwaukee Badgers	0
12/3	14	at Racine Legion	0

Score By Periods

	1	2	3	4	Tot
Packers	6	24	3	37	70
Opponents	9	26	7	12	54

INDIVIDUAL STATISTICS

Touchdown Passes

	No
Lambeau	3
Packers	**3**
Opponents	1

Scoring

	TDr	TDp	TDrt	PAT	FG	S	TP
Lambeau	3	0	0	3	1	0	24
Mathys	0	2	0	0	1	0	15
Buck	0	0	0	3	1	0	6
Cronin	0	1	0	0	0	0	6
Taugher	1	0	0	0	0	0	6
Usher	1	0	0	0	0	0	6
Wheeler	0	0	1	0	0	0	6
Packers	**5**	**3**	**1**	**7**	**3**	**0**	**70**
Opponents	5	1	0	3	5	0	54

NFL STANDINGS

	W	L	T	Pct
Canton Bulldogs	10	0	2	1.000
Chicago Bears	9	3	0	.750
Chicago Cardinals	8	3	0	.727
Toledo Maroons	5	2	2	.714
Rock Island Independents	4	2	1	.667
Racine Legion	6	4	1	.600
Dayton Triangles	4	3	1	.571
Green Bay Packers	**4**	**3**	**3**	**.571**
Buffalo All-Americans	5	4	1	.556
Akron Pros	3	5	2	.375
Milwaukee Badgers	2	4	3	.333
Oorang Indians	2	6	0	.250
Minneapolis Marines	1	3	0	.250
Louisville Brecks	1	3	0	.250
Evansville Crimson Giants	0	3	0	.000
Rochester Jeffersons	0	4	1	.000
Hammond Pros	0	5	1	.000
Columbus Panhandles	0	7	0	.000

ROSTER

Name	Pos	Ht	Wt	College
Buck, Howard (Cub)	T	6-3	250	Wisconsin
Cronin, Tommy	B	5-8	170	Marquette
Davis, Pahl	G	6-1	185	Marquette
Dunnigan, Walt	E	5-11	210	Minnesota
Earpe, Francis (Jug)	T	6-1	235	Monmouth
Faye, Allen	E	6-1	205	Marquette
Gardella, Gus	B	5-10	185	Holy Cross
Gardner, Milton (Moose)	G	6-2	224	Wisconsin
Glick, Eddie	B	5-11	165	Marquette
Hayes, Dave	E	5-11	165	Notre Dame
Howard, Lynn (Tubby)	B	5-11	210	Indiana
Lambeau, Earl (Curly)	B	6-0	190	Notre Dame
Lauer, Hal (Dutch)	E	5-11	184	Detroit
Lyle, Dewey	G	6-0	202	Minnesota
Mathys, Charlie	B	5-8	165	Indiana
Mills, Tommy	B	5-11	190	Penn State
Murray, Richard (Jab)	T	6-3	250	Marquette
Nadolney, Romanus (Peaches)	T	5-11	230	Notre Dame
Niemann, Walter	C	6-0	170	Michigan
Owens, Harry	G	6-0	210	Lake Forest
Regnier, Pete (Doc)	B	5-11	170	Minnesota
Secord, Joe	C	6-1	190	No college
Smith, Earl	E	6-0	195	Ripon
Smith, Rex	E	6-1	200	UW-LaCrosse
Taugher, Claude	B	5-10	185	Marquette
Usher, Eddie	B	6-0	195	Michigan
Wheeler, Lyle (Cowboy)	E	6-0	190	Ripon
Woodin, Howard (Whitey)	T	5-11	206	Marquette
Zoll, Carl	G	5-11	240	No college

A.B. Turnbull and three close friends, Leland H. Joannes, Dr. W. Webber Kelly and Gerald F. Clifford, along with others, had plans in December of 1922 to incorporate the Green Bay Packers and start a sale of stock. The first sale of stock failed, but a second, started in late summer, met with better success – enough so the team had the necessary resources to begin play. Turnbull, Joannes, Kelly, Clifford, and Curly Lambeau became known as the "**Hungry Five**" because of their determination to keep the team afloat. With Lambeau's promise to field a winner, the season began.

Only four players who had played in both 1921 and 1922 – Howard (Cub) Buck, Lambeau, Richard (Jab) Murray and Lyle (Cowboy) Wheeler – returned for a third go-around. Fritz Gavin and Wes Leaper returned after a years' absence. Lambeau brought in only four new faces – Myrt Basing, Jack Gray, Hal Hanson, and Norbert Hayes – to round out a roster that had shrunk considerably from a year ago.

Green Bay played its home games at Bellevue Park in 1923 because Hagemeister Park was dug up in order to build a new East High School. The Packers opened the season at Bellevue Park, where Basing scored two touchdowns. His efforts helped Green Bay knock off Minneapolis 12-0. A week later, the team missed four field goals and had to settle for a 0-0 tie with St. Louis. The Packers slipped to 1-1-1 after the Bears' Dutch Sternamann's second-quarter field goal sank them 3-0. Green Bay rebounded against Milwaukee, then watched as Racine used a Packer speciality – the pass – to score three touchdowns in a 24-3 Legion win.

Green Bay (2-2-1) then went on a tear, winning its final five games. Buck, who would score a field goal in six consecutive games beginning on October 21, kicked his third of the year to ignite the winning streak as the Packers beat St. Louis 3-0 on November 4. Also coming to the fore with big performances were Lambeau and Tommy Mills. In the final four games, the two men scored six of Green Bay's seven touchdowns. Charlie Mathys ran for the other as Green Bay downed Hammond 19-0 in the season finale. With that victory the Packers finished 7-2-1 to make good on Lambeau's promise to bring home a winner.

Stiller Photo

FRONT ROW: (L-R) Howard (Whitey) Woodin, Norbert Hayes, Fritz Gavin, Charlie Mathys, Tommy Mills, Lyle (Cowboy) Wheeler, Dewey Lyle.
BACK ROW: (L-R) Curly Lambeau, Richard (Jab) Murray, Francis (Jug) Earpe, Milton (Moose) Gardner, Walter Niemann, Howard (Cub) Buck, Myrt Basing, Coach Carey.

TEAM STATISTICS

Regular Season 7-2-1

Date	GB		OPP
9/30	12	Minneapolis Marines	0
10/7	0	St. Louis All-Stars	0
10/14	0	Chicago Bears	3
10/21	12	Milwaukee Badgers	0
10/28	3	Racine Legion	24
11/4	3	at St. Louis All-Stars	0
11/11	16	at Racine Legion	0
11/18	10	at Milwaukee Badgers	7
11/25	10	Duluth Eskimos	0
11/29	19	Hammond Pros	0

Score By Periods

	1	2	3	4	Total
Packers	18	10	36	21	85
Opponents	0	20	7	7	34

1923

INDIVIDUAL STATISTICS

Touchdown Passes

	No
Lambeau	3
Mathys	2
Packers	**5**
Opponents	3

Scoring

	TDr	TDp	TDrt	PAT	FG	S	TP
Buck	0	0	0	5	6	0	23
Lambeau	1	2	0	0	0	0	18
Mills	1	2	0	0	0	0	18
Basing	2	0	0	0	0	0	12
Mathys	1	0	0	0	0	0	6
Wheeler	0	1	0	0	0	0	6
Niemann	0	0	0	0	0	1	2
Packers	**5**	**5**	**0**	**5**	**6**	**1**	**85**
Opponents	1	3	0	4	2	0	34

NFL STANDINGS

	W	L	T	Pct
Canton Bulldogs	11	0	1	1.000
Chicago Bears	9	2	1	.818
Green Bay Packers	**7**	**2**	**1**	**.778**
Milwaukee Badgers	7	2	3	.778
Cleveland Indians	3	1	3	.750
Chicago Cardinals	8	4	0	.667
Duluth Kelleys	4	3	0	.571
Columbus Tigers	5	4	1	.556
Buffalo All-Americans	4	4	3	.500
Racine Legion	4	4	2	.500
Toledo Maroons	2	3	2	.400
Rock Island Independents	2	3	3	.400
St. Louis All-Stars	1	4	2	.200
Hammond Pros	1	5	1	.167
Akron Indians	1	6	0	.143
Dayton Triangles	1	6	1	.143
Oorang Indians	1	10	0	.091
Rochester Jeffersons	0	2	0	.000
Louisville Brecks	0	3	0	.000

ROSTER

Name	Pos	Ht	Wt	College
Basing, Myrt	B	6-0	200	Lawrence
Buck, Howard (Cub)	T	6-3	250	Wisconsin
Earpe, Francis (Jug)	T	6-1	235	Monmouth
Gardner, Milton (Moose)	G	6-2	224	Wisconsin
Gavin, Fritz	B	6-0	195	Marquette
Gray, Jack	E	5-11	180	No college
Hanson, Hal	B	6-3	220	Marquette
Hayes, Norbert	E	5-10	200	Marquette
Lambeau, Earl (Curly)	B	6-0	190	Notre Dame
Leaper, Wes	E	6-1	210	Wisconsin
Lyle, Dewey	E	6-0	220	Minnesota
Mathys, Charlie	B	5-8	165	Indiana
Mills, Tommy	B	5-11	190	Penn State
Murray, Richard (Jab)	T	6-3	250	Marquette
Niemann, Walter	C	6-0	170	Michigan
Wheeler, Lyle (Cowboy)	E	6-0	190	Ripon
Woodin, Howard (Whitey)	G	5-11	206	Marquette

1924

On September 21, the Packers defeated the Bears for the first time (5-0), but the game didn't count in the standings because the season hadn't officially started. To this day, the NFL does not recognize the game; instead, the league puts the start of the Packers 1924 season on September 28. On that day, the Packers gave up a fourth-quarter touchdown and lost 6-3 to the Duluth Kelleys. A week later, the Cardinals and Paddy Driscoll's field goal beat them 3-0. The team then returned home to Bellevue Park and embarked on a six-game winning streak. Two losses in the final three games left Green Bay with a final 7-4 mark.

Curly Lambeau made one major roster move. He signed Verne Lewellen from the University of Nebraska. Lewellen was a triple threat who, over a nine-year career, became especially well-known for his punting. The 6-2, 181-pound back scored 307 points in his stay with the Packers (51 touchdowns and an extra point). His 37 rushing touchdowns is still third best in club history, despite the passage of more than 60 years since his retirement in 1932.

Lewellen scored his first professional touchdown in the third quarter of the Packers first win of 1924, a 16-0 shutout of Kansas City. The following week, Green Bay evened its record (2-2) by beating Milwaukee 17-0 behind Lambeau who caught and threw a touchdown pass. Dutch Hendrian ran for a pair of scores in leading the team to its third straight win, 19-0 over Minneapolis. Win number four came at the expense of Racine where Lambeau's pass to Tillie Voss beat the Legion 6-3. A week later, Lambeau threw his fifth and sixth touchdown passes of the year and Duluth fell 13-0 in the Packers' final home game.

Now 5-2, the Packers completed their winning streak by defeating Milwaukee 17-10. A chance for a seventh straight win was wasted in Chicago when Hendrian lost a fumble in the third quarter and Dutch Sternamann kicked a field goal that allowed the Bears to squeak by 3-0. Green Bay rebounded with a 17-6 triumph in Kansas City before closing the year with a 7-0 setback at Racine on the last day in November.

Stiller Photo

FRONT ROW: (L-R) Curly Lambeau, Dick O'Donnell, Verne Lewellen, Dutch Hendrian, Charlie Mathys, Walter Neimann, Lester Hearden, Myrt Basing.
BACK ROW: (L-R) Walter (Tillie) Voss, Roman Rosatti, Milton (Moose) Gardner, Francis (Jug) Earpe, Howard (Whitey) Woodin, Howard (Cub) Buck, Wilfred Duford, Richard (Jab) Murray.

TEAM STATISTICS

NFL STANDINGS

Regular Season   7-4-0

Date	GB		OPP
9/28	3	at Duluth Kelleys	6
10/5	0	at Chicago Cardinals	3
10/12	16	Kansas City Blues	0
10/19	17	Milwaukee Badgers	0
10/26	19	Minneapolis Marines	0
11/2	6	Racine Legion	3
11/9	13	Duluth Kelleys	0
11/16	17	at Milwaukee Badgers	10
11/23	0	at Chicago Bears	3
11/27	17	at Kansas City Blues	6
11/30	0	at Racine Legion	7

Score By Periods

	1	2	3	4	Total
Packers	20	19	26	43	108
Opponents	6	10	3	19	38

INDIVIDUAL STATISTICS

Touchdown Passes

	No
Lambeau	8
Buck	1
Packers	**9**
Opponents	2

Scoring

	TDr	TDp	TDrt	PAT	FG	S	TP
Voss	0	5	0	0	0	0	30
Hendrian	3	0	0	0	1	0	21
Buck	0	0	0	8	3	0	17
Lewellen	2	0	0	0	0	0	12
Mathys	0	2	0	0	0	0	12
Lambeau	0	1	0	1	1	0	10
L. Hearden	0	1	0	0	0	0	6
Packers	**5**	**9**	**0**	**9**	**5**	**0**	**108**
Opponents	2	2	0	2	4	0	38

	W	L	T	Pct
Cleveland Bulldogs	7	1	1	.875
Chicago Bears	6	1	4	.857
Frankford Yellow Jackets	11	2	1	.846
Duluth Kelleys	5	1	0	.833
Rock Island Independents	6	2	2	.750
Green Bay Packers	**7**	**4**	**0**	**.636**
Racine Legion	4	3	3	.571
Chicago Cardinals	5	4	1	.556
Buffalo Bisons	6	5	0	.545
Columbus Tigers	4	4	0	.500
Hammond Pros	2	2	1	.500
Milwaukee Badgers	5	8	0	.385
Akron Indians	2	6	0	.333
Dayton Triangles	2	6	0	.333
Kansas City Blues	2	7	0	.222
Kenosha Maroons	0	5	1	.000
Minneapolis Marines	0	6	0	.000
Rochester Jeffersons	0	7	0	.000

ROSTER

Name	Pos	Ht	Wt	College
Basing, Myrt	B	6-0	200	Lawrence
Beasey, Jack	B	6-2	195	South Dakota
Buck, Howard (Cub)	T	6-3	250	Wisconsin
Buland, Walter	T	5-11	240	No college
Duford, Wilfred	B	5-10	200	Marquette
Earpe, Francis (Jug)	T	6-1	235	Monmouth
Gardner, Milton (Moose)	G	6-2	224	Wisconsin
Hearden, Lester	B	5-9	175	St. Ambrose
Hendrian, Dutch	B	5-10	200	Princeton
Lambeau, Earl (Curly)	B	6-0	190	Notre Dame
Lewellen, Verne	B	6-2	181	Nebraska
Mathys, Charlie	B	5-8	165	Indiana
Murray, Richard (Jab)	T	6-3	250	Marquette
Niemann, Walter	C	6-0	170	Michigan
O'Donnell, Dick	E	5-10	196	Minnesota
Rosatti, Roman	T	6-2	210	Michigan
Usher, Eddie	B	6-0	210	Michigan
Voss, Walter (Tillie)	E	6-4	190	Lake Forest
Woodin, Howard (Whitey)	G	5-11	206	Marquette

City Stadium opened in 1925 on the city's east side behind the new East High School with a seating capacity of between five and six thousand. A.B. Turnbull and the Green Bay Football Corporation had joined the city and local school board in building the structure. The field would be home of the Packers for the next 32 years, undergoing renovations and additions until it reached its peak capacity of 25,000 in the late '30s.

The stadium was opened just in time for the season opener on September 20 against Hammond. Verne Lewellen scored on a pass from Charlie Mathys and Myrt Basing added a touchdown to ensure a successful 14-10 debut. The Bears invaded next and again Mathys hit Lewellen with a scoring pass, this time in the fourth quarter, and Green Bay notched its first official win over Chicago, 14-10. After those victories, the Packers took to the road where they lost 3-0 to Rock Island.

Green Bay then returned home for three games and won all three. The first, a 31-0 blowout of Milwaukee, featured three touchdowns from Marty Norton. The second, a 20-0 shutout of Rock Island, was highlighted by two Basing scoring runs. The third, a 33-13 triumph over Rochester, saw both Norton and Basing each score twice.

The Packers won a fourth straight, in Milwaukee, 6-0 over the Badgers. The win pushed Green Bay to 6-1, but the Packers still trailed the Akron Pros (4-0-2), the Detroit Tigers (4-0-2) and Frankford (8-1).

Any ground the Packers could have gained disappeared when the team dropped four of its next five games. All four losses occurred on the road, the first in Chicago where the Cardinals' Paddy Driscoll kicked a late field goal to beat them 9-6 in early November. After a 7-0 win at home over Dayton, the team played three games within seven days losing first to the Bears who gained revenge 21-0. Pottsville then ran up 31 unanswered points and blanked the Packers. A third loss was ensured when a triple pass play in the fourth quarter, Henry Homan to Houston Stockton to George Sullivan, resulted in a touchdown which sank Green Bay 13-7 at Frankford.

Green Bay completed its Eastern swing with a 13-10 win over Providence. It was the team's eighth victory against five losses. The Packers wound up ninth in the standings, their lowest finish to that point.

Stiller Photo

FRONT ROW: (L-R) Charlie Mathys, Marty Norton, Eddie Kotal, Curly Lambeau, Jack Harris, George Vegara, Dick O'Donnell, Walter LeJeune.
BACK ROW: (L-R) George Abramson, Howard (Whitey) Woodin, Francis (Jug) Earpe, Milton (Moose) Gardner, Verne Lewellen, Howard (Cub) Buck, Fred (OJ) Larson, Myrt Basing.

TEAM STATISTICS

Regular Season 8-5-0

Date	GB		OPP
9/20	14	Hammond Pros	0
9/27	14	Chicago Bears	10
10/4	0	at Rock Island Independents	3
10/11	31	Milwaukee Badgers	0
10/18	20	Rock Island Independents	0
10/25	33	Rochester Jeffersons	13
11/1	6	at Milwaukee Badgers	0
11/8	6	at Chicago Cardinals	9
11/15	7	Dayton Triangles	0
11/22	0	at Chicago Bears	21
11/26	0	at Pottsville Maroons	31
11/28	7	at Frankford Yellow Jackets	13
12/6	13	at Providence Steam Roller	10

Score By Periods

	1	2	3	4	Total
Packers	3	41	27	80	151
Opponents	24	24	13	49	110

1925

INDIVIDUAL STATISTICS

Touchdown Passes

	No
Mathys	7
Lambeau	4
Packers	**11**
Opponents	7

Scoring

	TDr	TDp	TDrt	PAT	FG	S	TP
Basing	4	2	0	0	0	0	36
M. Norton	1	4	1	0	0	0	36
Lewellen	1	3	0	1	0	0	25
Abramson	0	0	0	2	2	0	8
Buck	0	0	0	8	0	0	8
Lambeau	0	0	0	5	1	0	8
Crowley	0	1	0	0	0	0	6
Gardner	0	0	1	0	0	0	6
Jack Harris	1	0	0	0	0	0	6
Kotal	0	0	1	0	0	0	6
O'Donnell	0	1	0	0	0	0	6
Packers	**7**	**11**	**3**	**16**	**3**	**0**	**151**
Opponents	6	7	1	11	5	0	110

NFL STANDINGS

	W	L	T	Pct
Chicago Cardinals	11	2	1	.846
Pottsville Maroons	10	2	0	.833
Detroit Panthers	8	2	2	.800
New York Giants	8	4	0	.667
Akron Indians	4	2	2	.667
Frankford Yellow Jackets	13	7	0	.667
Chicago Bears	9	5	3	.643
Rock Island Independents	5	3	3	.625
Green Bay Packers	**8**	**5**	**0**	**.615**
Providence Steam Roller	6	5	1	.545
Canton Bulldogs	4	4	0	.500
Cleveland Bulldogs	5	8	1	.385
Kansas City Cowboys	2	5	1	.286
Hammond Pros	1	4	0	.250
Buffalo Bisons	1	6	2	.143
Duluth Kelleys	0	3	0	.000
Rochester Jeffersons	0	6	1	.000
Milwaukee Badgers	0	6	0	.000
Dayton Triangles	0	7	1	.000
Columbus Tigers	0	9	0	.000

ROSTER

Name	Pos	Ht	Wt	College
Abramson, George	T	5-9	210	Minnesota
Basing, Myrt	B	6-0	200	Lawrence
Buck, Howard (Cub)	T	6-3	250	Wisconsin
Crowley, Jim	B	5-9	165	Notre Dame
Earpe, Francis (Jug)	T	6-1	235	Monmouth
Gardner, Milton (Moose)	G	6-2	224	Wisconsin
Harris, Jack	B	6-0	190	Wisconsin
Kotal, Eddie	B	5-10	165	Lawrence
Lambeau, Earl (Curly)	B	6-0	190	Notre Dame
Larson, Fred (OJ)	C	6-0	215	Notre Dame
LeJeune, Walter	G	6-0	242	Missouri
Lewellen, Verne	B	6-2	181	Nebraska
Mathys, Charlie	B	5-8	165	Indiana
Norton, Marty	B	5-8	165	Carleton
O'Donnell, Dick	E	5-10	196	Minnesota
Vegara, George	E	6-1	190	Notre Dame
Wilkins, Ted	E	5-10	195	Indiana
Woodin, Howard (Whitey)	G	5-11	206	Marquette

1926

Missing from the 1926 roster was Howard (Cub) Buck. For five years he had anchored one of the tackle spots, playing in the neighborhood of 250 to 265 pounds. Buck departed to coach at the University of Miami. Not until 1929, with the acquisition of Robert (Cal) Hubbard, would the Packers possess a lineman of such huge proportions.

Green Bay opened its season earlier than ever before, on September 19th. They faced the Detroit Panthers in City Stadium. There, Dick O'Donnell caught two touchdown passes from Curly Lambeau and Verne Lewellen snared one from Charlie Mathys to beat the Motor City team 21-0. The victory was the eighth consecutive at home for the Packers.

That winning streak, however, ended the very next week. The Bears tied Green Bay 6-6 when Lambeau's last-minute field goal attempt failed. Seven days later, Ernie Nevers and the Duluth Eskimos battled the Packers to a 0-0 standstill in a rainstorm. Following those two nondecisions, the Packers suffered their first regular season loss in City Stadium on October 10. Carl (Cully) Lidberg ran for a score, but the Cardinals prevailed 13-7.

After defeating Milwaukee 7-0 on October 17 behind Lewellen's scoring run, the Packers bounced the Racine Tornadoes, 35-0. Jack Harris scored twice in that game.

The Packers (3-1-2) had to play six of their last seven games on the road. First they faced the Cardinals who fell 3-0 compliments of Everett (Pid) Purdy's field goal. The following week, Lewellen contributed two scores in a 21-0 shutout of Milwaukee. Green Bay had been scheduled to host Racine in week nine, but the Legion folded. Instead, the Packers beat Louisville 14-0 at City Stadium.

Green Bay then faced a four-game road trip. Unfortunately, the team picked up only one win in the stretch drive. In Chicago, Paddy Driscoll returned a Lidberg fumble for a touchdown in the fourth quarter enabling his Bears to stop the Packers 19-13. Four days later, the Packers again stumbled in the fourth quarter. Houston Stockton passed to Henry Homan for a touchdown and a 20-14 Frankford win. Green Bay closed out November with a 7-0 win in Detroit, then tied the Bears 3-3 after a three-week layoff.

Stiller Photo

FRONT ROW: (L-R) Curly Lambeau, Dick O'Donnell, Verne Lewellen, Jack Harris, Everett (Pid) Purdy, Rex Enright, Jack MacAuliffe, Carl (Cully) Lidberg, Howard (Whitey) Woodin.
BACK ROW: (L-R) Dick Flaherty, George Abramson, Roman Rosatti, Francis (Jug) Earpe, Milton (Moose) Gardner, Walter LeJeune, Ivan Cahoon, Myrt Basing, Hector Cyre.

TEAM STATISTICS

Regular Season 7-3-3

Date	GB		OPP
9/19	21	Detroit Panthers	0
9/26	6	Chicago Bears	6
10/3	0	Duluth Eskimos	0
10/10	7	Chicago Cardinals	13
10/17	7	Milwaukee Badgers	0
10/24	35	Racine Tornadoes	0
10/31	3	at Chicago Cardinals	0
11/7	21	at Milwaukee Badgers	0
11/14	14	at Louisville Colonels	0
11/21	13	at Chicago Bears	19
11/25	14	at Frankford Yellow Jackets	20
11/28	7	at Detroit Panthers	0
12/19	3	at Chicago Bears	3

Score By Periods

	1	2	3	4	Total
Packers	30	28	37	56	151
Opponents	19	10	6	26	61

INDIVIDUAL STATISTICS

Touchdown Passes

	No
Lambeau	3
Mathys	2
Kotal	1
MacAuliffe	1
Purdy	1
Packers	**8**
Opponents	4

Scoring

	TDr	TDp	TDrt	PAT	FG	S	TP
Lewellen	3	3	1	0	0	0	42
Lidberg	4	0	0	0	0	0	24
Purdy	0	0	0	14	2	0	20
Flaherty	0	2	0	0	0	0	12
Jack Harris	2	0	0	0	0	0	12
Kotal	1	1	0	0	0	0	12
O'Donnell	0	2	0	0	0	0	12
Basing	1	0	0	0	0	0	6
Enright	1	0	0	0	0	0	6
Lambeau	0	0	0	4	0	0	4
Woodin	0	0	0	1	0	0	1
Packers	**12**	**8**	**1**	**19**	**2**	**0**	**151**
Opponents	2	4	1	4	5	0	61

NFL STANDINGS

	W	L	T	Pct
Frankford Yellow Jackets	14	1	1	.933
Chicago Bears	12	1	3	.923
Pottsville Maroons	10	2	1	.833
Kansas City Cowboys	8	3	0	.727
Green Bay Packers	**7**	**3**	**3**	**.700**
Los Angeles Buccaneers	6	3	1	.667
New York Giants	8	4	1	.667
Duluth Eskimos	6	5	3	.545
Buffalo Rangers	4	4	2	.500
Chicago Cardinals	5	6	1	.455
Providence Steam Roller	5	7	1	.417
Detroit Panthers	4	6	2	.400
Hartford Blues	3	7	0	.300
Brooklyn Lions	3	8	0	.273
Milwaukee Badgers	2	7	0	.222
Akron Pros	1	4	3	.200
Dayton Triangles	1	4	1	.200
Racine Tornadoes	1	4	0	.200
Columbus Tigers	1	6	0	.143
Canton Bulldogs	1	9	3	.100
Hammond Pros	0	4	0	.000
Louisville Colonels	0	4	0	.000

ROSTER

Name	Pos	Ht	Wt	College
Basing, Myrt	B	6-0	200	Lawrence
Bieberstein, Adolph	G	5-10	205	Wisconsin
Cahoon, Ivan	T	6-2	235	Gonzaga
Carlson, Wes	G	6-1	220	St. John's
Cyre, Hector	T	6-2	216	Gonzaga
Earpe, Francis (Jug)	T	6-1	235	Monmouth
Enright, Rex	B	5-11	195	Notre Dame
Flaherty, Dick	E	6-1	200	Marquette
Gardner, Milton (Moose)	G	6-2	224	Wisconsin
Harris, Jack	B	6-0	190	Wisconsin
Kotal, Eddie	B	5-10	165	Lawrence
Lambeau, Earl (Curly)	B	6-0	190	Notre Dame
LeJeune, Walter	G	6-0	242	Missouri
Lewellen, Verne	B	6-2	181	Nebraska
Lidberg, Carl (Cully)	B	6-0	200	Minnesota
MacAuliffe, Jack	B	5-10	155	Beloit
Mathys, Charlie	B	5-8	165	Indiana
McGaw, Walter	G	5-10	195	Beloit
O'Donnell, Dick	E	5-10	196	Minnesota
Purdy, Everett (Pid)	B	5-10	175	Beloit
Rosatti, Roman	T	6-2	210	Michigan
Rose, Bob	C	N/A	N/A	Ripon
Woodin, Howard (Whitey)	G	5-11	206	Marquette

1927

Curly Lambeau, now 29, began devoting more time to coaching and managing the team and less time to playing halfback. He signed a number of players in 1927 who would contribute greatly in the championship years ahead. From the dissolved Milwaukee Badgers, he picked up end LaVern (Lavvie) Dilweg and quarterback Joseph (Red) Dunn. From Alabama he acquired Claude Perry, a durable tackle who would play through 1935. All three were solid additions and their efforts helped bring the Packers in at 7-2-1, a record good enough for second place behind the New York Giants.

Though Green Bay finished behind New York in the standings, the Giants were not the team to give the Packers problems. The two never met. Instead, it was the Bears who handed Green Bay its only two losses and kept the Packers playing catchup.
After back-to-back wins over Dayton and Cleveland, respectively, the Packers played host to the Bears. The Chicagoans took an early 7-0 lead and held Green Bay scoreless throughout most of the game. Late in the fourth quarter, Dunn threw an apparent touchdown pass to Lambeau, but the officials ruled that Dunn was not five yards behind the line of scrimmage when he released the throw as was necessary in those days. In addition, the Bears were offside and so the play was nullified. Undaunted, the Packers scored three plays later when Lewellen ran across the goal. This time the touchdown held up, but Pid Purdy missed the extra point and the Bears slipped by 7-6.

The Bears, however, had not heard the last of Green Bay. Following the heartbreaking loss to Chicago, the Packers won three straight to bolster their record to 5-1 and remain a game behind the Bears, who were undefeated at 4-0. Right behind the Bears and Packers were the Giants at 4-1-1.

On November 6, the Packers tangled with the Cardinals. With his team down by six, Lewellen tied the score 6-6 in the fourth quarter with his run, but Bill Springsteen blocked Dunn's point after try. The Cardinals missed a late field goal themselves and the 6-6 score held up.

After beating Dayton 7-0, the Packers had a rematch with the Bears in Wrigley Field. Again Green Bay trailed late, 7-6. Dunn attempted a fourth-quarter field goal, but the Bears blocked it and subsequently drove the length of the field to put the Packers away 14-6. A week later, Dunn threw two touchdowns passes to beat Frankford 17-9. On November 24, New York (8-1-1) held a slight lead over the Bears (7-1-1) and Green Bay (7-2-1). While the Packers broke camp, the Giants and Bears played additional games. After the dust settled, the Packers had moved past the Bears into second place, the team's best finish to date.

Stiller photo

FRONT ROW: (L-R) Bruce Jones, Richard (Red) Smith, Howard (Whitey) Woodin, Eddie Kotal, Everett (Pid) Purdy, Thomas Hearden, Frank Mayer, Joseph (Red) Dunn, Claude Perry.
BACK ROW: (L-R) Roman Rosatti, Dick O'Donnell, Francis (Jug) Earpe, Verne Lewellen, Ivan Cahoon, Rex Enright, LaVern (Lavvie) Dilweg, Bernard (Boob) Darling, Curly Lambeau.

TEAM STATISTICS

Regular Season 7-2-1

Date	GB		OPP
9/18	14	Dayton Triangles	0
9/25	12	Cleveland Bulldogs	7
10/2	6	Chicago Bears	7
10/9	20	Duluth Eskimos	0
10/16	13	Chicago Cardinals	0
10/23	13	New York Yankees	0
11/6	6	at Chicago Cardinals	6
11/13	6	Dayton Triangles	0
11/20	6	at Chicago Bears	14
11/24	17	at Frankford Yellow Jackets	9

Score By Periods

	1	2	3	4	Total
Packers	7	32	28	46	113
Opponents	6	23	0	14	43

1927

INDIVIDUAL STATISTICS

Touchdown Passes

	No
Dunn	3
Lambeau	1
Packers	**4**
Opponents	4

Scoring

	TDr	TDp	TDrt	PAT	FG	S	TP
Lewellen	5	0	0	0	0	0	30
Enright	2	2	0	0	0	0	24
Dunn	0	1	0	7	0	0	13
L. Dilweg	0	1	1	0	0	0	12
Lambeau	2	0	0	0	0	0	12
Purdy	1	0	0	1	1	0	10
Cahoon	0	0	1	0	0	0	6
Kotal	1	0	0	0	0	0	6
Packers	**11**	**4**	**2**	**8**	**1**	**0**	**113**
Opponents	2	4	0	4	1	0	43

NFL STANDINGS

	W	L	T	Pct
New York Giants	11	1	1	.917
Green Bay Packers	**7**	**2**	**1**	**.778**
Chicago Bears	9	3	2	.750
Cleveland Bulldogs	8	4	1	.667
Providence Steam Roller	8	5	1	.615
New York Yankees	7	8	1	.467
Frankford Yellow Jackets	6	9	3	.400
Pottsville Maroons	5	8	0	.385
Chicago Cardinals	3	7	1	.300
Dayton Triangles	1	6	1	.143
Duluth Eskimos	1	8	0	.111
Buffalo Bisons	0	5	0	.000

ROSTER

Name	Pos	Ht	Wt	College
Basing, Myrt	B	6-0	200	Lawrence
Bross, Marty	B	5-9	170	Gonzaga
Cahoon, Ivan	T	6-2	235	Gonzaga
Darling, Bernard (Boob)	C	6-3	216	Beloit
Dilweg, LaVern (Lavvie)	E	6-3	202	Marquette
Dunn, Joseph (Red)	B	6-0	178	Marquette
Earpe, Francis (Jug)	T	6-1	235	Monmouth
Enright, Rex	B	5-11	195	Notre Dame
Hearden, Thomas	B	5-9	175	Notre Dame
Jones, Bruce	G	6-0	215	Alabama
Kotal, Eddie	B	5-10	165	Lawrence
Lambeau, Earl (Curly)	B	6-0	190	Notre Dame
Lewellen, Verne	B	6-2	181	Nebraska
Mayer, Frank	G	6-0	215	Notre Dame
O'Donnell, Dick	E	5-10	196	Minnesota
Perry, Claude	T	6-1	211	Alabama
Purdy, Everett (Pid)	B	5-10	175	Beloit
Rosatti, Roman	T	6-2	210	Michigan
Skeate, Gil	B	5-10	190	Gonzaga
Smith, Richard (Red)	G	5-10	225	Notre Dame
Tuttle, Dick	E	6-0	178	Minnesota
Woodin, Howard (Whitey)	G	5-11	206	Marquette

A slow start – two losses and a tie in the first three weeks – put a championship season on hold for yet another year. Highlights of 1928 included two victories over the Bears, both at Wrigley Field, and a 7-7 tie with the eventual NFL champion Providence Steam Roller. Two key additions to the roster were Tom Nash, a 6-3, 210 pound end who joined the team in time for the first Bear game, and Bo Molenda, who came aboard shortly before the second Pottsville skirmish.

As had become custom, Green Bay played most of its early-season games at City Stadium. As was not the custom, the Packers struggled there. Play commenced on September 23 against Frankford. Harry O'Boyle kicked a first-quarter field goal for an early 3-0 lead, but the Yellow Jackets scored 19 unanswered points and eventually won 19-9. O'Boyle had a chance to give Green Bay a win in week two against the Bears. His late field goal attempt, however, failed and two plays later the game ended 12-12. On October 7, the Packers met the defending New York Giants for the first time. Faye (Mule) Wilson, who would join the Packers in 1931, scored on a run in the third quarter to give the Giants a 6-0 victory.

After that disastrous start, Green Bay (0-2-1) got hot. Verne Lewellen ran for two scores to propel the Packers past the Cardinals 20-0 and get the Packers in the win column. The resurgence continued when the Packers defeated the unbeaten Bears, 16-6 for the first time since the second week of the 1925 campaign. Bruce Jones sealed the win with an interception return for a touchdown. Two more wins followed before a tie with the Yankees left Green Bay with a 4-2-2 record on the eve of its annual Eastern swing.

The Packers dispelled the notion they couldn't play with the big boys when they downed the Giants for the first time at the Polo Grounds on November 18. Verne Lewellen's run and Red Dunn's point after held up and the Packers exited with a 7-0 win. Then, uncharacteristically, Green Bay stumbled against a weak opponent, taking a 26-14 beating at the hands of the 1-7 Pottsville Maroons.

Lambeau, who rarely allowed the team to play poorly two games in a row, saw significant improvement in the final three games. Green Bay went toe-to-toe with Frankford, never allowing the Yellow Jackets to pierce its 30-yard line. Frankford won 2-0, because a snap from center went over Lewellen's head and wound up out of the end zone. Against the eventual champion Steamroller, the Packers blew a first-quarter scoring opportunity from the two-yard line when Lewellen threw the ball away on fourth down. The game ended 7-7 but Eddie Kotal and O'Boyle first had to block a Gus Sonneberg field goal try late in the fourth quarter. Green Bay finally got a win for its efforts by knocking off the Bears for a second time, 6-0. After the other teams completed play on December 16, Green Bay's 6-4-3 record was good for fourth place.

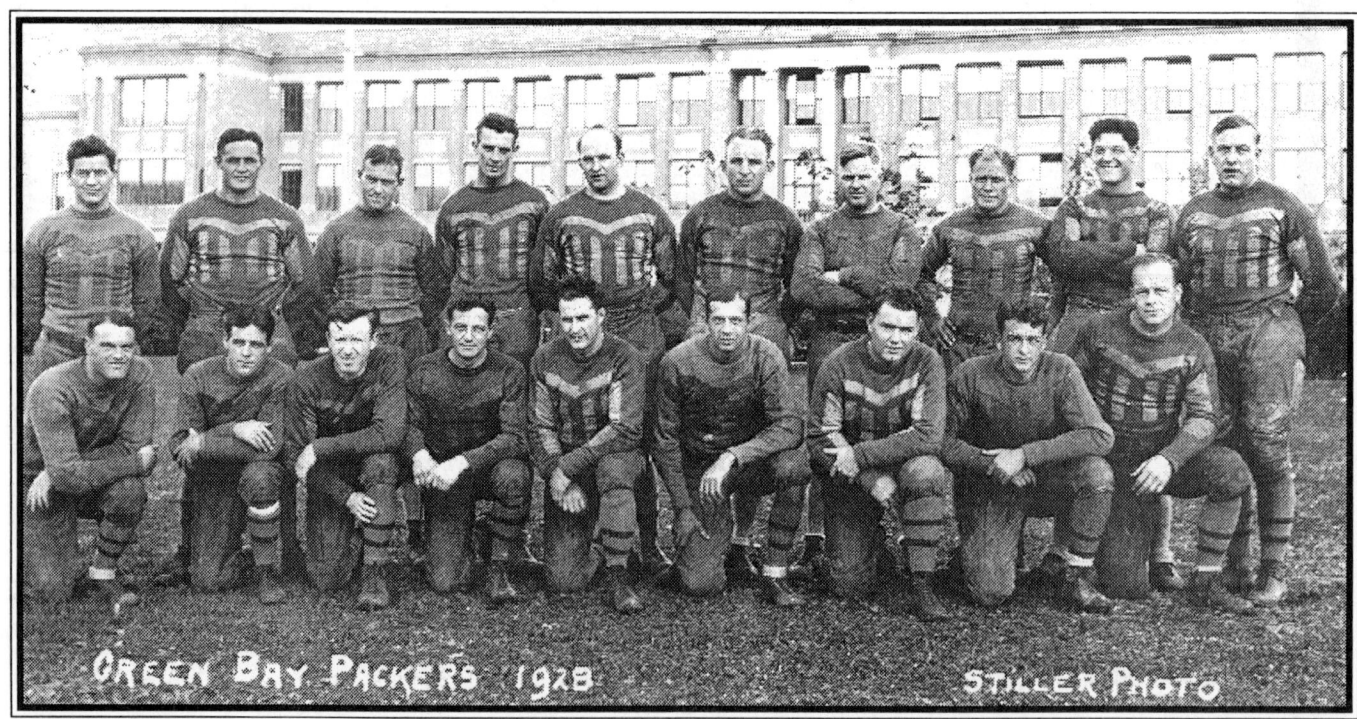

Stiller photo

FRONT ROW: (L-R) Roger Ashmore, Harry O'Boyle, Joseph (Red) Dunn, Eddie Kotal, Dick O'Donnell, Verne Lewellen, George Lollar, Bernard (Boob) Darling, Paul Minick.
BACK ROW: (L-R) Curly Lambeau, James Bowdoin, Larry Marks, LaVern (Lavvie) Dilweg, Ivan Cahoon, Claude Perry, Howard (Whitey) Woodin, Roy Baker, Bruce Jones, Francis (Jug) Earpe.

TEAM STATISTICS

Regular Season 6-4-3

Date	GB		OPP
9/23	9	Frankford Yellow Jackets	19
9/30	12	Chicago Bears	12
10/7	0	New York Giants	6
10/14	20	Chicago Cardinals	0
10/21	16	at Chicago Bears	6
10/28	17	Dayton Triangles	0
11/4	26	Pottsville Maroons	14
11/11	0	New York Yankees	0
11/18	7	at New York Giants	0
11/25	0	at Pottsville Maroons	26
11/29	0	at Frankford Yellow Jackets	2
12/2	7	at Providence Steam Roller	7
12/9	6	at Chicago Bears	0

Score By Periods

	1	2	3	4	Total
Packers	15	53	13	39	120
Opponents	26	20	26	20	92

1928

INDIVIDUAL STATISTICS

Touchdown Passes

	No
Dunn	4
Kotal	1
Lambeau	1
Lewellen	1
Packers	**7**
Opponents	6

Scoring

	TDr	TDp	TDrt	PAT	FG	S	TP
Lewellen	6	3	0	0	0	0	54
O'Boyle	1	0	0	8	3	0	23
Kotal	2	1	0	0	0	0	18
Marks	0	2	0	0	0	0	12
Bruce Jones	0	0	1	0	0	0	6
O'Donnell	0	1	0	0	0	0	6
Dunn	0	0	0	1	0	0	1
Packers	**9**	**7**	**1**	**9**	**3**	**0**	**120**
Opponents	6	6	2	6	0	1	92

NFL STANDINGS

	W	L	T	Pct
Providence Steam Roller	8	1	2	.889
Frankford Yellow Jackets	11	3	2	.786
Detroit Wolverines	7	2	1	.778
Green Bay Packers	**6**	**4**	**3**	**.600**
Chicago Bears	7	5	1	.583
New York Giants	4	7	2	.364
New York Yankees	4	8	1	.333
Pottsville Maroons	2	8	0	.200
Chicago Cardinals	1	5	0	.167
Dayton Triangles	0	7	0	.000

ROSTER

Name	Pos	Ht	Wt	College
Ashmore, Roger	T	6-1	212	Gonzaga
Baker, Roy	B	6-0	177	USC
Bowdoin, James	G	6-2	220	Alabama
Cahoon, Ivan	T	6-2	235	Gonzaga
Darling, Bernard (Boob)	C	6-3	216	Beloit
Dilweg, LaVern (Lavvie)	E	6-3	202	Marquette
Dunn, Joseph (Red)	B	6-0	178	Marquette
Earpe, Francis (Jug)	T	6-1	235	Monmouth
Griffin, Harold	C	6-3	238	Iowa
Hearden, Thomas	B	5-9	175	Notre Dame
Jones, Bruce	G	6-0	215	Alabama
Kotal, Eddie	B	5-10	165	Lawrence
Lambeau, Earl (Curly)	B	6-0	190	Notre Dame
Lewellen, Verne	B	6-2	181	Nebraska
Lollar, George	B	6-0	200	Howard
Marks, Larry	B	5-11	185	Indiana
Minick, Paul	G	5-11	210	Iowa
Molenda, Bo	B	5-11	208	Michigan
Nash, Tom	E	6-3	210	Georgia
O'Boyle, Harry	B	6-1	180	Notre Dame
O'Donnell, Dick	E	5-10	196	Minnesota
Perry, Claude	T	6-1	211	Alabama
Webber, Harry	E	6-0	185	Nebraska
Woodin, Howard (Whitey)	G	5-11	206	Marquette

Curly Lambeau's gift for recognizing and obtaining talent reached new heights in 1929 when he acquired three future Hall of Famers. Over the summer, the New York Yankees had folded and Lambeau plucked August (Mike) Michalske, a guard from Penn State, from the remains. From the Giants, Lambeau signed disgruntled Robert (Cal) Hubbard, a giant of a man at 6-5 and 250 pounds. His most colorful addition, however, was one Johnny (Blood) McNally, whose off-the-field exploits rivaled his on-the-field accomplishments. Blood could run, pass, and punt with the best of them, but perhaps more importantly, he was the best pass catching back in the league.

In addition to playing offense, these men enhanced an already solid defense, turning it into the best in the NFL. Green Bay held opponents scoreless eight times and gave up just 22 points over the course of a 13-game schedule. Just three teams were able to score a touchdown against the Packers virtually impenetrable wall of defenders.

The key to the entire season was a matchup with the New York Giants on November 24 at the Polo Grounds. Both teams had ripped through the competition with Green Bay (9-0) holding a slightly better record than the Giants (8-0-1). Since ties did not count in figuring position, the teams were essentially even going into the contest.

The game boiled down to a case of an immovable object meeting an unyielding force. Green Bay had given up just 16 points while the Giants had scored 204, tops in the league. Hurdis McCrary scored on a pass from Bo Molenda and Molenda kicked the extra point to give the Packers a 7-0 first-quarter lead. Bennie Friedman threw a touchdown pass to Tony Plansky, but his point after attempt sailed wide and the Packers clung to a one-point, 7-6 lead going into the fourth quarter. In that period, Green Bay established itself using scoring runs from Molenda and Blood to put the Giants away 20-6.

With three games remaining, the Packers tied Frankford before pounding Providence and the Bears by identical 25-0 scores to wrap up a 12-0-1 championship year.

Green Bay trailed only once in any game all year. After dispatching the Triangles and Bears to start the season, the Packers unexpectedly found themselves behind 2-0 at halftime in a game with the Cardinals. A field goal by Dunn and a touchdown run by Lewellen in the second half revived the team in time to post a 9-2 win.

Three weeks later the stubborn Cardinals again gave the Packers fits. After his team fell behind, Ernie Nevers passed for a touchdown to Chuck Kassel in the fourth quarter to cut the score 7-6. Nevers could not convert on the extra point try and Green Bay won 7-6.

Other than that, the Packers had smooth sailing until the showdown with New York. There, the little town from the midwest demonstrated again it belonged in the league. If anyone needed further convincing, they had only wait until 1930 when the Packers went to work on a second championship.

Stiller photo

FRONT ROW: (L-R) 20 Curly Lambeau, 25 Paul Minick, 27 Bo Molenda, 17 Roy Baker, 10 Eddie Kotal, 16 Joseph (Red) Dunn, 30 Dick O'Donnell, 36 August (Mike) Michalske, 33 William Kern, 23 Howard (Whitey) Woodin, 34 Carl (Cully) Lidberg.
BACK ROW: (L-R) 39 Robert (Cal) Hubbard, Hurdis McCrary, 19 Tom Nash, 29 Bernard (Boob) Darling, 26 Claude Perry, 15 Richard (Red) Smith, 31 Verne Lewellen, 35 Roger Ashmore, 24 Johnny (Blood) McNally, 32 James Bowdoin, 22 LaVerne (Lavvie) Dilweg, 38 Francis (Jug) Earpe.

TEAM STATISTICS

Regular Season   12-0-1

Date	GB		OPP
9/22	9	Dayton Triangles	0
9/29	23	Chicago Bears	0
10/6	9	Chicago Cardinals	2
10/13	14	Frankford Yellow Jackets	2
10/20	24	Minneapolis Red Jackets	0
10/27	7	at Chicago Cardinals	6
11/3	16	at Minneapolis Red Jackets	6
11/10	14	at Chicago Bears	0
11/17	12	at Chicago Cardinals	0
11/24	20	at New York Giants	6
11/28	0	at Frankford Yellow Jackets	0
12/1	25	at Providence Steam Roller	0
12/8	25	at Chicago Bears	0

Score By Periods

	1	2	3	4	Total
Packers	38	33	66	61	198
Opponents	2	0	14	6	22

1929

INDIVIDUAL STATISTICS

Touchdown Passes

	No
Dunn	5
Lewellen	4
Blood	1
McCrary	1
Molenda	1
Packers	**12**
Opponents	2

Scoring

	TDr	TDp	TDrt	PAT	FG	S	TP
Lewellen	6	1	1	0	0	0	48
Blood	3	2	0	0	0	0	30
McCrary	1	2	1	0	0	0	24
Molenda	3	0	0	3	0	0	21
L. Dilweg	0	3	0	0	0	0	18
Kotal	0	3	0	0	0	0	18
Dunn	0	0	0	11	2	0	17
Lidberg	2	0	0	0	0	0	12
Nash	0	1	0	0	0	0	6
team	0	0	0	0	0	2	4
Packers	**15**	**12**	**2**	**14**	**2**	**2**	**198**
Opponents	1	2	0	0	0	2	22

NFL STANDINGS

	W	L	T	Pct
Green Bay Packers	12	0	1	1.000
New York Giants	13	1	1	.929
Frankford Yellow Jackets	9	4	5	.692
Chicago Cardinals	6	6	1	.500
Boston Bulldogs	4	4	0	.500
Orange Tornadoes	3	4	4	.429
Staten Island Stapletons	3	4	3	.429
Providence Steam Roller	4	6	2	.400
Chicago Bears	4	9	2	.308
Buffalo Bisons	1	7	1	.125
Minneapolis Red Jackets	1	9	0	.100
Dayton Triangles	0	6	0	.000

ROSTER

Name	Pos	Ht	Wt	College
Ashmore, Roger	T	6-1	212	Gonzaga
Baker, Roy	B	6-0	177	USC
Bowdoin, James	G	6-2	220	Alabama
Cahoon, Ivan	T	6-2	235	Gonzaga
Darling, Bernard (Boob)	C	6-3	216	Beloit
Dilweg, LaVern (Lavvie)	E	6-3	202	Marquette
Dunn, Joseph (Red)	B	6-0	178	Marquette
Earpe, Francis (Jug)	T	6-1	235	Monmouth
Evans, Jack	B	6-0	195	California
Hill, Don	B	5-11	190	Stanford
Hubbard, Robert (Cal)	T	6-5	250	Geneva
Kern, William	T	6-0	187	Pittsburgh
Kotal, Eddie	B	5-10	165	Lawrence
Lambeau, Earl (Curly)	B	6-0	190	Notre Dame
Lewellen, Verne	B	6-2	181	Nebraska
Lidberg, Carl (Cully)	B	6-0	200	Minnesota
McCrary, Hurdis	B	6-2	205	Georgia
McNally (Blood), Johnny	B	6-0	190	St. John's
Michalske, August (Mike)	G	6-1	215	Penn State
Minick, Paul	G	5-11	210	Iowa
Molenda, Bo	B	5-11	208	Michigan
Nash, Tom	E	6-3	210	Georgia
O'Donnell, Dick	E	5-10	196	Minnesota
Perry, Claude	T	6-1	211	Alabama
Smith, Richard (Red)	B	5-10	225	Notre Dame
Woodin, Howard (Whitey)	G	5-11	206	Marquette
Young, Bill	G	6-1	200	Ohio State
Zuidmulder, Dave	B	6-1	184	St. Ambrose

1930

Ten of the 28 players on the 1929 championship team were let go and Curly Lambeau added 11 newcomers to fill their shoes. This large turnover, with the exception of Lambeau and rookie Arnie Herber, involved mainly lesser-known players. The solid core which had taken the Packers to the top remained. Lambeau retired from active duty on the playing field, having thrown 24 touchdown passes in a nine-year career. Herber, it was hoped, could take over where Lambeau had left off. The long ball passer from Regis College threw three touchdown passes in 1930, but his most productive years were still to come. Instead, Joseph (Red) Dunn came to the quarterbacking front, firing a then-team record 11 touchdown tosses.

As was the case last year, the team to beat was the New York Giants. The Packers and Giants met twice in 1930 and traded wins. On October 5, the Packers hosted the New Yorkers. Tom Nash scored on a pass from Verne Lewellen to give Green Bay a 7-0 lead. The Giants came back to tie on a pass from Bennie Friedman to Len Sedbrook. With time running out, Dunn threw his first scoring pass of the year (to Johnny (Blood) McNally) which gave the Packers a 14-7 win.

When the two met again on November 23, Green Bay was in first place with an 8-1 record while New York was second with a 10-2 mark. The Giants took a 13-0 lead as Friedman threw one touchdown pass and ran for a score in the third quarter. Lewellen also scored in the third period, but after Dunn missed the extra point, the Packers were shut out the rest of the way and lost 13-6. New York had taken over first place.

Both teams had four games remaining. Green Bay did away with Frankford 25-7 while Staten Island helped the Packers cause by beating the Giants 7-6. In the way of thanks, Green Bay turned around and clobbered Staten Island 37-7 three days later. Meanwhile, the Giants lost again, 7-6 to Brooklyn. The pair of wins improved Green Bay to 10-2 while the Giants slumped to 11-4. Despite losing to the Bears 21-0 and managing only a 6-6 deadlock with the Spartans, Green Bay (10-3-1) edged New York (13-4-0) by .004 of a percentage point (.769 to .765) to clinch its second straight championship.

Green Bay was fast gaining a reputation for being an offensive machine. In 1930, the Packers scored 234 points, a team record and second best in the league behind the Giants. The team scored 36 touchdowns and exploded for 47 points against Portsmouth on November 11. The defense, while still reliable, surrendered 111 points.

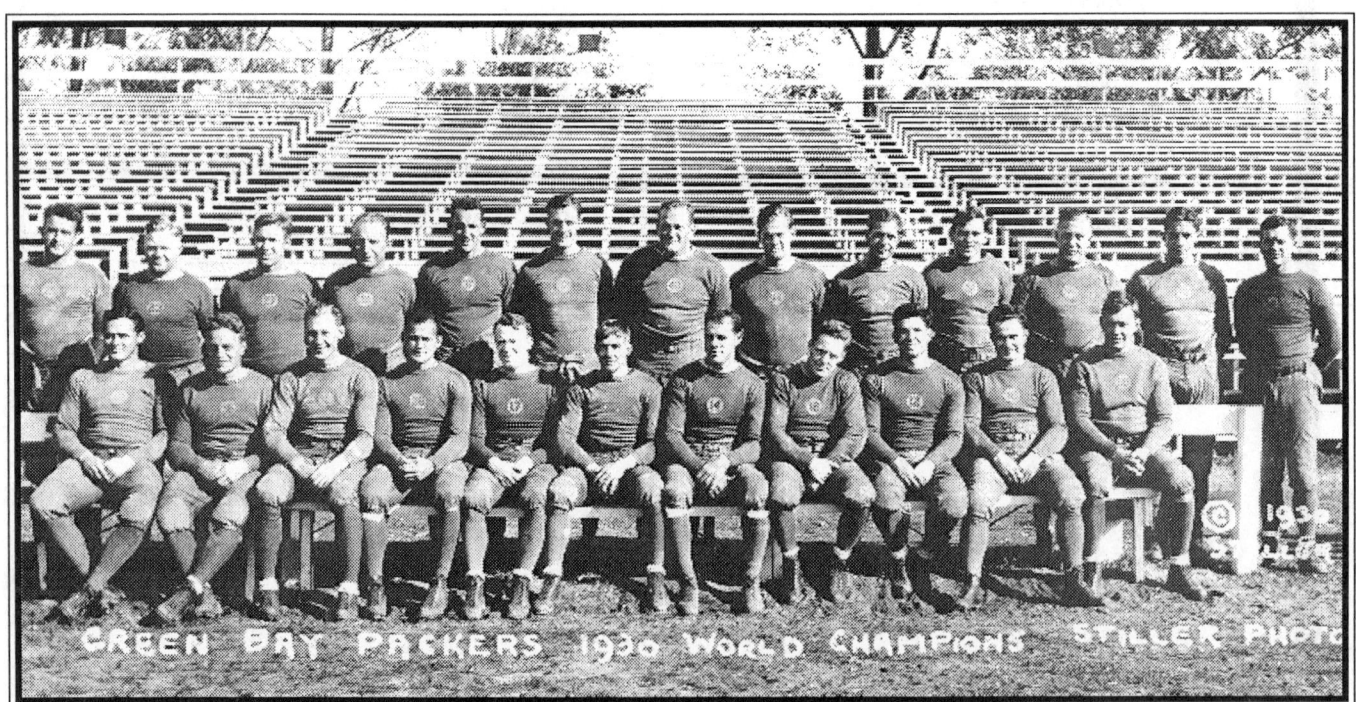

Stiller photo

FRONT ROW: (L-R) 32 James Bowdoin, 35 Ken Radick, 33 Wuert Engelmann, 28 Hurdis McCrary, 17 Joseph (Red) Dunn, Dave Zuidmulder, 14 Merle Zuver, 18 Paul Fitzgibbons, 12 Arnie Herber, 30 Dick O'Donnell, 38 Carl (Cully) Lidberg.
BACK ROW: (L-R) 29 Bernard (Boob) Darling, 23 Howard (Whitey) Woodin, 27 Bo Molenda, 26 Claude Perry, 37 Tom Nash, 22 LaVern (Lavvie) Dilweg, 40 Robert (Cal) Hubbard, 34 Elmer Sleight, 31 Verne Lewellen, 24 Johnny (Blood) McNally, 39 Francis (Jug) Earpe, 36 August (Mike) Michalske, 20 Curly Lambeau.

TEAM STATISTICS

Regular Season 10-3-1

Date	GB		OPP
9/21	14	Chicago Cardinals	0
9/28	7	Chicago Bears	0
10/5	14	New York Giants	7
10/12	27	Frankford Yellow Jackets	12
10/19	13	at Minneapolis Red Jackets	0
10/26	19	Minneapolis Red Jackets	0
11/2	47	Portsmouth Spartans	13
11/9	13	at Chicago Bears	12
11/16	6	at Chicago Cardinals	13
11/23	6	at New York Giants	13
11/27	25	at Frankford Yellow Jackets	7
11/30	37	at Staten Island Stapletons	7
12/7	0	at Chicago Bears	21
12/14	6	at Portsmouth Spartans	6

Score By Periods

	1	2	3	4	Total
Packers	58	64	52	60	234
Opponents	0	40	31	40	111

1930

INDIVIDUAL STATISTICS

Touchdown Passes

	No
Dunn	11
Herber	3
Lewellen	3
Packers	**17**
Opponents	9

Scoring

	TDr	TDp	TDrt	PAT	FG	S	TP
Lewellen	8	1	0	0	0	0	54
McCrary	4	2	0	0	0	0	36
Blood	0	5	0	0	0	0	30
Molenda	3	0	0	4	0	0	22
L. Dilweg	0	2	1	0	0	0	18
Engelmann	1	2	0	0	0	0	18
Fitzgibbons	1	2	0	0	0	0	18
Dunn	0	0	0	14	0	0	14
Herber	0	1	0	0	0	0	6
Hubbard	0	1	0	0	0	0	6
Lidberg	1	0	0	0	0	0	6
Nash	0	1	0	0	0	0	6
Packers	**18**	**17**	**1**	**18**	**0**	**0**	**234**
Opponents	8	9	0	9	0	0	111

NFL STANDINGS

	W	L	T	Pct
Green Bay Packers	**10**	**3**	**1**	**.769**
New York Giants	13	4	0	.765
Chicago Bears	9	4	1	.692
Brooklyn Dodgers	7	4	1	.636
Providence Steam Roller	6	4	1	.600
Staten Island Stapletons	5	5	2	.500
Chicago Cardinals	5	6	2	.455
Portsmouth Spartans	5	6	3	.455
Frankford Yellow Jackets	4	13	1	.222
Minneapolis Red Jackets	1	7	1	.125
Newark Tornadoes	1	10	1	.091

ROSTER

Name	Pos	Ht	Wt	College
Bloodgood, Elbert	B	6-1	175	Nebraska
Bowdoin, James	G	6-2	220	Alabama
Darling, Bernard (Boob)	C	6-3	216	Beloit
Dilweg, LaVern (Lavvie)	E	6-3	202	Marquette
Dunn, Joseph (Red)	B	6-0	178	Marquette
Earpe, Francis (Jug)	T	6-1	235	Monmouth
Engelmann, Wuert	B	6-2	191	South Dakota
Fitzgibbons, Paul	B	5-10	174	Creighton
Franta, Herb	T	6-0	220	St. Thomas (MN)
Hanny, Frank	T	6-0	200	Indiana
Haycraft, Ken	E	5-11	190	Minnesota
Herber, Arnie	B	5-11	208	Regis
Hubbard, Robert (Cal)	T	6-5	250	Geneva
Kern, William	T	6-0	187	Pittsburgh
Lewellen, Verne	B	6-2	181	Nebraska
Lidberg, Carl (Cully)	B	6-0	200	Minnesota
McCrary, Hurdis	B	6-2	205	Georgia
McNally (Blood), Johnny	B	6-0	190	St. John's
Michalske, August (Mike)	G	6-1	215	Penn State
Molenda, Bo	B	5-11	208	Michigan
Nash, Tom	E	6-3	210	Georgia
O'Donnell, Dick	E	5-10	196	Minnesota
Pape, Orrin	B	6-0	205	Iowa
Perry, Claude	T	6-1	211	Alabama
Radick, Ken	E	6-0	210	Marquette
Sleight, Elmer (Red)	T	6-2	228	Purdue
Woodin, Howard (Whitey)	G	5-11	206	Marquette
Zuidmulder, Dave	B	6-1	184	St. Ambrose
Zuver, Merle	C	6-2	198	Nebraska

1931

Once again, Coach Curly Lambeau refused to stand pat after a championship. He sent nine veterans packing and added 13 new bodies. He fine-tuned the line by adding former Giants Rudy Comstock and Dick Stahlman prior to opening day and center Nate Barrager from Frankford in late October after an injury to Verne Lewellen. Rookies of note included Hank Bruder, Roger Grove and Milt Gantenbein. Offensively, the Packers of 1931 hit a peak. The team scored 291 points and 44 touchdowns. The touchdown total would not be broken until the 1961 team scored 49.

Chances for a third straight championship appeared good when Green Bay roared out of the gate with nine consecutive wins. But the road to three-in-a-row was not without controversy. A 7-6 loss to the Bears on December 6 gave the Packers a 12-2 record, a game ahead of Portsmouth which sported an 11-3 mark. The two teams had not met during the year. The Spartans, however, claimed the Packers owed them a game on December 13 in Portsmouth. Green Bay refused to play, pointing out that the contest was penciled in only after the league schedule had been determined. Therefore, the game was not official and the Packers had no reason to honor the date. League president Joe Carr concurred and the Packers were assured of another title.

After outscoring Cleveland and Brooklyn 58-6 to start the year, the Packers ran into three tough foes: the Bears, Giants, and Cardinals. Verne Lewellen's run beat the Bears 7-0 and his two scores a week later helped set back the Giants 27-7. Green Bay then disposed of the Cardinals 26-7 behind Johnny (Blood) McNally's 18 points and improved to 5-0 with Portsmouth (4-0) keeping pace.

Green Bay continued to roll, downing Frankford 15-0 and then trouncing Providence 48-20. Wuert Engelmann scored 18 points, six on a kickoff return in the Steam Roller game. Mike Michalske then returned an interception for a touchdown as the Packers downed the Bears 6-2. The team recorded its ninth straight win by blanking Stapleton 26-0. Meanwhile, Portsmouth had dropped two and was now 8-2.

The Packers' two losses came in their final five games. As he had done last year, Ernie Nevers of the Cardinals turned in a brilliant performance against Green Bay, throwing for two scores and kicking three extra points. His team handed the Packers a 21-13 loss. The Bears then edged Green Bay 7-6 on the final weekend of play.

Though the Packers did not play Portsmouth in 1931, the Spartans did not fade from the scene. They would beat the Packers once in 1932 and again in 1933 before a move to Detroit gave them two opportunities a year to harass Green Bay, not as the Spartans, but as the Lions.

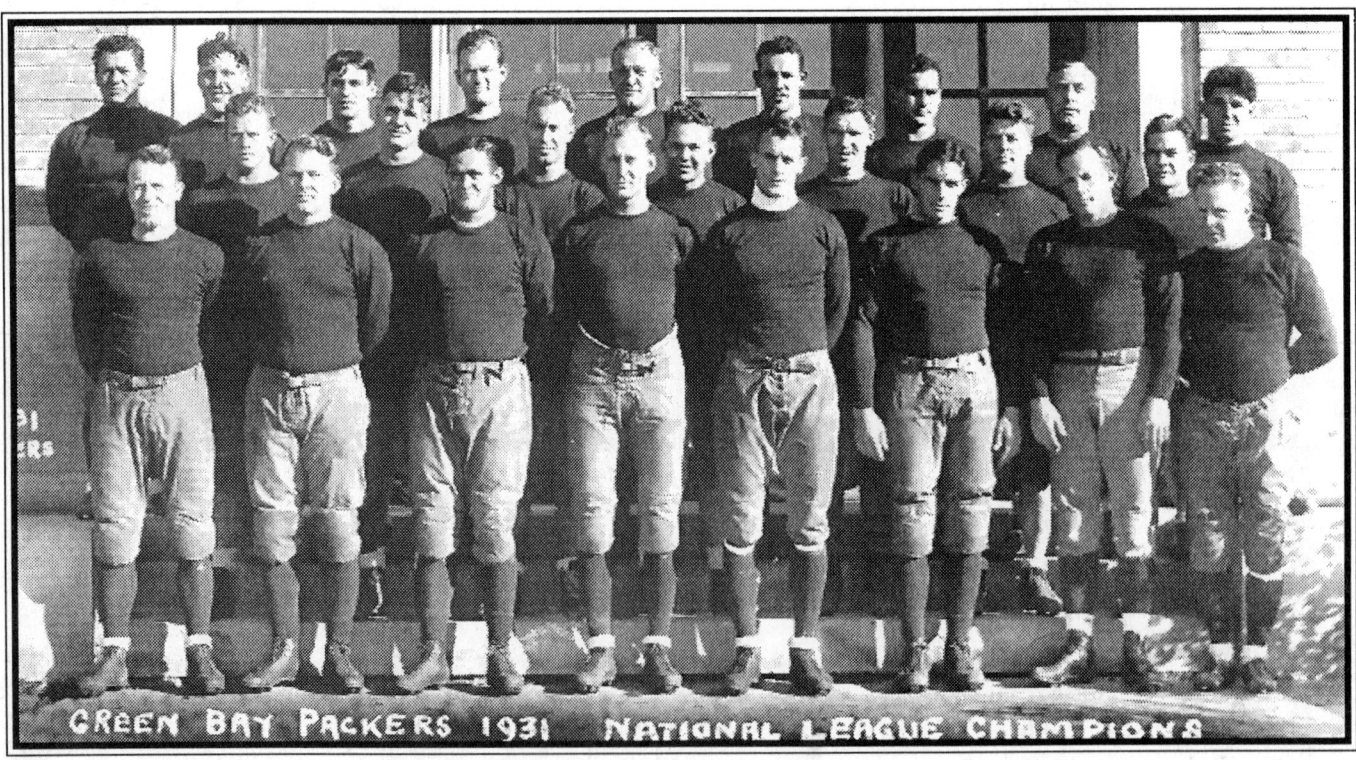

Stiller photo

FRONT ROW: (L-R) Joseph (Red) Dunn, Nate Barrager, James Bowdoin, Wuert Engelmann, LaVern (Lavvie) Dilweg, August (Mike) Michalske, Faye (Mule) Wilson, Paul Fitzgibbons.
MIDDLE ROW: (L-R) Roger Grove, Waldo DonCarlos, Hank Bruder, Milt Gantenbein, Bo Molenda, Rudy Comstock, Russell Saunders.
BACK ROW: (L-R) Curly Lambeau, Dick Stahlman, Johnny (Blood) McNally, Elmer (Red) Sleight, Robert (Cal) Hubbard, Tom Nash, Hurdis McCrary, Francis (Jug) Earpe, Arnie Herber.

TEAM STATISTICS

Regular Season 12-2-0

Date	GB		OPP
9/13	26	Cleveland Indians	0
9/20	32	Brooklyn Dodgers	6
9/27	7	Chicago Bears	0
10/4	27	New York Giants	7
10/11	26	Chicago Cardinals	7
10/18	15	Frankford Yellow Jackets	0
10/25	48	Providence Steam Roller	20
11/1	6	at Chicago Bears	2
11/8	26	Staten Island Stapletons	0
11/15	13	at Chicago Cardinals	21
11/22	14	at New York Giants	10
11/26	38	at Providence Steam Roller	7
11/29	7	at Brooklyn Dodgers	0
12/6	6	at Chicago Bears	7

Score By Periods

	1	2	3	4	Total
Packers	78	87	47	79	291
Opponents	28	24	22	13	87

1931

INDIVIDUAL STATISTICS

Touchdown Passes

	No
Dunn	8
Fitzgibbons	4
Molenda	4
Grove	2
Bruder	1
Saunders	1
F. Wilson	1
Packers	**21**
Opponents	7

Scoring

	TDr	TDp	TDrt	PAT	FG	S	TP
Blood	2	10	1	0	0	0	78
Lewellen	6	0	0	0	0	0	36
L. Dilweg	0	4	0	1	0	0	25
Engelmann	1	2	1	0	0	0	24
Molenda	3	0	0	3	0	0	21
Bruder	1	2	0	0	0	0	18
Dunn	0	0	0	15	0	0	15
F. Wilson	2	0	0	0	0	0	12
Woodin	0	0	1	3	0	0	9
Grove	0	1	0	2	0	0	8
F. Baker	0	1	0	0	0	0	6
Herber	1	0	0	0	0	0	6
Gantenbein	0	1	0	0	0	0	6
McCrary	1	0	0	0	0	0	6
Michalske	0	0	1	0	0	0	6
Nash	0	0	1	0	0	0	6
Saunders	1	0	0	0	0	0	6
team	0	0	0	0	0	1	2
Fitzgibbons	0	0	0	1	0	0	1
Packers	**18**	**21**	**5**	**25**	**0**	**1**	**291**
Opponents	4	7	1	10	1	1	87

NFL STANDINGS

	W	L	T	Pct
Green Bay Packers	12	2	0	.857
Portsmouth Spartans	11	3	0	.786
Chicago Bears	8	5	0	.615
Chicago Cardinals	5	4	0	.556
New York Giants	7	6	1	.538
Providence Steam Roller	4	4	3	.500
Staten Island Stapletons	4	6	1	.400
Cleveland Indians	2	8	0	.200
Brooklyn Dodgers	2	12	0	.143
Frankford Yellow Jackets	1	6	1	.143

ROSTER

Name	Pos	Ht	Wt	College
Baker, Frank	E	6-2	182	Northwestern
Barrager, Nate	C	6-0	210	USC
Bowdoin, James	G	6-2	220	Alabama
Bruder, Hank	B	6-0	190	Northwestern
Comstock, Rudy	G	5-11	198	Georgetown
Darling, Bernard (Boob)	C	6-3	216	Beloit
Davenport, Wayne	B		185	Hardin-Simmons
Dilweg, LaVern (Lavvie)	E	6-3	202	Marquette
DonCarlos, Waldo	C	6-2	190	Drake
Dunn, Joseph (Red)	B	6-0	178	Marquette
Earpe, Francis (Jug)	T	6-1	235	Monmouth
Engelmann, Wuert	B	6-2	191	South Dakota
Fitzgibbons, Paul	B	5-10	174	Creighton
Gantenbein, Milt	E	6-0	199	Wisconsin
Grove, Roger	B	6-0	175	Michigan State
Herber, Arnie	B	5-11	208	Regis
Hubbard, Robert (Cal)	T	6-5	250	Geneva
Jenison, Ray	T	6-2	220	South Dakota
Johnston, Chester (Swede)	B	5-10	200	Marquette
Lewellen, Verne	B	6-2	181	Nebraska
McCrary, Hurdis	B	6-2	205	Georgia
McNally (Blood), Johnny	B	6-0	190	St. John's
Michalske, August (Mike)	G	6-1	215	Penn State
Molenda, Bo	B	5-11	208	Michigan
Nash, Tom	E	6-3	210	Georgia
Perry, Claude	T	6-1	211	Alabama
Radick, Ken	E	6-0	210	Marquette
Saunders, Russell	B	5-10	175	USC
Sleight, Elmer (Red)	T	6-2	228	Purdue
Stahlman, Dick	T	6-3	221	Chicago
Wilson, Faye (Mule)	B	5-11	190	Texas A&M
Woodin, Howard (Whitey)	G	5-11	206	Marquette
Zuidmulder, Dave	B	6-1	184	St. Ambrose

Of the three losses incurred in 1932, the two costliest occurred on successive weekends in early December. Prior to the last month of the year, Green Bay was caught up in a three-way battle with the Portsmouth Spartans and the Chicago Bears. The Packers were 11-1-1 at the end of the November, while Portsmouth and Chicago were 5-1-4 and 4-1-6, respectively. Little matter that Green Bay had won more games than both teams combined. Portsmouth and Chicago had just one loss each which made the upcoming fortnight critical.

On December 4, Green Bay faced the Spartans in Portsmouth. Arnie Herber, the NFL's leading quarterback, tried unsuccessfully to mount a passing attack. He managed just one completion in better than a dozen tries and was intercepted three times. The Spartans jumped to a 13-0 lead and eventually won 19-0. The Bears also won that week, downing the Giants 6-0 and sending Green Bay into third place. Even so, the Packers could force a playoff with the Spartans, whose season had ended, if they could first get by the Bears.

The two met in Chicago in a snowstorm on December 11. The Packers blew two potential scoring opportunities in the second quarter. First, Herber fumbled away the ball at the Bear one-yard line. Then, on the team's next possession, Herber reached the Bears' eight-yard line only to have his gain negated by an offside penalty. The Packers went backwards after that and eventually Chicago wore them down, scoring nine fourth-quarter points to win 9-0.

The Bears (6-1-6) went on to defeat the Spartans (6-1-4) in a playoff on December 18 to secure the championship and deny the Packers a chance for a fourth straight crown. The game counted in the standings and the Spartans' loss moved Green Bay (10-3-1) into second place.

Green Bay's backfield underwent change. Joseph (Red) Dunn retired after 1931 and Bo Molenda was traded to New York after the second week in 1932. Roger Grove and Hank Bruder gained more playing time which relegated Verne Lewellen and Hurdis McCrary to backup roles. Only Johnny (Blood) McNally of the championship years still played on a regular basis. Perhaps the biggest change was the addition of Clarke Hinkle, a rough-and-tumble fullback from Bucknell. Hinkle would go on to spar with some of the greatest talents the game had to offer over the next 10 years, but his greatest individual battles would occur in clashes with Bronko Nagurski of the Chicago Bears.

Though the end of the season was not to the Packers' liking, the team did start impressively. Green Bay won eight of its first nine games and, after defeating Boston on November 13, was in sole possession of first place with an 8-0-1 record. Green Bay suffered its first loss in week 10 as the Giants beat them 6-0. The team bounced back with wins over Brooklyn and Staten Island but, unfortunately the Packers couldn't duplicate their early-season success in December and had to settle for second place.

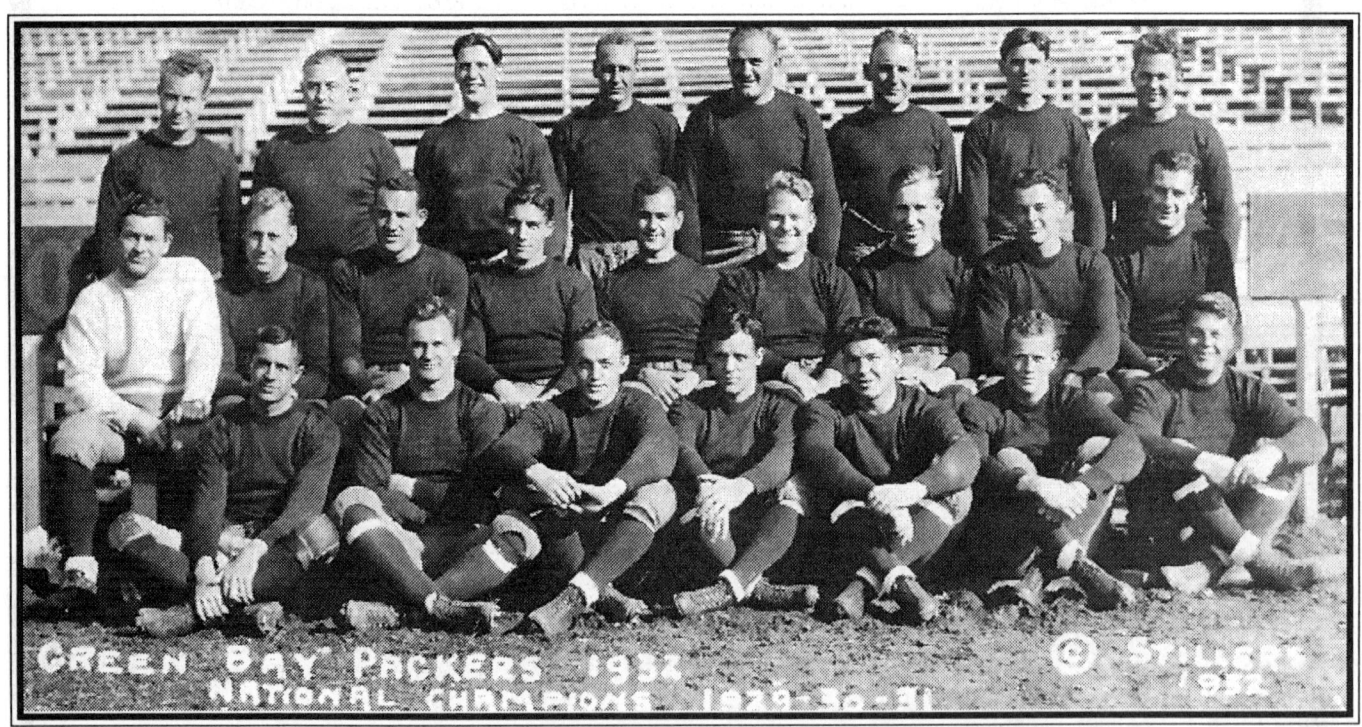

Stiller photo

FRONT ROW: (L-R) Verne Lewellen, Joe Zeller, Clarke Hinkle, Harry O'Boyle, Arnie Herber, Roger Grove, Rudy Comstock.
MIDDLE ROW: (L-R) Coach Curly Lambeau, Wuert Engelmann, Tom Nash, August (Mike) Michalske, Hurdis McCrary, Nate Barrager, Arthur (Red) Bultman, Lester Peterson, LaVern (Lavvie) Dilweg.
BACK ROW: (L-R) Hank Bruder, Francis (Jug) Earpe, Dick Stahlman, Al Rose, Robert (Cal) Hubbard, Claude Perry, Johnny (Blood) McNally, Milt Gantenbein.

TEAM STATISTICS

NFL STANDINGS

Regular Season 10-3-1

Date	GB		OPP
9/18	15	Chicago Cardinals	7
9/25	0	Chicago Bears	0
10/2	13	New York Giants	0
10/9	15	Portsmouth Spartans	10
10/16	2	at Chicago Bears	0
10/23	13	Brooklyn Dodgers	0
10/30	26	Staten Island Stapletons	0
11/6	19	at Chicago Cardinals	9
11/13	21	at Boston Braves	0
11/20	0	at New York Giants	6
11/24	7	at Brooklyn Dodgers	0
11/27	21	at Staten Island Stapletons	3
12/4	0	at Portsmouth Spartans	19
12/11	0	at Chicago Bears	9

Score By Periods

	1	2	3	4	Total
Packers	36	35	34	47	152
Opponents	7	22	10	24	63

INDIVIDUAL STATISTICS

Rushing

	Att	Yds	Avg	TD
Hinkle	95	331	3.5	3
Blood	27	130	4.8	0

Receiving

	No	Yds	Avg	TD
Blood	14	168	12.0	3

Passing

	Att	Com	Yds	Pct	TD	In	Rate
Herber	101	37	639	36.6	9	9	51.5

Scoring

	TDr	TDp	TDrt	PAT	FG	S	TP
Blood	0	3	1	0	0	0	24
Bruder	2	2	0	0	0	0	24
Grove	0	3	0	4	0	0	22
Hinkle	3	0	0	1	0	0	19
Herber	1	0	1	0	0	0	12
A. Rose	0	0	2	0	0	0	12
O'Boyle	0	0	0	8	0	0	8
Engelmann	0	0	1	0	0	0	6
Lewellen	0	1	0	0	0	0	6
McCrary	1	0	0	0	0	0	6
Michalske	0	0	1	0	0	0	6
Nash	0	0	0	0	0	2	4
team	0	0	0	0	0	1	2
L. Dilweg	0	0	0	1	0	0	1
Packers	7	9	6	14	0	3	152
Opponents	4	3	1	4	3	1	63

ROSTER

Name	Pos	Ht	Wt	College
Apsit, Marger	B	5-11	202	USC
Barrager, Nate	C	6-0	210	USC
Bruder, Hank	B	6-0	190	Northwestern
Bultman, Arthur (Red)	C	6-2	199	Marquette
Comstock, Rudy	G	5-11	198	Georgetown
Culver, Al	T	6-2	212	Notre Dame
Dilweg, LaVern (Lavvie)	E	6-3	202	Marquette
Earpe, Francis (Jug)	T	6-1	235	Monmouth
Engelmann, Wuert	B	6-2	191	South Dakota
Fitzgibbons, Paul	B	5-10	174	Creighton
Gantenbein, Milt	E	6-0	199	Wisconsin
Grove, Roger	B	6-0	175	Michigan State
Herber, Arnie	B	5-11	208	Regis
Hinkle, Clarke	FB	5-11	200	Bucknell
Hubbard, Robert (Cal)	T	6-5	250	Geneva
Lewellen, Verne	B	6-2	181	Nebraska
McCrary, Hurdis	B	6-2	205	Georgia
McNally (Blood), Johnny	B	6-0	190	St. John's
Michalske, August (Mike)	G	6-1	215	Penn State
Molenda, Bo	B	5-11	208	Michigan
Nash, Tom	E	6-3	210	Georgia
O'Boyle, Harry	B	5-9	180	Notre Dame
Perry, Claude	T	6-1	211	Alabama
Peterson, Lester	E	6-2	195	Texas
Rose, Al	E	6-3	195	Texas
Shelly, Dexter	B	5-11	192	Texas
Stahlman, Dick	T	6-3	221	Chicago
Van Sickle, Clyde	C	6-2	224	Arkansas
Zeller, Joe	G	6-1	198	Indiana

1933

In its first 12 seasons, Green Bay had never come away with more losses than wins. The Packers experienced their first losing season in 1933 and so disliked the taste, they waited 15 years before stumbling through another. The Packers weren't a bad team; they just could not beat the top teams as they had over the last four years. Five of the team's seven losses came courtesy of the Bears and Giants, who won their respective divisions. Boston and Portsmouth provided the other setbacks.

Green Bay's troubles involved more than wins and losses. The Packers had lost money in 1931 and 1932. In addition, a fan had fallen from a set of bleachers during the second game of 1931 and sued for $25,000. In 1933, he won a $5,200 judgement. To make matters worse, the Packers' insurance company had gone bankrupt in the interim and refused to pay the claim. Lee Joannes stepped in and loaned the Green Bay Packer Football Corporation $6,000, enough to pay its debts and allow play to continue into 1933.

Changes were made by both the team and the league. The NFL split into a Western and Eastern division for the first time. It would play in this format through 1966 after which the league realigned itself again. As for the Packers, they lost two key contributors who were getting up in years. Verne Lewellen and Francis (Jug) Earpe retired after successful careers. Coach Curly Lambeau added guard Lon Evans, fullback Charles (Buckets) Goldenberg and halfback Bob Monnett in an attempt to replace the departed men.

The Packers also made a historic decision concerning home games. For the first time, the team played a home game at State Fair Park in Milwaukee. A year later, the team was playing two there. Milwaukee, which had seen its Badgers go under after the 1926 season, now backed the Packers, strengthening the notion that the Packers were a state team.

Green Bay opened 1933 much like it had 1928. After tying Boston 7-7 in the opener, the Packers hosted the Bears. Green Bay led 7-0 going into the final period, but gave up a 40-yard touchdown pass and another score after Bill Hewitt blocked Arnie Herber's punt. Chicago won 14-7. The Giants then beat the Packers 10-7, dropping the team to 0-2-1 and last place.

Green Bay rallied to avoid the cellar but was never able to win more than two games in a row. A particularly rough stretch saw the Packers lose three in a row in mid-to-late November.

The Bears made sure the Packers went home with more losses than wins. Gene Ronzani, future Packers head coach, scored on a 23-yard pass from Keith Molesworth to give the Bears a 7-0 lead. Monnett then returned a punt 88 yards for a touchdown but Joe Zeller, last of the Packers in 1932, blocked Roger Grove's placekick and Green Bay fell 7-6 to close out a 5-7-1 season.

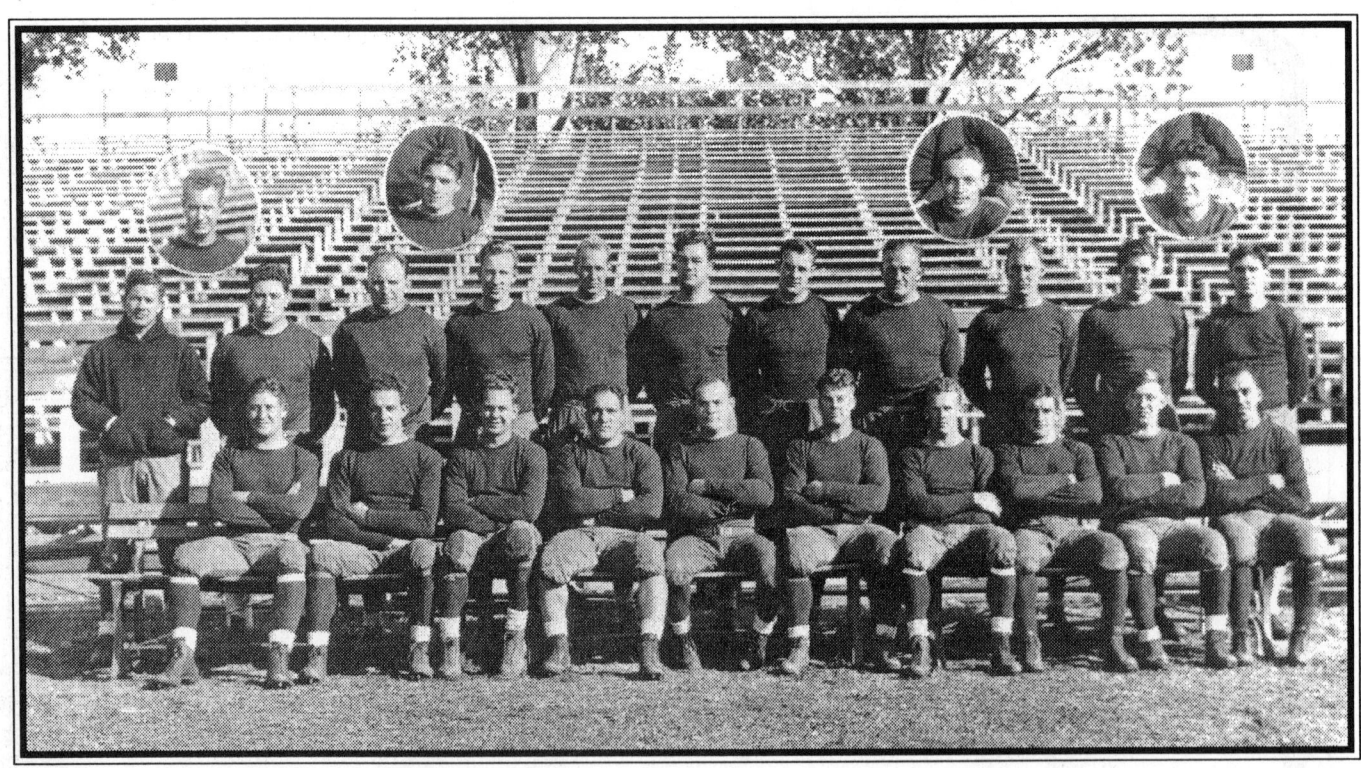

Stiller photo

INSETS: (L-R) Hank Bruder, August (Mike) Michalske, Clarke Hinkle, Arnie Herber.
FRONT ROW: (L-R) Lon Evans, Joe Kurth, Milt Gantenbein, Charles (Buckets) Goldenberg, Clyde Van Sickle, Rudy Comstock, Roger Grove, Bob Monnett, Norm Greeney, Larry Bettencourt.
BACK ROW: (L-R) Coach Curly Lambeau, Jess Quatse, Claude Perry, Arthur (Red) Bultman, Al Rose, Ben Smith, LaVern (Lavvie) Dilweg, Robert (Cal) Hubbard, Wuert Engelmann, Al Sarafiny, Johnny (Blood) McNally.

TEAM STATISTICS

	GB	OPP
Rushes	487	443
Yards Gained	1,513	1,226
Average Gain	3.11	2.77
Average Yards per Game	116.4	94.3
Passes Attempted	209	179
Completed	89	48
% Completed	42.58	26.82
Total Yards Gained	1,186	711
Yards Gained per Completion	13.33	14.81
Average Yards per Game	91.2	54.7
Laterals Attempted	9	7
Completed	3	6
Yards Gained	3	-8
Combined Yards Gained	2,702	1,929
Total Plays	705	629
Average Yards per Play	3.83	3.07
Average Yards per Game	207.8	148.4
Intercepted By	31	18
Total Points Scored	170	107
Total Touchdowns	24	14
Touchdowns Rushing	13	4
Touchdowns Passing	7	7
Touchdowns on Returns & Recoveries	4	3
Extra Points	20	12
Safeties	0	1
Field Goals Made	2	3

Regular Season 5-7-1

Date	GB		OPP
9/17	7	Boston Redskins	7
9/24	7	Chicago Bears	14
10/1	7	New York Giants (M)	10
10/8	17	Portsmouth Spartans	0
10/15	47	Pittsburgh Pirates	0
10/22	7	at Chicago Bears	10
10/29	35	Philadelphia Eagles	9
11/5	14	at Chicago Cardinals	6
11/12	0	at Portsmouth Spartans	7
11/19	7	at Boston Redskins	20
11/26	6	at New York Giants	17
12/3	10	at Philadelphia Eagles	0
12/10	6	at Chicago Bears	7

1933

Score By Periods

	1	2	3	4	Total
Packers	28	30	44	68	170
Opponents	10	27	32	38	107

INDIVIDUAL STATISTICS

Rushing

	Att	Yds	Avg	TD
Monnett	108	413	3.8	3
Hinkle	139	413	3.0	3
Bruder	77	250	3.2	3
Goldenberg	52	213	4.1	4
Engelmann	23	79	3.4	0
Herber	62	77	1.2	0
Blood	14	41	2.9	0
Mott	5	13	2.6	0
McCrary	6	10	1.7	0
Grove	1	4	4.0	0
Packers	487	1,513	3.1	13
Opponents	443	1,226	2.8	4

Receiving

	No	Yds	Avg	LG	TD
Grove	18	215	11.9		0
L. Dilweg	17	225	13.2		0
Blood	10	215	21.5	t38	3
Gantenbein	8	144	18.0		1
A. Rose	7	89	12.7		1
Monnett	6	44	7.3		0
Hinkle	6	38	6.3		0
Bruder	4	69	17.3	40	0
Engelmann	4	54	13.5	23	1
Goldenberg	4	43	10.8	18	1
Herber	3	27	9.0	25	0
Ben Smith	2	23	11.5	13	0
Packers	89	1,186	13.3		7
Opponents	48	711	14.8	t40	7

Passing

	Att	Com	Yds	Pct	TD	In	Rate
Herber	124	50	656	40.3	4	12	28.9
Monnett	46	23	325	50.0	3	3	67.8
Hinkle	27	12	147	44.4	0	3	22.2
Bruder	7	3	14	42.9	0	0	—
Grove	3	1	44	33.3	0	0	—
Blood	2	0	0	00.0	0	0	—
Packers	209	89	1,186	42.6	7	18	36.5
Opponents	179	48	711	26.8	7	31	17.1

Scoring

	TDr	TDp	TDrt	PAT	FG	S	TP
Goldenberg	4	1	2	0	0	0	42
Monnett	3	0	1	10	0	0	34
Hinkle	3	0	0	0	2	0	24
Blood	0	3	0	1	0	0	19
Bruder	3	0	0	0	0	0	18
Engelmann	0	1	1	0	0	0	12
Grove	0	0	0	8	0	0	8
Gantenbein	0	1	0	0	0	0	6
A. Rose	0	1	0	0	0	0	6
Herber	0	0	0	1	0	0	1
Packers	13	7	4	20	2	0	170
Opponents	4	7	3	12	3	1	107

NFL STANDINGS

Western Division

	W	L	T	Pct	PF	PA
Chicago Bears	10	2	1	.833	133	82
Portsmouth Spartans	6	5	0	.545	128	87
Green Bay Packers	5	7	1	.417	170	107
Cincinnati Reds	3	6	1	.333	38	110
Chicago Cardinals	1	9	1	.100	52	101

Eastern Division

	W	L	T	Pct	PF	PA
New York Giants	11	3	0	.786	244	101
Brooklyn Dodgers	5	4	1	.556	93	54
Boston Redskins	5	5	2	.500	103	57
Philadelphia Eagles	3	5	1	.375	77	158
Pittsburgh Pirates	3	6	2	.333	67	208

ROSTER

Name	Pos	Ht	Wt	College
Bettencourt, Larry	C	6-3	215	St. Mary's (CA)
Bruder, Hank	B	6-0	190	Northwestern
Bultman, Arthur (Red)	C	6-2	199	Marquette
Comstock, Rudy	G	5-11	198	Georgetown
Dilweg, LaVern (Lavvie)	E	6-3	202	Marquette
Engelmann, Wuert	B	6-2	191	South Dakota
Evans, Lon	G	6-2	225	TCU
Gantenbein, Milt	E	6-0	199	Wisconsin
Goldenberg, Charles (Buckets)	B	5-10	220	Wisconsin
Greeney, Norm	G	6-0	215	Notre Dame
Grove, Roger	B	6-0	175	Michigan State
Herber, Arnie	B	5-11	208	Regis
Hinkle, Clarke	FB	5-11	200	Bucknell
Hubbard, Robert (Cal)	T	6-5	250	Geneva
Kurth, Joe	T	6-3	202	Notre Dame
McCrary, Hurdis	B	6-2	205	Georgia
McNally (Blood), Johnny	B	6-0	190	St. John's
Michalske, August (Mike)	G	6-1	215	Penn State
Monnett, Bob	B	5-9	180	Michigan State
Mott, Norm (Buster)	B	5-11	190	Georgia
Perry, Claude	T	6-1	211	Alabama
Quatse, Jess	T	5-11	230	Pittsburgh
Rose, Al	E	6-3	195	Texas
Sarafiny, Al	C	6-3	240	St. Edward's
Smith, Ben	E	6-0	200	Alabama
Van Sickle, Clyde	C	6-2	224	Arkansas

1934

Green Bay continued its post-championship slump, but did make a slight improvement from 1933. The Packers were able to beat up on winless teams such as the Cincinnati Reds, a team so inept it changed its name and became the St. Louis Gunners for the last three games of the year. The Packers defeated that sorry version also (21-14) on the final weekend of play. But Green Bay couldn't handle the teams from Chicago and lost twice to both the Bears and Cardinals to finish with a 7-6 mark.

The Packers did score two big upsets, evidence that the team was on its way back. The first came in late September. The Packers were coming off a 24-10 loss to the Bears who fashioned a spectacular 13-0 record before losing 30-13 to the Giants in the NFL championship game. The Packers faced those same New Yorkers on September 30. Clarke Hinkle keyed a running attack that produced 163 yards. Bob Monnett kicked two field goals and Roger Grove and Charles (Buckets) Goldenberg ran for scores as the Packers triumphed 20-6 and improved to 2-1.

The second upset may have been even bigger. By the time Green Bay traveled to Detroit on November 25, the unbeaten Lions had ripped through 10 opponents, shutting out the first seven and outscoring all ten, 215-27. The Packers and Lions battled to a standstill for three quarters. Then, just after the fourth quarter opened, Hinkle kicked a 47-yard field goal. That score proved the difference as Green Bay held on for a 3-0 win.

Coach Curly Lambeau continued to bring in new talent. He signed rookies Joe Laws and Champ Seibold from Iowa and Wisconsin, respectively. Later in the year, he acquired Paul (Tiny) Engebretsen from Brooklyn, which made the retirement of Robert (Cal) Hubbard at season's start a little easier to take. Lambeau's penchant for making roster moves meant that only five members of the 1931 championship team would play a part in the 1936 drive to the title: Johnny (Blood) McNally, Hank Bruder, Milt Gantenbein, Arnie Herber and Chester (Swede) Johnston.

After Monnett's 16 points helped down Philadelphia 19-6, Bronko Nagurski made sure the Packers didn't win two in a row. He rushed for 90 yards and two scores in the Bears' 24-10 win. In the second Chicago go-round, the Packers ran into Beattie Feathers, the NFL's first 1,000 yard rusher. Feathers gained 155 yards and scored twice as the Bears pounded Green Bay 27-14. Three weeks later, the Cardinals handed the Packers their fifth loss, leaving the team at 5-5, too far back to challenge.

Stiller photo

FRONT ROW: (L-R) Bob Monnett, Milt Gantenbein, Nate Barrager, Clarke Hinkle, Roger Grove.
MIDDLE ROW: (L-R) Coach Curly Lambeau, Al Norgard, Lon Evans, Joe Laws, Arnie Herber, August (Mike) Michalske, Charles (Buckets) Goldenberg, Hank Bruder, Ade Schwammel, Claude Perry, Francis (Jug) Earpe.
BACK ROW: (L-R) Frank Butler, Arthur (Red) Bultman, Joe Kurth, LaVern (Lavvie) Dilweg, Carl Jorgensen, Champ Seibold, Lester Peterson, Robert Jones, Earl Witte.

TEAM STATISTICS

	GB	OPP
Rushes	456	517
Yards Gained	1,183	1,564
Average Gain	2.59	3.03
Average Yards per Game	91.0	120.3
Passes Attempted	197	173
Completed	74	56
% Completed	37.56	32.37
Total Yards Gained	1,165	676
Yards Gained per Completion	15.74	12.07
Average Yards per Game	89.6	52.0
Laterals Attempted	1	9
Completed	1	9
Yards Gained	-8	94
Combined Yards Gained	2,340	2,334
Total Plays	654	699
Average Yards per Play	3.58	3.34
Average Yards per Game	180.0	179.5
Intercepted By	25	19
Total Points Scored	156	112
Total Touchdowns	19	14
Touchdowns Rushing	8	8
Touchdowns Passing	10	3
Touchdowns on Returns & Recoveries	1	3
Extra Points	16	10
Safeties	1	0
Field Goals Made	8	6

Regular Season 7-6-0

Date	GB		OPP
9/16	19	Philadelphia Eagles	6
9/23	10	Chicago Bears	24
9/30	20	New York Giants (M)	6
10/7	0	Detroit Lions	3
10/14	41	Cincinnati Reds	0
10/21	15	Chicago Cardinals	0
10/28	14	at Chicago Bears	27
11/4	10	at Boston Redskins	0
11/11	3	at New York Giants	17
11/18	3	Chicago Cardinals (M)	9
11/25	3	at Detroit Lions	0
11/29	0	at Chicago Cardinals	6
12/2	21	at St. Louis Gunners	14

1934

Score By Periods

	1	2	3	4	Total
Packers	27	43	33	53	156
Opponents	19	6	47	40	112

INDIVIDUAL STATISTICS

Rushing

	Att	Yds	Avg	TD
Hinkle	144	359	2.5	1
Grove	62	262	4.2	1
Laws	46	155	3.4	1
Monnett	68	129	1.9	2
Bruder	48	106	2.2	1
Goldenberg	30	73	2.4	2
Herber	37	33	0.9	0
Johnston	7	23	3.3	0
Witte	8	22	2.8	0
Casper	4	19	4.8	0
Perry	1	2	2.0	0
L. Peterson	1	0	0.0	0
Packers	456	1,183	2.6	8
Opponents	517	1,564	3.0	8

Receiving

	No	Yds	Avg	LG	TD
Hinkle	12	113	9.4	t69	1
Gantenbein	11	155	14.1		0
Laws	9	165	18.3	61	1
L. Peterson	8	139	17.4		0
Bruder	7	104	14.9		1
Grove	6	125	20.8	37	3
A. Rose	6	117	19.5	36	2
L. Dilweg	5	135	27.0	39	2
Goldenberg	4	26	6.5	9	0
Norgard	3	29	9.7	22	0
Monnett	2	27	13.5	26	0
Unaccounted for	1	30	30.0	30	0
Packers	74	1,165	15.7	t69	10
Opponents	56	676	12.1	35	3

Passing

	Att	Com	Yds	Pct	TD	In	Rate
Herber	115	42	799	36.5	8	12	45.1
Monnett	43	16	223	37.2	2	4	31.4
Hinkle	19	9	87	47.4	0	2	21.1
Grove	10	5	34	50.0	0	0	57.9
Bruder	6	2	22	33.3	0	1	—
Blood	4	0	0	00.0	0	1	—
Packers	197	74	1,165	37.6	10	19	35.4
Opponents	173	56	676	32.4	3	25	11.5

Scoring

	TDr	TDp	TDrt	PAT	FG	S	TP
Monnett	2	0	0	6	4	0	30
Hinkle	1	1	0	5	3	0	26
Grove	1	3	0	1	0	0	25
Bruder	1	1	1	4	0	0	22
L. Dilweg	0	2	0	0	0	0	12
Goldenberg	2	0	0	0	0	0	12
Laws	1	1	0	0	0	0	12
A. Rose	0	2	0	0	0	0	12
Schwammel	0	0	0	0	1	0	3
team	0	0	0	0	0	1	2
Packers	8	10	1	16	8	1	156
Opponents	8	3	3	10	6	0	112

NFL STANDINGS

Western Division

	W	L	T	Pct	PF	PA
Chicago Bears	13	0	0	1.000	286	86
Detroit Lions	10	3	0	.769	238	59
Green Bay Packers	7	6	0	.538	156	112
Chicago Cardinals	5	6	0	.455	80	84
St. Louis Gunners	1	2	0	.333	27	61
Cincinnati Reds	0	8	0	.000	10	243

Eastern Division

	W	L	T	Pct	PF	PA
New York Giants	8	5	0	.615	147	107
Boston Redskins	6	6	0	.500	107	94
Brooklyn Dodgers	4	7	0	.364	61	153
Philadelphia Eagles	4	7	0	.364	127	85
Pittsburgh Pirates	2	10	0	.167	51	206

ROSTER

Name	Pos	Ht	Wt	College
Barrager, Nate	C	6-0	210	USC
Bruder, Hank	B	6-0	190	Northwestern
Bultman, Arthur (Red)	C	6-2	199	Marquette
Butler, Frank	C	6-3	246	Michigan State
Casper, Charles	B	6-0	195	TCU
Dilweg, LaVern (Lavvie)	E	6-3	202	Marquette
Engebretsen, Paul (Tiny)	G	6-1	235	Northwestern
Evans, Lon	G	6-2	225	TCU
Gantenbein, Milt	E	6-0	199	Wisconsin
Goldenberg, Charles (Buckets)	B	5-10	220	Wisconsin
Grove, Roger	B	6-0	175	Michigan State
Herber, Arnie	B	5-11	208	Regis
Hinkle, Clarke	FB	5-11	200	Bucknell
Johnston, Chester (Swede)	B	5-10	200	Marquette
Jones, Robert	G	6-0	216	Indiana
Jorgensen, Carl	T	6-2	200	St. Mary's (CA)
Kurth, Joe	T	6-3	202	Notre Dame
Laws, Joe	B	5-9	180	Iowa
Michalske, August (Mike)	G	6-1	215	Penn State
Monnett, Bob	B	5-9	180	Michigan State
Norgard, Al	E	6-0	193	Stanford
Perry, Claude	T	6-1	211	Alabama
Peterson, Lester	E	6-0	211	Texas
Rose, Al	E	6-3	195	Texas
Schwammel, Ade	T	6-2	230	Oregon State
Seibold, Champ	T	6-4	240	Wisconsin
Witte, Earl	B	6-1	187	Gustavus-Adolphus
Wunsch, Harry	G	5-11	210	Notre Dame

1935

1935 marked the professional debut of a 6-1, 185-pound end from Alabama. Though he played sparingly in the season opener against the Cardinals, his career really began with a bang on the second week when he gathered in his first pass and raced 83 yards to paydirt, a score which singlehandedly beat the Bears 7-0 and introduced Don Hutson to the National Football League. Before he retired, Hutson went on to catch another 98 touchdown passes, setting an NFL record that stood for 44 years.

The year also saw the Packers remain in contention for the Western Crown until week 11 when the Chicago Cardinals beat them for a third time, 9-7. The Cardinals eked out wins of one, two, and three points against the Packers and in doing so, completely ruined Green Bay's postseason hopes.

The Packers fared much better against the Lions and Giants, two teams that eventually met to decide the championship. Green Bay beat the Lions in two of three meetings and defeated the Giants 16-7 in week three. In addition, the Packers downed the Bears twice in 1935 to record their last sweep of the Monsters of the Midway until 1961.

For the first time since 1928, the Packers dropped a season opener, falling to the Cardinals 7-6 when Bob Monnett's second-quarter extra point drifted wide. Hutson's sensational catch followed and then in week three two interception returns for touchdowns helped the Packers past the Giants 16-7. Pittsburgh fell victim next (27-0) as Hutson registered the first individual 100-yard receiving performance in franchise history by catching four passes for 109 yards and two touchdowns.

After Paul Pardonner's 12-yard field goal beat Green Bay 3-0, the Packers won three straight. Those wins gave Green Bay a 6-2 mark and sole possession of first place. The Lions, however, finally figured out how to beat the Packers and did so 20-10 at the University of Detroit stadium. The loss was not fatal as the Packers (6-3) still owned the top spot over the Lions (5-3-1). The Cardinals, however, did provide the lethal blow two weeks later, pushing back Green Bay's title hopes for another year.

Lefebvre photo

FRONT ROW: (L-R) 33 August (Mike) Michalske, 36 Bob Tenner, 31 Nate Barrager, 50 Ade Schwammel, 43 George Svendsen, 46 Lon Evans, 25 George Sauer, 24 Bob O'Connor, 12 Bob Monnett, Trainer Dave Woodward.
MIDDLE ROW: (L-R) 44 Charles (Buckets) Goldenberg, 29 Joe Laws, 34 Paul (Tiny) Engebretsen, 30 Clarke Hinkle, 38 Arnie Herber, 11 Roger Grove, 27 Hank Bruder, 22 Milt Gantenbein, 4 Herm Schneidman, 15 Chester (Swede) Johnston.
BACK ROW: (L-R) Coach Curly Lambeau, 26 Johnny (Blood) McNally, 47 Al Rose, 48 Frank Butler, 52 Champ Seibold, 51 Robert (Cal) Hubbard, 49 Walt Kiesling, 32 Claude Perry, 14 Don Hutson, 45 Ernie Smith.

TEAM STATISTICS

	GB	OPP
First Downs	130	96
Rushes	447	448
Yards Gained	1,562	1,219
Average Gain	3.49	2.72
Average Yards per Game	130.2	101.6
Passes Attempted	230	191
Completed	93	61
% Completed	40.43	31.94
Total Yards Gained	1,449	837
Yards Gained per Completion	15.58	13.72
Average Yards per Game	120.8	69.8
Laterals Attempted	5	10
Completed	2	10
Yards Gained	10	35
Combined Yards Gained	3,021	2,091
Total Plays	682	649
Average Yards per Play	4.43	3.22
Average Yards per Game	251.8	174.3
Intercepted By	26	27
Yards Penalized	295	190
Fumbles	29	27
Recovered	21	24
Total Points Scored	181	96
Total Touchdowns	23	13
Touchdowns Rushing	7	5
Touchdowns Passing	11	7
Touchdowns on Returns & Recoveries	5	1
Extra Points	19	9
Safeties	0	0
Field Goals Made	8	3

Regular Season 8-4-0

Date	GB		OPP
9/15	6	Chicago Cardinals	7
9/22	7	Chicago Bears	0
9/29	16	New York Giants	7
10/6	27	Pittsburgh Pirates	0
10/13	0	Chicago Cardinals (M)	3
10/20	13	Detroit Lions (M)	9
10/27	17	at Chicago Bears	14
11/10	31	Detroit Lions	7
11/17	10	at Detroit Lions	20
11/24	34	at Pittsburgh Pirates	14
11/28	7	at Chicago Cardinals	9
12/8	13	at Philadelphia Eagles	6

1935

Score By Periods

	1	2	3	4	Total
Packers	26	53	37	65	181
Opponents	13	42	14	27	96

INDIVIDUAL STATISTICS

Rushing

	Att	Yds	Avg	TD
Monnett	68	336	4.9	1
Sauer	89	334	3.8	3
Hinkle	77	273	3.5	2
Johnston	52	176	3.4	0
Bruder	44	158	3.6	0
Blood	42	115	2.7	0
Laws	24	63	2.6	1
Goldenberg	15	52	3.5	0
Hutson	6	22	3.7	0
Grove	7	21	3.0	0
Schneidman	4	12	3.0	0
Herber	19	0	0.0	0
Packers	**447**	**1,562**	**3.5**	**7**
Opponents	448	1,219	2.7	5

Receiving

	No	Yds	Avg	LG	TD
Blood	25	404	16.2	t70	3
Hutson	18	420	23.3	t83	6
Gantenbein	13	168	12.9	—	1
A. Rose	8	91	11.4	—	0
Johnston	6	59	9.8	—	1
Laws	4	82	20.5	41	0
Bruder	4	67	16.8	30	0
Goldenberg	3	42	14.0	21	0
Tenner	3	38	12.7	29	0
Sauer	3	32	10.7	14	0
Herber	2	36	13.0	17	0
Schneidman	2	16	8.0	8	0
Monnett	1	8	8.0	8	0
Hinkle	1	-4	-4.0	-4	0
Packers	**93**	**1,449**	**15.6**	**t83**	**11**
Opponents	61	837	13.7	t44	7

Passing

	Att	Com	Yds	Pct	TD	In	Rate
Herber	106	40	729	37.7	8	14	47.8
Monnett	65	31	354	47.7	2	5	42.7
Sauer	21	9	177	42.9	1	5	49.2
Blood	33	11	164	33.3	0	3	12.7
Bruder	1	1	17	100.0	0	0	—
Laws	4	1	8	25.0	0	0	—
Packers	**230**	**93**	**1,449**	**40.4**	**11**	**27**	**38.4**
Opponents	191	61	837	31.9	7	26	19.6

Scoring

	TDr	TDp	TDrt	PAT	FG	S	TP
Hutson	0	6	1	1	0	0	43
Blood	0	3	1	0	0	0	24
Sauer	3	0	1	0	0	0	24
Hinkle	2	0	0	1	2	0	19
Schwammel	0	0	0	2	4	0	14
Ernie Smith	0	0	0	11	1	0	14
Monnett	1	0	0	2	1	0	11
Bruder	0	0	1	0	0	0	6
Gantenbein	0	1	0	0	0	0	6
Hubbard	0	0	1	0	0	0	6
Johnston	0	1	0	0	0	0	6
Laws	1	0	0	0	0	0	6
Engebretsen	0	0	0	1	0	0	1
Herber	0	0	0	1	0	0	1
Packers	**7**	**11**	**5**	**19**	**8**	**0**	**181**
Opponents	5	7	1	9	3	0	96

NFL STANDINGS

Western Division

	W	L	T	Pct	PF	PA
Detroit Lions	7	3	2	.700	191	111
Green Bay Packers	**8**	**4**	**0**	**.667**	**181**	**96**
Chicago Bears	6	4	2	.600	192	106
Chicago Cardinals	6	4	2	.600	99	97

Eastern Division

	W	L	T	Pct	PF	PA
New York Giants	9	3	0	.750	180	96
Brooklyn Dodgers	5	6	1	.455	90	141
Pittsburgh Pirates	4	8	0	.333	100	209
Boston Redskins	2	8	1	.200	65	123
Philadelphia Eagles	2	9	0	.182	60	179

ROSTER

No	Name	Pos	Ht	Wt	DOB	College
31	Barrager, Nate	C	6-0	210		USC
27	Bruder, Hank	B	6-0	197	11/22/07	Northwestern
48	Butler, Frank	C	6-3	230	05/03/09	Michigan State
34	Engebretsen, Paul (Tiny)	G	6-1	235	07/27/10	Northwestern
46	Evans, Lon	G	6-2	219	12/25/11	TCU
22	Gantenbein, Milt	E	6-0	193	05/31/10	Wisconsin
44	Goldenberg, Charles (Buckets)	G	5-10	215	03/10/11	Wisconsin
11	Grove, Roger	B	6-0	184	06/19/08	Michigan State
38	Herber, Arnie	B	5-11	203	04/02/10	Regis
30	Hinkle, Clarke	FB	5-11	205	04/10/12	Bucknell
51	Hubbard, Robert (Cal)	T	6-5	265	10/11/00	Geneva
14	Hutson, Don	E	6-1	189	01/31/13	Alabama
15	Johnston, Chester (Swede)	B	5-10	200	03/07/10	Marquette
49	Kiesling, Walt	G	6-3	260	05/27/03	St. Thomas (MN)
29	Laws, Joe	B	5-9	185	06/16/11	Iowa
28	Maddox, George (Buster)	T	6-3	240	11/04/11	Kansas State
42	McDonald, Dustin	G	5-4	202		Indiana
26	McNally (Blood), Johnny	B	6-0	190	11/27/03	St. John's
33	Michalske, August (Mike)	G	6-0	200	04/24/03	Penn State
3/12	Monnett, Bob	B	5-9	181	02/27/10	Michigan State
24	O'Connor, Bob	G	6-1	220	01/27/10	Stanford
32	Perry, Claude	T	6-1	211		Alabama
47	Rose, Al	E	6-3	195	01/26/07	Texas
25	Sauer, George	B	6-2	204	12/11/10	Nebraska
4	Schneidman, Herm	B	5-10	205	11/22/13	Iowa
33/50	Schwammel, Ade	T	6-2	230	10/14/08	Oregon State
37	Seibold, Champ	T	6-4	240	12/05/12	Wisconsin
45	Smith, Ernie	T	6-2	234	11/26/09	USC
43	Svendsen, George	C	6-4	214	03/22/13	Minnesota
36	Tenner, Bob	E	6-0	212	06/01/13	Minnesota
35	Vairo, Dominic	E	6-2	203	11/02/12	Notre Dame

1936

Green Bay lost only one game all season but did not lock up the Western Division title until it beat Detroit 26-17 on November 29, the same weekend the Bears lost 14-7 to the Chicago Cardinals. For most of the year the Packers and Bears fought it out for top honors, each knocking off the other on the others' home field. In the end, Green Bay prevailed and earned the right to face the Boston Redskins in the NFL Championship Game.

Coach Curly Lambeau had some preseason concerns regarding personnel. He needed to plug holes left by the departures of August (Mike) Michalske, Robert (Cal) Hubbard, Nate Barrager, Johnny (Blood) McNally and Claude Perry. Except for Blood, these men held down critical positions in the line. Hubbard and Michalske had been all-pro (Hubbard in 1931-33 and Michalske in 1931 and 1935). Fortunately, the talent pool was deep. Guard Lon Evans and tackle Ernie Smith in particular rose to the occasion, being honored with all-pro status themselves in 1936.

Blood's story was different. He didn't have any intentions of retiring, he just wanted more money. In what may have been the first contract holdout in Packers' history, Blood rejected the first offer sent him by management and demanded more money. The two sides dickered back and forth and Blood missed the first two games because of his holdout. Only after the Bears had throttled the Packers 30-3, did he end the stalemate and rejoin the team.

Prior to the rout suffered at the hands of the Bears, the Packers used a 25-yard, fourth-quarter field goal from Ernie Smith to beat the Cardinals 10-7. The two met again in week three in Milwaukee and this time Green Bay won 24-0. After beating Boston 31-2, the Packers faced a stiff challenge from defending champion Detroit.

The Lions came into the contest 3-0 and tied with the Bears for first place in the West. Arnie Herber threw a 46-yard touchdown pass to Blood early in the fourth quarter to give Green Bay a 17-15 lead. But, on its next possession, Detroit moved in for 28-yard, Dutch Clark field goal. Down by a point, the Packers rallied. Paul (Tiny) Engebretsen hit an 18-yard field goal and Hutson intercepted Clark's next pass to preserve a 20-18 victory.

Green Bay then won six in a row, including a 21-10 repayment to the Bears at Wrigley Field. A 0-0 tie with the Cardinals on December 6 was the only other blemish on the Packers' record. Following that, the team eagerly awaited its first ever postseason game, scheduled for December 13.

Tuffy Leemans (4) of the Giants is off on a 16-yard gain at the Polo Grounds in New York. The Packers won 26 - 14. Milt Gantenbein trails Leemans. Ade Schwammel (57) and Ernie Smith (61) can also be seen. Lon Evans (51) is crouched behind Schwammel.

TEAM STATISTICS

	GB	OPP
First Downs	148	136
Rushes	490	479
Yards Gained	1,664	1,494
Average Gain	3.40	3.12
Average Yards per Game	138.7	124.5
Passes Attempted	255	227
Completed	108	81
% Completed	42.35	35.68
Total Yards Gained	1,629	1,170
Yards Gained per Completion	15.08	14.44
Average Yards per Game	135.8	97.5
Laterals Attempted	5	7
Completed	5	6
Yards Gained	30	0
Combined Yards Gained	3,323	2,664
Total Plays	750	713
Average Yards per Play	4.43	3.74
Average Yards per Game	276.9	222.0
Intercepted By	31	19
Yards Penalized	478	386
Fumbles	23	29
Recovered	19	28
Total Points Scored	248	118
Total Touchdowns	31	14
Touchdowns Rushing	11	5
Touchdowns Passing	17	7
Touchdowns on Returns & Recoveries	3	2
Extra Points	30	12
Safeties	1	2
Field Goals Made	10	6

Regular Season   10-1-1

Date	GB		OPP
9/13	10	Chicago Cardinals	7
9/20	3	Chicago Bears	30
10/4	24	Chicago Cardinals (M)	0
10/11	31	Boston Redskins	2
11/18	20	Detroit Lions	18
10/25	42	Pittsburgh Pirates (M)	10
11/1	21	at Chicago Bears	10
11/8	7	at Boston Redskins	3
11/15	38	at Brooklyn Dodgers	7
11/22	26	at New York Giants	14
11/29	26	at Detroit Lions	17
12/6	0	at Chicago Cardinals	0

Postseason   1-0-0

12/13	21	Boston Redskins (Polo Grounds, NY)	6

1936

Score By Periods

	1	2	3	4	Total
Packers	40	86	76	46	248
Opponents	26	21	27	44	118

INDIVIDUAL STATISTICS

Rushing

	Att	Yds	Avg	TD
Hinkle	100	476	4.8	5
Sauer	94	305	3.2	3
Laws	50	296	5.9	1
P. Miller	52	227	4.4	1
Monnett	104	224	2.2	0
Johnston	42	110	2.6	1
Blood	13	65	5.0	0
Goldenberg	6	9	1.5	0
Mattos	1	2	2.0	0
Hutson	1	-3	-3.0	0
Bruder	4	-7	-1.7	0
Clemens	3	-8	-2.7	0
Herber	20	-32	-1.6	0
Packers	**490**	**1,664**	**3.4**	**11**
Opponents	479	1,494	3.1	5

Receiving

	No	Yds	Avg	LG	TD
Hutson	34	526	15.5	t58	8
Gantenbein	15	221	14.7		1
Monnett	13	169	13.0		0
Laws	10	132	13.2		2
P. Miller	8	113	14.1	34	2
Blood	7	147	21.0	t46	2
Sauer	6	110	18.3		0
Becker	5	66	13.2		1
Schneidman	3	68	22.7	t46	1
Bruder	2	25	12.5	23	0
Scherer	2	13	6.5	7	0
Johnston	2	11	5.5		0
Clemens	1	18	18.0	18	0
Packers	**108**	**1,629**	**15.1**	**t58**	**17**
Opponents	81	1,170	14.4	52	7

Passing

	Att	Com	Yds	Pct	TD	In	Rate
Herber	173	77	1,239	44.5	11	13	58.9
Monnett	52	20	280	38.5	4	2	66.2
Mattos	12	4	32	33.3	0	2	2.8
Sauer	4	2	26	50.0	0	1	—
Laws	4	1	22	25.0	0	1	—
Blood	6	3	20	50.0	1	0	—
Hinkle	2	1	10	50.0	0	0	—
Clemens	1	0	0	00.0	0	0	—
P. Miller	1	0	0	00.0	0	1	—
Packers	**255**	**108**	**1,629**	**42.4**	**17**	**19**	**60.7**
Opponents	227	81	1,170	35.7	7	31	24.0

Scoring

	TDr	TDp	TDrt	PAT	FG	S	TP
Hutson	0	8	1	0	0	0	54
Hinkle	5	0	0	1	0	0	31
Ernie Smith	0	0	0	17	4	0	29
Blood	0	2	1	1	0	0	19
Laws	1	2	0	0	0	0	18
P. Miller	1	2	0	0	0	0	18
Sauer	3	0	0	0	0	0	18
Engebretsen	0	0	0	2	5	0	17
Schwammel	0	0	0	5	1	0	8
Becker	0	1	0	0	0	0	6
Gantenbein	0	1	0	0	0	0	6
Johnston	1	0	0	0	0	0	6
Scherer	0	0	1	0	0	0	6
Schneidman	0	1	0	0	0	0	6
Monnett	0	0	0	3	0	0	3
team	0	0	0	0	0	1	2
Clemens	0	0	0	1	0	0	1
Packers	**11**	**17**	**3**	**30**	**10**	**1**	**248**
Opponents	5	7	2	12	6	2	118

NFL STANDINGS

Western Division

	W	L	T	Pct	PF	PA
Green Bay Packers	**10**	**1**	**1**	**.909**	**248**	**118**
Chicago Bears	9	3	0	.750	222	94
Detroit Lions	8	4	0	.667	235	102
Chicago Cardinals	3	8	1	.273	74	143

Eastern Division

	W	L	T	Pct	PF	PA
Boston Redskins	7	5	0	.583	149	110
Pittsburgh Pirates	6	6	0	.500	98	187
New York Giants	5	6	1	.455	115	163
Brooklyn Dodgers	3	8	1	.273	92	161
Philadelphia Eagles	1	11	0	.083	51	206

Lefebvre photo

FRONT ROW: (L-R) 39 Tony Paulekas, 52 Paul (Tiny) Engebretsen, 51 Lon Evans, 57 Ade Schwammel, 58 Champ Seibold, 59 Frank Butler, 33 Cal Clemens, 44 Charles (Buckets) Goldenberg. **SECOND ROW:** (L-R) 41 Clarke Hinkle, 40 Bernie Scherer, 18 Hank Bruder, 53 Lou Gordon, 43 George Svendsen, 60 Walt Kiesling, 55 Johnny (Blood) McNally, 54 Chester (Swede) Johnston.
THIRD ROW: (L-R) 38 Arnie Herber, 41 Herm Schneidman, 62 Russ Letlow, 3 Paul Miller, 14 Don Hutson, 22 Milt Gantenbein, 29 Joe Laws, 5 Bob Monnett. **FOURTH ROW:** (L-R) Coach Curly Lambeau, 25 George Sauer, 32 Wayland Becker, 61 Ernie Smith, Assistant Coach Richard (Red) Smith.

1936 ROSTER

No	Name	Pos	Ht	Wt	DOB	College
32	Becker, Wayland	E	6-0	183		Marquette
27/18	Bruder, Hank	B	6-0	197	11/22/07	Northwestern
48/59	Butler, Frank	C	6-3	246	05/03/09	Michigan State
33	Clemens, Cal	B	6-1	195		USC
34/52	Engebretsen, Paul (Tiny)	G	6-1	238	07/27/10	Northwestern
51	Evans, Lon	G	6-2	223	12/25/11	TCU
22	Gantenbein, Milt	E	6-0	208	05/31/10	Wisconsin
44	Goldenberg, Charles (Buckets)	G	5-10	212	03/10/11	Wisconsin
53	Gordon, Lou	T	6-5	235	07/15/06	Illinois
38	Herber, Arnie	B	5-11	195	04/02/10	Regis
41	Hinkle, Clarke	FB	5-11	202	04/10/12	Bucknell
14	Hutson, Don	E	6-1	180	01/31/13	Alabama
15/54	Johnston, Chester (Swede)	B	5-10	192	03/07/10	Marquette
49/60	Kiesling, Walt	G	6-3	248	05/27/03	St. Thomas (MN)
29	Laws, Joe	B	5-9	186	06/16/11	Iowa
46/62	Letlow, Russ	G	6-0	203	10/05/13	San Francisco
23	Mattos, Harry	B	6-0	201	04/07/11	St. Mary's (CA)
55	McNally (Blood), Johnny	B	6-0	190	11/27/03	St. John's
3	Miller, Paul	B	5-10	175	01/23/13	South Dakota State
12/5	Monnett, Bob	B	5-9	181	02/27/10	Michigan State
39	Paulekas, Tony	C	5-10	207	08/09/12	Wash.-Jefferson
47	Rose, Al	E	6-3	195	01/26/07	Texas
25	Sauer, George	B	6-2	208	12/11/10	Nebraska
40	Scherer, Bernie	E	6-1	183	01/28/13	Nebraska
4	Schneidman, Herm	B	5-10	205	11/22/13	Iowa
50/57	Schwammel, Ade	T	6-2	232	10/14/08	Oregon State
37/58	Seibold, Champ	T	6-4	230	12/05/12	Wisconsin
45/61	Smith, Ernie	T	6-2	221	11/26/09	USC
43	Svendsen, George	C	6-4	224	03/22/13	Minnesota

1936 DRAFT

Rnd	Name	Pos	College
1	Russ Letlow	G	San Francisco
2	J.W. Wheeler	T	Oklahoma
3	Bernie Scherer	E	Nebraska
4	Theron Ward	B	Idaho
5	Darrell Lester	C	TCU
6	Bob Reynolds	T	Stanford
7	Wally Fromhart	B	Notre Dame
8	Wally Cruice	B	Northwestern
9	J.C. Wetsel	G	SMU

Because Green Bay had won the NFL championship in 1936, it played the College All-Stars in Chicago on September 1, 1937. The game was created in 1934 and pitted the previous years' champion against the best players in college. Not only did the Packers become the first professional team to lose to the collegians (6-0), they also lost the services of Arnie Herber and Bob Monnett to shoulder injuries. Both missed the opener with the Cardinals and Herber was unable to participate in the subsequent Bears skirmish. With their two finest passers ailing, the Packers lost 14-7 and 14-2, respectively, to the two teams from Chicago. The slow start hurt. Green Bay was never able to catch the Bears, despite beating them 24-14 at Chicago November 7. The Packers then fell completely out of the race when they lost to the Giants and Redskins on the season's final two weekends.

City Stadium had been enlarged by approximately 6,000 seats by the time the Packers took the field against the Cardinals on September 12. Seven days later a record 16,658 fans attended the Bears game. That record fell when, two weeks later, 17,553 watched the Packers bounce Detroit 26-6.

The team enjoyed a 14-day break between the Bears game and Lions contest. The layoff helped Herber and Monnett recover. Herber was able to return for a limited engagement against Detroit and Monnett, by then back to his old form, threw for 115 yards and a touchdown. The win was the first of seven in a row.

After dispatching Detroit, Green Bay ran into the Cardinals for a second time. Led by Ed Jankowski's 96 yards on 13 carries, the Packers piled up 241 yards rushing and won 34-13. Four weeks later, they met their other nemesis from Chicago. There, Don Hutson caught five passes for 140 yards and a touchdown to spark a 24-14 victory.

One week later, the team pounded Philadelphia 37-7 to improve to 7-2. The Bears, however, still held first place with a 6-1-1 mark and had to lose at least once in order for the Packers to have any chance at all of claiming the title.

It wasn't to be. New York beat Green Bay 10-0 on November 21 and Washington followed suit 14-6 a week later. Monnett and Herber were intercepted a combined seven times in those final two games. The Bears, meanwhile, won their final three games and claimed the Western crown with a 9-1-1 effort.

Besides the four losses in the standings, the Packers also lost longtime guard August (Mike) Michalske. Michalske, who had returned after a year's absence, severely injured his back in the second Lion game and never did play again. He was the last player remaining from the triple championships of 1929-31.

Lefebvre photo

Bobby Monnett (5) turns the corner and shakes off Hal Pangle (21) for an 11-yard gain against the Cardinals in Milwaukee. Monnett struck through the air also, completing six of eight passes for 77 yards and a touchdown. The Packers won 34-13. Others in the photo include: Joe Laws (24), Lou Gordon (lying on the ground) and Milt Gantenbein (the head behind Gordon). Jack Robinson (49), Mike Michalske (36), Ernie Smith (45) and George Svendsen (43) can also be seen.

TEAM STATISTICS

	GB	OPP
First Downs	140	110
Rushes	483	400
Yards Gained	1,786	1,184
Average Gain	3.70	2.96
Average Yards per Game	162.4	107.6
Passes Attempted	216	197
Completed	95	70
% Completed	43.98	35.53
Total Yards Gained	1,398	1,115
Yards Gained per Completion	14.72	15.93
Average Yards per Game	127.1	101.4
Laterals Attempted	3	6
Completed	3	6
Yards Gained	17	0
Combined Yards Gained	3,201	2,299
Total Plays	702	603
Average Yards per Play	4.60	3.81
Average Yards per Game	291.0	209.0
Intercepted By	21	26
Yards Penalized	291	286
Fumbles	18	18
Recovered	11	9
Total Points Scored	220	122
Total Touchdowns	30	17
Touchdowns Rushing	10	8
Touchdowns Passing	17	7
Touchdowns on Returns & Recoveries	3	2
Extra Points	26	14
Safeties	1	0
Field Goals Made	4	2

Regular Season 7-4-0

Date	GB		OPP
9/12	7	Chicago Cardinals	14
9/19	2	Chicago Bears	14
10/3	26	Detroit Lions	6
10/10	34	Chicago Cardinals (M)	13
10/17	35	at Cleveland Rams	10
10/24	35	Cleveland Rams	7
10/31	14	at Detroit Lions	13
11/7	24	at Chicago Bears	14
11/14	37	Philadelphia Eagles (M)	7
11/21	0	at New York Giants	10
11/28	6	at Washington Redskins	14

Score By Periods

	1	2	3	4	Total
Packers	35	75	33	77	220
Opponents	7	26	62	27	122

1937

INDIVIDUAL STATISTICS

Rushing

	Att	Yds	Avg	TD
Hinkle	129	552	4.3	5
Jankowski	61	324	5.3	2
Laws	74	310	4.2	1
P. Miller	71	262	3.7	1
Monnett	87	161	1.9	1
Bruder	15	56	3.7	0
Banet	9	29	3.2	0
Hutson	14	26	1.9	0
Goldenberg	4	18	4.5	0
Schneidman	5	17	3.4	0
Sauer	7	17	2.4	0
Herber	5	9	1.8	0
Becker	2	5	2.5	0
Packers	483	1,786	3.7	10
Opponents	400	1,184	3.0	8

Receiving

	No	Yds	Avg	LG	TD
Hutson	41	552	13.5	t78	7
Gantenbein	12	237	19.8	t77	2
Laws	10	121	12.1	19	1
Hinkle	8	116	14.5	t49	2
Scherer	6	149	24.8	t78	2
P. Miller	6	66	11.0		1
Monnett	4	32	8.0	13	0
Jankowski	2	60	30.0	46	1
Schneidman	2	35	17.5	23	1
Becker	2	13	6.5	11	0
G. Svendsen	1	11	11.0	11	0
Banet	1	6	6.0	6	0
Packers	95	1,398	14.7	t78	17
Opponents	70	1,115	15.9	t86	7

Passing

	Att	Com	Yds	Pct	TD	In	Rate
Herber	104	47	684	45.2	7	10	50.0
Monnett	73	37	580	50.7	9	8	77.4
R. Peterson	6	3	47	50.0	0	0	—
Hinkle	3	2	43	66.7	0	0	—
Laws	11	5	42	45.5	1	2	46.6
Banet	7	1	2	14.3	0	2	—
Bruder	6	0	0	00.0	0	2	—
Hutson	4	0	0	00.0	0	1	—
Ed Smith	2	0	0	00.0	0	1	—
Packers	216	95	1,398	44.0	17	26	52.4
Opponents	197	70	1,115	35.5	7	21	27.5

Scoring

	TDr	TDp	TDrt	PAT	FG	S	TP
Hinkle	5	2	0	8	2	0	56
Hutson	0	7	0	0	0	0	42
Jankowski	2	1	1	1	0	0	25
Ernie Smith	0	0	0	12	1	0	15
Gantenbein	0	2	0	0	0	0	12
Laws	1	1	0	0	0	0	12
Scherer	0	2	0	0	0	0	12
Engebretsen	0	0	0	5	1	0	6
Bruder	1	0	0	0	0	0	6
Goldenberg	0	0	1	0	0	0	6
P. Miller	1	0	0	0	0	0	6
Monnett	1	0	0	0	0	0	6
Schammel	0	0	1	0	0	0	6
Schneidman	0	0	1	0	0	0	6
team	0	0	0	0	0	1	2
Packers	10	17	3	26	4	1	220
Opponents	8	7	2	14	2	0	122

NFL STANDINGS

Western Division

	W	L	T	Pct	PF	PA
Chicago Bears	9	1	1	.900	201	100
Green Bay Packers	7	4	0	.636	220	120
Detroit Lions	7	4	0	.636	180	105
Chicago Cardinals	5	5	1	.500	135	165
Cleveland Rams	1	10	0	.091	75	207

Eastern Division

	W	L	T	Pct	PF	PA
Washington Redskins	8	3	0	.727	195	120
New York Giants	6	3	2	.667	128	109
Pittsburgh Pirates	4	7	0	.364	122	145
Brooklyn Dodgers	3	7	1	.300	82	174
Philadelphia Eagles	2	8	1	.200	86	177

Lefebvre Photo

FRONT ROW: (L-R) Trainer Dave Woodward, 25 Ed Jankowski, 5 Bob Monnett, 22 Milt Gantenbein, 38 Arnie Herber, 3 Paul Miller, 45 Ernie Smith, 37 Francis (Zud) Schammel, 39 Lon Evans, 34 Paul (Tiny) Engebretsen, Assistant Trainer Carl (Bud) Jorgensen.
SECOND ROW: (L-R) Coach Curly Lambeau, 30 Clarke Hinkle, 44 Charles (Buckets) Goldenberg, 24 Joe Laws, 18 Hank Bruder, 11 Bernie Scherer, 46 Russ Letlow, 29 Darrell Lester, 17 George Sauer, 14 Don Hutson.
BACK ROW: (L-R) 47 Lou Gordon, 26 Lyle Sturgeon, 21 Herb Banet, 41 Champ Seibold, 40 Bill Lee, 43 George Svendsen, 4 Herm Schneidman, 7 Earl Svendsen, 32 Wayland Becker, Assistant Coach Richard (Red) Smith.

1937 ROSTER

No	Name	Pos	Ht	Wt	DOB	College
21	Banet, Herb	B	6-2	200	10/17/13	Manchester
32	Becker, Wayland	E	6-0	205		Marquette
18	Bruder, Hank	B	6-0	200	11/22/07	Northwestern
23	Daniell, Averell	T	6-3	210	11/06/14	Pittsburgh
34	Engebretsen, Paul (Tiny)	G	6-1	240	07/27/10	Northwestern
39	Evans, Lon	G	6-2	230	12/25/11	TCU
22	Gantenbein, Milt	E	6-0	200	05/31/10	Wisconsin
44	Goldenberg, Charles (Buckets)	G	5-10	220	03/10/11	Wisconsin
47	Gordon, Lou	T	6-5	230	07/15/06	Illinois
19/38	Herber, Arnie	B	5-11	195	04/02/10	Regis
30	Hinkle, Clarke	FB	5-11	205	04/10/12	Bucknell
14	Hutson, Don	E	6-1	180	01/31/13	Alabama
25	Jankowski, Ed	B	5-10	205	06/23/13	Wisconsin
15	Johnston, Chester (Swede)	B	5-10	195	03/07/10	Marquette
24	Laws, Joe	B	5-9	185	06/16/11	Iowa
40	Lee, Bill	T	6-3	225	10/19/11	Alabama
29	Lester, Darrell	C	6-3	220	04/29/14	TCU
46	Letlow, Russ	G	6-0	210	10/05/13	San Francisco
36	Michalske, August (Mike)	G	6-0	210	04/24/03	Penn State
3	Miller, Paul	B	5-10	180	01/23/13	South Dakota
5	Monnett, Bob	B	5-9	180	02/27/10	Michigan State
33	Peterson, Ray	B	6-0	190	06/27/13	San Francisco
17	Sauer, George	B	6-2	208	12/11/10	Nebraska
37	Schammel, Francis (Zud)	G	6-2	235		Iowa
11	Scherer, Bernie	E	6-1	190	01/28/13	Nebraska
4	Schneidman, Herm	B	5-10	200	11/22/13	Iowa
41	Seibold, Champ	T	6-4	235	12/05/12	Wisconsin
28	Smith, Ed	B	6-2	205		New York
45	Smith, Ernie	T	6-2	222	11/26/09	USC
26	Sturgeon, Lyle	T	6-3	250	02/07/15	North Dakota State
7	Svendsen, Earl	C	6-1	195	02/07/15	Minnesota
43	Svendsen, George	C	6-4	230	03/22/13	Minnesota

1937 DRAFT

Rnd	Name	Pos	College
1	Ed Jankowski	B	Wisconsin
2	Averill Daniell	T	Pittsburgh
3	Charles (Bud) Wilkinson	B	Minnesota
4	Earl Svendsen	C	Minnesota
5	Dave Gavin	T	Holy Cross
6	Merle Wendt	E	Ohio State
7	Dick Dahlgren	G	Michigan State
8	Dick Chapman	T	Tulsa
9	Marv Baldwin	G	TCU
10	Gibson DeWitt	T	Northwestern

1938

Arnie Herber turned 28 in April, certainly not old, but, following his eighth, often injury-plagued 1937 campaign, Coach Curly Lambeau turned to the draft and selected Cecil Isbell of Purdue on the first round. Isbell not only led the team in passing, but pounded out 445 yards rushing, tops for the team. He, Herber, and Bob Monnett threw 20 touchdown passes while guiding the league's number one offense.

Two other additions benefitted the Packers. Andy Uram, a back out of Minnesota, was taken with the fourth selection, and Buford (Baby) Ray, a giant 6-6, 280-pound tackle signed as a free agent. Uram reeled off a then-NFL record 97-yard run in 1939 and Ray became a mainstay on the line for the next 11 years.

Green Bay lost two of its first five games. The team, however, was never out of the race for the Western title. On October 24, the Packers shut out Pittsburgh 20-0. In doing so, they improved to 5-2 and moved into first place ahead of the Chicago Bears (4-2). Two weeks later, Green Bay defeated the Bears 24-17 in Chicago and followed up with a 28-7 triumph at Detroit which clinched a championship date with the New York Giants.

City Stadium was again expanded. The east end was filled-in to give the structure a horseshoe look. The press box was enlarged and a clock was placed near the field. Overall, 6,554 new seats were added which brought capacity from around 18,000 to well over 24,000. Opening day attendance (8,247) was surprisingly low. Those in the stands saw Herber throw three touchdown passes to Don Hutson as the Packers beat Cleveland 26-17. Terrible field conditions wreaked havoc with the Packers' and Bears' offenses the following week. The two combined for just 195 yards and a fourth-quarter safety proved the difference as Chicago prevailed 2-0.

The Packers suffered one more loss, in week five, before putting together a string of five wins. Detroit, before a City Stadium-record 21,968, beat Green Bay 17-7. The Packers then downed Brooklyn, beat Pittsburgh to move into first place, and topped Cleveland to solidify its position.

Green Bay won twice more, both key victories, the last of which clinched the division. In the first, the Bears fumbled six times, once each on their first two possessions. Bob Monnett threw touchdown passes, first to Clarke Hinkle and then to Hutson, to capitalize on the miscues and give the Packers a quick 14-0 lead. Though outgained in nearly every department, Green Bay prevailed 24-17.

The second, the Lions game, was almost anticlimatic. The team won handily, 28-7 to capture its second Western title in three years.

Lefebvre photo

Milt Gantenbein (22) is off after catching one of two pass receptions against the Cleveland Rams in the season opener. The Packers won 26-17. Gantenbein caught 12 passes in 1938 and, for the third year in a row, finished second to Don Hutson in receiving. The Rams shown are Vic Spadaccini (33), Ed Goddard (28) and Tom Hupke (22).

TEAM STATISTICS

	GB	OPP
First Downs	134	118
Rushes	454	372
Yards Gained	1,571	1,206
Average Gain	3.46	3.24
Average Yards per Game	142.8	109.6
Passes Attempted	210	232
Completed	91	92
% Completed	43.33	39.66
Total Yards Gained	1,466	1,343
Yards Gained per Completion	16.11	14.60
Average Yards per Game	133.3	122.1
Laterals Attempted	1	9
Completed	1	9
Yards Gained	0	45
Combined Yards Gained	3,037	2,594
Total Plays	665	613
Average Yards per Play	4.57	4.23
Average Yards per Game	276.1	235.8
Intercepted By	21	20
Yards Penalized	250	334
Fumbles	18	27
Lost	11	12
Own Recovered for TD	0	0
Opponent's Recovered by	12	11
Opponent's Recovered for TD	0	0
Total Points Scored	223	118
Total Touchdowns	30	15
Touchdowns Rushing	9	7
Touchdowns Passing	20	6
Touchdowns on Returns & Recoveries	1	2
Extra Points	28	12
Safeties	0	0
Field Goals Attempted	14	10
Field Goals Made	5	4
% Successful	35.71	40.00

Regular Season 8-3-0

Date	GB		OPP
9/11	26	Cleveland Rams	17
9/18	0	Chicago Bears	2
9/25	28	Chicago Cardinals (M)	7
9/28	24	Chicago Cardinals at Buffalo	22
10/9	7	Detroit Lions	17
10/16	35	Brooklyn Dodgers (M)	7
10/23	20	Pittsburgh Pirates	0
10/30	28	at Cleveland Rams	7
11/6	24	at Chicago Bears	17
11/13	28	at Detroit Lions	7
11/20	3	at New York Giants	15

1938

Postseason 0-1-0

12/11 .. 17 ... at New York Giants 23

Score By Periods

	1	2	3	4	Total
Packers	45	87	61	30	223
Opponents	16	27	44	31	118

INDIVIDUAL STATISTICS

Rushing

	Att	Yds	Avg	TD
Isbell	85	445	5.2	2
Hinkle	114	299	2.6	3
Laws	60	253	4.2	0
Monnett	75	225	3.0	0
Uram	28	145	5.2	2
Jankowski	44	124	2.8	2
P. Miller	20	48	2.4	0
Weisgerber	6	13	2.2	0
Schneidman	4	8	2.0	0
Howell	7	7	1.0	0
Bruder	2	6	3.0	0
Hutson	3	-1	-0.3	0
Herber	6	-1	-0.2	0
Packers	**454**	**1,571**	**3.5**	**9**
Opponents	372	1,206	3.2	7

Receiving

	No	Yds	Avg	LG	TD
Hutson	32	548	17.1	54	9
Gantenbein	12	164	13.7	29	1
Becker	7	166	23.7	49	0
Hinkle	7	98	14.0	32	4
Laws	6	55	9.2	17	1
Isbell	5	104	20.8	49	0
Herber	5	84	16.8	20	2
C. Mulleneaux	4	97	24.3	36	2
Uram	4	46	11.5		0
P. Miller	4	36	9.0	12	0
Scherer	2	31	15.5	16	1
Bruder	2	14	7.0		0
Monnett	1	23	23.0	23	0
Packers	**91**	**1,466**	**16.1**	**54**	**20**
Opponents	92	1,343	14.6	63	6

Passing

	Att	Com	Yds	Pct	TD	In	Rate
Isbell	91	37	659	40.7	7	10	52.2
Monnett	57	31	465	54.4	9	4	91.7
Herber	55	22	336	40.0	4	4	54.8
Hinkle	2	1	6	50.0	0	0	—
Laws	5	0	0	0.0	0	2	—
Packers	**210**	**91**	**1,466**	**43.3**	**20**	**20**	**59.4**
Opponents	232	92	1,343	39.7	6	21	30.2

Scoring

	TDr	TDp	TDrt	PAT	FG	S	TP
Hinkle	3	4	0	7/8	3/9	0	58
Hutson	0	9	0	3/3	0/0	0	57
Engebretsen	0	0	0	9/9	2/4	0	15
Jankowski	2	0	0	2/3	0/0	0	14
Herber	0	2	0	0/0	0/1	0	12
Isbell	2	0	0	0/0	0/0	0	12
Laws	0	1	1	0/0	0/0	0	12
C. Mulleneaux	0	2	0	0/0	0/0	0	12
Uram	2	0	0	0/0	0/0	0	12
Monnett	0	0	0	7/7	0/0	0	7
Gantenbein	0	1	0	0/0	0/0	0	6
Scherer	0	1	0	0/0	0/0	0	6
Packers	**9**	**20**	**1**	**28/30**	**5/14**	**0**	**223**
Opponents	7	6	2	12/15	4/10	0	118

NFL STANDINGS

Western Division

	W	L	T	Pct	PF	PA
Green Bay Packers	**8**	**3**	**0**	**.727**	**223**	**118**
Detroit Lions	7	4	0	.636	119	108
Chicago Bears	6	5	0	.545	194	148
Cleveland Rams	4	7	0	.364	131	215
Chicago Cardinals	2	9	0	.182	111	168

Eastern Division

	W	L	T	Pct	PF	PA
New York Giants	8	2	1	.800	194	79
Washington Redskins	6	3	2	.667	148	154
Brooklyn Dodgers	4	4	3	.500	131	161
Philadelphia Eagles	5	6	0	.455	154	164
Pittsburgh Pirates	2	9	0	.182	79	169

Lefebvre photo

FRONT ROW: (L-R) Trainer Dave Woodward, 30 Clarke Hinkle, 50 Bob Monnett, 22 Milt Gantenbein, 36 Bernie Scherer, 35 Frank Butler, 19 Carl (Moose) Mulleneaux, 40 Bill Lee, 51 Herm Schneidman, 48 Charles (Ookie) Miller, 41 Champ Seibold, 18 Lee Mulleneaux, Assistant Trainer Carl (Bud) Jorgensen. **MIDDLE ROW:** (L-R) Coach Curly Lambeau, 3 Paul Miller, 24 Joe Laws, 7 Ed Jankowski, 34 Paul (Tiny) Engebretsen, 37 Tom Jones, 14 Don Hutson, 5 Hank Bruder, 32 Wayland Becker, 11 Leo Katalinas, Assistant Coach Richard (Red) Smith. **BACK ROW:** (L-R) 33 Dick Weisgerber, 8 Andy Uram, 38 Arnie Herber, 46 Russ Letlow, 49 John Howell, 20 Buford (Baby) Ray, 29 Darrell Lester, 9 Tony (Fritz) Borak, 17 Cecil Isbell, 43 Charles (Buckets) Goldenberg, 21 Pete Tinsley.

1938 ROSTER

No	Name	Pos	Ht	Wt	DOB	College
32	Becker, Wayland	E	6-0	205		Marquette
9	Borak, Tony (Fritz)	E	6-1	190		Creighton
18/5	Bruder, Hank	B	6-0	200	11/22/07	Northwestern
35	Butler, Frank	T	6-3	246	05/03/09	Michigan State
34	Engebretsen, Paul (Tiny)	G	6-1	240	07/27/10	Northwestern
22	Gantenbein, Milt	E	6-0	200	05/31/10	Wisconsin
43	Goldenberg, Charles (Buckets)	G	5-10	225	03/10/11	Wisconsin
38	Herber, Arnie	B	5-11	200	04/02/10	Regis
30	Hinkle, Clarke	FB	5-11	205	04/10/12	Bucknell
49	Howell, John	B	5-11	185		Nebraska
14	Hutson, Don	E	6-1	185	01/31/13	Alabama
17	Isbell, Cecil	B	6-1	190	07/11/15	Purdue
7	Jankowski, Ed	B	5-10	195	06/23/13	Wisconsin
15	Johnston, Chester (Swede)	B	5-10	200	03/07/10	Marquette
37	Jones, Tom	G	5-11	230	10/15/09	Bucknell
11	Katalinas, Leo	T	6-2	240	02/04/15	Catholic University
24	Laws, Joe	B	5-9	185	06/16/11	Iowa
40	Lee, Bill	T	6-3	225	10/19/11	Alabama
29	Lester, Darrell	C	6-3	220	04/29/14	TCU
46	Letlow, Russ	G	6-0	212	10/05/13	San Francisco
48	Miller, Charles (Ookie)	C	6-1	215	11/11/09	Purdue
3	Miller, Paul	B	5-10	185	01/23/13	South Dakota
50	Monnett, Bob	B	5-9	180	02/27/10	Michigan State
19	Mulleneaux, Carl (Moose)	E	6-4	210	04/01/17	Utah State
18	Mulleneaux, Lee	C	6-2	225	09/16/14	Northern Arizona
44	Ray, Buford (Baby)	T	6-6	250	09/30/15	Vanderbilt
36	Scherer, Bernie	E	6-1	193	01/28/13	Nebraska
51	Schneidman, Herm	B	5-10	200	11/22/13	Iowa
42	Schoemann, Roy	C	6-1	195		Marquette
41	Seibold, Champ	T	6-4	240	12/05/12	Wisconsin
21	Tinsley, Pete	G	5-8	205	03/16/13	Georgia
8	Uram, Andy	B	5-10	187	03/22/15	Minnesota
33	Weisgerber, Dick	B	5-10	205	02/19/15	Williamette

1938 DRAFT

Rnd	Name	Pos	College
1	Cecil Isbell	B	Purdue
2	Marty Schreyer	T	Purdue
3	Chuck Sweeney	E	Notre Dame
4	Andy Uram	B	Minnesota
5	John Kovatch	E	Northwestern
6	Phil Ragazzo	T	Case Western Reserve
7	John Howell	B	Nebraska
8	Frank Barnhart	G	Northern Colorado
9	Pete Tinsley	G	Georgia
10	Tony Falkenstein	B	St. Mary's (CA)

1939

Two three-point losses kept the Packers from an undefeated season. As impressive as that may sound, the team rarely dominated. Green Bay's offense ranked third and its' defense fifth. Six of the Packers victories were by a touchdown or less. Yet the team managed to find ways to win. When the season closed on December 3, Green Bay was the Western Division champion for a second straight year, this time with a 9-2 record.

Two rookies who would be heard from for a long time to come joined the team. Charley Brock was plucked from Nebraska on the second round of the draft and Larry Craig was selected fourth. Brock, a 6-1 center, enjoyed a nine-year career in Green Bay while Craig played through 1949. Just as importantly, Coach Curly Lambeau decided to play Craig at end on defense in place of Don Hutson, freeing the fleet end to play safety. This move undoubtedly prolonged the 26-year-old's career, as he was no longer in on bruising line play.

One veteran, Arnie Herber, gained an additional $100 dollars in his contract when he weighed in at 199 pounds on August 12. Herber had been promised the incentive on July 3, at which time he was a hefty 227, if he could slim down to 200 pounds or less by mid-August. The quarterback's weight had been a concern almost from the day he first wore a uniform. It became such a concern that, prior to the 1941 season, Herber himself suggested he forfeit $50 if he weighed in at over 200 pounds on any Saturday before a game.

Two losses in the first seven games kept the Packers out of sole possession of first place until they clobbered Brooklyn 28-0 on November 19. Until then, the team was involved in a three-way race with the Bears and Detroit. On October 1, the Cleveland Rams beat Green Bay 27-24. The Rams intercepted Green Bay quarterbacks three times. Cleveland trailed by 10 going into the fourth quarter but scored 13 points in the last period - seven coming on a drive following an interception of Cecil Isbell - to down Green Bay by three. The Packers then won three straight, including a 26-7 pasting of the unbeaten Lions 26-7, before heading to Chicago.

In Chicago, the Bears defeated Green Bay on the first weekend in November as the Packers again blew a fourth-quarter lead. Herber hit Hutson with a 20-yard touchdown pass to give his team a 27-23 lead. But Bill Osmanski scored on a late, four-yard run, resulting in a 30-27 Chicago win.

After the Bears loss, the Packers (5-2-0) trailed Detroit (6-1-0) by a game. On November 12, the Packers piled up 376 yards and toppled the Eagles 23-16 in Philadelphia. At the same time, the Bears defeated Detroit 23-13 which allowed Green Bay to move into a tie with Detroit for first place. That tie was broken one week later when Green Bay shut out Brooklyn 28-0. That win, combined with Detroit's 14-3 loss to Cleveland, gave the Packers sole possession of first place, a spot they nailed down with two final wins, the last a 12-7 triumph at Detroit.

Tom Pigeon Collection

Joe Laws (24) scores on a five-yard run to give Green Bay a 10-0 second-quarter lead against the Cleveland Rams on October 1. The Packers, however, could not withstand a fourth-quarter Rams' rally and lost 27-24. Coming in a bit too late are Cleveland's Corby Davis (3), Gaylon Smith (10), Vic Spadaccini (33) and Art Lewis (11). Paul (Tiny) Engebretsen is on the ground at the two-yard line while Pete Tinsley (21) and Charles Schultz (60) can also be seen.

TEAM STATISTICS

	GB	OPP
First Downs	147	113
Rushing	73	40
Passing	66	64
Penalty	8	9
Rushes	500	333
Yards Gained	1,574	1,165
Average Gain	3.15	3.50
Average Yards per Game	143.1	105.9
Passes Attempted	248	239
Completed	101	106
% Completed	40.73	44.35
Total Yards Gained	1,871	1,602
Yards Gained per Completion	18.52	15.11
Average Yards per Game	170.1	145.6
Laterals Attempted	0	3
Completed	0	3
Yards Gained	0	3
Combined Yards Gained	3,445	2,770
Total Plays	748	575
Average Yards per Play	4.61	4.82
Average Yards per Game	313.2	251.8
Intercepted By	26	15
Punts	72	81
Yards Punted	2,866	3,263
Average Yards per Punt	39.81	40.28
Yards Penalized	259	315
Fumbles	16	27
Lost	7	9
Own Recovered for Touchdown	0	0
Opponent's Recovered by	9	7
Opponent's Recovered for Touchdown	2	0
Total Points Scored	233	153
Total Touchdowns	31	21
Touchdowns Rushing	13	12
Touchdowns Passing	14	9
Touchdowns on Returns & Recoveries	4	0
Extra Points	28	15
Safeties	2	0
Field Goals Attempted	18	10
Field Goals Made	5	4
% Successful	27.78	40.00

Regular Season   9-2-0

Date	GB		OPP	Att.
9/17	14	Chicago Cardinals	10	(11,792)
9/24	21	Chicago Bears	16	(19,192)
10/1	24	Cleveland Rams	27	(9,888)
10/8	27	Chicago Cardinals (M)	20	(18,965)
10/22	26	Detroit Lions	7	(22,558)
10/29	24	Washington Redskins (M)	14	(24,308)
11/5	27	at Chicago Bears	30	(40,537)
11/12	23	at Philadelphia Eagles	16	(23,000)
11/19	28	at Brooklyn Dodgers	0	(19,843)
11/26	7	at Cleveland Rams	6	(30,691)
12/3	12	at Detroit Lions	7	(30,699)

1939

Postseason   1-0-0

12/10 .. 27 ... New York Giants (M) 0 (32,279)

Score By Periods

	1	2	3	4	Total
Packers	51	78	58	46	233
Opponents	17	44	33	59	153

INDIVIDUAL STATISTICS

Rushing

	Att	Yds	Avg	TD
Isbell	132	407	3.1	2
Hinkle	135	381	2.8	5
Jankowski	75	278	3.7	2
Uram	52	272	5.2	1
Laws	55	162	2.9	2
Balazs	11	41	3.7	0
Hutson	5	26	5.2	0
C. Thompson	6	9	1.5	0
Craig	2	6	3.0	0
Buhler	5	3	0.6	0
Lawrence	4	0	0.0	0
Herber	18	-11	-0.6	1
Packers	**500**	**1,574**	**3.1**	**13**
Opponents	333	1,165	3.5	12

Receiving

	No	Yds	Avg	LG	TD
Hutson	34	846	24.9	t92	6
C. Mulleneaux	12	218	18.2	48	1
Laws	11	177	16.1	31	1
Isbell	9	71	7.9	20	0
Gantenbein	7	127	18.1	t32	1
Uram	7	93	13.3	t21	2
Jacunski	5	104	20.8	t29	2
Hinkle	4	70	17.5	25	0
Bruder	4	65	16.3	22	1
Craig	3	44	14.7	28	0
Lawrence	1	21	21.0	21	0
Herber	1	18	18.0	18	0
Balazs	1	11	11.0	11	0
Jankowski	1	5	5.0	5	0
C. Thompson	1	1	1.0	1	0
Packers	**101**	**1,871**	**18.5**	**t92**	**14**
Opponents	106	1,602	15.1	t61	9

Passing

	Att	Com	Yds	Pct	TD	In	Rate
Herber	139	57	1,107	41.0	8	9	61.6
Isbell	103	43	749	41.7	6	5	66.4
Lawrence	4	1	15	25.0	0	1	—
Laws	1	0	0	00.0	0	0	—
Uram	1	0	0	00.0	0	0	—
Packers	**248**	**101**	**1,871**	**40.7**	**14**	**15**	**61.1**
Opponents	239	106	1,602	44.4	9	26	39.9

Punting

	No	Yds	Avg	LG	HB
Hinkle	43	1,751	40.7	65	0
Herber	24	957	39.9	74	2
Isbell	4	123	30.8	39	0
Balazs	1	35	35.0	35	0
Packers	**72**	**2,866**	**39.8**	**74**	**2**
Opponents	81	3,263	40.3	70	0

Scoring

	TDr	TDp	TDrt	PAT	FG	S	TP
Hutson	0	6	0	2/2	0/0	0	38
Hinkle	5	0	0	0/0	0/0	0	35
Engebretsen	0	0	0	18/19	4/8	0	30
Laws	2	1	1	0/0	0/0	0	24
Uram	1	2	0	0/0	0/0	0	19
Isbell	2	0	0	3/3	0/0	0	15
Jacunski	0	2	0	0/0	0/0	0	12
Jankowski	2	0	0	0/0	0/0	0	12
C. Brock	0	0	1	0/0	0/0	0	6
Bruder	0	1	0	0/0	0/0	0	6
Gantenbein	0	1	0	0/0	0/0	0	6
Greenfield	0	0	1	0/0	0/0	0	6
Herber	1	0	0	0/0	0/0	0	6
C. Mulleneaux	0	1	0	0/0	0/0	0	6
E. Svendsen	0	0	1	0/0	0/0	0	6
team	0	0	0	0/0	0/0	2	4
Ernie Smith	0	0	0	0/0	3/4	0	3
Packers	**13**	**14**	**4**	**28/31**	**5/18**	**2**	**233**
Opponents	12	9	0	15/21	4/10	0	153

NFL STANDINGS

Western Division

	W	L	T	Pct	PF	PA
Green Bay Packers	9	2	0	.818	233	153
Chicago Bears	8	3	0	.727	298	157
Detroit Lions	6	5	0	.545	145	150
Cleveland Rams	5	5	1	.500	195	164
Chicago Cardinals	1	10	1	.091	84	254

Eastern Division

	W	L	T	Pct	PF	PA
New York Giants	9	1	1	.900	168	85
Washington Redskins	8	2	1	.800	242	92
Brooklyn Dodgers	4	6	1	.400	108	219
Philadelphia Eagles	1	9	1	.100	105	200
Pittsburgh Pirates	1	9	1	.100	114	216

Lefebvre photo

FRONT ROW: (L-R) 42 Andy Uram, 29 Charley Brock, 49 Don Wilson, 51 Herm Schneidman, 24 Joe Laws, 50 Clarence Thompson, 57 Dick Zoll, 62 Francis Twedell, 15 Chester (Swede) Johnston, 33 Dick Weisgerber, 21 Pete Tinsley, 32 John Biolo, 7 Ed Jankowski.
MIDDLE ROW: (L-R) Coach Curly Lambeau, 54 Larry Craig, 41 Paul Kell, 30 Clarke Hinkle, 22 Milt Gantenbein, 38 Arnie Herber, 53 Earl Svendsen, 40 Bill Lee, 17 Cecil Isbell, 43 Charles (Buckets) Goldenberg, 5 Hank Bruder, 18 Lee Mulleneaux, 46 Russ Letlow, 34 Paul (Tiny) Engebretsen.
BACK ROW: (L-R) 37 John Brennan, 35 Frank Balazs, 48 Harry Jacunski, 58 Warren Kilbourne, 36 Frank Steen, 56 Tom Greenfield, 44 Buford (Baby) Ray, 19 Carl (Moose) Mulleneaux, 52 Larry Buhler, 55 Allen Moore, 14 Don Hutson, 60 Charles Schultz, 10 Clarence Thompson, Assistant Coach Richard Smith.

1939 ROSTER

No	Name	Pos	Ht	Wt	DOB	College
35	Balazs, Frank	B	6-2	215	01/23/18	Iowa
32	Biolo, John	G	5-10	191	02/08/16	Lake Forest
37	Brennan, John	G	6-1	204		Michigan
29	Brock, Charley	C	6-1	195	03/15/16	Nebraska
5	Bruder, Hank	B	6-0	200	11/22/07	Northwestern
52	Buhler, Larry	B	6-2	204	05/28/17	Minnesota
54	Craig, Larry	E	6-0	205	06/27/16	South Carolina
34	Engebretsen, Paul (Tiny)	G	6-1	240	07/27/10	Northwestern
22	Gantenbein, Milt	E	6-0	195	05/31/10	Wisconsin
43	Goldenberg, Charles (Buckets)	G	5-10	222	03/10/11	Wisconsin
56	Greenfield, Tom	C	6-4	209	11/10/17	Arizona
38	Herber, Arnie	B	5-11	200	04/02/10	Regis
30	Hinkle, Clarke	FB	5-11	195	04/10/12	Bucknell
14	Hutson, Don	E	6-1	185	01/31/13	Alabama
17	Isbell, Cecil	B	6-1	190	07/11/15	Purdue
48	Jacunski, Harry	E	6-2	197	10/20/15	Fordham
7	Jankowski, Ed	B	5-10	200	06/23/13	Wisconsin
41	Kell, Paul	T	6-2	217	07/18/15	Notre Dame
58	Kilbourne, Warren	T	6-3	240		Minnesota
51	Lawrence, Jim	B	5-10	190	03/14/15	TCU
24	Laws, Joe	B	5-9	185	06/16/11	Iowa
40	Lee, Bill	T	6-3	225	10/19/11	Alabama
46	Letlow, Russ	G	6-0	212	10/05/13	San Francisco
55	Moore, Allen	E	6-2	218		Texas A&M
19	Mulleneaux, Carl (Moose)	E	6-4	206	04/01/17	Utah State
44	Ray, Buford (Baby)	T	6-6	240	09/30/15	Vanderbilt
51	Schneidman, Herm	B	5-10	200	11/22/13	Iowa
60	Schultz, Charles	T	6-3	230	10/08/16	Minnesota
45	Smith, Ernie	T	6-2	220	11/26/09	USC
36	Steen, Frank	E	6-1	190	10/05/13	Rice
53	Svendsen, Earl	C	6-1	185	02/07/15	Minnesota
50	Thompson, Clarence	B	5-11	170	09/28/14	Minnesota
21	Tinsley, Pete	G	5-8	205	03/16/13	Georgia
62	Twedell, Francis	G	5-11	220		Minnesota
42	Uram, Andy	B	5-10	187	03/22/15	Minnesota
33	Weisgerber, Dick	B	5-10	205	02/19/15	Williamette
63	Zarnas, Gus	G	5-10	225		Ohio State
57	Zoll, Dick	G	6-1	223	12/10/13	Indiana

1939 DRAFT

Rnd	Name	Pos	College
1	Larry Buhler	B	Minnesota
2	Charley Brock	C	Nebraska
3	Lynn Hovland	G	Wisconsin
4	Larry Craig	E	South Carolina
5	Francis Twedell	T	Minnesota
6	Paul Kell	T	Notre Dame
7	John Hall	B	TCU
8	Vince Gavre	B	Wisconsin
9	Charley Sprague	E	SMU
10	(Choice to Dodgers)		
11	Dan Elmer	C	Minnesota
12	Bill Badgett	T	Georgia
13	Tom Greenfield	C	Arizona
14	Roy Bellin	B	Wisconsin
15	John Yerby	E	Oregon
16	Frank Balazs	B	Iowa
17	John Brennan	G	Michigan
18	Charles Schultz	T	Minnesota
19	Willard Hofer	B	Notre Dame
20	Bill Gunther	B	Santa Clara

1940

Only once in the past 19 years had the Packers given up more than 30 points – 31 to Pottsville in 1925. Imagine the shock fans must have felt when the defending champion Packers were blasted 41-10 by the Chicago Bears in week two at City Stadium. The 31-point pasting, however, was as much the result of Packer ineptness as Bears power. Green Bay outgained the Bears and had more first downs, but turned the ball over nine times and gave up two touchdowns on kickoff returns. The loss, while unsettling, didn't discourage the team and it went on to win three of its next four games.

At that point, Green Bay (4-2-0) trailed the Bears (5-1-0) by a game. On November 3, the two met at Wrigley Field where the Bears took an early 7-0 lead. Arnie Herber threw a seven-yard scoring pass to Don Hutson to tie the game 7-7 early in the second quarter, but Gary Famiglietti's seven-yard touchdown run shortly thereafter proved the difference as the Bears won 14-7. It was this second, less dramatic loss, which closed the door on the Packers' chances of a third straight trip to the NFL Championship Game.

The Packers became the first professional football team to make use of the airlines when they boarded a pair of planes to fly from Chicago to New York City for a game with the Giants on November 17. Once there, the team managed one field goal and lost 7-3 in a defensive struggle. In contrast, one week later, seven different players scored as the team exploded for a 50-7 win over Detroit. Following that, the Packers tied Cleveland 13-13 on the final weekend of play which left the team with a 6-4-1 record. The six wins were the fewest since 1934.

Solid defensive play held the Philadelphia Eagles to minus-seven yards rushing in the season opener. Forced to the air, Davey O'Brien threw 40 passes, three for touchdowns. Green Bay withstood the charge and won 27-20. After the first Bears loss, the Packers intercepted six Cardinals' passes, aiding a 31-6 win. In week four, Cecil Isbell and Herber combined for 327 yards passing, including four touchdowns, a key reason why the Packers downed Cleveland 31-14. The duo, however, didn't sparkle a week later, combining to throw five of the Packers' seven interceptions in a 23-14 loss to Detroit. Green Bay then held Pittsburgh to 95 total yards in a 24-3 victory at Milwaukee before venturing south for the crucial rematch with the Bears.

Tom Pigeon collection

Hal Van Every (36) returns a punt 20 yards in the third quarter of the season opener, a 27-20 victory over the Philadelphia Eagles. Don Looney (30) makes the tackle while Ray George (23), Russ Thompson (25) and Charley Brock (29) approach.

TEAM STATISTICS

	GB	OPP
First Downs	154	120
Rushing	82	61
Passing	66	53
Penalty	6	6
Rushes	463	387
Yards Gained	1,604	1,040
Average Gain	3.46	2.69
Average Yards per Game	145.8	94.5
Passes Attempted	283	252
Completed	118	98
% Completed	41.70	38.89
Total Yards Gained	1,796	1,492
Yards Gained per Completion	15.22	15.22
Average Yards per Game	163.3	135.6
Laterals Attempted	0	0
Completed	0	0
Yards Gained	0	0
Combined Yards Gained	3,400	2,532
Total Plays	746	639
Average Yards per Play	4.56	3.96
Average Yards per Game	313.2	251.8
Intercepted By	40	26
Yards Returned	414	290
Returned for TD	1	1
Punts	57	76
Yards Punted	2,131	2,994
Average Yards per Punt	37.39	39.39
Yards Punt Returns	494	231
Returned for TD	0	0
Yards Kickoff Returns	381	995
Returned for TD	0	2
Yards Penalized	295	342
Fumbles	21	15
Lost	12	7
Own Recovered for Touchdown	0	0
Opponent's Recovered by	7	12
Opponent's Recovered for Touchdown	1	0
Total Points Scored	238	155
Total Touchdowns	30	22
Touchdowns Rushing	10	9
Touchdowns Passing	18	10
Touchdowns on Returns & Recoveries	2	3
Extra Points	28	17
Safeties	0	0
Field Goals Attempted	20	3
Field Goals Made	10	2
% Successful	50.00	66.67

Regular Season   6-4-1

Date	GB		OPP	Att.
9/15	27	Philadelphia Eagles	20	(11,657)
9/22	10	Chicago Bears	41	(22,557)
9/29	31	Chicago Cardinals (M)	6	(20,234)
10/13	31	Cleveland Rams	14	(16,299)
10/20	14	Detroit Lions	23	(21,001)
10/27	24	Pittsburgh Steelers (M)	3	(13,703)
11/3	7	at Chicago Bears	14	(45,434)
11/10	28	at Chicago Cardinals	7	(11,364)
11/17	3	at New York Giants	7	(28,262)
11/24	50	at Detroit Lions	7	(26,019)
12/1	13	at Cleveland Rams	13	(16,249)

Score By Periods

	1	2	3	4	Total
Packers	74	52	44	68	238
Opponents	24	54	30	47	155

1940

INDIVIDUAL STATISTICS

Rushing

	Att	Yds	Avg	TD
Hinkle	109	383	3.5	2
Uram	71	270	3.8	1
Isbell	97	270	2.8	4
Jankowski	48	211	4.4	2
Van Every	38	154	4.1	0
Buhler	36	118	3.3	0
Balazs	25	107	4.3	1
L. Brock	18	60	3.3	0
Laws	7	21	3.0	0
Feathers	4	19	4.8	0
Craig	3	9	3.0	0
Adkins	1	5	5.0	0
Herber	6	-23	-3.8	0
Packers	**463**	**1,604**	**3.5**	**10**
Opponents	387	1,040	2.7	9

Receiving

	No	Yds	Avg	LG	TD
Hutson	45	664	14.8	t36	7
C. Mulleneaux	16	288	18.0	t47	6
Riddick	11	148	13.5		0
Uram	10	188	18.8	44	2
Craig	6	67	11.2	24	0
L. Brock	5	97	19.4	33	0
Laws	5	60	12.0	24	1
Adkins	4	73	18.3	t55	1
Van Every	4	41	10.3	23	0
Hinkle	4	28	7.0	t12	1
D. Evans	2	40	20.0	30	0
Jacunski	2	29	14.5	17	0
Weisgerber	1	37	37.0	37	0
C. Berry	1	17	17.0	17	0
Gantenbein	1	12	12.0	12	0
Balazs	1	7	7.0	7	0
Packers	**118**	**1,796**	**15.2**	**t55**	**18**
Opponents	98	1,492	15.2	74	10

Passing

	Att	Com	Yds	Pct	TD	In	Rate
Isbell	150	68	1,037	45.3	9	12	55.3
Herber	89	38	560	42.7	5	7	49.8
Van Every	41	12	199	29.3	4	6	40.2
L. Brock	2	0	0	00.0	0	0	—
Balazs	1	0	0	00.0	0	1	—
Packers	**283**	**118**	**1,796**	**41.7**	**18**	**26**	**46.2**
Opponents	252	98	1,492	38.9	10	40	32.8

Punting

	No	Yds	Avg	LG	HB
Hinkle	22	819	37.2	59	0
Van Every	17	620	36.5	50	0
Herber	13	504	38.8	55	0
L. Brock	3	125	41.7	52	0
Isbell	2	63	31.5	37	0
Packers	**57**	**2,131**	**37.4**	**59**	**0**
Opponents	76	2,994	39.4	75	0

Interceptions

	No	Yds	Avg	LG	TD
Hutson	6	24	4.0		0
L. Brock	5	116	23.2	74	0
Weisgerber	4	51	12.8	24	0
Van Every	3	30	10.0		0
Uram	3	27	9.0	15	0
C. Brock	3	7	2.3	6	0
Buhler	2	58	29.0	32	0
Adkins	2	35	17.5	t35	1
Isbell	2	14	7.0	14	0
Hinkle	2	11	5.5	8	0
Herber	2	0	0.0		0
B. Lee	1	14	14.0	14	0
Balazs	1	11	11.0	11	0
G. Svendsen	1	6	6.0	6	0
Goldenberg	1	5	5.0	5	0
Greenfield	1	5	5.0	5	0
Craig	1	0	0.0		0
Packers	**40**	**414**	**10.4**	**74**	**1**
Opponents	26	290	11.2	28	1

Scoring

	TDr	TDp	TDrt	PAT	FG	S	TP
Hutson	0	7	0	15/16	0/0	0	57
Hinkle	2	1	0	3/3	9/14	0	48
C. Mulleneaux	0	6	1	0/0	0/0	0	42
Isbell	4	0	0	0/0	0/0	0	24
Uram	1	2	0	1/2	0/0	0	19
Adkins	0	1	1	1/1	0/1	0	13
Jankowski	2	0	0	0/0	0/0	0	12
Engebretsen	0	0	0	8/8	1/5	0	11
Balazs	1	0	0	0/0	0/0	0	6
Laws	0	1	0	0/0	0/0	0	6
Packers	**10**	**18**	**2**	**28/30**	**10/20**	**0**	**238**
Opponents	9	10	3	17/22	2/3	0	155

NFL STANDINGS

Western Division

	W	L	T	Pct	PF	PA
Chicago Bears	8	3	0	.727	238	152
Green Bay Packers	**6**	**4**	**1**	**.600**	**238**	**155**
Detroit Lions	5	5	1	.500	138	153
Cleveland Rams	4	6	1	.400	171	191
Chicago Cardinals	2	7	2	.222	139	222

Eastern Division

	W	L	T	Pct	PF	PA
Washington Redskins	9	2	0	.818	245	142
Brooklyn Dodgers	8	3	0	.727	186	120
New York Giants	6	4	1	.600	131	133
Pittsburgh Steelers	2	7	2	.222	60	178
Philadelphia Eagles	1	10	0	.091	111	211

1940 ROSTER

No	Name	Pos	Ht	Wt	DOB	College
55	Adkins, Robert	E	6-0	211	02/07/17	Marshall
35	Balazs, Frank	B	6-2	215	01/23/18	Iowa
37	Berry, Connie	E	6-3	210		North Carolina State
29	Brock, Charley	C	6-1	205	03/15/16	Nebraska
15	Brock, Lou	B	6-0	195	12/09/17	Purdue
52	Buhler, Larry	B	6-2	210	05/28/17	Minnesota
54	Craig, Larry	E	6-0	205	06/27/16	South Carolina
18	Disend, Leo	T	6-2	225	11/07/15	Albright
34	Engebretsen, Paul (Tiny)	G	6-1	245	07/27/10	Northwestern
53	Evans, Dick	E	6-3	195	05/31/18	Iowa
3	Feathers, Beattie	B	5-11	180	08/04/08	Tennessee
22	Gantenbein, Milt	E	6-0	200	05/31/10	Wisconsin
43	Goldenberg, Charles (Buckets)	G	5-10	225	03/10/11	Wisconsin
56	Greenfield, Tom	C	6-4	218	11/10/17	Arizona
38	Herber, Arnie	B	5-11	208	04/02/10	Regis
30	Hinkle, Clarke	FB	5-11	200	04/10/12	Bucknell
14	Hutson, Don	E	6-1	185	01/31/13	Alabama
17	Isbell, Cecil	B	6-1	191	07/11/15	Purdue
48	Jacunski, Harry	E	6-2	198	10/20/15	Fordham
7	Jankowski, Ed	B	5-10	205	06/23/13	Wisconsin
64	Johnson, Howard (Smiley)	G	5-10	200	09/22/16	Georgia
41	Kell, Paul	T	6-2	217	07/18/15	Notre Dame
24	Laws, Joe	B	5-9	186	06/16/11	Iowa
40	Lee, Bill	T	6-3	235	10/19/11	Alabama
46	Letlow, Russ	G	6-0	215	10/05/13	San Francisco
27	Midler, Lou	G	6-1	220	07/21/15	Minnesota
19	Mulleneaux, Carl (Moose)	E	6-4	205	04/01/17	Utah State
44	Ray, Buford (Baby)	T	6-6	248	09/30/15	Vanderbilt
5	Riddick, Ray	E	6-0	225	10/17/17	Fordham
60	Schultz, Charles	T	6-3	230	10/08/16	Minnesota
68	Seeman, George	E	6-0	194	04/03/16	Nebraska
57	Seibold, Champ	T	6-4	246	12/05/12	Wisconsin
18	Shirey, Fred	T	6-2	220		Nebraska
66	Svendsen, George	C	6-4	240	03/22/13	Minnesota
21	Tinsley, Pete	G	5-8	205	03/16/13	Georgia
42	Uram, Andy	B	5-10	188	03/22/15	Minnesota
36	Van Every, Hal	B	6-0	195	02/10/18	Minnesota
33	Weisgerber, Dick	B	5-10	194	02/19/15	Williamette
	Woods, Bobby	T	6-1	235		Alabama
63	Zarnas, Gus	G	5-10	225		Ohio State

1940 DRAFT

Rnd	Name	Pos	College
1	Hal Van Every	B	Minnesota
2	Lou Brock	B	Purdue
3	Esco Sarkkinen	E	Ohio State
4	Dick Cassiano	B	Pittsburgh
5	Millard White	T	Tulane
6	George Seeman	E	Nebraska
7	J.R. Manley	G	Oklahoma
8	Jack Brown	B	Purdue
9	Don Guritz	G	Northwestern
10	Phil Gaspar	B	USC
11	Ambrose Schindler	B	USC
12	Bill Kerr	E	Notre Dame
13	Mel Brewer	G	Illinois
14	Ray Andrus	B	Vanderbilt
15	Archie Kodros	C	Michigan
16	Jim Gillette	B	Virginia
17	Al Matuza	C	Georgetown
18	Jim Reeder	T	Illinois
19	Vince Eichler	B	Cornell
20	Henry Luebcke	T	Iowa

1940 GREEN BAY PACKERS

FRONT ROW: (L-R) 5 Ray Riddick, 63 Gus Zarnas, 40 Bill Lee, 42 Andy Uram, 33 Dick Weisgerber, 7 Ed Jankowski, 38 Arnie Herber, 54 Larry Craig, 19 Carl (Moose) Mulleneaux, 29 Charley Brock.

SECOND ROW: (L-R) Coach Curly Lambeau, 43 Charles (Buckets) Goldenberg, 24 Joe Laws, 3 Beattie Feathers, 48 Harry Jacunski, 66 George Svendsen, 44 Buford (Baby) Ray, 34 Paul (Tiny) Engebretsen, 37 Connie Berry, Assistant Coach Richard (Red) Smith.

THIRD ROW: (L-R) 68 George Seeman, 22 Milt Gantenbein, 64 Howard (Smiley) Johnson, 21 Pete Tinsley, 30 Clarke Hinkle, 14 Don Hutson, 55 Robert Adkins, 46 Russ Letlow, 17 Cecil Isbell, 15 Lou Brock.

BACK ROW: (L-R) 53 Dick Evans, 41 Paul Kell, 56 Tom Greenfield, 27 Lou Midler, 60 Charles Schultz, 52 Larry Buhler, 18 Leo Disend, 57 Champ Seibold, 36 Hal Van Every.

After the Chicago Bears had destroyed the Washington Redskins 73-0 in the 1940 NFL Championship Game, some in the football world believed the Monsters of the Midway were invincible. The Bears did nothing to shake that image when they opened 1941 and overran their first five foes 209-52, including a 25-17 triumph at Green Bay. With each win, the Chicagoans added a new group of believers. One notable exception hailed from Green Bay: Packers Coach Curly Lambeau.

Having survived the 25-17 setback on September 28, Lambeau and his team regrouped and quietly won four in a row. On November 2, the Packers (6-1) traveled to Wrigley Field, den of the Bears, where Chicago (5-0) had not lost since 1939. The Packers jumped to a 16-0 lead after three quarters, but Chicago fought back and scored twice. Green Bay, however, held on for a 16-14 win, proving the Bears were only human after all.

Still, the Bears had the last laugh. Both teams continued to win after the face-off in Chicago. When the season ended, the two boasted identical 10-1 records. A divisional playoff game followed in Chicago where the Bears took revenge 33-14 and sent the Packers home for Christmas.

Two players who had played major roles in the championship era of the 1930s departed. Milt Gantenbein retired after 10 seasons and Arnie Herber was released in a surprising move just before the beginning of the regular season. Gantenbein had toiled in relative obscurity, overshadowed by the exploits of Don Hutson. Herber, the first master of the bomb, had played on four championship teams and exited having thrown for more yards than any other in NFL history to that point.

While both would be missed, the team nonetheless got off to a good start with wins over Detroit and Cleveland. The Packers limited the Lions to 132 total yards and a week later Green Bay rushed 62 times for 235 yards to top the Rams 24-7.

In week three, the Bears completed only one pass —a 44-yarder for a touchdown— but beat Green Bay 25-17. From that point the Packers caught fire and closed out with eight consecutive victories.

Cecil Isbell in particular, came to the front. He threw at least one touchdown pass in every game while completing an amazing 56.8 percent of his passes. He ran for a touchdown and passed 36 yards to Lou Brock for another to help beat the Bears in week eight. In addition, he engineered the biggest comeback in Packer history to that point, on the final weekend of the regular season.

On November 30, Green Bay fell behind the Redskins and trailed 17-0 at halftime. In the second half, Isbell threw three touchdown passes – all to Don Hutson – to spark an attack that scored 22 points and subdued Washington 22-17. Without the win, the Packers would never have had a third shot at the Bears and a chance for another championship berth.

Green Bay Press-Gazette photo

Clarke Hinkle (30) and Charles (Buckets) Goldenberg (43) provide escort for Andy Uram (42) in a game against Cleveland. The Packers triumphed 24-7 before 18,463 at State Fair Park in Milwaukee. Uram went on to return a punt 90 yards for a touchdown against Brooklyn and finished the year third in rushing behind Hinkle and Cecil Isbell.

TEAM STATISTICS

	GB	OPP
First Downs	166	124
Rushing	82	78
Passing	69	49
Penalty	15	11
Rushes	467	356
Yards Gained	1,550	1,221
Average Gain	3.32	3.43
Average Yards per Game	140.9	111.0
Passes Attempted	253	233
Completed	133	104
% Completed	52.57	44.64
Total Yards Gained	1,731	1,343
Yards Gained per Completion	13.02	12.91
Average Yards per Game	157.4	122.1
Laterals Attempted	1	15
Completed	1	14
Yards Gained	13	22
Combined Yards Gained	3,294	2,586
Total Plays	721	604
Average Yards per Play	4.57	4.28
Average Yards per Game	299.5	235.1
Intercepted By	25	13
Yards Returned	455	170
Returned for TD	1	0
Punts	53	58
Yards Punted	2,232	2,367
Average Yards per Punt	42.11	40.81
Punt Returns	41	31
Yards Returned	487	432
Average Yards per Return	11.88	13.94
Returned for TD	1	1
Kickoff Returns	28	39
Yards Returned	567	880
Average Yards per Return	20.25	22.56
Returned for TD	0	0
Penalties	47	63
Yards Penalized	509	539
Fumbles	20	41
Lost	11	23
Own Recovered for Touchdown	0	0
Opponent's Recovered by	23	11
Opponent's Recovered for Touchdown	1	0
Total Points Scored	258	120
Total Touchdowns	33	16
Touchdowns Rushing	13	7
Touchdowns Passing	17	8
Touchdowns on Returns & Recoveries	3	1
Extra Points	28	12
Safeties	1	0
Field Goals Attempted	20	12
Field Goals Made	10	4
% Successful	50.00	33.33

Regular Season 10-1-0

Date	GB		OPP		Att.
9/14	23	Detroit Lions	0		(16,734)
9/21	24	Cleveland Rams (M)	7		(18,463)
9/28	17	Chicago Bears	25		(24,876)
10/5	14	Chicago Cardinals (M)	13		(10,000)
10/12	30	Brooklyn Dodgers (M)	7		(15,621)
10/19	17	at Cleveland Rams	14		(13,086)
10/26	24	at Detroit Lions	7		(30,269)
11/2	16	at Chicago Bears	14		(46,484)
11/16	17	Chicago Cardinals	9		(15,495)
11/23	54	at Pittsburgh Steelers	7		(15,202)
11/30	22	at Washington Redskins	17		(35,594)

Postseason 0-1-0

12/14	14	at Chicago Bears	33		(43,425)

Score By Periods

	1	2	3	4	Total
Packers	54	58	54	92	258
Opponents	39	23	20	38	120

INDIVIDUAL STATISTICS

Rushing

	Att	Yds	Avg	LG	TD
Hinkle	129	393	3.0	20	5
Isbell	72	317	4.4	24	1
Uram	49	258	5.3	61	0
Canadeo	43	137	3.2	16	3
Van Every	25	127	5.1	t31	2
Paskvan	38	116	3.1	12	0
Jankowski	47	65	1.4	13	0
Laws	21	58	2.8	10	0
L. Brock	14	44	3.1	14	0
Hutson	4	22	5.5	t18	2
Frutig	1	11	11.0	11	0
Rohrig	21	2	0.1	18	0
Craig	1	1	1.0	1	0
Balazs	2	-1	-0.5	1	0
Packers	**467**	**1,550**	**3.3**	**61**	**13**
Opponents	356	1,221	3.4	31	7

Receiving

	No	Yds	Avg	LG	TD
Hutson	58	738	12.7	t45	10
L. Brock	22	307	14.0	t36	2
Rohrig	11	58	5.3	19	0
C. Mulleneaux	9	216	24.0	56	2
Hinkle	8	78	9.8	28	1
Uram	6	124	20.7	44	0
Jacunski	4	48	12.0	27	0
Laws	4	48	12.0	t18	1
Riddick	3	33	11.0	16	0
Frutig	2	40	20.0	34	0
Urban	2	26	13.0	14	1
Craig	2	13	6.5	12	0
Van Every	1	3	3.0	3	0
Isbell	1	-1	-1.0	-1	0
Packers	**133**	**1,731**	**13.0**	**56**	**17**
Opponents	104	1,343	12.9	t80	8

Passing

	Att	Com	Yds	Pct	TD	In	Rate
Isbell	206	117	1,479	56.8	15	11	81.4
Van Every	30	11	195	36.7	0	2	31.9
Canadeo	16	4	54	25.0	2	0	80.7
Rohrig	1	1	3	100.0	0	0	—
Packers	**253**	**133**	**1,731**	**52.6**	**17**	**13**	**75.4**
Opponents	233	104	1,343	44.6	8	25	35.2

Punting

	No	Yds	Avg	LG	HB
Hinkle	22	980	44.5	63	0
Van Every	13	505	38.8	65	0
Canadeo	10	405	40.5	62	0
Rohrig	5	214	42.8	52	0
L. Brock	3	128	42.7	48	0
Packers	**53**	**2,232**	**42.1**	**65**	**0**
Opponents	58	2,367	40.8	74	1

Kickoff Returns

	No	Yds	Avg	LG	TD
Canadeo	4	110	27.5	55	0
Van Every	4	99	24.8	31	0
L. Brock	4	94	23.5	36	0
Laws	3	75	25.0	26	0
Rohrig	3	60	20.0	29	0
Hinkle	3	38	12.7	16	0
Isbell	2	32	16.0	20	0
Uram	2	27	13.5	14	0
Riddick	1	14	14.0	14	0
Buhler	1	10	10.0	10	0
Hutson	1	8	8.0	8	0
Packers	**28**	**567**	**20.3**	**55**	**0**
Opponents	39	880	22.6	51	0

Punt Returns

	No	Yds	Avg	LG	TD
L. Brock	15	153	10.2	45	0
Uram	7	121	17.3	t90	1
Van Every	4	58	14.5	20	0
Rohrig	4	46	11.5	14	0
Canadeo	4	26	6.5	10	0
Isbell	3	19	6.3	7	0
Hinkle	2	61	30.5	36	0
Laws	2	3	1.5	3	0
Packers	**41**	**487**	**11.9**	**t90**	**1**
Opponents	31	432	13.9	t77	1

Interceptions

	No	Yds	Avg	LG	TD
Van Every	3	104	34.7	t91	1
Adkins	2	79	39.5	54	0
Uram	2	37	18.5	28	0
Laws	2	36	18.0	36	0
Canadeo	2	30	15.0	22	0
Paskvan	2	6	3.0	4	0
L. Brock	2	3	1.5	3	0
G. Svendsen	1	42	42.0	42	0
Jankowski	1	33	33.0	33	0
Hutson	1	32	32.0	32	0
Tinsley	1	24	24.0	24	0
Rohrig	1	17	17.0	17	0
H. Johnson	1	10	10.0	10	0
Hinkle	1	2	2.0	2	0
Goldenberg	1	0	0.0	0	0
Isbell	1	0	0.0	0	0
Pannell	1	0	0.0	0	0
Packers	**25**	**455**	**18.2**	**t91**	**1**
Opponents	13	170	13.1	56	0

Scoring

	TDr	TDp	TDrt	PAT	FG	S	TP
Hutson	2	10	0	20/24	1/1	0	95
Hinkle	5	1	0	2/2	6/14	0	56
Canadeo	3	6	0	0/0	0/0	0	18
Van Every	2	0	1	0/0	0/0	0	18
L. Brock	0	2	0	0/0	0/0	0	12
C. Mulleneaux	0	2	0	0/0	0/0	0	12
Isbell	1	0	0	0/0	0/0	0	6
Laws	0	1	0	0/0	0/0	0	6
Pannell	0	0	1	0/0	0/0	0	6
Uram	0	0	1	0/0	0/0	0	6
Urban	0	1	0	0/0	0/0	0	6
Rohrig	0	0	0	1/1	1/1	0	4
Jankowski	0	0	0	1/2	1/1	0	4
Adkins	0	0	0	3/3	0/0	0	3
Engebretsen	0	0	0	0/0	1/3	0	3
team	0	0	0	0/0	0/0	1	2
Balasz	0	0	0	1/1	0/0	0	1
Packers	**13**	**17**	**3**	**28/33**	**10/20**	**1**	**258**
Opponents	7	8	1	12/16	4/12	0	120

NFL STANDINGS

Western Division

	W	L	T	Pct	PF	PA
Chicago Bears	10	1	0	.909	396	147
Green Bay Packers	10	1	0	.909	258	120
Detroit Lions	4	6	1	.400	121	195
Chicago Cardinals	3	7	1	.300	127	197
Cleveland Rams	2	9	0	.182	116	244

Eastern Division

	W	L	T	Pct	PF	PA
New York Giants	9	3	0	.727	238	114
Brooklyn Dodgers	7	4	0	.636	158	127
Washington Redskins	6	5	0	.545	176	174
Philadelphia Eagles	2	8	1	.200	119	218
Pittsburgh Steelers	1	9	1	.100	103	276

1941 ROSTER

No	Name	Pos	Ht	Wt	DOB	College
55	Adkins, Robert	E	6-0	211	02/07/17	Marshall
35	Balazs, Frank	FB	6-2	205	01/23/18	Iowa
29	Brock, Charley	C	6-1	207	03/15/16	Nebraska
16	Brock, Lou	HB	6-0	196	12/09/17	Purdue
33	Bucchianeri, Amadeo (Mike)	G	5-10	210	09/01/17	Indiana
52	Buhler, Larry	HB	6-2	210	05/28/17	Minnesota
3	Canadeo, Tony	HB	6-0	190	05/05/19	Gonzaga
54	Craig, Larry	E	6-0	210	06/27/16	South Carolina
34	Engebretsen, Paul (Tiny)	G	6-1	245	07/27/10	Northwestern
51	Frutig, Ed	E	6-1	190	08/19/20	Michigan
43	Goldenberg, Charles (Buckets)	G	5-10	230	03/10/11	Wisconsin
56	Greenfield, Tom	C	6-4	219	11/10/17	Arizona
30	Hinkle, Clarke	FB	5-11	205	04/10/12	Bucknell
14	Hutson, Don	E	6-1	180	01/31/13	Alabama
17	Isbell, Cecil	HB	6-1	190	07/11/15	Purdue
48	Jacunski, Harry	E	6-2	202	10/20/15	Fordham
7	Jankowski, Ed	FB	5-10	195	06/23/13	Wisconsin
50	Johnson, Bill	E	6-1	195	10/04/16	Minnesota
64	Johnson, Howard (Smiley)	G	5-10	195	09/22/16	Georgia
45	Kuusisto, William	G	6-0	235	04/26/18	Minnesota
24	Laws, Joe	HB	5-9	190	06/16/11	Iowa
40	Lee, Bill	T	6-3	240	10/19/11	Alabama
46	Letlow, Russ	G	6-0	220	10/05/13	San Francisco
15	Lyman, Del	T	6-2	225	07/09/18	UCLA
37	McLaughlin, Lee	T	6-1	225	02/28/17	Virginia
19	Mulleneaux, Carl (Moose)	E	6-4	205	04/01/17	Utah State
22	Pannell, Ernie	T	6-3	215	02/02/17	Texas A&M
68	Paskvan, George	FB	6-0	190	04/01/18	Wisconsin
44	Ray, Buford (Baby)	T	6-6	250	09/30/15	Vanderbilt
5	Riddick, Ray	E	6-0	220	10/17/17	Fordham
8	Rohrig, Herman	HB	5-9	187	03/19/18	Nebraska
60	Schultz, Charles	T	6-3	235	10/08/16	Minnesota
66	Svendsen, George	C	6-4	240	03/22/13	Minnesota
21	Tinsley, Pete	G	5-8	200	03/16/13	Georgia
42	Uram, Andy	HB	5-10	188	03/22/15	Minnesota
23	Urban, Alex	E	6-3	199	07/16/17	South Carolina
36	Van Every, Hal	HB	6-0	195	02/10/18	Minnesota

1941 DRAFT

Rnd	Name	Pos	College
1	George Paskvan	B	Wisconsin
2	Robert Paffrath	B	Minnesota
3	Ed Frutig	E	Michigan
4	Herman Rohrig	B	Nebraska
5	Bill Telesmanic	E	San Francisco
6	William Kuusisto	G	Minnesota
7	Tony Canadeo	B	Gonzaga
8	Mike Byelene	B	Purdue
9	Paul Hiemenz	C	Northwestern
10	Mike Enich	T	Iowa
11	Ed Heffernan	B	St. Mary's (CA)
12	Del Lyman	T	UCLA
13	John Frieberger	E	Arkansas
14	Ernie Pannell	T	Texas A&M
15	Bob Saggau	B	Notre Dame
16	Heige Pukema	G	Minnesota
17	Robert Hayes	E	Toledo
18	James Strasbaugh	B	Ohio State
19	Joe Bailey	C	Kentucky
20	Bruno Malinowski	B	Holy Cross

1941 GREEN BAY PACKERS

FRONT ROW: (L-R) 8 Herman Rohrig, 54 Larry Craig, 30 Clarke Hinkle, 42 Andy Uram, 7 Ed Jankowski, 24 Joe Laws, 33 Amadeo (Mike) Bucchianeri, 40 Bill Lee, 14 Don Hutson.
SECOND ROW: (L-R) 51 Ed Frutig, 3 Tony Canadeo, 34 Paul (Tiny) Engebretsen, 64 Howard (Smiley) Johnson, 55 Bob Adkins, 17 Cecil Isbell, 5 Ray Riddick, 29 Charley Brock, 43 Charles (Buckets) Goldenberg.
THIRD ROW: (L-R) 68 George Paskvan, Lou Brock, 50 Bill Johnson, 36 Hal Van Every, 56 Tom Greenfield, 48 Harry Jacunski, 23 Alex Urban, 52 Larry Buhler, 21 Pete Tinsley, 45 William Kuusisto.
BACK ROW: (L-R) 15 Del Lyman, 35 Frank Balazs, 19 Carl (Moose) Mulleneaux, 66 George Svendsen, 44 Buford (Baby) Ray, 22 Ernie Pannell, 37 Lee McLaughlin.

The Packers had long been a proponent of the passing game. From the start, quarterbacks Curly Lambeau, Charlie Mathys and Joseph (Red) Dunn turned to the air to move the ball. Arnie Herber and Bobby Monnett continued the trend, throwing in particular to Don Hutson. All played a role in transforming the passing game into an effective weapon.

Perhaps the greatest display of Packer passing power occurred in 1942. Cecil Isbell and Hutson turned in record-breaking performances. Isbell became the first quarterback to throw for 2,000 yards in a single season. His 24 touchdown passes also set a then-NFL record. Hutson shattered a number of receiving marks —many his own— by catching 74 passes for 1,211 yards and 17 touchdowns. Their efforts and those of others, such as Andy Uram and Lou Brock, provided the Packers with the league's top passing offense.

The only team the Packers could not beat in 1942 was the Bears. Then again, nobody was able to defeat them during the regular season as Chicago raced to an 11-0 mark. The Bears exploded for 17 fourth-quarter points to knock off Green Bay 44-28 in week one and then rudely bounced them 38-7 in the return trip in Chicago. Those two losses left the Packers with an 8-2-1 record, good for second place.

Clarke Hinkle, whose running would have helped in the losses, was called to the Coast Guard. Although he turned 30 in 1942, Hinkle was not past his prime. He left the game as the NFL's top rusher to that point, having gained 3,860 yards.

Even though the Bears set Green Bay back in week one, the team snapped back with six straight wins. Great passing and receiving efforts played a part in at least three of them. On October 11, Don Hutson caught five passes for 149 yards and two touchdowns in a 38-7 pounding of Detroit. The following week, he set then-team records with 13 catches for 209 yards plus two scores as Green Bay beat the Rams 45-28. He registered his second 200-yard day with five catches for 207 yards and three touchdowns on November 1. In that game Uram also caught four passes for 174 yards and another three touchdowns as the Packers destroyed the Cardinals 55-24.

As far as quarterbacks went, Isbell threw for 15 touchdowns during the six-game winning streak. Perhaps his best game came against the Cardinals when he completed 10 of 21 passes for 333 yards and five touchdowns.

The Bears put a stop to the Packers' good fortune and essentially their season with a 38-7 win on November 15. Though Chicago could not completely shut down the Packers' passing game, they did not allow a completion of more than 20 yards and intercepted three tosses, one of which was returned for a touchdown.

Green Bay Press-Gazette photo

Don Hutson (14) hauls in one of 13 passes he caught in a 45-28 triumph over the Cleveland Rams on October 18. Hutson's receptions, good for 209 yards, set team and NFL marks at the time. On the year, he caught 74 passes for 1,211 yards and 17 touchdowns, numbers which again established then-NFL records.

TEAM STATISTICS

	GB	OPP
First Downs	176	147
Rushing	65	79
Passing	97	59
Penalty	14	9
Rushes	422	376
Yards Gained	1,374	1,549
Average Gain	3.26	4.12
Average Yards per Game	124.9	140.8
Passes Attempted	330	242
Completed	172	100
% Completed	52.12	41.32
Total Yards Gained	2,407	1,471
Yards Gained per Completion	13.99	14.71
Average Yards per Game	218.8	133.7
Laterals Attempted	3	4
Completed	3	4
Yards Gained	9	56
Combined Yards Gained	3,790	3,076
Total Plays	755	622
Average Yards per Play	5.02	4.95
Average Yards per Game	344.5	279.6
Intercepted By	33	18
Yards Returned	352	282
Returned for TD	1	2
Punts	58	56
Yards Punted	2,175	2,088
Average Yards per Punt	37.50	37.29
Punt Returns	32	38
Yards Returned	327	396
Average Yards per Return	10.22	10.42
Returned for TD	0	0
Kickoff Returns	37	45
Yards Returned	789	1,044
Average Yards per Return	21.32	23.20
Returned for TD	1	1
Penalties	38	63
Yards Penalized	312	539
Fumbles	13	22
Lost	8	15
Own Recovered for Touchdown	0	0
Opponent's Recovered by	15	8
Opponent's Recovered for Touchdown	1	2
Total Points Scored	300	215
Total Touchdowns	41	28
Touchdowns Rushing	10	14
Touchdowns Passing	28	8
Touchdowns on Returns & Recoveries	3	6
Extra Points	39	27
Safeties	0	1
Field Goals Attempted	10	7
Field Goals Made	5	6
% Successful	50.00	85.71

Regular Season 8-2-1

Date	GB		OPP	Att.
9/27	28	Chicago Bears	44	(20,007)
10/4	17	at Chicago Cardinals	13	(24,897)
10/11	38	Detroit Lions (M)	7	(19,500)
10/18	45	Cleveland Rams	28	(12,847)
10/25	28	at Detroit Lions	7	(19,097)
11/1	55	Chicago Cardinals	24	(14,782)
11/8	30	at Cleveland Rams	12	(16,473)
11/15	7	at Chicago Bears	38	(42,787)
11/22	21	at New York Giants	21	(30,246)
11/29	7	at Philadelphia Eagles	0	(13,700)
12/6	24	Pittsburgh Steelers (M)	21	(5,138)

Score By Periods

	1	2	3	4	Total
Packers	57	90	48	105	300
Opponents	45	61	43	66	215

INDIVIDUAL STATISTICS

Rushing

	Att	Yds	Avg	LG	TD
Fritsch	74	323	4.4	55	0
Canadeo	89	272	3.1	t50	3
Sample	57	255	4.5	31	4
L. Brock	95	237	2.5	24	2
Laws	29	100	3.4	17	0
Isbell	36	83	2.3	32	1
Uram	24	75	3.1	8	0
Weisgerber	5	21	4.2	6	0
Hutson	3	4	1.3	9	0
Bob Kahler	8	4	0.5	13	0
Craig	2	0	0.0	4	0
Packers	422	1,374	3.3	55	10
Opponents	376	1,549	4.1	54	14

Receiving

	No	Yds	Avg	LG	TD
Hutson	74	1,211	16.4	t73	17
Uram	21	420	20.0	t64	4
L. Brock	20	139	7.0	29	1
Canadeo	10	66	6.6	15	0
Fritsch	9	60	6.7	21	0
Jacunski	8	125	15.6	t49	1
J. Mason	7	86	12.3	19	0
Riddick	6	104	17.3	t24	1
Laws	6	96	16.0	28	1
Sample	6	35	5.8	t10	1
Bob Kahler	2	21	10.5	12	0
Joe Carter	2	19	9.5	t10	1
Ranspot	1	25	25.0	t25	1
Packers	172	2,407	14.0	t73	28
Opponents	100	1,471	14.7	t67	8

Passing

	Att	Com	Yds	Pct	TD	In	Rate
Isbell	268	146	2,021	54.5	24	14	87.0
Canadeo	59	24	310	40.7	3	4	46.6
Laws	3	2	76	66.7	1	0	—
Packers	330	172	2,407	52.1	28	18	81.5
Opponents	242	100	1,471	41.3	8	33	33.3

Punting

	No	Yds	Avg	LG	HB
L. Brock	32	1,226	38.3	52	2
Canadeo	18	643	35.7	47	0
Isbell	4	141	35.3	46	0
Fritsch	3	122	40.7	54	0
Starret	1	43	43.0	43	0
Packers	58	2,175	37.5	54	2
Opponents	56	2,088	37.3	67	1

Kickoff Returns

	No	Yds	Avg	LG	TD
L. Brock	9	179	19.9	26	0
Uram	8	208	26.0	t98	1
Canadeo	6	137	22.8	35	0
Isbell	4	64	16.0	20	0
Sample	3	91	30.3	35	0
Fritsch	2	43	21.5	23	0
Laws	2	36	18.0	18	0
Craig	2	24	12.0	16	0
Berezney	1	7	7.0	7	0
Packers	37	789	21.3	t98	1
Opponents	45	1,044	23.2	t95	1

Punt Returns

	No	Yds	Avg	LG	TD
L. Brock	8	86	10.8	22	0
Canadeo	7	76	10.9	26	0
Laws	7	56	8.0	15	0
Uram	7	50	7.1	24	0
Fritsch	1	31	31.0	31	0
Isbell	1	31	31.0	31	0
Bob Kahler	1	14	14.0	14	0
Packers	32	327	10.2	31	0
Opponents	38	396	10.4	44	0

Interceptions

	No	Yds	Avg	LG	TD
Hutson	7	71	10.1	27	0
Isbell	6	47	7.8	19	0
C. Brock	6	25	4.2	16	0
Goldenberg	4	31	7.8	15	0
Laws	3	67	22.3	38	0
L. Brock	2	32	16.0	19	0
Uram	2	18	9.0	18	0
Canadeo	1	35	35.0	35	0
Ingalls	1	23	23.0	t23	1
Tinsley	1	3	3.0	3	0
Packers	33	352	10.7	38	1
Opponents	18	282	15.7	t54	2

Scoring

	TDr	TDp	TDrt	PAT	FG	S	TP
Hutson	0	17	0	33/34	1/4	0	138
Uram	0	4	1	1/1	0/0	0	31
Sample	4	1	0	0/0	0/0	0	30
L. Brock	2	1	0	2/2	0/1	0	20
Canadeo	3	0	0	0/0	0/0	0	18
Fritsch	0	0	0	1/1	4/5	0	13
C. Brock	0	0	1	0/0	0/0	0	6
Joe Carter	0	1	0	0/0	0/0	0	6
Ingalls	0	0	1	0/0	0/0	0	6
Jacunski	0	1	0	0/0	0/0	0	6
Laws	0	1	0	0/0	0/0	0	6
Ranspot	0	1	0	0/0	0/0	0	6
Riddick	0	1	0	0/0	0/0	0	6
Weisgerber	0	0	0	2/2	0/0	0	2
Packers	10	28	3	39/41	5/10	0	300
Opponents	14	8	6	27/28	6/7	1	215

NFL STANDINGS

Western Division

	W	L	T	Pct	PF	PA
Chicago Bears	11	0	0	1.000	376	84
Green Bay Packers	8	2	1	.800	300	215
Cleveland Rams	5	6	0	.455	150	207
Chicago Cardinals	3	8	0	.273	98	209
Detroit Lions	0	11	0	.000	38	263

Eastern Division

	W	L	T	Pct	PF	PA
Washington Redskins	10	1	0	.909	227	102
Pittsburgh Steelers	7	4	0	.636	167	119
New York Giants	5	5	1	.500	155	139
Brooklyn Dodgers	3	8	0	.273	100	168
Philadelphia Eagles	2	9	0	.182	134	239

1942 ROSTER

No	Name	Pos	Ht	Wt	DOB	College
19	Albrecht, Art	C	6-1	200	12/29/21	Wisconsin
47	Berezney, Paul	T	6-2	220	09/25/16	Fordham
29	Brock, Charley	C	6-1	209	03/15/16	Nebraska
16	Brock, Lou	HB	6-0	192	12/09/17	Purdue
3	Canadeo, Tony	HB	6-0	195	05/05/19	Gonzaga
58	Carter, Joe	E	6-1	200	07/23/12	SMU
54	Craig, Larry	E	6-0	205	06/27/16	South Carolina
75	Croft, Milburn (Tiny)	T	6-4	300	11/07/20	Ripon
35	Flowers, Bob	C	6-1	205	08/06/17	Texas Tech
64	Fritsch, Ted	FB	5-10	205	10/31/20	Stevens Point
43	Goldenberg, Charles (Buckets)	G	5-10	220	03/10/11	Wisconsin
15	Hinte, Harold	E	6-1	195	01/25/20	Pittsburgh
14	Hutson, Don	E	6-1	178	01/31/13	Alabama
53	Ingalls, Bob	C	6-3	200	01/17/19	Michigan
17	Isbell, Cecil	HB	6-1	190	07/11/15	Purdue
48	Jacunski, Harry	E	6-2	202	10/20/15	Fordham
8	Kahler, Bob	HB	6-3	200	02/13/17	Nebraska
72	Kahler, Royal	T	6-3	225	03/22/18	Nebraska
45	Kuusisto, William	G	6-0	225	04/26/18	Minnesota
24	Laws, Joe	HB	5-9	182	06/16/11	Iowa
40	Lee, Bill	T	6-3	240	10/19/11	Alabama
46	Letlow, Russ	G	6-0	220	10/05/13	San Francisco
7	Mason, Joel	E	6-0	198	03/12/13	Western Michigan
23	Ohlgren, Earl	E	6-3	210	02/21/18	Minnesota
22	Pannell, Ernie	T	6-3	220	02/02/17	Texas A&M
27	Ranspot, Keith	E	6-0	190	12/11/14	SMU
44	Ray, Buford (Baby)	T	6-6	245	09/30/15	Vanderbilt
5	Riddick, Ray	E	6-0	220	10/17/17	Fordham
38	Sample, Chuck	FB	5-9	202	01/05/20	Toledo
63	Starret, Ben	B	5-11	210	11/19/17	St. Mary's (CA)
51	Stonebreaker, John	E	6-3	200	04/25/18	USC
21	Tinsley, Pete	G	5-8	200	03/16/13	Georgia
42	Uram, Andy	HB	5-10	188	03/22/15	Minnesota
18	Vant Hull, Fred	T	6-0	213	08/21/20	Minnesota
33	Weisgerber, Dick	HB	5-10	198	02/19/15	Williamette

1942 DRAFT

Rnd	Name	Pos	College
1	Urban Odson	T	Minnesota
2	Ray Frankowski	G	Washington
3	Bill Green	B	Iowa
4	Joe Krivonak	G	South Carolina
5	Preston Johnson	B	SMU
6	Joe Rogers	E	Michigan
7	Phil Langdale	T	Alabama
8	Gene Flick	C	Minnesota
9	Tom Farris	B	Wisconsin
10	Jimmy Richardson	B	Marquette
11	Bruce Smith	B	Minnesota
12	Bill Applegate	G	South Carolina
13	Jim Trimble	T	Indiana
14	Tom Kinkade	B	Ohio State
15	Fred Preston	E	Nebraska
16	Bob Ingalls	C	Michigan
17	George Benson	B	Northwestern
18	Horace Young	B	SMU
19	Henry Woronicz	E	Boston College
20	Woody Adams	T	TCU

1942 GREEN BAY PACKERS

FRONT ROW: (L-R) Coach Curly Lambeau, Assistant Coach Richard (Red) Smith, 30 Tony Canadeo, 23 Earl Ohlgren, 40 Bill Lee, 43 Charles (Buckets) Goldenberg, 29 Charley Brock, 46 Russ Letlow, 44 Buford (Baby) Ray, 14 Don Hutson, 47 Paul Berezney, Trainer Carl (Bud) Jorgensen.
MIDDLE ROW: (L-R) 24 Joe Laws, 53 Bob Ingalls, 17 Cecil Isbell, 58 Joe Carter, 15 Tex Hinte, 27 Don Miller, 18 Fred Vant Hull, 7 Joel Mason, 54 Larry Craig, 42 Andy Uram,
21 Pete Tinsley, Assistant Coach Eddie Kotal.
BACK ROW: (L-R) 16 Lou Brock, 19 Art Albrecht, 22 Ernie Pannell, 35 Bob Flowers, 51 John Stonebreaker, 75 Milburn (Tiny) Croft, 8 Bob Kahler, 45 William Kuusisto,
64 Ted Fritsch, 63 Ben Starret, 38 Chuck Sample, 72 James Finley.

1943

The two best teams in the league in the early '40s were the Chicago Bears and the Washington Redskins. The two clashed in the 1940, 1942 and 1943 NFL Championship Games with the Bears winning in 1940 and 1943. The Bears also took the title in 1941 by defeating the New York Giants.

The Packers fit in right below this upper echelon. Green Bay suffered five losses in the three-year span from 1941-43. The Bears handed the Packers four of them and the other came courtesy of the Redskins. Most weeks the Packers hardly worked up a sweat in defeating an opponent, but a tie and a loss to Chicago and a loss in Washington kept Green Bay in second place for the fourth straight year, this time with a 7-2-1 record.

Cecil Isbell left to take a football coaching job at Purdue University. He exited at the peak of his career rather than risk being asked to retire by Lambeau a few years down the road. With Isbell gone, Tony Canadeo and Irv Comp were left to shoulder the passing game, which slipped from first to second behind the Bears.

Don Hutson again threatened retirement. Over the past few years, the receiving ace had hinted at calling it quits but always returned. This year was no different and Hutson waited until August before signing. Despite learning of the deaths of his brother (killed in action in the South Pacific) and father less than a week before the season opener, Hutson was ready for the Bears on September 26.

Because of the war, the league shortened its schedule to 10 games. The NFL used the abbreviated format through 1945.

The Bears had opened their season against the Packers for the past three years and did so again in 1943 but failed to win as they had done in 1940-42. Hutson caught only two passes, but the second, a 26-yarder from Canadeo late in the fourth quarter, counted a touchdown and secured a 21-21 tie.

Sammy Baugh was next to give Green Bay problems. After piling up 339 and then 445 yards in dispatching the Cardinals and Lions 28-7 and 35-14, respectively, the Packers hosted the Redskins at State Fair Park in Milwaukee. There, Baugh fired four touchdown passes in engineering a 33-7 win. The loss dropped the Packers to 2-1-1.

The Bears again prevented Green Bay from building a head of steam. After two wins over the Lions and Giants, the Packers once again invaded Wrigley Field. Canadeo, Comp, Lou Brock, Andy Uram, and Hutson all took turns throwing but could complete only six of 23 passes. With that avenue shut off, the Packers were unable to mount an effective attack and lost 21-7.

Following the frustrating setback, Green Bay posted 104 points in beating its final three foes. Even though the Bears did stumble against Washington, Chicago (8-1-1) earned the right to a face the Redskins (6-3-1) in the championship game.

Green Bay Press-Gazette photo

Andy Uram looks for an opening against the Washington Redskins in Milwaukee on October 17. Open field was hard to come by and the Packers lost 33-7. Uram, who held the NFL record for longest run from scrimmage (97 yards) for many years, gained just 53 yards rushing all year. He enlisted in the Navy once the season came to a close.

TEAM STATISTICS

	GB	OPP
First Downs	134	122
Rushing	60	62
Passing	66	56
Penalty	8	4
Rushes	397	350
Yards Gained	1,442	1,112
Average Gain	3.63	3.18
Average Yards per Game	144.2	111.2
Passes Attempted	253	242
Completed	114	111
% Completed	45.06	45.87
Total Yards Gained	1,909	1,420
Yards Gained per Completion	16.75	12.79
Average Yards per Game	190.9	142.0
Laterals Attempted	2	15
Completed	1	14
Yards Gained	0	175
Combined Yards Gained	3,351	2,707
Total Plays	652	607
Average Yards per Play	5.14	4.46
Average Yards per Game	335.1	270.7
Intercepted By	42	19
Yards Returned	599	188
Returned for TD	2	0
Punts	52	55
Yards Punted	1,870	2,017
Average Yards per Punt	35.96	36.67
Punt Returns	32	28
Yards Returned	371	330
Average Yards per Return	11.59	11.79
Returned for TD	0	0
Kickoff Returns	28	31
Yards Returned	661	606
Average Yards per Return	23.61	19.55
Returned for TD	0	0
Penalties	52	51
Yards Penalized	403	391
Fumbles	15	22
Lost	6	9
Own Recovered for Touchdown	0	0
Opponent's Recovered by	9	6
Opponent's Recovered for Touchdown	0	0
Total Points Scored	264	172
Total Touchdowns	36	25
Touchdowns Rushing	13	9
Touchdowns Passing	21	15
Touchdowns on Returns & Recoveries	2	1
Extra Points	36	22
Safeties	0	0
Field Goals Attempted	15	3
Field Goals Made	4	0
% Successful	26.67	00.00

Regular Season   7-2-1

Date	GB		OPP	Att.
9/26	21	Chicago Bears	21	(23,675)
10/3	28	at Chicago Cardinals	7	(15,563)
10/10	35	Detroit Lions	14	(21,396)
10/17	7	Washington Redskins (M)	33	(23,058)
10/24	27	at Detroit Lions	6	(41,463)
10/31	35	at New York Giants	21	(46,208)
11/7	7	at Chicago Bears	21	(43,425)
11/14	35	Chicago Cardinals (M)	14	(10,831)
11/21	31	Brooklyn Dodgers	7	(18,992)
12/5	38	at Phil-Pitt Steagles	28	(34,294)

Score By Periods

	1	2	3	4	Total
Packers	80	62	56	66	264
Opponents	47	28	34	63	172

INDIVIDUAL STATISTICS

Rushing

	Att	Yds	Avg	LG	TD
Canadeo	94	489	5.2	t35	3
Laws	43	232	5.4	31	0
Falkenstein	58	198	3.4	59	1
Comp	77	182	2.4	27	3
Fritsch	54	169	3.1	14	4
L. Brock	45	67	1.5	9	2
Uram	15	53	3.5	9	0
Hutson	6	41	6.8	16	0
Bob Kahler	1	5	5.0	5	0
Craig	1	3	3.0	3	0
Lankas	2	2	1.0	1	0
Starret	1	1	1.0	1	0
Packers	**397**	**1,442**	**3.6**	**59**	**13**
Opponents	350	1,112	3.2	47	9

Receiving

	No	Yds	Avg	LG	TD
Hutson	47	776	16.5	t79	11
Jacunski	24	528	22.0	t86	3
Uram	10	212	21.2	51	2
J. Mason	8	107	13.4	21	2
D. Evans	8	71	8.9	13	0
Laws	5	33	6.6	22	0
L. Brock	4	57	14.3	32	1
Falkenstein	3	39	13.0	18	0
Canadeo	3	31	10.3	t13	2
Fritsch	2	55	27.5	32	0
Packers	**114**	**1,909**	**16.7**	**t86**	**21**
Opponents	111	1,420	12.8	t66	15

Passing

	Att	Com	Yds	Pct	TD	In	Rate
Canadeo	129	56	875	43.4	9	12	51.0
Comp	92	46	662	50.0	7	4	81.0
L. Brock	22	9	274	40.9	3	1	108.7
Uram	6	2	60	33.3	1	1	—
Hutson	4	1	38	25.0	1	1	—
Packers	**253**	**114**	**1,909**	**45.1**	**21**	**19**	**67.4**
Opponents	242	111	1,420	45.9	15	42	45.8

Punting

	No	Yds	Avg	LG	HB
L. Brock	32	1,164	36.4	72	1
Comp	12	453	37.8	46	0
Fritsch	5	151	30.2	47	0
Canadeo	3	102	34.0	39	0
Packers	**52**	**1,870**	**36.0**	**72**	**1**
Opponents	55	2,017	36.7	60	1

Kickoff Returns

	No	Yds	Avg	LG	TD
Canadeo	10	242	24.2	43	0
L. Brock	5	112	22.4	40	0
Fritsch	4	99	24.8	32	0
Comp	4	81	20.3	24	0
Falkenstein	2	47	23.5	24	0
Laws	2	47	23.5	24	0
Jacunski	1	33	33.0	33	0
Packers	**28**	**661**	**23.6**	**43**	**0**
Opponents	31	606	19.5	37	0

Punt Returns

	No	Yds	Avg	LG	TD
Laws	10	84	8.4	19	0
L. Brock	8	126	15.8	32	0
Canadeo	8	93	11.6	22	0
Uram	5	48	9.6	17	0
Comp	1	20	20.0	20	0
Packers	**32**	**371**	**11.6**	**32**	**0**
Opponents	28	330	11.8	22	0

Interceptions

	No	Yds	Avg	LG	TD
Comp	10	149	14.9	35	1
Hutson	8	197	24.6	t84	1
Laws	7	67	9.6	17	0
C. Brock	4	60	15.0	41	0
Uram	2	40	20.0	22	0
Goldenberg	2	37	18.5	30	0
Canadeo	2	15	7.5	15	0
Fries	2	6	3.0	4	0
L. Brock	1	9	9.0	9	0
Tinsley	1	8	8.0	8	0
Jacunski	1	7	7.0	7	0
Starret	1	4	4.0	4	0
Flowers	1	0	0.0	0	0
Packers	**42**	**599**	**14.3**	**184**	**2**
Opponents	19	188	9.9	24	0

Scoring

	TDr	TDp	TDrt	PAT	FG	S	TP
Hutson	0	11	1	36/36	3/5	0	117
Canadeo	3	2	0	0/0	0/0	0	30
Comp	3	0	1	0/0	0/0	0	24
Fritsch	4	0	0	0/0	0/2	0	24
L. Brock	2	1	0	0/0	0/0	0	18
Jacunski	0	3	0	0/0	0/0	0	18
J. Mason	0	2	0	0/0	0/0	0	12
Uram	0	2	0	0/0	0/0	0	12
Falkenstein	1	0	0	0/0	0/0	0	6
Adams	0	0	0	0/0	1/6	0	3
Sorenson	0	0	0	0/0	0/2	0	0
Packers	**13**	**21**	**2**	**36/36**	**4/15**	**0**	**264**
Opponents	9	15	1	22/25	0/3	0	172

NFL STANDINGS

Western Division

	W	L	T	Pct	PF	PA
Chicago Bears	8	1	1	.889	303	157
Green Bay Packers	7	2	1	.778	264	172
Detroit Lions	3	6	1	.333	178	218
Chicago Cardinals	0	10	0	.000	95	238

Eastern Division

	W	L	T	Pct	PF	PA
Washington Redskins	6	3	1	.667	229	137
New York Giants	6	3	1	.667	197	170
Phil-Pitt Steagles	5	4	1	.556	225	230
Brooklyn Dodgers	2	8	0	.200	65	234

1943 ROSTER

No	Name	Pos	Ht	Wt	DOB	College
27	Adams, Chet	T	6-3	240	10/24/16	Ohio State
47	Berezney, Paul	T	6-2	220	09/25/16	Fordham
29	Brock, Charley	C	6-1	210	03/15/16	Nebraska
16	Brock, Lou	HB	6-0	195	12/09/17	Purdue
3	Canadeo, Tony	HB	6-0	195	05/05/19	Gonzaga
51	Comp, Irv	HB	6-3	192	05/17/19	St. Benedict
54	Craig, Larry	E	6-0	208	06/27/16	South Carolina
75	Croft, Milburn (Tiny)	T	6-4	298	11/07/20	Ripon
22	Evans, Dick	E	6-3	210	05/31/18	Iowa
18	Falkenstein, Tony	FB	5-10	210	02/16/15	St. Mary's (CA)
35	Flowers, Bob	C	6-1	215	08/06/17	Texas Tech
46	Fries, Sherwood	G	6-1	238	11/24/20	Colorado State
64	Fritsch, Ted	FB	5-10	205	10/31/20	Stevens Point
43	Goldenberg, Charles (Buckets)	G	5-10	220	03/10/11	Wisconsin
14	Hutson, Don	E	6-1	178	01/31/13	Alabama
48	Jacunski, Harry	E	6-2	198	10/20/15	Fordham
8	Kahler, Bob	HB	6-3	200	02/13/17	Nebraska
45	Kuusisto, William	G	6-0	230	04/26/18	Minnesota
23	Lankas, Jim	FB	6-2	215	08/26/18	St. Mary's (CA)
24	Laws, Joe	HB	5-9	188	06/16/11	Iowa
7	Mason, Joel	E	6-0	198	03/12/13	Western Michigan
72	McPherson, Forrest	C	5-11	248	10/22/11	Nebraska
58	Perkins, Don	FB	6-0	195	09/18/17	Platteville
44	Ray, Buford (Baby)	T	6-6	250	09/30/15	Vanderbilt
40	Schwammel, Ade	T	6-2	215	10/14/08	Oregon State
33	Sorenson, Glen	G	6-0	225	02/29/20	Utah State
63	Starret, Ben	B	5-11	215	11/19/17	St. Mary's (CA)
21	Tinsley, Pete	G	5-8	200	03/16/13	Georgia
42	Uram, Andy	HB	5-10	190	03/22/15	Minnesota

1943 DRAFT

Rnd	Name	Pos	College
1	Dick Wildung	T	Minnesota
2	Irv Comp	B	St. Benedict
3	Roy McKay	B	Texas
4	Nick Susseoff	E	Washington State
5	Ken Snelling	B	UCLA
6	Lester Gatewood	C	Baylor
7	Norm Verry	T	USC
8	Solon Barnett	G	Baylor
9	Bob Forte	B	Arkansas
10	Van Davis	E	Georgia
11	Tom Brock	C	Notre Dame
12	Ralph Tate	B	Oklahoma A&M
13	Don Carlson	T	Denver
14	Mike Welch	B	Minnesota
15	Ron Thomas	G	USC
16	James Powers	T	St. Mary's (CA)
17	Harold (Ace) Prescott	E	Hardin-Simmons
18	Ed Forrest	C	Santa Clara
19	Lloyd Wasserbach	T	Wisconsin
20	Mark Hoskins	B	Wisconsin
21	Earl Bennett	G	Hardin-Simmons
22	George Zellick	E	Oregon State
23	Gene Bierhaus	E	Minnesota
24	George Makris	G	Wisconsin
25	Pete Susick	B	Washington
26	Bud Hasse	E	Northwestern
27	Dick Thornally	T	Wisconsin
28	Bob Ray	B	Wisconsin
29	Brunnel Christensen	T	California
30	Ken Roskie	B	USC

1943 GREEN BAY PACKERS

FRONT ROW: (L-R) 72 Forrest McPherson, 24 Joe Laws, 42 Andy Uram, 43 Charles (Buckets) Goldenberg, 21 Pete Tinsley, 18 Tony Falkenstein, 16 Lou Brock, 3 Tony Canadeo, 14 Don Hutson.
MIDDLE ROW: (L-R) Coach Curly Lambeau, 33 Glen Sorenson, 8 Bob Kahler, 48 Harry Jacunski, 27 Chet Adams, 44 Buford (Baby) Ray, 75 Milburn (Tiny) Croft, 46 Sherwood Fries, 7 Joel Mason, 45 William Kuusisto, Assistant Coach Richard (Red) Smith.
BACK ROW: (L-R) Trainer Gust Seaburg, 23 Jim Lankas, 35 Bob Flowers, 50 Ade Schwammel, 22 Dick Evans, 47 Paul Berezney, 51 Irv Comp, 54 Larry Craig, 63 Ben Starret, 64 Ted Fritsch, Trainer Carl (Bud) Jorgensen.

1944

The Packers were shutout twice in one year for the first time since 1934. The Bears clubbed them 21-0 in week seven and two weeks later the Giants followed suit 24-0. The losses were particularly disturbing because they came against clubs the Packers needed to beat if a sixth NFL title was to become reality; the Bears in the Western conference standings, and, provided that came to pass, the Giants in the championship game.

Fortunately, the Chicagoans got off to a slow start (1-2-1) thanks in part to a 42-28 setback in Green Bay on September 24. Even after the Bears rolled over them five weeks later, the Packers (6-1-0) still held first place ahead of Chicago (3-2-1). By the time the Giants handed Green Bay its second loss, the Bears had fallen to Detroit for their third setback. With a 35-20 win over Card-Pitt on the season's final weekend, the Packers clinched the division crown and headed to the Polo Grounds to take revenge on the Giants in the title game.

Two veterans took their time deciding if they wanted a piece of the championship pie. Don Hutson again threatened retirement and didn't sign until September 1. Charles (Buckets) Goldenberg, by this time a Milwaukee restaurant owner, waited a bit longer. He came out of voluntary retirement in time for the first Bears clash after missing the opener.

Green Bay opened for the first time at State Fair Park in Milwaukee. Milwaukee had been a good second home for the Packers; they had won 17 of their last 18 games there, including 16 straight between 1935-42. Overall, the team was 18-4 in Milwaukee since it began playing home games there in 1933. Green Bay continued its run of good fortune with a 14-7 victory over Brooklyn on September 17.

The Packers then reeled off five more wins, the first coming against the Bears. Lou Brock scored on a 42-yard run and Ted Fritsch counted on a 50-yard interception return in the fourth quarter to break a 28-28 tie and lead Green Bay to a 42-28 win. A week later, the two combined for 127 yards rushing in a 27-6 conquest of Detroit. The Packers then picked up victories over Card-Pitt, Cleveland and Detroit to round out the winning streak. Hutson had 11 catches for 207 yards and a pair of touchdowns in the Card-Pitt contest.

Both Chicago and New York shut out the Packers once during the next three weeks. The two stymied the Packers' passing attack and intercepted nine passes, five by the Giants. The Giants skirmish also was noteworthy because Arnie Herber directed the New York attack. He completed just one pass in six attempts, albeit a 36-yard score.

The Packers regrouped on the last weekend in November. They held Card-Pitt to 19 yards rushing, intercepted three passes and rolled to a 35-20 win. Three weeks later, the Packers again tangled with the Giants, this time for the NFL crown.

Green Bay Press-Gazette photo

Lou Brock is on the run against Card-Pitt in Green Bay on October 8. Brock scored on a 25-yard run in the fourth quarter to give the Packers a 27-0 lead. Green Bay went on to beat the "Carpets" 34-7 for its fourth win of the season. Brock gained 200 yards on the ground in 1944, good for third place behind Ted Fritsch and Don Perkins.

TEAM STATISTICS

	GB	OPP
First Downs	147	114
Rushing	70	56
Passing	63	49
Penalty	14	9
Rushes	395	357
Yards Gained	1,517	1,130
Average Gain	3.84	3.17
Average Yards per Game	151.7	113.0
Passes Attempted	253	227
Completed	105	89
% Completed	41.50	39.21
Total Yards Gained	1,471	1,229
Yards Gained per Completion	14.01	13.81
Average Yards per Game	147.1	122.9
Laterals Attempted	3	8
Completed	3	6
Yards Gained	36	58
Combined Yards Gained	3,024	2,417
Total Plays	651	592
Average Yards per Play	4.65	4.08
Average Yards per Game	302.4	241.7
Intercepted By	29	24
Yards Returned	454	344
Returned for TD	3	1
Punts	48	56
Yards Punted	1,774	2,083
Average Yards per Punt	36.96	37.20
Punt Returns	27	18
Yards Returned	241	192
Average Yards per Return	8.93	10.67
Returned for TD	0	0
Kickoff Returns	30	35
Yards Returned	610	828
Average Yards per Return	20.33	23.66
Returned for TD	0	0
Penalties	62	88
Yards Penalized	558	700
Fumbles	11	25
Lost	7	12
Own Recovered for Touchdown	0	0
Opponent's Recovered by	12	7
Opponent's Recovered for Touchdown	0	0
Total Points Scored	238	141
Total Touchdowns	34	20
Touchdowns Rushing	16	9
Touchdowns Passing	15	11
Touchdowns on Returns & Recoveries	3	1
Extra Points	32	18
Safeties	1	0
Field Goals Attempted	5	2
Field Goals Made	0	1
% Successful	00.00	50.00

Regular Season   8-2-0

Date	GB		OPP	Att.
9/17	14	Brooklyn Dodgers (M)	7	(12,994)
9/24	42	Chicago Bears	28	(24,362)
10/1	27	Detroit Lions (M)	6	(18,556)
10/8	34	Card-Pitt Carpets	7	(16,535)
10/22	30	Cleveland Rams	21	(18,780)
10/29	14	at Detroit Lions	0	(30,844)
11/5	0	at Chicago Bears	21	(45,553)
11/12	42	at Cleveland Rams	7	(17,166)
11/19	0	at New York Giants	24	(56,481)
11/26	35	at Card-Pitt Carpets	20	(7,158)

Postseason   1-0-0

12/17	14	at New York Giants	7	(46,016)

Score By Periods

	1	2	3	4	Total
Packers	56	77	41	64	238
Opponents	34	27	38	42	141

INDIVIDUAL STATISTICS

Rushing

	Att	Yds	Avg	LG	TD
Fritsch	94	322	3.4	18	4
Perkins	58	207	3.6	26	0
L. Brock	36	200	5.6	t42	3
Laws	45	200	4.4	20	3
Duhart	51	183	3.6	16	2
Canadeo	31	149	4.8	34	0
Comp	52	134	2.6	28	2
Hutson	12	87	7.3	27	0
Starret	10	21	2.1	8	2
McKay	5	12	2.4	11	0
Urban	1	2	2.0	2	0
Packers	**395**	**1,517**	**3.8**	**t42**	**16**
Opponents	357	1,130	3.2	t75	8

1944

Receiving

	No	Yds	Avg	LG	TD
Hutson	58	866	14.9	t55	9
Duhart	9	176	19.6	32	2
Jacunski	9	151	16.8	48	0
Laws	7	61	8.7	t29	1
Wheba	6	67	11.2	17	0
L. Brock	4	74	18.5	t52	2
Fritsch	3	5	1.7	13	0
Craig	2	17	8.5	9	0
Comp	2	16	8.0	t11	1
Canadeo	1	12	12.0	12	0
Urban	1	10	10.0	10	0
J. Mason	1	9	9.0	9	0
Starret	1	6	6.0	6	0
Perkins	1	1	1.0	1	0
Packers	**105**	**1,471**	**14.0**	**t55**	**15**
Opponents	89	1,229	13.8	t72	11

Passing

	Att	Com	Yds	Pct	TD	In	Rate
Comp	177	80	1,159	45.2	12	21	50.0
L. Brock	21	5	94	23.8	2	0	77.5
Canadeo	20	9	89	45.0	0	0	58.1
McKay	14	6	72	42.9	1	2	43.5
Duhart	13	4	42	30.8	0	0	41.2
Laws	4	1	15	25.0	0	1	—
Hutson	3	0	0	00.0	0	0	—
Bilda	1	0	0	00.0	0	0	—
Packers	**253**	**105**	**1,471**	**41.5**	**15**	**24**	**41.1**
Opponents	227	89	1,229	39.2	11	29	33.9

Punting

	No	Yds	Avg	LG	HB
L. Brock	14	494	35.3	50	0
Canadeo	13	479	36.8	46	0
Fritsch	10	408	40.8	54	0
McKay	8	297	37.1	55	0
Starret	2	65	32.5	43	0
Perkins	1	31	31.0	31	0
Packers	**48**	**1,774**	**37.0**	**55**	**0**
Opponents	56	2,083	37.2	73	0

Kickoff Returns

	No	Yds	Avg	LG	TD
Fritsch	11	288	26.2	44	0
Laws	8	132	16.5	25	0
L. Brock	2	41	20.5	21	0
Comp	2	35	17.5	18	0
Perkins	2	34	17.0	18	0
Urban	1	20	20.0	20	0
Duhart	1	18	18.0	18	0
Craig	1	17	17.0	17	0
Starret	1	13	13.0	13	0
Canadeo	1	12	12.0	12	0
Packers	**30**	**610**	**20.3**	**44**	**0**
Opponents	35	828	23.7	44	0

Punt Returns

	No	Yds	Avg	LG	TD
Laws	15	118	7.9	23	0
L. Brock	4	36	9.0	22	0
Duhart	3	32	10.7	18	0
Comp	2	32	16.0	18	0
McKay	2	19	9.5	17	0
Canadeo	1	4	4.0	4	0
Packers	**27**	**241**	**8.9**	**23**	**0**
Opponents	18	192	10.7	20	0

Interceptions

	No	Yds	Avg	LG	TD
Fritsch	6	115	19.2	t50	1
Comp	6	54	9.0	43	0
Hutson	4	50	12.5	43	0
Duhart	4	23	5.8	14	0
Laws	3	36	12.0	16	0
Perkins	2	123	61.5	t83	2
Bilda	1	25	25.0	25	0
Craig	1	20	20.0	20	0
Wheba	1	7	7.0	7	0
C. Brock	1	1	1.0	1	0
Packers	**29**	**454**	**15.7**	**t83**	**3**
Opponents	24	344	14.3	48	1

Scoring

	TDr	TDp	TDrt	PAT	FG	S	TP
Hutson	0	9	0	31/33	0/3	0	85
L. Brock	3	2	0	0/0	0/0	0	30
Fritsch	4	0	1	0/0	0/0	0	30
Duhart	2	2	0	0/0	0/0	0	24
Laws	3	1	0	0/0	0/0	0	24
Comp	2	1	0	0/0	0/0	0	18
Perkins	0	0	2	0/0	0/0	0	12
Starret	2	0	0	0/0	0/0	0	12
team	0	0	0	0/0	0/0	1	2
Sorenson	0	0	0	1/1	0/2	0	1
Packers	**16**	**15**	**3**	**32/34**	**0/5**	**1**	**238**
Opponents	8	11	1	18/20	1/2	0	141

NFL STANDINGS

Western Division

	W	L	T	Pct	PF	PA
Green Bay Packers	8	2	0	.800	238	141
Chicago Bears	6	3	1	.667	258	172
Detroit Lions	6	3	1	.667	216	151
Cleveland Rams	4	6	0	.400	188	224
Card-Pitt Carpets	0	10	0	.000	108	328

Eastern Division

	W	L	T	Pct	PF	PA
New York Giants	8	1	1	.889	206	75
Philadelphia Eagles	7	1	2	.875	267	131
Washington Redskins	6	3	1	.667	169	180
Boston Yanks	2	8	0	.200	82	233
Brooklyn Tigers	0	10	0	.000	69	166

1944 ROSTER

No	Name	Pos	Ht	Wt	DOB	College
47	Berezney, Paul	T	6-2	220	09/25/16	Fordham
22	Bilda, Dick	HB	6-1	200	05/17/19	Marquette
29	Brock, Charley	C	6-1	210	03/15/16	Nebraska
16	Brock, Lou	HB	6-0	195	12/09/17	Purdue
19	Bucchianeri, Amadeo (Mike)	G	5-10	215	09/01/17	Indiana
3	Canadeo, Tony	HB	6-0	195	05/05/19	Gonzaga
51	Comp, Irv	HB	6-3	192	05/17/19	St. Benedict
54	Craig, Larry	E	6-0	208	06/27/16	South Carolina
75	Croft, Milburn (Tiny)	T	6-4	298	11/07/20	Ripon
42	Duhart, Paul	HB	6-0	180	12/30/20	Florida
35	Flowers, Bob	C	6-1	215	08/06/17	Texas Tech
64	Fritsch, Ted	FB	5-10	205	10/31/20	Stevens Point
43	Goldenberg, Charles (Buckets)	G	5-10	220	03/10/11	Wisconsin
14	Hutson, Don	E	6-1	180	01/31/13	Alabama
48	Jacunski, Harry	E	6-2	198	10/20/15	Fordham
8	Kahler, Bob	HB	6-3	200	02/13/17	Nebraska
18	Kercher, Bob	E	6-2	195	01/14/19	Georgetown
45	Kuusisto, William	G	6-0	230	04/26/18	Minnesota
24	Laws, Joe	HB	5-9	188	06/16/11	Iowa
7	Mason, Joel	E	6-0	200	03/12/13	Western Michigan
3	McKay, Roy	HB	6-0	195	02/02/20	Texas
72	McPherson, Forrest	C	5-11	248	10/22/11	Nebraska
23	Perkins, Don	FB	6-0	195	09/18/17	Platteville
44	Ray, Buford (Baby)	T	6-6	250	09/30/15	Vanderbilt
58	Schwammel, Ade	T	6-2	215	10/14/08	Oregon State
33	Sorenson, Glen	G	6-0	225	02/29/20	Utah State
63	Starret, Ben	B	5-11	215	11/19/17	St. Mary's (CA)
21	Tinsley, Pete	G	5-8	200	03/16/13	Georgia
46	Tollefson, Charles	G	6-0	218	02/28/16	Iowa
18	Urban, Alex	E	6-2	200	07/16/17	South Carolina
17	Wheba, Ray	E	6-0	210		USC

1944 DRAFT

Rnd	Name	Pos	College	Rnd	Name	Pos	College
1	Merv Pregulman	G	Michigan	16	Hugh Cox	B	North Carolina
2	Tom Kuzma	B	Michigan	17	Kermit Davis	E	Mississippi State
3	Bill McPartland	T	St. Mary's (CA)	18	Bob Johnson	C	Purdue
4	Mickey McCardle	B	USC	19	Jim Cox	T	Stanford
5	Jack Tracy	E	Washington	20	Cliff Anderson	E	Minnesota
6	Alex Agase	G	Illinois	21	John Perry	B	Duke
7	Don Whitmire	T	Alabama	22	Pete DeMaria	G	Purdue
8	Bob Koch	B	Oregon	23	Len Liss	T	Marquette
9	Virgil Johnson	E	Arkansas	24	Ray Jordan	B	North Carolina
10	Roy Giusti	B	St. Mary's (CA)	25	Al Grubaugh	T	Nebraska
11	Bill Baughman	C	Alabama	26	O.B. Howard	E	Mississippi State
12	Don Griffin	B	Illinois	27	Paul Paladino	G	Arkansas
13	Bert Gissler	E	Nebraska	28	Bob Butchofsky	B	Texas A&M
14	Lou Shelton	B	Oregon State	29	Russ Deal	G	Indiana
15	Charles Cusick	G	Oregon	30	Abel Gonzales	B	SMU

1944 GREEN BAY PACKERS

1944 WORLD CHAMPIONS

FRONT ROW: (L-R) 43 Charles (Buckets) Goldenberg, 42 Paul Duhart, 63 Ben Starret, 21 Pete Tinsley, 72 Forrest McPherson, 54 Larry Craig, 29 Charley Brock, 16 Lou Brock, 3 Roy McKay, 24 Joe Laws.
MIDDLE ROW: (L-R) Trainer Carl (Bud) Jorgensen, 45 William Kuusisto, 17 Ray Wheba, 33 Glen Sorenson, 35 Bob Flowers, 48 Harry Jacunski, 64 Ted Fritsch, 23 Don Perkins, 46 Charles Tollefson, 7 Joel Mason, Trainer Gust Seaburg.
BACK ROW: (L-R) Coach Curly Lambeau, 14 Don Hutson, 47 Paul Berezney, 58 Ade Schwammel, 51 Irv Comp, 75 Milburn (Tiny) Croft, 18 Bob Kercher, 8 Bob Kahler, 44 Buford (Baby) Ray, Amadeo (Mike) Bucchianeri, Assistant Coach George (Brute) Trafton.

1945

An era came to an end in Detroit on a cold day in early December. Green Bay's three remaining players from the championship teams of 1936, 1939 and 1944 hung up their cleats for good and passed into Packer legend. First among them was Don Hutson, at the time the NFL's all-time leading receiver with 488 passes for 7,991 yards and 99 touchdowns. Joining him in retirement were Joe Laws, a gutsy running back who had toiled a dozen years in Green Bay, and guard Charles (Buckets) Goldenberg who had played 13, more than any Packer to that point.

Unfortunately, a championship sendoff was not in the cards. The Packers (6-4) finished a disappointing third behind Detroit and Cleveland. Green Bay let halftime leads of one, three and three points slip away in three of the season's four losses. Not big leads certainly, but over the years Curly Lambeau's men did not lose games they led at halftime, no matter how small the advantage. Prior to 1945, the Packers were 143-6 in games in which they led at intermission. Only once (1939) did the team blow two such leads in a single year.

The Packers remained in the hunt throughout the first half of the year. At the six-game mark, the Packers (4-2-0) trailed the Rams (5-1-0) and Lions (5-1-0) by just one game. Green Bay and the Rams tangled in League Park on November 11 to settle differences. Earlier, the Rams had beaten the Packers 27-14 and again wasted no time in gaining the upper hand. Fred Gehrke scored on runs of 72 and 42 yards to give Cleveland a quick 13-0 lead. Rookie Clyde Goodnight then scored on a 75-yard pass from Irv Comp to close 13-7. But Bob Waterfield fired an 84-yard strike to Jim Benton for a 20-7 advantage. Though the game was only a quarter old, neither team added to its score and the Rams, with their first sweep of the Packers, were on the way to their first ever championship game appearance.

The Packers of 1945 represented the "silver anniversary" edition of the team. The Lions, Kiwanis and Rotary clubs honored the organization with a dinner at the Beaumont Hotel on August 9. Approximately 300 attended, including a number of players who had worked out that morning in the first practice session of the year.

Green Bay began a decline in 1945 that worsened each year through 1949. The team and Hutson in particular, did have one last shining moment. On October 7, the Packers rang up 57 points —a team record— and hammered the Lions 57-21. Hutson, 32 years old and in his 11th season, caught four touchdown passes and kicked five extra points in the second quarter alone, to set an NFL record that still stands today. He kicked two more PATs in the game and left professional football having scored a team and then-NFL record 823 points.

Green Bay Press-Gazette photo

Don Hutson (14) looks to gain yardage against the Rams in City Stadium on October 14. Though he caught seven passes for 110 yards, he never did find the end zone and the Packers came up short 27-14. Hutson led the team in receptions for a 10th straight season and the league for a fifth consecutive time. He caught 47 passes in 1945 good for 834 yards and nine touchdowns.

TEAM STATISTICS

	GB	OPP
First Downs	131	137
Rushing	73	65
Passing	44	57
Penalty	14	15
Rushes	377	388
Yards Gained	1,325	1,349
Average Gain	3.51	3.48
Average Yards per Game	132.5	134.9
Passes Attempted	218	231
Completed	81	111
% Completed	37.16	48.05
Total Yards Gained	1,536	1,708
Yards Gained per Completion	18.96	15.39
Average Yards per Game	153.6	170.8
Laterals Attempted	1	9
Completed	1	9
Yards Gained	8	59
Combined Yards Gained	2,869	3,116
Total Plays	596	628
Average Yards per Play	4.81	4.96
Average Yards per Game	286.9	311.6
Intercepted By	24	24
Yards Returned	464	376
Returned for TD	5	0
Punts	46	59
Yards Punted	1,839	2,210
Average Yards per Punt	39.98	37.46
Punt Returns	35	25
Yards Returned	317	284
Average Yards per Return	9.06	11.36
Returned for TD	0	0
Kickoff Returns	33	39
Yards Returned	670	737
Average Yards per Return	20.30	18.90
Returned for TD	0	0
Penalties	69	68
Yards Penalized	723	701
Fumbles	21	31
Lost	8	17
Own Recovered for Touchdown	0	0
Opponent's Recovered by	17	8
Opponent's Recovered for Touchdown	1	0
Total Points Scored	258	173
Total Touchdowns	35	25
Touchdowns Rushing	15	16
Touchdowns Passing	14	9
Touchdowns on Returns & Recoveries	6	0
Extra Points	31	23
Safeties	1	0
Field Goals Attempted	13	2
Field Goals Made	5	0
% Successful	38.46	00.00

Regular Season 6-4-0

Date	GB		OPP	Att.
9/30	31	Chicago Bears	21	(24,525)
10/7	57	Detroit Lions (M)	21	(23,500)
10/14	14	Cleveland Rams	27	(24,607)
10/21	38	Boston Yanks (M)	14	(20,846)
10/28	33	Chicago Cardinals	14	(19,122)
11/4	24	at Chicago Bears	28	(45,527)
11/11	7	at Cleveland Rams	20	(28,686)
11/18	28	at Boston Yanks	0	(33,748)
11/25	23	at New York Giants	14	(52,681)
12/2	3	at Detroit Lions	14	(23,468)

Score By Periods

	1	2	3	4	Total
Packers	52	116	56	34	258
Opponents	40	42	35	56	173

INDIVIDUAL STATISTICS

Rushing

	Att	Yds	Avg	LG	TD
Fritsch	88	282	3.2	31	7
McKay	71	231	3.3	41	2
L. Brock	46	196	4.3	28	3
Perkins	36	192	5.3	49	1
Bruce Smith	21	94	4.5	27	0
Laws	16	82	5.1	20	0
Comp	57	75	1.3	18	1
Hutson	8	60	7.5	18	1
Mosley	16	49	3.1	9	0
Starret	5	26	5.2	13	0
Goodnight	8	26	3.3	12	0
Snelling	3	10	3.3	8	0
Sample	2	2	1.0	3	0
Packers	**377**	**1,325**	**3.5**	**49**	**15**
Opponents	388	1,349	3.5	t72	16

Receiving

	No	Yds	Avg	LG	TD
Hutson	47	834	17.7	t75	9
Luhn	10	151	15.1	t44	1
Goodnight	7	283	40.4	t75	3
L. Brock	4	87	21.8	46	0
C. Mulleneaux	3	31	10.3	13	0
Fritsch	3	13	4.3	9	0
Laws	2	11	5.5	7	0
Perkins	2	11	5.5	10	0
Urban	1	55	55.0	55	0
Comp	1	50	50.0	t50	1
Mosley	1	10	10.0	10	0
Packers	**81**	**1,536**	**19.0**	**t75**	**14**
Opponents	111	1,708	15.4	t84	9

Passing

	Att	Com	Yds	Pct	TD	In	Rate
Comp	106	44	865	41.5	7	11	53.1
McKay	89	32	520	36.0	5	9	35.5
L. Brock	22	5	151	22.7	2	4	46.4
Mosley	1	0	0	00.0	0	0	—
Packers	**218**	**81**	**1,536**	**37.2**	**14**	**24**	**44.2**
Opponents	231	111	1,708	48.1	9	24	46.3

Punting

	No	Yds	Avg	LG	HB
McKay	44	1,814	41.2	73	0
Perkins	1	13	13.0	13	0
Keuper	1	12	12.0	12	0
Packers	**46**	**1,839**	**40.0**	**73**	**0**
Opponents	59	2,210	37.5	56	0

Kickoff Returns

	No	Yds	Avg	LG	TD
Fritsch	8	279	34.9	79	0
Comp	5	110	22.0	31	0
Laws	4	72	18.0	29	0
McKay	4	67	16.8	26	0
Hutson	4	37	9.3	12	0
Bruce Smith	2	46	23.0	26	0
J. Mason	1	15	15.0	15	0
L. Brock	1	12	12.0	12	0
Craig	1	11	11.0	11	0
Pannell	1	10	10.0	10	0
Goodnight	1	8	8.0	8	0
Starret	1	3	3.0	3	0
Packers	**33**	**670**	**20.3**	**79**	**0**
Opponents	39	737	18.9	36	0

Punt Returns

	No	Yds	Avg	LG	TD
Laws	12	78	6.5	21	0
McKay	7	66	9.4	17	0
Bruce Smith	6	67	11.2	20	0
L. Brock	4	37	9.3	18	0
Comp	4	36	9.0	15	0
J. Mason	1	20	20.0	20	0
Mosley	1	13	13.0	13	0
Packers	**35**	**317**	**9.1**	**21**	**0**
Opponents	25	284	11.4	32	0

Interceptions

	No	Yds	Avg	LG	TD
C. Brock	4	122	30.5	38	2
Hutson	4	15	3.8	15	0
Laws	3	60	20.0	35	0
L. Brock	3	33	11.0	33	0
McKay	3	33	11.0	18	0
Comp	2	67	33.5	t54	1
Fritsch	1	69	69.0	t69	1
Starret	1	27	27.0	27	0
Mosley	1	20	20.0	20	0
Crimmins	1	12	12.0	t12	1
Tinsley	1	6	6.0	6	0
Packers	**24**	**464**	**19.3**	**t69**	**5**
Opponents	24	376	15.7	55	0

Scoring

	TDr	TDp	TDrt	PAT	FG	S	TP
Hutson	1	9	0	31/35	2/4	0	97
Fritsch	7	0	1	0/0	3/8	0	57
L. Brock	3	0	0	0/0	0/0	0	18
Comp	1	1	1	0/0	0/0	0	18
Goodnight	0	3	0	0/0	0/0	0	18
C. Brock	0	0	2	0/0	0/0	0	12
McKay	2	0	0	0/0	0/0	0	12
Craig	0	0	1	0/0	0/0	0	6
Crimmins	0	0	1	0/0	0/0	0	6
Luhn	0	1	0	0/0	0/0	0	6
Perkins	1	0	0	0/0	0/0	0	6
team	0	0	0	0/0	0/0	1	2
Sorenson	0	0	0	0/0	0/1	0	—
Packers	**15**	**14**	**6**	**31/35**	**5/13**	**1**	**258**
Opponents	16	9	0	23/25	0/2	0	173

Fumbles

	Fum	Ow	Op	Yds	Tot
Adkins	1	1	0	0	1
C. Brock	0	0	5	52	5
L. Brock	1	0	0	0	0
Comp	5	3	1	-1	4
Craig	0	0	2	18	2
Fritsch	2	1	1	0	2
Goodnight	1	1	0	8	1
Hutson	1	0	0	0	0
Keuper	0	0	1	0	1
Laws	2	1	0	2	1
Lipscomb	0	0	3	0	3
J. Mason	0	0	1	0	1
McKay	4	3	0	12	3
Perkins	0	0	1	15	1
Ray	0	0	1	0	1
Snelling	1	0	0	0	0
Bruce Smith	2	1	0	-2	1
Sorenson	0	0	1	0	1
Starret	1	1	0	0	1
Packers	**21**	**12**	**17**	**104**	**29**

NFL STANDINGS

Western Division

	W	L	T	Pct	PF	PA
Cleveland Rams	9	1	0	.900	244	136
Detroit Lions	7	3	0	.700	195	194
Green Bay Packers	**6**	**4**	**0**	**.600**	**258**	**173**
Chicago Bears	3	7	0	.300	192	235
Chicago Cardinals	1	9	0	.100	98	228

Eastern Division

	W	L	T	Pct	PF	PA
Washington Redskins	8	2	0	.800	209	121
Philadelphia Eagles	7	3	0	.700	272	133
New York Giants	3	6	1	.333	179	198
Boston Yanks	3	6	1	.333	123	211
Pittsburgh Steelers	2	8	0	.200	79	220

1945 ROSTER

No	Name	Pos	Ht	Wt	DOB	College	G
79	Adkins, Bob	B	6-0	220	02/07/17	Marshall	4
72	Barnett, Solon	T	6-1	235	03/30/21	Baylor	4
29	Brock, Charley	C	6-1	210	03/15/16	Nebraska	10
16	Brock, Lou	HB	6-0	195	12/09/17	Purdue	10
19	Bucchianeri, Amadeo (Mike)	G	5-10	210	09/01/17	Indiana	5
51	Comp, Irv	HB	6-3	192	05/17/19	St. Benedict	9
54	Craig, Larry	E	6-0	215	06/27/16	South Carolina	10
76	Crimmins, Bernard	G	5-11	195	04/14/19	Notre Dame	6
75	Croft, Milburn (Tiny)	T	6-4	285	11/07/20	Ripon	9
35	Flowers, Bob	C	6-1	210	08/06/17	Texas Tech	10
15	Frankowski, Ray	G	5-11	220	09/14/19	Washington	2
64	Fritsch, Ted	FB	5-10	210	10/31/20	Stevens Point	10
51	Frutig, Ed	E	6-1	185	08/19/20	Michigan	1
43	Goldenberg, Charles (Buckets)	G	5-10	220	03/10/11	Wisconsin	4
23	Goodnight, Clyde	E	6-1	195	03/03/24	Tulsa	10
14	Hutson, Don	E	6-1	180	01/31/13	Alabama	10
18	Keuper, Ken	HB	6-0	215	11/14/18	Georgia	9
45	Kuusisto, William	G	6-0	230	04/26/18	Minnesota	10
24	Laws, Joe	HB	5-9	185	06/16/11	Iowa	10
47	Lipscomb, Paul	T	6-5	230	01/13/23	Tennessee	10
38	Luhn, Nolan	E	6-3	200	07/27/21	Tulsa	9
7	Mason, Joel	E	6-0	200	03/12/13	Western Michigan	10
3	McKay, Roy	HB	6-0	195	02/02/20	Texas	10
72	McPherson, Forrest	C	5-11	240	10/22/11	Nebraska	5
8	Mosley, Russ	HB	5-10	170	07/22/18	Alabama	6
19	Mulleneaux, Carl (Moose)	E	6-4	210	04/01/17	Utah State	5
58	Neal, Ed	T	6-4	287	12/31/18	Tulane	9
22	Pannell, Ernie	T	6-3	220	02/02/17	Texas A&M	7
48	Perkins, Don	FB	6-0	198	09/18/17	Platteville	7
44	Ray, Buford (Baby)	T	6-6	256	09/30/15	Vanderbilt	10
38	Sample, Chuck	FB	5-9	210	01/05/20	Toledo	1
42	Smith, Bruce	HB	6-0	197	02/08/20	Minnesota	3
52	Snelling, Ken	FB	6-0	210		UCLA	2
33	Sorenson, Glen	G	6-0	210	02/29/20	Utah State	10
63	Starret, Ben	B	5-11	220	11/19/17	St. Mary's (CA)	8
21	Tinsley, Pete	G	5-8	205	03/16/13	Georgia	10
46	Tollefson, Charles	G	6-0	215	02/28/16	Iowa	9
79	Urban, Alex	E	6-2	210	07/16/17	South Carolina	1

1945 DRAFT

Rnd	Name	Pos	College
1	Walt Schlinkman	B	Texas Tech
2	Clyde Goodnight	E	Tulsa
3	Joseph Graham	E	Florida
4	Don Wells	T	Georgia
5	Casey Stephenson	B	Tennessee
6	Wilder Collins	T	Tulsa
7	Lamar Dingler	E	Arkansas
8	Harold Helscher	B	LSU
9	Ralph Hammond	C	Pittsburgh
10	Edward Podgorski	T	Lafayette
11	William Hackett	G	Ohio State
12	Marvin Lindsey	B	Arkansas
13	Bob McClure	T	Nevada
14	Harry Pieper	C	California
15	Robert Kula	B	Minnesota
16	Frank Hazard	G	Nebraska
17	Ed Jeffers	T	Oklahoma State
18	William Prentice	B	Santa Clara
19	Warren Fuller	E	Fordham
20	Fred Neilsen	T	San Francisco
21	Robert Gilmore	B	Washington
22	Lloyd Baxter	C	SMU
23	Nolan Luhn	E	Tulsa
24	Nestor Blanco	G	Colorado Mines
25	Bill Chestnut	B	Kansas
26	Jim Thompson	B	Washington State
27	John Evans	E	Idaho
28	Hamilton Nichols	G	Rice
29	John Friday	B	Ohio State
30	Billy Joe Aldridge	B	Oklahoma State

1945 GREEN BAY PACKERS

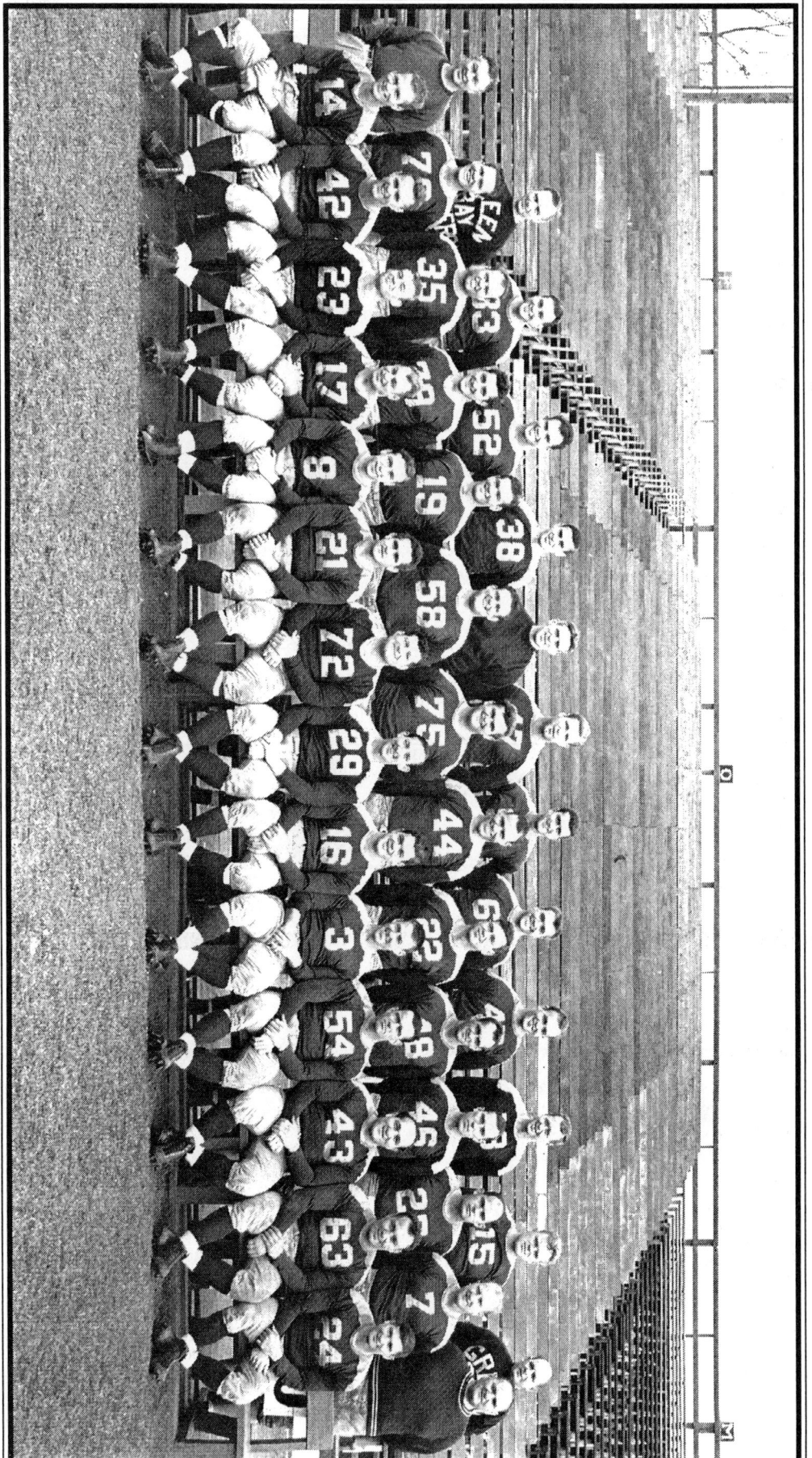

FRONT ROW: (L-R) 14 Don Hutson, 42 Bruce Smith, 23 Clyde Goodnight, 17 Amadeo (Mike) Bucchianeri, 8 Russ Mosley, 21 Pete Tinsley, 72 Forrest McPherson, 29 Charley Brock, 16 Lou Brock, 3 Roy McKay, 54 Larry Craig, 43 Charles (Buckets) Goldenberg, 24 Joe Laws.
MIDDLE ROW: (L-R) Coach Curly Lambeau, 76 Bernie Crimmins, 35 Bob Flowers, 79 Bob Adkins, 19 Carl (Moose) Mulleneaux, 58 Ed Neal, 75 Milburn (Tiny) Croft, 44 Buford (Baby) Ray, 22 Ernie Pannell, 48 Don Perkins, 46 Charles Tollefson, 27 Solon Barnett, 7 Joel Mason, Assistant Coach Walt Kiesling.
BACK ROW: (L-R) Trainer Carl (Bud) Jorgensen, 33 Glen Sorenson, 52 Ken Snelling, 38 Nolan Luhn, Johnny (Blood) McNally, 47 Paul Lipscomb, 51 Irv Comp, 64 Ted Fritsch, 45 William Kuusisto, 18 Ken Keuper, 15 Ray Frankowski, Trainer John Proski.

1946

Don Hutson had departed and he took with him much of the Packers' passing game. Though some still held out hope he would don his uniform in time for the opening Bears game as he had done in 1945, Hutson remained on the sidelines as an assistant coach unable to help a sick aerial attack. Six men —Irv Comp, Cliff Aberson, Tony Canadeo, Herman Rohrig, Bob Forte and Bob Nussbaumer— took turns throwing and combined for just four touchdowns against 18 interceptions. The group completed a miserable 30.3 percent of its throws and Green Bay's air game sank to dead last in the NFL.

With no one to throw, the Packers lived and died by the run. Keying this department were Canadeo, Ted Fritsch, and rookie Walt Schlinkman. The team ran often —four times rushing more than 60 times in a single game— culminating in a 64-attempt, 301-yard performance at Washington on December 1. Four times Green Bay rushed for more than 200 yards and four times they won.

Even with such a one-sided attack, the Packers were still in the race for almost half the season. After losing to the Bears and Rams in the first two weeks, Green Bay battled back, winning three in a row. The Packers (3-2-0) faced a crucial rematch with division-leading Chicago (3-1-1) on November 3. For two quarters the two battled to a standstill, although Green Bay had had opportunities. Fritsch missed two field goals from 45 and 34 yards in the first half. Then, in the third quarter, Fritsch fumbled at the Packers' 30-yard line where Ed Sprinkle scooped it up and raced in for a touchdown. The Bears added a field goal, hung on to win 10-7 and all but eliminated the Packers from the race.

In addition to the Bears, the Packers faced a challenge from another front. The All-American Football Conference (AAFC) began play in 1946. Competition from the new league drove players' salaries up, caused bidding for drafted talent and in some cases, lured veterans from established clubs. Fritsch, Green Bay's fullback for the past four seasons, was signed by the Cleveland Browns during the winter of 1945-46. Only after some maneuvering on the part of the Packers and Los Angeles Rams was he able to return to Green Bay. Once back, he proved a scoring force, registering 100 of the team's 148 points.

The Packers purchased Rockwood Lodge, located 15 miles northeast of the city, for its practice and training facilities. The former religious retreat became home for training camp until it burned to the ground in 1950.

Rumors concerning a possible move of the Packers to Milwaukee or elsewhere, though aired in the past, grew in volume in 1946. Such talk continued to be heard throughout the rest of the decade despite reassurances from NFL commisioner Bert Bell, Curly Lambeau and others. Though Green Bay's on-the-field performances had suffered, hometown fans were far from ready to give up their Packers to another city.

Green Bay Press-Gazette photo

Roy McKay scores on a six-yard run in the fourth quarter against the Chicago Bears on opening day. He also added the point after, but Green Bay never challenged, falling 30-7 to the Bears. In his four years with the Packers, McKay was used primarily as a punter and led the team in that department in 1945-46. He was traded to the Redskins following the 1947 season.

TEAM STATISTICS

	GB	OPP
First Downs	160	158
Rushing	112	84
Passing	34	59
Penalty	14	15
Rushes	560	367
Yards Gained	1,765	1,372
Average Gain	3.15	3.74
Average Yards per Game	160.5	124.7
Passes Attempted	178	214
Completed	54	94
% Completed	30.34	43.93
Total Yards Gained	841	1,288
Yards Gained per Completion	15.57	13.70
Average Yards per Game	76.5	117.1
Laterals Attempted	3	7
Completed	3	5
Yards Gained	12	1
Combined Yards Gained	2,618	2,661
Total Plays	741	4.53
Average Yards per Play	3.53	4.53
Average Yards per Game	238.0	241.9
Intercepted By	24	18
Yards Returned	399	275
Returned for TD	0	1
Punts	65	60
Yards Punted	2,787	2,513
Average Yards per Punt	42.88	41.88
Punt Returns	28	35
Yards Returned	284	414
Average Yards per Return	10.14	11.83
Returned for TD	0	0
Kickoff Returns	34	28
Yards Returned	740	683
Average Yards per Return	21.76	24.39
Returned for TD	0	0
Penalties	82	76
Yards Penalized	693	628
Fumbles	24	45
Lost	11	28
Own Recovered for Touchdown	0	0
Opponent's Recovered by	28	11
Opponent's Recovered for Touchdown	0	2
Total Points Scored	148	158
Total Touchdowns	17	21
Touchdowns Rushing	13	12
Touchdowns Passing	4	6
Touchdowns on Returns & Recoveries	0	3
Extra Points	15	20
Safeties	2	0
Field Goals Attempted	17	7
Field Goals Made	9	4
% Successful	52.94	57.14

Regular Season   6-5-0

Date	GB		OPP	Att.
9/29	7	Chicago Bears	30	(25,049)
10/6	17	Los Angeles Rams (M)	21	(27,049)
10/13	19	at Philadelphia Eagles	7	(36,127)
10/20	17	Pittsburgh Steelers	7	(22,588)
10/27	10	Detroit Lions (M)	7	(23,564)
11/3	7	at Chicago Bears	10	(46,321)
11/10	19	at Chicago Cardinals	7	(30,681)
11/17	9	at Detroit Lions	0	(22,950)
11/24	6	Chicago Cardinals	24	(16,150)
12/1	20	at Washington Redskins	7	(33,691)
12/8	17	at Los Angeles Rams	38	(46,838)

Score By Periods

	1	2	3	4	Total
Packers	13	47	33	55	148
Opponents	24	38	45	51	158

INDIVIDUAL STATISTICS

Rushing

	Att	Yds	Avg	LG	TD
Canadeo	122	476	3.9	27	0
Fritsch	128	444	3.5	32	9
Schlinkman	97	379	3.9	44	2
Aberson	48	161	3.4	13	0
Bruce Smith	22	119	5.4	36	0
B. Forte	17	73	4.3	20	0
Comp	61	62	1.0	29	1
Nussbaumer	29	43	1.5	16	0
McKay	21	34	1.6	9	1
Craig	1	-3	-3.0	-3	0
Rohrig	14	-23	-1.6	15	0
Packers	**560**	**1,765**	**3.2**	**44**	**13**
Opponents	367	1,372	3.7	t61	12

Receiving

	No	Yds	Avg	LG	TD
Goodnight	16	308	19.8	t51	1
Luhn	16	224	14.0	36	2
Nussbaumer	10	143	14.3	35	0
D. Wells	2	74	37.0	65	0
Rohrig	2	36	18.0	21	0
Canadeo	2	25	12.5	15	0
Fritsch	2	13	6.5	t12	1
B. Forte	2	5	2.5	4	0
Prescott	1	8	8.0	8	0
Schlinkman	1	5	5.0	5	0
Packers	**54**	**841**	**15.6**	**65**	**4**
Opponents	94	1,288	13.7	54	6

Passing

	Att	Com	Yds	Pct	TD	In	Rate
Comp	94	27	333	28.7	1	8	9.9
Aberson	41	14	184	34.1	0	5	9.7
Canadeo	27	7	189	25.9	1	3	29.0
Rohrig	8	2	97	25.0	1	1	—
B. Forte	7	3	28	42.9	1	1	—
Nussbaumer	1	1	10	100.0	0	0	—
Packers	**178**	**54**	**841**	**30.3**	**4**	**18**	**15.0**
Opponents	214	94	1,288	43.9	6	24	33.5

Punting

	No	Yds	Avg	LG	HB
McKay	64	2,735	42.7	64	1
Fritsch	1	52	52.0	52	0
Packers	**65**	**2,787**	**42.9**	**64**	**1**
Opponents	60	2,513	41.9	69	0

Kickoff Returns

	No	Yds	Avg	LG	TD
Canadeo	6	163	27.2	38	0
Nussbaumer	6	148	24.7	44	0
Rohrig	5	106	21.2	27	0
Aberson	3	69	23.0	26	0
Fritsch	3	68	22.7	37	0
Schlinkman	2	43	21.5	23	0
McKay	2	41	20.5	22	0
Luhn	2	28	14.0	17	0
Craig	2	18	9.0	11	0
Comp	1	29	29.0	29	0
Bruce Smith	1	21	21.0	21	0
Keuper	1	6	6.0	6	0
Packers	**34**	**740**	**21.8**	**44**	**0**
Opponents	28	683	24.4	51	0

Punt Returns

	No	Yds	Avg	LG	TD
Nussbaumer	12	98	8.2	21	0
Rohrig	8	98	12.3	18	0
Canadeo	6	76	12.7	22	0
Bruce Smith	2	12	6.0	8	0
Packers	**28**	**284**	**10.1**	**22**	**0**
Opponents	35	414	11.8	70	0

Interceptions

	No	Yds	Avg	LG	TD
Rohrig	5	134	26.8	51	0
Aberson	3	53	17.7	33	0
Nussbaumer	3	31	10.3	16	0
Keuper	3	22	7.3	10	0
Comp	2	38	19.0	21	0
B. Forte	2	23	11.5	16	0
Canadeo	1	23	23.0	23	0
McKay	1	20	20.0	20	0
Mosley	1	20	20.0	20	0
Mitchell	1	18	18.0	18	0
Fritsch	1	15	15.0	15	0
Ray	1	2	2.0	2	0
Packers	**24**	**399**	**16.6**	**51**	**0**
Opponents	18	275	15.3	t85	1

Scoring

	TDr	TDp	TDrt	PAT	FG	S	TP
Fritsch	9	1	0	13/15	9/17	0	100
Luhn	0	2	0	0/0	0/0	0	12
Schlinkman	2	0	0	0/0	0/0	0	12
McKay	1	0	0	2/2	0/0	0	8
Comp	1	0	0	0/0	0/0	0	6
Goodnight	0	1	0	0/0	0/0	0	6
Odson	0	0	0	0/0	0/0	1	2
team	0	0	0	0/0	0/0	1	2
Packers	**13**	**4**	**0**	**15/17**	**9/17**	**2**	**148**
Opponents	12	6	3	20/21	4/7	0	158

Fumbles

	Fum	Ow	Op	Yds	Tot
Aberson	2	0	1	0	1
C. Brock	0	1	5	31	6
Canadeo	3	0	0	0	3
Comp	6	4	0	0	4
Craig	0	2	4	3	6
Croft	0	0	3	16	3
B. Forte	1	0	1	0	1
Fritsch	3	3	0	-9	3
Keuper	0	0	1	0	1
Lipscomb	0	0	5	0	5
Luhn	1	0	0	0	0
McKay	2	1	0	-2	1
Nussbaumer	1	1	0	0	1
Odson	0	0	1	0	1
Ray	0	0	2	0	2
Rohrig	2	0	1	0	1
Schlinkman	2	0	0	0	1
Bruce Smith	1	0	0	0	0
D. Wells	0	0	3	47	3
Wildung	0	0	1	0	1
Packers	**24**	**13**	**28**	**86**	**41**

NFL STANDINGS

Western Division

	W	L	T	Pct	PF	PA
Chicago Bears	8	2	1	.800	289	193
Los Angeles Rams	6	4	1	.600	277	257
Green Bay Packers	6	5	0	.545	148	158
Chicago Cardinals	6	5	0	.545	260	198
Detroit Lions	1	10	0	.091	142	310

Eastern Division

	W	L	T	Pct	PF	PA
New York Giants	7	3	1	.700	236	162
Philadelphia Eagles	6	5	0	.545	231	220
Washington Redskins	5	5	1	.500	171	191
Pittsburgh Steelers	5	5	1	.500	136	117
Boston Yanks	2	8	1	.200	189	273

1946 ROSTER

No	Name	Pos	Ht	Wt	DOB	College	G
78	Aberson, Cliff	HB	6-1	195	08/28/21	No college	10
72	Barnett, Solon	T	6-1	235	03/30/21	Baylor	1
15	Bennett, Earl	G	5-8	190	02/27/20	Hardin-Simmons	3
29	Brock, Charley	C	6-1	210	03/15/16	Nebraska	11
3	Canadeo, Tony	HB	6-0	190	05/05/19	Gonzaga	11
51	Comp, Irv	HB	6-3	205	05/17/19	St. Benedict	11
54	Craig, Larry	E	6-0	218	06/27/16	South Carolina	11
75	Croft, Milburn (Tiny)	T	6-4	285	11/07/20	Ripon	11
35	Flowers, Bob	C	6-1	210	08/06/17	Texas Tech	10
8	Forte, Bob	HB	6-0	195	07/15/22	Arkansas	9
64	Fritsch, Ted	FB	5-10	210	10/31/20	Stevens Point	11
33	Gatewood, Lester	C	6-2	195	05/30/21	Baylor	11
23	Goodnight, Clyde	E	6-1	195	03/03/24	Tulsa	8
18	Keuper, Ken	HB	6-0	205	11/14/18	Georgia	10
52	Kuusisto, William	G	6-0	225	04/26/18	Minnesota	4
40	Lee, Bill	T	6-3	225	10/19/11	Alabama	4
46	Letlow, Russ	G	6-0	218	10/05/13	San Francisco	5
47	Lipscomb, Paul	T	6-5	240	01/13/23	Tennessee	11
38	Luhn, Nolan	E	6-3	200	07/27/21	Tulsa	11
3	McKay, Roy	HB	6-0	195	02/02/20	Texas	11
76	Miller, Tom	E	6-2	208	05/23/18	Hampden-Sydney	2
16	Mitchell, Charles	HB	6-0	190	12/28/20	Tulsa	2
8	Mosley, Russ	HB	5-10	170	07/22/18	Alabama	2
19	Mulleneaux, Carl (Moose)	E	6-4	210	04/01/17	Utah State	1
58	Neal, Ed	T	6-4	290	12/31/18	Tulane	10
48	Nussbaumer, Bob	HB	5-11	175	04/23/24	Michigan	10
63	Odson, Urban	T	6-3	255	11/17/18	Minnesota	6
17	Pregulman, Merv	G	6-3	215	10/10/22	Michigan	11
31	Prescott, Harold (Ace)	E	6-2	210	10/18/20	Hardin-Simmons	2
44	Ray, Buford (Baby)	T	6-6	250	09/30/15	Vanderbilt	11
19	Riddick, Ray	E	6-0	220	10/17/17	Fordham	2
80	Rohrig, Herman	HB	5-9	190	03/19/18	Nebraska	8
7	Schlinkman, Walt	FB	5-9	190	05/02/22	Texas Tech	11
42	Smith, Bruce	HB	6-0	197	02/08/20	Minnesota	6
21	Sparlis, Al	G	5-11	185	05/20/20	UCLA	3
27	Tollefson, Charles	G	6-0	215	02/28/16	Iowa	2
43	Wells, Don	E	6-2	200	07/12/22	Georgia	11
45	Wildung, Dick	G	6-0	220	08/16/21	Minnesota	11
25	Zupek, Al	B	6-1	205	01/12/23	Lawrence	3

1946 DRAFT

Rnd	Name	Pos	College
1	Johnny Strzykalski	B	Marquette
2	Bob Nussbaumer	B	Michigan
3	Ed Cody	B	Purdue
4	John Ferraro	T	USC
5	Art Renner	E	Michigan
6	Bert Cole	T	Oklahoma State
7	Grant Darnell	G	Texas A&M
8	Joe McAfee	B	Holy Cross
9	Steve Conroy	B	Holy Cross
10	Bill Hildebrand	E	Mississippi
11	Tom Hand	C	Iowa
12	George Hills	G	Georgia Tech
13	Jim Hough	B	Clemson
14	Dean Gaines	T	Georgia Tech
15	J.P. Miller	G	Georgia
16	Boyd Morse	E	Arizona
17	Joe Bradford	C	USC
18	Bill DeRosa	B	Boston College
19	Ralph Grant	B	Bucknell
20	Howard Brown	G	Indiana
21	Andy Kosmac	C	LSU
22	Maurice Stacy	B	Washington
23	Chick Davidson	T	Cornell
24	John Norton	B	Washington
25	Ed Holtsinger	B	Georgia Tech
26	Joe Campbell	E	Holy Cross
27	Francis Saunders	T	Clemson
28	Al Sparlis	G	UCLA
29	Ralph Clymer	G	Purdue
30	Joervin Henderson	C	Missouri

1946 GREEN BAY PACKERS

FRONT ROW: (L-R) 8 Bob Forte, 76 Tom Miller, 42 Bruce Smith, 29 Charley Brock, 15 Earl Bennett, 48 Bob Nussbaumer, 22 Roy McKay, 3 Tony Canadeo, 80 Herman Rohrig, 7 Walt Schlinkman, 46 Russ Letlow, 54 Larry Craig, 38 Nolan Luhn.
MIDDLE ROW: (L-R) Coach Curly Lambeau, 19 Ray Riddick, 78 Cliff Aberson, 40 Bill Lee, 43 Don Wells, 79 Bob Adkins, 17 Marv Pregulman, 58 Ed Neal, 47 Paul Lipscomb, 35 Bob Flowers, 21 Al Sparlis, 16 Charles Mitchell, 23 Clyde Goodnight, Assistant Coaches Walt Kiesling, Don Hutson.
BACK ROW: (L-R) Trainer Carl (Bud) Jorgensen, Assistant Trainer Tim O'Brien, 64 Ted Fritsch, 33 Lester Gatewood, 51 Irv Comp, 63 Urban Odson, 75 Milburn (Tiny) Croft, 44 Buford (Baby) Ray, 25 Al Zupek, 52 William Kuusisto, 18 Ken Keuper, 45 Dick Wildung.

1947

"Close but no cigar" summed up Green Bay's 1947 campaign. The Packers dropped five games, four by narrow margins. The Steelers and Cardinals each shaded them by a point, the Bears were a field goal better and the Cardinals beat the Packers by four the first time around. Three stung particularly hard, coming as they did all in midseason. In that span, Green Bay fell from first place to third, a spot they hung onto for the remainder of the year. After Philadelphia dumped them 28-14 at season's end, Green Bay returned home with a 6-5-1 record, third best behind the Bears and Cardinals.

To its credit, the team did boast a very potent running game, even with the retirement of two key lineman, tackle Bill Lee and guard Russ Letlow. Tony Canadeo and Walt Schlinkman headed a cast which accumulated 2,149 yards, second only to the Rams 2,171. The team piled up at least 120 yards on the ground every week, save one, and set the franchise record on October 26. On that day, the Packers rushed 50 times for 366 yards, sparked by Ed Cody's 111 on nine carries. Cody scored twice to lead Green Bay to a 34-17 win over Detroit.

Unfortunately, after hitting such a high note, the team's fortunes changed. The Detroit win pushed Green Bay's record to 4-1-0—the same as the front running Cardinals— but the Packers' stay at the top was short-lived. The Steelers, Bears and Cardinals took turns frustrating the NFL's smallest city. First, Pittsburgh tackle Ralph Calcogni tackled Jack Jacobs in the end zone for a fourth-quarter safety which put his team up 18-10, a margin too large for a late Jacobs to Luhn scoring pass to overcome. A week later, Jim Gillette and Irv Comp fumbled away chances to score from inside the Bears eight-yard line and Ward Cuff had a field goal attempt blocked by Noah Mullins with 20 seconds left as Green Bay fell 20-17. To complete the misery, the Packers traveled to Comiskey Park where 40,086 saw Green Bay blow a 20-7 lead and Cuff miss a field goal with 31 seconds remaining. The 21-20 setback dropped the Packers (4-4-0) and third place behind the Bears (6-2-0) and Cardinals (7-1-0).

Off the field, Packers president Lee Joannes resigned on July 23. Joannes had held his post since 1930. For 18 years he had provided solid leadership, playing a major role in guiding the organization through the depression and the financial difficulties of the early '30s. He was replaced by Emil R. Fischer.

After the three-game skid, the Packers were able to put together two more wins, 30-10 over the Rams and 35-14 at Detroit. In doing so, Green Bay was able to finish with a winning record, a feat not duplicated until Vince Lombardi arrived on the scene in 1959.

Green Bay Press-Gazette photo

Bruce Smith (42) dashes around right end for a 16-yard gain in the second quarter of the Packers' 34-17 victory over Detroit. The win allowed Green Bay to keep pace with the front-running Cardinals. Smith carried just twice in a record-setting ground attack (366 yards), but gained 51 yards. Such performances allowed him to average a team-leading 7.0 yards per carry .

TEAM STATISTICS

	GB	OPP
First Downs	206	193
Rushing	105	96
Passing	82	71
Penalty	19	26
Rushes	510	433
Yards Gained	2,149	1,606
Average Gain	4.21	3.71
Average Yards per Game	179.1	133.8
Passes Attempted	253	277
Completed	112	122
% Completed	44.27	44.04
Total Yards Gained	1,724	1,790
Yards Lost	104	190
Net Yards Gained	1,620	1,600
Yards Gained per Completion	15.39	14.67
Average Yards per Game	143.6	149.2
Laterals Attempted	0	2
Completed	0	1
Yards Gained	0	0
Combined Yards Gained	3,873	3,396
Total Plays	763	712
Average Yards per Play	5.08	4.77
Average Yards per Game	322.8	283.0
Intercepted By	30	19
Yards Returned	428	293
Returned for TD	1	1
Punts	65	65
Yards Punted	2,831	2,830
Average Yards per Punt	43.55	43.54
Punt Returns	45	44
Yards Returned	563	483
Average Yards per Return	12.51	10.98
Returned for TD	0	0
Kickoff Returns	42	48
Yards Returned	874	1,034
Average Yards per Return	20.81	21.54
Returned for TD	0	0
Penalties	104	88
Yards Penalized	1,019	759
Fumbles	24	41
Lost	13	20
Own Recovered for Touchdown	0	0
Opponent's Recovered by	20	13
Opponent's Recovered for Touchdown	0	0
Total Points Scored	274	210
Total Touchdowns	33	28
Touchdowns Rushing	14	13
Touchdowns Passing	17	14
Touchdowns on Returns & Recoveries	2	1
Extra Points	33	25
Safeties	2	1
Field Goals Attempted	29	11
Field Goals Made	13	5
% Successful	44.83	45.45

Regular Season 6-5-1

Date	GB		OPP	Att.
9/28	29	Chicago Bears	20	(25,461)
10/5	17	Los Angeles Rams (M)	14	(31,613)
10/12	10	Chicago Cardinals	14	(25,502)
10/19	27	Washington Redskins (M)	10	(28,572)
10/26	34	Detroit Lions	17	(25,179)
11/2	17	Pittsburgh Steelers (M)	18	(30,073)
11/9	17	at Chicago Bears	20	(46,112)
11/16	20	at Chicago Cardinals	21	(40,086)
11/23	24	at New York Giants	24	(27,939)
11/30	30	at Los Angeles Rams	10	(31,040)
12/7	35	at Detroit Lions	14	(14,055)
12/14	14	at Philadelphia Eagles	28	(24,216)

Score By Periods

	1	2	3	4	Total
Packers	49	61	85	79	274
Opponents	37	57	58	58	210

INDIVIDUAL STATISTICS

Rushing

	Att	Yds	Avg	LG	TD
Canadeo	103	464	4.5	35	2
Schlinkman	115	439	3.8	20	2
Bruce Smith	47	288	7.0	37	1
Cody	56	263	4.7	t32	2
Fritsch	68	247	3.6	48	6
Gillette	50	207	4.1	26	0
B. Forte	29	80	2.4	12	0
J. Jacobs	18	64	3.6	t15	1
Comp	5	46	9.2	34	0
Rohrig	7	22	3.1	6	0
Keuper	6	14	2.3	8	0
McKay	3	11	3.7	5	0
Cuff	1	7	7.0	7	0
Goodnight	1	-1	-1.0	-1	0
G. Wilson	1	-2	-2.0	-2	0
Packers	**510**	**2,149**	**4.2**	**48**	**14**
Opponents	433	1,606	3.7	41	13

Receiving

	No	Yds	Avg	LG	TD
Luhn	42	696	16.5	44	7
Goodnight	38	593	15.6	t69	6
Gillette	12	224	18.6	50	1
B. Forte	7	80	11.4	t22	2
Bruce Smith	4	50	12.5	t36	1
G. Wilson	3	34	11.3	15	0
Keuper	2	37	18.5	26	0
Schlinkman	2	-6	-3.0	-1	0
Craig	1	14	14.0	14	0
Cody	1	2	2.0	2	0
Packers	**112**	**1,724**	**15.4**	**t69**	**17**
Opponents	122	1,790	14.7	t66	14

Passing

	Att	Com	Yds	Pct	TD	In	YL	Rate
J. Jacobs	242	108	1,615	44.6	16	17	104	59.8
Canadeo	8	3	101	37.5	1	1	0	—
B. Forte	2	1	8	50.0	0	0	0	—
Comp	1	0	0	00.0	0	1	0	—
Packers	**253**	**112**	**1,724**	**44.3**	**17**	**19**	**104**	**58.5**
Opponents	277	122	1,790	44.0	14	30	190	43.0

Punting

	No	Yds	Avg	LG	HB
J. Jacobs	57	2,481	43.5	74	1
McKay	8	350	43.8	54	0
Packers	**65**	**2,831**	**43.5**	**74**	**1**
Opponents	65	2,830	43.5	86	0

Kickoff Returns

	No	Yds	Avg	LG	TD
Canadeo	15	312	20.8	35	0
Cody	10	269	26.9	39	0
Fritsch	5	100	20.0	25	0
Gillette	3	66	22.0	29	0
Bruce Smith	3	61	20.3	23	0
Luhn	2	30	15.0	18	0
B. Forte	2	28	14.0	23	0
Rohrig	1	15	15.0	15	0
Goodnight	1	7	7.0	7	0
Packers	**42**	**874**	**20.8**	**39**	**0**
Opponents	48	1,034	21.5	40	0

Punt Returns

	No	Yds	Avg	LG	TD
Rohrig	18	213	11.8	28	0
Gillette	11	168	15.3	26	0
Canadeo	10	111	11.1	24	0
Cody	2	30	15.0	20	0
Bruce Smith	1	22	22.0	22	0
B. Forte	1	15	15.0	15	0
J. Jacobs	1	4	4.0	4	0
Comp	1	0	0.0	0	0
Packers	**45**	**563**	**12.5**	**28**	**0**
Opponents	44	483	11.0	35	0

Interceptions

	No	Yds	Avg	LG	TD
B. Forte	8	140	17.5	t68	1
Rohrig	5	80	16.0	28	0
Comp	5	54	10.8	30	0
J. Jacobs	4	64	16.0	29	0
Keuper	2	41	20.5	26	0
C. Brock	2	14	7.0	7	0
Bruce Smith	2	11	5.5	11	0
Flowers	1	12	12.0	12	0
Fritsch	1	12	12.0	12	0
Packers	**30**	**428**	**14.3**	**t68**	**1**
Opponents	19	293	15.4	t63	1

Scoring

	TDr	TDp	TDrt	PAT	FG	S	TP
Fritsch	6	0	0	2/2	6/13	0	56
Cuff	0	0	0	30/30	7/16	0	51
Luhn	0	7	0	0/0	0/0	0	42
Goodnight	0	6	0	0/0	0/0	0	36
B. Forte	0	2	1	0/0	0/0	0	18
Bruce Smith	1	1	0	0/0	0/0	1	14
Canadeo	2	0	0	0/0	0/0	0	12
Cody	2	0	0	0/0	0/0	0	12
Schlinkman	2	0	0	0/0	0/0	0	12
Gillette	0	1	0	0/0	0/0	0	6
J. Jacobs	1	0	0	0/0	0/0	0	6
E. Neal	0	0	1	0/0	0/0	0	6
Wildung	0	0	0	0/0	0/0	1	2
McKay	0	0	0	1/1	0/0	0	1
Packers	**14**	**17**	**2**	**33/33**	**13/29**	**2**	**274**
Opponents	13	14	1	25/28	5/11	1	210

Fumbles

	Fum	Ow	Op	Yds	Tot
C. Brock	0	1	1	0	2
Canadeo	0	0	2	0	1
Cody	2	1	0	0	1
Comp	2	1	1	-5	2
Craig	0	0	1	0	1
Flowers	0	0	1	0	1
A. Forte	0	0	2	1	2
B. Forte	1	0	2	0	2
Fritsch	1	0	0	0	0
Gatewood	0	1	0	0	2
Gillette	2	0	0	0	0
J. Jacobs	5	1	0	1	1
Keuper	0	0	1	0	1
Lipscomb	0	1	0	1	1
Luhn	1	0	1	4	1
Ray	0	0	3	5	3
Rohrig	2	2	1	-2	3
Schlinkman	8	2	0	10	2
Skoglund	0	0	2	0	2
D. Wells	0	0	1	0	1
Wildung	0	0	3	1	3
Packers	**24**	**11**	**21**	**17**	**32**

NFL STANDINGS

Western Division

	W	L	T	Pct	PF	PA
Chicago Cardinals	9	3	0	.750	306	231
Chicago Bears	8	4	0	.667	363	241
Green Bay Packers	**6**	**5**	**1**	**.545**	**274**	**210**
Los Angeles Rams	6	6	0	.500	259	214
Detroit Lions	3	9	0	.250	231	305

Eastern Division

	W	L	T	Pct	PF	PA
Philadelphia Eagles	8	4	0	.667	308	242
Pittsburgh Steelers	8	4	0	.667	240	259
Boston Yanks	4	7	1	.364	168	256
Washington Redskins	4	8	0	.333	295	367
New York Giants	2	8	2	.200	190	309

1947 ROSTER

No	Name	Pos	Ht	Wt	DOB	College	G
82	Bell, Edward	G	6-1	233	09/20/21	Indiana	11
29	Brock, Charley	C	6-1	210	03/15/16	Nebraska	12
3	Canadeo, Tony	HB	6-0	190	05/05/19	Gonzaga	12
46	Clemons, Raymond	G	5-10	200	04/02/21	St. Mary's (CA)	9
17	Cody, Ed	FB	5-9	190	02/27/23	Purdue	10
51	Comp, Irv	HB	6-3	205	05/17/19	St. Benedict	12
54	Craig, Larry	E	6-0	218	06/27/16	South Carolina	12
75	Croft, Milburn (Tiny)	T	6-4	280	11/07/20	Ripon	10
21	Cuff, Ward	HB	6-1	192	08/13/14	Marquette	10
66	Davis, Ralph	G	5-11	205	05/30/22	Wisconsin	11
35	Flowers, Bob	C	6-1	210	08/06/17	Texas Tech	12
40	Forte, Aldo	G	6-0	215	01/20/18	Montana	10
8	Forte, Bob	HB	6-0	195	07/15/22	Arkansas	12
64	Fritsch, Ted	FB	5-10	210	10/31/20	Stevens Point	12
33	Gatewood, Lester	C	6-2	200	05/30/21	Baylor	12
16	Gillette, Jim	HB	6-1	185	12/19/17	Virginia	10
23	Goodnight, Clyde	E	6-1	195	03/03/24	Tulsa	11
27	Jacobs, Jack	QB	6-2	190	08/07/19	Oklahoma	12
18	Keuper, Ken	HB	6-0	205	11/14/18	Georgia	12
76	Kovatch, John	E	6-3	200	07/21/20	Notre Dame	3
47	Lipscomb, Paul	T	6-5	245	01/13/23	Tennessee	12
38	Luhn, Nolan	E	6-3	200	07/27/21	Tulsa	12
19	McDougal, Robert	FB	6-2	205	03/19/21	Miami (FL)	1
22	McKay, Roy	HB	6-0	195	02/02/20	Texas	11
58	Neal, Ed	T	6-4	290	12/31/18	Tulane	12
63	Odson, Urban	T	6-3	250	11/17/18	Minnesota	11
44	Ray, Buford (Baby)	T	6-6	250	09/30/15	Vanderbilt	11
80	Rohrig, Herman	HB	5-9	190	03/19/18	Nebraska	7
7	Schlinkman, Walt	FB	5-9	190	05/02/22	Texas Tech	12
52	Skoglund, Robert	E	6-1	198	07/29/25	Notre Dame	9
42	Smith, Bruce	HB	6-0	197	02/08/20	Minnesota	10
15	Tassos, Damon	G	6-1	225	12/05/23	Texas A&M	3
43	Wells, Don	E	6-2	200	07/12/22	Georgia	12
45	Wildung, Dick	G	6-0	220	08/16/21	Minnesota	3
65	Wilson, Gene	E	5-10	175	06/24/26	SMU	9

1947 DRAFT

Rnd	Name	Pos	College	Rnd	Name	Pos	College
1	Ernie Case	B	UCLA	16	Jim Goodman	T	Indiana
2	Burr Baldwin	E	UCLA	17	Dick Miller	G	Lawrence
3	Paul (Buddy) Burris	G	Oklahoma	18	Brad Ecklund	C	Oregon
4	Gene Wilson	E	SMU	19	Bob West	B	Colorado
5	Dick Connors	B	Northwestern	20	Tex Reilly	B	Colorado
6	Monte Moncrief	T	Texas A&M	21	Ron Sockolov	T	California
7	Robert McDougal	B	Miami	22	Herb St. John	G	Georgia
8	Bob Kelly	B	Notre Dame	23	Fred Redeker	B	Cincinnati
9	Tom Moulton	C	Oklahoma State	24	Herm Lubker	E	Arkansas
10	George Hills	G	Georgia Tech	25	Bob Palladino	B	Notre Dame
11	Bob Skoglund	E	Notre Dame	26	Jerrell Baxter	T	North Carolina
12	Jack Mitchell	B	Oklahoma	27	Ray Sellers	E	Georgia
13	Denver Crawford	T	Tennessee	28	Jerry Carle	B	Northwestern
14	Jim Callahan	E	USC	29	Bill Hogan	B	Kansas
15	Ted Scalissi	B	Ripon	30	Ralph Olsen	E	Utah

1947 GREEN BAY PACKERS

FRONT ROW: (L–R) Assistant Trainer Tim O'Brien, 22 Roy McKay, 65 Gene Wilson, 3 Tony Canadeo, 17 Ed Cody, 80 Herman Rohrig, 29 Charley Brock, 7 Walt Schlinkman, 43 Don Wells, 23 Clyde Goodnight, 54 Larry Craig, Trainer Carl (Bud) Jorgensen.
MIDDLE ROW: (L–R) 46 Bill McPartland, 66 Ralph Davis, 64 Ted Fritsch, 8 Bob Forte, 18 Ken Keuper, 35 Bob Flowers, 38 Nolan Luhn, 33 Lester Gatewood, 40 Aldo Forte, 16 Jim Gillette, 27 Jack Jacobs, 15 Damon Tassos, Assistant Coach Don Hutson.
BACK ROW: (L–R) Assistant Coach Walt Kiesling, 42 Bruce Smith, 52 Robert Skoglund, 75 Milburn (Tiny) Croft, 58 Ed Neal, 47 Paul Lipscomb, 44 Buford (Baby) Ray, 63 Urban Odson, 51 Irv Comp, 82 Edward Bell, 45 Dick Wildung, Coach Curly Lambeau.

Don Hutson, Joe Laws and Charles (Buckets) Goldenberg departed in 1945. Bill Lee, Russ Letlow and Carl (Moose) Mulleneaux left a year later. In 1947, Charley Brock and Milburn (Tiny) Croft called it quits. Just six players remained from the 1944 championship team heading into 1948: Tony Canadeo, Irv Comp, Larry Craig, Bob Flowers, Ted Fritsch and Buford (Baby) Ray. Losing such talent was problem enough. Replacing it proved impossible.

The draft hadn't been the answer. Only two choices from 1946 and 1947 played in 1948: Ed Cody, a third-round selection in '46, and Gene Wilson, the fourth pick a year later. The 1944 draft was such a washout that only one player from it ever played for the Packers —Merv Pregulman— who lasted but a year. To top it off, Green Bay lost its number-one choices in a bidding war to the AAFC in both 1946 and 1947.

With the draft a dead-end, Lambeau tried to get talent wherever he could find it. He signed cast-offs Ted Cook and Ted Cremer from Detroit, obtained Don Deeks from Washington, lured James Kekeris from the Eagles, acquired Pat West from the Rams and even gave Ken Roskie, last of the AAFC's 49ers in 1946, a shot at fullback. Of those six, only Cook went on to play with the Packers in 1949. Of all the players Lambeau added from 1946 to 1948, either by the draft or other means, only three, Cook, Earl (Jug) Girard and Jay Rhodemyre would outlast Lambeau in Green Bay. The fiery coach, once able to gather the likes of Robert (Cal) Hubbard, Clarke Hinkle and Don Hutson from various sources, was now coming up empty in his quest for talent.

The turning point of the year occurred after the Cardinals defeated the Packers 17-7 in week four at Milwaukee. Prior to that game, the Packers were 2-1-0 and still a part of the race. After the loss, Lambeau fined each player a half game's pay for what he considered indifferent, spiritless play and waived Bruce Smith outright.

After finding their checks lacking on Tuesday, the players turned around that Sunday and handed the Rams a 16-0 loss at City Stadium. Following that effort, the men expected an extra large check – pay for the Rams game plus the missing pay from the Cardinals contest. Lambeau, however, did not return the fines and morale hit rock bottom. The team lost its final seven games to finish 3-9, a game ahead of the cellar-dwelling Lions. Only after the season was over did Lambeau return the missing money, and by then the damage had been done.

Perhaps statistics can best illustrate Green Bay's slide. The Packers gave up 77 first downs in the first five games then turned around and allowed 145 in the final seven. Opponents gained 728 rushing yards before October 24, then piled up 1,425 the rest of the way. And finally, after having surrendered just 83 points, the team gave up a whopping 207 down the stretch.

Never before had a Packer team sunk so low. Unfortunately such dreary performances, long the exception in the past, would become the norm in the following decade.

Green Bay Press-Gazette photo

Bob Forte (8) intercepts a Bob Waterfield pass in front of Don Currivan to end a Ram threat in Green Bay on October 17. Packer defenders intercepted seven throws in posting a 16-0 win. The victory, however, was the last of 1948. Green Bay closed out its campaign with seven straight losses and finished with a losing record for the first time since 1933.

TEAM STATISTICS

	GB	OPP
First Downs	172	222
Rushing	89	132
Passing	58	74
Penalty	25	16
Rushes	446	537
Yards Gained	1,759	2,153
Average Gain	3.94	4.01
Average Yards per Game	146.6	179.4
Passes Attempted	274	260
Completed	109	134
% Completed	39.78	51.54
Total Yards Gained	1,364	1,626
Yards Lost	293	112
Net Yards Gained	1,071	1,514
Yards Gained per Completion	12.51	12.13
Average Yards per Game	113.7	135.5
Laterals Attempted	1	5
Completed	1	5
Yards Gained	12	69
Combined Yards Gained	3,135	3,848
Total Plays	721	802
Average Yards per Play	4.35	4.80
Average Yards per Game	261.3	320.7
Intercepted By	29	29
Yards Returned	405	457
Returned for TD	0	2
Punts	78	70
Yards Punted	3,140	3,029
Average Yards per Punt	40.26	43.27
Punt Returns	47	38
Yards Returned	527	473
Average Yards per Return	11.21	12.45
Returned for TD	0	1
Kickoff Returns	47	22
Yards Returned	926	611
Average Yards per Return	19.70	27.77
Returned for TD	0	1
Penalties	104	91
Yards Penalized	941	771
Fumbles	30	23
Lost	19	15
Own Recovered for Touchdown	0	0
Opponent's Recovered by	15	19
Opponent's Recovered for Touchdown	1	0
Total Points Scored	154	290
Total Touchdowns	20	39
Touchdowns Rushing	11	21
Touchdowns Passing	8	13
Touchdowns on Returns & Recoveries	1	5
Extra Points	16	38
Safeties	0	0
Field Goals Attempted	16	14
Field Goals Made	6	6
% Successful	37.50	42.86

Regular Season 3-9-0

Date	GB		OPP	Att.
9/17	31	at Boston Yanks	0	(15,443)
9/26	7	Chicago Bears	45	(25,546)
10/3	33	Detroit Lions	21	(24,206)
10/10	7	Chicago Cardinals (M)	17	(34,369)
10/17	16	Los Angeles Rams	0	(25,119)
10/24	7	Washington Redskins (M)	23	(13,433)
10/31	20	at Detroit Lions	24	(16,174)
11/7	7	at Pittsburgh Steelers	38	(26,058)
11/14	6	at Chicago Bears	7	(48,113)
11/21	3	at New York Giants (M)	49	(12,639)
11/28	10	at Los Angeles Rams	24	(23,874)
12/5	7	at Chicago Cardinals	42	(26,072)

Score By Periods

	1	2	3	4	Total
Packers	40	44	20	50	154
Opponents	55	90	59	86	290

INDIVIDUAL STATISTICS

Rushing

	Att	Yds	Avg	LG	TD
Canadeo	123	589	4.8	49	4
Schlinkman	106	441	4.2	19	4
Fritsch	37	173	4.7	30	0
Earhart	30	140	4.7	t72	1
Provo	29	90	3.1	28	0
O.E. Smith	27	85	3.1	10	0
J. Jacobs	24	73	3.0	23	1
Cody	26	58	2.2	10	0
B. Forte	12	30	2.5	9	0
Roskie	5	28	5.6	9	1
Girard	13	26	2.0	7	0
Bruce Smith	6	21	3.5	20	0
Comp	3	3	1.0	2	0
Moss	5	2	0.4	3	0
Packers	**446**	**1,759**	**3.9**	**t72**	**11**
Opponents	537	2,153	4.0	t72	21

1948

Receiving

	No	Yds	Avg	LG	TD
Goodnight	28	448	16.0	57	3
Luhn	17	285	16.8	40	2
Earhart	17	194	11.4	t64	2
T. Cook	13	156	12.0	23	0
O.E. Smith	12	121	10.1	49	0
Canadeo	9	81	9.0	32	0
B. Forte	6	63	10.5	19	1
Provo	4	-9	-2.3	3	0
G. Wilson	2	23	11.5	14	0
Girard	1	2	2.0	2	0
Packers	**109**	**1,364**	**12.5**	**t64**	**8**
Opponents	134	1,626	12.1	t61	13

Passing

	Att	Com	Yds	Pct	TD	In	YL	Rate
J. Jacobs	184	82	848	44.6	5	21	169	27.9
Comp	49	16	335	32.7	1	7	76	25.0
Girard	14	4	117	28.6	1	1	29	56.0
Canadeo	8	2	24	25.0	0	0	0	—
Moss	17	4	20	23.5	0	0	19	39.6
Provo	1	1	20	100.0	0	0	0	—
Bruce Smith	1	0	0	00.0	0	0	0	—
Packers	**274**	**109**	**1,364**	**39.8**	**8**	**29**	**293**	**26.1**
Opponents	260	134	1,626	51.5	13	29	112	48.2

Punting

	No	Yds	Avg	LG	HB
J. Jacobs	69	2,782	40.3	78	1
Girard	8	320	40.0	49	0
Canadeo	1	38	38.0	38	0
Packers	**78**	**3,140**	**40.3**	**78**	**1**
Opponents	70	3,029	43.3	88	0

Kickoff Returns

	No	Yds	Avg	LG	TD
O.E. Smith	12	287	23.9	36	0
Provo	10	205	20.5	28	0
Canadeo	9	166	18.4	28	0
Schlinkman	4	89	22.3	34	0
Luhn	3	18	6.0	11	0
Earhart	2	51	25.5	27	0
Cody	2	31	15.5	20	0
B. Forte	2	30	15.0	17	0
Girard	1	20	20.0	20	0
Fritsch	1	17	17.0	17	0
Goodnight	1	12	12.0	12	0
Packers	**47**	**926**	**19.7**	**36**	**0**
Opponents	22	611	27.8	t96	1

Punt Returns

	No	Yds	Avg	LG	TD
Provo	18	208	11.6	40	0
Earhart	11	137	12.5	27	0
O.E. Smith	8	71	8.9	27	0
Canadeo	4	55	13.8	20	0
Comp	3	35	11.7	16	0
T. Cook	2	18	9.0	14	0
J. Jacobs	1	3	3.0	3	0
Packers	**47**	**527**	**11.2**	**40**	**0**
Opponents	38	473	12.5	t49	1

Interceptions

	No	Yds	Avg	LG	TD
T. Cook	6	81	13.5	27	0
Comp	5	86	17.2	28	0
B. Forte	5	56	11.2	40	0
Flowers	4	21	5.3	19	0
Canadeo	3	26	8.7	25	0
G. Wilson	2	13	6.5	13	0
Fritsch	1	52	52.0	52	0
Girard	1	34	34.0	34	0
Rhodemyre	1	24	24.0	24	0
Roskie	1	12	12.0	12	0
Packers	**29**	**405**	**14.0**	**52**	**0**
Opponents	29	457	15.8	t82	2

Scoring

	TDr	TDp	TDrt	PAT	FG	S	TP
Fritsch	0	0	1	5/6	6/16	0	29
Canadeo	4	0	0	0/0	0/0	0	24
Schlinkman	4	0	0	0/0	0/0	0	24
Earhart	1	2	0	0/0	0/0	0	18
Goodnight	0	3	0	0/0	0/0	0	18
Luhn	0	2	0	0/0	0/0	0	12
Cody	0	0	0	11/13	0/0	0	11
B. Forte	0	1	0	0/0	0/0	0	6
J. Jacobs	1	0	0	0/0	0/0	0	6
Roskie	1	0	0	0/0	0/0	0	6
Packers	**11**	**8**	**1**	**16/20**	**6/16**	**0**	**154**
Opponents	21	13	5	38/39	6/14	0	290

Fumbles

	Fum	Ow	Op	Yds	Tot
Baxter	0	0	1	0	1
Canadeo	5	0	0	0	0
Cody	2	0	0	0	0
Comp	3	1	2	5	3
T. Cook	1	0	0	0	0
Craig	0	0	1	0	1
Cremer	0	0	1	0	1
Earhart	0	0	1	0	1
Flowers	0	1	0	0	1
B. Forte	1	0	1	0	1
Fritsch	2	0	4	8	4
Girard	2	0	0	0	0
Goodnight	2	1	0	0	1
J. Jacobs	1	1	0	-3	1
Lipscomb	0	0	2	0	2
Moss	3	1	0	-1	1
E. Neal	0	0	1	0	1
Olsonoski	0	2	0	0	2
Provo	0	0	1	0	1
Schlinkman	4	0	0	0	0
Bruce Smith	1	0	0	0	0
O.E. Smith	2	0	0	0	0
Vogds	0	0	1	0	1
Wildung	0	1	1	5	2
G. Wilson	0	0	1	0	1
Packers	**30**	**11**	**15**	**15**	**26**

NFL STANDINGS

Western Division

	W	L	T	Pct	PF	PA
Chicago Cardinals	11	1	0	.917	395	226
Chicago Bears	10	2	0	.833	375	151
Los Angeles Rams	6	5	1	.545	327	269
Green Bay Packers	**3**	**9**	**0**	**.250**	**154**	**290**
Detroit Lions	2	10	0	.167	200	407

Eastern Division

	W	L	T	Pct	PF	PA
Philadelphia Eagles	9	2	1	.818	376	156
Washington Redskins	7	5	0	.583	291	287
New York Giants	4	8	0	.333	297	388
Pittsburgh Steelers	4	8	0	.333	200	243
Boston Yanks	3	9	0	.250	174	372

1948 ROSTER

No	Name	Pos	Ht	Wt	DOB	College	G
33	Baxter, Lloyd	C	6-2	210	01/18/23	SMU	11
82	Bell, Edward	G	6-1	233	09/20/21	Indiana	12
3	Canadeo, Tony	HB	6-0	190	05/05/19	Gonzaga	12
17	Cody, Ed	FB	5-9	190	02/27/23	Purdue	10
51	Comp, Irv	HB	6-3	205	05/17/19	St. Benedict	11
48	Cook, Ted	E	6-2	195	02/06/22	Alabama	12
54	Craig, Larry	E	6-0	218	06/27/16	South Carolina	12
	Cremer, Ted	E	6-2	210	03/16/19	Auburn	3
66	Davis, Ralph	G	5-11	205	05/30/22	Wisconsin	11
85	Deeks, Donald	G	6-4	245	02/10/23	Washington	8
41	Earhart, Ralph	HB	5-10	165	03/29/23	Texas Tech	12
35	Flowers, Bob	C	6-1	210	08/06/17	Texas Tech	11
8	Forte, Bob	HB	6-0	195	07/15/22	Arkansas	12
64	Fritsch, Ted	FB	5-10	210	10/31/20	Stevens Point	12
36	Girard, Earl (Jug)	HB	5-11	175	01/25/27	Wisconsin	10
23	Goodnight, Clyde	E	6-1	195	03/03/24	Tulsa	8
27	Jacobs, Jack	QB	6-2	190	08/07/19	Oklahoma	12
72	Kekeris, James	T	6-1	257	10/17/23	Missouri	5
47	Lipscomb, Paul	T	6-5	245	01/13/23	Tennessee	12
38	Luhn, Nolan	E	6-3	200	07/27/21	Tulsa	12
10	Moss, Perry	QB	5-10	170	08/04/26	Illinois	6
58	Neal, Ed	T	6-4	290	12/31/18	Tulane	12
63	Odson, Urban	T	6-3	250	11/17/18	Minnesota	12
72	Olsonoski, Larry	G	6-2	215	09/10/25	Minnesota	12
80	Provo, Fred	HB	5-9	185	04/17/22	Washington	9
44	Ray, Buford (Baby)	T	6-6	250	09/30/15	Vanderbilt	12
22	Rhodemyre, Jay	C	6-1	210	12/16/22	Kentucky	9
34	Roskie, Ken	FB	6-1	220	11/29/21	South Carolina	6
7	Schlinkman, Walt	FB	5-9	190	05/02/22	Texas Tech	11
42	Smith, Bruce	HB	6-0	197	02/08/20	Minnesota	4
21	Smith, Oscar E.	HB	6-0	185	07/20/23	Texas-El Paso	12
15	Tassos, Damon	G	6-1	225	12/05/23	Texas A&M	11
79	Vogds, Evan	G	5-10	215	02/10/23	Wisconsin	12
43	Wells, Don	E	6-2	200	07/12/22	Georgia	12
25	West, Pat	FB	6-0	201	02/21/23	USC	3
45	Wildung, Dick	G	6-0	220	08/16/21	Minnesota	12
65	Wilson, Gene	E	5-10	180	06/24/26	SMU	12

1948 DRAFT

Rnd	Name	Pos	Ht	Wt	College
1	Earl (Jug) Girard	B	5-11	180	Wisconsin
2	Oscar E. Smith	B	6-0	190	Texas-El Paso
3	Wayman Sellers	E	6-1	190	Georgia
4	Larry Olsonoski	G	6-2	215	Minnesota
5a	Don Richards	T	6-2	245	Arkansas
	(Choice from Lions)				
5b	Jay Rhodemyre	C	6-1	210	Kentucky
6	Bob Cunz	T	5-10	220	Illinois
7	(Choice to Giants)				
8	George Walmsley	B	5-8	170	Rice
9	Bob Hodges	T	6-2	230	Bradley
10	Bob Rennebohm	E	6-0	195	Wisconsin
11	Perry Moss	B	5-10	190	Illinois
12	Fred Provo	B	5-9	185	Washington
13	Lou Agase	E-T	6-1	198	Illinois
14	Travis Raven	B	5-11	190	Texas
15	(Choice to Redskins)				
16	Ken Balge	E	6-2	210	Michigan State
17	Charley Tatom	T	6-5	236	Texas
18	Floyd Thomas	C	6-3	205	Arkansas
19	Herb St. John	G	5-10	210	Georgia
20	Don Anderson	B	5-11	190	Rice
21	Fred Kling	B	6-2	190	Missouri
22	Clyde Biggers	T	6-6	240	Catawba
23	Stan Heath	B	6-1	190	Nevada-Reno
24	Aubrey Allen	T	6-1	246	Colorado
25	Stan Gorski	E	6-2	193	Northwestern
26	Don Sharp	C	6-3	228	Tulsa
27	John Panelli	B	5-11	198	Notre Dame
28	Clarence (Clink) McGeary	T	6-5	250	N. Dakota State
29	Mike Mills	E	6-1	200	Brigham Young
30	Ralph Earhart	B	5-10	165	Texas Tech

1948 GREEN BAY PACKERS

TOP ROW: (L-R) Buford (Baby) Ray, Larry Craig, Tony Canadeo, Ted Fritsch, Bob Flowers, Irv Comp, Ed Neal, Clyde Goodnight, Paul Lipscomb, Nolan Luhn.
SECOND ROW: (L-R) Dick Wildung, Don Wells, Bob Forte, Urban Odson, Walt Schlinkman, Gene Wilson, Damon Tassos, Edward Bell, Ed Cody.
THIRD ROW: (L-R) Ralph Davis, Robert Skoglund, Jack Jacobs, Fred Provo, Ted Cook, Earl (Jug) Girard.
FOURTH ROW: (L-R) Lloyd Baxter, Perry Moss, Larry Olsonoski, Oscar E. Smith, Donald Deeks.
BOTTOM ROW: (L-R) Evan Vogds, Ralph Earhart, Jay Rhodemyre, Coach Curly Lambeau, Assistant Coach Don Hutson, Line Coach Walt Kiesling, Backfield Coach Bo Molenda, Trainer Carl (Bud) Jorgensen, Assistant Trainer Tim O'Brien.

Unlike any other, 1949 was a year of transition. The team dropped 10 games, battled bankruptcy, lost the only coach it had ever known and awaited word from the league in early December as to its future. From the opening of training camp in early August, to the intrasquad game staged on Thanksgiving, to the resignation of Curly Lambeau in late January, the season was filled with changes.

Lambeau surprised virtually everyone when he turned his on-the-field coaching duties over to assistants Tom Stidham, Bob Snyder and Charley Brock following a 17-0 season-opening loss to the Bears. The three were to prepare the team each week with Lambeau offering advice as needed. More often than not, Lambeau watched the games from the press box, though on occasion he observed from the sidelines.

The move didn't help the Packers, who won but two games all year. They defeated the New York Bulldogs handily 19-0 in week three for one win, but found the road more difficult against Detroit on the final weekend in October. In that game, Green Bay led 16-7 late in the fourth quarter. Bill Dudley raced 80 yards for a score on fourth-and-one from his own 20. Evan Vogds then bobbled the subsequent onside kick and the Lions moved in for a field goal try. Dudley, however, botched his fourth field goal attempt of the day and the Packers held on 16-14.

Tony Canadeo provided the season's other highlights. He piled up 1,052 yards rushing on 208 attempts to become just the third player in NFL history to surpass 1,000 yards in a single season. He dueled Philadelphia's Steve Van Buren for the rushing title and was out front until Van Buren passed him in late November.

At the same time the team struggled to win games, it fought to stay alive financially. The situation deteriorated to the point where the team staged an intrasquad contest on Thanksgiving to raise $50,000. At game time, $42,174 in cash had been raised and nearly $8,000 more had been pledged. A crowd of about 15,000 watched the Veteran Blues, quarterbacked by Earl (Jug) Girard, defeat the Newcomer Golds (35-31), led by first-round draft choice Stan Heath. Along with the game, a new sale of stock was authorized.

As on and off-the-field difficulties worsened, the voices calling for Lambeau's dismissal grew louder. Even so, the board of directors renewed his contract for another two years in late November. They never did present the pact to the head coach, who continued on even after his current obligation expired on December 31.

After that, rumors began to swirl as to where Lambeau might be headed. On January 31, 1950, Lambeau submitted his letter of resignation to Emil R. Fisher, Packer president. The only man the Packers had called coach moved on to take the head coaching position of the Chicago Cardinals.

While Green Bay struggled with its problems, the NFL smoothed over its grievances with the AAFC. The two agreed to a merger, then immediately set out to plan for the future. Thirteen teams emerged from the unification including Green Bay which was renominated and granted a spot in the post-merger National Football League.

Green Bay Press-Gazette photo

Tony Canadeo (3) reels off a 37-yard run in the second quarter of a 17-0 season opening loss to the Chicago Bears. Canadeo gained 92 yards on 11 attempts. By season's end he joined Beattie Feathers and Steve Van Buren as the only men to gain 1,000 yards rushing in a year. Bob Forte (8), lying on the ground behind Ed Sprinkle (7), threw a key block to free Canadeo.

TEAM STATISTICS

	GB	OPP
First Downs	182	218
Rushing	99	110
Passing	68	89
Penalty	15	19
Rushes	503	501
Yards Gained	2,061	2,077
Average Gain	4.10	4.15
Average Yards per Game	171.8	173.1
Passes Attempted	299	292
Completed	91	138
% Completed	30.43	47.26
Total Yards Gained	1,291	2,123
Yards Lost	233	244
Net Yards Gained	1,058	1,879
Yards Gained per Completion	14.19	15.38
Average Yards per Game	107.6	176.9
Laterals Attempted	0	7
Completed	0	6
Yards Gained	0	43
Combined Yards Gained	3,352	4,243
Total Plays	802	800
Average Yards per Play	4.18	5.30
Average Yards per Game	279.3	353.6
Intercepted By	20	29
Yards Returned	187	406
Returned for TD	0	4
Punts	87	68
Yards Punted	3,500	2,708
Average Yards per Punt	40.23	39.82
Punt Returns	37	50
Yards Returned	310	932
Average Yards per Return	8.38	18.64
Returned for TD	1	3
Kickoff Returns	42	29
Yards Returned	815	583
Average Yards per Return	19.40	20.10
Returned for TD	0	0
Penalties	76	91
Yards Penalized	722	836
Fumbles	32	23
Lost	16	15
Own Recovered for Touchdown	0	0
Opponent's Recovered by	15	16
Opponent's Recovered for Touchdown	0	0
Total Points Scored	114	329
Total Touchdowns	14	42
Touchdowns Rushing	7	20
Touchdowns Passing	5	15
Touchdowns on Returns & Recoveries	2	7
Extra Points	12	40
Safeties	0	2
Field Goals Attempted	22	26
Field Goals Made	6	11
% Successful	27.27	42.31

Regular Season 2-10-0

Date	GB		OPP	Att.
9/25	0	Chicago Bears	17	(25,571)
10/2	7	Los Angeles Rams	48	(24,308)
10/7	19	at New York Bulldogs	0	(5,099)
10/16	17	Chicago Cardinals (M)	39	(18,464)
10/23	7	at Los Angeles Rams	35	(37,546)
10/30	16	Detroit Lions (M)	14	(10,855)
11/6	3	at Chicago Bears	24	(47,218)
11/13	10	New York Giants	30	(20,151)
11/20	7	Pittsburgh Steelers (M)	30	(5,483)
11/27	21	at Chicago Cardinals	41	(16,787)
12/4	0	at Washington Redskins	30	(23,200)
12/11	7	at Detroit Lions	21	(12,576)

Score By Periods

	1	2	3	4	Total
Packers	6	47	26	35	114
Opponents	95	47	83	104	329

INDIVIDUAL STATISTICS

Rushing

	Att	Yds	Avg	LG	TD
Canadeo	208	1,052	5.1	54	4
Fritsch	69	227	3.3	27	1
Girard	45	198	4.4	35	1
Schlinkman	47	196	4.2	37	0
B. Forte	40	135	3.4	25	0
Summerhays	29	101	3.5	14	0
Earhart	20	54	2.7	14	0
Cifers	23	52	2.3	19	0
Heath	10	25	2.5	18	1
O.E. Smith	9	15	1.7	11	0
Kirby	3	6	2.0	8	0
Packers	503	2,061	4.1	54	7
Opponents	501	2,077	4.2	t80	20

Receiving

	No	Yds	Avg	LG	TD
T. Cook	25	442	17.7	50	1
Kelley	17	222	13.1	32	1
Luhn	15	169	11.3	30	1
B. Forte	7	85	12.1	28	0
Pritko	6	94	15.7	24	2
Fritsch	6	81	13.5	35	0
Earhart	5	109	21.8	50	0
Orlich	4	39	9.8	12	0
Canadeo	3	-2	-0.7	3	0
Summerhays	1	34	34.0	34	0
Girard	1	13	13.0	13	0
Cifers	1	5	5.0	5	0
Packers	91	1,291	14.2	50	5
Opponents	138	2,123	15.4	t64	15

Passing

	Att	Com	Yds	Pct	TD	In	YL	Rate
Girard	175	62	881	35.4	4	12	193	31.6
Heath	106	26	355	24.5	1	14	40	4.6
J. Jacobs	16	3	55	18.8	0	3	0	1.8
B. Forte	1	0	0	00.0	0	0	0	—
Fritsch	1	0	0	00.0	0	0	0	—
Packers	299	91	1,291	30.4	5	29	233	11.4
Opponents	292	138	2,123	47.3	15	20	244	60.3

Punting

	No	Yds	Avg	LG	HB
Girard	69	2,694	39.0	72	3
J. Jacobs	17	757	44.5	58	0
Cifers	1	49	49.0	49	0
Packers	87	3,500	40.2	72	3
Opponents	68	2,708	39.8	82	1

Kickoff Returns

	No	Yds	Avg	LG	TD
Kirby	14	315	22.5	34	0
Earhart	11	187	17.0	30	0
B. Forte	7	159	22.7	36	0
Girard	2	45	22.5	24	0
O.E. Smith	2	36	18.0	21	0
Canadeo	2	20	10.0	12	0
Fritsch	1	23	23.0	23	0
Schlinkman	1	23	23.0	23	0
T. Cook	1	7	7.0	7	0
Vogds	1	0	0.0	0	0
Packers	42	815	19.4	36	0
Opponents	29	583	20.1	48	0

Punt Returns

	No	Yds	Avg	LG	TD
Earhart	14	161	11.5	t57	1
Girard	11	70	6.4	11	0
Kirby	8	48	6.0	13	0
O.E. Smith	2	9	4.5	9	0
B. Forte	1	13	13.0	13	0
J. Jacobs	1	9	9.0	9	0
Packers	37	310	8.4	t57	1
Opponents	50	932	18.6	85	3

Interceptions

	No	Yds	Avg	LG	TD
T. Cook	5	52	10.4	30	0
Rhodemyre	4	12	3.0	9	0
Comp	3	24	8.0	14	0
J. Jacobs	2	26	13.0	26	0
B. Forte	2	17	8.5	17	0
Girard	1	41	41.0	41	0
Tassos	1	10	10.0	10	0
Harding	1	5	5.0	5	0
Burris	1	0	0.0	0	0
Packers	20	187	9.4	41	0
Opponents	29	406	14.0	68	4

Scoring

	TDr	TDp	TDrt	PAT	FG	S	TP
Fritsch	1	0	0	11/13	5/20	0	32
Canadeo	4	0	0	0/0	0/0	0	24
Pritko	0	2	0	0/0	0/0	0	12
T. Cook	0	1	0	0/0	0/0	0	6
Earhart	0	0	1	0/0	0/0	0	6
Girard	1	0	0	0/0	0/0	0	6
Heath	1	0	0	0/0	0/0	0	6
G. Johnson	0	0	1	0/0	0/0	0	6
Kelley	0	1	0	0/0	0/0	0	6
Luhn	0	1	0	0/0	0/0	0	6
Ethridge	0	0	0	1/1	1/2	0	4
Packers	7	5	2	12/14	6/22	0	114
Opponents	20	15	7	40/42	11/26	2	329

Fumbles

	Fum	Ow	Op	Yds	Tot
E. Bell	0	1	0	0	1
Burris	0	0	1	0	1
Canadeo	6	1	0	0	1
Cifers	0	1	0	5	1
T. Cook	0	0	1	2	1
Craig	0	0	1	0	1
Earhart	5	1	0	0	1
Ethridge	0	1	0	0	1
Ferry	0	0	2	0	2
B. Forte	1	1	1	3	2
Fritsch	2	0	0	0	0
Girard	4	2	0	5	2
Harding	2	0	0	0	1
Heath	2	0	0	0	0
J. Jacobs	0	0	1	0	1
Kelley	1	0	0	0	0
Kirby	3	0	0	0	0
Kranz	0	0	1	7	1
Luhn	0	1	0	0	1
E. Neal	1	2	1	0	3
Odson	0	0	2	0	2
Olsen	0	1	0	0	1
Rhodemyre	0	0	1	0	1
Schlinkman	6	2	0	0	2
Summerhays	1	0	0	0	0
Tassos	0	0	2	0	2
D. Wells	0	0	1	0	1
Wildung	0	1	0	0	1
Packers	32	16	15	22	31

NFL STANDINGS

Western Division

	W	L	T	Pct	PF	PA
Los Angeles Rams	8	2	2	.800	360	239
Chicago Bears	9	3	0	.750	332	218
Chicago Cardinals	6	5	1	.545	360	301
Detroit Lions	4	8	0	.333	237	259
Green Bay Packers	2	10	0	.167	114	329

Eastern Division

	W	L	T	Pct	PF	PA
Philadelphia Eagles	11	1	0	.917	364	134
Pittsburgh Steelers	6	5	1	.545	224	214
New York Giants	6	6	0	.500	287	298
Washington Redskins	4	7	1	.364	268	339
New York Bulldogs	1	10	1	.091	153	365

1949 ROSTER

No	Name	Pos	Ht	Wt	DOB	College	G
82	Bell, Edward	G	6-1	233	09/20/21	Indiana	12
33	Burris, Paul (Buddy)	G	5-11	215	01/20/23	Oklahoma	10
3	Canadeo, Tony	HB	6-0	190	05/05/19	Gonzaga	12
16	Cifers, Bob	HB	5-11	210	09/05/20	Tennessee	9
51	Comp, Irv	HB	6-3	205	05/17/19	St. Benedict	7
48	Cook, Ted	E	6-2	195	02/06/22	Alabama	11
54	Craig, Larry	E	6-0	218	06/27/16	South Carolina	12
41	Earhart, Ralph	HB	5-10	165	03/29/23	Texas Tech	12
40	Eason, Roger	G	6-2	230	07/31/18	Oklahoma	12
85	Ethridge, Joe	T	6-0	230	04/15/28	SMU	12
18	Ferry, Louis	T	6-2	233	12/01/27	Villanova	12
35	Flowers, Bob	C	6-1	210	08/06/17	Texas Tech	1
8	Forte, Bob	HB	6-0	195	07/15/22	Arkansas	12
64	Fritsch, Ted	FB	5-10	210	10/31/20	Stevens Point	12
36	Girard, Earl (Jug)	HB	5-11	175	01/25/27	Wisconsin	12
23	Clyde Goodnight	E	6-1	195	03/03/24	Tulsa	1
31	Harding, Roger	C	6-2	215	06/11/23	California	6
39	Heath, Stan	QB	6-1	190	03/05/27	Nevada-Reno	12
27	Jacobs, Jack	QB	6-2	190	08/07/19	Oklahoma	12
35	Johnson, Glen	T	6-4	265		Temple Tech	8
26	Kelley, Bill	E	6-2	195	08/23/26	Texas Tech	12
43	Kirby, Jack	HB	5-11	185	09/21/22	USC	6
42	Kranz, Kenneth	HB	5-11	187	09/12/23	Wisconsin-Milwaukee	7
47	Lipscomb, Paul	T	6-5	245	01/13/23	Tennessee	12
38	Luhn, Nolan	E	6-3	200	07/27/21	Tulsa	12
58	Neal, Ed	T	6-4	290	12/31/18	Tulane	12
63	Odson, Urban	T	6-3	250	11/17/18	Minnesota	10
46	Olsonoski, Larry	G	6-2	215	09/10/25	Minnesota	4
19	Olsen, Ralph	E	6-4	220	04/10/24	Utah	4
49	Orlich, Dan	E	6-5	215	12/21/24	Nevada-Reno	12
23	Pritko, Steve	E	6-2	215	12/25/21	Villanova	8
22	Rhodemyre, Jay	C	6-1	210	12/16/22	Kentucky	12
7	Schlinkman, Walt	FB	5-9	190	05/02/22	Texas Tech	12
21	Smith, Oscar E.	HB	6-0	185	07/20/23	Texas-El Paso	2
77	Summerhays, Bob	FB	6-1	207	03/19/27	Utah	12
15	Tassos, Damon	G	6-1	225	12/05/23	Texas A&M	12
79	Vogds, Evan	G	5-10	215	02/10/23	Wisconsin	12
43	Wells, Don	E	6-2	200	07/12/22	Georgia	2
45	Wildung, Dick	G	6-0	220	08/16/21	Minnesota	12

1949 DRAFT

Rnd	Name	Pos	Ht	Wt	College	Rnd	Name	Pos	Ht	Wt	College
1	Stan Heath	B	6-1	190	Nevada-Reno	14	Bobby Williams	C	6-2	202	Texas Tech
2	Dan Dworsky	C	6-0	205	Michigan	15	Ken Cooper	G	6-0	205	Vanderbilt
3	Louis Ferry	T	6-2	232	Villanova	16	Gene Remenar	T	6-2	225	West Virginia
4	Bob Summerhays	B	6-1	207	Utah	17	Paul Devine	B	5-11	185	Heidelberg
5	Glenn Lewis	B	5-11	190	Texas Tech	18	Floyd Lewis	G	5-11	210	SMU
6	Joe Ethridge	T	6-0	230	SMU	19	Bobby Folsom	E	6-1	190	SMU
7	(Choice to Rams)					20	Larry Cooney	B	5-11	185	Penn State
8	Dan Orlich	E	6-5	215	Nevada-Reno	21	Kenneth Kranz	B	5-11	187	Wis.-Milwaukee
9	Everett Faunce	B	5-11	178	Minneosta	22	John Kordick	B	5-11	190	USC
10	(Choice to Rams through Lions)					23	Bill Kelley	E	6-2	195	Texas Tech
11	Harry Larche	T	6-1	220	Arkansas State	24	Jimmy Ford	B	5-8	158	Tulsa
12	Rebel Steiner	E	6-0	190	Alabama	25	Frank Lambright	G	5-11	205	Arkansas
13	Al Mastrangeli	C	6-1	202	Illinois						

1949 GREEN BAY PACKERS

LEFT GROUP KNEELING: (L-R) 38 Nolan Luhn, 47 Paul Lipscomb, 15 Damon Tassos, 33 Paul (Buddy) Burris, 45 Dick Wildung, 44 Buford (Baby) Ray, 23 Clyde Goodnight.
LEFT GROUP STANDING: (L-R) 21 Oscar E. Smith, 64 Ted Fritsch, 42 Kenneth Kranz, 27 Jack Jacobs.
MIDDLE GROUP STANDING: (L-R) 85 Joe Ethridge, 79 Evan Vogds, 77 Bob Summerhays, 66 Ralph Davis, unidentified, 16 Bob Cifers, 8 Bob Forte, 3 Tony Canadeo, 48 Ted Cook, 28 unidentified, 22 Jay Rhodemyre, 82 Edward Bell.
RIGHT GROUP KNEELING: (L-R) 43 Don Wells, 63 Urban Odson, 40 Roger Eason, 35 Bob Flowers, 58 Ed Neal, 75 Milburn (Tiny) Croft, 25 Eugene Canada.
RIGHT GROUP STANDING: (L-R) 18 Louis Ferry, 80 Glenn Lewis, 7 Walt Schlinkman, 51 Irv Comp.

ROCKWOOD LODGE

1950

Green Bay lost 38-7 to the Cleveland Browns in a preseason game on August 12. In attendance was Curly Lambeau whose Cardinals were to meet the Packers that Wednesday. After his former club had been polished off, Lambeau remarked, "Just like 1949–no effort." Using that remark as fuel, Green Bay bounced the Cardinals 17-14 at City Stadium in mid-week to silence Lambeau. But by season's end, when the 3-9 Packers limped home ahead of only the lowly Baltimore Colts, his assessment appeared all the more accurate.

In fairness, new Packers Coach Gene Ronzani inherited a team in disarray, due in no small part to the failings of its previous leader. Ronzani was faced with the task of breathing life into a team which had had its worst finish in history to that point. The passing game lacked a strong leader and the defense leaked horribly, allowing 329 points and 353.6 yards per game in 1949.

The former Bears assistant added 25 new players to try and rectify the situation. Eight came from the old AAFC. Of those eight, Al Baldwin, last of the Buffalo Bills, led the team in receptions while Billy Grimes, a former Los Angeles Don, accounted for 1,896 all-purpose yards, a Packer and then-NFL record.

Tobin Rote, the team's second pick, was expected to solidify the passing game. A 6-3, 200-pounder, Rote could run as well as pass. He brought stability to the position and, though he often was afforded less than adequate protection, never missed a game in seven years. In addition, he led the team in rushing in 1951-52 and 1956.

Aside from Rote, the team had no quarterback. With Jack Jacobs and Stan Heath departed for the Canadian Football League, Earl (Jug) Girard remained as the only holdover, and he was more suited to halfback than quarterback. At season's start, Tom O'Malley backed up Rote and suffered six interceptions in 15 attempts in the opener after Rote damaged his shoulder. That performance was his last in Green Bay.

With Rote ailing, Ronzani quickly engineered a trade with the Cardinals for Paul Christman. Christman had run the show when Chicago won the NFL title in 1947. His stock had declined – he had shared duties with Jim Hardy in 1949 – and thus Ronzani was able to land him. The 32-year old Missouri alum completed 51 of 126 passes in 1950 and was able to avoid the interception better than Rote, who threw 24 of the team's league-high 37.

Ronzani's other concern never got better. Green Bay's defense allowed 406 points and an average of nearly 400 yards a game. It was a major reason why the Packers, in a five-way tie for first place after three weeks, fell completely out of the race with eight losses in their last nine games.

Billy Grimes (22) is enroute to a 26-yard gain against the Yanks in Green Bay on October 8. The Packers lost 44-31. Grimes accounted for 226 all-purpose yards in the game, including a then team-record 167 rushing on 10 carries. The former Los Angeles Don led the team in rushing, kickoff returns, punt returns and scoring. He set a team record with 1,896 all-purpose yards in 1950.

TEAM STATISTICS

	GB	OPP
First Downs	174	220
Rushing	82	91
Passing	70	110
Penalty	22	19
Rushes	398	422
Yards Gained	1,706	1,855
Average Gain	4.29	4.47
Average Yards per Game	142.2	157.1
Passes Attempted	367	379
Completed	140	185
% Completed	38.15	48.81
Total Yards Gained	1,831	2,818
Yards Lost	327	230
Net Yards Gained	1,504	2,588
Yards Gained per Completion	13.08	15.23
Average Yards per Game	152.6	234.8
Combined Yards Gained	3,537	4,703
Total Plays	765	801
Average Yards per Play	4.62	5.87
Average Yards per Game	294.8	391.9
Intercepted By	27	37
Yards Returned	337	575
Returned for TD	2	5
Punts	74	72
Yards Punted	2,822	2,891
Average Yards per Punt	38.14	40.15
Punt Returns	44	49
Yards Returned	729	372
Average Yards per Return	16.57	7.59
Returned for TD	2	0
Kickoff Returns	56	41
Yards Returned	1,233	845
Average Yards per Return	22.02	20.61
Returned for TD	0	0
Penalties	85	95
Yards Penalized	757	919
Fumbles	35	34
Lost	20	15
Own Recovered for Touchdown	0	1
Opponent's Recovered by	15	20
Opponent's Recovered for Touchdown	1	3
Total Points Scored	244	406
Total Touchdowns	34	56
Touchdowns Rushing	15	24
Touchdowns Passing	14	24
Touchdowns on Returns & Recoveries	5	8
Extra Points	31	50
Safeties	0	1
Field Goals Attempted	17	13
Field Goals Made	3	6
% Successful	17.65	46.15

Regular Season 3-9-0

Date	GB		OPP	Att.
9/17	7	Detroit Lions	45	(22,096)
9/24	35	Washington Redskins (M)	21	(14,109)
10/1	31	Chicago Bears	21	(24,893)
10/8	31	New York Yankees	44	(23,871)
10/15	14	at Chicago Bears	28	(51,065)
10/19	17	at New York Yankees	35	(13,661)
11/5	21	at Baltimore Colts	41	(12,971)
11/12	14	Los Angeles Rams (M)	45	(20,456)
11/19	21	at Detroit Lions	24	(17,752)
11/26	25	San Francisco 49ers	21	(13,196)
12/3	14	at Los Angeles Rams	51	(39,323)
12/10	14	at San Francisco 49ers	30	(20,797)

Score By Periods

	1	2	3	4	Total
Packers	41	58	77	68	244
Opponents	53	123	127	103	406

INDIVIDUAL STATISTICS

Rushing

	Att	Yds	Avg	LG	TD
Grimes	84	480	5.7	t73	5
Reid	87	394	4.5	57	1
Coutre	41	283	6.9	53	1
Canadeo	93	247	2.7	15	4
Rote	27	158	5.9	29	0
Cloud	18	52	2.9	13	3
Girard	14	39	2.8	11	0
Christman	7	18	2.6	4	1
Boedecker	8	16	2.0	8	0
Fritsch	7	13	1.9	5	0
B. Forte	9	13	1.4	11	0
Cannava	1	2	2.0	2	0
Dreyer	1	0	0.0	0	0
O'Malley	1	-9	-9.0	-9	0
Packers	**398**	**1,706**	**4.3**	**t73**	**15**
Opponents	422	1,885	4.5	t96	24

Receiving

	No	Yds	Avg	LG	TD
Baldwin	28	555	19.8	t85	3
Grimes	17	261	15.4	t96	1
Coutre	17	206	12.1	t77	2
Pritko	17	125	7.4	14	2
T. Cook	16	182	11.4	t21	3
Reid	11	120	10.9	144	2
Canadeo	10	54	5.4	20	0
B. Mann	6	89	14.8	40	1
Manley	5	66	13.2	18	0
Girard	4	89	22.3	55	0
Cloud	3	19	6.3	13	0
Wimberly	2	18	9.0	10	0
B. Forte	2	9	4.5	10	0
Cannava	1	28	28.0	28	0
Boedecker	1	10	10.0	10	0
Packers	**140**	**1,831**	**13.1**	**t96**	**14**
Opponents	185	2,818	15.2	t74	24

Passing

	Att	Com	Yds	Pct	TD	In	YL	Rate
Rote	224	83	1,231	37.1	7	24	153	26.7
Christman	126	51	545	40.5	7	7	132	49.2
O'Malley	15	4	31	26.7	0	6	42	0.0
B. Forte	2	2	24	100.0	0	0	0	—
Packers	**367**	**140**	**1,831**	**38.2**	**14**	**37**	**327**	**27.8**
Opponents	379	185	2,818	48.8	24	27	230	65.2

Punting

	No	Yds	Avg	LG	HB
Girard	71	2,715	38.2	63	2
B. Forte	3	107	35.7	39	0
Packers	**74**	**2,822**	**38.1**	**63**	**2**
Opponents	72	2,891	40.2	65	1

Kickoff Returns

	No	Yds	Avg	LG	TD
Grimes	26	600	23.1	36	0
Canadeo	16	411	25.7	48	0
B. Forte	3	73	24.3	34	0
DiPierro	3	42	14.0	26	0
Burris	3	18	6.0	11	0
Fritsch	2	34	17.0	19	0
Girard	1	25	25.0	25	0
Boedecker	1	20	20.0	20	0
Cannava	1	10	10.0	10	0
Packers	**56**	**1,233**	**22.0**	**48**	**0**
Opponents	41	845	20.6	50	0

Punt Returns

	No	Yds	Avg	LG	TD
Grimes	29	555	19.1	t85	2
Canadeo	5	68	13.6	21	0
Boedecker	5	49	9.8	12	0
Dreyer	3	48	16.0	22	0
Cannava	2	9	4.5	9	0
Packers	**44**	**729**	**16.6**	**t85**	**2**
Opponents	49	372	7.6	29	0

Interceptions

	No	Yds	Avg	LG	TD
Steiner	7	190	27.1	t94	1
Dreyer	5	62	12.4	34	1
Baldwin	5	35	7.0	22	0
Wizbicki	2	38	19.0	34	0
Girard	1	6	6.0	6	0
B. Forte	1	5	5.0	5	0
Tonnemaker	1	1	1.0	1	0
Orlich	1	0	0.0	0	0
Schuette	1	0	0.0	0	0
J. Spencer	1	0	0.0	0	0
Summerhays	1	0	0.0	0	0
Wimberly	1	0	0.0	0	0
Packers	**27**	**337**	**12.5**	**t94**	**2**
Opponents	37	575	15.5	t56	5

Scoring

	TDr	TDp	TDrt	PAT	FG	S	TP
Grimes	5	1	2	0/0	0/0	0	48
Fritsch	0	0	0	30/33	3/17	0	39
Canadeo	4	0	0	0/0	0/0	0	24
Baldwin	0	3	0	0/0	0/0	0	18
Cloud	3	0	0	0/0	0/0	0	18
T. Cook	0	3	0	0/0	0/0	0	18
Coutre	1	2	0	0/0	0/0	0	18
Reid	1	2	0	0/0	0/0	0	18
Pritko	0	2	0	0/0	0/0	0	12
Christman	1	0	0	0/0	0/0	0	6
Dreyer	0	0	1	0/0	0/0	0	6
B. Mann	0	1	0	0/0	0/0	0	6
Orlich	0	1	0	0/0	0/0	0	6
Steiner	0	0	1	0/0	0/0	0	6
Tonnemaker	0	0	0	1/1	0/0	0	1
Packers	**15**	**14**	**5**	**31/34**	**3/17**	**0**	**244**
Opponents	24	24	8	50/56	6/13	1	406

Fumbles

	Fum	Ow	Op	Yds	Tot
Baldwin	3	1	0	-3	1
Canadeo	4	2	0	0	2
Cannava	1	0	0	0	0
Christman	2	0	0	0	0
Cloud	1	0	0	0	0
T. Cook	1	0	0	0	0
Coutre	1	0	0	0	0
Girard	1	0	0	0	0
Grimes	8	3	0	0	3
McGeary	0	1	0	0	1
E. Neal	0	1	0	0	1
Orlich	0	0	3	37	3
Pritko	1	0	0	0	0
Reid	3	0	0	0	0
Rote	9	3	0	-21	3
Schuette	0	0	3	8	3
J. Spencer	0	1	1	0	2
Stansauk	0	0	2	0	2
Summerhays	0	0	1	0	1
Szafaryn	0	1	1	0	2
Wildung	0	2	0	1	2
Wimberly	0	0	2	0	2
Wizbicki	0	0	2	12	2
Packers	**35**	**15**	**15**	**34**	**30**

NFL STANDINGS

National Conference

	W	L	T	Pct	PF	PA
Los Angeles Rams	9	3	0	.750	466	309
Chicago Bears	9	3	0	.750	279	207
New York Yanks	7	5	0	.583	366	367
Detroit Lions	6	6	0	.500	321	285
Green Bay Packers	**3**	**9**	**0**	**.250**	**244**	**406**
San Francisco 49ers	3	9	0	.250	213	300
Baltimore Colts	1	11	0	.083	213	462

American Conference

	W	L	T	Pct	PF	PA
Cleveland Browns	10	2	0	.833	310	144
New York Giants	10	2	0	.833	268	150
Philadelphia Eagles	6	6	0	.500	254	141
Pittsburgh Steelers	6	6	0	.500	180	195
Chicago Cardinals	5	7	0	.417	233	287
Washington Redskins	3	9	0	.250	232	326

1950 ROSTER

No	Name	Pos	Ht	Wt	DOB	College	G
19	Baldwin, Al	E	6-2	210	02/21/25	Arkansas	12
31	Boedecker, Bill	HB	5-11	195	03/07/24	Kalamazoo	9
33	Burris, Paul (Buddy)	G	5-11	215	01/20/23	Oklahoma	12
3	Canadeo, Tony	HB	6-0	190	05/05/19	Gonzaga	12
42	Cannava, Al	HB	5-10	180	05/24/24	Boston College	1
28	Christman, Paul	QB	6-0	200	03/05/18	Missouri	11
82	Cloud, Jack	FB	5-10	220	01/01/25	William and Mary	9
48	Cook, Ted	E	6-2	195	02/06/22	Alabama	12
27	Coutre, Larry	HB	5-10	175	04/11/28	Notre Dame	12
21	DiPierro, Ray	G	5-11	210	08/22/26	Ohio State	12
42	Dreyer, Wally	HB	5-10	170	02/25/23	Wisconsin	12
18	Drulis, Charles	G	5-10	220	03/08/18	Temple	11
55	Ecker, Ed	T	6-7	270	01/21/23	John Carroll	12
8	Forte, Bob	HB	6-0	205	07/15/22	Arkansas	12
64	Fritsch, Ted	FB	5-10	210	10/31/20	Stevens Point	12
36	Girard, Earl (Jug)	HB	5-11	175	01/25/27	Wisconsin	12
22	Grimes, Billy	HB	6-1	197	07/27/27	Oklahoma State	12
90	Manley, Leon	G-T	6-2	210	05/20/26	Oklahoma	12
31	Mann, Bob	E	5-11	175	04/08/24	Michigan	3
44	McGeary, Clarence	T	6-5	250	08/08/26	North Dakota	12
58	Neal, Ed	T	6-4	275	12/31/18	Tulane	12
76	O'Malley, Tom	QB	5-11	185		Cincinnati	1
49	Orlich, Dan	E	6-5	215	12/21/24	Nevada-Reno	12
23	Pritko, Steve	E	6-2	210	12/25/21	Villanova	12
80	Reid, Floyd (Breezy)	HB	5-11	187	09/04/27	Georgia	11
38	Rote, Tobin	QB	6-3	200	01/18/28	Rice	12
7	Schlinkman, Walt	FB	5-9	190	05/02/22	Texas Tech	1
17	Schuette, Carl	C	6-1	210	04/04/22	Marquette	12
34	Spencer, Joe	T	6-3	240	08/15/23	Oklahoma State	12
63	Stansauk, Don	T	6-2	255	03/16/26	Denver	11
74	Steiner, Rebel	DB	6-0	185	08/27/27	Alabama	12
77	Summerhays, Bob	FB	6-1	207	03/19/27	Utah	11
51	Szafaryn, Len	G	6-2	229	01/19/28	North Carolina	12
35	Tonnemaker, Clayton	C	6-2	235	08/08/28	Minnesota	12
45	Wildung, Dick	T	6-0	220	08/16/21	Minnesota	12

1950 DRAFT

Rnd	Name	Pos	Ht	Wt	College
1	Clayton Tonnemaker	C	6-2	235	Minnesota
2	Tobin Rote	QB	6-3	200	Rice
3	Gordy Soltau	E	6-2	215	Minnesota
4	Larry Coutre	RB	5-10	175	Notre Dame
5	(Choice to Steelers)				
6	Jack Cloud	B	5-10	220	William and Mary
7	Leon Manley	T	6-2	220	Oklahoma
8	Harry Szulborski	B	5-10	175	Purdue
9	Roger Wilson	E	6-1	210	South Carolina
10	Bob Mealey	T	6-2	225	Minnesota
11	Gene Lorendo	E	6-0	205	Georgia
12	Andy Pavich	E	6-0	196	Denver
13	Carlton Elliott	E	6-4	215	Virginia
14	Fred Leon	T	6-0	220	Nevada-Reno
15	Gene Huebner	C	6-4	230	Baylor
16	Frank Kuzma	B	6-0	200	Minnesota
17	Hal Otterback	G	6-2	210	Wisconsin
18	Arnold Galiffa	QB	6-2	190	Army
19	Earl T. Rowan	T	5-11	240	Hardin-Simmons
20	Jim Howe	B	6-2	190	Kentucky
21	Gene Evans	B	5-7	165	Wisconsin
22	Chuck Beatty	C	6-1	215	Penn State
23	George Mattey	G	5-10	225	Ohio State
24	Don Delph	B	6-0	190	Dayton
25	Frank Waters	B	6-0	202	Michigan State
26	Claude Radtke	E	6-3	196	Lawrence
27	Bill Osbourne	B	6-1	205	Nevada-Reno
28	Herm Hering	B	6-2	195	Rutgers
29	Ben Zaranka	E	6-4	191	Kentucky
30	Ray Mallouf	B	6-0	185	SMU

1950 GREEN BAY PACKERS

FRONT ROW: (L-R) 18 Charles Drulis, 16 Abner Wimberly, 21 Ray DiPierro, 63 Don Stansauk, 36 Earl (Jug) Girard, 22 Billy Grimes, 82 Jack Cloud, 58 Ed Neal, 64 Ted Fritsch, 3 Tony Canadeo.
SECOND ROW: (L-R) 17 Carl Schuette, 44 Clarence (Clink) McGeary, 33 Paul (Buddy) Burris, 74 Rebel Steiner, 25 Alex Wizbicki, 31 Bill Boedecker, 35 Clayton Tonnemaker, 27 Larry Coutre, 42 Wally Dreyer.
THIRD ROW: (L-R) 55 Ed Ecker, 77 Bob Summerhays, 51 Len Szafaryn, 49 Dan Orlich, 90 Leon Manley, 38 Tobin Rote, 19 Al Baldwin, 34 Joe Spencer.
FOURTH ROW: (L-R) Property Man Dick Geniesse, 23 Steve Pritko, 28 Paul Christman, 8 Bob Forte, 45 Dick Wildung, 48 Ted Cook, 80 Floyd (Breezy) Reid, Trainer Carl (Bud) Jorgensen.
BACK ROW: (L-R) Head Coach Gene Ronzani, Backfield Coach Ray Nolting, End Coach Dick Plasman, Line Coach John (Tarzan) Taylor.

Green Bay turned to the air as never before in 1951. More than two-thirds of the team's offense came from the arms of quarterbacks Tobin Rote and Bobby Thomason. The Packers threw a then-record 478 passes and completed 231 for 2,846 yards – single season team-highs that would stand until the 16-game schedules of the late '70s.

On the receiving end of the barrage were Bob Mann, Ray Pelfrey and Carlton Elliott. The trio caught 123 passes for 1,475 yards and 18 touchdowns. Mann became the first black player to join the Packers and the first individual since Don Hutson to catch 50 passes in a single season. Pelfrey was a 17th-round pick in 1951 while Elliott was the team's 13th-round selection in 1950.

With such an emphasis on passing, the running game was virtually ignored. Three times the Packers failed to gain even 50 yards rushing, and over the course of the season averaged less than 100 yards per contest. Only Rote gained more than 200 yards and he scored three of the team's league-low eight rushing touchdowns.

The Korean War entered its second year in 1951 and many NFL players were called to duty. Going into the draft, the Packers specifically singled out players who were either 4-F or who had already fulfilled their service obligations. Drafting for available bodies rather than talent hurt. Only four draftees – Fred Cone, Albin (Rip) Collins, Dick Afflis, and Ray Pelfrey – made the team. (Top pick Bob Gain chose the Canadian Football League (CFL) over Green Bay.) Of those, only Cone and Afflis lasted more than two years.

The Packers bid farewell to one of the last two players remaining from the 1944 championship team. Fullback Ted Fritsch, a nine-year veteran, was waived on the final September 25 cutdown. That move left Tony Canadeo as the only holdover from the championship team.

As would be the case for the next decade or so, military service robbed the Packers of a number of veterans. Bob Forte, Clayton Tonnemaker, Larry Coutre and Len Szafaryn were given orders to report. All but Forte missed the 1952 season as well.

As they had done in 1950, the Packers opened well. After absorbing a 31-20 setback at the hands of the Bears, Green Bay defeated Pittsburgh and Philadelphia to move into a five-way tie for first place. One of those first-place teams, the Rams, clobbered the Packers 28-0 in week four to start a skid that saw Green Bay lose eight of its last nine games.

One highlight in the long tailspin was the celebration of Don Hutson day on December 2. The former great had his jersey number officially retired. That provided the only bright spot in a day that saw the Packers lose 31-28 to the winless New York Yanks.

Green Bay Press-Gazette photo

Bob Mann (31) readies to receive a five-yard pass from Bobby Thomason, a pass which Mann turned into a touchdown in the first quarter of the Packers 37-24 win over Philadelphia in mid-October. Mann caught five passes for 93 yards in the game and reached the end zone three times. Behind Mann are Eagles Joe Sutton (45) and Pete Pihos (35).

TEAM STATISTICS

	GB	OPP
First Downs	218	236
Rushing	75	127
Passing	115	95
Penalty	28	14
Rushes	313	496
Yards Gained	1,196	2,152
Average Gain	3.82	4.34
Average Yards per Game	99.7	179.3
Passes Attempted	478	313
Completed	231	157
% Completed	48.33	50.16
Total Yards Gained	2,846	2,535
Yards Lost	289	217
Net Yards Gained	2,557	2,318
Yards Gained per Completion	12.32	16.15
Average Yards per Game	237.2	211.3
Combined Yards Gained	4,042	4,687
Total Plays	791	809
Average Yards per Play	5.11	5.79
Average Yards per Game	336.8	390.6
Intercepted By	22	29
Yards Returned	292	387
Returned for TD	1	1
Punts	61	62
Yards Punted	2,504	2,333
Average Yards per Punt	41.05	37.63
Punt Returns	29	38
Yards Returned	213	564
Average Yards per Return	7.34	14.84
Returned for TD	0	2
Kickoff Returns	60	40
Yards Returned	1,449	741
Average Yards per Return	24.15	18.53
Returned for TD	0	0
Penalties	90	99
Yards Penalized	790	924
Fumbles	23	23
Lost	15	13
Own Recovered for Touchdown	0	0
Opponent's Recovered by	13	15
Opponent's Recovered for Touchdown	0	0
Total Points Scored	254	375
Total Touchdowns	35	50
Touchdowns Rushing	8	22
Touchdowns Passing	26	25
Touchdowns on Returns & Recoveries	1	3
Extra Points	29	49
Safeties	0	1
Field Goals Attempted	8	17
Field Goals Made	5	8
% Successful	62.50	47.06

Regular Season 3-9-0

Date	GB		OPP	Att.
9/30	20	Chicago Bears	31	(24,666)
10/7	35	Pittsburgh Steelers (M)	33	(8,324)
10/14	37	Philadelphia Eagles	24	(18,489)
10/21	0	Los Angeles Rams (M)	28	(21,393)
10/28	29	at New York Yankees	27	(7,351)
11/4	17	Detroit Lions	24	(18,800)
11/11	7	at Pittsburgh Steelers	28	(20,080)
11/18	13	at Chicago Bears	24	(36,771)
11/22	35	at Detroit Lions	52	(33,452)
12/2	28	New York Yankees	31	(14,297)
12/9	19	at San Francisco 49ers	31	(18,681)
12/16	14	at Los Angeles Rams	42	(23,698)

Score By Periods

	1	2	3	4	Total
Packers	62	56	37	99	254
Opponents	68	96	86	125	375

INDIVIDUAL STATISTICS

Rushing

	Att	Yds	Avg	LG	TD
Rote	76	523	6.9	t55	3
Cone	56	190	3.4	16	1
Canadeo	54	131	2.4	15	1
Grimes	44	123	2.8	t18	1
Reid	23	73	3.2	33	0
Cloud	29	61	2.1	19	1
Pelfrey	3	44	14.7	24	0
Moselle	12	23	1.9	7	1
Girard	4	20	5.0	32	0
B. Mann	2	9	4.5	9	0
A. Collins	5	4	0.8	6	0
Thomason	5	-5	-1.0	10	0
Packers	**313**	**1,196**	**3.8**	**t55**	**8**
Opponents	496	2,152	4.3	t85	22

Receiving

	No	Yds	Avg	LG	TD
B. Mann	50	696	13.9	52	8
Pelfrey	38	462	12.2	49	5
Elliott	35	317	9.1	33	5
Cone	28	315	11.3	49	0
Canadeo	22	226	10.3	46	2
Grimes	15	170	11.3	t38	1
Moselle	14	233	16.6	85	2
Girard	10	220	22.0	t75	2
Reid	9	115	12.8	29	0
Cloud	3	16	5.3	t6	1
H. Davis	1	15	15.0	15	0
Moje	1	11	11.0	11	0
Wimberly	1	10	10.0	10	0
Loomis	1	9	9.0	9	0
Orlich	1	9	9.0	9	0
Jansante	1	6	6.0	6	0
A. Collins	1	5	5.0	5	0
Rote	0	11	—	11	0
Packers	**231**	**2,846**	**12.3**	**85**	**26**
Opponents	157	2,535	16.2	t81	22

Passing

	Att	Com	Yds	Pct	TD	In	YL	Rate
Rote	256	106	1,540	41.4	15	20	143	48.6
Thomason	221	125	1,306	56.6	11	9	146	73.5
Reid	1	0	0	00.0	0	0	0	—
Packers	**478**	**231**	**2,846**	**48.3**	**26**	**29**	**289**	**60.0**
Opponents	313	157	2,535	50.2	25	22	217	75.0

Punting

	No	Yds	Avg	LG	HB
Girard	52	2,101	40.4	66	0
Pelfrey	5	220	44.0	46	0
A. Collins	2	81	40.5	49	0
Rote	1	55	55.0	55	0
Cone	1	47	47.0	47	0
Packers	**61**	**2,504**	**41.1**	**66**	**0**
Opponents	62	2,333	37.6	72	0

Kickoff Returns

	No	Yds	Avg	LG	TD
Grimes	23	582	25.3	47	0
Moselle	20	547	27.4	44	0
W. Michaels	5	86	17.2	26	0
Canadeo	4	101	25.3	48	0
Martinkovic	2	34	17.0	31	0
Wimberly	2	4	2.0	3	0
A. Collins	1	40	40.0	40	0
Summerhays	1	21	21.0	21	0
Cone	1	20	20.0	20	0
Elliott	1	14	14.0	14	0
Packers	**60**	**1,449**	**24.2**	**48**	**0**
Opponents	40	741	18.5	41	0

Punt Returns

	No	Yds	Avg	LG	TD
Grimes	16	100	6.3	26	0
Moselle	9	80	8.9	17	0
H. Davis	2	21	10.5	17	0
Girard	1	9	9.0	9	0
Nussbaumer	1	3	3.0	3	0
Packers	**29**	**213**	**7.3**	**26**	**0**
Opponents	38	564	14.8	t89	2

Interceptions

	No	Yds	Avg	LG	TD
Girard	5	25	5.0	15	0
Loomis	4	103	25.8	66	0
H. Davis	4	37	9.3	25	0
Steiner	3	4	1.3	3	0
Summerhays	2	112	56.0	t88	1
A. Collins	2	0	0.0	0	0
Ruetz	1	11	11.0	11	0
Moselle	1	0	0.0	0	0
Packers	**22**	**292**	**13.3**	**t88**	**1**
Opponents	29	387	13.3	40	1

Scoring

	TDr	TDp	TDrt	PAT	FG	S	TP
Cone	1	0	0	29/35	5/7	0	50
B. Mann	0	8	0	0/0	0/0	0	48
Elliott	0	5	0	0/0	0/0	0	30
Pelfrey	0	5	0	0/0	0/0	0	30
Canadeo	1	2	0	0/0	0/0	0	18
Moselle	1	2	0	0/0	0/0	0	18
Rote	3	0	0	0/0	0/0	0	18
Cloud	1	1	0	0/0	0/0	0	12
Girard	0	2	0	0/0	0/0	0	12
Grimes	1	1	0	0/0	0/0	0	12
Summerhays	0	0	1	0/0	0/0	0	6
W. Michaels	0	0	0	0/1	0	0	0
Packers	**8**	**26**	**1**	**29/35**	**5/8**	**0**	**254**
Opponents	22	25	3	49/50	8/17	1	375

Fumbles

	Fum	Ow	Op	Yds	Tot
Burris	0	1	0	0	1
Canadeo	2	0	0	0	0
Cloud	2	1	0	0	1
Cone	1	1	0	0	1
H. Davis	0	0	1	0	1
Girard	1	1	1	0	2
Grimes	5	0	0	0	0
Loomis	0	0	2	0	2
Martinkovic	0	0	2	10	2
Moselle	4	1	1	0	2
Orlich	0	0	1	31	1
Reid	1	0	0	0	0
Rhodemyre	0	0	1	0	1
Rote	4	1	0	0	1
Ruetz	0	0	1	0	1
Summerhays	0	0	2	0	2
Thomason	2	0	0	0	0
Wildung	0	0	2	0	2
Wimberly	1	1	0	0	1
Packers		**23**	**8**	**13**	**41**	**21**

NFL STANDINGS

National Conference

	W	L	T	Pct	PF	PA
Los Angeles Rams	8	4	0	.667	392	261
Detroit Lions	7	4	1	.636	336	259
San Francisco 49ers	7	4	1	.636	255	205
Chicago Bears	7	5	0	.583	286	282
Green Bay Packers	**3**	**9**	**0**	**.250**	**254**	**375**
New York Yanks	1	9	2	.100	241	382

American Conference

	W	L	T	Pct	PF	PA
Cleveland Browns	11	1	0	.917	331	152
New York Giants	9	2	1	.818	254	161
Washington Redskins	5	7	0	.417	183	296
Pittsburgh Steelers	4	7	1	.364	183	235
Philadelphia Eagles	4	8	0	.333	234	264
Chicago Cardinals	3	9	0	.250	210	287

1951 ROSTER

No	Name	Pos	Ht	Wt	DOB	College	G
15	Afflis, Dick	G	6-0	252	06/27/29	Nevada	12
33	Burris, Paul (Buddy)	G	5-11	215	01/20/23	Oklahoma	7
3	Canadeo, Tony	HB	6-0	190	05/05/19	Gonzaga	12
82	Cloud, Jack	FB	5-10	220	01/01/25	William and Mary	4
65	Collins, Albin (Rip)	HB	5-11	190	09/27/27	LSU	7
66	Cone, Fred	FB	5-11	197	06/21/26	Clemson	12
25	Davis, Harper	HB	5-11	172	12/11/25	Mississippi State	12
21	DiPierro, Ray	G	5-11	210	08/22/26	Ohio State	6
55	Ecker, Ed	T	6-7	270	01/21/23	John Carroll	7
40	Elliott, Carlton	E	6-4	215	11/12/27	Virginia	12
36	Girard, Earl (Jug)	HB	5-11	175	01/25/27	Wisconsin	12
22	Grimes, Billy	HB	6-1	197	07/27/27	Oklahoma State	12
23	Jansante, Val	E	6-1	190	09/27/21	Duquesne	3
7	Loomis, Ace	HB	6-1	190	06/12/28	Wisconsin-LaCrosse	12
90	Manley, Leon	G-T	6-2	225	05/20/26	Oklahoma	12
31	Mann, Bob	E	5-11	175	04/08/24	Michigan	11
39	Martinkovic, John	DE	6-3	235	02/04/27	Xavier	12
79	Moje, Dick	E	6-3	210		Loyola (Los Angeles)	2
35	Michaels, Walt	G	6-0	225	10/16/29	Washington and Lee	12
93	Moselle, Dom	HB	6-0	192	06/03/26	Wisconsin-Superior	12
58	Neal, Ed	T	6-4	275	12/31/18	Tulane	1
46	Nichols, Hamilton	G	5-11	215	10/18/24	Rice	9
23	Nussbaumer, Bob	HB	5-11	175	04/23/24	Michigan	4
49	Orlich, Dan	E	6-5	215	12/21/24	Nevada-Reno	12
8	Pelfrey, Ray	E	6-0	190	01/11/28	Eastern Kentucky	12
80	Reid, Floyd (Breezy)	HB	5-10	180	09/04/27	Georgia	12
85	Rhodemyre, Jay	C	6-1	210	12/16/22	Kentucky	12
38	Rote, Tobin	QB	6-3	200	01/18/28	Rice	12
75	Ruetz, Howard	T	6-3	265	08/18/27	Loras	12
86	Schroll, Charles	G	6-0	218	01/24/26	LSU	12
17	Schuette, Carl	C	6-1	210	04/04/22	Marquette	12
34	Spencer, Joe	T	6-3	240	08/15/23	Oklahoma State	12
63	Stansauk, Don	T	6-2	255	03/16/26	Denver	4
74	Steiner, Rebel	DB	6-0	185	08/27/27	Alabama	12
44	Stephenson, Dave	G	6-2	235	10/22/25	West Virginia	12
77	Summerhays, Bob	FB	6-1	215	03/19/27	Utah	12
28	Thomason, Bobby	QB	6-1	197	03/26/28	Virginia Military	11
45	Wildung, Dick	T	6-0	220	08/16/21	Minnesota	12
16	Wimberly, Abner	E	6-1	210	05/04/26	LSU	12

1951 DRAFT

Rnd	Name	Pos	Ht	Wt	College
1	Bob Gain	T	6-3	235	Kentucky
2	Albin (Rip) Collins	HB	5-11	190	LSU
3	Fred Cone	FB	5-10	197	Clemson
4	(Choice to Browns)				
5	Wade Stinson	HB	5-11	180	Kansas
6	Sidmund Holowenko	T	6-3	240	John Carroll
7	Bill Sutherland	E	6-2	210	St. Vincent
8	(Choice to Browns)				
9	Dick McWilliams	T	6-3	242	Michigan
10	Bob Noppinger	E	6-3	215	Georgetown
11	George Rooks	FB	6-0	215	Morgan State
12	Carl Kreager	C	6-1	215	Michigan
13	Ed Stephens	HB	5-11	182	Missouri
14	Ray Bauer	E	6-1	190	Montana
15	Joe Ernst	QB	6-0	185	Tulane
16	Dick Afflis	T	5-11	252	Nevada
17	Ray Pelfrey	HB	6-0	190	Eastern Kentucky
18	Ed Petela	FB	5-10	200	Boston College
19	Jim Liber	HB	5-8	175	Xavier
20	Dick Johnson	T	6-1	225	Virginia
21	Art Edling	E	6-2	200	Minnesota
22	Art Felker	E	6-2	205	Marquette
23	Tubba Chamberlain	T	6-3	285	Wis.-Eau Claire
24	Dick Christie	FB	5-11	190	Nebraska-Omaha
25	Charles Monte	HB	6-1	195	Hillsdale
26	Bill Miller	T	6-1	225	Ohio State
27	Bob Bossons	C	6-0	198	Georgia Tech
28	Bill Ayre	HB	5-11	192	Abilene Christian
29	Ralph Fieler	E	6-5	230	Miami (FL)
30	Ed Withers	HB	6-0	188	Wisconsin

1951 GREEN BAY PACKERS

FRONT ROW: (L-R) 66 Fred Cone, 21 Ray DiPierro, 36 Earl (Jug) Girard, 93 Dom Moselle, 8 Ray Pelfrey, 3 Tony Canadeo, 74 Rebel Steiner, 65 Albin (Rip) Collins, 31 Bob Mann, 25 Harper Davis, 80 Floyd (Breezy) Reid.

MIDDLE ROW: (L-R) Tubby Bero, 7 Ace Loomis, 85 Jay Rhodemyre, 17 Carl Schuette, 16 Abner Wimberly, 77 Bob Summerhays, 86 Charles Schroll, 28 Bobby Thomason, 22 Billy Grimes, 23 Val Jansante, 35 Walt Michaels, 15 Dick Afflis, Line Coach Charles Drulis.

BACK ROW: (L-R) Head Coach Gene Ronzani, Line Coach John (Tarzan) Taylor, Backfield Coach Ray (Scooter) McLean, 45 Dick Wildung, 44 Dave Stephenson, 90 Leon Manley, 34 Joe Spencer, 19 Dan Orlich, 55 Ed Ecker, 40 Carlton Elliott, 38 Tobin Rote, 39 John Martinkovic, 75 Howard Ruetz, End Coach Dick Plasman, Trainer Carl (Bud) Jorgensen, Assistant Trainer John Proski.

1952

The Packers posted a non-losing record for the first time in five years. In fact, nine weeks into the season the Packers (6-3) stood alongside the Lions, Rams and 49ers in first place. Just as importantly, Green Bay could control its own destiny as it faced those very three teams in the season's final weeks. The Packers went out and lost all three, capping a promising start with a disappointing finish.

One reason for the early resurgence could be traced to the draft. Green Bay changed its philosophy from a year ago and selected the best athletes available. Future Pro Bowlers Bill Howton, Bobby Dillon, Dave Hanner and Deral Teteak were chosen in the first nine rounds. First round pick Vito (Babe) Parilli also reached the Pro Bowl, but did it with the Boston Patriots of the American Football League (AFL) in the mid-sixties.

The five newcomers turned in excellent performances in 1952. Howton caught 53 passes for 1,231 yards and 13 touchdowns, all then-NFL-rookie bests. Dillon shared the team lead in interceptions with four. Parilli threw for 1,416 yards, tops on the team, while Hanner and Teteak strengthened a defense that improved from 10th to fifth overall.

The defense was key. Six times the Packers held opponents to fewer than 300 total yards. Six times the team won. During a four-game winning streak in November – the longest since 1944 – Green Bay held each of its adversaries under 200 yards. Philadelphia could manage only a mere 74 yards at Milwaukee on November 2.

Green Bay's brief rise to the top began with that Eagles game. The team had just absorbed a 52-17 shellacking at the hands of Detroit in City Stadium, but bounced back a week later in Milwaukee. Midway through the fourth quarter, Green Bay trailed the Eagles 10-6. When Adrian Burk went to punt from his own 23-yard line, Teteak crashed through and blocked the kick. John Martinkovic scooped up the ball and rumbled seven yards for a touchdown. Although Fred Cone missed the point after, the Packers pulled out a 12-10 win, the first of four in a row.

A week later, the Packers downed the Bears in Chicago for the first time in 11 years. That 41-28 triumph was followed by a 17-3 win at New York against the Giants. Tony Canadeo Day followed, and the Packers defeated the Dallas Texans 42-14 at home to complete the streak and move into a tie for first place.

The Packers' stay at the top ended after just four days. On Thanksgiving Day, Detroit again handled the Packers, this time 48-24. The loss was followed by setbacks to Los Angeles and San Francisco which left Green Bay in fourth place behind the three teams it had failed to beat in the last weeks of the season.

Green Bay Press-Gazette photo

Bill Howton (86) is about to take a pass from Tobin Rote in the second quarter of the Packers' 52-17 loss to Detroit at City Stadium. Howton caught seven passes for 151 yards, including a 78-yarder for a score. Howton led the Packers in every receiving category and the NFL in yards gained. Green Bay turned the ball over nine times in the loss.

- 92 -

TEAM STATISTICS

	GB	OPP
First Downs	197	202
Rushing	84	87
Passing	95	97
Penalty	18	18
Rushes	405	415
Yards Gained	1,485	1,507
Average Gain	3.67	3.63
Average Yards per Game	123.8	125.6
Passes Attempted	337	340
Completed	161	162
% Completed	47.77	47.65
Total Yards Gained	2,688	2,205
Yards Lost	314	443
Net Yards Gained	2,374	1,762
Yards Gained per Completion	16.70	13.61
Average Net Yards per Game	197.8	146.8
Combined Net Yards Gained	3,859	3,269
Total Plays	742	755
Average Yards per Play	5.20	4.33
Average Net Yards per Game	321.6	272.4
Intercepted By	22	25
Yards Returned	254	339
Returned for TD	1	3
Punts	65	72
Yards Punted	2,645	2,808
Average Yards per Punt	40.69	39.00
Punt Returns	38	36
Yards Returned	370	281
Average Yards per Return	9.74	7.81
Returned for TD	0	1
Kickoff Returns	52	51
Yards Returned	1,085	1,312
Average Yards per Return	20.87	25.73
Returned for TD	0	2
Penalties	83	96
Yards Penalized	739	752
Fumbles	40	28
Lost	31	19
Own Recovered for Touchdown	0	1
Opponent's Recovered by	19	31
Opponent's Recovered for Touchdown	1	0
Total Points Scored	295	312
Total Touchdowns	40	40
Touchdowns Rushing	11	16
Touchdowns Passing	26	17
Touchdowns on Returns & Recoveries	3	7
Extra Points	37	39
Safeties	0	0
Field Goals Attempted	21	20
Field Goals Made	6	11
% Successful	28.57	55.00

Regular Season 6-6-0

Date	GB		OPP	Att.
9/28	14	Chicago Bears	24	(24,656)
10/5	35	Washington Redskins (M)	20	(9,657)
10/12	28	Los Angeles Rams (M)	30	(21,693)
10/18	24	at Dallas Texans	14	(14,000)
10/26	17	Detroit Lions	52	(24,656)
11/2	12	Philadelphia Eagles (M)	10	(10,149)
11/9	41	at Chicago Bears	28	(41,751)
11/16	17	at New York Giants	3	(26,723)
11/23	42	Dallas Texans	14	(16,340)
11/27	24	at Detroit Lions	48	(39,101)
12/7	27	at Los Angeles Rams	45	(49,822)
12/14	14	at San Francisco 49ers	24	(18,006)

Score By Periods

	1	2	3	4	Total
Packers	51	97	80	67	295
Opponents	58	75	77	102	312

INDIVIDUAL STATISTICS

Rushing

	Att	Yds	Avg	LG	TD
Rote	58	313	5.4	30	2
Cone	70	276	3.9	t30	2
Floyd	61	236	3.9	17	1
Canadeo	65	191	2.9	35	2
Reid	58	156	2.7	14	2
Reichardt	39	121	3.1	14	1
Parilli	32	106	3.3	19	1
Grimes	17	59	3.5	31	0
B. Robinson	3	4	1.3	4	0
Pearson	2	2	1.0	2	0
Self	0	21	—	21	0
Packers	**405**	**1,485**	**3.7**	**35**	**11**
Opponents	415	1,507	3.6	74	16

Receiving

	No	Yds	Avg	LG	TD
Howton	53	1,231	23.2	t90	13
B. Mann	30	517	17.2	42	6
Keane	18	191	10.6	t29	1
Reid	12	250	20.8	t81	2
Elliott	12	114	9.5	15	1
Floyd	11	129	11.7	44	0
Canadeo	9	86	9.6	t21	1
Cone	8	98	12.3	37	1
Reichardt	5	18	3.6	12	0
Rote	1	28	28.0	t28	1
Pearson	1	16	16.0	16	0
Pelfrey	1	10	10.0	10	0
Packers	**161**	**2,688**	**16.7**	**t90**	**26**
Opponents	162	2,205	13.6	t78	17

Passing

	Att	Com	Yds	Pct	TD	In	YL	Rate
Parilli	177	77	1,416	43.5	13	17	127	56.6
Rote	157	82	1,268	52.2	13	8	187	85.6
B. Forte	2	2	4	100.0	0	0	0	—
Canadeo	1	0	0	00.0	0	0	0	—
Packers	**337**	**161**	**2,688**	**47.8**	**26**	**25**	**314**	**69.9**
Opponents	340	162	2,205	47.7	17	22	443	58.5

Punting

	No	Yds	Avg	LG	HB
Parilli	65	2,645	40.7	63	0
Packers	**65**	**2,645**	**40.7**	**63**	**0**
Opponents	72	2,808	39.0	68	2

Kickoff Returns

	No	Yds	Avg	LG	TD
Grimes	18	422	23.4	34	0
Loomis	10	207	20.7	34	0
Moselle	5	83	16.6	26	0
Floyd	5	75	15.0	26	0
Self	3	85	28.3	33	0
Canadeo	2	62	31.0	40	0
B. Robinson	2	49	24.5	26	0
Cone	2	23	11.5	13	0
Pelfrey	1	26	26.0	26	0
Dees	1	20	20.0	20	0
Reichardt	1	19	19.0	19	0
Schmidt	1	14	14.0	14	0
Martinkovic	1	0	0.0	0	0
Packers	**52**	**1,085**	**20.9**	**40**	**0**
Opponents	51	1,312	25.7	t89	2

Punt Returns

	No	Yds	Avg	LG	TD
Grimes	18	179	9.9	72	0
Loomis	8	83	10.4	31	0
Moselle	7	77	11.0	24	0
Dillon	2	22	11.0	13	0
Sandifer	2	5	2.5	5	0
Canadeo	1	4	4.0	4	0
Packers	**38**	**370**	**9.7**	**72**	**0**
Opponents	36	281	7.8	t65	1

Interceptions

	No	Yds	Avg	LG	TD
Loomis	4	115	28.8	t45	1
B. Forte	4	50	12.5	25	0
Dillon	4	35	8.8	17	0
Moselle	3	2	0.7	2	0
Sandifer	2	25	12.5	17	0
M. Johnson	2	22	11.0	22	0
Wimberly	1	5	5.0	5	0
Self	1	0	0.0	0	0
Teteak	1	0	0.0	0	0
Packers	**22**	**254**	**11.5**	**t45**	**1**
Opponents	25	339	13.6	t80	3

Scoring

	TDr	TDp	TDrt	PAT	FG	S	TP
Howton	0	13	0	0/0	0/0	0	78
Cone	2	1	0	32/34	1/1	0	53
B. Mann	0	6	0	0/0	0/0	0	36
Reichardt	1	0	0	5/5	5/20	0	26
Reid	2	2	0	0/0	0/0	0	24
Canadeo	2	1	0	0/0	0/0	0	18
Rote	2	1	0	0/0	0/0	0	18
Martinkovic	0	0	2	0/0	0/0	0	12
Elliott	0	1	0	0/0	0/0	0	6
Floyd	1	0	0	0/0	0/0	0	6
Keane	0	1	0	0/0	0/0	0	6
Loomis	0	0	1	0/0	0/0	0	6
Parilli	1	0	0	0/0	0/0	0	6
Packers	**11**	**26**	**3**	**37/40**	**6/21**	**0**	**295**
Opponents	16	17	7	39/40	11/20	0	312

Fumbles

	Fum	Ow	Op	Yds	Tot
Canadeo	3	1	0	0	1
Cone	6	1	0	0	1
Faverty	0	0	3	0	3
Floyd	5	1	0	0	1
B. Forte	0	1	3	0	4
Grimes	5	2	0	0	2
Howton	1	0	0	0	0
Loomis	2	0	0	0	0
Martinkovic	0	0	4	19	4
Parilli	4	0	0	0	0
Pelfrey	1	0	0	0	0
Reichardt	1	0	0	0	0
Reid	1	0	0	0	0
Rote	10	1	0	0	1
Ruetz	0	0	1	0	1
Ruzich	1	2	0	0	2
Self	0	0	3	10	3
Serini	0	0	3	0	3
Wimberly	0	0	2	0	2
Packers	**40**	**9**	**19**	**29**	**28**

NFL STANDINGS

National Conference

	W	L	T	Pct	PF	PA
Detroit Lions	9	3	0	.750	344	192
Los Angeles Rams	9	3	0	.750	349	234
San Francisco 49ers	7	5	0	.583	285	221
Green Bay Packers	6	6	0	.500	295	312
Chicago Bears	5	7	0	.417	245	326
Dallas Texans	1	11	0	.083	182	427

American Conference

	W	L	T	Pct	PF	PA
Cleveland Browns	8	4	0	.667	310	213
New York Giants	7	5	0	.583	234	231
Philadelphia Eagles	7	5	0	.583	252	271
Pittsburgh Steelers	5	7	0	.417	300	273
Chicago Cardinals	4	8	0	.333	172	221
Washington Redskins	4	8	0	.333	240	287

1952 ROSTER

No	Name	Pos	Ht	Wt	DOB	College	G
62	Afflis, Dick	G	6-0	252	06/27/29	Nevada	12
63	Bray, Ray	G	6-0	240	02/01/17	Western Michigan	12
3	Canadeo, Tony	HB	6-0	190	05/05/19	Gonzaga	12
31	Cone, Fred	FB	5-11	197	06/21/26	Clemson	10
76	Dees, Robert	T	6-4	245	09/26/29	Southwest Missouri State	9
44	Dillon, Bobby	DB	6-1	185	02/23/30	Texas	12
70	Dowden, Steve	T	6-2	235	02/24/29	Baylor	12
80	Elliott, Carlton	E	6-4	215	11/12/27	Virginia	12
51	Faverty, Hal	DE	6-2	220	09/26/27	Wisconsin	11
33	Floyd, Bobby Jack	FB	6-0	210	12/08/29	TCU	12
8	Forte, Bob	LB	6-0	205	07/15/22	Arkansas	12
22	Grimes, Billy	HB	6-1	195	07/27/27	Oklahoma State	12
77	Hanner, Dave	DT	6-2	245	05/20/30	Arkansas	12
86	Howton, Bill	E	6-2	185	07/05/30	Rice	12
41	Johnson, Marvin	DB	5-11	185	04/13/27	San Jose State	5
72	Johnson, Tom	DT	6-2	230	01/19/31	Michigan	8
81	Keane, Jim	E	6-4	215	01/11/24	Iowa	11
67	Logan, Dick	DT	6-2	225	05/04/30	Ohio State	7
43	Loomis, Ace	DB	6-1	190	06/12/28	Wisconsin-LaCrosse	11
87	Mann, Bob	E	5-11	170	04/08/24	Michigan	12
83	Martinkovic, John	DE	6-3	235	02/04/27	Xavier	12
47	Moselle, Dom	HB	6-0	192	06/03/26	Wisconsin-Superior	8
15	Parilli, Vito (Babe)	QB	6-1	190	05/07/30	Kentucky	12
26	Pearson, Lindell	HB	6-0	200	03/06/29	Oklahoma	2
8	Pelfrey, Ray	E	6-0	190	01/11/28	Eastern Kentucky	1
37	Reichardt, Bill	FB	5-11	210	06/24/30	Iowa	12
24	Reid, Floyd (Breezy)	HB	5-10	185	09/04/27	Georgia	12
50	Rhodemyre, Jay	C	6-1	210	12/16/22	Kentucky	12
41	Robinson, Bill	HB	6-0	195		Lincoln	2
18	Rote, Tobin	QB	6-3	200	01/18/28	Rice	12
75	Ruetz, Howard	DT	6-3	265	08/18/27	Loras	3
61	Ruzich, Steve	G	6-2	225	12/24/28	Ohio State	12
20	Sandifer, Dan	DB	6-2	190	03/01/29	LSU	12
54	Schmidt, George	C	6-2	220	10/28/27	Lewis	7
28	Self, Clarence	HB	5-9	180	10/10/25	Wisconsin	12
73	Serini, Washington	DT	6-2	240	03/09/24	Kentucky	11
69	Stephenson, Dave	G	6-2	235	10/22/25	West Virginia	11
66	Teteak, Deral	LB	5-10	210	12/11/29	Wisconsin	12
85	Wimberly, Abner	DE	6-1	215	05/04/26	LSU	12

1952 DRAFT

Rnd	Name	Pos	Ht	Wt	College
1	Vito (Babe) Parilli	QB	6-1	190	Kentucky
2	Bill Howton	E	6-2	185	Rice
3	Bobby Dillon	DB	6-1	185	Texas
4	(Choice to Browns)				
5	Dave Hanner	DT	6-2	245	Arkansas
6	Tom Johnson	T	6-2	230	Michigan
7	Bill Reichardt	FB	5-11	210	Iowa
8	Mel Becket	C	6-3	220	Indiana
9	Deral Teteak	G	5-10	210	Wisconsin
10a	Art Kleinschmidt	G	6-1	230	Tulane
10b	Bud Roffler	HB	6-1	185	Washington State
	(Choice from Bears)				
11	Billy Burkhalter	HB	5-10	180	Rice
12	Bill Wilson	E	6-2	205	Texas
13	Billy Hair	HB	6-0	178	Clemson
14	Jack Morgan	T	6-2	235	Michigan State
15	Bobby Jack Floyd	FB	6-0	210	TCU
16	Johnny Coatta	QB	5-11	180	Wisconsin
17	Don Peterson	HB	5-11	180	Michigan
18	Howard Tisdale	T	6-3	250	Stephen A. Austin
19	John Pont	HB	5-8	170	Miami (OH)
20	Charles Boerio	C	5-11	198	Illinois
21	Herb Zimmerman	G	6-0	220	TCU
22	Karl Kluckhorn	E	6-2	195	Colgate
23	Frank Kapral	G	5-10	210	Michigan State
24	John Schuetzner	E	6-3	220	North Carolina
25	Charles LaPradd	T	6-3	222	Florida
26	Charles Stokes	C	6-2	210	Tennessee
27	I.D. Russell	B	6-1	210	SMU
28	Bill Barrett	HB	5-9	180	Notre Dame
29	Bill Stratton	B	6-0	210	Lewis
30	Jack Fulkerson	T	6-2	230	Mississippi Southern

1952 GREEN BAY PACKERS

FRONT ROW: (L-R) Line Coach John (Tarzan) Taylor, Line Coach Charles Drulis, Head Coach Gene Ronzani, Backfield Coach Ray (Scooter) McLean, End Coach Dick Plasman.
SECOND ROW: (L-R) Trainer Carl (Bud) Jorgensen, 86 Bill Howton, 72 Tom Johnson, 8 Bob Forte, 83 John Martinkovic, 73 Washington Serini, 80 Carlton Elliott, 81 Jim Keane, 54 George Schmidt, 41 Bill Robinson, 76 Robert Dees, 77 Dave Hanner, Assistant Trainer John Proski.
THIRD ROW: (L-R) 70 Steve Dowden, 51 Hal Faverty, 61 Steve Ruzich, 67 Dick Logan, 18 Tobin Rote, 85 Abner Wimberly, 20 Dan Sandifer, 22 Billy Grimes, 69 Dave Stephenson, 63 Ray Bray, 50 Jay Rhodemyre, 43 Ace Loomis.
BACK ROW: (L-R) 15 Vito (Babe) Parilli, 37 Bill Reichardt, 62 Dick Afflis, 24 Floyd (Breezy) Reid, 3 Tony Canadeo, 66 Deral Teteak, 87 Bob Mann, 47 Dom Moselle, 31 Fred Cone, 44 Bobby Dillon, 28 Clarence Self, 33 Bobby Jack Floyd.

1953

The strides made the previous season all but disappeared in 1953. Green Bay dropped its first three games, won two of its next three, then failed to win in the last six weeks. So inept were the Packers that they could only defeat the Baltimore Colts —back after a two-year hiatus— yet still finish a half-game behind the Colts at the bottom of the Western Conference with a 2-9-1 record. Two weeks before the end —November 27— Gene Ronzani was released, marking the only time a Packer head coach was dismissed in the midst of a season. Assistants Hugh Devore and Ray (Scooter) McLean took over as co-coaches. (Chuck Drulis was a third co-coach for a few days.)

A major reason for the step back was the deterioration of the passing game. Tobin Rote and Vito (Babe) Parilli had thrown an NFL-leading 26 touchdown passes in 1952 and Bill Howton had caught 13 of them. In 1953, the quarterbacking duo managed nine – lowest in the league – while tossing an NFL-high 34 interceptions. Howton missed the first four games with a chest injury, suffered in the team's preseason wind-up against Cleveland, and caught just 25 passes for four scores when he returned.

Good news came in the form of a television contract the NFL signed with ABC and the Dumont networks. The $1.3 million deal called for a game to be played and televised on Saturday nights. With the growing popularity of the medium and the sport, a fan could now watch out-of-town teams go at it on Saturday and then catch the home team on Sunday in person.

The Packers played twice on consecutive Saturday evenings in 1953. It wasn't their first Saturday showing; they lost to Frankford 13-7 on November 28, 1925. But then that game wasn't televised. On October 24, Green Bay lost to Pittsburgh 31-14 and a week later, beat Baltimore 35-24.

Al Carmichael, Bill Forester, Roger Zatkoff and Jim Ringo were selected in the first seven rounds of the draft. Carmichael, the team's first pick, blossomed into one of the best kickoff return men in league history. Forester played 11 years for the Packers, while Zatkoff played in three Pro Bowls from 1955-57. Ringo made a habit of it, enjoying Pro-Bowl berths in 1957 and 1959-63.

Though the Packers were only able to defeat the Colts in 1953, they played the Bears tough. With his team up 13-10 early in the fourth quarter, Val Joe Walker intercepted Steve Romanik and returned 20 yards to the Bears' two-yard line. There, Green Bay picked up a five yard penalty and on first-and-goal from the seven, Rote fumbled and Frank Dempsey recovered for the Bears. Rote would be intercepted by Jack Hoffman after reaching the Chicago 18 with less than two minutes left. The Bears prevailed 17-13.

The second meeting on November 8 ended in a 21-21 tie. Parilli threw 23 yards to Howton for the tying score.

Less than three weeks later, Ronzani was gone. A 34-15 loss to Detroit on Thanksgiving was the final straw. For the second time in four years, the Packers began searching for a head coach.

Green Bay Press-Gazette photo

Al Carmichael, the team's number one draft choice, picks up seven yards against the Colts in Green Bay October 18. The Packers defeated Baltimore twice, first 37-14 and then 35-24 on Halloween. Carmichael led the team in kickoff and punt returns. Colts in the picture include Tom Finnin (77), Barney Poole (83), Alex Agase (62) and future Colts Head Coach Don Shula (25).

TEAM STATISTICS

	GB	OPP
First Downs	189	199
Rushing	93	95
Passing	79	91
Penalty	17	13
Rushes	424	407
Yards Gained	1,665	1,746
Average Gain	3.93	4.29
Average Yards per Game	138.8	145.5
Passes Attempted	352	312
Completed	147	144
% Completed	41.76	46.15
Total Yards Gained	1,833	2,341
Yards Lost	278	236
Net Yards Gained	1,555	2,105
Yards Gained per Completion	12.47	16.26
Average Net Yards per Game	129.6	175.4
Combined Net Yards Gained	3,220	3,851
Total Plays	776	719
Average Yards per Play	4.15	5.36
Average Net Yards per Game	268.3	320.9
Intercepted By	28	34
Yards Returned	351	407
Returned for TD	2	2
Punts	80	66
Yards Punted	3,005	2,750
Average Yards per Punt	37.56	41.67
Punt Returns	39	41
Yards Returned	348	232
Average Yards per Return	8.92	5.66
Returned for TD	1	1
Kickoff Returns	56	40
Yards Returned	1,197	851
Average Yards per Return	21.38	21.28
Returned for TD	0	0
Penalties	67	84
Yards Penalized	624	617
Fumbles	29	28
Lost	14	19
Own Recovered for Touchdown	0	0
Opponent's Recovered by	19	14
Opponent's Recovered for Touchdown	0	0
Total Points Scored	200	338
Total Touchdowns	27	44
Touchdowns Rushing	14	24
Touchdowns Passing	9	15
Touchdowns on Returns & Recoveries	4	5
Extra Points	23	41
Safeties	0	0
Field Goals Attempted	16	22
Field Goals Made	5	11
% Successful	31.25	50.00

Regular Season 2-9-1

Date	GB		OPP	Att.
9/27	0	Cleveland Browns (M)	27	(22,604)
10/4	13	Chicago Bears	17	(24,835)
10/11	20	Los Angeles Rams (M)	38	(23,352)
10/18	37	Baltimore Colts	14	(18,713)
10/24	14	at Pittsburgh Steelers	31	(22,918)
10/31	35	at Baltimore Colts	24	(33,797)
11/8	21	at Chicago Bears	21	(39,889)
11/15	7	Detroit Lions	14	(20,834)
11/22	7	San Francisco 49ers (M)	37	(16,378)
11/26	15	at Detroit Lions	34	(52,547)
12/6	14	at San Francisco 49ers	48	(35,837)
12/12	17	at Los Angeles Rams	33	(23,069)

Score By Periods

	1	2	3	4	Total
Packers	52	62	31	55	200
Opponents	98	76	92	72	338

INDIVIDUAL STATISTICS

Rushing

	Att	Yds	Avg	LG	TD
Reid	95	492	5.2	43	3
Cone	92	301	3.3	t41	5
Carmichael	49	199	4.1	t41	1
Rote	33	180	5.5	21	0
Parilli	42	171	4.1	19	4
Ferguson	52	134	2.6	12	0
Papit	6	44	7.3	21	1
Barton	7	40	5.7	14	0
Coutre	22	39	1.8	8	0
Bailey	13	29	2.2	13	0
Boone	7	24	3.4	24	0
G. Dawson	5	18	3.6	18	0
Rush	1	-6	-6.0	-6	0
Packers	424	1,665	3.9	43	14
Opponents	407	1,746	4.3	58	24

Receiving

	No	Yds	Avg	LG	TD
Howton	25	463	18.5	t80	4
B. Mann	23	327	14.2	42	2
Cone	18	165	9.2	30	1
Ferguson	15	86	5.7	23	0
Rush	14	190	13.6	24	0
Elliott	13	150	11.5	19	0
Carmichael	12	131	10.9	52	0
Reid	10	100	10.0	26	0
Bailey	8	119	14.9	50	0
Boone	6	55	9.2	18	1
Barton	2	51	25.5	t42	1
Coutre	1	-4	-4.0	-4	0
Packers	147	1,833	12.5	t80	9
Opponents	144	2,341	16.3	t97	15

Passing

	Att	Com	Yds	Pct	TD	In	YL	Rate
Rote	185	72	1,005	38.9	5	15	117	32.4
Parilli	166	74	830	44.6	4	19	161	28.5
Boone	1	1	-2	100.0	0	0	0	—
Packers	352	147	1,833	41.8	9	34	278	27.5
Opponents	312	144	2,341	46.2	15	28	236	50.4

Punting

	No	Yds	Avg	LG	HB
Rush	60	2,262	37.7	60	0
Parilli	19	686	36.1	58	0
Rote	1	57	57.0	57	0
Packers	80	3,005	37.6	60	0
Opponents	66	2,750	41.7	60	1

Kickoff Returns

	No	Yds	Avg	LG	TD
Carmichael	26	641	24.7	43	0
Ferguson	7	123	17.6	30	0
G. Dawson	4	102	25.5	33	0
Reid	4	82	20.5	23	0
Coutre	3	52	17.3	27	0
Teteak	2	62	31.0	47	0
Papit	2	38	19.0	21	0
Bailey	2	34	17.0	21	0
Martinkovic	2	12	6.0	8	0
Loomis	1	19	19.0	19	0
Barton	1	14	14.0	14	0
Forester	1	12	12.0	12	0
Wildung	1	6	6.0	6	0
Packers	56	1,197	21.4	47	0
Opponents	40	851	21.3	47	0

Punt Returns

	No	Yds	Avg	LG	TD
Carmichael	20	199	10.0	52	0
G. Dawson	7	72	10.3	t60	1
Boone	5	24	4.8	9	0
Sandifer	3	35	11.7	23	0
Barton	2	13	6.5	9	0
Coutre	1	5	5.0	5	0
B. Aldridge	1	0	0.0	0	0
Packers	39	348	8.9	t60	1
Opponents	41	232	5.7	t71	1

Interceptions

	No	Yds	Avg	LG	TD
Dillon	9	112	12.4	t49	1
B. Aldridge	5	85	17.0	34	0
V.J. Walker	4	74	18.5	t54	1
M. Johnson	4	39	9.8	36	0
Loomis	4	39	9.8	27	0
Hanner	1	2	2.0	2	0
Forester	1	0	0.0	0	0
Packers	28	351	12.5	t54	2
Opponents	34	407	12.0	t67	2

Scoring

	TDr	TDp	TDrt	PAT	FG	S	TP
Cone	5	1	0	23/25	5/16	0	74
Howton	0	4	0	0/0	0/0	0	24
Parilli	4	0	0	0/0	0/0	0	24
Reid	3	0	0	0/0	0/0	0	18
B. Mann	0	2	0	0/0	0/0	0	12
Barton	0	1	0	0/0	0/0	0	6
Boone	0	1	0	0/0	0/0	0	6
Carmichael	1	0	0	0/0	0/0	0	6
G. Dawson	0	0	1	0/0	0/0	0	6
Dillon	0	0	1	0/0	0/0	0	6
Elliott	0	0	1	0/0	0/0	0	6
Papit	1	0	0	0/0	0/0	0	6
V.J. Walker	0	0	1	0/0	0/0	0	6
Packers	14	9	4	23/27	5/16	0	200
Opponents	24	15	5	41/44	11/22	0	338

Fumbles

	Fum	Ow	Op	Yds	Tot
B. Aldridge	0	0	2	0	2
Bailey	1	0	0	0	0
Boone	1	1	0	0	1
Bill Brown	0	1	1	0	2
Carmichael	3	0	0	0	0
Cifelli	0	1	0	0	1
Cone	2	0	0	5	2
G. Dawson	1	0	0	0	0
Dillon	0	0	1	0	1
Elliott	0	0	1	17	1
Ferguson	4	1	0	0	1
Forester	0	0	2	0	2
B. Forte	0	0	1	0	1
Howton	1	0	0	0	0
M. Johnson	0	0	1	0	1
Dick Logan	0	1	0	0	1
Loomis	0	0	3	0	3
Martinkovic	0	0	1	3	1
Parilli	8	3	0	0	3
Reid	5	4	0	2	4
Rote	2	0	0	0	0
Ruetz	0	0	1	13	1
Rush	1	0	0	0	0
Ruzich	0	0	1	0	1
Szafaryn	0	1	0	0	1
V.J. Walker	0	0	3	0	3
Zatkoff	0	0	1	0	1
Packers	29	15	19	40	34

NFL STANDINGS

Western Conference

	W	L	T	Pct	PF	PA
Detroit Lions	10	2	0	.833	271	205
San Francisco 49ers	9	3	0	.750	372	237
Los Angeles Rams	8	3	1	.727	366	236
Chicago Bears	3	8	1	.273	218	262
Baltimore Colts	3	9	0	.250	182	350
Green Bay Packers	2	9	1	.182	200	338

Eastern Conference

	W	L	T	Pct	PF	PA
Cleveland Browns	11	1	0	.917	348	162
Philadelphia Eagles	7	4	1	.636	352	215
Washington Redskins	6	5	1	.545	208	215
Pittsburgh Steelers	6	6	0	.500	211	263
New York Giants	3	9	0	.250	179	277
Chicago Cardinals	1	10	1	.091	190	337

1953 ROSTER

No	Name	Pos	Ht	Wt	DOB	College	G
72	Afflis, Dick	G	6-0	250	06/27/29	Nevada	12
40	Aldridge, Ben	DB	6-1	195		Oklahoma State	8
20	Bailey, Byron	HB	5-11	198	10/12/30	Washington State	9
43	Barton, Don	HB	5-11	175	05/29/30	Texas	5
22	Boone, J.R.	HB	5-9	167	07/28/25	Tulsa	8
62	Brown, Bill (Buddy)	G	6-1	220	10/19/26	Arkansas	11
42	Carmichael, Al	HB	6-1	190	11/10/28	USC	12
73	Cifelli, Gus	T	6-4	250	02/03/26	Notre Dame	12
31	Cone, Fred	FB	5-11	197	06/21/26	Clemson	12
27	Coutre, Larry	HB	5-10	180	04/11/28	Notre Dame	7
26	Dawson, Gib	HB	5-11	180	08/27/30	Texas	7
44	Dillon, Bobby	DB	6-1	180	02/23/30	Texas	10
80	Elliott, Carlton	E	6-4	220	11/12/27	Virginia	12
37	Ferguson, Howie	FB	6-2	210	08/05/30	No college	11
69	Forester, Bill	DT	6-3	230	08/09/32	SMU	12
8	Forte, Bob	LB	6-0	205	07/15/22	Arkansas	11
77	Hanner, Dave	DT	6-2	250	05/20/30	Arkansas	12
88	Hays, George	DE	6-2	215	08/29/25	St. Bonaventure	9
86	Howton, Bill	E	6-2	188	07/05/30	Rice	8
41	Johnson, Marvin	DB	5-11	185	04/13/27	San Jose State	7
67	Logan, Dick	DT	6-2	230	05/04/30	Ohio State	12
48	Loomis, Ace	DB	6-1	190	06/12/28	Wisconsin-LaCrosse	10
87	Mann, Bob	E	5-11	175	04/08/24	Michigan	10
83	Martinkovic, John	DE	6-3	240	02/04/27	Xavier	12
22	Papit, Johnny	HB	6-0	190	07/25/28	Virginia	4
15	Parilli, Vito (Babe)	QB	6-1	190	05/07/30	Kentucky	12
24	Reid, Floyd (Breezy)	HB	5-10	185	09/04/27	Georgia	12
51	Ringo, Jim	C	6-1	225	11/21/32	Syracuse	5
18	Rote, Tobin	QB	6-3	200	01/18/28	Rice	12
75	Ruetz, Howard	DT	6-3	250	08/18/27	Loras	5
81	Rush, Clive	E	6-2	197	02/14/31	Miami (OH)	11
61	Ruzich, Steve	G	6-2	225	12/24/28	Ohio State	12
23	Sandifer, Dan	DB	6-2	190	03/01/29	LSU	1
53	Stephenson, Dave	G	6-2	225	10/22/25	West Virginia	12
68	Szafaryn, Len	G	6-2	230	01/19/28	North Carolina	7
66	Teteak, Deral	LB	5-10	210	12/11/29	Wisconsin	7
58	Tonnemaker, Clayton	LB	6-2	235	06/08/28	Minnesota	12
47	Walker, Val Joe	DB	6-1	179	01/07/30	SMU	12
70	Wildung, Dick	T	6-0	230	08/16/21	Minnesota	12
74	Zatkoff, Roger	T	6-2	215	03/25/31	Michigan	12

1953 DRAFT

Rnd	Name	Pos	Ht	Wt	College
1	Al Carmichael	HB	6-1	190	USC
2	Gil Reich	HB	6-0	188	Kansas
3	Bill Forester	DT	6-3	235	SMU
4	Gib Dawson	HB	5-11	175	Texas
5	Roger Zatkoff	T	6-2	210	Michigan
6	Bob Kennedy	G	5-11	225	Wisconsin
7	Jim Ringo	C	6-1	225	Syracuse
8	Lauren Hargrove	HB	6-1	193	Georgia
9	Floyd Harrawood	T	6-4	240	Tulsa
10	Victor Rimkus	G	6-1	220	Holy Cross
*11	Joe Johnson	HB	6-0	185	Boston College
*12	Dick Curran	HB	6-0	185	Arizona State
*13	Bob Orders	C	6-3	230	West Virginia
*14	Charles Wrenn	T	6-3	250	TCU
15	Gene Helwig	HB	6-1	190	Tulsa
16	John Hlay	FB	6-1	218	Ohio State
17	Bill Georges	E	6-1	195	Texas
18	Jim Philbee	HB	6-2	185	Bradley
*19	Bill Lucky	T	6-2	230	Baylor
20	John Harville	HB	6-2	200	TCU
21	Bob Conway	HB	6-0	185	Alabama
22	Bill Turnbeaugh	T	6-3	265	Auburn
23	Bill Murray	E	6-2	215	American International
24	Jim Haslam	T	6-3	210	Tennessee
25	Ike Jones	E	5-11	185	UCLA
*26	George Bozanic	HB	6-2	210	USC
27	James McConaughey	E	6-3	215	Houston
28	Zack Jordan	HB	6-1	190	Colorado
29	Henry O'Brien	E	6-1	240	Boston College
30	Al Barry	G	6-2	222	USC

*   denotes juniors

1953 GREEN BAY PACKERS

FRONT ROW: (L–R) Property Man Toby Sylvester, 88 George Hays, 69 Bill Forester, 43 Don Barton, 47 Val Joe Walker, 53 Dave Stephenson, 26 Gib Dawson, 27 Larry Coutre, 67 Dick Logan, Trainer Carl (Bud) Jorgensen.
SECOND ROW: (L–R) 83 John Martinkovic, 74 Roger Zatkoff, 41 Marvin Johnson, 61 Steve Ruzich, 72 Dick Afflis, 87 Bob Mann, 15 Vito (Babe) Parilli, 42 Al Carmichael, 20 Byron Bailey, 37 Howie Ferguson, 40 Ben Aldridge, 58 Clayton Tonnemaker.
THIRD ROW: (L–R) 81 Clive Rush, 62 Bill (Buddy) Brown, 75 Dave Hanner, 51 Jim Ringo, 18 Tobin Rote, 68 Len Szafaryn, 80 Carlton Elliott, 73 Gus Cifelli, 23 Dan Sandifer, 86 Bill Howton, 48 Ace Loomis, 44 Bobby Dillon, 70 Dick Wildung, 8 Bob Forte.
BACK ROW: (L–R) Head Coach Gene Ronzani, Backfield Coach Ray (Scooter) McLean, 22 J.R. Boone, 24 Floyd (Breezy) Reid, 31 Fred Cone, 66 Deral Teteak, End Coach Hugh Devore, Line Coach Charles Drulis.

- 99 -

1954

As Gene Ronzani had done four years previous, Lisle Blackbourn geared up for the challenge of bringing the Packers back to the top. The team finished far from it – its 4-8 record was good for fifth place ahead of only the Baltimore Colts – but Blackbourn had his men playing hard. Seven of the eight losses were by eight points or less and Green Bay led at one point or another in all but two of its games. Only San Francisco blew out the Packers (35-0) on the second-to-last weekend of the year.

The Blackbourn regime began with a blockbuster trade. On August 6, the Packers traded Vito (Babe) Parilli and second round pick Bob Fleck to the Browns for four players. Green Bay acquired quarterback Bob Garrett, guard John Bauer, defensive back Don Miller and Chester Giarola. Garrett was the Browns bonus pick and Bauer its first-round pick in the 1954 draft. The trade looked good at the time – the Packers had already lost Parilli's services to the Air Force for two years in mid-July – but only Garrett and Miller made the team and they played but one year. Parilli was eventually traded back to Green Bay prior to the 1957 season.

Three consecutive fourth-quarter collapses cost the Packers victories in the first three weeks. First, Pittsburgh beat Green Bay 21-20 when Jim Finks passed 38 yards to Ray Matthews for a touchdown with about five minutes remaining. A week later, Tobin Rote lost a fumble on the first play of the fourth quarter; a turnover George Blanda and Billy Stone turned into seven points with a five-yard pass three plays later. Blanda added a 23-yard field goal and the Bears prevailed 10-3. Then, in week three, a long pass from Y.A. Tittle to Hugh McElhenny set up Tittle's 2-yard touchdown run with 3:23 left. The 49ers handed Green Bay its third straight loss, 23-17.

In those first games, the Packers were without the services of Bob Mann and Deral Teteak. Teteak sustained an ankle fracture in a mid-August practice and didn't return to the active roster until late October. Mann, who saw action briefly in the Bears loss, was injured in a preseason game with the Eagles. He was waived at the same time Teteak was activated.

While the 1954 draft was not as strong as the previous two, one player in particular made an instant impact. Max McGee, an end from Tulane, caught 36 passes for 614 yards and nine touchdowns. His efforts helped mitigate the loss of Mann.

The Packers roared to life in midseason. After the initial three-game losing streak, Green Bay won four of its next five games. The one loss, to the Bears 28-23, mirrored the team's earlier fourth-quarter breakdowns. The Packers led 23-14 with just over ten minutes remaining, but a fumble by Veryl Switzer and a pass to Jack Hoffman from Blanda led to touchdowns.

In keeping with a pattern established over the last seven years, Green Bay lost its last four games in 1954. Since 1948, the Packers record in November and December games was a pitiful 6-36-1. The team had not won in December since a 35-14 triumph at Detroit on December 7, 1947.

Green Bay Press-Gazette photo

Veryl Switzer (27) goes after John Hoffman in a game at City Stadium on October 3. Hoffman had just taken a pass from George Blanda in the fourth quarter. The Bears scored 10 points in the period to defeat the Packers 10-3. Green Bay blew fourth-quarter leads in four of its eight losses. Clayton Tonnemaker (58), Val Joe Walker (47) and Gene White (88) can also be seen.

TEAM STATISTICS

	GB	OPP
First Downs	207	228
Rushing	79	101
Passing	112	119
Penalty	16	8
Rushes	321	403
Yards Gained	1,328	1,871
Average Gain	4.14	4.64
Average Yards per Game	110.7	155.9
Passes Attempted	412	374
Completed	195	208
% Completed	47.33	55.61
Total Yards Gained	2,454	2,690
Yards Lost	295	211
Net Yards Gained	2,159	2,479
Yards Gained per Completion	12.58	12.93
Average Net Yards per Game	179.9	206.6
Combined Net Yards Gained	3,487	4,350
Total Plays	733	777
Average Yards per Play	4.76	5.60
Average Net Yards per Game	290.6	362.5
Intercepted By	19	19
Yards Returned	285	380
Returned for TD	1	1
Punts	72	64
Yards Punted	2,999	2,568
Average Yards per Punt	41.65	40.13
Punt Returns	40	43
Yards Returned	394	290
Average Yards per Return	9.85	6.74
Returned for TD	1	1
Kickoff Returns	49	45
Yards Returned	1,193	832
Average Yards per Return	24.35	18.49
Returned for TD	0	0
Penalties	57	72
Yards Penalized	522	666
Fumbles	21	22
Lost	12	14
Own Recovered for Touchdown	0	0
Opponent's Recovered by	14	12
Opponent's Recovered for Touchdown	1	1
Total Points Scored	234	251
Total Touchdowns	30	33
Touchdowns Rushing	13	13
Touchdowns Passing	14	17
Touchdowns on Returns & Recoveries	3	3
Extra Points	27	32
Safeties	0	0
Field Goals Attempted	16	14
Field Goals Made	9	7
% Successful	56.25	50.00

Regular Season 4-8-0

Date	GB		OPP	Att.
9/26	20	Pittsburgh Steelers	21	(20,675)
10/3	3	Chicago Bears	10	(24,414)
10/10	17	San Francisco 49ers (M)	23	(15,571)
10/17	35	Los Angeles Rams (M)	17	(17,455)
10/24	7	at Baltimore Colts	6	(28,680)
10/30	37	at Philadelphia Eagles	14	(25,378)
11/7	23	at Chicago Bears	28	(47,038)
11/13	24	Baltimore Colts (M)	13	(19,786)
11/21	17	Detroit Lions	21	(20,767)
11/25	24	at Detroit Lions	28	(55,532)
12/5	0	at San Francisco 49ers	35	(33,712)
12/12	27	at Los Angeles Rams	35	(38,839)

Score By Periods

	1	2	3	4	Total
Packers	38	70	77	49	234
Opponents	72	73	34	72	251

INDIVIDUAL STATISTICS

Rushing

	Att	Yds	Avg	LG	TD
Reid	99	507	5.1	t69	5
Rote	67	301	4.5	30	8
Ferguson	83	276	3.3	25	0
Carmichael	33	130	3.9	23	0
Switzer	15	59	3.9	33	0
J. Johnson	7	31	4.4	10	0
Cone	15	18	1.2	11	0
McGee	1	9	9.0	9	0
B. Garrett	1	-3	-3.0	-3	0
Packers	321	1,328	4.1	t69	13
Opponents	403	1,871	4.6	44	13

1954

Receiving

	No	Yds	Avg	LG	TD
Howton	52	768	14.8	59	2
Ferguson	41	398	9.7	49	0
McGee	36	614	17.1	t82	9
Carmichael	18	251	13.9	45	0
Switzer	17	166	9.8	28	2
Reid	14	129	9.2	25	0
J. Johnson	10	72	7.2	17	1
Cone	4	19	4.8	13	0
Knafelc	3	37	12.3	15	0
Packers	195	2,454	12.6	t82	14
Opponents	208	2,690	12.9	t71	17

Passing

	Att	Com	Yds	Pct	TD	In	YL	Rate
Rote	382	180	2,311	47.1	14	18	295	59.1
B. Garrett	30	15	143	50.0	0	1	0	49.7
Packers	412	195	2,454	47.3	14	19	295	58.5
Opponents	374	208	2,690	55.6	17	19	211	72.4

Punting

	No	Yds	Avg	LG	HB
McGee	72	2,999	41.7	63	0
Packers	72	2,999	41.7	63	0
Opponents	64	2,568	40.1	72	0

Kickoff Returns

	No	Yds	Avg	LG	TD
Carmichael	20	531	26.6	49	0
Switzer	20	500	25.0	88	0
J. Johnson	4	91	22.8	28	0
Ferguson	2	31	15.5	22	0
Cone	1	22	22.0	22	0
Forester	1	18	18.0	18	0
Bill Brown	1	0	0.0	0	0
Packers	49	1,193	24.3	88	0
Opponents	45	832	18.5	35	0

Punt Returns

	No	Yds	Avg	LG	TD
Switzer	24	306	12.8	t93	1
Carmichael	9	43	4.8	14	0
J. Johnson	5	38	7.6	9	0
Dillon	1	7	7.0	7	0
Psaltis	1	0	0.0	0	0
Packers	40	394	9.9	t93	1
Opponents	43	290	6.7	t61	1

Interceptions

	No	Yds	Avg	LG	TD
Dillon	7	111	15.9	t59	1
V.J. Walker	4	83	20.8	44	0
Self	2	23	11.5	23	0
Teteak	1	23	23.0	23	0
Forester	1	21	21.0	21	0
White	1	20	20.0	20	0
Afflis	1	3	3.0	3	0
Tonnemaker	1	1	1.0	1	0
Zatkoff	1	0	0.0	0	0
Packers	19	285	15.0	t59	1
Opponents	19	380	20.0	57	1

Scoring

	TDr	TDp	TDrt	PAT	FG	S	TP
Cone	0	0	0	27/29	9/16	0	54
McGee	0	9	0	0/0	0/0	0	54
Rote	8	0	0	0/0	0/0	0	48
Reid	5	0	0	0/0	0/0	0	30
Switzer	0	2	2	0/0	0/0	0	24
Howton	0	2	0	0/0	0/0	0	12
Dillon	0	0	1	0/0	0/0	0	6
J. Johnson	0	1	0	0/0	0/0	0	6
Packers	13	14	3	27/30	9/16	0	234
Opponents	13	17	3	32/33	7/14	0	251

Fumbles

	Fum	Ow	Op	Yds	Tot
Carmichael	2	1	0	0	1
Cone	1	0	0	0	0
Dillon	1	0	0	0	0
Elliott	0	0	1	0	1
Ferguson	8	1	0	0	1
B. Garrett	2	1	0	0	1
Hanner	0	0	1	0	1
Helluin	0	0	2	0	2
Howton	0	1	0	0	1
A. Hunter	0	0	1	0	1
G. Knutson	0	0	1	0	1
Martinkovic	0	0	1	0	1
Psaltis	0	0	1	0	1
Reid	0	1	0	0	1
Rote	4	2	0	0	2
Self	0	0	1	0	1
Switzer	3	1	1	0	2
V.J. Walker	0	0	1	3	1
White	0	0	1	0	1
Zatkoff	0	0	3	0	3
Packers	21	9	14	3	23

NFL STANDINGS

Western Conference

	W	L	T	Pct	PF	PA
Detroit Lions	9	2	1	.818	337	189
Chicago Bears	8	4	0	.667	301	279
San Francisco 49ers	7	4	1	.636	313	251
Los Angeles Rams	6	5	1	.545	314	285
Green Bay Packers	4	8	0	.333	234	251
Baltimore Colts	3	9	0	.250	131	279

Eastern Conference

	W	L	T	Pct	PF	PA
Cleveland Browns	9	3	0	.750	336	162
Philadelphia Eagles	7	4	1	.636	284	230
New York Giants	7	5	0	.583	293	184
Pittsburgh Steelers	5	7	0	.417	219	263
Washington Redskins	3	9	0	.250	207	432
Chicago Cardinals	2	10	0	.167	183	347

1954 ROSTER

No	Name	Pos	Ht	Wt	DOB	College	G
75	Afflis, Dick	G	6-0	250	06/27/29	Nevada	12
63	Barry, Al	G	6-2	225	12/24/30	USC	12
62	Brown, Bill (Buddy)	G	6-1	225	10/19/26	Arkansas	12
42	Carmichael, Al	HB	6-1	190	11/10/28	USC	10
31	Cone, Fred	FB	5-11	200	06/21/26	Clemson	12
44	Dillon, Bobby	DB	6-1	180	02/23/30	Texas	12
80	Elliott, Carlton	E	6-4	230	11/12/27	Virginia	12
37	Ferguson, Howie	FB	6-2	210	08/05/30	No college	12
69	Forester, Bill	LB	6-3	235	08/09/32	SMU	12
15	Garrett, Bob	QB	6-1	198	08/16/32	Stanford	9
77	Hanner, Dave	DT	6-2	260	05/20/30	Arkansas	12
72	Helluin, Jerry	DT	6-2	280	08/08/29	Tulane	12
86	Howton, Bill	E	6-2	190	07/05/30	Rice	12
70	Hunter, Art	T	6-4	240	04/24/33	Notre Dame	12
40	Johnson, Joe	HB	6-0	185	11/03/29	Boston College	12
84	Knafelc, Gary	E	6-4	205	01/02/32	Colorado	8
81	Knutson, Gene	E	6-2	205	11/10/32	Michigan	12
87	Mann, Bob	E	5-11	175	04/08/24	Michigan	1
83	Martinkovic, John	DE	6-3	245	02/04/27	Xavier	12
85	McGee, Max	E	6-3	203	07/16/32	Tulane	12
41	Mihajlovich, Lou	E	5-11	175		Indiana	3
20	Miller, Don	DB	6-2	195	05/24/32	SMU	1
48	Psaltis, Jim	HB	6-1	190	12/14/27	USC	11
24	Reid, Floyd (Breezy)	HB	5-10	190	09/04/27	Georgia	12
51	Ringo, Jim	C	6-1	230	11/21/32	Syracuse	12
18	Rote, Tobin	QB	6-3	205	01/18/28	Rice	12
61	Ruzich, Steve	G	6-2	230	12/24/28	Ohio State	12
28	Self, Clarence	DB	5-9	185	10/25/25	Wisconsin	12
53	Stephenson, Dave	G	6-2	225	10/22/25	West Virginia	12
27	Switzer, Veryl	HB	5-11	190	08/06/32	Kansas State	12
68	Szafaryn, Len	G	6-2	225	01/19/28	North Carolina	12
66	Teteak, Deral	LB	5-10	210	12/11/29	Wisconsin	6
58	Tonnemaker, Clayton	LB	6-2	240	06/08/28	Minnesota	12
47	Walker, Val Joe	DB	6-1	179	01/07/30	SMU	10
88	White, Gene	DE	6-2	205	06/21/30	Georgia	8
74	Zatkoff, Roger	LB	6-2	215	03/25/31	Michigan	12

1954 DRAFT

Rnd	Name	Pos	Ht	Wt	College
1a	Art Hunter	T	6-2	240	Notre Dame
1b	Veryl Switzer	HB	5-11	190	Kansas State
	(Choice from Giants)				
2	Bob Fleck	T	6-2	260	Syracuse
3	George Timberlake	G	6-1	220	USC
4a	(Choice to Redskins for Johnny Papit)				
4b	Tom Allman	FB	6-0	210	West Virginia
	(Choice from Colts)				
5	Max McGee	E	6-2	203	Tulane
6	(Choice to Lions for Gus Cifelli)				
7	Sam Marshall	T	6-2	240	Florida A&M
8	Jimmie Williams	T	6-3	220	Texas Tech
9	Dave Davis	E	6-4	210	Georgia Tech
10	Gene Knutson	E	6-2	205	Michigan
11	Ken Hall	E	6-1	200	North Texas State
12	Bill Oliver	HB	6-2	190	Alabama
13	Mike Takacs	G	6-0	240	Ohio State
14	Dave Johnson (Kosse)	HB	6-0	180	Rice
15	(Choice to 49ers for Ben Aldridge)				
16	Desmond Koch	HB	6-0	205	USC
17	J.D. Roberts	G	5-10	210	Oklahoma
18	Emery Barnes	E	6-6	215	Oregon
19	Ken Hall	C	6-0	220	Springfield
20	Herbert Lowell	G	5-11	215	Pacific
21	Art Liebscher	HB	5-11	180	Pacific
22	Bill Buford	T	6-1	235	Morgan State
23	Clint Sathrum	QB	6-1	195	St. Olaf
24	Marvin Tennefoss	E	6-2	210	Stanford
25	Jack Smalley	T	6-3	225	Alabama
*26	Ralph Baierl	T	6-3	220	Maryland
27	Hosea Sims	E	6-0	192	Marquette
28	Evan Slonac	FB	5-8	175	Michigan State
29	Jerry Dufek	T	6-3	210	St. Norbert
30	Terry Campbell	QB	6-2	172	Washington State
*	denotes juniors				

1954 GREEN BAY PACKERS

FRONT ROW: (L–R) 84 Gary Knafelc, 69 Bill Forester, 37 Howie Ferguson, 61 Steve Ruzich, 68 Len Szafaryn, 88 Gene White, 40 Joe Johnson, Property Man Toby Sylvester.
SECOND ROW: (L–R) 42 Al Carmichael, 70 Art Hunter, 74 Roger Zatkoff, 66 Deral Teteak, 47 Val Joe Walker, 28 Clarence Self, 44 Bobby Dillon, 27 Veryl Switzer, 41 Lou Mihajlovich, Trainer Carl (Bud) Jorgensen.
THIRD ROW: (L–R) Head Coach Lisle Blackbourn, Line Coach Lou Rymkus, 83 John Martinkovic, 86 Bill Howton, 15 Bob Garrett, 53 Dave Stephenson, 75 Dick Afflis, 31 Fred Cone, 63 Al Barry, End Coach Tom Hearden.
BACK ROW: (L–R) 79 Dave Hanner, 62 Bill (Buddy) Brown, 81 Gene Knutson, 85 Max McGee, 80 Carlton Elliott, 72 Jerry Helluin, 58 Clayton Tonnemaker, 18 Tobin Rote, 51 Jim Ringo, 48 Jim Psaltis, Backfield Coach Ray (Scooter) McLean.

- 103 -

1955

The 1955 season opened with a bang – two actually – when the Packers defeated the 1954 Western Conference champion Detroit Lions 20-17 and then followed up with a 24-3 thrashing of the Chicago Bears. Jubilant fans poured onto City Stadium's playing field after both victories. The strong start was followed by another shocker, a 30-28 last-second win over Los Angeles in Milwaukee on October 16. The wins kept the Packers on pace with the Rams and Colts for the first third of the season. Unfortunately, the promising start couldn't be maintained. By the first week of November, the Packers had settled into third place behind the Rams and Bears, a spot they nailed down with a 6-6 mark.

The initial three wins came in dramatic fashion. Gary Knafelc scored on an 18-yard pass from Tobin Rote with 20 seconds left to beat Detroit in the opener. He scored again on a pass from Rote in the final quarter against the Bears, but by then the Packers were out in front 17-3, thanks to a strong rushing game led by Howie Ferguson's 153 yards on 15 carries. Two weeks later, Fred Cone kicked a 25-yard field goal with 24 seconds remaining to edge the Rams by two points.

The Packers could well have been 4-0 instead of 3-1. In week three, Rote was unable to get the ball to Bill Howton from the Colts' 16-yard line on the game's last play and Green Bay fell short 24-20. Nevertheless, the Packers still shared first place after four weeks with the Colts and Rams.

Outstanding performances from some veterans keyed the team's two-game improvement from a year ago. Ferguson, who joined the team in 1953, gained 859 yards rushing, second best in the league behind Alan Ameche's 961. Rote threw 17 touchdown passes which tied Y.A. Tittle's output for the most in the league. Bobby Dillon sparked a defense that led the NFL in interceptions with 31 by stealing nine himself. And Al Carmichael topped the pros with a 29.9 average on 14 kickoff returns; a mark aided by a then-Packer record 100-yard return for a touchdown against Cleveland on October 23.

On area of concern for Coach Lisle Blackbourn was punting. Max McGee had been called up for military service, leaving the team without its regular punter. Blackbourn brought in Dick Deschaine, who had not played football in college, to fill in for McGee. The move proved profitable. Deschaine averaged well over 42 yards for the Packers for the next three years. Though he also could play offensive end, Deschaine was the team's first true kicking specialist.

Another change which brought the game closer to its modern counterpart was the addition of hash marks on City Stadium's playing field. The stripes aided ball placement and made statistical play-by-play easier.

After the early euphoria wore off, the Packers again faced the Lions, Bears and Rams, this time on the road. Green Bay lost all three by a combined 107-58 score, evidence the team was far from back.

Green Bay Press-Gazette photo

Fred Cone (31) kicks a 34-yard field goal in the second quarter of the Packers' thrilling, season-opening, 20-17 win over Detroit. Cone's 25-yard boot with just 25 seconds left beat the Rams 30-28 three weeks later. The fullback converted 30 of 30 extra point trys and made 16 of 24 field goals to lead the team in scoring with 78 points. Holding for Cone is Tobin Rote (18). Leon Hart (82) reaches skyward in a futile attempt to block the kick.

TEAM STATISTICS

	GB	OPP
First Downs	213	196
Rushing	106	118
Passing	95	71
Penalty	12	7
Rushes	433	475
Yards Gained	1,883	2,174
Average Gain	4.35	4.58
Average Yards per Game	156.9	181.2
Passes Attempted	348	259
Completed	159	118
% Completed	45.69	45.56
Total Yards Gained	2,004	1,768
Yards Lost	225	80
Net Yards Gained	1,779	1,688
Yards Gained per Completion	12.60	14.98
Average Net Yards per Game	148.3	140.7
Combined Net Yards Gained	3,662	3,862
Total Plays	781	734
Average Yards per Play	4.69	5.26
Average Net Yards per Game	305.2	321.8
Intercepted By	31	19
Yards Returned	400	268
Returned for TD	0	1
Punts	56	52
Yards Punted	2,420	2,174
Average Yards per Punt	43.21	41.81
Punt Returns	36	36
Yards Returned	280	223
Average Yards per Return	7.78	6.19
Returned for TD	1	1
Kickoff Returns	39	48
Yards Returned	1,002	1,157
Average Yards per Return	25.69	24.10
Returned for TD	1	0
Penalties	41	56
Yards Penalized	401	490
Fumbles	37	27
Lost	25	18
Own Recovered for Touchdown	0	0
Opponent's Recovered by	18	25
Opponent's Recovered for Touchdown	0	3
Total Points Scored	258	276
Total Touchdowns	30	36
Touchdowns Rushing	11	18
Touchdowns Passing	17	13
Touchdowns on Returns & Recoveries	2	5
Extra Points	30	36
Safeties	0	0
Field Goals Attempted	24	17
Field Goals Made	16	8
% Successful	66.67	47.06

Regular Season 6-6-0

Date	GB		OPP	Att.
9/25	20	Detroit Lions	17	(22,217)
10/2	24	Chicago Bears	3	(24,662)
10/8	20	Baltimore Colts (M)	24	(40,199)
10/16	30	Los Angeles Rams (M)	28	(26,960)
10/23	10	at Cleveland Browns	41	(51,482)
10/29	10	at Baltimore Colts	14	(34,411)
11/6	31	at Chicago Bears	52	(48,890)
11/13	31	Chicago Cardinals	14	(20,104)
11/20	27	San Francisco 49ers (M)	21	(19,099)
11/24	10	at Detroit Lions	24	(51,685)
12/4	28	at San Francisco 49ers	7	(34,527)
12/11	17	at Los Angeles Rams	31	(90,535)

Score By Periods

	1	2	3	4	Total
Packers	40	101	45	72	258
Opponents	77	59	58	82	276

INDIVIDUAL STATISTICS

Rushing

	Att	Yds	Avg	LG	TD
Ferguson	192	859	4.5	57	4
Rote	74	332	4.5	49	5
Reid	83	303	3.7	28	2
J. Johnson	49	210	4.3	21	0
Switzer	16	101	6.3	38	0
Carmichael	6	45	7.5	20	0
Cone	12	25	2.1	14	0
Held	1	8	8.0	8	0
Packers	**433**	**1,883**	**4.4**	**57**	**11**
Opponents	475	2,174	4.6	t55	18

1955

Receiving

	No	Yds	Avg	LG	TD
Howton	44	697	15.8	60	5
Knafelc	40	613	15.3	48	8
Ferguson	22	153	7.0	16	0
Carmichael	16	222	13.9	32	1
Switzer	14	103	7.4	22	1
Reid	13	138	10.6	t60	1
J. Johnson	9	71	7.9	30	1
Cone	1	7	7.0	7	0
Packers	**159**	**2,004**	**12.6**	**t60**	**17**
Opponents	118	1,768	15.0	t98	13

Passing

	Att	Com	Yds	Pct	TD	In	YL	Rate
Rote	342	157	1,977	45.9	17	19	218	57.8
Held	4	2	27	50.0	0	0	0	—
Brackins	2	0	0	00.0	0	0	7	—
Packers	**348**	**159**	**2,004**	**45.7**	**17**	**19**	**225**	**57.7**
Opponents	259	118	1,768	45.6	13	31	80	45.6

Punting

	No	Yds	Avg	LG	HB
Deschaine	56	2,420	43.2	73	0
Packers	**56**	**2,420**	**43.2**	**73**	**0**
Opponents	52	2,174	41.8	55	1

Kickoff Returns

	No	Yds	Avg	LG	TD
Switzer	17	445	26.2	57	0
Carmichael	14	418	29.9	t100	1
Forester	3	52	17.3	20	0
J. Johnson	2	46	23.0	27	0
Reid	2	21	10.5	17	0
Ferguson	1	20	20.0	20	0
Packers	**39**	**1,002**	**25.7**	**t100**	**1**
Opponents	48	1,157	24.1	81	0

Punt Returns

	No	Yds	Avg	LG	TD
Switzer	24	158	6.6	38	0
Carmichael	10	89	8.9	40	0
Szafaryn	1	28	28.0	t28	1
J. Johnson	1	5	5.0	5	0
Packers	**36**	**280**	**7.8**	**40**	**1**
Opponents	36	223	6.2	t55	1

Interceptions

	No	Yds	Avg	LG	TD
Dillon	9	153	17.0	61	0
V.J. Walker	6	77	12.8	36	0
Nix	5	33	6.6	12	0
Forester	4	32	8.0	17	0
Zatkoff	3	25	8.3	15	0
Teteak	2	41	20.5	32	0
Bookout	2	39	19.5	27	0
Packers	**31**	**400**	**12.9**	**61**	**0**
Opponents	19	268	14.1	36	1

Scoring

	TDr	TDp	TDrt	PAT	FG	S	TP
Cone	0	0	0	30/30	16/24	0	78
Knafelc	0	8	0	0/0	0/0	0	48
Howton	0	5	0	0/0	0/0	0	30
Rote	5	0	0	0/0	0/0	0	30
Ferguson	4	0	0	0/0	0/0	0	24
Reid	2	1	0	0/0	0/0	0	18
Carmichael	0	1	1	0/0	0/0	0	12
J. Johnson	0	1	0	0/0	0/0	0	6
Switzer	0	1	0	0/0	0/0	0	6
Szafaryn	0	0	1	0/0	0/0	0	6
Packers	**11**	**17**	**2**	**30/30**	**16/24**	**0**	**258**
Opponents	18	13	5	36/36	8/17	0	276

Fumbles

	Fum	Ow	Op	Yds	Tot
Bookout	0	1	2	0	3
Borden	0	0	3	0	3
Bill Brown	0	1	0	0	1
Cone	0	0	1	0	1
Dillon	0	0	1	0	1
Ferguson	8	1	0	0	1
Forester	1	0	0	0	0
Helluin	0	0	1	0	1
Howton	0	0	1	0	1
Jennings	0	0	1	0	1
J. Johnson	4	0	0	0	0
Martinkovic	0	0	1	0	1
Nix	0	0	1	0	1
Reid	4	2	0	0	2
Ringo	0	0	1	0	1
Rote	10	2	0	0	2
Switzer	6	3	0	0	3
Teteak	0	0	3	0	3
V.J. Walker	1	0	1	0	3
Zatkoff	1	0	1	0	1
Packers	**37**	**12**	**18**	**0**	**30**

NFL STANDINGS

Western Conference

	W	L	T	Pct	PF	PA
Los Angeles Rams	8	3	1	.727	260	231
Chicago Bears	8	4	0	.667	294	251
Green Bay Packers	6	6	0	.500	258	276
Baltimore Colts	5	6	1	.455	214	239
San Francisco 49ers	4	8	0	.333	216	298
Detroit Lions	3	9	0	.250	230	275

Eastern Conference

	W	L	T	Pct	PF	PA
Cleveland Browns	9	2	1	.818	349	218
Washington Redskins	8	4	0	.667	246	222
New York Giants	6	5	1	.545	267	223
Chicago Cardinals	4	7	1	.364	224	252
Philadelphia Eagles	4	7	1	.364	248	231
Pittsburgh Steelers	4	8	0	.333	195	285

1955 ROSTER

No	Name	Pos	Ht	Wt	DOB	College	G
58	Bettis, Tom	LB	6-2	225	03/17/33	Purdue	12
20	Bookout, Billy	DB	5-11	180	06/01/32	Austin	12
87	Borden, Nate	DE	6-0	205	09/22/32	Indiana	12
15	Brackins, Charles	QB	6-2	202	01/12/32	Prairie View A&M	7
62	Brown, Bill (Buddy)	G	6-1	225	10/19/26	Arkansas	12
67	Bullough, Hank	G	6-0	220	01/24/34	Michigan State	12
23	Capuzzi, Jim	DB	6-0	190	03/12/32	Cincinnati	3
48	Carmichael, Al	HB	6-1	190	11/10/28	USC	12
33	Clemens, Bob	FB	6-2	200	08/03/33	Georgia	2
31	Cone, Fred	FB	5-11	200	06/21/26	Clemson	12
78	Dahms, Tom	T	6-5	240	04/19/27	San Diego	12
80	Deschaine, Dick	P	6-0	190	04/28/32	No college	12
44	Dillon, Bobby	DB	6-1	180	02/23/30	Texas	12
37	Ferguson, Howie	FB	6-2	212	08/05/30	No college	12
69	Forester, Bill	LB	6-3	235	08/09/32	SMU	12
79	Hanner, Dave	DT	6-2	250	05/20/30	Arkansas	12
15	Held, Paul	QB	6-2	194	10/20/28	San Diego	5
72	Helluin, Jerry	DT	6-2	280	08/08/29	Tulane	12
86	Howton, Bill	E	6-2	190	07/05/30	Rice	12
85	Jennings, Jim	E	6-3	195	11/14/33	Missouri	6
40	Johnson, Joe	HB	6-0	180	11/03/29	Boston College	12
84	Knafelc, Gary	E	6-4	215	01/02/32	Colorado	12
71	Lucky, Bill	DT	6-3	250	08/24/31	Baylor	12
83	Martinkovic, John	DE	6-3	245	02/04/27	Xavier	12
41	Nix, Doyle	DB	6-1	188	05/30/33	SMU	12
81	O'Donahue, Pat	DE	6-2	215	10/07/30	Wisconsin	12
24	Reid, Floyd (Breezy)	HB	5-10	190	09/04/27	Georgia	12
51	Ringo, Jim	C	6-1	230	11/21/32	Syracuse	12
23	Romine, Al	HB	6-2	190	03/10/32	North Alabama	4
18	Rote, Tobin	QB	6-3	215	01/18/28	Rice	12
28	Self, Clarence	DB	5-9	180	10/25/25	Wisconsin	2
63	Skibinski, Joe	G	5-11	228	12/23/28	Purdue	12
61	Spinks, Jack	G	6-1	240	02/04/30	Alcorn State	6
53	Stephenson, Dave	C	6-2	230	10/22/25	West Virginia	2
27	Switzer, Veryl	HB	5-11	190	08/06/32	Kansas State	12
68	Szafaryn, Len	G	6-2	230	01/19/28	North Carolina	12
66	Teteak, Deral	LB	5-10	210	12/11/29	Wisconsin	12
53	Timberlake, George	G	6-1	220	11/03/32	USC	6
47	Walker, Val Joe	DB	6-1	179	01/07/30	SMU	12
74	Zatkoff, Roger	LB	6-2	215	03/25/31	Michigan	12

1955 DRAFT

Rnd	Name	Pos	Ht	Wt	College
1	Tom Bettis	LB	6-2	225	Purdue
2	Jim Temp	DE	6-4	230	Wisconsin
3	John Leake	HB	6-0	185	Oklahoma
4	(Choice to Browns for Jerry Helluin)				
5	Hank Bullough	G	6-2	220	Michigan State
6	Norm Amundsen	G	5-11	222	Wisconsin
7	Bob Clemens	FB	6-0	212	Georgia
8	John Crouch	HB	6-2	195	TCU
9	Ed Culpepper	T	6-1	245	Alabama
*10	George Rogers	T	6-5	247	Auburn
11	Ron Clark	HB	5-11	180	Nebraska
12	Art Walker	T	5-11	220	Michigan
13	Ed Adams	FB	6-2	225	North Carolina
14	Fred Baer	HB	5-11	190	Michigan
15	George Machoukas	C	6-2	220	Toledo
16	Charles Brackins	QB	6-2	202	Prairie View
*17	Ed Beightol	QB	6-1	185	Maryland
18	Doyle Nix	DB	6-1	188	SMU
19	Robert Carter	T	6-3	250	Grambling
20a	Carl Bolt	HB	6-1	185	Southern Mississippi
20b	Bob Antkowiak	T	6-5	240	Bucknell
	(Choice from Giants for John Bauer)				
*21	Lavell Isbell	T	6-3	220	Houston
*22	Bill Brunner	FB	6-3	220	Arkansas Tech
*23	Elton Shaw	T	6-3	225	LSU
24	Charles Bryant	G	6-0	197	Nebraska
25	Nate Borden	DE	6-0	205	Indiana
26	Jim Jennings	E	6-3	205	Missouri
27	Bob Peringer	E	6-3	195	Washington State
28	Jack Spears	T	6-4	230	Tennessee-Chattanooga
29	Sam Pino	FB	5-8	197	Boston U
*30	Bob Sala	FB	6-0	195	Tulane

* denotes juniors

1955 GREEN BAY PACKERS

FRONT ROW: (L-R) 84 Gary Knafelc, 40 Joe Johnson, 23 Jim Capuzzi, 15 Paul Held, 86 Bill Howton, 41 Doyle Nix, 31 Fred Cone, 80 Dick Deschaine.
SECOND ROW: (L-R) 48 Al Carmichael, 37 Howie Ferguson, 24 Floyd (Breezy) Reid, 47 Val Joe Walker, 44 Bobby Dillon, 62 Bill (Buddy) Brown, 74 Roger Zatkoff, 20 Billy Bookout, 27 Veryl Switzer, 66 Deral Teteak.
THIRD ROW: (L-R) Backfield Coach Ray (Scooter) McLean, Line Coach Lou Rymkus, 83 John Martinkovic, 87 Nate Borden, 78 Tom Dahms, 71 Bill Lucky, 72 Jerry Helluin, 81 Pat O'Donahue, End Coach Tom Hearden, Head Coach Lisle Blackbourn.
BACK ROW: (L-R) 68 Len Szafaryn, 61 Jack Spinks, 58 Tom Bettis, 63 Joe Skibinski, 67 Hank Bullough, 69 Bill Forester, 51 Jim Ringo, 79 Dave Hanner, Trainer Carl (Bud) Jorgensen, Equipment Manager Toby Sylvester.

- 107 -

Hopes were especially high going into the 1956 season. The team was coming off its best year since 1952. The Packers produced a 4-1 preaseason record which included a 21-20 triumph over the NFL champion Browns. And finally, most of the players who had pushed Green Bay to first place after nine weeks a year ago returned, bolstered by a good crop of rookies that included tackle Forrest Gregg and defensive back Hank Gremminger.

For four weeks the Packers were able to stay in the race. After beating the Rams 42-17 in Milwaukee, Green Bay (2-2) trailed only Detroit (4-0) and the Bears (3-1). A four-game losing streak followed, however. When it finally ended on Thanksgiving Day, the Packers had been mathematically eliminated.

A major trouble spot was Green Bay's defense. Ranked sixth a year ago, it dropped to last. No team gave up more first downs, more yardage or more rushing yardage than the Packers. Green Bay gave up yards at the rate of 392.5 per game, a dubious feat that included the team's most generous day in history. On December 16, the Rams piled up 611 yards and walloped the Packers 49-21.

Offensively, the Packers improved from seventh to fifth on the strength of a passing game that ranked second only to the Rams. Tobin Rote led the league in passing yards with 2,203 and again in touchdown passes, this time with 18. Bill Howton finished second to Billy Wilson of the 49ers with 55 receptions, but Howton's 1,188 yards and 12 touchdowns led the league.

Rote and Howton keyed an attack that, when it outgained opponents, was able to win. The Packers generated more yards than the Colts, Rams, Lions, and Cardinals and won all four games.

Of the four victories, one stood out. On November 22, the Packers beat Detroit 24-20. The win was the first the Packers earned against the Lions on Thanksgiving Day. Rote hit Howton with a 13-yard pass for the deciding score with just over a minute-and-a-half remaining and Bobby Dillon intercepted Bobby Layne with 38 seconds left to kill any final Detroit hopes.

Besides the porous defense, Coach Lisle Blackbourn had another worry early. Fred Cone, the NFL's leading field goal kicker in 1955, annouced his retirement during the off-season. Blackbourn looked high and wide but nobody could fill Cone's shoes. In the early weeks of camp, fullback Bob Laugherty looked like the best bet, but he called it quits following an intrasquad game on August 4 and the Packers were left virtually without a kicker. Fortunately, Blackbourn was able to talk Cone back into football a few days later. The veteran fullback went on to tie Howton for scoring honors with 72 points.

The team lost eight games in 1956 and finished in a tie with the Lions for last place. One of those losses, a narrow 17-16 setback to the 49ers on November 18, closed another chapter in Packers' history. On that day, before 17,986 fans, Green Bay played its final game at old City Stadium. Al Carmichael, Howie Ferguson and Rote all lost fumbles in the final six minutes to insure that the Packers' last game in the old wooden structure was less than memorable.

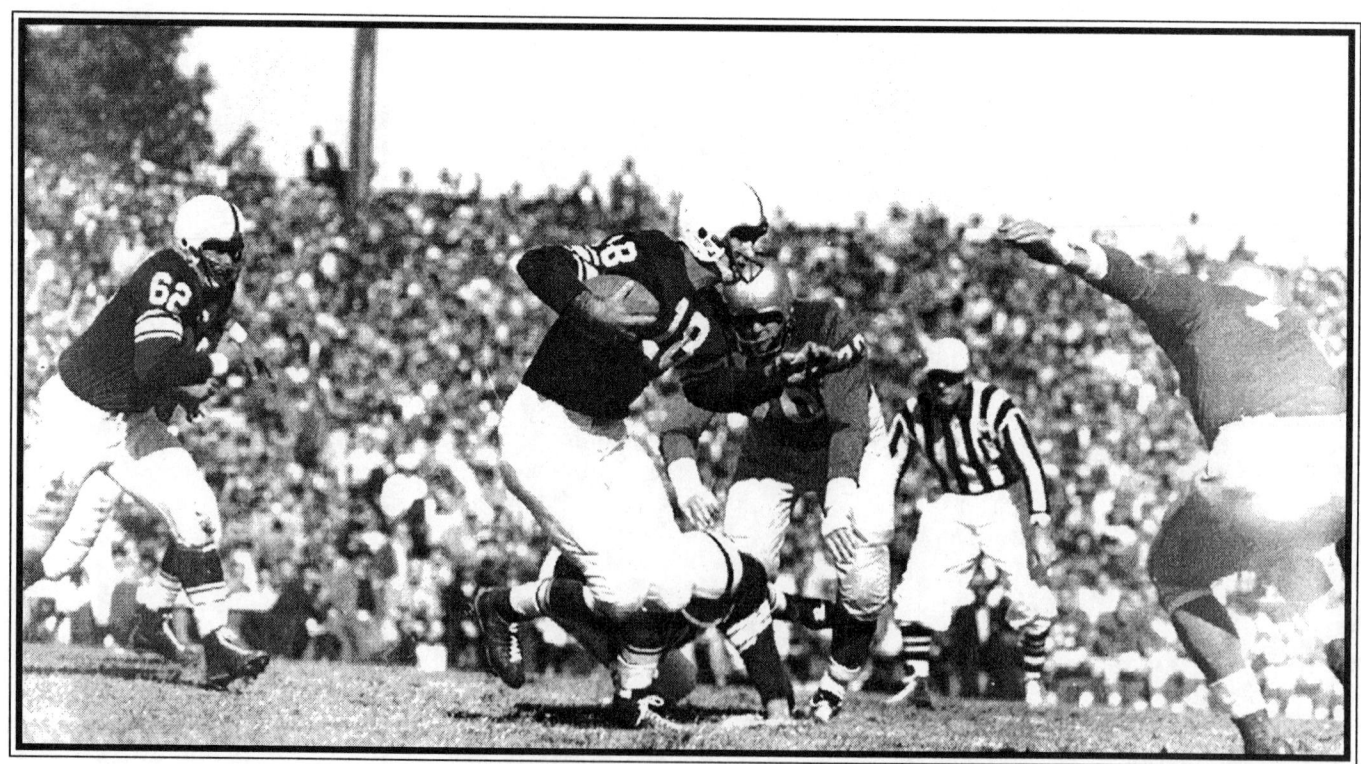

Green Bay Press-Gazette photo

Tobin Rote (18) scrambles for yardage against the Lions in Green Bay on September 30. Rote, who led the NFL with 2,203 yards passing and 18 touchdowns, gained 30 yards on nine carries in the 20-16 loss. Rote went on to throw for 301 yards in the rematch, a 24-20 victory on Thanksgiving Day. Bill (Buddy) Brown (62) trails Rote.

TEAM STATISTICS

	GB	OPP
First Downs	212	246
Rushing	86	129
Passing	112	104
Penalty	14	13
Rushes	337	512
Yards Gained	1,421	2,619
Average Gain	4.22	5.12
Average Yards per Game	118.4	218.3
Passes Attempted	353	260
Completed	171	144
% Completed	48.44	55.38
Total Yards Gained	2,591	2,166
Yards Lost	193	75
Net Yards Gained	2,398	2,091
Yards Gained per Completion	15.15	15.04
Average Net Yards per Game	199.8	174.3
Combined Net Yards Gained	3,819	4,710
Total Plays	690	772
Average Yards per Play	5.53	6.10
Average Net Yards per Game	318.3	392.5
Intercepted By	21	18
Yards Returned	406	312
Returned for TD	1	3
Punts	62	50
Yards Punted	2,649	2,040
Average Yards per Punt	42.73	40.80
Punt Returns	30	49
Yards Returned	239	280
Average Yards per Return	7.97	5.71
Returned for TD	0	1
Kickoff Returns	59	48
Yards Returned	1,442	924
Average Yards per Return	24.44	19.25
Returned for TD	1	0
Penalties	42	52
Yards Penalized	393	493
Fumbles	24	17
Lost	11	8
Own Recovered for Touchdown	0	0
Opponent's Recovered by	8	11
Opponent's Recovered for Touchdown	0	2
Total Points Scored	264	342
Total Touchdowns	36	44
Touchdowns Rushing	13	21
Touchdowns Passing	21	17
Touchdowns on Returns & Recoveries	2	6
Extra Points	33	42
Safeties	0	0
Field Goals Attempted	8	18
Field Goals Made	5	12
% Successful	62.50	66.67

Regular Season 4-8-0

Date	GB		OPP	Att.
9/30	16	Detroit Lions	20	(24,668)
10/7	21	Chicago Bears	37	(24,668)
10/14	38	Baltimore Colts (M)	33	(24,214)
10/21	42	Los Angeles Rams (M)	17	(24,200)
10/28	21	at Baltimore Colts	28	(40,086)
11/4	7	Cleveland Browns (M)	24	(28,590)
11/11	14	at Chicago Bears	38	(49,172)
11/18	16	San Francisco 49ers	17	(17,986)
11/22	24	at Detroit Lions	20	(54,087)
12/2	24	at Chicago Cardinals	21	(22,620)
12/8	20	at San Francisco 49ers	38	(32,436)
12/16	21	at Los Angeles Rams	49	(45,209)

Score By Periods

	1	2	3	4	Total
Packers	51	61	62	90	264
Opponents	78	125	54	85	342

INDIVIDUAL STATISTICS

Rushing

	Att	Yds	Avg	LG	TD
Rote	84	398	4.7	39	11
Ferguson	99	367	3.7	24	0
Cone	49	211	4.3	21	2
Carmichael	32	199	6.2	35	0
J. Johnson	35	129	3.7	14	0
Losch	19	43	2.3	8	0
Reid	14	39	2.8	11	0
Starr	5	35	7.0	14	0
Packers	**337**	**1,421**	**4.2**	**39**	**13**
Opponents	512	2,619	5.1	t86	21

Receiving

	No	Yds	Avg	LG	TD
Howton	55	1,188	21.6	t66	12
Knafelc	30	418	13.9	38	6
J. Johnson	28	258	9.2	20	0
Ferguson	22	214	9.7	25	0
Carmichael	13	180	13.8	63	1
Cone	12	218	18.2	t69	2
Losch	7	85	12.1	43	0
Reid	3	16	5.3	12	0
Roberts	1	14	14.0	14	0
Packers	**171**	**2,591**	**15.2**	**t69**	**21**
Opponents	144	2,166	15.0	t70	17

Passing

	Att	Com	Yds	Pct	TD	In	YL	Rate
Rote	308	146	2,203	47.4	18	15	177	70.6
Starr	44	24	325	54.5	2	3	16	65.1
Losch	1	1	63	100.0	1	0	0	—
Packers	**353**	**171**	**2,591**	**48.4**	**21**	**18**	**193**	**71.6**
Opponents	260	144	2,166	55.4	17	21	75	71.1

Punting

	No	Yds	Avg	LG	HB
Deschaine	62	2,649	42.7	57	0
Packers	**62**	**2,649**	**43.2**	**57**	**0**
Opponents	50	2,040	40.8	56	0

Kickoff Returns

	No	Yds	Avg	LG	TD
Carmichael	33	927	28.1	t106	1
Losch	15	390	26.0	51	0
Ferguson	5	83	16.6	34	0
Forester	4	56	9.0	17	0
Gremminger	1	6	6.0	6	0
Borden	1	0	0.0	0	0
Packers	**59**	**1,442**	**24.4**	**t106**	**1**
Opponents	48	924	19.3	45	0

Punt Returns

	No	Yds	Avg	LG	TD
Carmichael	21	165	7.9	22	0
Losch	8	74	9.3	58	0
Reid	1	0	0.0	0	0
Packers	**30**	**239**	**8.0**	**58**	**0**
Opponents	49	280	5.7	t90	1

Interceptions

	No	Yds	Avg	LG	TD
Dillon	7	244	34.9	45	1
Forester	4	35	8.8	13	0
Capuzzi	2	65	32.5	65	0
Gremminger	2	36	18.0	21	0
Teteak	2	20	10.0	18	0
Gorgal	2	2	1.0	2	0
Bookout	1	4	4.0	4	0
V.J. Walker	1	0	0.0	0	0
Packers	**21**	**406**	**19.3**	**65**	**1**
Opponents	18	312	17.3	t95	3

Scoring

	TDr	TDp	TDrt	PAT	FG	S	TP
Cone	2	2	0	33/35	5/8	0	72
Howton	0	12	0	0/0	0/0	0	72
Rote	11	0	0	0/0	0/0	0	66
Knafelc	0	6	0	0/0	0/0	0	36
Carmichael	0	1	1	0/0	0/0	0	12
Dillon	0	0	1	0/0	0/0	0	6
Packers	**13**	**21**	**2**	**33/36**	**5/8**	**0**	**264**
Opponents	21	17	6	42/44	12/18	0	342

Fumbles

	Fum	Ow	Op	Yds	Tot
Capuzzi	0	0	1	0	1
Carmichael	6	1	0	0	1
Cone	2	1	1	0	2
Dillon	0	0	1	0	1
Ferguson	6	3	0	0	3
Forester	0	0	1	0	1
Hanner	0	0	1	0	1
J. Johnson	1	0	0	0	0
Losch	3	3	0	0	3
Martinkovic	0	0	1	0	1
Reid	0	0	0	0	0
Ringo	0	2	0	0	2
Rote	5	1	0	0	1
Szafaryn	0	1	1	0	1
Teteak	0	0	2	0	2
Zatkoff	0	0	1	0	1
Packers	**24**	**13**	**8**	**0**	**21**

NFL STANDINGS

Western Conference

	W	L	T	Pct	PF	PA
Chicago Bears	9	2	1	.818	363	246
Detroit Lions	9	3	0	.750	300	188
San Francisco 49ers	5	6	1	.455	233	284
Baltimore Colts	5	7	0	.417	270	322
Green Bay Packers	**4**	**8**	**0**	**.333**	**264**	**342**
Los Angeles Rams	4	8	0	.333	291	307

Eastern Conference

	W	L	T	Pct	PF	PA
New York Giants	8	3	1	.727	264	197
Chicago Cardinals	7	5	0	.583	240	182
Washington Redskins	6	6	0	.500	183	225
Cleveland Browns	5	7	0	.417	167	177
Pittsburgh Steelers	5	7	0	.417	217	250
Philadelphia Eagles	3	8	1	.273	143	215

1956 ROSTER

No	Name	Pos	Ht	Wt	DOB	College	G
85	Barnes, Emery	DE	6-6	235	12/15/29	Oregon	2
65	Bettis, Tom	LB	6-2	230	03/17/33	Purdue	12
20	Bookout, Billy	DB	5-11	180	06/01/32	Austin	7
87	Borden, Nate	DE	6-0	225	09/22/32	Indiana	12
62	Brown, Bill (Buddy)	G	6-1	225	10/19/26	Arkansas	12
26	Capuzzi, Jim	DB	6-0	190	03/12/32	Cincinnati	7
48	Carmichael, Al	HB	6-1	190	11/10/28	USC	12
31	Cone, Fred	FB	5-11	200	06/21/26	Clemson	12
80	Deschaine, Dick	P	6-0	210	04/28/32	No college	12
44	Dillon, Bobby	DB	6-1	180	02/23/30	Texas	12
37	Ferguson, Howie	FB	6-2	215	08/05/30	No college	11
69	Forester, Bill	LB	6-3	235	08/09/32	SMU	12
26	Gorgal, Ken	DB	6-2	210	02/13/29	Purdue	5
75	Gregg, Forrest	G	6-4	240	10/18/33	SMU	11
46	Gremminger, Hank	DB	6-1	195	09/01/33	Baylor	12
79	Hanner, Dave	DT	6-2	255	05/20/30	Arkansas	12
72	Helluin, Jerry	DT	6-2	265	08/08/29	Tulane	12
86	Howton, Bill	E	6-2	190	07/05/30	Rice	12
40	Johnson, Joe	HB	6-0	180	11/03/29	Boston College	11
70	King, Don	DT	6-3	265	03/11/29	Kentucky	6
84	Knafelc, Gary	E	6-4	215	01/02/32	Colorado	12
81	Knutson, Gene	E	6-2	230	11/10/32	Michigan	6
58	Lauer, Larry	C	6-3	235	08/27/29	Alabama	6
25	Losch, John	HB	6-1	205	08/13/34	Miami (FL)	12
83	Martinkovic, John	DE	6-3	245	02/04/27	Xavier	12
24	Reid, Floyd (Breezy)	HB	5-10	190	09/04/27	Georgia	7
51	Ringo, Jim	C	6-1	235	11/21/32	Syracuse	12
22	Roberts, Bill	HB	6-0	200	09/11/29	Dartmouth	4
18	Rote, Tobin	QB	6-3	215	01/18/28	Rice	12
77	Sandusky, John	DT	6-1	250	12/28/25	Villanova	12
63	Skibinski, Joe	G	5-11	230	12/23/28	Purdue	12
76	Skoronski, Bob	T	6-3	250	03/05/34	Indiana	12
61	Smith, Jerry	G	6-0	230	09/09/30	Wisconsin	3
61	Spinks, Jack	G	6-1	240	02/04/30	Alcorn State	1
15	Starr, Bart	QB	6-1	200	01/09/34	Alabama	9
68	Szafaryn, Len	G	6-2	225	01/19/28	North Carolina	12
66	Teteak, Deral	LB	5-10	210	12/11/29	Wisconsin	12
47	Walker, Val Joe	DB	6-1	180	01/07/30	SMU	12
23	Young, Glenn	DB	6-2	205	12/22/30	Purdue	4
74	Zatkoff, Roger	LB	6-2	215	03/25/31	Michigan	12

1956 DRAFT

Rnd	Name	Pos	Ht	Wt	College
1	John Losch	HB	6-1	205	Miami (FL)
2	Forrest Gregg	T	6-4	240	SMU
3	(Choice to Rams in Tom Dahms deal)				
4	Cecil Morris	G	6-2	230	Oklahoma
5	Bob Skoronski	T	6-3	250	Indiana
6	Bob Burris	HB	6-0	190	Oklahoma
7	Hank Gremminger	E	6-1	195	Baylor
8	Russ Dennis	E	6-3	215	Maryland
9	Gordon Duvall	FB	6-0	200	USC
10	Bob Laugherty	FB	6-0	210	Maryland
*11	Mike Hudock	C	6-2	220	Miami (FL)
12	Max Burnett	HB	6-0	190	Arizona
13	James Mense	C	6-1	220	Notre Dame
14	Charlie Thomas	FB	5-11	217	Wisconsin
15	Buddy Allison Vaughn	G	6-0	210	Mississippi
16	Curtis Lynch	T	6-3	230	Alabama
17	Bart Starr	QB	6-1	200	Alabama
18	Stan Intihar	E	6-3	220	Cornell
*19	Ken Vakey	E	6-3	200	Texas Tech
*20	Clyde Letbetter	G	6-2	225	Baylor
21	Hal O'Brien	FB	6-0	200	SMU
22	John Popson	HB	6-1	195	Furman
*23	Jesse Birchfield	G	6-2	220	Duke
24	Don Wilson	C	6-3	215	Rice
25	Franz Koeneke	E	6-2	220	Minnesota
26	Dick Goehe	T	6-4	225	Mississippi
27	Dick Kolian	E	6-2	212	Wisconsin
28	Bob Lance	QB	6-1	185	Florida
29	Vester Newcomb	C	6-2	200	Southwest Jr. College
30	Rod Hermes	QB	6-2	202	Beloit

* denotes juniors

1956 GREEN BAY PACKERS

FRONT ROW: (L-R) 83 John Martinkovic, 69 Bill Forester, 26 Jim Capuzzi, 80 Dick Deschaine, 84 Gary Knafelc, 86 Bill Howton, 66 Deral Teteak, 47 Val Joe Walker, 44 Bobby Dillon, 37 Howie Ferguson, 24 Floyd (Breezy) Reid, 61 Jerry Smith, 58 Larry Lauer.

MIDDLE ROW: (L-R) Propertyman Gerald (Dad) Braisher, Head Coach Lisle Blackbourn, Defensive Line Coach Earl Klapstein, 74 Roger Zatkoff, 68 Len Szafaryn, 48 Al Carmichael, 31 Fred Cone, 46 Hank Gremminger, 25 John Losch, 63 Joe Skibinski, 40 Joe Johnson, 22 Bill Roberts, Backfield Coach Ray (Scooter) McLean, Offensive Line Coach Lou Rymkus, Trainer Carl (Bud) Jorgensen.

BACK ROW: (L-R) Defensive Backfield Coach Emmett (Abe) Stuber, 51 Jim Ringo, 79 Dave Hanner, 62 Bill (Buddy) Brown, 81 Gene Knutson, 72 Jerry Helluin, 15 Bart Starr, 18 Tobin Rote, 77 John Sandusky, 23 Glenn Young, 65 Tom Bettis, 87 Nate Borden, 76 Bob Skoronski, 75 Forrest Gregg, 20 Billy Bookout.

1957

On September 29, 1957, the Packers inaugurated play in new City Stadium. A crowd of 32,132 turned out to see the Packers upend the Bears 21-17. Vito (Babe) Parilli, who completed nine of 17 passes for 197 yards, passed six yards to Gary Knafelc for the winning touchdown with 8:21 left. Knafelc caught 4 passes for 70 yards while Bill Howton snagged 8 for 165.

The game put the finishing touches on a weekend that saw James Arness, *Gunsmoke's* Matt Dillon, Miss America Marilyn Elaine Van Derbur and Vice-President Richard M. Nixon come to town. A parade was staged the Saturday before the game as well as a farewell ceremony to the old stadium. That evening, 20 or so lighted yachts graced the Fox River in a Venetian Nights display.

Unfortunately, after that initial excitement, the season bogged down. The Packers lost six of their next seven games and settled into last place. The team's final 3-9 record tied the Cardinals for worst in the league and cost Coach Lisle Blackbourn his job.

Blackbourn, who had begun his tenure with a large trade, worked three major deals in his final year. In April he sent Roger Zatkoff and Bobby Garrett to Cleveland for Carlton Massey, John Macerelli, Sam Palumbo, Parilli, John Petitbon and Billy Kinard. In July, Tobin Rote and Val Joe Walker were shipped to the Lions for Oliver Spencer, Norm Masters, Jim Salsbury and Don McIlhenny. Then in September, Blackbourn traded John Martinkovic to the Giants for a third-round draft choice.

Of the four teams involved in the trades, the Lions appeared to benefit the most. Rote led the Lions to the NFL title after Bobby Layne broke his leg late in the year.

But the Packers profited also. All but Macerelli made the team. McIlhenny lasted three years at fullback and Masters went on to play tackle for eight years. Perhaps the most significant result of the trades was the pick obtained for Martinkovic. The Packers used it to select Ray Nitschke in 1958.

The Packers also owned the bonus pick in 1957. With it they selected Paul Hornung, the Heisman trophy quarterback from Notre Dame. Though he gained 319 yards rushing in his rookie year, his biggest contributions were yet to come.

After beating Pittsburgh on November 24, Green Bay lost its last three games. Blackbourn was released in early January.

Green Bay Press-Gazette photo

Bobby Dillon (44) intercepts a pass intended for Harlon Hill (87) and ends the Bears last threat with just under four minutes remaining in the first game played at new City Stadium, September 29. Green Bay defenders intercepted five Chicago passes and the Packers prevailed 21-17. Dillon and John Symank shared the team lead in interceptions with nine. Gene Schroeder (88) and John Petitbon (20) witness the action.

TEAM STATISTICS

	GB	OPP
First Downs	179	226
Rushing	72	117
Passing	90	97
Penalty	17	12
Rushes	380	462
Yards Gained	1,441	2,159
Average Gain	3.79	4.67
Average Yards per Game	120.1	179.9
Passes Attempted	325	314
Completed	157	153
% Completed	48.31	48.73
Total Yards Gained	2,157	2,185
Yards Lost	366	147
Net Yards Gained	1,791	2,038
Yards Gained per Completion	13.74	14.28
Average Net Yards per Game	149.3	169.8
Combined Net Yards Gained	3,232	4,197
Total Plays	705	776
Average Yards per Play	4.58	5.41
Average Net Yards per Game	269.3	349.8
Intercepted By	30	23
Yards Returned	561	252
Returned for TD	1	2
Punts	63	50
Yards Punted	2,645	2,151
Average Yards per Punt	41.98	43.02
Punt Returns	36	40
Yards Returned	256	149
Average Yards per Return	7.11	3.73
Returned for TD	0	0
Kickoff Returns	58	42
Yards Returned	1,261	897
Average Yards per Return	21.74	21.36
Returned for TD	0	0
Penalties	43	75
Yards Penalized	516	709
Fumbles	28	26
Lost	18	17
Own Recovered for Touchdown	0	0
Opponent's Recovered by	17	18
Opponent's Recovered for Touchdown	0	0
Total Points Scored	218	311
Total Touchdowns	26	39
Touchdowns Rushing	13	18
Touchdowns Passing	12	18
Touchdowns on Returns & Recoveries	1	3
Extra Points	26	39
Safeties	0	1
Field Goals Attempted	21	22
Field Goals Made	12	12
% Successful	57.14	54.55

Regular Season 3-9-0

Date	GB		OPP	Att.
9/29	21	Chicago Bears	17	(32,132)
10/6	14	Detroit Lions	24	(32,120)
10/13	17	Baltimore Colts (M)	45	(26,322)
10/20	14	San Francisco 49ers (M)	24	(18,919)
10/27	24	at Baltimore Colts	21	(48,510)
11/3	24	New York Giants	31	(32,070)
11/10	14	at Chicago Bears	21	(47,183)
11/17	27	Los Angeles Rams (M)	31	(19,540)
11/24	27	at Pittsburgh Steelers	10	(29,701)
11/28	6	at Detroit Lions	18	(54,301)
12/8	17	at Los Angeles Rams	42	(70,572)
12/15	20	at San Francisco 49ers	27	(59,522)

Score By Periods

	1	2	3	4	Total
Packers	30	99	7	82	218
Opponents	72	61	84	94	311

INDIVIDUAL STATISTICS

Rushing

	Att	Yds	Avg	LG	TD
McIlhenny	100	384	3.8	t40	1
Hornung	60	319	5.3	72	3
Ferguson	59	216	3.7	t40	1
Cone	53	135	2.5	t26	2
Carmichael	37	118	3.2	10	1
Starr	31	98	3.2	16	3
Parilli	24	83	3.5	20	2
McGee	5	40	8.0	24	0
Purnell	5	22	4.4	7	0
Howton	4	20	5.0	11	0
J. Johnson	2	6	3.0	3	0
Packers	380	1,441	3.8	72	13
Opponents	462	2,159	4.7	76	18

1957

Receiving

	No	Yds	Avg	LG	TD
Howton	38	727	19.1	t77	5
R. Kramer	28	337	12.0	31	0
McIlhenny	18	210	11.7	t28	2
McGee	17	273	16.1	49	1
Ferguson	15	107	7.1	17	1
Carmichael	13	184	14.2	39	0
Knafelc	9	164	18.2	53	2
J. Johnson	7	75	10.7	14	1
Hornung	6	34	5.7	16	0
Cone	4	30	7.5	10	0
Purnell	2	16	8.0	15	0
Packers	157	2,157	13.7	t77	12
Opponents	153	2,185	14.3	t61	18

Passing

	Att	Com	Yds	Pct	TD	In	YL	Rate
Starr	215	117	1,489	54.4	8	10	231	69.3
Parilli	102	39	669	38.2	4	12	125	34.8
Hornung	6	1	-1	16.7	0	0	10	—
Ferguson	1	0	0	00.0	0	0	0	—
R. Kramer	1	0	0	00.0	0	1	0	—
Packers	325	157	2,157	48.3	12	23	366	52.8
Opponents	314	153	2,185	48.7	18	30	147	51.2

Punting

	No	Yds	Avg	LG	HB
Deschaine	63	2,645	42.0	71	2
Packers	63	2,645	42.0	71	2
Opponents	50	2,151	43.0	66	0

Kickoff Returns

	No	Yds	Avg	LG	TD
Carmichael	31	690	22.3	33	0
McIlhenny	14	362	25.9	53	0
Cone	5	83	16.6	25	0
McGee	4	69	17.3	32	0
Forester	4	57	14.3	27	0
Packers	58	1,261	21.7	53	0
Opponents	42	897	21.4	46	0

Punt Returns

	No	Yds	Avg	LG	TD
Carmichael	25	190	7.6	48	0
J. Johnson	4	39	9.8	13	0
Kinard	3	19	6.3	19	0
Symank	3	0	0.0	0	0
Dillon	1	8	8.0	8	0
Packers	36	256	7.1	48	0
Opponents	40	149	3.7	22	0

Interceptions

	No	Yds	Avg	LG	TD
Symank	9	198	22.0	36	0
Dillon	9	180	20.0	t55	1
Gremminger	5	93	18.6	45	0
Forester	4	79	19.8	37	0
Palumbo	1	11	11.0	11	0
Helluin	1	0	0.0	0	0
Petitbon	1	0	0.0	0	0
Packers	30	561	18.7	t55	1
Opponents	23	252	11.0	t52	2

Scoring

	TDr	TDp	TDrt	PAT	FG	S	TP
Cone	2	0	0	26/26	12/17	0	74
Howton	0	5	0	0/0	0/0	0	30
Hornung	3	0	0	0/0	0/4	0	18
McIlhenny	1	2	0	0/0	0/0	0	18
Starr	3	0	0	0/0	0/0	0	18
Ferguson	1	1	0	0/0	0/0	0	12
Knafelc	0	2	0	0/0	0/0	0	12
Parilli	2	0	0	0/0	0/0	0	12
Carmichael	1	0	0	0/0	0/0	0	6
Dillon	0	0	1	0/0	0/0	0	6
J. Johnson	0	1	0	0/0	0/0	0	6
McGee	0	1	0	0/0	0/0	0	6
Packers	13	12	1	26/26	12/21	0	218
Opponents	18	18	3	39/39	12/22	1	311

Fumbles

	Fum	Ow	Op	Yds	Tot
Bettis	0	0	1	0	1
Borden	0	0	2	0	2
Carmichael	3	1	0	0	1
Cone	2	1	0	0	1
Danjean	0	0	1	0	1
Ferguson	2	0	0	0	0
Forester	1	1	3	45	4
Gremminger	1	0	0	0	0
Helluin	0	0	3	0	3
Hornung	2	0	0	0	0
Howton	1	0	0	0	0
Kinard	0	0	1	3	1
R. Kramer	1	0	0	0	0
Lauer	0	0	1	0	1
Masters	0	1	0	0	1
McIlhenny	4	1	0	0	1
Parilli	3	1	0	0	1
Petitbon	0	0	1	0	1
Purnell	1	0	0	0	1
Salsbury	0	0	1	0	1
O. Spencer	0	0	1	0	1
Starr	4	1	0	0	1
Symank	1	0	2	0	2
Temp	0	1	1	4	2
Packers	28	10	17	52	27

NFL STANDINGS

Western Conference

	W	L	T	Pct	PF	PA
Detroit Lions	8	4	0	.667	251	231
San Francisco 49ers	8	4	0	.667	260	264
Baltimore Colts	7	5	0	.583	303	235
Los Angeles Rams	6	6	0	.500	307	278
Chicago Bears	5	7	0	.417	203	211
Green Bay Packers	3	9	0	.250	218	311

Eastern Conference

	W	L	T	Pct	PF	PA
Cleveland Browns	9	2	1	.818	269	172
New York Giants	7	5	0	.583	254	211
Pittsburgh Steelers	6	6	1	.455	251	230
Philadelphia Eagles	4	8	0	.333	173	230
Chicago Cardinals	3	9	0	.250	200	299

1957 ROSTER

No	Name	Pos	Ht	Wt	DOB	College	G
62	Amundsen, Norm	G	5-11	245	09/28/32	Wisconsin	12
66	Barry, Al	G	6-2	235	12/24/30	USC	12
65	Bettis, Tom	LB	6-2	235	03/17/33	Purdue	12
87	Borden, Nate	DE	6-0	235	09/22/32	Indiana	9
48	Carmichael, Al	HB	6-1	190	11/10/28	USC	12
31	Cone, Fred	FB	5-11	205	06/21/26	Clemson	12
64	Danjean, Ernest	LB	6-0	230	03/05/34	Auburn	12
80	Deschaine, Dick	P	6-0	215	04/28/32	No college	12
44	Dillon, Bobby	DB	6-1	180	02/23/30	Texas	12
37	Ferguson, Howie	FB	6-2	220	08/05/30	No college	12
69	Forester, Bill	LB	6-3	235	08/09/32	SMU	12
46	Gremminger, Hank	DB	6-1	195	09/01/33	Baylor	12
79	Hanner, Dave	DT	6-2	250	05/20/30	Arkansas	12
72	Helluin, Jerry	DT	6-2	265	08/08/29	Tulane	12
5	Hornung, Paul	HB	6-2	215	12/23/35	Notre Dame	12
86	Howton, Bill	E	6-2	190	07/05/30	Rice	12
40	Johnson, Joe	HB	6-0	180	11/03/29	Boston College	12
25	Kinard, Billy	DB	6-0	185	12/16/33	Mississippi	12
84	Knafelc, Gary	E	6-4	215	01/02/32	Colorado	3
88	Kramer, Ron	E	6-3	220	06/24/35	Michigan	11
58	Lauer, Larry	C	6-3	235	08/27/29	Alabama	12
81	Massey, Carlton	DE	6-4	225	01/17/30	Texas	12
78	Masters, Norm	T	6-2	240	09/19/33	Michigan State	12
85	McGee, Max	E	6-3	205	07/16/32	Tulane	12
42	McIlhenny, Don	HB	6-0	200	11/22/34	SMU	12
53	Palumbo, Sam	LB	6-2	230	06/07/32	Notre Dame	9
10	Parilli, Vito (Babe)	QB	6-1	190	05/07/30	Kentucky	12
20	Petitbon, John	DB	5-11	190	06/04/31	Notre Dame	12
33	Purnell, Frank	FB	5-11	230	04/05/33	Alcorn State	9
51	Ringo, Jim	C	6-1	230	11/21/32	Syracuse	12
67	Salsbury, Jim	G	6-0	235	08/08/32	UCLA	12
77	Spencer, Ollie	T	6-2	250	04/17/31	Kansas	12
15	Starr, Bart	QB	6-1	200	01/09/34	Alabama	12
27	Symank, John	DB	5-11	180	08/31/35	Florida	12
82	Temp, Jim	DE	6-4	230	10/14/33	Wisconsin	12
74	Vereen, Carl	T	6-2	247	01/27/36	Georgia Tech	12

1957 DRAFT

Rnd	Name	Pos	Ht	Wt	College
**	Paul Hornung	HB	6-2	215	Notre Dame
1	Ron Kramer	E	6-3	220	Michigan
2	Joel Wells	HB	6-1	198	Clemson
3	Dalton Truax	T	6-2	230	Tulane
4	Carl Vereen	T	6-2	247	Georgia Tech
5	(Choice to Browns for Don King)				
6a	(Choice to Browns for John Sandusky)				
6b	Jack Nisby	G	6-0	230	Pacific
	(Choice from Cardinals for Tom Dahms)				
7	Frank Gilliam	HB	6-2	185	Iowa
8	George Belotti	T	6-3	240	USC
9	Ken Wineburg	HB	5-11	185	TCU
10	Gary Gustafson	HB	6-1	193	Gustavus Adolphus
11	Jim Roseboro	HB	5-11	180	Ohio State
*12a	Ed Sullivan	C	6-1	190	Notre Dame
12b	Glenn Bestor	B	6-2	215	Wisconsin
	(Choice from Giants for Jack Spinks)				
13	Jim Morse	HB	5-11	185	Notre Dame
14	Rudy Schoendorf	T	6-1	245	Miami (OH)
15	Pat Hinton	G	6-2	230	Louisiana Tech
16	Ed Buckingham	T	6-4	250	Minnesota
*17	Don Boudreaux	T	6-3	220	Houston
18	Credell Grenn	HB	5-10	200	Washington
19	Ernest Danjean	G	6-0	230	Auburn
20	Percy Oliver	G	6-1	205	Illinois
21	Charles Mehrer	T	6-3	230	Missouri
22	Ron Quillian	QB	6-2	205	Tulane
23	John Symank	DB	5-11	180	Florida
24	Charles Leyendecker	T	6-2	220	SMU
*25	Jerry Johnson	T	6-3	250	St. Norbert
26	Buddy Bass	B	6-1	190	Duke
27	Martin Booher	T	6-1	240	Wisconsin
*28	Dave Herbold	G	5-10	225	Minnesota
*29	Howard Dare	RB	6-1	180	Maryland

* denotes juniors
** bonus choice

1957 GREEN BAY PACKERS

FRONT ROW: (L-R) 37 Howie Ferguson, 20 Billy Bookout, 42 Don McIlhenny, 86 Bill Howton, 40 Joe Johnson, 44 Bobby Dillon, 66 Al Barry, 69 Bill Forester, 31 Fred Cone, 84 Gary Knafelc.

SECOND ROW: (L-R) 5 Paul Hornung, 27 John Symank, 46 Hank Gremminger, 15 Bart Starr, 10 Vito (Babe) Parilli, 67 Jim Salsbury, 33 Frank Purnell, 53 Sam Palumbo, 25 Billy Kinard, 81 Carlton Massey, 85 Max McGee.

THIRD ROW: (L-R) Trainer Carl (Bud) Jorgensen, 64 Ernest Danjean, 62 Norm Amundsen, 78 Norm Masters, 88 Ron Kramer, 77 Ollie Spencer, 58 Larry Lauer, 74 Carl Vereen, 87 Nate Borden, Assistant Trainer Gerald (Dad) Braisher.

BACK ROW: (L-R) Backfield Coach Ray (Scooter) McLean, Head Coach Lisle Blackbourn, 63 Joe Skibinski, 72 Jerry Helluin, 65 Tom Bettis, 51 Jim Ringo, 79 Dave Hanner, Offensive Line Coach Lou Rymkus, Defensive Line Coach Jack Morton.

1958

Never before had the Packers spent the entire season in the cellar. That happened in 1958. From the last week of September when the Bears squashed them 34-20, to the second weekend in December when the Rams topped them by the same score, Green Bay held down the lowest spot in the Western Conference.

Amazingly, 17 of the Packers who made up the 1961 championship team were in already in place. But this 1958 team was a far cry from that level. Seven times Green Bay gave up more than 30 points. The Packers allowed every opponent except Detroit at least 300 yards per game and wound up the league's second-from-last defense. Only a tie with the Lions and a narrow three-point win against Philadelphia kept the 1-10-1 Packers from a winless season.

Ray (Scooter) McLean, backfield coach since 1951, became head coach. His relaxation of rules and affable personality were taken advantage of by certain players. In some cases, performance suffered because there was no one to reign them in. Though McLean may have been one of the more popular coaches with players, he didn't endear himself to the fans and was fired at the end of the year.

Green Bay had to hold on just to win its only game. For a while, it looked like the Eagles might stage one of the greatest comebacks in NFL history. Vito (Babe) Parilli threw four touchdown passes in helping the Packers to a 38-14 lead. But Philadelphia scored 21 fourth-quarter points and closed to 38-35 with 54 seconds left. Only after rookie Ray Nitschke recovered the Eagles' subsequent onside kick were the Packers able to nail down the win.

The season's lone win was followed by the most lopsided loss in team history. On November 2, the Packers traveled to Baltimore, where the Colts proceeded to humiliate them 56-0. The Colts ran up 30 first downs to the Packers' eight. Baltimore outgained Green Bay 390-142. Its defense intercepted five Packers' passes while its own quarterbacks passed for five touchdowns. Never before had the Packers been beaten so soundly.

In such a down year, bright spots were hard to find. One rookie who rated a second look was Jim Taylor, the team's second-round pick. Taylor gained 137 yards rushing in 22 trips against the 49ers on the season's second-to-last weekend. He followed with 99 yards a week later in Los Angeles; two solid outings that hinted at better things to come.

Green Bay Press-Gazette photo

In a dismal 1-10-1 season, Max McGee (85) provided some relief. Here he's about to score on a 34-yard pass from Vito (Babe) Parilli in the first quarter of the Packers-Eagles game. McGee's catch put Green Bay in front 10-0. The Packers held on for a 38-35 win, their only of the year. McGee caught six passes for 100 yards and two scores against Philadelphia.

TEAM STATISTICS

	GB	OPP
First Downs	177	236
Rushing	76	109
Passing	87	111
Penalty	14	16
Rushes	345	427
Yards Gained	1,421	2,040
Average Gain	4.12	4.78
Average Yards per Game	118.4	170.0
Passes Attempted	348	336
Completed	161	175
% Completed	46.26	52.08
Total Yards Gained	2,118	2,653
Yards Lost	298	78
Net Yards Gained	1,820	2,575
Yards Gained per Completion	13.16	15.16
Average Net Yards per Game	151.7	214.6
Combined Net Yards Gained	3,241	4,615
Total Plays	693	763
Average Yards per Play	4.68	6.05
Average Net Yards per Game	270.1	384.6
Intercepted By	13	27
Yards Returned	174	371
Returned for TD	1	1
Punts	62	42
Yards Punted	2,625	1,747
Average Yards per Punt	42.34	41.60
Punt Returns	33	46
Yards Returned	179	268
Average Yards per Return	5.42	5.83
Returned for TD	0	0
Kickoff Returns	60	32
Yards Returned	1,309	710
Average Yards per Return	21.82	22.19
Returned for TD	0	0
Penalties	52	72
Yards Penalized	545	657
Fumbles	26	31
Lost	17	19
Own Recovered for Touchdown	0	0
Opponent's Recovered by	19	17
Opponent's Recovered for Touchdown	0	1
Total Points Scored	193	382
Total Touchdowns	23	50
Touchdowns Rushing	7	24
Touchdowns Passing	15	24
Touchdowns on Returns & Recoveries	1	2
Extra Points	22	46
Safeties	0	0
Field Goals Attempted	21	25
Field Goals Made	11	12
% Successful	52.38	48.00

Regular Season 1-10-1

Date	GB		OPP	Att.
9/28	20	Chicago Bears	34	(32,150)
10/5	13	Detroit Lions	13	(32,053)
10/12	17	Baltimore Colts (M)	24	(24,553)
10/19	21	at Washington Redskins	37	(25,228)
10/26	38	Philadelphia Eagles	35	(31,043)
11/2	0	at Baltimore Colts	56	(51,333)
11/9	10	at Chicago Bears	24	(48,424)
11/16	7	Los Angeles Rams	20	(28,051)
11/23	12	San Francisco 49ers (M)	33	(19,786)
11/27	14	at Detroit Lions	24	(50,971)
12/7	21	at San Francisco 49ers	48	(50,792)
12/14	20	at Los Angeles Rams	34	(54,634)

Score By Periods

	1	2	3	4	Total
Packers	63	44	41	45	193
Opponents	77	113	93	99	382

INDIVIDUAL STATISTICS

Rushing

	Att	Yds	Avg	LG	TD
Hornung	69	310	4.5	55	2
Ferguson	59	268	4.5	29	1
J. Taylor	52	247	4.8	25	1
McIlhenny	74	239	3.2	36	1
Francis	24	153	6.4	20	1
Starr	25	113	4.5	20	1
Shanley	23	30	1.3	5	0
Carmichael	9	21	2.3	8	0
Parilli	8	15	1.9	5	0
Ringo	0	13	—	13	0
McGee	1	9	9.0	9	0
Salsbury	0	3	—	3	0
Romine	1	0	0.0	0	0
Packers	**345**	**1,421**	**4.1**	**55**	**7**
Opponents	427	2,040	4.8	t80	24

Receiving

	No	Yds	Avg	LG	TD
McGee	37	655	17.7	t80	7
Howton	36	507	14.1	50	2
McIlhenny	20	154	7.7	t55	1
Hornung	15	137	9.1	39	0
Meilinger	13	139	10.7	19	1
Ferguson	12	121	10.1	27	0
J. Johnson	10	176	17.6	61	1
Knafelc	8	118	14.8	40	1
J. Taylor	4	72	18.0	t31	1
Carmichael	3	26	8.7	t14	1
Shanley	3	13	4.3	7	0
Packers	**161**	**2,118**	**13.2**	**t80**	**15**
Opponents	175	2,653	15.2	t93	24

Passing

	Att	Com	Yds	Pct	TD	In	YL	Rate
Parilli	157	68	1,068	43.3	10	13	89	53.3
Starr	157	78	875	49.7	3	12	147	41.2
Francis	31	15	175	48.4	2	2	62	60.6
Ferguson	1	0	0	00.0	0	0	0	—
Hornung	1	0	0	00.0	0	0	0	—
McGee	1	0	0	00.0	0	0	0	—
Packers	**348**	**161**	**2,118**	**46.3**	**15**	**27**	**298**	**48.0**
Opponents	336	175	2,653	52.1	24	13	78	86.1

Punting

	No	Yds	Avg	LG	HB
McGee	62	2,625	42.3	61	0
Packers	**62**	**2,625**	**42.3**	**61**	**0**
Opponents	42	1,747	41.6	61	0

Kickoff Returns

	No	Yds	Avg	LG	TD
Carmichael	29	700	24.1	60	0
Hornung	10	248	24.8	39	0
J. Taylor	7	185	26.4	47	0
McIlhenny	7	146	20.9	45	0
Currie	2	14	7.0	7	0
Massey	1	10	10.0	10	0
Forester	1	6	6.0	6	0
J. Kramer	1	0	0.0	0	0
Nitschke	1	0	0.0	0	0
Temp	1	0	0.0	0	0
Packers	**60**	**1,309**	**21.8**	**60**	**0**
Opponents	32	710	22.2	50	0

Punt Returns

	No	Yds	Avg	LG	TD
Carmichael	15	67	4.5	51	0
Shanley	14	105	7.5	26	0
Romine	2	7	3.5	7	0
McIlhenny	1	0	0.0	0	0
Symank	1	0	0.0	0	0
Packers	**33**	**179**	**5.4**	**51**	**0**
Opponents	46	268	5.8	38	0

Interceptions

	No	Yds	Avg	LG	TD
Dillon	6	134	22.3	46	1
Gremminger	3	15	5.0	14	0
Symank	1	23	23.0	23	0
Nitschke	1	2	2.0	2	0
Romine	1	0	0.0	0	0
Whittenton	1	0	0.0	0	0
Packers	**13**	**174**	**13.4**	**46**	**1**
Opponents	27	371	13.7	69	1

Scoring

	TDr	TDp	TDrt	PAT	FG	S	TP
Hornung	2	0	0	22/23	11/21	0	67
McGee	0	7	0	0/0	0/0	0	42
Howton	0	2	0	0/0	0/0	0	12
McIlhenny	1	1	0	0/0	0/0	0	12
J. Taylor	1	1	0	0/0	0/0	0	12
Carmichael	0	1	0	0/0	0/0	0	6
Dillon	0	0	1	0/0	0/0	0	6
Ferguson	1	0	0	0/0	0/0	0	6
Francis	1	0	0	0/0	0/0	0	6
J. Johnson	0	1	0	0/0	0/0	0	6
Knafelc	0	1	0	0/0	0/0	0	6
Meilinger	0	1	0	0/0	0/0	0	6
Starr	1	0	0	0/0	0/0	0	6
Packers	**7**	**15**	**1**	**22/23**	**11/21**	**0**	**193**
Opponents	24	24	2	46/50	12/25	0	382

Fumbles

	Fum	Ow	Op	Yds	Tot
Bettis	0	0	2	0	2
Borden	0	0	1	0	1
Bullough	0	0	1	0	1
Carmichael	2	0	0	0	0
Ferguson	1	1	0	0	1
Ford	0	0	1	5	1
Forester	0	0	1	0	1
Francis	3	0	0	0	0
Gregg	0	1	0	0	1
Hanner	0	0	2	0	2
Hornung	1	0	1	0	2
J. Johnson	1	0	0	0	0
Kimmel	0	0	1	0	1
Kinard	0	0	1	11	1
Massey	0	0	1	0	1
McGee	1	0	0	0	0
McIlhenny	8	2	0	0	2
Nitschke	0	0	2	0	2
Parilli	4	0	0	0	0
Ringo	0	2	0	0	2
Salsbury	0	0	1	0	1
Shanley	1	0	0	0	0
Starr	2	0	0	0	0
Symank	1	0	3	37	3
J. Taylor	1	0	0	0	0
Whittenton	0	0	2	2	2
Packers	**26**	**9**	**19**	**56**	**28**

NFL STANDINGS

Western Conference

	W	L	T	Pct	PF	PA
Baltimore Colts	9	3	0	.750	381	203
Chicago Bears	8	4	0	.667	298	230
Los Angeles Rams	8	4	0	.667	344	278
San Francisco 49ers	6	6	0	.500	257	324
Detroit Lions	4	7	1	.364	261	276
Green Bay Packers	**1**	**10**	**1**	**.091**	**193**	**382**

Eastern Conference

	W	L	T	Pct	PF	PA
New York Giants	9	3	0	.750	246	183
Cleveland Browns	9	3	0	.750	302	217
Pittsburgh Steelers	7	4	1	.636	261	230
Washington Redskins	4	7	1	.364	214	268
Chicago Cardinals	2	9	1	.182	261	356
Philadelphia Eagles	2	9	1	.182	235	306

1958 ROSTER

No	Name	Pos	Ht	Wt	DOB	College	G
65	Bettis, Tom	LB	6-2	225	03/17/33	Purdue	12
87	Borden, Nate	DE	6-0	240	09/22/32	Indiana	12
61	Bullough, Hank	G	6-0	240	01/24/34	Michigan State	8
48	Carmichael, Al	HB	6-1	195	11/10/28	USC	12
58	Currie, Dan	LB	6-3	235	06/27/35	Michigan State	12
44	Dillon, Bobby	DB	6-1	189	02/23/30	Texas	12
37	Ferguson, Howie	FB	6-2	213	08/05/30	No college	7
83	Ford, Len	DE	6-5	251	02/18/26	Michigan	11
69	Forester, Bill	LB	6-3	240	08/09/32	SMU	12
20	Francis, Joe	QB	6-1	194	04/21/36	Oregon State	12
75	Gregg, Forrest	G	6-4	245	10/18/33	SMU	12
46	Gremminger, Hank	DB	6-1	201	09/01/33	Baylor	12
79	Hanner, Dave	DT	6-2	266	05/20/30	Arkansas	12
5	Hornung, Paul	HB	6-2	211	12/23/35	Notre Dame	12
86	Howton, Bill	E	6-2	195	07/05/30	Rice	12
40	Johnson, Joe	HB	6-0	188	11/03/29	Boston College	6
72	Kimmel, J.D.	DT	6-4	250	09/30/29	Houston	12
25	Kinard, Billy	DB	6-0	202	12/16/33	Mississippi	12
84	Knafelc, Gary	E	6-4	217	01/02/32	Colorado	6
64	Kramer, Jerry	G	6-3	235	01/23/36	Idaho	12
81	Massey, Carlton	DE	6-4	225	01/17/30	Texas	2
78	Masters, Norm	T	6-2	250	09/19/33	Michigan State	12
63	Matuszak, Marv	LB	6-3	235	09/12/31	Tulsa	3
85	McGee, Max	E	6-3	196	07/16/32	Tulane	12
42	McIlhenny, Don	HB	6-0	200	11/22/34	SMU	12
80	Meilinger, Steve	E	6-2	230	12/12/30	Kentucky	12
33	Nitschke, Ray	LB	6-3	220	12/29/36	Illinois	12
10	Parilli, Vito (Babe)	QB	6-1	196	05/07/30	Kentucky	12
51	Ringo, Jim	C	6-1	236	11/21/32	Syracuse	12
23	Romine, Al	HB	6-2	184	03/10/32	North Alabama	12
67	Salsbury, Jim	G	6-0	241	08/08/32	UCLA	12
22	Shanley, Jim	HB	5-9	174	07/27/36	Oregon	12
77	Spencer, Ollie	T	6-2	245	04/17/31	Kansas	12
15	Starr, Bart	QB	6-1	200	01/09/34	Alabama	12
27	Symank, John	DB	5-11	180	08/31/35	Florida	12
31	Taylor, Jim	FB	6-0	205	09/20/35	LSU	12
82	Temp, Jim	DE	6-4	250	10/14/33	Wisconsin	12
47	Whittenton, Jesse	DB	6-0	195	05/09/34	Texas-El Paso	8

1958 DRAFT

Rnd	Name	Pos	Ht	Wt	College
1	Dan Currie	C	6-3	240	Michigan State
2	Jim Taylor	FB	6-0	205	LSU
3a	Dick Christy	HB	5-10	190	North Carolina State
3b	Ray Nitschke	LB	6-3	220	Illinois
	(Choice from Giants for John Martinkovic)				
4	Jerry Kramer	G	6-3	235	Idaho
5	Joe Francis	QB	6-1	194	Oregon State
6	Ken Gray	T	6-2	235	Howard Payne
7	Doug Maison	QB	6-3	200	Hillsdale
8	Mike Bill	C	6-3	225	Syracuse
9	Norm Jarock	HB	6-0	195	St. Norbert
*10	Carl Johnson	T	6-3	230	Illinois
11	Harry Horton	E	6-3	220	Wichita
12	Wayne Miller	E	6-2	195	Baylor
13	Gene Cook	E	6-2	205	Toledo
14	Harry Hauffe	T	6-4	240	South Dakota
*15	Tom Newell	HB	6-2	195	Drake
*16	Arley Finley	T	6-4	240	Georgia Tech
17	Joe Reese	E	6-3	197	Arkansas Tech
18	Charles Strid	G	6-1	225	Syracuse
19	(Choice to Bears for Lee Hermsen)				
20	John Duboise	HB	6-0	150	Trinity (TX)
21	Jerry Kershner	T	6-4	220	Oregon
22	Dick Maggard	HB	5-11	205	College of Idaho
**23	Jack Ashton	G	6-1	220	South Carolina
**24	John Jereck	T	6-4	250	Detroit
25	Larry Plenty	HB	6-1	210	Boston College
26	Esker Harris	G	6-1	210	UCLA
27	Neil Habig	C	6-0	210	Purdue
**28	Dave Crowell	G	6-3	225	Washington State
29	Robert Haynes	T	6-3	240	Sam Houston State
30	John Peters	G	6-2	240	Houston

*   denotes juniors
**   denotes sophomores

1958 GREEN BAY PACKERS

FRONT ROW: (L–R) Head Coach Ray (Scooter) McLean, 46 Hank Gremminger, 80 Steve Meilinger, 86 Bill Howton, 84 Gary Knafelc, 44 Bobby Dillon, 27 John Symank, 25 Billy Kinard, Backfield Coach Floyd (Breezy) Reid.
SECOND ROW: (L–R) Offensive Line Coach Nick Skorich, 48 Al Carmichael, 58 Dan Currie, 47 Jesse Whittenton, 85 Max McGee, 5 Paul Hornung, 37 Howie Ferguson, 22 Jim Shanley, 42 Don McIlhenny, 31 Jim Taylor, 69 Bill Forester, Defense Coach Ray Richards.
THIRD ROW: (L–R) Trainer Carl (Bud) Jorgensen, 83 Len Ford, 23 Al Romine, 77 Ollie Spencer, 64 Jerry Kramer, 10 Vito (Babe) Parilli, 15 Bart Starr, 20 Joe Francis, 33 Ray Nitschke, 40 Joe Johnson, Defensive Line Coach Jack Morton.
BACK ROW: (L–R) Assistant Trainer Gerald (Dad) Braisher, 81 Carlton Massey, 61 Hank Bullough, 72 J.D. Kimmel, 65 Tom Bettis, 78 Norm Masters, 82 Jim Temp, 75 Forrest Gregg, 67 Jim Salsbury, 79 Dave Hanner, 51 Jim Ringo, 87 Nate Borden.

1959

First-year Coach Vince Lombardi faced many challenges in his quest to turn the Packers around. One of his earliest priorities was to end the attitude of defeatism that had sunk in over the past decade. How this state of mind had come about was no mystery. Over the 11-year span from 1948 to 1958, the Packers had finished last or second-to-last in their respective conference or division nine times. Gene Ronzani, Lisle Blackbourn and Ray (Scooter) McLean had all been chosen to return the team to the top and all had failed. Why should the hiring of a former Giants' assistant instill in anyone a feeling of optimism?

From the start, changes were evident. On April 24, Lombardi traded Bill Howton, second only to Don Hutson in Packers receptions, to the Browns for Bill Quinlan and Lew Carpenter. A month later, he acquired Lamar McHan from the Cardinals for a third-round draft choice. After veteran defensive back Bobby Dillon announced his retirement in early June, Lombardi obtained Emlen Tunnell from the Giants. Lombardi also picked up Fred (Fuzzy) Thurston from the Colts in exchange for Marv Matuszak and Henry Jordan from Cleveland for a fourth-round pick.

Although Dillon returned for one last season, three big names of the last decade didn't last through camp. Howie Ferguson, bothered by shoulder, back and leg problems, retired. Al Carmichael and Vito (Babe) Parilli, former first-round draftees, were waived in August and September, respectively. In all, 16 veterans from the previous year were sent packing.

Lombardi became one of the first professional football coaches to film practices. In addition, he added wind sprints and grass drills to the long list of activities at camp. He took conditioning to a level rarely seen before. Veterans returning from service, such as Ron Kramer, often remarked that drills in the armed forces were less strenuous.

Green Bay opened against the Bears for the third consecutive year. The Packers held Chicago to 164 yards but didn't get the lead until 7:45 remained in the fourth quarter. Jim Taylor scored on five-yard run to put Green Bay ahead 7-6. Dave Hanner later tackled Ed Brown in the end zone for a safety for the game's final points. Lombardi was mobbed by fans in the wake of the team's 9-6 win.

The results of Lombardi's approach were dramatic. After three weeks, his 3-0 Packers stood as the only unbeaten team in the league. When all the early success seem destined to be wiped out by a five-game losing streak, Green Bay bounced back to win its last four games and produce a 7-5 season, the first winner since 1947. After the team's final 479-yard outburst at San Francisco on December 13, an attitude of defeatism was but a distant memory.

Green Bay Press-Gazette photo

Lamar McHan (17) directed the Packers' offense in the first half of 1959. Here he gets protection from Forrest Gregg (75), Don McIlhenny (42), Jim Taylor (31), Jerry Kramer (64), Jim Ringo (51), Fred (Fuzzy) Thurston (63) and Norm Masters (78). McHan threw four touchdown passes to lead Green Bay past Detroit 28-10. Darris McCord (78), Alex Karras (71), Gil Mains (72) and Gene Cronin (85) provide the enemy rush.

TEAM STATISTICS

	GB	OPP
First Downs	212	215
Rushing	109	101
Passing	87	102
Penalty	16	12
Rushes	421	430
Yards Gained	1,907	1,770
Average Gain	4.53	4.12
Average Yards per Game	158.9	147.5
Passes Attempted	268	329
Completed	128	169
% Completed	47.76	51.37
Total Yards Gained	1,963	2,030
Yards Lost	131	248
Net Yards Gained	1,832	1,782
Yards Gained per Completion	15.34	12.01
Average Net Yards per Game	152.7	148.5
Combined Net Yards Gained	3,739	3,552
Total Plays	689	759
Average Yards per Play	5.43	4.68
Average Net Yards per Game	311.6	296.0
Intercepted By	14	17
Yards Returned	231	227
Returned for TD	0	1
Punts	64	56
Yards Punted	2,716	2,481
Average Yards per Punt	42.44	44.30
Punt Returns	33	40
Yards Returned	316	291
Average Yards per Return	9.58	7.28
Returned for TD	1	1
Kickoff Returns	43	40
Yards Returned	949	917
Average Yards per Return	22.07	22.93
Returned for TD	0	0
Penalties	49	51
Yards Penalized	435	450
Fumbles	24	28
Lost	16	15
Own Recovered for Touchdown	0	0
Opponent's Recovered by	15	16
Opponent's Recovered for Touchdown	0	0
Total Points Scored	248	246
Total Touchdowns	32	30
Touchdowns Rushing	15	14
Touchdowns Passing	16	14
Touchdowns on Returns & Recoveries	1	2
Extra Points	31	28
Safeties	2	1
Field Goals Attempted	17	22
Field Goals Made	7	12
% Successful	41.18	54.55

Regular Season 7-5-0

Date	GB		OPP	Att.
9/27	9	Chicago Bears	6	(32,150)
10/4	28	Detroit Lions	10	(32,150)
10/11	21	San Francisco 49ers	20	(32,150)
10/18	6	Los Angeles Rams (M)	45	(36,194)
10/25	21	at Baltimore Colts	38	(57,557)
11/1	3	at New York Giants	20	(68,837)
11/8	17	at Chicago Bears	28	(46,205)
11/15	24	Baltimore Colts (M)	28	(25,521)
11/22	21	Washington Redskins	0	(31,853)
11/26	24	at Detroit Lions	17	(49,221)
12/6	38	at Los Angeles Rams	20	(61,044)
12/13	36	at San Francisco 49ers	14	(55,997)

Score By Periods

	1	2	3	4	Total
Packers	55	82	44	67	248
Opponents	66	68	75	37	246

INDIVIDUAL STATISTICS

Rushing

	Att	Yds	Avg	LG	TD
Hornung	152	681	4.5	63	7
J. Taylor	120	452	3.8	21	6
Carpenter	60	322	5.4	t55	1
McIlhenny	47	231	4.9	46	1
Starr	16	83	5.2	39	0
McHan	16	64	4.0	19	0
B. Butler	7	49	7.0	16	0
Dowler	1	20	20.0	20	0
Francis	2	5	2.5	8	0
Packers	**421**	**1,907**	**4.5**	**63**	**15**
Opponents	430	1,770	4.1	t49	14

1959

Receiving

	No	Yds	Avg	LG	TD
Dowler	32	549	17.2	35	4
McGee	30	695	23.2	t81	5
Knafelc	27	384	14.2	38	4
Hornung	15	113	7.5	19	0
J. Taylor	9	71	7.9	t20	2
McIlhenny	8	95	11.9	30	1
Carpenter	5	47	9.4	23	0
A.D. Williams	1	11	11.0	11	0
B. Butler	1	-2	-2.0	-2	0
Packers	**128**	**1,963**	**15.3**	**t81**	**16**
Opponents	169	2,030	12.0	t75	14

Passing

	Att	Com	Yds	Pct	TD	In	YL	Rate
Starr	134	70	972	52.2	6	7	30	69.0
McHan	108	48	805	44.4	8	9	94	60.1
Francis	18	5	91	27.8	0	1	7	25.0
Hornung	8	5	95	62.5	2	0	0	—
Packers	**268**	**128**	**1,963**	**47.8**	**16**	**17**	**131**	**65.9**
Opponents	329	169	2,030	51.4	14	14	248	67.1

Punting

	No	Yds	Avg	LG	HB
McGee	64	2,716	42.4	61	1
Packers	**64**	**2,716**	**42.4**	**61**	**1**
Opponents	56	2,481	44.3	61	0

Kickoff Returns

	No	Yds	Avg	LG	TD
B. Butler	21	472	22.5	35	0
Symank	14	338	24.1	39	0
McIlhenny	3	50	16.7	24	0
Francis	2	52	26.0	28	0
Nitschke	2	13	6.5	10	0
Carpenter	1	24	24.0	24	0
Packers	**43**	**949**	**22.1**	**39**	**0**
Opponents	40	917	22.9	85	0

Punt Returns

	No	Yds	Avg	LG	TD
B. Butler	18	163	9.1	t61	1
Carpenter	13	150	11.5	51	0
Tunnell	1	3	3.0	3	0
Symank	1	0	0.0	0	0
Packers	**33**	**316**	**9.6**	**t61**	**1**
Opponents	40	291	7.3	t71	1

Interceptions

	No	Yds	Avg	LG	TD
Forester	2	48	24.0	34	0
Symank	2	46	23.0	25	0
Freeman	2	22	11.0	22	0
Tunnell	2	20	10.0	18	0
Gremminger	1	45	45.0	45	0
Currie	1	25	25.0	25	0
Temp	1	13	13.0	13	0
Dillon	1	7	7.0	7	0
Quinlan	1	5	5.0	5	0
Bettis	1	0	0.0	0	0
Packers	**14**	**231**	**16.5**	**45**	**0**
Opponents	17	227	13.4	49	1

Scoring

	TDr	TDp	TDrt	PAT	FG	S	TP
Hornung	7	0	0	31/32	7/17	0	94
J. Taylor	6	2	0	0/0	0/0	0	48
McGee	0	5	0	0/0	0/0	0	30
Dowler	0	4	0	0/0	0/0	0	24
Knafelc	0	4	0	0/0	0/0	0	24
McIlhenny	1	1	0	0/0	0/0	0	12
B. Butler	0	0	1	0/0	0/0	0	6
Carpenter	1	0	0	0/0	0/0	0	6
Forester	0	0	0	0/0	0/0	1	2
Hanner	0	0	0	0/0	0/0	1	2
Packers	**15**	**16**	**1**	**31/32**	**7/17**	**2**	**248**
Opponents	14	14	2	28/30	12/22	1	246

Fumbles

	Fum	Ow	Op	Yds	Tot
Bettis	0	0	1	0	1
Borden	0	0	1	0	1
B. Butler	1	1	0	0	1
Carpenter	3	0	0	0	0
Dittrich	0	0	1	0	1
Forester	1	0	3	0	3
Hanner	0	0	1	0	1
Hornung	7	0	0	0	0
H. Jordan	0	0	2	0	2
Knafelc	0	1	0	0	1
McHan	3	0	0	0	0
McIlhenny	1	1	0	0	1
Nitschke	0	1	1	10	2
Ringo	0	0	1	0	1
Starr	2	2	0	-8	2
Symank	0	0	2	0	3
J. Taylor	2	1	0	0	1
Whittenton	0	0	2	45	2
Packers	**24**	**8**	**15**	**47**	**23**

NFL STANDINGS

Western Conference

	W	L	T	Pct	PF	PA
Baltimore Colts	9	3	0	.750	374	251
Chicago Bears	8	4	0	.667	252	196
Green Bay Packers	7	5	0	.583	248	246
San Francisco 49ers	7	5	0	.583	255	237
Detroit Lions	3	8	1	.273	203	275
Los Angeles Rams	2	10	0	.167	242	315

Eastern Conference

	W	L	T	Pct	PF	PA
New York Giants	10	2	0	.833	284	170
Cleveland Browns	7	5	0	.583	270	214
Philadelphia Eagles	7	5	0	.583	268	278
Pittsburgh Steelers	6	5	1	.545	257	216
Washington Redskins	3	9	0	.250	185	350
Chicago Cardinals	2	10	0	.167	234	324

1959 ROSTER

No	Name	Pos	Ht	Wt	DOB	College	G
73	Beck, Ken	DT	6-2	240	09/03/35	Texas A&M	12
65	Bettis, Tom	LB	6-2	225	03/17/33	Purdue	12
87	Borden, Nate	DE	6-0	240	09/22/32	Indiana	12
25	Brown, Tim	HB	5-10	195	05/24/37	Ball State	1
22	Butler, Bill	HB	5-10	180	07/10/37	Chattanooga	11
33	Carpenter, Lew	FB	6-2	210	01/12/32	Arkansas	12
58	Currie, Dan	LB	6-3	235	06/27/35	Michigan State	12
44	Dillon, Bobby	DB	6-1	180	02/23/30	Texas	12
68	Dittrich, John	G	6-1	235	05/07/33	Wisconsin	12
86	Dowler, Boyd	E	6-5	225	10/18/37	Colorado	12
69	Forester, Bill	LB	6-3	240	08/09/32	SMU	12
20	Francis, Joe	QB	6-1	195	04/21/36	Oregon State	12
41	Freeman, Bob	DB	6-1	205	10/19/32	Auburn	12
75	Gregg, Forrest	G	6-4	245	10/18/33	SMU	12
46	Gremminger, Hank	DB	6-1	205	09/01/33	Baylor	12
79	Hanner, Dave	DT	6-2	260	05/20/30	Arkansas	12
5	Hornung, Paul	HB	6-2	215	12/23/35	Notre Dame	12
74	Jordan, Henry	DT	6-3	250	01/26/35	Virginia	12
84	Knafelc, Gary	E	6-4	220	01/02/32	Colorado	12
64	Kramer, Jerry	G	6-3	245	01/23/36	Idaho	12
88	Kramer, Ron	E	6-3	230	06/24/35	Michigan	12
78	Masters, Norm	T	6-2	250	09/19/33	Michigan State	12
85	McGee, Max	E	6-3	205	07/16/32	Tulane	12
17	McHan, Lamar	QB	6-1	205	12/16/32	Arkansas	12
42	McIlhenny, Don	HB	6-0	200	11/22/34	SMU	12
66	Nitschke, Ray	LB	6-3	230	12/29/36	Illinois	12
83	Quinlan, Bill	DE	6-3	250	06/19/32	Michigan State	12
51	Ringo, Jim	C	6-1	230	11/21/32	Syracuse	12
76	Skoronski, Bob	T	6-3	250	03/05/34	Indiana	12
15	Starr, Bart	QB	6-1	200	01/09/34	Alabama	12
27	Symank, John	DB	5-11	180	08/31/35	Florida	12
31	Taylor, Jim	FB	6-0	212	09/20/35	LSU	12
82	Temp, Jim	DE	6-4	250	10/14/33	Wisconsin	12
63	Thurston, Fred (Fuzzy)	G	6-1	245	05/07/35	Valparaiso	12
45	Tunnell, Emlen	DB	6-1	215	03/29/25	Iowa	12
47	Whittenton, Jesse	DB	6-0	195	05/09/34	Texas-El Paso	12

1959 DRAFT

Rnd	Name	Pos	Ht	Wt	College
1	Randy Duncan	QB	6-0	190	Iowa
2	Alex Hawkins	HB	6-1	195	South Carolina
3	Boyd Dowler	E	6-5	225	Colorado
4	(Choice to Browns for Len Ford)				
5a	(Choice to Redskins for J.D. Kimmel)				
5b	Andy Cvercko	G	6-0	235	Northwestern
	(Choice from Steelers for Dick Christy)				
6	Willie Taylor	C	6-0	232	Florida A&M
7a	Bobby Jackson	HB	6-1	185	Alabama
7b	Gary Raid	T	6-2	255	Williamette
	(Choice from Giants for Al Barry)				
8a	Buddy Mayfield	E	6-2	190	South Carolina
8b	Bob Laraba	HB	6-2	190	Texas-El Paso
	(Choice from Browns for Dick Deschaine)				
9	George Dixon	HB	6-1	195	Bridgeport
10	Sam Tuccio	G-T	6-2	248	Southern Mississippi
11	Bob Webb	QB	6-0	204	St. Ambrose
12	Larry Hall	G	6-0	235	Missouri Valley
*13	Jim Hurd	FB	6-1	220	Albion
14	Jim Kerr	G	6-2	265	Arizona State
15	Dick Teteak	C	6-0	212	Wisconsin
16	Dan Edgington	E	6-2	191	Florida
17	Tom Secules	HB	6-3	200	William and Mary
18	Dick Nearents	T	6-2	265	Eastern Washington
19	Bill Butler	HB	5-10	180	Chattanooga
*20	Chuck Sample	FB	6-3	208	Arkansas
21	Dave Smith	FB	6-1	201	Ripon
22	Charles Anderson	E	6-5	235	Drake
*23	Orville Lawver	T	6-3	280	Lewis and Clark
24	Joe Hergert	C	6-2	215	Florida
25	Leroy Hardee	HB	6-0	180	Florida A&M
*26	Tom Higginbotham	E	6-3	201	Trinity (TX)
27	Tim Brown	HB	5-10	195	Ball State
28	Jerry Epps	G	6-1	230	West Texas State
29	John Flara	HB	5-11	182	Pittsburgh
30	Dick Emerich	T	6-2	230	West Chester

* denotes juniors

1959 GREEN BAY PACKERS

FRONT ROW: (L-R) 66 Ray Nitschke, 74 Henry Jordan, 81 A.D. Williams, 41 Bob Freeman, 47 Jesse Whittenton, 27 John Symank, 25 Tim Brown.
SECOND ROW: (L-R) 67 Andy Cvercko, 15 Bart Starr, 42 Don McIlhenny, 69 Bill Forester, 44 Bobby Dillon, 33 Lew Carpenter, 84 Gary Knafelc, 88 Ron Kramer, 46 Hank Gremminger.
THIRD ROW: (L-R) 75 Forrest Gregg, 45 Emlen Tunnell, 20 Joe Francis, 68 John Dittrich, 17 Lamar McHan, 86 Boyd Dowler, 58 Dan Currie, 83 Bill Quinlan, 63 Fred (Fuzzy) Thurston, 31 Jim Taylor.
BACK ROW: (L-R) 64 Jerry Kramer, 76 Bob Skoronski, 87 Nate Borden, 82 Jim Temp, 85 Max McGee, 5 Paul Hornung, 65 Tom Bettis, 78 Norm Masters, 51 Jim Ringo, 79 Dave Hanner.

1960

The vast improvement began in 1959 continued in 1960. Lombardi added halfback Tom Moore from the draft, obtained Willie Davis from Cleveland for A.D. Williams and signed three free agents, most notably safety Willie Wood. Jim Taylor emerged as one of the league's best backs, gaining 1,101 yards to break Tony Canadeo's team record. Paul Hornung, shifted to halfback last year, scored an NFL-record 176 points. And Moore returned 12 kickoffs at a league-leading pace of 33.1 yards per return.

Such performances helped propel the Packers to the top of the Western Conference. Green Bay won seven of its first nine contests, including a 35-21 downing of the 1959 champion Colts. After back-to-back losses threatened to leave Green Bay an also-ran, the Packers turned around and knocked off the Bears, 49ers and Rams to claim the title.

Three men who had played important roles in the team's history passed away in 1960. *Green Bay Press-Gazette* publisher and first Packers president A.B. Turnbull died on October 17 at age 76. Thirteen days later, H.S. Atkinson, team physician from 1945-59, died. Then on November 27, business manager and chief talent scout Jack Vainisi succumbed to rheumatic fever at age 33. Vainisi had been instrumental in uncovering and bringing some of the best talent in football to town. Sadly, he would never see the championship contributions of future Hall of Famers Hornung, Taylor, Nitschke, Ringo and others.

Since the merger of the NFL and AAFC in 1950, the only competition the league faced had come from the CFL. That changed on September 9 when the AFL began play. Like the AAFC before it, the AFL lured talent away from the established league, competed for college players, and drove up salaries. From its modest beginnings, the upstart league grew in stature and eventually merged with the NFL in the late '60s.

After a heartbreaking 17-14 season-opening loss to the Bears which saw the team blow a 14-0 fourth-quarter lead, the Packers won four straight. The fourth, a 19-13 win over Pittsburgh, pushed Green Bay (4-1) to the top ahead of Baltimore (4-2).

The Colts and Packers squared off the following week. Green Bay spotted Baltimore a 21-0 lead then battled back and tied the game 24-24 with touchdown runs by Hornung and Taylor and a field goal by Hornung. The Colts, however, scored two touchdowns in the last four minutes to take the game 38-24 and conference lead.

After welcoming the Dallas Cowboys to the league 41-7, the Packers lost two straight including a 23-10 setback to Detroit on Thanksgiving. That loss pushed Green Bay (5-4) to third place behind the Colts (6-2) and Bears (4-3-1). The Packers would get a crack at the Bears, but needed help with the Colts.

Green Bay did its part. Bart Starr, who had been sharing the quarterbacking duties with Lamar McHan, took over. He completed 31 of 49 passes for 469 yards and four touchdowns as the Packers beat the Bears 41-13, the 49ers 13-0 and finally the Rams 35-21.

As for Baltimore, it lost its last four games, opening the door for the Packers' first Division title since 1944.

Green Bay Press-Gazette photo

Emlen Tunnell (45) returns his 78th career interception against the Colts in Green Bay on October 9. The Packers stole four Baltimore passes on the way to a 35-21 win. Tunnell, who began his career as a free agent in 1948 with the Giants, came to Green Bay in 1959. Tunnell retired after 1961 with more interceptions (79) than any other player.

TEAM STATISTICS

	GB	OPP
First Downs	237	199
Rushing	135	74
Passing	86	110
Penalty	16	15
Rushes	463	350
Yards Gained	2,150	1,285
Average Gain	4.64	3.67
Average Yards per Game	179.2	107.1
Passes Attempted	279	365
Completed	137	192
% Completed	49.10	52.60
Total Yards Gained	1,993	2,432
Yards Lost	118	275
Net Yards Gained	1,875	2,157
Yards Gained per Completion	14.55	12.67
Average Net Yards per Game	156.3	179.8
Combined Net Yards Gained	4,025	3,442
Total Plays	742	715
Average Yards per Play	5.42	4.81
Average Net Yards per Game	335.4	286.8
Intercepted By	22	13
Yards Returned	358	185
Returned for TD	1	0
Punts	49	66
Yards Punted	2,020	2,600
Average Yards per Punt	41.22	39.39
Punt Returns	26	22
Yards Returned	172	144
Average Yards per Return	6.62	6.55
Returned for TD	0	0
Kickoff Returns	35	57
Yards Returned	852	1,158
Average Yards per Return	24.34	20.32
Returned for TD	0	0
Penalties	64	61
Yards Penalized	578	636
Fumbles	18	23
Lost	12	15
Own Recovered for Touchdown	0	0
Opponent's Recovered by	15	12
Opponent's Recovered for Touchdown	0	0
Total Points Scored	332	209
Total Touchdowns	41	26
Touchdowns Rushing	29	7
Touchdowns Passing	9	19
Touchdowns on Returns & Recoveries	3	0
Extra Points	41	24
Safeties	0	1
Field Goals Attempted	28	13
Field Goals Made	15	9
% Successful	53.57	69.23

Regular Season 8-4-0

Date	GB		OPP	Att.
9/25	14	Chicago Bears	17	(32,150)
10/2	28	Detroit Lions	9	(32,150)
10/9	35	Baltimore Colts	21	(32,150)
10/23	41	San Francisco 49ers (M)	14	(39,914)
10/30	19	at Pittsburgh Steelers	13	(30,155)
11/6	24	at Baltimore Colts	38	(57,808)
11/13	41	Dallas Cowboys	7	(32,294)
11/20	31	Los Angeles Rams (M)	33	(35,763)
11/24	10	at Detroit Lions	23	(51,123)
12/4	41	at Chicago Bears	13	(46,406)
12/11	13	at San Francisco 49ers	0	(53,612)
12/18	35	at Los Angeles Rams	21	(53,445)

Postseason 0-1-0

12/26	13	at Philadelphia Eagles	17	(67,325)

Score By Periods

	1	2	3	4	Total
Packers	47	98	69	118	332
Opponents	40	53	34	82	209

INDIVIDUAL STATISTICS

Rushing

	Att	Yds	Avg	LG	TD
J. Taylor	230	1,101	4.8	32	11
Hornung	160	671	4.2	37	13
T. Moore	45	237	5.3	t59	4
McHan	8	67	8.4	t35	1
Carpenter	1	24	24.0	24	0
Hickman	7	22	3.1	4	0
Starr	7	12	1.7	13	0
McGee	2	11	5.5	16	0
Dowler	1	8	8.0	8	0
Winslow	2	-3	-1.5	3	0
Packers	**463**	**2,150**	**4.6**	**t59**	**29**
Opponents	350	1,285	3.7	35	7

Receiving

	No	Yds	Avg	LG	TD
McGee	38	787	20.7	t57	4
Dowler	30	505	16.8	t91	2
Hornung	28	257	9.2	33	2
J. Taylor	15	121	8.1	27	0
Knafelc	14	164	11.7	23	0
T. Moore	5	40	8.0	t12	1
R. Kramer	4	55	13.8	18	0
Meilinger	2	43	21.5	23	0
Carpenter	1	21	21.0	21	0
Packers	**137**	**1,993**	**14.6**	**t91**	**9**
Opponents	192	2,432	12.7	58	19

Passing

	Att	Com	Yds	Pct	TD	In	YL	Rate
Starr	172	98	1,358	57.0	4	8	78	70.8
McHan	91	33	517	36.3	3	5	33	44.1
Hornung	16	6	118	37.5	2	0	7	103.6
Packers	**279**	**137**	**1,993**	**49.1**	**9**	**13**	**118**	**64.1**
Opponents	365	192	2,432	52.6	19	22	275	65.9

Punting

	No	Yds	Avg	LG	HB
McGee	31	1,291	41.6	58	1
Dowler	18	729	40.5	61	2
Packers	**49**	**2,020**	**41.2**	**61**	**3**
Opponents	66	2,600	39.4	59	1

Kickoff Returns

	No	Yds	Avg	LG	TD
T. Moore	12	397	33.1	84	0
Carpenter	12	249	20.8	29	0
Symank	4	103	25.8	32	0
Hickman	3	54	18.0	27	0
Nitschke	2	33	16.5	17	0
Temp	1	16	16.0	16	0
Meilinger	1	0	0.0	0	0
Packers	**35**	**852**	**24.3**	**84**	**0**
Opponents	57	1,158	20.3	42	0

Punt Returns

	No	Yds	Avg	LG	TD
Wood	16	106	6.6	33	0
Carpenter	9	59	6.6	12	0
Forester	1	7	7.0	7	0
Packers	**26**	**172**	**6.6**	**33**	**0**
Opponents	22	144	6.6	15	0

Interceptions

	No	Yds	Avg	LG	TD
Whittenton	6	101	16.8	52	0
Currie	4	75	18.8	33	0
Nitschke	3	90	30.0	t43	1
Gremminger	3	52	17.3	21	0
Tunnell	3	22	7.3	22	0
Forester	2	18	9.0	15	0
Symank	1	0	0.0	0	0
Packers	**22**	**358**	**16.3**	**52**	**1**
Opponents	13	185	14.2	44	0

Scoring

	TDr	TDp	TDrt	PAT	FG	S	TP
Hornung	13	2	0	41/41	15/28	0	176
J. Taylor	11	0	0	0/0	0/0	0	66
T. Moore	4	1	0	0/0	0/0	0	30
McGee	0	4	0	0/0	0/0	0	24
Dowler	0	2	0	0/0	0/0	0	12
W. Davis	0	0	1	0/0	0/0	0	6
McHan	1	0	0	0/0	0/0	0	6
Nitschke	0	0	1	0/0	0/0	0	6
Winslow	0	0	1	0/0	0/0	0	6
Packers	**29**	**9**	**3**	**41/41**	**15/28**	**0**	**332**
Opponents	7	19	0	24/26	9/13	1	209

Fumbles

	Fum	Ow	Op	Yds	Tot
Bettis	0	0	1	4	1
Carpenter	4	0	0	0	0
Currie	0	0	1	0	1
W. Davis	0	0	1	0	1
Gremminger	0	0	2	0	2
Hornung	3	0	0	0	0
H. Jordan	0	1	4	0	5
McGee	1	0	0	0	0
T. Moore	0	1	0	0	1
Nitschke	0	0	1	0	1
Starr	3	2	0	0	2
Symank	0	0	2	13	2
J. Taylor	5	2	0	1	2
Tunnell	0	0	1	0	1
Whittenton	0	0	2	0	2
Wood	2	0	0	0	0
Packers	**18**	**6**	**15**	**18**	**21**

NFL STANDINGS

Western Conference

	W	L	T	Pct	PF	PA
Green Bay Packers	8	4	0	.667	332	209
Detroit Lions	7	5	0	.583	239	212
San Francisco 49ers	7	5	0	.583	208	205
Baltimore Colts	6	6	0	.500	288	234
Chicago Bears	5	6	1	.455	194	299
Los Angeles Rams	4	7	1	.364	265	297
Dallas Cowboys	0	11	1	.000	177	369

Eastern Conference

	W	L	T	Pct	PF	PA
Philadelphia Eagles	10	2	0	.833	321	246
Cleveland Browns	8	3	1	.727	362	217
New York Giants	6	4	2	.600	271	261
St. Louis Cardinals	6	5	1	.545	288	230
Pittsburgh Steelers	5	6	1	.455	240	275
Washington Redskins	1	9	2	.100	178	309

1960 ROSTER

No	Name	Pos	Ht	Wt	DOB	College	G
73	Beck, Ken	DT	6-2	250	09/03/35	Texas A&M	12
65	Bettis, Tom	LB	6-2	225	03/17/33	Purdue	12
33	Carpenter, Lew	FB	6-2	215	01/12/32	Arkansas	12
58	Currie, Dan	LB	6-3	240	06/27/35	Michigan State	12
62	Cvercko, Andy	G	6-0	240	11/06/37	Northwestern	12
87	Davis, Willie	DE	6-3	240	07/24/34	Grambling	12
86	Dowler, Boyd	E	6-5	220	10/18/37	Colorado	12
71	Forester, Bill	LB	6-3	240	08/09/32	SMU	12
75	Gregg, Forrest	G	6-4	250	10/18/33	SMU	12
46	Gremminger, Hank	DB	6-1	205	09/01/33	Baylor	12
40	Hackbarth, Dale	DB	6-3	200	07/21/38	Wisconsin	12
79	Hanner, Dave	DT	6-2	260	05/20/30	Arkansas	12
37	Hickman, Larry	FB	6-1	230	10/10/35	Baylor	12
5	Hornung, Paul	HB	6-2	215	12/23/35	Notre Dame	12
53	Iman, Ken	C	6-1	230	02/08/39	Southeast Missouri State	12
74	Jordan, Henry	DT	6-3	250	01/26/35	Virginia	12
84	Knafelc, Gary	E	6-4	220	01/02/32	Colorado	12
64	Kramer, Jerry	G	6-3	250	01/23/36	Idaho	12
88	Kramer, Ron	E	6-3	230	06/24/35	Michigan	12
78	Masters, Norm	T	6-2	250	09/19/33	Michigan State	12
85	McGee, Max	E	6-3	205	07/16/32	Tulane	12
17	McHan, Lamar	QB	6-1	210	12/16/32	Arkansas	12
80	Meilinger, Steve	E	6-2	230	12/12/30	Kentucky	12
72	Miller, John	T	6-5	260	02/01/34	Boston College	5
25	Moore, Tom	HB	6-2	215	07/17/38	Vanderbilt	12
66	Nitschke, Ray	LB	6-3	235	12/29/36	Illinois	12
48	Pesonen, Dick	DB	6-0	190	06/10/38	Minnesota-Duluth	12
83	Quinlan, Bill	DE	6-3	250	06/19/32	Michigan State	12
51	Ringo, Jim	C	6-1	235	11/21/32	Syracuse	12
76	Skoronski, Bob	T	6-3	250	03/05/34	Indiana	12
15	Starr, Bart	QB	6-1	200	01/09/34	Alabama	12
27	Symank, John	DB	5-11	180	08/31/35	Florida	12
31	Taylor, Jim	FB	6-0	215	09/20/35	LSU	12
82	Temp, Jim	DE	6-4	250	10/14/33	Wisconsin	7
63	Thurston, Fred (Fuzzy)	G	6-1	250	05/07/35	Valparaiso	12
45	Tunnell, Emlen	DB	6-1	210	03/29/25	Iowa	12
47	Whittenton, Jesse	DB	6-0	195	05/09/34	Texas-El Paso	12
23	Winslow, Paul	HB	5-11	200	02/28/38	North Carolina Central	12
24	Wood, Willie	DB	5-10	185	12/23/36	USC	12

1960 DRAFT

Rnd	Name	Pos	Ht	Wt	College
1	Tom Moore	HB	6-2	212	Vanderbilt
2	Bob Jeter	HB	6-1	185	Iowa
3	(Choice to Cardinals for Lamar McHan)				
4	(Choice to Browns for Henry Jordan)				
5a	Dale Hackbarth	DB	6-3	200	Wisconsin
	(Choice from Lions for Ollie Spencer)				
5b	(Choice to Browns for Bob Freeman)				
6	Mike Wright	T	6-3	235	Minnesota
7	Kirk Phares	G	6-2	235	South Carolina
8	Don Hitt	C	6-3	235	Oklahoma State
*9	Frank Brixius	T	6-5	265	Minnesota
10	(Choice to Cardinals for Ken Beck)				
11	Ron Ray	T	6-4	234	Howard Payne
12	Harry Hall	T	6-1	235	Boston College
13	Paul Winslow	HB	5-11	200	North Carolina Central
14	Jon Gilliam	C	6-2	210	East Texas State
15	Garney Henley	HB	5-11	177	Huron
*16	John Littlejohn	HB	6-1	190	Kansas State
17	Joe Gomes	HB	6-1	200	South Carolina
18	Royce Whittington	T	6-2	265	Southwestern Louisiana
19	Rich Brooks	E	6-3	195	Purdue
20	Gilmer Lewis	T	6-4	215	Oklahoma

* denotes juniors

1960 GREEN BAY PACKERS

FRONT ROW: (L-R) 67 Andy Cvercko, 53 Ken Iman, 40 Dale Hackbarth, 23 Paul Winslow, 48 Dick Pesonen, 24 Willie Wood, 25 Tom Moore.
SECOND ROW: (L-R) 71 Bill Forester, 27 John Symank, 64 Jerry Kramer, 63 Fred (Fuzzy) Thurston, 46 Hank Gremminger, 47 Jesse Whittenton, 31 Jim Taylor, 58 Dan Currie, 33 Lew Carpenter, 88 Ron Kramer, 80 Steve Meilinger.
THIRD ROW: (L-R) Equipment Manager Gerald (Dad) Braisher, 15 Bart Starr, 76 Bob Skoronski, 84 Gary Knafelc, 51 Jim Ringo, 82 Jim Temp, 78 Norm Masters, 74 Henry Jordan, 79 Dave Hanner, 72 John Miller, 86 Boyd Dowler, 37 Larry Hickman, Trainer Carl (Bud) Jorgensen.
BACK ROW: (L-R) 75 Forrest Gregg, 45 Emlen Tunnell, 66 Ray Nitschke, 73 Ken Beck, 20 Joe Francis, 17 Lamar McHan, 83 Bill Quinlan, 87 Willie Davis, 65 Tom Bettis, 5 Paul Hornung, 85 Max McGee.

- 127 -

1961

Seventeen years after Ted Fritsch scored his two touchdowns in the championship game, the Packers were once again the NFL's best. Green Bay featured the league's top running game with backs Jim Taylor, Paul Hornung and sophomore Tom Moore. Its passing attack was the most accurate in the NFL. Its quarterbacks were sacked for fewer yards than any other team's, thanks to a stalwart line composed of Jerry Kramer, Fred (Fuzzy) Thurston, Bob Skoronski, Forrest Gregg and Jim Ringo. Defensively, only the New York Giants allowed fewer points than the Packers.

Green Bay bolted to a 6-1 record in the first half of an expanded 14-game schedule. Then, despite the interference of Uncle Sam and some key injuries, the Packers won five of their last seven —including a muddy battle with Detroit on Thanksgiving— to outdistance the Lions and Bears and claim the Western Conference title.

Packers' management was so pleased with Coach Vince Lombardi that it gave him a new five-year contract even before his club finished 11-3. The pact, signed in August, superseded his previous commitment and locked up his services through February 1, 1966.

Detroit provided Green Bay with its only defeat in the opening half of the year. Nick Pietrosante scored twice to give the Lions a 14-7 lead. Jim Martin then kicked a 44-yard field goal to seal the win 17-13.

After shrugging off that misstep, the Packers won their next six games by no fewer than 18 points each. Notable wins included the team's first shutout of the Bears (24-0) since 1935 and its first regular-season victory over the Cleveland Browns. But, just when things were going so well, injuries and the U.S. Army intervened. Hornung and Ray Nitschke were ordered to active duty on October 17. Nine days later, Boyd Dowler got the call. Green Bay then lost the services of Jerry Kramer after he shattered his ankle.

Army weekend passes saved the Packers. Though rarely able to practice, Hornung and Nitschke missed only two games each while Dowler was able to get away and play in all 14. Even though the Packers didn't completely lose the services of those three starters, the weekly wait-and-see who's available dilemma didn't help.

With Hornung's availibility uncertain and backup kicker Jerry Kramer out, Green Bay obtained Ben Agajanian from the AFL's Dallas Texans. The oldest man ever to play in a regular-season game for the Packers hit eight of eight extra points and made one of two field goals in his three-game stint.

On November 23, the Packers (8-2) met the second-place Lions (6-3-1) in Tiger Stadium. Hornung, Nitschke and Dowler were able to join the team for the annual Thanksgiving Day clash. The Packers intercepted four passes and beat the Lions 17-9 in a downpour.

A week later, the Packers defeated the Giants 20-17 in Milwaukee to clinch the Western crown. On New Years' Eve, the two met again in the NFL Championship Game.

Green Bay Press-Gazette photo

Jim Taylor (31) scores from three yards out to put the Packers ahead of the Bears 16-0 on October 1. Paul Hornung (5) added the point after and Green Bay shut out Chicago (24-0) for the first time in 26 years. Taylor ran for 130 yards on 19 carries and finished second to Cleveland's Jim Brown in the rushing race.

TEAM STATISTICS

	GB	OPP
First Downs	274	245
Rushing	142	110
Passing	115	117
Penalty	17	18
Rushes	474	412
Yards Gained	2,350	1,694
Average Gain	4.96	4.11
Average Yards per Game	167.9	121.0
Passes Attempted	306	414
Completed	177	218
% Completed	57.84	52.66
Total Yards Gained	2,502	2,630
Yards Lost	138	273
Net Yards Gained	2,364	2,357
Yards Gained per Completion	14.14	12.06
Average Net Yards per Game	168.9	168.4
Combined Net Yards Gained	4,714	4,051
Total Plays	780	826
Average Yards per Play	6.04	4.90
Average Net Yards per Game	336.7	289.4
Intercepted By	29	16
Yards Returned	446	238
Returned for TD	2	0
Punts	51	49
Yards Punted	2,194	1,851
Average Yards per Punt	43.02	37.78
Punt Returns	20	25
Yards Returned	355	313
Average Yards per Return	17.75	12.52
Returned for TD	2	1
Kickoff Returns	41	69
Yards Returned	1,077	1,597
Average Yards per Return	26.27	23.14
Returned for TD	0	0
Penalties	66	52
Yards Penalized	647	609
Fumbles	18	30
Lost	10	17
Own Recovered for Touchdown	0	0
Opponent's Recovered by	17	10
Opponent's Recovered for Touchdown	0	0
Total Points Scored	391	223
Total Touchdowns	49	26
Touchdowns Rushing	27	12
Touchdowns Passing	18	13
Touchdowns on Returns & Recoveries	4	1
Extra Points	49	26
Safeties	0	1
Field Goals Attempted	24	21
Field Goals Made	16	13
% Successful	66.67	61.90

Regular Season   11-3-0

Date	GB		OPP	Att.
9/17	13	Detroit Lions (M)	17	(44,307)
9/24	30	San Francisco 49ers	10	(38,669)
10/1	24	Chicago Bears	0	(38,669)
10/8	45	Baltimore Colts	7	(38,669)
10/15	49	at Cleveland Browns	17	(75,042)
10/22	33	at Minnesota Vikings	7	(42,007)
10/29	28	Minnesota Vikings (M)	10	(44,116)
11/5	21	at Baltimore Colts	45	(57,641)
11/12	31	at Chicago Bears	28	(49,711)
11/19	35	Los Angeles Rams	17	(38,669)
11/23	17	at Detroit Lions	9	(55,662)
12/3	20	New York Giants (M)	17	(47,012)
12/10	21	at San Francisco 49ers	22	(55,722)
12/17	24	at Los Angeles Rams	17	(49,169)

Postseason   1-0-0

12/31	37	New York Giants	0	(39,029)

Score By Periods

	1	2	3	4	Total
Packers	100	123	44	124	391
Opponents	45	81	39	58	223

INDIVIDUAL STATISTICS

Rushing

	Att	Yds	Avg	LG	TD
J. Taylor	243	1,307	5.4	53	15
Hornung	127	597	4.7	t54	8
T. Moore	61	302	5.0	69	1
E. Pitts	23	75	3.3	t17	1
Starr	12	56	4.7	t21	1
R. Kramer	5	13	2.6	12	0
Carpenter	1	5	5.0	5	0
Roach	2	-5	-2.5	t1	1
Packers	**474**	**2,350**	**5.0**	**69**	**27**
Opponents	412	1,694	4.1	t55	12

Receiving

	No	Yds	Avg	LG	TD
McGee	51	883	17.3	53	7
Dowler	36	633	17.6	t78	3
R. Kramer	35	559	16.0	t53	4
J. Taylor	25	175	7.0	18	1
Hornung	15	145	9.7	t34	2
T. Moore	8	41	5.1	11	1
Knafelc	3	32	10.7	13	0
Carpenter	3	29	9.7	16	0
E. Pitts	1	5	5.0	5	0
Packers	**177**	**2,502**	**14.1**	**t78**	**18**
Opponents	218	2,630	12.1	t51	13

Passing

	Att	Com	Yds	Pct	TD	In	YL	Rate
Starr	295	172	2,418	58.3	16	16	138	80.3
Hornung	5	3	42	60.0	1	0	0	—
T. Moore	2	2	42	100.0	1	0	0	—
Roach	4	0	0	0.0	0	0	0	—
Packers	**306**	**177**	**2,502**	**57.8**	**18**	**16**	**138**	**82.2**
Opponents	414	218	2,630	52.7	13	29	273	53.7

Punting

	No	Yds	Avg	LG	HB
Dowler	38	1,674	44.1	75	0
McGee	13	520	40.0	51	0
Packers	**51**	**2,194**	**43.0**	**75**	**0**
Opponents	49	1,851	37.8	61	0

Kickoff Returns

	No	Yds	Avg	LG	TD
Adderley	18	478	26.6	61	0
T. Moore	15	409	27.3	60	0
Symank	4	121	30.3	38	0
Forester	3	55	18.3	20	0
E. Pitts	1	14	14.0	14	0
Packers	**41**	**1,077**	**26.3**	**61**	**0**
Opponents	69	1,597	23.1	64	0

Punt Returns

	No	Yds	Avg	FC	LG	TD
Wood	14	225	16.1	11	t72	2
Carpenter	6	130	21.7	5	48	0
Packers	**20**	**355**	**17.8**	**16**	**t72**	**2**
Opponents	25	313	12.5	4	t90	1

Interceptions

	No	Yds	Avg	LG	TD
Symank	5	99	19.8	41	0
Whittenton	5	98	19.6	t41	1
Gremminger	5	54	10.8	41	0
Wood	5	52	10.4	21	0
Currie	3	59	19.7	t21	1
Nitschke	2	41	20.5	27	0
Forester	2	33	16.5	33	0
Adderley	1	9	9.0	9	0
Hanner	1	1	1.0	1	0
Packers	**29**	**446**	**15.4**	**t41**	**2**
Opponents	16	238	14.9	63	0

Scoring

	TDr	TDp	TDrt	PAT	FG	S	TP
Hornung	8	2	0	41/41	15/22	0	146
J. Taylor	15	1	0	0/0	0/0	0	96
McGee	0	7	0	0/0	0/0	0	42
R. Kramer	0	4	0	0/0	0/0	0	24
Dowler	0	3	0	0/0	0/0	0	18
T. Moore	1	1	0	0/0	0/0	0	12
Wood	0	0	2	0/0	0/0	0	12
Agajanian	0	0	0	8/8	1/2	0	11
Currie	0	0	1	0/0	0/0	0	6
E. Pitts	1	0	0	0/0	0/0	0	6
Roach	1	0	0	0/0	0/0	0	6
Starr	1	0	0	0/0	0/0	0	6
Whittenton	0	0	1	0/0	0/0	0	6
Packers	**27**	**18**	**4**	**49/49**	**16/24**	**0**	**391**
Opponents	12	13	1	26/26	13/21	1	223

1961

Fumbles

	Fum	Ow	Op	Yds	Tot
Adderley	1	0	0	0	0
Currie	0	0	2	0	2
W. Davis	0	0	3	0	3
Gremminger	0	0	1	0	1
Hanner	0	0	2	0	2
Hornung	1	0	0	0	0
Masters	0	2	0	0	2
McGee	1	0	0	0	0
T. Moore	2	1	0	0	1
Nitschke	0	0	1	0	1
Quinlan	0	0	1	0	1
Roach	1	0	0	0	0
Starr	1	0	0	0	2
Symank	1	0	2	0	2
J. Taylor	2	1	0	0	1
Toburen	0	1	0	0	1
Whittenton	0	0	1	0	1
Wood	1	1	4	0	5
Packers	**18**	**8**	**17**	**2**	**25**

NFL STANDINGS

Western Conference

	W	L	T	Pct	PF	PA
Green Bay Packers	**11**	**3**	**0**	**.786**	**391**	**223**
Detroit Lions	8	5	1	.615	270	258
Baltimore Colts	8	6	0	.571	302	307
Chicago Bears	8	6	0	.571	326	302
San Francisco 49ers	7	6	1	.538	346	272
Los Angeles Rams	4	10	0	.286	263	333
Minnesota Vikings	3	11	0	.214	285	407

Eastern Conference

	W	L	T	Pct	PF	PA
New York Giants	10	3	1	.769	368	220
Philadelphia Eagles	10	4	0	.714	361	297
Cleveland Browns	8	5	1	.615	319	270
St. Louis Cardinals	7	7	0	.500	279	267
Pittsburgh Steelers	6	8	0	.429	295	287
Dallas Cowboys	4	9	1	.308	236	380
Washington Redskins	1	12	1	.077	174	392

1961 ROSTER

No	Name	Pos	Ht	Wt	DOB	College	G
26	Adderley, Herb	CB	6-1	205	06/08/39	Michigan State	14
3	Agajanian, Ben	K	6-0	220	08/28/19	New Mexico	3
65	Bettis, Tom	LB	6-2	225	03/17/33	Purdue	12
33	Carpenter, Lew	FB	6-2	215	01/12/32	Arkansas	14
58	Currie, Dan	LB	6-3	240	06/27/35	Michigan State	14
72	Davidson, Ben	DE	6-8	275	06/14/40	Washington	14
87	Davis, Willie	DE	6-3	240	07/24/34	Grambling	14
86	Dowler, Boyd	E	6-5	220	10/18/37	Colorado	14
81	Folkins, Lee	DE	6-5	220	07/04/39	Washington	14
71	Forester, Bill	LB	6-3	240	08/09/32	SMU	14
75	Gregg, Forrest	T	6-4	250	10/18/33	SMU	14
46	Gremminger, Hank	DB	6-1	205	09/01/33	Baylor	14
79	Hanner, Dave	DT	6-2	260	05/20/30	Arkansas	13
5	Hornung, Paul	HB	6-2	215	12/23/35	Notre Dame	12
53	Iman, Ken	C	6-1	230	02/08/39	Southeast Missouri State	14
74	Jordan, Henry	DT	6-3	250	01/26/35	Virginia	14
84	Knafelc, Gary	E	6-4	220	01/02/32	Colorado	13
77	Kostelnik, Ron	DT	6-4	260	01/14/40	Cincinnati	14
64	Kramer, Jerry	G	6-3	250	01/23/36	Idaho	7
88	Kramer, Ron	E	6-3	230	06/24/35	Michigan	14
78	Masters, Norm	T	6-2	250	09/19/33	Michigan State	14
85	McGee, Max	E	6-3	205	07/16/32	Tulane	13
25	Moore, Tom	HB	6-2	215	07/17/38	Vanderbilt	13
66	Nitschke, Ray	LB	6-3	235	12/29/36	Illinois	12
22	Pitts, Elijah	HB	6-1	200	02/03/39	Philander Smith	14
83	Quinlan, Bill	DE	6-3	250	06/19/32	Michigan State	14
51	Ringo, Jim	C	6-1	235	11/21/32	Syracuse	14
10	Roach, John	QB	6-4	200	03/26/33	SMU	7
76	Skoronski, Bob	T	6-3	250	03/05/34	Indiana	13
15	Starr, Bart	QB	6-1	200	01/09/34	Alabama	14
27	Symank, John	DB	5-11	180	08/31/35	Florida	14
31	Taylor, Jim	FB	6-0	215	09/20/35	LSU	14
63	Thurston, Fred (Fuzzy)	G	6-1	250	05/07/35	Valparaiso	14
61	Toburen, Nelson	LB	6-3	235	11/24/38	Wichita	14
45	Tunnell, Emlen	DB	6-1	210	03/29/25	Iowa	13
47	Whittenton, Jesse	DB	6-0	195	05/09/34	Texas-El Paso	14
24	Wood, Willie	DB	5-10	185	12/23/36	USC	14

1961 DRAFT

Rnd	Name	Pos	Ht	Wt	College
1	Herb Adderley	DB	6-1	205	Michigan State
2	Ron Kostelnik	T	6-4	260	Cincinnati
3	Phil Nugent	QB	6-1	192	Tulane
*4a	Paul Dudley	HB	6-0	195	Arkansas
4b	Joe LeSage	G	6-2	235	Tulane
	(Choice from Eagles for Bob Freeman)				
5	Jack Novak	G	6-2	225	Miami (FL)
6	Lee Folkins	DE	6-5	220	Washington
7	Lewis Johnson	HB	6-1	195	Florida A&M
8	(Choice to Browns for Bob Jarus)				
9	Vester Flanagan	T	6-4	250	Humboldt
10a	Roger Hagberg	FB	6-1	212	Minnesota
	(Choice from Cowboys for Fred Cone)				
10b	Terry McLeod	T	6-3	230	Baylor
11	Val Keckin	QB	6-3	210	Southern Mississippi
*12	John Denvir	T	6-2	230	Colorado
13	Elijah Pitts	HB	6-1	200	Philander Smith
14	Nelson Toburen	LB	6-3	230	Wichita
*15	Ray Lardani	T	6-3	265	Miami (FL)
16	Clarence Mason	E	6-2	185	Bowling Green
17	Jim Brewington	T	6-5	270	North Carolina Central
18	Randy Sims	B	6-0	190	Texas A&M
19	Leland Bondhus	T	6-3	230	South Dakota State
20	Ray Ratkowski	HB	6-1	185	Notre Dame

* denotes juniors

1961 GREEN BAY PACKERS

FRONT ROW: (L-R) 26 Herb Adderley, 72 Ben Davidson, 22 Elijah Pitts, 81 Lee Folkins, 77 Ron Kostelnik, 61 Nelson Toburen.
SECOND ROW: (L-R) 53 Ken Iman, 24 Willie Wood, 46 Hank Gremminger, 25 Tom Moore, 64 Jerry Kramer, 63 Fred (Fuzzy) Thurston, 47 Jesse Whittenton, 27 John Symank, 65 Tom Bettis.
THIRD ROW: (L-R) Trainer Carl (Bud) Jorgensen, 76 Bob Skoronski, 15 Bart Starr, 84 Gary Knafelc, 51 Jim Ringo, 78 Norm Masters, 58 Dan Currie, 87 Willie Davis, 10 John Roach, 33 Lew Carpenter, Equipment Manager Gerald (Dad) Braisher.
BACK ROW: (L-R) 83 Bill Quinlan, 75 Forrest Gregg, 45 Emlen Tunnell, 66 Ray Nitschke, 79 Dave Hanner, 74 Henry Jordan, 86 Boyd Dowler, 31 Jim Taylor, 88 Ron Kramer, 71 Bill Forester, 5 Paul Hornung, 85 Max McGee.

1962

In 1961, Green Bay fielded the best team in the league. In 1962, the Packers assembled one of the greatest teams in NFL history.

If the Packers were good in 1961, they dominated in 1962. One loss kept the Green and Gold from an unbeaten season. The team scored a league-leading 415 points while holding opponents to an NFL-low 148. The circuit's top running attack exploded for an NFL-record 36 touchdowns. Led by ball-hawking Willie Wood and Herb Adderley, the defense intercepted more passes (31) than any other.

From start to finish, the Packers perched themselves atop the Western Conference and never wavered. The team reeled off 10 straight wins to start the season, then ran off three more to close with a flourish. Green Bay registered three shutouts along the way to a 13-1 record and third consecutive Western Conference championship.

A pair of 49-0 blowouts displayed Packer power at its finest. On September 30, Green Bay piled up 244 yards rushing, intercepted five passes and held the Bears to seven first downs. A month-and-a-half later against the Eagles, the team set club records for total yards (628), first downs (37) and touchdowns rushing (six). Nine weeks into the season, Green Bay's opponents had managed to score a mere 61 points.

Not everything went according to plan. The Lions gave Green Bay all the trouble they could handle and then some. The two were unbeaten (3-0) when they met on October 7. The Lions built a 7-6 lead in rain-soaked City Stadium and clung to it with 1:25 left in the fourth quarter. But Herb Adderley intercepted Milt Plum on third down and returned the theft 40 yards to set up Hornung's 21-yard field goal with 33 seconds left. Green Bay escaped with a 9-7 win.

The rematch took place on Thanksgiving and this time the Packers weren't so fortunate. The Lions (8-2) sacked Bart Starr nine times for 93 yards in losses. They intercepted him twice and recovered three Green Bay fumbles. In one well-executed ambush, Detroit crushed the Packers 26-14 and moved to within a game of the frontrunning Pack.

Green Bay bounced back. They blew out the Rams 41-10, then beat both West Coast clubs on the road to end the year two games ahead of the second-place Lions.

Jim Taylor, the team's bruising fullback, had his best year in 1962. He wrested the rushing title from Cleveland's Jim Brown, surpassing him for the lead in week three. Taylor finished with a team-record 1,474 yards on 272 carries. He also scored a then-NFL record 19 rushing touchdowns.

Taylor supplanted Hornung as the league's top scorer with 114 points. Hornung's point production suffered in part because he missed five games after damaging his knee in a 48-21 win at Minnesota. He sat out five of the next six contests and gained only 53 yards rushing after he returned. Oddly enough, a healthy Hornung was unable to help the Packers in their quest for a third straight championship in 1963.

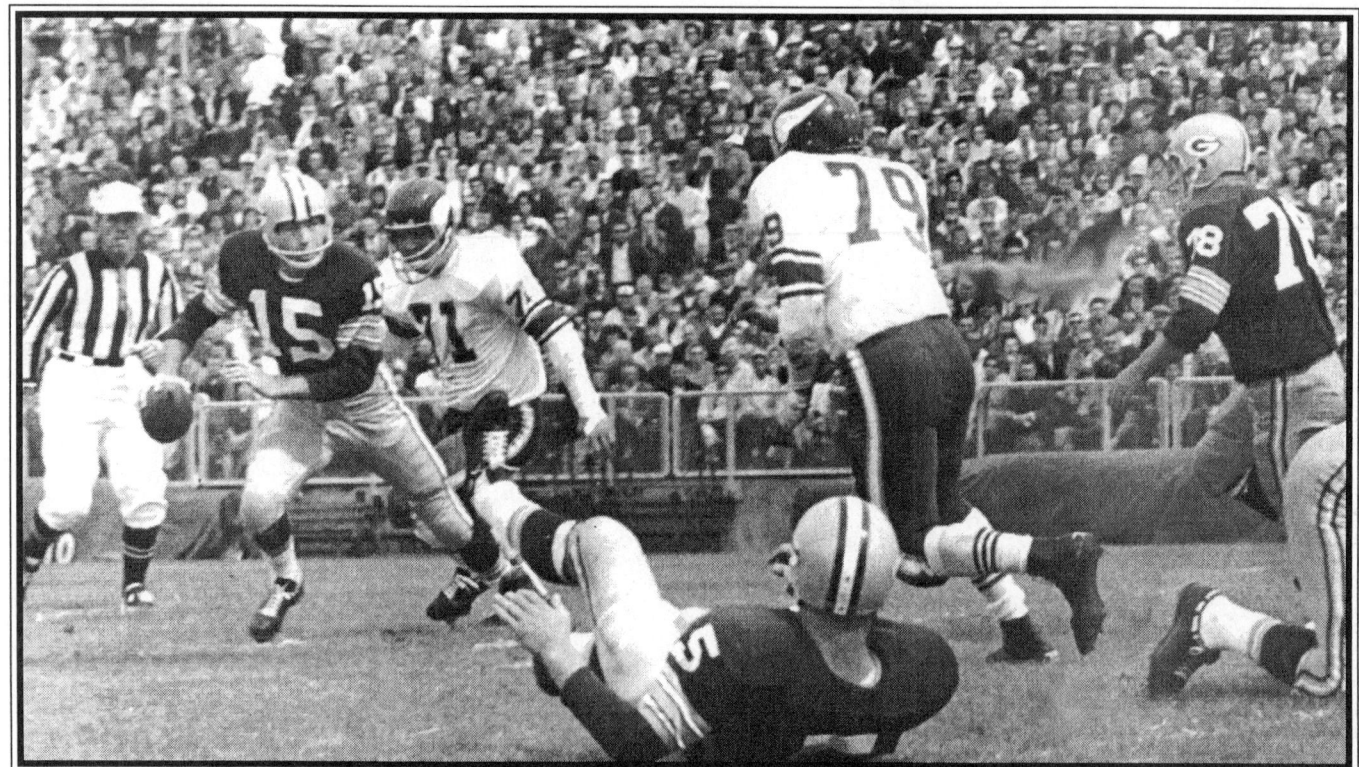

Green Bay Press-Gazette photo

Bart Starr (15) breaks away from Larry Bowie (71) for a nine-yard gain in the first quarter of a 34-7 triumph over the Vikings, September 16. Starr completed seven of 14 passes for 108 yards in the game. Number 15 wound up the as the league's leading passer and completed a remarkable 62.5 percent of his throws. Number 79 is Jim Prestel.

TEAM STATISTICS

	GB	OPP
First Downs	281	191
Rushing	145	88
Passing	120	94
Penalty	16	9
Rushes	518	404
Yards Gained	2,460	1,531
Average Gain	4.75	3.79
Average Yards per Game	175.7	109.4
Passes Attempted	311	355
Completed	187	187
% Completed	60.13	52.68
Total Yards Gained	2,621	2,084
Yards Lost	290	338
Net Yards Gained	2,331	1,746
Yards Gained per Completion	14.02	11.14
Average Net Yards per Game	166.5	124.7
Combined Net Yards Gained	4,791	3,277
Total Plays	829	759
Average Yards per Play	5.78	4.32
Average Net Yards per Game	342.2	234.1
Intercepted By	31	13
Yards Returned	452	122
Returned for TD	1	1
Punts	50	58
Yards Punted	2,046	2,506
Average Yards per Punt	40.92	43.21
Punt Returns	31	20
Yards Returned	290	183
Average Yards per Return	9.35	9.15
Returned for TD	0	1
Kickoff Returns	30	76
Yards Returned	716	1,524
Average Yards per Return	23.87	20.05
Returned for TD	1	0
Penalties	59	54
Yards Penalized	617	611
Fumbles	29	28
Lost	15	19
Own Recovered for Touchdown	1	0
Opponent's Recovered by	19	15
Opponent's Recovered for Touchdown	0	1
Total Points Scored	415	148
Total Touchdowns	53	17
Touchdowns Rushing	36	4
Touchdowns Passing	14	10
Touchdowns on Returns & Recoveries	3	3
Extra Points	52	17
Safeties	0	1
Field Goals Attempted	21	22
Field Goals Made	15	9
% Successful	71.43	40.91

Regular Season   13-1-0

Date	GB		OPP		Att.
9/16	34	Minnesota Vikings	7		(38,669)
9/23	17	St. Louis Cardinals (M)	0		(44,885)
9/30	49	Chicago Bears	0		(38,669)
10/7	9	Detroit Lions	7		(38,669)
10/14	48	at Minnesota Vikings	21		(41,475)
10/21	31	San Francisco 49ers (M)	13		(46,010)
10/28	17	at Baltimore Colts	6		(57,966)
11/4	38	at Chicago Bears	7		(48,753)
11/11	49	at Philadelphia Eagles	0		(60,671)
11/18	17	Baltimore Colts	13		(38,669)
11/22	14	at Detroit Lions	26		(57,578)
12/2	41	Los Angeles Rams (M)	10		(46,833)
12/9	31	at San Francisco 49ers	21		(53,769)
12/16	20	at Los Angeles Rams	17		(60,353)

Postseason   1-0-0

12/30	16	at New York Giants	7		(64,892)

Score By Periods

	1	2	3	4	Total
Packers	71	115	93	136	415
Opponents	26	71	16	35	148

INDIVIDUAL STATISTICS

Rushing

	Att	Yds	Avg	LG	TD
J. Taylor	272	1,474	5.4	51	19
T. Moore	112	377	3.4	t32	7
Hornung	57	219	3.8	t37	5
Gros	29	155	5.3	26	2
E. Pitts	22	110	5.0	t26	2
Starr	21	72	3.4	18	1
McGee	3	52	17.3	36	0
Roach	1	5	5.0	5	0
R. Kramer	1	-4	-4.0	-4	0
Packers	**518**	**2,460**	**4.8**	**51**	**36**
Opponents	404	1,531	3.8	40	4

1962

Receiving

	No	Yds	Avg	LG	TD
McGee	49	820	16.7	64	3
Dowler	49	724	14.8	41	2
R. Kramer	37	555	15.0	t54	7
J. Taylor	22	106	4.8	25	0
T. Moore	11	100	9.1	34	0
Hornung	9	168	18.7	t83	2
Carpenter	7	104	14.9	22	0
E. Pitts	3	44	14.7	29	0
Packers	**187**	**2,621**	**14.0**	**t83**	**14**
Opponents	187	2,084	11.1	63	10

Passing

	Att	Com	Yds	Pct	TD	In	YL	Rate
Starr	285	178	2,438	62.5	12	9	286	90.7
Hornung	6	4	80	66.7	0	2	0	—
T. Moore	5	2	70	40.0	2	1	0	—
Hornung	12	3	33	25.0	0	0	4	39.6
E. Pitts	2	0	0	00.0	0	0	0	—
McGee	1	0	0	00.0	0	1	0	—
Packers	**311**	**187**	**2,621**	**60.1**	**14**	**13**	**290**	**84.9**
Opponents	355	187	2,084	52.7	10	31	338	43.4

Punting

	No	Yds	Avg	LG	HB
Dowler	36	1,550	43.1	75	0
McGee	14	496	35.4	56	0
Packers	**50**	**2,046**	**40.9**	**75**	**0**
Opponents	58	2,506	43.2	80	0

Kickoff Returns

	No	Yds	Avg	LG	TD
Adderley	15	418	27.9	t103	1
T. Moore	13	284	21.8	28	0
Gros	1	7	7.0	7	0
Nitschke	1	7	7.0	7	0
Packers	**30**	**716**	**23.9**	**t103**	**1**
Opponents	76	1,524	20.1	47	0

Punt Returns

	No	Yds	Avg	FC	LG	TD
Wood	23	273	11.9	9	65	0
E. Pitts	7	17	2.4	3	7	0
Kostelnik	1	0	0.0	0	0	0
Packers	**31**	**290**	**9.4**	**12**	**65**	**0**
Opponents	20	183	9.2	6	t85	1

Interceptions

	No	Yds	Avg	LG	TD
Wood	9	132	14.7	37	0
Adderley	7	132	18.9	t50	1
Gremminger	5	88	17.6	35	0
Nitschke	4	56	14.0	28	0
Whittenton	3	40	13.3	36	0
Quinlan	1	4	4.0	4	0
Hanner	1	0	0.0	0	0
H. Jordan	1	0	0.0	0	0
Packers	**31**	**452**	**14.6**	**t50**	**1**
Opponents	13	122	9.4	35	1

Scoring

	TDr	TDp	TDrt	PAT	FG	S	TP
J. Taylor	19	0	0	0/0	0/0	0	114
Hornung	5	2	0	14/14	6/10	0	74
J. Kramer	0	0	0	38/39	9/11	0	65
R. Kramer	0	7	0	0/0	0/0	0	42
T. Moore	7	0	0	0/0	0/0	0	42
McGee	0	3	0	0/0	0/0	0	18
Adderley	0	0	2	0/0	0/0	0	12
Dowler	0	2	0	0/0	0/0	0	12
Gros	2	0	0	0/0	0/0	0	12
E. Pitts	2	0	0	0/0	0/0	0	12
W. Davis	0	0	1	0/0	0/0	0	6
Starr	1	0	0	0/0	0/0	0	6
Packers	**36**	**14**	**3**	**52/53**	**15/21**	**0**	**415**
Opponents	4	10	3	17/17	9/22	1	148

Fumbles

	Fum	Ow	Op	Yds	Tot
Adderley	2	3	1	15	4
Carpenter	0	0	1	0	1
Currie	0	0	1	0	1
W. Davis	0	1	2	0	3
Dowler	1	0	0	0	0
Forester	0	0	2	0	2
Gremminger	0	0	1	0	1
Gros	1	0	0	0	1
Hanner	0	0	1	0	1
Hornung	1	0	0	0	0
Iman	0	0	1	0	1
H. Jordan	0	0	1	7	1
J. Kramer	0	2	0	13	2
McGee	2	3	0	16	3
T. Moore	4	2	0	0	2
Nitschke	1	1	3	0	4
E. Pitts	2	0	0	0	1
Quinlan	1	0	1	0	1
Ringo	0	0	1	0	1
Roach	1	0	0	0	0
Starr	8	1	0	0	1
J. Taylor	5	1	0	0	1
Whittenton	0	0	2	0	2
Wood	0	0	0	36	0
Packers	**29**	**14**	**19**	**87**	**33**

NFL STANDINGS

Western Conference

	W	L	T	Pct	PF	PA
Green Bay Packers	13	1	0	.929	415	148
Detroit Lions	11	3	0	.786	315	177
Chicago Bears	9	5	0	.643	321	287
Baltimore Colts	7	7	0	.500	293	288
San Francisco 49ers	6	8	0	.429	282	331
Minnesota Vikings	2	11	1	.154	254	410
Los Angeles Rams	1	12	1	.077	220	334

Eastern Conference

	W	L	T	Pct	PF	PA
New York Giants	12	2	0	.857	398	283
Pittsburgh Steelers	9	5	0	.643	312	363
Cleveland Browns	7	6	1	.538	291	257
Washington Redskins	5	7	2	.417	305	376
Dallas Cowboys	5	8	1	.385	398	402
St. Louis Cardinals	4	9	1	.308	287	361
Philadelphia Eagles	3	10	1	.231	282	356

1962 ROSTER

No	Name	Pos	Ht	Wt	DOB	College	G
26	Adderley, Herb	CB	6-1	205	06/08/39	Michigan State	14
80	Barnes, Gary	E	6-4	210	09/13/39	Clemson	13
60	Blaine, Ed	G	6-2	240	01/30/40	Missouri	14
33	Carpenter, Lew	FB	6-2	215	01/12/32	Arkansas	14
58	Currie, Dan	LB	6-3	240	06/27/35	Michigan State	12
87	Davis, Willie	DE	6-3	240	07/24/34	Grambling	14
86	Dowler, Boyd	E	6-5	225	10/18/37	Colorado	14
71	Forester, Bill	LB	6-3	240	08/09/32	SMU	14
73	Gassert, Ron	DT	6-3	260	07/22/40	Virginia	11
75	Gregg, Forrest	T	6-4	250	10/18/33	SMU	14
46	Gremminger, Hank	DB	6-1	205	09/01/33	Baylor	14
40	Gros, Earl	FB	6-3	230	08/29/40	Louisiana	14
79	Hanner, Dave	DT	6-2	260	05/20/30	Arkansas	14
5	Hornung, Paul	HB	6-2	215	12/23/35	Notre Dame	9
53	Iman, Ken	C	6-1	230	02/08/39	Southeast Missouri State	14
74	Jordan, Henry	DT	6-3	250	01/26/35	Virginia	14
84	Knafelc, Gary	E	6-4	220	01/02/32	Colorado	11
77	Kostelnik, Ron	DT	6-4	260	01/14/40	Cincinnati	14
64	Kramer, Jerry	G	6-3	255	01/23/36	Idaho	14
88	Kramer, Ron	E	6-3	240	06/24/35	Michigan	14
78	Masters, Norm	T	6-2	250	09/19/33	Michigan State	14
85	McGee, Max	E	6-3	205	07/16/32	Tulane	14
25	Moore, Tom	HB	6-2	215	07/17/38	Vanderbilt	14
66	Nitschke, Ray	LB	6-3	235	12/29/36	Illinois	14
22	Pitts, Elijah	HB	6-1	200	02/03/39	Philander Smith	14
83	Quinlan, Bill	DE	6-3	250	06/19/32	Michigan State	14
51	Ringo, Jim	C	6-1	235	11/21/32	Syracuse	14
10	Roach, John	QB	6-4	200	03/26/33	SMU	8
76	Skoronski, Bob	T	6-3	250	03/05/34	Indiana	13
15	Starr, Bart	QB	6-1	200	01/09/34	Alabama	14
27	Symank, John	DB	5-11	180	08/31/35	Florida	14
31	Taylor, Jim	FB	6-0	215	09/20/35	LSU	14
63	Thurston, Fred (Fuzzy)	G	6-1	250	05/07/35	Valparaiso	14
61	Toburen, Nelson	LB	6-3	235	11/24/38	Wichita	10
47	Whittenton, Jesse	DB	6-0	195	05/09/34	Texas-El Paso	14
29	Williams, Howard	DB	6-1	190	12/04/37	Howard J.C.	3
24	Wood, Willie	DB	5-10	185	12/23/36	USC	14

1962 DRAFT

Rnd	Name	Pos	Ht	Wt	College
1	Earl Gros	FB	6-3	230	LSU
2	Ed Blaine	G	6-2	240	Missouri
3a	Gary Barnes	E	6-4	210	Clemson
	(Choice from Giants for Joel Wells)				
3b	(Choice to Browns for John Roach)				
4	Ron Gassert	DT	6-3	260	Virginia
*5a	Chuck Morris	HB	6-1	195	Mississippi
	(Choice from Colts for Lamar McHan)				
5b	Jon Schopf	G	6-2	240	Michigan
6a	John Sutro	T	6-4	250	San Jose State
	(Choice from Redskins for Dale Hackbarth)				
6b	Oscar Donahue	E	6-3	205	San Jose State
7	Gary Cutsinger	T	6-4	230	Oklahoma State
*8	James Tulis	HB	6-3	195	Florida A&M
9	Pete Schenk	DB	6-2	200	Washington State
10	Gale Weidener	QB	6-1	195	Colorado
*11	Jim Thrush	E	6-4	230	Xavier
12a	Joe Thorne	HB	6-1	195	South Dakota State
	(Choice from Cowboys for Steve Meilinger)				
12b	Tom Pennington	K	6-2	210	Georgia
13	Tom Kepner	T	6-3	245	Villanova
14	Ernest Green	HB	6-2	205	Louisville
15	Roger Holdinsky	HB	5-11	185	West Virginia
*16	James Field	DB	6-1	190	LSU
17	Junias Buchanon	T	6-5	246	Grambling
18	Bob Joiner	QB	6-1	205	Presbyterian
19	Jerry Scatini	DB	6-2	200	California
20	Mike Snodgrass	C	6-2	220	Western Michigan

* denotes juniors

1962 GREEN BAY PACKERS

FRONT ROW: (L–R) 22 Elijah Pitts, 60 Ed Blaine, 40 Earl Gros, 80 Gary Barnes, 73 Ron Gassert, 89 Oscar Donahue, 77 Ron Kostelnik.
SECOND ROW: (L–R) 24 Willie Wood, 27 John Symank, 46 Hank Gremminger, 58 Dan Currie, 26 Herb Adderley, 61 Nelson Toburen, 10 John Roach, 75 Forrest Gregg.
THIRD ROW: (L–R) 51 Jim Ringo, 15 Bart Starr, 84 Gary Knafelc, 64 Jerry Kramer, 63 Fred (Fuzzy) Thurston, 47 Jesse Whittenton, 33 Lew Carpenter, 25 Tom Moore.
FOURTH ROW: (L–R) Property Manager Gerald (Dad) Braisher, 76 Bob Skoronski, 66 Ray Nitschke, 53 Ken Iman, 87 Willie Davis, 74 Henry Jordan, Trainer Carl (Bud) Jorgensen.
BACK ROW: (L–R) 83 Bill Quinlan, 78 Norm Masters, 86 Boyd Dowler, 31 Jim Taylor, 88 Ron Kramer, 71 Bill Forester, 79 Dave Hanner, 5 Paul Hornung.

1963

One team kept the Packers from a fourth straight Western Conference title and a shot at a third straight championship: the Chicago Bears. Green Bay's ungracious neighbor to the south used its top-ranked defense to shut down the Packers 10-3 on opening day. They then thumped the Green and Gold 26-7 in the return engagement in mid-November. In between, both teams went undefeated and quickly outdistanced the other conference members. In the end, the Bears (11-1-2) edged the Packers (11-2-1) by the slimmest of margins.

Except for the finish in the standings, Green Bay hardly slipped at all in 1963. Its rushing attack fell to second behind Cleveland. Defensively, the team dropped to second. The Giants scored more points and the Bears allowed fewer. But, except for Chicago, nobody could beat the Packers.

Two events upset Packerdom even before the season began. On April 17, Commissioner Pete Rozelle suspended Paul Hornung and the Lions' Alex Karras indefinitely for gambling. The two had placed bets, ranging from $50 to $200, on a number of games over the past few years. Five other players, all from Detroit, were fined $2,000 for placing one-time wagers on the 1962 Championship game. The men did not bet against their teams and no evidence of point shaving was found.

The second event, a 20-17 loss to the College All-Stars, was unsettling because of its rarity. It marked the first time since 1959 that Green Bay had lost a preseason game.

In midsummer, the NFL honored 17 of its finest at Canton, Ohio. Four Packers were among the charter members inducted into the Hall of Fame. Earl (Curly) Lambeau, Johnny (Blood) McNally, Robert (Cal) Hubbard and Don Hutson were enshrined.

On September 15, the Packers hosted the Bears. Green Bay was held to 150 yards and Chicago 231. Joe Marconi's one-yard run in the third quarter broke a 3-3 tie and gave the Bears a 10-3 win.

The fierce rivals then each won eight straight. The Packers were thrown a scare in the middle of their streak when Bart Starr endured a hairline fracture on his passing hand in the team's 30-7 win at St. Louis. He was outfitted with a splint and missed the subsequent Baltimore game completely. He returned only to hold for field goals in the next two games.

John Roach filled in for the ailing Starr and led the team to three straight wins. Nevertheless, Coach Vince Lombardi obtained Zeke Bratkowski as insurance from the Rams for the waiver price of $100.

By the time the Bears rematch rolled around, Starr was ready if needed. Lombardi made his decision to stick with Roach a few days prior to the game. In the end, it didn't matter who quarterbacked. The Bears ran up 26 points and routed the Packers 26-7.

With that loss, the Packers needed help to win the conference. Unfortunately, no one was able to topple the Bears and Green Bay was out of championship play for the first time since 1959.

Green Bay Press-Gazette photo

Ray Nitschke (66) and Herb Adderley (26) attempt to break up a pass intended for the Rams' Jim Phillips (82) in Green Bay on October 6. The Packers won 42-10. Adderley returned a kickoff 98 yards for a touchdown to start the days' scoring. Adderley led the team in kickoff returns and shared the interception lead with Willie Wood (24).

TEAM STATISTICS

	GB	OPP
First Downs	258	193
Rushing	114	92
Passing	126	87
Penalty	18	14
Rushes	504	428
Yards Gained	2,248	1,586
Average Gain	4.46	3.71
Average Yards per Game	160.6	113.3
Passes Attempted	345	378
Completed	179	180
% Completed	51.88	47.62
Total Yards Gained	2,711	2,340
Times Sacked	20	39
Yards Lost	178	327
Net Yards Gained	2,533	2,013
Yards Gained per Completion	15.15	13.00
Net Yards per Attempt	6.94	4.83
Average Net Yards per Game	180.9	143.8
Combined Net Yards Gained	4,781	3,599
Total Plays	869	845
Average Yards per Play	5.50	4.26
Average Net Yards per Game	341.5	257.1
Intercepted By	22	21
Yards Returned	312	297
Returned for TD	0	1
Punts	51	59
Yards Punted	2,279	2,558
Average Yards per Punt	44.69	43.36
Punt Returns	26	29
Yards Returned	229	220
Average Yards per Return	8.81	7.59
Returned for TD	0	0
Kickoff Returns	46	69
Yards Returned	1,122	1,331
Average Yards per Return	24.39	19.29
Returned for TD	1	0
Penalties	53	59
Yards Penalized	517	568
Fumbles	30	31
Lost	20	21
Own Recovered for Touchdown	0	0
Opponent's Recovered by	21	20
Opponent's Recovered for Touchdown	0	2
Total Points Scored	369	206
Total Touchdowns	46	23
Touchdowns Rushing	22	11
Touchdowns Passing	22	9
Touchdowns on Returns & Recoveries	2	3
Extra Points	43	23
Safeties	1	0
Field Goals Attempted	34	33
Field Goals Made	16	15
% Successful	47.06	45.45

Regular Season 11-2-1

Date	GB		OPP	Att.
9/15	3	Chicago Bears	10	(42,327)
9/22	31	Detroit Lions (M)	10	(45,912)
9/29	31	Baltimore Colts	20	(42,327)
10/6	42	Los Angeles Rams	10	(42,327)
10/13	37	at Minnesota Vikings	28	(42,567)
10/20	30	at St. Louis Cardinals	7	(32,224)
10/27	34	at Baltimore Colts	20	(60,065)
11/3	33	Pittsburgh Steelers (M)	14	(46,293)
11/10	28	Minnesota Vikings	7	(42,327)
11/17	7	at Chicago Bears	26	(49,166)
11/24	28	San Francisco 49ers (M)	10	(45,905)
11/28	13	at Detroit Lions	13	(54,016)
12/7	31	at Los Angeles Rams	14	(52,357)
12/14	21	at San Francisco 49ers	17	(31,031)

Score By Periods

	1	2	3	4	Total
Packers	66	97	92	114	369
Opponents	47	47	44	68	206

INDIVIDUAL STATISTICS

Rushing

	Att	Yds	Avg	LG	TD
J. Taylor	248	1,018	4.1	t40	9
T. Moore	132	658	5.0	t77	6
E. Pitts	54	212	3.9	t34	5
Gros	48	203	4.2	t19	2
Starr	13	116	8.9	20	0
Roach	3	31	10.3	22	0
Carpenter	2	8	4.0	5	0
Mestnik	1	4	4.0	4	0
J. Norton	2	0	0.0	4	0
Bratkowski	1	-2	-2.0	-2	0
Packers	**504**	**2,248**	**4.5**	**t77**	**22**
Opponents	428	1,586	3.7	t52	11

1963

Receiving

	No	Yds	Avg	LG	TD
Dowler	53	901	17.0	t53	6
McGee	39	749	19.2	64	6
R. Kramer	32	537	16.8	49	4
T. Moore	23	237	10.3	t45	2
J. Taylor	13	68	5.2	t27	1
E. Pitts	9	54	6.0	21	1
Fleming	7	132	18.9	33	2
Gros	1	19	19.0	19	0
Carpenter	1	12	12.0	12	0
Jeter	1	2	2.0	2	0
Packers	**179**	**2,711**	**15.1**	**64**	**22**
Opponents	180	2,340	13.0	62	9

Passing

	Att	Com	Yds	Pct	TD	In	Tk/Yds	Rate
Starr	244	132	1,855	54.1	15	10	11/109	82.3
Roach	84	38	620	45.2	4	8	7/53	46.8
T. Moore	4	3	99	75.0	1	0	1/6	—
Bratkowski	11	4	96	36.4	1	3	0/0	59.5
E. Pitts	2	2	41	100.0	1	0	0/0	—
J. Taylor	0	0	0	00.0	0	1	1/10	—
Packers	**345**	**179**	**2,711**	**51.9**	**22**	**21**	**20/178**	**74.0**
Opponents	378	180	2,340	47.6	9	22	39/327	51.2

Punting

	No	Yds	Avg	LG	HB
J. Norton	51	2,279	44.7	61	0
Packers	**51**	**2,279**	**44.7**	**61**	**0**
Opponents	59	2,558	43.4	68	0

Kickoff Returns

	No	Yds	Avg	LG	TD
Adderley	20	597	29.9	t98	1
Gros	17	430	25.3	51	0
Carpenter	5	75	15.0	24	0
Wood	1	20	20.0	20	0
Fleming	1	0	0.0	0	0
J. Kramer	1	0	0.0	0	0
Mestnik	1	0	0.0	0	0
Packers	**46**	**1,122**	**24.4**	**t98**	**1**
Opponents	69	1,331	19.3	93	0

Punt Returns

	No	Yds	Avg	FC	LG	TD
Wood	19	169	8.9	9	41	0
E. Pitts	7	60	8.6	7	20	0
Packers	**26**	**229**	**8.8**	**16**	**41**	**0**
Opponents	29	220	7.6	10	32	0

Interceptions

	No	Yds	Avg	LG	TD
Adderley	5	86	17.2	35	0
Wood	5	67	13.4	22	0
Whittenton	4	90	22.5	33	0
Gremminger	3	25	8.3	16	0
Nitschke	2	8	4.0	5	0
Currie	1	23	23.0	23	0
Forester	1	13	13.0	13	0
Hanner	1	0	0.0	0	0
Packers	**22**	**312**	**14.2**	**35**	**0**
Opponents	21	297	14.1	t47	1

Scoring

	TDr	TDp	TDrt	PAT	FG	S	TP
J. Kramer	0	0	0	43/46	16/34	0	91
J. Taylor	9	1	0	0/0	0/0	0	60
T. Moore	6	2	0	0/0	0/0	0	48
Dowler	0	6	0	0/0	0/0	0	36
McGee	0	6	0	0/0	0/0	0	36
E. Pitts	5	1	0	0/0	0/0	0	36
R. Kramer	0	4	0	0/0	0/0	0	24
Fleming	0	2	0	0/0	0/0	0	12
Gros	2	0	0	0/0	0/0	0	12
Adderley	0	0	1	0/0	0/0	0	6
Gremminger	0	0	1	0/0	0/0	0	6
W. Davis	0	0	0	0/0	0/0	1	2
Packers	**22**	**22**	**2**	**43/46**	**16/34**	**1**	**369**
Opponents	11	9	3	23/23	15/33	0	206

Fumbles

	Fum	Ow	Op	Yds	Tot
Adderley	1	0	0	0	0
L. Aldridge	0	0	1	0	1
Carpenter	0	0	1	0	1
Currie	0	0	1	0	1
W. Davis	0	0	4	10	4
Dowler	4	0	0	0	1
Fleming	0	0	1	0	1
Forester	0	0	2	0	2
Gregg	0	2	0	0	2
Gremminger	0	0	1	0	1
Gros	6	1	0	0	1
H. Jordan	0	0	4	0	4
R. Kramer	1	1	0	0	1
Mestnik	0	0	1	0	1
T. Moore	2	0	0	0	0
Nitschke	1	1	0	0	1
E. Pitts	2	0	0	0	0
Roach	2	1	0	0	1
Starr	5	3	0	0	3
J. Taylor	5	1	0	0	1
Whittenton	0	0	1	0	1
Wood	0	0	4	0	4
Packers	**30**	**10**	**20**	**10**	**31**

NFL STANDINGS

Western Conference

	W	L	T	Pct	PF	PA
Chicago Bears	11	1	2	.917	301	144
Green Bay Packers	11	2	1	.846	369	206
Baltimore Colts	8	6	0	.571	316	285
Detroit Lions	5	8	1	.385	326	265
Minnesota Vikings	5	8	1	.385	309	390
Los Angeles Rams	5	9	0	.357	210	350
San Francisco 49ers	2	12	0	.143	198	391

Eastern Conference

	W	L	T	Pct	PF	PA
New York Giants	11	3	0	.786	448	280
Cleveland Browns	10	4	0	.714	343	262
St. Louis Cardinals	9	5	0	.643	341	283
Pittsburgh Steelers	7	4	3	.636	321	295
Dallas Cowboys	4	10	0	.286	305	378
Washington Redskins	3	11	0	.214	279	398
Philadelphia Eagles	2	10	2	.167	242	381

1963 ROSTER

No	Name	Pos	Ht	Wt	DOB	College	G
26	Adderley, Herb	CB	6-1	210	06/08/39	Michigan State	14
62	Aldridge, Lionel	DE	6-4	245	02/18/41	Utah State	14
82	Barrett, Jan	E	6-3	230	11/13/39	Fresno State	3
12	Bratkowski, Zeke	QB	6-3	200	10/20/31	Georgia	6
33	Carpenter, Lew	FB	6-2	215	01/12/32	Arkansas	14
58	Currie, Dan	LB	6-3	240	06/27/35	Michigan State	14
87	Davis, Willie	DE	6-3	245	07/24/34	Grambling	14
86	Dowler, Boyd	E	6-5	225	10/18/37	Colorado	14
81	Fleming, Marv	TE	6-4	230	01/02/42	Utah	14
71	Forester, Bill	LB	6-3	240	08/09/32	SMU	14
75	Gregg, Forrest	T	6-4	250	10/18/33	SMU	14
46	Gremminger, Hank	DB	6-1	200	09/01/33	Baylor	14
67	Grimm, Dan	G	6-3	245	02/07/41	Colorado	14
40	Gros, Earl	FB	6-3	230	08/29/40	Louisiana	13
79	Hanner, Dave	DT	6-2	260	05/20/30	Arkansas	14
83	Henry, Urban	DE-DT	6-4	265	06/07/35	Georgia Tech	14
65	Holler, Ed	LB	6-2	235	01/23/40	South Carolina	2
53	Iman, Ken	C	6-1	230	02/08/39	Southeast Missouri State	14
21	Jeter, Bob	E	6-1	205	05/09/37	Iowa	13
74	Jordan, Henry	DT	6-3	250	01/26/35	Virginia	14
77	Kostelnik, Ron	DT	6-4	260	01/14/40	Cincinnati	13
64	Kramer, Jerry	G	6-3	245	01/23/36	Idaho	14
88	Kramer, Ron	E	6-3	240	06/24/35	Michigan	12
78	Masters, Norm	T	6-2	250	09/19/33	Michigan State	14
85	McGee, Max	E	6-3	205	07/16/32	Tulane	14
35	Mestnik, Frank	FB	6-2	220	02/23/38	Marquette	11
25	Moore, Tom	HB	6-2	210	07/17/38	Vanderbilt	12
66	Nitschke, Ray	LB	6-3	240	12/29/36	Illinois	12
23	Norton, Jerry	P	5-11	195	05/16/31	SMU	14
22	Pitts, Elijah	HB	6-1	205	02/03/39	Philander Smith	14
51	Ringo, Jim	C	6-1	235	11/21/32	Syracuse	14
10	Roach, John	QB	6-4	200	03/26/33	SMU	8
89	Robinson, Dave	LB	6-3	245	05/03/41	Penn State	14
76	Skoronski, Bob	T	6-3	250	03/05/34	Indiana	14
15	Starr, Bart	QB	6-1	200	01/09/34	Alabama	13
31	Taylor, Jim	FB	6-0	215	09/20/35	LSU	14
63	Thurston, Fred (Fuzzy)	G	6-1	245	05/07/35	Valparaiso	14
47	Whittenton, Jesse	DB	6-0	195	05/09/34	Texas-El Paso	14
29	Williams, Howard	DB	6-1	190	12/04/37	Howard J.C.	7
24	Wood, Willie	DB	5-10	190	12/23/36	USC	14

1963 DRAFT

Rnd	Name	Pos	Ht	Wt	College
1	Dave Robinson	DE	6-3	245	Penn State
2	Tom Brown	DB	6-1	195	Maryland
*3a	Dennis Claridge	QB	6-3	210	Nebraska
	(Choice from Steelers for Tom Bettis)				
3b	Tony Liscio	T	6-4	250	Tulsa
4a	Lionel Aldridge	G	6-4	245	Utah State
	(Choice from Giants for Paul Dudley)				
4b	Carlton Simons	C	6-2	230	Stanford
*5a	Jack Cverko	G	6-1	240	Northwestern
	(Choice from Redskins for Ben Davidson)				
5b	Dan Grimm	T	6-3	240	Colorado
*6a	John Simmons	E	6-3	205	Tulsa
	(Choice from Cowboys)				
6b	Jan Barrett	E	6-3	230	Fresno State
7a	Gary Kroner	HB	6-1	198	Wisconsin
	(Choice from Browns for Ernie Green)				
7b	Olin Hill	T	6-4	240	Furman
	(Choice from Steelers)				
*7c	Turnley Todd	LB	6-2	225	Virginia

Rnd	Name	Pos	Ht	Wt	College
8a	Keith Kinderman	HB	6-0	210	Florida State
	(Choice from Cowboys)				
8b	Louis Rettino	FB	6-1	225	Villanova
*9	Bill Freeman	T	6-4	225	Mississippi Southern
10	Earl McQuiston	G	6-2	240	Iowa
11	Marv Fleming	E	6-4	230	Utah
12	Daryle Lamonica	QB	6-2	205	Notre Dame
*13	Bill Kellum	T	6-4	237	Tulane
14	Ed Holler	LB	6-2	235	South Carolina
*15	Gene Breen	LB	6-2	215	Virginia Tech
16	Coolidge Hunt	FB	6-2	215	Texas Tech
17	Thurman Walker	E	6-2	200	Illinois
18	Louis Hernandez	G	6-1	255	Texas-El Paso
*19	Herman Hamp	HB	5-11	195	Fresno State
20	Bobby Brezina	HB	6-1	205	Houston

* denotes futures

1963 GREEN BAY PACKERS

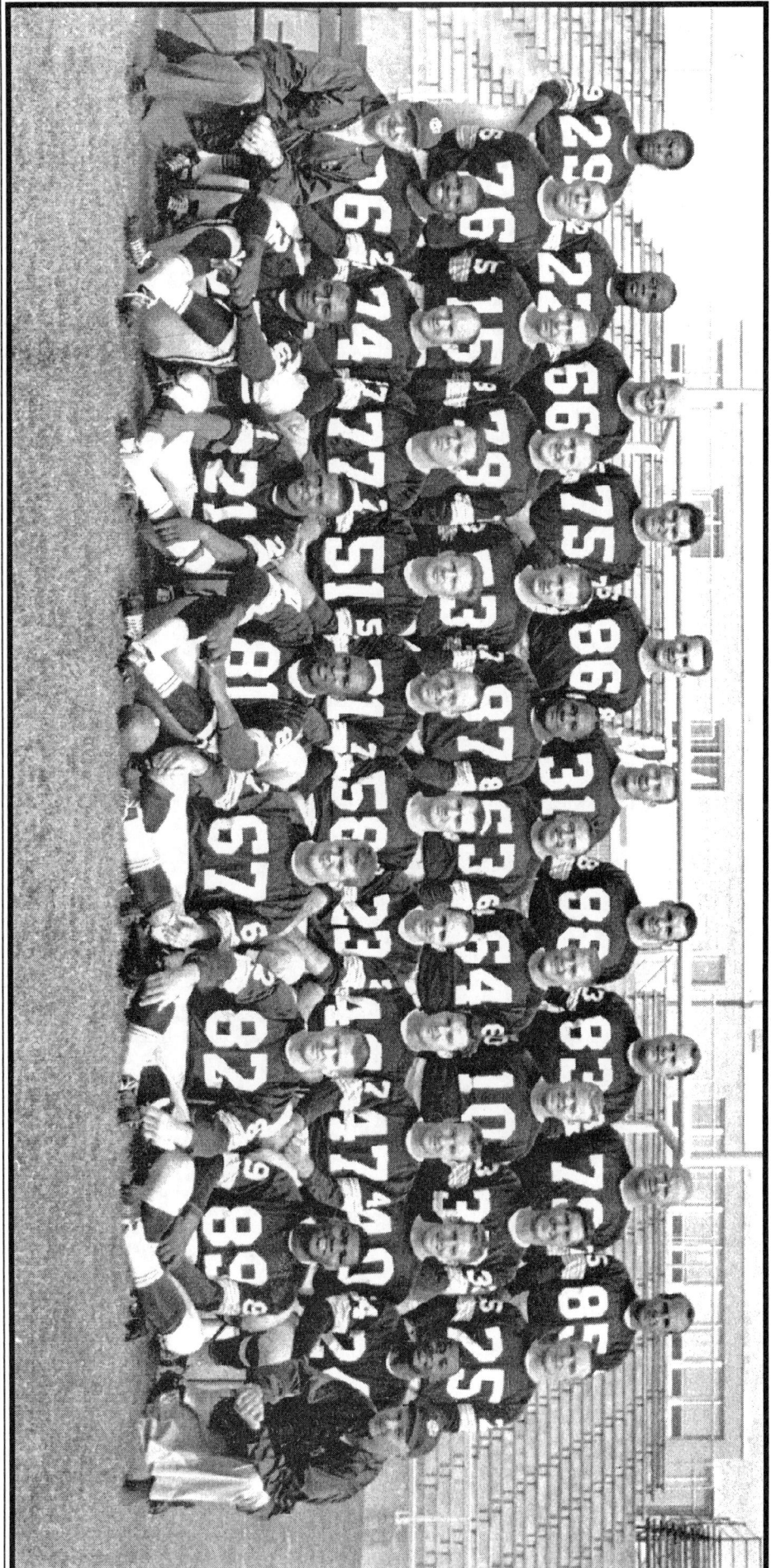

FRONT ROW: (L-R) Property Manager Gerald (Dad) Braisher, 62 Lionel Aldridge, 21 Bob Jeter, 81 Marv Fleming, 67 Dan Grimm, 82 Jan Barrett, 89 Dave Robinson, Trainer Carl (Bud) Jorgensen.
SECOND ROW: (L-R) 26 Herb Adderley, 74 Henry Jordan, 77 Ron Kostelnik, 51 Jim Ringo, 71 Bill Forester, 58 Dan Currie, 23 Jerry Norton, 46 Hank Gremminger, 47 Jesse Whittenton, 40 Earl Gros, 24 Willie Wood.
THIRD ROW: (L-R) 76 Bob Skoronski, 15 Bart Starr, 78 Norm Masters, 53 Ken Iman, 87 Willie Davis, 63 Fred (Fuzzy) Thurston, 64 Jerry Kramer, 10 John Roach, 33 Lew Carpenter, 25 Tom Moore.
BACK ROW: (L-R) 29 Howard Williams, 22 Elijah Pitts, 66 Ray Nitschke, 75 Forrest Gregg, 86 Boyd Dowler, 31 Jim Taylor, 88 Ron Kramer, 83 Urban Henry, 79 Dave Hanner, 85 Max McGee.

Consider. In 1964, Green Bay had the NFL's top-ranked defense – including the number one pass defense – for the first time since 1947. The Packers created 34 fumbles and recovered a league-high 25. Green Bay boasted pro football's most productive running attack. And Bart Starr did not have any interceptions after the third game, despite attempting 219 passes in the final 11 games.

Despite those sparkling numbers, the Green and Gold dropped five games. The Packers climbed into first place just twice – after beating the Bears 23-12 in the opener and after downing Detroit 14-10 in week three. At the season's halfway point, Green Bay (3-4) was lodged in fourth place. With the Packers struggling, the Colts quickly ran away with the Western Conference title. A 5-1-1 second-half surge helped Green Bay claim second place with an 8-5-1 mark.

The Packers' kicking game was a major problem. Paul Hornung returned but left his kicking leg behind. The former bonus pick botched extra point tries in one-point losses to the Colts and Vikings. He missed four field goals in a 24-14 loss at San Francisco. He really got the attention of Coach Vince Lombardi when he blew five tries in a 24-21 return engagement against Baltimore. After that display, Lombardi summoned Ben Agajanian to "tutor" Hornung.

Jerry Kramer missed most of the year. Early in the season, he complained of stomach pain. He underwent exploratory surgery after the first Colts game. Doctors discovered an inflammed abcess beneath his abdomen. More surgery, in the off-season, revealed three wooden splinters lodged there as the result of a childhood accident. Kramer, who came back after a shattered ankle in 1961, was lucky this time to escape with his life.

Small, nagging injuries also caused concern. Starters Henry Jordan (groin), Herb Adderley (muscle pull), Fred (Fuzzy) Thurston (shoulder), Jim Taylor (shoulder) and Dave Robinson (knee) missed a combined 10 games. Furthermore, Starr was knocked out of the San Francisco loss early with a concussion.

"We'll sink or swim with Hornung," Lombardi predicted in a preseason article in the *Green Bay Press-Gazette*. On the surface, Hornung seemed to prove Lombardi right. But Hornung's dismal kicking alone cannot be blamed for the team's sub-par year. In the first Colts game, Starr threw two fourth-quarter interceptions in Baltimore territory. In the Minnesota loss, Fran Tarkenton overcame a fourth-and-22 from his 35-yard line with a minute remaining to set up Fred Cox's game-winning, 27-yard field goal. Finally, in the second Baltimore loss, Lenny Moore scored the decisive touchdown from the five-yard line after a questionable pass interference call on Adderley put the ball there.

A trio of wins demonstrated the Packers were far from dead. Green Bay posted two victories over the defending champion Bears and managed a 28-21 win over the eventual 1964 champion Browns; accomplishments that indicated the Packers were still a team to be reckoned with.

Green Bay Press-Gazette

Max McGee (85) extends himself to snatch an 11-yard pass from Bart Starr in front of the Bears' Dave Whitsell (23). The first quarter score put Green Bay ahead of the Bears 7-0 in the season opener. The Packers gained revenge on last season's NFL champions 23-12. McGee led the team with six touchdowns receiving, but the nine-year veteran was reduced to playing backup in 1965.

TEAM STATISTICS

	GB	OPP
First Downs	250	197
Rushing	133	95
Passing	106	91
Penalty	11	11
Rushes	495	417
Yards Gained	2,276	1,532
Average Gain	4.60	3.67
Average Yards per Game	162.6	109.4
Passes Attempted	321	318
Completed	186	173
% Completed	57.94	54.40
Total Yards Gained	2,474	1,980
Times Sacked	47	45
Yards Lost	369	333
Net Yards Gained	2,105	1,647
Yards Gained per Completion	13.30	11.45
Net Yards per Attempt	5.72	4.54
Average Net Yards per Game	150.4	117.6
Combined Net Yards Gained	4,381	3,179
Total Plays	863	780
Average Yards per Play	5.08	4.08
Average Net Yards per Game	312.9	227.1
Intercepted By	16	6
Yards Returned	263	58
Returned for TD	1	0
Punts	56	72
Yards Punted	2,365	3,131
Average Yards per Punt	42.23	43.49
Punt Returns	34	31
Yards Returned	443	397
Average Yards per Return	13.03	12.81
Returned for TD	1	2
Kickoff Returns	45	60
Yards Returned	1,160	1,320
Average Yards per Return	25.78	22.00
Returned for TD	0	0
Penalties	50	56
Yards Penalized	576	521
Fumbles	25	34
Lost	17	25
Own Recovered for Touchdown	1	0
Opponent's Recovered by	25	17
Opponent's Recovered for Touchdown	2	1
Total Points Scored	342	245
Total Touchdowns	44	30
Touchdowns Rushing	23	15
Touchdowns Passing	16	11
Touchdowns on Returns & Recoveries	5	4
Extra Points	42	29
Safeties	0	0
Field Goals Attempted	39	23
Field Goals Made	12	12
% Successful	30.77	52.17

Regular Season 8-5-1

Date	GB		OPP	Att.
9/13	23	Chicago Bears	12	(42,327)
9/20	20	Baltimore Colts	21	(42,327)
9/28	14	at Detroit Lions	10	(59,203)
10/4	23	Minnesota Vikings	24	(42,327)
10/11	24	San Francisco 49ers (M)	14	(47,380)
10/18	21	at Baltimore Colts	24	(60,213)
10/25	17	Los Angeles Rams (M)	27	(46,617)
11/1	42	at Minnesota Vikings	13	(44,278)
11/8	30	Detroit Lions	7	(42,327)
11/15	14	at San Francisco 49ers	24	(38,483)
11/22	28	Cleveland Browns (M)	21	(48,065)
11/29	45	at Dallas Cowboys	21	(44,975)
12/5	17	at Chicago Bears	3	(43,636)
12/13	24	at Los Angeles Rams	24	(40,735)

Score By Periods

	1	2	3	4	Total
Packers	63	132	65	82	342
Opponents	49	92	57	47	245

INDIVIDUAL STATISTICS

Rushing

	Att	Yds	Avg	LG	TD
J. Taylor	235	1,169	5.0	t84	12
Hornung	103	415	4.0	40	5
T. Moore	102	371	3.6	35	2
Starr	24	165	6.9	28	3
E. Pitts	27	127	4.7	27	1
J. Norton	1	24	24.0	24	0
Crutcher	1	5	5.0	5	0
Bratkowski	2	0	0.0	0	0
Packers	495	2,276	4.6	t84	23
Opponents	417	1,532	3.7	t53	11

1964

Receiving

	No	Yds	Avg	LG	TD
Dowler	45	623	13.8	t50	5
J. Taylor	38	354	9.3	t35	3
R. Kramer	34	551	16.2	55	0
McGee	31	592	19.1	55	6
T. Moore	17	140	8.2	t33	2
Hornung	9	98	10.9	40	0
E. Pitts	6	38	6.3	22	0
Fleming	4	36	9.0	10	0
Jeter	1	23	23.0	23	0
Long	1	19	19.0	19	0
Packers	186	2,474	13.3	55	16
Opponents	173	1,980	11.4	t95	11

Passing

	Att	Com	Yds	Pct	TD	In	Tk/Yds	Rate
Starr	272	163	2,144	59.9	15	4	42/323	97.1
Bratkowski	36	19	277	52.8	1	1	5/46	75.8
Hornung	10	3	25	30.0	0	1	0/0	0.0
T. Moore	3	1	28	33.3	0	0	0/0	—
Packers	321	186	2,474	57.9	16	6	47/369	91.3
Opponents	318	173	1,980	54.4	11	16	45/333	63.9

Punting

	No	Yds	Avg	LG	HB
J. Norton	56	2,365	42.2	61	0
Packers	56	2,365	42.2	61	0
Opponents	72	3,131	43.5	66	0

Kickoff Returns

	No	Yds	Avg	LG	TD
Adderley	19	508	26.7	43	0
T. Moore	16	431	26.9	55	0
T. Brown	7	167	23.9	34	0
Crutcher	2	54	27.0	37	0
Caffey	1	0	0.0	0	0
Packers	45	1,160	25.8	55	0
Opponents	60	1,320	22.0	53	0

Punt Returns

	No	Yds	Avg	FC	LG	TD
Wood	19	252	13.3	11	64	0
E. Pitts	15	191	12.7	7	t65	1
Packers	34	443	13.0	18	t65	1
Opponents	31	397	12.8	9	t70	2

Interceptions

	No	Yds	Avg	LG	TD
Adderley	4	56	14.0	35	0
Wood	3	73	24.3	t42	1
Nitschke	2	36	18.0	18	0
Currie	2	11	5.5	10	0
Caffey	1	44	44.0	44	0
T. Brown	1	30	30.0	30	0
Gremminger	1	13	13.0	13	0
Hart	1	0	0.0	0	0
Whittenton	1	0	0.0	0	0
Packers	16	263	16.4	44	1
Opponents	6	58	9.7	23	0

Scoring

	TDr	TDp	TDrt	PAT	FG	S	TP
Hornung	5	0	0	41/43	12/38	0	107
J. Taylor	12	3	0	0/0	0/0	0	90
McGee	0	6	1	0/0	0/0	0	42
Dowler	0	5	0	0/0	0/0	0	30
T. Moore	2	2	0	0/0	0/0	0	24
Starr	3	0	0	0/0	0/0	0	18
E. Pitts	1	0	1	0/0	0/0	0	12
Wood	0	0	1	1/1	0/1	0	7
L. Aldridge	0	0	1	0/0	0/0	0	6
H. Jordan	0	0	1	0/0	0/0	0	6
Packers	23	16	5	42/44	12/39	0	342
Opponents	15	11	4	29/30	12/23	0	245

Fumbles

	Fum	Ow	Op	Yds	Tot
Adderley	1	0	1	18	1
L. Aldridge	0	0	5	29	5
Bowman	1	1	0	0	1
Bratkowski	2	1	0	0	1
Caffey	0	0	1	0	1
Currie	0	0	1	0	1
W. Davis	0	0	2	0	2
Dowler	1	0	0	0	0
Gremminger	0	0	2	0	2
Hanner	0	0	1	0	1
Hart	0	0	1	0	1
Hornung	4	1	0	0	1
H. Jordan	0	0	3	60	3
Kostelnik	0	0	3	0	3
R. Kramer	1	0	0	0	0
Masters	0	1	0	0	1
McDowell	0	0	1	0	1
McGee	1	1	0	27	1
Nitschke	0	0	2	0	2
E. Pitts	1	0	1	0	1
Starr	7	2	0	0	2
J. Taylor	6	0	0	0	0
Wood	1	1	1	0	2
Packers	25	8	25	134	33

NFL STANDINGS

Western Conference

	W	L	T	Pct	PF	PA
Baltimore Colts	12	2	0	.857	428	225
Green Bay Packers	**8**	**5**	**1**	**.615**	**342**	**245**
Minnesota Vikings	8	5	1	.615	355	296
Detroit Lions	7	5	2	.583	280	260
Los Angeles Rams	5	7	2	.417	283	339
Chicago Bears	5	9	0	.357	260	379
San Francisco 49ers	4	10	0	.286	236	330

Eastern Conference

	W	L	T	Pct	PF	PA
Cleveland Browns	10	3	1	.769	415	293
St. Louis Cardinals	9	3	2	.750	357	331
Philadelphia Eagles	6	8	0	.429	312	313
Washington Redskins	6	8	0	.429	307	305
Dallas Cowboys	5	8	1	.385	250	289
Pittsburgh Steelers	5	9	0	.357	253	315
New York Giants	2	10	2	.167	241	399

1964 ROSTER

No	Name	Pos	Ht	Wt	DOB	College	G
26	Adderley, Herb	CB	6-1	210	06/08/39	Michigan State	13
82	Aldridge, Lionel	DE	6-4	245	02/18/41	Utah State	14
57	Bowman, Ken	C	6-3	230	12/15/42	Wisconsin	14
12	Bratkowski, Zeke	QB	6-3	200	10/20/31	Georgia	5
61	Breen, Gene	LB	6-2	230	06/21/41	Virginia Tech	6
40	Brown, Tom	DB	6-1	190	12/12/40	Maryland	14
60	Caffey, Lee Roy	LB	6-3	250	06/03/41	Texas A&M	14
37	Crutcher, Tommy	LB	6-3	230	08/10/41	TCU	14
58	Currie, Dan	LB	6-3	240	06/27/35	Michigan State	14
87	Davis, Willie	DE	6-3	245	07/24/34	Grambling	14
86	Dowler, Boyd	WR	6-5	225	10/18/37	Colorado	14
81	Fleming, Marv	TE	6-4	235	01/02/42	Utah	14
75	Gregg, Forrest	T	6-4	250	10/18/33	SMU	14
46	Gremminger, Hank	DB	6-1	200	09/01/33	Baylor	13
67	Grimm, Dan	G	6-3	245	02/07/41	Colorado	14
79	Hanner, Dave	DT	6-2	260	05/20/30	Arkansas	11
43	Hart, Doug	DB	6-0	190	06/03/39	Arlington State	14
5	Hornung, Paul	HB	6-2	215	12/23/35	Notre Dame	14
21	Jeter, Bob	WR	6-1	205	05/09/37	Iowa	13
74	Jordan, Henry	DT	6-3	250	01/26/35	Virginia	12
77	Kostelnik, Ron	DT	6-4	260	01/14/40	Cincinnati	14
64	Kramer, Jerry	G	6-3	245	01/23/36	Idaho	2
88	Kramer, Ron	E	6-3	240	06/24/35	Michigan	14
80	Long, Bob	WR	6-3	190	06/16/42	Wichita	7
78	Masters, Norm	T	6-2	250	09/19/33	Michigan State	14
73	McDowell, John	G-T	6-3	260	02/12/42	St. John's (MN)	12
85	McGee, Max	E	6-3	205	07/16/32	Tulane	13
25	Moore, Tom	HB	6-2	210	07/17/38	Vanderbilt	14
66	Nitschke, Ray	LB	6-3	240	12/29/36	Illinois	14
23	Norton, Jerry	P	5-11	195	05/16/31	SMU	14
22	Pitts, Elijah	HB	6-1	205	02/03/39	Philander Smith	14
89	Robinson, Dave	LB	6-3	245	05/03/41	Penn State	11
76	Skoronski, Bob	T	6-3	250	03/05/34	Indiana	14
15	Starr, Bart	QB	6-1	200	01/09/34	Alabama	14
31	Taylor, Jim	FB	6-0	215	09/20/35	LSU	13
63	Thurston, Fred (Fuzzy)	G	6-1	245	05/07/35	Valparaiso	11
71	Voss, Lloyd	T	6-4	260	02/13/42	Nebraska	14
47	Whittenton, Jesse	DB	6-0	195	05/09/34	Texas-El Paso	14
24	Wood, Willie	DB	5-10	190	12/23/36	USC	14
72	Wright, Steve	T	6-6	250	07/18/42	Alabama	14

1964 DRAFT

Rnd	Name	Pos	Ht	Wt	College
1	Lloyd Voss	T	6-4	245	Nebraska
2	Jon Morris	C	6-3	228	Holy Cross
3a	Ode Burrell	HB	6-0	180	Mississippi State
	(Choice from Colts)				
3b	Joe O'Donnell	G	6-2	250	Michigan
	(Choice from Giants as part of Bill Quinlan, John Symank deal)				
3c	Tommy Crutcher	LB	6-3	230	TCU
4a	Bob Long	WR	6-3	190	Wichita
	(Choice from Eagles for Ed Blaine)				
*4b	Paul Costa	HB	6-4	232	Notre Dame
5a	Duke Carlisle	HB	6-1	180	Texas
	(Choice from Cowboys for Gary Barnes)				
5b	Steve Wright	T	6-6	250	Alabama
6	(Choice to Cowboys for Jerry Norton)				
*7	Dick Herzing	T	6-4	250	Drake
8	Ken Bowman	C	6-3	230	Wisconsin
9	John McDowell	T	6-3	260	St. John's (MN)
*10	Allen Jacobs	HB	6-1	210	Utah
11	Jack Peterson	T	6-6	275	Omaha
12	Dwaine Bean	HB	6-0	205	Texas State
13	Jack Mauro	T	6-2	247	Northern Michigan
14	Tom O'Grady	WR	6-4	205	Northwestern
*15	Alex Zenko	T	6-5	250	Kent State
*16	Andrew Ireland	HB	6-1	195	Utah
17	Leonard St. Jean	E	6-0	240	Northern Michigan
18	Mike Hicks	G	6-3	235	Marshall
19	John Baker	E	6-4	235	Virginia Union
*20	Bill Curry	C	6-2	225	Georgia Tech

* denotes futures

1964 GREEN BAY PACKERS

FRONT ROW: (L-R) 82 Lionel Aldridge, 78 Norm Masters, 23 Jerry Norton, 43 Doug Hart, 46 Hank Gremminger, 76 Bob Skoronski, 37 Tommy Crutcher, 47 Jesse Whittenton, 21 Bob Jeter, 81 Marv Fleming.

SECOND ROW: (L-R) Equipment Manager Gerald (Dad) Braisher, Jerry Kramer, 89 Dave Robinson, 15 Bart Starr, 22 Elijah Pitts, 58 Dan Currie, 87 Willie Davis, 74 Henry Jordan, 25 Tom Moore, 26 Herb Adderley, 24 Willie Wood, Trainer Carl (Bud) Jorgensen.

THIRD ROW: (L-R) Assistant Trainer Domenic Gentile, 73 John McDowell, 40 Tom Brown, 57 Ken Bowman, 66 Ray Nitschke, 63 Fred (Fuzzy) Thurston, 67 Dan Grimm, 60 Lee Roy Caffey, 79 Dave Hanner, 72 Steve Wright, 80 Bob Long.

BACK ROW: (L-R) 10 Dennis Claridge, 71 Lloyd Voss, 12 Zeke Bratkowski, 77 Ron Kostelnik, 86 Boyd Dowler, 75 Forrest Gregg, 31 Jim Taylor, 88 Ron Kramer, 5 Paul Hornung, 85 Max McGee.

Often outgained and occasionally outplayed, the Packers of 1965 relied on savvy and experience in order to stay in the Western Conference race. The running game, the very essence of Green and Gold football the past five years, all but vanished. Consequently, the offense sagged to 12th place, ahead of only Detroit and Pittsburgh. During a four-game spell starting in late October, Green Bay managed just 36 points and dropped back-to-back decisions to the Bears and Lions. The losses knocked the Packers (6-2) from the unbeaten ranks and into second place behind the Colts (6-1-1).

Then, late in the season, the lowly Rams (1-9) threw a big scare into the Packers' championship hopes. Bruce Gossett kicked four field goals, Deacon Jones sacked Zeke Bratkowski in the end zone and Ben Wilson scored on a four-yard run as Los Angeles upset Green Bay 21-10. The Packers (8-3) slipped a game-and-a-half behind the Colts (9-1-1) with just three games remaining. Although the two would meet on December 12, Green Bay had to hope either the Bears or the Rams could handle Baltimore.

The Bears obliged, shutting out the Colts 13-0 and knocking quarterback Johnny Unitas from the rest of the season. The Packers, meanwhile, edged the Vikings 24-19 to set up the crucial rematch.

With the season in the balance, Paul Hornung reached back for one more golden performance. The Notre Dame alumnus rolled up a team-record five touchdowns and led the Packers to a convincing 42-27 triumph over the Colts. Hornung scored on three short runs and on pass plays of 50 and 65 yards. Bart Starr hit Boyd Dowler with a 10-yard pass for the other touchdown.

Once in the driver's seat, Green Bay blew its chance to clinch the Western Conference outright by managing only a tie with the 49ers on the season's final weekend. Meanwhile, Baltimore beat the Rams 20-17 and moved into a first-place tie with the Packers. As a result, the two met one week later in a playoff game to decide who would play the Browns for the NFL championship.

Vince Lombardi, frustrated with last year's kicking game, acquired Don Chandler from the Giants. A fifth-round choice in 1956, Chandler converted 17 of 26 field goal tries, including a last-second effort that beat the Rams 6-3 on November 14.

In early November, Lombardi's contract was again renewed and extended. The extension he had signed in 1961 had been ripped up in early 1964, at which time he signed another agreement. Now that pact gave way to a contract that locked up his services through January 31, 1974.

Lombardi's contract spoke to the future. The death of Curly Lambeau on June 1, gave pause to reflect on the team's roots. The Packers' first coach was felled by a massive heart attack in Door County, Wisconsin. In his honor, City Stadium was renamed Lambeau Field prior to the first preseason game with New York on August 14.

Green Bay Press-Gazette photo

Bob Long (80) grabs a pass from Bart Starr in the second quarter of the Packers' 23-14 win over the Chicago Bears. Long turned the catch into a 48-yard touchdown which put Green Bay ahead 20-0. A fourth-round pick in 1964, Long enjoyed his best season in 1965. He hauled in 13 passes for 304 yards and four touchdowns.

TEAM STATISTICS

	GB	OPP
First Downs	201	240
Rushing	85	115
Passing	103	111
Penalty	13	14
Rushes	432	480
Yards Gained	1,488	1,988
Average Gain	3.44	4.14
Average Yards per Game	106.3	142.0
Passes Attempted	306	383
Completed	166	187
% Completed	54.25	48.83
Total Yards Gained	2,508	2,316
Times Sacked	43	44
Yards Lost	395	335
Net Yards Gained	2,113	1,981
Yards Gained per Completion	15.11	12.39
Net Yards per Attempt	6.05	4.64
Average Net Yards per Game	150.9	141.5
Combined Net Yards Gained	3,601	3,969
Total Plays	781	907
Average Yards per Play	4.61	4.38
Average Net Yards per Game	257.2	283.5
Intercepted By	27	14
Yards Returned	561	209
Returned for TD	4	1
Punts	74	60
Yards Punted	3,176	2,523
Average Yards per Punt	42.92	42.05
Punt Returns	22	36
Yards Returned	65	290
Average Yards per Return	2.95	8.06
Returned for TD	0	0
Kickoff Returns	50	52
Yards Returned	1,040	1,216
Average Yards per Return	20.80	23.38
Returned for TD	0	0
Penalties	48	67
Yards Penalized	529	677
Fumbles	18	37
Lost	12	23
Own Recovered for Touchdown	0	0
Opponent's Recovered by	23	12
Opponent's Recovered for Touchdown	1	0
Total Points Scored	316	224
Total Touchdowns	38	22
Touchdowns Rushing	14	10
Touchdowns Passing	19	11
Touchdowns on Returns & Recoveries	5	1
Extra Points	37	22
Safeties	0	2
Field Goals Attempted	26	33
Field Goals Made	17	22
% Successful	65.38	66.67

Regular Season   10-3-1

Date	GB		OPP	Att.
9/19	41	at Pittsburgh Steelers	9	(38,383)
9/26	20	Baltimore Colts (M)	17	(48,130)
10/3	23	Chicago Bears	14	(50,852)
10/10	27	San Francisco 49ers	10	(50,852)
10/17	31	at Detroit Lions	21	(56,712)
10/24	13	Dallas Cowboys (M)	3	(48,311)
10/31	10	at Chicago Bears	31	(45,664)
11/7	7	Detroit Lions	12	(50,852)
11/14	6	Los Angeles Rams (M)	3	(48,485)
11/21	38	at Minnesota Vikings	13	(47,426)
11/28	10	at Los Angeles Rams	21	(39,733)
12/5	24	Minnesota Vikings	19	(50,852)
12/12	42	at Baltimore Colts	27	(60,238)
12/19	24	at San Francisco 49ers	24	(45,710)

Postseason   2-0

12/26	13	Baltimore Colts (OT)	10	(50,484)
1/2	23	Cleveland Browns	12	(50,777)

Score By Periods

	1	2	3	4	Total
Packers	65	66	82	103	316
Opponents	40	85	37	62	224

INDIVIDUAL STATISTICS

Rushing

	Att	Yds	Avg	LG	TD
J. Taylor	207	734	3.5	35	4
Hornung	89	299	3.4	17	5
Starr	18	169	9.4	38	1
T. Moore	51	124	2.4	13	0
E. Pitts	54	122	2.3	12	4
Chandler	1	27	27.0	27	0
Coffey	3	12	4.0	10	0
A. Jacobs	3	5	1.7	2	0
Bratkowski	4	-1	-0.3	1	0
Claridge	2	-3	-1.5	1	0
Packers	432	1,488	3.4	38	14
Opponents	480	1,988	4.1	43	10

Receiving

	No	Yds	Avg	LG	TD
Dowler	44	610	13.9	t47	4
Dale	20	382	19.1	t77	2
J. Taylor	20	207	10.4	41	0
Hornung	19	336	17.7	t65	3
Fleming	14	141	10.1	t31	2
Long	13	304	23.4	t62	4
E. Pitts	11	182	16.5	t80	1
McGee	10	154	15.4	t37	1
B. Anderson	8	105	13.1	t27	1
T. Moore	7	87	12.4	t31	1
Packers	166	2,508	15.1	t80	19
Opponents	187	2,316	12.4	t65	11

Passing

	Att	Com	Yds	Pct	TD	In	Tk/Yds	Rate
Starr	251	140	2,055	55.8	16	9	34/303	89.0
Bratkowski	48	21	348	43.8	3	4	8/79	54.9
E. Pitts	2	1	51	50.0	0	0	0/0	—
T. Moore	2	2	22	100.0	0	0	0/0	—
Hornung	2	1	19	50.0	0	1	1/13	—
Claridge	1	1	13	100.0	0	0	0/0	—
Packers	306	166	2,508	54.2	19	14	43/395	83.1
Opponents	383	187	2,316	48.8	11	27	44/335	48.2

Punting

	No	Yds	Avg	LG	HB
Chandler	74	3,176	42.9	90	0
Packers	74	3,176	42.9	90	0
Opponents	60	2,523	42.1	63	0

Kickoff Returns

	No	Yds	Avg	LG	TD
E. Pitts	20	396	19.8	29	0
T. Moore	15	361	24.1	52	0
Adderley	10	221	22.1	33	0
Crutcher	3	53	17.7	21	0
Coffey	1	9	9.0	9	0
Grimm	1	0	0.0	0	0
Packers	50	1,040	20.8	52	0
Opponents	52	1,216	23.4	68	0

Punt Returns

	No	Yds	Avg	FC	LG	TD
Wood	13	38	2.9	10	14	0
E. Pitts	8	27	3.4	6	12	0
Adderley	1	0	0.0	0	0	0
T. Brown	0	0	0.0	1	0	0
Packers	22	65	3.0	17	14	0
Opponents	36	290	8.1	11	62	0

Interceptions

	No	Yds	Avg	LG	TD
Adderley	6	175	29.2	t44	3
Wood	6	65	10.8	28	0
Hart	4	29	7.3	24	0
D. Robinson	3	141	47.0	87	0
T. Brown	3	42	14.0	27	0
Caffey	1	42	42.0	42	1
W. Davis	1	21	21.0	21	0
Jeter	1	21	21.0	21	0
Nitschke	1	21	21.0	21	0
Crutcher	1	4	4.0	4	0
Packers	27	561	20.8	87	4
Opponents	14	209	14.9	t36	1

Scoring

	TDr	TDp	TDrt	PAT	FG	S	TP
Chandler	0	0	0	37/38	17/26	0	88
Hornung	5	3	0	0/0	0/0	0	48
E. Pitts	4	1	0	0/0	0/0	0	30
Dowler	0	4	0	0/0	0/0	0	24
Long	0	4	0	0/0	0/0	0	24
J. Taylor	4	0	0	0/0	0/0	0	24
Adderley	0	0	3	0/0	0/0	0	18
Dale	0	2	0	0/0	0/0	0	12
Fleming	0	2	0	0/0	0/0	0	12
B. Anderson	0	1	0	0/0	0/0	0	6
Caffey	0	0	1	0/0	0/0	0	6
Hart	0	0	1	0/0	0/0	0	6
McGee	0	1	0	0/0	0/0	0	6
T. Moore	0	1	0	0/0	0/0	0	6
Starr	1	0	0	0/0	0/0	0	6
Packers	14	19	5	37/38	17/26	0	316
Opponents	10	11	1	22/22	22/33	2	224

Fumbles

	Fum	Ow	Op	Yds	Tot
Adderley	1	0	3	2	3
L. Aldridge	0	0	2	0	2
Bratkowski	1	1	0	0	1
T. Brown	0	0	1	0	1
Claridge	1	0	0	0	0
Coffey	0	0	1	0	1
Curry	0	1	1	0	1
Dale	1	0	0	0	0
W. Davis	0	0	2	0	2
Dowler	1	0	0	0	0
Gregg	0	1	0	0	1
Grimm	0	0	1	0	1
Hart	0	0	1	20	1
Hornung	2	0	0	0	0
H. Jordan	0	0	3	0	3
Kostelnik	0	0	1	0	1
Marshall	0	0	1	0	1
T. Moore	4	0	0	0	0
Nitschke	0	0	3	18	3
E. Pitts	2	1	0	0	1
D. Robinson	0	0	2	2	2
Starr	2	0	0	0	0
J. Taylor	3	1	0	0	1
Wood	0	0	2	0	2
S. Wright	0	1	0	0	1
Packers	18	6	23	42	29

NFL STANDINGS

Western Conference

	W	L	T	Pct	PF	PA
Green Bay Packers	**10**	**3**	**1**	**.769**	**316**	**224**
Baltimore Colts	10	3	1	.769	389	284
Chicago Bears	9	5	0	.643	409	275
San Francisco 49ers	7	6	1	.538	421	402
Minnesota Vikings	7	7	0	.500	383	403
Detroit Lions	6	7	1	.462	257	295
Los Angeles Rams	4	10	0	.286	269	328

Eastern Conference

	W	L	T	Pct	PF	PA
Cleveland Browns	11	3	0	.786	363	325
Dallas Cowboys	7	7	0	.500	325	280
New York Giants	7	7	0	.500	270	338
Washington Redskins	6	8	0	.429	257	301
Philadelphia Eagles	5	9	0	.357	363	359
St. Louis Cardinals	5	9	0	.357	296	309
Pittsburgh Steelers	2	12	0	.143	202	397

1965 ROSTER

No	Name	Pos	Ht	Wt	DOB	College	G
26	Adderley, Herb	CB	6-1	210	06/08/39	Michigan State	14
82	Aldridge, Lionel	DE	6-4	245	02/18/41	Utah State	14
88	Anderson, Bill	TE	6-3	216	07/16/36	Tennessee	14
57	Bowman, Ken	C	6-3	230	12/15/42	Wisconsin	14
12	Bratkowski, Zeke	QB	6-3	200	10/20/31	Georgia	6
40	Brown, Tom	DB	6-1	190	12/12/40	Maryland	14
60	Caffey, Lee Roy	LB	6-3	250	06/03/41	Texas A&M	14
34	Chandler, Don	K	6-2	210	09/05/34	Florida	14
10	Claridge, Dennis	QB	6-3	225	08/18/41	Nebraska	1
41	Coffey, Junior	HB	6-1	210	03/21/42	Washington	13
56	Crutcher, Tommy	LB	6-3	230	08/10/41	TCU	14
50	Curry, Bill	C	6-2	235	10/21/42	Georgia Tech	14
84	Dale, Carroll	WR	6-2	200	04/24/38	Virginia Tech	13
87	Davis, Willie	DE	6-3	245	07/24/34	Grambling	14
86	Dowler, Boyd	WR	6-5	225	10/18/37	Colorado	14
81	Fleming, Marv	TE	6-4	235	01/02/42	Utah	13
75	Gregg, Forrest	T	6-4	250	10/18/33	SMU	14
46	Gremminger, Hank	DB	6-1	200	09/01/33	Baylor	8
67	Grimm, Dan	G	6-3	245	02/07/41	Colorado	14
43	Hart, Doug	DB	6-0	190	06/03/39	Arlington State	14
5	Hornung, Paul	HB	6-2	215	12/23/35	Notre Dame	12
35	Jacobs, Allen	HB	6-1	215	05/19/41	Utah	14
21	Jeter, Bob	DB	6-1	205	05/09/37	Iowa	13
74	Jordan, Henry	DT	6-3	250	01/26/35	Virginia	14
77	Kostelnik, Ron	DT	6-4	260	01/14/40	Cincinnati	14
64	Kramer, Jerry	G	6-3	245	01/23/36	Idaho	14
80	Long, Bob	WR	6-3	190	06/16/42	Wichita	13
70	Marshall, Rich	DT	6-5	270	09/12/41	Stephen A. Austin	14
85	McGee, Max	E	6-3	205	07/16/32	Tulane	12
25	Moore, Tom	HB	6-2	210	07/17/38	Vanderbilt	13
66	Nitschke, Ray	LB	6-3	240	12/29/36	Illinois	12
22	Pitts, Elijah	HB	6-1	205	02/03/39	Philander Smith	14
89	Robinson, Dave	LB	6-3	245	05/03/41	Penn State	14
76	Skoronski, Bob	T	6-3	250	03/05/34	Indiana	14
15	Starr, Bart	QB	6-1	200	01/09/34	Alabama	14
31	Taylor, Jim	FB	6-0	215	09/20/35	LSU	13
63	Thurston, Fred (Fuzzy)	G	6-1	245	05/07/35	Valparaiso	14
71	Voss, Lloyd	T	6-4	260	02/13/42	Nebraska	14
24	Wood, Willie	DB	5-10	190	12/23/36	USC	14
72	Wright, Steve	T	6-6	250	07/18/42	Alabama	14

1965 DRAFT

Rnd	Name	Pos	Ht	Wt	College
*1a	Donny Anderson	HB	6-3	210	Texas Tech
	(Choice from Eagles as part of Jim Ringo, Earl Gros, Lee Roy Caffey deal)				
1b	Larry Elkins	WR	6-1	190	Baylor
2	Alphonse Dotson	T	6-4	260	Grambling
3a	(Choice to Giants)				
3b	Allen Brown	E	6-4	230	Mississippi
4	Wally Mahle	HB	6-3	195	Syracuse
*5a	James Harvey	T	6-4	240	Mississippi
	(Choice from Steelers)				
5b	Doug Goodwin	FB	6-3	220	Maryland State
6a	Rick Koeper	T	6-4	245	Oregon State
	(Choice from Steelers)				
6b	Bill Symons	HB	6-1	196	Colorado
7a	Jerry Roberts	E	6-4	205	Baldwin-Wallace
	(Choice from Giants for Turnley Todd)				
7b	Roger Jacobazzi	T	6-3	250	Wisconsin
	(Choice from 49ers)				
7c	Junior Coffey	HB	6-1	210	Washington
*8	Mike Shinn	E	6-3	220	Kansas
9	Larry Bulaich	HB	6-2	200	TCU
10	Rick Marshall	T	6-5	270	Stephen A. Austin
*11	Jim Weatherwax	T	6-7	260	Los Angeles State
12	Eugene Jeter	HB	6-3	200	Arkansas-Pine Bluff
*13	Roy Schmidt	G	6-3	240	Long Beach State
14	John Putman	FB	6-3	234	Drake
15	Chuck Hurston	T	6-5	220	Auburn
*16	Phil Vandersea	FB	6-3	225	Massachusetts
17	Steve Clark	K	6-2	210	Oregon State
*18	Jeff White	E	6-3	185	Texas Tech
*19	Len Sears	T	6-5	240	South Carolina
20	James Chandler	HB	6-4	206	Benedict
*	denotes futures				

1965 GREEN BAY PACKERS

FRONT ROW: (L-R) 89 Dave Robinson, 34 Don Chandler, 82 Lionel Aldridge, 43 Doug Hart, 46 Hank Gremminger, 77 Ron Kostelnik, 24 Willie Wood, 26 Herb Adderley, 21 Bob Jeter, 81 Marv Fleming.
SECOND ROW: (L-R) Trainer Carl (Bud) Jorgensen, 71 Lloyd Voss, 84 Carroll Dale, 15 Bart Starr, 22 Elijah Pitts, 88 Bill Anderson, 12 Zeke Bratkowski, 67 Dan Grimm, 25 Tom Moore, 80 Bob Long, 40 Tom Brown, Equipment Manager Gerald (Dad) Braisher.
THIRD ROW: (L-R) Assistant Trainer Domenic Gentile, 50 Bill Curry, 56 Tommy Crutcher, 41 Junior Coffey, 74 Henry Jordan, 64 Jerry Kramer, 63 Fred (Fuzzy) Thurston, 76 Bob Skoronski, 87 Willie Davis, 66 Ray Nitschke, Assistant Equipment Manager Bob Noel.
BACK ROW: (L-R) 35 Allen Jacobs, 70 Rich Marshall, 10 Dennis Claridge, 57 Ken Bowman, 86 Boyd Dowler, 75 Forrest Gregg, 72 Steve Wright, 31 Jim Taylor, 5 Paul Hornung, 85 Max McGee.

Sports Illustrated was right. In its September 12 issue, the magazine's Tex Maule predicted the Packers and Cowboys would meet for the NFL title at the end of the season. Green Bay did its part, holding down the top spot in the West from the get-go and finishing 12-2. Dallas won the Eastern Conference on the strength of a 10-3-1 record. On January 1, 1967 the two clashed in a Cotton Bowl thriller that saw the Packers emerge a 34-27 winner and claim their second consecutive NFL championship.

A one-point loss to the 49ers and a three-point setback to the Vikings kept Green Bay from a perfect season. Against the 49's, Don Chandler missed a 26-yard field goal with 6:57 left and the Packers, who didn't get the ball back until 30 seconds remained, bowed out 21-20. Against Minnesota, Bill Brown scored on a one-yard run with 6:53 remaining to give the Vikings a 20-17 win.

The Packers handed out approximately $1,000,000 to sign All-America running backs Donny Anderson and Jim Grabowski. Anderson, who received about $600,000, was a junior eligible selected in 1965 while Grabowski was the team's first pick in 1966. The two were expected to bolster the running game. Some hoped the tandem would blossom into the next Jim Taylor and Paul Hornung.

With attention focused on the two rookies, Bart Starr began to quietly fill the air with footballs. Starr led the league in passing as he did in 1962 and 1964 and was voted the league's MVP. For the record, he completed 62.2 percent of his throws, gave up only three interceptions and crafted a whopping 105.0 passer rating.

The Packers defense, on the other hand, excelled at shutting down the pass. For the third year in a row, Green Bay defenders led the NFL in pass defense. Henry Jordan, Lionel Aldridge, Ron Kostelnik and Willie Davis spearheaded a charge that sacked enemy quarterbacks 47 times. Bob Jeter and Dave Robinson collected 10 of the team's 28 interceptions, a total second only to Cleveland's 30. Green Bay gave up just seven touchdown passes, fewest in the league since Cleveland allowed the same number in 1956.

The real Taylor and Hornung were approaching the end of their careers. Hornung, bothered by a pinched nerve in his neck, missed five games. His 2.6 average and 200 yards rushing were personal lows. Taylor announced he was playing out his option following the Packers' 13-6 win over the Bears. He became a free agent on May 1, 1967.

In the middle of the year, Green Bay unleashed a sample of its power at the expense of newcomer Atlanta. The expansion club, coached by former Packers assistant Norb Hecker, was routed 56-3. The 53 points is still the largest margin of victory in team history.

The Packers eliminated one final obstacle in their path on the second weekend in December. Baltimore (8-4) still had a slight chance of catching the Packers (10-2). For much of the game it appeared the Colts' 10-7 lead might hold up. Elijah Pitts changed that with a fourth-quarter touchdown run that not only won the game 14-10, but clinched the Western Conference crown.

Green Bay Press-Gazette photo

Tom Brown (40) intercepts a pass intended for his former teammate Ron Kramer (88). The theft ended a Detroit drive just before halftime. The Packers won the early-October matchup 23-14. Brown's biggest interception of the year occurred approximately three months later when his steal ended a late-Dallas drive in the NFL Championship Game.

TEAM STATISTICS

	GB	OPP
First Downs	231	211
Rushing	98	90
Passing	115	106
Penalty	18	15
Rushes	475	446
Yards Gained	1,673	1,644
Average Gain	3.52	3.69
Average Yards per Game	119.5	117.4
Passes Attempted	318	390
Completed	193	202
% Completed	60.69	51.79
Total Yards Gained	2,831	2,316
Times Sacked	31	47
Yards Lost	229	357
Net Yards Gained	2,602	1,959
Yards Gained per Completion	14.67	11.47
Net Yards per Attempt	7.46	4.48
Average Net Yards per Game	185.9	139.9
Combined Net Yards Gained	4,275	3,603
Total Plays	824	883
Average Yards per Play	5.19	4.08
Average Net Yards per Game	305.4	257.4
Intercepted By	28	5
Yards Returned	547	75
Returned for TD	6	0
Punts	62	69
Yards Punted	2,541	2,850
Average Yards per Punt	40.98	41.30
Punt Returns	37	30
Yards Returned	215	171
Average Yards per Return	5.81	5.70
Returned for TD	1	0
Kickoff Returns	42	52
Yards Returned	903	1,213
Average Yards per Return	21.50	23.33
Returned for TD	0	0
Penalties	57	67
Yards Penalized	544	745
Fumbles	23	26
Lost	19	14
Own Recovered for Touchdown	0	0
Opponent's Recovered by	14	19
Opponent's Recovered for Touchdown	0	1
Total Points Scored	335	163
Total Touchdowns	43	17
Touchdowns Rushing	18	9
Touchdowns Passing	18	7
Touchdowns on Returns & Recoveries	7	1
Extra Points	41	16
Safeties	0	0
Field Goals Attempted	28	27
Field Goals Made	12	15
% Successful	42.86	55.56

Regular Season   12-2-0

Date	GB		OPP	Att.
9/10	24	Baltimore Colts (M)	3	(48,650)
9/18	21	at Cleveland Browns	20	(83,943)
9/25	24	Los Angeles Rams	13	(50,861)
10/2	23	Detroit Lions	14	(50,861)
10/9	20	at San Francisco 49ers	21	(39,290)
10/16	17	at Chicago Bears	0	(48,573)
10/23	56	Atlanta Falcons (M)	3	(48,623)
10/30	31	at Detroit Lions	7	(56,954)
11/6	17	Minnesota Vikings	20	(50,861)
11/20	13	Chicago Bears	6	(50,861)
11/27	28	at Minnesota Vikings	16	(47,426)
12/4	20	San Francisco 49ers	7	(48,725)
12/10	14	at Baltimore Colts	10	(60,238)
12/18	27	at Los Angeles Rams	23	(72,416)

Postseason   2-0

1/1	34	at Dallas Cowboys	27	(74,152)
1/15	35	Chiefs at LA Coliseum	10	(61,946)

Score By Periods

	1	2	3	4	Total
Packers	62	117	54	102	335
Opponents	13	66	23	61	163

INDIVIDUAL STATISTICS

Rushing

	Att	Yds	Avg	LG	TD
J. Taylor	204	705	3.5	19	4
E. Pitts	115	393	3.4	20	7
Hornung	76	200	2.6	9	2
Grabowski	29	127	4.4	t36	1
Starr	21	104	5.0	21	2
D. Anderson	25	104	4.2	15	2
Chandler	1	33	33.0	33	0
Bratkowski	4	7	1.8	4	0
Packers	**475**	**1,673**	**3.5**	**t36**	**18**
Opponents	446	1,644	3.7	38	9

Receiving

	No	Yds	Avg	LG	TD
J. Taylor	41	331	8.1	21	2
Dale	37	876	23.7	t83	7
Fleming	31	361	11.6	t53	2
Dowler	29	392	13.5	40	0
E. Pitts	26	460	17.7	t80	3
Hornung	14	192	13.7	t44	3
McGee	4	91	22.8	29	1
Grabowski	4	13	3.3	7	0
Long	3	68	22.7	42	0
D. Anderson	2	33	16.5	22	0
B. Anderson	2	14	7.0	8	0
Packers	**193**	**2,831**	**14.7**	**t83**	**18**
Opponents	202	2,316	11.5	t65	7

Passing

	Att	Com	Yds	Pct	TD	In	Tk/Yds	Rate
Starr	251	156	2,257	62.2	14	3	26/183	105.0
Bratkowski	64	36	569	56.3	4	2	5/46	93.8
Hornung	1	1	5	100.0	0	0	0/0	—
E. Pitts	2	0	0	00.0	0	0	0/0	—
Packers	**318**	**193**	**2,831**	**60.7**	**18**	**5**	**31/229**	**102.1**
Opponents	390	202	2,316	51.8	7	28	47/357	46.1

Punting

	No	Yds	Avg	LG	HB
Chandler	60	2,452	40.9	58	0
D. Anderson	2	89	44.5	49	0
Packers	**62**	**2,541**	**41.0**	**58**	**0**
Opponents	69	2,850	41.3	58	1

Kickoff Returns

	No	Yds	Avg	LG	TD
D. Anderson	23	533	23.2	61	0
Adderley	14	320	22.9	65	0
Vandersea	3	50	16.7	21	0
E. Pitts	1	0	0.0	0	0
Wood	1	0		0	0
Packers	**42**	**903**	**21.5**	**65**	**0**
Opponents	52	1,213	23.3	51	0

Punt Returns

	No	Yds	Avg	FC	LG	TD
Wood	22	82	3.7	9	13	0
E. Pitts	7	9	1.3	4	6	0
D. Anderson	6	124	20.7	1	t77	1
T. Brown	2	0	0.0	1	0	0
Packers	**37**	**215**	**5.8**	**15**	**t77**	**1**
Opponents	30	171	5.7	15	29	0

Interceptions

	No	Yds	Avg	LG	TD
Jeter	5	142	28.4	t75	2
D. Robinson	5	60	12.0	23	0
Adderley	4	125	31.3	t68	1
T. Brown	4	21	5.3	15	0
Caffey	3	62	20.7	t52	1
Wood	3	38	12.7	t20	1
Nitschke	2	44	22.0	22	0
Hart	1	40	40.0	t40	1
Crutcher	1	15	15.0	15	0
Packers	**28**	**547**	**19.5**	**t75**	**6**
Opponents	5	75	15.0	44	0

Scoring

	TDr	TDp	TDrt	PAT	FG	S	TP
Chandler	0	0	0	41/43	12/28	0	77
E. Pitts	7	3	0	0/0	0/0	0	60
Dale	0	7	0	0/0	0/0	0	42
J. Taylor	4	2	0	0/0	0/0	0	36
Hornung	2	3	0	0/0	0/0	0	30
D. Anderson	2	0	1	0/0	0/0	0	18
Fleming	0	2	0	0/0	0/0	0	12
Jeter	0	0	2	0/0	0/0	0	12
Starr	2	0	0	0/0	0/0	0	12
Adderley	0	0	1	0/0	0/0	0	6
Caffey	0	0	1	0/0	0/0	0	6
Grabowski	1	0	0	0/0	0/0	0	6
Hart	0	0	1	0/0	0/0	0	6
McGee	0	1	0	0/0	0/0	0	6
Wood	0	0	1	0/0	0/0	0	6
Packers	**18**	**18**	**7**	**41/43**	**12/28**	**0**	**335**
Opponents	9	7	1	16/17	15/27	0	163

Fumbles

	Fum	Ow	Op	Yds	Tot
Adderley	1	1	1	0	2
L. Aldridge	0	0	2	3	2
D. Anderson	3	0	0	0	0
Bratkowski	0	1	0	0	1
T. Brown	0	0	2	5	2
Caffey	0	0	1	0	1
Dale	0	1	0	0	1
W. Davis	0	0	2	0	2
Dowler	1	0	0	0	0
Fleming	0	1	0	0	1
Grabowski	2	0	0	0	0
Hart	0	0	1	0	1
Hornung	1	0	0	0	0
Jeter	0	0	1	0	1
Kostelnik	0	0	2	0	2
E. Pitts	4	0	0	0	0
D. Robinson	0	0	2	7	2
Starr	7	0	0	0	0
J. Taylor	4	0	0	0	0
Packers	**23**	**4**	**14**	**15**	**18**

NFL STANDINGS

Western Conference

	W	L	T	Pct	PF	PA
Green Bay Packers	12	2	0	.857	335	163
Baltimore Colts	9	5	0	.643	314	226
Los Angeles Rams	8	6	0	.571	289	212
San Francisco 49ers	6	6	2	.500	320	325
Chicago Bears	5	7	2	.417	234	272
Detroit Lions	4	9	1	.308	206	317
Minnesota Vikings	4	9	1	.308	292	304

Eastern Conference

	W	L	T	Pct	PF	PA
Dallas Cowboys	10	3	1	.769	445	239
Cleveland Browns	9	5	0	.643	403	259
Philadelphia Eagles	9	5	0	.643	326	340
St. Louis Cardinals	8	5	1	.615	264	265
Washington Redskins	7	7	0	.500	351	355
Pittsburgh Steelers	5	8	1	.385	316	347
Atlanta Falcons	3	11	0	.214	204	437
New York Giants	1	12	1	.077	263	501

1966 ROSTER

No	Name	Pos	Ht	Wt	DOB	College	G
26	Adderley, Herb	CB	6-1	200	06/08/39	Michigan State	14
82	Aldridge, Lionel	DE	6-4	245	02/18/41	Utah State	13
88	Anderson, Bill	TE	6-3	225	07/16/36	Tennessee	10
44	Anderson, Donny	RB	6-3	210	05/16/43	Texas Tech	14
57	Bowman, Ken	C	6-3	230	12/15/42	Wisconsin	4
12	Bratkowski, Zeke	QB	6-3	210	10/20/31	Georgia	8
83	Brown, Allen	TE	6-5	235	03/02/43	Mississippi	5
78	Brown, Bob	DE	6-5	260	02/23/40	Arkansas-Pine Bluff	14
40	Brown, Tom	DB	6-1	190	12/12/40	Maryland	14
60	Caffey, Lee Roy	LB	6-3	250	06/03/41	Texas A&M	14
34	Chandler, Don	K	6-2	210	09/05/34	Florida	14
56	Crutcher, Tommy	LB	6-3	230	08/10/41	TCU	14
50	Curry, Bill	C	6-2	235	10/21/42	Georgia Tech	14
84	Dale, Carroll	WR	6-2	200	04/24/38	Virginia Tech	14
87	Davis, Willie	DE	6-3	245	07/24/34	Grambling	14
86	Dowler, Boyd	WR	6-5	225	10/18/37	Colorado	14
81	Fleming, Marv	TE	6-4	235	01/02/42	Utah	14
68	Gillingham, Gale	G	6-3	255	02/03/44	Minnesota	14
33	Grabowski, Jim	RB	6-2	220	09/09/44	Illinois	14
75	Gregg, Forrest	T	6-4	250	10/18/33	SMU	14
43	Hart, Doug	DB	6-0	190	06/03/39	Arlington State	14
45	Hathcock, Dave	DB	6-0	195	07/20/43	Memphis State	14
5	Hornung, Paul	HB	6-2	215	12/23/35	Notre Dame	9
21	Jeter, Bob	DB	6-1	205	05/09/37	Iowa	14
74	Jordan, Henry	DT	6-3	250	01/26/35	Virginia	14
77	Kostelnik, Ron	DT	6-4	260	01/14/40	Cincinnati	14
64	Kramer, Jerry	G	6-3	245	01/23/36	Idaho	14
80	Long, Bob	WR	6-3	205	06/16/42	Wichita	5
27	Mack, Red	WR	5-10	185	06/19/37	Notre Dame	9
85	McGee, Max	E	6-3	210	07/16/32	Tulane	12
66	Nitschke, Ray	LB	6-3	240	12/29/36	Illinois	14
22	Pitts, Elijah	HB	6-1	205	02/03/39	Philander Smith	14
89	Robinson, Dave	LB	6-3	240	05/03/41	Penn State	14
76	Skoronski, Bob	T	6-3	245	03/05/34	Indiana	14
15	Starr, Bart	QB	6-1	190	01/09/34	Alabama	14
31	Taylor, Jim	FB	6-0	215	09/20/35	LSU	14
63	Thurston, Fred (Fuzzy)	G	6-1	245	05/07/35	Valparaiso	12
37	Vandersea, Phil	LB	6-3	235	02/25/43	Massachusetts	14
73	Weatherwax, Jim	DT	6-7	260	01/09/43	Cal State-Los Angeles	14
24	Wood, Willie	DB	5-10	190	12/23/36	USC	14
72	Wright, Steve	T	6-6	250	07/18/42	Alabama	14

1966 DRAFT

Rnd	Name	Pos	Ht	Wt	College
1a	Jim Grabowski	FB	6-2	225	Illinois
	(Choice from Lions for Ron Kramer)				
1b	Gale Gillingham	T	6-3	250	Minnesota
*2	Tom Cichowski	T	6-4	238	Maryland
3a	Fred Heron	T	6-5	250	San Jose State
	(Choice from Browns)				
3b	Tony Jeter	E	6-4	238	Nebraska
*4	John Roderick	HB	6-1	171	SMU
5	(Choice to Rams)				
6	(Choice to Redskins for Bill Anderson)				
*7	Ray Miller	E	6-4	250	Idaho
8	Ken McLean	HB	6-0	191	Texas A&M
9	Ron Rector	HB	5-11	196	Northwestern
10	Sam Montgomery	HB	6-1	200	Southern
11	Ralph Wenzel	C	6-3	240	San Diego State
*12	Jim Mankins	FB	6-1	238	Florida State
*13	Ed King	LB	6-2	220	USC
14	Ron Hanson	E	6-3	200	North Dakota State
15	Grady Bolton	T	6-2	250	Mississippi State
16	Robert Schultz	T	6-3	255	Wisconsin-Stevens Point
17	Dave Hathcock	DB	6-0	195	Memphis State
18	Jim Jones	DT	6-3	260	Omaha
19	Dave Norton	TE	6-0	220	USC
20	Ed Maras	E	6-2	220	South Dakota State

* denotes futures

- 150 -

1966 GREEN BAY PACKERS

FRONT ROW: (L-R) 89 Dave Robinson, 22 Elijah Pitts, 82 Lionel Aldridge, 43 Doug Hart, 21 Bob Jeter, 87 Willie Davis, 76 Bob Skoronski, 26 Herb Adderley, 45 Dave Hathcock, 81 Marv Fleming.

SECOND ROW: (L-R) Trainer Carl (Bud) Jorgensen, 12 Zeke Bratkowski, 84 Carroll Dale, 15 Bart Starr, 78 Bob Brown, 77 Ron Kostelnik, 74 Henry Jordan, 33 Jim Grabowski, 88 Bill Anderson, 44 Donny Anderson, Equipment Manager Gerald (Dad) Braisher.

THIRD ROW: (L-R) 24 Willie Wood, 27 Red Mack, 66 Ray Nitschke, 50 Bill Curry, 56 Tommy Crutcher, 60 Lee Roy Caffey, 63 Fred (Fuzzy) Thurston, 64 Jerry Kramer, 57 Ken Bowman, 75 Forrest Gregg, 80 Bob Long, 37 Phil Vandersea, Assistant Equipment Manager Bob Noel.

BACK ROW: (L-R) 40 Tom Brown, 73 Jim Weatherwax, 34 Don Chandler, 83 Allen Brown, 86 Boyd Dowler, 72 Steve Wright, 31 Jim Taylor, 5 Paul Hornung, 85 Max McGee.

1967

At a Packers recognition luncheon at St. Norbert College in early September, Vince Lombardi announced that the Packers "have the wherewithal to win a third straight National Football League championship." Though injuries to Bart Starr and the running corps made the going rough, Lombardi's statement stood the test of time. On November 26, Starr completed 11 of 17 passes for 202 yards and a touchdown to lead Green Bay past the Bears 17-13. That victory clinched the Central Division title and sent the Packers on their way to a third straight NFL championship.

An unsettled situation at running back dogged the team all year. Jim Taylor played out his option and was finally traded to the expansion New Orleans Saints in early July. Paul Hornung was selected by the same team on February 10 as the infant franchise stocked itself with players from other clubs. To soften the losses, Lombardi obtained Ben Wilson from the Rams at the same time he traded Taylor.

Fullback Jim Grabowski and Elijah Pitts at halfback were tabbed as the starters in the revamped backfield. But Grabowski twisted a knee and Pitts tore his Achilles tendon in a 13-10 loss to Baltimore in the season's eighth week. Pitts was lost for the year but Grabowski played again briefly in the second Bears game.

With Pitts out and Grabowski ailing, Lombardi signed Chuck Mercein from the Redskins' taxi squad on November 9. The Yale graduate backed up Wilson, who took over for Grabowski. Donny Anderson slipped into the halfback duties ahead of rookie Travis Willliams, the NFL's leading kickoff returner.

While Lombardi scrambled to find healthy ballcarriers, he didn't need to tamper with the defensive unit. Green Bay had the league's stingiest defense. Especially potent was its pass defense which held nine opponents to less than 75 yards passing. The Packers gave up a miserly 98.4 yards passing per game, the best since the Browns allowed 91.5 in 1956.

The Packers reported a record $827,439.18 in profits for the year 1966. This figure was made public at the annual stockholders meeting on June 5. The amount, which more than doubled the previous record of $404,730 in 1964, was a far cry from earlier seasons when the team was happy just to survive financially.

On October 1, Starr suffered a bruised right shoulder when Atlanta's defensive back Bob Riggle and linebacker Tommy Nobis tackled him early in Green Bay's 23-0 win. Already ailing from thumb and rib injuries sustained in the preseason, Starr was relieved by Zeke Bratkowski for the next two weeks.

After the Packers' decisive win at Chicago, Green Bay edged the Vikings and then lost to both the Rams and Steelers. Green Bay hadn't lost two games in a row at the end of a season since 1958. No one expected the Packers' play to slump back to that level, but the losses signaled the end of Green Bay's days at the top.

Green Bay Press-Gazette photo

Don Chandler kicks a 28-yard field goal with 1:28 left to forge a 17-17 tie with the Lions on September 17. His kick with just over a minute left, beat the Bears 13-10 a week later. He booted another game-winner at Minnesota in early December. In all, Chandler made 19 of 29 field goals and led the team in scoring for a third straight year.

TEAM STATISTICS

	GB	OPP
First Downs	243	183
Rushing	115	98
Passing	112	78
Penalty	16	7
Rushes	474	443
Yards Gained	1,915	1,923
Average Gain	4.04	4.34
Average Yards per Game	136.8	137.4
Passes Attempted	331	337
Completed	182	155
% Completed	54.98	45.99
Total Yards Gained	2,758	1,644
Times Sacked	41	29
Yards Lost	394	267
Net Yards Gained	2,364	1,377
Yards Gained per Completion	15.15	10.61
Net Yards per Attempt	6.35	3.76
Average Net Yards per Game	168.9	98.4
Combined Net Yards Gained	4,279	3,300
Total Plays	846	809
Average Yards per Play	5.06	4.08
Average Net Yards per Game	305.6	235.7
Intercepted By	26	27
Yards Returned	284	370
Returned for TD	2	3
Punts	66	75
Yards Punted	2,409	3,119
Average Yards per Punt	36.50	41.59
Punt Returns	39	13
Yards Returned	157	22
Average Yards per Return	4.03	1.69
Returned for TD	0	0
Kickoff Returns	46	59
Yards Returned	1,241	1,276
Average Yards per Return	26.98	21.63
Returned for TD	4	0
Penalties	48	55
Yards Penalized	531	482
Fumbles	19	23
Lost	10	14
Own Recovered for Touchdown	0	0
Opponent's Recovered by	14	10
Opponent's Recovered for Touchdown	0	1
Total Points Scored	332	209
Total Touchdowns	39	24
Touchdowns Rushing	18	7
Touchdowns Passing	15	13
Touchdowns on Returns & Recoveries	6	4
Extra Points	39	23
Safeties	1	0
Field Goals Attempted	29	28
Field Goals Made	19	14
% Successful	65.52	50.00

Regular Season   9-4-1

Date	GB		OPP	Att.
9/17	17	Detroit Lions	17	(50,861)
9/24	13	Chicago Bears	10	(50,861)
10/1	23	Atlanta Falcons (M)	0	(49,467)
10/8	27	at Detroit Lions	17	(57,877)
10/15	7	Minnesota Vikings (M)	10	(49,601)
10/22	48	at New York Giants	21	(62,585)
10/30	31	at St. Louis Cardinals	23	(49,792)
11/5	10	at Baltimore Colts	13	(60,238)
11/12	55	Cleveland Browns (M)	7	(50,074)
11/19	13	San Francisco 49ers	0	(50,861)
11/26	17	at Chicago Bears	13	(47,513)
12/3	30	at Minnesota Vikings	27	(47,693)
12/9	24	at Los Angeles Rams	27	(76,637)
12/17	17	Pittsburgh Steelers	24	(50,861)

Postseason   3-0

12/23	28	Los Angeles Rams (M)	7	(49,861)
12/31	21	Dallas Cowboys	17	(50,861)
1/14	33	Raiders at Orange Bowl	14	(75,546)

Score By Periods

	1	2	3	4	Total
Packers	76	93	53	110	332
Opponents	40	69	30	70	209

1967

INDIVIDUAL STATISTICS

Rushing

	Att	Yds	Avg	LG	TD
Grabowski	120	466	3.9	24	2
B. Wilson	103	453	4.4	40	2
D. Anderson	97	402	4.1	40	6
E. Pitts	77	247	3.2	30	6
T. Williams	35	188	5.4	37	1
Starr	21	90	4.3	23	0
Mercein	14	56	4.0	15	1
Dale	1	9	9.0	9	0
Bratkowski	5	6	1.2	4	0
Horn	1	-2	-2.0	-2	0
Packers	**474**	**1,915**	**4.0**	**40**	**18**
Opponents	443	1,923	4.3	t59	7

Receiving

	No	Yds	Avg	LG	TD
Dowler	54	836	15.5	t57	4
Dale	35	738	21.9	t86	5
D. Anderson	22	331	15.0	37	3
E. Pitts	15	210	14.0	84	0
B. Wilson	14	88	6.3	21	0
Grabowski	12	171	14.3	53	1
Fleming	10	126	12.6	19	1
Long	8	96	12.3	21	0
T. Williams	5	80	16.0	t29	1
Allen Brown	3	43	14.3	17	0
McGee	3	33	11.0	13	0
Mercein	1	6	6.0	6	0
Packers	**182**	**2,758**	**15.2**	**t86**	**15**
Opponents	155	1,644	10.6	t49	13

Passing

	Att	Com	Yds	Pct	TD	In	Tk/Yds	Rate
Starr	210	115	1,823	54.8	9	17	34/322	64.4
Bratkowski	94	53	724	56.4	5	9	6/64	59.3
Horn	24	12	171	50.0	1	1	1/8	70.0
E. Pitts	1	1	21	100.0	0	0	0/0	—
D. Anderson	2	1	19	50.0	0	0	0/0	—
Packers	**331**	**182**	**2,758**	**55.0**	**15**	**27**	**41/394**	**63.7**
Opponents	337	155	1,644	46.0	13	26	29/267	41.5

Punting

	No	Yds	Avg	LG	HB
D. Anderson	65	2,378	36.6	63	1
Chandler	1	31	31.0	31	0
Packers	**66**	**2,409**	**36.5**	**63**	**1**
Opponents	75	3,119	41.6	78	0

Kickoff Returns

	No	Yds	Avg	LG	TD
T. Williams	18	739	41.1	t104	4
D. Anderson	11	226	20.5	30	0
Adderley	10	207	20.7	37	0
Crutcher	3	48	16.0	23	0
Allen Brown	1	13	13.0	13	0
Hart	1	8	8.0	8	0
D. Robinson	1	0	0.0	0	0
Wood	1	0	0.0	0	0
Packers	**46**	**1,241**	**27.0**	**t104**	**4**
Opponents	59	1,276	21.6	50	0

Punt Returns

	No	Yds	Avg	FC	LG	TD
Wood	12	3	0.3	6	8	0
D. Anderson	9	98	10.9	3	43	0
T. Brown	9	40	4.4	1	12	0
E. Pitts	9	16	1.8	3	10	0
Packers	**39**	**157**	**4.0**	**13**	**43**	**0**
Opponents	13	22	1.7	27	10	0

Interceptions

	No	Yds	Avg	LG	TD
Jeter	8	78	9.8	25	0
Wood	4	60	15.0	25	0
Adderley	4	16	4.0	t12	1
D. Robinson	4	16	4.0	12	0
Nitschke	3	35	11.7	t20	1
Caffey	2	28	14.0	24	0
T. Brown	1	51	51.0	51	0
Packers	**26**	**284**	**10.9**	**51**	**2**
Opponents	27	370	13.7	37	3

Scoring

	TDr	TDp	TDrt	PAT	FG	S	TP
Chandler	0	0	0	39/39	19/29	0	96
D. Anderson	6	3	0	0/0	0/0	0	54
E. Pitts	6	0	0	0/0	0/0	0	36
T. Williams	1	1	4	0/0	0/0	0	36
Dale	0	5	0	0/0	0/0	0	30
Dowler	0	4	0	0/0	0/0	0	24
Grabowski	2	1	0	0/0	0/0	0	18
B. Wilson	2	0	0	0/0	0/0	0	12
Adderley	0	0	1	0/0	0/0	0	6
Fleming	0	1	0	0/0	0/0	0	6
Mercein	1	0	0	0/0	0/0	0	6
Nitschke	0	0	1	0/0	0/0	0	6
W. Davis	0	0	0	0/0	0/0	1	2
Packers	**18**	**15**	**6**	**39/39**	**19/29**	**1**	**332**
Opponents	7	13	4	23/24	14/28	0	209

Fumbles

	Fum	Ow	Op	Yds	Tot
Adderley	0	1	0	0	1
L. Aldridge	0	0	1	0	1
D. Anderson	3	0	0	0	0
Bowman	0	1	0	0	1
Bratkowski	2	0	0	0	1
T. Brown	0	0	2	0	2
Flanigan	0	0	1	0	1
Grabowski	3	0	0	0	0
Gregg	0	1	0	0	1
Hart	0	0	1	0	1
Horn	1	0	0	0	0
Jeter	0	0	1	7	1
J. Kramer	0	1	0	0	1
Mercein	1	0	0	0	1
Nitschke	0	0	1	0	1
E. Pitts	1	0	0	0	0
D. Robinson	0	0	1	0	1
Rowser	0	0	1	0	1
Skoronski	0	1	0	0	1
Starr	3	1	0	0	1
Weatherwax	0	0	1	0	1
T. Williams	1	0	0	0	0
B. Wilson	4	2	0	0	2
S. Wright	0	0	3	0	3
Packers	**19**	**9**	**14**	**7**	**23**

NFL STANDINGS

Western Conference

Coastal Division

	W	L	T	Pct	PF	PA
Los Angeles Rams	11	1	2	.917	398	196
Baltimore Colts	11	1	2	.917	394	198
San Francisco 49ers	7	7	0	.500	273	337
Atlanta Falcons	1	12	1	.077	175	422

Central Division

	W	L	T	Pct	PF	PA
Green Bay Packers	**9**	**4**	**1**	**.692**	**332**	**209**
Chicago Bears	7	6	1	.538	239	218
Detroit Lions	5	7	2	.417	260	259
Minnesota Vikings	3	8	3	.273	233	294

Eastern Conference

Capitol Division

	W	L	T	Pct	PF	PA
Dallas Cowboys	9	5	0	.643	342	268
Philadelphia Eagles	6	7	1	.462	351	409
Washington Redskins	5	6	3	.455	347	353
New Orleans Saints	3	11	0	.214	233	379

Century Division

	W	L	T	Pct	PF	PA
Cleveland Browns	9	5	0	.643	334	297
New York Giants	7	7	0	.500	369	379
St. Louis Cardinals	6	7	1	.462	333	356
Pittsburgh Steelers	4	9	1	.308	281	320

1967 ROSTER

No	Name	Pos	Ht	Wt	DOB	College	G
26	Adderley, Herb	CB	6-1	200	06/08/39	Michigan State	14
82	Aldridge, Lionel	DE	6-4	245	02/18/41	Utah State	12
44	Anderson, Donny	RB	6-3	210	05/16/43	Texas Tech	14
57	Bowman, Ken	C	6-3	230	12/15/42	Wisconsin	13
12	Bratkowski, Zeke	QB	6-3	210	10/20/31	Georgia	6
83	Brown, Allen	TE	6-5	235	03/02/43	Mississippi	14
78	Brown, Bob	DE	6-5	260	02/23/40	Arkansas-Pine Bluff	14
40	Brown, Tom	DB	6-1	190	12/12/40	Maryland	14
60	Caffey, Lee Roy	LB	6-3	250	06/03/41	Texas A&M	13
88	Capp, Dick	TE	6-3	235	04/09/42	Boston College	2
34	Chandler, Don	K	6-2	210	09/05/34	Florida	14
56	Crutcher, Tommy	LB	6-3	230	08/10/41	TCU	14
84	Dale, Carroll	WR	6-2	200	04/24/38	Virginia Tech	14
87	Davis, Willie	DE	6-3	245	07/24/34	Grambling	14
86	Dowler, Boyd	WR	6-5	225	10/18/37	Colorado	14
55	Flanigan, Jim	LB	6-3	240	04/15/45	Pittsburgh	12
81	Fleming, Marv	TE	6-4	235	01/02/42	Utah	14
68	Gillingham, Gale	G	6-3	255	02/03/44	Minnesota	14
33	Grabowski, Jim	RB	6-2	220	09/09/44	Illinois	9
75	Gregg, Forrest	T	6-4	250	10/18/33	SMU	14
43	Hart, Doug	DB	6-0	190	06/03/39	Arlington State	14
13	Horn, Don	QB	6-2	195	03/09/45	San Diego State	3
50	Hyland, Bob	C-G	6-5	250	07/21/45	Boston College	14
27	James, Claudis	WR	6-2	190	11/07/43	Jackson State	1
21	Jeter, Bob	DB	6-1	205	05/09/37	Iowa	14
74	Jordan, Henry	DT	6-3	250	01/26/35	Virginia	14
77	Kostelnik, Ron	DT	6-4	260	01/14/40	Cincinnati	14
64	Kramer, Jerry	G	6-3	245	01/23/36	Idaho	14
80	Long, Bob	WR	6-3	205	06/16/42	Wichita	10
85	McGee, Max	WR	6-3	210	07/16/32	Tulane	10
30	Mercein, Chuck	RB	6-3	230	04/09/43	Yale	7
66	Nitschke, Ray	LB	6-3	240	12/29/36	Illinois	14
22	Pitts, Elijah	HB	6-1	205	02/03/39	Philander Smith	8
89	Robinson, Dave	LB	6-3	240	05/03/41	Penn State	14
45	Rowser, John	DB	6-1	180	04/24/44	Michigan	14
76	Skoronski, Bob	T	6-3	245	03/05/34	Indiana	14
15	Starr, Bart	QB	6-1	190	01/09/34	Alabama	14
63	Thurston, Fred (Fuzzy)	G	6-1	245	05/07/35	Valparaiso	9
73	Weatherwax, Jim	DT	6-7	260	01/09/43	Cal State-Los Angeles	14
23	Williams, Travis	RB	6-1	210	01/14/46	Arizona State	14
36	Wilson, Ben	RB	6-0	225	03/09/40	USC	14
24	Wood, Willie	DB	5-10	190	12/23/36	USC	14
72	Wright, Steve	T	6-6	250	07/18/42	Alabama	14

1967 DRAFT

Rnd	Name	Pos	Ht	Wt	College
1a	Bob Hyland (9)	C-G	6-5	255	Boston College
	(Choice from Steelers as part of Tony Jeter, Lloyd Voss deal)				
1b	Don Horn (25)	QB	6-2	195	San Diego State
2a	Dave Dunaway (41)	WR	6-2	205	Duke
	(Choice from Rams for Tom Moore)				
2b	Jim Flanigan (51)	LB	6-3	240	Pittsburgh
3	John Rowser (78)	DB	6-1	180	Michigan
4a	Travis Williams (93)	RB	6-1	210	Arizona State
	(Choice from Redskins for Ron Rector)				
4b	(Choice (105) traded to Cardinals for Cardinals No. 3 in 1968)				
5a	Dwight Hood (116)	DE	6-5	240	Baylor
	(Choice from Steelers for Ron Smith)				
5b	Dick Tate (130)	DB	6-0	185	Utah
	(Choice from Cowboys for Hank Gremminger)				
5c	Jay Bachman (132)	C	6-3	240	Cincinnati
6	Stew Williams (158)	FB	6-1	240	Bowling Green
7a	Bob Ziolkowski (161)	T	6-5	270	Iowa
	(Choice from Giants for Allen Jacobs)				
7b	Bill Powell (184)	G-LB	6-1	240	Missouri
8	Clarence Mills (210)	DT	6-6	280	Trinity
9	Harland Reed (236)	TE	6-2	220	Mississippi State
10	Bill Shear (262)	K	5-10	175	Cortland State
11	Dave Bennett (287)	QB	6-4	200	Springfield
12	Mike Bass (314)	DB	6-0	190	Michigan
13	Keith Brown (340)	WR	6-5	215	Central Missouri
14	Claudis James (366)	HB	6-2	190	Jackson State
15	James Schneider (392)	DT	6-5	230	Colgate
16	Fred Cassidy (418)	HB	6-1	200	Miami (FL)
17	Jeff Elias (444)	TE	6-5	230	Kansas

1967 GREEN BAY PACKERS

FRONT ROW: (L–R) 89 Dave Robinson, 22 Elijah Pitts, 82 Lionel Aldridge, 43 Doug Hart, 21 Bob Jeter, 76 Bob Skoronski, 87 Willie Davis, 26 Herb Adderley, 24 Willie Wood, 81 Marv Fleming.
SECOND ROW: (L–R) Trainer Carl (Bud) Jorgensen, 40 Tom Brown, 66 Ray Nitschke, 12 Zeke Bratkowski, 84 Carroll Dale, 15 Bart Starr, 77 Ron Kostelnik, 74 Henry Jordan, 34 Don Chandler, 13 Don Horn, 45 John Rowser, 80 Bob Long, Equipment Manager Gerald (Dad) Braisher.
THIRD ROW: (L–R) Assistant Trainer Domenic Gentile, 78 Bob Brown, 57 Ken Bowman, 33 Jim Grabowski, 64 Jerry Kramer, 63 Fred (Fuzzy) Thurston, 36 Ben Wilson, 68 Gale Gillingham, 50 Bob Hyland, 27 Claudis James, Assistant Equipment Manager Bob Noel.
BACK ROW: (L–R) 44 Donny Anderson, 73 Jim Weatherwax, 56 Tommy Crutcher, 55 Jim Flanigan, 83 Allen Brown, 86 Boyd Dowler, 75 Forrest Gregg, 60 Lee Roy Caffey, 72 Steve Wright, 88 Dick Capp, 23 Travis Williams, 85 Max McGee.

Carroll Dale was 30; Boyd Dowler 31; Jerry Kramer, Ray Nitschke and Willie Wood 32. Henry Jordan turned 33; Willie Davis, Bart Starr and Bob Skoronski 34; Forrest Gregg 35 and Zeke Bratkowski 37. Max McGee, Fred (Fuzzy) Thurston and Don Chandler retired. Vince Lombardi no longer prowled the sidelines and practice field exhorting maximum effort from his squad, having withdrawn to the position of general manager. So began the coaching reign of Phil Bengtson.

Bengtson claimed, "There is no age problem as far as we're concerned." Indeed, a number of veterans turned in respectable performances. Starr, when his arm was healthy, completed 63.7 percent of his throws. Dowler caught 45 passes to lead the team. And Wood, Gregg and Dale played in the Pro Bowl.

The defense, third overall, was number one against the pass for a record fifth time. Opponents gained more yards rushing than passing against the Packers.

With the exception of losing Lombardi to the front office, the loss of Chandler probably hurt the most. Kramer began the year as Chandler's replacement but missed five straight field goals after hitting his first four. Chuck Mercein took a turn, but after he went one-for-three and Kramer injured his knee on October 21, Errol Mann was called up from the taxi squad. Mann blew three attempts and gave way to Mike Mercer, who ended up as the only kicker to better 50 percent. Overall, the Packers converted 45 percent (13 of 29).

Also missing was the Packers' ability to pull out close games. Seven games were decided by a touchdown or less and Green Bay won only one at Chicago, 28-27 and then that win came only after the Packers had been eliminated from the division race.

In spite of a final 6-7-1 record, the Packers stayed at or near the top of the Central Division standings for a dozen weeks. The team recorded its biggest win of the year when it downed the unbeaten Cowboys in week seven. Starr, who had pulled a tendon in his passing arm in pregame warmups against the Rams two weeks earlier, returned and passed for four touchdowns to lead Green Bay past Dallas 28-17. That win moved the Packers (3-3-1) into a first-place tie with Detroit.

Unfortunately, Green Bay was unable to build on the upset. A week later, the Bears edged the Packers 13-10 on Mac Percival's last-second free kick and then Bill Brown ran for two touchdowns as Minnesota shaded Green Bay 14-10. The losses dropped the team (3-5-1) behind the division-leading Vikings (5-4).

The up-and-down Packers then won two of their next three to stay close. With just two games remaining, Green Bay (5-6-1) had to get past Baltimore and Chicago and hope Minnesota (6-6) lost at least once. Late in the Packers-Colts game, however, it became apparent such a scenario would not unfold. With the Vikings leading San Francisco on the West Coast, and the final period winding down at Lambeau Field with Green Bay in arrears 16-3, band director Wilner Burke approached the microphone. "For years these Packers have given some great thrills. How about a standing ovation for them." The entire stadium arose and joined together to honor the team that had delivered an incredible five championships over the past seven years.

Green Bay Press-Gazette photo

Willie Davis (87) zeros in on the Lions' Mel Farr (24) in the Packers' 23-17 loss to Detroit on September 29. Davis came to Green Bay from Cleveland in 1960 and he went on to play in 138 consecutive games for the Packers before retiring after the 1969 season.

TEAM STATISTICS

	GB	OPP
First Downs	240	213
Rushing	96	105
Passing	130	92
Penalty	14	16
Rushes	450	476
Yards Gained	1,749	1,800
Average Gain	3.89	3.78
Average Yards per Game	124.9	128.6
Passes Attempted	318	327
Completed	188	157
% Completed	59.12	48.01
Total Yards Gained	2,651	2,031
Times Sacked	41	28
Yards Lost	376	235
Net Yards Gained	2,275	1,796
Yards Gained per Completion	14.10	12.94
Net Yards per Attempt	6.34	5.06
Average Net Yards per Game	162.5	128.3
Combined Net Yards Gained	4,024	3,596
Total Plays	809	831
Average Yards per Play	4.97	4.33
Average Net Yards per Game	287.4	256.9
Intercepted By	17	15
Yards Returned	244	150
Returned for TD	0	0
Punts	59	77
Yards Punted	2,359	3,049
Average Yards per Punt	39.98	39.60
Punt Returns	43	19
Yards Returned	238	66
Average Yards per Return	5.53	3.47
Returned for TD	1	0
Kickoff Returns	48	56
Yards Returned	1,007	1,211
Average Yards per Return	20.98	21.63
Returned for TD	0	0
Penalties	64	60
Yards Penalized	653	541
Fumbles	31	28
Lost	18	17
Own Recovered for Touchdown	0	0
Opponent's Recovered by	17	18
Opponent's Recovered for Touchdown	1	0
Total Points Scored	281	227
Total Touchdowns	35	25
Touchdowns Rushing	12	11
Touchdowns Passing	21	14
Touchdowns on Returns & Recoveries	2	0
Extra Points	32	24
Safeties	0	1
Field Goals Attempted	29	26
Field Goals Made	13	17
% Successful	44.83	65.38

Regular Season 6-7-1

Date	GB		OPP	Att.
9/15	30	Philadelphia Eagles	13	(50,861)
9/22	13	Minnesota Vikings (M)	26	(49,346)
9/29	17	Detroit Lions	23	(50,861)
10/6	38	at Atlanta Falcons	7	(58,850)
10/13	14	Los Angeles Rams (M)	16	(49,646)
10/20	14	at Detroit Lions	14	(57,302)
10/28	28	at Dallas Cowboys	17	(74,604)
11/3	10	Chicago Bears	13	(50,861)
11/10	10	at Minnesota Vikings	14	(47,644)
11/17	29	New Orleans Saints	7	(49,644)
11/24	27	at Washington Redskins	7	(50,621)
12/1	20	at San Francisco 49ers	27	(47,218)
12/7	3	Baltimore Colts	16	(50,861)
12/15	28	at Chicago Bears	27	(46,435)

Score By Periods

	1	2	3	4	Total
Packers	68	61	95	57	281
Opponents	55	69	40	63	227

INDIVIDUAL STATISTICS

Rushing

	Att	Yds	Avg	LG	TD
D. Anderson	170	761	4.5	42	5
Grabowski	135	518	3.8	25	3
E. Pitts	72	264	3.7	14	2
T. Williams	33	63	1.9	9	0
Starr	11	62	5.6	15	1
Mercein	17	49	2.9	8	1
Bratkowski	8	24	3.0	13	0
James	1	15	15.0	15	0
Horn	3	-7	-2.3	1	0
Packers	**450**	**1,749**	**3.9**	**42**	**12**
Opponents	476	1,800	3.8	63	11

Receiving

	No	Yds	Avg	LG	TD
Dowler	45	668	14.8	t72	6
Dale	42	818	19.5	t63	8
D. Anderson	25	333	13.3	t47	1
Fleming	25	278	11.1	t32	3
Grabowski	18	210	11.7	t67	1
E. Pitts	17	142	8.4	19	0
James	8	148	18.5	24	2
T. Williams	5	48	9.6	17	0
Mercein	3	6	2.0	9	0
Packers	**188**	**2,651**	**14.1**	**t72**	**21**
Opponents	157	2,031	12.9	t60	14

Passing

	Att	Com	Yds	Pct	TD	In	Tk/Yds	Rate
Starr	171	109	1,617	63.7	15	8	29/261	104.3
Bratkowski	126	68	835	54.0	3	7	11/107	59.5
Horn	16	10	187	62.5	2	0	1/8	142.4
D. Anderson	3	1	12	33.3	1	0	0/0	—
Stevens	2	0	0	00.0	0	0	0/0	—
Packers	**318**	**188**	**2,651**	**59.1**	**21**	**15**	**41/376**	**88.4**
Opponents	327	157	2,031	48.0	14	17	28/235	60.6

Punting

	No	Yds	Avg	LG	HB
D. Anderson	59	2,359	40.0	65	0
Packers	**59**	**2,359**	**40.0**	**65**	**0**
Opponents	77	3,049	39.6	62	0

Kickoff Returns

	No	Yds	Avg	LG	TD
T. Williams	28	599	21.4	60	0
Adderley	14	331	23.6	50	0
E. Pitts	2	40	20.0	27	0
D. Robinson	2	29	14.5	19	0
Vandersea	1	8	8.0	8	0
Winkler	1	0	0.0	0	0
Packers	**48**	**1,007**	**21.0**	**60**	**0**
Opponents	56	1,211	21.6	46	0

Punt Returns

	No	Yds	Avg	FC	LG	TD
Wood	26	126	4.8	11	16	0
T. Brown	16	111	6.9	5	t52	1
E. Pitts	1	1	1.0	1	1	0
Packers	**43**	**238**	**5.5**	**17**	**t52**	**1**
Opponents	19	66	3.5	20	16	0

Interceptions

	No	Yds	Avg	LG	TD
T. Brown	4	66	16.5	25	0
Jeter	3	35	11.7	29	0
Adderley	3	27	9.0	17	0
Wood	2	54	27.0	35	0
Nitschke	2	20	10.0	11	0
D. Robinson	2	18	9.0	18	0
Hart	1	24	24.0	24	0
Packers	**17**	**244**	**14.4**	**35**	**0**
Opponents	15	150	10.0	36	0

Scoring

	TDr	TDp	TDrt	PAT	FG	S	TP
Dale	0	8	0	0/0	0/0	0	48
D. Anderson	5	1	0	0/0	0/0	0	36
Dowler	0	6	0	0/0	0/0	0	36
Mercer	0	0	0	12/14	7/12	0	33
Grabowski	3	1	0	0/0	0/0	0	24
J. Kramer	0	0	0	9/9	4/9	0	21
Mercein	1	0	0	7/7	2/5	0	19
Fleming	0	3	0	0/0	0/0	0	18
T. Brown	0	0	2	0/0	0/0	0	12
James	0	2	0	0/0	0/0	0	12
E. Pitts	2	0	0	0/0	0/0	0	12
Starr	1	0	0	0/0	0/0	0	6
E. Mann	0	0	0	4/4	0/3	0	4
Packers	**12**	**21**	**2**	**32/35**	**13/29**	**0**	**281**
Opponents	11	14	0	24/25	17/26	1	227

Fumbles

	Fum	Ow	Op	Yds	Tot
Adderley	2	0	2	25	2
L. Aldridge	1	0	2	12	2
D. Anderson	7	0	0	0	0
Bowman	0	1	0	0	1
Bratkowski	4	1	0	0	1
T. Brown	0	0	1	22	1
Caffey	0	0	1	0	1
Carr	0	0	1	0	1
Carroll	0	1	0	0	1
Dale	1	0	0	0	0
W. Davis	0	0	3	9	3
Gillingham	0	1	0	0	1
Grabowski	6	1	0	0	1
Gregg	0	2	0	0	2
Horn	1	0	0	0	0
James	2	0	0	0	0
H. Jordan	0	1	1	0	2
Kostelnik	0	0	1	0	1
Nitschke	0	0	3	6	3
E. Pitts	0	1	0	0	1
D. Robinson	1	0	1	0	1
Starr	2	1	0	0	1
T. Williams	3	1	0	0	2
Winkler	0	0	1	0	1
Wood	0	0	0	0	0
Packers	**31**	**13**	**17**	**74**	**30**

NFL STANDINGS

Western Conference

Coastal Division

	W	L	T	Pct	PF	PA
Baltimore Colts	13	1	0	.929	402	144
Los Angeles Rams	10	3	1	.769	312	200
San Francisco 49ers	7	6	1	.538	303	310
Atlanta Falcons	2	12	0	.143	170	389

Central Division

	W	L	T	Pct	PF	PA
Minnesota Vikings	8	6	0	.571	282	242
Chicago Bears	7	7	0	.500	250	333
Green Bay Packers	6	7	1	.462	281	227
Detroit Lions	4	8	2	.333	207	241

Eastern Conference

Capitol Division

	W	L	T	Pct	PF	PA
Dallas Cowboys	12	2	0	.857	431	186
New York Giants	7	7	0	.500	294	325
Washington Redskins	5	9	0	.357	249	358
Philadelphia Eagles	2	12	0	.143	202	351

Century Division

	W	L	T	Pct	PF	PA
Cleveland Browns	10	4	0	.714	394	273
St. Louis Cardinals	9	4	1	.692	325	289
New Orleans Saints	4	9	1	.308	246	327
Pittsburgh Steelers	2	11	1	.154	244	397

1968 ROSTER

No	Name	Pos	Ht	Wt	DOB	College	G
26	Adderley, Herb	CB	6-1	200	06/08/39	Michigan State	14
82	Aldridge, Lionel	DE	6-4	245	02/18/41	Utah State	14
44	Anderson, Donny	RB	6-3	210	05/16/43	Texas Tech	14
57	Bowman, Ken	C	6-3	230	12/15/42	Wisconsin	14
12	Bratkowski, Zeke	QB	6-3	210	10/20/31	Georgia	10
78	Brown, Bob	DE	6-5	260	02/23/40	Arkansas-Pine Bluff	6
40	Brown, Tom	DB	6-1	190	12/12/40	Maryland	14
60	Caffey, Lee Roy	LB	6-3	250	06/03/41	Texas A&M	14
53	Carr, Fred	LB	6-5	238	08/19/46	Texas-El Paso	14
67	Carroll, Leo	DE	6-7	250	02/16/44	San Diego State	6
70	Crenshaw, Leon	DT	6-6	280	07/14/43	Tuskegee	10
84	Dale, Carroll	WR	6-2	200	04/24/38	Virginia Tech	14
87	Davis, Willie	DE	6-3	245	07/24/34	Grambling	14
86	Dowler, Boyd	WR	6-5	225	10/18/37	Colorado	14
29	Dunaway, Dave	WR	6-2	205	01/19/45	Duke	2
55	Flanigan, Jim	LB	6-3	240	04/15/45	Pittsburgh	13
81	Fleming, Marv	TE	6-4	235	01/02/42	Utah	14
68	Gillingham, Gale	G	6-3	255	02/03/44	Minnesota	14
33	Grabowski, Jim	RB	6-2	220	09/09/44	Illinois	14
75	Gregg, Forrest	T	6-4	250	10/18/33	SMU	14
43	Hart, Doug	DB	6-0	190	06/03/39	Arlington State	14
72	Himes, Dick	T	6-4	244	05/25/46	Ohio State	14
13	Horn, Don	QB	6-2	195	03/09/45	San Diego State	1
50	Hyland, Bob	C-G	6-5	250	07/21/45	Boston College	14
27	James, Claudis	WR	6-2	190	11/07/43	Jackson State	14
21	Jeter, Bob	DB	6-1	205	05/09/37	Iowa	12
74	Jordan, Henry	DT	6-3	250	01/26/35	Virginia	14
77	Kostelnik, Ron	DT	6-4	260	01/14/40	Cincinnati	13
64	Kramer, Jerry	G	6-3	245	01/23/36	Idaho	14
62	Lueck, Bill	G	6-3	235	04/07/46	Arizona	11
39	Mann, Errol	K	6-0	203	06/27/41	North Dakota	2
30	Mercein, Chuck	RB	6-3	230	04/09/43	Yale	11
38	Mercer, Mike	K	6-0	217	11/21/35	Arizona State	6
66	Nitschke, Ray	LB	6-3	235	12/29/36	Illinois	14
71	Peay, Francis	T	6-5	250	05/23/44	Missouri	14
22	Pitts, Elijah	HB	6-1	205	02/03/39	Philander Smith	14
80	Pope, Bucky	WR	6-5	200	03/23/41	Catawba	3
89	Robinson, Dave	LB	6-3	240	05/03/41	Penn State	14
45	Rowser, John	CB	6-1	180	04/24/44	Michigan	14
47	Rule, Gordon	S	6-2	180	03/01/46	Dartmouth	1
76	Skoronski, Bob	T	6-3	245	03/05/34	Indiana	14
15	Starr, Bart	QB	6-1	190	01/09/34	Alabama	13
10	Stevens, Bill	QB	6-3	195	08/27/45	Texas-El Paso	1
83	Vandersea, Phil	LB	6-3	235	02/25/43	Massachusetts	10
23	Williams, Travis	RB	6-1	210	01/14/46	Arizona State	14
58	Winkler, Francis	DE	6-3	230	10/20/46	Memphis State	7
24	Wood, Willie	DB	5-10	190	12/23/36	USC	14

1968 DRAFT

Rnd	Name	Pos	Ht	Wt	College
1a	Fred Carr (5)	LB	6-5	238	Texas-El Paso
	(Choice from Saints for Jim Taylor)				
1b	Bill Lueck (26)	G	6-3	235	Arizona
2	(Choice (53) to Rams in Ben Wilson deal)				
3a	Bill Stevens (67)	QB	6-3	195	Texas-El Paso
	(Choice from Cardinals for Fred Heron)				
3b	Dick Himes (81)	T	6-4	244	Ohio State
4a	Brendan McCarthy (92)	FB	6-3	217	Boston College
	(Choice from Steelers for Dick Arndt)				
4b	John Robinson (108)	WR	6-2	196	Tennessee State
5a	Steve Duich (121)	T	6-3	248	San Diego State
	(Choice from Steelers for Kent Nix)				
5b	Francis Winkler (137)	DE	6-3	230	Memphis State
6	Walter Chadwick (164)	HB	6-0	205	Tennessee
7	Andy Beath (191)	DB	6-2	192	Duke
8	Tom Owens (218)	G	6-3	240	Missouri-Rolla
9	Bob Apisa (245)	FB	6-2	225	Michigan State
10a	Richard Cash (260)	T	6-5	260	NE Missouri State
	(Choice from Giants for Dave Hathcock)				
10b	Ron Worthen (272)	C	6-5	235	Arkansas State
11	Gordon Rule (299)	DB	6-2	180	Dartmouth
12	Dennis Porter (325)	DT	6-4	242	Northern Michigan
13	Frank Geiselman (353)	WR	6-2	207	Rhode Island
14	John Farler (380)	WR	6-1	208	Colorado
15	Ridley Gibson (407)	DB	6-2	200	Baylor
16	Al Groves (434)	DT	6-4	270	St. Norbert
17	Ken Rota (461)	HB	6-2	200	North Dakota State

1968 GREEN BAY PACKERS

FRONT ROW: (L-R) 89 Dave Robinson, 82 Lionel Aldridge, 43 Doug Hart, 57 Ken Bowman, 21 Bob Jeter, 76 Bob Skoronski, 87 Willie Davis, 40 Tom Brown, 26 Herb Adderley, 24 Willie Wood, 81 Marv Fleming.

SECOND ROW: (L-R) Trainer Carl (Bud) Jorgensen, 15 Bart Starr, 84 Carroll Dale, 12 Zeke Bratkowski, 77 Ron Kostelnik, 74 Henry Jordan, 45 John Rowser, 83 Phil Vandersea, 27 Claudis James, 50 Bob Hyland, 22 Elijah Pitts, Equipment Manager Gerald (Dad) Braisher.

THIRD ROW: (L-R) Assistant Trainer Domenic Gentile, 66 Ray Nitschke, 36 Ben Wilson, 33 Jim Grabowski, 44 Donny Anderson, 68 Gale Gillingham, 64 Jerry Kramer, 30 Chuck Mercein, 29 Dave Dunaway, 67 Leo Carroll, 78 Bob Brown, 70 Leon Crenshaw, Assistant Equipment Manager Bob Noel.

BACK ROW: (L-R) 23 Travis Williams, 53 Fred Carr, 73 Jim Weatherwax, 60 Lee Roy Caffey, 86 Boyd Dowler, 75 Forrest Gregg, 55 Jim Flanigan, 71 Francis Peay, 58 Francis Winkler, 62 Bill Lueck, 72 Dick Himes.

For seven weeks it appeared the Pack might be back. The Green and Gold whipped the Bears 17-0 to start the year, followed up with a 14-7 victory over the 49ers, then chalked up three more wins in the next five games. At midseason, Green Bay (5-2) owned second place in the Central Division behind the Vikings (6-1).

Baltimore was next on the schedule before the Packers got a second shot at the Vikings. (Minnesota had beaten Green Bay 19-7 on October 5.) Johnny Unitas fired a pair of touchdown passes to lead the Colts past Green Bay 14-6. Then, in Milwaukee on November 16, Bobby Bryant intercepted a Bart Starr pass intended for Dave Hampton on the Vikings' five-yard line with 1:22 remaining to seal a 9-7 Minnesota win. A week later, after Minnesota trounced Pittsburgh 52-14 and Green Bay lost 16-10 to Detroit, the Packers were mathematically eliminated from the playoff race.

Six more players from the Lombardi era departed. Bob Skoronski, Jerry Kramer, Zeke Bratkowski and Forrest Gregg retired, while Ron Kostelnik and Tom Brown were traded to the Colts and Redskins, respectively. Bratkowski and Gregg remained in Green Bay as assistant coaches, though the door remained open for them to return to active duty. Gregg did come out of retirement on September 2 and ran his string of consecutive games played to 173.

Lombardi himself ended up in Washington, D.C. Off-season rumors had him going to the Eagles, the Giants, the Redskins or becoming major league baseball's next commissioner. On February 4, he made it known he wanted a head coaching job in the nation's capitol. At a special meeting held, strangely enough in the Lombardi Room of the Forum Supper Club, the Packers Board of Directors released the general manager from his contract. The last winning coach in Packers history moved on to become head coach, executive vice-president and part-owner of the Redskins.

Phil Bengtson, who became general manager after meeting with team president President Dominic Olejniczak at Olejniczak's home on March 6, had more to worry about than just replacing retired players. He had a sore-armed quarterback in Bart Starr and an erratic reliever in Don Horn. He had an offense that could explode – 38 points in a thriller at Pittsburgh and 45 in a passing clinic versus St. Louis – but one that lost an NFL-high 21 fumbles.

Most troubling of all, Bengtson had no reliable field-goal kicker. Last year's derby featured five hopefuls. In 1969, Bengtson auditioned just two – holdover Mike Mercer and Booth Lusteg. Mercer lasted nine games and connected on five of 17 attempts with six blocked. Lusteg made a lone 28-yarder in five attempts. He had one blocked.

The NFL's most successful team of the '60s closed out the decade with a flourish on December 21 at home against the Cardinals. With Starr out because of injuries, Horn completed 22 of 31 passes for a then-team record 410 yards. His five touchdowns passes in the 45-28 win tied Cecil Isbell's team record.

Green Bay Press-Gazette photo

Jim Grabowski (33) rambles on a fourth-quarter draw play in the season opener. Green Bay shut out the Bears 17-0, then followed up with a 14-7 triumph over San Francisco; victories that placed the Packers in sole possession of first place in the Central Division. Grabowski led all runners with 85 yards on 16 carries in the Bears contest but, like his team, lost steam in the second half of the year. He wound up fourth in rushing with 261 yards.

TEAM STATISTICS

	GB	OPP
First Downs	242	224
Rushing	95	103
Passing	122	107
Penalty	25	14
Rushes	432	485
Yards Gained	1,692	1,982
Average Gain	3.92	4.09
Average Yards per Game	120.9	141.6
Passes Attempted	319	360
Completed	182	177
% Completed	57.05	49.17
Total Yards Gained	2,678	2,133
Times Sacked	34	36
Yards Lost	302	288
Net Yards Gained	2,376	1,845
Yards Gained per Completion	14.71	12.05
Net Yards per Attempt	6.73	4.66
Average Net Yards per Game	169.7	131.8
Combined Net Yards Gained	4,068	3,827
Total Plays	785	881
Average Yards per Play	5.18	4.34
Average Net Yards per Game	290.6	273.4
Intercepted By	19	17
Yards Returned	428	256
Returned for TD	2	1
Punts	59	72
Yards Punted	2,363	2,855
Average Yards per Punt	40.05	39.65
Punt Returns	32	18
Yards Returned	287	62
Average Yards per Return	8.97	3.44
Returned for TD	1	0
Kickoff Returns	50	51
Yards Returned	1,165	1,078
Average Yards per Return	23.30	21.14
Returned for TD	2	1
Penalties	63	65
Yards Penalized	602	733
Fumbles	31	23
Lost	21	7
Own Recovered for Touchdown	0	0
Opponent's Recovered by	7	21
Opponent's Recovered for Touchdown	0	1
Total Points Scored	269	221
Total Touchdowns	36	23
Touchdowns Rushing	11	7
Touchdowns Passing	20	13
Touchdowns on Returns & Recoveries	5	3
Extra Points	35	23
Safeties	0	0
Field Goals Attempted	22	34
Field Goals Made	6	20
% Successful	27.27	58.82

Regular Season   8-6-0

Date	GB		OPP	Att.
9/21	17	Chicago Bears	0	(50,861)
9/28	14	San Francisco 49ers (M)	7	(48,184)
10/5	7	at Minnesota Vikings	19	(60,740)
10/12	28	at Detroit Lions	17	(58,384)
10/19	21	at Los Angeles Rams	34	(78,947)
10/26	28	Atlanta Falcons	10	(50,861)
11/2	38	at Pittsburgh Steelers	34	(46,403)
11/9	6	at Baltimore Colts	14	(63,238)
11/16	7	Minnesota Vikings (M)	9	(48,321)
11/23	2	Detroit Lions	16	(50,861)
11/30	20	New York Giants (M)	10	(48,156)
12/7	7	at Cleveland Browns	20	(82,102)
12/14	21	at Chicago Bears	3	(45,216)
12/21	45	St. Louis Cardinals	28	(50,861)

Score By Periods

	1	2	3	4	Total
Packers	48	72	59	90	269
Opponents	53	87	55	26	221

INDIVIDUAL STATISTICS

Rushing

	Att	Yds	Avg	LG	TD
T. Williams	129	536	4.2	t39	4
Hampton	80	365	4.6	53	4
D. Anderson	87	288	3.3	116	1
Grabowski	73	261	3.6	22	1
E. Pitts	35	134	3.8	13	0
Starr	7	60	8.6	18	0
P. Williams	18	55	3.1	13	0
Horn	3	-7	-2.3	t2	1
Packers	**432**	**1,692**	**3.9**	**53**	**11**
Opponents	485	1,982	4.1	52	7

1969

Receiving

	No	Yds	Avg	LG	TD
Dale	45	879	19.5	48	6
Dowler	31	477	15.4	45	4
T. Williams	27	275	10.2	t60	3
Fleming	18	226	12.6	23	2
Hampton	15	216	14.4	50	2
D. Anderson	14	308	22.0	51	1
Grabowski	12	98	8.2	25	1
E. Pitts	9	47	5.2	t21	1
Spilis	7	89	12.7	16	0
P. Williams	4	63	15.8	24	0
Packers	**182**	**2,678**	**14.7**	**t60**	**20**
Opponents	177	2,133	12.1	t80	13

Passing

	Att	Com	Yds	Pct	TD	In	Tk/Yds	Rate
Horn	168	89	1,505	53.0	11	11	10/85	78.1
Starr	148	92	1,161	62.2	9	6	24/217	89.9
Stevens	3	1	12	33.3	0	0	0/0	—
Packers	**319**	**182**	**2,678**	**57.1**	**20**	**17**	**34/302**	**83.3**
Opponents	360	177	2,133	49.2	13	19	36/288	57.8

Punting

	No	Yds	Avg	LG	HB
D. Anderson	58	2,329	40.2	58	0
Dowler	1	34	34.0	34	0
Packers	**59**	**2,363**	**40.1**	**58**	**0**
Opponents	72	2,855	39.7	66	0

Kickoff Returns

	No	Yds	Avg	LG	TD
Hampton	22	582	26.5	t87	1
T. Williams	21	517	24.6	t96	1
D. Robinson	3	31	10.3	15	0
E. Pitts	1	22	22.0	22	0
Gillingham	1	13	13.0	13	0
Hyland	1	0	0.0	0	0
P. Williams	1	0	0.0	0	0
Packers	**50**	**1,165**	**23.3**	**t96**	**2**
Opponents	51	1,078	21.1	t100	1

Punt Returns

	No	Yds	Avg	FC	LG	TD
E. Pitts	16	60	3.8	8	10	0
T. Williams	8	189	23.6	3	t83	1
Wood	8	38	4.8	6	13	0
Packers	**32**	**287**	**9.0**	**17**	**t83**	**1**
Opponents	18	62	3.4	25	15	0

Interceptions

	No	Yds	Avg	LG	TD
Adderley	5	169	33.8	t80	1
Hart	3	156	52.0	t85	1
Wood	3	40	13.3	21	0
Jeter	3	30	10.0	30	0
Nitschke	2	32	16.0	32	0
Caffey	2	1	0.5	1	0
W. Davis	1	0	0.0	0	0
Packers	**19**	**428**	**22.5**	**t85**	**2**
Opponents	17	256	15.1	44	1

Scoring

	TDr	TDp	TDrt	PAT	FG	S	TP
T. Williams	4	3	2	0/0	0/0	0	54
Hampton	4	2	1	0/0	0/0	0	42
Mercer	0	0	0	23/23	5/17	0	38
Dale	0	6	0	0/0	0/0	0	36
Dowler	0	4	0	0/0	0/0	0	24
Lusteg	0	0	0	12/12	1/5	0	15
D. Anderson	1	1	0	0/0	0/0	0	12
Fleming	0	2	0	0/0	0/0	0	12
Grabowski	1	1	0	0/0	0/0	0	12
Adderley	0	0	1	0/0	0/0	0	6
Hart	0	0	1	0/0	0/0	0	6
Horn	1	0	0	0/0	0/0	0	6
E. Pitts	0	1	0	0/0	0/0	0	6
Packers	**11**	**20**	**5**	**35/36**	**6/22**	**0**	**269**
Opponents	7	13	3	23/23	20/34	0	221

Fumbles

	Fum	Ow	Op	Yds	Tot
L. Aldridge	0	0	1	0	1
D. Anderson	4	2	0	0	2
Caffey	0	0	1	0	1
W. Davis	0	0	2	0	2
Fleming	0	1	0	0	1
Gillingham	0	1	0	0	1
Grabowski	2	0	0	0	0
Hampton	7	2	0	0	2
Horn	6	1	0	0	1
Lueck	0	1	0	0	1
R. Moore	0	0	1	0	1
E. Pitts	2	1	0	0	1
D. Robinson	0	0	1	0	1
Starr	4	0	0	0	0
P. Williams	1	0	0	0	0
T. Williams	5	1	0	0	1
Wood	0	0	1	0	1
Packers	**31**	**10**	**7**	**0**	**17**

NFL STANDINGS

Western Conference

Coastal Division

	W	L	T	Pct	PF	PA
Los Angeles Rams	11	3	0	.786	320	243
Baltimore Colts	8	5	1	.615	279	268
Atlanta Falcons	6	8	0	.429	276	268
San Francisco 49ers	4	8	2	.333	277	319

Central Division

	W	L	T	Pct	PF	PA
Minnesota Vikings	12	2	0	.857	379	133
Detroit Lions	9	4	1	.692	259	188
Green Bay Packers	8	6	0	.571	269	221
Chicago Bears	1	13	0	.071	210	339

Eastern Conference

Capitol Division

	W	L	T	Pct	PF	PA
Dallas Cowboys	11	2	1	.846	369	223
Washington Redskins	7	5	2	.583	307	319
New Orleans Saints	5	9	0	.357	311	393
Philadelphia Eagles	4	9	1	.308	279	377

Century Division

	W	L	T	Pct	PF	PA
Cleveland Browns	10	3	1	.769	351	300
New York Giants	6	8	0	.429	264	298
St. Louis Cardinals	4	9	1	.308	314	389
Pittsburgh Steelers	1	13	0	.071	218	404

1969 ROSTER

No	Name	Pos	Ht	Wt	DOB	College	G
26	Adderley, Herb	CB	6-1	200	06/08/39	Michigan State	14
82	Aldridge, Lionel	DE	6-4	245	02/18/41	Utah State	14
44	Anderson, Donny	RB	6-3	210	05/16/43	Texas Tech	14
57	Bowman, Ken	C	6-3	230	12/15/42	Wisconsin	14
61	Bradley, Dave	G	6-4	245	02/13/47	Penn State	4
78	Brown, Bob	DE	6-5	260	02/23/40	Arkansas-Pine Bluff	14
60	Caffey, Lee Roy	LB	6-3	250	06/03/41	Texas A&M	14
53	Carr, Fred	LB	6-5	238	08/19/46	Texas-El Paso	14
84	Dale, Carroll	WR	6-2	200	04/24/38	Virginia Tech	14
87	Davis, Willie	DE	6-3	245	07/24/34	Grambling	14
86	Dowler, Boyd	WR	6-5	225	10/18/37	Colorado	14
55	Flanigan, Jim	LB	6-3	240	04/15/45	Pittsburgh	4
81	Fleming, Marv	TE	6-4	235	01/02/42	Utah	12
68	Gillingham, Gale	G	6-3	255	02/03/44	Minnesota	14
33	Grabowski, Jim	RB	6-2	220	09/09/44	Illinois	14
75	Gregg, Forrest	T	6-4	250	10/18/33	SMU	14
25	Hampton, Dave	RB	6-0	210	05/07/47	Wyoming	14
43	Hart, Doug	DB	6-0	190	06/03/39	Arlington State	14
77	Hayhoe, Bill	T	6-8	258	10/06/46	USC	14
72	Himes, Dick	T	6-4	244	05/25/46	Ohio State	14
13	Horn, Don	QB	6-2	195	03/09/45	San Diego State	9
50	Hyland, Bob	C-G	6-5	250	07/21/45	Boston College	14
21	Jeter, Bob	CB	6-1	205	05/09/37	Iowa	14
88	Jones, Ron	TE	6-3	220	07/17/47	Texas-El Paso	6
74	Jordan, Henry	DT	6-3	250	01/26/35	Virginia	5
62	Lueck, Bill	G	6-3	235	04/07/46	Arizona	14
32	Lusteg, Booth	K	5-11	190	05/08/39	Connecticut	4
30	Mercein, Chuck	RB	6-3	230	04/09/43	Yale	5
38	Mercer, Mike	K	6-0	217	11/21/35	Arizona State	10
70	Moore, Rich	DT	6-6	285	04/26/47	Villanova	14
66	Nitschke, Ray	LB	6-3	235	12/29/36	Illinois	14
71	Peay, Francis	T	6-5	250	05/23/44	Missouri	14
22	Pitts, Elijah	HB	6-1	205	02/03/39	Philander Smith	14
89	Robinson, Dave	LB	6-3	240	05/03/41	Penn State	14
45	Rowser, John	CB	6-1	180	04/24/44	Michigan	14
47	Rule, Gordon	S	6-2	180	03/01/46	Dartmouth	14
85	Spilis, John	WR	6-3	205	10/14/47	Northern Illinois	12
15	Starr, Bart	QB	6-1	190	01/09/34	Alabama	12
10	Stevens, Bill	QB	6-3	195	08/27/45	Texas-El Paso	1
83	Vandersea, Phil	LB	6-3	235	02/25/43	Massachusetts	14
73	Weatherwax, Jim	DT	6-7	260	01/09/43	Cal State-Los Angeles	6
31	Williams, Perry	RB	6-2	219	12/11/46	Purdue	14
23	Williams, Travis	RB	6-1	210	01/14/46	Arizona State	13
58	Winkler, Francis	DE	6-3	230	10/20/46	Memphis State	14
24	Wood, Willie	S	5-10	190	12/23/36	USC	14

1969 DRAFT

Rnd	Name	Pos	Ht	Wt	College
1	Rich Moore (12)	DT	6-6	285	Villanova
2	Dave Bradley (38)	T	6-4	255	Penn State
3	John Spilis (64)	WR	6-3	205	Northern Illinois
4	Perry Williams (90)	FB	6-2	219	Purdue
5	Bill Hayhoe (116)	T	6-8	258	USC
6a	Ron Jones (134)	TE	6-3	220	Texas-El Paso
	(Choice from Cardinals through Steelers in Dick Capp trade)				
6b	Ken Vinyard (142)	K	5-10	180	Texas Tech
7	Larry Agajanian (168)	DT	6-3	250	UCLA
8	Doug Gosnell (194)	DT	6-4	250	Utah State
9	Dave Hampton (220)	RB	6-0	210	Wyoming
10	Bruce Nelson (246)	T	6-4	225	North Dakota State
11	Leon Harden (272)	DB	5-11	197	Texas-El Paso
12	Tom Buckman (298)	TE	6-4	230	Texas A&M
13	Craig Koinzan (324)	LB	6-4	238	Doane
14	Rich Voltzke (350)	HB	6-2	206	Minnesota
15	Dan Eckstein (376)	S	5-10	180	Presbyterian
16	Dick Hewins (402)	WR	6-1	180	Drake
17	John Mack (428)	RB	6-3	230	Central Missouri State

1969 GREEN BAY PACKERS

FRONT ROW: (L-R) 89 Dave Robinson, 22 Elijah Pitts, 82 Lionel Aldridge, 43 Doug Hart, 21 Bob Jeter, 57 Ken Bowman, 75 Forrest Gregg, 87 Willie Davis, 26 Herb Adderley, 24 Willie Wood, 74 Henry Jordan, 81 Marv Fleming.

SECOND ROW: (L-R) Assistant Trainer Domenic Gentile, 23 Travis Williams, 88 Ron Jones, 53 Fred Carr, 66 Ray Nitschke, 84 Carroll Dale, 15 Bart Starr, 45 John Rowser, 25 Dave Hampton, 38 Mike Mercer, 47 Gordon Rule, 50 Bob Hyland, 70 Rich Moore, Equipment Manager Gerald (Dad) Braisher.

THIRD ROW: (L-R) 71 Francis Peay, 73 Jim Weatherwax, 61 Dave Bradley, 78 Bob Brown, 44 Donny Anderson, 68 Gale Gillingham, 33 Jim Grabowski, 13 Don Horn, 30 Chuck Mercein, 83 Phil Vandersea, 55 Jim Flanigan, 56 Larry Agajanian, Assistant Equipment Manager Bob Noel.

BACK ROW: (L-R) Trainer Carl (Bud) Jorgensen, 85 John Spilis, 31 Perry Williams, 10 Bill Stevens, 60 Lee Roy Caffey, 86 Boyd Dowler, 77 Bill Hayhoe, 72 Dick Himes, 58 Francis Winkler, 27 Claudis James, 62 Bill Lueck, 28 Leon Harden.

Trouble between management and the National Football League Players Association (NFLPA) cast an air of uncertainty over the 1970 season. On July 9, the NFLPA sent letters to its members ordering them not to report to training camp. In response, owners barred veterans from camp less than a week later. Negotiations continued, but as July turned to August the fate of the preseason hung in the balance.

The rift came just five months after the once warring NFL and AFL officially completed their merger. The 16 NFL and 10 AFL clubs banded together to form two 13-team conferences. The American Football Conference (AFC) consisted of the AFL franchises and Baltimore, Cleveland and Pittsburgh. Green Bay and the remaining 12 NFL teams made up the National Football Conference (NFC). While some teams found themselves in new surroundings, the Packers, Bears, Lions and Vikings continued to play in the Central Division.

Center Ken Bowman, a member of the NFLPA's negotiating committee, represented the Packers in their struggle with management. He, president John Mackey of the Colts, and four others locked horns with the owners, led by Tex Schramm, Ralph Wilson and Rankin Smith, in an effort to improve working conditions and pension pay.

The owners ended the lockout on July 29 and invited veterans to return. With no resolution in sight, the players stayed out. Not until Commissioner Pete Rozelle stepped in and accomplished what federal mediators had been unable to do did football return to normal. Rozelle brought together representatives from all 26 clubs and the NFLPA committee. In a 22-hour session that ended on August 3, the two sides finally agreed on a four-year pact.

While the midsummer contract dispute raged on, former Coach Vince Lombardi was in and out of Georgetown Hospital. He underwent an operation on June 27 in which a tumor, thought to be non-malignant, and two feet of his colon were removed. Though weakened, Lombardi left the hospital on July 13 and attended NFL meetings and watched the Redskins rookie game. He returned for a second operation in late July after which his condition deteriorated. On September 3, Lombardi died of cancer at age 57.

When the season did get underway, the Packers endured one of their worst beatings. Detroit clubbed them 40-0 on September 20 holding them to five first downs and 114 total yards. Not satisfied, the Lions pounced on the Packers again 20-0 to end the year.

In between, Green Bay won six games and wound up 6-8. The team reached the top of the Central Division standings once. After beating San Diego 22-20, the Packers (3-1) forged a three-way, first-place tie with the Lions and Vikings. Green Bay then lost five of its next seven.

Seven more from the championship era exited prior to 1970. Willie Davis, Boyd Dowler and Henry Jordan retired. Herb Adderley, Lee Roy Caffey, Marv Fleming and Elijah Pitts were traded. One other key figure departed. Two days after the 1970 season ended, Bengtson, the molder of some of the league's best defenses in the '60s, resigned.

Green Bay Press-Gazette photo

Carroll Dale (84) outsprints the Falcons' secondary on the way to an 89-yard touchdown reception that beat Atlanta 27-24 in week two. Dale caught four passes for 186 yards and two touchdowns in the game and led the team in receiving for a second straight year.

TEAM STATISTICS

	GB	OPP
First Downs	194	202
Rushing	69	88
Passing	110	102
Penalty	15	12
Rushes	453	453
Yards Gained	1,595	1,829
Average Gain	3.52	4.04
Average Yards per Game	113.9	130.6
Passes Attempted	351	369
Completed	177	177
% Completed	50.43	47.97
Total Yards Gained	2,196	2,496
Times Sacked	43	32
Yards Lost	382	270
Net Yards Gained	1,814	2,226
Yards Gained per Completion	12.41	14.10
Net Yards per Attempt	4.60	5.55
Average Net Yards per Game	129.6	159.0
Combined Net Yards Gained	3,409	4,055
Total Plays	847	854
Average Yards per Play	4.02	4.75
Average Net Yards per Game	243.5	289.6
Intercepted By	20	24
Yards Returned	398	421
Returned for TD	1	3
Punts	87	71
Yards Punted	3,501	2,845
Average Yards per Punt	40.24	40.07
Punt Returns	25	40
Yards Returned	98	338
Average Yards per Return	3.92	8.45
Returned for TD	0	0
Kickoff Returns	63	36
Yards Returned	1,422	888
Average Yards per Return	22.57	24.67
Returned for TD	2	0
Penalties	76	63
Yards Penalized	691	686
Fumbles	34	29
Lost	17	17
Own Recovered for Touchdown	0	0
Opponent's Recovered by	17	17
Opponent's Recovered for Touchdown	0	1
Total Points Scored	196	293
Total Touchdowns	22	30
Touchdowns Rushing	8	14
Touchdowns Passing	11	13
Touchdowns on Returns & Recoveries	3	3
Extra Points	19	29
Safeties	0	0
Field Goals Attempted	28	42
Field Goals Made	15	28
% Successful	53.57	66.67

Regular Season 6-8-0

Date	GB		OPP	Att.
9/20	0	Detroit Lions	40	(56,263)
9/27	27	Atlanta Falcons	24	(56,263)
10/4	13	Minnesota Vikings (M)	10	(47,967)
10/12	22	at San Diego Chargers	20	(53,064)
10/18	21	Los Angeles Rams	31	(56,263)
10/25	30	Philadelphia Eagles (M)	17	(48,022)
11/1	10	at San Francisco 49ers	26	(59,335)
11/9	10	Baltimore Colts	13	(48,063)
11/15	20	Chicago Bears	19	(56,263)
11/22	3	at Minnesota Vikings	10	(47,900)
11/26	3	at Dallas Cowboys	16	(67,182)
12/6	20	at Pittsburgh Steelers	12	(46,418)
12/13	17	at Chicago Bears	35	(44,957)
12/20	0	at Detroit Lions	20	(57,387)

Score By Periods

	1	2	3	4	Total
Packers	51	47	29	69	196
Opponents	47	49	73	124	293

INDIVIDUAL STATISTICS

Rushing

	Att	Yds	Avg	LG	TD
D. Anderson	222	853	3.8	54	5
T. Williams	74	276	3.7	37	1
Grabowski	67	210	3.1	17	1
Hampton	48	115	2.4	14	0
Starr	12	62	5.2	15	1
P. Williams	17	44	2.6	4	0
Krause	2	13	6.5	12	0
Dale	2	9	4.5	8	0
Patrick	2	5	2.5	3	0
Horn	5	4	0.8	4	0
McGeorge	1	3	3.0	3	0
Livingston	1	1	1.0	1	0
Packers	**453**	**1,595**	**3.5**	**54**	**8**
Opponents	453	1,829	4.0	76	14

Receiving

	No	Yds	Avg	LG	TD
Dale	49	814	16.6	t89	2
D. Anderson	36	414	11.5	34	0
Hilton	25	350	14.0	t65	4
Grabowski	19	83	4.4	19	0
Clancy	16	244	15.3	t33	2
T. Williams	12	127	10.6	t55	1
Hampton	7	23	3.3	12	0
Spilis	6	76	12.7	18	0
P. Williams	3	11	3.7	6	0
McGeorge	2	32	16.0	t16	2
Krause	2	22	11.0	11	0
Packers	**177**	**2,196**	**12.4**	**t89**	**11**
Opponents	177	2,496	14.1	187	13

Passing

	Att	Com	Yds	Pct	TD	In	Tk/Yds	Rate
Starr	255	140	1,645	54.9	8	13	29/252	63.9
Horn	76	28	428	36.8	2	10	6/59	25.4
R. Norton	5	3	64	60.0	1	0	2/16	—
Patrick	14	6	59	42.9	0	1	6/55	25.6
D. Anderson	1	0	0	00.0	0	0	0/0	—
Packers	**351**	**177**	**2,196**	**50.4**	**11**	**24**	**43/382**	**52.1**
Opponents	369	177	2,496	48.0	13	20	32/270	59.4

Punting

	No	Yds	Avg	LG	HB
D. Anderson	81	3,302	40.4	62	0
Livingston	6	199	33.2	52	0
Packers	**87**	**3,501**	**40.2**	**62**	**0**
Opponents	71	2,845	40.1	65	0

Kickoff Returns

	No	Yds	Avg	LG	TD
K. Ellis	22	451	20.5	48	0
Krause	18	513	28.5	t100	1
T. Williams	10	203	20.3	28	0
Hampton	6	188	31.3	t101	1
M.P. McCoy	3	22	7.3	10	0
Gregg	2	21	10.5	16	0
P. Williams	1	20	20.0	20	0
Himes	1	4	4.0	4	0
Packers	**63**	**1,422**	**22.6**	**t101**	**2**
Opponents	36	888	24.7	82	0

Punt Returns

	No	Yds	Avg	FC	LG	TD
Wood	11	58	5.3	18	12	0
K. Ellis	7	27	3.9	0	8	0
T. Williams	4	20	5.0	2	11	0
Harden	2	-7	-3.5	0	0	0
C. Williams	1	0	0.0	0	0	0
Packers	**25**	**98**	**3.9**	**20**	**12**	**0**
Opponents	40	338	8.5	11	65	0

Interceptions

	No	Yds	Avg	LG	TD
Wood	7	110	15.7	24	0
Hart	3	114	38.0	t76	1
K. Ellis	3	69	23.0	60	0
Jeter	3	27	9.0	18	0
Carr	2	45	22.5	28	0
D. Robinson	2	33	16.5	20	0
Packers	**20**	**398**	**19.9**	**t76**	**1**
Opponents	24	421	17.5	70	3

Scoring

	TDr	TDp	TDrt	PAT	FG	S	TP
Livingston	0	0	0	19/21	15/28	0	64
D. Anderson	5	0	0	0/0	0/0	0	30
Hilton	0	4	0	0/0	0/0	0	24
Clancy	0	2	0	0/0	0/0	0	12
Dale	0	2	0	0/0	0/0	0	12
McGeorge	0	2	0	0/0	0/0	0	12
T. Williams	1	1	0	0/0	0/0	0	12
Grabowski	1	0	0	0/0	0/0	0	6
Hampton	0	0	1	0/0	0/0	0	6
Hart	0	0	1	0/0	0/0	0	6
Krause	0	0	1	0/0	0/0	0	6
Starr	1	0	0	0/0	0/0	0	6
Packers	**8**	**11**	**3**	**19/22**	**15/28**	**0**	**196**
Opponents	14	13	3	29/30	28/42	0	293

Fumbles

	Fum	Ow	Op	Yds	Tot
L. Aldridge	0	0	1	0	1
D. Anderson	8	2	0	0	2
Bowman	1	0	0	-4	0
Bradley	0	0	1	0	1
Carr	0	0	3	0	3
Jim Carter	0	0	1	0	1
Dale	2	0	0	0	0
K. Ellis	3	1	1	5	2
Gregg	0	0	1	0	1
Hampton	3	1	0	0	1
L. Harden	1	0	0	0	0
Hart	0	0	1	0	1
Hilton	1	2	0	0	2
Horn	3	2	0	0	2
Krause	2	0	0	0	0
Al Matthews	0	0	1	0	1
M.P. McCoy	1	1	0	0	1
McGeorge	1	0	0	0	0
Nitschke	0	0	2	0	2
R. Norton	0	0	1	0	1
Peay	0	0	1	0	1
Starr	6	3	0	0	3
M. Walker	0	1	1	4	2
C. Williams	1	0	2	0	2
P. Williams	1	0	0	0	0
Wood	1	0	1	0	1
Packers	**34**	**15**	**17**	**5**	**32**

NFL STANDINGS

National Conference

Eastern Division

	W	L	T	Pct	PF	PA
Dallas Cowboys	10	4	0	.714	299	221
New York Giants	9	5	0	.643	301	270
St. Louis Cardinals	8	5	1	.615	325	228
Washington Redskins	6	8	0	.429	297	314
Philadelphia Eagles	3	10	1	.231	241	332

Central Division

	W	L	T	Pct	PF	PA
Minnesota Vikings	12	2	0	.857	335	143
Detroit Lions	10	4	0	.714	347	202
Chicago Bears	6	8	0	.429	256	261
Green Bay Packers	**6**	**8**	**0**	**.429**	**196**	**293**

Western Division

	W	L	T	Pct	PF	PA
San Francisco 49ers	10	3	1	.769	352	267
Los Angeles Rams	9	4	1	.692	325	202
Atlanta Falcons	4	8	2	.333	206	261
New Orleans Saints	2	11	1	.154	172	347

American Conference

Eastern Division

	W	L	T	Pct	PF	PA
Baltimore Colts	11	2	1	.846	321	234
Miami Dolphins	10	4	0	.714	297	228
New York Jets	4	10	0	.286	255	286
Buffalo Bills	3	10	1	.231	204	337
Boston Patriots	2	12	0	.143	149	361

Central Division

	W	L	T	Pct	PF	PA
Cincinnati Bengals	8	6	0	.571	312	255
Cleveland Browns	7	7	0	.500	286	265
Pittsburgh Steelers	5	9	0	.357	210	272
Houston Oilers	3	10	1	.231	217	352

Western Division

	W	L	T	Pct	PF	PA
Oakland Raiders	8	4	2	.667	300	293
Kansas City Chiefs	7	5	2	.583	272	244
San Diego Chargers	5	6	3	.455	282	278
Denver Broncos	5	8	1	.385	253	264

1970 ROSTER

No	Name	Pos	Ht	Wt	DOB	College	G
82	Aldridge, Lionel	DE	6-4	245	02/18/41	Utah State	14
87	Amsler, Marty	DE	6-5	255	10/26/42	Evansville	9
44	Anderson, Donny	RB	6-3	210	05/16/43	Texas Tech	14
57	Bowman, Ken	C	6-3	230	12/15/42	Wisconsin	10
61	Bradley, Dave	G	6-4	245	02/13/47	Penn State	4
78	Brown, Bob	DE	6-5	260	02/23/40	Arkansas-Pine Bluff	14
53	Carr, Fred	LB	6-5	238	08/19/46	Texas-El Paso	14
50	Carter, Jim	LB	6-3	235	10/18/48	Minnesota	10
36	Carter, Mike	WR	6-1	210	02/18/48	Sacramento State	3
80	Clancy, Jack	WR	6-1	195	06/18/44	Michigan	14
84	Dale, Carroll	WR	6-2	200	04/24/38	Virginia Tech	14
48	Ellis, Ken	CB	5-10	190	09/27/47	Southern University	14
55	Flanigan, Jim	LB	6-3	240	04/15/45	Pittsburgh	11
68	Gillingham, Gale	G	6-3	255	02/03/44	Minnesota	14
33	Grabowski, Jim	RB	6-2	220	09/04/44	Illinois	14
75	Gregg, Forrest	T	6-4	250	10/18/33	SMU	14
25	Hampton, Dave	RB	6-0	210	05/07/47	Wyoming	6
28	Harden, Leon	DB	5-11	195	08/17/47	Texas-El Paso	8
73	Hardy, Kevin	DT	6-5	260	07/28/45	Notre Dame	14
43	Hart, Doug	DB	6-0	190	06/03/39	Arlington State	14
77	Hayhoe, Bill	T	6-8	258	10/06/46	USC	14
86	Hilton, John	TE	6-5	225	03/12/42	Richmond	14
72	Himes, Dick	T	6-4	244	05/25/46	Ohio State	11
13	Horn, Don	QB	6-2	195	03/09/45	San Diego State	9
45	Hunt, Ervin	DB	6-2	190	07/01/47	Fresno State	7
21	Jeter, Bob	CB	6-1	205	05/09/37	Iowa	14
30	Krause, Larry	RB	6-0	208	04/22/48	St. Norbert	14
59	Kuechenberg, Rudy	LB	6-2	215	02/07/43	Indiana	6
37	Livingston, Dale	K	6-1	210	03/12/45	Western Michigan	14
62	Lueck, Bill	G	6-3	235	04/07/46	Arizona	14
29	Matthews, Al	DB	5-11	190	11/07/47	Texas A&I	14
76	McCoy, Mike P.	DT	6-5	284	09/06/48	Notre Dame	14
81	McGeorge, Rich	TE	6-4	235	09/14/48	Elon	14
70	Moore, Rich	T	6-6	280	04/26/47	Villanova	6
66	Nitschke, Ray	LB	6-3	235	12/29/36	Illinois	14
11	Norton, Rick	QB	6-2	190	11/16/43	Kentucky	3
10	Patrick, Frank	QB	6-7	225	03/11/47	Nebraska	14
71	Peay, Francis	T	6-5	250	05/23/44	Missouri	14
89	Robinson, Dave	LB	6-3	245	05/03/41	Penn State	4
85	Spilis, John	WR	6-3	205	10/14/47	Northern Illinois	14
15	Starr, Bart	QB	6-1	190	01/09/34	Alabama	14
52	Walker, Cleo	LB	6-3	219	02/07/48	Louisville	14
54	Walker, Malcolm	C-T	6-4	250	05/24/43	Rice	14
83	Williams, Clarence	DE	6-5	255	09/03/46	Prairie View	14
31	Williams, Perry	RB	6-2	219	12/11/46	Purdue	14
23	Williams, Travis	RB	6-1	210	01/14/46	Arizona State	8
24	Wood, Willie	S	5-10	190	12/23/36	USC	14

1970 DRAFT

Rnd	Name	Pos	Ht	Wt	College
1a	Mike P. McCoy (2)	DT	6-5	284	Notre Dame
	(Choice from Bears in Lee Roy Caffey, Elijah Pitts, Bob Hyland trade)				
1b	Rich McGeorge (16)	TE	6-4	235	Elon
2	Al Matthews (41)	DB	5-11	190	Texas A&I
3	Jim Carter (68)	LB	6-3	240	Minnesota
4a	Ken Ellis (93)	WR	5-10	190	Southern
4b	Skip Butler (96)	K	6-1	198	Texas-Arlington
	(Choice from Colts for Ron Kostelnik)				
5	Cecil Pryor (120)	DE	6-5	240	Michigan
6	Ervin Hunt (145)	DB	6-2	190	Fresno State
7	Cleo Walker (172)	C-LB	6-3	219	Louisville
8	Tim Mjos (197)	HB	6-2	205	North Dakota State
9	Bob Reinhard (224)	G	6-2	230	Stanford
10a	Russ Melby (248)	DT	6-4	250	Weber State
10b	Frank Patrick (251)	TE	6-7	225	Nebraska
	(Choice from Redskins for Leo Carroll)				
11	Dan Hook (276)	LB	6-3	215	Cal State-Humboldt
12	Frank Foreman (300)	WR	6-2	204	Michigan State
13	Dave Smith (328)	RB	6-1	210	Utah
14	Bob Lints (353)	G	6-3	250	Eastern Michigan
15	Mike Carter (380)	WR	6-1	208	Cal State-Sacramento
16	Jim Heacock (405)	DB	6-2	180	Muskingum
17	Larry Krause (432)	HB	6-0	208	St. Norbert

1970 GREEN BAY PACKERS

FRONT ROW: (L-R) 53 Fred Carr, 23 Travis Williams, 82 Lionel Aldridge, 43 Doug Hart, 21 Bob Jeter, 57 Ken Bowman, 24 Willie Wood, 68 Gale Gillingham, 78 Bob Brown, 48 Ken Ellis, 37 Dale Livingston, 75 Forrest Gregg.

SECOND ROW: (L-R) Trainer Domenic Gentile, 36 Mike Carter, 52 Cleo Walker, 66 Ray Nitschke, 15 Bart Starr, 84 Carroll Dale, 30 Larry Krause, 13 Don Horn, 62 Bill Lueck, 80 Jack Clancy, Equipment Manager Gerald (Dad) Braisher, Assistant Equipment Manager Bob Noel.

THIRD ROW: (L-R) 29 Al Matthews, 83 Clarence Williams, 71 Francis Peay, 85 John Spilis, 44 Donny Anderson, 33 Jim Grabowski, 86 John Hilton, 10 Frank Patrick, 31 Perry Williams, 61 Dave Bradley, 70 Rich Moore.

BACK ROW: (L-R) Trainer Carl (Bud) Jorgensen, 39 Jerry Warren, 45 Ervin Hunt, 81 Rich McGeorge, 73 Kevin Hardy, 77 Bill Hayhoe, 54 Malcolm Snyder, 87 Marty Amsler, 72 Dick Himes, 55 Jim Flanigan, 76 Mike P. McCoy, 50 Jim Carter, 28 Leon Harden.

1971

To replace Phil Bengtson, the Packers hired Dan Devine from the University of Missouri. The Devine era got off to inauspicious start when Green Bay scored 40 points in the opener and not only failed to win the game, but lost its head coach when he was run over by a group of players and broke his leg. Devine was taken to St. Vincent's Hospital, where he listened to the fourth quarter on radio. Even though the Packers scored 16 points in the final period, they wound up 42-40 losers to the Giants.

Defensive Line Coach Dave Hanner took over for the incapacitated Devine. He directed the final minutes of the Giants game and conducted Tuesday's practice. By Wednesday, Devine and his wheel chair were back on the field in a golf cart-like set-up. Even so, Hanner handled the on-the-field operation for the second game, a 34-13 win over Denver, while Devine watched from the County Stadium press box. By the third game, Devine no longer needed a wheel chair and watched from the sidelines on crutches as Dave Robinson and Willie Wood stopped Ken Anderson on fourth down in the final minutes to deny Cincinnati 20-17 and bring Green Bay a second straight win.

Just when the Packers fortunes were looking up, the team entered a nine-game stretch in which it won just once. By the time the slide ended with a 31-10 win over the Bears, the season was a week from completion. On December 19, Green Bay dropped a 27-6 decision at Miami and returned home with a 4-8-2 record, its worst since 1958.

On the positive side, rookie John Brockington ran wild. The fullback set a then-NFL rookie record with 1,105 yards rushing. At the same time, Dave Hampton came within three yards of Bobby Jancik's league record. Hampton returned 46 kickoffs for 1,314 yards, both team marks.

While Brockington and Hampton were at the beginning of their careers, two others neared the end. Bart Starr underwent surgery in late June and again in July to repair a shredded bicipital tendon in his passing arm. He remained on the team's taxi squad before being activated for the Atlanta contest. Although he didn't play, he did start three of the final four games, the exception being the Bears game in which rookie Scott Hunter opened.

After attending a pre-training camp in April and then part of training camp, Starr announced his retirement in late July, 1972. He exited after having worn the Green and Gold a record 16 years.

The other "senior citizen", Ray Nitschke, rambled through a 14th season in an unfamiliar role: that of a backup. Early in the year Devine replaced him with the younger Jim Carter. Number 66 did start at middle linebacker once more though. Wisconsin Govenor Patrick J. Lucey declared December 12, Ray Nitschke Day. Devine moved Carter to the outside so that Nitschke could prowl for Bear once again from his old spot. The finest middle linebacker in the first 50 years of professional football still had one year of football left in him. Nitschke returned in 1972 for one more campaign and a welcome taste of playoff action.

Green Bay Press-Gazette photo

Dave Robinson (89) returns a second-quarter interception 20 yards with Willie Wood (24) as escort. Led by Ken Ellis' three, the Packers intercepted six passes and beat Denver 34-13 for their first win of the year. Robinson, who missed 10 games in 1970 because of abdominal surgery, had three interceptions in 1971 to finish second in that department behind Ellis.

TEAM STATISTICS

	GB	OPP
First Downs	208	230
Rushing	115	104
Passing	87	110
Penalty	6	16
Rushes	500	489
Yards Gained	2,229	1,707
Average Gain	4.46	3.49
Average Yards per Game	159.2	121.9
Passes Attempted	254	353
Completed	121	186
% Completed	47.64	52.69
Total Yards Gained	1,842	2,469
Times Sacked	18	19
Yards Lost	157	168
Net Yards Gained	1,685	2,301
Yards Gained per Completion	15.22	13.27
Net Yards per Attempt	6.19	6.19
Average Net Yards per Game	120.4	164.4
Combined Net Yards Gained	3,914	4,008
Total Plays	772	861
Average Yards per Play	5.07	4.66
Average Net Yards per Game	279.6	286.3
Intercepted By	16	24
Yards Returned	205	449
Returned for TD	0	2
Punts	56	61
Yards Punted	2,238	2,448
Average Yards per Punt	39.96	40.13
Punt Returns	38	23
Yards Returned	177	169
Average Yards per Return	4.66	7.35
Returned for TD	0	0
Kickoff Returns	58	56
Yards Returned	1,546	1,248
Average Yards per Return	26.66	22.29
Returned for TD	1	0
Penalties	61	60
Yards Penalized	568	514
Fumbles	29	33
Lost	20	16
Own Recovered for Touchdown	0	0
Opponent's Recovered by	16	20
Opponent's Recovered for Touchdown	0	3
Total Points Scored	274	298
Total Touchdowns	33	34
Touchdowns Rushing	18	7
Touchdowns Passing	12	21
Touchdowns on Returns & Recoveries	3	6
Extra Points	32	32
Safeties	1	1
Field Goals Attempted	26	37
Field Goals Made	14	20
% Successful	53.85	54.05

Regular Season 4-8-2

Date	GB		OPP	Att.
9/19	40	New York Giants	42	(56,263)
9/26	34	Denver Broncos (M)	13	(47,957)
10/3	20	Cincinnati Bengals	17	(56,263)
10/10	28	at Detroit Lions	31	(54,418)
10/17	13	Minnesota Vikings	24	(56,263)
10/24	13	at Los Angeles Rams	30	(75,351)
11/1	14	Detroit Lions (M)	14	(47,961)
11/7	17	at Chicago Bears	14	(55,049)
11/14	0	at Minnesota Vikings	3	(49,784)
11/22	21	at Atlanta Falcons	28	(58,850)
11/28	21	New Orleans Saints (M)	29	(48,035)
12/5	16	at St. Louis Cardinals	16	(50,443)
12/12	31	Chicago Bears	10	(56,263)
12/19	6	at Miami Dolphins	27	(76,812)

Score By Periods

	1	2	3	4	Total
Packers	41	85	64	84	274
Opponents	57	72	78	91	298

INDIVIDUAL STATISTICS

Rushing

	Att	Yds	Avg	LG	TD
Brockington	216	1,105	5.1	t52	4
D. Anderson	186	757	4.1	31	5
Hampton	67	307	4.6	41	3
S. Hunter	21	50	2.4	16	4
Starr	3	11	3.7	9	1
P. Williams	3	4	1.3	3	0
Bratkowski	1	1	1.0	t1	1
Krause	3	-6	-2.0	2	0
Packers	500	2,229	4.5	t52	18
Opponents	489	1,707	3.5	42	7

1971

Receiving

	No	Yds	Avg	LG	TD
Dale	31	598	19.3	t77	4
McGeorge	27	463	17.1	50	4
D. Anderson	26	306	11.8	39	1
Spilis	14	281	20.1	39	1
Brockington	14	98	7.0	29	1
D. Davis	6	59	9.8	20	0
Hampton	3	37	12.3	t19	1
Packers	121	1,842	15.2	t77	12
Opponents	186	2,469	13.3	t81	21

Passing

	Att	Com	Yds	Pct	TD	In	Tk/Yds	Rate
S. Hunter	163	75	1,210	46.0	7	17	11/81	46.1
Starr	45	24	286	53.3	0	3	6/64	45.2
Bratkowski	37	19	298	51.4	4	3	1/12	80.7
Patrick	5	1	39	20.0	0	1	0/0	—
D. Anderson	4	2	9	50.0	1	0	0/0	—
Packers	254	121	1,842	47.6	12	24	18/157	48.4
Opponents	353	186	2,469	52.7	21	16	19/168	76.1

Punting

	No	Yds	Avg	LG	HB
D. Anderson	50	2,022	40.4	58	0
Duncan	6	216	36.0	47	0
Packers	56	2,238	40.0	58	0
Opponents	61	2,448	40.1	63	0

Kickoff Returns

	No	Yds	Avg	LG	TD
Hampton	46	1,314	28.6	t90	1
Krause	5	101	20.2	29	0
E. Pitts	2	41	20.5	22	0
P. Williams	2	41	20.5	21	0
D. Davis	1	22	22.0	22	0
K. Ellis	1	22	22.0	22	0
Jim Carter	1	5	5.0	5	0
Packers	58	1,546	26.7	t90	1
Opponents	56	1,248	22.3	82	0

Punt Returns

	No	Yds	Avg	FC	LG	TD
K. Ellis	22	107	4.9	1	30	0
D. Davis	6	36	6.0	0	19	0
E. Pitts	5	13	2.6	2	5	0
Wood	4	21	5.3	2	9	0
A. Randolph	1	0	0.0	0	0	0
Packers	38	177	4.7	5	30	0
Opponents	23	169	7.3	12	38	0

Interceptions

	No	Yds	Avg	LG	TD
K. Ellis	6	10	1.7	5	0
D. Robinson	3	44	14.7	23	0
Hart	2	73	36.5	69	0
A. Randolph	1	34	34.0	34	0
Al Matthews	1	20	20.0	20	0
Jim Carter	1	16	16.0	16	0
Wood	1	8	8.0	8	0
Nitschke	1	0	0.0	0	0
Packers	16	205	12.8	69	0
Opponents	24	449	18.7	t65	2

Scoring

	TDr	TDp	TDrt	PAT	FG	S	TP
L. Michaels	0	0	0	19/20	8/14	0	43
D. Anderson	5	1	0	0/0	0/0	0	36
Brockington	4	1	0	0/0	0/0	0	30
Hampton	3	1	1	0/0	0/0	0	30
Webster	0	0	0	8/8	6/11	0	26
Dale	0	4	0	0/0	0/0	0	24
S. Hunter	4	0	0	0/0	0/0	0	24
McGeorge	0	4	0	0/0	0/0	0	24
Hart	0	0	1	0/0	0/0	1	8
Bratkowski	1	0	0	0/0	0/0	0	6
K. Ellis	0	0	1	0/0	0/0	0	6
Spilis	0	1	0	0/0	0/0	0	6
Starr	1	0	0	0/0	0/0	0	6
Conway	0	0	0	5/5	0/1	0	5
Packers	18	12	3	32/33	14/26	1	274
Opponents	7	21	6	32/34	20/37	1	298

Fumbles

	Fum	Ow	Op	Yds	Tot
L. Aldridge	0	0	1	0	1
D. Anderson	6	1	0	-5	1
Bratkowski	1	0	0	0	0
Brockington	4	2	0	0	2
Carr	0	0	2	34	2
Jim Carter	0	0	1	0	1
D. Davis	1	0	0	18	1
Hampton	7	1	0	0	1
S. Hunter	7	1	0	-11	1
Krause	0	0	1	0	1
M.P. McCoy	0	0	2	17	2
McGeorge	0	1	0	0	1
Nitschke	0	0	1	0	1
A. Randolph	1	0	0	0	2
D. Robinson	0	0	1	0	1
Roche	0	0	2	0	2
Spilis	1	0	0	0	0
Starr	1	0	0	0	0
C. Williams	0	0	2	0	2
Wood	0	0	1	3	1
Packers	29	7	16	56	23

NFL STANDINGS

National Conference

Eastern Division

	W	L	T	Pct	PF	PA
Dallas Cowboys	11	3	0	.786	406	222
Washington Redskins	9	4	1	.692	276	190
Philadelphia Eagles	6	7	1	.462	221	302
St. Louis Cardinals	4	9	1	.308	231	279
New York Giants	4	10	0	.286	228	362

Central Division

	W	L	T	Pct	PF	PA
Minnesota Vikings	11	3	0	.786	245	139
Detroit Lions	7	6	1	.538	341	286
Chicago Bears	6	8	0	.429	185	276
Green Bay Packers	4	8	2	.333	274	298

Western Division

	W	L	T	Pct	PF	PA
San Francisco 49ers	9	5	0	.643	300	216
Los Angeles Rams	8	5	1	.615	313	260
Atlanta Falcons	7	6	1	.538	274	277
New Orleans Saints	4	8	2	.333	266	347

American Conference

Eastern Division

	W	L	T	Pct	PF	PA
Miami Dolphins	10	3	1	.769	315	174
Baltimore Colts	10	4	0	.714	313	140
New England Patriots	6	8	0	.429	238	325
New York Jets	6	8	0	.429	212	299
Buffalo Bills	1	13	0	.071	184	394

Central Division

	W	L	T	Pct	PF	PA
Cleveland Browns	9	5	0	.643	285	273
Pittsburgh Steelers	6	8	0	.429	246	292
Houston Oilers	4	9	1	.308	251	330
Cincinnati Bengals	4	10	0	.286	284	265

Western Division

	W	L	T	Pct	PF	PA
Kansas City Chiefs	10	3	1	.769	302	208
Oakland Raiders	8	4	2	.667	344	278
San Diego Chargers	6	8	0	.429	311	341
Denver Broncos	4	9	1	.308	203	275

1971 ROSTER

No	Name	Pos	Ht	Wt	DOB	College	G
82	Aldridge, Lionel	DE	6-4	245	02/18/41	Utah State	14
44	Anderson, Donny	RB	6-3	210	05/16/43	Texas Tech	14
57	Bowman, Ken	C	6-3	230	12/15/42	Wisconsin	14
61	Bradley, Dave	G	6-4	245	02/13/47	Penn State	6
12	Bratkowski, Zeke	QB	6-3	210	10/20/31	Georgia	6
42	Brockington, John	RB	6-1	225	09/07/48	Ohio State	14
78	Brown, Bob	DE	6-5	260	02/23/40	Arkansas-Pine Bluff	14
53	Carr, Fred	LB	6-5	238	08/19/46	Texas-El Paso	14
50	Carter, Jim	LB	6-3	235	10/18/48	Minnesota	10
35	Conway, Dave	K	6-0	195	01/06/45	Texas	1
56	Crutcher, Tommy	LB	6-3	230	08/10/41	TCU	14
84	Dale, Carroll	WR	6-2	200	04/24/38	Virginia Tech	14
47	Davis, Dave	WR	6-0	175	07/05/48	Tennessee State	14
79	DeLisle, Jim	DT	6-4	255	01/20/49	Wisconsin	9
18	Duncan, Ken	P	6-2	200	02/28/46	Tulsa	3
48	Ellis, Ken	CB	5-10	190	09/27/47	Southern University	14
88	Garrett, Len	TE	6-3	225	12/18/47	New Mexico Highlands	14
68	Gillingham, Gale	G	6-3	255	02/03/44	Minnesota	14
21	Hall, Charlie	CB	6-1	195	03/31/48	Pittsburgh	14
25	Hampton, Dave	RB	6-0	210	05/07/47	Wyoming	13
43	Hart, Doug	DB	6-0	190	06/03/39	Arlington State	14
77	Hayhoe, Bill	T	6-8	258	10/06/46	USC	14
72	Himes, Dick	T	6-4	244	05/25/46	Ohio State	14
16	Hunter, Scott	QB	6-2	205	11/19/47	Alabama	14
30	Krause, Larry	RB	6-0	208	04/22/48	St. Norbert	9
62	Lueck, Bill	G	6-3	235	04/07/46	Arizona	14
29	Matthews, Al	DB	5-11	190	11/07/47	Texas A&I	14
76	McCoy, Mike P.	DT	6-5	284	09/06/48	Notre Dame	14
81	McGeorge, Rich	TE	6-4	235	09/14/48	Elon	14
75	Michaels, Lou	K	6-2	250	09/28/36	Kentucky	10
66	Nitschke, Ray	LB	6-3	235	12/29/36	Illinois	14
10	Patrick, Frank	QB	6-7	225	03/11/47	Nebraska	14
71	Peay, Francis	T	6-5	250	05/23/44	Missouri	14
22	Pitts, Elijah	RB	6-1	205	02/03/39	Philander Smith	6
27	Randolph, Al	S	6-2	205	07/08/44	Iowa	14
89	Robinson, Dave	LB	6-3	245	05/03/41	Penn State	14
87	Roche, Alden	DE	6-4	255	04/09/45	Southern University	14
74	Smith, Donnell	DE	6-4	245	05/25/49	Southern University	5
85	Spilis, John	WR	6-3	205	10/14/47	Northern Illinois	14
15	Starr, Bart	QB	6-1	190	01/09/34	Alabama	5
38	Webster, Tim	K	6-0	195	09/11/49	Arkansas	4
83	Williams, Clarence	DE	6-5	255	09/03/46	Prairie View	14
31	Williams, Perry	RB	6-2	219	12/11/46	Purdue	14
63	Winkler, Randy	G	6-4	260	07/18/43	Tarleton State	5
52	Winther, Wimpy	C	6-4	260	10/22/47	Mississippi	11
74	Withrow, Cal	C	6-0	240	08/04/45	Kentucky	14
24	Wood, Willie	S	5-10	190	12/23/36	USC	14

1971 DRAFT

Rnd	Name	Pos	Ht	Wt	College
1a	John Brockington (9)	FB	6-1	225	Ohio State
	(Packers traded own choice (12) and Don Horn for Broncos (9) and Alden Roche)				
1b	(Choice (12) to Broncos in deal above)				
2a	(Choice (37) to 49ers for Kevin Hardy)				
2b	Virgil Robinson (46)	WR-CB	5-11	195	Grambling
	(Choice from Rams as part of Travis Williams deal)				
3	Charlie Hall (62)	CB	6-1	195	Pittsburgh
4	(Choice (90) to Rams as part of Travis Williams deal)				
5a	(Choice (115) to Chargers for Jacque MacKinnon)				
5b	Donnell Smith (116)	DE	6-4	245	Southern University
	(Choice from Redskins, deferred payment for Tom Brown)				
5c	Jim Stillwagon (124)	LB	6-0	230	Ohio State
	(Choice from Rams through Redskins for rights to Boyd Dowler)				

Rnd	Name	Pos	Ht	Wt	College
6	Scott Hunter (140)	QB	6-2	205	Alabama
7a	Dave Davis (168)	WR	6-0	175	Tennessee State
7b	James Johnson (175)	WR	5-10	175	Bishop
	(Choice from Raiders for Jacque MacKinnon)				
8	Win Headley (193)	C	6-3	255	Wake Forest
9	Barry Mayer (218)	RB	6-2	215	Minnesota
10	Kevin Hunt (246)	T	6-5	250	Doane
11	John Lanier (271)	RB-TE	6-2	235	Parsons
12	Greg Hendren (296)	G-C	6-2	240	California
13	Jack Martin (324)	RB	6-2	205	Angelo State
14	Leroy Spears (348)	DE	6-5	225	Moorhead State
15	Len Garrett (374)	TE	6-3	210	New Mexico Highlands
16	Jack O'Donnell (402)	G	6-1	245	Central Oklahoma State
17	Monty Johnson (427)	S	5-11	190	Oklahoma

1971 GREEN BAY PACKERS

FRONT ROW: (L-R) 89 Dave Robinson, 22 Elijah Pitts, 82 Lionel Aldridge, 43 Doug Hart, 57 Ken Bowman, 56 Tommy Crutcher, 68 Gale Gillingham, 24 Willie Wood, 78 Bob Brown, 48 Ken Ellis, 53 Fred Carr, 29 Al Matthews.
SECOND ROW: (L-R) 66 Ray Nitschke, 12 Zeke Bratkowski, 84 Carroll Dale, 15 Bart Starr, 21 Charlie Hall, 44 Donny Anderson, 47 Dave Davis, 54 Wimpy Winther, 75 Lou Michaels, 18 Ken Duncan.
THIRD ROW: (L-R) 61 Dave Bradley, 36 Mike Carter, 81 Rich McGeorge, 85 John Spilis, 42 John Brockington, 16 Scott Hunter, 25 Dave Hampton, 30 Larry Krause, 58 Cal Withrow, 62 Bill Lueck, 27 Al Randolph, 80 Sam Dickerson.
BACK ROW: (L-R) 71 Francis Peay, 83 Clarence Williams, 88 Len Garrett, 31 Perry Williams, 10 Frank Patrick, 63 Randy Winkler, 72 Dick Himes, 77 Bill Hayhoe, 74 Donnell Smith, 79 Jim DeLisle, 76 Mike P. McCoy, 50 Jim Carter.

1972

From start to finish, Green Bay never relinquished its hold on first place in the Central Division and wound up winning the title with a 10-4 mark. This was no easy feat considering its schedule, based on opponents' 1971 records (.579), was fourth toughest in the league. In addition, the Packers faced five 1971 playoff opponents, six if the Vikings were counted twice. But Green Bay defeated four of the five, including close wins over NFC champion runner-up San Francisco and 1971 Super Bowl champion Dallas. So powerful were the Packers that they lost but one game in the second half of the year, 21-16 to the Redskins.

Many factors figured into the resurgence but four stood out. First, the rushing game. Dan Devine traded Donny Anderson to St. Louis for MacArthur Lane. Lane and John Brockington paired for 1,848 yards and 11 touchdowns to become the league's most productive tandem short of Miami's Larry Csonka and Mercury Morris.

First-round pick Willie Buchanon joined Ken Ellis, Jim Hill and Al Matthews to form one of the better secondaries in the league. The quartet had 14 of the Packers' 17 interceptions and spearheaded a defense that allowed a league-low seven touchdown passes.

Another top pick, Chester Marcol, brought reliability to a kicking game that had floundered since the retirement of Don Chandler. Marcol led the NFL in scoring with 128 points. He made 33 field goals in 48 attempts and won three games outright with his kicks.

Finally, the Packers were able to overcome injuries; some minor, some major. Oakland came to Lambeau Field in the season's second week. Not only did the Raiders win 20-14, aided by a controversial 104-yard return of a fumble by Jack Tatum, but they also physically beat the Packers. Later in the week NFL supervisor of officials Art McNally declared what Packers' fans already knew: the fumble was actually a muff and thus not advanceable. But McNally could do nothing to ease the injury situation. The walking wounded included Scott Hunter (back), Brockington (neck), Bill Lueck (shoulder), Ike Thomas (ribs) and Francis Peay (knee). Those five would return. Rich McGeorge and Gale Gillingham (both knees) were lost for the year.

Gillingham was a prime example of how the Packers shuffled successfully in the face of injuries. The massive offensive guard was switched to defensive tackle in training camp after Mike P. McCoy was lost because of a broken bone in his right foot.

To its credit, Green Bay snapped back from the Raider thumping and found the resolve and determination needed to stay at the top. In week three in Milwaukee, the Packers forced five Cowboy turnovers, Marcol kicked three field goals and the defense allowed just one touchdown as Green Bay beat the World Champions 16-13.

Five weeks later, after back-to-back losses to Atlanta and Minnesota, the team similarly bounced back against the 49ers 34-24. That win opened the second half of the season in which the Packers lost only once, to the Redskins. The Washington game offered a preview of the postseason that awaited the once again playoff-bound Green and Gold.

Green Bay Press-Gazette photo

John Brockington (42) eludes Cornell Green (34) and Lee Roy Jordan (55) for a gain in the fourth quarter of the Packers' 16-13 victory over the Dallas Cowboys. Brockington scored once and rushed for 91 yards on 26 carries, but it took a 22-yard Chester Marcol field goal with 10:54 remaining to beat the visiting Texans. Brockington led the Packers with 1,027 yards rushing, fourth best in the NFC.

TEAM STATISTICS

	GB	OPP
First Downs	195	209
Rushing	109	85
Passing	72	109
Penalty	14	15
Rushes	544	443
Yards Gained	2,127	1,517
Average Gain	3.91	3.42
Average Yards per Game	151.9	108.4
Passes Attempted	237	340
Completed	101	174
% Completed	42.62	51.18
Total Yards Gained	1,536	2,209
Times Sacked	17	29
Yards Lost	124	252
Net Yards Gained	1,412	1,957
Yards Gained per Completion	15.21	12.70
Net Yards per Attempt	5.56	5.30
Average Net Yards per Game	100.9	139.8
Combined Net Yards Gained	3,539	3,474
Total Plays	798	812
Average Yards per Play	4.43	4.28
Average Net Yards per Game	252.8	248.1
Third Down Efficiency	72/204	72/183
Percentage	35.29	39.34
Intercepted By	17	9
Yards Returned	223	69
Returned for TD	1	2
Punts	65	66
Yards Punted	2,714	2,732
Average Yards per Punt	41.75	41.39
Punt Returns	25	32
Yards Returned	364	225
Average Yards per Return	14.56	7.03
Returned for TD	2	0
Kickoff Returns	49	46
Yards Returned	1,141	932
Average Yards per Return	23.29	20.26
Returned for TD	0	0
Penalties	63	50
Yards Penalized	610	446
Fumbles	22	35
Lost	10	19
Own Recovered for Touchdown	1	0
Opponent's Recovered by	19	10
Opponent's Recovered for Touchdown	1	1
Total Points Scored	304	226
Total Touchdowns	29	26
Touchdowns Rushing	17	14
Touchdowns Passing	7	7
Touchdowns on Returns & Recoveries	5	5
Extra Points	29	25
Safeties	1	0
Field Goals Attempted	48	27
Field Goals Made	33	15
% Successful	68.75	55.56

Regular Season   10-4-0

Date	GB		OPP	Att.
9/17	26	at Cleveland Browns	10	(75,771)
9/24	14	Oakland Raiders	20	(56,263)
10/1	16	Dallas Cowboys (M)	13	(47,103)
10/8	20	Chicago Bears	17	(56,263)
10/16	24	at Detroit Lions	23	(54,418)
10/22	9	Atlanta Falcons (M)	10	(47,967)
10/29	13	Minnesota Vikings	27	(56,263)
11/5	34	San Francisco 49ers (M)	24	(47,897)
11/12	23	at Chicago Bears	17	(55,701)
11/19	23	at Houston Oilers	10	(41,752)
11/26	16	at Washington Redskins	21	(53,039)
12/3	33	Detroit Lions	7	(56,263)
12/10	23	at Minnesota Vikings	7	(49,784)
12/17	30	at New Orleans Saints	20	(65,881)

Postseason   0-1-0

12/24	3	at Washington Redskins	16	(53,140)

Score By Periods

	1	2	3	4	Total
Packers	80	95	63	66	304
Opponents	37	68	49	72	226

INDIVIDUAL STATISTICS

Rushing

	Att	Yds	Avg	LG	TD
Brockington	274	1,027	3.7	t30	8
Lane	177	821	4.6	41	3
P. Williams	33	139	4.2	14	0
B. Hudson	15	62	4.1	17	0
Kopay	10	39	3.9	20	0
S. Hunter	22	37	1.7	15	5
Glass	2	13	6.5	13	0
D. Davis	2	0	0.0	7	0
Tagge	8	-3	-0.4	-8	0
Staggers	1	-8	-8.0	-8	0
Packers	**544**	**2,127**	**3.9**	**41**	**17**
Opponents	443	1,517	3.4	26	14

Receiving

	No	Yds	Avg	LG	TD
Lane	26	285	11.0	49	0
Brockington	19	243	12.8	t48	1
Dale	16	317	19.8	48	1
Glass	15	261	17.4	31	1
Staggers	8	123	15.4	t48	1
D. Davis	4	119	29.8	t68	1
L. Garrett	4	66	16.5	21	0
McGeorge	4	50	12.5	t23	2
Kopay	3	19	6.3	8	0
Nitschke	1	34	34.0	34	0
Lammons	1	19	19.0	19	0
Packers	**101**	**1,536**	**15.2**	**t68**	**7**
Opponents	174	2,209	12.7	t62	7

Passing

	Att	Com	Yds	Pct	TD	In	Tk/Yds	Rate
S. Hunter	199	86	1,252	43.2	6	9	13/86	55.5
Tagge	29	10	154	34.5	0	0	3/27	52.9
Widby	2	2	102	100.0	1	0	0/0	—
Lane	2	2	19	100.0	0	0	0/0	—
Patrick	4	1	9	25.0	0	0	1/11	—
Staggers	1	0	0	00.0	0	0	0/0	—
Packers	**237**	**101**	**1,536**	**42.6**	**7**	**9**	**17/124**	**58.6**
Opponents	340	174	2,209	51.2	7	17	29/252	57.8

Punting

	No	Yds	Avg	LG	HB
Widby	65	2,714	41.8	64	2
Packers	**65**	**2,714**	**41.8**	**64**	**2**
Opponents	66	2,732	41.4	61	0

Kickoff Returns

	No	Yds	Avg	LG	TD
I. Thomas	21	572	27.2	89	0
Staggers	11	260	23.6	39	0
B. Hudson	11	247	22.5	55	0
Kroll	1	23	23.0	23	0
D. Robinson	1	20	20.0	20	0
K. Ellis	1	10	10.0	10	0
P. Williams	1	9	9.0	9	0
L. Garrett	1	0	0.0	0	0
Wortman	1	0	0.0	0	0
Packers	**49**	**1,141**	**23.3**	**89**	**0**
Opponents	46	932	20.3	37	0

Punt Returns

	No	Yds	Avg	FC	LG	TD
K. Ellis	14	215	15.4	1	t80	1
Staggers	9	148	16.4	20	t85	1
Glass	1	1	1.0	0	1	0
B. Hudson	1	0	0.0	2	0	0
Packers	**25**	**364**	**14.6**	**23**	**t85**	**2**
Opponents	32	225	7.0	6	33	0

Interceptions

	No	Yds	Avg	LG	TD
K. Ellis	4	106	26.5	40	1
Buchanon	4	62	15.5	26	0
J. Hill	4	37	9.3	21	0
D. Robinson	2	10	5.0	7	0
Al Matthews	2	8	4.0	8	0
Jim Carter	1	0	0.0	0	0
Packers	**17**	**223**	**13.1**	**40**	**1**
Opponents	9	69	7.7	t32	2

Scoring

	TDr	TDp	TDrt	PAT	FG	S	TP
Marcol	0	0	0	29/29	33/48	0	128
Brockington	8	1	0	0/0	0/0	0	54
S. Hunter	5	0	0	0/0	0/0	0	30
Lane	3	0	0	0/0	0/0	0	18
K. Ellis	0	0	2	0/0	0/0	0	12
McGeorge	0	2	0	0/0	0/0	0	12
Staggers	0	1	1	0/0	0/0	0	12
Buchanon	0	0	1	0/0	0/0	0	6
Dale	0	1	0	0/0	0/0	0	6
D. Davis	0	1	0	0/0	0/0	0	6
Glass	0	1	0	0/0	0/0	0	6
Tagge	1	0	0	0/0	0/0	0	6
C. Williams	0	0	1	0/0	0/0	0	6
Bob Brown	0	0	0	0/0	0/0	1	2
Packers	**17**	**7**	**5**	**29/29**	**33/48**	**1**	**304**
Opponents	14	7	5	25/26	15/27	0	226

Fumbles

	Fum	Ow	Op	Yds	Tot
Brockington	4	0	0	0	0
Bob Brown	0	0	1	0	1
Buchanon	0	0	3	0	3
Carr	0	0	2	30	2
Jim Carter	0	0	1	0	1
K. Ellis	2	1	1	0	2
L. Garrett	0	0	1	0	1
Glass	0	0	1	0	1
Hayhoe	0	0	1	0	1
J. Hill	0	0	1	15	1
Himes	0	1	0	1	1
B. Hudson	1	0	0	0	0
S. Hunter	5	3	0	0	3
Kopay	1	0	0	0	0
Kroll	0	0	1	0	1
Lammons	0	0	1	0	1
Lane	6	1	0	0	1
Al Matthews	0	0	2	-7	2
M.P. McCoy	0	0	1	0	1
D. Robinson	0	0	1	14	1
Roche	0	0	1	0	1
Staggers	2	0	0	0	0
I. Thomas	0	1	0	0	1
C. Williams	0	0	2	21	2
P. Williams	1	0	0	0	0
Withrow	0	0	1	0	1
Packers	**22**	**11**	**19**	**74**	**30**

NFL STANDINGS

National Conference

Eastern Division

	W	L	T	Pct	PF	PA
Washington Redskins	11	3	0	.786	336	218
Dallas Cowboys	10	4	0	.714	319	240
New York Giants	8	6	0	.571	331	247
St. Louis Cardinals	4	9	1	.321	193	303
Philadelphia Eagles	2	11	1	.179	145	352

Central Division

	W	L	T	Pct	PF	PA
Green Bay Packers	**10**	**4**	**0**	**.714**	**304**	**226**
Detroit Lions	8	5	1	.607	339	290
Minnesota Vikings	7	7	0	.500	301	252
Chicago Bears	4	9	1	.321	225	275

Western Division

	W	L	T	Pct	PF	PA
San Francisco 49ers	8	5	1	.607	353	249
Atlanta Falcons	7	7	0	.500	269	274
Los Angeles Rams	6	7	1	.464	291	286
New Orleans Saints	2	11	1	.179	215	361

American Conference

Eastern Division

	W	L	T	Pct	PF	PA
Miami Dolphins	14	0	0	1.000	385	171
New York Jets	7	7	0	.500	367	324
Baltimore Colts	5	9	0	.357	235	252
Buffalo Bills	4	9	1	.321	257	377
New England Patriots	3	11	0	.214	192	446

Central Division

	W	L	T	Pct	PF	PA
Pittsburgh Steelers	11	3	0	.786	343	175
Cleveland Browns	10	4	0	.714	268	249
Cincinnati Bengals	8	6	0	.571	299	229
Houston Oilers	1	13	0	.071	164	380

Western Division

	W	L	T	Pct	PF	PA
Oakland Raiders	10	3	1	.750	365	248
Kansas City Chiefs	8	6	0	.571	287	254
Denver Broncos	5	9	0	.357	325	350
San Diego Chargers	4	9	1	.321	264	344

1972 ROSTER

No	Name	Pos	Ht	Wt	DOB	College	G
57	Bowman, Ken	C	6-3	230	12/15/42	Wisconsin	14
42	Brockington, John	RB	6-1	225	09/07/48	Ohio State	14
78	Brown, Bob	DE	6-5	260	02/23/40	Arkansas-Pine Bluff	14
28	Buchanon, Willie	CB	6-0	190	11/04/50	San Diego State	14
53	Carr, Fred	LB	6-5	238	08/19/46	Texas-El Paso	14
50	Carter, Jim	LB	6-3	235	10/18/48	Minnesota	14
56	Crutcher, Tommy	LB	6-3	230	08/10/41	TCU	12
84	Dale, Carroll	WR	6-2	200	04/24/38	Virginia Tech	14
47	Davis, Dave	WR	6-0	175	07/05/48	Tennessee State	14
48	Ellis, Ken	CB	5-10	190	09/27/47	Southern University	14
88	Garrett, Len	TE	6-3	230	12/18/47	New Mexico Highlands	14
41	Gibson, Paul	S	6-2	195	06/20/48	Texas-El Paso	1
68	Gillingham, Gale	G	6-3	255	02/03/44	Minnesota	2
46	Glass, Leland	WR	6-0	185	11/05/50	Oregon	14
21	Hall, Charlie	CB	6-1	195	03/31/48	Pittsburgh	14
77	Hayhoe, Bill	T	6-8	258	10/06/46	USC	14
51	Hefner, Larry	LB	6-2	215	08/02/49	Clemson	2
39	Hill, Jim	S	6-2	190	10/21/46	Texas A&I	14
72	Himes, Dick	T	6-4	244	05/25/46	Ohio State	14
23	Hudson, Bob	RB	5-11	210	03/21/48	Southeast Oklahoma	12
64	Hunt, Kevin	T	6-5	260	11/29/48	Doane	3
16	Hunter, Scott	QB	6-2	205	11/19/47	Alabama	14
40	Kopay, Dave	RB	6-0	218	06/28/42	Washington	14
44	Kroll, Bob	S	6-1	195	06/09/50	Northern Michigan	5
86	Lammons, Pete	TE	6-3	228	10/20/43	Texas	12
36	Lane, MacArthur	RB	6-1	220	03/16/42	Utah State	14
62	Lueck, Bill	G	6-3	235	04/07/46	Arizona	14
13	Marcol, Chester	K	6-0	190	10/24/49	Hillsdale	14
29	Matthews, Al	DB	5-11	190	11/07/47	Texas A&I	14
76	McCoy, Mike P.	DT	6-5	284	09/06/48	Notre Dame	12
81	McGeorge, Rich	TE	6-4	235	09/14/48	Elon	2
66	Nitschke, Ray	LB	6-3	235	12/29/36	Illinois	11
10	Patrick, Frank	QB	6-7	225	03/11/47	Nebraska	2
71	Peay, Francis	T	6-5	250	05/23/44	Missouri	6
75	Pureifory, Dave	DE	6-1	260	07/12/49	Eastern Michigan	14
89	Robinson, Dave	LB	6-3	245	05/03/41	Penn State	14
87	Roche, Alden	DE	6-4	255	04/09/45	Southern University	14
67	Snider, Malcolm	G	6-4	251	04/05/47	Stanford	14
22	Staggers, Jon	WR	5-10	180	12/14/48	Missouri	14
17	Tagge, Jerry	QB	6-2	220	04/12/50	Nebraska	4
37	Thomas, Ike	CB	6-2	193	11/04/47	Bishop	12
73	Vanoy, Vernon	DT	6-8	270	12/31/46	Kansas	13
26	Walsh, Ward	RB	6-0	208	11/21/49	Montana	2
20	Widby, Ron	P	6-4	210	03/09/45	Tennessee	14
83	Williams, Clarence	DE	6-5	255	09/03/46	Prairie View	14
31	Williams, Perry	RB	6-2	219	12/11/46	Purdue	14
58	Withrow, Cal	C	6-0	240	08/04/45	Kentucky	14
65	Wortman, Keith	G	6-2	245	07/20/50	Nebraska	13

1972 DRAFT

Rnd	Name	Pos	Ht	Wt	College
1a	Willie Buchanon (7)	CB	6-0	190	San Diego State
1b	Jerry Tagge (11)	QB	6-2	220	Nebraska
	(Choice from Chargers for Kevin Hardy)				
2	Chester Marcol (34)	K	6-0	190	Hillsdale
3	(Choice (59) to Vikings for Zeke Bratkowski)				
4	Eric Patton (86)	LB	6-3	240	Notre Dame
5	(Choice (111) to Saints for Wimpy Winther)				
6a	Nate Ross (138)	CB	6-1	195	Bethune-Cookman
6b	Dave Pureifory (142)	LB	6-1	240	Eastern Michigan
	(Choice from Bears for Bob Jeter)				
6c	Bob Hudson (147)	RB	5-11	210	NE Oklahoma
	(Choice from Rams as part of Travis Williams trade)				
7	Bill Bushong (163)	DT	6-3	250	Kentucky
8	Leland Glass (190)	WR	6-0	185	Oregon
9	(Choice (215) to Colts)				
10	Keith Wortman (242)	G	6-2	245	Nebraska
11	Dave Bailey (266)	WR	6-1	195	Alabama
12	Mike Rich (294)	RB	6-2	210	Florida
13	Jesse Lakes (319)	RB	5-11	195	Central Michigan
14	Larry Hefner (346)	LB	6-2	215	Clemson
15	Rick Thone (371)	S	6-1	200	Arkansas Tech
16	Charles Burrell (398)	DT	6-0	290	Arkansas-Pine Bluff
17	(Choice (423) to Chargers for Cal Withrow)				

1972 GREEN BAY PACKERS

FRONT ROW: (L-R) 57 Ken Bowman, 58 Cal Withrow, 62 Bill Lueck, 72 Dick Himes, 39 Jim Hill, 66 Ray Nitschke, 89 Dave Robinson, 68 Gale Gillingham, 29 Al Matthews, 48 Ken Ellis, 31 Perry Williams, 40 Dave Kopay, 53 Fred Carr.

SECOND ROW: (L-R) Trainer Domenic Gentile, Assistant Trainer Dan Davis, 17 Jerry Tagge, 20 Ron Widby, 78 Bob Brown, 36 MacArthur Lane, Offensive Line Coach Rollie Dotsch, Offensive Backfield Coach John (Red) Cochran, Quarterbacks Coach Bart Starr, Head Coach Dan Devine, Defensive Coordinator Dave Hanner, Receivers Coach John Polonchek, Defensive Backfield Coach Don Doll, 33 Charlie Pittman, 11 Charlie Napper, 44 Bob Kroll, Equipment Manager Gerald (Dad) Braisher, Assistant Equipment Manager Bob Noel.

THIRD ROW: (L-R) 88 Len Garrett, 71 Francis Peay, 81 Rich McGeorge, 56 Tommy Crutcher, 84 Carroll Dale, 16 Scott Hunter, 21 Charlie Hall, 42 John Brockington, 28 Willie Buchanon, 30 Larry Krause, 76 Mike P. McCoy, 47 Dave Davis, 37 Ike Thomas.

BACK ROW: (L-R) 87 Alden Roche, 67 Malcolm Snider, 10 Frank Patrick, 64 Kevin Hunt, 73 Vernon Vanoy, 83 Clarence Williams, 77 Bill Hayhoe, 65 Keith Wortman, 75 Dave Pureifory, 13 Chester Marcol, 23 Bob Hudson, 46 Leland Glass, 51 Larry Hefner, 50 Jim Carter.

- 175 -

1973

Talk again of playoffs, fueled by last year's postseason trip to the nation's capitol on Christmas Eve, was quickly put to rest after Green Bay invaded Los Angeles on October 21 to face the unbeaten Rams. Until then, the Packers (2-1-2) had maintained second place behind the fast-charging Vikings (5-0). The game against Los Angeles would provide a good litmus test for the Green and Gold.

Unfortunately, nearly everything went wrong. Willie Buchanon broke his left leg in two places while covering Jack Snow in the second quarter and was lost for the season. The Packers reached enemy territory just once all afternoon and converted only one of nine third downs. Defensive end Fred Dryer twice blew by Malcolm Snider, who filled in at tackle for the injured Bill Hayhoe, to register safeties. Dryer first sacked Scott Hunter in the end zone and then did the same to Jim Del Gaizo five minutes later. Green Bay picked up a scant six first downs, 63 total yards and a number of injuries in addition to Buchanon's.

Unlike a year ago, Green Bay failed to right itself. Detroit (1-4-1) rocked them 34-0 the following week, and then Bobby Douglass and the Bears (2-5) dealt the team a 31-17 setback on the strength of Douglass's four rushing touchdowns. By the time Green Bay recovered with a narrow 25-21 win over St. Louis (3-4-1), the Packers (3-4-2) had been eliminated from the Central Division race.

Coach Dan Devine couldn't decide on a quarterback. For the first eight weeks he wavered between Hunter and Del Gaizo, the latter acquired in an August 23 trade. Neither made more than two consecutive starts and in all but the opener, the starter was pulled because of injury or ineffectiveness. Jerry Tagge started the last six games but even he couldn't help a passing attack that managed 1,283 net yards, the lowest Packer total since 1946.

In mid-September, Congress passed a bill that allowed home games to be televised locally if sold out 72 hours in advance. The NFL opposed the legislation fearing ticket sales would be affected. Such fears proved unfounded. But some fans with tickets did stay home for late-season contests in cold weather sites. For the first time the league kept track of the "no-show".

The Lombardi era faded further into the past when Ray Nitschke announced his retirement and Carroll Dale was placed on waivers. Nitschke made his final Packer appearance against the Bears in the first preseason game and then retired approximately three weeks later. Dale was released to make room for defensive back Perry Smith.

The disappointing season closed on a high note. John Brockington and MacArthur Lane each rushed for over 100 yards to pace a 298-yard output, fifth highest in team history. Surprisingly, neither Brockington (22 carries-142 yards) nor Lane (19-101) scored, but Jon Staggers caught two touchdown passes to lead the Packers past the Bears 21- 0.

Green Bay Press-Gazette photo

Jerry Tagge (17) sizes up the Saints's defense in Milwaukee on December 2. Tagge completed nine of 13 passes for 109 yards to lead Green Bay past New Orleans 30-10. The former Green Bay West High School star started the final six games of 1973, but faded into the background once John Hadl was acquired in 1974. Tagge was cut prior to the 1975 campaign.

TEAM STATISTICS

	GB	OPP
First Downs	187	230
Rushing	98	114
Passing	72	101
Penalty	17	15
Rushes	527	506
Yards Gained	1,973	1,999
Average Gain	3.74	3.95
Average Yards per Game	140.9	142.8
Passes Attempted	255	327
Completed	119	180
% Completed	46.67	55.05
Total Yards Gained	1,503	2,050
Times Sacked	27	25
Yards Lost	220	228
Net Yards Gained	1,283	1,822
Yards Gained per Completion	12.63	11.39
Net Yards per Attempt	4.55	5.18
Average Net Yards per Game	91.6	130.1
Combined Net Yards Gained	3,256	3,821
Total Plays	809	858
Average Yards per Play	4.02	4.45
Average Net Yards per Game	232.6	272.9
Third Down Efficiency	60/194	71/192
Percentage	30.93	36.98
Intercepted By	15	17
Yards Returned	220	256
Returned for TD	3	1
Punts	68	67
Yards Punted	2,787	2,605
Average Yards per Punt	40.99	38.88
Punt Returns	30	41
Yards Returned	137	300
Average Yards per Return	4.57	7.32
Returned for TD	0	0
Kickoff Returns	53	40
Yards Returned	1,189	817
Average Yards per Return	22.43	20.43
Returned for TD	0	0
Penalties	68	54
Yards Penalized	653	483
Fumbles	23	34
Lost	12	18
Own Recovered for Touchdown	0	0
Opponent's Recovered by	18	12
Opponent's Recovered for Touchdown	0	0
Total Points Scored	202	259
Total Touchdowns	20	28
Touchdowns Rushing	10	13
Touchdowns Passing	7	14
Touchdowns on Returns & Recoveries	3	1
Extra Points	19	28
Safeties	0	3
Field Goals Attempted	35	27
Field Goals Made	21	19
% Successful	60.00	70.37

Regular Season 5-7-2

Date	GB		OPP	Att.
9/17	23	New York Jets (M)	7	(47,124)
9/23	13	Detroit Lions	13	(55,495)
9/30	3	at Minnesota Vikings	11	(48,176)
10/7	16	at New York Giants	14	(70,050)
10/14	10	Kansas City Chiefs (M)	10	(46,583)
10/21	7	at Los Angeles Rams	24	(80,558)
10/28	0	at Detroit Lions	34	(43,616)
11/4	17	Chicago Bears	31	(53,231)
11/11	25	St. Louis Cardinals	21	(52,922)
11/18	24	at New England Patriots	33	(60,525)
11/26	6	at San Francisco 49ers	20	(49,244)
12/2	30	New Orleans Saints	10	(46,092)
12/8	7	Minnesota Vikings	31	(53,830)
12/16	21	at Chicago Bears	0	(29,157)

Score By Periods

	1	2	3	4	Total
Packers	51	78	30	43	202
Opponents	52	64	40	103	259

INDIVIDUAL STATISTICS

Rushing

	Att	Yds	Avg	LG	TD
Brockington	265	1,144	4.3	53	3
Lane	170	528	3.1	20	1
Goodman	18	88	4.9	19	1
P. Williams	32	87	2.7	9	1
Tagge	15	62	4.1	t41	2
Staggers	4	33	8.3	t20	1
Staroba	1	11	11.0	11	0
Krause	1	8	8.0	8	0
Highsmith	7	7	1.0	4	0
Barry Smith	1	5	5.0	5	0
S. Hunter	8	3	0.4	6	1
Del Gaizo	4	1	0.3	3	0
D. Gordon	1	-4	-4.0	-4	0
Packers	**527**	**1,973**	**3.7**	**53**	**10**
Opponents	506	1,999	4.0	t50	13

1973

Receiving

	No	Yds	Avg	LG	TD
Lane	27	255	9.4	30	1
Staggers	25	412	16.5	50	3
McGeorge	16	260	16.3	44	1
Brockington	16	128	8.0	37	0
Barry Smith	15	233	15.5	24	2
Glass	11	119	10.8	23	0
P. Williams	5	44	8.8	14	0
Goodman	2	19	9.5	12	0
Staroba	1	23	23.0	23	0
Donohoe	1	10	10.0	10	0
Packers	**119**	**1,503**	**12.6**	**50**	**7**
Opponents	180	2,050	11.4	t63	14

Passing

	Att	Com	Yds	Pct	TD	In	Tk/Yds	Rate
Tagge	106	56	720	52.8	2	7	9/54	53.2
Hunter	84	35	442	41.7	2	4	10/89	46.8
Del Gaizo	62	27	318	43.5	2	6	8/77	30.9
Lane	2	1	23	50.0	1	0	0/0	—
Brockington	1	0	0	00.0	0	0	0/0	—
Packers	**255**	**119**	**1,503**	**46.7**	**7**	**17**	**27/220**	**46.9**
Opponents	327	180	2,050	55.0	14	15	25/228	69.2

Punting

	No	Yds	Avg	LG	HB
Widby	56	2,414	43.1	60	0
Staroba	12	373	31.1	49	0
Packers	**68**	**2,787**	**41.0**	**60**	**0**
Opponents	67	2,605	38.9	58	1

Kickoff Returns

	No	Yds	Avg	LG	TD
I. Thomas	23	527	22.9	34	0
K. Ellis	12	319	26.6	84	0
Krause	11	244	22.2	30	0
Aaron Brown	3	26	8.7	12	0
Lane	2	31	15.5	29	0
P. Williams	1	24	24.0	24	0
Highsmith	1	18	18.0	18	0
Packers	**53**	**1,189**	**22.4**	**84**	**0**
Opponents	40	817	20.4	45	0

Punt Returns

	No	Yds	Avg	FC	LG	TD
Staggers	19	90	4.7	12	26	0
K. Ellis	11	47	4.3	7	23	0
Packers	**30**	**137**	**4.6**	**19**	**26**	**0**
Opponents	41	300	7.3	13	72	0

Interceptions

	No	Yds	Avg	LG	TD
K. Ellis	3	53	17.7	t47	1
J. Hill	3	53	17.7	20	0
Jim Carter	3	44	14.7	t42	1
Al Matthews	2	58	29.0	t58	1
MacLeod	2	8	4.0	8	0
Hefner	1	3	3.0	3	0
Toner	1	1	1.0	1	0
Packers	**15**	**220**	**14.7**	**t58**	**3**
Opponents	17	256	15.1	t46	1

Scoring

	TDr	TDp	TDrt	PAT	FG	S	TP
Marcol	0	0	0	19/20	21/35	0	82
Staggers	1	3	0	0/0	0/0	0	24
Brockington	3	0	0	0/0	0/0	0	18
Lane	1	1	0	0/0	0/0	0	12
Barry Smith	0	2	0	0/0	0/0	0	12
Tagge	2	0	0	0/0	0/0	0	12
Jim Carter	0	0	1	0/0	0/0	0	6
K. Ellis	0	0	1	0/0	0/0	0	6
Goodman	1	0	0	0/0	0/0	0	6
S. Hunter	1	0	0	0/0	0/0	0	6
Al Matthews	0	0	1	0/0	0/0	0	6
McGeorge	0	1	0	0/0	0/0	0	6
P. Williams	1	0	0	0/0	0/0	0	6
Packers	**10**	**7**	**3**	**19/20**	**21/35**	**0**	**202**
Opponents	13	14	1	28/28	19/27	3	259

Fumbles

	Fum	Ow	Op	Yds	Tot
Bowman	1	0	0	-24	0
Brockington	4	2	0	0	2
Buchanon	0	0	1	0	1
Carr	0	0	2	0	2
Jim Carter	0	0	1	0	1
Del Gaizo	3	2	0	0	2
Donohoe	0	1	0	2	1
K. Ellis	1	0	0	0	0
Goodman	2	0	0	0	0
Hefner	0	0	1	4	1
Highsmith	1	0	0	0	0
J. Hille	0	0	4	0	4
S. Hunter	1	1	0	0	1
Krause	1	0	0	0	0
Lane	4	1	0	0	1
MacLeod	0	0	2	0	2
Al Matthews	0	0	2	0	2
M.P. McCoy	0	0	2	0	2
Roche	0	0	1	0	1
Staggers	1	1	0	0	1
Tagge	1	0	0	0	0
I. Thomas	2	2	0	0	2
C. Williams	0	0	1	0	1
P. Williams	1	0	0	0	0
Packers	**23**	**10**	**18**	**-18**	**28**

NFL STANDINGS

National Conference

Eastern Division

	W	L	T	Pct	PF	PA
Dallas Cowboys	10	4	0	.714	382	203
Washington Redskins	10	4	0	.714	325	198
Philadelphia Eagles	5	8	1	.393	310	393
St. Louis Cardinals	4	9	1	.321	286	365
New York Giants	2	11	1	.179	226	362

Central Division

	W	L	T	Pct	PF	PA
Minnesota Vikings	12	2	0	.857	296	168
Detroit Lions	6	7	1	.464	271	247
Green Bay Packers	5	7	2	.429	202	259
Chicago Bears	3	11	0	.214	195	334

Western Division

	W	L	T	Pct	PF	PA
Los Angeles Rams	12	2	0	.857	388	178
Atlanta Falcons	9	5	0	.643	318	224
New Orleans Saints	5	9	0	.357	163	312
San Francisco 49ers	5	9	0	.357	262	319

American Conference

Eastern Division

	W	L	T	Pct	PF	PA
Miami Dolphins	12	2	0	.857	343	150
Buffalo Bills	9	5	0	.643	259	230
New England Patriots	5	9	0	.357	258	300
Baltimore Colts	4	10	0	.286	226	341
New York Jets	4	10	0	.286	240	306

Central Division

	W	L	T	Pct	PF	PA
Cincinnati Bengals	10	4	0	.714	286	231
Pittsburgh Steelers	10	4	0	.714	347	210
Cleveland Browns	7	5	2	.571	234	255
Houston Oilers	1	13	0	.071	199	447

Western Division

	W	L	T	Pct	PF	PA
Oakland Raiders	9	4	1	.679	292	175
Denver Broncos	7	5	2	.571	354	296
Kansas City Chiefs	7	5	2	.571	231	192
San Diego Chargers	2	11	1	.179	188	386

1973 ROSTER

No	Name	Pos	Ht	Wt	DOB	College	G
27	Austin, Hise	CB	6-4	195	09/08/50	Prairie View	9
57	Bowman, Ken	C	6-3	245	12/15/42	Wisconsin	14
71	Branstetter, Kent	T	6-3	260	02/03/49	Houston	9
42	Brockington, John	RB	6-1	230	09/07/48	Ohio State	14
74	Brown, Aaron	DE	6-5	270	11/16/43	Minnesota	8
78	Brown, Bob	DE	6-5	280	02/23/40	Arkansas-Pine Bluff	14
28	Buchanon, Willie	CB	6-0	190	11/04/50	San Diego State	6
53	Carr, Fred	LB	6-5	240	08/19/46	Texas-El Paso	14
50	Carter, Jim	LB	6-3	245	10/18/48	Minnesota	14
12	Del Gaizo, Jim	QB	6-1	198	05/31/47	Tampa	8
86	Donohoe, Mike	TE	6-3	230	05/06/45	San Francisco	13
48	Ellis, Ken	CB	5-10	195	09/27/47	Southern University	14
88	Garrett, Len	TE	6-3	230	12/18/47	New Mexico Highlands	2
68	Gillingham, Gale	G	6-3	265	02/03/44	Minnesota	14
46	Glass, Leland	WR	6-0	185	11/05/50	Oregon	12
25	Goodman, Les	RB	5-11	206	09/01/50	Yankton	6
85	Gordon, Dick	WR	5-11	190	01/01/44	Michigan State	2
21	Hall, Charlie	CB	6-1	190	03/31/48	Pittsburgh	13
77	Hayhoe, Bill	T	6-8	260	10/06/46	USC	6
51	Hefner, Larry	LB	6-2	230	08/02/49	Clemson	14
32	Highsmith, Don	RB	6-0	200	03/12/48	Michigan State	7
39	Hill, Jim	S	6-2	195	10/21/46	Texas A&I	13
72	Himes, Dick	T	6-4	260	05/25/46	Ohio State	14
16	Hunter, Scott	QB	6-2	210	11/19/47	Alabama	8
55	Jenke, Noel	LB	6-1	225	12/17/47	Minnesota	2
30	Krause, Larry	RB	6-0	208	04/22/48	St. Norbert	14
36	Lane, MacArthur	RB	6-1	220	03/16/42	Utah State	13
62	Lueck, Bill	G	6-3	235	04/07/46	Arizona	14
13	Marcol, Chester	K	6-0	190	10/24/49	Hillsdale	14
29	Matthews, Al	DB	5-11	190	11/07/47	Texas A&I	14
56	MacLeod, Tom	LB	6-3	225	01/10/51	Minnesota	11
24	McBride, Ron	RB	6-0	200	10/12/48	Missouri	1
54	McCarren, Larry	C	6-3	240	11/09/51	Illinois	5
76	McCoy, Mike P.	DT	6-5	285	09/06/48	Notre Dame	14
81	McGeorge, Rich	TE	6-4	230	09/14/48	Elon	14
73	Oats, Carleton	DT	6-3	260	04/24/42	Florida A&M	8
75	Pureifory, Dave	DE	6-1	250	07/12/49	Eastern Michigan	13
87	Roche, Alden	DE	6-4	255	04/09/45	Southern University	13
80	Smith, Barry	WR	6-1	190	01/15/51	Florida State	14
45	Smith, Perry	CB	6-1	195	03/29/51	Colorado State	8
67	Snider, Malcolm	G	6-4	250	04/05/47	Stanford	14
22	Staggers, Jon	WR	5-10	180	12/14/48	Missouri	14
85	Staroba, Paul	WR	6-3	204	01/20/49	Michigan	2
17	Tagge, Jerry	QB	6-2	215	04/12/50	Nebraska	7
37	Thomas, Ike	CB	6-2	195	11/04/47	Bishop	13
59	Toner, Tom	LB	6-3	235	01/25/50	Idaho State	14
20	Widby, Ron	P	6-4	220	03/09/45	Tennessee	12
83	Williams, Clarence	DE	6-5	255	09/03/46	Prairie View	14
31	Williams, Perry	RB	6-2	225	12/11/46	Purdue	14
58	Withrow, Cal	C	6-0	230	08/04/45	Kentucky	14
65	Wortman, Keith	G	6-2	250	07/20/50	Nebraska	8

1973 DRAFT

Rnd	Name	Pos	Ht	Wt	College
1	Barry Smith (21)	WR	6-1	185	Florida State
2	(Choice (46) to Cowboys for Ike Thomas and Ron Widby)				
3	Tom MacLeod (74)	LB	6-3	221	Minnesota
4	(Choice (99) to Rams for Tommy Crutcher)				
5	(Choice (124) to Raiders as part of Carleton Oats trade)				
6	Tom Toner (152)	LB	6-3	225	Idaho State
7	John Muller (177)	G-T	6-3	260	Iowa
8	Hise Austin (202)	CB	6-4	187	Prairie View
9	Rick Brown (230)	LB	6-3	225	USC
10	Larry Allen (255)	S-LB	6-1	214	Illinois
11	Phil Engle (280)	G	6-2	270	South Dakota State
12	Larry McCarren (308)	C	6-3	242	Illinois
13	Tim Alderson (333)	S	6-2	193	Minnesota
14	Jim Anderson (358)	DT	6-5	250	Northwestern
15	Reggie Echols (386)	WR	6-2	185	UCLA
16	Keith Pretty (411)	TE	6-4	229	Western Michigan
17	Harold Sampson (436)	DT	6-5	268	Southern University

1973 GREEN BAY PACKERS

FRONT ROW: Equipment Manager Gerald (Dad) Braisher, Assistant Equipment Manager Bob Noel, 12 Jim Del Gaizo, 57 Ken Bowman, 58 Cal Withrow, 72 Dick Himes, 68 Gale Gillingham, 31 Perry Williams, 50 Jim Carter, 29 Al Matthews, 48 Ken Ellis, 39 Jim Hill, 28 Willie Buchanon, 53 Fred Carr, 51 Larry Hefner.

SECOND ROW: (L-R) Assistant Trainer Dan Davis, Trainer Domenic Gentile, 20 Ron Widby, 30 Larry Krause, 76 Mike P. McCoy, 78 Bob Brown, 36 MacArthur Lane, 59 Tom Toner, 21 Charlie Hall, 16 Scott Hunter, 42 John Brockington, 87 Alden Roche, Offensive Backfield Coach John (Red) Cochran, Receivers Coach John Polonchek, Head Coach Dan Devine, Defensive Secondary Coach Don Doll, Defensive Coordinator Dave Hanner.

THIRD ROW: (L-R) Offensive Line Coach Rollie Dotsch, Linebackers Coach Burt Gustafson, 25 Les Goodman, 88 Len Garrett, 83 Clarence Williams, 81 Rich McGeorge, 32 Don Highsmith, 17 Jerry Tagge, 13 Chester Marcol, 80 Barry Smith, 22 Jon Staggers, 37 Ike Thomas, 46 Leland Glass, Special Teams Coach Hank Kuhlmann, Pro Scout Bill Tobin.

BACK ROW: (L-R) 86 Mike Donohoe, 54 Larry McCarren, 45 Perry Smith, 56 Tom MacLeod, 27 Hise Austin, 77 Bill Hayhoe, 67 Malcolm Snyder, 62 Bill Lueck, 65 Keith Wortman, 75 Dave Pureifory, 74 Aaron Brown, 73 Carleton Oats.

At the midpoint of the season when Green Bay's record stood at 3-4, its quarterbacks had thrown just one touchdown pass. Only once before had the team thrown that few in its first seven games (1923), and then that team started 4-2-1. Dan Devine, who shipped two second-round picks to Miami for Jim Del Gaizo in 1973, and a fifth-round selection for Jack Concannon in July, again went looking for a quarterback. He settled on the Rams' John Hadl but paid an unbelievable price. To get the rights to the 34-year old signal caller, Devine gave up two firsts, two seconds and a third-round pick. Hadl started the final seven games and tossed three touchdown passes but the results were the same. The Packers second-half record matched its first-half mark and Green Bay finished 6-8, ahead of only the Bears in the Central Division.

For the second time in four years, pro football was hit by a players' strike. This time the main issue of contention was free agency. Players wanted the freedom to sign with a team of their choice after their initial contract expired. Management balked. Veterans went on strike July 1.

The Chargers' camp opened first and in turn was the first to have a picket line. Jim Hill and Willie Buchanon represented the Packers in the group toting signs in San Diego. The Houston Oilers became the second team to sprout a picket line and soon Green Bay followed suit.

In an attempt to keep rookies from the strikers, Packers assistant coaches arranged for draft choices to disembark on the field at Austin Straubel airport rather than enter the terminal. A chain-link fence prevented the veterans from approaching the rookies, who were quickly whisked off to team headquarters in waiting cars. The team did allow one 50-minute meeting between the two groups, then returned to keeping the veterans away.

On July 18, linebackers Jim Carter and Larry Hefner became the first Packers veterans to cross the picket line. Five days later, Chester Marcol joined them. A handful more returned but the first two preseason games against the Bills and Cardinals were played mostly with rookies.

After the second weekend of exhibitions games, the NFLPA suspended its strike and entered a self-imposed 14-day cooling off period during which veterans were to report to camp. Even though no agreement was reached during those two weeks, the players decided not to go back on strike. Not until February, 1977, was a collective bargaining agreement reached.

A number of rule changes were made in 1974 that included moving the goal posts back to the end of the end zone where they had been prior to 1934. A sudden-death period was added. Kickoffs were moved from the 40-yard to the 35-yard line and other modifications were made.

One final change occurred at season's end. On December 16, Devine resigned for the head coaching position at Notre Dame. Eight days later, Bart Starr was named his successor, and though he promised no miracles, images of the Glory Years resurfaced.

Green Bay Press-Gazette photo

Clarence Williams (83) draws a bead on Los Angeles quarterback John Hadl (21) in Milwaukee on October 13. Hadl was sacked twice as the Packers gained a measure of revenge for last year by beating the Rams 17-6. Ten days after the win, Hadl was in a Packers' uniform, the result of a trade. He led Green Bay with 1,072 yards passing but threw only three touchdown passes.

TEAM STATISTICS

	GB	OPP
First Downs	214	218
Rushing	87	93
Passing	108	106
Penalty	19	19
Rushes	482	465
Yards Gained	1,571	1,641
Average Gain	3.26	3.53
Average Yards per Game	112.2	117.2
Passes Attempted	385	383
Completed	187	188
% Completed	48.57	49.09
Total Yards Gained	2,162	2,254
Times Sacked	17	28
Yards Lost	126	254
Net Yards Gained	2,036	2,000
Yards Gained per Completion	11.56	11.99
Net Yards per Attempt	5.06	4.87
Average Net Yards per Game	145.4	142.9
Combined Net Yards Gained	3,607	3,641
Total Plays	884	876
Average Yards per Play	4.08	4.16
Average Net Yards per Game	257.6	260.1
Third Down Efficiency	68/207	77/203
Percentage	32.85	37.93
Intercepted By	23	21
Yards Returned	278	289
Returned for TD	1	1
Punts	69	84
Yards Punted	2,648	3,074
Average Yards per Punt	38.38	36.60
Punt Returns	42	48
Yards Returned	416	356
Average Yards per Return	9.90	7.42
Returned for TD	2	0
Kickoff Returns	49	55
Yards Returned	1,022	1,156
Average Yards per Return	20.86	21.02
Returned for TD	0	0
Penalties	55	88
Yards Penalized	536	715
Fumbles	25	19
Lost	16	12
Own Recovered for Touchdown	0	0
Opponent's Recovered by	12	16
Opponent's Recovered for Touchdown	1	2
Total Points Scored	210	206
Total Touchdowns	19	23
Touchdowns Rushing	10	10
Touchdowns Passing	5	10
Touchdowns on Returns & Recoveries	4	3
Extra Points	19	17
Safeties	1	0
Field Goals Attempted	39	26
Field Goals Made	25	17
% Successful	64.10	65.38

Regular Season   6-8-0

Date	GB		OPP	Att.
9/15	17	Minnesota Vikings	32	(55,131)
9/22	20	at Baltimore Colts	13	(35,873)
9/29	21	Detroit Lions (M)	19	(45,970)
10/6	7	Buffalo Bills	27	(51,919)
10/13	17	Los Angeles Rams (M)	6	(45,938)
10/21	9	at Chicago Bears	10	(50,623)
10/27	17	at Detroit Lions	19	(51,775)
11/3	6	Washington Redskins	17	(55,288)
11/10	20	Chicago Bears (M)	3	(46,567)
11/17	19	at Minnesota Vikings	7	(47,924)
11/24	34	San Diego Chargers	0	(50,321)
12/1	14	at Philadelphia Eagles	36	(42,030)
12/8	6	at San Francisco 49ers	7	(47,475)
12/15	3	at Atlanta Falcons	10	(10,020)

Score By Periods

	1	2	3	4	Total
Packers	12	78	59	61	210
Opponents	48	61	40	57	206

INDIVIDUAL STATISTICS

Rushing

	Att	Yds	Avg	LG	TD
Brockington	266	883	3.3	33	5
Lane	137	362	2.6	20	3
Goodman	20	101	5.1	47	0
Odom	6	66	11.0	28	1
Torkelson	13	60	4.6	21	0
Tagge	18	58	3.2	12	0
Barty Smith	9	19	2.1	4	0
R. Walker	1	18	18.0	18	0
Concannon	3	7	2.3	6	1
Leigh	1	0	0.0	0	0
Hadl	8	-3	-0.4	6	0
Packers	**482**	**1,571**	**3.3**	**47**	**10**
Opponents	465	1,641	3.5	27	10

Receiving

	No	Yds	Avg	LG	TD
Brockington	43	314	7.3	29	0
Lane	34	315	9.3	t68	3
Staggers	32	450	14.1	63	0
McGeorge	30	440	14.7	51	0
Barry Smith	20	294	14.7	t27	1
Odom	15	249	16.6	57	1
Payne	5	63	12.6	18	0
Goodman	5	19	3.8	12	0
Torkelson	2	10	5.0	8	0
Donohoe	1	8	8.0	8	0
Packers	**187**	**2,162**	**11.6**	**t68**	**5**
Opponents	188	2,254	12.0	t57	10

Passing

	Att	Com	Yds	Pct	TD	In	Tk/Yds	Rate
Hadl	184	89	1,072	48.4	3	8	9/70	54.0
Tagge	146	70	709	47.9	1	10	5/35	36.0
Concannon	54	28	381	51.9	1	3	3/21	57.7
Lane	1	0	0	00.0	0	0	0/0	—
Packers	**385**	**187**	**2,162**	**48.6**	**5**	**21**	**17/126**	**47.6**
Opponents	383	188	2,254	49.1	10	23	28/254	51.2

Punting

	No	Yds	Avg	LG	HB
R. Walker	69	2,648	38.4	58	0
Packers	**69**	**2,648**	**38.4**	**58**	**0**
Opponents	84	3,074	36.6	52	2

Kickoff Returns

	No	Yds	Avg	LG	TD
Odom	31	713	23.0	52	0
Leigh	9	201	22.3	30	0
Goodman	4	49	12.3	20	0
Okoniewski	2	11	5.5	11	0
Van Valkenburg	1	22	22.0	22	0
Torkelson	1	20	20.0	20	0
Krause	1	6	6.0	6	0
Packers	**49**	**1,022**	**20.9**	**52**	**0**
Opponents	55	1,156	21.0	43	0

Punt Returns

	No	Yds	Avg	FC	LG	TD
Staggers	22	222	10.1	6	t68	1
Odom	15	191	12.7	2	t95	1
K. Ellis	3	3	1.0	0	9	0
Hefner	1	0	0.0	0	0	0
Torkelson	1	0	0.0	0	0	0
Packers	**42**	**416**	**9.9**	**8**	**t95**	**2**
Opponents	48	356	7.4	2	26	0

Interceptions

	No	Yds	Avg	LG	TD
Hendricks	5	74	14.8	44	0
Buchanon	4	10	2.5	8	0
K. Ellis	3	56	18.7	t38	1
Al Matthews	3	41	13.7	32	0
J. Hill	2	47	23.5	24	0
C. Hall	2	22	11.0	19	0
C. Williams	1	23	23.0	23	0
M.P. McCoy	1	5	5.0	5	0
Carr	1	0	0.0	0	0
Jim Carter	1	0	0.0	0	0
Packers	**23**	**278**	**12.1**	**44**	**1**
Opponents	21	289	13.8	45	1

Scoring

	TDr	TDp	TDrt	PAT	FG	S	TP
Marcol	0	0	0	19/19	25/39	0	94
Lane	3	3	0	0/0	0/0	0	36
Brockington	5	0	0	0/0	0/0	0	30
Odom	1	1	1	0/0	0/0	0	18
Concannon	1	0	0	0/0	0/0	0	6
K. Ellis	0	0	1	0/0	0/0	0	6
Barry Smith	0	1	0	0/0	0/0	0	6
Staggers	0	0	1	0/0	0/0	0	6
Torkelson	0	0	1	0/0	0/0	0	6
Hendricks	0	0	0	0/0	0/0	1	2
Packers	**10**	**5**	**4**	**19/19**	**25/39**	**1**	**210**
Opponents	10	10	3	17/23	17/26	0	206

Fumbles

	Fum	Ow	Op	Yds	Tot
Brockington	6	0	0	0	0
Buchanon	0	0	1	0	1
Carr	0	0	2	0	1
Jim Carter	0	0	1	19	1
K. Ellis	1	0	0	0	0
Goodman	1	0	0	0	0
Hadl	4	0	0	0	0
Hefner	0	1	0	0	0
Hendricks	0	0	1	0	1
Himes	0	0	1	0	1
Lane	3	0	0	0	0
D. Mason	0	0	1	19	1
M.P. McCoy	0	0	2	0	2
McGeorge	0	1	0	0	1
Odom	5	2	0	0	2
Roche	0	0	1	0	1
H. Schuh	0	2	0	0	2
P. Smith	0	0	1	0	1
Tagge	5	1	0	-6	1
Torkelson	0	0	1	29	1
C. Williams	0	0	1	0	1
Packers	**25**	**8**	**12**	**61**	**20**

NFL STANDINGS

National Conference

Eastern Division

	W	L	T	Pct	PF	PA
St. Louis Cardinals	10	4	0	.714	285	218
Washington Redskins	10	4	0	.714	320	196
Dallas Cowboys	8	6	0	.571	297	235
Philadelphia Eagles	7	7	0	.500	242	217
New York Giants	2	12	0	.143	195	299

Central Division

	W	L	T	Pct	PF	PA
Minnesota Vikings	10	4	0	.714	310	195
Detroit Lions	7	7	0	.500	256	270
Green Bay Packers	6	8	0	.429	210	206
Chicago Bears	4	10	0	.286	152	279

Western Division

	W	L	T	Pct	PF	PA
Los Angeles Rams	10	4	0	.714	263	181
San Francisco 49ers	6	8	0	.429	226	236
New Orleans Saints	5	9	0	.357	166	263
Atlanta Falcons	3	11	0	.214	111	271

American Conference

Eastern Division

	W	L	T	Pct	PF	PA
Miami Dolphins	11	3	0	.786	327	216
Buffalo Bills	9	5	0	.643	264	244
New England Patriots	7	7	0	.500	348	289
New York Jets	7	7	0	.500	279	300
Baltimore Colts	2	12	0	.143	190	329

Central Division

	W	L	T	Pct	PF	PA
Pittsburgh Steelers	10	3	1	.750	305	189
Cincinnati Bengals	7	7	0	.500	283	259
Houston Oilers	7	7	0	.500	236	282
Cleveland Browns	4	10	0	.286	251	344

Western Division

	W	L	T	Pct	PF	PA
Oakland Raiders	12	2	0	.857	355	228
Denver Broncos	7	6	1	.536	302	294
Kansas City Chiefs	5	9	0	.357	233	293
San Diego Chargers	5	9	0	.357	212	285

1974 ROSTER

No	Name	Pos	Ht	Wt	DOB	College	G
52	Acks, Ron	LB	6-2	225	10/03/44	Illinois	13
71	Basinger, Mike	DE	6-3	258	12/11/51	California-Riverside	1
42	Brockington, John	RB	6-1	225	09/07/48	Ohio State	14
74	Brown, Aaron	DE	6-5	270	11/16/43	Minnesota	2
28	Buchanon, Willie	CB	6-0	190	11/04/50	San Diego State	14
53	Carr, Fred	LB	6-5	240	08/19/46	Texas-El Paso	14
50	Carter, Jim	LB	6-3	245	10/18/48	Minnesota	14
10	Concannon, Jack	QB	6-3	200	02/25/43	Boston College	14
58	Cooney, Mark	LB	6-4	222	06/02/51	Colorado	13
86	Donohoe, Mike	TE	6-3	230	05/06/45	San Francisco	14
48	Ellis, Ken	CB	5-10	195	09/27/47	Southern University	14
71	Fanucci, Mike	DE	6-4	242	09/25/49	Arizona State	13
68	Gillingham, Gale	G	6-3	265	02/03/44	Minnesota	14
25	Goodman, Les	RB	5-11	206	09/01/50	Yankton	13
12	Hadl, John	QB	6-1	214	02/15/40	Kansas	7
21	Hall, Charlie	CB	6-1	190	03/31/48	Pittsburgh	13
51	Hefner, Larry	LB	6-2	230	08/02/49	Clemson	14
56	Hendricks, Ted	LB	6-7	220	11/01/47	Miami	14
39	Hill, Jim	S	6-2	195	10/21/46	Texas A&I	14
72	Himes, Dick	T	6-4	260	05/25/46	Ohio State	14
55	Jenke, Noel	LB	6-1	225	12/17/47	Minnesota	8
30	Krause, Larry	RB	6-0	208	04/22/48	St. Norbert	14
36	Lane, MacArthur	RB	6-1	220	03/16/42	Utah State	14
23	Leigh, Charlie	RB	5-11	206	10/30/45	No college	12
62	Lueck, Bill	G	6-3	235	04/07/46	Arizona	9
13	Marcol, Chester	K	6-0	190	10/24/49	Hillsdale	14
43	Mason, Dave	DB	6-0	195	11/02/49	Nebraska	12
29	Matthews, Al	DB	5-11	190	11/07/47	Texas A&I	14
54	McCarren, Larry	C	6-3	240	11/09/51	Illinois	14
76	McCoy, Mike P.	DT	6-5	285	09/06/48	Notre Dame	14
81	McGeorge, Rich	TE	6-4	230	09/14/48	Elon	14
70	Nystrom, Lee	T	6-5	258	10/30/51	MacAlester	13
84	Odom, Steve	WR	5-8	165	09/05/52	Utah	14
73	Okoniewski, Steve	DT	6-4	252	08/22/49	Montana	14
85	Payne, Ken	WR	6-1	185	10/06/50	Langston	12
75	Pureifory, Dave	DE	6-1	250	07/12/49	Eastern Michigan	13
87	Roche, Alden	DE	6-4	255	04/09/45	Southern University	14
52	Schmitt, John	C	6-4	250	11/12/42	Hofstra	14
79	Schuh, Harry	T	6-3	260	09/25/42	Memphis State	14
80	Smith, Barry	WR	6-1	190	01/15/51	Florida State	14
33	Smith, Barty	FB	6-3	240	03/23/52	Richmond	8
45	Smith, Perry	CB	6-1	195	03/29/51	Colorado State	12
67	Snider, Malcolm	G	6-4	250	04/05/47	Stanford	14
22	Staggers, Jon	WR	5-10	180	12/14/48	Missouri	14
17	Tagge, Jerry	QB	6-2	215	04/12/50	Nebraska	6
26	Torkelson, Eric	RB	6-2	194	03/03/52	Connecticut	14
40	Van Valkenburg, Pete	RB	6-2	205	05/19/50	BYU	6
78	Wafer, Carl	T	6-3	250	01/17/51	Tennessee State	1
18	Walker, Randy	P	5-10	177	08/29/51	Northwestern State (LA)	14
49	Wicks, Bob	WR	6-3	205	07/24/50	Utah State	1
83	Williams, Clarence	DE	6-5	255	09/03/46	Prairie View	14
65	Wortman, Keith	G	6-2	250	07/20/50	Nebraska	12

1974 DRAFT

Rnd	Name	Pos	Ht	Wt	College
1	Barty Smith (12)	FB	6-3	240	Richmond
2	(Choice (38) to Dolphins in Jim Del Gaizo trade)				
3	(Choice (64) to Vikings through Chargers in Jim Hill trade)				
4	(Choice (90) to 49ers for Al Randolph)				
5	Steve Odom (116)	WR	5-8	165	Utah
6a	Don Woods (134)	RB	6-1	191	New Mexico
	(Choice from Bears for rights to Zeke Bratkowski)				
6b	Ken Payne (142)	WR	6-1	185	Langston
7	Bart Purvis (168)	G	6-4	240	Maryland
8a	Monte Doris (194)	LB	6-2	245	USC
8b	Ned Guillet (200)	S	6-1	183	Boston College
	(Choice from Falcons through Saints for Len Garrett)				
9	Harold Holton (220)	G	6-2	242	Texas-El Paso
10	Doug Troszak (246)	DT	6-3	248	Michigan
11	Eric Torkelson (272)	RB	6-2	194	Connecticut
12	Randy Walker (298)	P	5-10	177	Northwestern State (LA)
13	Emanuel Armstrong (324)	LB	6-3	222	San Jose State
14	Andy Neloms (350)	DT	6-4	260	Kentucky State
15	Dave Wannstedt (376)	T	6-4	245	Pittsburgh
16	Mark Cooney (402)	LB	6-4	222	Colorado
17	Randy Woodfield (428)	WR	6-0	170	Portland State

1974 GREEN BAY PACKERS

FRONT ROW: (L-R) 76 Mike P. McCoy, 30 Larry Krause, 80 Barry Smith, 51 Larry Hefner, 50 Jim Carter, 68 Gale Gillingham, 17 Jerry Tagge, 48 Ken Ellis, 39 Jim Hill, 29 Al Matthews, 28 Willie Buchanon, 53 Fred Carr.
SECOND ROW: (L-R) Assistant Trainer Dave Davis, Trainer Domenic Gentile, 36 MacArthur Lane, 10 Jack Concannon, 21 Charlie Hall, 42 John Brockington, 40 Pete Van Valkenburg, 57 Ron Acks, Assistant Equipment Manager Bob Noel, Equipment Manager Gerald (Dad) Braisher.
THIRD ROW: (L-R) 84 Steve Odom, 33 Barty Smith, 23 Charlie Leigh, 13 Chester Marcol, 45 Perry Smith, 18 Randy Walker, 25 Les Goodman, 75 Dave Pureifory, 22 Jon Staggers.
FOURTH ROW: (L-R) 62 Bill Lueck, 65 Keith Wortman, 52 John Schmitt, 78 Carl Wafer, 54 Larry McCarren, 73 Steve Okoniewski, 71 Mike Fanucci, 26 Eric Torkelson, 79 Harry Schuh.
BACK ROW: (L-R) 85 Ken Payne, 86 Mike Donohoe, 12 Dean Carlson, 87 Alden Roche, 58 Mark Cooney, 83 Clarence Williams, 56 Ted Hendricks, 67 Malcolm Snyder, 70 Lee Nystrom, 81 Rich McGeorge, 72 Dick Himes.

Bart Starr had guided Green Bay to five NFL championships and two Super Bowl victories as a player. If he fared just half as well as head coach, Packerdom would be ecstatic. Starr, however, had two strikes against him. He had little coaching experience and just three choices in the first six rounds of the draft.

Once he settled into his new position a flood of challenges faced him. Ted Hendricks, the all-pro linebacker who had blocked seven kicks in 1974, became a free agent and could not come to terms on a contract. Ken Ellis, unhappy with his pact, walked out of camp twice. And Bill Lueck requested to be traded at the end of August.

Starr dealt with all three. He sent Hendricks to the Raiders and received two first-round draft choices in compensation. Ellis was fined and suspended for a week but returned to play. Lueck was shipped to the Eagles for a fourth-round choice in 1976.

More difficulties arose once the season got underway. The Packers lost their opener 30-16 to Detroit on September 21. The Lions blocked three of Steve Broussard's nine punts to set an NFL record. Chester Marcol tore a quadricep muscle in his leg and was lost for the year. A week later, Willie Buchanon had his season come to an end when he broke his leg against Denver. In addition to the injuries, John Brockington's production dropped off markedly. And no one in the NFC threw more interceptions than John Hadl.

Starr replaced Marcol with Joe Danelo, Broussard with David Beverly and Buchanon with Perry Smith. No doubt, he would have loved to replace the team's start, worst in franchise history to that point. After the Lions defeated Green Bay, the Broncos and then Dolphins beat up on the Packers. Next, the winless Saints took their turn, edging the Packers 20-19 in week four. Following that loss, the Green and Gold had the distinction of being ranked number one in Steve Harvey's "Bottom Ten". The syndicated columnist wrote, "Packer Coach Bart Starr (0-4) is off to his worst start since 1955 when he helped quarterback Alabama to an 0-10 season."

Green Bay was not about to remain without a victory. On October 19 in Dallas, the Packers staged one of their bigger upsets in history. Hadl passed 26 yards to Rich McGeorge for a touchdown with 1:52 remaining to give the 17-point underdog Packers a 19-17 win and drop the Cowboys from the ranks of the unbeaten. Willard Harrell, Johnnie Gray, Steve Luke and Tom Toner recovered Dallas fumbles while Perry Smith added an interception.

The following week, the Packers played eventual Super Bowl champion Pittsburgh even until Roy Gerela's 29-yard fourth-quarter field goal sank them 16-13. Green Bay then lost five of its last eight to finish 4-10.

Green Bay Press-Gazette photo

Steve Odom (84) and Gerald Tinker (82) celebrate Odom's 14-yard touchdown catch amid the snowflakes in a late-November game at Lambeau Field. Halfback Willard Harrell passed to Odom for the score which put Green Bay up 21-0. The Packers went on to beat the Bears 28-7 for their third win of the year. A dejected Doug Plank (46) is at left.

TEAM STATISTICS

	GB	OPP
First Downs	211	260
Rushing	84	132
Passing	112	112
Penalty	15	16
Rushes	431	580
Yards Gained	1,547	2,339
Average Gain	3.59	4.03
Average Yards per Game	110.5	167.1
Passes Attempted	394	369
Completed	212	192
% Completed	53.81	52.03
Total Yards Gained	2,400	2,474
Times Sacked	42	32
Yards Lost	328	302
Net Yards Gained	2,072	2,172
Yards Gained per Completion	11.32	12.89
Net Yards per Attempt	4.75	5.42
Average Net Yards per Game	148.0	155.1
Combined Net Yards Gained	3,619	4,511
Total Plays	867	981
Average Yards per Play	4.17	4.60
Average Net Yards per Game	258.5	322.2
Third Down Efficiency	58/202	87/220
Percentage	28.71	39.55
Intercepted By	14	22
Yards Returned	174	388
Returned for TD	0	2
Punts	95	70
Yards Punted	3,404	2,776
Average Yards per Punt	35.83	39.66
Punt Returns	30	45
Yards Returned	190	221
Average Yards per Return	6.33	4.91
Returned for TD	0	0
Kickoff Returns	63	49
Yards Returned	1,398	1,020
Average Yards per Return	22.19	20.82
Returned for TD	1	1
Penalties	72	72
Yards Penalized	606	544
Fumbles	31	44
Lost	16	27
Own Recovered for Touchdown	0	0
Opponent's Recovered by	27	16
Opponent's Recovered for Touchdown	1	0
Total Points Scored	226	285
Total Touchdowns	27	32
Touchdowns Rushing	14	14
Touchdowns Passing	11	13
Touchdowns on Returns & Recoveries	2	5
Extra Points	22	30
Safeties	3	0
Field Goals Attempted	17	31
Field Goals Made	12	21
% Successful	70.59	67.74

Regular Season 4-10-0

Date	GB		OPP	Att.
9/21	16	Detroit Lions (M)	30	(50,781)
9/29	13	at Denver Broncos	23	(52,491)
10/5	7	Miami Dolphins	31	(55,396)
10/12	19	at New Orleans Saints	20	(51,371)
10/19	19	at Dallas Cowboys	17	(64,189)
10/26	13	Pittsburgh Steelers (M)	16	(52,258)
11/2	17	Minnesota Vikings	28	(55,378)
11/9	14	at Chicago Bears	27	(48,738)
11/16	10	at Detroit Lions	13	(76,356)
11/23	40	New York Giants (M)	14	(50,150)
11/30	28	Chicago Bears	7	(46,821)
12/7	3	at Minnesota Vikings	24	(46,147)
12/14	5	at Los Angeles Rams	22	(59,312)
12/21	22	Atlanta Falcons	13	(38,565)

Score By Periods

	1	2	3	4	Total
Packers	53	64	40	69	226
Opponents	64	77	79	65	285

INDIVIDUAL STATISTICS

Rushing

	Att	Yds	Avg	LG	TD
Brockington	144	434	3.0	19	7
Harrell	121	359	3.0	t26	1
Barty Smith	60	243	4.1	17	4
Torkelson	42	226	5.4	29	2
T. Wells	33	139	4.2	25	0
Odom	5	55	11.0	27	0
Hadl	20	47	2.4	9	0
Milan	4	41	10.3	15	0
Tinker	1	5	5.0	5	0
Payne	1	-2	-2.0	-2	0
Packers	**431**	**1,547**	**3.6**	**29**	**14**
Opponents	580	2,339	4.0	34	14

1975

Receiving

	No	Yds	Avg	LG	TD
Payne	58	766	13.2	54	0
Harrell	34	261	7.7	t36	2
Brockington	33	242	7.3	21	1
McGeorge	32	458	14.3	43	1
Barty Smith	16	140	8.8	33	1
Odom	15	299	19.9	56	4
Barry Smith	6	77	12.8	20	1
Torkelson	6	37	6.2	12	0
T. Wells	6	11	1.8	4	0
Tinker	4	84	21.0	t35	1
Askson	2	25	12.5	18	0
Packers	**212**	**2,400**	**11.3**	**56**	**11**
Opponents	192	2,474	12.9	t58	13

Passing

	Att	Com	Yds	Pct	TD	In	Tk/Yds	Rate
Hadl	353	191	2,095	54.1	6	21	35/284	52.8
Milan	32	15	181	46.9	1	1	7/44	62.1
C. Brown	4	3	63	75.0	1	0	0/0	—
Harrell	5	3	61	60.0	3	0	0/0	—
Packers	**394**	**212**	**2,400**	**53.8**	**11**	**22**	**42/328**	**58.3**
Opponents	369	192	2,474	52.0	13	14	32/302	69.3

Punting

	No	Yds	Avg	LG	HB
Beverly	66	2,482	37.6	55	0
Broussard	29	922	31.8	51	3
Packers	**95**	**3,404**	**35.8**	**55**	**3**
Opponents	70	2,776	39.7	67	1

Kickoff Returns

	No	Yds	Avg	LG	TD
Odom	42	1,034	24.6	t93	1
Luke	6	91	15.2	21	0
Torkelson	5	89	17.8	22	0
Barty Smith	4	53	13.3	18	0
Harrell	3	78	26.0	39	0
T. Wells	1	26	26.0	26	0
McGeorge	1	17	17.0	17	0
Bain	1	10	10.0	10	0
Packers	**63**	**1,398**	**22.2**	**t93**	**1**
Opponents	49	1,020	20.8	t94	1

Punt Returns

	No	Yds	Avg	FC	LG	TD
Harrell	21	136	6.5	5	25	0
K. Ellis	6	27	4.5	2	12	0
J. Gray	1	27	27.0	0	27	0
C. Hall	1	0	0.0	0	0	0
Odom	1	0	0.0	0	0	0
Packers	**30**	**190**	**6.3**	**7**	**27**	**0**
Opponents	45	221	4.9	14	31	0

Interceptions

	No	Yds	Avg	LG	TD
P. Smith	6	97	16.2	61	0
Carr	3	28	9.3	21	0
Al Matthews	2	42	21.0	40	0
J. Gray	1	7	7.0	7	0
K. Ellis	1	0	0.0	0	0
Toner	1	0	0.0	0	0
Packers	**14**	**174**	**12.4**	**61**	**0**
Opponents	22	388	17.6	t76	2

Scoring

	TDr	TDp	TDrt	PAT	FG	S	TP
Danelo	0	0	0	20/23	11/16	0	53
Brockington	7	1	0	0/0	0/0	0	48
Odom	0	4	1	0/0	0/0	0	30
Barty Smith	4	1	0	0/0	0/0	0	30
Harrell	1	2	0	0/0	0/0	0	18
Torkelson	2	0	0	0/0	0/0	0	12
M.P. McCoy	0	0	1	0/0	0/0	0	6
McGeorge	0	1	0	0/0	0/0	0	6
Barry Smith	0	1	0	0/0	0/0	0	6
Tinker	0	1	0	0/0	0/0	0	6
Pureifory	0	0	0	2/4	0/0	1	4
Marcol	0	0	0	0/0	1/1	0	3
Toner	0	0	1	0/0	0/0	0	6
team	0	0	0	0/0	0/0	1	2
Packers	**14**	**11**	**2**	**22/27**	**12/17**	**3**	**226**
Opponents	14	13	5	30/32	21/31	0	285

Fumbles

	Fum	Ow	Op	Yds	Tot
Askson	0	0	1	0	1
Brockington	2	2	0	0	2
C. Brown	1	1	0	-2	1
Buchanon	0	0	1	9	1
Carr	0	0	2	0	2
K. Ellis	0	0	2	6	2
J. Gray	0	0	4	0	4
Hadl	7	3	0	-12	3
C. Hall	1	1	0	0	1
Harrell	11	2	1	0	3
Luke	1	0	2	0	2
Al Matthews	0	0	2	0	2
M.P. McCoy	0	0	2	19	2
McGeorge	1	1	1	0	2
Milan	1	0	0	0	0
Odom	2	2	0	0	2
Payne	1	1	0	0	1
Pureifory	0	0	2	11	2
Roche	0	0	3	17	3
Scales	0	0	1	0	1
Barty Smith	2	2	0	0	0
Tinker	0	0	1	0	1
Toner	0	0	2	0	2
Torkelson	0	1	0	0	1
T. Wells	0	0	1	0	0
Packers	**31**	**14**	**27**	**48**	**41**

NFL STANDINGS

National Conference

Eastern Division

	W	L	T	Pct	PF	PA
St. Louis Cardinals	11	3	0	.786	356	276
Dallas Cowboys	10	4	0	.714	350	268
Washington Redskins	8	6	0	.571	325	276
New York Giants	5	9	0	.357	216	306
Philadelphia Eagles	4	10	0	.286	225	302

Central Division

	W	L	T	Pct	PF	PA
Minnesota Vikings	12	2	0	.857	377	180
Detroit Lions	7	7	0	.500	245	262
Chicago Bears	4	10	0	.286	191	379
Green Bay Packers	**4**	**10**	**0**	**.286**	**226**	**285**

Western Division

	W	L	T	Pct	PF	PA
Los Angeles Rams	12	2	0	.857	312	135
San Francisco 49ers	5	9	0	.357	255	286
Atlanta Falcons	4	10	0	.286	240	289
New Orleans Saints	2	12	0	.143	165	360

American Conference

Eastern Division

	W	L	T	Pct	PF	PA
Baltimore Colts	10	4	0	.714	395	269
Miami Dolphins	10	4	0	.714	357	222
Buffalo Bills	8	6	0	.571	420	355
New England Patriots	3	11	0	.214	258	358
New York Jets	3	11	0	.214	258	433

Central Division

	W	L	T	Pct	PF	PA
Pittsburgh Steelers	12	2	0	.857	373	162
Cincinnati Bengals	11	3	0	.786	340	246
Houston Oilers	10	4	0	.714	293	226
Cleveland Browns	3	11	0	.214	218	372

Western Division

	W	L	T	Pct	PF	PA
Oakland Raiders	11	3	0	.786	375	255
Denver Broncos	6	8	0	.429	254	307
Kansas City Chiefs	5	9	0	.357	282	341
San Diego Chargers	2	12	0	.143	189	345

1975 ROSTER

No	Name	Pos	Ht	Wt	DOB	College	G
57	Acks, Ron	LB	6-2	225	10/03/44	Illinois	14
88	Askson, Bert	TE	6-2	225	12/18/45	Texas Southern	14
69	Bain, Bill	G	6-4	269	08/09/52	USC	14
11	Beverly, David	P	6-2	180	08/19/50	Auburn	10
42	Brockington, John	RB	6-1	225	09/07/48	Ohio State	14
11	Broussard, Steve	P	6-0	200	07/19/49	SMU	4
19	Brown, Carlos	QB	6-3	210	07/31/52	Pacific	13
28	Buchanon, Willie	CB	6-0	190	11/04/50	San Diego State	2
53	Carr, Fred	LB	6-5	240	08/19/46	Texas-El Paso	14
50	Carter, Jim	LB	6-3	245	10/18/48	Minnesota	12
78	Cooke, Bill	T	6-5	251	02/26/51	Massachusetts	5
18	Danelo, Joe	K	5-9	166	09/02/53	Washington State	12
48	Ellis, Ken	CB	5-10	195	09/27/47	Southern University	14
86	Gaydos, Kent	WR	6-6	228	09/08/49	Florida State	4
24	Gray, Johnnie	S	5-11	185	12/18/53	Cal State-Fullerton	14
12	Hadl, John	QB	6-1	214	02/15/40	Kansas	14
44	Hall, Charlie	CB	6-1	190	03/31/48	Pittsburgh	14
40	Harrell, Willard	RB	5-9	182	09/16/52	Pacific	14
51	Hefner, Larry	LB	6-2	230	08/02/49	Clemson	4
72	Himes, Dick	T	6-4	260	05/25/46	Ohio State	14
55	Hull, Tom	LB	6-3	230	06/30/52	Penn State	12
63	Janet, Ernie	G	6-4	255	07/22/49	Washington	1
46	Luke, Steve	DB	6-2	205	09/04/53	Ohio State	14
13	Marcol, Chester	K	6-0	190	10/24/49	Hillsdale	1
62	Matson, Pat	G	6-1	245	07/22/44	Oregon	14
29	Matthews, Al	S	5-11	190	11/07/47	Texas A&I	14
58	McCaffrey, Bob	C	6-3	245	04/16/52	USC	13
54	McCarren, Larry	C	6-3	248	11/09/51	Illinois	14
76	McCoy, Mike P.	DT	6-5	275	09/06/48	Notre Dame	14
81	McGeorge, Rich	TE	6-4	230	09/14/48	Elon	14
70	McMillan, Ernie	T	6-5	265	02/21/38	Illinois	12
12	Milan, Don	QB	6-3	196	01/12/49	Cal-Poly-SLO	7
84	Odom, Steve	WR	5-8	174	09/05/52	Utah	14
73	Okoniewski, Steve	DT	6-4	272	08/22/49	Montana	14
85	Payne, Ken	WR	6-1	185	10/06/50	Langston	14
75	Pureifory, Dave	DE	6-1	255	07/12/49	Eastern Michigan	14
87	Roche, Alden	DE	6-4	255	04/09/45	Southern University	14
74	Roller, Dave	DT	6-2	270	10/28/49	Kentucky	6
38	Scales, Hurles	DB	6-1	200	12/01/50	North Texas State	7
80	Smith, Barry	WR	6-1	190	01/15/51	Florida State	13
33	Smith, Barty	FB	6-3	240	03/23/52	Richmond	14
45	Smith, Perry	CB	6-1	195	03/29/51	Colorado State	14
82	Tinker, Gerald	WR	5-9	170	01/19/51	Kent State	6
59	Toner, Tom	LB	6-3	235	01/25/50	Idaho State	14
26	Torkelson, Eric	RB	6-2	194	03/03/52	Connecticut	14
61	Van Dyke, Bruce	G	6-2	255	08/06/44	Missouri	14
89	Wade, Charley	WR	5-10	163	02/23/50	Tennessee State	2
52	Weaver, Gary	LB	6-1	225	03/13/49	Fresno State	14
37	Wells, Terry	RB	5-11	195	04/20/51	Southern Mississippi	13
83	Williams, Clarence	DE	6-5	255	09/03/46	Prairie View	14
65	Wortman, Keith	G	6-2	250	07/20/50	Nebraska	14

1975 DRAFT

Rnd	Name	Pos	Ht	Wt	College
1	(Choice (9) to Rams for John Hadl)				
2a	(Choice (28) from Colts for Tom MacLeod to Rams for John Hadl)				
2b	(Choice (36) to Dolphins for Jim Del Gaizo)				
2c	Bill Bain (47)	G	6-4	269	USC
	(Choice from Redskins for Dave Robinson)				
3a	Willard Harrell (58)	RB	5-8	182	Pacific
	(Choice from Chargers for Bob Brown)				
3b	(Choice (61) to Rams for John Hadl)				
4	Steve Luke (88)	DB	6-1	205	Ohio State
5	(Choice (113) to Cowboys for Jack Concannon)				
6	(Choice (140) to Rams for Harry Schuh)				
7	Tony Giaquinto (165)	WR	6-3	188	Cent. Connecticut St.
8	(Choice (192) to Colts for Ted Hendricks)				
9	Jay Lynn Hodgin (217)	RB	5-11	205	South Carolina
10	Bill Cooke (244)	DE	6-5	251	Massachusetts
11	Bob Martin (269)	DE	6-4	242	Washington
12	Carlos Brown (296)	QB	6-3	210	Pacific
13	Bob Fuhriman (321)	S	6-2	185	Utah State
14	Stan Blackmon (348)	TE	6-7	230	North Texas State
15	Randy Allen (373)	WR	6-2	180	Southern University
16	Bob McCaffrey (400)	C	6-3	245	USC
17	Tom Ray (425)	DB	5-11	180	Central Michigan

1975 GREEN BAY PACKERS

FRONT ROW: (L-R) 76 Mike P. McCoy, 72 Dick Himes, 84 Steve Odom, 13 Chester Marcol, 53 Fred Carr, 48 Ken Ellis, 29 Al Matthews, 75 Dave Pureifory, 62 Pat Matson, 57 Ron Acks, 61 Bruce Van Dyke, 21 John Hadl.

SECOND ROW: (L-R) Defensive Backs Coach Jim Colbert, Defensive Coordinator Dave Hanner, Quarterbacks Coach Zeke Bratkowski, Receivers Coach Lew Carpenter, Offensive Line Coach Leon McLaughlin, Head Coach Bart Starr, Offensive Coordinator Paul Roach, Special Teams Coach Bob Lord, Billy Kinard, Research and Development, Linebackers Coach John Meyer.

THIRD ROW: (L-R) 80 Barry Smith, 11 Steve Broussard, 59 Tom Toner, 44 Charlie Hall, Assistant Trainer Dan Davis, Equipment Assistants Jack and Bob Noel, Equipment Manager Gerald (Dad) Braisher, Trainer Domenic Gentile, 42 John Brockington, 46 Steve Luke, 18 Joe Danelo, 24 Johnnie Gray.

FOURTH ROW: (L-R) 45 Perry Smith, 37 Terry Wells, 12 Don Milan, 19 Carlos Brown, 73 Steve Okoniewski, 58 Bob McCaffrey, 54 Larry McCarren, 65 Keith Wortman, 33 Barty Smith, 26 Eric Torkelson, 52 Gary Weaver.

BACK ROW: (L-R) 85 Ken Payne, 40 Willard Harrell, 88 Bert Askson, 55 Tom Hull, 87 Alden Roche, 83 Clarence Williams, 70 Ernie McMillan, 86 Kent Gaydos, 81 Rich McGeorge, 69 Bill Bain, 51 Larry Hefner, 50 Jim Carter.

Except for a four-game stretch beginning in the fourth week, the Packers of 1976 were as pitiful as their counterparts of a year ago. The team's fortunes went with its running game. In 13 of the Packers 14 games, the team that ran for more yards won. Minnesota ignored this trend and beat Green Bay anyway 17-10 on November 21, despite being out-rushed 146-100. A 24-20 victory at Atlanta on the season's final weekend left the Green and Gold with a 5-9 record, a slight improvement from a year ago.

Bart Starr recognized it was time to acquire a young quarterback whom he could mold into a leader. On April 2, he sent Ken Ellis, who had played out his option in 1975, and John Hadl to Houston along with a fourth- and third-round pick for backup Lynn Dickey. The move was a gamble in the sense that the Packers again turned over high picks for a quarterback, one that nearly had his career wiped out in 1972 by a hip injury. Dickey declared himself fit and did an adequate job until a shoulder separation against the Bears in week 10 sidelined him for the rest of the year.

Just as last year, sailing was never smooth during the preseason. In addition to matching the 2-4 record of a year ago, problems arose with a few veterans. Ellis demanded to be traded and was as part of the Dickey trade. Bill Bain walked out of camp after a film session and was traded at his request less than 24 hours later. He was upset at what he perceived to be unfair criticism that had been on-going for some time. The *Milwaukee Sentinel* revealed that John Brockington had asked to be traded. His struggles continued in 1976 after the Packers found little or no interest in him league-wide.

After dropping its first three games by a combined 83-21 score, Green Bay suddenly caught fire. The team piled up 212 yards rushing, bolstered by Willard Harrell's 111 on 17 carries, and buried Detroit 24-14. A week later, Barty Smith gained 84 yards on 20 attempts to lead a 187-yard rushing explosion. Harrell scored on a six-yard sweep with 2:42 left for a 27-20 win over the expansion Seahawks. On October 17, Smith rushed for two scores and Harrell caught a 69-yard pass from Dickey as the Packers beat the Eagles 28-13.

The three wins pushed the team into a tie with the Bears (3-3) for second place in the Central Division. Green Bay looked to improve its position in week seven in Oakland. Dickey threw for 303 yards on 22 completions, but the Raiders squeezed by 18-14.

The Packers then lost five of their next six. They also lost Barty Smith to a knee injury in the second Lions game. Two weeks later, Dickey went down. Brockington took over for Smith, and Carlos Brown and then Randy Johnson replaced Dickey. Johnson threw for 165 yards and Brockington rushed for 89 in a successful 24-20 finale at Atlanta.

Green Bay Press-Gazette photo

Johnnie Gray (24) waits for blocking on a punt return against the Saints in Milwaukee on November 7. Providing interference are Tom Perko (56), Steve Wagner (21), Bob Barber (70) and Jim Gueno (51). Gray returned three punts for 58 yards in Green Bay's 32-27 win over New Orleans. Gray, who made the team as a free agent in 1975, led the team in punt returns as well as interceptions.

TEAM STATISTICS

	GB	OPP
First Downs	210	262
Rushing	99	132
Passing	94	107
Penalty	17	23
Rushes	485	546
Yards Gained	1,722	2,288
Average Gain	3.55	4.19
Average Yards per Game	123.0	163.4
Passes Attempted	357	354
Completed	164	196
% Completed	45.94	55.37
Total Yards Gained	2,105	2,192
Times Sacked	41	43
Yards Lost	375	357
Net Yards Gained	1,730	1,835
Yards Gained per Completion	12.84	11.18
Net Yards per Attempt	4.35	4.62
Average Net Yards per Game	123.6	131.1
Combined Net Yards Gained	3,452	4,123
Total Plays	883	943
Average Yards per Play	3.91	4.37
Average Net Yards per Game	246.6	294.5
Third Down Efficiency	79/223	77/212
Percentage	35.43	36.32
Intercepted By	11	22
Yards Returned	197	362
Returned for TD	2	3
Punts	84	77
Yards Punted	3,074	2,966
Average Yards per Punt	36.60	38.52
Punt Returns	40	48
Yards Returned	300	268
Average Yards per Return	7.50	5.58
Returned for TD	0	0
Kickoff Returns	65	44
Yards Returned	1,361	784
Average Yards per Return	20.94	17.82
Returned for TD	0	0
Penalties	87	104
Yards Penalized	791	914
Fumbles	37	27
Lost	23	15
Own Recovered for Touchdown	0	0
Opponent's Recovered by	15	23
Opponent's Recovered for Touchdown	0	0
Total Points Scored	218	299
Total Touchdowns	27	34
Touchdowns Rushing	15	17
Touchdowns Passing	10	13
Touchdowns on Returns & Recoveries	2	4
Extra Points	24	29
Safeties	1	0
Field Goals Attempted	19	33
Field Goals Made	10	22
% Successful	52.63	66.67

Regular Season 5-9-0

Date	GB		OPP	Att.
9/12	14	San Francisco 49ers	26	(54,628)
9/19	0	at St. Louis Cardinals	29	(48,842)
9/26	7	at Cincinnati Bengals	28	(44,103)
10/3	24	Detroit Lions	14	(54,758)
10/10	27	Seattle Seahawks (M)	20	(54,983)
10/17	28	Philadelphia Eagles	13	(55,115)
10/24	14	at Oakland Raiders	18	(52,232)
10/31	6	at Detroit Lions	27	(74,582)
11/7	32	New Orleans Saints (M)	27	(52,936)
11/14	13	at Chicago Bears	24	(52,907)
11/21	10	Minnesota Vikings (M)	17	(53,104)
11/28	10	Chicago Bears	16	(56,267)
12/5	9	at Minnesota Vikings	20	(43,700)
12/12	24	at Atlanta Falcons	20	(23,116)

Score By Periods

	1	2	3	4	Total
Packers	60	50	34	74	218
Opponents	46	128	60	65	299

INDIVIDUAL STATISTICS

Rushing

	Att	Yds	Avg	LG	TD
Harrell	130	435	3.3	56	3
Brockington	117	406	3.5	29	2
Barty Smith	97	355	3.7	16	5
Torkelson	88	289	3.3	15	2
Odom	4	78	19.5	28	0
C. Brown	12	49	4.1	21	0
C. Taylor	14	47	3.4	17	1
R. Johnson	5	25	5.0	11	0
Dickey	11	19	1.7	12	1
Osborn	6	16	2.7	6	0
Zimmerman	1	3	3.0	3	0
Packers	**485**	**1,722**	**3.6**	**56**	**15**
Opponents	546	2,288	4.2	59	17

Receiving

	No	Yds	Avg	LG	TD
Payne	33	467	14.2	t57	4
McGeorge	24	278	11.6	28	1
Odom	23	456	19.8	t66	2
O. Smith	20	364	18.2	47	1
Torkelson	19	140	7.4	31	0
Harrell	17	201	11.8	t69	1
Barty Smith	11	88	8.0	35	0
Brockington	11	49	4.5	20	0
C. Taylor	2	21	10.5	18	0
C. Hall	1	18	18.0	18	0
Zimmerman	1	13	13.0	13	0
M. Jackson	1	8	8.0	8	0
Askson	1	2	2.0	t2	1
Packers	**164**	**2,105**	**12.8**	**t69**	**10**
Opponents	196	2,192	11.2	t88	13

Passing

	Att	Com	Yds	Pct	TD	In	Tk/Yds	Rate
Dickey	243	115	1,465	47.3	7	14	28/279	52.2
C. Brown	74	26	333	35.1	2	6	10/66	25.3
R. Johnson	35	21	249	60.0	0	1	2/23	69.8
Harrell	4	1	40	25.0	1	1	1/7	—
Beverly	1	1	18	100.0	0	0	0/0	—
Packers	**357**	**164**	**2,105**	**45.9**	**10**	**22**	**41/375**	**48.6**
Opponents	354	196	2,192	55.4	13	11	43/357	73.3

Punting

	No	Yds	Avg	In20	TB	LG	HB
Beverly	83	3,074	37.0	14	5	60	1
Packers	**84**	**3,074**	**36.6**	**14**	**5**	**60**	**1**
Opponents	77	2,966	38.5	13	12	57	0

Kickoff Returns

	No	Yds	Avg	LG	TD
Odom	29	610	21.0	88	0
M.C. McCoy	18	457	25.4	65	0
Torkelson	6	123	20.5	29	0
C. Taylor	3	59	19.7	23	0
Hyland	3	31	10.3	11	0
Osborn	3	19	6.3	10	0
S. Wagner	1	27	27.0	27	0
J. Gray	1	23	23.0	23	0
O. Smith	1	12	12.0	12	0
Packers	**65**	**1,361**	**20.9**	**88**	**0**
Opponents	44	784	17.8	59	0

Punt Returns

	No	Yds	Avg	FC	LG	TD
J. Gray	37	307	8.3	7	27	0
Harrell	3	-7	-2.3	1	1	0
Packers	**40**	**300**	**7.5**	**8**	**27**	**0**
Opponents	48	268	5.6	10	19	0

Interceptions

	No	Yds	Avg	LG	TD
J. Gray	4	101	20.3	67	1
Luke	2	30	15.0	15	0
Buchanon	2	28	14.0	22	0
Toner	1	28	28.0	28	0
Carr	1	10	10.0	t10	1
P. Smith	1	0	0.0	0	0
Packers	**11**	**197**	**17.9**	**67**	**2**
Opponents	22	362	16.5	t53	3

Scoring

	TDr	TDp	TDrt	PAT	FG	S	TP
Marcol	0	0	0	24/27	10/19	0	54
Barty Smith	5	0	0	0/0	0/0	0	30
Harrell	3	1	0	0/0	0/0	0	24
Payne	0	4	0	0/0	0/0	0	24
Brockington	2	0	0	0/0	0/0	0	12
Odom	0	2	0	0/0	0/0	0	12
Torkelson	2	0	0	0/0	0/0	0	12
Askson	0	1	0	0/0	0/0	0	6
Carr	0	0	1	0/0	0/0	0	6
Dickey	1	0	0	0/0	0/0	0	6
J. Gray	0	0	1	0/0	0/0	0	6
R. Johnson	1	0	0	0/0	0/0	0	6
McGeorge	0	1	0	0/0	0/0	0	6
O. Smith	0	1	0	0/0	0/0	0	6
C. Taylor	1	0	0	0/0	0/0	0	6
team	0	0	0	0/0	0/0	1	2
Packers	**15**	**10**	**2**	**24/27**	**10/19**	**1**	**218**
Opponents	17	13	4	29/34	22/33	0	299

Fumbles

	Fum	Ow	Op	Yds	Tot
Brockington	3	0	0	0	0
C. Brown	2	2	0	0	2
Carr	0	0	1	0	1
Dickey	7	3	0	-8	3
J. Gray	0	0	4	0	4
Gueno	0	1	1	0	2
Harrell	9	0	0	0	0
Hyland	1	0	0	0	0
R. Johnson	2	1	0	-4	1
M.C. McCoy	1	0	0	0	0
M.P. McCoy	0	0	3	0	3
McGeorge	0	0	1	0	1
Odom	2	1	0	0	1
Payne	1	0	0	0	0
Pureifory	0	0	1	0	1
Roller	0	0	2	-2	2
Barty Smith	4	1	0	0	1
O. Smith	2	0	0	0	0
Torkelson	3	2	0	0	2
Van Dyke	0	0	1	0	1
S. Wagner	0	0	2	0	2
Weaver	0	0	1	0	1
Packers	**37**	**14**	**15**	**-14**	**29**

NFL STANDINGS

National Conference

Eastern Division

	W	L	T	Pct	PF	PA
Dallas Cowboys	11	3	0	.786	296	194
Washington Redskins	10	4	0	.714	291	217
St. Louis Cardinals	10	4	0	.714	309	267
Philadelphia Eagles	4	10	0	.286	165	286
New York Giants	3	11	0	.214	170	250

Central Division

	W	L	T	Pct	PF	PA
Minnesota Vikings	11	2	1	.821	305	176
Chicago Bears	7	7	0	.500	253	216
Detroit Lions	6	8	0	.429	262	220
Green Bay Packers	5	9	0	.357	218	299

Western Division

	W	L	T	Pct	PF	PA
Los Angeles Rams	10	3	1	.750	351	190
San Francisco 49ers	8	6	0	.571	270	190
Atlanta Falcons	4	10	0	.286	172	312
New Orleans Saints	4	10	0	.286	253	346
Seattle Seahawks	2	12	0	.143	229	429

American Conference

Eastern Division

	W	L	T	Pct	PF	PA
Baltimore Colts	11	3	0	.786	417	246
New England Patriots	11	3	0	.786	376	236
Miami Dolphins	6	8	0	.429	263	264
New York Jets	3	11	0	.214	169	383
Buffalo Bills	2	12	0	.143	245	363

Central Division

	W	L	T	Pct	PF	PA
Pittsburgh Steelers	10	4	0	.714	342	138
Cincinnati Bengals	10	4	0	.714	335	210
Cleveland Browns	9	5	0	.643	267	287
Houston Oilers	5	9	0	.357	222	273

Western Division

	W	L	T	Pct	PF	PA
Oakland Raiders	13	1	0	.929	350	237
Denver Broncos	9	5	0	.643	315	206
San Diego Chargers	6	8	0	.429	248	285
Kansas City Chiefs	5	9	0	.357	290	376
Tampa Bay Buccaneers	0	14	0	.000	125	412

1976 ROSTER

No	Name	Pos	Ht	Wt	DOB	College	G
57	Acks, Ron	LB	6-2	225	10/03/44	Illinois	13
88	Askson, Bert	TE	6-2	225	12/18/45	Texas Southern	14
70	Barber, Bob	DE	6-3	240	12/26/51	Grambling	14
11	Beverly, David	P	6-2	180	08/19/50	Auburn	14
42	Brockington, John	RB	6-1	225	09/07/48	Ohio State	14
19	Brown, Carlos	QB	6-3	210	07/31/52	Pacific	13
28	Buchanon, Willie	CB	6-0	190	11/04/50	San Diego State	14
41	Burrow, Jim	S	5-11	180	11/29/53	Montana	3
53	Carr, Fred	LB	6-5	240	08/19/46	Texas-El Paso	14
10	Dickey, Lynn	QB	6-4	210	10/19/49	Kansas State	10
67	Enderle, Dick	G	6-2	250	11/06/47	Minnesota	3
68	Gillingham, Gale	G	6-3	265	02/03/44	Minnesota	14
24	Gray, Johnnie	S	5-11	185	12/18/53	Cal State-Fullerton	14
51	Gueno, Jim	LB	6-2	220	01/15/54	Tulane	14
44	Hall, Charlie	CB	6-1	190	03/31/48	Pittsburgh	14
58	Hansen, Don	LB	6-2	228	08/20/44	Illinois	12
40	Harrell, Willard	RB	5-9	182	09/16/52	Pacific	13
72	Himes, Dick	T	6-4	260	05/25/46	Ohio State	14
55	Hyland, Bob	C	6-5	255	07/25/45	Boston College	14
71	Jackson, Mel	G	6-1	267	05/05/54	USC	13
16	Johnson, Randy	QB	6-3	205	06/17/44	Texas A&I	3
60	Knutson, Steve	T	6-3	254	10/05/51	USC	12
79	Koncar, Mark	T	6-5	268	05/05/53	Colorado	14
58	Lally, Bob	LB	6-2	230	02/12/52	Cornell	2
46	Luke, Steve	S	6-2	205	09/04/53	Ohio State	14
13	Marcol, Chester	K	6-0	190	10/24/49	Hillsdale	14
54	McCarren, Larry	C	6-3	248	11/09/51	Illinois	14
29	McCoy, Mike C.	CB	5-11	183	08/16/53	Colorado	14
76	McCoy, Mike P.	DT	6-5	275	09/06/48	Notre Dame	14
81	McGeorge, Rich	TE	6-4	230	09/14/48	Elon	14
84	Odom, Steve	WR	5-8	174	09/05/52	Utah	12
41	Osborn, Dave	RB	6-0	208	03/18/43	North Dakota	6
85	Payne, Ken	WR	6-1	185	10/06/50	Langston	14
56	Perko, Tom	LB	6-3	233	06/17/54	Pittsburgh	14
75	Pureifory, Dave	DE	6-1	255	07/12/49	Eastern Michigan	14
87	Roche, Alden	DE	6-4	255	04/09/45	Southern University	14
74	Roller, Dave	DT	6-2	270	10/28/49	Kentucky	14
33	Smith, Barty	FB	6-3	240	03/23/52	Richmond	8
89	Smith, Ollie	WR	6-3	200	03/08/49	Tennessee State	13
45	Smith, Perry	CB	6-1	195	03/29/51	Colorado State	13
32	Starch, Ken	RB	5-11	219	03/05/54	Wisconsin	6
27	Taylor, Cliff	RB	6-0	195	05/10/52	Memphis State	7
59	Toner, Tom	LB	6-3	235	01/25/50	Idaho State	11
26	Torkelson, Eric	RB	6-2	194	03/03/52	Connecticut	14
61	Van Dyke, Bruce	G	6-2	255	08/06/44	Missouri	14
21	Wagner, Steve	S	6-2	208	04/18/54	Wisconsin	11
52	Weaver, Gary	LB	6-1	225	03/13/49	Fresno State	14
83	Williams, Clarence	DE	6-5	255	09/03/46	Prairie View	14
80	Zimmerman, Don	WR	6-3	195	11/22/49	Northeast Louisiana	2

1976 DRAFT

Rnd	Name	Pos	Ht	Wt	College
1a	(Choice (8) to Rams for John Hadl)				
1b	Mark Koncar (23)	T	6-4	268	Colorado
	(Choice from Raiders for Ted Hendricks)				
2	(Choice (39) to Rams for John Hadl)				
3a	(Choice (70) to Steelers for Bruce Van Dyke)				
3b	Mike C. McCoy (72)	DB	5-11	183	Colorado
	(Choice from Chiefs for MacArthur Lane)				
3c	(Choice (74) from Giants for Jim Del Gaizo to Chiefs for Dean Carlson)				
4a	Tom Perko (101)	LB	6-3	233	Pittsburgh
4b	(Choice (117) from Eagles for Bill Lueck to Oilers for Lynn Dickey)				
5	Aundra Thompson (132)	RB	6-0	202	East Texas State
6	(Choice (166) to Oilers for Paul Robinson)				
7	(Choice (192) to Bengals for Pat Matson)				
8	Jim Burrow (218)	DB	5-11	181	Nebraska
9	Jim Gueno (245)	LB	6-2	220	Tulane
10	Jessie Green (274)	WR	5-11	180	Tulsa
11	Curtis Leak (301)	WR	5-11	180	Johnson C. Smith
12	Mel Jackson (328)	G	6-1	267	USC
13	Bradley Bowman (355)	DB	5-11	195	Southern Mississippi
14	John Henson (386)	RB	6-1	226	Cal Poly-SLO
15	Jerry Dandridge (413)	LB	6-1	222	Memphis State
16	Mike Timmermans (440)	G	6-1	240	Northern Iowa
17	Ray Hall (467)	TE	6-6	231	Cal Poly-SLO

1976 GREEN BAY PACKERS

FRONT ROW: (L–R) 19 Carlos Brown, 13 Chester Marcol, 84 Steve Odom, 53 Fred Carr, 40 Willard Harrell, 45 Perry Smith, 28 Willie Buchanon, 46 Steve Luke, 24 Johnnie Gray, 29 Mike C. McCoy.

SECOND ROW: (L–R) 57 Ron Acks, 71 Mel Jackson, 11 David Beverly, 52 Gary Weaver, 61 Bruce Van Dyke, 88 Bert Askson, 75 Dave Pureifory, 33 Barty Smith, 89 Ollie Smith, 10 Lynn Dickey, 85 Ken Payne, 51 Jim Gueno.

THIRD ROW: (L–R) Team Physician Dr. Eugene Brusky, Assistant Equipment Manager Bob Noel, Film Director Al Treml, Quarterbacks Coach Zeke Bratkowski, Offensive Coordinator Paul Roach, Offensive Line Coach Leon McLaughlin, Passing Game Coach Lew Carpenter, Head Coach Bart Starr, Assistant Head Coach/Defensive Coordinator Dave Hanner, Defensive Backfield Coach Dick LeBeau, Special Teams Coach Bob Lord, Linebackers Coach John Meyer, Equipment Manager Gerald (Dad) Braisher.

FOURTH ROW: (L–R) Assistant Trainer Dan Davis, 87 Alden Roche, 58 Don Hansen, 54 Larry McCarren, 59 Tom Toner, 21 Steve Wagner, 74 Dave Roller, 44 Charlie Hall, 42 John Brockington, 27 Cliff Taylor, 26 Eric Torkelson, Pro Player Personnel Director Dick Corrick.

BACK ROW: (L–R) Jim Huxford, 55 Bob Hyland, 56 Tom Perko, 70 Bob Barber, 68 Gale Gillingham, 72 Dick Himes, 76 Mike P. McCoy, 81 Rich McGeorge, 79 Mark Koncar, 83 Clarence Williams, 60 Steve Knutson, Trainer Domenic Gentile.

Since the 1970 AFL-NFL merger, Green Bay had struggled to produce a respectable offense. Only once during that time did the Packers offense not finish among the league's bottom ten, coming in at 16th or 11th from the basement in 1971. In 1977, the Packers produced the NFL's second worst offense, ahead of only Tampa Bay. So ineffective was it that in all but two games, the Green and Gold could not score more than a single touchdown. The running game produced 1,464 yards – fewest since 1958, 134 points – a 28-year low, and 3,212 total yards – fewest since 1948. With such numbers, Green Bay was fortunate to finish 4-10.

Signs of trouble were there as early as August. New England manhandled the Packers 38-3 in Milwaukee. Bart Starr accused Patriots Coach Chuck Fairbanks of running up the score by having his quarterbacks run play-action passes late in the game. Seven days later, the Buccaneers, who had won just once in 22 pre- and regular season tries, edged Green Bay 10-7. The Packers lost two more preseason skirmishes before salvaging a 24-16 decision against the Eagles on September 9.

It was during this time that Mike P. McCoy was switched from defensive tackle to left guard. The move lasted two weeks and was prompted in part because the team was not happy with McCoy's play. On September 7, Alden Roche was traded to the Colts and McCoy rejoined the defensive line. Less than a week later, he was traded to Oakland for defensive tackle Herb McMath, six years his junior, and two draft choices.

John Brockington followed on the heels of McCoy. He gained 25 yards on 11 carries in the opener which pushed him beyond the 5,000 yard mark for his career. He surpassed the milestone on his first carry, a five-yard jaunt in the second quarter. Nevertheless, the team's second all-time leading ground gainer was placed on waivers the following Tuesday to make room for rookie running back Jim Culbreath. Though no team claimed Brockington from the wire, he did join the Chiefs later in the year.

A third veteran of note departed in unusual circumstances. Ken Payne was first suspended and then fined for insubordination on the Tuesday after the Packers 17-7 loss to the Bengals. Payne was asked by assistant coach Bob Lord to move closer to the team's bench in the closing minutes of the game. The receiver ignored Lord at first, then responded in an obscene manner. He was fined $1,000 and suspended for one week but never served the suspension. By mutual agreement, Payne was waived Friday and claimed by the Eagles that Monday.

To further the team's problems, linebacker Gary Weaver and quarterback Lynn Dickey were lost to injuries, the latter for the second year in a row. Weaver banged up his knee in the first Lions game and missed the final nine games. Dickey broke his leg on the final play in the Rams game and not only sat out the remainder of 1977, but missed the entire 1978 season as well.

Green Bay Press-Gazette photo

Mike C. McCoy (29), Willie Buchanon (28), Steve Luke (46) and Bob Barber (70) celebrate Luke's third-quarter interception against the Lions on December 4. The steal was the fourth of the year for the strong safety who, along with McCoy, led the team in interceptions. Green Bay edged Detroit 10-9 to register its third win of the season.

TEAM STATISTICS

	GB	OPP
First Downs	195	261
Rushing	81	140
Passing	91	105
Penalty	23	16
Rushes	469	582
Yards Gained	1,464	2,314
Average Gain	3.12	3.98
Average Yards per Game	104.6	165.3
Passes Attempted	327	319
Completed	164	186
% Completed	50.15	58.31
Total Yards Gained	2,013	2,042
Times Sacked	32	37
Yards Lost	265	323
Net Yards Gained	1,748	1,719
Yards Gained per Completion	12.27	10.98
Net Yards per Attempt	4.87	4.83
Average Net Yards per Game	124.9	122.8
Combined Net Yards Gained	3,212	4,033
Total Plays	828	938
Average Yards per Play	3.88	4.30
Average Net Yards per Game	229.4	288.1
Third Down Efficiency	66/209	89/211
Percentage	31.58	42.18
Intercepted By	13	21
Yards Returned	89	349
Returned for TD	1	1
Punts	86	76
Yards Punted	3,391	2,776
Average Yards per Punt	39.43	36.53
Punt Returns	38	53
Yards Returned	321	311
Average Yards per Return	8.45	5.87
Returned for TD	1	0
Kickoff Returns	51	39
Yards Returned	947	786
Average Yards per Return	18.57	20.15
Returned for TD	1	0
Penalties	82	101
Yards Penalized	690	799
Fumbles	24	27
Lost	9	11
Own Recovered for Touchdown	0	0
Opponent's Recovered by	11	9
Opponent's Recovered for Touchdown	0	0
Total Points Scored	134	219
Total Touchdowns	14	27
Touchdowns Rushing	5	16
Touchdowns Passing	6	10
Touchdowns on Returns & Recoveries	3	1
Extra Points	11	22
Safeties	0	1
Field Goals Attempted	21	23
Field Goals Made	13	11
% Successful	61.90	47.83
Average Time of Possession	27:47	32:13

Regular Season   4-10-0

Date	GB		OPP	Att.
9/18	24	at New Orleans Saints	20	(56,250)
9/25	10	Houston Oilers	16	(55,071)
10/2	7	at Minnesota Vikings	19	(47,143)
10/9	7	Cincinnati Bengals (M)	17	(53,653)
10/16	6	at Detroit Lions	10	(78,087)
10/23	13	at Tampa Bay Buccaneers	0	(47,635)
10/30	0	Chicago Bears	26	(56,002)
11/6	10	at Kansas City Chiefs	20	(62,687)
11/13	6	Los Angeles Rams (M)	24	(52,948)
11/21	9	at Washington Redskins	10	(51,498)
11/27	6	Minnesota Vikings	13	(50,000)
12/4	10	Detroit Lions	9	(50,000)
12/11	10	at Chicago Bears	21	(33,557)
12/18	16	San Francisco 49ers (M)	14	(44,902)

Score By Periods

	1	2	3	4	Total
Packers	53	49	22	10	134
Opponents	44	76	21	78	219

INDIVIDUAL STATISTICS

Rushing

	Att	Yds	Avg	LG	TD
Barty Smith	166	554	3.3	11	2
Torkelson	103	309	3.0	29	1
N. Simpson	60	204	3.4	40	0
Harrell	60	140	2.3	9	1
Middleton	35	97	2.8	16	0
Whitehurst	14	55	3.9	19	1
Culbreath	12	53	4.4	18	0
Brockington	11	25	2.3	8	0
Dickey	5	24	4.8	10	0
Odom	1	6	6.0	6	0
Beverly	2	-3	-1.5	0	0
Packers	469	1,464	3.1	40	5
Opponents	582	2,314	4.0	58	16

Receiving

	No	Yds	Avg	LG	TD
Barty Smith	37	340	9.2	42	1
Odom	27	549	20.3	t95	3
O. Smith	22	357	16.2	41	0
Harrell	19	194	10.2	48	0
McGeorge	17	142	8.4	18	1
Torkelson	11	107	9.7	14	0
Vataha	10	109	10.9	20	0
Payne	7	99	14.1	45	1
N. Simpson	5	19	3.8	14	0
Askson	2	51	25.5	34	0
Aundra Thompson	2	12	6.0	14	0
Culbreath	2	6	3.0	5	0
Brockington	2	1	0.5	6	0
Middleton	1	27	27.0	27	0
Packers	164	2,013	12.3	t95	6
Opponents	186	2,042	11.0	t59	10

Passing

	Att	Com	Yds	Pct	TD	In	Tk/Yds	Rate
Dickey	220	113	1,346	51.4	5	14	21/187	51.4
Whitehurst	105	50	634	47.6	1	7	10/68	42.3
Harrell	1	1	33	100.0	0	0	1/10	—
Dowling	1	0	0	00.0	0	0	0/0	—
Packers	327	164	2,013	50.2	6	21	32/265	48.9
Opponents	319	186	2,042	58.3	16	13	37/323	77.1

Punting

	No	Yds	Avg	In20	TB	LG	HB
Beverly	85	3,391	39.9	16	9	59	1
Packers	86	3,391	39.4	16	9	59	1
Opponents	76	2,776	36.5	17	4	57	2

Kickoff Returns

	No	Yds	Avg	LG	TD
Odom	23	468	20.3	37	0
S. Wagner	6	62	10.3	20	0
Culbreath	5	82	16.4	30	0
Middleton	4	141	35.3	t85	1
Aundra Thompson	4	82	20.5	30	0
Harrell	3	48	16.0	24	0
Torkelson	2	36	18.0	25	0
Moresco	1	15	15.0	15	0
Gofourth	1	13	13.0	13	0
Gueno	1	0	0.0	0	0
N. Simpson	1	0	0.0	0	0
Packers	51	947	18.6	t96	1
Opponents	39	786	20.2	68	0

Punt Returns

	No	Yds	Avg	FC	LG	TD
Harrell	28	253	9.0	10	t75	1
J. Gray	10	68	6.8	3	24	0
Packers	38	321	8.4	13	t75	1
Opponents	53	311	5.9	4	18	0

Interceptions

	No	Yds	Avg	LG	TD
Luke	4	9	2.3	7	0
M.C. McCoy	4	2	0.5	2	0
Buchanon	2	41	20.5	t29	1
Carr	1	15	15.0	15	0
J. Gray	1	12	12.0	12	0
Toner	1	10	10.0	10	0
Packers	13	89	6.8	t29	1
Opponents	21	349	16.6	t95	1

Scoring

	TDr	TDp	TDrt	PAT	FG	S	TP
Marcol	0	0	0	11/14	13/21	0	50
Odom	0	3	0	0/0	0/0	0	18
Barty Smith	2	1	0	0/0	0/0	0	18
Harrell	1	0	1	0/0	0/0	0	12
Buchanon	0	0	1	0/0	0/0	0	6
McGeorge	0	1	0	0/0	0/0	0	6
Middleton	0	0	1	0/0	0/0	0	6
Payne	0	1	0	0/0	0/0	0	6
Torkelson	1	0	0	0/0	0/0	0	6
Whitehurst	1	0	0	0/0	0/0	0	6
Packers	5	6	3	11/14	13/21	0	134
Opponents	16	10	1	22/27	11/23	1	219

Fumbles

	Fum	Ow	Op	Yds	Tot
Barber	0	0	2	0	2
Beverly	1	1	0	0	1
Buchanon	1	0	1	0	1
M. Butler	0	0	1	0	1
Culbreath	1	2	0	0	2
Dickey	1	0	0	0	0
J. Gray	0	0	2	0	2
Gueno	0	1	0	0	1
Harrell	3	0	0	0	0
Himes	0	1	0	0	1
E. Johnson	0	0	1	0	1
Koncar	0	1	0	0	1
Luke	0	0	1	0	1
McGeorge	1	1	0	0	1
Middleton	4	1	0	0	1
Pureifory	0	0	1	0	1
Roller	0	1	0	0	1
N. Simpson	4	1	0	0	1
Barty Smith	1	1	0	0	1
O. Smith	0	0	1	0	1
Torkelson	4	1	0	0	1
S. Wagner	0	0	1	0	1
Whitehurst	0	0	0	0	0
Packers	24	12	11	0	23

NFL STANDINGS

National Conference

Eastern Division

	W	L	T	Pct	PF	PA
Dallas Cowboys	12	2	0	.857	345	212
Washington Redskins	9	5	0	.643	196	189
St. Louis Cardinals	7	7	0	.500	272	287
Philadelphia Eagles	5	9	0	.357	220	207
New York Giants	5	9	0	.357	181	265

Central Division

	W	L	T	Pct	PF	PA
Minnesota Vikings	9	5	0	.643	231	227
Chicago Bears	9	5	0	.643	255	253
Detroit Lions	6	8	0	.429	183	252
Green Bay Packers	4	10	0	.286	134	219
Tampa Bay Buccaneers	2	12	0	.143	103	223

Western Division

	W	L	T	Pct	PF	PA
Los Angeles Rams	10	4	0	.714	302	146
Atlanta Falcons	7	7	0	.500	179	129
San Francisco 49ers	5	9	0	.357	220	260
New Orleans Saints	3	11	0	.214	232	336

American Conference

Eastern Division

	W	L	T	Pct	PF	PA
Baltimore Colts	10	4	0	.714	295	221
Miami Dolphins	10	4	0	.714	313	197
New England Patriots	9	5	0	.643	278	217
New York Jets	3	11	0	.214	191	300
Buffalo Bills	3	11	0	.214	160	313

Central Division

	W	L	T	Pct	PF	PA
Pittsburgh Steelers	9	5	0	.643	283	243
Houston Oilers	8	6	0	.571	299	230
Cincinnati Bengals	8	6	0	.571	238	235
Cleveland Browns	6	8	0	.429	269	267

Western Division

	W	L	T	Pct	PF	PA
Denver Broncos	12	2	0	.857	274	148
Oakland Raiders	11	3	0	.786	351	230
San Diego Chargers	7	7	0	.500	222	205
Seattle Seahawks	5	9	0	.357	282	373
Kansas City Chiefs	2	12	0	.143	225	349

1977 ROSTER

No	Name	Pos	Ht	Wt	DOB	College	G
88	Askson, Bert	TE	6-2	225	12/18/45	Texas Southern	14
70	Barber, Bob	DE	6-3	240	12/26/51	Grambling	14
11	Beverly, David	P	6-2	180	08/19/50	Auburn	14
42	Brockington, John	RB	6-1	225	09/07/48	Ohio State	1
28	Buchanon, Willie	CB	6-0	190	11/04/50	San Diego State	14
77	Butler, Mike	DE	6-5	265	04/04/54	Kansas	14
53	Carr, Fred	LB	6-5	240	08/19/46	Texas-El Paso	14
50	Carter, Jim	LB	6-3	245	10/18/48	Minnesota	14
31	Culbreath, Jim	RB	6-0	210	10/21/52	Oklahoma	13
10	Dickey, Lynn	QB	6-4	210	10/19/49	Kansas State	9
12	Dowling, Brian	QB	6-2	200	04/01/47	Yale	5
57	Gofourth, Derrel	C	6-3	260	03/20/55	Oklahoma State	14
24	Gray, Johnnie	S	5-11	185	12/18/53	Cal State-Fullerton	14
51	Gueno, Jim	LB	6-2	220	01/15/54	Tulane	14
58	Hansen, Don	LB	6-2	228	08/20/44	Illinois	13
40	Harrell, Willard	RB	5-9	182	09/16/52	Pacific	13
82	Hartwig, Keith	WR	6-0	186	12/10/53	Arizona	7
62	Havig, Dennis	G	6-3	255	05/06/49	Colorado	9
72	Himes, Dick	T	6-4	260	05/25/46	Ohio State	14
71	Jackson, Mel	G	6-1	267	05/05/54	USC	13
78	Johnson, Ezra	DE	6-4	240	10/02/55	Morris Brown	14
60	Knutson, Steve	T	6-3	254	10/05/51	USC	13
68	Koch, Greg	T	6-4	265	06/14/55	Arkansas	14
79	Koncar, Mark	T	6-5	268	05/05/53	Colorado	13
67	Kowalkowski, Bob	G	6-3	245	11/05/43	Virginia	9
46	Luke, Steve	S	6-2	205	09/04/53	Ohio State	14
13	Marcol, Chester	K	6-0	190	10/24/49	Hillsdale	14
54	McCarren, Larry	C	6-3	248	11/09/51	Illinois	14
29	McCoy, Mike C.	CB	5-11	183	08/16/53	Colorado	14
81	McGeorge, Rich	TE	6-4	230	09/14/48	Elon	14
61	McMath, Herb	DT	6-4	250	09/06/54	Morningside	9
34	Middleton, Terdell	HB	6-0	195	04/08/55	Memphis State	14
37	Moresco, Tim	S	5-10	176	10/03/54	Syracuse	14
84	Odom, Steve	WR	5-8	174	09/05/52	Utah	14
85	Payne, Ken	WR	6-1	185	10/06/50	Langston	4
75	Pureifory, Dave	DE	6-1	255	07/12/49	Eastern Michigan	12
23	Randolph, Terry	CB	6-0	184	07/17/55	American International	14
74	Roller, Dave	DT	6-2	270	10/28/49	Kentucky	13
48	Simpson, Nate	RB	5-11	190	11/30/54	Tennessee State	12
33	Smith, Barty	FB	6-3	240	03/23/52	Richmond	14
56	Smith, Blane	G	6-3	238	07/13/54	Purdue	1
89	Smith, Ollie	WR	6-3	200	03/08/49	Tennessee State	12
43	Thompson, Aundra	WR	6-0	186	01/02/53	East Texas State	14
59	Toner, Tom	LB	6-3	235	01/25/50	Idaho State	14
26	Torkelson, Eric	RB	6-2	194	03/03/52	Connecticut	14
18	Vataha, Randy	WR	5-10	170	12/04/48	Stanford	6
21	Wagner, Steve	S	6-2	208	04/18/54	Wisconsin	14
52	Weaver, Gary	LB	6-1	225	03/13/49	Fresno State	5
17	Whitehurst, David	QB	6-2	204	04/27/55	Furman	7
83	Williams, Clarence	DE	6-5	255	09/03/46	Prairie View	13

1977 DRAFT

Rnd	Name	Pos	Ht	Wt	College
1a	Mike Butler (9)	DE	6-5	265	Kansas
1b	Ezra Johnson (28)	DE	6-4	240	Morris Brown
	(Choice from Raiders for Ted Hendricks)				
2	Greg Koch (39)	G-T	6-4	265	Arkansas
3a	(Choice (66) to Oilers for Lynn Dickey)				
3b	Rick Scribner (74)	G	6-4	257	Idaho State
	(Choice from Broncos for Bill Bain)				
3c	Terdell Middleton (80)	RB	6-0	195	Memphis State
	(Choice from Cardinals for Perry Smith)				
4	(Choice (94) to Steelers for Bob Barber)				
Rnd	Name	Pos	Ht	Wt	College
5	Nate Simpson (122)	RB	5-10	190	Tennessee State
6	Tim Moresco (149)	DB	5-10	176	Syracuse
7a	Derrel Gofourth (172)	C	6-3	260	Oklahoma State
	(Choice from Giants for Joe Danelo)				
7b	Rell Tipton (176)	G	6-4	245	Baylor
8	David Whitehurst (206)	QB	6-2	204	Furman
9	Joel Mullins (233)	T	6-4	260	Arkansas State
10	Jim Culbreath (260)	RB	6-0	209	Oklahoma
11	Terry Randolph (290)	DB	6-0	184	American International
12	(Choice (317) to Raiders for Ollie Smith)				

1977 GREEN BAY PACKERS

FRONT ROW: (L-R) 24 Johnnie Gray, 46 Steve Luke, 29 Mike C. McCoy, 28 Willie Buchanon, 13 Chester Marcol, 40 Willard Harrell, 53 Fred Carr, 72 Dick Himes, 75 Dave Pureifory, 74 Dave Roller, 67 Bob Kowalkowski, 60 Steve Knutson, 84 Steve Odom.

SECOND ROW: (L-R) Groundskeeper Earl DuChateau, Film Director Al Treml, Equipment Assistant Jack Noel, Assistant Equipment Manager Bob Noel, Quarterbacks Coach Zeke Bratkowski, Passing Game Coach Lew Carpenter, Special Teams Coach Burt Gustafson, Head Coach Bart Starr, Assistant Head Coach/Defensive Coordinator Dave Hanner, Defensive Backfield Coach Dick LeBeau, Offensive Line Coach Bill Curry, Offensive Backfield Coach Bob Lord, Linebackers Coach John Meyer, Pro Player Personnel Director Dick Corrick.

THIRD ROW: (L-R) Team Physcian Dr. Eugene Brusky, 52 Gary Weaver, 18 Randy Vataha, 59 Tom Toner, 34 Terdell Middleton, 43 Aundra Thompson, 88 Bert Askson, 11 David Beverly, 71 Mel Jackson, 89 Ollie Smith, 10 Lynn Dickey, 48 Nate Simpson, Jim Huxford.

FOURTH ROW: (L-R) Trainer Domenic Gentile, 51 Jim Gueno, 58 Don Hansen, 57 Derrel Gofourth, 77 Mike Butler, 23 Terry Randolph, 31 Jim Culbreath, 68 Greg Koch, 17 David Whitehurst, 37 Tim Moresco, Assistant Trainer Greg Vergamini.

BACK ROW: (L-R) 62 Dennis Havig, 54 Larry McCarren, 83 Clarence Williams, 81 Rich McGeorge, 33 Barty Smith, 26 Eric Torkelson, 78 Ezra Johnson, 21 Steve Wagner, 70 Bob Barber, 79 Mark Koncar, 50 Jim Carter.

Just when all the prognosticators had written off the Packers for another year, Green Bay roared from the opening gun to post a 6-1 mark. Youth and an aggressive defense sparked the team as it moved three full games ahead of the second-place Vikings, Lions and Bears after seven weeks. Second-year quarterback David Whitehurst threw to first-round sensation James Lofton and handed off to sophomore halfback Terdell Middleton with great success. Last year's top picks, Ezra Johnson and Mike Butler, formed bookends on a defensive line that sacked opposing quarterbacks a team-record 48 times. Rookie linebackers John Anderson, Mike Hunt and Mike Douglass settled into starting spots and formed a solid wall behind the defensive line. The Pack was back, if only for a short time.

Unfortunately, in the final nine games Green Bay went 2-6-1. Down the stretch the team blew chances, most notably against the Eagles (4-5) and Bears (5-9), to solidify its hold on first place. As a result, Green Bay needed to defeat the playoff-bound Rams on the season's final weekend in order to have any shot at postseason play. The Packers' journey to the West Coast did not prove fruitful as Los Angeles handled them 31-14. Both Minnesota and Green Bay wound up 8-7-1 but the Vikings clinched the division because of a better head-to-head mark against the Packers.

The team's 6-1 start, best since 1966, caught everyone by surprise and was the result of some solid performances. Whitehurst threw more touchdown passes (10) than any Packer since Don Horn's 11 in 1969. Middleton became just the fourth Packer to surpass 1,000 yards rushing in a single year, picking up 1,116. Ezra Johnson piled up 20 1/2 sacks. Willie Buchanon tied a league record with four interceptions against the Chargers and led the NFC with nine.

The Packers' turnover ratio illustrated how the team was able to bolt to the top of the Central Division standings and then stumble down the stretch. The defense, nicknamed Gang Green by the fans, created 30 turnovers in the first seven games. The offense gave up 16. In the final nine contests, the defense produced just 17 takeaways while the offense turned the ball over 26 times.

After the heady start began to erode and Minnesota slowly closed the gap, a rematch with the Vikings on November 26 loomed large. The two sat tied for first place in the Central Division with 7-5 records. Fran Tarkenton, who had given the Packers headaches for 18 years, fired a five-yard touchdown pass to Ahmad Rashad over Mike C. McCoy and threw the game into overtime. The two teams battled to a standstill for the next fifteen minutes. The resulting 10-10 tie provided the Vikings with a tiebreaking edge over the Packers who missed the playoffs for a sixth consecutive year.

Green Bay Press-Gazette photo

Terdell Middleton (34) gallops 76 yards for a touchdown against the Lions in Milwaukee on October 1. Middleton rushed 11 times for 148 yards and a touchdown. Detroit's Luther Bradley (27) gives chase. Green Bay beat Detroit 35-14. Middleton became the fourth Packer to rush for 1,000 yards in a single season. He amassed 1,116 yards and made the Pro Bowl.

TEAM STATISTICS

	GB	OPP
First Downs	226	302
Rushing	105	137
Passing	101	143
Penalty	20	22
Rushes	550	620
Yards Gained	2,023	2,439
Average Gain	3.68	3.93
Average Yards per Game	126.4	152.4
Passes Attempted	357	463
Completed	180	254
% Completed	50.42	54.86
Total Yards Gained	2,358	2,910
Times Sacked	37	48
Yards Lost	274	386
Net Yards Gained	2,084	2,524
Yards Gained per Completion	13.10	11.46
Net Yards per Attempt	5.29	4.94
Average Net Yards per Game	130.3	157.8
Combined Net Yards Gained	4,107	4,963
Total Plays	944	1,131
Average Yards per Play	4.35	4.39
Average Net Yards per Game	256.7	310.2
Third Down Efficiency	65/226	102/269
Percentage	28.76	37.92
Intercepted By	27	18
Yards Returned	344	262
Returned for TD	2	1
Punts	106	90
Yards Punted	3,759	3,411
Average Yards per Punt	35.46	37.90
Punt Returns	46	51
Yards Returned	393	286
Average Yards per Return	8.54	5.61
Returned for TD	0	0
Kickoff Returns	52	52
Yards Returned	1,085	1,015
Average Yards per Return	20.87	19.52
Returned for TD	1	0
Penalties	99	116
Yards Penalized	776	949
Fumbles	35	40
Lost	24	20
Own Recovered for Touchdown	0	0
Opponent's Recovered by	20	24
Opponent's Recovered for Touchdown	0	0
Total Points Scored	249	269
Total Touchdowns	31	36
Touchdowns Rushing	16	19
Touchdowns Passing	11	16
Touchdowns on Returns & Recoveries	4	1
Extra Points	30	36
Safeties	0	1
Field Goals Attempted	19	18
Field Goals Made	11	5
% Successful	57.89	27.78
Average Time of Possession	28:16	31:44

Regular Season 8-7-1

Date	GB		OPP	Att.
9/3	13	at Detroit Lions	7	(51,187)
9/10	28	New Orleans Saints (M)	14	(52,646)
9/17	3	Oakland Raiders	28	(55,903)
9/24	24	at San Diego Chargers	3	(42,755)
10/1	35	Detroit Lions (M)	14	(54,606)
10/8	24	Chicago Bears	14	(55,352)
10/15	45	Seattle Seahawks (M)	28	(52,712)
10/22	7	at Minnesota Vikings	21	(47,411)
10/29	9	Tampa Bay Buccaneers	7	(55,108)
11/5	3	at Philadelphia Eagles	10	(64,214)
11/12	14	Dallas Cowboys (M)	42	(55,256)
11/19	3	at Denver Broncos	16	(74,743)
11/26	10	Minnesota Vikings (OT)	10	(51,354)
12/3	17	at Tampa Bay Bucaneers	7	(67,754)
12/10	0	at Chicago Bears	14	(34,306)
12/17	14	at Los Angeles Rams	31	(42,500)

Score By Periods

	1	2	3	4	Total
Packers	77	58	66	48	249
Opponents	20	84	83	82	269

INDIVIDUAL STATISTICS

Rushing

	Att	Yds	Avg	LG	TD
Middleton	284	1,116	3.9	t76	11
Barty Smith	154	567	3.7	33	4
Culbreath	30	92	3.1	15	0
Whitehurst	28	67	2.4	18	1
N. Simpson	27	58	2.1	11	0
Landers	7	40	5.7	10	0
B. Douglass	4	27	6.8	17	0
Aundra Thompson	4	25	6.3	13	0
Torkelson	6	18	3.0	6	0
Lofton	3	13	4.3	15	0
Beverly	1	0	0.0	0	0
Sproul	2	0	0.0	0	0
Packers	**550**	**2,023**	**3.7**	**t76**	**16**
Opponents	620	2,439	3.9	t33	19

Receiving

	No	Yds	Avg	LG	TD
Lofton	46	818	17.8	t58	6
Barty Smith	37	256	6.9	24	0
Middleton	34	332	9.8	50	1
Aundra Thompson	26	527	20.3	57	2
McGeorge	23	247	10.7	25	1
Culbreath	7	78	11.1	19	0
Odom	4	60	15.0	18	1
Torkelson	2	36	18.0	31	0
N. Simpson	1	4	4.0	4	0
Packers	**180**	**2,358**	**13.1**	**t58**	**11**
Opponents	254	2,910	11.5	53	16

Passing

	Att	Com	Yds	Pct	TD	In	Tk/Yds	Rate
Whitehurst	328	168	2,093	51.2	10	17	35/258	59.9
B. Douglass	12	5	90	41.7	1	1	1/9	61.1
Beverly	2	2	88	100.0	0	0	0/0	—
Sproul	13	5	87	38.5	0	0	1/7	62.0
Lofton	2	0	0	00.0	0	0	0/0	—
Packers	**357**	**180**	**2,358**	**50.4**	**11**	**18**	**37/274**	**60.9**
Opponents	463	254	2,910	54.9	16	27	48/386	61.2

Punting

	No	Yds	Avg	In20	TB	LG	HB
Beverly	106	3,759	35.5	20	9	57	0
Packers	**106**	**3,759**	**35.5**	**20**	**9**	**57**	**0**
Opponents	90	3,411	37.9	24	6	61	1

Kickoff Returns

	No	Yds	Avg	LG	TD
Odom	25	677	27.1	t95	1
Aundra Thompson	6	124	20.7	31	0
S. Wagner	6	84	14.0	17	0
Culbreath	4	58	14.5	20	0
Hood	3	74	24.7	33	0
Sampson	1	23	23.0	23	0
Middleton	1	22	22.0	22	0
E. Johnson	1	14	14.0	14	0
Gueno	1	9	9.0	9	0
Landers	1	0	0.0	0	0
Lofton	1	0	0.0	0	0
McGeorge	1	0	0.0	0	0
Barty Smith	1	0	0.0	0	0
Packers	**52**	**1,085**	**20.9**	**t95**	**1**
Opponents	52	1,015	19.5	32	0

Punt Returns

	No	Yds	Avg	FC	LG	TD
Odom	33	298	9.0	7	48	0
J. Gray	11	95	8.6	6	22	0
Sampson	1	0	0.0	0	0	0
Tullis	1	0	0.0	0	0	0
Packers	**46**	**393**	**8.5**	**13**	**48**	**0**
Opponents	51	286	5.6	22	16	0

Interceptions

	No	Yds	Avg	LG	TD
Buchanon	9	93	10.3	t77	1
J. Anderson	5	27	5.4	12	0
J. Gray	3	66	22.0	66	0
M.C. McCoy	3	34	11.3	23	0
Hood	3	18	6.0	18	0
Luke	2	91	45.5	t63	1
M. Hunt	1	10	10.0	10	0
Barzilauskas	1	5	5.0	5	0
Packers	**27**	**344**	**12.7**	**t77**	**2**
Opponents	18	262	14.6	t44	1

Scoring

	TDr	TDp	TDrt	PAT	FG	S	TP
Middleton	11	1	0	0/0	0/0	0	72
Marcol	0	0	0	30/30	11/19	0	63
Lofton	0	6	0	0/0	0/0	0	36
Barty Smith	4	0	0	0/0	0/0	0	24
Odom	0	1	1	0/0	0/0	0	12
Aundra Thompson	0	2	0	0/0	0/0	0	12
Buchanon	0	0	1	0/0	0/0	0	6
Landers	1	0	0	0/0	0/0	0	6
Luke	0	0	1	0/0	0/0	0	6
McGeorge	0	1	0	0/0	0/0	0	6
Whitehurst	1	0	0	0/0	0/0	0	6
Packers	**16**	**11**	**4**	**30/31**	**11/19**	**0**	**249**
Opponents	19	16	1	36/36	5/18	1	269

Fumbles

	Fum	Ow	Op	Yds	Tot
J. Anderson	0	0	1	0	1
Barber	0	0	1	0	1
Beverly	1	0	0	-11	0
Buchanon	0	0	1	0	1
Jim Carter	0	0	2	0	2
Culbreath	1	0	0	0	0
M. Douglass	0	0	2	0	2
J. Gray	0	0	2	0	2
Hood	0	0	1	0	1
M. Hunt	0	0	1	0	1
E. Johnson	0	0	2	0	2
Lofton	2	0	0	0	0
Luke	0	0	2	0	2
M.C. McCoy	2	0	1	0	1
Middleton	8	0	0	0	0
Nuzum	0	0	1	15	1
Odom	2	1	0	0	1
Roller	0	1	1	-2	2
Sampson	1	0	0	0	0
N. Simpson	1	0	0	0	0
Barty Smith	5	1	0	0	1
Sproul	2	1	0	-5	1
Aundra Thompson	1	1	0	0	1
Torkelson	0	0	1	0	1
Weaver	0	0	1	0	1
Whitehurst	8	2	0	-28	0
Packers	**35**	**7**	**20**	**-31**	**27**

NFL STANDINGS

National Conference

Eastern Division

	W	L	T	Pct	PF	PA
Dallas Cowboys	12	4	0	.750	384	208
Philadelphia Eagles	9	7	0	.563	270	250
Washington Redskins	8	8	0	.500	273	283
St. Louis Cardinals	6	10	0	.375	248	296
New York Giants	6	10	0	.375	264	298

Central Division

	W	L	T	Pct	PF	PA
Minnesota Vikings	8	7	1	.531	294	306
Green Bay Packers	**8**	**7**	**1**	**.531**	**249**	**269**
Detroit Lions	7	9	0	.438	290	300
Chicago Bears	7	9	0	.438	253	274
Tampa Bay Buccaneers	5	11	0	.313	241	259

Western Division

	W	L	T	Pct	PF	PA
Los Angeles Rams	12	4	0	.750	316	245
Atlanta Falcons	9	7	0	.563	240	290
New Orleans Saints	7	9	0	.438	281	298
San Francisco 49ers	2	14	0	.125	219	350

American Conference

Eastern Division

	W	L	T	Pct	PF	PA
New England Patriots	11	5	0	.688	358	286
Miami Dolphins	11	5	0	.688	372	254
New York Jets	8	8	0	.500	359	364
Buffalo Bills	5	11	0	.313	302	354
Baltimore Colts	5	11	0	.313	239	421

Central Division

	W	L	T	Pct	PF	PA
Pittsburgh Steelers	14	2	0	.875	356	195
Houston Oilers	10	6	0	.625	283	298
Cleveland Browns	8	8	0	.500	334	356
Cincinnati Bengals	4	12	0	.250	252	284

Western Division

	W	L	T	Pct	PF	PA
Denver Broncos	10	6	0	.625	282	198
Oakland Raiders	9	7	0	.563	311	283
Seattle Seahawks	9	7	0	.563	345	358
San Diego Chargers	9	7	0	.563	355	309
Kansas City Chiefs	4	12	0	.250	243	327

1978 ROSTER

No	Name	Pos	Ht	Wt	DOB	College	G
60	Anderson, John	LB	6-3	221	02/14/56	Michigan	13
70	Barber, Bob	DE	6-3	240	12/26/51	Grambling	16
75	Barzilauskas, Carl	DT	6-6	265	03/19/51	Indiana	16
11	Beverly, David	P	6-2	180	08/19/50	Auburn	16
85	Boyd, Elmo	WR	6-0	188	06/15/54	Eastern Kentucky	2
28	Buchanon, Willie	CB	6-0	190	11/04/50	San Diego State	16
77	Butler, Mike	DE	6-5	265	04/04/54	Kansas	16
50	Carter, Jim	LB	6-3	245	10/18/48	Minnesota	14
53	Chesley, Francis	LB	6-3	219	07/14/55	Wyoming	1
82	Coffman, Paul	TE	6-3	218	03/29/56	Kansas State	16
31	Culbreath, Jim	RB	6-0	210	10/21/52	Oklahoma	12
19	Douglass, Bobby	QB	6-4	225	06/22/48	Kansas	12
65	Douglass, Mike	LB	6-0	224	03/15/55	San Diego State	16
57	Gofourth, Derrel	C	6-3	260	03/20/55	Oklahoma State	16
24	Gray, Johnnie	S	5-11	185	12/18/53	Cal State-Fullerton	16
51	Gueno, Jim	LB	6-2	220	01/15/54	Tulane	15
69	Harris, Leotis	G	6-1	267	06/28/55	Arkansas	13
38	Hood, Estus	CB	5-11	180	11/14/55	Illinois State	16
55	Hunt, Mike	LB	6-2	240	10/06/56	Minnesota	16
71	Jackson, Mel	G	6-1	267	05/05/54	USC	16
58	Johnson, Danny	LB	6-1	216	05/07/55	Tennessee State	16
78	Johnson, Ezra	DE	6-4	240	10/02/55	Morris Brown	16
63	Jones, Terry	DT	6-2	259	11/08/56	Alabama	16
68	Koch, Greg	T	6-4	265	06/14/55	Arkansas	16
42	Landers, Walt	FB	6-0	214	07/04/53	Clark	4
80	Lofton, James	WR	6-3	187	07/05/56	Stanford	16
46	Luke, Steve	S	6-2	205	09/04/53	Ohio State	16
13	Marcol, Chester	K	6-0	190	10/24/49	Hillsdale	16
54	McCarren, Larry	C	6-3	248	11/09/51	Illinois	16
29	McCoy, Mike C.	CB	5-11	183	08/16/53	Colorado	16
81	McGeorge, Rich	TE	6-4	230	09/14/48	Elon	16
34	Middleton, Terdell	HB	6-0	195	04/08/55	Memphis State	16
56	Nuzum, Rick	C	6-4	238	06/30/52	Kentucky	16
84	Odom, Steve	WR	5-8	174	09/05/52	Utah	12
74	Roller, Dave	DT	6-2	270	10/28/49	Kentucky	16
66	Rudzinski, Paul	LB	6-1	220	07/28/56	Michigan State	16
36	Sampson, Howard	DB	5-10	185	07/07/56	Arkansas	15
48	Simpson, Nate	RB	5-11	190	11/30/54	Tennessee State	16
73	Skinner, Gerald	T	6-4	260	01/12/54	Arkansas	16
33	Smith, Barty	FB	6-3	240	03/23/52	Richmond	16
16	Sproul, Dennis	QB	6-2	210	07/17/56	Arizona	6
76	Stokes, Tim	T	6-5	252	03/16/50	Oregon	16
89	Taylor, Willie	WR	6-1	179	12/09/55	Pittsburgh	1
43	Thompson, Aundra	WR	6-0	186	01/02/53	East Texas State	16
26	Torkelson, Eric	RB	6-2	194	03/03/52	Connecticut	14
20	Tullis, Walter	WR	6-0	170	04/12/53	Delaware State	16
21	Wagner, Steve	S	6-2	208	04/18/54	Wisconsin	16
52	Weaver, Gary	LB	6-1	225	03/13/49	Fresno State	16
17	Whitehurst, David	QB	6-2	204	04/27/55	Furman	16

1978 DRAFT

Rnd	Name	Pos	Ht	Wt	College
1a	James Lofton (6)	WR	6-3	187	Stanford
1b	John Anderson (26)	LB	6-3	221	Michigan
	(Choice from Raiders for Mike P. McCoy)				
2	Mike Hunt (34)	LB	6-2	240	Minnesota
3	Estus Hood (62)	DB	5-11	180	Illinois State
4	(Choice declared forfeit by comissioner Pete Rozelle for scouting violations)				
5a	Mike Douglass (116)	LB	6-0	224	San Diego State
5b	Willie Wilder (128)	RB	6-1	200	Florida
	(Choice from Steelers in Dave Pureifory trade)				

Rnd	Name	Pos	Ht	Wt	College
6	Leotis Harris (144)	G	6-1	267	Arkansas
7	George Plasketes (172)	LB	6-0	220	Mississippi
8	Dennis Sproul (200)	QB	6-2	210	Arizona State
9	Keith Myers (228)	QB	6-2	190	Utah State
10a	Larry Key (256)	RB	5-9	193	Florida State
10b	Mark Totten (259)	C	6-3	288	Florida
	(Choice from Giants in Joe Danelo deal)				
11	Terry Jones (284)	DT	6-2	259	Alabama
12	Eason Ramson (312)	TE	6-2	221	Washington State

1978 GREEN BAY PACKERS

FRONT ROW: (L-R) 38 Estus Hood, 29 Mike C. McCoy, 24 Johnnie Gray, 46 Steve Luke, 28 Willie Buchanon, 20 Walter Tullis, 13 Chester Marcol, 84 Steve Odom, 43 Aundra Thompson, 48 Nate Simpson, 42 Walt Landers, 36 Howard Sampson.

SECOND ROW: (L-R) Equipment Assistant Jack Noel, Team Physician Dr. Eugene Brusky, Trainer Domenic Gentile, Equipment Manager Bob Noel, Quarterbacks Coach Zeke Bratkowski, Offensive Line Assistant Ernie McMillan, Head Coach Bart Starr, Assistant Head Coach/Defensive Coordinator Dave Hanner, Passing Game Coach Lew Carpenter, Defensive Backfield Coach Dick LeBeau, Linebackers Coach John Meyer, Offensive Line Coach Bill Curry, Offensive Backfield Coach Bob Lord.

THIRD ROW: (L-R) Film Director Al Treml, Groundskeeper Earl DuChateau, 71 Mel Jackson, 79 Mark Koncar, 54 Larry McCarren, 57 Derrel Gofourth, 65 Mike Douglass, 16 Dennis Sproul, 55 Mike Hunt, 19 Bobby Douglass, 17 David Whitehurst, Assistant Trainer Jim Popp, Special Teams Coach Burt Gustafson.

FOURTH ROW: (L-R) 69 Leotis Harris, 26 Eric Torkelson, 81 Rich McGeorge, 33 Barty Smith, 80 James Lofton, 74 Dave Roller, 66 Paul Rudzinski, 51 Jim Gueno, 21 Steve Wagner, 60 John Anderson, 63 Terry Jones.

BACK ROW: (L-R) 34 Terdell Middleton, 73 Gerald Skinner, 68 Greg Koch, 76 Tim Stokes, 78 Ezra Johnson, 77 Mike Butler, 75 Carl Barzilauskas, 70 Bob Barber, 56 Rick Nuzum, 82 Paul Coffman, 52 Gary Weaver, 50 Jim Carter.

On September 2 in Chicago, first-round pick Eddie Lee Ivery made his professional football debut. The rookie running back flashed some real promise, gaining 24 yards in three carries. Unfortunately, the former Georgia Tech standout tore up his left knee the third time he handled the ball. After breaking through the line on a draw play in the second quarter, Ivery veered to the outside then planted his foot to break upfield. Instead of turning an 11-yard gain into something bigger, No. 40 fell to the artificial turf, fumbled and held on to his leg in agony. Torn cartilage and damage to the anterior cruciate ligament in his knee ended his year.

The loss of Ivery and the game (6-3) was followed by a rash of injuries. Before the season ended, Mike Hunt, Barty Smith, Bobby Kimball and Steve Atkins fell victim to season-ending knee injuries. Mark Koncar (ankle), John Anderson (broken arm), Terdell Middleton (separated shoulder), Ezra Johnson (ankle) and Mike Butler (dislocated elbow) were just some of the others who missed more than one game because of physical ailments.

The fourth losing season under Starr was not without its stressful moments. James Lofton had a run-in with the coach after the team played it safe at Minnesota by calling three running plays in the last 1:41 of regulation only to lose 27-21 in overtime without getting another shot at the ball. Weeks later, Lofton made an obscene gesture to the crowd after being booed for dropping passes and fumbling away a potential score in a 27-22 loss to the Jets. Earlier, David Whitehurst's comeback ability had come under fire following a 21-10 setback to Tampa Bay, seething Starr. In addition, the *Milwaukee Journal's* Dave Begel profiled the head coach as unfeeling and out of touch with his players.

To its credit, the team stuck together and even put together a thrilling weekend or two of football. Green Bay hosted its first Monday Night Football game on October 1. Few gave the 1-3 Packers much of a chance against New England, 1978's AFC Eastern Division champions. Undaunted, a fired-up defense forced six turnovers and paved the way for a 27-14 upset.

Just over a month later, the Packers defeated the Vikings 19-7 in Milwaukee. Middleton registered the final 100-yard rushing game (27-135) of his career and Green Bay defeated Minnesota for the first time since 1974.

Defense was the Packers' biggest weakness. Opponents ran at will (639 times for 2,885 yards) and piled up 5,647 total yards. Green Bay gave up more than 400 yards five times, and in all but four contests, the Packers were outgained.

Defensive coordinator Dave Hanner paid the price for the defensive woes. In late December, the man who had spent 28 years with the organization was fired by Starr after declining to tender his resignation. The former defensive tackle had logged more years as a Packers player and coach than any other, short of Curly Lambeau himself.

Green Bay Press-Gazette photo

Paul Coffman (82) heads for the end zone in a 24-16 victory over Detroit in Milwaukee. His 13-yard, third-quarter reception gave the Packers a 17-9 lead. Coffman led all Green Bay receivers with 56 catches in 1979. He made the team in 1978 as a free agent after practically having to beg for a tryout. By the time he departed, Coffman had moved into fifth place on the team's all-time receiving list.

TEAM STATISTICS

	GB	OPP
First Downs	279	327
Rushing	121	162
Passing	133	146
Penalty	25	19
Rushes	483	639
Yards Gained	1,861	2,885
Average Gain	3.85	4.51
Average Yards per Game	116.3	180.3
Passes Attempted	444	440
Completed	240	249
% Completed	54.05	56.59
Total Yards Gained	3,057	3,041
Times Sacked	47	35
Yards Lost	376	279
Net Yards Gained	2,681	2,762
Yards Gained per Completion	12.74	12.21
Net Yards per Attempt	5.46	5.81
Average Net Yards per Game	167.6	172.6
Combined Net Yards Gained	4,542	5,647
Total Plays	974	1,114
Average Yards per Play	4.66	5.07
Average Net Yards per Game	283.9	352.9
Third Down Efficiency	85/224	114/248
Percentage	37.95	45.97
Intercepted By	18	22
Yards Returned	243	247
Returned for TD	0	2
Punts	69	64
Yards Punted	2,785	2,516
Average Yards per Punt	40.36	39.31
Punt Returns	28	43
Yards Returned	141	305
Average Yards per Return	5.04	7.09
Returned for TD	0	0
Kickoff Returns	61	50
Yards Returned	1,295	999
Average Yards per Return	21.23	20.00
Returned for TD	1	0
Penalties	93	106
Yards Penalized	681	912
Fumbles	37	30
Lost	22	14
Own Recovered for Touchdown	0	0
Opponent's Recovered by	14	22
Opponent's Recovered for Touchdown	1	0
Total Points Scored	246	316
Total Touchdowns	31	37
Touchdowns Rushing	14	14
Touchdowns Passing	15	21
Touchdowns on Returns & Recoveries	2	2
Extra Points	24	32
Safeties	0	1
Field Goals Attempted	20	33
Field Goals Made	12	20
% Successful	60.00	60.60
Average Time of Possession	27:55	32:05

Regular Season   5-11-0

Date	GB		OPP		Att.
9/2	3	at Chicago Bears	6		(56,515)
9/9	28	New Orleans Saints (M)	19		(53,184)
9/16	10	Tampa Bay Buccaneers	21		(55,498)
9/23	21	at Minnesota Vikings (OT)	27		(46,524)
10/1	27	New England Patriots	14		(52,842)
10/7	7	at Atlanta Falcons	25		(56,184)
10/14	24	Detroit Lions (M)	16		(53,950)
10/21	3	at Tampa Bay Buccaneers	21		(67,186)
10/28	7	at Miami Dolphins	27		(47,741)
11/4	22	New York Jets	27		(54,201)
11/11	19	Minnesota Vikings (M)	7		(52,706)
11/18	12	at Buffalo Bills	19		(39,679)
11/25	10	Philadelphia Eagles	21		(50,023)
12/2	21	at Washington Redskins	38		(51,682)
12/9	14	Chicago Bears	15		(54,207)
12/15	18	at Detroit Lions	13		(57,376)

Score By Periods

	1	2	3	4	OT	Total
Packers	35	79	64	48	0	246
Opponents	61	90	68	91	6	316

INDIVIDUAL STATISTICS

Rushing

	Att	Yds	Avg	LG	TD
Middleton	131	495	3.8	28	2
Torkelson	98	401	4.1	15	3
Atkins	42	239	5.7	60	1
N. Simpson	66	235	3.6	22	1
Barty Smith	57	201	3.5	23	3
Patton	37	134	3.6	14	0
Whitehurst	18	73	4.1	17	4
Landers	17	41	2.4	14	0
Ivery	3	24	8.0	11	0
Wagner	1	16	16.0	16	0
Dickey	5	13	2.6	8	0
Culbreath	5	8	1.6	6	0
Lofton	1	-1	-1.0	-1	0
Aundra Thompson	2	-18	-9.0	-7	0
Packers	483	1,861	3.9	60	14
Opponents	639	2,885	4.5	80	14

1979

Receiving

	No	Yds	Avg	LG	TD
Coffman	56	711	12.7	t78	4
Lofton	54	968	17.9	52	4
Aundra Thompson	25	395	15.8	50	3
Barty Smith	19	155	8.2	22	1
Torkelson	19	139	7.3	14	0
Middleton	18	155	8.6	29	1
N. Simpson	11	46	4.2	10	0
Tullis	10	173	17.3	t52	1
Atkins	10	89	8.9	19	0
Cassidy	6	102	17.0	23	0
Patton	6	41	6.8	9	0
Landers	5	60	12.0	t55	1
Gueno	1	23	23.0	23	0
Packers	240	3,057	12.7	t78	15
Opponents	249	3,041	12.2	t50	21

Passing

	Att	Com	Yds	Pct	TD	In	Tk/Yds	Rate
Whitehurst	322	179	2,247	55.6	10	18	32/256	64.5
Dickey	119	60	787	50.4	5	4	15/120	71.7
Beverly	2	1	23	50.0	0	0	0/0	—
Lofton	1	0	0	00.0	0	0	0/0	—
Packers	444	240	3,057	54.1	15	22	47/376	66.4
Opponents	440	249	3,041	56.6	21	18	35/279	76.9

Punting

	No	Yds	Avg	In20	TB	LG	HB
Beverly	69	2,785	40.4	11	4	65	0
Packers	69	2,785	40.4	11	4	65	0
Opponents	64	2,516	39.3	21	10	68	0

Kickoff Returns

	No	Yds	Avg	LG	TD
Odom	29	622	21.4	31	0
Aundra Thompson	15	346	23.1	t100	1
M.C. McCoy	11	248	22.5	41	0
Sampson	4	61	15.3	21	0
Wellman	1	10	10.0	10	0
S. Wagner	1	8	8.0	8	0
Packers	61	1,295	21.2	t100	1
Opponents	50	999	20.0	69	0

Punt Returns

	No	Yds	Avg	FC	LG	TD
Odom	15	80	5.3	5	19	0
J. Gray	13	61	4.7	8	18	0
Packers	28	141	5.0	13	19	0
Opponents	43	305	7.1	7	19	0

Interceptions

	No	Yds	Avg	LG	TD
J. Gray	5	66	13.2	35	0
M. Douglass	3	73	24.3	46	0
M.C. McCoy	3	60	20.0	38	0
Wingo	2	13	6.5	13	0
Hood	2	8	4.0	6	0
M. Hunt	1	13	13.0	13	0
Luke	1	10	10.0	10	0
Charles Johnson	1	0	0.0	0	0
Packers	18	243	13.5	46	0
Opponents	22	247	11.2	66	2

Scoring

	TDr	TDp	TDrt	PAT	FG	S	TP
Birney	0	0	0	7/10	7/9	0	28
Marcol	0	0	0	16/18	4/10	0	28
Coffman	0	4	0	0/0	0/0	0	24
Lofton	0	4	0	0/0	0/0	0	24
Barty Smith	3	1	0	0/0	0/0	0	24
Aundra Thompson	0	3	1	0/0	0/0	0	24
Whitehurst	4	0	0	0/0	0/0	0	24
Middleton	2	1	0	0/0	0/0	0	18
Torkelson	3	0	0	0/0	0/0	0	18
Atkins	1	0	0	0/0	0/0	0	6
M. Butler	0	0	1	0/0	0/0	0	6
Landers	0	1	0	0/0	0/0	0	6
N. Simpson	1	0	0	0/0	0/0	0	6
Tullis	0	1	0	0/0	0/0	0	6
J. Anderson	0	0	0	0/2	1/1	0	4
Packers	14	15	2	24/31	12/20	0	246
Opponents	14	21	2	32/36	20/33	1	316

Fumbles

	Fum	Ow	Op	Yds	Tot
J. Anderson	0	0	1	0	1
Atkins	1	0	0	0	0
Barber	0	0	1	0	1
Barzilauskas	0	0	1	0	1
M. Butler	0	0	1	70	1
Coffman	4	0	0	0	0
Culbreath	0	0	1	0	1
Dickey	2	1	0	-1	1
J. Gray	3	1	3	0	4
L. Harris	0	0	1	0	1
Ivery	1	0	0	0	0
Charles Johnson	0	0	1	0	1
Terry Jones	0	0	1	0	1
Lathrop	0	1	0	0	1
Lofton	5	0	0	0	0
Luke	0	0	1	0	1
M.C. McCoy	1	0	2	0	2
Middleton	2	0	0	0	0
Odom	4	0	0	0	0
Patton	1	0	0	0	0
N. Simpson	1	0	1	0	1
Barty Smith	1	0	0	0	0
Aundra Thompson	3	1	0	0	1
J. Thompson	3	2	0	0	2
Weaver	0	0	1	0	1
Whitehurst	9	0	0	0	0
Wingo	0	0	1	0	1
Packers	37	11	14	69	25

NFL STANDINGS

National Conference

Eastern Division

	W	L	T	Pct	PF	PA
Dallas Cowboys	11	5	0	.688	371	313
Philadelphia Eagles	11	5	0	.688	339	282
Washington Redskins	10	6	0	.625	348	295
New York Giants	6	10	0	.375	237	323
St. Louis Cardinals	5	11	0	.313	307	358

Central Division

	W	L	T	Pct	PF	PA
Tampa Bay Buccaneers	10	6	0	.625	273	237
Chicago Bears	10	6	0	.625	306	249
Minnesota Vikings	7	9	0	.438	259	337
Green Bay Packers	5	11	0	.313	246	316
Detroit Lions	2	14	0	.125	219	365

Western Division

	W	L	T	Pct	PF	PA
Los Angeles Rams	9	7	0	.563	323	309
New Orleans Saints	8	8	0	.500	370	360
Atlanta Falcons	6	10	0	.375	300	388
San Francisco 49ers	2	14	0	.125	308	416

American Conference

Eastern Division

	W	L	T	Pct	PF	PA
Miami Dolphins	10	6	0	.625	341	257
New England Patriots	9	7	0	.563	411	326
New York Jets	8	8	0	.500	337	383
Buffalo Bills	7	9	0	.438	268	279
Baltimore Colts	5	11	0	.313	271	351

Central Division

	W	L	T	Pct	PF	PA
Pittsburgh Steelers	12	4	0	.750	416	262
Houston Oilers	11	5	0	.688	362	331
Cleveland Browns	9	7	0	.563	359	352
Cincinnati Bengals	4	12	0	.250	337	421

Western Division

	W	L	T	Pct	PF	PA
San Diego Chargers	12	4	0	.750	411	246
Denver Broncos	10	6	0	.625	289	262
Seattle Seahawks	9	7	0	.563	378	372
Oakland Raiders	9	7	0	.563	365	337
Kansas City Chiefs	7	9	0	.438	238	262

1979 ROSTER

No	Name	Pos	Ht	Wt	DOB	College	G
59	Anderson, John	LB	6-3	221	02/14/56	Michigan	7
32	Atkins, Steve	RB	6-0	216	06/22/56	Maryland	7
70	Barber, Bob	DE	6-3	240	12/26/51	Grambling	16
75	Barzilauskas, Carl	DT	6-6	265	03/19/51	Indiana	5
11	Beverly, David	P	6-2	180	08/19/50	Auburn	16
19	Birney, Tom	K	6-4	220	08/11/56	Michigan	6
77	Butler, Mike	DE	6-5	265	04/04/54	Kansas	14
88	Cassidy, Ron	WR	6-0	175	07/23/57	Utah State	8
82	Coffman, Paul	TE	6-3	218	03/29/56	Kansas State	16
31	Culbreath, Jim	RB	6-0	210	10/21/52	Oklahoma	4
10	Dickey, Lynn	QB	6-4	220	10/19/49	Kansas State	5
53	Douglass, Mike	LB	6-0	224	03/15/55	San Diego State	16
73	Edwards, Earl	DT	6-6	260	03/17/46	Wichita State	9
57	Gofourth, Derrel	C	6-3	260	03/20/55	Oklahoma State	16
24	Gray, Johnnie	S	5-11	185	12/18/53	Cal State-Fullerton	16
51	Gueno, Jim	LB	6-2	220	01/15/54	Tulane	16
69	Harris, Leotis	G	6-1	267	06/28/55	Arkansas	15
38	Hood, Estus	CB	5-11	180	11/14/55	Illinois State	16
55	Hunt, Mike	LB	6-2	240	10/06/56	Minnesota	3
40	Ivery, Eddie Lee	RB	6-1	210	07/30/57	Georgia Tech	1
71	Jackson, Mel	G	6-1	267	05/05/54	USC	16
99	Johnson, Charles	DT	6-1	262	06/29/57	Maryland	16
90	Johnson, Ezra	DE	6-4	240	10/02/55	Morris Brown	11
39	Johnson, Sammy	RB	6-1	226	09/22/52	North Carolina	3
63	Jones, Terry	DT	6-2	259	11/08/56	Alabama	12
85	Kimball, Bobby	WR	6-1	190	03/12/57	Oklahoma	7
68	Koch, Greg	T	6-4	265	06/14/55	Arkansas	16
79	Koncar, Mark	T	6-5	268	05/05/53	Colorado	12
42	Landers, Walt	FB	6-0	214	07/04/53	Clark	9
72	Lathrop, Kit	DT	6-5	253	05/10/56	Arizona State	2
80	Lofton, James	WR	6-3	187	07/05/56	Stanford	16
46	Luke, Steve	S	6-2	205	09/04/53	Ohio State	16
13	Marcol, Chester	K	6-0	190	10/24/49	Hillsdale	10
54	McCarren, Larry	C	6-3	248	11/09/51	Illinois	16
29	McCoy, Mike C.	CB	5-11	183	08/16/53	Colorado	16
62	McLaughlin, Joe	LB	6-1	235	07/01/57	Massachusetts	3
78	Merrill, Casey	DE	6-4	255	07/16/57	California-Davis	11
34	Middleton, Terdell	HB	6-0	195	04/08/55	Memphis State	14
84	Odom, Steve	WR	5-8	174	09/05/52	Utah	9
30	Patton, Ricky	RB	5-11	189	04/06/54	Jackson State	6
66	Rudzinski, Paul	LB	6-1	220	07/28/56	Michigan State	11
36	Sampson, Howard	CB	5-10	185	07/07/56	Arkansas	16
61	Simmons, Davie	LB	6-4	218	01/19/57	North Carolina	16
48	Simpson, Nate	RB	5-11	190	11/30/54	Tennessee State	15
33	Smith, Barty	FB	6-3	240	03/23/52	Richmond	6
58	Stewart, Steve	LB	6-3	215	05/01/56	Minnesota	3
76	Stokes, Tim	T	6-5	252	03/16/50	Oregon	16
89	Thompson, Aundra	WR	6-0	186	01/02/53	East Texas State	15
83	Thompson, John	TE	6-3	228	01/18/57	Utah State	16
26	Torkelson, Eric	RB	6-2	194	03/03/52	Connecticut	14
87	Tullis, Walter	WR	6-0	170	04/12/53	Delaware State	16
20	Turner, Wylie	CB	5-10	182	04/19/57	Angelo State	12
21	Wagner, Steve	S	6-2	208	04/18/54	Wisconsin	16
52	Weaver, Gary	LB	6-1	225	03/13/49	Fresno State	14
65	Wellman, Mike	C	6-3	253	07/15/56	Kansas	16
17	Whitehurst, David	QB	6-2	204	04/27/55	Furman	13
50	Wingo, Rich	LB	6-1	230	07/16/56	Alabama	16

1979 DRAFT

Rnd	Name	Pos	Ht	Wt	College
1	Eddie Lee Ivery (15)	RB	6-0	210	Georgia Tech
2	Steve Atkins (44)	RB	6-0	216	Maryland
3	Charles Johnson (71)	DT	6-1	262	Maryland
4a	(Choice (98) to Jets as part of Carl Barzilauskas deal)				
4b	(Choice (103) from Raiders for Mike P. McCoy to Redskins for Tim Stokes)				
5	(Choice (125) to Jets as part of Carl Barzilauskas deal)				
6	Davie Simmons (153)	LB	6-4	218	North Carolina
7a	Henry Monroe (180)	DB	5-10	180	Mississippi State
7b	Rich Wingo (184)	LB	6-1	230	Alabama
	(Choice from Chargers as part of Willie Buchanon deal)				
8a	Ron Cassidy (193)	WR	6-0	175	Utah State
	(Choice from 49ers for Steve Knutson)				
8b	Rick Partridge (208)	P	6-1	175	Utah
9	John Thompson (235)	TE	6-3	228	Utah State
10	Frank Lockett (264)	WR	5-11	192	Nebraska
11	Mark Thorson (290)	DB	5-10	188	Ottawa
12	Bill Moats (318)	P	5-11	177	South Dakota

1979 GREEN BAY PACKERS

FRONT ROW: (L-R) 48 Nate Simpson, 71 Mel Jackson, 79 Mark Koncar, 77 Mike Butler, 55 Mike Hunt, 11 David Beverly, 34 Terdell Middleton, 58 Steve Stewart, 89 Aundra Thompson, 84 Steve Odom, 54 Larry McCarren, 33 Barty Smith, 26 Eric Torkelson, 13 Chester Marcol.

SECOND ROW: (L-R) Equipment Assistant Jack Noel, Equipment Manager Bob Noel, Offensive Backfield Coach Zeke Bratkowski, Special Assistant Dick Rehbein, Special Teams Coach Fred vonAppen, Passing Game Coach Lew Carpenter, Assistant Head Coach/Defensive Coordinator Dave Hanner, Head Coach Bart Starr, Linebackers Coach John Meyer, Offensive Line Assistant Ernie McMillan, Defensive Backfield Coach Dick LeBeau, Offensive Line Coach Bill Curry, Orthopedic Consultant Dr. James W. Nellen, Assistant Trainer Jim Popp.

THIRD ROW: (L-R) 46 Steve Luke, 38 Estus Hood, 29 Mike C. McCoy, 40 Eddie Lee Ivery, 42 Walt Landers, 43 Henry Monroe, 36 Howard Sampson, 50 Rich Wingo, 85 Bobby Kimball, 24 Johnnie Gray, 82 Paul Coffman, 17 David Whitehurst, 52 Gary Weaver.

FOURTH ROW: (L-R) Groundskeeper Earl DuChateau, 31 Jim Culbreath, 88 Ron Cassidy, 65 Mike Wellman, 61 Davie Simmons, 63 Terry Jones, 87 Walter Tullis, 80 James Lofton, 53 Mike Douglass, 99 Charles Johnson, 51 Jim Gueno, 21 Steve Wagner, 59 John Anderson, 32 Steve Atkins, Film Director Al Treml.

BACK ROW: (L-R) Team Physician Dr. Eugene Brusky, 78 Casey Merrill, 57 Derrel Gofourth, 76 Tim Stokes, 68 Greg Koch, 10 Lynn Dickey, 90 Ezra Johnson, 75 Carl Barzilauskas, 69 Leotis Harris, 70 Bob Barber, 83 John Thompson, Trainer Domenic Gentile.

Opening day. After 60 minutes of play, the Bears and Packers were deadlocked 6-6. Six minutes into overtime, the Packers' Chester Marcol lined up for his third field goal try only to have it blocked. Amazingly, the ball bounced back into his arms and he hot-footed 25 yards to the endzone to give his team a 12-6 win.

Marcol, who was swarmed under by his teammates, didn't last the season. Aside from the bizarre opener, there was precious little to celebrate in a year that included a 51-21 beating in Los Angeles and a 61-7 trouncing in the rematch with the Bears. After Green Bay finished 5-10-1, Bart Starr was stripped of his general manager duties.

Warning signs appeared shortly after draft day. First-round draft choice Bruce Clark shunned Green Bay for the Toronto Argonauts of the CFL. The team's other top pick, George Cumby, underwent knee surgery on August 1 and was lost until midseason. David Whitehurst stretched knee ligaments at about the same time and the Packers scrambled to land a backup quarterback, trading for the likes of Randy Dean and Mark Miller. Then, Green Bay stumbled through a winless preseason for the first time since 1946.

Under fire for the 0-4-1 preseason exhibition, Starr vowed not to resign and got a vote of confidence from team president Dominic Olejniczak. Instead, it was defensive line coach Fred von Appen who quit. Ezra Johnson, who answered to von Appen, caused a stir by casually eating a hot dog on the bench in the second half of a 38-0 loss to Denver. Though Johnson apologized and was fined, von Appen resigned on September 3.

The euphoria of the initial Bears win quickly evaporated. Three lopsided losses followed as the Packers were pounded in order by the Lions (29-7), Rams (51-21) and Cowboys (28-7). The Rams loss had Lynn Dickey questioning whether or not he was "the guy for the quarterback job."

As it turned out, Dickey had little reason to doubt his ability. Relatively injury free and able to play a full season for the first time since arriving in Green Bay, he set then-team records with 278 completions in 478 attempts for 3,529 yards. In a 14-14 tie with Tampa Bay on October 12, he set single-game marks of 418 yards on 35 completions.

The Packers used the 3-4 as its primary defensive formation for the first time. First-year coordinator John Meyer was particularly upset with the results. Green Bay surrendered 5,782 yards, second most in franchise history.

Marcol was waived on October 8. His replacement Tom Birney proved unreliable, so Starr brought in the venerable Jan Stenerud. Stenerud, who became the most efficient kicker in team history, blew a game-tying 45-yarder against Tampa Bay with 21 seconds left. As a result, Green Bay couldn't force overtime, lost 20-17 and blew a chance to move a half-game behind the Central Division-leading Lions and Vikings.

After bungling its shot to move within striking distance of the division leaders, the team came full circle and endured three beatings reminiscent of its early struggles. On Pearl Harbor Day, the Bears destroyed Green Bay 61-7 and the Packers then bowed out with losses to Houston and Detroit. On December 27, the board of directors relieved Starr of his general manager duties.

Green Bay Press-Gazette photo

Chester Marcol (13) has his 24-yard field goal try blocked in the season-opener against the Chicago Bears in Lambeau Field. The ball shot back into Marcol's arms and he returned it 25 yards for the decisive touchdown in the Packers' 12-6 overtime win. Marcol was released in early October but not before he had ascended to fourth place on the team's all-time scoring list with 521 points.

TEAM STATISTICS

	GB	OPP
First Downs	307	316
Rushing	119	136
Passing	164	166
Penalty	24	14
Rushes	493	565
Yards Gained	1,806	2,399
Average Gain	3.66	4.25
Average Yards per Game	112.9	149.9
Passes Attempted	511	460
Completed	289	259
% Completed	56.56	56.30
Total Yards Gained	3,651	3,617
Times Sacked	43	34
Yards Lost	360	234
Net Yards Gained	3,291	3,383
Yards Gained per Completion	12.63	13.97
Net Yards per Attempt	5.94	6.85
Average Net Yards per Game	205.7	211.4
Combined Net Yards Gained	5,097	5,782
Total Plays	1,047	1,059
Average Yards per Play	4.87	5.46
Average Net Yards per Game	318.6	361.4
Third Down Efficiency	91/234	102/237
Percentage	38.89	43.04
Intercepted By	13	29
Yards Returned	92	483
Returned for TD	0	4
Punts	87	83
Yards Punted	3,327	3,247
Average Yards per Punt	38.24	39.12
Punt Returns	37	50
Yards Returned	297	342
Average Yards per Return	8.03	6.84
Returned for TD	0	0
Kickoff Returns	73	52
Yards Returned	1,415	902
Average Yards per Return	19.38	17.35
Returned for TD	0	0
Penalties	84	109
Yards Penalized	697	872
Fumbles	36	27
Lost	12	14
Own Recovered for Touchdown	0	0
Opponent's Recovered by	14	12
Opponent's Recovered for Touchdown	0	1
Total Points Scored	231	371
Total Touchdowns	29	43
Touchdowns Rushing	13	19
Touchdowns Passing	15	19
Touchdowns on Returns & Recoveries	1	5
Extra Points	24	36
Safeties	0	1
Field Goals Attempted	20	27
Field Goals Made	11	25
% Successful	55.00	92.59
Average Time of Possession	30:15	29:45

Regular Season   5-10-1

Date	GB		OPP	Att.
9/7	12	Chicago Bears (OT)	6	(54,381)
9/14	7	Detroit Lions (M)	29	(53,099)
9/21	21	at Los Angeles Rams	51	(63,850)
9/28	7	Dallas Cowboys (M)	28	(54,776)
10/5	14	Cincinnati Bengals	9	(55,006)
10/12	14	at TB Buccaneers (OT)	14	(64,854)
10/19	21	at Cleveland Browns	26	(75,548)
10/26	16	Minnesota Vikings	3	(55,361)
11/2	20	at Pittsburgh Steelers	22	(52,165)
11/9	23	San Francisco 49ers	16	(54,475)
11/16	21	at New York Giants	27	(72,368)
11/23	25	at Minnesota Vikings	13	(47,234)
11/30	17	Tampa Bay Buccaneers (M)	20	(54,225)
12/7	7	at Chicago Bears	61	(57,176)
12/14	3	Houston Oilers	22	(53,201)
12/21	3	at Detroit Lions	24	(75,111)

Score By Periods

	1	2	3	4	OT	Total
Packers	21	91	33	80	6	231
Opponents	64	135	65	107	0	371

INDIVIDUAL STATISTICS

Rushing

	Att	Yds	Avg	LG	TD
Ivery	202	831	4.1	t38	3
G. Ellis	126	545	4.3	22	5
Atkins	67	216	3.2	16	1
Middleton	56	155	2.8	15	2
Beverly	6	21	3.5	11	0
Huckleby	6	11	1.8	9	1
Dickey	19	11	0.6	t7	1
V. R. Anderson	4	5	1.3	4	0
Aundra Thompson	5	5	1.0	16	0
Coffman	1	3	3.0	3	0
Barty Smith	1	3	3.0	3	0
Packers	**493**	**1,806**	**3.7**	**38**	**13**
Opponents	565	2,399	4.2	48	19

Receiving

	No	Yds	Avg	LG	TD
Lofton	71	1,226	17.3	47	4
Ivery	50	481	9.6	t46	1
G. Ellis	48	496	10.3	t69	3
Coffman	42	496	11.8	25	3
Aundra Thompson	40	609	15.2	55	2
Middleton	13	59	4.5	17	0
Atkins	7	47	6.7	16	1
Cassidy	5	109	21.8	43	0
Nixon	4	78	19.5	32	0
B. Larson	4	37	9.3	21	1
Huckleby	3	11	3.7	8	0
V. R. Anderson	2	2	1.0	2	0
Packers	**289**	**3,651**	**12.6**	**t69**	**15**
Opponents	259	3,617	14.0	t87	19

Passing

	Att	Com	Yds	Pct	TD	In	Tk/Yds	Rate
Dickey	478	278	3,529	58.2	15	25	37/314	70.0
Whitehurst	15	5	55	33.3	0	1	3/19	17.4
Troup	12	4	48	33.3	0	3	2/20	6.9
Pisarkiewicz	5	2	19	40.0	0	0	1/7	—
Beverly	1	0	0	00.0	0	0	0/0	—
Packers	**511**	**289**	**3,651**	**56.6**	**15**	**29**	**43/360**	**65.1**
Opponents	460	259	3,617	56.3	19	13	34/234	83.8

Punting

	No	Yds	Avg	In20	TB	LG	HB
Beverly	86	3,294	38.3	18	6	55	0
Marcol	1	33	33.0	0	1	33	0
Packers	**87**	**3,327**	**38.2**	**18**	**7**	**55**	**0**
Opponents	83	3,247	39.1	23	11	61	1

Kickoff Returns

	No	Yds	Avg	LG	TD
M. Lee	30	589	19.6	35	0
Aundra Thompson	15	283	18.9	57	0
M.C. McCoy	14	261	18.6	32	0
Nixon	6	160	26.7	54	0
J. Gray	5	63	12.6	18	0
Huckleby	3	59	19.7	21	0
Packers	**73**	**1,415**	**19.4**	**57**	**0**
Opponents	52	902	17.3	59	0

Punt Returns

	No	Yds	Avg	FC	LG	TD
Cassidy	17	139	8.2	5	20	0
Nixon	11	85	7.7	2	16	0
M. Lee	5	32	6.4	0	17	0
J. Gray	4	41	10.3	2	16	0
Packers	**37**	**297**	**8.0**	**9**	**20**	**0**
Opponents	50	342	6.8	12	21	0

Interceptions

	No	Yds	Avg	LG	TD
J. Gray	5	54	10.8	21	0
W. Turner	2	13	6.5	13	0
Jolly	2	2	1.0	2	0
Rudzinski	1	14	14.0	14	0
Luke	1	9	9.0	9	0
Hood	1	0	0.0	0	0
M.C. McCoy	1	0	0.0	0	0
Packers	**13**	**92**	**7.1**	**21**	**0**
Opponents	29	483	16.7	t99	4

Scoring

	TDr	TDp	TDrt	PAT	FG	S	TP
G. Ellis	5	3	0	0/0	0/0	0	48
Birney	0	0	0	14/18	6/12	0	32
Ivery	3	1	0	0/0	0/0	0	24
Lofton	0	4	0	0/0	0/0	0	24
Marcol	0	0	1	7/7	2/3	0	19
Coffman	0	3	0	0/0	0/0	0	18
Atkins	1	1	0	0/0	0/0	0	12
Middleton	2	0	0	0/0	0/0	0	12
Stenerud	0	0	0	3/3	3/5	0	12
Aundra Thompson	0	2	0	0/0	0/0	0	12
Dickey	1	0	0	0/0	0/0	0	6
Huckleby	1	0	0	0/0	0/0	0	6
B. Larson	0	1	0	0/0	0/0	0	6
Packers	**13**	**15**	**1**	**24/29**	**11/20**	**0**	**231**
Opponents	19	19	5	36/43	25/27	1	371

Fumbles

	Fum	Ow	Op	Yds	Tot
J. Anderson	0	0	1	0	1
V. R. Anderson	1	0	0	0	0
Atkins	1	1	0	0	1
Aydelette	1	0	0	-28	0
Beverly	1	1	0	-5	1
Ken Brown	1	0	0	-37	0
Cassidy	1	0	0	0	0
Dickey	13	5	0	-7	5
M. Douglass	0	0	2	0	2
G. Ellis	7	5	0	0	5
J. Gray	0	0	4	30	4
Gueno	0	1	0	0	1
L. Harris	0	0	1	0	1
Hood	0	0	1	0	1
Ivery	3	2	0	0	2
C. Johnson	0	0	1	0	1
Jolly	0	0	1	0	1
T. Jones	0	0	1	0	1
Lathrop	0	0	1	0	1
M. Lee	1	0	0	0	0
McCarren	0	0	1	0	1
M.C. McCoy	1	0	0	0	0
C. Merrill	0	0	1	0	1
Middleton	1	0	0	0	0
Nixon	1	0	0	0	0
E. O'Neil	0	0	2	26	2
Stokes	0	0	1	0	1
Aundra Thompson	2	2	0	5	2
Whitehurst	1	0	0	0	0
Packers	**36**	**22**	**14**	**-16**	**36**

NFL STANDINGS

National Conference

Eastern Division

	W	L	T	Pct	PF	PA
Philadelphia Eagles	12	4	0	.750	384	222
Dallas Cowboys	12	4	0	.750	454	311
Washington Redskins	6	10	0	.375	261	293
St. Louis Cardinals	5	11	1	.313	299	350
New York Giants	4	12	0	.250	249	425

Central Division

	W	L	T	Pct	PF	PA
Minnesota Vikings	9	7	0	.563	317	308
Detroit Lions	9	7	0	.563	334	272
Chicago Bears	7	9	0	.438	304	264
Tampa Bay Buccaneers	5	10	1	.344	271	341
Green Bay Packers	5	10	1	.344	231	371

Western Division

	W	L	T	Pct	PF	PA
Atlanta Falcons	12	4	0	.750	405	272
Los Angeles Rams	11	5	0	.688	424	289
San Francisco 49ers	6	10	0	.375	320	415
New Orleans Saints	1	15	0	.063	291	487

American Conference

Eastern Division

	W	L	T	Pct	PF	PA
Buffalo Bills	11	5	0	.688	320	260
New England Patriots	10	6	0	.625	441	325
Miami Dolphins	8	8	0	.500	266	305
Baltimore Colts	7	9	0	.438	355	387
New York Jets	4	12	0	.250	302	395

Central Division

	W	L	T	Pct	PF	PA
Cleveland Browns	11	5	0	.688	357	310
Houston Oilers	11	5	0	.688	295	251
Pittsburgh Steelers	9	7	0	.563	352	313
Cincinnati Bengals	6	10	0	.375	244	312

Western Division

	W	L	T	Pct	PF	PA
San Diego Chargers	11	5	0	.688	418	327
Oakland Raiders	11	5	0	.688	364	306
Kansas City Chiefs	8	8	0	.500	319	336
Denver Broncos	8	8	0	.500	310	323
Seattle Seahawks	4	12	0	.250	291	408

1980 ROSTER

No	Name	Pos	Ht	Wt	DOB	College	G
60	Allerman, Kurt	LB	6-2	222	08/30/55	Penn State	13
59	Anderson, John	LB	6-3	221	02/14/56	Michigan	9
44	Anderson, Vickey Ray	HB	6-0	205	05/03/56	Oklahoma	7
32	Atkins, Steve	RB	6-0	216	06/22/56	Maryland	9
62	Aydelette, Buddy	T	6-4	250	08/19/56	Alabama	9
58	Beekley, Bruce	LB	6-2	225	12/15/56	Oregon	15
11	Beverly, David	P	6-2	180	08/19/50	Auburn	16
19	Birney, Tom	K	6-4	220	08/11/56	Michigan	7
74	Brown, Ken	C	6-1	245	04/19/54	New Mexico	6
77	Butler, Mike	DE	6-5	265	04/04/54	Kansas	16
65	Cabral, Brian	LB	6-1	224	06/23/56	Colorado	7
88	Cassidy, Ron	WR	6-0	185	07/23/57	Utah State	15
82	Coffman, Paul	TE	6-3	218	03/29/56	Kansas State	16
52	Cumby, George	LB	6-0	215	07/05/56	Oklahoma	9
12	Dickey, Lynn	QB	6-4	220	10/19/49	Kansas State	16
92	Dimler, Rich	DT	6-6	260	07/18/56	USC	3
53	Douglass, Mike	LB	6-0	224	03/15/55	San Diego State	16
31	Ellis, Gerry	FB	5-11	216	11/12/57	Missouri	15
57	Gofourth, Derrel	C	6-3	260	03/20/55	Oklahoma State	16
24	Gray, Johnnie	S	5-11	185	12/18/53	Cal State-Fullerton	16
51	Gueno, Jim	LB	6-2	220	01/15/54	Tulane	16
69	Harris, Leotis	G	6-1	267	06/28/55	Arkansas	16
38	Hood, Estus	CB	5-11	180	11/14/55	Illinois State	15
25	Huckleby, Harlan	HB	6-1	199	12/30/57	Michigan	16
55	Hunt, Mike	LB	6-2	240	10/06/56	Minnesota	3
40	Ivery, Eddie Lee	RB	6-1	210	07/30/57	Georgia Tech	16
71	Jackson, Mel	G	6-1	267	05/05/54	USC	6
99	Johnson, Charles	DT	6-1	262	06/29/57	Maryland	15
90	Johnson, Ezra	DE	6-4	240	10/02/55	Morris Brown	15
21	Jolly, Mike	S	6-3	185	03/19/58	Michigan	16
63	Jones, Terry	DT	6-2	259	11/08/56	Alabama	15
85	Kimball, Bobby	WR	6-1	190	03/12/57	Oklahoma	1
64	Kitson, Syd	G	6-4	252	09/27/58	Wake Forest	14
68	Koch, Greg	T	6-4	265	06/14/55	Arkansas	16
79	Koncar, Mark	T	6-5	268	05/05/53	Colorado	1
87	Larson, Bill	TE	6-4	225	10/07/53	Colorado State	9
72	Lathrop, Kit	DT	6-5	253	05/10/56	Arizona State	15
22	Lee, Mark	CB	5-11	187	03/20/58	Washington	15
66	Lewis, Mike	DT	6-4	260	07/14/49	Arkansas A&M	10
80	Lofton, James	WR	6-3	187	07/05/56	Stanford	16
46	Luke, Steve	S	6-2	205	09/04/53	Ohio State	16
13	Marcol, Chester	K	6-0	190	10/24/49	Hillsdale	5
54	McCarren, Larry	C	6-3	248	11/09/51	Illinois	16
29	McCoy, Mike C.	CB	5-11	183	08/16/53	Colorado	16
78	Merrill, Casey	DE	6-4	255	07/16/57	California-Davis	16
34	Middleton, Terdell	HB	6-0	195	04/08/55	Memphis State	13
37	Murphy, Mark	S	6-2	199	04/22/58	West Liberty State	1
84	Nixon, Fred	WR	5-11	191	09/22/58	Oklahoma	15
56	O'Neil, Ed	LB	6-3	235	09/08/52	Penn State	12
19	Pisarkewicz, Steve	QB	6-2	205	11/10/53	Missouri	1
70	Rudzinski, Paul	LB	6-1	220	07/28/56	Michigan State	6
33	Smith, Barty	FB	6-3	240	03/23/52	Richmond	1
10	Stenerud, Jan	K	6-2	190	11/26/43	Montana State	4
76	Stokes, Tim	T	6-5	252	03/16/50	Oregon	15
67	Swanke, Karl	T	6-6	251	12/29/57	Boston College	16
89	Thompson, Aundra	WR	6-0	186	01/02/53	East Texas State	15
83	Thompson, John	TE	6-3	228	01/18/57	Utah State	7
10	Troup, Bill	QB	6-5	215	04/02/51	South Carolina	2
20	Turner, Wylie	CB	5-10	182	04/19/57	Angelo State	12
65	Wellman, Mike	C	6-3	253	07/15/56	Kansas	4
17	Whitehurst, David	QB	6-2	204	04/27/55	Furman	2

1980 DRAFT

Rnd	Name	Pos	Ht	Wt	College
1a	Bruce Clark (4)	DT	6-2	255	Penn State
1b	George Cumby (26)	LB	6-0	215	Oklahoma
	(Choice from Chargers in Willie Buchanon deal)				
2	Mark Lee (34)	DB	5-11	187	Washington
3	Syd Kitson (61)	G	6-4	252	Wake Forest
4	Fred Nixon (87)	WR	5-11	191	Oklahoma
5	(Choice (116) to Rams for Rick Nuzum)				
6	Karl Swanke (143)	T-C	6-6	251	Boston College
7	Buddy Aydelette (169)	T	6-4	250	Alabama
8	Tim Smith (199)	S	6-1	194	Oregon State
9	Kelly Saalfeld (226)	C	6-3	246	Nebraska
10	Jafus White (253)	S	6-2	195	Texas A&I
11	Ricky Skiles (283)	LB	6-3	220	Louisville
12	James Stewart (310)	DB	5-11	186	Memphis State

1980 GREEN BAY PACKERS

FRONT ROW: (L–R) 57 Derrel Gofourth, 79 Mark Koncar, 71 Mel Jackson, 29 Mike C. McCoy, 12 Lynn Dickey, 24 Johnnie Gray, 11 David Beverly, 89 Aundra Thompson, 34 Terdell Middleton,
55 Mike Hunt, 56 Ed O'Neil, 13 Chester Marcol, 54 Larry McCarren, 33 Barty Smith, 26 Eric Torkelson.
SECOND ROW: (L–R) 50 Rich Wingo, 88 Ron Cassidy, 65 Mike Wellman, 64 Syd Kitson, 51 Jim Gueno, 59 John Anderson, 25 Harlan Huckleby, 31 Gerry Ellis, 69 Leotis Harris,
68 Greg Koch, 82 Paul Coffman, 17 David Whitehurst.
THIRD ROW: (L–R) 38 Estus Hood, 46 Steve Luke, 60 Kurt Allerman, 20 Wylie Turner, 62 Buddy Aydelette, 40 Eddie Lee Ivery, 58 Bruce Beekley, 83 John Thompson, 19 Steve Pisarkiewicz,
66 Mike Lewis, 99 Charles Johnson, 63 Terry Jones.
FOURTH ROW: (L–R) 72 Kit Lathrop, 76 Tim Stokes, 67 Karl Swanke, 84 Fred Nixon, 52 George Cumby, 53 Mike Douglass, 80 James Lofton, 32 Steve Atkins, 77 Mike Butler,
90 Ezra Johnson, 96 Troy Thomas, 22 Mark Lee.
BACK ROW: (L–R) 85 Bobby Kimball, 21 Mike Jolly, 10 Bill Troup, 37 Mark Murphy, 44 Vickey Ray Anderson, 43 Calvin Perkins, 18 Mark Miller, 61 Davie Simmons, 78 Casey Merrill.

1981

Green Bay's play the past two years had rarely been deserving of a standing ovation. But such a display was just what the team received in Lambeau Field at the end of the third quarter in week two. The Packers had a comfortable 17-0 lead over the visiting Falcons and apparently were poised to go 2-0 on the year. Enthused because of a 3-1 preseason and the team's first seven regular-season quarters, fans envisioned a successful start such as that of 1978. Instead, the faithful witnessed a tremendous collapse. Green Bay not only blew the game 31-17, but floundered hopelessly for the next six weeks – a period in which, it turned out, one additional win would have meant a trip to the playoffs.

Green Bay staged its version of Jekyll and Hyde, albeit in reverse order. In the first eight games, the Packers won just two games. In the second half of the season, Green Bay lost but twice. Surprisingly, the team gained more yards, registered more first downs and punted fewer times in the first eight contests. Why the turnaround? Two reasons. The Packers blew leads – ranging from two to 17 points – in five of their first eight games. After midseason, Green Bay won all six games in which it held a lead. In addition, the team's turnover ratio, a minus three in the first half, was a +15 in the final eight games.

Eddie Lee Ivery, Lynn Dickey and Mark Koncar took some lumps in 1981. Just as in 1979, the Packers lost Ivery to a knee injury in the opener at Chicago. Later in the year, Lynn Dickey was speared in the back on a late hit by the Lions' William Gay, who was fined $2,000 for the offense. Dickey missed three games. Koncar went AWOL prior to the October 11 Buccaneers game. The oft-injured tackle fled the Thursday before, after having been heavily criticized by Bart Starr in a team meeting. Koncar returned the Monday after the team's 21-10 loss.

After the Packers lost their sixth game, 31-27 to Detroit, Starr appealed to the fans. He sought to regain the backing so evident early in the season. He got it. For the Seattle game on November 1, the Green Bay Area Visitor and Convention Bureau, with the help of business and civic leaders, organized a Packer Support Sunday. Pre-game festivities included performances by a number of bands and cheerleaders and were followed by organized cheers during the game. Green Bay beat Seattle 34-24 and linebacker Rich Wingo showed his appreciation for the support by tossing his fourth-quarter interception into the stands.

The rebirth, with the exception of a 37-3 setback at Tampa Bay, continued unabated until the season's last weekend. At that time, with a playoff berth on the line, the Packers completely fell apart and gave up nine sacks in dropping a 28-3 decision to the Jets. Though the team failed to qualify for postseason action for the seventh time under Starr, he was awarded a two-year contract extension.

Green Bay Press-Gazette photo

John Jefferson, acquired in a trade with the Chargers on September 17, dips low to catch a pass during the third quarter of the Vikings game in Milwaukee September 27. Jefferson caught seven passes for 121 yards in his first game as a Packer. No. 83 pulled in 39 passes for 632 yards in 1981. Walt Williams (44) closes in.

TEAM STATISTICS

	GB	OPP
First Downs	308	326
Rushing	104	140
Passing	174	168
Penalty	30	18
Rushes	478	546
Yards Gained	1,670	2,098
Average Gain	3.49	3.84
Average Yards per Game	104.4	131.1
Passes Attempted	514	505
Completed	286	284
% Completed	55.64	56.24
Total Yards Gained	3,576	3,353
Times Sacked	52	36
Yards Lost	387	266
Net Yards Gained	3,189	3,087
Yards Gained per Completion	12.50	11.81
Net Yards per Attempt	5.63	5.71
Average Net Yards per Game	199.3	192.9
Combined Net Yards Gained	4,859	5,185
Total Plays	1,044	1,087
Average Net Yards per Play	4.65	4.77
Average Net Yards per Game	303.7	324.1
Third Down Efficiency	72/210	103/230
Percentage	34.29	44.78
Intercepted By	30	24
Yards Returned	495	475
Returned for TD	1	3
Punts	84	69
Yards Punted	3,330	2,738
Average Yards per Punt	39.64	39.68
Punt Returns	40	50
Yards Returned	306	511
Average Yards per Return	7.65	10.22
Returned for TD	1	0
Kickoff Returns	58	70
Yards Returned	1,066	1,183
Average Yards per Return	18.38	16.90
Returned for TD	0	0
Penalties	84	108
Yards Penalized	687	907
Fumbles	31	42
Lost	17	24
Own Recovered for Touchdown	0	0
Opponent's Recovered by	24	17
Opponent's Recovered for Touchdown	0	3
Total Points Scored	324	361
Total Touchdowns	37	45
Touchdowns Rushing	11	21
Touchdowns Passing	24	18
Touchdowns on Returns & Recoveries	2	6
Extra Points	36	43
Safeties	0	0
Field Goals Attempted	24	24
Field Goals Made	22	16
% Successful	91.67	66.67
Average Time of Possession	29:23	30:37

Regular Season   8-8-0

Date	GB		OPP	Att.
9/6	16	at Chicago Bears	9	(62,411)
9/13	17	Atlanta Falcons	31	(55,382)
9/20	23	at Los Angeles Rams	35	(61,286)
9/27	13	Minnesota Vikings (M)	30	(55,012)
10/4	27	at New York Giants	14	(73,684)
10/11	10	Tampa Bay Buccaneers	21	(55,264)
10/18	3	San Francisco 49ers (M)	13	(50,171)
10/25	27	at Detroit Lions	31	(76,063)
11/1	34	Seattle Seahawks	24	(54,099)
11/8	26	New York Giants (M)	24	(54,138)
11/15	21	Chicago Bears	17	(55,338)
11/22	3	at Tampa Bay Buccaneers	37	(63,251)
11/29	35	at Minnesota Vikings	23	(46,025)
12/6	31	Detroit Lions	17	(54,481)
12/13	35	at New Orleans Saints	7	(45,518)
12/20	3	at New York Jets	28	(56,340)

Score By Periods

	1	2	3	4	OT	Total
Packers	89	108	64	63	0	324
Opponents	51	127	81	102	0	361

INDIVIDUAL STATISTICS

Rushing

	Att	Yds	Avg	LG	TD
G. Ellis	196	860	4.4	29	4
Huckleby	139	381	2.7	22	5
Middleton	53	181	3.4	34	0
J. Jensen	27	79	2.9	15	0
Ivery	14	72	5.1	28	1
Whitehurst	15	51	3.4	15	1
J. Jefferson	2	22	11.0	15	0
Atkins	11	12	1.1	6	0
Dickey	19	6	0.3	13	0
Torkelson	1	4	4.0	4	0
Aundra Thompson	1	2	2.0	2	0
Packers	**478**	**1,670**	**3.5**	**34**	**11**
Opponents	546	2,098	3.8	t35	21

Receiving

	No	Yds	Avg	LG	TD
Lofton	71	1,294	18.2	t75	8
G. Ellis	65	499	7.7	t46	3
Coffman	55	687	12.5	29	4
J. Jefferson	39	632	16.2	41	4
Huckleby	27	221	8.2	t39	3
Middleton	12	86	7.2	27	1
J. Jensen	5	49	9.8	16	0
G. Lewis	3	31	10.3	15	0
Aundra Thompson	2	30	15.0	25	0
Nixon	2	27	13.5	19	0
Ivery	2	10	5.0	8	0
Cassidy	1	6	6.0	6	0
Atkins	1	2	2.0	2	0
Swanke	1	2	2.0	t2	1
Packers	**286**	**3,576**	**12.5**	**t75**	**24**
Opponents	284	3,353	11.8	t50	18

Passing

	Att	Com	Yds	Pct	TD	In	Tk/Yds	Rate
Dickey	354	204	2,593	57.6	17	15	40/298	79.0
Whitehurst	128	66	792	51.6	7	5	10/78	72.8
Campbell	30	15	168	50.0	0	4	2/11	27.5
G. Ellis	2	1	23	50.0	0	0	0/0	—
Packers	**514**	**286**	**3,576**	**55.6**	**24**	**24**	**52/387**	**73.5**
Opponents	505	284	3,353	56.2	18	30	36/266	63.7

Punting

	No	Yds	Avg	In20	TB	LG	HB
Stachowicz	82	3,330	40.6	16	9	72	2
Packers	**84**	**3,330**	**39.6**	**16**	**9**	**72**	**2**
Opponents	69	2,738	39.7	14	5	58	0

Kickoff Returns

	No	Yds	Avg	LG	TD
M. Lee	14	270	19.3	31	0
Nixon	12	222	18.5	25	0
M.C. McCoy	11	221	20.1	36	0
Huckleby	7	134	19.1	27	0
Middleton	6	100	16.7	30	0
Coffman	3	77	25.7	52	0
J. Gray	2	24	12.0	19	0
J. Jensen	1	15	15.0	15	0
J. Jefferson	1	3	3.0	3	0
Braggs	1	0	0.0	0	0
Packers	**58**	**1,066**	**18.4**	**52**	**0**
Opponents	70	1,183	16.9	42	0

Punt Returns

	No	Yds	Avg	FC	LG	TD
M. Lee	20	187	9.4	1	t94	1
Nixon	15	118	7.9	4	17	0
Whitaker	2	1	0.5	0	1	0
Cassidy	2	0	0.0	4	0	0
J. Gray	1	0	0.0	1	0	0
Packers	**40**	**306**	**7.7**	**10**	**t94**	**1**
Opponents	50	511	10.2	4	56	0

Interceptions

	No	Yds	Avg	LG	TD
Harvey	6	217	36.2	53	0
M. Lee	6	50	8.3	25	0
Hood	3	59	19.7	t41	1
M. Murphy	3	57	19.0	50	0
Cumby	3	22	7.3	17	0
M. Douglass	3	20	6.7	13	0
J. Anderson	3	12	4.0	8	0
M.C. McCoy	2	20	10.0	16	0
Wingo	1	38	38.0	38	0
Packers	**30**	**495**	**16.5**	**53**	**1**
Opponents	24	475	19.8	t81	3

Scoring

	TDr	TDp	TDrt	PAT	FG	S	TP
Stenerud	0	0	0	35/36	22/24	0	101
Huckleby	5	3	0	0/0	0/0	0	48
Lofton	0	8	0	0/0	0/0	0	48
G. Ellis	4	3	0	0/0	0/0	0	42
Coffman	0	4	0	0/0	0/0	0	24
J. Jefferson	0	4	0	0/0	0/0	0	24
Hood	0	0	1	0/0	0/0	0	6
Ivery	1	0	0	0/0	0/0	0	6
M. Lee	0	0	1	0/0	0/0	0	6
Middleton	0	1	0	0/0	0/0	0	6
Swanke	0	1	0	0/0	0/0	0	6
Whitehurst	1	0	0	0/0	0/0	0	6
Wingo	0	0	0	1/0	0/0	0	1
Packers	**11**	**24**	**2**	**36/37**	**22/24**	**0**	**324**
Opponents	21	18	6	43/45	16/24	0	361

Fumbles

	Fum	Ow	Op	Yds	Tot
Allerman	0	0	1	0	1
J. Anderson	0	0	4	22	4
Ane	0	1	1	0	2
Atkins	1	0	0	0	0
Cassidy	1	0	0	0	0
Coffman	1	0	1	0	1
Cumby	0	0	2	70	2
Dickey	8	3	0	-36	3
M. Douglass	0	0	3	0	3
G. Ellis	5	1	0	0	1
Gofourth	0	1	0	0	1
J. Gray	0	0	1	0	1
L. Harris	0	0	1	0	1
Harvey	1	1	1	0	3
Huckleby	3	0	0	0	0
J. Jensen	1	0	0	0	0
T. Jones	0	0	2	0	2
Koncar	0	1	0	0	1
M. Lee	0	0	1	0	1
Lofton	0	1	0	0	1
McCarren	0	1	0	0	1
M.C. McCoy	1	0	0	0	1
C. Merrill	0	0	3	0	3
Middleton	2	1	0	0	1
M. Murphy	0	0	2	0	2
Nixon	2	0	0	0	0
Arland Thompson	0	0	1	0	1
Whitaker	0	0	1	0	1
Whitehurst	4	1	0	-2	1
Packers	**31**	**14**	**24**	**54**	**38**

NFL STANDINGS

National Conference

Eastern Division

	W	L	T	Pct	PF	PA
Dallas Cowboys	12	4	0	.750	367	277
Philadelphia Eagles	10	6	0	.625	368	221
New York Giants	9	7	0	.563	295	257
Washington Redskins	8	8	0	.500	347	349
St. Louis Cardinals	7	9	0	.438	315	408

Central Division

	W	L	T	Pct	PF	PA
Tampa Bay Buccaneers	9	7	0	.563	315	268
Detroit Lions	8	8	0	.500	397	322
Green Bay Packers	**8**	**8**	**0**	**.500**	**324**	**361**
Minnesota Vikings	7	9	0	.438	325	369
Chicago Bears	6	10	0	.375	253	324

Western Division

	W	L	T	Pct	PF	PA
San Francisco 49ers	13	3	0	.813	357	250
Atlanta Falcons	7	9	0	.438	426	355
Los Angeles Rams	6	10	0	.375	303	351
New Orleans Saints	4	12	0	.250	207	378

American Conference

Eastern Division

	W	L	T	Pct	PF	PA
Miami Dolphins	11	4	1	.719	345	275
New York Jets	10	5	1	.656	355	287
Buffalo Bills	10	6	0	.625	311	276
Baltimore Colts	2	14	0	.125	259	533
New England Patriots	2	14	0	.125	322	370

Central Division

	W	L	T	Pct	PF	PA
Cincinnati Bengals	12	4	0	.750	421	304
Pittsburgh Steelers	8	8	0	.500	356	297
Houston Oilers	7	9	0	.438	281	355
Cleveland Browns	5	11	0	.313	276	375

Western Division

	W	L	T	Pct	PF	PA
San Diego Chargers	10	6	0	.625	478	390
Denver Broncos	10	6	0	.625	321	289
Kansas City Chiefs	9	7	0	.563	343	290
Oakland Raiders	7	9	0	.438	273	343
Seattle Seahawks	6	10	0	.375	322	388

1981 ROSTER

No	Name	Pos	Ht	Wt	DOB	College	G
60	Allerman, Kurt	LB	6-2	222	08/30/55	Penn State	16
59	Anderson, John	LB	6-3	221	02/14/56	Michigan	16
61	Ane, Charlie	C	6-1	237	08/12/52	Michigan State	16
32	Atkins, Steve	RB	6-0	216	06/22/56	Maryland	3
73	Braggs, Byron	NT	6-4	290	10/10/59	Alabama	16
77	Butler, Mike	DE	6-5	265	04/04/54	Kansas	16
19	Campbell, Rich	QB	6-4	224	12/22/58	California	2
88	Cassidy, Ron	WR	6-0	185	07/23/57	Utah State	11
82	Coffman, Paul	TE	6-3	218	03/29/56	Kansas State	16
52	Cumby, George	LB	6-0	215	07/05/56	Oklahoma	16
12	Dickey, Lynn	QB	6-4	220	10/19/49	Kansas State	13
53	Douglass, Mike	LB	6-0	224	03/15/55	San Diego State	16
31	Ellis, Gerry	FB	5-11	216	11/12/57	Missouri	15
57	Gofourth, Derrel	C	6-3	260	03/20/55	Oklahoma State	15
24	Gray, Johnnie	S	5-11	185	12/18/53	Cal State-Fullerton	9
69	Harris, Leotis	G	6-1	267	06/28/55	Arkansas	16
23	Harvey, Maurice	S	5-10	190	01/14/56	Ball State	16
38	Hood, Estus	CB	5-11	180	11/14/55	Illinois State	16
25	Huckleby, Harlan	HB	6-1	199	12/30/57	Michigan	16
74	Huffman, Tim	T	6-5	277	08/31/59	Notre Dame	4
40	Ivery, Eddie Lee	RB	6-1	210	07/30/57	Georgia Tech	1
83	Jefferson, John	WR	6-1	198	02/03/56	Arizona State	13
33	Jensen, Jim	RB	6-3	235	11/28/53	Iowa	15
90	Johnson, Ezra	DE	6-4	240	10/02/55	Morris Brown	16
63	Jones, Terry	NT	6-2	259	11/08/56	Alabama	16
64	Kitson, Syd	G	6-4	252	09/27/58	Wake Forest	11
68	Koch, Greg	T	6-4	265	06/14/55	Arkansas	16
79	Koncar, Mark	T	6-5	268	05/05/53	Colorado	14
22	Lee, Mark	CB	5-11	187	03/20/58	Washington	16
56	Lewis, Cliff	LB	6-1	226	11/09/59	Southern Mississippi	16
81	Lewis, Gary	TE	6-5	234	12/30/58	Texas-Arlington	16
80	Lofton, James	WR	6-3	187	07/05/56	Stanford	16
54	McCarren, Larry	C	6-3	248	11/09/51	Illinois	16
29	McCoy, Mike C.	CB	5-11	183	08/16/53	Colorado	16
78	Merrill, Casey	DE	6-4	255	07/16/57	California-Davis	16
34	Middleton, Terdell	HB	6-0	195	04/08/55	Memphis State	12
37	Murphy, Mark	S	6-2	199	04/22/58	West Liberty State	16
84	Nixon, Fred	WR	5-11	191	09/22/56	Oklahoma	8
47	Petway, David	S	6-2	207	10/17/55	Northern Illinois	5
51	Prather, Guy	LB	6-2	230	03/28/58	Grambling	16
55	Scott, Randy	LB	6-1	220	01/31/59	Alabama	16
16	Stachowicz, Ray	P	5-11	185	03/06/59	Michigan State	16
10	Stenerud, Jan	K	6-2	190	11/26/43	Montana State	16
76	Stokes, Tim	T	6-5	252	03/16/50	Oregon	7
67	Swanke, Karl	T	6-6	251	12/29/57	Boston College	4
71	Thompson, Arland	G	6-2	265	09/19/57	Baylor	10
89	Thompson, Aundra	WR	6-0	186	01/02/53	East Texas State	3
87	Thompson, John	TE	6-3	228	01/18/57	Utah State	2
26	Torkelson, Eric	RB	6-2	210	03/03/52	Connecticut	8
75	Turner, Rich	NT	6-2	260	02/14/59	Oklahoma	16
30	Whitaker, Bill	S	6-0	182	11/18/59	Missouri	16
17	Whitehurst, David	QB	6-2	204	04/27/55	Furman	2
50	Wingo, Rich	LB	6-1	230	07/16/56	Alabama	16

1981 DRAFT

Rnd	Name	Pos	Ht	Wt	College
1	Rich Campbell (6)	QB	6-4	224	California
2	Gary Lewis (35)	TE	6-5	234	Texas-Arlington
3	Ray Stachowicz (62)	P	5-11	185	Michigan State
4a	(Choice (90) traded to Redskins for Redskins' 4th round pick (105) and 5th round pick (117))				
4b	Richard Turner (105)	DT	6-2	260	Oklahoma
	(Choice from Redskins through the Rams in draft pick exchange)				
5	Byron Braggs (117)	DT	6-4	290	Alabama
	(Choice (117) to Rams for Mike Wellman, subsequently traded through a separate deal by the Rams to the Redskins, who turned choice back to Green Bay for position exchange)				
6	(Choice (145) to Giants for Randy Dean)				
7	Bill Whitaker (182)	DB	6-0	182	Missouri
8	Larry Werts (200)	LB	6-2	231	Jackson State
9	Tim Huffman (227)	T	6-5	277	Notre Dame
10	Nickie Hall (255)	QB	6-4	205	Tulane
11	Forrest Valora (282)	LB	6-0	236	Oklahoma
12	Cliff Lewis (311)	LB	6-1	226	Southern Mississippi

1981 GREEN BAY PACKERS

FRONT ROW: (L-R) 79 Mark Koncar, 57 Derrel Gofourth, 24 Johnnie Gray, 29 Mike C. McCoy, 83 John Jefferson, 84 Fred Nixon, 34 Terdell Middleton, 78 Casey Merrill, 33 Jim Jensen, 12 Lynn Dickey, 26 Eric Torkelson, 54 Larry McCarren.

SECOND ROW: (L-R) Equipment Assistant Dick Zoll, Equipment Manager Bob Noel, Director of Player Personnel Burt Gustafson, Defensive Backfield Coach Ross Fichtner, Special Teams Coach Dick Rehbein, Offensive Backfield Coach Zeke Bratkowski, Receivers Coach Lew Carpenter, Head Coach Bart Starr, Special Assistant Pete Kettela, Defensive Coordinator John Meyer, Linebackers Coach John Marshall, Offensive Line Coach Ernie McMillan, Defensive Line Coach Richard (Doc) Urich, Trainer Domenic Gentile.

THIRD ROW: (L-R) 67 Karl Swanke, 40 Eddie Lee Ivery, 62 Buddy Aydelette, 64 Syd Kitson, 37 Mark Murphy, 55 Randy Scott, 48 Willard Reaves, 60 Kurt Allerman, 59 John Anderson, 25 Harlan Huckleby, 75 Richard Turner, 98 Chris Godfrey, 23 Maurice Harvey, 63 Terry Jones.

FOURTH ROW: (L-R) Groundskeeper Earl DuChateau, 10 Jan Stenerud, 61 Charlie Ane, 74 Tim Huffman, 19 Rich Campbell, 16 Ray Stachowicz, 51 Guy Prather, 52 George Cumby, 80 James Lofton, 53 Mike Douglass, 69 Leotis Harris, 68 Greg Koch, 82 Paul Coffman, 17 David Whitehurst, 71 Arland Thompson, Assistant Trainer Jim Popp, 38 Estus Hood, Equipment Assistant Jack Noel.

BACK ROW: (L-R) Film Director Al Treml, 30 Bill Whitaker, 88 Ron Cassidy, 50 Rich Wingo, 58 Paul Rudzinski, 21 Mike Jolly, 56 Cliff Lewis, 11 Nickie Hall, 31 Gerry Ellis, 77 Mike Butler, 90 Ezra Johnson, 81 Gary Lewis, 76 Tim Stokes, 87 John Thompson, 22 Mark Lee, 73 Byron Braggs.

1982

With the Packers down 23-0 at halftime in Milwaukee against the Rams on opening day, discontented fans braced themselves for another loss. After all, in the past 61 years no Green Bay team had ever come back from more than 18 points to win and the club that did that captured the NFL title in 1965. Certainly the Packers of 1982 couldn't be expected to mount such a championship effort, despite the strong finish of a year ago.

In the second half of the opener, the Green and Gold woke up. Dickey threw a pair of touchdown passes to Paul Coffman and another to James Lofton. Eddie Lee Ivery scampered for a game-high 109 yards, scoring on runs of three and 24 yards. John Jefferson didn't reach the end zone but caught six passes for 116 yards. The Packers rang up 35 points while holding the Rams scoreless and forged their greatest ever come-from-behind win, 35-23.

A week later, the Packers again turned the trick, although in a less dramatic fashion. Green Bay rallied from a 19-7 deficit to beat the Giants 27-19 on Monday night.

But the promising start had to be put on hold. The league's collective bargaining agreement of 1977 expired, and the NFLPA had made plans to strike on the Tuesday after the Packers-Giants game. As the stadium in East Rutherford went dark, so too did the outlook for the 1982 season.

In March, the NFL had annouced the signing of a $2.1 billion contract with the three television networks. Part of the players' demands centered on sharing the windfall. Led by executive director Ed Garvey and president Gene Upshaw, the union called for owners to set aside 55 percent of gross revenues from all sources for player's salaries. The organization had a list of other lesser demands, including free agency, but did not stress the latter as in the past.

For 57 days the nation was without NFL action. A pair of all-star games sponsored by the union were played on the weekend of October 17 and 18. Other than that, fans had to settle for Canadian or college football to fill their weekends.

A tentative agreement was reached on November 16 and although the actual contract was not signed until December 11, play resumed. The season was shortened to nine games and the playoffs expanded to include 16 berths. The additional spots gave unbeaten Green Bay (2-0) its best chance in years of returning to the playoffs.

Unlike some teams, the Packers had held informal practices (at St. Norbert College) during the two-month layoff. The benefits of that solidarity were displayed when Green Bay crushed Minnesota 26-7 on the first weekend back. Though the Lions dealt them a pair of losses and the lowly Colts tied them 20-20, the Packers clinched their first playoff slot in a decade with a rousing 38-7 win at Atlanta in the season's eighth week.

Green Bay Press-Gazette photo

Eddie Lee Ivery (40) caps the days' scoring with a 24-yard jaunt in Milwaukee on September 12. Ivery picked up 109 yards rushing on 17 trips and was instrumental in engineering the team's second-half comeback effort. Green Bay defeated Los Angeles 35-23. Also shown are Pat Thomas (27) and James Lofton (80).

TEAM STATISTICS

	GB	OPP
First Downs	175	164
Rushing	59	58
Passing	97	96
Penalty	19	10
Rushes	283	275
Yards Gained	1,081	932
Average Gain	3.82	3.39
Average Yards per Game	120.1	103.6
Passes Attempted	267	327
Completed	143	177
% Completed	53.56	54.13
Total Yards Gained	2,068	1,950
Times Sacked	32	20
Yards Lost	239	175
Net Yards Gained	1,829	1,775
Yards Gained per Completion	14.46	11.02
Net Yards per Attempt	6.12	5.12
Average Net Yards per Game	203.2	197.2
Combined Net Yards Gained	2,910	2,707
Total Plays	582	622
Average Yards per Play	5.00	4.35
Average Net Yards per Game	323.3	300.8
Third Down Efficiency	50/121	53/138
Percentage	41.32	38.41
Intercepted By	12	15
Yards Returned	174	146
Returned for TD	0	0
Punts	42	46
Yards Punted	1,687	1,925
Average Yards per Punt	40.17	41.85
Punt Returns	26	27
Yards Returned	198	286
Average Yards per Return	7.62	10.59
Returned for TD	0	0
Kickoff Returns	34	45
Yards Returned	664	875
Average Yards per Return	19.53	19.44
Returned for TD	0	1
Penalties	42	72
Yards Penalized	343	629
Fumbles	20	26
Lost	11	11
Own Recovered for Touchdown	2	0
Opponent's Recovered by	11	11
Opponent's Recovered for Touchdown	1	0
Total Points Scored	226	169
Total Touchdowns	27	19
Touchdowns Rushing	12	9
Touchdowns Passing	12	9
Touchdowns on Returns & Recoveries	3	1
Extra Points	25	17
Safeties	0	1
Field Goals Attempted	18	18
Field Goals Made	13	12
% Successful	72.22	66.67
Average Time of Possession	29:40	30:20

Regular Season   5-3-1

Date	GB		OPP	Att.
9/12	35	Los Angeles Rams (M)	23	(53,694)
9/20	27	at New York Giants	19	(68,405)
9/26	*	Miami Dolphins		
10/3	*	Philadelphia Eagles (M)		
10/10	*	at Chicago Bears		
10/17	*	Tampa Bay Buccaneers		
10/24	*	at Minnesota Vikings		
10/31	*	Chicago Bears		
11/7	*	at Tampa Bay Buccaneers		
11/14	**	at Detroit Lions		
11/21	26	Minnesota Vikings (M)	7	(44,681)
11/28	13	at New York Jets	15	(53,872)
12/5	33	Buffalo Bills (M)	21	(46,655)
12/12	10	Detroit Lions	30	(51,875)
12/19	20	at Baltimore Colts (OT)	20	(25,920)
12/26	38	at Atlanta Falcons	7	(50,245)
1/2	24	at Detroit Lions	27	(64,377)

* game cancelled because of players' strike
** game played on January 2

Postseason   1-1-0

1/8	41	St. Louis Cardinals	16	(54,282)
1/16	26	at Dallas Cowboys	37	(63,972)

Score By Periods

	1	2	3	4	OT	Total
Packers	26	65	64	71	0	226
Opponents	59	46	29	35	0	169

1982

INDIVIDUAL STATISTICS

Rushing

	Att	Yds	Avg	LG	TD
Ivery	127	453	3.6	32	9
G. Ellis	62	228	3.7	29	1
Rodgers	46	175	3.8	13	1
Lofton	4	101	25.3	t83	1
Meade	14	42	3.0	19	0
J. Jensen	9	28	3.1	10	0
Dickey	13	19	1.5	11	0
Huckleby	4	19	4.8	7	0
J. Jefferson	2	16	8.0	11	0
Stachowicz	2	0	0.0	0	0
Packers	**283**	**1,081**	**3.8**	**t83**	**12**
Opponents	275	932	3.4	36	9

Receiving

	No	Yds	Avg	LG	TD
Lofton	35	696	19.9	t80	4
J. Jefferson	27	452	16.7	50	0
Coffman	23	287	12.5	42	2
G. Ellis	18	140	7.8	20	0
Ivery	16	186	11.6	62	1
Epps	10	226	22.6	50	2
Rodgers	3	23	7.7	16	0
G. Lewis	3	21	7.0	12	0
J. Jensen	3	18	6.0	11	1
Meade	3	-5	-1.7	-1	0
J. Thompson	2	24	12.0	t23	2
Packers	**143**	**2,068**	**14.5**	**t80**	**12**
Opponents	177	1,950	11.0	44	9

Passing

	Att	Com	Yds	Pct	TD	In	Tk/Yds	Rate
Dickey	218	124	1,790	56.9	12	14	25/196	75.3
Whitehurst	47	18	235	38.3	0	1	7/43	46.0
Lofton	1	1	43	100.0	0	0	0/0	—
Ivery	1	0	0	00.0	0	0	0/0	—
Packers	**267**	**143**	**2,068**	**53.6**	**12**	**15**	**32/239**	**70.6**
Opponents	327	177	1,950	44.1	9	12	20/175	65.9

Punting

	No	Yds	Avg	In20	TB	LG	HB
Stachowicz	42	1,687	40.2	7	2	53	0
Packers	**42**	**1,687**	**40.2**	**7**	**2**	**53**	**0**
Opponents	46	1,925	41.8	11	4	55	0

Kickoff Returns

	No	Yds	Avg	LG	TD
Rodgers	20	436	21.8	76	0
Huckleby	5	89	17.8	26	0
A. Clark	4	75	18.8	30	0
Meade	2	31	15.5	17	0
J. Gray	2	29	14.5	25	0
C. Lewis	1	4	4.0	4	0
Packers	**34**	**664**	**19.5**	**76**	**0**
Opponents	45	875	19.4	t96	1

Punt Returns

	No	Yds	Avg	FC	LG	TD
Epps	20	150	7.5	5	35	0
J. Epps	6	48	8.0	1	15	0
Packers	**26**	**198**	**7.6**	**6**	**35**	**0**
Opponents	27	286	10.6	3	58	0

Interceptions

	No	Yds	Avg	LG	TD
J. Anderson	3	22	7.3	9	0
M. Douglass	2	55	27.5	30	0
Harvey	2	32	16.0	17	0
M. Lee	1	40	40.0	40	0
J. Gray	1	21	21.0	21	0
Cumby	1	4	4.0	4	0
Hood	1	0	0.0	0	0
Wingo	1	0	0.0	0	0
Packers	**12**	**174**	**14.5**	**40**	**0**
Opponents	15	146	9.7	36	0

Scoring

	TDr	TDp	TDrt	PAT	FG	S	TP
Stenerud	0	0	0	25/27	13/18	0	64
Ivery	9	1	0	0/0	0/0	0	60
Lofton	1	4	0	0/0	0/0	0	30
Rodgers	1	0	2	0/0	0/0	0	18
Coffman	0	2	0	0/0	0/0	0	12
Epps	0	2	0	0/0	0/0	0	12
J. Thompson	0	2	0	0/0	0/0	0	12
G. Ellis	1	0	0	0/0	0/0	0	6
Harvey	0	0	1	0/0	0/0	0	6
J. Jensen	0	1	0	0/0	0/0	0	6
Packers	**12**	**12**	**3**	**25/27**	**13/18**	**0**	**226**
Opponents	9	9	1	17/19	12/18	1	169

Fumbles

	Fum	Ow	Op	Yds	Tot
J. Anderson	0	0	2	0	2
R. Brown	0	0	1	0	1
M. Butler	0	0	1	0	1
Cumby	0	0	1	0	1
Dickey	5	2	0	-1	2
M. Douglass	0	0	1	6	1
G. Ellis	6	0	0	0	0
Epps	1	0	0	0	0
Gofourth	0	1	0	0	1
Harvey	0	0	3	25	3
Ivery	2	0	0	0	0
J. Jensen	1	0	0	0	0
M.C. McCoy	0	0	1	0	1
Prather	0	0	1	0	1
Rodgers	2	0	0	0	2
Rubens	1	0	0	-15	0
Stachowicz	1	1	0	-10	0
Stokes	0	1	0	0	1
Swanke	0	1	0	0	1
A. Clark	1	1	0	0	1
Packers	**20**	**8**	**11**	**5**	**19**

Quarterback Sacks

	No
E. Johnson	5.5
C. Merrill	4.0
M. Douglass	3.0
T. Jones	3.0
M. Butler	2.0
Harvey	1.0
Wingo	1.0
J. Anderson	0.5
Packers	**20.0**
Opponents	32.0

NFL STANDINGS

National Conference

	W	L	T	Pct	PF	PA
Washington Redskins	8	1	0	.889	190	128
Dallas Cowboys	6	3	0	.667	226	145
Green Bay Packers	**5**	**3**	**1**	**.611**	**226**	**169**
Minnesota Vikings	5	4	0	.556	187	198
Atlanta Falcons	5	4	0	.556	183	199
St. Louis Cardinals	5	4	0	.556	135	170
Tampa Bay Buccaneers	5	4	0	.556	158	178
Detroit Lions	4	5	0	.444	181	176
New Orleans Saints	4	5	0	.444	129	160
New York Giants	4	5	0	.444	164	160
San Francisco 49ers	3	6	0	.333	209	206
Chicago Bears	3	6	0	.333	141	174
Philadelphia Eagles	3	6	0	.333	191	195
Los Angeles Rams	2	7	0	.222	200	250

American Conference

	W	L	T	Pct	PF	PA
Los Angeles Raiders	8	1	0	.889	260	200
Miami Dolphins	7	2	0	.778	198	131
Cincinnati Bengals	7	2	0	.778	232	177
Pittsburgh Steelers	6	3	0	.667	204	146
San Diego Chargers	6	3	0	.667	288	221
New York Jets	6	3	0	.667	245	166
New England Patriots	5	4	0	.556	143	157
Cleveland Browns	4	5	0	.444	140	182
Buffalo Bills	4	5	0	.444	150	154
Seattle Seahawks	4	5	0	.444	127	147
Kansas City Chiefs	3	6	0	.333	176	184
Denver Broncos	2	7	0	.222	148	226
Houston Oilers	1	8	0	.111	136	245
Baltimore Colts	0	8	1	.056	113	236

1982 ROSTER

No	Name	Pos	Ht	Wt	DOB	College	G
59	Anderson, John	LB	6-3	221	02/14/56	Michigan	9
73	Braggs, Byron	NT	6-4	290	10/10/59	Alabama	9
93	Brown, Robert	DE	6-2	238	05/21/60	Virginia Tech	9
77	Butler, Mike	DE	6-5	265	04/04/54	Kansas	9
19	Campbell, Rich	QB	6-4	224	12/22/58	California	1
34	Clark, Allan	RB	5-10	186	06/08/57	Northern Arizona	4
82	Coffman, Paul	TE	6-3	218	03/29/56	Kansas State	9
52	Cumby, George	LB	6-0	215	07/05/56	Oklahoma	9
12	Dickey, Lynn	QB	6-4	220	10/19/49	Kansas State	9
53	Douglass, Mike	LB	6-0	224	03/15/55	San Diego State	9
31	Ellis, Gerry	FB	5-11	216	11/12/57	Missouri	9
85	Epps, Phillip	WR	5-10	165	11/11/58	TCU	9
57	Gofourth, Derrel	C	6-3	260	03/20/55	Oklahoma State	9
24	Gray, Johnnie	S	5-11	185	12/18/53	Cal State-Fullerton	9
65	Hallstrom, Ron	G	6-6	286	06/11/59	Iowa	7
69	Harris, Leotis	G	6-1	267	06/28/55	Arkansas	9
23	Harvey, Maurice	S	5-10	190	01/14/56	Ball State	9
38	Hood, Estus	CB	5-11	180	11/14/55	Illinois State	9
25	Huckleby, Harlan	HB	6-1	199	12/30/57	Michigan	9
74	Huffman, Tim	T	6-5	277	08/31/59	Notre Dame	9
40	Ivery, Eddie Lee	RB	6-1	210	07/30/57	Georgia Tech	9
83	Jefferson, John	WR	6-1	198	02/03/56	Arizona State	8
33	Jensen, Jim	RB	6-3	235	11/28/53	Iowa	9
90	Johnson, Ezra	DE	6-4	240	10/02/55	Morris Brown	9
21	Jolly, Mike	S	6-3	185	03/19/58	Michigan	7
63	Jones, Terry	NT	6-2	259	11/08/56	Alabama	9
68	Koch, Greg	T	6-4	265	06/14/55	Arkansas	9
60	Laslavic, Jim	LB	6-2	236	10/24/51	Penn State	6
22	Lee, Mark	CB	5-11	187	03/20/58	Washington	9
56	Lewis, Cliff	LB	6-1	226	11/09/59	Southern Mississippi	9
81	Lewis, Gary	TE	6-5	234	12/30/58	Texas-Arlington	9
80	Lofton, James	WR	6-3	187	07/05/56	Stanford	9
54	McCarren, Larry	C	6-3	248	11/09/51	Illinois	9
29	McCoy, Mike C.	CB	5-11	183	08/16/53	Colorado	9
39	Meade, Mike	RB	5-10	228	02/12/60	Penn State	2
78	Merrill, Casey	DE	6-4	255	07/16/57	California-Davis	9
62	Merrill, Mark	LB	6-3	234	05/05/55	Minnesota	2
37	Murphy, Mark	S	6-2	199	04/22/58	West Liberty State	9
51	Prather, Guy	LB	6-2	230	03/28/58	Grambling	9
35	Rodgers, Del	RB	5-10	197	06/22/60	Utah	9
58	Rubens, Larry	C	6-1	253	01/25/59	Montana State	9
55	Scott, Randy	LB	6-1	220	01/31/59	Alabama	9
16	Stachowicz, Ray	P	5-11	185	03/06/59	Michigan State	9
10	Stenerud, Jan	K	6-2	190	11/26/43	Montana State	9
76	Stokes, Tim	T	6-5	252	03/16/50	Oregon	9
67	Swanke, Karl	T	6-6	251	12/29/57	Boston College	8
87	Thompson, John	TE	6-3	228	01/18/57	Utah State	9
75	Turner, Rich	NT	6-2	260	02/14/59	Oklahoma	9
30	Whitaker, Bill	S	6-0	182	11/18/59	Missouri	9
17	Whitehurst, David	QB	6-2	204	04/27/55	Furman	3
50	Wingo, Rich	LB	6-1	230	07/16/56	Alabama	5

1982 DRAFT

Rnd	Name	Pos	Ht	Wt	College
1a	(Choice (13) to Chargers in John Jefferson trade)				
1b	Ron Hallstrom (22)	G	6-6	286	Iowa
	(Choice from Chargers in John Jefferson trade)				
2	(Choice (40) to Chargers in John Jefferson trade)				
3	Del Rodgers (71)	RB	5-10	197	Utah
4	Robert Brown (98)	LB	6-2	238	Virginia Tech
5	Mike Meade (126)	RB	5-10	228	Penn State
6	Chet Parlavecchio (152)	LB	6-2	225	Penn State
7	Joe Whitley (183)	DB	5-11	177	Texas-El Paso
8	Thomas Boyd (210)	LB	6-2	210	Alabama
9	Charles Riggins (237)	DE	6-3	245	Bethune-Cookman
10	Eddie Garcia (264)	K	5-8	188	SMU
11	John Macaulay (294)	C	6-3	254	Stanford
12	Phillip Epps (321)	WR	5-10	165	TCU

1982 GREEN BAY PACKERS

FRONT ROW: (L-R) 24 Johnnie Gray, 29 Mike C. McCoy, 34 Allan Clark, 22 Mark Lee, 85 Phillip Epps, 83 John Jefferson, 31 Gerry Ellis, 12 Lynn Dickey, 30 Bill Whitaker, 78 Casey Merrill, 54 Larry McCarren.

SECOND ROW: (L-R) Adminstrative Assistant Paul Rudzinski, Defensive Secondary Coach Ross Fichtner, Special Teams Coach Dick Rehbein, Offensive Backfield Coach Pete Kettela, Receivers Coach Lew Carpenter, Offensive Line Assistant Bill Meyers, Head Coach Bart Starr, Offensive Coordinator Bob Schnelker, Offensive Line Coach Ernie McMillan, Linebackers Coach John Marshall, Defensive Line Coach Richard (Doc) Urich, Defensive Coordinator John Meyer, Director of Pro Personnel Burt Gustafson.

THIRD ROW: (L-R) 51 Guy Prather, 23 Maurice Harvey, 35 Del Rodgers, 33 Jim Jensen, 25 Harlan Huckleby, 80 James Lofton, 53 Mike Douglass, 40 Eddie Lee Ivery, 87 Angelo Fields, 63 Terry Jones.

FOURTH ROW: (L-R) 39 Mike Meade, 57 Derrel Gofourth, 58 Larry Rubens, 62 Mark Merrill, 60 Jim Laslavic, 59 John Anderson, 55 Randy Scott, 50 Rich Wingo, 16 Ray Stachowicz, 10 Jan Stenerud.

FIFTH ROW: (L-R) 38 Estus Hood, 56 Cliff Lewis, 65 Ron Hallstrom, 19 Rich Campbell, 67 Karl Swanke, 76 Tim Stokes, 69 Leotis Harris, 68 Greg Koch, 82 Paul Coffman, 17 David Whitehurst.

SIXTH ROW: (L-R) 74 Tim Huffman, 93 Robert Brown, 90 Ezra Johnson, 77 Mike Butler, 81 Gary Lewis, 75 Richard Turner, 37 Mark Murphy, 21 Mike Jolly, 73 Byron Braggs.

BACK ROW: (L-R) Film Director Al Treml, Team Physician Dr. Eugene Brusky, Equipment Assistant Dick Zoll, Head Trainer Domenic Gentile, Equipment Manager Bob Noel, Groundskeeper Earl DuChateau, Assistant Film Director Bob Eckberg, Equipment Assistant Jack Noel, Assistant Trainer Jim Popp.

1983

The Packers of 1983 represented the best and worst professional football had to offer. Its offense ranked among the NFL's elite while its defense rated last place in the league. Quarterback Lynn Dickey, wideouts James Lofton and John Jefferson, and tight end Paul Coffman spearheaded a unit that piled up a team-record 6,172 yards – second to San Diego (6,197) – and a franchise-best 429 points. Unfortunately, Green Bay's defense acted as a neutralizing agent and gave up 6,403 yards and 439 points, both team records. The result. The Packers finished an even 8-8.

Starting with the team's inability to sign defensive end Mike Butler, to the waiving of starter Maurice Harvey, to the season-ending injuries to linebacker Randy Scott and nose tackle Rich Turner, Green Bay's defense gave up more yards than any other team in NFL history with the exception of Baltimore (6,793) in 1981. Eight times opponents gained more than 400 yards against Green Bay, with a high of 552 rung up by Washington on October 17.

With the offense and defense at odds with one another, the Packers were unable to win more than two games in a row. Even so, the Packers had a shot at the playoffs if they could first get past the Bears at Chicago on the season's final weekend. Green Bay led 21-20 with time winding down and the Bears moving into field goal range. Starr refused to use his remaining timeouts as Chicago inched closer to a potential game-winning field goal. As a result, after Bob Thomas successfully booted a 22-yard field goal, the Packers had a mere 10 —instead of a possible 60— seconds to work with. Johnnie Gray then fumbled the ensuing kickoff and Green Bay exited a 23-21 loser. Packers President Robert J. Parins fired Starr the next day.

Such a dismal scenario was far from anyone's mind on opening day in Houston where Dickey launched a season filled with individual and team highlights. Though he was unable to finish the game because of a severe headache, the 33-year old signal caller fired five touchdown passes. Dickey completed 27 of 31 passes, including a team-record 18 straight, and accounted for 333 of the team's 479 yards. The Packers prevailed 41-38 in overtime.

Over the course of the year, Dickey set team records with 289 completions in 484 attempts for 4,458 yards and 32 touchdowns. His primary target, Lofton, established a then-club record with 1,300 yards receiving on 58 catches. He led the NFL with a 22.4 yard average per catch.

Team highs were reached with a 55-14 thrashing of Tampa Bay and a high-powered 48-47 showdown with the Washington Redskins on Monday night.

Season lowlights included the release of Harvey on September 30 for what Starr described as "a lousy attitude," Eddie Lee Ivery's absence for half the year because of cocaine dependency and Starr's dismissal. In nine years at the helm, the Hall-of-Fame quarterback had fashioned a 53-77-3 mark, simply not good enough in the cold, bottom-line business of professional football.

Green Bay Press-Gazette photo

Lynn Dickey (12) releases a pass in Lambeau Field on September 11. The red-hot Kansan completed 14 of 20 passes for 290 yards and three touchdowns against the visiting Steelers, but his efforts were not enough. Pittsburgh beat Green Bay 25-21. Dickey led the NFL in four categories: yards thrown (4,458), yards per attempt (9.21), touchdown passes (32) and interceptions (29).

TEAM STATISTICS

	GB	OPP
First Downs	340	366
Rushing	99	171
Passing	214	187
Penalty	27	8
Rushes	439	597
Yards Gained	1,807	2,641
Average Gain	4.12	4.42
Average Yards per Game	112.9	165.1
Passes Attempted	526	518
Completed	311	300
% Completed	59.13	57.92
Total Yards Gained	4,688	4,033
Times Sacked	42	41
Yards Lost	323	271
Net Yards Gained	4,365	3,762
Yards Gained per Completion	15.07	13.44
Net Yards per Attempt	7.68	6.73
Average Net Yards per Game	272.8	235.1
Combined Net Yards Gained	6,172	6,403
Total Plays	1,007	1,156
Average Yards per Play	6.13	5.54
Average Net Yards per Game	385.8	400.2
Third Down Efficiency	72/189	111/239
Percentage	38.10	46.44
Intercepted By	19	32
Yards Returned	227	337
Returned for TD	1	4
Punts	70	78
Yards Punted	2,869	3,052
Average Yards per Punt	40.99	39.13
Punt Returns	41	43
Yards Returned	329	384
Average Yards per Return	8.02	8.93
Returned for TD	1	1
Kickoff Returns	79	78
Yards Returned	1,339	1,429
Average Yards per Return	16.95	18.32
Returned for TD	0	0
Penalties	80	110
Yards Penalized	648	965
Fumbles	37	32
Lost	18	12
Own Recovered for Touchdown	0	1
Opponent's Recovered by	12	18
Opponent's Recovered for Touchdown	2	1
Total Points Scored	429	439
Total Touchdowns	52	55
Touchdowns Rushing	15	28
Touchdowns Passing	33	20
Touchdowns on Returns & Recoveries	4	7
Extra Points	52	50
Safeties	1	1
Field Goals Attempted	26	29
Field Goals Made	21	19
% Successful	80.77	65.52
Average Time of Possession	27:01	32:59

Regular Season   8-8-0

Date	GB		OPP	Att.
9/4	41	at Houston Oilers (OT)	38	(44,073)
9/11	21	Pittsburgh Steelers	25	(55,154)
9/18	27	Los Angeles Rams (M)	24	(54,037)
9/26	3	at New York Giants	27	(75,308)
10/2	55	Tampa Bay Buccaneers	14	(54,272)
10/9	14	at Detroit Lions	38	(67,738)
10/17	48	Washington Redskins	47	(55,255)
10/23	17	Minnesota Vikings (OT)	20	(55,236)
10/30	14	at Cincinnati Bengals	34	(53,349)
11/6	35	Cleveland Browns (M)	21	(54,089)
11/13	29	at Minnesota Vikings	21	(60,113)
11/20	20	Detroit Lions (M) (OT)	23	(50,050)
11/27	41	at Atlanta Falcons (OT)	47	(35,688)
12/4	31	Chicago Bears	28	(51,147)
12/12	12	at Tampa Bay Buccaneers (OT)9		(50,763)
12/18	21	at Chicago Bears	23	(35,807)

Score By Periods

	1	2	3	4	OT	Total
Packers	120	147	44	112	6	429
Opponents	74	105	109	139	12	439

INDIVIDUAL STATISTICS

Rushing

	Att	Yds	Avg	LG	TD
G. Ellis	141	696	4.9	71	4
Ivery	86	340	4.0	21	2
J. Clark	71	328	4.6	42	0
Meade	55	201	3.7	15	1
Huckleby	50	182	3.6	20	4
Lofton	9	36	4.0	13	0
G. Lewis	4	16	4.0	11	1
Dickey	21	12	0.6	4	3
Whitehurst	2	-4	-2.0	0	0
Packers	**439**	**1,807**	**4.1**	**71**	**15**
Opponents	597	2,641	4.4	43	28

Receiving

	No	Yds	Avg	LG	TD
Lofton	58	1,300	22.4	174	8
J. Jefferson	57	830	14.6	36	7
Coffman	54	814	15.1	74	11
G. Ellis	52	603	11.6	56	2
Epps	18	313	17.4	45	0
J. Clark	18	279	15.5	t75	1
Ivery	16	139	8.7	17	1
Meade	16	110	6.9	t31	2
G. Lewis	11	204	18.5	49	1
Huckleby	10	87	8.7	14	0
Kitson	1	9	9.0	9	0
Packers	**311**	**4,688**	**15.1**	**t75**	**33**
Opponents	300	4,033	13.4	t87	20

Passing

	Att	Com	Yds	Pct	TD	In	Tk/Yds	Rate
Dickey	484	289	4,458	59.7	32	29	40/307	87.3
Whitehurst	35	18	149	51.4	0	2	2/16	38.9
Ivery	2	2	50	100.0	0	0	0/0	—
G. Ellis	5	2	31	40.0	1	1	0/0	—
Packers	**526**	**311**	**4,688**	**59.1**	**33**	**32**	**42/323**	**84.1**
Opponents	518	300	4,033	57.9	20	19	41/271	80.4

Punting

	No	Yds	Avg	In20	TB	LG	HB
Scribner	69	2,869	41.6	11	7	70	1
Packers	**70**	**2,869**	**41.0**	**11**	**7**	**70**	**1**
Opponents	78	3,052	39.1	19	7	59	0

Kickoff Returns

	No	Yds	Avg	LG	TD
Huckleby	41	757	18.5	57	0
T. Lewis	20	358	17.9	30	0
J. Gray	11	178	16.2	26	0
Winters	3	28	9.3	12	0
Ivery	1	17	17.0	17	0
Drechsler	1	1	1.0	1	0
Kitson	1	0	0.0	0	0
M. Lee	1	0	0.0	0	0
Packers	**79**	**1,339**	**16.9**	**57**	**0**
Opponents	78	1,429	18.3	41	0

Punt Returns

	No	Yds	Avg	FC	LG	TD
Epps	36	324	9.0	13	t90	1
J. Gray	2	9	4.5	0	5	0
Hood	1	0	0.0	0	0	0
C. Lewis	1	0	0.0	0	0	0
M. Lee	1	-4	-4.0	0	-4	0
Packers	**41**	**329**	**8.0**	**13**	**t90**	**1**
Opponents	43	384	8.9	8	t59	1

Interceptions

	No	Yds	Avg	LG	TD
T. Lewis	5	111	22.2	46	0
J. Anderson	5	54	10.8	t27	1
M. Lee	4	23	5.8	15	0
J. Gray	2	5	2.5	5	0
Laughlin	1	22	22.0	22	0
R. Scott	1	12	12.0	12	0
Jolly	1	0	0.0	0	0
Packers	**19**	**227**	**11.9**	**46**	**1**
Opponents	32	337	10.5	58	4

Scoring

	TDr	TDp	TDrt	PAT	FG	S	TP
Stenerud	0	0	0	52/52	21/26	0	115
Coffman	0	11	0	0/0	0/0	0	66
Lofton	0	8	0	0/0	0/0	0	48
J. Jefferson	0	7	0	0/0	0/0	0	42
G. Ellis	4	2	0	0/0	0/0	0	36
Huckleby	4	0	0	0/0	0/0	0	24
Dickey	3	0	0	0/0	0/0	0	18
Ivery	2	1	0	0/0	0/0	0	18
Meade	1	2	0	0/0	0/0	0	18
M. Douglass	0	0	2	0/0	0/0	0	12
G. Lewis	1	1	0	0/0	0/0	0	12
J. Anderson	0	0	1	0/0	0/0	0	6
J. Clark	0	1	0	0/0	0/0	0	6
Epps	0	0	1	0/0	0/0	0	6
G. Boyd	0	0	0	0/0	0/0	1	2
Packers	**15**	**33**	**4**	**52/52**	**21/26**	**1**	**429**
Opponents	28	20	7	50/55	19/29	1	439

Fumbles

	Fum	Ow	Op	Yds	Tot
J. Anderson	0	0	1	0	1
Braggs	0	0	2	0	2
J. Clark	2	1	0	0	1
Coffman	1	0	0	0	0
Dickey	9	6	0	0	6
M. Douglass	0	0	4	57	4
G. Ellis	7	1	0	0	1
Epps	2	0	0	0	0
J. Gray	2	1	0	0	1
Huckleby	4	1	0	0	1
Ivery	1	1	0	0	1
J. Jefferson	1	0	0	0	0
E. Johnson	0	0	2	0	2
M. Lee	1	0	1	15	1
G. Lewis	0	1	0	0	1
T. Lewis	3	1	0	0	1
Meade	2	1	0	0	1
M. Murphy	0	0	1	0	1
Rubens	0	0	1	0	1
Swanke	0	2	0	0	2
Whitehurst	2	1	0	0	1
Packers	**37**	**16**	**12**	**72**	**28**

Quarterback Sacks

	No
E. Johnson	14.5
Braggs	5.5
M. Douglass	5.5
J. Anderson	4.5
C. Johnson	3.5
G. Boyd	2.0
Cumby	2.0
C. Lewis	2.0
R. Turner	1.0
Spears	0.5
Packers	**41.0**
Opponents	42.0

NFL STANDINGS

National Conference

Eastern Division

	W	L	T	Pct	PF	PA
Washington Redskins	14	2	0	.875	541	332
Dallas Cowboys	12	4	0	.750	479	360
St. Louis Cardinals	8	7	1	.531	374	428
Philadelphia Eagles	5	11	0	.313	233	322
New York Giants	3	12	1	.219	267	347

Central Division

	W	L	T	Pct	PF	PA
Detroit Lions	9	7	0	.563	347	286
Green Bay Packers	**8**	**8**	**0**	**.500**	**429**	**439**
Chicago Bears	8	8	0	.500	311	301
Minnesota Vikings	8	8	0	.500	316	348
Tampa Bay Buccaneers	2	14	0	.125	241	380

Western Division

	W	L	T	Pct	PF	PA
San Francisco 49ers	10	6	0	.625	432	293
Los Angeles Rams	9	7	0	.563	361	344
New Orleans Saints	8	8	0	.500	319	337
Atlanta Falcons	7	9	0	.438	370	389

American Conference

Eastern Division

	W	L	T	Pct	PF	PA
Miami Dolphins	12	4	0	.750	389	250
New England Patriots	8	8	0	.500	274	289
Buffalo Bills	8	8	0	.500	283	351
Baltimore Colts	7	9	0	.438	264	354
New York Jets	7	9	0	.438	313	331

Central Division

	W	L	T	Pct	PF	PA
Pittsburgh Steelers	10	6	0	.625	355	303
Cleveland Browns	9	7	0	.563	356	342
Cincinnati Bengals	7	9	0	.438	346	302
Houston Oilers	2	14	0	.125	288	460

Western Division

	W	L	T	Pct	PF	PA
Los Angeles Raiders	12	4	0	.750	442	338
Seattle Seahawks	9	7	0	.563	403	397
Denver Broncos	9	7	0	.563	302	327
San Diego Chargers	6	10	0	.375	358	462
Kansas City Chiefs	6	10	0	.375	386	367

1983 ROSTER

No	Name	Pos	Ht	Wt	DOB	College	G
59	Anderson, John	LB	6-3	229	02/14/56	Michigan	16
72	Boyd, Greg	DE	6-6	280	09/15/53	San Diego State	12
73	Braggs, Byron	NT	6-4	270	10/10/59	Alabama	16
93	Brown, Robert	DE	6-2	250	05/21/60	Virginia Tech	16
19	Campbell, Rich	QB	6-4	219	12/22/58	California	1
88	Cassidy, Ron	WR	6-0	180	07/23/57	Utah State	16
33	Clark, Jessie	FB	6-0	233	01/03/60	Arkansas	16
82	Coffman, Paul	TE	6-3	225	03/29/56	Kansas State	16
52	Cumby, George	LB	6-0	224	07/05/56	Oklahoma	15
57	Curcio, Mike	LB	6-1	232	01/24/57	Temple	14
12	Dickey, Lynn	QB	6-4	203	10/19/49	Kansas State	16
53	Douglass, Mike	LB	6-0	214	03/15/55	San Diego State	15
61	Drechsler, Dave	G	6-3	264	07/18/60	North Carolina	16
31	Ellis, Gerry	FB	5-11	225	11/12/57	Missouri	15
85	Epps, Phillip	WR	5-10	165	11/11/58	TCU	16
11	Garcia, Eddie	K	5-8	178	04/15/59	SMU	12
77	Getty, Charlie	T	6-4	270	07/24/52	Penn State	16
24	Gray, Johnnie	S	5-11	202	12/18/53	Cal State-Fullerton	16
65	Hallstrom, Ron	G	6-6	283	06/11/59	Iowa	16
69	Harris, Leotis	G	6-1	265	06/28/55	Arkansas	6
23	Harvey, Maurice	S	5-10	190	01/14/56	Ball State	4
38	Hood, Estus	CB	5-11	189	11/14/55	Illinois State	16
25	Huckleby, Harlan	HB	6-1	201	12/30/57	Michigan	16
74	Huffman, Tim	T	6-5	282	08/31/59	Notre Dame	15
40	Ivery, Eddie Lee	RB	6-1	214	07/30/57	Georgia Tech	8
83	Jefferson, John	WR	6-1	204	02/03/56	Arizona State	16
99	Johnson, Charles	NT	6-2	265	06/29/57	Maryland	15
90	Johnson, Ezra	DE	6-4	259	10/02/55	Morris Brown	16
21	Jolly, Mike	S	6-3	185	03/19/58	Michigan	12
63	Jones, Terry	NT	6-2	253	11/08/56	Alabama	1
64	Kitson, Syd	G	6-4	264	09/27/58	Wake Forest	14
68	Koch, Greg	T	6-4	276	06/14/55	Arkansas	15
62	Laughlin, Jim	LB	6-1	222	07/05/58	Ohio State	15
22	Lee, Mark	CB	5-11	188	03/20/58	Washington	16
56	Lewis, Cliff	LB	6-1	224	11/09/59	Southern Mississippi	16
81	Lewis, Gary	TE	6-5	234	12/30/58	Texas-Arlington	16
26	Lewis, Tim	CB	5-11	191	12/18/61	Pittsburgh	16
80	Lofton, James	WR	6-3	197	07/05/56	Stanford	16
54	McCarren, Larry	C	6-3	251	11/09/51	Illinois	16
29	McCoy, Mike C.	CB	5-11	190	08/16/53	Colorado	9
39	Meade, Mike	RB	5-10	224	02/12/60	Penn State	16
78	Merrill, Casey	DE	6-4	255	07/16/57	California-Davis	5
37	Murphy, Mark	S	6-2	201	04/22/58	West Liberty State	16
44	O'Steen, Dwayne	CB	6-1	195	12/20/54	San Jose State	7
57	Parlavecchio, Chet	LB	6-2	225	02/14/60	Penn State	3
51	Prather, Guy	LB	6-2	229	03/28/58	Grambling	16
58	Rubens, Larry	C	6-1	250	01/25/59	Montana State	16
70	Sams, Ron	G	6-3	269	04/12/61	Pittsburgh	5
55	Scott, Randy	LB	6-1	222	01/31/59	Alabama	6
13	Scribner, Bucky	P	6-0	202	07/11/60	Kansas	16
91	Skaugstad, Daryle	NT	6-5	268	04/08/57	California	9
79	Spears, Ron	DE	6-6	255	11/23/59	San Diego State	13
10	Stenerud, Jan	K	6-2	190	11/26/43	Montana State	16
67	Swanke, Karl	T	6-6	262	12/29/57	Boston College	16
75	Turner, Rich	NT	6-2	261	02/14/59	Oklahoma	6
17	Whitehurst, David	QB	6-2	205	04/27/55	Furman	4
50	Wingo, Rich	LB	6-1	227	07/16/56	Alabama	16
20	Winters, Chet	RB	5-11	204	10/22/61	Oklahoma	4

1983 DRAFT

Rnd	Name	Pos	Ht	Wt	College
1a	Tim Lewis (11)	DB	5-11	192	Pittsburgh
	(Choice from Saints for Bruce Clark)				
1b	(Choice (20) to Chargers in John Jefferson trade)				
2	Dave Drechsler (48)	G	6-3	264	North Carolina
3	(Choice (76) to Oilers for Angelo Fields)				
4	Mike Miller (104)	WR	5-11	182	Tennessee
5	Bryan Thomas (132)	RB	5-10	198	Pittsburgh
6	Ron Sams (160)	G	6-3	265	Pittsburgh
7	Jessie Clark (188)	RB	6-0	226	Arkansas
8	Carlton Briscoe (216)	DB	6-0	180	McNeese State
9	Robin Ham (243)	C	6-2	252	West Texas State
10a	Byron Williams (253)	WR	6-1	180	Texas-Arlington
	(Choice from Oilers in Mark Koncar trade)				
10b	Jimmy Thomas (271)	DB	6-3	190	Indiana
11	Bucky Scribner (299)	P	6-0	203	Kansas
12	John Harvey (327)	LB	6-2	236	USC

1983 GREEN BAY PACKERS

FRONT ROW: (L-R) 29 Mike C. McCoy, 88 Ron Cassidy, 19 Rich Campbell, 12 Lynn Dickey, 85 Phillip Epps, 31 Gerry Ellis, 10 Jan Stenerud, 59 John Anderson, 38 Estus Hood, 54 Larry McCarren.

SECOND ROW: (L-R) 79 Ron Spears, 91 Daryle Skaugstad, 65 Ron Hallstrom, 75 Rich Turner, 26 Tim Lewis, 83 John Jefferson, 22 Mark Lee, 40 Eddie Lee Ivery, 35 Del Rodgers, 69 Leotis Harris.

THIRD ROW: (L-R) 51 Guy Prather, 57 Mike Curcio, 74 Tim Huffman, 81 Gary Lewis, 64 Syd Kitson, 21 Mike Jolly, 37 Mark Murphy, 55 Randy Scott, 63 Terry Jones.

FOURTH ROW: (L-R) 56 Cliff Lewis, 93 Robert Brown, 77 Charlie Getty, 67 Karl Swanke, 80 James Lofton, 53 Mike Douglass, 68 Greg Koch, 82 Paul Coffman, 17 David Whitehurst.

FIFTH ROW: (L-R) 99 Charles Johnson, 13 Bucky Scribner, 90 Ezra Johnson, 52 George Cumby, 50 Rich Wingo, 58 Larry Rubens, 70 Ron Sams.

SIXTH ROW: (L-R) 62 Jim McLaughlin, 11 Eddie Garcia, 39 Mike Meade, 33 Jessie Clark, 25 Harlan Huckleby, 61 Dave Drechsler, 24 Johnnie Gray, 20 Chet Winters, 72 Greg Boyd, 73 Byron Braggs.

BACK ROW: (L-R) Offensive Backfield Coach John Brunner, Receivers Coach Lew Carpenter, Pro Player Personnel Director Burt Gustafson, Special Teams Coach Dick Rehbein, Defensive Backfield Coach Ross Fichtner, Defensive Line Coach Richard (Doc) Urich, Offensive Line Coach Bill Meyers, Head Coach Bart Starr, Offensive Coordinator Bob Schnelker, Offensive Line Coach Ernie McMillan, Defensive Coordinator John Meyer, Linebackers Coach Monte Kiffin.

1984

Two seasons in one. It happened in 1981 and again in a slightly more dramatic fashion in 1984. Coach Forrest Gregg assumed command and his men edged St. Louis 24-23 on opening day. Seven straight losses followed, the most in a row in a single season since 1958. On October 28, Eddie Lee Ivery regained full strength and ran for 116 yards on nine carries to spark a 41-9 blowout of Detroit. With him healthy, the Packers won seven of their last eight and wound up 8-8 for the second straight year.

Five factors contributed to the resurgence. First, Ivery, who missed the first six games with a recurring knee problem, returned to rejuvenate a rushing attack that was averaging 94 yards per game. His 552, second-half output helped Green Bay average 158 per game in the season's second half.

After a 9-7 loss to the Bears in week three, Gregg pulled guards Dave Drechsler and Syd Kitson from the starting lineup. He replaced the pair with jumbo-sized Ron Hallstrom and Tim Huffman. Kitson was released on October 23 to make room for guard Keith Uecker while Drechsler lasted the year as a backup. After having allowed 31 sacks at midseason, the line jelled and surrendered just 11 the rest of the way.

A third factor that coincided with the improved line play was a startling transformation in the team's turnover ratio. A minus nine figure was followed by a +14 in the second half. Rookie Tom Flynn contributed to the turnaround by intercepting nine passes, eight after midseason. Tim Lewis picked off seven, including one for a team-record 99 yards and a touchdown against the Rams.

Next, a change in the kicking game proved profitable. Gregg had traded the nearly-automatic Jan Stenerud to Minnesota in the off-season. But Eddie Garcia, the heir apparent, hit just three of nine field goals. After Garcia botched two tries in a 17-14 loss to Denver in a snow storm, Gregg turned to Al Del Greco who connected on nine of twelve down the stretch.

And finally, the defense improved. Hank Bullough had been scheduled to rebuild the unit, but he departed in May for the United States Football League (USFL). Instead, Dick Modzelewski crafted the defense, which rose from last to 16th in 1984.

Any playoff hopes the team may have had disappeared in Detroit on Thanksgiving. The Packers had won four straight, the last a 31-6 whipping of the playoff-bound Los Angeles Rams. Against the Lions however, Green Bay blew a 21-7 lead, gave up 518 yards and closed the door on any chance for postseason play.

The contest was also notable in that it marked the first time in 162 games that the Packers were without center Larry McCarren. A pinched nerve in his neck kept him out for that and the final three games. He attempted to come back in 1985 but announced his retirement that August. "The Rock" as he was known, had anchored the line longer than Charley Brock, Jim Ringo, or Ken Bowman; a very select group in whose company McCarren belonged.

Green Bay Press-Gazette photo

James Lofton (80) one-hands a 20-yard touchdown pass from Lynn Dickey in the first quarter of the Packers 30-24 loss to Seattle on October 21. Lofton caught five passes for 162 yards and opened the day's scoring with his other touchdown catch, a 79-yarder. The former Stanford standout led the team in receiving for the fifth year in a row, this time collecting 62 passes for 1,361 yards.

TEAM STATISTICS

	GB	OPP
First Downs	315	323
Rushing	120	136
Passing	168	166
Penalty	27	21
Rushes	461	545
Yards Gained	2,019	2,145
Average Gain	4.38	3.94
Average Yards per Game	126.2	134.1
Passes Attempted	506	551
Completed	281	315
% Completed	55.53	57.17
Total Yards Gained	3,740	3,470
Times Sacked	42	44
Yards Lost	310	324
Net Yards Gained	3,430	3,146
Yards Gained per Completion	13.31	11.02
Net Yards per Attempt	6.26	5.29
Average Net Yards per Game	214.4	196.6
Combined Net Yards Gained	5,449	5,291
Total Plays	1,009	1,140
Average Yards per Play	5.40	4.64
Average Net Yards per Game	340.6	330.7
Third Down Efficiency	75/205	89/243
Percentage	36.59	36.63
Intercepted By	27	30
Yards Returned	338	317
Returned for TD	2	2
Punts	85	89
Yards Punted	3,596	3,643
Average Yards per Punt	42.31	40.93
Punt Returns	48	46
Yards Returned	351	368
Average Yards per Return	7.31	8.00
Returned for TD	0	0
Kickoff Returns	67	73
Yards Returned	1,362	1,171
Average Yards per Return	20.33	16.04
Returned for TD	1	0
Penalties	110	145
Yards Penalized	915	1,129
Fumbles	17	33
Lost	7	15
Own Recovered for Touchdown	0	0
Opponent's Recovered by	15	7
Opponent's Recovered for Touchdown	0	2
Total Points Scored	390	309
Total Touchdowns	51	34
Touchdowns Rushing	18	14
Touchdowns Passing	30	16
Touchdowns on Returns & Recoveries	3	4
Extra Points	48	33
Safeties	0	0
Field Goals Attempted	21	31
Field Goals Made	12	24
% Successful	57.14	77.42
Average Time of Possession	26:48	33:12

Regular Season 8-8-0

Date	GB		OPP	Att.
9/2	24	St. Louis Cardinals	23	(53,738)
9/9	7	at Los Angeles Raiders	28	(46,269)
9/16	7	Chicago Bears	9	(55,942)
9/23	6	at Dallas Cowboys	20	(64,222)
9/30	27	at TB Buccaneers (OT)	30	(47,487)
10/7	28	San Diego Chargers	34	(54,045)
10/15	14	at Denver Broncos	17	(62,546)
10/21	24	Seattle Seahawks (M)	30	(52,286)
10/28	41	Detroit Lions	9	(54,289)
11/4	23	at New Orleans Saints	13	(57,426)
11/11	45	Minnesota Vikings (M)	17	(52,931)
11/18	31	Los Angeles Rams (M)	6	(52,031)
11/22	28	at Detroit Lions	31	(63,698)
12/2	27	Tampa Bay Buccaneers	14	(46,800)
12/9	20	at Chicago Bears	14	(59,374)
12/16	38	at Minnesota Vikings	14	(51,197)

Score By Periods

	1	2	3	4	OT	Total
Packers	79	121	108	82	0	390
Opponents	72	88	65	81	3	309

INDIVIDUAL STATISTICS

Rushing

	Att	Yds	Avg	LG	TD
G. Ellis	123	581	4.7	50	4
Ivery	99	552	5.6	49	6
J. Clark	87	375	4.3	t43	4
Crouse	53	169	3.2	14	0
Huckleby	35	145	4.1	23	0
Rodgers	25	94	3.8	15	0
Lofton	10	82	8.2	26	0
R. Wright	8	11	1.4	5	0
Dickey	18	6	0.3	9	3
Campbell	2	2	1.0	5	1
E. West	1	2	2.0	t2	1
Packers	**461**	**2,019**	**4.4**	**50**	**18**
Opponents	545	2,145	3.9	39	14

1984

Receiving

	No	Yds	Avg	LG	TD
Lofton	62	1,361	22.0	t79	7
Coffman	43	562	13.1	t44	9
G. Ellis	36	312	8.7	22	2
J. Clark	29	234	8.1	20	2
Epps	26	435	16.7	56	3
J. Jefferson	26	339	13.0	33	0
Ivery	19	141	7.4	18	1
Crouse	9	93	10.3	25	1
Huckleby	8	65	8.1	13	0
E. West	6	54	9.0	t29	4
Rodgers	5	56	11.2	22	0
Childs	4	32	8.0	17	0
G. Lewis	4	29	7.3	15	0
Cassidy	2	16	8.0	10	0
L. Taylor	1	8	8.0	8	0
Blake Moore	1	3	3.0	t3	1
Packers	**281**	**3,740**	**13.3**	**t79**	**30**
Opponents	315	3,470	11.0	50	16

Passing

	Att	Com	Yds	Pct	TD	In	Tk/Yds	Rate
Dickey	401	237	3,195	59.1	25	19	32/244	85.6
R. Wright	62	27	310	43.5	2	6	4/17	30.4
R. Campbell	38	16	218	42.1	3	5	5/46	47.8
G. Ellis	4	1	17	25.0	0	0	1/3	—
Scribner	1	0	0	00.0	0	0	0/0	—
Packers	**506**	**281**	**3,740**	**55.5**	**30**	**30**	**42/310**	**74.2**
Opponents	551	315	3,470	57.2	16	27	44/324	65.2

Punting

	No	Yds	Avg	In20	TB	LG	HB
Scribner	85	3,596	42.3	18	12	61	0
Packers	**85**	**3,596**	**42.3**	**18**	**12**	**61**	**0**
Opponents	89	3,643	40.9	13	4	63	0

Kickoff Returns

	No	Yds	Avg	LG	TD
Rodgers	39	843	21.6	t97	1
Huckleby	14	261	18.6	54	0
Epps	12	232	19.3	47	0
D. Jones	1	19	19.0	19	0
Prather	1	7	7.0	7	0
Packers	**67**	**1,362**	**20.3**	**t97**	**1**
Opponents	73	1,171	16.0	51	0

Punt Returns

	No	Yds	Avg	FC	LG	TD
Epps	29	199	6.9	10	39	0
Flynn	15	128	8.5	4	20	0
G. Hayes	4	24	6.0	0	10	0
M. Murphy	0	0	0.0	2	0	0
Packers	**48**	**351**	**7.3**	**16**	**39**	**0**
Opponents	46	368	8.0	5	22	0

Interceptions

	No	Yds	Avg	LG	TD
Flynn	9	106	11.8	31	0
T. Lewis	7	151	21.6	t99	1
M. Lee	3	33	11.0	14	0
J. Anderson	3	24	8.0	22	0
Hood	1	8	8.0	8	0
Cumby	1	7	7.0	7	0
R. Brown	1	5	5.0	t5	1
M. Murphy	1	4	4.0	4	0
McLeod	1	0	0.0	0	0
Packers	**27**	**338**	**12.5**	**t99**	**2**
Opponents	30	317	10.6	t53	2

Scoring

	TDr	TDp	TDrt	PAT	FG	S	TP
Del Greco	0	0	0	34/34	9/12	0	61
Coffman	0	9	0	0/0	0/0	0	54
Ivery	6	1	0	0/0	0/0	0	42
Lofton	0	7	0	0/0	0/0	0	42
J. Clark	4	2	0	0/0	0/0	0	36
G. Ellis	4	2	0	0/0	0/0	0	36
E. West	1	4	0	0/0	0/0	0	30
Garcia	0	0	0	14/15	3/9	0	23
Dickey	3	0	0	0/0	0/0	0	18
Epps	0	3	0	0/0	0/0	0	18
R. Brown	0	0	1	0/0	0/0	0	6
Crouse	0	1	0	0/0	0/0	0	6
T. Lewis	0	0	1	0/0	0/0	0	6
Blake Moore	0	1	0	0/0	0/0	0	6
Rodgers	0	0	1	0/0	0/0	0	6
Packers	**18**	**30**	**3**	**48/51**	**12/21**	**0**	**390**
Opponents	14	16	4	33/34	24/31	0	309

Fumbles

	Fum	Ow	Op	Yds	Tot
J. Anderson	0	0	1	0	1
R. Campbell	1	0	0	0	0
J. Clark	2	0	0	0	0
Coffman	1	1	0	0	1
Cumby	0	0	2	0	2
Dickey	3	1	0	-11	1
M. Douglass	0	0	1	0	2
G. Ellis	2	0	0	0	0
Epps	1	0	0	0	1
Flynn	0	0	3	3	3
Hallstrom	0	2	0	1	2
Huckleby	1	1	0	0	1
Ivery	1	0	0	0	0
D. Jones	0	1	2	0	3
T. Jones	0	0	1	0	1
M. Lee	0	0	2	0	2
Lofton	1	0	0	0	0
McLeod	1	0	0	0	1
M. Murphy	1	0	1	2	1
Prather	0	0	1	0	1
Rodgers	1	0	0	0	0
E. West	0	1	0	0	1
R. Wright	1	1	0	0	1
Packers	**17**	**10**	**15**	**-5**	**25**

Quarterback Sacks

	No
M. Douglass	9.0
E. Johnson	7.0
R. Brown	5.0
T. Jones	4.0
J. Anderson	3.5
Carreker	3.0
C. Martin	3.0
R. Scott	3.0
Cumby	2.5
M. Murphy	2.0
Humphrey	1.0
Neill	1.0
Packers	**44.0**
Opponents	42.0

NFL STANDINGS

National Conference

Eastern Division

	W	L	T	Pct	PF	PA
Washington Redskins	11	5	0	.688	426	310
New York Giants	9	7	0	.563	299	301
St. Louis Cardinals	9	7	0	.563	423	345
Dallas Cowboys	9	7	0	.563	308	308
Philadelphia Eagles	6	9	1	.406	278	320

Central Division

	W	L	T	Pct	PF	PA
Chicago Bears	10	6	0	.625	325	248
Green Bay Packers	8	8	0	.500	390	309
Tampa Bay Buccaneers	6	10	0	.375	335	380
Detroit Lions	4	11	1	.281	283	408
Minnesota Vikings	3	13	0	.188	276	484

Western Division

	W	L	T	Pct	PF	PA
San Francisco 49ers	15	1	0	.938	475	227
Los Angeles Rams	10	6	0	.625	346	316
New Orleans Saints	7	9	0	.438	298	361
Atlanta Falcons	4	12	0	.250	281	382

American Conference

Eastern Division

	W	L	T	Pct	PF	PA
Miami Dolphins	14	2	0	.875	513	298
New England Patriots	9	7	0	.563	362	352
New York Jets	7	9	0	.438	332	364
Indianapolis Colts	4	12	0	.250	239	414
Buffalo Bills	2	14	0	.125	250	454

Central Division

	W	L	T	Pct	PF	PA
Pittsburgh Steelers	9	7	0	.563	387	310
Cincinnati Bengals	8	8	0	.500	339	339
Cleveland Browns	5	11	0	.313	250	297
Houston Oilers	3	13	0	.188	240	437

Western Division

	W	L	T	Pct	PF	PA
Denver Broncos	13	3	0	.813	353	241
Seattle Seahawks	12	4	0	.750	418	282
Los Angeles Raiders	11	5	0	.688	368	278
Kansas City Chiefs	8	8	0	.500	314	324
San Diego Chargers	7	9	0	.438	394	413

1984 ROSTER

No	Name	Pos	Ht	Wt	DOB	College	G
59	Anderson, John	LB	6-3	229	02/14/56	Michigan	16
93	Brown, Robert	DE	6-2	250	05/21/60	Virginia Tech	16
19	Campbell, Rich	QB	6-4	219	12/22/58	California	3
58	Cannon, Mark	C	6-3	258	06/14/62	Texas-Arlington	16
76	Carreker, Alphonso	DE	6-6	260	05/25/62	Florida State	14
88	Cassidy, Ron	WR	6-0	180	07/23/57	Utah State	15
89	Childs, Henry	TE	6-2	220	04/16/51	Kansas State	3
33	Clark, Jessie	FB	6-0	233	01/03/60	Arkansas	11
82	Coffman, Paul	TE	6-3	225	03/29/56	Kansas State	14
21	Crouse, Ray	RB	5-11	214	03/16/59	Nevada-Las Vegas	16
52	Cumby, George	LB	6-0	224	07/05/56	Oklahoma	16
10	Del Greco, Al	K	5-10	195	03/02/62	Auburn	9
98	DeLuca, Tony	NT	6-4	250	11/16/60	Rhode Island	1
12	Dickey, Lynn	QB	6-4	203	10/19/49	Kansas State	15
99	Dorsey, John	LB	6-2	235	08/31/60	Connecticut	16
53	Douglass, Mike	LB	6-0	214	03/15/55	San Diego State	16
61	Drechsler, Dave	G	6-3	264	07/18/60	North Carolina	16
31	Ellis, Gerry	FB	5-11	225	11/12/57	Missouri	16
85	Epps, Phillip	WR	5-10	165	11/11/58	TCU	16
41	Flynn, Tom	S	6-0	195	03/24/62	Pittsburgh	15
11	Garcia, Eddie	K	5-8	178	04/15/59	SMU	7
65	Hallstrom, Ron	G	6-6	283	06/11/59	Iowa	16
27	Hayes, Gary	CB	5-10	180	08/19/57	Fresno State	16
78	Hoffman, Gary	T	6-7	282	09/28/61	Santa Clara	1
38	Hood, Estus	CB	5-11	189	11/14/55	Illinois State	16
25	Huckleby, Harlan	HB	6-1	201	12/30/57	Michigan	16
74	Huffman, Tim	T	6-5	282	08/31/59	Notre Dame	16
79	Humphrey, Donnie	DE	6-3	275	04/20/61	Auburn	16
40	Ivery, Eddie Lee	RB	6-1	214	07/30/57	Georgia Tech	10
83	Jefferson, John	WR	6-1	204	02/03/56	Arizona State	13
90	Johnson, Ezra	DE	6-4	259	10/02/55	Morris Brown	13
71	Jones, Boyd	T	6-3	272	05/30/61	Texas Southern	2
43	Jones, Daryll	S	6-0	190	03/23/62	Georgia	16
63	Jones, Terry	NT	6-2	253	11/08/56	Alabama	16
64	Kitson, Syd	G	6-4	264	09/27/58	Wake Forest	8
68	Koch, Greg	T	6-4	276	06/14/55	Arkansas	15
22	Lee, Mark	CB	5-11	188	03/20/58	Washington	16
56	Lewis, Cliff	LB	6-1	224	11/09/59	Southern Mississippi	16
81	Lewis, Gary	TE	6-5	234	12/30/58	Texas-Arlington	3
26	Lewis, Tim	CB	5-11	191	12/18/61	Pittsburgh	16
80	Lofton, James	WR	6-3	197	07/05/56	Stanford	16
94	Martin, Charles	DE	6-4	270	08/31/59	Livingston	16
54	McCarren, Larry	C	6-3	263	11/09/51	Illinois	12
28	McLeod, Mike	S	6-0	180	05/04/58	Montana State	11
60	Moore, Blake	C	6-5	272	05/08/58	Wooster	11
37	Murphy, Mark	S	6-2	201	04/22/58	West Liberty State	16
77	Neill, Bill	NT	6-4	255	03/15/59	Pittsburgh	16
44	O'Steen, Dwayne	CB	6-1	195	12/20/54	San Jose State	4
51	Prather, Guy	LB	6-2	229	03/28/58	Grambling	16
35	Rodgers, Del	RB	5-10	202	06/22/60	Utah	14
55	Scott, Randy	LB	6-1	222	01/31/59	Alabama	16
13	Scribner, Bucky	P	6-0	202	07/11/60	Kansas	16
67	Swanke, Karl	T	6-6	262	12/29/57	Boston College	15
84	Taylor, Lenny	WR	5-10	179	02/15/61	Tennessee	2
70	Uecker, Keith	G	6-5	270	06/29/60	Auburn	6
49/86	West, Ed	TE	6-1	242	08/02/61	Auburn	16
50	Wingo, Rich	LB	6-1	227	07/16/56	Alabama	16
16	Wright, Randy	QB	6-2	194	01/12/61	Wisconsin	8

1984 DRAFT

Rnd	Name	Pos	Ht	Wt	College
1	Alphonso Carreker (12)	DE	6-6	260	Florida State
2	(Choice (39) to Chargers in John Jefferson trade)				
3	Donnie Humphrey (72)	DE	6-3	275	Auburn
4	John Dorsey (99)	LB	6-2	235	Connecticut
5	Tom Flynn (126)	S	6-0	195	Pittsburgh
6	Randy Wright (153)	QB	6-2	194	Wisconsin
7	Daryll Jones (181)	DB	6-0	190	Georgia
8	(Choice (207) to Broncos for Greg Boyd)				
9	(Choice (240) to Chiefs for Charlie Getty)				
10	Gary Hoffman (267)	T	6-7	282	Santa Clara
11	Mark Cannon (294)	C	6-3	258	Texas-Arlington
12a	Lenny Taylor (313)	WR	5-10	179	Tennessee
	(Choice from Chargers for Derrel Gofourth)				
12b	Mark Emans (323)	LB	6-3	223	Bowling Green

1984 GREEN BAY PACKERS

FRONT ROW: (L-R) 11 Eddie Garcia, 12 Lynn Dickey, 13 Bucky Scribner, 16 Randy Wright, 19 Rich Campbell, 21 Ray Crouse, 22 Mark Lee, 24 Johnnie Gray, 25 Harlan Huckleby.

SECOND ROW: (L-R) 26 Tim Lewis, 27 Gary Hayes, 29 Mike C. McCoy, 31 Gerry Ellis, 33 Jessie Clark, 35 Del Rodgers, 37 Mark Murphy, 38 Estus Hood, 40 Eddie Lee Ivery, 41 Tom Flynn.

THIRD ROW: (L-R) 42 Lenny Taylor, 43 Daryll Jones, 44 Dwayne O'Steen, 50 Rich Wingo, 51 Guy Prather, 52 George Cumby, 53 Mike Douglass, 54 Larry McCarren, 55 Randy Scott.

FOURTH ROW: (L-R) 56 Cliff Lewis, 58 Mark Cannon, 59 John Anderson, 61 Dave Drechsler, 63 Terry Jones, 64 Syd Kitson, 65 Ron Hallstrom, 67 Karl Swanke, 68 Greg Koch, 69 Leotis Harris.

FIFTH ROW: (L-R) 74 Tim Huffman, 76 Alphonso Carreker, 77 Bill Neill, 78 Gary Hoffman, 79 Donnie Humphrey, 80 James Lofton, 81 Gary Lewis, 82 Paul Coffman, 83 John Jefferson, 85 Phillip Epps.

SIXTH ROW: (L-R) Equipment Manager Bob Noel, 86 Ed West, 88 Ron Cassidy, 89 Henry Childs, 90 Ezra Johnson, 93 Robert Brown, 94 Charles Martin, 95 Ken Walter, 99 John Dorsey, Equipment Assistant Jack Noel.

BACK ROW: (L-R) Special Teams/Linebackers Coach Chuck Priefer, Trainer Domenic Gentile, Receivers Coach Lew Carpenter, Offensive Line Coach Jerry Wampfler, Linebackers/Special Teams Coach Herb Paterra, Offensive Coordinator Bob Schnelker, Head Coach Forrest Gregg, Strength-Conditioning Coach Virgil Knight, Secondary Coach Ken Riley, Defensive Coordinator/Line Coach Dick Modzelewski, Offensive Backfield Coach George Sefcik, Director of Pro Personnel Burt Gustafson.

1985

For the third year in a row and the fourth time in the last five seasons, Green Bay finished 8-8. A strong second-half showing (five wins) enabled the team to do that. But the second-half victories all came against opponents with losing records. Down the stretch, the Packers couldn't beat the playoff-bound Bears, Rams or Dolphins. That fact, when taken into account with the team's poor start, explains why Green Bay didn't come close to a postseason berth.

An unsettled situation at quarterback, unseen since the days of Dan Devine, didn't help matters. Lynn Dickey entered the campaign as the starter but benched himself prior to the St. Louis game in week four. Though he came back in relief after his team had fallen behind the Cardinals 26-0 and threw three touchdown passes, the team was without a clearcut starter for the remainder of the season. Dickey, Jim Zorn and Randy Wright all took a turn at the helm with no better than adequate results.

Also reminiscent of the Devine era was the team's rushing attack. Not since John Brockington piled up 1,105 yards as a rookie had the Packers gained more yards on the ground than the 2,208 churned out in 1985. Eddie Lee Ivery, Jessie Clark and Gerry Ellis combined for 1,840 yards and an impressive 4.8 average per carry. The Packers were 7-2 in games in which they outrushed their opponents.

Green Bay threatened to begin 1985 as it had done 1984. Except for a narrow 23-20 win over the New York Giants in week two, the Packers couldn't find the win column and were 1-3 in the season's first quarter.

Green Bay came to life with a 43-10 pasting of the Lions in week five. James Lofton caught 10 passes for 151 yards and the team put together its most potent attack of the year, 227 yards passing and 285 rushing.

Unfortunately, the team slipped back into inconsistency. After edging Minnesota 20-17 on the strength of Al Del Greco's 22-yard field goal with seven seconds left, Green Bay was smothered by the Bears 23-7. The next week, the lowly (2-5) Colts stunned the Packers 37-10. A flareup involving assistant coach Virgil Knight and linebacker Mike Douglass occurred as the team reached the locker room. Frustrations continued when the Bears again beat the Packers in week nine and dropped Green Bay to 3-6. By then, playoff hopes had all but vanished.

A Dec. 1 game played in blizzard conditions at Lambeau Field against the visiting warm-weather Buccaneers, provided some late-season fun. The "Snow Bowl," as it was dubbed, turned into a 21-0 rout of Tampa Bay. Both Ellis (9-101) and Ivery (13-109) surpassed the 100-yard rushing mark and Lofton caught six passes for 106 yards. Green Bay mushed its way to 512 yards while holding Tampa Bay to a paltry 65 before 19,856 diehard fans.

Sadly, the game was the last of Dickey's career. On the following Thursday he injured his neck while working out on a nautilus machine and never played again. Dickey departed having thrown for more yards in a Packers uniform than any one short of the coach who brought him to Green Bay in the first place: Bart Starr.

Green Bay Press-Gazette photo

Gerry Ellis (31) stiff arms Bob Brudzinski (59) on the way to a gain against the Dolphins in Green Bay. The Packers lost the early-December matchup 34-24. Ellis picked up 50 yards rushing on five carries to pace the ground game. At season's end, he placed third among Green Bay's backs with 571 yards on 104 carries for a healthy 5.5 yards per carry.

TEAM STATISTICS

	GB	OPP
First Downs	318	310
Rushing	114	111
Passing	172	178
Penalty	32	21
Rushes	470	494
Yards Gained	2,208	2,047
Average Gain	4.70	4.14
Average Yards per Game	138.0	127.9
Passes Attempted	513	509
Completed	267	295
% Completed	52.05	57.96
Total Yards Gained	3,552	3,509
Times Sacked	50	48
Yards Lost	389	383
Net Yards Gained	3,163	3,126
Yards Gained per Completion	13.30	11.89
Net Yards per Attempt	5.62	5.61
Average Net Yards per Game	197.7	195.4
Combined Net Yards Gained	5,371	5,173
Total Plays	1,033	1,051
Average Yards per Play	5.20	4.92
Average Net Yards per Game	335.7	323.3
Third Down Efficiency	66/200	80/213
Percentage	33.00	37.56
Fourth Down Efficiency	6/12	6/15
Percentage	50.00	40.00
Intercepted By	15	27
Yards Returned	262	326
Returned for TD	2	1
Punts	82	77
Yards Punted	3,262	3,290
Average Yards per Punt	39.78	42.73
Punt Returns	38	46
Yards Returned	370	411
Average Yards per Return	9.74	8.93
Returned for TD	0	0
Kickoff Returns	67	71
Yards Returned	1,318	1,570
Average Yards per Return	19.67	22.11
Returned for TD	0	2
Penalties	101	102
Yards Penalized	798	797
Fumbles	39	44
Lost	18	25
Own Recovered for Touchdown	0	0
Opponent's Recovered by	25	18
Opponent's Recovered for Touchdown	1	1
Total Points Scored	337	355
Total Touchdowns	40	43
Touchdowns Rushing	16	17
Touchdowns Passing	21	22
Touchdowns on Returns & Recoveries	3	4
Extra Points	38	41
Safeties	1	4
Field Goals Attempted	26	31
Field Goals Made	19	16
% Successful	73.08	51.61
Average Time of Possession	28:59	31:01

Regular Season 8-8-0

Date	GB		OPP	Att.
9/8	20	at New England Patriots	26	(49,488)
9/15	23	New York Giants	20	(56,149)
9/22	3	New York Jets (M)	24	(53,667)
9/29	28	at St. Louis Cardinals	43	(48,598)
10/6	43	Detroit Lions	10	(55,914)
10/13	20	Minnesota Vikings	17	(54,674)
10/21	7	at Chicago Bears	23	(65,095)
10/27	10	at Indianapolis Colts	37	(59,708)
11/3	10	Chicago Bears	16	(56,895)
11/10	27	at Minnesota Vikings	17	(59,970)
11/17	38	New Orleans Saints (M)	14	(52,104)
11/24	17	at Los Angeles Rams	34	(52,710)
12/1	21	Tampa Bay Buccaneers	0	(19,856)
12/8	24	Miami Dolphins	34	(52,671)
12/15	26	at Detroit Lions	23	(49,379)
12/22	20	at Tampa Bay Buccaneers	17	(33,992)

Score By Periods

	1	2	3	4	OT	Total
Packers	50	82	89	116	0	337
Opponents	68	109	66	112	0	355

INDIVIDUAL STATISTICS

Rushing

	Att	Yds	Avg	LG	TD
Ivery	132	636	4.8	34	2
J. Clark	147	633	4.3	80	5
G. Ellis	104	571	5.5	t39	5
Ellerson	32	205	6.4	t37	2
Epps	5	103	20.6	34	1
Huckleby	8	41	5.1	15	0
Lofton	4	14	3.5	21	0
Zorn	10	9	0.9	8	0
R. Wright	8	8	1.0	8	0
Prather	1	0	0.0	0	0
E. West	1	0	0.0	0	0
Dickey	18	-12	-0.7	3	1
Packers	**470**	**2,208**	**4.7**	**80**	**16**
Opponents	494	2,047	4.1	t65	17

Receiving

	No	Yds	Avg	LG	TD
Lofton	69	1,153	16.7	t56	4
Coffman	49	666	13.6	32	6
Epps	44	683	15.5	63	3
Ivery	28	270	9.6	24	2
J. Clark	24	252	10.5	t55	2
G. Ellis	24	206	8.6	35	0
Dennard	13	182	14.0	34	2
E. West	8	95	11.9	30	1
Huckleby	5	27	5.4	8	0
Ellerson	2	15	7.5	11	0
Blake Moore	1	3	3.0	13	1
Packers	**267**	**3,552**	**13.3**	**63**	**21**
Opponents	295	3,509	11.9	t61	22

Passing

	Att	Com	Yds	Pct	TD	In	Tk/Yds	Rate
Dickey	314	172	2,206	54.8	15	17	30/226	70.4
Zorn	123	56	794	45.5	4	6	11/89	57.4
R. Wright	74	39	552	52.7	2	4	8/67	63.6
G. Ellis	1	0	0	00.0	0	0	0/0	—
Ivery	1	0	0	00.0	0	0	1/7	—
Packers	**513**	**267**	**3,552**	**52.0**	**21**	**27**	**50/389**	**66.0**
Opponents	509	295	3,509	58.0	22	15	48/383	81.2

Punting

	No	Yds	Avg	In20	TB	LG	HB
Prokop	56	2,210	39.5	9	6	66	0
Bracken	26	1,052	40.5	1	2	54	0
Packers	**82**	**3,262**	**39.8**	**10**	**8**	**66**	**0**
Opponents	77	3,290	42.7	24	11	68	0

Kickoff Returns

	No	Yds	Avg	LG	TD
Ellerson	29	521	18.0	32	0
G. Ellis	13	247	19.0	40	0
Epps	12	279	23.3	48	0
Stanley	9	212	23.6	36	0
Flynn	1	20	20.0	20	0
J. Anderson	1	14	14.0	14	0
Stills	1	14	14.0	14	0
D. Jones	1	11	11.0	11	0
Packers	**67**	**1,318**	**19.7**	**48**	**0**
Opponents	71	1,570	22.1	t98	2

Punt Returns

	No	Yds	Avg	FC	LG	TD
Epps	15	146	9.7	3	46	0
Stanley	14	179	12.8	1	27	0
Flynn	7	41	5.9	4	13	0
M. Murphy	1	4	4.0	0	4	0
G. Hayes	1	0	0.0	2	0	0
Packers	**38**	**370**	**9.7**	**10**	**46**	**0**
Opponents	46	411	8.9	10	47	0

Interceptions

	No	Yds	Avg	LG	TD
T. Lewis	4	4	1.0	4	0
M. Douglass	2	126	63.0	t80	1
M. Murphy	2	50	25.0	t50	1
R. Scott	2	50	25.0	30	0
J. Anderson	2	2	1.0	2	0
M. Lee	1	23	23.0	23	0
Flynn	1	7	7.0	7	0
Cade	1	0	0.0	0	0
Packers	**15**	**262**	**17.5**	**180**	**2**
Opponents	27	326	12.1	67	1

Scoring

	TDr	TDp	TDrt	PAT	FG	S	TP
Del Greco	0	0	0	38/40	19/26	0	95
J. Clark	5	2	0	0/0	0/0	0	42
Coffman	0	6	0	0/0	0/0	0	36
G. Ellis	5	0	0	0/0	0/0	0	30
Epps	1	3	0	0/0	0/0	0	24
Ivery	2	2	0	0/0	0/0	0	24
Lofton	0	4	0	0/0	0/0	0	24
Dennard	0	2	0	0/0	0/0	0	12
Ellerson	2	0	0	0/0	0/0	0	12
Dickey	1	0	0	0/0	0/0	0	6
M. Douglass	0	0	1	0/0	0/0	0	6
T. Lewis	0	0	1	0/0	0/0	0	6
Blake Moore	0	1	0	0/0	0/0	0	6
M. Murphy	0	0	1	0/0	0/0	0	6
E. West	0	1	0	0/0	0/0	0	6
R. Brown	0	0	0	0/0	0/0	1	2
Packers	**16**	**21**	**3**	**38/40**	**19/26**	**1**	**337**
Opponents	17	22	4	41/43	16/31	4	355

Fumbles

	Fum	Ow	Op	Yds	Tot
J. Anderson	0	0	1	0	1
R. Brown	0	0	4	0	4
Cade	0	0	1	0	1
Cannon	0	2	0	0	2
J. Clark	4	2	0	0	2
Coffman	1	0	0	0	0
Dennard	1	0	0	0	0
Dickey	8	5	0	-18	5
J. Dorsey	0	0	2	0	2
Ellerson	3	2	1	0	3
G. Ellis	2	1	0	0	0
Epps	1	0	0	0	0
Flynn	0	1	0	0	1
Hallstrom	0	1	1	2	3
G. Hayes	1	1	0	0	1
Ivery	1	0	0	0	1
E. Johnson	0	0	2	0	2
Koch	0	1	0	0	1
T. Lewis	0	0	1	6	1
Lofton	3	0	0	0	0
C. Martin	0	1	0	0	1
Blake Moore	1	0	0	0	0
M. Murphy	0	0	1	0	1
Prather	0	1	0	0	1
R. Scott	0	0	5	31	5
Stanley	2	0	0	0	0
Uecker	0	1	0	0	1
E. West	1	0	0	0	0
R. Wright	5	2	0	-6	2
Zorn	3	2	0	-1	2
Packers	**39**	**20**	**25**	**12**	**45**

Quarterback Sacks

	No
E. Johnson	9.5
Carreker	9.0
J. Anderson	6.0
M. Murphy	4.0
R. Brown	3.0
C. Martin	3.0
Noble	3.0
R. Scott	3.0
M. Butler	2.0
Humphrey	2.0
Prather	2.0
M. Douglass	1.5
Packers	**48.0**
Opponents	50.0

NFL STANDINGS

National Conference

Eastern Division

	W	L	T	Pct	PF	PA
Dallas Cowboys	10	6	0	.625	357	333
New York Giants	10	6	0	.625	399	283
Washington Redskins	10	6	0	.625	297	312
Philadelphia Eagles	7	9	0	.438	286	310
St. Louis Cardinals	5	11	0	.313	278	414

Central Division

	W	L	T	Pct	PF	PA
Chicago Bears	15	1	0	.938	456	198
Green Bay Packers	**8**	**8**	**0**	**.500**	**337**	**355**
Minnesota Vikings	7	9	0	.438	346	359
Detroit Lions	7	9	0	.438	307	366
Tampa Bay Buccaneers	2	14	0	.125	294	448

Western Division

	W	L	T	Pct	PF	PA
Los Angeles Rams	11	5	0	.688	340	277
San Francisco 49ers	10	6	0	.625	411	263
New Orleans Saints	5	11	0	.313	294	401
Atlanta Falcons	4	12	0	.250	282	452

American Conference

Eastern Division

	W	L	T	Pct	PF	PA
Miami Dolphins	12	4	0	.750	428	320
New York Jets	11	5	0	.688	393	264
New England Patriots	11	5	0	.688	362	290
Indianapolis Colts	5	11	0	.313	320	386
Buffalo Bills	2	14	0	.125	200	381

Central Division

	W	L	T	Pct	PF	PA
Cleveland Browns	8	8	0	.500	287	294
Cincinnati Bengals	7	9	0	.438	441	437
Pittsburgh Steelers	7	9	0	.438	379	355
Houston Oilers	5	11	0	.313	284	412

Western Division

	W	L	T	Pct	PF	PA
Los Angeles Raiders	12	4	0	.750	354	308
Denver Broncos	11	5	0	.688	380	329
Seattle Seahawks	8	8	0	.500	349	303
San Diego Chargers	8	8	0	.500	467	435
Kansas City Chiefs	6	10	0	.375	317	360

1985 ROSTER

No	Name	Pos	Ht	Wt	DOB	College	G
59	Anderson, John	LB	6-3	229	02/14/56	Michigan	16
17	Bracken, Don	P	6-0	205	02/16/62	Michigan	7
93	Brown, Robert	DE	6-2	270	05/21/60	Virginia Tech	16
39	Burgess, Ronnie	DB	5-11	175	03/07/63	Wake Forest	11
77	Butler, Mike	DE	6-5	269	04/04/54	Kansas	12
24	Cade, Mossy	CB	6-1	195	12/26/61	Texas	14
58	Cannon, Mark	C	6-3	268	06/14/62	Texas-Arlington	16
76	Carreker, Alphonso	DE	6-6	270	05/25/62	Florida State	16
23	Clanton, Chuck	DB	5-11	192	05/15/62	Auburn	3
33	Clark, Jessie	FB	6-0	233	01/03/60	Arkansas	16
82	Coffman, Paul	TE	6-3	225	03/29/56	Kansas State	16
52	Cumby, George	LB	6-0	224	07/05/56	Oklahoma	16
95	Degrate, Tony	DE	6-3	280	04/25/62	Texas	1
10	Del Greco, Al	K	5-10	195	03/02/62	Auburn	16
88	Dennard, Preston	WR	6-1	183	11/28/55	New Mexico	16
12	Dickey, Lynn	QB	6-4	210	10/19/49	Kansas State	12
99	Dorsey, John	LB	6-2	235	08/31/60	Connecticut	16
53	Douglass, Mike	LB	6-0	214	03/15/55	San Diego State	16
42	Ellerson, Gary	RB	5-11	220	07/17/63	Wisconsin	15
31	Ellis, Gerry	FB	5-11	225	11/12/57	Missouri	16
85	Epps, Phillip	WR	5-10	165	11/11/58	TCU	16
41	Flynn, Tom	S	6-0	195	03/24/62	Pittsburgh	15
65	Hallstrom, Ron	G	6-6	289	06/11/59	Iowa	16
27	Hayes, Gary	CB	5-10	180	08/19/57	Fresno State	16
25	Huckleby, Harlan	HB	6-1	201	12/30/57	Michigan	11
74	Huffman, Tim	T	6-5	280	08/31/59	Notre Dame	2
79	Humphrey, Donnie	DE	6-3	275	04/20/61	Auburn	16
40	Ivery, Eddie Lee	RB	6-1	210	07/30/57	Georgia Tech	15
90	Johnson, Ezra	DE	6-4	259	10/02/55	Morris Brown	16
43	Jones, Daryll	S	6-0	195	03/23/62	Georgia	8
68	Koch, Greg	T	6-4	276	06/14/55	Arkansas	16
22	Lee, Mark	CB	5-11	188	03/20/58	Washington	14
89	Lewis, Mark	TE	6-2	237	05/05/61	Texas A&M	1
26	Lewis, Tim	CB	5-11	191	12/18/61	Pittsburgh	16
80	Lofton, James	WR	6-3	197	07/05/56	Stanford	16
94	Martin, Charles	DE	6-4	282	08/31/59	Livingston	16
28	McLeod, Mike	S	6-0	180	05/04/58	Montana State	8
60	Moore, Blake	C	6-5	272	05/08/58	Wooster	16
57	Moran, Rich	G	6-2	272	03/19/62	San Diego State	16
37	Murphy, Mark	S	6-2	201	04/22/58	West Liberty State	14
91	Noble, Brian	LB	6-3	237	09/06/62	Arizona State	16
51	Prather, Guy	LB	6-2	229	03/28/58	Grambling	16
11	Prokop, Joe	P	6-3	225	07/07/60	Cal Poly-Pomona	9
75	Ruettgers, Ken	T	6-5	267	08/20/62	USC	16
55	Scott, Randy	LB	6-1	228	01/31/59	Alabama	16
71	Shumate, Mark	NT	6-5	265	03/30/60	Wisconsin	3
87	Stanley, Walter	WR	5-9	180	11/05/62	Mesa	14
29	Stills, Ken	S	5-10	185	09/06/63	Wisconsin	8
67	Swanke, Karl	T	6-6	275	12/29/57	Boston College	15
20	Turner, Maurice	RB	5-11	199	09/10/60	Utah State	13
70	Uecker, Keith	G	6-5	270	06/29/60	Auburn	8
86	West, Ed	TE	6-1	236	08/02/61	Auburn	16
61	Wingle, Blake	G	6-2	260	04/17/60	UCLA	2
16	Wright, Randy	QB	6-2	194	01/12/61	Wisconsin	7
18	Zorn, Jim	QB	6-2	200	05/10/53	Cal Poly-Pomona	13

1985 DRAFT

Rnd	Name	Pos	Ht	Wt	College
1	Ken Ruettgers (7)	T	6-5	267	USC
	(Traded positions with Bills, 14th choice to 7th)				
2	(Choice (42) to Bills for position switch)				
3	Rich Moran (71)	G	6-2	272	San Diego State
4	Walter Stanley (98)	WR	5-9	180	Mesa (CO)
5	Brian Noble (125)	LB	6-3	237	Arizona State
6	Mark Lewis (155)	TE	6-2	237	Texas A&M
7a	Eric Wilson (171)	LB	6-1	247	Maryland
	(Choice from Vikings for Jan Stenerud)				
7b	Gary Ellerson (182)	RB	5-11	220	Wisconsin
8	Ken Stills (209)	DB	5-10	185	Wisconsin
9	Morris Johnson (239)	G	6-3	317	Alabama A&M
10	Ronnie Burgess (266)	CB	5-11	174	Wake Forest
11	Joe Shield (294)	QB	6-1	185	Trinity (CT)
12	Jim Meyer (323)	P	6-4	204	Arizona State

1985 GREEN BAY PACKERS

FRONT ROW: 10 Al Del Greco, 11 Joe Prokop, 12 Lynn Dickey, 16 Randy Wright, 17 Joe Shield, 22 Mark Lee, 24 Mossy Cade, 25 Harlan Huckleby.
SECOND ROW: (L-R) 26 Tim Lewis, 27 Gary Hayes, 28 Mike McLeod, 31 Gerry Ellis, 33 Jessie Clark, 35 Del Rodgers, 37 Mark Murphy, 39 Ronnie Burgess, 40 Eddie Lee Ivery.
THIRD ROW: (L-R) 41 Tom Flynn, 42 Gary Ellerson, 43 Daryll Jones, 50 Rich Wingo, 51 Guy Prather, 52 George Cumby, 53 Mike Douglass, 55 Randy Scott, 57 Rich Moran, 58 Mark Cannon.
FOURTH ROW: (L-R) 59 John Anderson, 60 Blake Moore, 63 Terry Jones, 65 Ron Hallstrom, 67 Karl Swanke, 68 Greg Koch, 70 Keith Uecker, 74 Tim Huffman, 75 Ken Ruettgers.
FIFTH ROW: (L-R) 76 Alphonso Carreker, 77 Mike Butler, 79 Donnie Humphrey, 80 James Lofton, 82 Paul Coffman, 85 Phillip Epps, 86 Ed West, 87 Walter Stanley, 88 Preston Dennard, 89 Mark Lewis.
SIXTH ROW: (L-R) Equipment Assistant Jack Noel, Trainer Domenic Gentile, 90 Ezra Johnson, 91 Brian Noble, 93 Robert Brown, 94 Charles Martin, 99 John Dorsey, Administrative Assistant Burt Gustafson, Equipment Manager Bob Noel.
BACK ROW: (L-R) Special Teams Coach Chuck Priefer, Offensive Coordinator Bob Schnelker, Linebackers Coach Herb Paterra, Receivers Coach Lew Carpenter, Head Coach Forrest Gregg, Strength-Conditioning Coach Virgil Knight, Offensive Line Coach Jerry Wampfler, Defensive Coordinator/Line Coach Dick Modzelewski, Offensive Backfield George Sefcik, Secondary Coach Ken Riley.

1986

Tired of .500 football, Coach Forrest Gregg released a number of the veterans who had contributed to the string of 8-8 years. Missing in 1986 were defensive end Mike Butler, tight end Paul Coffman, linebackers Mike Douglass and George Cumby, and tackle Greg Koch. In addition, offensive coordinator Bob Schnelker was dropped resulting in an offense run by committee. This "younger team," as expected, experienced growing pains. The club dropped its first six games – the worst start in Packers' history, was 1-9 after 10 games and limped home with a final 4-12 tally.

Trouble dogged the Packers on and off the field. Cornerback Tim Lewis suffered a career-ending neck injury when he tackled Willie Gault during the first Bears game. John Anderson missed 12 games and Phillip Epps four when they fractured the fibula in their left legs. Punter Don Bracken dislocated his elbow on an icy practice field and was replaced by Bill Renner who had three punts blocked in the last three games. The team had a total of five blocked, an NFL single-season record. In addition, defensive end Charles Martin was suspended for two games by Commissioner Pete Rozelle after spiking Bears' quarterback Jim McMahon once play had stopped. And finally, James Lofton saw his distinguished career come to an end in Green Bay. He was kept from the finale after second-degree sexual assault charges were filed against him. He was cleared of the charges, but was traded to the Los Angeles Raiders for a third-round choice in 1987, nonetheless.

In orchestrating the worst start in franchise history, Green Bay gave up the football 19 times in its first six games while forcing just nine opponents' turnovers. The running attack was non-existent. The Packers failed to score a rushing touchdowns in their first four games and counted just two in the opening six-game drought. In that same span, the Packers were outrushed 885-388 and never did pick up more than 82 yards in a single game.

Finally, on October 19, things improved. Randy Wright completed 21 of 27 passes for 277 yards. His only touchdown pass, a 47-yarder to Epps in the third quarter, propelled the Packers past Cleveland 17-14. The game also marked the first start by linebacker Tim Harris. A week later, Green Bay dominated statistically, outgaining San Francisco 464-222 and out-possessing them 41:10 to 18:50. But two fourth-quarter interception returns for touchdowns by Ronnie Lott and Tory Nixon, sank the Packers 31-17.

The Packers discovered the winning formula three times in the last six games. Walter Stanley provided the late-season highlights with 287 all-purpose yards against the Lions. His electrifying 83-yard punt return for a touchdown with 41 seconds remaining allowed the Packers to post a thrilling 44-40 Thanksgiving Day win.

Green Bay Press-Gazette photo

Randy Wright (16) readies to throw against the Bengals in Milwaukee in early October. Afforded good protection by the likes of Ron Hallstrom (65), Wright threw for 276 yards on 19 completions in 31 attempts. Wright took over for the departed Lynn Dickey and became the first Packer since Dickey to throw for 3,000 yards in a single season.

TEAM STATISTICS

	GB	OPP
First Downs	286	313
Rushing	96	135
Passing	172	151
Penalty	18	27
Rushes	424	565
Yards Gained	1,614	2,095
Average Gain	3.81	3.71
Average Yards per Game	100.9	130.9
Passes Attempted	565	448
Completed	305	267
% Completed	53.98	59.60
Total Yards Gained	3,708	3,142
Times Sacked	37	28
Yards Lost	261	222
Net Yards Gained	3,447	2,920
Yards Gained per Completion	12.16	11.77
Net Yards per Attempt	5.73	6.13
Average Net Yards per Game	215.4	182.5
Combined Net Yards Gained	5,061	5,015
Total Plays	1,026	1,041
Average Yards per Play	4.93	4.82
Average Net Yards per Game	316.3	313.4
Third Down Efficiency	79/222	94/217
Percentage	35.59	43.32
Fourth Down Efficiency	13/25	7/14
Percentage	52.00	50.00
Intercepted By	20	27
Yards Returned	147	357
Returned for TD	1	3
Punts	75	70
Yards Punted	2,825	2,769
Average Yards per Punt	37.67	39.56
Punt Returns	33	44
Yards Returned	316	287
Average Yards per Return	9.58	6.52
Returned for TD	1	0
Kickoff Returns	76	62
Yards Returned	1,470	1,181
Average Yards per Return	19.34	19.05
Returned for TD	0	0
Penalties	128	79
Yards Penalized	949	657
Fumbles	35	32
Lost	18	12
Own Recovered for Touchdown	0	0
Opponent's Recovered by	12	18
Opponent's Recovered for Touchdown	0	0
Total Points Scored	254	418
Total Touchdowns	29	52
Touchdowns Rushing	8	16
Touchdowns Passing	18	31
Touchdowns on Returns & Recoveries	3	5
Extra Points	29	48
Safeties	0	2
Field Goals Attempted	27	25
Field Goals Made	17	18
% Successful	62.96	72.00
Average Time of Possession	28:11	31:49

Regular Season 4-12-0

Date	GB		OPP	Att.
9/7	3	Houston Oilers	31	(54,065)
9/14	10	at New Orleans Saints	24	(46,383)
9/22	12	Chicago Bears	25	(55,527)
9/28	7	at Minnesota Vikings	42	(60,478)
10/5	28	Cincinnati Bengals (M)	34	(51,230)
10/12	14	Detroit Lions	21	(52,290)
10/19	17	at Cleveland Browns	14	(76,438)
10/26	17	San Francisco 49ers (M)	31	(50,557)
11/2	3	at Pittsburgh Steelers	27	(52,831)
11/9	7	Washington Redskins	16	(47,728)
11/16	31	Tampa Bay Buccaneers (M)	7	(48,271)
11/23	10	at Chicago Bears	12	(59,291)
11/27	44	at Detroit Lions	40	(61,199)
12/7	6	Minnesota Vikings	32	(47,637)
12/14	21	at Tampa Bay Buccaneers	7	(30,099)
12/20	24	at New York Giants	55	(71,351)

Score By Periods

	1	2	3	4	OT	Total
Packers	57	80	65	52	0	254
Opponents	124	106	78	110	0	418

INDIVIDUAL STATISTICS

Rushing

	Att	Yds	Avg	LG	TD
K. Davis	114	519	4.6	50	0
G. Ellis	84	345	4.1	24	2
Carruth	81	308	3.8	42	2
Ellerson	90	287	3.2	18	3
J. Clark	18	41	2.3	9	0
R. Wright	18	41	2.3	18	1
Ivery	4	25	6.3	15	0
Stanley	1	19	19.0	19	0
Epps	4	18	4.5	20	0
Fusina	7	11	1.6	6	0
Ferragamo	1	0	0.0	0	0
Renner	1	0	0.0	0	0
Swanke	1	0	0.0	0	0
Packers	**424**	**1,614**	**3.8**	**50**	**8**
Opponents	565	2,095	3.7	t41	16

Receiving

	No	Yds	Avg	LG	TD
Lofton	64	840	13.1	36	4
Epps	49	612	12.5	t53	4
Stanley	35	723	20.7	62	2
Ivery	31	385	12.4	42	1
G. Ellis	24	258	10.8	29	0
Carruth	24	134	5.6	19	2
K. Davis	21	142	6.8	18	1
Ross	17	143	8.4	16	1
E. West	15	199	13.3	t46	1
Ellerson	12	130	10.8	32	0
J. Clark	6	41	6.8	12	0
Moffitt	4	87	21.8	34	0
M. Lewis	2	7	3.5	t4	2
Franz	1	7	7.0	7	0
Packers	**305**	**3,708**	**12.2**	**62**	**18**
Opponents	267	3,142	11.8	84	31

Passing

	Att	Com	Yds	Pct	TD	In	Tk/Yds	Rate
R. Wright	492	263	3,247	53.5	17	23	33/243	66.2
Ferragamo	40	23	283	57.5	1	3	3/15	56.6
Fusina	32	19	178	59.4	0	1	1/3	61.7
Lofton	1	0	0	00.0	0	0	0/0	—
Packers	**565**	**305**	**3,708**	**54.0**	**18**	**27**	**37/261**	**65.1**
Opponents	448	267	3,142	59.6	31	20	28/222	85.4

Punting

	No	Yds	Avg	In20	TB	LG	HB
Bracken	55	2,203	40.1	6	5	63	2
Renner	15	622	41.5	2	1	50	3
Packers	**75**	**2,825**	**37.7**	**8**	**6**	**63**	**5**
Opponents	70	2,769	39.6	16	13	61	2

Kickoff Returns

	No	Yds	Avg	LG	TD
Stanley	28	559	20.0	55	0
Watts	12	239	19.9	40	0
K. Davis	12	231	19.3	35	0
Stills	10	209	20.9	38	0
Ellerson	7	154	22.0	57	0
Carruth	4	40	10.0	20	0
Epps	1	21	21.0	21	0
E. Berry	1	16	16.0	16	0
Noble	1	1	1.0	1	0
Packers	**76**	**1,470**	**19.3**	**57**	**0**
Opponents	62	1,181	19.0	64	0

Punt Returns

	No	Yds	Avg	FC	LG	TD
Stanley	33	316	9.6	7	t83	1
Packers	**33**	**316**	**9.6**	**7**	**t83**	**1**
Opponents	44	287	6.5	5	17	0

Interceptions

	No	Yds	Avg	LG	TD
M. Lee	9	33	3.7	11	0
Cade	4	26	6.5	18	0
Greene	2	0	0.0	0	0
Stills	1	58	58.0	t58	1
Leopold	1	21	21.0	21	0
Watts	1	6	6.0	6	0
J. Anderson	1	3	3.0	3	0
Flynn	1	0	0.0	0	0
Packers	**20**	**147**	**7.4**	**t58**	**1**
Opponents	27	357	13.2	t88	3

Scoring

	TDr	TDp	TDrt	PAT	FG	S	TP
Del Greco	0	0	0	29/29	17/27	0	80
Carruth	2	2	0	0/0	0/0	0	24
Epps	0	4	0	0/0	0/0	0	24
Lofton	0	4	0	0/0	0/0	0	24
Ellerson	3	0	0	0/0	0/0	0	18
Stanley	0	2	1	0/0	0/0	0	18
G. Ellis	2	0	0	0/0	0/0	0	12
M. Lewis	0	2	0	0/0	0/0	0	12
K. Davis	0	1	0	0/0	0/0	0	6
Ivery	0	1	0	0/0	0/0	0	6
Ross	0	1	0	0/0	0/0	0	6
Simmons	0	0	1	0/0	0/0	0	6
Stills	0	0	1	0/0	0/0	0	6
E. West	0	1	0	0/0	0/0	0	6
R. Wright	1	0	0	0/0	0/0	0	6
Packers	**8**	**18**	**3**	**29/29**	**17/27**	**0**	**254**
Opponents	16	31	5	48/52	18/25	2	418

Fumbles

	Fum	Ow	Op	Yds	Tot
E. Berry	0	1	0	0	1
R. Brown	0	0	1	0	1
Carreker	0	0	2	0	2
Carruth	0	0	0	0	0
Cherry	1	0	0	-23	0
J. Clark	1	0	0	0	0
K. Davis	2	0	0	0	0
J. Dorsey	0	0	2	0	2
Ellerson	3	0	0	0	0
G. Ellis	4	1	0	0	1
Ferragamo	3	0	0	-8	0
Fusina	4	4	0	-1	4
T. Harris	0	0	1	0	1
Humphrey	0	0	1	0	1
Ivery	1	0	0	0	1
Koart	0	0	1	0	1
M. Lee	0	0	1	0	1
Lofton	3	2	0	8	2
C. Martin	0	0	1	0	1
Ruettgers	0	1	0	0	1
R. Scott	0	0	1	0	1
Stanley	1	0	0	0	0
Stills	0	0	1	0	1
Swanke	3	0	0	-4	0
Veingrad	0	1	0	0	1
E. West	0	0	1	0	1
R. Wright	8	3	0	-4	3
Packers	**35**	**14**	**12**	**-32**	**26**

Quarterback Sacks

	No
T. Harris	8.0
Greenwood	3.0
E. Johnson	3.0
Carreker	2.5
R. Brown	2.0
Noble	2.0
Leopold	1.5
Cade	1.0
Greene	1.0
C. Martin	1.0
R. Scott	1.0
B. Thomas	1.0
Watts	1.0
Packers	**28.0**
Opponents	37.0

NFL STANDINGS

National Conference

Eastern Division

	W	L	T	Pct	PF	PA
New York Giants	14	2	0	.875	371	236
Washington Redskins	12	4	0	.750	368	296
Dallas Cowboys	7	9	0	.438	346	337
Philadelphia Eagles	5	10	1	.344	256	312
St. Louis Cardinals	4	11	1	.281	218	351

Central Division

	W	L	T	Pct	PF	PA
Chicago Bears	14	2	0	.875	352	187
Minnesota Vikings	9	7	0	.563	398	273
Detroit Lions	5	11	0	.313	277	326
Green Bay Packers	**4**	**12**	**0**	**.250**	**254**	**418**
Tampa Bay Buccaneers	2	14	0	.125	239	473

Western Division

	W	L	T	Pct	PF	PA
San Francisco 49ers	10	5	1	.656	374	247
Los Angeles Rams	10	6	0	.625	309	267
Atlanta Falcons	7	8	1	.469	280	280
New Orleans Saints	7	9	0	.438	288	287

American Conference

Eastern Division

	W	L	T	Pct	PF	PA
New England Patriots	11	5	0	.688	412	307
New York Jets	10	6	0	.625	364	386
Miami Dolphins	8	8	0	.500	430	405
Buffalo Bills	4	12	0	.250	287	348
Indianapolis Colts	3	13	0	.188	229	400

Central Division

	W	L	T	Pct	PF	PA
Cleveland Browns	12	4	0	.750	391	310
Cincinnati Bengals	10	6	0	.625	409	394
Pittsburgh Steelers	6	10	0	.375	307	336
Houston Oilers	5	11	0	.313	274	329

Western Division

	W	L	T	Pct	PF	PA
Denver Broncos	11	5	0	.688	378	327
Kansas City Chiefs	10	6	0	.625	358	326
Seattle Seahawks	10	6	0	.625	366	293
Los Angeles Raiders	8	8	0	.500	323	346
San Diego Chargers	4	12	0	.250	335	396

1986 ROSTER

No	Name	Pos	Ht	Wt	DOB	College	G
59	Anderson, John	LB	6-3	228	02/14/56	Michigan	4
20	Berry, Ed	DB	5-10	183	09/28/63	Utah State	16
61	Boyarsky, Jerry	NT	6-3	290	05/15/59	Pittsburgh	2
17	Bracken, Don	P	6-0	211	02/16/62	Michigan	13
93	Brown, Robert	DE	6-2	267	05/21/60	Virginia Tech	16
24	Cade, Mossy	CB	6-1	198	12/26/61	Texas	16
58	Cannon, Mark	C	6-3	268	06/14/62	Texas-Arlington	7
76	Carreker, Alphonso	DE	6-6	271	05/25/62	Florida State	16
30	Carruth, Paul Ott	RB	6-1	220	07/22/61	Alabama	16
69	Cherry, Bill	C	6-4	277	01/05/61	Mid Tenn. State	16
33	Clark, Jessie	FB	6-0	228	01/03/60	Arkansas	5
36	Davis, Kenneth	RB	5-10	209	04/16/62	TCU	16
10	Del Greco, Al	K	5-10	191	03/02/62	Auburn	16
56	Dent, Burnell	LB	6-1	236	03/16/63	Tulane	16
99	Dorsey, John	LB	6-2	243	08/31/60	Connecticut	16
42	Ellerson, Gary	RB	5-11	219	07/17/63	Wisconsin	16
31	Ellis, Gerry	FB	5-11	235	11/12/57	Missouri	16
85	Epps, Phillip	WR	5-10	165	11/11/58	TCU	12
77	Feasel, Greg	T	6-7	301	11/07/58	Abilene Christian	15
5	Ferragamo, Vince	QB	6-3	217	04/24/54	Nebraska	3
41	Flynn, Tom	S	6-0	195	03/24/62	Pittsburgh	7
84	Franz, Nolan	WR	6-2	183	09/11/59	Tulane	1
4	Fusina, Chuck	QB	6-1	195	05/31/57	Penn State	7
23	Greene, George (Tiger)	DB	6-0	194	02/15/62	Western Carolina	13
49	Greenwood, David	S	6-3	210	03/25/60	Wisconsin	9
65	Hallstrom, Ron	G	6-6	290	06/11/59	Iowa	16
97	Harris, Tim	LB	6-5	235	09/10/64	Memphis State	16
27	Hayes, Gary	CB	5-10	180	08/19/57	Fresno State	10
79	Humphrey, Donnie	DE	6-3	295	04/20/61	Auburn	16
40	Ivery, Eddie Lee	RB	6-1	206	07/30/57	Georgia Tech	12
90	Johnson, Ezra	DE	6-4	264	10/02/55	Morris Brown	16
92	Koart, Matt	DE	6-5	256	09/28/63	USC	6
22	Lee, Mark	CB	5-11	189	03/20/58	Washington	16
53	Leopold, Bobby	LB	6-1	224	10/18/57	Notre Dame	12
89	Lewis, Mark	TE	6-2	237	05/05/61	Texas A&M	16
26	Lewis, Tim	CB	5-11	191	12/18/61	Pittsburgh	3
80	Lofton, James	WR	6-3	197	07/05/56	Stanford	15
94	Martin, Charles	DE	6-4	280	08/31/59	Livingston	14
88	McConkey, Phil	WR	5-10	170	02/24/57	Navy	4
62	Mendoza, Ruben	G	6-3	278	05/10/63	Wayne State	6
82	Moffitt, Mike	WR	6-4	211	07/28/63	Fresno State	4
57	Moran, Rich	G	6-2	275	03/19/62	San Diego State	5
72	Neville, Tom	G	6-5	306	09/04/61	Fresno State	16
91	Noble, Brian	LB	6-3	252	09/06/62	Arizona State	16
71	Ploeger, Kurt	DE	6-5	260	12/01/62	Gus. Adolphus	1
13	Renner, Bill	P	6-0	198	05/23/59	Virginia Tech	3
81	Ross, Dan	TE	6-4	240	02/09/57	Northeastern	15
75	Ruettgers, Ken	T	6-5	280	08/20/62	USC	16
54	Schuh, Jeff	LB	6-3	234	05/22/58	Minnesota	12
55	Scott, Randy	LB	6-1	228	01/31/59	Alabama	15
18	Shield, Joe	QB	6-1	185	06/26/62	Trinity College	3
32	Simmons, John	CB	5-11	192	12/01/58	SMU	6
87	Stanley, Walter	WR	5-9	179	11/05/62	Mesa	16
29	Stills, Ken	S	5-10	186	09/06/63	Wisconsin	16
38	Sullivan, John	S	6-1	190	10/15/61	California	6
67	Swanke, Karl	T	6-6	280	12/29/57	Boston College	10
92	Thomas, Ben	DE	6-4	275	07/02/61	Auburn	9
53	Turpin, Mike	LB	6-4	230	05/15/64	California	1
73	Veingrad, Alan	T	6-5	277	07/24/63	E. Texas State	16
28	Watts, Elbert	CB	6-1	205	03/20/63	USC	9
52	Weddington, Mike	LB	6-2	245	10/09/60	Oklahoma	3
86	West, Ed	TE	6-1	243	08/02/61	Auburn	16
16	Wright, Randy	QB	6-2	203	01/12/61	Wisconsin	16

1986 DRAFT

Rnd	Name	Pos	Ht	Wt	College
1	(Choice (14) to Chargers for Mossy Cade)				
2	Kenneth Davis (41)	RB	5-10	209	TCU
3	Robbie Bosco (72)	QB	6-3	200	Brigham Young
4a	Tim Harris (84)	LB	6-5	235	Memphis State
	(Choice from Bills in first round switch of 1985)				
4b	Dan Knight (98)	T	6-5	280	San Diego State
5	Matt Koart (125)	DT	6-5	256	USC
6a	Burnell Dent (143)	LB	6-1	230	Tulane
	(Choice from Cardinals for Scott Brunner)				
6b	(Choice (151) to Broncos for Scott Brunner)				
7	Ed Berry (183)	DB	5-10	176	Utah State
8	Michael Cline (210)	NT	6-3	265	Arkansas State
9	Brent Moore (236)	LB	6-5	242	USC
10	Gary Spann (263)	LB	6-2	220	TCU
11	(Choice (294) to Bengals for Mike Obrovac)				
12	(Choice (331) to Bills for Preston Dennard)				

1986 GREEN BAY PACKERS

FRONT ROW: (L-R) 5 Vince Ferragamo, 10 Al Del Greco, 11 Robbie Bosco, 16 Randy Wright, 17 Don Bracken, 20 Ed Berry, 22 Mark Lee, 24 Mossy Cade, 26 Tim Lewis, 27 Gary Hayes.

SECOND ROW: (L-R) 29 Ken Stills, 30 Paul Ott Carruth, 31 Gerry Ellis, 33 Jessie Clark, 34 Mike Moffitt, 36 Kenneth Davis, 37 Mark Murphy, 38 John Sullivan, 39 Freddie Parker, 40 Eddie Lee Ivery, 41 Tom Flynn.

THIRD ROW: (L-R) 42 Gary Ellerson, 52 Mike Weddington, 54 Jeff Schuh, 55 Randy Scott, 56 Burnell Dent, 57 Rich Moran, 58 Mark Cannon, 59 John Anderson, 62 Ruben Mendoza, 65 Ron Hallstrom.

FOURTH ROW: (L-R) 67 Karl Swanke, 69 Bill Cherry, 70 Keith Uecker, 72 Tom Neville, 73 Alan Veingrad, 74 Dan Knight, 75 Ken Ruettgers, 76 Alphonso Carreker, 77 Greg Feasel, 79 Donnie Humphrey, 80 James Lofton.

FIFTH ROW: (L-R) 81 Dan Ross, 84 Nolan Franz, 85 Phillip Epps, 86 Ed West, 87 Walter Stanley, 88 Phil McConkey, 89 Mark Lewis, 90 Ezra Johnson, 91 Brian Noble, 92 Matt Koart.

SIXTH ROW: (L-R) Medical Assistant Derick Brock, Trainer Domenic Gentile, 93 Robert Brown, 94 Charles Martin, 97 Tim Harris, 98 Brent Moore, 99 John Dorsey, Equipment Manager Bob Noel, Equipment Assistant Jack Noel, Assistant Equipment Manager Bryan Nehring.

BACK ROW: (L-R) Passing Game/Receivers Coach Tom Coughlin, Administrative Assistant Forrest Gregg, Jr., Defensive Backfield Coach Dick Jauron, Strength-Conditioning/Offensive Line Coach Virgil Knight, Linebackers Coach Dale Lindsey, Head Coach Forrest Gregg, Special Teams/Offensive Line Coach Jerry Wampfler, Defensive Coordinator/Line Coach Dick Modzelewski, Quarterbacks Coach George Sefcik.

In an attempt to avoid the miserable starts that had plagued the Packers the past three seasons, the team adopted a self-proclaimed "operation quickstart." Win early, and records such as the 1-7, 3-5 and 1-7 getaways of recent years would become a thing of the past. Early optimism faded as the Packers dropped four preseason games and were pounded 20-0 by the Raiders on opening day. Yet thanks in part to a players' strike, the fourth in 18 years, Green Bay sported a 3-2-1 mark six weeks into the year. But this time the team could not win down the stretch. Shortly after the strike-shortened 5-9-1 year ended, Coach Forrest Gregg departed for Southern Methodist University.

On January 31, the Packers hired Tom Braatz from the Falcons to fill a newly created position of executive vice-president of football operations. His duties included but were not limited to: conducting the draft in conjunction with the head coach, handling trades and waivers, and negotiating players' contracts. Braatz's hiring marked the first time since the days of Ray (Scooter) McLean, that a Packers head coach was not in total control of the team.

A number of veterans such as Eddie Lee Ivery, Gerry Ellis, Karl Swanke and Randy Scott saw their careers come to an end during training camp. Ivery, a receiver in 1986, missed the entire year after he underwent surgery to repair a disc problem in his lower back. Ellis ruptured an Achilles' tendon in the off-season, had surgery, failed his physical and was waived in early August. Swanke retired and Scott was cut just before the season-opener.

More often than not, Gregg filled departing player's spots with journeyman free agents such as linebacker Clayton Weishuhn and running back Kelly Cook. Fourteen free agents made the squad in 1987 after 13 had a year earlier.

Again the Packers had their share of problems. Quarterback Randy Wright held out until for 15 days, didn't sign until mid-August then looked anything but sharp in the opener. Defensive end Charles Martin, battling a drinking problem, was waived September 23 after participating in a fight in a local night club. First-round draft choice Brent Fullwood missed 18 practices and 12 days of work before signing and then disappointed with a measly 274 yards rushing. Cornerback Mossy Cade was sentenced to two years in prison on August 3 after having been found guilty of second-degree sexual assault. Even the team's eleventh-round pick, wide receiver Patrick Scott, held out into August for more money.

Perhaps the biggest distraction came in the form of a player's strike. The NFLPA again presented owners with a list of grievances and its members then walked out after the second weekend of games. Owners staged three games in October with replacement players. The union ended its 24-day strike on October 15 without reaching an agreement.

Green Bay's first post-strike opponent was Detroit, whom the Packers hung on to beat 34-33 despite blowing a 24-0 lead. Unfortunately, the team won but twice more. The final victory of Gregg's tenure came in Milwaukee where Kenneth Davis scored on a seven-yard run with 1:09 left to beat the playoff-bound Vikings 16-10.

Green Bay Press-Gazette

Brent Fullwood (21) scores on a three-yard run behind the blocking of Ron Hallstrom (65) and Ken Ruettgers (75) in Milwaukee. Fullwood gained 57 yards on 13 carries as the Packers tied Denver 17-17. At season's end, the team's number-one draft pick had gained 274 yards, a total that ranked second to team-leader Kenneth Davis' 413.

TEAM STATISTICS

	GB	OPP
First Downs	248	296
Rushing	97	118
Passing	133	152
Penalty	18	26
Rushes	464	521
Yards Gained	1,801	1,920
Average Gain	3.88	3.69
Average Yards per Game	120.1	128.0
Passes Attempted	455	469
Completed	234	279
% Completed	51.43	59.49
Total Yards Gained	2,977	3,200
Times Sacked	45	34
Yards Lost	296	197
Net Yards Gained	2,681	3,003
Yards Gained per Completion	12.72	11.47
Net Yards per Attempt	5.36	5.97
Average Net Yards per Game	178.7	200.2
Combined Net Yards Gained	4,482	4,923
Total Plays	964	1,024
Average Yards per Play	4.65	4.81
Average Net Yards per Game	298.8	328.2
Third Down Efficiency	68/217	86/220
Percentage	31.34	39.09
Fourth Down Efficiency	2/8	10/14
Percentage	25.00	71.43
Intercepted By	18	17
Yards Returned	220	115
Returned for TD	0	1
Punts	93	77
Yards Punted	3,659	3,084
Average Yards per Punt	39.34	40.05
Punt Returns	35	54
Yards Returned	245	422
Average Yards per Return	7.00	7.81
Returned for TD	0	0
Kickoff Returns	59	61
Yards Returned	1,032	1,140
Average Yards per Return	17.49	18.69
Returned for TD	0	0
Penalties	135	104
Yards Penalized	1,103	852
Fumbles	35	42
Lost	18	24
Own Recovered for Touchdown	0	0
Opponent's Recovered by	24	18
Opponent's Recovered for Touchdown	0	0
Total Points Scored	255	300
Total Touchdowns	28	31
Touchdowns Rushing	13	15
Touchdowns Passing	15	14
Touchdowns on Returns & Recoveries	0	2
Extra Points	24	29
Safeties	0	2
Field Goals Attempted	29	36
Field Goals Made	21	27
% Successful	72.41	75.00
Average Time of Possession	29:02	30:58

Regular Season 5-9-1

Date	GB		OPP	Att.
9/13	0	Los Angeles Raiders	20	(54,983)
9/20	17	Denver Broncos (M) (OT)	17	(50,624)
9/27	**	at Tampa Bay Buccaneers		
10/4	*23	at Minnesota Vikings	16	(13,911)
10/11	*16	Detroit Lions (OT)	19	(35,779)
10/18	*16	Philadelphia Eagles (OT)	10	(35,842)
10/25	34	at Detroit Lions	33	(27,278)
11/1	17	Tampa Bay Buccaneers (M)	23	(50,308)
11/8	24	Chicago Bears	26	(53,320)
11/15	13	at Seattle Seahawks	24	(60,963)
11/22	23	at Kansas City Chiefs	3	(34,611)
11/29	10	at Chicago Bears	23	(61,638)
12/6	12	San Francisco 49ers	23	(51,118)
12/13	16	Minnesota Vikings (M)	10	(47,059)
12/19	10	at New York Giants	20	(51,013)
12/27	24	at New Orleans Saints	33	(68,364)

* replacement games
** game cancelled because of players' strike

Score By Periods

	1	2	3	4	OT	Total
Packers	80	75	42	52	6	255
Opponents	40	98	71	88	3	300

INDIVIDUAL STATISTICS

Rushing

	Att	Yds	Avg	LG	TD
K. Davis	109	413	3.8	t39	3
Fullwood	84	274	3.3	18	5
Willhite	53	251	4.7	61	0
J. Clark	56	211	3.8	57	0
Carruth	64	192	3.0	23	3
Majkowski	15	127	8.5	33	0
R. Wright	13	70	5.4	27	0
Risher	11	64	5.8	15	1
Hargrove	11	38	3.5	7	0

1987

Rushing (cont.)

	Att	Yds	Avg	LG	TD
Stanley	4	38	9.5	24	0
Parker	8	33	4.1	17	0
Weigel	10	26	2.6	7	0
Sterling	5	20	4.0	9	0
L. Thomas	5	19	3.8	5	0
Larry Morris	8	18	2.3	10	0
K. Cook	2	3	1.5	2	0
P. Scott	1	2	2.0	2	0
Lee Morris	2	2	1.0	4	0
Epps	1	0	0.0	0	0
T. Hunter	1	0	0.0	0	0
F. Neal	1	0	0.0	0	0
Packers	**464**	**1,801**	**3.9**	**61**	**13**
Opponents	521	1,920	3.7	t57	15

Receiving

	No	Yds	Avg	LG	TD
Stanley	38	672	17.7	t70	3
F. Neal	36	420	11.7	38	3
Epps	34	516	15.2	40	2
J. Clark	22	119	5.4	19	1
E. West	19	261	13.7	40	1
Lee Morris	16	259	16.2	t46	1
K. Davis	14	110	7.9	35	0
Paskett	12	188	15.7	t47	1
Carruth	10	78	7.8	19	1
P. Scott	8	79	9.9	16	0
Summers	7	83	11.9	17	1
Willhite	6	37	6.2	12	0
Parker	3	22	7.3	13	0
L. Thomas	2	52	26.0	t30	1
D. Harden	2	29	14.5	15	0
Fullwood	2	11	5.5	12	0
Redick	1	18	18.0	18	0
Weigel	1	17	17.0	17	0
Hargrove	1	6	6.0	6	0
Packers	**234**	**2,977**	**12.7**	**t70**	**15**
Opponents	279	3,200	11.5	t63	14

Passing

	Att	Com	Yds	Pct	TD	In	Tk/Yds	Rate
R. Wright	247	132	1,507	53.4	6	11	20/128	61.6
Majkowski	127	55	875	43.3	5	3	10/77	70.2
Risher	74	44	564	59.5	3	3	12/77	80.0
Gillus	5	2	28	40.0	0	0	3/14	—
Carruth	1	1	3	100.0	1	0	0/0	—
F. Neal	1	0	0	00.0	0	0	0/0	—
Packers	**455**	**234**	**2,977**	**51.4**	**15**	**17**	**45/296**	**67.6**
Opponents	469	279	3,200	59.5	14	18	34/197	74.0

Punting

	No	Yds	Avg	In20	TB	LG	HB
Bracken	72	2,947	40.9	13	5	65	1
Renner	20	712	35.6	4	1	49	0
Packers	**93**	**3,659**	**39.3**	**17**	**6**	**65**	**1**
Opponents	77	3,084	40.1	22	11	71	0

Kickoff Returns

	No	Yds	Avg	LG	TD
Fullwood	24	510	21.3	46	0
K. Cook	10	147	14.7	38	0
Lee Morris	6	104	17.3	28	0
D. Harden	4	72	18.0	20	0
F. Neal	4	44	11.0	18	0
Stanley	3	47	15.7	29	0
N. Jefferson	2	30	15.0	18	0
P. Scott	2	32	16.0	23	0
Carruth	1	8	8.0	8	0
Weishuhn	1	1	1.0	1	0
Cherry	1	0	0.0	0	0
Sterling	1	0	0.0	0	0
Willhite	0	37	—	37	0
Packers	**59**	**1,032**	**17.5**	**46**	**0**
Opponents	61	1,140	18.7	74	0

Punt Returns

	No	Yds	Avg	FC	LG	TD
Stanley	28	173	6.2	4	48	0
P. Scott	6	71	11.8	2	36	0
Lee Morris	1	1	1.0	0	1	0
Packers	**35**	**245**	**7.0**	**6**	**48**	**0**
Opponents	54	422	7.8	8	37	0

Interceptions

	No	Yds	Avg	LG	TD
J.B. Morris	3	135	45.0	73	0
D. Brown	3	16	5.3	11	0
J. Anderson	2	22	11.0	13	0
Holland	2	4	2.0	4	0
Mansfield	1	14	14.0	14	0
Greene	1	11	11.0	11	0
Noble	1	10	10.0	10	0
Carreker	1	6	6.0	6	0
K. Johnson	1	2	2.0	2	0
A. Harrison	1	0	0.0	0	0
M. Lee	1	0	0.0	0	0
Melka	1	0	0.0	0	0
Packers	**18**	**220**	**12.2**	**73**	**0**
Opponents	17	115	6.8	t35	1

Scoring

	TDr	TDp	TDrt	PAT	FG	S	TP
Zendejas	0	0	0	13/15	16/19	0	61
Fullwood	5	0	0	0/0	0/0	0	30
Del Greco	0	0	0	11/11	5/10	0	26
Carruth	3	1	0	0/0	0/0	0	24
K. Davis	3	0	0	0/0	0/0	0	18
F. Neal	0	3	0	0/0	0/0	0	18
Stanley	0	3	0	0/0	0/0	0	18
Epps	0	2	0	0/0	0/0	0	12
J. Clark	0	1	0	0/0	0/0	0	6
Hargrove	1	0	0	0/0	0/0	0	6
Lee Morris	0	1	0	0/0	0/0	0	6
Paskett	0	1	0	0/0	0/0	0	6
Risher	1	0	0	0/0	0/0	0	6
Summers	0	1	0	0/0	0/0	0	6
L. Thomas	0	1	0	0/0	0/0	0	6
E. West	0	1	0	0/0	0/0	0	6
Packers	**13**	**15**	**0**	**24/27**	**21/29**	**0**	**255**
Opponents	15	14	2	29/31	27/36	2	300

Quarterback Sacks

	No
T. Harris	7.0
J. Anderson	4.0
Carreker	4.0
R. Brown	3.0
Boyarsky	2.0
Drost	2.0
E. Johnson	2.0
M. Murphy	2.0
Browner	1.0
Holland	1.0
K. Johnson	1.0
K. Jordan	1.0
C. Martin	1.0
J.B. Morris	1.0
Noble	1.0
Caldwell	0.5
C. Sullivan	0.5
Packers	**34.0**
Opponents	45.0

NFL STANDINGS

National Conference

Eastern Division

	W	L	T	Pct	PF	PA
Washington Redskins	11	4	0	.733	379	285
Dallas Cowboys	7	8	0	.467	340	348
St. Louis Cardinals	7	8	0	.467	362	368
Philadelphia Eagles	7	8	0	.467	337	380
New York Giants	6	9	0	.400	280	312

Central Division

	W	L	T	Pct	PF	PA
Chicago Bears	11	4	0	.733	356	282
Minnesota Vikings	8	7	0	.533	336	335
Green Bay Packers	5	9	1	.367	255	300
Tampa Bay Buccaneers	4	11	0	.267	286	360
Detroit Lions	4	11	0	.267	269	384

Western Division

	W	L	T	Pct	PF	PA
San Francisco 49ers	13	2	0	.867	459	253
New Orleans Saints	12	3	0	.800	422	283
Los Angeles Rams	6	9	0	.400	317	361
Atlanta Falcons	3	12	0	.200	205	436

American Conference

Eastern Division

	W	L	T	Pct	PF	PA
Indianapolis Colts	9	6	0	.600	300	238
New England Patriots	8	7	0	.533	320	293
Miami Dolphins	8	7	0	.533	362	335
Buffalo Bills	7	8	0	.467	270	305
New York Jets	6	9	0	.400	334	360

Central Division

	W	L	T	Pct	PF	PA
Cleveland Browns	10	5	0	.667	390	239
Houston Oilers	9	6	0	.600	345	349
Pittsburgh Steelers	8	7	0	.533	285	299
Cincinnati Bengals	4	11	0	.267	285	370

Western Division

	W	L	T	Pct	PF	PA
Denver Broncos	10	4	1	.700	379	288
Seattle Seahawks	9	6	0	.600	371	314
San Diego Chargers	8	7	0	.533	253	317
Los Angeles Raiders	5	10	0	.333	301	289
Kansas City Chiefs	4	11	0	.267	273	388

1987 "UNION" ROSTER

No	Name	Pos	Ht	Wt	DOB	College	G
59	Anderson, John	LB	6-3	228	02/14/56	Michigan	12
61	Boyarsky, Jerry	NT	6-3	290	05/15/59	Pittsburgh	12
17	Bracken, Don	P	6-0	211	02/16/62	Michigan	12
32	Brown, Dave	CB	6-1	197	01/16/53	Michigan	12
93	Brown, Robert	DE	6-2	267	05/21/60	Virginia Tech	12
79	Browner, Ross	DE	6-3	265	03/22/54	Notre Dame	11
58	Cannon, Mark	C	6-3	270	06/14/62	Texas-Arlington	12
76	Carreker, Alphonso	DE	6-6	271	05/25/62	Florida State	12
30	Carruth, Paul Ott	RB	6-1	220	07/22/61	Alabama	12
69	Cherry, Bill	C	6-4	277	01/05/61	Middle Tennessee State	12
33	Clark, Jessie	FB	6-0	228	01/03/60	Arkansas	12
64	Collier, Steve*	T	6-7	342	04/19/63	Bethune-Cookman	7
20	Cook, Kelly	RB	5-10	225	08/20/62	Oklahoma State	11
36	Davis, Kenneth	RB	5-10	209	04/16/62	TCU	10
10	Del Greco, Al	K	5-10	191	03/02/62	Auburn	5
56	Dent, Burnell	LB	6-1	236	03/16/63	Tulane	9
99	Dorsey, John	LB	6-2	243	08/31/60	Connecticut	12
85	Epps, Phillip	WR	5-10	165	11/11/58	TCU	10
21	Fullwood, Brent	FB	5-11	209	10/10/63	Auburn	11
23	Greene, George (Tiger)	DB	6-0	194	02/15/62	Western Carolina	11
89	Hackett, Joey	TE	6-5	267	09/29/58	Elon	11
65	Hallstrom, Ron	G	6-6	290	06/11/59	Iowa	12
97	Harris, Tim	LB	6-5	235	09/10/64	Memphis State	12
50	Holland, Johnny	LB	6-2	221	03/11/65	Texas A&M	12
38	Jefferson, Norman	DB	5-10	183	08/07/64	LSU	12
90	Johnson, Ezra	DE	6-4	264	10/02/55	Morris Brown	6
39	Johnson, Kenneth	CB	6-0	185	12/28/63	Mississippi State	12
22	Lee, Mark	CB	5-11	189	03/20/58	Washington	12
89	Lewis, Mark	TE	6-2	237	05/05/61	Texas A&M	1
94	Logan, Dave	NT	6-2	250	10/25/56	Pittsburgh	2
5	Majkowski, Don	QB	6-2	197	02/25/64	Virginia	7
44	Mandeville, Chris	S	6-1	213	02/01/65	California-Davis	4
94	Martin, Charles	DE	6-4	280	08/31/59	Livingston	2
98	Moore, Brent	LB	6-5	242	01/09/63	USC	4
57	Moran, Rich	G	6-2	275	03/19/62	San Diego State	12
47	Morris, Jim Bob*	S	6-3	211	05/17/61	Kansas State	8
81	Morris, Lee*	WR	5-10	180	07/14/64	Oklahoma	2
37	Murphy, Mark	S	6-2	201	04/22/58	West Liberty	12
80	Neal, Frankie	WR	6-1	202	10/01/65	Fort Hays State	12
72	Neville, Tom	G	6-5	306	09/04/61	Fresno State	12
91	Noble, Brian	LB	6-3	252	09/06/62	Arizona State	12
82	Paskett, Keith	WR	5-11	180	12/07/64	Western Kentucky	12
77	Robison, Tommy	G	6-4	290	11/17/61	Texas A&M	3
75	Ruettgers, Ken	T	6-5	280	08/20/62	USC	12
83	Scott, Patrick*	WR	5-10	170	09/13/64	Grambling	5
87	Stanley, Walter	WR	5-9	179	11/05/62	Mesa	12
54	Stephen, Scott	LB	6-2	232	06/18/64	Arizona State	8
29	Stills, Ken	S	5-10	186	09/06/63	Wisconsin	11
70	Uecker, Keith*	G	6-5	284	06/29/60	Auburn	7
73	Veingrad, Alan	T	6-5	277	07/24/63	East Texas State	11
52	Weddington, Mike	LB	6-4	245	10/09/60	Oklahoma	12
51	Weishuhn, Clayton	LB	6-1	218	10/07/59	Angelo State	9
86	West, Ed	TE	6-1	243	08/02/61	Auburn	12
16	Wright, Randy	QB	6-2	203	01/12/61	Wisconsin	9
8	Zendejas, Max*	K	5-11	184	09/02/63	Arizona	7

* also played in replacement games

1987 DRAFT

Rnd	Name	Pos	Ht	Wt	College
1	Brent Fullwood (4)	RB	5-11	209	Auburn
2a	(Traded positions with Falcons, 31st choice to 41st and an extra 3rd round selection)				
2b	Johnny Holland (41)	LB	6-2	221	Texas A&M
	(Choice from Falcons for position switch)				
3a	Dave Croston (61)	T	6-5	280	Iowa
3b	Scott Stephen (69)	LB	6-2	232	Arizona State
	(Choice from Falcons for position switch)				
3c	Frankie Neal (71)	WR	6-1	202	Fort Hays State
	(Choice from Raiders in James Lofton trade)				
4	Lorenzo Freeman (89)	DT	6-5	255	Pittsburgh
5	(Choice (115) to Chargers for Mossy Cade)				
6	Willie Marshall (145)	WR	6-1	190	Temple
7a	Tony Leiker (172)	DT	6-5	250	Stanford
7b	Bill Smith (191)	P	6-3	222	Mississippi
	(Choice from Browns for John Jefferson)				
8	Jeff Drost (198)	DT	6-5	286	Iowa
9	Gregg Harris (228)	G	6-4	279	Wake Forest
10	Don Majkowski (255)	QB	6-2	197	Virginia
11	Patrick Scott (282)	WR	5-10	170	Grambling
12a	(Choice (312) to Seahawks for Dan Ross)				
12b	Norman Jefferson (335)	DB	5-10	183	LSU
	(Choice from Giants in Phil McConkey trade)				

1987 "REPLACEMENT" ROSTER

No	Name	Pos	Ht	Wt	DOB	College	G
53	Anderson, Aric	LB	6-2	220	04/09/65	Iona	3
63	Anderson, Curtis	DE	6-7	265	05/16/57	Central State (OR)	3
72/98	Auer, Todd	LB	6-1	230	01/08/65	Western Illinois	3
72	Bone, Warren	DE	6-4	265	11/04/64	Texas Southern	1
73	Caldwell, David	NT	6-1	261	02/28/65	TCU	3
57	Choate, Putt	LB	6-0	225	12/11/56	SMU	2
92/70/74	Collier, Steve*	T	6-7	342	04/19/63	Bethune-Cookman	3
41	Compton, Chuck	DB	5-10	190	01/13/65	Boise State	2
71	Drost, Jeff	DT	6-5	286	01/27/64	Iowa	2
27	Elliott, Tony	DB	5-10	195	01/10/64	Central Michigan	1
79	Estep, Mike	G	6-4	265	12/29/63	Bowling Green	1
89	Fitzgerald, Kevin	TE	6-3	235	06/30/64	Wisconsin-Eau Claire	1
5	Gillus, Willie	QB	6-4	215	09/01/63	Norfolk State	1
69	Gruber, Bob	T	6-5	280	06/07/58	Pittsburgh	1
82	Harden, Derrick	WR	6-1	175	04/21/64	East New Mexico	3
20	Hargrove, James	RB	6-2	232	11/13/58	Wake Forest	2
46	Harrison, Anthony	DB	6-1	195	09/26/65	Georgia Tech	3
63	Hartnett, Perry	G	6-5	285	04/28/60	SMU	1
78	Hobbins, Jim	T	6-6	275	06/04/64	Minnesota	3
31	Hunter, Tony	RB	5-9	215	02/24/63	Minnesota	1
26/81	Jay, Craig	TE	6-4	257	02/05/63	Mt. Senario	3
54/60	Jensen, Greg	OL	6-3	266	01/23/62	No college	1
55	Jordan, Kenneth	LB	6-2	235	04/29/64	Tuskegee	3
40	King, David	DB	5-9	175	05/19/63	Auburn	3
17/32	King, Don	DB	6-0	200	02/10/64	SMU	1
68	Konopasek, Ed	T	6-6	289	04/12/64	Ball State	3
96	Leiker, Tony	DT	6-5	250	09/26/64	Stanford	1
60/54	Malancon, Rydell	LB	6-2	230	01/10/62	LSU	3
44	Mansfield, Von	DB	5-11	183	07/12/60	Wisconsin	3
94	Mataele, Stan	DL	6-2	278	06/24/63	Arizona	2
61	McGarry, John	OL	6-5	288	11/24/63	St. Joseph's	2
77	McGrew, Sylvester	DE	6-4	257	02/27/60	Tulane	3
52	Melka, James	LB	6-1	235	01/15/62	Wisconsin	1
62	Meyer, Jim	T	6-5	290	06/09/63	Illinois State	2
97	Miller, John	LB	6-2	218		Mississippi State	1
51	Monaco, Ron	LB	6-2	240	05/03/63	South Carolina	2
47	Morris, Jim Bob*	DB	6-3	211	05/17/61	Kansas State	3
43	Morris, Larry	RB	5-7	207	02/27/62	Syracuse	2
48/85	Morris, Lee*	WR	5-10	180	07/14/64	Oklahoma	3
39	Parker, Freddie	RB	5-10	215	07/06/62	Mississippi Valley	1
56	Pointer, John	LB	6-2	225	01/16/58	Vanderbilt	3
50	Rafferty, Vince	C-G	6-4	285	08/06/61	Colorado	3
34	Rash, Lou	DB	5-10	190	06/05/60	Mississippi Valley	3
87	Redick, Cornelius	WR	6-0	185	01/07/64	Cal State Fullerton	1
13	Renner, Bill	P	6-0	198	05/23/59	Virginia Tech	3
11	Risher, Alan	QB	6-2	190	05/06/61	LSU	3
83	Scott, Patrick*	WR	5-10	170	09/13/64	Grambling	3
67	Simpson, Travis	OL	6-3	272	11/19/63	Oklahoma	3
84	Smith, Wes	WR	6-0	190	06/24/63	East Texas	1
33	Sterling, John	RB	6-2	203	09/15/64	Central State Oklahoma	2
95	Sullivan, Carl	DE	6-4	248	04/30/62	San Jose State	3
86	Summer, Don	TE	6-4	235	02/22/61	Boise State	3
45	Thomas, Lavale	RB	6-0	205	12/12/63	Fresno State	1
70	Uecker, Keith*	G	6-5	284	06/29/60	Auburn	3
64	Villanucci, Vince	NT	6-2	265	05/30/64	Bowling Green	2
93	Wallace, Calvin	DE	6-2	230	04/17/65	West VA Tech	1
18/38	Washington, Chuck	DB	5-11	186	01/09/64	Arkansas	3
25	Weigel, Lee	RB	5-11	220	11/15/63	Wisconsin-Eau Claire	2
35	Willhite, Kevin	RB	5-11	208	05/04/63	Oregon	3
8	Zendejas, Max*	K	5-11	184	09/02/63	Arizona	3

* also played in union games

Fumbles

	Fum	Ow	Op	Yds	Tot
J. Anderson	0	0	3	0	3
R. Brown	0	0	4	0	4
Cannon	1	0	0	-8	0
Choate	0	0	1	4	1
K. Davis	2	0	0	0	0
Epps	1	0	0	0	0
Fullwood	2	1	0	0	1
Greene	0	0	2	0	2
Hallstrom	0	0	1	0	1
D. Harden	1	0	0	0	0
A. Harrison	0	0	1	0	1
Hobbins	0	0	1	0	1

Fumbles (cont.)

	Fum	Ow	Op	Yds	Tot
Holland	0	0	1	0	1
N. Jefferson	2	0	1	0	1
Majkowski	5	0	0	0	0
V. Mansfield	1	0	0	0	0
Moran	1	1	0	3	1
Lee Morris	1	2	0	0	2
M. Murphy	0	0	2	0	2
F. Neal	1	0	0	0	0
Neville	0	1	0	0	1
Noble	0	0	5	0	5
Pointer	0	0	1	0	1
Risher	4	1	0	0	1

Fumbles (cont.)

	Fum	Ow	Op	Yds	Tot
P. Scott	2	2	0	0	2
Stanley	5	3	0	0	3
Stills	0	1	0	0	1
L. Thomas	0	0	1	3	2
C. Washington	0	1	0	0	1
Weddington	0	0	1	0	1
Willhite	2	0	0	0	0
R. Wright	3	1	0	-4	1
Sterling	1	0	0	0	0
Packers	**35**	**16**	**24**	**-2**	**40**

James Hargrove scores the game-winning touchdown against the Philadelphia Eagles on October 18.

A BRIEF MOMENT IN THE SUN

Don Summer (86) and Patrick Scott.

THREE WEEKS IN OCTOBER

Sunday, October 4
   Packers 23, Vikings 16

Sunday, October 11
   Packers 16, **Lions 19** (OT)

Sunday, October 18
   Packers 16, Eagles 10 (OT)

On Monday, September 21, 1987, players union leader Gene Upshaw announced that following the completion of the New York Jets - New England Patriots game, NFL players would be on strike. NFL owners were determined to continue the season with "replacement players."

The Packers had prepared for such a walkout and by Thursday, the 24th the franchise was conducting practice with more than 40 such players. At that first practice, Packers veterans, stationed outside the fences surrounding the practice field, hurled verbal insults at the strikebreakers.

But Packers fans embraced the new team and its competitive fire. The collection of cast-offs won two games and lost a third in overtime to the Detroit Lions. By contrast, the regulars were only able to muster three wins in 12 tries.

On October 15, the union ended its 24-day walkout. The replacements played their final game that weekend and Green Bay knocked off the Eagles 16-10. While some of the replacement players were retained, most faded quietly from the scene, their moment in the sun over.

REPLACEMENT TEAM RECORDS

San Diego Chargers 3-0
San Francisco 49ers 3-0
Washington Redskins 3-0
Chicago Bears 2-1
Cleveland Browns 2-1
Dallas Cowboys 2-1
Denver Broncos 2-1
Green Bay Packers 2-1
Houston Oilers 2-1
Indianapolis Colts 2-1
New England Patriots 2-1
New Orleans Saints 2-1
Pittsburgh Steelers 2-1
Seattle Seahawks 2-1
Tampa Bay Buccaneers 2-1
Atlanta Falcons 1-2
Buffalo Bills 1-2
Cincinnati Bengals 1-2
Detroit Lions 1-2
Los Angeles Raiders 1-2
Los Angeles Rams 1-2
Miami Dolphins 1-2
New York Jets 1-2
St. Louis Cardinals 1-2
Kansas City Chiefs 0-3
Minnesota Vikings 0-3
New York Giants 0-3
Philadelphia Eagles 0-3

1987 GREEN BAY PACKERS

FRONT ROW: (L-R) 5 Don Majkowski, 6 Robbie Bosco, 8 Max Zendejas, 10 Al Del Greco, 16 Randy Wright, 17 Don Bracken, 20 Kelly Cook, 21 Brent Fullwood, 22 Mark Lee, 23 George (Tiger) Greene, 28 Elbert Watts, 29 Ken Stills.

SECOND ROW: (L-R) 30 Paul Ott Carruth, 32 Dave Brown, 33 Jessie Clark, 35 Kevin Willhite, 36 Kenneth Davis, 37 Mark Murphy, 38 Norman Jefferson, 39 Kenneth Johnson, 44 Chris Mandeville, 45 Lavale Thomas, 47 Jim Bob Morris, 48 Don Summers.

THIRD ROW: (L-R) 49 David Greenwood, 50 Johnny Holland, 51 Clayton Weishuhn, 52 Mike Weddington, 54 Scott Stephen, 56 Burnell Dent, 57 Rich Moran, 58 Mark Cannon, 59 John Anderson, 60 Dave Croston, 61 Jerry Boyarsky.

FOURTH ROW: (L-R) 63 Gregg Harris, 64 Steve Collier, 65 Ron Hallstrom, 69 Bill Cherry, 70 Keith Uecker, 72 Tom Neville, 73 Alan Veingrad, 75 Alphonso Carreker, 77 Tommy Robison.

FIFTH ROW: (L-R) 79 Ross Browner, 80 Frankie Neal, 81 Lee Morris, 82 Keith Paskett, 83 Patrick Scott, 85 Phillip Epps, 86 Ed West, 87 Walter Stanley, 89 Joey Hackett, 90 Ezra Johnson.

BACK ROW: (L-R) Team Physician Eugene Brusky, Medical Assistant Bob Kunz, Medical Assistant Larry Lemberger, 91 Brian Noble, 93 Robert Brown, 97 Tim Harris, 98 Brent Moore, 99 John Dorsey, Administrative Assistant Burt Gustafson, Equipment Manager Bob Noel, Trainer Domenic Gentile, Equipment Assistant Jack Noel, Assistant Equipment Manager Bryan Nehring.

1988

A new coach, a new system, terrible place-kicking, injuries, an anemic running attack and holdouts all contributed to Coach Lindy Infante's 4-12 record in his first year in Green Bay. As had become the script in recent years, the Packers were thumped in the opener (34-7 by the Rams), floundered to a poor start (0-5), then showed signs of improvement late with victories over Minnesota and Phoenix.

Infante, offensive coordinator and quarterbacks coach of the Browns in 1986-87, brought with him a ball-control, passing offense. A half dozen quarterbacks, including former Raider Marc Wilson, Randy Wright and Don Majkowski, attempted to lead the complex attack. Wright got the nod and guided the struggling team to five losses before a groin pull knocked him out. Majkowski then took over and the Packers put together impressive wins over New England and Minnesota before sliding into a seven-game losing streak.

As difficult as it was to master, the passing game caused less headaches than did the team's kicking. Max Zendejas, who had hit 16 of 19 field goals in 1987, went nine of 16 and was released after missing a game-tying 24-yarder against the Redskins in week eight. A parade of kickers followed, none of whom were adequate. Dale Dawson, Dean Dorsey and Curtis Burrow combined to make four of nine field goals and six of 10 extra points.

The receiving corps was hit with injuries. Phillip Epps broke his wrist in the second week and missed four games. Walter Stanley separated his left shoulder and was lost for the final nine games. While those two recovered, first-round pick Sterling Sharpe and free agent Perry Kemp established themselves as starters. Sharpe broke Bill Howton's 36-year old rookie record with 55 catches.

Fullwood, last year's top draft choice, led a virtually non-existent ground game. The Packers failed to gain 100 yards on a dozen occasions and averaged less than 90 yards per game for the first time in team history. Only against New England (207 yards and five touchdowns) did the Packers running game click.

As late as August, six veterans remained unsigned. Rich Moran, Ron Hallstrom, Mark Cannon, Epps, Stanley and Brian Noble were without contracts. All but Noble signed prior to the opener. The fourth-year linebacker became the longest holdout in team annals to that point, missing 67 days before agreeing to terms.

With only four wins and an offense ranked 24th overall, bright spots were hard to uncover. One of the brightest roamed free on a defense which wound up a respectable seventh. Tim Harris registered 13 1/2 sacks, two safeties and a blocked punt that went for a touchdown. Such exploits were only the beginning for the 6'5 linebacker who became every quarterback's nightmare in 1989.

Green Bay Press-Gazette photo

Sterling Sharpe (84) outsprints Mike Richardson (27) with one of his seven receptions against the Bears in Green Bay. Sharpe gained 137 yards receiving in the Packers' 24-6 loss. The team's top pick led the team in receiving with 55 catches for 791 yards.

TEAM STATISTICS

	GB	OPP
First Downs	280	281
Rushing	77	130
Passing	176	136
Penalty	27	15
Rushes	385	514
Yards Gained	1,379	2,110
Average Gain	3.58	4.11
Average Yards per Game	86.2	131.9
Passes Attempted	582	474
Completed	319	256
% Completed	54.81	54.01
Total Yards Gained	3,609	2,949
Times Sacked	51	30
Yards Lost	324	216
Net Yards Gained	3,285	2,733
Yards Gained per Completion	11.31	11.52
Net Yards per Attempt	5.19	5.42
Average Net Yards per Game	205.3	170.8
Combined Net Yards Gained	4,664	4,843
Total Plays	1,018	1,018
Average Yards per Play	4.58	4.76
Average Net Yards per Game	291.5	302.7
Third Down Efficiency	77/215	76/215
Percentage	35.81	35.35
Fourth Down Efficiency	7/14	8/16
Percentage	50.00	50.00
Intercepted By	20	24
Yards Returned	224	386
Returned for TD	0	4
Punts	86	76
Yards Punted	3,287	2,859
Average Yards per Punt	38.22	37.62
Punt Returns	35	39
Yards Returned	208	314
Average Yards per Return	5.94	8.05
Returned for TD	1	0
Kickoff Returns	64	49
Yards Returned	1,181	966
Average Yards per Return	18.45	19.71
Returned for TD	0	0
Penalties	94	112
Yards Penalized	785	903
Fumbles	44	33
Lost	26	21
Own Recovered for Touchdown	0	0
Opponent's Recovered by	21	26
Opponent's Recovered for Touchdown	0	1
Total Points Scored	240	315
Total Touchdowns	29	34
Touchdowns Rushing	14	17
Touchdowns Passing	13	12
Touchdowns on Returns & Recoveries	2	5
Extra Points	23	34
Safeties	2	1
Field Goals Attempted	25	35
Field Goals Made	13	25
% Successful	52.00	71.43
Average Time of Possession	29:16	30:44

Regular Season   4-12-0

Date	GB		OPP	Att.
9/4	7	Los Angeles Rams	34	(53,769)
9/11	10	Tampa Bay Buccaneers	13	(52,984)
9/18	17	at Miami Dolphins	24	(54,409)
9/25	6	Chicago Bears	24	(56,492)
10/2	24	at Tampa Bay Buccaneers	27	(40,003)
10/9	45	New England Patriots (M)	3	(51,932)
10/16	34	at Minnesota Vikings	14	(59,053)
10/23	17	Washington Redskins (M)	20	(51,767)
10/30	0	at Buffalo Bills	28	(79,176)
11/6	0	at Atlanta Falcons	20	(29,952)
11/13	13	Indianapolis Colts	20	(53,942)
11/20	9	Detroit Lions (M)	19	(44,327)
11/27	0	at Chicago Bears	16	(62,026)
12/4	14	at Detroit Lions	30	(28,124)
12/11	18	Minnesota Vikings	6	(48,892)
12/18	26	at Phoenix Cardinals	17	(44,586)

Score By Periods

	1	2	3	4	OT	Total
Packers	58	58	47	77	0	240
Opponents	78	131	38	68	0	315

INDIVIDUAL STATISTICS

Rushing

	Att	Yds	Avg	LG	TD
Fullwood	101	483	4.8	t33	7
Majkowski	47	225	4.8	24	1
Woodside	83	195	2.3	10	3
L. Mason	48	194	4.0	17	0
K. Davis	39	121	3.1	27	1
Carruth	49	114	2.3	14	0
R. Wright	8	43	5.4	19	2
Aubrey Matthews	3	3	1.0	4	0
P. Collins	2	2	1.0	2	0
Stanley	1	1	1.0	1	0
Sharpe	4	-2	-0.5	5	0
Packers	**385**	**1,379**	**3.6**	**t33**	**14**
Opponents	514	2,110	4.1	t80	17

Receiving

	No	Yds	Avg	LG	TD
Sharpe	55	791	14.4	51	1
Kemp	48	620	12.9	36	0
Woodside	39	352	9.0	t49	2
E. West	30	276	9.2	35	3
Stanley	28	436	15.6	56	0
Carruth	24	211	8.8	31	0
P. Scott	20	275	13.8	41	1
Fullwood	20	128	6.4	t30	0
Aubrey Matthews	15	167	11.1	25	2
Epps	11	99	9.0	25	0
K. Davis	11	81	7.4	11	0
L. Mason	8	84	10.5	39	1
Didier	5	37	7.4	15	1
Bolton	2	33	16.5	18	0
P. Collins	2	17	8.5	9	0
Hackett	1	2	2.0	t2	1
Packers	**319**	**3,609**	**11.3**	**56**	**13**
Opponents	256	2,949	11.5	t46	12

Passing

	Att	Com	Yds	Pct	TD	In	Tk/Yds	Rate
Majkowski	336	178	2,119	53.0	9	11	31/176	67.8
R. Wright	244	141	1,490	57.8	4	13	20/148	58.9
Carruth	2	0	0	00.0	0	0	0/0	—
Packers	**582**	**319**	**3,609**	**54.8**	**13**	**24**	**51/324**	**63.9**
Opponents	474	256	2,949	54.0	12	20	30/216	63.9

Punting

	No	Yds	Avg	In20	TB	LG	HB
Bracken	85	3,287	38.7	20	12	62	1
Packers	**86**	**3,287**	**38.2**	**20**	**12**	**62**	**1**
Opponents	76	2,859	37.6	22	5	69	1

Kickoff Returns

	No	Yds	Avg	LG	TD
Fullwood	21	421	20.0	31	0
Woodside	19	343	18.1	29	0
P. Scott	12	207	17.3	27	0
N. Jefferson	4	116	29.0	46	0
Stanley	2	39	19.5	22	0
R. Pitts	1	17	17.0	17	0
Sharpe	1	17	17.0	17	0
Hackett	1	9	9.0	9	0
Winter	1	7	7.0	7	0
Stills	1	4	4.0	4	0
N. Hill	1	1	1.0	1	0
Packers	**64**	**1,181**	**18.5**	**46**	**0**
Opponents	49	966	19.7	37	0

Punt Returns

	No	Yds	Avg	FC	LG	TD
Stanley	12	52	4.3	3	15	0
R. Pitts	9	93	10.3	6	t63	1
Sharpe	9	48	5.3	7	14	0
N. Jefferson	5	15	3.0	2	9	0
Packers	**35**	**208**	**5.9**	**18**	**t63**	**1**
Opponents	39	314	8.1	14	46	0

Interceptions

	No	Yds	Avg	LG	TD
M. Murphy	5	19	3.8	9	0
Cecil	4	56	14.0	33	0
M. Lee	3	37	12.3	27	0
Stills	3	29	9.7	17	0
D. Brown	3	27	9.0	15	0
R. Pitts	2	56	28.0	31	0
Packers	**20**	**224**	**11.2**	**33**	**0**
Opponents	24	386	16.1	t90	4

Scoring

	TDr	TDp	TDrt	PAT	FG	S	TP
Fullwood	7	1	0	0/0	0/0	0	48
Zendejas	0	0	0	17/19	9/16	0	44
Woodside	3	2	0	0/0	0/0	0	30
E. West	0	3	0	0/0	0/0	0	18
Aubrey Matthews	0	2	0	0/0	0/0	0	12
R. Wright	2	0	0	0/0	0/0	0	12
D. Dawson	0	0	0	1/2	3/5	0	10
T. Harris	0	0	1	0/0	0/0	2	10
K. Davis	1	0	0	0/0	0/0	0	6
Didier	0	1	0	0/0	0/0	0	6
D. Dorsey	0	0	0	3/4	1/3	0	6
Hackett	0	1	0	0/0	0/0	0	6
Majkowski	1	0	0	0/0	0/0	0	6
L. Mason	0	1	0	0/0	0/0	0	6
R. Pitts	0	0	1	0/0	0/0	0	6
P. Scott	0	1	0	0/0	0/0	0	6
Sharpe	0	1	0	0/0	0/0	0	6
C. Burrow	0	0	0	2/4	0/1	0	2
Packers	**14**	**13**	**2**	**23/29**	**13/25**	**2**	**240**
Opponents	17	12	5	34/34	25/35	1	315

Fumbles

	Fum	Ow	Op	Yds	Tot
Cannon	2	0	0	-31	0
Carreker	0	0	1	0	1
Carruth	4	0	0	0	0
Cecil	0	0	1	0	1
Dent	0	0	1	0	1
Didier	1	0	0	4	1
Fullwood	6	1	0	0	1
Holland	0	0	1	0	1
N. Jefferson	3	0	1	0	1
Kemp	3	0	0	0	0
M. Lee	0	0	1	0	1
Majkowski	8	3	0	0	3
M. Murphy	0	0	4	0	4
Noble	0	0	1	0	1
Patterson	0	0	1	0	1
R. Pitts	1	2	2	0	4
Ruettgers	0	1	0	0	1
Sharpe	3	1	0	0	1
Stanley	3	1	0	0	1
Stills	0	1	2	4	3
Uecker	0	1	1	0	2
Weddington	0	0	2	0	2
E. West	1	0	0	0	0
Winter	0	0	2	0	2
Woodside	3	1	0	0	1
R. Wright	6	3	0	-5	3
Packers	**44**	**16**	**21**	**-28**	**37**

Quarterback Sacks

	No
T. Harris	13.5
Winter	5.0
Patterson	4.0
R. Brown	1.5
J. Anderson	1.0
Dent	1.0
Greene	1.0
Stephens	1.0
Stills	1.0
Boyarsky	0.5
Noble	0.5
Packers	**30.0**
Opponents	51.0

NFL STANDINGS

National Conference

Eastern Division

	W	L	T	Pct	PF	PA
Philadelphia Eagles	10	6	0	.625	379	319
New York Giants	10	6	0	.625	359	387
Washington Redskins	7	9	0	.438	345	387
Phoenix Cardinals	7	9	0	.438	344	398
Dallas Cowboys	3	13	0	.188	265	381

Central Division

	W	L	T	Pct	PF	PA
Chicago Bears	12	4	0	.750	312	215
Minnesota Vikings	11	5	0	.688	406	233
Tampa Bay Buccaneers	5	11	0	.313	261	350
Detroit Lions	4	12	0	.250	220	313
Green Bay Packers	**4**	**12**	**0**	**.250**	**240**	**315**

Western Division

	W	L	T	Pct	PF	PA
San Francisco 49ers	10	6	0	.625	369	294
Los Angeles Rams	10	6	0	.625	407	293
New Orleans Saints	10	6	0	.625	312	283
Atlanta Falcons	5	11	0	.313	244	315

American Conference

Eastern Division

	W	L	T	Pct	PF	PA
Buffalo Bills	12	4	0	.750	329	237
Indianapolis Colts	9	7	0	.563	354	315
New England Patriots	9	7	0	.563	250	284
New York Jets	8	7	1	.531	372	354
Miami Dolphins	6	10	0	.375	319	380

Central Division

	W	L	T	Pct	PF	PA
Cincinnati Bengals	12	4	0	.750	448	329
Cleveland Browns	10	6	0	.625	304	288
Houston Oilers	10	6	0	.625	424	365
Pittsburgh Steelers	5	11	0	.313	336	421

Western Division

	W	L	T	Pct	PF	PA
Seattle Seahawks	9	7	0	.563	339	329
Denver Broncos	8	8	0	.500	327	352
Los Angeles Raiders	7	9	0	.438	325	369
San Diego Chargers	6	10	0	.375	231	332
Kansas City Chiefs	4	11	1	.281	254	320

1988 ROSTER

No	Name	Pos	Ht	Wt	DOB	College	G
59	Anderson, John	LB	6-3	228	02/14/56	Michigan	14
88	Bell, Albert	WR	6-0	170	04/23/64	Alabama	5
82	Bolton, Scott	WR	6-0	188	01/04/65	Auburn	4
61	Boyarsky, Jerry	NT	6-3	290	05/15/59	Pittsburgh	2
17	Bracken, Don	P	6-0	205	02/16/62	Michigan	16
32	Brown, Dave	CB	6-1	197	01/16/53	Michigan	16
93	Brown, Robert	DE	6-2	267	05/21/60	Virginia Tech	16
5	Burrow, Curtis	K	5-11	185	12/11/62	Central Arkansas	1
58	Cannon, Mark	C	6-3	270	06/14/62	Texas-Arlington	16
76	Carreker, Alphonso	DE	6-6	271	05/25/62	Florida State	14
30	Carruth, Paul Ott	RB	6-1	220	07/22/61	Alabama	15
26	Cecil, Chuck	S	6-0	184	11/08/64	Arizona	16
25	Collins, Pat	RB	5-9	188	08/04/66	Oklahoma	6
53	Corker, John	LB	6-5	240	12/29/58	Oklahoma State	2
60	Croston, Dave	T	6-5	280	11/10/63	Iowa	16
36	Davis, Kenneth	RB	5-10	209	04/16/62	TCU	9
4	Dawson, Dale	K	6-1	212	11/02/64	Eastern Kentucky	4
56	Dent, Burnell	LB	6-1	236	03/16/63	Tulane	10
80	Didier, Clint	TE	6-5	240	04/04/59	Portland State	15
9	Dorsey, Dean	K	5-11	195	03/15/57	Toronto	3
99	Dorsey, John	LB	6-2	243	08/31/60	Connecticut	16
85	Epps, Phillip	WR	5-10	165	11/11/58	TCU	6
21	Fullwood, Brent	FB	5-11	209	10/10/63	Auburn	14
23	Greene, George (Tiger)	DB	6-0	194	02/15/62	Western Carolina	16
89	Hackett, Joey	TE	6-5	267	09/29/58	Elon	9
74	Haley, Darryl	T	6-5	265	02/16/61	Utah	13
65	Hallstrom, Ron	G	6-5	290	06/11/59	Iowa	16
97	Harris, Tim	LB	6-5	235	09/10/64	Memphis State	16
90	Hill, Nate	DE	6-4	273	02/22/66	Auburn	3
50	Holland, Johnny	LB	6-2	221	03/11/65	Texas A&M	13
38	Jefferson, Norman	DB	5-10	183	08/07/64	LSU	2
62	Kauahi, Kani	C	6-2	271	09/06/59	Hawaii	16
81	Kemp, Perry	WR	5-11	170	12/31/61	California State (PA)	16
22	Lee, Mark	CB	5-11	189	03/20/58	Washington	15
7	Majkowski, Don	QB	6-2	197	02/25/64	Virginia	13
34	Mason, Larry	RB	5-11	205	05/21/61	Troy State	15
88	Matthews, Aubrey	WR	5-7	165	09/15/62	Delta State	7
57	Moran, Rich	G	6-2	275	03/19/62	San Diego State	16
37	Murphy, Mark	S	6-2	201	04/22/58	West Liberty	14
79	Nelson, Bob	NT	6-4	275	03/03/59	Miami	14
72	Neville, Tom	G	6-5	300	09/04/61	Fresno State	2
91	Noble, Brian	LB	6-3	252	09/06/62	Arizona State	12
96	Patterson, Shawn	DE	6-5	261	04/06/65	Arizona State	15
28	Pitts, Ron	DB	5-10	175	10/14/62	UCLA	14
46	Richard, Gary	CB	5-9	171	10/09/65	Pittsburgh	10
75	Ruettgers, Ken	T	6-5	280	08/20/62	USC	15
83	Scott, Patrick	WR	5-10	170	09/13/64	Grambling	16
84	Sharpe, Sterling	WR	5-11	202	04/06/65	South Carolina	16
51	Simpkins, Ron	LB	6-1	234	04/02/58	Michigan	7
87	Stanley, Walter	WR	5-9	179	11/05/62	Mesa	7
54	Stephen, Scott	LB	6-2	232	06/18/64	Arizona State	8
29	Stills, Ken	S	5-10	186	09/06/63	Wisconsin	14
45	Thomas, Lavale	RB	6-0	205	12/12/63	Fresno State	1
70	Uecker, Keith	G	6-5	284	06/29/60	Auburn	16
52	Weddington, Mike	LB	6-4	245	10/09/60	Oklahoma	16
86	West, Ed	TE	6-1	243	08/02/61	Auburn	16
68	Winter, Blaise	DE	6-3	275	01/31/62	Syracuse	16
33	Woodside, Keith	RB	5-11	203	07/29/64	Texas A&M	16
16	Wright, Randy	QB	6-2	203	01/12/61	Wisconsin	8
8	Zendejas, Max	K	5-11	184	09/02/63	Arizona	8

1988 DRAFT

Rnd	Name	Pos	Ht	Wt	College
1	Sterling Sharpe (7)	WR	5-11	202	South Carolina
2	Shawn Patterson (34)	DT	6-5	261	Arizona State
3	Keith Woodside (61)	RB	5-11	203	Texas A&M
4a	Rollin Putzier (88)	NT	6-4	279	Oregon
	(Choice from Raiders in James Lofton trade)				
4b	Chuck Cecil (89)	FS	6-0	184	Arizona
5	Darrell Reed (116)	LB	6-1	225	Oklahoma
6	Nate Hill (144)	DE	6-4	273	Auburn
7	Gary Richard (173)	CB	5-9	172	Pittsburgh
8	Patrick Collins (200)	HB	5-9	188	Oklahoma
9	Neal Wilkinson (228)	TE	6-5	226	James Madison
10	Bud Keyes (256)	QB	6-2	211	Wisconsin
11	(Choice (284) to Seahawks in Dave Brown trade)				
12	Scott Bolton (312)	WR	6-0	188	Auburn

1988 GREEN BAY PACKERS

FRONT ROW: (L-R) 7 Don Majkowski, 8 Max Zendejas, 16 Randy Wright, 17 Don Bracken, 20 Kelly Cook, 21 Brent Fullwood, 22 Mark Lee, 23 George (Tiger) Greene, 25 Pat Collins, 26 Chuck Cecil, 27 Tony Elliott.

SECOND ROW: (L-R) 28 Ron Pitts, 29 Ken Stills, 30 Paul Ott Carruth, 31 Joe Armentrout, 32 Dave Brown, 33 Keith Woodside, 34 Larry Mason, 36 Kenneth Davis, 37 Mark Murphy, 38 Norman Jefferson, 39 Kenneth Johnson.

THIRD ROW: (L-R) 42 Scott Bolton, 45 Lavale Thomas, 46 Gary Richard, 50 Johnny Holland, 51 Ron Simpkins, 52 Mike Weddington, 54 Scott Stephen, 56 Burnell Dent, 57 Rich Moran, 58 Mark Cannon, 59 John Anderson.

FOURTH ROW: (L-R) 60 Dave Croston, 61 Jerry Boyarsky, 62 Kani Kauahi, 64 Steve Collier, 65 Ron Hallstrom, 68 Blaise Winter, 70 Keith Uecker, 74 Darryl Haley, 75 Ken Ruettgers, 76 Alphonso Carreker, 77 Tommy Robison.

FIFTH ROW: (L-R) 79 Bob Nelson, 80 Clint Didier, 81 Perry Kemp, 82 Keith Paskett, 83 Patrick Scott, 84 Sterling Sharpe, 85 Phillip Epps, 86 Ed West, 87 Walter Stanley, 88 Albert Bell, 89 Joey Hackett.

SIXTH ROW: (L-R) Assistant Video Director Bob Eckburg, Training Room Assistant Tim Wall, Training Room Assistant Kurt Fielding, Trainer Domenic Gentile, 93 Robert Brown, 96 Shawn Patterson, 97 Tim Harris, 99 John Dorsey, Team Physician Dr. Eugene Brusky, Equipment Manager Bob Noel, Equipment Assistant Jack Noel, Assistant Equipment Manager Bryan Nehring.

BACK ROW: (L-R) Defensive Line Coach Greg Blache, Outside Linebackers Coach Dick Moseley, Receivers Coach Wayne (Buddy) Geis, Defensive Backfield Coach Dick Jauron, Strength-Conditioning/Tight Ends Coach Virgil Knight, Offensive Backfield Coach Willie Peete, Head Coach Lindy Infante, Special Teams Coach Howard Tippett, Offensive Line Coach Charlie Davis, Defensive Coordinator Hank Bullough, Administrative Assistant Burt Gustafson, Video Director Al Treml.

1989. The year of "Majik." Of excitement. Of comebacks and close games galore. A sweep of the Bears and a share of the NFC Central Division title. More than any Packers team in recent memory, the 1989 edition provided thrills and entertainment by the minute. To get a seat on this rollercoaster of a season, one needed nerves of steel and a never-say-die attitude. The team came from behind to win seven times and set an NFL record with four one-point wins.

Unfortunately, the dizzying ride came to an end on Christmas Day when Minnesota defeated Cincinnati 29-21. With the win, the Vikings matched Green Bay's 10-6 record and claimed a share of the Central Division title. Since the Vikings owned a better division record than the Packers, they and not the Packers journeyed to the playoffs.

Swept along by its high-powered offense, Green Bay wasted no time in putting fans on the edge of their seats. The team trailed New Orleans 24-7 in the season's second week but, with Don "Majik" Majkowski hitting 16 straight passes to open the second half, shot back to defeat the Saints 35-34. The following week, Green Bay faced an even bigger halftime deficit against the Rams (38-7). Had Brent Fullwood not fumbled away a scoring opportunity from the one-yard line, the Packers might have prevailed instead of falling 41-38. One week later, the team trailed Atlanta by 15 points heading into the fourth quarter, but put away the Falcons 23-21.

Green Bay's resurgence gained legitimacy when it downed the Bears 14-13 and upset the defending Super Bowl champion 49ers 21-17 in San Francisco two weeks later. The Bears win tasted particularly sweet but the outcome rested in the hands of the officials for several minutes. Sterling Sharpe caught an apparent 14-yard touchdown pass from Majkowski with 32 seconds left but an official on the field ruled that the ball had crossed the line of scrimmage before being released. Pandemonium reigned after replay official Bill Parkinson upheld the score by overruling the original call on the field.

Majkowski, Sharpe, Tim Harris, Brent Fullwood and Chris Jacke were at the heart of the rebirth. Majkowski set club records with 599 attempts and 353 completions. Sharpe led the NFL with 90 catches, the first Packer to do so since Don Hutson's 47 topped the circuit in 1945. Fullwood contributed 821 rushing yards. Harris, with 19 1/2 sacks, became the first defensive player since Ezra Johnson in 1978 to make the Pro Bowl. And Jacke won five games in the last two minutes with his kicks and led the team in scoring with 108 points.

The Packers signed a league-high 20 Plan B players. Nine played in at least one game and of those, Carl Bland, Blair Bush, Michael Haddix and Van Jakes saw action in all 16.

On November 26, the Packers (6-5) faced the Vikings (7-4) in Milwaukee. In the first meeting Minnesota had dominated 26-14. This time with Majkowski connecting on 26 of 35 passes for 276 yards and Sharpe hauling 10 passes, Green Bay turned back the visitors 20-19. Even so, the outcome was up in the air until wily Dave Brown intercepted Wade Wilson twice in the closing minutes.

Green Bay Press-Gazette photo

Don Majkowski (7) directs the resurgent Pack Attack in 1989. The tenth-round choice in 1987 set a host of season records with his passing and became the first Packers quarterback to make the Pro Bowl since Bart Starr in 1966.

TEAM STATISTICS

	GB	OPP
First Downs	342	307
Rushing	114	116
Passing	207	179
Penalty	21	12
Rushes	397	460
Yards Gained	1,732	2,008
Average Gain	4.36	4.37
Average Yards per Game	108.3	125.5
Passes Attempted	600	476
Completed	354	302
% Completed	59.00	63.45
Total Yards Gained	4,325	3,553
Times Sacked	48	34
Yards Lost	277	214
Net Yards Gained	4,048	3,339
Yards Gained per Completion	12.22	11.76
Net Yards per Attempt	6.25	6.55
Average Net Yards per Game	253.0	208.7
Combined Net Yards Gained	5,780	5,347
Total Plays	1,045	970
Average Yards per Play	5.53	5.51
Average Net Yards per Game	361.3	334.2
Third Down Efficiency	93/204	86/191
Percentage	45.59	45.03
Fourth Down Efficiency	8/12	5/6
Percentage	66.67	83.33
Intercepted By	25	20
Yards Returned	232	321
Returned for TD	0	2
Punts	66	65
Yards Punted	2,682	2,644
Average Yards per Punt	40.64	40.68
Punt Returns	35	30
Yards Returned	289	416
Average Yards per Return	8.26	13.87
Returned for TD	0	0
Kickoff Returns	69	63
Yards Returned	1,239	1,389
Average Yards per Return	17.96	22.05
Returned for TD	0	0
Penalties	81	105
Yards Penalized	666	851
Fumbles	35	28
Lost	13	15
Own Recovered for Touchdown	2	0
Opponent's Recovered by	15	13
Opponent's Recovered for Touchdown	0	2
Total Points Scored	362	356
Total Touchdowns	42	41
Touchdowns Rushing	13	15
Touchdowns Passing	27	22
Touchdowns on Returns & Recoveries	2	4
Extra Points	42	39
Safeties	1	1
Field Goals Attempted	28	30
Field Goals Made	22	23
% Successful	78.57	76.67
Average Time of Possession	30:21	29:39

Regular Season 10-6-0

Date	GB		OPP	Att.
9/10	21	Tampa Bay Buccaneers	23	(55,650)
9/17	35	New Orleans Saints	34	(55,809)
9/24	38	at Los Angeles Rams	41	(57,701)
10/1	23	Atlanta Falcons (M)	21	(54,647)
10/8	31	Dallas Cowboys	13	(56,656)
10/15	14	at Minnesota Vikings	26	(62,075)
10/22	20	at Miami Dolphins	23	(56,624)
10/29	23	Detroit Lions (M) (OT)	20	(53,731)
11/5	14	Chicago Bears	13	(56,556)
11/12	22	at Detroit Lions	31	(44,324)
11/19	21	at San Francisco 49ers	17	(62,219)
11/26	20	Minnesota Vikings (M)	19	(55,592)
12/3	17	at Tampa Bay Buccaneers	16	(58,120)
12/10	3	Kansas City Chiefs	21	(56,694)
12/17	40	at Chicago Bears	28	(44,781)
12/24	20	at Dallas Cowboys	10	(41,265)

Score By Periods

	1	2	3	4	OT	Total
Packers	71	74	89	125	3	362
Opponents	77	157	70	52	0	356

INDIVIDUAL STATISTICS

Rushing

	Att	Yds	Avg	LG	TD
Fullwood	204	821	4.0	38	5
Majkowski	75	358	4.8	20	5
Woodside	46	273	5.9	t68	0
Haddix	44	135	3.1	10	0
Fontenot	17	69	4.1	19	1
Kemp	5	43	8.6	14	0
Sharpe	2	25	12.5	26	0
Workman	4	8	2.0	3	1
Packers	**397**	**1,732**	**4.4**	**t68**	**13**
Opponents	460	2,008	4.4	73	15

Receiving

	No	Yds	Avg	LG	TD
Sharpe	90	1,423	15.8	t79	12
Woodside	59	527	8.9	33	0
Kemp	48	611	12.7	39	2
Fontenot	40	372	9.3	t38	3
Query	23	350	15.2	45	2
E. West	22	269	12.2	31	5
Fullwood	19	214	11.3	67	0
Aubrey Matthews	18	200	11.1	25	0
Haddix	15	111	7.4	23	1
Bland	11	164	14.9	t46	1
Didier	7	71	10.1	t24	1
Spagnola	2	13	6.5	14	0
Packers	**354**	**4,325**	**12.2**	**t79**	**27**
Opponents	302	3,553	11.8	61	22

Passing

	Att	Com	Yds	Pct	TD	In	Tk/Yds	Rate
Majkowski	599	353	4,318	58.9	27	20	47/268	82.3
A. Dilweg	1	1	7	100.0	0	0	0/0	—
Fontenot	0	0	0		0	0	1/9	—
Packers	**600**	**354**	**4,325**	**59.0**	**27**	**20**	**48/277**	**82.4**
Opponents	476	302	3,553	63.4	22	25	34/214	79.6

Punting

	No	Yds	Avg	In20	TB	LG	HB
Bracken	66	2,682	40.6	17	11	63	0
Packers	**66**	**2,682**	**40.6**	**17**	**11**	**63**	**0**
Opponents	65	2,644	40.7	16	1	55	0

Kickoff Returns

	No	Yds	Avg	LG	TD
Workman	30	527	16.6	46	0
Bland	13	256	19.7	37	0
Fullwood	11	243	22.1	35	0
Query	6	125	20.8	28	0
Woodside	2	38	19.0	23	0
Fontenot	2	30	15.0	20	0
Didier	1	0	0.0	0	0
Mandarich	1	0	0.0	0	0
Packers	**69**	**1,239**	**18.0**	**46**	**0**
Opponents	63	1,389	22.0	90	0

Punt Returns

	No	Yds	Avg	FC	LG	TD
Query	30	247	8.2	7	15	0
Sutton	5	42	8.4	1	17	0
R. Pitts	0	0	0.0	1	0	0
Packers	**35**	**289**	**8.3**	**9**	**17**	**0**
Opponents	30	416	13.9	11	74	0

Interceptions

	No	Yds	Avg	LG	TD
D. Brown	6	12	2.0	12	0
M. Murphy	3	31	10.3	20	0
Stills	3	20	6.7	12	0
Stephen	2	16	8.0	8	0
M. Lee	2	10	5.0	10	0
Noble	2	10	5.0	10	0
Dent	1	53	53.0	53	0
R. Pitts	1	37	37.0	37	0
Holland	1	26	26.0	26	0
Cecil	1	16	16.0	16	0
J. Anderson	1	1	1.0	1	0
Greene	1	0	0.0	0	0
Jakes	1	0	0.0	0	0
Packers	**25**	**232**	**9.3**	**53**	**0**
Opponents	20	321	16.1	t81	2

Scoring

	TDr	TDp	TDrt	PAT	FG	S	TP
Jacke	0	0	0	42/42	22/28	0	108
Sharpe	0	12	1	0/0	0/0	0	78
Fullwood	5	0	0	0/0	0/0	0	30
Majkowski	5	0	0	0/0	0/0	0	30
E. West	0	5	0	0/0	0/0	0	30
Fontenot	1	3	0	0/0	0/0	0	24
Bland	0	1	1	0/0	0/0	0	12
Kemp	0	2	0	0/0	0/0	0	12
Query	0	2	0	0/0	0/0	0	12
Didier	0	1	0	0/0	0/0	0	6
Haddix	0	1	0	0/0	0/0	0	6
Woodside	1	0	0	0/0	0/0	0	6
Workman	1	0	0	0/0	0/0	0	6
team	0	0	0	0/0	0/0	1	2
Packers	**13**	**27**	**2**	**42/42**	**22/28**	**1**	**362**
Opponents	15	22	4	39/41	23/30	1	356

Fumbles

	Fum	Ow	Op	Yds	Tot
Bland	0	2	1	4	3
Bush	0	1	0	0	1
Fontenot	0	1	1	0	2
Fullwood	6	1	0	0	1
Greene	1	0	1	0	1
Haddix	2	0	0	0	0
T. Harris	0	0	3	0	3
Holland	0	0	3	0	3
Kemp	3	1	0	0	1
Majkowski	15	6	0	-13	6
McGruder	0	1	1	0	1
Moran	0	0	1	0	1
M. Murphy	0	0	1	0	1
B. Nelson	0	0	1	0	1
Noble	0	0	1	0	1
Query	1	0	1	0	1
Ruettgers	0	2	0	0	2
Sharpe	1	1	0	5	1
Stephen	0	0	1	76	1
Sutton	1	1	0	0	0
Weddington	0	0	1	0	1
Woodside	4	1	0	0	1
Workman	1	1	0	0	1
Packers	**35**	**19**	**15**	**72**	**34**

Quarterback Sacks

	No
T. Harris	19.5
R. Brown	3.0
Greene	2.0
Noble	2.0
Winter	2.0
M. Hall	1.0
M. Murphy	1.0
B. Nelson	1.0
Stephen	1.0
Weddington	1.0
Patterson	0.5
Packers	**34.0**
Opponents	48.0

NFL STANDINGS

National Conference

Eastern Division

	W	L	T	Pct	PF	PA
New York Giants	12	4	0	.750	348	252
Philadelphia Eagles	11	5	0	.688	342	274
Washington Redskins	10	6	0	.625	386	308
Phoenix Cardinals	5	11	0	.313	258	377
Dallas Cowboys	1	15	0	.063	204	393

Central Division

	W	L	T	Pct	PF	PA
Minnesota Vikings	10	6	0	.625	351	275
Green Bay Packers	**10**	**6**	**0**	**.625**	**362**	**356**
Detroit Lions	7	9	0	.438	312	364
Chicago Bears	6	10	0	.375	358	377
Tampa Bay Buccaneers	5	11	0	.313	320	419

Western Division

	W	L	T	Pct	PF	PA
San Francisco 49ers	14	2	0	.875	442	253
Los Angeles Rams	11	5	0	.688	426	344
New Orleans Saints	9	7	0	.563	386	301
Atlanta Falcons	3	13	0	.188	279	437

American Conference

Eastern Division

	W	L	T	Pct	PF	PA
Buffalo Bills	9	7	0	.563	409	317
Indianapolis Colts	8	8	0	.500	298	301
Miami Dolphins	8	8	0	.500	331	379
New England Patriots	5	11	0	.313	297	391
New York Jets	4	12	0	.250	253	411

Central Division

	W	L	T	Pct	PF	PA
Cleveland Browns	9	6	1	.594	334	254
Houston Oilers	9	7	0	.563	365	412
Pittsburgh Steelers	9	7	0	.563	265	326
Cincinnati Bengals	8	8	0	.500	404	285

Western Division

	W	L	T	Pct	PF	PA
Denver Broncos	11	5	0	.688	362	226
Kansas City Chiefs	8	7	1	.531	318	286
Los Angeles Raiders	8	8	0	.500	315	297
Seattle Seahawks	7	9	0	.438	241	327
San Diego Chargers	6	10	0	.375	266	290

1989 ROSTER

No	Name	Pos	Ht	Wt	DOB	College	G
59	Anderson, John	LB	6-3	228	02/14/56	Michigan	14
67	Ard, Billy	G	6-3	270	03/12/59	Wake Forest	15
76	Ariey, Mike	T	6-5	285	03/12/64	San Diego State	1
83	Bland, Carl	WR	5-11	182	08/17/61	Virginia Union	16
61	Boyarsky, Jerry	NT	6-3	290	05/15/59	Pittsburgh	13
17	Bracken, Don	P	6-0	211	02/16/62	Michigan	16
62	Brock, Matt	DE	6-4	267	01/14/66	Oregon	7
32	Brown, Dave	CB	6-1	197	01/16/53	Michigan	16
93	Brown, Robert	DE	6-2	270	05/21/60	Virginia Tech	16
51	Bush, Blair	C	6-3	272	11/25/56	Washington	16
63	Campen, James	C	6-3	270	06/11/64	Tulane	15
58	Cannon, Mark	C	6-3	270	06/14/62	Texas-Arlington	15
26	Cecil, Chuck	S	6-0	184	11/08/64	Arizona	9
56	Dent, Burnell	LB	6-1	236	03/16/63	Tulane	16
80	Didier, Clint	TE	6-5	240	04/04/59	Portland State	16
8	Dilweg, Anthony	QB	6-3	215	03/28/65	Duke	1
27	Fontenot, Herman	RB	6-0	206	09/12/63	LSU	16
21	Fullwood, Brent	FB	5-11	209	10/10/63	Auburn	15
23	Greene, George (Tiger)	DB	6-0	194	02/15/62	Western Carolina	16
35	Haddix, Michael	RB	6-1	227	12/27/61	Mississippi State	16
72	Hall, Mark	DE	6-4	285	08/21/65	Southwestern Louisiana	7
65	Hallstrom, Ron	G	6-6	290	06/11/59	Iowa	16
97	Harris, Tim	LB	6-5	235	09/10/64	Memphis State	16
50	Holland, Johnny	LB	6-2	221	03/11/65	Texas A&M	16
13	Jacke, Chris	K	6-0	197	03/12/66	Texas-El Paso	16
24	Jakes, Van	CB	6-0	190	05/10/61	Kent State	16
81	Kemp, Perry	WR	5-11	170	12/31/61	California State (PA)	14
22	Lee, Mark	CB	5-11	189	03/20/58	Washington	12
7	Majkowski, Don	QB	6-2	197	02/25/64	Virginia	16
77	Mandarich, Tony	T	6-5	315	09/23/66	Michigan State	14
88	Matthews, Aubrey	WR	5-7	165	09/15/62	Delta State	13
20	McGruder, Michael	DB	5-11	180	08/25/64	Kent State	2
57	Moran, Rich	G	6-2	275	03/19/62	San Diego State	16
37	Murphy, Mark	S	6-2	201	04/22/58	West Liberty	16
79	Nelson, Bob	NT	6-4	275	03/03/59	Miami	16
91	Noble, Brian	LB	6-3	252	09/06/62	Arizona State	16
96	Patterson, Shawn	DE	6-5	261	04/06/65	Arizona State	6
28	Pitts, Ron	DB	5-10	175	10/14/62	UCLA	14
85	Query, Jeff	WR	5-11	165	03/07/67	Millikin	16
75	Ruettgers, Ken	T	6-5	280	08/20/62	USC	16
84	Sharpe, Sterling	WR	5-11	202	04/06/65	South Carolina	16
89	Spagnola, John	TE	6-4	242	08/01/57	Yale	6
54	Stephen, Scott	LB	6-2	232	06/18/64	Arizona State	16
29	Stills, Ken	S	5-10	186	09/06/63	Wisconsin	16
49	Sutton, Mickey	CB	5-9	172	08/28/60	Montana	3
73	Veingrad, Alan	T	6-5	277	07/24/63	East Texas State	16
52	Weddington, Mike	LB	6-4	245	10/09/60	Oklahoma	15
86	West, Ed	TE	6-1	243	08/02/61	Auburn	13
68	Winter, Blaise	DE	6-3	275	01/31/62	Syracuse	16
33	Woodside, Keith	RB	5-11	213	07/29/64	Texas A&M	16
46	Workman, Vince	RB	5-10	193	05/09/68	Ohio State	15

1989 DRAFT

Rnd	Name	Pos	Ht	Wt	College
1	Tony Mandarich (2)	T	6-5	315	Michigan State
2	(Packers traded 2nd round choice (31) and 5th round selection (114) to Browns for Browns' No. 1 pick in 1990 and Browns' 3rd and 5th round choices in 1989 plus Herman Fontenot)				
3a	Matt Brock (58)	DE	6-4	267	Oregon
3b	Anthony Dilweg (74)	QB	6-3	215	Duke
	(Choice from Browns in deal mentioned above)				
4	Jeff Graham (87)	QB	6-4	205	Long Beach State
	(Packers then traded Graham to Redskins for Erik Affholter plus Redskins' 5th and 8th round choices in 1989)				
5a	(Choice (114) to Browns in deal mentioned above)				
5b	Jeff Query (124)	WR	5-11	167	Millikin
	(Choice from Redskins in deal mentioned above)				
5c	Vince Workman (127)	RB	5-10	195	Ohio State
	(Choice from Browns in deal mentioned above)				
6	Chris Jacke (142)	K	6-0	197	Texas-El Paso
7	Mark Hall (169)	DT	6-4	285	SW Louisiana
8a	Thomas King (198)	DB	6-1	198	SW Louisiana
8b	Brian Shulman (206)	P	5-10	185	Auburn
	(Choice from Redskins in deal mentioned above)				
9	Scott Kirby (225)	T	6-6	290	Arizona State
10	Ben Jessie (254)	DB	6-0	205	SW Texas State
11	Cedric Stallworth (281)	DB	6-0	180	Georgia Tech
12	Stan Shiver (310)	DB	6-1	208	Florida State

1989 GREEN BAY PACKERS

FRONT ROW: (L-R) 7 Don Majkowski, 8 Anthony Dilweg, 10 Blair Kiel, 13 Chris Jacke, 17 Don Bracken, 20 Michael McGruder, 21 Brent Fullwood, 22 Mark Lee, 23 George (Tiger) Greene, 24 Van Jakes, 26 Chuck Cecil.
SECOND ROW: (L-R) 27 Herman Fontenot, 28 Ron Pitts, 29 Ken Stills, 32 Dave Brown, 33 Keith Woodside, 35 Michael Haddix, 36 George Cooper, 37 Mark Murphy, 38 Stan Shiver, 40 Cedric Gordon, 46 Vince Workman, 50 Johnny Holland.
THIRD ROW: (L-R) 51 Blair Bush, 52 Mike Weddington, 54 Scott Stephen, 56 Burnell Dent, 57 Rich Moran, 58 Mark Cannon, 59 John Anderson, 60 Dave Croston, 61 Jerry Boyarsky, 62 Matt Brock, 63 James Campen.
FOURTH ROW: (L-R) Team Physician Dr. Eugene Brusky, 64 Scott Kirby, 65 Ron Hallstrom, 67 Billy Ard, 68 Blaise Winter, 70 Keith Uecker, 72 Mark Hall, 73 Alan Veingrad, 75 Ken Ruettgers, 76 Mike Ariey, 77 Tony Mandarich, Trainer Domenic Gentile.
FIFTH ROW: (L-R) Equipment Assistant Jack Noel, Equipment Manager Bob Noel, 79 Bob Nelson, 80 Clint Didier, 81 Perry Kemp, 82 Erik Affholter, 83 Carl Bland, 84 Sterling Sharpe, 85 Jeff Query, Assistant Video Director Bob Eckberg, Video Director Al Treml.
SIXTH ROW: (L-R) Trainer Intern Larry Lemberger, Assistant Equipment Manager Bryan Nehring, 86 Ed West, 88 Aubrey Matthews, 89 John Spagnola, 91 Brian Noble, 93 Robert Brown, 96 Shawn Patterson, 97 Tim Harris,
99 John Dorsey, Trainer Intern Greg Everts, Trainer Intern John Bray.
BACK ROW: (L-R) Defensive Line Coach Greg Blache, Defensive Backs Coach Dick Jauron, Offensive Backfield Coach Willie Peete, Outside Linebackers Coach Dick Moseley, Strength-Conditioning/Tight Ends Coach Virgil Knight, Head Coach Lindy Infante,
Special Teams Coach Howard Tippett, Defensive Coordinator Hank Bullough, Receivers Coach Wayne (Buddy) Geis, Offensive Line Coach Charlie Davis, General Offensive Assistant Joe Clark, Administrative Assistant Jesse Kaye.

Green Bay's 10-6 record last year was better than four 1989 AFC playoff teams. After the NFL added a third wild card team for each conference in 1990, it was noted that had such a situation existed a year ago, the Packers would have earned a postseason berth. A three-game winning streak in midseason shot the team into playoff contention but the optimism that accompanied it had to be tempered when Don Majkowski went down with a season-ending injury. With their flamboyant leader sidelined, the Packers stumbled and dropped five straight. As it turned out, had the team been able to beat the cellar-dwelling Lions and Broncos on the season's final two weekends, it could have claimed the third wildcard spot. Instead, Green Bay lost both and narrowly avoided the basement itself.

High expectations fell apart as holdouts, offensive line woes and a weak running game hindered the team's progress. Eighteen players, the majority of them starters, missed the first day of training camp because of contract troubles. Alan Veingrad (15), Ken Ruettgers (25), Rich Moran (29) and Ron Hallstrom (32) – in other words four fifths of 1989's starting offensive line – missed a combined 101 days of practice. While Ruettgers regained his left tackle spot, Moran and Hallstrom were replaced by Billy Ard and Keith Uecker, respectively, for most of the season. Tony Mandarich, the team's number-one pick in 1989, moved ahead of Veingrad but did little to distinguish himself.

The missed practice time, new faces and nagging injuries kept the offensive unit from meshing. Green Bay gave up a team-record 62 sacks and put together its worst ever rushing output on a per game average (85.6 yards).

Neither of those dubious achievements were entirely the line's fault, especially the lack of a ground game. Lindy Infante waited in vain for a back to take charge and seize control of the running game. Michael Haddix wound up the ground-gaining leader with 311 yards, the fewest by a team leader since Paul Hornung's 310 in 1958.

As far as quarterbacks went, down they went. Majkowski held out 45 days before signing a club-record $1.5 million contract. He regained starter status after the first Bears game, but didn't completely recapture his touch until orchestrating a last-second 24-21 comeback at Detroit. Against the Cardinals six weeks later, he was flushed from the pocket and sacked by defensive end Freddie Joe Nunn. His injury was diagnosed as a deep bruise. Majkowski endured nearly four weeks of severe soreness and even attempted to practice. Finally, Majkowski sought a second opinion. Dr. Gary Losse of San Diego discovered a torn rotator cuff and repaired the injury on December 13.

Anthony Dilweg finished off the Cardinals 24-21 with an 11-point comeback. He then was knocked from the Eagles game with a sprained arch. Blair Kiel, inactive for nearly three years, took over but wasn't the answer.

The team staged its best performance of the year on November 11. Majkowski was in top form, Chris Jacke kicked a team-record five field goals and Green Bay notched its first regular-season win over the Raiders 29-16. Vietnam veteran Bob Wieland inspired the team with his pre-game speech. Shortly thereafter, the team hired the double amputee as a strength and conditioning consultant for the duration of the year.

Green Bay Press-Gazette photo

Herman Fontenot (27) scores on an eight-yard pass from Don Majkowski at Tampa Bay on October 14. Green Bay lost to the Buccaneers 26-14. Fontenot caught 31 passes for 293 yards in 1990.

TEAM STATISTICS

	GB	OPP
First Downs	276	286
Rushing	72	113
Passing	183	160
Penalty	21	13
Rushes	350	475
Yards Gained	1,369	2,059
Average Gain	3.91	4.33
Average Yards per Game	85.6	128.7
Passes Attempted	541	479
Completed	302	256
% Completed	55.82	53.44
Total Yards Gained	3,696	3,555
Times Sacked	62	27
Yards Lost	390	172
Net Yards Gained	3,306	3,383
Yards Gained per Completion	12.24	13.89
Net Yards per Attempt	5.48	6.69
Average Net Yards per Game	206.6	211.4
Combined Net Yards Gained	4,675	5,442
Total Plays	953	981
Average Yards per Play	4.91	5.54
Average Net Yards per Game	292.2	340.1
Third Down Efficiency	76/196	85/210
Percentage	38.78	40.48
Fourth Down Efficiency	5/14	3/9
Percentage	35.71	33.33
Intercepted By	16	21
Yards Returned	154	293
Returned for TD	1	2
Punts	65	69
Yards Punted	2,431	2,698
Average Yards per Punt	37.40	39.10
Punt Returns	32	34
Yards Returned	308	266
Average Yards per Return	9.63	7.82
Returned for TD	0	0
Kickoff Returns	63	56
Yards Returned	1,303	1,125
Average Yards per Return	20.68	20.09
Returned for TD	1	0
Penalties	84	109
Yards Penalized	674	854
Fumbles	37	26
Lost	22	14
Own Recovered for Touchdown	0	0
Opponent's Recovered by	14	22
Opponent's Recovered for Touchdown	1	2
Total Points Scored	271	347
Total Touchdowns	29	40
Touchdowns Rushing	5	16
Touchdowns Passing	20	20
Touchdowns on Returns & Recoveries	4	4
Extra Points	28	39
Safeties	0	1
Field Goals Attempted	30	34
Field Goals Made	23	22
% Successful	76.67	64.71
Average Time of Possession	29:34	30:26

Regular Season   6-10-0

Date	GB		OPP	Att.
9/9	36	Los Angeles Rams	24	(57,685)
9/16	13	Chicago Bears	31	(58,938)
9/23	3	Kansas City Chiefs	17	(58,817)
9/30	24	at Detroit Lions	21	(64,509)
10/7	13	at Chicago Bears	27	(59,929)
10/14	14	at Tampa Bay Buccaneers	26	(67,472)
10/28	24	Minnesota Vikings (M)	10	(55,155)
11/4	20	San Francisco 49ers	24	(58,835)
11/11	29	at Los Angeles Raiders	16	(50,855)
11/18	24	at Phoenix Cardinals	21	(46,878)
11/25	20	Tampa Bay Buccaneers (M)	10	(53,677)
12/2	7	at Minnesota Vikings	23	(62,058)
12/9	14	Seattle Seahawks (M)	20	(52,015)
12/16	0	at Philadelphia Eagles	31	(65,627)
12/22	17	Detroit Lions	24	(46,700)
12/30	13	at Denver Broncos	22	(46,943)

Score By Periods

	1	2	3	4	OT	Total
Packers	36	76	57	102	0	271
Opponents	64	103	88	92	0	347

INDIVIDUAL STATISTICS

Rushing

	Att	Yds	Avg	LG	TD
Haddix	98	311	3.2	13	0
D. Thompson	76	264	3.5	37	1
Majkowski	29	186	6.4	24	1
Woodside	46	182	4.0	21	1
Fullwood	44	124	2.8	16	1
A. Dilweg	21	114	5.4	22	0
Fontenot	17	76	4.5	18	0
Workman	8	51	6.4	31	0
Query	3	39	13.0	18	0
Sharpe	2	14	7.0	10	0
Kiel	5	9	1.8	7	0
Kemp	1	-1	-1.0	-1	0
Packers	**350**	**1,369**	**3.9**	**37**	**5**
Opponents	475	2,059	4.3	52	16

Receiving

	No	Yds	Avg	LG	TD
Sharpe	67	1,105	16.5	t76	6
Kemp	44	527	12.0	29	2
Query	34	458	13.5	t47	2
Weathers	33	390	11.8	29	1
Fontenot	31	293	9.5	59	1
E. West	27	356	13.2	50	5
Woodside	24	184	7.7	25	0
Haddix	13	94	7.2	28	2
J. Harris	12	157	13.1	26	0
C. Wilson	7	84	12.0	18	0
Workman	4	30	7.5	9	1
Fullwood	3	17	5.7	10	0
D. Thompson	3	1	0.3	1	0
Packers	**302**	**3,696**	**12.2**	**t76**	**20**
Opponents	256	3,555	13.9	74	20

Passing

	Att	Com	Yds	Pct	TD	In	Tk/Yds	Rate
Majkowski	264	150	1,925	56.8	10	12	32/178	73.5
A. Dilweg	192	101	1,267	52.6	8	7	22/150	72.1
Kiel	85	51	504	60.0	2	2	8/62	74.8
Packers	**541**	**302**	**3,696**	**55.8**	**20**	**21**	**62/390**	**73.2**
Opponents	479	256	3,555	53.4	20	16	27/172	77.5

Punting

	No	Yds	Avg	In20	TB	LG	HB
Bracken	64	2,431	38.0	17	2	59	1
Packers	**65**	**2,431**	**37.4**	**17**	**2**	**59**	**1**
Opponents	69	2,698	39.1	16	10	61	2

Kickoff Returns

	No	Yds	Avg	LG	TD
C. Wilson	35	798	22.8	36	0
Workman	14	210	15.0	26	0
Bland	7	104	14.9	24	0
D. Thompson	3	103	34.3	t76	1
Fontenot	3	88	29.3	50	0
E. West	1	0	0.0	0	0
Packers	**63**	**1,303**	**20.7**	**t76**	**1**
Opponents	56	1,125	20.1	87	0

Punt Returns

	No	Yds	Avg	FC	LG	TD
Query	32	308	9.6	7	25	0
R. Pitts	0	0	—	2	0	0
Packers	**32**	**308**	**9.6**	**9**	**25**	**0**
Opponents	34	266	7.8	13	30	0

Interceptions

	No	Yds	Avg	LG	TD
L. Butler	3	42	14.0	28	0
Holmes	3	39	13.0	24	0
M. Murphy	3	6	2.0	4	0
Stephen	2	26	13.0	26	0
Holland	1	32	32.0	32	0
Patterson	1	9	9.0	t9	1
Cecil	1	0	0.0	0	0
M. Lee	1	0	0.0	0	0
R. Pitts	1	0	0.0	0	0
Packers	**16**	**154**	**9.6**	**32**	**1**
Opponents	21	293	14.0	47	2

Scoring

	TDr	TDp	TDrt	PAT	FG	S	TP
Jacke	0	0	0	28/29	23/30	0	97
Sharpe	0	6	0	0/0	0/0	0	36
E. West	0	5	0	0/0	0/0	0	30
Query	0	2	1	0/0	0/0	0	18
Haddix	0	2	0	0/0	0/0	0	12
Kemp	0	2	0	0/0	0/0	0	12
D. Thompson	1	0	1	0/0	0/0	0	12
Fontenot	0	1	0	0/0	0/0	0	6
Fullwood	1	0	0	0/0	0/0	0	6
Greene	0	0	1	0/0	0/0	0	6
Kiel	1	0	0	0/0	0/0	0	6
Majkowski	1	0	0	0/0	0/0	0	6
Patterson	0	0	1	0/0	0/0	0	6
Weathers	0	1	0	0/0	0/0	0	6
Woodside	1	0	0	0/0	0/0	0	6
Workman	0	1	0	0/0	0/0	0	6
Packers	**5**	**20**	**4**	**28/29**	**23/30**	**0**	**271**
Opponents	16	20	4	39/40	22/34	1	347

Fumbles

	Fum	Ow	Op	Yds	Tot
Bennett	0	0	1	0	1
Bland	0	0	1	0	1
R. Brown	0	0	1	0	1
Campen	2	0	0	-21	0
A. Dilweg	10	4	0	-9	4
Fontenot	1	0	0	0	1
Fullwood	1	0	0	0	0
Haddix	3	0	0	0	0
T. Harris	0	0	2	28	2
Holland	0	0	1	0	1
Holmes	0	0	3	44	3
Kemp	2	0	0	0	0
Kiel	2	1	0	0	1
Majkowski	6	3	0	-10	3
Mandarich	0	1	0	0	1
Pitts	0	0	1	0	1
Query	3	2	1	0	3
Ruettgers	0	0	1	0	1
Stephen	0	0	2	15	2
D. Thompson	1	0	0	0	0
E. West	3	0	0	0	0
Woodside	0	0	0	0	0
Packers	**37**	**12**	**14**	**47**	**26**

Quarterback Sacks

	No
T. Harris	7.0
M. Brock	4.0
Patterson	4.0
Bennett	3.0
R. Brown	3.0
Dent	1.0
Holmes	1.0
M. Murphy	1.0
B. Nelson	1.0
Noble	1.0
Stephen	1.0
Packers	**27.0**
Opponents	62.0

NFL STANDINGS

National Conference

Eastern Division

	W	L	T	Pct	PF	PA
New York Giants	13	3	0	.813	335	211
Philadelphia Eagles	10	6	0	.625	396	299
Washington Redskins	10	6	0	.625	381	301
Dallas Cowboys	7	9	0	.438	244	308
Phoenix Cardinals	5	11	0	.313	268	396

Central Division

	W	L	T	Pct	PF	PA
Chicago Bears	11	5	0	.688	348	280
Tampa Bay Buccaneers	6	10	0	.375	264	367
Detroit Lions	6	10	0	.375	373	413
Green Bay Packers	**6**	**10**	**0**	**.375**	**271**	**347**
Minnesota Vikings	6	10	0	.375	351	326

Western Division

	W	L	T	Pct	PF	PA
San Francisco 49ers	14	2	0	.875	353	239
New Orleans Saints	8	8	0	.500	274	275
Los Angeles Rams	5	11	0	.313	345	412
Atlanta Falcons	5	11	0	.313	348	365

American Conference

Eastern Division

	W	L	T	Pct	PF	PA
Buffalo Bills	13	3	0	.813	428	263
Miami Dolphins	12	4	0	.750	336	242
Indianapolis Colts	7	9	0	.438	281	353
New York Jets	6	10	0	.375	295	345
New England Patriots	1	15	0	.063	181	446

Central Division

	W	L	T	Pct	PF	PA
Cincinnati Bengals	9	7	0	.563	360	352
Houston Oilers	9	7	0	.563	405	307
Pittsburgh Steelers	9	7	0	.563	292	240
Cleveland Browns	3	13	0	.188	228	462

Western Division

	W	L	T	Pct	PF	PA
Los Angeles Raiders	12	4	0	.750	337	268
Kansas City Chiefs	11	5	0	.688	369	257
Seattle Seahawks	9	7	0	.563	306	286
San Diego Chargers	6	10	0	.375	315	281
Denver Broncos	5	11	0	.313	331	374

1990 ROSTER

No	Name	Pos	Ht	Wt	DOB	College	G
74	Archambeau, Lester	DE	6-4	270	06/27/67	Stanford	4
67	Ard, Billy	G	6-3	273	03/12/59	Wake Forest	15
90	Bennett, Tony	LB	6-2	233	07/01/67	Mississippi	14
83	Bland, Carl	WR	5-11	179	08/17/61	Virginia Union	14
17	Bracken, Don	P	6-0	218	02/16/62	Michigan	16
62	Brock, Matt	DE	6-4	285	01/14/66	Oregon	16
93	Brown, Robert	DE	6-2	270	05/21/60	Virginia Tech	16
51	Bush, Blair	C	6-3	273	11/25/56	Washington	16
36	Butler, LeRoy	CB	6-0	192	07/19/68	Florida State	16
63	Campen, James	C	6-3	275	06/11/64	Tulane	16
26	Cecil, Chuck	S	6-0	188	11/08/64	Arizona	9
56	Dent, Burnell	LB	6-1	234	03/16/63	Tulane	15
8	Dilweg, Anthony	QB	6-3	198	03/28/65	Duke	9
27	Fontenot, Herman	RB	6-0	205	09/12/63	LSU	14
21	Fullwood, Brent	FB	5-11	209	10/10/63	Auburn	5
23	Greene, George (Tiger)	DB	6-0	192	02/15/62	Western Carolina	16
35	Haddix, Michael	RB	6-1	230	12/27/61	Mississippi State	16
72	Hall, Mark	DE	6-4	280	08/21/65	Southwestern Louisiana	3
65	Hallstrom, Ron	G	6-6	297	06/11/59	Iowa	16
80	Harris, Jackie	TE	6-3	240	01/04/68	Northeast Louisiana	16
97	Harris, Tim	LB	6-5	258	09/10/64	Memphis State	16
89	Harris, William	TE	6-5	255	02/10/65	Bishop	4
50	Holland, Johnny	LB	6-2	233	03/11/65	Texas A&M	16
44	Holmes, Jerry	CB	6-1	176	12/22/57	West Virginia	16
60	Houston, Bobby	LB	6-2	234	10/26/67	North Carolina State	1
13	Jacke, Chris	K	6-0	197	03/12/66	Texas-El Paso	16
81	Kemp, Perry	WR	5-11	170	12/31/61	California State (PA)	16
10	Kiel, Blair	QB	6-0	205	11/29/61	Notre Dame	3
22	Lee, Mark	CB	5-11	189	03/20/58	Washington	16
7	Majkowski, Don	QB	6-2	208	02/25/64	Virginia	9
77	Mandarich, Tony	T	6-5	295	09/23/66	Michigan State	16
57	Moran, Rich	G	6-2	283	03/19/62	San Diego State	16
37	Murphy, Mark	S	6-2	203	04/22/58	West Liberty	16
79	Nelson, Bob	NT	6-4	275	03/03/59	Miami	16
91	Noble, Brian	LB	6-3	243	09/06/62	Arizona State	14
96	Patterson, Shawn	DE	6-5	265	04/06/65	Arizona State	11
95	Paup, Bryce	LB	6-4	245	02/29/68	Northern Iowa	5
28	Pitts, Ron	DB	5-10	183	10/14/62	UCLA	16
85	Query, Jeff	WR	5-11	167	03/07/67	Millikin	16
75	Ruettgers, Ken	T	6-5	288	08/20/62	USC	11
84	Sharpe, Sterling	WR	5-11	202	04/06/65	South Carolina	16
54	Stephen, Scott	LB	6-2	243	06/18/64	Arizona State	16
39	Thompson, Darrell	FB	6-0	215	11/23/67	Minnesota	16
70	Uecker, Keith	G	6-5	295	06/29/60	Auburn	13
73	Veingrad, Alan	T	6-5	281	07/24/63	East Texas State	16
87	Weathers, Clarence	WR	5-8	182	01/10/62	Delaware State	14
52	Weddington, Mike	LB	6-4	243	10/09/60	Oklahoma	6
86	West, Ed	TE	6-1	240	08/02/61	Auburn	16
88	Wilson, Charles	WR	5-9	174	0701/68	Memphis State	15
68	Winter, Blaise	DE	6-3	282	01/31/62	Syracuse	13
29	Woods, Jerry	S	5-8	193	02/13/66	Northern Michigan	16
33	Woodside, Keith	RB	5-11	200	07/29/64	Texas A&M	16
46	Workman, Vince	RB	5-10	195	05/09/68	Ohio State	15

1990 DRAFT

Rnd	Name	Pos	Ht	Wt	College
1a	Tony Bennett (18)	LB	6-2	233	Mississippi
	(Choice from Browns completing 1989 trade involving draft choices and Herman Fontenot)				
1b	Darrell Thompson (19)	FB	6-0	215	Minnesota
2	LeRoy Butler (48)	CB	5-11	192	Florida State
3	Bobby Houston (75)	LB	6-2	234	North Carolina State
4	Jackie Harris (102)	TE	6-3	240	Northeast Louisiana
5	Charles Wilson (132)	WR	5-9	174	Memphis State
6	Bryce Paup (154)	LB	6-4	245	Northern Iowa
7	Lester Archambeau (186)	DE	6-4	270	Stanford
8	Roger Brown (215)	CB	6-0	196	Virginia Tech
9	Kirk Baumgartner (242)	QB	6-3	210	Wisconsin-Stevens Point
10	Jerome Martin (269)	S	6-0	222	Western Kentucky
11	Harry Jackson (299)	FB	5-11	220	St. Cloud State
12	Kirk Maggio (325)	P	5-11	157	UCLA

1990 GREEN BAY PACKERS

FRONT ROW: (L-R) 7 Don Majkowski, 8 Anthony Dilweg, 10 Blair Kiel, 13 Chris Jacke, 17 Don Bracken, 21 Brent Fullwood, 22 Mark Lee, 23 George (Tiger) Greene, 26 Chuck Cecil, 27 Herman Fontenot.

SECOND ROW: (L-R) 28 Ron Pitts, 29 Jerry Woods, 32 Dave Brown, 33 Keith Woodside, 35 Michael Haddix, 36 LeRoy Butler, 37 Mark Murphy, 39 Darrell Thompson, 44 Jerry Holmes, 46 Vince Workman, 50 Johnny Holland.

THIRD ROW: (L-R) 51 Blair Bush, 52 Mike Weddington, 54 Scott Stephen, 56 Burnell Dent, 57 Rich Moran, 60 Bobby Houston, 62 Matt Brock, 63 James Campen, 65 Ron Hallstrom, 67 Billy Ard.

FOURTH ROW: (L-R) Trainer Domenic Gentile, 68 Blaise Winter, 70 Keith Uecker, 72 Mark Hall, 73 Alan Veingrad, 74 Lester Archambeau, 75 Ken Ruettgers, 77 Tony Mandarich, 79 Bob Nelson, 80 Jackie Harris.

FIFTH ROW: (L-R) Dr. Eugene Brusky, 81 Perry Kemp, 82 Erik Affholter, 83 Carl Bland, 84 Sterling Sharpe, 85 Jeff Query, 86 Ed West, 87 Clarence Weathers, 88 Charles Wilson, Assistant Video Director Bob Eckberg, Video Director Al Treml.

SIXTH ROW: (L-R) Equipment Assistant Jack Noel, Assistant Equipment Manager Bryan Nehring, Equipment Manager Bob Noel, 90 Tony Bennett, 91 Brian Noble, 93 Robert Brown, 95 Bryce Paup, 96 Shawn Patterson, 97 Tim Harris, Trainer Intern Kurt Fielding, Trainer Intern Michael Van Veghel, Trainer Intern Larry Lemberger.

BACK ROW: (L-R) Defensive Backfield Coach Dick Jauron, Defensive Coordinator Hank Bullough, Defensive Line Coach Greg Blache, Outside Linebackers Coach Dick Moseley, Receivers Coach Wayne (Buddy) Geis, Head Coach Lindy Infante, Special Teams Coach Howard Tippett, Offensive Line Coach Charlie Davis, Strength-Conditioning/Tight Ends Coach Virgil Knight, Offensive Backfield Coach Willie Peete, Assistant Offensive Line Coach Joe Clark, Administrative Assistant/Pro Scout Jesse Kaye.

Yet another losing season had everyone on edge. Quarterback Don Majkowski dinged an ambulance with his helmet after an early-season loss to the Lions. Tim Harris held out, then fired parting shots at the city after an October trade sent him to San Francisco. And a larger-than-usual number of Packers faithful were arrested after a frustrating 10-0 loss at home to the Bears on national television.

But the spotlight burned brightest on vice-president of football operations Tom Braatz and head coach Lindy Infante. Both sweated out the mounting losses with an eye on job security. Braatz went first, fired by Bob Harlan on November 20. Infante lasted the year but was dismissed by Braatz's replacement, the day after Green Bay's season-ending 27-7 win at Minnesota. Voted the greatest coach in team history in a telepoll just one year earlier, Infante departed having fashioned an uninspiring 24-40 record in Green Bay.

The team gave quick notice of which direction it was headed. Philadelphia and Detroit whipped the Packers to start the year. The team then eked out a 15-13 decision over the winless Buccaneers, but followed up with four straight losses. Only the finale in Minnesota kept the team from a team-record 13 losses.

For a stretch, Green Bay was at its generous best. The gift-giving began in earnest in week four when Majkowski, his team up 13-6 in the fourth quarter, dropped the ball in his end zone. Nose tackle Chuck Klingbeil recovered and his touchdown and Pete Stoyanovich's subsequent 31-yard field goal gave Don Shula his 300th career win. A week later, two Packers fumbles allowed the Rams to score 14 points in a span of seven seconds. That 23-21 loss was followed by a 20-17 setback to the Cowboys who turned a pair of Green Bay miscues into 14 second-quarter points in a matter of 37 seconds.

Though the team stumbled often, it never was blown out, thanks in part to a solid defense. Even without Tim Harris, sent to the 49ers on September 30, the unit finished 10th overall. Green Bay allowed opponents just 3.33 yards per rush (2nd to the Eagles) and 96.6 yards rushing per game (lowest since the 1940 club yielded 94.5 per game). A younger, quicker line featuring rookie nose tackle Esera Tuaolo and end Lester Archambeau, was bolstered by linebackers Tony Bennett and Bryce Paup. The result: 45 sacks, up from 27 in 1990.

A week after Braatz was let go, the Packers named the Jets' Ron Wolf general manager. Wolf was given total control of football operations, a luxury Braatz never enjoyed. Wolf fired Infante on December 22 and a 21-day search for a coach ensued. Former Giants Coach Bill Parcells and 49ers assistant Mike Holmgren emerged as frontrunners for the position. After Parcells reconsidered and decided not to return to coaching, the door was left open for Holmgren to became the Packers 11th head coach on January 11.

Green Bay Press-Gazette photo

Linebacker Tony Bennett (90) basks in the Tampa sun, site of Green Bay's second win of 1991. Bennett led the Packers in sacks (13), two of which came in the team's 27-0 win over the Buccaneers.

TEAM STATISTICS

	GB	OPP
First Downs	259	298
Rushing	88	99
Passing	150	177
Penalty	21	22
Rushes	381	457
Yards Gained	1,389	1,546
Average Gain	3.65	3.38
Average Yards per Game	86.8	96.6
Passes Attempted	514	531
Completed	272	305
% Completed	52.92	57.44
Total Yards Gained	3,213	3,573
Times Sacked	45	45
Yards Lost	270	307
Net Yards Gained	2,943	3,266
Yards Gained per Completion	11.81	11.71
Net Yards per Attempt	5.26	5.67
Average Net Yards per Game	183.9	204.1
Combined Net Yards Gained	4,332	4,812
Total Plays	940	1,033
Average Yards per Play	4.61	4.66
Average Net Yards per Game	270.8	300.8
Third Down Efficiency	77/207	85/220
Percentage	37.20	38.64
Fourth Down Efficiency	8/14	10/19
Percentage	57.14	52.63
Intercepted By	15	19
Yards Returned	234	185
Returned for TD	0	1
Punts	86	76
Yards Punted	3,473	3,199
Average Yards per Punt	40.38	42.09
Punt Returns	41	35
Yards Returned	396	375
Average Yards per Return	9.66	10.71
Returned for TD	0	1
Kickoff Returns	60	46
Yards Returned	1,197	942
Average Yards per Return	19.96	20.48
Returned for TD	1	0
Penalties	98	106
Yards Penalized	834	777
Fumbles	41	31
Lost	17	14
Own Recovered for Touchdown	0	0
Opponent's Recovered by	14	17
Opponent's Recovered for Touchdown	1	3
Total Points Scored	273	313
Total Touchdowns	31	35
Touchdowns Rushing	12	10
Touchdowns Passing	17	20
Touchdowns on Returns & Recoveries	2	5
Extra Points	31	35
Safeties	1	0
Field Goals Attempted	24	31
Field Goals Made	18	23
% Successful	75.00	74.19
Average Time of Possession	28:15	31:45

Regular Season 4-12-0

Date	GB		OPP	Att.
9/1	3	Philadelphia Eagles	20	(58,991)
9/8	14	at Detroit Lions	23	(43,132)
9/15	15	Tampa Bay Buccaneers	13	(58,114)
9/22	13	at Miami Dolphins	16	(56,583)
9/29	21	at Los Angeles Rams	23	(54,736)
10/6	17	Dallas Cowboys (M)	20	(53,695)
10/17	0	Chicago Bears	10	(58,435)
10/27	27	at Tampa Bay Buccaneers	0	(40,275)
11/3	16	at New York Jets (OT)	19	(67,435)
11/10	24	Buffalo Bills (M)	34	(52,175)
11/17	21	Minnesota Vikings	35	(57,614)
11/24	14	Indianapolis Colts (M)	10	(42,132)
12/1	31	at Atlanta Falcons	35	(43,270)
12/8	13	at Chicago Bears	27	(62,353)
12/15	17	Detroit Lions	21	(43,881)
12/21	27	at Minnesota Vikings	7	(52,860)

Score By Periods

	1	2	3	4	OT	Total
Packers	68	78	55	72	0	273
Opponents	47	102	49	112	3	313

INDIVIDUAL STATISTICS

Rushing

	Att	Yds	Avg	LG	TD
D. Thompson	141	471	3.3	t40	1
Woodside	84	326	3.9	29	1
Workman	71	237	3.3	t30	7
Majkowski	25	108	4.3	15	2
Rice	30	100	3.3	21	0
Tomczak	17	93	5.5	48	1
Kiel	4	46	11.5	26	0
Sharpe	4	4	1.0	12	0
C. Wilson	3	3	1.0	5	0
J. Harris	1	1	1.0	1	0
McJulien	1	0	0.0	0	0
Packers	**381**	**1,389**	**3.6**	**48**	**12**
Opponents	457	1,546	3.4	27	10

Receiving

	No	Yds	Avg	LG	TD
Sharpe	69	961	13.9	t58	4
Workman	46	371	8.1	25	4
Kemp	42	583	13.9	39	2
J. Harris	24	264	11.0	35	3
Woodside	22	185	8.4	28	0
C. Wilson	19	305	16.1	t75	1
E. West	15	151	10.1	21	3
Weathers	12	150	12.5	22	0
Query	7	94	13.4	26	0
D. Thompson	7	71	10.1	18	0
Affholter	7	68	9.7	20	0
Rice	2	10	5.0	7	0
Packers	**272**	**3,213**	**11.8**	**t75**	**17**
Opponents	305	3,573	11.7	t87	20

Passing

	Att	Com	Yds	Pct	TD	In	Tk/Yds	Rate
Tomczak	238	128	1,490	53.8	11	9	13/105	72.6
Majkowski	226	115	1,362	50.9	3	8	30/152	59.3
Kiel	50	29	361	58.0	3	2	2/13	83.8
Packers	**514**	**272**	**3,213**	**52.9**	**17**	**19**	**45/270**	**67.9**
Opponents	531	305	3,573	57.4	20	15	45/307	78.8

Punting

	No	Yds	Avg	In20	TB	LG	HB
McJulien	86	3,473	40.4	22	7	62	0
Packers	**86**	**3,473**	**40.4**	**22**	**7**	**62**	**0**
Opponents	76	3,199	42.1	19	9	61	0

Kickoff Returns

	No	Yds	Avg	LG	TD
C. Wilson	23	522	22.7	t82	1
Sikahema	15	325	21.7	35	0
Workman	8	139	17.4	26	0
D. Thompson	7	127	18.1	30	0
Rice	3	36	12.0	15	0
Webb	2	40	20.0	23	0
Davey	1	8	8.0	8	0
Dean	1	0	0.0	0	0
Packers	**60**	**1,197**	**20.0**	**t82**	**1**
Opponents	46	942	20.5	56	0

Punt Returns

	No	Yds	Avg	FC	LG	TD
Sikahema	26	239	9.2	4	62	0
Query	14	157	11.2	3	28	0
Workman	1	0	0.0	0	0	0
Packers	**41**	**396**	**9.7**	**7**	**62**	**0**
Opponents	35	375	10.7	24	t78	1

Interceptions

	No	Yds	Avg	LG	TD
Cecil	3	76	25.3	32	0
Murphy	3	27	9.0	16	0
L. Butler	3	6	2.0	6	0
V. Clark	2	42	21.0	22	0
D. Brown	1	37	37.0	37	0
Stephen	1	23	23.0	23	0
Tuaolo	1	23	23.0	23	0
Holmes	1	0	0.0	0	0
Packers	**15**	**234**	**15.6**	**37**	**0**
Opponents	19	185	9.7	t65	1

Scoring

	TDr	TDp	TDrt	PAT	FG	S	TP
Jacke	0	0	0	31/31	18/24	0	85
Workman	7	4	0	0/0	0/0	0	66
Sharpe	0	4	0	0/0	0/0	0	24
J. Harris	0	3	0	0/0	0/0	0	18
E. West	0	3	0	0/0	0/0	0	18
Kemp	0	2	0	0/0	0/0	0	12
Majkowski	2	0	0	0/0	0/0	0	12
C. Wilson	0	1	1	0/0	0/0	0	12
Noble	0	0	1	0/0	0/0	0	6
D. Thompson	1	0	0	0/0	0/0	0	6
Tomczak	1	0	0	0/0	0/0	0	6
Woodside	1	0	0	0/0	0/0	0	6
Paup	0	0	0	0/0	0/0	1	2
Packers	**12**	**17**	**2**	**31/31**	**18/24**	**1**	**273**
Opponents	10	20	5	34/35	23/31	0	313

Fumbles

	Fum	Ow	Op	Yds	Tot
Ard	0	2	0	0	2
R. Brown	0	0	1	0	1
Bush	0	0	1	0	1
L. Butler	0	0	1	0	1
Dean	1	0	0	0	0
Dent	0	0	1	0	1
Hallstrom	0	1	0	0	1
J. Harris	1	0	1	0	1
Hauck	0	0	1	0	1
Holland	0	0	4	3	4
Holmes	0	0	1	12	1
Kemp	2	0	0	0	0
Kiel	2	1	0	0	1
Majkowski	10	4	0	-3	4
McJulien	1	1	0	-2	1
Murphy	0	0	1	0	1
Noble	0	0	1	1	1
Query	1	1	0	0	1
Rice	2	0	0	0	0
Ruettgers	0	0	1	0	1
Sharpe	1	2	0	0	2
Sikahema	3	0	0	0	0
Stephen	0	0	1	0	1
D. Thompson	1	1	0	0	1
Tomczak	5	2	0	-1	2
Weathers	1	0	0	0	0
C. Wilson	4	1	0	0	1
Woodside	3	1	0	0	1
Workman	3	4	2	9	4
Packers	**41**	**22**	**14**	**19**	**36**

Quarterback Sacks

	No
Bennett	13.0
Paup	7.5
Archambeau	4.5
D. Brown	4.0
Tuaolo	3.5
M. Brock	2.5
Noble	2.5
Dent	1.5
Patterson	1.5
Stephen	1.5
R. Mitchell	1.0
Murphy	1.0
team	1.0
Packers	**45.0**
Opponents	45.0

NFL STANDINGS

National Conference

Eastern Division

	W	L	T	Pct	PF	PA
Washington Redskins	14	2	0	.875	485	224
Dallas Cowboys	11	5	0	.688	342	310
Philadelphia Eagles	10	6	0	.625	285	244
New York Giants	8	8	0	.500	281	297
Phoenix Cardinals	4	12	0	.250	196	344

Central Division

	W	L	T	Pct	PF	PA
Detroit Lions	12	4	0	.750	339	295
Chicago Bears	11	5	0	.688	299	269
Minnesota Vikings	8	8	0	.500	301	306
Green Bay Packers	4	12	0	.250	273	313
Tampa Bay Buccaneers	3	13	0	.188	199	365

Western Division

	W	L	T	Pct	PF	PA
New Orleans Saints	11	5	0	.688	341	211
Atlanta Falcons	10	6	0	.625	361	338
San Francisco 49ers	10	6	0	.625	393	239
Los Angeles Rams	3	13	0	.188	234	390

American Conference

Eastern Division

	W	L	T	Pct	PF	PA
Buffalo Bills	13	3	0	.813	458	318
New York Jets	8	8	0	.500	314	293
Miami Dolphins	8	8	0	.500	343	349
New England Patriots	6	10	0	.375	211	305
Indianapolis Colts	1	15	0	.063	143	381

Central Division

	W	L	T	Pct	PF	PA
Houston Oilers	11	5	0	.688	386	251
Pittsburgh Steelers	7	9	0	.438	292	344
Cleveland Browns	6	10	0	.375	293	298
Cincinnati Bengals	3	13	0	.188	263	435

Western Division

	W	L	T	Pct	PF	PA
Denver Broncos	12	4	0	.750	304	235
Kansas City Chiefs	10	6	0	.625	322	252
Los Angeles Raiders	9	7	0	.563	298	297
Seattle Seahawks	7	9	0	.438	276	261
San Diego Chargers	4	12	0	.250	274	342

1991 ROSTER

No	Name	Pos	Ht	Wt	DOB	College	G
82	Affholter, Erik	WR	6-0	187	04/10/66	USC	4
74	Archambeau, Lester	DE	6-4	270	06/27/67	Stanford	16
67	Ard, Billy	G	6-3	273	03/12/59	Wake Forest	5
32	Avery, Steve	FB	6-1	225	08/18/66	Northern Michigan	1
90	Bennett, Tony	LB	6-2	233	07/01/67	Mississippi	16
62	Brock, Matt	DE	6-4	285	01/14/66	Oregon	16
93	Brown, Robert	DE	6-2	270	05/21/60	Virginia Tech	16
55	Burnette, Reggie	LB	6-1	240	10/04/68	Houston	3
51	Bush, Blair	C	6-3	273	11/25/56	Washington	16
36	Butler, LeRoy	CB	6-0	192	07/19/68	Florida State	16
63	Campen, James	C	6-3	275	06/11/64	Tulane	13
26	Cecil, Chuck	S	6-0	188	11/08/64	Arizona	16
78	Cheek, Louis	G/T	6-7	286	10/06/64	Texas A&M	12
55	Clark, Greg	LB	6-2	226	03/05/65	Arizona State	2
25	Clark, Vinnie	CB	6-0	194	01/22/69	Ohio State	16
99	Davey, Don	DE	6-4	273	04/08/68	Wisconsin	16
42	Dean, Walter	FB	5-10	216	05/01/68	Grambling	9
56	Dent, Burnell	LB	6-1	234	03/16/63	Tulane	14
21	Fuller, Joe	CB	5-10	186	09/25/64	Northern Iowa	16
72	Gabbard, Steve	G/T	6-3	290	07/19/66	Florida State	4
65	Hallstrom, Ron	G	6-6	297	06/11/59	Iowa	16
80	Harris, Jackie	TE	6-3	240	01/04/68	Northeast Louisiana	16
24	Hauck, Tim	S	5-10	181	12/20/66	Montana	16
50	Holland, Johnny	LB	6-2	233	03/11/65	Texas A&M	16
44	Holmes, Jerry	CB	6-1	176	12/22/57	West Virginia	13
13	Jacke, Chris	K	6-0	197	03/12/66	Texas-El Paso	16
71	Jones, Scott	T	6-6	284	03/20/66	Washington	2
92	Jurkovic, John	NT	6-2	297	08/18/67	Eastern Illinois	4
81	Kemp, Perry	WR	5-11	170	12/31/61	California State (PA)	16
10	Kiel, Blair	QB	6-0	205	11/29/61	Notre Dame	4
59	Larson, Kurt	LB	6-4	241	02/25/66	Michigan State	13
7	Majkowski, Don	QB	6-2	208	02/25/64	Virginia	9
77	Mandarich, Tony	T	6-5	295	09/23/66	Michigan State	15
16	McJulien, Paul	P	5-10	210	02-24-65	Jackson State	16
47	Mitchell, Roland	CB	5-11	198	03/15/64	Texas Tech	16
57	Moran, Rich	G	6-2	283	03/19/62	San Diego State	16
37	Murphy, Mark	S	6-2	203	04/22/58	West Liberty	16
91	Noble, Brian	LB	6-3	243	09/06/62	Arizona State	16
96	Patterson, Shawn	DE	6-5	265	04/06/65	Arizona State	12
95	Paup, Bryce	LB	6-4	245	02/29/68	Northern Iowa	12
85	Query, Jeff	WR	5-11	167	03/07/67	Millikin	16
31	Rice, Allen	RB	5-10	206	04/05/62	Baylor	6
75	Ruettgers, Ken	T	6-5	288	08/20/62	USC	4
84	Sharpe, Sterling	WR	5-11	202	04/06/65	South Carolina	16
45	Sikahema, Vai	RB/KR	5-8	196	08/29/62	BYU	11
54	Stephen, Scott	LB	6-2	243	06/18/64	Arizona State	16
39	Thompson, Darrell	FB	6-0	215	11/23/67	Minnesota	13
18	Tomczak, Mike	QB	6-1	204	10/23/62	Ohio State	12
98	Tuaolo, Esera	NT	6-2	284	07/11/68	Oregon State	16
70	Uecker, Keith	G	6-5	295	04/29/60	Auburn	14
87	Weathers, Clarence	WR	5-8	182	01/10/62	Delaware State	14
30	Webb, Chuck	FB	5-9	201	11/17/69	Tennessee	2
86	West, Ed	TE	6-1	240	08/02/61	Auburn	16
88	Wilson, Charles	WR	5-9	174	0701/68	Memphis State	15
33	Woodside, Keith	RB	5-11	200	07/29/64	Texas A&M	16
46	Workman, Vince	RB	5-10	195	05/09/68	Ohio State	16

1991 DRAFT

Rnd	Name	Pos	Ht	Wt	College
1b	Vinnie Clark (19)	CB	6-0	194	Ohio State

(Traded positions with Eagles, 8th choice for 19th and Eagles' 1st round pick in 1992)

Rnd	Name	Pos	Ht	Wt	College
2	Esera Tuaolo	NT	6-2	284	Oregon State
3a	Don Davey (67)	DE	6-4	273	Wisconsin

(Traded 3rd round pick (63) to Jets for Jets' 3rd (67) and 5th (121) round picks)

Rnd	Name	Pos	Ht	Wt	College
3b	Chuck Webb (81)	FB	5-9	201	Tennessee

(Traded 4th (95) and 5th (122) round picks to 49ers for 3rd (81) round pick)

Rnd					
4	(Choice (95) to 49ers for 49ers 3rd (81) round pick)				
5a	(Choice (121) from Jets to Dolphins for Dolphins 5th (135) and 6th (164) round picks)				
5b	(Choice (122) to 49ers for 49ers 3rd (81) round pick)				

Rnd	Name	Pos	Ht	Wt	College
5c	Jeff Fite (135)	P	6-0	206	Memphis State

(Choice from Miami for Packers 5th (121) round pick from Jets)

Rnd	Name	Pos	Ht	Wt	College
6a	Walter Dean (149)	FB	5-10	216	Grambling
6b	Joe Garten (164)	C/G	6-2	286	Colorado

(Choice from Miami for Packers 5th (121) round pick from Jets)

Rnd	Name	Pos	Ht	Wt	College
7a	Frank Blevins (169)	LB	6-4	232	Oklahoma

(Choice from Browns for Brent Fullwood)

Rnd	Name	Pos	Ht	Wt	College
7b	Reggie Burnette (176)	LB	6-1	240	Houston
8	Johnny Walker (203)	WR	5-11	188	Texas
9	Dean Witkowski (229)	LB	6-1	238	North Dakota
10	Rapier Porter (262)	TE	6-3	275	AK-Pine Bluff
11	J.J. Wierenga (289)	DE	6-3	276	Central Michigan
12	Linzy Collins (316)	WR	6-0	185	Missouri

1991 GREEN BAY PACKERS

FRONT ROW: (L-R) 7 Don Majkowski, 10 Blair Kiel, 13 Chris Jacke, 16 Paul McJulien, 18 Mike Tomczak, 21 Joe Fuller, 24 Tim Hauck, 25 Vinnie Clark, 26 Chuck Cecil, 30 Chuck Webb, 31 Allen Rice.

SECOND ROW: (L-R) 33 Keith Woodside, 36 LeRoy Butler, 37 Mark Murphy, 39 Darrell Thompson, 42 Walter Dean, 44 Jerry Holmes, 45 Vai Sikahema, 46 Vince Workman, 47 Roland Mitchell, 49 Ray Porter, 50 Johnny Holland, 51 Blair Bush.

THIRD ROW: (L-R) 54 Scott Stephen, 55 Greg Clark, 56 Burnell Dent, 57 Rich Moran, 59 Kurt Larson, 62 Matt Brock, 63 James Campen, 65 Ron Hallstrom, 67 Billy Ard, 69 Reggie Burnette, 70 Keith Uecker, 51 Blair Bush.

FOURTH ROW: (L-R) 71 Scott Jones, 72 Steve Gabbard, 74 Lester Archambeau, 75 Ken Ruettgers, 77 Tony Mandarich, 78 Louis Cheek, 80 Jackie Harris, 81 Perry Kemp, 82 Erik Affholter, 83 Johnny Walker, 84 Sterling Sharpe.

FIFTH ROW: (L-R) Administrative Assistant Jesse Kaye, Administrative Assistant John Johnson, 85 Jeff Query, 86 Ed West, 87 Clarence Weathers, 88 Charles Wilson, 90 Tony Bennett, 91 Brian Noble, 92 John Jurkovic, Assistant Video Director Bob Eckberg, Video Director Al Treml.

SIXTH ROW: (L-R) Assistant Equipment Manager Bryan Nehring, Equipment Manager Bob Noel, Equipment Assistant Jack Noel, 93 Robert Brown, 95 Bryce Paup, 96 Shawn Patterson, 98 Esera Tuaolo, 99 Don Davey, Trainer Domenic Gentile, Team Physician Dr. Clarence Novotny, Assistant Trainer Kurt Fielding, Assistant Trainer Larry Lemberger.

BACK ROW: (L-R) Defensive Backfield Coach Dick Jauron, Outside Linebackers Coach Dick Moseley, Defensive Coordinator Hank Bullough, Defensive Line Coach Greg Blache, Receivers Coach Buddy Geis, Special Teams Coach Howard Tippett, Head Coach Lindy Infante, Offensive Line Coach Virgil Knight, Strength and Conditioning Coach Russ Riederer, Offensive Backfield Coach Willie Peete, Assistant Offensive Line Coach Joe Clark.

- 253 -

Nearly 35 years ago, a highly successful NFL assistant named Vince Lombardi seized the coaching reins in Green Bay and called for an end to an "attitude of defeatism" that had taken hold after a decade of losing. A generation-and-a-half later, a similar message echoed throughout Packerdom as another first-year coach, Mike Holmgren, prescribed "an attitude change" for his outfit. Both saw their clubs respond. In 1992, Green Bay surprised with a 9-7 record and Holmgren became the first Packers coach since Lombardi to post a winning season as a rookie.

The Packers began improving their cause long before the season began. Holmgren and General Manager Ron Wolf never stopped tinkering with their product. Any chance the duo saw for improvement was explored.

Wolf replaced half the scouting staff, let go all but two assistants from Lindy Infante's regime, and sent nearly half the roster from 1991 packing. In February, Wolf traded a first-round draft choice to the Atlanta Falcons for quarterback Brett Favre. He bolstered the offensive line by acquiring mammoth Tootie Robbins from Phoenix for a sixth-round choice. And he selected a brash Terrell Buckley with the fifth pick overall in the draft.

Holmgren brought Sherman Lewis and Ray Rhodes with him from the 49ers and made them his offensive and defensive coordinators, respectively. Holmgren installed a low-risk offensive, eschewing the big play for a constant moving of the chains. Perhaps just as importantly, the native Californian proved particularly adept at handling the distractions that can overwhelm a first-year coach.

The players responded. Favre passed his way to the Pro Bowl. His favorite target, Sterling Sharpe, caught an NFL-record 108 passes and joined Favre in Hawaii. Jackie Harris emerged at tight end and snagged 55 passes. Robbins and the line gave up 43 sacks, the fewest in six years. And Vince Workman was heading for 1,000 yards before a shoulder injury knocked him out in week 10.

Defensively, Chuck Cecil, Johnny Holland and Tony Bennett had outstanding seasons. Cecil led the team in interceptions and was the third Packer to make the Pro Bowl. Holland topped the team in tackles with 122 total, despite missing the final two games after suffering a career-threatening neck injury. Bennett sacked opposing quarterbacks 13 1/2 times and forced three fumbles.

The Packers stumbled out of the gate with only three wins in their first nine games. But a 27-24 last-minute victory over the Eagles, spawned a six-game winning streak, the club's longest since Lombardi's Packers of 1965. After the Raiders defeated the Redskins on December 26, the playoffs became a possibility for Green Bay, if they could first get by Minnesota. And even though the Norsemen triumphed with a 27-7 win, the Vikings couldn't squelch a growing feeling in Green Bay that the Pack, might just indeed, be back.

Green Bay Press-Gazette photo

Sterling Sharpe, shown maneuvering here against Detroit in November, caught an NFL-record 108 passes in 1992. He also led the league in receiving yards and touchdowns. Art Monk had held the previous best single-season reception mark with 106.

TEAM STATISTICS

	GB	OPP
First Downs	291	277
Rushing	101	89
Passing	171	170
Penalty	19	18
Rushes	420	406
Yards Gained	1,556	1,821
Average Gain	3.70	4.49
Average Yards per Game	97.3	113.8
Passes Attempted	527	483
Completed	340	277
% Completed	64.52	57.35
Total Yards Gained	3,498	3,496
Times Sacked	43	34
Yards Lost	268	219
Net Yards Gained	3,230	3,277
Yards Gained per Completion	10.29	12.62
Net Yards per Attempt	6.13	6.78
Average Net Yards per Game	201.9	204.8
Combined Net Yards Gained	4,786	5,098
Total Plays	990	923
Average Yards per Play	4.83	5.52
Average Net Yards per Game	299.1	318.6
Third Down Efficiency	91/214	71/189
Percentage	42.52	37.57
Fourth Down Efficiency	6/11	7/16
Percentage	54.54	43.75
Intercepted By	15	15
Yards Returned	222	198
Returned for TD	1	1
Punts	68	68
Yards Punted	2,608	2,941
Average Yards per Punt	38.35	43.25
Punt Returns	35	26
Yards Returned	315	230
Average Yards per Return	9.00	8.85
Returned for TD	1	1
Kickoff Returns	54	57
Yards Returned	1,017	901
Average Yards per Return	18.83	15.81
Returned for TD	0	0
Penalties	88	98
Yards Penalized	749	830
Fumbles	42	32
Lost	21	19
Own Recovered for Touchdown	0	0
Opponent's Recovered by	19	21
Opponent's Recovered for Touchdown	1	1
Total Points Scored	276	296
Total Touchdowns	30	32
Touchdowns Rushing	7	12
Touchdowns Passing	20	16
Touchdowns on Returns & Recoveries	3	4
Extra Points	30	32
Safeties	0	0
Field Goals Attempted	29	27
Field Goals Made	22	24
% Successful	75.86	88.89
Average Time of Possession	32:30	27:30

Regular Season   9-7-0

Date	GB		OPP	Att.
9/6	20	Minnesota Vikings (OT)	23	(58,617)
9/13	3	at Tampa Bay Buccaneers	31	(50,051)
9/20	24	Cincinnati Bengals	23	(57,272)
9/27	17	Pittsburgh Steelers	3	(58,724)
10/4	10	at Atlanta Falcons	24	(63,769)
10/18	6	at Cleveland Browns	17	(69,268)
10/25	10	Chicago Bears	30	(59,435)
11/01	27	at Detroit Lions	13	(60,594)
11/08	7	at New York Giants	27	(72,038)
11/15	27	Philadelphia Eagles (M)	24	(52,689)
11/22	17	at Chicago Bears	3	(56,170)
11/29	19	Tampa Bay Buccaneers (M)	14	(52,347)
12/6	38	Detroit Lions (M)	10	(49,469)
12/13	16	at Houston Oilers	14	(57,285)
12/20	28	Los Angeles Rams	13	(57,796)
12/27	7	at Minnesota Vikings	27	(61,461)

Score By Periods

	1	2	3	4	OT	Total
Packers	48	115	25	88	0	276
Opponents	73	73	71	76	3	296

INDIVIDUAL STATISTICS

Rushing

	Att	Yds	Avg	LG	TD
Workman	159	631	4.0	44	2
D. Thompson	76	255	3.4	33	2
E. Bennett	61	214	3.5	18	0
Favre	47	198	4.2	19	1
Sydney	51	163	3.2	19	2
Majkowski	8	33	4.1	8	0
B. McGee	8	19	2.4	4	0
Brooks	2	14	7.0	8	0
McNabb	2	11	5.5	8	0
C. Harris	2	10	5.0	7	0
Sharpe	4	8	2.0	14	0
Packers	**420**	**1,556**	**3.7**	**44**	**7**
Opponents	406	1,821	4.5	71	12

Receiving

	No	Yds	Avg	LG	TD
Sharpe	108	1,461	13.5	t76	13
J. Harris	55	595	10.8	40	2
Sydney	49	384	7.8	20	1
Workman	47	290	6.2	21	0
Beach	17	122	7.2	20	1
R. Lewis	13	152	11.7	27	0
D. Thompson	13	129	9.9	43	1
E. Bennett	13	93	7.2	22	0
Brooks	12	126	10.5	18	1
B. McGee	6	60	10.0	15	0
E. West	4	30	7.5	10	0
K. Taylor	2	63	31.5	t35	1
Favre	1	-7	-7	-7.0	0
Packers	**340**	**3,498**	**10.3**	**t76**	**20**
Opponents	277	3,496	12.6	t75	16

Passing

	Att	Com	Yds	Pct	TD	In	Tk/Yds	Rate
Favre	471	302	3,227	64.1	18	13	34/208	85.3
Majkowski	55	38	271	69.1	2	2	9/60	77.2
McJulien	1	0	0	0.00	0	0	0/0	39.6
Packers	**527**	**340**	**3,498**	**64.5**	**20**	**15**	**43/268**	**84.3**
Opponents	483	277	3,496	57.3	16	15	34/219	78.1

Punting

	No	Yds	Avg	In20	TB	LG	HB
McJulien	36	1,386	38.5	8	4	67	2
B. Wagner	30	1,222	40.7	10	5	52	0
Packers	**68**	**2,608**	**38.4**	**18**	**9**	**67**	**2**
Opponents	68	2,941	43.3	14	16	71	0

Kickoff Returns

	No	Yds	Avg	LG	TD
C. Harris	23	485	21.1	50	0
Brooks	18	338	18.8	30	0
E. Bennett	5	104	20.8	33	0
Jurkovic	3	39	13.0	14	0
Workman	1	17	17.0	17	0
McNabb	1	15	15.0	15	0
Sims	1	11	11.0	11	0
Davey	1	8	8.0	8	0
E. West	1	0	0.0	0	0
Packers	**54**	**1,017**	**18.8**	**50**	**0**
Opponents	57	901	15.8	48	0

Punt Returns

	No	Yds	Avg	FC	LG	TD
Buckley	21	211	10.0	5	t58	1
Brooks	11	102	9.3	1	22	0
Hauck	1	2	2.0	0	2	0
Cecil	1	0	0.0	0	0	0
V. Clark	1	0	0.0	0	0	0
Packers	**35**	**315**	**9.0**	**6**	**t58**	**1**
Opponents	26	230	8.8	10	t95	1

Interceptions

	No	Yds	Avg	LG	TD
Cecil	4	52	13.0	29	0
Buckley	3	33	11.0	t33	1
Holland	3	27	9.0	22	0
V. Clark	2	70	35.0	43	0
R. Mitchell	2	40	20.0	35	0
L. Butler	1	0	0.0	0	0
Packers	**15**	**222**	**14.8**	**43**	**1**
Opponents	15	198	13.2	t69	1

Scoring

	TDr	TDp	TDrt	PAT	FG	S	TP
Jacke	0	0	0	30/30	22/29	0	96
Sharpe	0	13	0	0/0	0/0	0	78
Sydney	2	1	0	0/0	0/0	0	18
D. Thompson	2	1	0	0/0	0/0	0	18
Buckley	0	0	2	0/0	0/0	0	12
J. Harris	0	2	0	0/0	0/0	0	12
Workman	2	0	0	0/0	0/0	0	12
Beach	0	1	0	0/0	0/0	0	6
T. Bennett	0	0	1	0/0	0/0	0	6
Brooks	0	1	0	0/0	0/0	0	6
Favre	1	0	0	0/0	0/0	0	6
K. Taylor	0	1	0	0/0	0/0	0	6
Packers	**7**	**20**	**3**	**30/30**	**22/29**	**0**	**276**
Opponents	12	16	4	32/32	24/27	0	296

Fumbles

	Fum	Ow	Op	Yds	Tot
Beach	1	0	1	0	1
E. Bennett	2	0	0	0	0
T. Bennett	0	0	2	18	2
Billups	0	0	1	0	1
M. Brock	0	0	2	34	2
R. Brown	0	0	1	0	1
Buckley	7	3	1	0	4
L. Butler	0	0	1	17	1
Campen	0	1	0	0	1
Cecil	1	0	0	0	0
Favre	12	3	0	-7	3
J. Harris	1	0	0	0	0
Holland	2	1	2	0	3
Koonce	0	0	1	0	1
Majkowski	4	3	0	0	3
McJulien	0	0	1	0	1
Millard	0	0	1	0	1
R. Mitchell	0	0	1	0	1
Moran	0	0	1	0	1
Noble	0	0	2	0	2
Paup	0	0	2	0	2
Sharpe	2	1	0	0	1
Sydney	2	2	0	-5	2
D. Thompson	2	0	0	0	0
Winters	1	0	0	0	0
Workman	4	2	0	0	2
team	0	1	0	0	1
Packers	**41**	**19**	**18**	**57**	**37**

Quarterback Sacks

	No
T. Bennett	13.5
Paup	6.5
M. Brock	4.0
Jurkovic	2.0
Noble	2.0
Koonce	1.5
Archambeau	1.0
R. Brown	1.0
Dent	1.0
Tuaolo	1.0
Holland	0.5
Packers	**34.0**
Opponents	43.0

NFL STANDINGS

National Conference

Eastern Division

	W	L	T	Pct	PF	PA
Dallas Cowboys	13	3	0	.813	409	243
Philadelphia Eagles	11	5	0	.688	354	245
Washington Redskins	9	7	0	.563	300	255
N.Y. Giants	6	10	0	.375	306	367
Phoenix Cardinals	4	12	0	.250	243	332

Central Division

	W	L	T	Pct	PF	PA
Minnesota Vikings	11	5	0	.688	374	249
Green Bay Packers	**9**	**7**	**0**	**.563**	**276**	**296**
Tampa Bay Buccaneers	5	11	0	.313	267	365
Chicago Bears	5	11	0	.313	295	361
Detroit Lions	5	11	0	.313	273	332

Western Division

	W	L	T	Pct	PF	PA
San Francisco 49ers	14	2	0	.875	431	236
New Orleans Saints	12	4	0	.750	330	202
Atlanta Falcons	6	10	0	.375	327	414
Los Angeles Rams	6	10	0	.375	313	383

American Conference

Eastern Division

	W	L	T	Pct	PF	PA
Miami Dolphins	11	5	0	.688	340	281
Buffalo Bills	11	5	0	.688	381	283
Indianapolis Colts	9	7	0	.563	216	302
New York Jets	4	12	0	.250	220	315
New England Patriots	2	14	0	.125	205	363

Central Division

	W	L	T	Pct	PF	PA
Pittsburgh Steelers	11	5	0	.688	299	225
Houston Oilers	10	6	0	.625	352	258
Cleveland Browns	7	9	0	.438	272	275
Cincinnati Bengals	5	11	0	.313	274	364

Western Division

	W	L	T	Pct	PF	PA
San Diego Chargers	11	5	0	.688	335	241
Kansas City Chiefs	10	6	0	.625	348	282
Denver Broncos	8	8	0	.500	262	329
Los Angeles Raiders	7	9	0	.438	249	281
Seattle Seahawks	2	14	0	.125	140	312

1992 ROSTER

No	Name	Pos	Ht	Wt	DOB	College	G
74	Archambeau, Lester	DE	6-4	270	06/27/67	Stanford	16
67	Barrie, Sebastian	DE	6-2	270	05/26/70	Liberty University	3
82	Beach, Sanjay	WR	6-1	194	02/21/66	Colorado State	16
34	Bennett, Edgar	RB	6-0	223	02/15/69	Florida State	16
90	Bennett, Tony	LB	6-2	243	07/01/67	Mississippi	16
22	Billups, Lewis	CB	5-11	182	10/10/63	North Alabama	5
51	Brady, Jeff	LB	6-1	235	11/09/68	Kentucky	8
62	Brock, Matt	DE	6-4	290	01/14/66	Oregon	16
87	Brooks, Robert	WR	6-0	171	06/23/70	South Carolina	16
93	Brown, Robert	DE	6-2	280	05/21/60	Virginia Tech	16
27	Buckley, Terrell	CB	5-9	174	06/07/71	Florida State	14
36	Butler, LeRoy	S	6-0	200	07/19/68	Florida State	15
63	Campen, James	C	6-3	280	06/11/64	Tulane	13
21	Carter, Carl	CB	5-11	190	03/07/64	Texas Tech	7
26	Cecil, Chuck	S	6-0	190	11/08/64	Arizona	16
25	Clark, Vinnie	CB	6-0	194	01/22/69	Ohio State	16
55	Collins, Brett	LB	6-1	226	10/08/68	Washington	11
99	Davey, Don	DE	6-4	280	04/08/68	Wisconsin	9
56	Dent, Burnell	LB	6-1	238	03/16/63	Tulane	15
58	D'Onofrio, Mark	LB	6-2	235	03/17/69	Penn State	2
4	Favre, Brett	QB	6-2	220	10/10/69	Southern Mississippi	15
71	Gray, Cecil	T	6-4	292	02/16/68	North Carolina	2
65	Hallstrom, Ron	G	6-6	310	06/11/59	Iowa	16
81	Harris, Corey	WR	5-11	195	10/25/69	Vanderbilt	10
80	Harris, Jackie	TE	6-3	243	01/04/68	North Louisiana	16
24	Hauck, Tim	S	5-10	181	12/20/66	Montana	16
50	Holland, Johnny	LB	6-2	235	03/11/65	Texas A&M	14
88	Ingram, Darryl	TE	6-3	250	05/02/66	California	16
13	Jacke, Chris	K	6-0	197	03/12/66	Texas-El Paso	16
40	Jackson, Johnnie	S	6-1	204	01/11/67	Houston	1
92	Jurkovic, John	NT	6-2	300	08/18/67	Eastern Illinois	16
53	Koonce, George	LB	6-1	238	10/15/68	East Carolina	16
85	Lewis, Ron	WR	5-11	180	03/25/68	Florida State	6
7	Majkowski, Don	QB	6-2	203	02/25/64	Virginia	14
23	McCloughan, Dave	CB	6-1	185	11/20/66	Colorado	5
31	McGee, Buford	RB	6-0	210	08/16/60	Mississippi	4
16	McJulien, Paul	P	5-10	210	02/24/65	Jackson State	9
45	McNabb, Dexter	FB	6-1	245	07/09/69	Florida	16
77	Millard, Keith	DT	6-5	268	03/18/62	Washington State	2
47	Mitchell, Roland	CB	5-11	195	03/15/64	Texas Tech	15
57	Moran, Rich	G	6-2	280	03/19/62	San Diego State	8
61	Neville, Tom	G	6-5	288	09/04/61	Fresno State	8
91	Noble, Brian	LB	6-3	250	09/06/62	Arizona State	13
97	Noonan, Danny	NT	6-4	275	07/14/65	Nebraska	6
98	Oglesby, Alfred	NT	6-3	285	01/27/67	Houston	7
95	Paup, Bryce	LB	6-4	247	02/29/68	Northern Iowa	16
73	Robbins, Tootie	T	6-5	315	06/02/58	East Carolina	15
75	Ruettgers, Ken	T	6-5	286	08/20/62	USC	16
72	Salem, Harvey	T	6-6	289	01/15/61	California	4
84	Sharpe, Sterling	WR	5-11	205	04/06/65	South Carolina	16
68	Sims, Joe	OL	6-3	294	03/01/69	Nebraska	15
42	Sydney, Harry	FB	6-0	217	06/29/59	Kansas	16
85	Taylor, Kittrick	WR	5-11	189	07/22/64	Washington State	10
39	Thompson, Darrell	RB	6-0	222	11/23/67	Minnesota	7
98	Tuaolo, Esera	NT	6-2	284	07/11/68	Oregon State	4
76	Viaene, David	OL	6-5	300	07/14/65	Minnesota-Duluth	1
9	Wagner, Bryan	P	6-2	200	03/28/62	Cal State-Northridge	7
86	West, Ed	TE	6-1	244	08/02/61	Auburn	16
38	White, Adrian	S	6-0	205	04/06/64	Florida	15
29	Wilson, Marcus	RB	6-1	210	04/16/68	Virginia	6
52	Winters, Frank	OL	6-3	290	01/23/64	West Illinois	16
46	Workman, Vince	RB	5-10	205	05/09/68	Ohio State	10

1992 DRAFT

Rnd	Name	Pos	Ht	Wt	College
1a.	Terrell Buckley (5)	DB	5-9	174	Florida State
1b.	(Choice (17) from Eagles in 1991 position exchange. Choice traded to Falcons for Brett Favre)				
2a.	Mark D'Onofrio (34)	LB	6-2	235	Penn State
2b.	(Choice (45) from 49ers for Tim Harris. Choice returned to 49ers for right to hire Mike Holmgren)				
3	Robert Brooks (62)	WR	6-0	171	South Carolina
4a.	(Choice (89) and 8th round pick (203) to 49ers for 49ers' 4th round pick (103), 5th round pick (130) and 6th round pick (157))				
4b	Edgar Bennett (103)	RB	6-0	223	Florida State
	(Choice from 49ers in exchange mentioned above)				
5a	Dexter McNabb (119)	FB	6-1	245	Florida
5b	Orlando McKay (130)	WR	5-10	175	Washington
	(Choice from 49ers in exchange mentioned above)				
6a	(Choice (146) to Phoenix for Tootie Robbins)				
6b	Mark Chmura (157)	TE	6-5	240	Boston College
	(Choice from 49ers in exchange mentioned above)				
7a	(Choice (173) to the Raiders for Raiders' 7th round choice (190) and 9th round choice (240))				
7b	Chris Holder (190)	WR	6-0	182	Tuskegee
	(Choice from Raiders in exchange mentioned above)				
8	(Choice (203) to 49ers in exchange mentioned above)				
9a	Ty Detmer (230)	QB	5-9	183	BYU
9b	Shazzon Bradley (240)	NT	6-1	272	Tennessee
	(Choice from Raiders in exchange mentioned above)				
10	Andrew Oberg (257)	T	6-6	300	North Carolina
11	Gabe Mokwuah (287)	LB	6-1	254	Am. International
12	Brett Collins (314)	LB	6-1	226	Washington

1992 GREEN BAY PACKERS

FRONT ROW: (L-R)4 Brett Favre, 7 Don Majkowski, 11 Ty Detmer, 13 Chris Jacke, 16 Paul McJulien, 22 Lewis Billups, 23 Dave McCloughan, 24 Tim Hauck, 25 Vinnie Clark, 26 Chuck Cecil, 27 Terrell Buckley.

SECOND ROW: (L-R) 29 Marcus Wilson, 31 Buford McGee, 34 Edgar Bennett, 36 LeRoy Butler, 38 Adrian White, 39 Darrell Thompson, 42 Harry Sydney, 45 Dexter McNabb, 46 Vince Workman, 47 Roland Mitchell, 50 Johnny Holland, 51 Jeff Brady.

THIRD ROW: (L-R) 52 Frank Winters, 53 George Koonce, 55 Brett Collins, 56 Burnell Dent, 57 Rich Moran, 62 Matt Brock, 63 James Campen, 65 Ron Hallstrom, 68 Joe Sims, 69 Joe Garten, 72 Harvey Salem.

FOURTH ROW: (L-R) 73 Tootie Robbins, 74 Lester Archambeau, 75 Ken Ruettgers, 79 Tony Mandarich, 80 Jackie Harris, 82 Sanjay Beach, 83 Orlando McKay, 84 Sterling Sharpe, 85 Kitrick Taylor, 86 Ed West, 87 Robert Brooks.

FIFTH ROW: (L-R) 88 Darryl Ingram, 89 Mark Chmura, 90 Tony Bennett, 91 Brian Noble, 92 John Jurkovic, 93 Robert Brown, 94 Mark D'Onofrio, 95 Bryce Paup, 96 Shawn Patterson, 97 Danny Noonan, 98 Esera Tuaolo.

SIXTH ROW: (L-R) Defensive Assistant/Quality Control Jim Lind, Tight Ends/Assistant Offensive Line Coach Andy Reid, Offensive Line Coach Tom Lovat, Quarterbacks Coach Steve Mariucci, Special Teams Coach Nolan Cromwell, Offensive Coordinator Sherman Lewis, Head Coach Mike Holmgren, Defensive Coordinator Ray Rhodes, Defensive Line Coach Greg Blache, Linebackers Coach Bob Valesente, Offensive Assistant/Quality Control Jon Gruden, Strength and Conditioning Kent Johnston, Defensive Backs Coach Dick Jauron, Running Backs Coach Gil Haskell.

BACK ROW: (L-R) Equipment Assistant Jack Noel, Assistant Equipment Manager Bryan Nehring, Equipment Manager Bob Noel, Administrative Assistant John Johnson, Head Trainer Domenic Gentile, Assistant Trainer Kurt Fielding, Assistant Trainer Jay Davide, Training Room Intern Sam Ramsden, Staff Orthopedist Dr. Patrick J. McKenzie, Team Physician Dr. Clarence G. Novotny, Assistant Video Director Bob Eckberg, Video Director Al Treml.

- 257 -

1993

In 1993, the Packers became the first professional football team to mark 75 seasons of operation. That alone was enough to stir interest in the club, but a spate of offseason signings and a solid draft had fans eagerly anticipating the upcoming year. The team did not disappoint. After a slow start, the club won eight of its final 12 games to ensure a second consecutive winning season and a trip to the playoffs for the first time in 11 years.

The Packers opened against the Rams with 13 new faces in their starting lineup. At least one change was due to injury (Frank Winters for Rich Moran at right guard) and another because of a holdout (Bryce Paup for Tony Bennett at outside linebacker), but most newcomers were there because the team sought out new talent in the offseason. Some of the new starters arrived via free agency: guard Harry Galbreath, safety Mike Prior, and, of course perennial Pro Bowler Reggie White. Others were traded for: Mark Clayton and John Stephens. The end result was a team quite different from its counterpart of 1992, but one just as hungry for victory.

Green Bay got off on the right foot when it mauled the Rams 36-6 in the season opener in Milwaukee. A fired-up defense held Jim Everett and company to 228 yards, including a mere 53 on the ground. Paup and George Koonce tackled Cleveland Gary in the end zone for a 2-0 lead and the Packers never looked back.

Two heartbreakers and a rout followed. In week two, the Eagles rallied for 13 fourth-quarter points and exited Lambeau Field with a 20-17 win. In week three, Jim McMahon passed 45 yards to Eric Guliford with six seconds remaining to allow Faud Reveiz to kick a 22-yard field goal and seal a 15-13 Vikings' win. One week later, the Cowboys ran up 393 yards on the Packers and discharged them from Irving Stadium on the wrong end of a 36-14 count.

The turnaround came in front of a national television audience on October 10. Green Bay rolled up a 30-7 halftime lead over the visiting Broncos. When John Elway threatened to pull the game out late, White sacked him on back-to-back plays to end the threat and preserve a 30-27 win.

Said safety LeRoy Butler: "That's what we brought Reggie here for. That's the biggest turnaround of the season."

Indeed. The Packers went on to bounce the Buccaneers 37-14 and the Bears 17-3. After a slip in Kansas City, they edged the Saints 19-17, the Lions 26-17, and the Buccaneers 13-10.

By Christmas time it became apparent that the team could clinch its first playoff spot since 1982 if it could get past the Raiders in Green Bay. On December 26 with a wind chill of minus-22 degrees, the Packers did just that. The foursome of White, John Jurkovic, Tony Bennett, and Paup combined to sack Raiders' quarterbacks eight times. The Packers defense gave up just 46 yards rushing and 182 yards overall. The 28-0 victory earned Green Bay a second straight winning season and a long-awaited return trip to the playoffs.

Vernon Beiver photo

Reggie White (92) chases the Rams' Jim Everett in the season opener in Milwaukee. White led the team in quarterback sacks with 13 in 1993 and was voted to the Pro Bowl at season's end.

TEAM STATISTICS

	GB	OPP
First Downs	282	261
Rushing	98	88
Passing	166	157
Penalty	18	16
Rushes	448	424
Yards Gained	1,619	1,582
Average Gain	3.61	3.73
Average Yards per Game	101.2	98.9
Passes Attempted	528	529
Completed	322	290
% Completed	60.98	54.82
Total Yards Gained	3,330	3,201
Times Sacked	30	46
Yards Lost	199	301
Net Yards Gained	3,131	2,900
Yards Gained per Completion	10.34	11.04
Net Yards per Attempt	5.61	5.04
Average Net Yards per Game	195.7	181.3
Combined Net Yards Gained	4,750	4,482
Total Plays	1,006	999
Average Yards per Play	4.72	4.49
Average Net Yards per Game	296.9	280.1
Third Down Efficiency	81/218	70/217
Percentage	37.16	32.26
Fourth Down Efficiency	9/16	3/19
Percentage	56.25	15.79
Intercepted By	18	24
Yards Returned	255	437
Returned for TD	0	3
Punts	74	79
Yards Punted	3,174	3,176
Average Yards per Punt	42.89	40.20
Punt Returns	45	38
Yards Returned	404	350
Average Yards per Return	8.98	9.21
Returned for TD	0	0
Kickoff Returns	60	70
Yards Returned	1,483	1,407
Average Yards per Return	24.72	20.10
Returned for TD	1	0
Penalties	85	85
Yards Penalized	734	712
Fumbles	26	33
Lost	10	15
Own Recovered for Touchdown	0	0
Opponent's Recovered by	15	10
Opponent's Recovered for Touchdown	1	2
Total Points Scored	340	282
Total Touchdowns	35	27
Touchdowns Rushing	14	6
Touchdowns Passing	19	16
Touchdowns on Returns & Recoveries	2	5
Extra Points	35	27
Safeties	1	0
Field Goals Attempted	37	40
Field Goals Made	31	31
% Successful	83.78	77.50
Average Time of Possession	30:53	29:07

Regular Season   9-7-0

Date	GB		OPP	Att.
9/5	36	Los Angeles Rams (M)	6	(54,648)
9/12	17	Philadelphia Eagles	20	(59,061)
9/26	13	at Minnesota Vikings	15	(61,077)
10/3	14	at Dallas Cowboys	36	(63,568)
10/10	30	Denver Broncos	27	(58,943)
10/24	37	at Tampa Bay Buccaneers	14	(47,354)
10/31	17	Chicago Bears	3	(58,945)
11/8	16	at Kansas City Chiefs	23	(76,742)
11/14	19	at New Orleans Saints	17	(69,043)
11/21	26	Detroit Lions (M)	17	(55,119)
11/28	13	Tampa Bay Buccaneers	10	(56,995)
12/5	17	at Chicago Bears	30	(62,236)
12/12	20	at San Diego Chargers	13	(57,930)
12/19	17	Minnesota Vikings (M)	21	(54,773)
12/26	28	Los Angeles Raiders	0	(54,482)
1/2	20	at Detroit Lions	30	(77,510)

Postseason   1-1-0

1/8	28	at Detroit Lions	24	(68,479)
1/16	17	at Dallas Cowboys	27	(64,790)

Score By Periods

	1	2	3	4	OT	Total
Packers	97	95	77	71	0	340
Opponents	29	76	90	87	0	282

INDIVIDUAL STATISTICS

Rushing

	Att	Yds	Avg	LG	TD
D. Thompson	169	654	3.9	t60	3
E. Bennett	159	550	3.5	19	9
Favre	58	216	3.7	27	1
J. Stephens	48	173	3.6	22	1
Brooks	3	17	5.7	21	0
Sharpe	4	8	2.0	5	0
M. Wilson	6	3	0.5	5	0
Detmer	1	-2	-2.0	-2	0
Packers	**448**	**1,619**	**3.6**	**t60**	**14**
Opponents	424	1,582	3.7	60	6

Receiving

	No	Yds	Avg	LG	TD
Sharpe	112	1,274	11.4	54	11
E. Bennett	59	457	7.7	t39	1
J. Harris	42	604	14.4	t66	4
Clayton	32	331	10.3	32	3
West	25	253	10.1	24	0
Brooks	20	180	9.0	25	0
D. Thompson	18	129	7.2	34	0
J. Stephens	5	31	6.2	10	0
R. Lewis	2	21	10.5	17	0
M. Wilson	2	18	9.0	11	0
Chmura	2	13	6.5	7	0
C. Harris	2	11	5.5	6	0
Morgan	1	8	8.0	8	0
Packers	**322**	**3,330**	**10.3**	**t66**	**19**
Opponents	290	3,201	11.0	t67	16

Passing

	Att	Com	Yds	Pct	TD	In	Tk/Yds	Rate
Favre	522	318	3,303	60.9	19	24	30/199	72.2
Detmer	5	3	26	60.0	0	0	0/0	73.8
Sharpe	1	1	1	100.0	0	0	0/0	79.2
Packers	**528**	**322**	**3,330**	**61.0**	**19**	**24**	**30/199**	**72.2**
Opponents	529	290	3,201	54.8	16	18	46/301	68.9

Punting

	No	Yds	Avg	In20	TB	LG	HB
Wagner	74	3,174	42.9	19	7	60	0
Packers	**74**	**3,174**	**42.9**	**19**	**7**	**60**	**0**
Opponents	79	3,176	40.2	20	3	58	0

Kickoff Returns

	No	Yds	Avg	LG	TD
Brooks	23	611	26.6	t95	1
C. Harris	16	482	30.1	65	0
D. Thompson	9	171	19.0	42	0
M. Wilson	9	197	21.9	37	0
Jurkovic	2	22	11.0	13	0
Chmura	1	0	0.0	0	0
Packers	**60**	**1,483**	**24.7**	**t95**	**1**
Opponents	70	1,407	20.1	68	0

Punt Returns

	No	Yds	Avg	FC	LG	TD
Prior	17	194	11.4	3	24	0
Brooks	16	135	8.4	4	35	0
Buckley	11	76	6.9	5	39	0
Teague	1	-1	-1.0	0	-1	0
Packers	**45**	**404**	**9.0**	**12**	**39**	**0**
Opponents	38	350	9.2	12	35	0

Interceptions

	No	Yds	Avg	LG	TD
L. Butler	6	131	21.8	39	0
Holland	2	41	20.5	30	0
Buckley	2	31	15.5	31	0
Simmons	2	21	10.5	19	0
Teague	1	22	22.0	22	0
Paup	1	8	8.0	8	0
Prior	1	1	1.0	1	0
M. Brock	1	0	0.0	0	0
D. Evans	1	0	0.0	0	0
Mitchell	1	0	0.0	0	0
Packers	**18**	**255**	**14.2**	**39**	**0**
Opponents	24	437	18.2	t86	3

Scoring

	TDr	TDp	TDrt	PAT	FG	S	TP
Jacke	0	0	0	35/35	31/37	0	128
Sharpe	0	11	0	0/0	0/0	0	66
E. Bennett	9	1	0	0/0	0/0	0	60
J. Harris	0	4	0	0/0	0/0	0	24
Clayton	0	3	0	0/0	0/0	0	18
D. Thompson	3	0	0	0/0	0/0	0	18
Brooks	0	0	1	0/0	0/0	0	6
L. Butler	0	0	1	0/0	0/0	0	6
Favre	1	0	0	0/0	0/0	0	6
J. Stephens	1	0	0	0/0	0/0	0	6
team	0	0	0	0/0	0/0	1	2
Packers	**14**	**19**	**2**	**35/35**	**31/37**	**1**	**340**
Opponents	6	16	5	27/27	31/40	0	282

Fumbles

	Fum	Ow	Op	Yds	Tot
E. Bennett	0	1	0	0	1
M. Brock	0	0	1	0	1
Brooks	1	0	0	0	1
Buckley	1	0	0	0	0
L. Butler	0	0	1	25	1
Campen	0	1	0	0	1
Chmura	1	0	0	0	1
Coleman	0	0	1	0	1
D. Evans	0	0	2	0	2
Favre	14	2	0	-1	2
Hauck	1	0	0	0	1
Holland	2	0	2	0	2
Koonce	0	0	1	0	1
Morrissey	0	0	1	0	1
Noble	0	0	1	0	1
Prior	3	2	0	0	2
Ruettgers	0	2	0	0	2
Sharpe	1	0	0	0	0
Simmons	0	0	1	0	1
J. Stephens	0	1	0	0	1
Teague	0	0	2	0	2
D. Thompson	2	1	0	0	1
R. White	0	0	1	10	2
Willis	0	1	0	0	1
M. Wilson	1	0	0	0	1
Packers	**26**	**15**	**15**	**34**	**30**

Quarterback Sacks

	No
R. White	13.0
Paup	11.0
T. Bennett	6.5
Jurkovic	5.5
Koonce	3.0
M. Brock	2.0
Holland	2.0
L. Butler	1.0
Patterson	1.0
Simmons	1.0
Packers	**46.0**
Opponents	30.0

NFL STANDINGS

National Conference

Eastern Division

	W	L	T	Pct	PF	PA
Dallas Cowboys	12	4	0	.750	376	229
New York Giants	11	5	0	.688	288	205
Philadelphia Eagles	8	8	0	.500	293	315
Phoenix Cardinals	7	9	0	.438	326	269
Washington Redskins	4	12	0	.250	230	345

Central Division

	W	L	T	Pct	PF	PA
Detroit Lions	10	6	0	.625	298	292
Minnesota Vikings	9	7	0	.563	277	290
Green Bay Packers	9	7	0	.563	340	282
Chicago Bears	7	9	0	.438	234	230
Tampa Bay Buccaneers	5	11	0	.313	237	376

Western Division

	W	L	T	Pct	PF	PA
San Francisco 49ers	10	6	0	.625	473	295
New Orleans Saints	8	8	0	.500	317	343
Atlanta Falcons	6	10	0	.375	316	385
Los Angeles Rams	5	11	0	.313	221	367

American Conference

Eastern Division

	W	L	T	Pct	PF	PA
Buffalo Bills	12	4	0	.750	329	242
Miami Dolphins	9	7	0	.563	349	351
New York Jets	8	8	0	.500	270	247
New England Patriots	5	11	0	.313	238	286
Indianapolis Colts	4	12	0	.250	189	378

Central Division

	W	L	T	Pct	PF	PA
Houston Oilers	12	4	0	.750	368	238
Pittsburgh Steelers	9	7	0	.563	308	281
Cleveland Browns	7	9	0	.438	304	307
Cincinnati Bengals	3	13	0	.188	187	319

Western Division

	W	L	T	Pct	PF	PA
Kansas City Chiefs	11	5	0	.688	328	291
Los Angeles Raiders	10	6	0	.625	306	326
Denver Broncos	9	7	0	.563	373	284
San Diego Chargers	8	8	0	.500	322	290
Seattle Seahawks	6	10	0	.375	280	314

1993 ROSTER

No	Name	Pos	Ht	Wt	DOB	College	G
34	Bennett, Edgar	RB	6-0	224	02/15/69	Florida State	16
90	Bennett, Tony	LB	6-2	243	07/01/67	Mississippi	10
62	Brock, Matt	DE	6-4	290	01/14/66	Oregon	16
87	Brooks, Robert	WR	6-0	175	06/23/70	South Carolina	14
93	Brown, Gilbert	NT	6-2	330	02/22/71	Kansas	2
27	Buckley, Terrell	CB	5-9	176	06/07/71	Florida State	16
36	Butler, LeRoy	S	6-0	197	07/19/68	Florida State	16
63	Campen, James	C	6-3	280	06/11/64	Tulane	4
89	Chmura, Mark	TE	6-5	245	02/22/69	Boston College	14
83	Clayton, Mark	WR	5-9	185	04/08/61	Louisville	16
54	Coleman, Keo	LB	6-1	245	05/01/70	Mississippi State	12
55	Collins, Brett	LB	6-1	234	10/08/68	Washington	4
81	Collins, Shawn	WR	6-2	205	02/20/67	Northern Arizona	4
99	Davey, Don	DE	6-4	270	04/08/68	Wisconsin	9
11	Detmer, Ty	QB	6-0	186	10/30/67	BYU	3
72	Dotson, Earl	T	6-3	310	12/17/70	Texas A&I	13
33	Evans, Doug	CB	6-1	188	05/13/70	Louisiana Tech	16
4	Favre, Brett	QB	6-2	222	10/10/69	Southern Mississippi	16
76	Galbreath, Harry	G	6-1	285	01/01/65	Tennessee	16
70	Grant, David	NT	6-4	275	09/17/65	West Virginia	7
30	Harris, Corey	CB	5-11	195	10/25/69	Vanderbilt	11
80	Harris, Jackie	TE	6-3	243	01/04/68	North Louisiana	12
24	Hauck, Tim	S	5-10	187	12/20/66	Montana	13
50	Holland, Johnny	LB	6-2	235	03/11/65	Texas A&M	16
67	Hutchins, Paul	T	6-4	335	02/11/70	Western Michigan	1
79	Ilkin, Tunch	T	6-3	272	09/23/57	Indiana State	1
88	Ingram, Darryl	TE	6-3	245	05/02/66	California	2
13	Jacke, Chris	K	6-0	200	03/12/66	Texas-El Paso	16
64	Jurkovic, John	NT	6-2	290	08/18/67	Eastern Illinois	16
53	Koonce, George	LB	6-1	240	10/15/68	East Carolina	15
85	Lewis, Ron	WR	5-11	192	03/25/68	Florida State	9
77	Maas, Bill	NT	6-5	282	03/02/62	Pittsburgh	14
45	McNabb, Dexter	FB	6-1	245	07/09/69	Florida	16
47	Mitchell, Roland	CB	5-11	195	03/15/64	Texas Tech	16
57	Moran, Rich	G	6-2	280	03/19/62	San Diego State	3
81	Morgan, Anthony	WR	6-1	195	11/15/67	Tennessee	2
51	Morrissey, Jim	LB	6-3	225	12/24/62	Michigan State	6
55	Mott, Joe	LB	6-4	255	10/06/65	Iowa	2
91	Noble, Brian	LB	6-3	245	09/06/62	Arizona State	2
25	Oliver, Muhammad	CB	5-11	180	03/12/69	Oregon	2
96	Patterson, Shawn	DE	6-5	270	06/13/64	Arizona State	5
95	Paup, Bryce	LB	6-4	247	02/29/68	Northern Iowa	15
38	Pickens, Bruce	CB	5-11	190	05/09/68	Nebraska	2
45	Prior, Mike	S	6-0	215	11/14/63	Illinois State	16
73	Robbins, Tootie	T	6-5	315	06/02/58	East Carolina	12
75	Ruettgers, Ken	T	6-5	290	08/20/62	USC	16
84	Sharpe, Sterling	WR	5-11	210	04/06/65	South Carolina	16
59	Simmons, Wayne	LB	6-2	245	12/15/69	Clemson	14
68	Sims, Joe	OL	6-3	310	03/01/69	Nebraska	13
32	Stephens, John	RB	6-1	215	02/23/66	Northwestern (LA) State	5
31	Teague, George	S	6-1	187	02/18/71	Alabama	16
39	Thompson, Darrell	RB	6-0	217	11/23/67	Minnesota	16
97	Traylor, Keith	DE	6-2	290	09/03/69	Central Oklahoma	5
9	Wagner, Bryan	P	6-2	200	03/28/62	Cal State-Northridge	16
23	Walker, Sammy	CB	5-11	200	01/20/69	Texas Tech	8
86	West, Ed	TE	6-1	245	08/02/61	Auburn	16
92	White, Reggie	DE	6-5	295	12/19/61	Tennessee	16
74	Widdell, Doug	G	6-4	287	09/23/66	Boston College	16
20	Williams, Kevin	RB	6-1	215	02/17/70	UCLA	3
56	Willis, James	LB	6-1	238	09/02/72	Auburn	13
29	Wilson, Marcus	RB	6-1	210	04/16/68	Virginia	16
52	Winters, Frank	OL	6-3	290	01/23/64	West Illinois	16
60	Zeno, Lance	C	6-4	279	04/15/67	UCLA	5

1993 DRAFT

Rnd	Name	Pos	Ht	Wt	Colllege
1a.	Wayne Simmons (15)	LB	6-1	236	Louisiana Tech
1b.	George Teague (29)	DB	6-1	185	Alabama

(Packers traded two 2nd-round choices (46 & 54), a 4th-round pick (94) and an 8th round pick (213) to the Cowboys for the Cowboys' 1st-round choice (29) and 4th round pick (112))

2a. (Choice (46) traded to Cowboys in deal mentioned above)

2b. (Choice (54) from 49ers for Tim Harris. To Cowboys in deal mentioned above)

3a. (Choice (72) to Raiders for Raiders' 3rd round pick (81) and 6th-round pick (152))

3b.	Earl Dotson (81)	T	6-3	318	Texas A&I

(Choice from Raiders in deal mentioned above)

4a. (Choice (94) from Falcons for Vinnie Clark. To Cowboys in deal mentioned above)

4b. (Choice (99) to Patriots for John Stephens)

4c. (Choice (112) from Cowboys in deal mentioned above. To Bears for Bears' 5th-round pick (118) and 6th-round pick (156))

Rnd	Name	Pos	Ht	Wt	Colllege
5a.	Mark Brunell (118)	QB	6-1	206	Washington

(Choice from Bears in deal mentioned above)

5b.	James Willis (119)	LB	6-1	230	Auburn

(Choice from Buccaneers for signing Vince Workman)

5c. (Choice (129) to Jets for Ken O'Brien)

6a.	Doug Evans (141)	CB	6-1	186	Louisiana Tech

(Choice from Seahawks for Doug McCloughan)

6b.	Paul Hutchins (152)	T	6-4	347	Western Michigan

(Choice from Raiders in deal mentioned above)

6c.	Tim Watson (156)	SS	6-2	215	Howard

(Choice (156) traded to Colts for Dave McCloughan. Colts then traded choice to Bears who traded it back to Packers in the deal mentioned above)

7	Robert Kuberski (183)	DT	6-4	281	Naval Academy

8 (Choice (213) to Cowboys in deal mentioned above)

1993 GREEN BAY PACKERS

FRONT ROW: (L-R)4 Brett Favre, 8 Mark Brunell, 9 Bryan Wagner, 11 Ty Detmer, 13 Chris Jacke, 24 Tim Hauck, 25 Tim Watson, 27 Terrell Buckley, 29 Marcus Wilson, 30 Corey Harris, 31 George Teague.
SECOND ROW: (L-R) Tight Ends/Assistant Offensive Line Coach Andy Reid, Offensive Line Coach Tom Lovat, Wide Receivers Coach Jon Gruden, Running Backs Coach Gil Haskell, Quarterbacks Coach Steve Mariucci, Offensive Coordinator Sherman Lewis, Head Coach Mike Holmgren, Defensive Coordinator Ray Rhodes, Defensive Line Coach Greg Blache, Linebackers Coach Bob Valesente, Defensive Backs Coach Dick Jauron, Defensive Assistant/Quality Control Jim Lind, Strength and Conditioning
Kent Johnston, Special Teams Coach Nolan Cromwell.
THIRD ROW: (L-R) 32 John Stephens, 33 Doug Evans, 34 Edgar Bennett, 36 LeRoy Butler, 39 Darrell Thompson, 44 Dexter McNabb, 45 Mike Prior, 47 Roland Mitchell, 50 Johnny Holland, 52 Frank Winters, 53 George Koonce, 54 Keo Coleman.
FOURTH ROW: (L-R) 55 Brett Collins, 56 James Willis, 57 Rich Moran, 59 Wayne Simmons, 62 Matt Brock, 63 James Campen, 64 John Jurkovic, 68 Joe Sims, 71 Gilbert Brown.
FIFTH ROW: (L-R) 72 Earl Dotson, 73 Tootie Robbins, 74 Doug Widell, 75 Ken Ruettgers, 76 Harry Galbreath, 77 Bill Maas, 79 Tunch Ilkin, 80 Jackie Harris, 81 Shawn Collins, 82 Sanjay Beach.
SIXTH ROW: (L-R) 83 Mark Clayton, 84 Sterling Sharpe, 86 Ed West, 87 Robert Brooks, 89 Mark Chmura, 91 Brian Noble, 92 Reggie White, 95 Bryce Paup, 96 Shawn Patterson, 98 David Grant, 99 Don Davey.
BACK ROW: (L-R) Corporate Security Officer Jerry Parins, Strength/Conditioning Intern Craig Kodanko, Assoc. Team Physician Dr. John Gray, Team Physician Dr. Patrick J. McKenzie, Head Trainer Pepper Burrus, Assistant Trainer Sam Ramsden, Assistant Trainer Kurt Fielding, Training Room Intern Geoff Kaplan, Equipment Manager Bryan Nehring, Equipment Assistant Jack Noel, Assistant to Head Coach Gary Reynolds, Video Assistant Chris Kirby, Assistant Video Director Bob Eckberg, Video Director Al Treml.

1994

If one play can turn a season around, that play occured in Milwaukee on December 18. Two straight winning seasons and a trip to the playoffs in 1993 had fans, coaches, and players alike aiming for a division championship in 1994. But a rough, three-game road trip in late November and early December dropped the team's record to 6-7 and threatened to turn the year into a wash. Enter quarterback Brett Favre. His nine-yard touchdown run with virtually no time left not only sank the Falcons 21-17, but it assured the Packers a postseason berth provided they could get past the lowly Buccaneers a week later. They did, thus delivering a third straight winning season (9-7) and a return engagement against the Lions in the playoffs.

For half a season, the Packers had the best defense in the NFL. After eight games, the Green and Gold had surrendered a paltry 2,082 yards or 22 fewer than defending champion Dallas. Likewise, for half a season, Green Bay had one of the top offenses in the league. Brett Favre and Sterling Sharpe combined for 13 touchdowns in the final six games. Problem was, the offense and defense never seemed to click at the same time.

Injuries were also a problem. In a June minicamp, top draft pick guard Aaron Taylor was lost for the year after he suffered a ruptured patellar tendon in a one-on-one blocking drill. The team's other top pick, running back LeShon Johnson, was slowed by a hamstring pull. Guard Guy McIntyre missed six weeks with a blood clot in his leg and LeRoy Butler missed three games because of a severe bout with pneumonia. Even though Sterling Sharpe and Edgar Bennett each played 16 games, they were hampered by a hamstring problem and separated shoulder, respectively, throughout much of the year.

Good news came in many forms. Off the field, the Don Hutson Practice facility debuted in July; Favre signed a long-term deal prior to training camp; the organization extended general manager Ron Wolf's contract through 1999 and did the same for coach Mike Holmgren. On the field, the team hammered the Bears 33-6 and 40-3 and beat the Vikings 16-10 for the first time under Holmgren's guidance.

In October, the club announced it was pulling out of Milwaukee. With additional luxury boxes becoming available in 1995 at Lambeau Field, the team stood to loose millions in the years ahead if it continued to operate to the south.

The season began with Sharpe threatening to sit out the season if his contract was not reworked. The Packers accommodated him and then got to the business of playing football. Despite a formidable defense, nicknamed "The Wolf Pack" later in the year, the Packers were unable to string wins together until they met the Bears on a rainy Monday night in Chicago. There Bennett, Favre, Reggie Cobb and LeShon Johnson racked up 223 yards rushing, the team's highest total in five years. Wins over the Jets and Lions followed.

Road losses in Buffalo, Dallas, and Detroit dropped Green Bay's record to 6-7. Two weeks later, in the last game to be played in Milwaukee, with the season in the balance,facing third down with 21 seconds left, Favre scrambled to pay dirt and salvaged a season.

Vernon Biever photo

Brett Favre, with only seconds left inthe game, scores a touchdown and a win against the Falcons in the Packers last game in Milwaukee. Favre's touchdown plus a win the following week in Tampa Bay secured the Packers a playoff berth for a second straight year.

TEAM STATISTICS

	GB	OPP
First Downs	314	281
Rushing	88	82
Passing	205	182
Penalty	21	17
Rushes	417	381
Yards Gained	1,543	1,363
Average Gain	3.70	3.58
Average Yards per Game	96.4	85.2
Passes Attempted	609	605
Completed	375	337
% Completed	61.58	55.70
Total Yards Gained	3,977	3,677
Times Sacked	33	37
Yards Lost	204	276
Net Yards Gained	3,773	3,401
Yards Gained per Completion	10.61	10.91
Net Yards per Attempt	5.88	5.30
Average Net Yards per Game	235.8	212.6
Combined Net Yards Gained	5,316	4,764
Total Plays	1,059	1,023
Average Yards per Play	5.02	4.66
Average Net Yards per Game	332.3	297.8
Third Down Efficiency	97/225	79/222
Percentage	43.11	35.59
Fourth Down Efficiency	6/14	9/18
Percentage	42.86	50.00
Intercepted By	21	14
Yards Returned	232	193
Returned for TD	1	0
Punts	81	88
Yards Punted	3,351	3,491
Average Yards per Punt	41.37	39.67
Punt Returns	49	36
Yards Returned	414	272
Average Yards per Return	8.45	7.56
Returned for TD	1	0
Kickoff Returns	56	75
Yards Returned	1,168	1,380
Average Yards per Return	20.86	18.40
Returned for TD	1	1
Penalties	85	82
Yards Penalized	760	675
Fumbles	25	32
Lost	8	12
Own Recovered for Touchdown	0	1
Opponent's Recovered by	12	8
Opponent's Recovered for Touchdown	0	1
Total Points Scored	382	287
Total Touchdowns	47	32
Touchdowns Rushing	11	9
Touchdowns Passing	33	20
Touchdowns on Returns & Recoveries	3	3
Extra Points (kicked)	41	24
Safeties	0	1
Field Goals Attempted	26	25
Field Goals Made	19	21
% Successful	73.08	84.00
Average Time of Possession	30:56	29:04

Regular Season 9-7-0

Date	GB		OPP	Att.
9/4	16	Minnesota Vikings	10	(59,487)
9/11	14	Miami Dolphins (M)	24	(55,011)
9/18	7	at Philadelphia Eagles	13	(63,922)
9/25	30	Tampa Bay Buccaneers	3	(58,551)
10/2	16	at New England Patriots	17	(57,522)
10/9	24	Los Angeles Rams	17	(58,911)
10/20	10	at Minnesota Vikings (OT)	13	(63,041)
10/31	33	at Chicago Bears	6	(47,381)
11/6	38	Detroit Lions (M)	30	(54,995)
11/13	17	New York Jets	10	(58,307)
11/20	20	at Buffalo Bills	29	(79,029)
11/24	31	at Dallas Cowboys	42	(64,597)
12/4	31	at Detroit Lions	34	(76,338)
12/11	40	Chicago Bears	3	(57,927)
12/18	21	Atlanta Falcons (M)	17	(54,885)
12/24	34	at Tampa Bay Buccaneers	19	(65,076)

Postseason 1-1-0

12/31	16	Detroit Lions	12	(58,125)
1/8	9	at Dallas Cowboys	35	(64,745)

Score By Periods

	1	2	3	4	OT	Total
Packers	89	129	92	72	0	382
Opponents	40	96	65	83	3	287

INDIVIDUAL STATISTICS

Rushing

	Att	Yds	Avg	LG	TD
E. Bennett	178	623	3.5	t39	5
Cobb	153	579	3.8	30	3
Favre	42	202	4.8	t36	2
L. Johnson	26	99	3.8	43	0
Levens	5	15	3.0	5	0
Sharpe	3	15	5.0	8	0
Brunell	6	7	1.2	t5	1
Jordan	1	5	5.0	5	0
Brooks	1	0	0.0	0	0
D. Thompson	2	-2	-1.0	2	0
Packers	**417**	**1,543**	**3.7**	**43**	**11**
Opponents	381	1,363	3.6	63	9

Receiving

	No	Yds	Avg	LG	TD
Sharpe	94	1,119	11.9	49	18
E. Bennett	78	546	7.0	40	4
Brooks	58	648	11.2	35	4
Cobb	35	299	8.5	t37	1
West	31	377	12.2	26	2
Morgan	28	397	14.2	t47	4
Chmura	14	165	11.8	27	0
L. Johnson	13	168	12.9	33	0
R. Lewis	7	108	15.4	38	0
Reg. Johnson	7	79	11.3	24	0
Wilner	5	31	6.2	9	0
Mickens	4	31	7.8	11	0
Levens	1	9	9.0	9	0
Packers	**375**	**3,977**	**10.6**	**49**	**33**
Opponents	337	3,677	10.9	68	20

Passing

	Att	Com	Yds	Pct	TD	In	Tk/Yds	Rate
Favre	582	363	3,882	62.4	33	14	31/188	90.7
Brunell	27	12	95	44.4	0	0	2/16	53.8
Packers	**609**	**375**	**3,977**	**61.6**	**33**	**14**	**33/204**	**89.1**
Opponents	605	337	3,677	55.7	20	21	37/276	70.4

Punting

	No	Yds	Avg	In20	TB	LG	HB
Hentrich	81	3,351	41.4	24	10	70	0
Packers	**81**	**3,351**	**41.4**	**24**	**10**	**70**	**0**
Opponents	88	3,491	39.7	21	5	60	0

Kickoff Returns

	No	Yds	Avg	LG	TD
C. Harris	29	618	21.3	59	0
Brooks	9	260	28.9	t96	1
Jordan	5	115	23.0	33	0
Jurkovic	4	57	14.3	16	0
D. Thompson	4	67	16.8	19	0
Levens	2	31	15.5	16	0
M. Wilson	2	14	7.0	14	0
Davey	1	6	6.0	6	0
Packers	**56**	**1,168**	**20.9**	**t96**	**1**
Opponents	75	1,380	18.4	t91	1

Punt Returns

	No	Yds	Avg	FC	LG	TD
Brooks	40	352	8.8	13	t85	1
Prior	8	62	7.8	4	16	0
Jordan	1	0	0.0	1	0	0
Packers	**49**	**414**	**8.4**	**18**	**t85**	**1**
Opponents	36	272	7.6	10	25	0

Interceptions

	No	Yds	Avg	LG	TD
Buckley	5	38	7.6	26	0
L. Butler	3	68	22.7	51	0
Paup	3	47	15.7	30	1
Teague	3	33	11.0	16	0
Willis	2	20	10.0	17	0
McGill	2	16	8.0	16	0
Strickland	1	7	7.0	7	0
KeShon Johnson	1	3	3.0	3	0
D. Evans	1	0	0.0	0	0
Packers	**21**	**232**	**11.0**	**51**	**1**
Opponents	14	193	13.8	36	0

Scoring

	TDr	TDp	TDrt	PAT	FG	S	TP
Sharpe	0	18	0	0/0	0/0	0	108
Jacke	0	0	0	41/43	19/26	0	98
E. Bennett	5	4	0	0/0	0/0	0	54
Brooks	0	4	2	0/0	0/0	0	36
Cobb	3	1	0	0/0	0/0	0	24
Morgan	0	4	0	0/0	0/0	0	24
West	0	2	0	2¹	0/0	0	14
Favre	2	0	0	0/0	0/0	0	12
Brunell	1	0	0	0/0	0/0	0	6
Paup	0	0	1	0/0	0/0	0	6
Packers	**11**	**33**	**3**	**41/43**	**19/26**	**0**	**382**
Opponents	9	20	3	24/24	21/25	0	287

¹ West scored on a 2-point conversion
Packers made 1 of 4 2-point conversions
Opponents made 3 of 8 2-point conversions

Fumbles

	Fum	Ow	Op	Yds	Tot
E. Bennett	1	1	0	0	1
Brooks	4	1	0	0	1
Brunell	1	0	0	-2	0
Buckley	0	0	1	0	1
Cobb	1	0	0	0	0
D. Evans	0	0	1	3	1
Favre	7	1	0	0	1
C. Harris	1	1	0	0	1
KeShon Johnson	0	0	1	0	1
S. Jones	0	0	3	0	3
Jordan	1	0	0	0	0
Koonce	0	0	2	0	2
McMichael	0	0	1	0	1
Morgan	1	1	0	0	0
Paup	0	0	2	0	2
Prior	3	2	0	0	2
Ruettgers	0	1	0	0	1
Sharpe	1	0	0	0	0
Sims	0	0	1	0	1
Strickland	0	0	1	0	1
West	1	0	0	0	0
R. White	0	0	1	0	1
M. Williams	0	0	1	0	1
Willis	1	1	0	0	1
M. Wilson	1	1	0	0	0
Winters	1	0	0	-2	1
Packers	**25**	**12**	**12**	**-1**	**24**

Quarterback Sacks

	No
S. Jones	10.5
R. White	8.0
Paup	7.5
Gi. Brown	3.0
McMichael	2.5
Davey	1.5
L. Butler	1.0
D. Evans	1.0
Koonce	1.0
Wilkins	1.0
Packers	**37.0**
Opponents	33.0

NFL STANDINGS

National Conference

Eastern Division

	W	L	T	Pct	PF	PA
Dallas Cowboys	12	4	0	.750	414	248
New York Giants	9	7	0	.563	279	305
Arizona Cardinals	8	8	0	.500	235	267
Philadelphia Eagles	7	9	0	.438	308	308
Washington Redskins	3	13	0	.188	320	412

Central Division

	W	L	T	Pct	PF	PA
Minnesota Vikings	10	6	0	.625	356	314
Green Bay Packers	9	7	0	.563	382	287
Detroit Lions	9	7	0	.563	357	342
Chicago Bears	9	7	0	.563	271	307
Tampa Bay Buccaneers	6	10	0	.375	251	351

Western Division

	W	L	T	Pct	PF	PA
San Francisco 49ers	13	3	0	.813	505	296
New Orleans Saints	7	9	0	.438	348	407
Atlanta Falcons	7	9	0	.438	317	385
Los Angeles Rams	4	12	0	.250	286	365

American Conference

Eastern Division

	W	L	T	Pct	PF	PA
Miami Dolphins	10	6	0	.625	389	327
New England Patriots	10	6	0	.625	351	312
Indianapolis Colts	8	8	0	.500	307	320
Buffalo Bills	7	9	0	.438	340	356
New York Jets	6	10	0	.375	264	320

Central Division

	W	L	T	Pct	PF	PA
Pittsburgh Steelers	12	4	0	.750	316	234
Cleveland Browns	11	5	0	.688	340	204
Cincinnati Bengals	3	13	0	.188	276	406
Houston Oilers	2	14	0	.125	226	352

Western Division

	W	L	T	Pct	PF	PA
San Diego Chargers	11	5	0	.688	381	306
Kansas City Chiefs	9	7	0	.563	319	298
Los Angeles Raiders	9	7	0	.563	303	327
Denver Broncos	7	9	0	.438	347	396
Seattle Seahawks	6	10	0	.375	287	323

1994 ROSTER

No	Name	Pos	Ht	Wt	DOB	College	G
34	Bennett, Edgar	RB	6-0	224	02/15/69	Florida State	16
94	Brock, Matt	DE	6-4	290	01/14/66	Oregon	5
87	Brooks, Robert	WR	6-0	175	06/23/70	South Carolina	16
93	Brown, Gary	T	6-4	288	06/25/71	Georgia Tech	1
93	Brown, Gilbert	NT	6-2	330	02/22/71	Kansas	13
8	Brunell, Mark	QB	6-1	208	09/17/70	Washington	2
27	Buckley, Terrell	CB	5-9	176	06/07/71	Florida State	16
36	Butler, LeRoy	S	6-0	197	07/19/68	Florida State	13
89	Chmura, Mark	TE	6-5	245	02/22/69	Boston College	14
32	Cobb, Reggie	RB	6-0	215	07/07/68	Tennessee	16
99	Davey, Don	DE	6-4	270	04/08/68	Wisconsin	16
72	Dotson, Earl	T	6-3	310	12/17/70	Texas A&I	4
21	Duckett, Forey	CB	6-3	195	02/05/70	Nevada-Reno	3
63	Dukes, Jamie	C	6-1	295	06/14/64	Florida State	6
33	Evans, Doug	CB	6-1	188	05/13/70	Louisiana Tech	16
4	Favre, Brett	QB	6-2	222	10/10/69	Southern Mississippi	16
76	Galbreath, Harry	G	6-1	285	01/01/65	Tennessee	16
58	Hamilton, Ruffin	LB	6-1	230	03/02/71	Tulane	5
30	Harris, Corey	CB	5-11	195	10/25/69	Vanderbilt	11
80	Harris, Jackie	TE	6-3	243	01/04/68	North Louisiana	16
24	Hauck, Tim	S	5-10	187	12/20/66	Montana	13
17	Hentrich, Craig	P	6-3	200	05/18/71	Notre Dame	16
70	Hope, Charles	G	6-3	303	03/12/70	Central State	6
67	Hutchins, Paul	T	6-4	335	02/11/70	Western Michigan	16
13	Jacke, Chris	K	6-0	200	03/12/66	Texas-El Paso	16
37	Johnson, KeShon	CB	5-10	179	07/17/70	Arizona	7
42	Johnson, LeShon	RB	5-11	200	01/15/71	Northern Illinois	12
82	Johnson, Reggie	TE	6-2	256	01/27/68	Florida State	9
96	Jones, Sean	DE	6-7	275	12/19/62	Northeastern	16
80	Jordan, Charles	WR	5-10	175	10/09/69	Long Beach City College	10
64	Jurkovic, John	NT	6-2	290	08/18/67	Eastern Illinois	16
53	Koonce, George	LB	6-1	240	10/15/68	East Carolina	16
48	Levens, Dorsey	RB	6-1	235	05/21/70	Georgia Tech	14
85	Lewis, Ron	WR	5-11	192	03/25/68	Florida State	6
22	McGill, Lenny	CB	6-1	194	05/31/71	Arizona State	6
62	McIntyre, Guy	G	6-3	265	02/17/61	Georgia	10
90	McMichael, Steve	DT	6-2	270	10/17/57	Texas	16
88	Mickens, Terry	WR	6-0	200	02/21/71	Florida A&M	12
47	Mitchell, Roland	CB	5-11	195	03/15/64	Texas Tech	1
81	Morgan, Anthony	WR	6-1	195	11/15/67	Tennessee	16
95	Paup, Bryce	LB	6-4	247	02/29/68	Northern Iowa	16
39	Prior, Mike	S	6-0	215	11/14/63	Illinois State	16
75	Ruettgers, Ken	T	6-5	290	08/20/62	USC	16
84	Sharpe, Sterling	WR	5-11	210	04/06/65	South Carolina	16
59	Simmons, Wayne	LB	6-2	245	12/15/69	Clemson	12
68	Sims, Joe	OL	6-3	310	03/01/69	Nebraska	15
55	Strickland, Fred	LB	6-2	250	08/15/66	Purdue	16
31	Teague, George	S	6-1	187	02/18/71	Alabama	16
26	Thompson, Darrell	RB	6-0	217	11/23/67	Minnesota	8
86	West, Ed	TE	6-1	245	08/02/61	Auburn	14
92	White, Reggie	DE	6-5	295	12/19/61	Tennessee	16
98	Wilkens, Gabe	DE	6-4	300	09/01/71	Gardner-Webb	15
51	Williams, Mark	LB	6-3	240	05/17/71	Ohio State	16
56	Willis, James	LB	6-1	238	09/02/72	Auburn	12
83	Wilner, Jeff	TE	6-4	250	12/31/71	Wesleyan	11
29	Wilson, Marcus	RB	6-1	210	04/16/68	Virginia	12
35	Wilson, Ray	S	6-2	202	08/26/71	New Mexico	3
52	Winters, Frank	OL	6-3	290	01/23/64	West Illinois	16

1994 DRAFT

Rnd	Name	Pos	Ht	Wt	College
1a.	Aaron Taylor (16)	G	6-4	300	Notre Dame

(Packers traded 1st-round (20) and 3rd-round (89) picks to Dolphins for Dolphins' 1st-round pick (16))

1b.	(Choice (20) to Dolphins in deal mentioned above)				

2. (Choice (53) to 49ers for 49ers' 3rd-round (84), 5th-round (149), and two 6th-round picks (175) and (190))

3a.	LeShon Johnson (84)	RB	5-11	200	Northern Illinois

(Choice from 49ers in deal mentioned above)

3b. (Choice (89) to Dolphins in deal mentioned above)

4a. (Choice (120) to Raiders for Raiders' 4th-round (126) and 6th-round (169) picks)

4b.	Gabe Wilkins (126)	DE	6-4	300	Gardner-Webb
5a.	Terry Mickens (146)	WR	6-0	200	Florida A&M
5b.	Dorsey Levens (149)	RB	6-1	235	Georgia Tech

(Choice from 49ers in deal mentioned above)

6a.	Jay Kearney (169)	WR	6-1	195	West Virginia

(Choice from Raiders in deal mentioned earlier)

6b.	Ruffin Hamilton (175)	LB	6-1	230	Tulane

(Choice from 49ers in deal mentioned earlier)

6c.	Bill Schroeder (181)	WR	6-1	195	UW-La-Crosse
6d.	Paul Duckworth (190)	LB	6-1	245	Connecticut

(Choice from 49ers in deal mentioned earlier)

7. (Choice (212) to Broncos for Doug Widell)

1994 GREEN BAY PACKERS

FRONT ROW: (L-R) 4 Brett Favre, 8 Mark Brunell, 11 Ty Detmer, 13 Chris Jacke, 17 Craig Hentrich, 22 Lenny McGill, 24 Tim Hauck, 25 Dorsey Levens, 26 Darrell Thompson, 27 Terrell Buckley, 29 Marcus Wilson.
SECOND ROW: (L-R) Special Teams Coach Nolan Cromwell, Tight Ends/Assistant Offensive Line Coach Andy Reid, Offensive Line Coach Tom Lovat, Wide Receivers Coach Jon Gruden, Quarterbacks Coach Steve Mariucci, Running Backs Coach Gil Haskell, Offensive Coordinator Sherman Lewis, Head Coach Mike Holmgren, Defensive Coordinator Fritz Shurmur, Defensive Line Coach Larry Brooks, Linebackers Coach Bob Valesente, Defensive Backs Coach Dick Jauron, Defensive Assistant/Quality Control Jim Lind, Strength and Conditioning Kent Johnston, General Assistant Coach Harry Sydney.
THIRD ROW: (L-R) 30 Corey Harris, 31 George Teague, 32 Reggie Cobb, 33 Doug Evans, 34 Edgar Bennett, 36 LeRoy Butler, 39 Mike Prior, 42 LeShon Johnson, 47 Roland Mitchell, 51 Mark Williams, 52 Frank Winters.
FOURTH ROW: (L-R) 53 George Koonce, 55 Fred Strickland, 56 James Willis, 58 Ruffin Hamilton, 59 Wayne Simmons, 62 Guy McIntyre, 63 Jamie Dukes, 64 John Jurkovic, 67 Paul Hutchins, 68 Joe Sims.
FIFTH ROW: (L-R) 71 Gary Brown, 72 Earl Dotson, 75 Ken Ruettgers, 76 Harry Galbreath, 79 Aaron Taylor, 80 Charles Jordan, 81 Anthony Morgan, 83 Jeff Wilner, 85 Ron Lewis, 86 Ed West, 87 Robert Brooks.
SIXTH ROW: (L-R) 88 Terry Mickens, 89 Mark Chmura, 90 Steve McMichael, 92 Reggie White, 93 Gilbert Brown, 94 Matt Brock, 95 Bryce Paup, 96 Sean Jones, 98 Gabe Wilkins, 99 Don Davey.
BACK ROW: (L-R) Corporate Security Officer Jerry Parins, Administrative Assistant to Head Coach Gary Reynolds, Training Room Intern Omar Ross, Assistant Trainer Sam Ramsden, Assistant Trainer Kurt Fielding, Head Trainer Pepper Burrus, Associate Team Physician Dr. John Gray, Team Physician Dr. Patrick J. McKenzie, Equipment Manager Gordon (Red) Batty, Assistant Equipment Manager Bryan Nehring, Assistant Equipment Manager Tom Bakken, Equipment Assistant Gary Poels, Video Assistant Chris Kirby, Assistant Video Director Bob Eckberg, Video Director Al Treml.

1995 OUTLOOK

In his first year in Green Bay, coach Mike Holmgren led the Packers to a record of nine wins and seven losses. The following year, the team again posted nine wins against seven losses but returned to the playoffs for the first time in over a decade. Last year, however, signs of progress were hard to detect as the club once again finished 9-7 and advanced no further in postseason play than it had the year previous. If 1994 represented "a step sideways," as defensive end Don Davey summarized after the 35-9 loss to the Cowboys, then 1995, unfortunately, will result in a step backward.

This past offseason has been uninspiring at best. More exits than entrances have marked the months since the curtain dropped in Dallas. Sterling Sharpe's neck injury cost him his career. All-Pro linebacker Bryce Paup signed with the Buffalo Bills. Special teams standouts Tim Hauck, Corey Harris, and Marcus Wilson departed. Offensive lineman Joe Sims, cornerback Terrell Buckley, and running back Reggie Cobb are three other starters who will not return in 1995. At least 15 players from the final 1994 roster won't be back this year.

So whom did the Packers lure to Green Bay? They obtained Mark Ingram from Miami in a trade, but the receiver failed to show at two of the team's three minicamps. They used a second-round draft choice to land tight end Mark Jackson in a swap with the Dolphins, but the 30-year-old veteran will likely retire. And that's it. The club went after other "big name" free agents such as receivers Andre Rison and Haywood Jeffires and tight ends Eric Green and Jay Novacek, but each time the player in question turned down the overtures from the north. And aside from cornerback Craig Newsome, who's expected to slide into Buckley's left cornerback slot, the draft didn't provide any surefire starters.

Thus, if the team is to improve in 1995, it will have to extract better performances from the holdovers. Offensively, Robert Brooks has to catch more than the career-best 59 balls he did in 1994. Mark Chmura has to use his size (6-5, 250) and improved speed (4.68 seconds in the 40) to make Packers fans forget Jackie Harris. Edgar Bennett needs to get the ball 20 times a game in order to amass 1,000 yards on the season. And Brett Favre needs to duplicate his success of a year ago.

Defensively, Sean Jones needs to match or better his team-leading sack total of 10-1/2 in 1994. Youngsters such as Gilbert Jones, Gabe Wilkins, and third-round pick Darius Holland are expected to add depth. Athletic Wayne Simmons has to fill Paup's spot and a young secondary consisting of LeRoy Butler, George Teague, Newsome, and Doug Evans has to jell and do so quickly.

Green Bay will struggle in 1995 because of its losses in the offseason, a slow start (again) to the regular season, and a tough six-week stretch in the schedule that pits them against five Central Division opponents and the Cowboys in Dallas. The Packers were just good enough to get over the .500 hump the past three years. This year they'll come up just short of it. **FORECAST: 7-9.**

Green Bay Press-Gazette photo   *Vernon Biever photo*   *Vernon Biever photo*

The Packers will need big performances from the likes of Lenny McGill (22), LeRoy Butler (36), and Wayne Simmons (59) in order to achieve success in 1995.

1995 OUTLOOK

SCHEDULE

PRESEASON

Date	Opponent	Site	Time
Sat., Aug. 5	New Orleans	Madison	Noon
Sun., Aug. 13	Pittsburgh	Pittsburgh	Noon
Sat., Aug. 19	Indianapolis	Green Bay	Noon
Fri., Aug. 25	Washington	Green Bay	6 p.m.

REGULAR SEASON

Date	Opponent	Site	Time
Sun., Sept. 3	St. Louis	Green Bay	Noon
Mon., Sept. 11	Chicago	Chicago	8 p.m.
Sun., Sept. 17	N.Y. Giants	Green Bay	Noon
Sun., Sept. 24	Jacksonville	Jacksonville	7 p.m.
Sun., Oct. 1	Bye Week		
Sun., Oct. 8	Dallas	Dallas	Noon
Sun., Oct. 15	Detroit	Green Bay	Noon
Sun., Oct. 22	Minnesota	Green Bay	Noon
Sun., Oct. 29	Detroit	Detroit	Noon
Sun., Nov. 5	Minnesota	Minnesota	Noon
Sun., Nov. 12	Chicago	Green Bay	Noon
Sun., Nov. 19	Cleveland	Cleveland	Noon
Sun., Nov. 26	Tampa Bay	Green Bay	Noon
Sun., Dec. 3	Cincinnati	Green Bay	Noon
Sun., Dec. 10	Tampa Bay	Tampa Bay	7 p.m.
Sat., Dec. 16	New Orleans	New Orleans	3 p.m.
Sun., Dec. 24	Pittsburgh	Green Bay	Noon

LOOK FOR IN 1995

1. Brett Favre needs just 17 completions to become the third quarterback in Packers history to complete 1,000 or more passes. Bart Starr (1,808) and Lynn Dickey (1,592) are the others. Favre, with 10,412 yards passing, needs to throw for 1,123 yards to move past Don Majkowski (10,870) and Tobin Rote (11,535) into third place behind Starr (24,718) and Dickey (21,369) on the team's all-time list.

2. Edgar Bennett needs 50 receptions to become the 11th Packer to reach 200 career receptions. Bennett's 150 catches rank him 17th on the team's all-time receiving list.

3. Chris Jacke could become the first Packer to lead the team in field goals made for a seventh straight year. Jacke, Fred Cone, Ted Fritsch, and Chester Marcol are the only players to have lead the team in that category on six different occasions.

4. With 33 returns, Robert Brooks will become just the fourth player in team history to have returned 100 or more punts. The others are Willie Wood (187), Phillip Epps (100) and Al Carmichael (100).

Green Bay Press-Gazette photo

First-round pick Craig Newsome faces the media.

DRAFT

Rnd	Name	Pos	Ht	Wt	College
1A.	(Packers traded its 1st-round choice (22) and 6th-round choice (188) to Panthers for Panthers' 1st-round (32), 3rd-round (65), and 6th-round (173) picks)				
1B.	Craig Newsome (32)	DB	5-11	185	Arizona State
	(Choice from Panthers in deal above)				
2.	(Choice (53) traded to Dolphins for Keith Jackson)				
3A.	Darius Holland (65)	DT	6-4	310	Colorado
	(Choice from Panthers in deal above)				
3B.	William Henderson (66)	FB	6-1	246	North Carolina
	(Choice from Jaguars for Mark Brunell)				
3C.	Brian Williams (73)	LB	6-1	238	USC
	(Compensation from Seahawks for Corey Harris)				
3D.	(Choice (84) to Browns for Browns' 3rd-round (90) and 5th-round (160) picks)				
3E.	Antonio Freeman (90)	WR	6-0	185	Virginia Tech
	(Choice from Browns in deal above)				
4.	Jeff Miller (117)	T	6-3	303	Mississippi
5A.	Jay Barker (160)	QB	6-2	212	Alabama
	(Choice from Browns in deal above)				
5B.	Travis Jervey (170)	RB	6-1	210	The Citadel
	(Choice to Raiders for Charles Jordan; from Jaguars for Mark Brunell)				
6A.	Charlie Simmons (173)	WR	6-3	202	Georgia Tech
	(Choice from Panthers in deal above)				
6B.	(Choice (188) to Panthers in deal above)				
7.	Adam Timmerman (230)	G	6-3	289	So. Dakota St.

Annual Individual Leaders

RUSHING

(leaders determined by total yards)

Year	Name	Att	Yds	Avg	LG	TD
1932	Clarke Hinkle	95	331	3.5	—	3
1933	Bob Monnett	108	413	3.8	—	3
	Clarke Hinkle	139	413	3.0	—	3
1934	Clarke Hinkle	144	359	2.5	—	1
1935	Bob Monnett	68	336	4.9	—	1
1936	Clarke Hinkle	100	476	4.8	—	5
1937	Clarke Hinkle	129	552	4.3	—	5
1938	Cecil Isbell	85	445	5.2	—	2
1939	Cecil Isbell	132	407	3.1	—	2
1940	Clarke Hinkle	109	383	3.5	—	2
1941	Clarke Hinkle	129	393	3.0	20	5
1942	Ted Fritsch	74	323	4.4	55	0
1943	Tony Canadeo	94	489	5.2	t35	3
1944	Ted Fritsch	94	322	3.4	18	4
1945	Ted Fritsch	88	282	3.2	31	7
1946	Tony Canadeo	122	476	3.9	27	0
1947	Tony Canadeo	103	464	4.5	35	2
1948	Tony Canadeo	123	589	4.8	49	4
1949	Tony Canadeo	208	1,052	5.1	54	4
1950	Billy Grimes	84	480	5.7	t73	5
1951	Tobin Rote	76	523	6.9	t55	3
1952	Tobin Rote	58	313	5.4	30	2
1953	Floyd (Breezy) Reid	95	492	5.2	43	3
1954	Floyd (Breezy) Reid	99	507	5.1	t69	5
1955	Howie Ferguson	192	859	4.5	57	4
1956	Tobin Rote	84	398	4.7	39	11
1957	Don McIlhenny	100	384	3.8	t40	1
1958	Paul Hornung	69	310	4.5	55	2
1959	Paul Hornung	152	681	4.5	63	7
1960	Jim Taylor	230	1,101	4.8	32	11
1961	Jim Taylor	243	1,307	5.4	53	15
1962	Jim Taylor	272	1,474	5.4	51	19
1963	Jim Taylor	248	1,018	4.1	t40	9
1964	Jim Taylor	235	1,169	5.0	t84	12
1965	Jim Taylor	207	734	3.5	35	4
1966	Jim Taylor	204	705	3.5	19	4
1967	Jim Grabowski	120	466	3.9	24	2
1968	Donny Anderson	170	761	4.5	42	5
1969	Travis Williams	129	536	4.2	t39	4
1970	Donny Anderson	222	853	3.8	54	5
1971	John Brockington	216	1,105	5.1	t52	4
1972	John Brockington	274	1,027	3.7	t30	8
1973	John Brockington	265	1,144	4.3	53	3
1974	John Brockington	266	883	3.3	33	5
1975	John Brockington	144	434	3.0	19	7
1976	Willard Harrell	130	435	3.3	56	3
1977	Barty Smith	166	554	3.3	11	2
1978	Terdell Middleton	284	1,116	3.9	t76	11
1979	Terdell Middleton	131	495	3.8	28	2
1980	Eddie Lee Ivery	202	831	4.1	t38	3
1981	Gerry Ellis	196	860	4.4	29	4
1982	Eddie Lee Ivery	127	453	3.6	32	9
1983	Gerry Ellis	141	696	4.9	71	4
1984	Gerry Ellis	123	581	4.7	50	4
1985	Eddie Lee Ivery	132	636	4.8	34	2
1986	Kenneth Davis	114	519	4.6	50	0
1987	Kenneth Davis	109	413	3.8	t39	3
1988	Brent Fullwood	101	483	4.8	t33	7
1989	Brent Fullwood	204	821	4.0	38	5
1990	Michael Haddix	98	311	3.2	13	0
1991	Darrell Thompson	141	471	3.3	t40	1
1992	Vince Workman	159	631	4.0	44	2
1993	Darrell Thompson	169	654	3.9	t60	3
1994	Edgar Bennett	178	623	3.5	t39	5

RECEIVING

(leaders determined by number of receptions)

Year	Name	No	Yds	Avg	LG	TD
1932	Johnny (Blood) McNally	14	168	12.0	—	3
1933	Roger Grove	18	215	11.9	—	0
1934	Clarke Hinkle	12	113	9.4	t69	1
1935	Johnny (Blood) McNally	25	404	16.2	t70	3
1936	Don Hutson	34	526	15.5	t58	8
1937	Don Hutson	41	552	13.5	t78	7
1938	Don Hutson	32	548	17.1	54	9
1939	Don Hutson	34	846	24.9	t92	6
1940	Don Hutson	45	664	14.8	t36	7
1941	Don Hutson	58	738	12.7	t45	10
1942	Don Hutson	74	1,211	16.4	t73	17
1943	Don Hutson	47	776	16.5	t79	11
1944	Don Hutson	58	866	14.9	t55	9
1945	Don Hutson	47	834	17.7	t75	9
1946	Clyde Goodnight	16	308	19.3	t51	1
	Nolan Luhn	16	224	14.0	36	2
1947	Nolan Luhn	42	696	16.5	44	7
1948	Clyde Goodnight	28	448	16.0	57	3
1949	Ted Cook	25	442	17.7	50	1
1950	Al Baldwin	28	555	19.8	t85	3
1951	Bob Mann	50	696	13.9	52	8
1952	Bill Howton	53	1,231	23.2	t90	13
1953	Bill Howton	25	463	18.5	t80	4
1954	Bill Howton	52	768	14.8	59	2
1955	Bill Howton	44	697	15.8	60	5
1956	Bill Howton	55	1,188	21.6	t66	12
1957	Bill Howton	38	727	19.1	t77	5
1958	Max McGee	37	655	17.7	t80	7
1959	Boyd Dowler	32	549	17.2	35	4
1960	Max McGee	38	787	20.7	t57	4
1961	Max McGee	51	883	17.3	53	7
1962	Max McGee	49	820	16.7	64	3
	Boyd Dowler	49	724	14.8	41	2
1963	Boyd Dowler	53	901	17.0	t53	6
1964	Boyd Dowler	45	623	13.8	t50	5
1965	Boyd Dowler	44	610	13.9	t47	4
1966	Jim Taylor	41	331	8.1	21	2
1967	Boyd Dowler	54	836	15.5	t57	4
1968	Boyd Dowler	45	668	14.8	t72	6
1969	Carroll Dale	45	879	19.5	48	6
1970	Carroll Dale	49	814	16.6	t89	2
1971	Carroll Dale	31	598	19.3	t77	4
1972	MacArthur Lane	26	285	11.0	49	0
1973	MacArthur Lane	27	255	9.4	30	1
1974	John Brockington	43	314	7.3	29	0
1975	Ken Payne	58	766	13.2	54	0
1976	Ken Payne	33	467	14.2	t57	4
1977	Barty Smith	37	340	9.2	42	1
1978	James Lofton	46	818	17.8	t58	6
1979	Paul Coffman	56	711	12.7	t78	4
1980	James Lofton	71	1,226	17.3	47	4
1981	James Lofton	71	1,294	18.2	t75	8
1982	James Lofton	35	696	19.9	t80	4
1983	James Lofton	58	1,300	22.4	t74	8
1984	James Lofton	62	1,361	22.0	t79	7
1985	James Lofton	69	1,153	16.7	t56	4
1986	James Lofton	64	840	13.1	36	4
1987	Walter Stanley	38	672	17.7	t70	3
1988	Sterling Sharpe	55	791	14.4	51	1
1989	Sterling Sharpe	90	1,423	15.8	t79	12
1990	Sterling Sharpe	67	1,105	16.5	t76	6
1991	Sterling Sharpe	69	961	13.9	t58	4
1992	Sterling Sharpe	108	1,461	13.5	t76	13
1993	Sterling Sharpe	112	1,274	11.4	54	11
1994	Sterling Sharpe	94	1,119	11.9	49	18

PASSING

(leaders determined by total yards)

Year	Name	Att	Com	Yds	Pct	TD	In	Rate
1932	Arnie Herber	101	37	637	45.5	9	9	51.5
1933	Arnie Herber	124	50	656	40.3	4	12	28.9
1934	Arnie Herber	115	42	799	36.5	8	12	45.1
1935	Arnie Herber	106	40	729	37.7	8	14	47.8
1936	Arnie Herber	173	77	1,239	44.5	11	13	58.9
1937	Arnie Herber	104	47	684	45.2	7	10	50.0
1938	Cecil Isbell	91	37	659	40.7	7	10	52.2
1939	Arnie Herber	139	57	1,107	41.0	8	9	61.6
1940	Cecil Isbell	150	68	1,037	45.3	9	12	55.3
1941	Cecil Isbell	206	117	1,479	56.8	15	11	81.4
1942	Cecil Isbell	268	146	2,021	54.5	24	14	87.0
1943	Tony Canadeo	129	56	875	43.4	9	12	51.0
1944	Irv Comp	177	80	1,159	45.2	12	21	50.0
1945	Irv Comp	106	44	865	41.5	7	11	53.1
1946	Irv Comp	94	27	333	28.7	1	8	9.9
1947	Jack Jacobs	242	108	1,615	44.6	16	17	59.8
1948	Jack Jacobs	184	82	848	44.6	5	21	27.9
1949	Earl (Jug) Girard	175	881	881	35.4	4	12	31.6
1950	Tobin Rote	224	83	1,231	37.1	7	24	26.7
1951	Tobin Rote	256	106	1,540	41.4	15	20	48.6
1952	Vito (Babe) Parilli	177	77	1,416	43.5	13	17	56.6
1953	Tobin Rote	185	72	1,005	38.9	5	15	32.4
1954	Tobin Rote	382	180	2,311	47.1	14	18	59.1
1955	Tobin Rote	342	157	1,977	45.9	17	19	57.8
1956	Tobin Rote	308	146	2,203	47.4	18	15	70.6
1957	Bart Starr	215	117	1,489	54.4	8	10	69.3
1958	Vito (Babe) Parilli	157	68	1,068	43.3	10	13	53.3
1959	Bart Starr	134	70	972	52.2	6	7	69.0
1960	Bart Starr	172	98	1,358	57.0	4	8	70.8
1961	Bart Starr	295	172	2,418	58.3	16	16	80.3
1962	Bart Starr	285	178	2,438	62.5	12	9	90.7
1963	Bart Starr	244	132	1,855	54.1	15	10	82.3
1964	Bart Starr	272	163	2,144	59.9	15	4	97.1
1965	Bart Starr	251	140	2,055	55.8	16	9	89.0
1966	Bart Starr	251	156	2,257	62.2	14	3	105.0
1967	Bart Starr	210	115	1,823	54.8	9	17	64.4
1968	Bart Starr	171	109	1,617	63.7	15	8	104.3
1969	Don Horn	168	89	1,505	53.0	11	11	78.1
1970	Bart Starr	255	140	1,645	54.9	8	13	63.9
1971	Scott Hunter	163	75	1,210	46.0	7	17	46.1
1972	Scott Hunter	199	86	1,252	43.2	6	9	55.5
1973	Jerry Tagge	106	56	720	52.8	2	7	53.2
1974	John Hadl	184	89	1,072	48.4	3	8	54.0
1975	John Hadl	353	191	2,095	54.1	6	21	52.8
1976	Lynn Dickey	243	115	1,465	47.3	7	14	52.2
1977	Lynn Dickey	220	113	1,346	51.4	5	14	51.4
1978	David Whitehurst	328	168	2,093	51.2	10	17	59.9
1979	David Whitehurst	322	179	2,247	55.6	10	18	64.5
1980	Lynn Dickey	478	278	3,529	58.2	15	25	70.0
1981	Lynn Dickey	354	204	2,593	57.6	17	15	79.0
1982	Lynn Dickey	218	124	1,790	56.9	12	14	75.3
1983	Lynn Dickey	484	289	4,458	59.7	32	29	87.3
1984	Lynn Dickey	401	237	3,195	59.1	25	19	85.6
1985	Lynn Dickey	314	172	2,206	54.8	15	17	70.4
1986	Randy Wright	492	263	3,247	53.5	17	23	66.2
1987	Randy Wright	247	132	1,507	53.4	6	11	61.6
1988	Don Majkowski	336	178	2,119	53.0	9	11	67.8
1989	Don Majkowski	599	353	4,318	58.9	27	20	82.3
1990	Don Majkowski	264	150	1,925	56.8	10	12	73.5
1991	Mike Tomczak	238	128	1,490	53.8	11	9	72.6
1992	Brett Favre	471	302	3,227	64.1	18	13	85.3
1993	Brett Favre	522	318	3,303	60.9	19	24	72.2
1994	Brett Favre	582	363	3,882	62.4	33	14	90.7

PUNTING

(leaders determined by number of punts)

Year	Name	No	Yds	Avg	LG	HB
1939	Clarke Hinkle	43	1,751	40.7	65	0
1940	Clarke Hinkle	22	819	37.2	59	0
1941	Clarke Hinkle	22	980	44.5	63	0
1942	Lou Brock	32	1,226	38.3	52	2
1943	Lou Brock	32	1,164	36.4	72	1
1944	Lou Brock	14	494	35.3	50	0
1945	Roy McKay	44	1,814	41.2	73	0
1946	Roy McKay	64	2,735	42.7	64	1
1947	Jack Jacobs	57	2,481	43.5	74	1
1948	Jack Jacobs	69	2,782	40.3	78	1
1949	Earl (Jug) Girard	69	2,694	39.0	72	3
1950	Earl (Jug) Girard	71	2,715	38.2	63	2
1951	Earl (Jug) Girard	52	2,101	40.4	66	0
1952	Vito (Babe) Parilli	65	2,645	40.7	63	0
1953	Clive Rush	60	2,262	37.7	60	0
1954	Max McGee	72	2,999	41.7	63	0
1955	Dick Deschaine	56	2,420	43.2	73	0
1956	Dick Deschaine	62	2,649	42.7	57	0
1957	Dick Deschaine	63	2,645	42.0	71	2
1958	Max McGee	62	2,625	42.3	61	0
1959	Max McGee	64	2,716	42.4	61	1
1960	Max McGee	31	1,291	41.6	58	1
1961	Boyd Dowler	38	1,674	44.1	75	0
1962	Boyd Dowler	36	1,550	43.1	75	0
1963	Jerry Norton	51	2,279	44.7	61	0
1964	Jerry Norton	56	2,365	42.2	61	0
1965	Don Chandler	74	3,176	42.9	90	0
1966	Don Chandler	60	2,452	40.9	58	0
1967	Donny Anderson	65	2,378	36.6	63	1
1968	Donny Anderson	59	2,359	40.0	65	0
1969	Donny Anderson	58	2,329	40.2	58	0
1970	Donny Anderson	81	3,302	40.4	62	0
1971	Donny Anderson	50	2,022	40.4	58	0
1972	Ron Widby	65	2,714	41.8	64	2
1973	Ron Widby	56	2,414	43.1	60	0
1974	Randy Walker	69	2,648	38.4	58	0
1975	David Beverly	66	2,482	37.6	55	0
1976	David Beverly	83	3,074	37.0	60	1
1977	David Beverly	85	3,391	39.9	59	1
1978	David Beverly	106	3,759	35.5	57	0
1979	David Beverly	69	2,785	40.4	65	0
1980	David Beverly	86	3,294	38.3	55	0
1981	Ray Stachowicz	82	3,330	40.6	72	2
1982	Ray Stachowicz	42	1,687	40.2	53	0
1983	Bucky Scribner	69	2,869	41.6	70	1
1984	Bucky Scribner	85	3,596	42.3	61	0
1985	Joe Prokop	56	2,210	39.8	66	0
1986	Don Bracken	55	2,203	40.1	63	2
1987	Don Bracken	72	2,947	40.9	65	1
1988	Don Bracken	85	3,287	38.7	62	1
1989	Don Bracken	66	2,662	40.6	63	0
1990	Don Bracken	64	2,431	38.0	59	1
1991	Paul McJulien	86	3,473	40.4	62	0
1992	Paul McJulien	36	1,386	38.5	67	2
1993	Bryan Wagner	74	3,174	42.9	60	0
1994	Craig Hentrich	81	3,351	41.4	70	0

KICKOFF RETURNS

(Leaders determined by number of returns)

Year	Name	No	Yds	Avg	LG	TD
1941	Tony Canadeo	4	110	27.5	55	0
	Hal Van Every	4	99	24.8	31	0
	Lou Brock	4	94	23.5	36	0
1942	Lou Brock	9	179	19.9	26	0
1943	Tony Canadeo	10	242	24.2	43	0
1944	Ted Fritsch	11	288	26.2	44	0
1945	Ted Fritsch	8	279	34.9	79	0
1946	Tony Canadeo	6	163	27.2	38	0
	Bob Nussbaumer	6	148	24.7	44	0
1947	Tony Canadeo	15	312	20.8	35	0
1948	O.E. Smith	12	287	23.9	36	0
1949	Jack Kirby	14	315	22.5	34	0
1950	Billy Grimes	26	600	23.1	36	0
1951	Billy Grimes	23	582	25.3	47	0
1952	Billy Grimes	18	422	23.4	34	0
1953	Al Carmichael	26	641	24.7	43	0
1954	Al Carmichael	20	531	26.6	49	0
	Veryl Switzer	20	500	25.0	88	0
1955	Veryl Switzer	17	445	26.2	57	0
1956	Al Carmichael	33	927	28.1	t106	1
1957	Al Carmichael	31	690	22.3	33	0
1958	Al Carmichael	29	700	24.1	60	0
1959	Bill Butler	21	472	22.5	35	0
1960	Tom Moore	12	397	33.1	84	0
	Lew Carpenter	12	249	20.8	29	0
1961	Herb Adderley	18	478	26.6	61	0
1962	Herb Adderley	15	418	27.9	t103	1
1963	Herb Adderley	20	597	29.9	t98	1
1964	Herb Adderley	19	508	26.7	43	0
1965	Elijah Pitts	20	396	19.8	29	0
1966	Donny Anderson	23	533	23.2	61	0
1967	Travis Williams	18	739	41.1	t104	4
1968	Travis Williams	28	599	21.4	60	0
1969	Dave Hampton	22	582	26.5	t87	1
1970	Ken Ellis	22	451	20.5	48	0
1971	Dave Hampton	46	1,314	28.6	t90	1
1972	Ike Thomas	21	572	27.2	89	0
1973	Ike Thomas	23	527	22.9	34	0
1974	Steve Odom	31	713	23.0	52	0
1975	Steve Odom	42	1,034	24.6	t93	1
1976	Steve Odom	29	610	21.0	88	0
1977	Steve Odom	23	468	20.3	37	0
1978	Steve Odom	25	677	27.1	t95	1
1979	Steve Odom	29	622	21.4	31	0
1980	Mark Lee	30	589	19.6	35	0
1981	Mark Lee	14	270	19.3	31	0
1982	Del Rodgers	20	436	21.8	76	0
1983	Harlan Huckleby	41	757	18.5	57	0
1984	Del Rodgers	39	843	21.6	t97	1
1985	Gary Ellerson	29	521	18.0	32	0
1986	Walter Stanley	28	559	20.0	55	0
1987	Brent Fullwood	24	510	21.3	46	0
1988	Brent Fullwood	21	421	20.0	31	0
1989	Vince Workman	33	547	16.6	46	0
1990	Charles Wilson	35	798	22.8	36	0
1991	Charles Wilson	23	522	22.7	t82	1
1992	Corey Harris	23	485	21.1	50	0
1993	Robert Brooks	23	611	26.6	t95	1
1994	Corey Harris	29	618	21.3	59	0

PUNT RETURNS

(Leaders determined by number of returns)

Year	Name	No	Yds	Avg	LG	TD
1941	Lou Brock	15	153	10.2	45	0
1942	Lou Brock	8	86	10.8	22	0
1943	Joe Laws	10	84	8.4	19	0
1944	Joe Laws	15	118	7.9	23	0
1945	Joe Laws	12	78	6.5	21	0
1946	Bob Nussbaumer	12	98	8.2	21	0
1947	Herman Rohrig	18	213	11.8	28	0
1948	Fred Provo	18	208	11.6	40	0
1949	Ralph Earhart	14	161	11.5	t57	1
1950	Billy Grimes	29	555	19.1	t85	2
1951	Billy Grimes	16	100	6.3	26	0
1952	Billy Grimes	18	179	9.9	72	0
1953	Al Carmichael	20	199	10.0	52	0
1954	Veryl Switzer	24	306	12.8	t93	1
1955	Veryl Switzer	24	158	6.6	38	0
1956	Al Carmichael	21	165	7.9	22	0
1957	Al Carmichael	25	190	7.6	48	0
1958	Al Carnichael	15	67	4.5	51	0
1959	Bill Butler	18	163	9.1	t61	1
1960	Willie Wood	16	106	6.6	33	0
1961	Willie Wood	14	225	16.1	t72	2
1962	Willie Wood	23	273	11.9	65	0
1963	Willie Wood	19	169	8.9	41	0
1964	Willie Wood	19	252	13.3	64	0
1965	Willie Wood	13	38	2.9	14	0
1966	Willie Wood	22	82	3.7	13	0
1967	Willie Wood	12	3	0.3	8	0
1968	Willie Wood	26	126	4.8	16	0
1969	Elijah Pitts	16	60	3.8	10	0
1970	Willie Wood	11	58	5.3	12	0
1971	Ken Ellis	22	107	4.9	30	0
1972	Ken Ellis	14	215	15.4	t80	1
1973	Jon Staggers	19	90	4.7	26	0
1974	Jon Staggers	22	222	10.1	t68	1
1975	Willard Harrell	21	136	6.5	25	0
1976	Johnnie Gray	37	307	8.3	27	0
1977	Willard Harrell	28	253	9.0	t75	1
1978	Steve Odom	33	298	9.0	48	0
1979	Steve Odom	15	80	5.3	19	0
1980	Ron Cassidy	17	139	8.2	20	0
1981	Mark Lee	20	187	9.4	t94	1
1982	Phil Epps	20	150	7.5	35	0
1983	Phil Epps	36	324	9.0	t90	1
1984	Phil Epps	29	199	6.9	39	0
1985	Phil Epps	15	146	9.7	46	0
1986	Walter Stanley	33	316	9.6	t83	1
1987	Walter Stanley	28	173	6.2	48	0
1988	Walter Stanley	12	52	4.3	15	0
1989	Jeff Query	30	247	8.2	15	0
1990	Jeff Query	32	308	9.6	25	0
1991	Vai Sikahema	26	239	9.2	62	0
1992	Terrell Buckley	21	211	10.0	t58	1
1993	Mike Prior	17	194	11.4	24	0
1994	Robert Brooks	40	352	8.8	t85	1

INTERCEPTIONS

(leaders determined by number of interceptions)

Year	Name	No	Yds	Avg	LG	TD
1940	Don Hutson	6	24	4.0	—	0
1941	Hal Van Every	3	104	34.7	t91	1
1942	Don Hutson	7	71	10.1	27	0
1943	Irv Comp	10	149	14.9	35	1
1944	Ted Fritsch	6	115	19.2	t50	1
	Irv Comp	6	54	9.0	43	0
1945	Charley Brock	4	122	30.5	38	2
	Don Hutson	4	15	3.8	15	0
1946	Herman Rohrig	5	134	26.8	51	0
1947	Bob Forte	8	140	17.5	t68	1
1948	Ted Cook	6	81	13.5	27	0
1949	Ted Cook	5	52	10.4	30	0
1950	Rebel Steiner	7	190	27.1	t94	1
1951	Earl (Jug) Girard	5	25	5.0	15	0
1952	Ace Loomis	4	115	28.8	t45	1
	Bob Forte	4	50	12.5	25	0
	Bobby Dillon	4	35	8.8	17	0
1953	Bobby Dillon	9	112	12.4	t49	1
1954	Bobby Dillon	7	111	15.9	t59	1
1955	Bobby Dillon	9	153	17.0	61	0
1956	Bobby Dillon	7	244	34.9	45	1
1957	John Symank	9	198	22.0	36	0
	Bobby Dillon	9	180	20.0	t55	1
1958	Bobby Dillon	6	134	22.3	46	1
1959	Bill Forester	2	48	24.0	34	0
	John Symank	2	46	23.0	25	0
	Bob Freeman	2	22	11.0	22	0
	Emlen Tunnell	2	20	10.0	18	0
1960	Jess Whittenton	6	101	16.8	52	0
1961	John Symank	5	99	19.8	41	0
	Jess Whittenton	5	98	19.6	t41	1
	Hank Gremminger	5	54	10.8	41	0
	Willie Wood	5	52	10.4	21	0
1962	Willie Wood	9	132	14.7	37	0
1963	Herb Adderley	5	86	17.2	35	0
	Willie Wood	5	67	13.4	22	0
1964	Herb Adderley	4	56	14.0	35	0
1965	Herb Adderley	6	175	29.2	t44	3
	Willie Wood	6	65	10.8	28	0
1966	Bob Jeter	5	142	28.4	t75	2
	Dave Robinson	5	60	12.0	23	0
1967	Bob Jeter	8	78	9.8	25	0
1968	Tom Brown	4	66	16.5	25	0
1969	Herb Adderley	5	169	33.8	t80	1
1970	Willie Wood	7	110	15.7	24	0
1971	Ken Ellis	6	10	1.7	5	0
1972	Ken Ellis	4	106	26.5	40	1
	Willie Buchanon	4	62	15.5	26	0
	Jim Hill	4	37	9.3	21	0
1973	Ken Ellis	3	53	17.7	t47	1
	Jim Hill	3	53	17.7	20	0
	Jim Carter	3	44	14.7	t42	1
1974	Ted Hendricks	5	74	14.8	44	0
1975	Perry Smith	6	97	16.2	61	0
1976	Johnnie Gray	4	101	25.3	67	1
1977	Steve Luke	4	9	2.3	7	0
	Mike C. McCoy	4	2	0.5	2	0
1978	Willie Buchanon	9	93	10.3	t77	1
1979	Johnnie Gray	5	66	13.2	35	0
1980	Johnnie Gray	5	54	10.8	21	0
1981	Maurice Harvey	6	217	36.2	53	0
	Mark Lee	6	50	8.3	25	0
1982	John Anderson	3	22	7.3	9	0
1983	Tim Lewis	5	111	22.2	46	0
	John Anderson	5	54	10.8	t27	1
1984	Tom Flynn	9	106	11.8	31	0
1985	Tim Lewis	4	4	1.0	4	0
1986	Mark Lee	9	33	3.7	11	0
1987	Jim Bob Morris	3	135	45.0	73	0
	Dave Brown	3	16	5.3	11	0
1988	Mark Murphy	5	19	3.8	9	0
1989	Dave Brown	6	12	2.0	12	0
1990	LeRoy Butler	3	42	14.0	28	0
	Jerry Holmes	3	39	13.0	24	0
	Mark Murphy	3	6	2.0	4	0
1991	Chuck Cecil	3	76	25.3	32	0
	Mark Murphy	3	27	9.0	16	0
	LeRoy Butler	3	6	2.0	6	0
1992	Chuck Cecil	4	52	13.0	29	0
1993	LeRoy Butler	6	131	21.8	39	0
1994	Terrell Buckley	5	38	7.6	26	0

SCORING

(leaders determined by total points)

Year	Name	TDr	TDp	TDrt	PAT	FG	S	TP
1921	Earl (Curly) Lambeau	2	0	0	7	3	0	28
1922	Earl (Curly) Lambeau	3	0	0	3	1	0	24
1923	Howard (Cub) Buck	0	0	0	5	6	0	23
1924	Walter (Tillie) Voss	0	5	0	0	0	0	30
1925	Myrt Basing	4	2	0	0	0	0	36
	Marty Norton	1	4	1	0	0	0	36
1926	Verne Lewellen	3	3	1	0	0	0	42
1927	Verne Lewellen	5	0	0	0	0	0	30
1928	Verne Lewellen	6	3	0	0	0	0	54
1929	Verne Lewellen	6	1	1	0	0	0	48
1930	Verne Lewellen	8	1	0	0	0	0	54
1931	Johnny (Blood) McNally	2	10	1	0	0	0	78
1932	Johnny (Blood) McNally	0	3	1	0	0	0	24
	Hank Bruder	0	3	1	0	0	0	24
1933	Charles Goldenberg	4	1	2	0	0	0	42
1934	Bob Monnett	2	0	0	6	4	0	30
1935	Don Hutson	0	6	1	1	0	0	43
1936	Don Hutson	0	8	1	0	0	0	54
1937	Clarke Hinkle	5	2	0	8	2	0	56
1938	Clarke Hinkle	3	4	0	7/8	3/9	0	58
1939	Don Hutson	0	6	0	2/2	0/0	0	38
1940	Don Hutson	0	7	0	15/16	0/0	0	57
1941	Don Hutson	2	10	0	20/24	1/1	0	95
1942	Don Hutson	0	17	0	33/34	1/4	0	138
1943	Don Hutson	0	11	1	36/36	3/5	0	117
1944	Don Hutson	0	9	0	31/33	0/3	0	85
1945	Don Hutson	1	9	0	31/35	2/4	0	97
1946	Ted Fritsch	9	1	0	13/15	9/17	0	100
1947	Ted Fritsch	6	0	0	2/2	6/13	0	56
1948	Ted Fritsch	0	0	1	5/6	6/16	0	29
1949	Ted Fritsch	1	0	0	11/13	5/20	0	32
1950	Billy Grimes	5	1	2	0/0	0/0	0	48
1951	Fred Cone	1	0	0	29/35	5/7	0	50
1952	Bill Howton	0	13	0	0/0	0/0	0	78
1953	Fred Cone	5	1	0	23/25	5/16	0	74
1954	Fred Cone	0	0	0	27/29	9/16	0	54
	Max McGee	0	9	0	0/0	0/0	0	54
1955	Fred Cone	0	0	0	30/30	16/24	0	78
1956	Fred Cone	2	2	0	33/35	5/8	0	72
	Bill Howton	0	12	0	0/0	0/0	0	72
1957	Fred Cone	2	0	0	26/26	12/17	0	74
1958	Paul Hornung	2	0	0	22/23	11/21	0	67
1959	Paul Hornung	7	0	0	31/32	7/17	0	94
1960	Paul Hornung	13	2	0	41/41	15/28	0	176
1961	Paul Hornung	8	2	0	41/41	15/22	0	146
1962	Jim Taylor	19	0	0	0/0	0/0	0	114
1963	Jerry Kramer	0	0	0	43/46	16/34	0	91
1964	Paul Hornung	5	0	0	41/43	12/38	0	107
1965	Don Chandler	0	0	0	37/38	17/26	0	88
1966	Don Chandler	0	0	0	41/43	12/28	0	77
1967	Don Chandler	0	0	0	39/39	19/29	S	96
1968	Carroll Dale	0	8	0	0/0	0/0	0	48
1969	Travis Williams	4	3	2	0/0	0/0	0	54
1970	Dale Livingston	0	0	0	19/21	15/28	0	64
1971	Lou Michaels	0	0	0	19/20	8/14	0	43
1972	Chester Marcol	0	0	0	29/29	33/48	0	128
1973	Chester Marcol	0	0	0	19/20	21/35	0	82
1974	Chester Marcol	0	0	0	19/19	25/39	0	94
1975	Joe Danelo	0	0	0	20/23	11/16	0	53
1976	Chester Marcol	0	0	0	24/27	10/19	0	54
1977	Chester Marcol	0	0	0	11/14	13/21	0	50
1978	Terdell Middleton	11	1	0	0/0	0/0	0	72
1979	Tom Birney	0	0	0	7/10	7/9	0	28
	Chester Marcol	0	0	0	16/18	4/10	0	28
1980	Gerry Ellis	5	3	0	0/0	0/0	0	48
1981	Jan Stenerud	0	0	0	35/36	22/24	0	101
1982	Jan Stenerud	0	0	0	25/27	13/18	0	64
1983	Jan Stenerud	0	0	0	52/52	21/26	0	115
1984	Al Del Greco	0	0	0	34/34	9/12	0	61
1985	Al Del Greco	0	0	0	38/40	19/26	0	95
1986	Al Del Greco	0	0	0	29/29	17/27	0	80
1987	Max Zendejas	0	0	0	13/15	16/19	0	61
1988	Brent Fullwood	7	1	0	0/0	0/0	0	48
1989	Chris Jacke	0	0	0	42/42	22/28	0	108
1990	Chris Jacke	0	0	0	28/29	23/30	0	97
1991	Chris Jacke	0	0	0	31/31	18/24	0	85
1992	Chris Jacke	0	0	0	30/30	22/29	0	96
1993	Chris Jacke	0	0	0	35/35	31/37	0	128
1994	Sterling Sharpe	0	18	0	0/0	0/0	0	108

QUARTERBACK SACKS

(leaders determined by number of sacks)

Year	Name	No
1982	Ezra Johnson	5.5
1983	Ezra Johnson	14.5
1984	Mike Douglass	9.0
1985	Ezra Johnson	9.5
1986	Tim Harris	8.0
1987	Tim Harris	7.0
1988	Tim Harris	13.5
1989	Tim Harris	19.5
1990	Tim Harris	7.0
1991	Tony Bennett	13.0
1992	Tony Bennett	13.5
1993	Reggie White	13.0
1994	Sean Jones	10.5

COMBINED NET YARDS

(leaders determined by total yards)

Year	Name	Rush	Rec	P-rt	K-rt	Int	Fum	Tot
1933	Bob Monnett	413	44	—	—	—	—	457
1934	Clarke Hinkle	359	113	—	—	—	—	472
1935	Johnny Blood	115	404	—	—	—	—	519
1936	Don Hutson	-3	526	—	—	—	—	523
1937	Clarke Hinkle	552	116	—	—	—	—	668
1938	Cecil Isbell	445	104	—	—	—	—	549
1939	Don Hutson	26	846	—	—	—	—	872
1940	Don Hutson	0	664	—	—	24	—	688
1941	Don Hutson	22	738	0	8	32	—	800
1942	Don Hutson	4	1,211	0	0	71	—	1,285
1943	Don Hutson	41	776	0	0	197	—	1,014
1944	Don Hutson	87	866	0	0	50	—	1,003
1945	Don Hutson	60	834	0	37	15	0	946
1946	Tony Canadeo	476	25	76	163	23	0	763
1947	Tony Canadeo	464	0	111	312	0	2	889
1948	Tony Canadeo	598	81	55	166	26	0	926
1949	Tony Canadeo	1,052	-2	0	20	0	0	1,070
1950	Billy Grimes	480	261	555	600	0	0	1,896
1951	Billy Grimes	123	170	100	582	0	0	975
1952	Bill Howton	0	1,231	0	0	0	0	1,231
1953	Al Carmichael	199	131	199	641	0	0	1,170
1954	Veryl Switzer	59	166	306	500	0	0	1,031
1955	Howie Ferguson	859	153	0	20	0	0	1,032
1956	Al Carmichael	199	180	165	927	0	0	1,471
1957	Al Carmichael	118	184	190	690	0	0	1,182
1958	Al Carmichael	21	26	67	700	0	0	814
1959	Paul Hornung	681	113	0	0	0	0	794
1960	Jim Taylor	1,101	121	0	0	0	1	1,223
1961	Jim Taylor	1,307	175	0	0	0	0	1,482
1962	Jim Taylor	1,474	106	0	0	0	0	1,580
1963	Jim Taylor	1,018	68	0	0	0	0	1,086
1964	Jim Taylor	1,169	354	0	0	0	0	1,523
1965	Jim Taylor	734	207	0	0	0	0	941
1966	Jim Taylor	705	331	0	0	0	0	1,036
1967	Donny Anderson	402	331	98	226	0	0	1,057
1968	Donny Anderson	761	333	0	0	0	0	1,094
1969	Travis Williams	536	275	189	517	0	0	1,517
1970	Donny Anderson	853	414	0	0	0	0	1,267
1971	Dave Hampton	307	37	0	1,314	0	0	1,658
1972	John Brockington	1,027	243	0	0	0	0	1,270
1973	John Brockington	1,144	128	0	0	0	0	1,272
1974	Steve Odom	66	249	191	713	0	0	1,219
1975	Steve Odom	55	299	0	1,034	0	0	1,388
1976	Steve Odom	78	456	0	610	0	0	1,144
1977	Steve Odom	6	549	0	468	0	0	1,023
1978	Terdell Middleton	1,116	332	0	22	0	0	1,470
1979	James Lofton	-1	968	0	0	0	0	967
1980	Eddie Lee Ivery	831	481	0	0	0	0	1,312
1981	Gerry Ellis	860	499	0	0	0	0	1,359
1982	James Lofton	101	696	0	0	0	0	797
1983	James Lofton	36	1,300	0	0	0	0	1,336
1984	James Lofton	82	1,361	0	0	0	0	1,443
1985	James Lofton	14	1,153	0	0	0	0	1,167
1986	Walter Stanley	19	723	316	559	0	0	1,617
1987	Walter Stanley	38	672	173	47	0	0	930
1988	Brent Fullwood	483	128	0	421	0	0	1,032
1989	Sterling Sharpe	25	1,423	0	0	0	5	1,453
1990	Sterling Sharpe	14	1,105	0	0	0	0	1,119
1991	Sterling Sharpe	4	961	0	0	0	0	965
1992	Sterling Sharpe	8	1,461	0	0	0	0	1,469
1993	Sterling Sharpe	8	1,274	0	0	0	0	1,282
1994	Robert Brooks	0	648	352	260	0	0	1,260

Al Carmichael (42) is on the move against the Bears in City Stadium, October 4, 1953.

Green Bay Press-Gazette photo

TOP SINGLE-GAME PERFORMANCES

100 OR MORE YARDS RUSHING (114)

Date	Name	Att	Yds	Avg	LG	TD
12-3-33	Clarke Hinkle	15	116	7.7	—	0
11-28-35	Bobby Monnett	12	107	8.9	—	1
11-1-36	Clarke Hinkle	13	109	8.4	—	1
10-8-39	Andy Uram	2	108	54.0	t97	1
11-10-40	Cecil Isbell	11	118	10.7	—	0
10-26-41	Andy Uram	7	103	14.7	61	0
11-22-42	Ted Fritsch	9	111	12.3	55	0
10-31-43	Tony Canadeo	18	122	6.8	t35	1
10-22-44	Tony Canadeo	12	107	8.9	34	0
10-26-47	Ed Cody	9	111	12.3	t32	2
10-3-48	Tony Canadeo	17	118	6.9	49	1
10-17-48	Tony Canadeo	16	105	6.6	36	0
10-7-49	Tony Canadeo	16	100	6.3	27	1
10-23-49	Tony Canadeo	26	122	4.7	45	0
10-30-49	Tony Canadeo	21	117	5.6	30	1
11-20-49	Tony Canadeo	21	116	5.5	25	0
11-27-49	Tony Canadeo	20	122	6.1	54	1
10-1-50	Larry Coutre	8	101	12.6	53	0
10-8-50	Billy Grimes	10	167	16.7	t61	1
11-18-51	Tobin Rote	14	150	10.7	32	0
11-22-51	Tobin Rote	15	131	8.7	23	1
12-12-52	Tobin Rote	14	106	7.6	30	0
10-31-53	Floyd (Breezy) Reid	9	120	13.3	t38	1
11-13-54	Howie Ferguson	15	112	7.5	25	0
10-2-55	Howie Ferguson	15	153	10.2	57	0
11-6-55	Howie Ferguson	17	120	7.1	24	2
11-3-57	Paul Hornung	16	112	7.0	72	0
10-19-58	Howie Ferguson	11	100	9.1	29	0
12-7-58	Jim Taylor	22	137	6.2	25	0
10-11-59	Paul Hornung	28	138	4.9	14	1
12-13-59	Lew Carpenter	16	113	7.1	26	0
10-2-60	Jim Taylor	26	151	5.8	27	1
10-30-60	Jim Taylor	25	105	4.2	18	1
11-13-60	Jim Taylor	15	121	8.1	t28	3
11-20-60	Tom Moore	11	105	9.5	t59	1
12-4-60	Jim Taylor	24	140	5.8	29	1
12-11-60	Jim Taylor	27	161	6.0	25	0
10-1-61	Jim Taylor	19	130	6.8	53	1
10-8-61	Paul Hornung	11	111	10.1	t54	3
10-15-61	Jim Taylor	21	158	7.5	t45	4
10-22-61	Tom Moore	16	159	9.9	69	0
12-3-61	Jim Taylor	27	186	6.9	43	2
12-10-61	Jim Taylor	22	122	5.5	23	1
9-23-62	Jim Taylor	23	122	5.3	12	0
9-30-62	Jim Taylor	17	126	7.4	26	3
10-14-62	Jim Taylor	17	164	9.6	31	0
10-21-62	Jim Taylor	17	160	9.4	27	2
11-4-62	Jim Taylor	25	124	5.0	51	4
11-11-62	Jim Taylor	25	141	5.6	26	4
12-16-62	Jim Taylor	23	156	6.8	t28	1
9-22-63	Tom Moore	17	122	7.2	t77	2
10-27-63	Jim Taylor	26	107	4.1	t16	2
11-3-63	Jim Taylor	30	141	4.7	21	1
11-24-63	Jim Taylor	15	119	7.9	t34	1
12-7-63	Jim Taylor	17	113	6.6	t40	1
10-11-64	Jim Taylor	23	133	5.8	t27	2
11-1-64	Jim Taylor	17	108	6.4	16	1
11-8-64	Jim Taylor	19	145	7.6	t84	2
12-13-64	Jim Taylor	17	165	9.7	65	1
11-21-65	Jim Taylor	25	111	4.4	13	0
9-24-67	Jim Grabowski	32	111	3.5	9	1
10-22-67	Jim Grabowski	21	123	5.9	14	1
11-12-67	Ben Wilson	16	100	6.3	19	0
10-6-68	Donny Anderson	15	101	6.7	18	1
10-26-69	Donny Anderson	18	114	6.3	t16	1
10-12-70	Travis Williams	21	109	5.2	37	0
11-1-70	Donny Anderson	15	105	7.0	54	0
10-3-71	John Brockington	19	120	6.3	29	0
11-1-71	John Brockington	16	111	6.9	41	0
11-7-71	John Brockington	30	142	4.7	22	1
11-14-71	John Brockington	23	149	6.5	31	0
11-5-72	John Brockington	24	133	5.5	t30	2
11-19-72	MacArthur Lane	16	126	7.9	t36	1
12-10-72	John Brockington	25	114	4.6	19	0
9-23-73	John Brockington	22	118	5.4	26	0
10-14-73	John Brockington	15	106	7.1	33	0
11-11-73	John Brockington	28	137	4.9	16	1
12-8-73	John Brockington	27	124	4.6	29	0
12-16-73	John Brockington	22	142	6.5	53	0
12-16-73	MacArthur Lane	19	101	6.3	18	0
11-17-74	John Brockington	32	137	4.3	23	0
11-30-75	John Brockington	26	111	4.3	19	3
10-3-76	Willard Harrell	17	111	6.5	56	0
9-10-78	Terdell Middleton	19	114	6.0	34	0
10-1-78	Terdell Middleton	11	148	13.5	t76	1
10-15-78	Terdell Middleton	23	121	5.3	25	4
11-26-78	Terdell Middleton	39	110	2.8	11	1
9-9-79	Steve Atkins	12	110	9.2	60	1
10-14-79	Nate Simpson	19	121	6.4	22	0
11-11-79	Terdell Middleton	27	135	5.0	28	0
11-23-80	Gerry Ellis	15	101	6.7	19	1
11-23-80	Eddie Lee Ivery	24	145	6.0	t38	1
11-1-81	Gerry Ellis	23	127	5.5	19	0
9-12-82	Eddie Lee Ivery	17	109	6.4	32	2
12-4-83	Gerry Ellis	18	141	7.8	71	1
10-28-84	Eddie Lee Ivery	9	116	12.9	49	0
11-11-84	Gerry Ellis	10	107	10.7	50	1
9-29-85	Jessie Clark	9	112	12.4	80	0
11-10-85	Eddie Lee Ivery	15	111	7.4	34	0
12-1-85	Gerry Ellis	9	101	11.2	t35	1
12-1-85	Eddie Lee Ivery	13	109	8.4	24	0
10-18-87	Kevin Willhite	16	100	6.3	61	0
10-25-87	Kenneth Davis	23	129	5.6	t39	2
10-9-88	Brent Fullwood	14	118	8.4	t33	3
9-17-89	Brent Fullwood	18	125	6.9	38	2
10-8-89	Brent Fullwood	28	119	4.3	13	0
12-17-89	Keith Woodside	10	116	11.6	t68	1
11-1-92	Vince Workman	23	101	4.4	14	0
11-22-92	Edgar Bennett	29	107	3.7	9	0
10-24-93	Darrell Thompson	21	105	5.0	22	0
12-26-93	Darrell Thompson	21	101	4.8	t60	1
10-31-94	Edgar Bennett	26	105	4.0	21	2
12-11-94	Edgar Bennett	22	106	4.8	28	1
12-24-94	Edgar Bennett	21	100	4.8	t39	1

100 OR MORE YARDS RECEIVING (206)

Date	Name	No	Yds	Avg	LG	TD
10-6-35	Don Hutson	4	109	27.3	t43	2
10-27-35	Don Hutson	5	103	20.6	t69	2
11-10-35	Johnny (Blood) McNally	3	100	33.3	t70	2
11-7-37	Don Hutson	5	140	28.0	t78	1
10-30-38	Don Hutson	6	148	24.7	t53	3
10-8-39	Don Hutson	3	126	42.0	t92	2
10-22-39	Don Hutson	2	111	55.5	t60	2
11-12-39	Don Hutson	5	112	22.4	—	0
11-19-39	Don Hutson	3	149	49.7	t69	1
10-13-40	Carl (Moose) Mulleneaux	4	111	27.8	t47	2
10-12-41	Don Hutson	8	126	15.8	t32	1
11-30-41	Don Hutson	9	135	15.0	t40	3
9-27-42	Don Hutson	8	147	18.4	t40	2
10-11-42	Don Hutson	5	149	29.8	t69	2
10-18-42	Don Hutson	13	209	16.1	33	2
11-1-42	Don Hutson	5	207	41.4	t73	3
11-1-42	Andy Uram	4	174	43.5	t64	3
11-15-42	Don Hutson	10	117	11.7	20	1
11-22-42	Don Hutson	14	134	9.6	19	2
10-31-43	Don Hutson	8	103	12.9	t19	2
10-31-43	Harry Jacunski	5	124	24.8	48	1
11-14-43	Harry Jacunski	3	120	40.0	t86	1
11-21-43	Don Hutson	8	237	29.6	t79	2
10-8-44	Don Hutson	11	207	18.8	t55	2
11-12-44	Don Hutson	5	107	21.4	t35	2
10-7-45	Don Hutson	6	144	24.0	t59	4
10-14-45	Don Hutson	7	110	15.7	25	0
10-21-45	Don Hutson	6	169	28.2	t75	2
10-28-45	Don Hutson	7	141	20.1	t59	2
10-19-47	Nolan Luhn	9	140	15.6	32	1
11-30-47	Clyde Goodnight	5	107	21.4	38	1
12-14-47	Nolan Luhn	8	135	16.9	44	1
10-24-48	Clyde Goodnight	5	117	23.4	57	1
10-19-50	Al Baldwin	3	106	35.3	t85	1
10-28-51	Earl (Jug) Girard	4	130	32.5	t75	1
12-16-51	Bob Mann	11	123	11.2	52	0
10-5-52	Bill Howton	3	128	42.7	t90	1
10-12-52	Bill Howton	5	156	31.2	t69	1
10-26-52	Bill Howton	7	151	21.6	t78	1
11-27-52	Bill Howton	7	123	17.6	t54	3
12-7-52	Bill Howton	6	200	33.3	76	0
12-14-52	Bill Howton	8	162	20.3	t90	2
10-4-53	Byron Bailey	4	100	25.0	50	0
10-11-53	Clive Rush	7	101	14.4	24	0
11-8-53	Bob Mann	6	101	16.8	45	0
10-3-54	Bill Howton	4	100	25.0	44	0
10-17-54	Bill Howton	5	105	21.0	42	1
10-24-54	Bill Howton	11	147	13.4	59	0
10-30-54	Max McGee	3	104	34.7	t49	3
11-21-54	Bill Howton	7	101	14.4	29	0
12-12-54	Max McGee	9	105	11.7	t22	1
10-16-55	Bill Howton	8	158	19.8	t57	1
10-21-56	Bill Howton	7	257	36.7	t63	2
11-11-56	Bill Howton	4	151	37.8	t53	1
11-18-56	Bill Howton	3	121	40.3	45	1
11-22-56	Howie Ferguson	7	106	15.1		0
9-29-57	Bill Howton	8	165	20.6	41	1
11-3-57	Bill Howton	4	111	27.8	t77	1
10-19-58	Bill Howton	5	130	26.0	50	0
10-26-58	Max McGee	6	100	16.7	t34	2

Date	Name	No	Yds	Avg	LG	TD
10-4-59	Max McGee	3	124	41.3	47	2
10-25-59	Max McGee	3	110	36.7	t81	1
11-15-59	Boyd Dowler	8	147	18.4	34	0
11-26-59	Boyd Dowler	4	107	26.8	35	0
10-23-60	Max McGee	5	110	22.0	30	1
12-4-60	Max McGee	6	121	20.2	46	1
12-18-60	Max McGee	4	125	31.3	t57	2
9-17-61	Max McGee	7	127	18.1	29	0
10-15-61	Max McGee	5	120	24.0	t48	1
10-22-61	Boyd Dowler	2	100	50.0	t78	1
10-29-61	Boyd Dowler	5	121	24.2	48	0
10-29-61	Max McGee	6	102	17.0	29	1
10-14-62	Boyd Dowler	7	124	17.7	41	1
10-14-62	Max McGee	10	159	15.9	t55	2
11-11-62	Boyd Dowler	7	101	14.4	25	1
11-11-62	Max McGee	7	174	24.9	64	0
11-10-63	Boyd Dowler	8	134	16.8	49	1
11-28-63	Boyd Dowler	9	178	19.8	49	0
12-7-63	Max McGee	7	105	15.0	t25	3
12-14-63	Boyd Dowler	8	188	23.5	t53	2
10-4-64	Boyd Dowler	6	128	21.3	t50	2
10-18-64	Max McGee	4	123	30.8	t42	1
11-15-64	Max McGee	6	139	23.2	t44	2
9-19-65	Boyd Dowler	6	104	17.3	31	0
10-17-65	Carroll Dale	3	108	36.0	t77	1
10-17-65	Bob Long	4	106	26.5	t62	1
11-28-65	Elijah Pitts	4	111	27.8	t80	1
12-12-65	Paul Hornung	2	115	57.5	t65	2
12-19-65	Boyd Dowler	6	117	19.5	t43	1
10-23-66	Carroll Dale	4	110	27.5	t51	1
12-4-66	Carroll Dale	3	142	47.3	t83	1
12-18-66	Carroll Dale	3	121	40.3	74	1
9-17-67	Carroll Dale	4	109	27.3	51	0
10-1-67	Boyd Dowler	8	105	13.1	18	0
10-12-67	Donny Anderson	5	103	20.6	37	1
11-26-67	Boyd Dowler	6	105	17.5	42	1
12-3-67	Boyd Dowler	3	100	33.3	t57	1
9-15-68	Boyd Dowler	5	110	22.0	t55	1
9-29-68	Carroll Dale	6	205	34.2	t63	2
11-17-68	Carroll Dale	8	161	20.1	t47	1
12-15-68	Boyd Dowler	6	182	30.3	t72	1
10-12-69	Carroll Dale	7	167	23.9	t40	2
10-19-69	Boyd Dowler	6	100	16.7	33	1
11-2-69	Carroll Dale	7	134	19.1	t43	1
12-21-69	Carroll Dale	9	195	21.7	44	2
12-21-69	Boyd Dowler	6	102	17.0	t43	2
9-27-70	Carroll Dale	4	186	46.5	t89	2
12-13-70	Carroll Dale	8	128	16.0	33	0
10-17-71	Carroll Dale	8	151	18.9	t56	1
9-29-75	Ken Payne	12	167	13.9	29	0
11-23-75	Ken Payne	4	103	25.8	54	0
10-24-76	Ken Payne	6	120	20.0	t57	1
11-28-76	Ollie Smith	4	121	30.3	47	0
11-13-77	Steve Odom	4	115	28.8	t65	1
9-10-78	James Lofton	3	107	35.7	t47	3
10-1-78	Aundra Thompson	3	111	37.0	49	2
10-21-79	Paul Coffman	7	106	15.1	21	0
10-28-79	Paul Coffman	5	116	23.2	t78	1
11-4-79	James Lofton	6	114	19.0	45	0
11-18-79	James Lofton	4	112	28.0	44	1
12-9-79	James Lofton	6	112	18.7	40	0
10-5-80	James Lofton	8	114	14.3	23	0
10-12-80	Paul Coffman	9	109	12.1	18	1
10-12-80	Eddie Lee Ivery	11	128	11.6	31	0
10-12-80	Aundra Thompson	7	102	14.6	36	0

Date	Name	No	Yds	Avg	LG	TD
10-19-80	James Lofton	8	136	17.0	31	1
11-2-80	Gerry Ellis	7	106	15.1	t69	2
11-9-80	James Lofton	8	146	18.3	37	0
11-16-80	James Lofton	8	175	21.9	47	1
12-7-80	James Lofton	6	111	18.5	24	1
9-13-81	James Lofton	8	179	22.4	53	0
9-27-81	John Jefferson	7	121	17.3	24	0
9-27-81	James Lofton	8	101	12.6	27	1
11-22-81	James Lofton	6	102	17.0	21	0
11-29-81	James Lofton	7	159	22.7	t47	1
12-6-81	John Jefferson	8	113	14.1	22	0
9-12-82	John Jefferson	6	116	19.3	50	0
9-20-82	James Lofton	4	101	25.3	36	0
12-19-82	John Jefferson	5	101	20.2	43	0
12-26-82	James Lofton	3	146	48.7	t80	2
1-2-83	James Lofton	7	128	18.3	30	1
9-4-83	James Lofton	8	154	19.3	t74	1
9-11-83	James Lofton	5	169	33.8	t73	3
10-2-83	James Lofton	4	112	28.0	t57	1
10-17-83	Paul Coffman	6	124	20.7	t36	2
10-17-83	Gerry Ellis	4	105	26.3	56	0
11-6-83	John Jefferson	7	102	14.6	28	1
11-27-83	James Lofton	7	161	23.0	41	1
12-4-83	James Lofton	6	120	20.0	67	0
12-18-83	Paul Coffman	4	122	30.5	74	1
9-2-84	James Lofton	7	134	19.1	43	0
10-7-84	Paul Coffman	8	104	13.0	42	1
10-7-84	James Lofton	5	158	31.6	46	1
10-15-84	James Lofton	11	206	18.7	t54	1
10-21-84	James Lofton	5	162	32.4	t79	2
11-11-84	James Lofton	4	119	29.8	t63	1
11-18-84	James Lofton	6	129	21.5	51	0
10-6-85	James Lofton	10	151	15.1	27	0
10-21-85	James Lofton	7	103	14.7	t27	1
11-10-85	Phillip Epps	6	118	19.7	63	0
12-1-85	James Lofton	6	106	17.7	27	0
9-14-86	James Lofton	8	100	12.5	21	1
10-5-86	James Lofton	7	109	15.6	24	1
11-23-86	Ed West	5	103	20.6	t46	1
11-27-86	Walter Stanley	4	124	31.0	62	2
10-18-87	Lee Morris	6	132	22.0	t46	1
10-25-87	Walter Stanley	6	150	25.0	t70	1
11-8-87	Phillip Epps	6	139	23.2	40	1
12-27-87	Walter Stanley	4	109	27.3	t39	2
9-25-88	Sterling Sharpe	7	137	19.6	51	0
10-2-88	Walter Stanley	6	107	17.8	56	0
10-16-88	Walter Stanley	5	101	20.2	43	0
11-20-88	Sterling Sharpe	8	124	15.5	27	0
12-11-88	Perry Kemp	6	108	18.0	29	0
9-17-89	Sterling Sharpe	8	107	13.4	39	1
9-24-89	Sterling Sharpe	8	164	20.5	57	1
10-8-89	Sterling Sharpe	6	132	22.0	t79	1
10-29-89	Sterling Sharpe	7	105	15.0	28	1
11-26-89	Sterling Sharpe	10	157	15.7	t34	2
12-3-89	Sterling Sharpe	8	169	21.1	t55	2
10-7-90	Sterling Sharpe	5	129	25.8	t76	1
10-14-90	Sterling Sharpe	7	139	19.9	35	0
11-18-90	Sterling Sharpe	10	157	15.7	t54	1
12-22-90	Ed West	7	103	14.7	22	0
11-10-91	Sterling Sharpe	8	133	16.6	t58	1
9-20-92	Sterling Sharpe	7	109	15.6	42	1
10-4-92	Sterling Sharpe	9	107	11.9	24	1
10-25-92	Sterling Sharpe	9	144	16.0	45	1
11-8-92	Sterling Sharpe	11	160	14.5	43	0
11-15-92	Sterling Sharpe	7	116	16.6	34	1
12-6-92	Sterling Sharpe	6	107	17.8	t65	2
12-20-92	Sterling Sharpe	8	110	13.8	18	2
9-5-93	Sterling Sharpe	7	120	17.1	t50	1
10-10-93	Jackie Harris	5	128	25.6	t66	1
10-24-93	Sterling Sharpe	10	147	14.7	t32	4
12-5-93	Sterling Sharpe	10	114	11.4	t18	1
12-19-93	Sterling Sharpe	6	106	17.7	42	1
12-26-93	Sterling Sharpe	7	119	17.0	26	1
9-18-94	Sterling Sharpe	6	108	18.0	48	0
10-2-94	Sterling Sharpe	9	132	14.7	30	1
11-24-94	Sterling Sharpe	9	122	13.6	t36	4
12-4-93	Sterling Sharpe	10	115	11.5	29	1
12-4-93	Anthony Morgan	6	103	17.2	t47	2
12-11-94	Robert Brooks	6	105	17.5	35	1
12-18-94	Edgar Bennett	8	101	12.6	40	0
12-24-94	Sterling Sharpe	9	132	14.7	49	3

300 OR MORE YARDS PASSING (41)

Date	Name	Att	Com	Yds	Pct	TD	In
11-1-42	Cecil Isbell	21	10	333	47.6	5	1
12-16-51	Tobin Rote	40	20	335	50.0	2	2
11-22-56	Tobin Rote	40	21	301	52.5	2	3
10-12-58	Bart Starr	46	26	320	56.5	1	4
10-29-61	Bart Starr	24	18	311	75.0	2	0
12-14-63	Bart Starr	27	17	306	63.0	2	0
10-17-65	Bart Starr	23	15	301	65.2	3	1
9-17-67	Bart Starr	23	14	321	60.9	0	4
12-21-69	Don Horn	31	22	410	71.0	5	1
10-24-76	Lynn Dickey	34	22	303	64.7	1	2
10-12-80	Lynn Dickey	51	35	418	68.6	1	2
11-16-80	Lynn Dickey	36	20	331	55.6	2	2
12-14-80	Lynn Dickey	37	18	309	48.6	0	3
9-13-81	Lynn Dickey	44	30	342	71.4	2	3
9-4-83	Lynn Dickey	31	27	333	87.1	5	1
10-17-83	Lynn Dickey	31	22	387	71.0	3	1
10-23-83	Lynn Dickey	41	23	383	56.1	2	3
11-27-83	Lynn Dickey	37	25	366	67.6	3	3
12-4-83	Lynn Dickey	34	16	345	47.1	1	1
10-7-84	Lynn Dickey	39	25	384	64.1	3	2
10-15-84	Lynn Dickey	37	27	371	73.0	1	1
10-21-84	Lynn Dickey	38	24	364	63.2	3	3
11-11-84	Lynn Dickey	40	22	303	55.0	4	1
11-17-85	Lynn Dickey	35	22	302	62.9	2	2
10-26-86	Randy Wright	54	30	328	55.6	1	3
10-25-87	Don Majkowski	29	19	323	65.5	1	1
10-2-88	Randy Wright	51	28	321	54.9	1	2
11-20-88	Don Majkowski	43	30	327	69.8	1	1
9-17-89	Don Majkowski	32	25	354	78.1	3	1
9-24-89	Don Majkowski	43	25	335	58.1	2	3
10-8-89	Don Majkowski	32	21	313	65.6	4	0
10-29-89	Don Majkowski	45	29	367	64.4	2	1
11-12-89	Don Majkowski	59	34	357	57.6	1	2
12-3-89	Don Majkowski	53	25	331	47.2	2	2
10-14-90	Don Majkowski	42	25	355	59.5	1	5
11-10-91	Mike Tomczak	38	23	317	60.5	2	2
12-5-93	Brett Favre	54	36	402	66.7	2	3
9-11-94	Brett Favre	51	31	362	60.8	2	1
9-25-94	Brett Favre	39	30	306	76.9	3	0
12-4-94	Brett Favre	43	29	366	67.4	3	2
12-18-94	Brett Favre	44	29	321	65.9	2	1

TWELVE OUTSTANDING SEASONS

RECEIVING - DON HUTSON, 1942

Hutson set the standard with this record-setting season.

Date	Opponent	No	Yds	Avg	LG	TD
9/27	Chicago Bears	8	147	18.4	t40	2
10/4	Chicago Cardinals	2	19	9.5	14	1
10/11	Detroit Lions	5	149	29.8	t69	2
10/18	Cleveland Rams	13	209	16.1	33	2
10/25	Detroit Lions	5	88	17.6	34	0
11/1	Chicago Cardinals	5	207	41.4	t73	3
11/8	Cleveland Rams	9	96	10.7	t15	3
11/15	Chicago Bears	10	117	11.7	20	1
11/22	New York Giants	14	134	9.6	19	2
11/29	Philadelphia Eagles	2	38	19.0	t31	1
12/6	Pittsburgh Steelers	1	7	7.0	7	0
	Totals	**74**	**1,211**	**16.4**	**t73**	**17**

INTERCEPTIONS - IRV COMP, 1943

No Packer has intercepted as many passes as did Irv Comp in 1943.

Date	Opponent	No	Yds	Avg	LG	TD
9/26	Chicago Bears	0	0	0.0	0	0
10/3	Chicago Cardinals	2	23	11.5	12	0
10/10	Detroit Lions	0	0	0.0	0	0
10/17	Washington Redskins	0	0	0.0	0	0
10/24	Detroit Lions	1	17	17.0	17	0
10/31	New York Giants	DID NOT PLAY				
11/7	Chicago Bears	1	35	35.0	35	0
11/14	Chicago Cardinals	1	0	0.0	0	0
11/21	Brooklyn Dodgers	3	28	9.3	—	1
12/5	Card-Pitt Carpets	2	46	23.0	—	1
	Totals	**10**	**149**	**14.9**	**35**	**1**

RUSHING - TONY CANADEO, 1949

Canadeo became the first Packer and just the third player in the NFL to produce 1,000 yards rushing.

Date	Opponent	Att	Yds	Avg	LG	TD
9/25	Chicago Bears	11	92	8.4	37	0
10/2	Cleveland Rams	12	43	3.6	18	0
10/7	New York Bulldogs	16	100	6.3	27	1
10/16	Chicago Cardinals	14	75	5.4	18	1
10/23	Los Angeles Rams	26	122	4.7	45	0
10/30	Detroit Lions	21	117	5.6	30	0
11/6	Chicago Bears	21	95	4.5	22	0
11/13	New York Giants	14	71	5.1	16	0
11/20	Pittsburgh Steelers	21	116	5.5	25	0
11/27	Chicago Cardinals	20	122	6.1	54	1
12/4	Washington Redskins	15	29	1.9	5	0
12/11	Detroit Lions	17	70	4.1	16	0
	Totals	**208**	**1,052**	**5.1**	**54**	**4**

PUNT RETURNS - BILLY GRIMES, 1950

He returned punts for more yards than any other Packer in history and Grimes did it with a franchise-best 19.1 average per return.

Date	Opponent	No	Yds	Avg	LG	TD
9/17	Detroit Lions	3	43	14.3	18	0
9/24	Washington Redskins	1	85	85.0	t85	1
10/1	Chicago Bears	4	102	25.5	t68	1
10/8	New York Yanks	2	17	8.5	10	0
10/15	Chicago Bears	0	0	0.0	0	0
10/19	New York Yanks	4	80	20.0	51	0
11/5	Baltimore Colts	5	75	15.0	44	0
11/12	Los Angeles Rams	3	56	18.7	30	0
11/19	Detroit Lions	4	66	16.5	20	0
11/26	San Francisco 49ers	1	4	4.0	4	0
12/3	Los Angeles Rams	2	27	13.5	18	0
12/10	San Francisco 49ers	0	0	0.0	0	0
	Totals	**29**	**555**	**19.1**	**t85**	**2**

RECEIVING - BILL HOWTON, 1952

No rookie receiver had done what Howton did in 1952. His 53 catches, 1,231 yards, and 13 touchdowns remained rookie bests for years to come.

Date	Opponent	No	Yds	Avg	LG	TD
9/28	Chicago Bears	3	72	24.0	t40	1
10/5	Washington Redskins	3	128	42.7	t90	1
10/12	Los Angeles Rams	5	156	31.2	t69	1
10/18	Dallas Texans	3	36	12.0	t21	2
10/26	Detroit Lions	7	151	21.6	t78	1
11/2	Philadelphia Eagles	3	59	19.7	42	0
11/9	Chicago Bears	5	65	13.0	20	1
11/16	New York Giants	1	6	6.0	6	0
11/23	Dallas Texans	2	73	36.5	t50	1
11/27	Detroit Lions	7	123	17.6	t54	3
12/7	Los Angeles Rams	6	200	33.3	76	0
12/14	San Francisco 49ers	8	162	20.3	t90	2
	Totals	**53**	**1,231**	**23.2**	**t90**	**13**

KICKOFF RETS - AL CARMICHAEL, 1956

Carmichael set then NFL marks with 927 yards returned and a 106-yard return for a touchdown against the Chicago Bears.

Date	Opponent	No	Yds	Avg	LG	TD
9/30	Detroit Lions	2	57	28.5	32	0
10/7	Chicago Bears	5	189	37.8	t106	1
10/14	Baltimore Colts	3	51	17.0	23	0
10/21	Los Angeles Rams	2	30	15.0	20	0
10/28	Baltimore Colts	0	0	0.0	0	0
11/4	Cleveland Browns	2	76	38.0	57	0
11/11	Chicago Bears	2	109	54.5	73	0
11/18	San Francisco 49ers	2	54	27.0	28	0
11/22	Detroit Lions	2	35	17.5	18	0
12/2	Chicago Cardinals	2	33	16.5	18	0
12/9	San Francisco 49ers	5	147	29.4	37	0
12/16	Los Angeles Rams	6	146	24.3	36	0
	Totals	**33**	**927**	**28.1**	**t106**	**1**

SCORING - PAUL HORNUNG, 1960

Hornung set the NFL mark for most points in a season.

Date	Opponent	TDr	TDp	FG	PAT	Tot
9/25	Chicago Bears	1	0	0/2	2/2	8
10/2	Detroit Lions	1	1	0/0	4/4	16
10/9	Baltimore Colts	0	0	0/1	5/5	5
10/23	San Francisco 49ers	2	0	2/3	5/5	23
10/30	Pittsburgh Steelers	0	0	4/6	1/1	13
11/6	Baltimore Colts	2	0	1/2	3/3	18
11/13	Dallas Cowboys	1	0	2/3	5/5	17
11/20	Los Angeles Rams	2	0	1/3	4/4	19
11/24	Detroit Lions	1	0	1/1	1/1	10
12/4	Chicago Bears	1	1	2/2	5/5	23
12/10	San Francisco 49ers	1	0	2/3	1/1	13
12/17	Los Angeles Rams	1	0	0/2	5/5	11
Totals		**13**	**2**	**15/28**	**41/41**	**176**

RUSHING - JIM TAYLOR, 1962

Taylor bested the great Jim Brown with this NFL-leading effort.

Date	Opponent	Att	Yds	Avg	LG	TD
9/16	Minnesota Vikings	17	75	4.4	14	0
9/23	St. Louis Cardinals	23	122	5.3	12	0
9/30	Chicago Bears	17	126	7.4	26	3
10/7	Detroit Lions	20	95	4.8	27	0
10/14	Minnesota Vikings	17	164	9.6	31	0
10/21	San Francisco 49ers	17	160	9.4	27	2
10/28	Baltimore Colts	16	68	4.3	t37	1
11/4	Chicago Bears	25	124	5.0	51	4
11/11	Philadelphia Eagles	25	141	5.6	26	4
11/18	Baltimore Colts	19	46	2.4	16	0
11/22	Detroit Lions	13	47	3.6	20	1
12/2	Los Angeles Rams	16	71	4.4	18	2
12/9	San Francisco 49ers	24	79	3.3	19	1
12/16	Los Angeles Rams	23	156	6.8	t28	1
Totals		**272**	**1,474**	**5.4**	**51**	**19**

KICKOFF RETS - DAVE HAMPTON, 1971

Hampton set Packers records with 1,314 yards on 46 returns.

Date	Opponent	Att	Yds	Avg	LG	TD
9/19	New York Giants	6	194	32.3	72	0
9/26	Denver Broncos	1	34	34.0	34	0
10/3	Cincinnati Bengals	2	115	57.5	80	0
10/10	Detroit Lions	6	140	23.3	31	0
10/17	Minnesota Vikings	DID NOT PLAY				
10/24	Los Angeles Rams	5	125	25.0	30	0
11/1	Detroit Lions	2	53	26.5	30	0
11/7	Chicago Bears	2	85	42.5	62	0
11/14	Minnesota Vikings	1	34	34.0	34	0
11/22	Atlanta Falcons	5	87	17.4	26	0
11/28	New Orleans Saints	5	189	37.8	t90	1
12/5	St. Louis Cardinals	4	103	25.8	32	0
12/12	Chicago Bears	3	73	24.3	32	0
12/19	Miami Dolphins	4	82	20.5	31	0
Totals		**46**	**1,314**	**28.6**	**t90**	**1**

FIELD GOALS - CHESTER MARCOL, 1972

A team record 33 field goals helped Marcol to the NFL scoring title.

Date	Opponent	FG	PAT	Tot
9/17	Cleveland Browns	4/6	2/2	14
9/24	Oakland Raiders	0/0	2/2	2
10/1	Dallas Cowboys	3/6	1/1	10
10/8	Chicago Bears	2/3	2/2	8
10/16	Detroit Lions	1/2	3/3	6
10/22	Atlanta Falcons	3/4	0/0	9
10/29	Minnesota Vikings	2/3	1/1	7
11/5	San Francisco 49ers	2/2	4/4	10
11/12	Chicago Bears	3/3	2/2	11
11/19	Houston Oilers	0/0	3/3	3
11/26	Washington Redskins	3/4	1/1	10
12/3	Detroit Lions	4/6	3/3	15
12/10	Minnesota Vikings	3/4	2/2	11
12/17	New Orleans Saints	3/4	3/3	12
Totals		**33/48**	**29/29**	**128**

PASSING - LYNN DICKEY, 1983

Dickey set a host of team records and led the NFC with 4,458 yards passing.

Date	Opponent	Att	Com	Yds	TD	In
9/4	Houston Oilers	31	27	333	5	1
9/11	Pittsburgh Steelers	20	14	290	3	0
9/18	Los Angeles Rams	36	22	288	1	3
9/26	New York Giants	28	16	283	0	1
10/2	Tampa Bay Buccaneers	15	10	267	3	1
10/9	Detroit Lions	37	21	214	1	2
10/17	Washington Redskins	31	22	387	3	1
10/23	Minnesota Vikings	41	23	383	2	3
10/30	Cincinnati Bengals	31	16	231	0	2
11/6	Cleveland Browns	33	20	228	4	3
11/13	Minnesota Vikings	27	13	180	2	1
11/20	Detroit Lions	17	10	123	2	0
11/27	Atlanta Falcons	37	25	366	3	3
12/4	Chicago Bears	34	16	345	1	1
12/12	Tampa Bay Buccaneers	36	24	278	0	3
12/18	Chicago Bears	30	10	262	2	4
Totals		**484**	**289**	**4,458**	**32**	**29**

RECEIVING - STERLING SHARPE, 1992

Sharpe set both a team and NFL record with 108 catches.

Date	Opponent	No	Yds	Avg	LG	TD
9/6	Minnesota Vikings	8	99	12.4	32	1
9/13	Tampa Bay Buccaneers	5	62	12.4	20	0
9/20	Cincinnati Bengals	7	109	15.6	42	1
9/27	Pittsburgh Steelers	2	93	46.5	t76	1
10/4	Atlanta Falcons	9	107	11.9	24	1
10/18	Cleveland Browns	4	48	12.0	20	0
10/25	Chicago Bears	9	144	16.0	45	1
11/1	Detroit Lions	6	84	14.0	t30	1
11/8	New York Giants	11	160	14.5	43	0
11/15	Philadelphia Eagles	7	116	16.6	34	1
11/22	Chicago Bears	5	79	15.8	t49	1
11/29	Tampa Bay Buccaneers	9	52	5.8	13	0
12/6	Detroit Lions	6	107	17.8	t65	2
12/13	Houston Oilers	6	46	7.7	13	1
12/20	Los Angeles Rams	8	110	13.8	18	2
12/27	Minnesota Vikings	6	45	7.5	11	0
Totals		**108**	**1,461**	**13.5**	**t76**	**13**

ALL-TIME RUSHERS

(Statistic kept since 1933; rankings based on total yards)

TOP TEN

Name	Att	Yds	Avg	LG	TD	100
Jim Taylor, 1958-66	1,811	8,207	4.53	t84	81	26
John Brockington, 1971-77	1,293	5,024	3.89	53	29	13
Tony Canadeo, 1941-44, 46-52	1,025	4,197	4.09	54	26	9
Clarke Hinkle, 1932-41	1,171	3,860	3.30	57	34	2
Gerry Ellis, 1980-86	836	3,826	4.58	71	25	5
Paul Hornung, 1957-62, 64-66	893	3,711	4.16	72	50	3
Donny Anderson, 1966-71	787	3,165	4.02	54	24	3
Eddie Lee Ivery, 1979-86	667	2,933	4.40	49	23	5
Tobin Rote, 1950-56	419	2,205	5.26	t55	29	3
Ted Fritsch, 1942-50	619	2,200	3.55	55	31	1

Name	Att	Yds	Avg	LG	TD	100
Howie Ferguson, 1953-58	544	2,120	3.90	57	6	4
Tom Moore, 1960-65	503	2,069	4.11	t77	20	3
Terdell Middleton, 1977-81	559	2,044	3.66	t76	15	5
Floyd Reid, 1950-56	459	1,964	4.28	t69	13	1
Barty Smith, 1974-80	544	1,942	3.57	33	18	0
Joe Laws, 1934-45	470	1,932	4.11		9	0
MacArthur Lane, 1972-74	484	1,711	3.54	41	7	2
Brent Fullwood, 1987-90	433	1,702	3.93	38	18	3
Elijah Pitts, 1961-69, 71	479	1,684	3.52	t34	28	0
Darrell Thompson, 1990-94	464	1,642	3.54	t60	7	2
Jessie Clark, 1983-87	379	1,588	4.19	80	9	1
Jim Grabowski, 1966-70	424	1,582	3.73	t36	8	2
Cecil Isbell, 1938-42	422	1,522	3.61		10	1
Bob Monnett, 1933-38	510	1,488	2.92		7	1
Walt Schlinkman, 1946-50	365	1,455	3.99	44	8	0
Edgar Bennett, 1992-94	398	1,387	3.48	t39	14	4
Bart Starr, 1956-71	247	1,308	5.30	39	15	0
Eric Torkelson, 1974-79, 81	351	1,307	3.72	29	8	0
Fred Cone, 1951-57	347	1,156	3.33	t41	12	0
Andy Uram, 1938-43	239	1,073	4.49	t97	4	2
Travis Williams, 1967-70	271	1,063	3.92	t39	6	1
Kenneth Davis, 1986-88	262	1,053	4.02	50	4	1
Don Majkowski, 1987-92	199	1,037	5.21	33	9	0
Ed Jankowski, 1937-41	275	1,002	3.64		8	0
Keith Woodside, 1988-91	259	976	3.77	t68	6	1
Willard Harrell, 1975-77	311	934	3.00	56	5	1
Vince Workman, 1989-92	242	927	3.83	44	10	1
Don McIlhenny, 1957-59	221	854	3.86	46	3	0
Lou Brock, 1940-45	254	804	3.17		10	0
Dave Hampton, 1969-71	195	787	4.04	53	7	0
Harlan Huckleby, 1980-85	242	779	3.22	23	10	0
Al Carmichael, 1953-58	166	712	4.29	t41	2	0
Billy Grimes, 1950-52	145	662	4.57	t73	6	1
George Sauer, 1935-37	190	656	3.45		6	0
Brett Favre, 1992-94	147	616	4.19	t36	4	0
Paul Ott Carruth, 1986-88	194	614	3.16	42	5	0
Reggie Cobb, 1994	153	579	3.78	30	3	0
Hank Bruder, 1931-39	190	569	2.99		5	0
Paul Miller, 1936-38	143	537	3.76		1	0
Bruce Smith, 1945-48	96	522	5.44	37	1	0
Irv Comp, 1943-49	255	502	1.97	34	7	0
Nate Simpson, 1977-79	153	497	3.25	40	1	1
Gary Ellerson, 1985-86	122	492	4.03	t37	5	0
Steve Atkins, 1979-81	120	467	3.89	60	2	1
Ben Wilson, 1967	103	453	4.40	40	2	1
Michael Haddix, 1989-90	142	446	3.14	13	0	0
Don Perkins, 1943-45	94	399	4.24	49	1	0
Joe Johnson, 1954-58	93	376	4.04	21	0	0
Vito (Babe) Parilli, 1952-53, 57-58	106	375	3.54	20	7	0
Charles Goldenberg, 1933-45	107	365	3.41		6	0
Lew Carpenter, 1959-63	64	359	5.61	t55	1	1
Earl Gros, 1962-63	77	358	4.65	26	4	0
Johnny Blood, 1929-33, 35-36	96	351	3.66		0	0
Bob Forte, 1946-50, 52-53	107	331	3.09	25	0	0
Perry Williams, 1969-73	103	329	3.19	14	1	0
Larry Coutre, 1950, 53	63	322	5.11	53	1	1
Ed Cody, 1947-48	82	321	3.91	t32	2	1
Chester Johnston, 1931, 34-37	101	309	3.06		1	0
Roy McKay, 1944-47	100	288	2.88	41	3	0
Roger Grove, 1931-35	70	287	4.10		1	0
Don Hutson, 1935-45	62	284	4.58	27	3	0
Earl (Jug) Girard, 1948-51	76	283	3.72	35	1	0
Hal Van Every, 1940-41	63	281	4.46		4	0
Del Rodgers, 1982, 84	71	269	3.79	15	1	0
Chuck Sample, 1942, 45	59	257	4.36	31	4	0

Name	Att	Yds	Avg	LG	TD	100
Kevin Willhite, 1987	53	251	4.74	61	0	1
James Lofton, 1978-86	31	245	7.90	t83	1	0
Mike Meade, 1982-83	69	243	3.52	19	1	0
David Whitehurst, 1977-83	77	242	3.14	19	7	0
Bobby Jack Floyd, 1952	61	236	3.87	17	1	0
Jim Gillette, 1947	50	207	4.14	26	0	0
Steve Odom, 1974-79	16	205	12.81	28	1	0
Tony Falkenstein, 1943	58	198	3.41	59	1	0
Larry Mason, 1988	48	194	4.04	17	0	0
Ralph Earhart, 1948-49	50	194	3.88	t72	1	0
Les Goodman, 1973-74	38	189	4.97	47	1	0
Paul Duhart, 1944	51	183	3.59	16	2	0
John Stephens, 1993	48	173	3.60	22	1	0
Randy Wright, 1984-88	55	173	3.15	27	3	0
Ray Crouse, 1984	53	169	3.19	14	0	0
Harry Sydney, 1992	51	163	3.20	19	2	0
Cliff Aberson, 1946	48	161	3.35	13	0	0
Veryl Switzer, 1954-55	31	160	5.16	38	0	0
Joe Francis, 1958-59	26	158	6.08	20	1	0
Jim Culbreath, 1977-79	47	153	3.26	18	0	0
Frank Balazs, 1939-41	38	147	3.87		1	0
Herman Fontenot, 1989-90	34	145	4.26	19	1	0
Terry Wells, 1975	33	139	4.21	25	0	0
Jack Jacobs, 1947-49	42	137	3.26	23	2	0
Ricky Patton, 1979	37	134	3.62	14	0	0
Lamar McHan, 1959-60	24	131	5.46	t35	1	0
Phillip Epps, 1982-88	10	121	12.10	34	1	0
Max McGee, 1954, 57-67	12	121	10.08	36	0	0
Bill Reichardt, 1952	39	121	3.10	14	1	0
Larry Buhler, 1939-41	41	121	2.95		0	0
Jerry Tagge, 1972-74	41	117	2.85	t41	3	0
George Paskvan, 1941	38	116	3.05	12	0	0
Anthony Dilweg, 1989-90	21	114	5.43	22	0	0
Jack Cloud, 1950-51	47	113	2.40	19	4	0
Jim Jensen, 1981-82	36	107	2.97	15	0	0
Chuck Mercein, 1967-69	31	105	3.39	15	2	0
Bob Summerhays, 1949-51	29	101	3.48	14	0	0
Allen Rice, 1991	30	100	3.33	21	0	0
Oscar E. Smith, 1948-49	36	100	2.78	11	0	0
LeShon Johnson, 1994	26	99	3.81	43	0	0
Lynn Dickey, 1976-77, 79-85	129	98	0.76	13	9	0
Mike Tomczak, 1991	17	93	5.47	48	1	0
Fred Provo, 1948	29	90	3.10	28	0	0
Scott Hunter, 1971-73	51	90	1.76	16	10	0
Walt Landers, 1978-79	24	81	3.38	14	0	0
Wuert Engelmann, 1930-33	23	79	3.43		0	0
Sterling Sharpe, 1988-94	23	72	3.13	26	0	0
Alan Risher, 1987	11	64	5.82	15	1	0
Bob Hudson, 1972	15	62	4.13	17	0	0
Don Chandler, 1965-67	2	60	30.00	33	0	0
Walter Stanley, 1985-88	6	58	9.67	24	0	0
Blair Kiel, 1990-91	9	55	6.11	26	1	0
Bob Cifers, 1949	23	52	2.26	19	0	0
Arnie Herber, 1930-40	173	52	0.30		1	0
Bill Butler, 1959	7	49	7.00	16	0	0
Carlos Brown, 1975-76	12	49	4.08	21	0	0
Russ Mosely, 1945-46	16	49	3.06	9	0	0
Ben Starret, 1942-45	16	48	3.00	13	2	0
Cliff Taylor, 1976	14	47	3.36	17	1	0
Ray Pelfrey, 1951-52	3	44	14.67	24	0	0
Johnny Papit, 1953	6	44	7.33	21	1	0
John Hadl, 1974-75	28	44	1.57	19	0	0
John Losch, 1956	19	43	2.26	8	0	0
Bob Nussbaumer, 1946, 51	29	43	1.48	16	0	0
Perry Kemp, 1988-91	6	42	7.00	14	0	0

Name	Att	Yds	Avg	LG	TD	100
Don Milan, 1975	4	41	10.25	15	0	0
Don Barton, 1953	7	40	5.71	14	0	0
Jeff Query, 1989-91	3	39	13.00	18	0	0
Dave Kopay, 1972	10	39	3.90	20	0	0
John Jefferson, 1981-84	4	38	9.50	15	0	0
James Hargrove, 1987	11	38	3.45	t7	1	0
Herm Schneidman, 1935-39	13	37	2.85		0	0
Zeke Bratkowski, 1963-68, 71	25	35	1.40	13	1	0
Dick Weisgerber, 1938-40, 42	11	34	3.09		0	0
Freddie Parker, 1987	8	33	4.13	17	0	0
Robert Brooks, 1992-94	6	31	5.17	21	0	0
John Roach, 1961-63	6	31	5.17	22	1	0
Jim Shanley, 1958	23	30	1.30	5	0	0
Herb Banet, 1937	9	29	3.22		0	0
Byron Bailey, 1953	13	29	2.23	13	0	0
Boyd Dowler, 1959-69	2	28	14.00	20	0	0
Ken Roskie, 1948	5	28	5.60	9	1	0
Bobby Douglass, 1978	4	27	6.25	17	0	0
Lee Weigel, 1987	10	26	2.60	7	0	0
Randy Johnson, 1976	5	25	5.00	11	0	0
Jon Staggers, 1972-74	5	25	5.00	t20	1	0
Clyde Goodnight, 1945-49	9	25	2.78	12	0	0
Stan Heath, 1949	10	25	2.50	18	1	0
Jerry Norton, 1963-64	3	24	8.00	24	0	0
J.R. Boone, 1953	7	24	3.43	24	0	0
Dom Moselle, 1951-52	12	23	1.92	7	1	0
Frank Purnell, 1957	5	22	4.40	7	0	0
Larry Hickman, 1960	7	22	3.14	4	0	0
Earl Witte, 1934	8	22	2.75		0	0
Clarence Self, 1952, 54-55	0	21	—	21	0	0
Bill Howton, 1952-58	4	20	5.00	11	0	0
John Sterling, 1987	5	20	4.00	9	0	0
Charles Casper, 1934	4	19	4.75		0	0
Beattie Feathers, 1940	4	19	4.75		0	0
Lavale Thomas, 1987	5	19	3.80	5	0	0
Buford McGee, 1992	8	19	2.38	4	0	0
Randy Walker, 1974	1	18	18.00	18	0	0
Carroll Dale, 1965-72	3	18	6.00	9	0	0
Gib Dawson, 1953	5	18	3.60	18	0	0
Paul Christman, 1950	7	18	2.57	4	1	0
Larry Morris, 1987	8	18	2.25	10	0	0
David Beverly, 1975-80	9	18	2.00	11	0	0
Steve Wagner, 1976-79	1	16	16.00	16	0	0
Gary Lewis, 1981-84	4	16	4.00	11	1	0
Dave Osborn, 1976	6	16	2.67	6	0	0
Bill Boedecker, 1950	8	16	2.00	8	0	0
Larry Craig, 1939-49	10	16	1.60	4	0	0
Claudis James, 1967-69	1	15	15.00	15	0	0
Dorsey Levens, 1994	5	15	3.00	5	0	0
Larry Krause, 1970-74	6	15	2.50	12	0	0
Ken Keuper, 1945-47	6	14	2.33	8	0	0
Aundra Thompson, 1977-81	12	14	1.17	16	0	0
Jim Ringo, 1953-63	0	13	—	13	0	0
Leland Glass, 1972-73	2	13	6.50	13	0	0
Norm (Buster) Mott, 1933	5	13	2.60		0	0
Junior Coffey, 1965	3	12	4.00	10	0	0
Ed Frutig, 1941, 45	1	11	11.00	11	0	0
Paul Staroba, 1973	1	11	11.00	11	0	0
Dexter McNabb, 1992-93	2	11	5.50	8	0	0
Chuck Fusina, 1986	7	11	1.57	6	0	0
Corey Harris, 1992	2	10	5.00	7	0	0
Ken Snelling, 1945	3	10	3.33	8	0	0
Hurdis McCrary, 1929-33	6	10	1.67		0	0
Bob Mann, 1950-54	2	9	4.50	9	0	0
Ron Kramer, 1957, 59-64	6	9	1.50	12	0	0
Clarence Thompson, 1939	6	9	1.50		0	0
Bob Kahler, 1942-44	9	9	1.00	13	0	0
Jim Zorn, 1985	10	9	0.90	8	0	0
Paul Held, 1955	1	8	8.00	8	0	0
Ward Cuff, 1947	1	7	7.00	7	0	0
Jack Concannon, 1974	3	7	2.33	6	1	0
Mark Brunell, 1994	6	7	1.17	t5	1	0
Don Highsmith, 1973	7	7	1.00	4	0	0
John Howell, 1938	7	7	1.00		0	0
John Kirby, 1949	3	6	2.00	8	0	0
Bob Adkins, 1940-41, 45	1	5	5.00	5	0	0
Tommy Crutcher, 1964-67, 71-72	1	5	5.00	5	0	0
Charles Jordan, 1994	1	5	5.00	5	0	0
Barry Smith, 1974-75	1	5	5.00	5	0	0
Gerald Tinker, 1975	1	5	5.00	5	0	0
Wayland Becker, 1936-38	2	5	2.50	3	0	0
Frank Patrick, 1970-72	2	5	2.50	3	0	0
Allen Jacobs, 1965	3	5	1.60	2	0	0
Vickey Ray Anderson, 1980	4	5	1.25	4	0	0
Frank Mestnick, 1963	1	4	4.00	4	0	0
Bill Robinson, 1952	3	4	1.33	4	0	0
Albin (Rip) Collins, 1951	5	4	0.80	6	0	0
Jim Salsbury, 1957-58	0	3	—	3	0	0
Paul Coffman, 1978-85	1	3	3.00	3	0	0
Rich McGeorge, 1970-78	1	3	3.00	3	0	0
Don Zimmerman, 1976	1	3	3.00	3	0	0
Kelly Cook, 1987	2	3	1.50	2	0	0
Aubrey Matthews, 1988	3	3	1.00	4	0	0
Charles Wilson, 1990-91	3	3	1.00	5	0	0
Marcus Wilson, 1992-94	6	3	0.50	5	0	0
Al Cannava, 1950	1	2	2.00	2	0	0
Harry Mattos, 1936	1	2	2.00	2	0	0
Claude Perry, 1927-35	1	2	2.00	2	0	0
Patrick Scott, 1987-88	1	2	2.00	2	0	0
Alex Urban, 1941, 44-45	1	2	2.00	2	0	0
Rich Campbell, 1981-84	2	2	1.00	5	0	0
Patrick Collins, 1988	2	2	1.00	1	0	0
Jim Lankas, 1943	2	2	1.00	1	0	0
Lee Morris, 1987	2	2	1.00	4	0	0
Lindell Pearson, 1952	2	2	1.00	2	0	0
Ed West, 1984-92	2	2	1.00	t2	1	0
Perry Moss, 1948	5	2	0.40	2	0	0
Jackie Harris, 1990-92	1	1	1.00	1	0	0
Dale Livingston, 1970	1	1	1.00	1	0	0
Jim Del Gaizo, 1973	4	1	0.25	3	0	0
Herman Rohrig, 1941, 46-47	42	1	0.02	18	0	0
Wally Dreyer, 1950	1	0	0.00	0	0	0
Vince Ferragamo, 1986	1	0	0.00	0	0	0
Tony Hunter, 1987	1	0	0.00	0	0	0
Charlie Leigh, 1974	1	0	0.00	0	0	0
Paul McJulien, 1991-92	1	0	0.00	0	0	0
Frankie Neal, 1987	1	0	0.00	0	0	0
Lester Peterson, 1932, 34	1	0	0.00	0	0	0
Guy Prather, 1981-85	1	0	0.00	0	0	0
Bill Renner, 1986-87	1	0	0.00	0	0	0
Al Romine, 1955, 58	1	0	0.00	0	0	0
Karl Swanke, 1980-86	1	0	0.00	0	0	0
Dave Davis, 1971-72	2	0	0.00	0	0	0
Dennis Sproul, 1978	2	0	0.00	0	0	0
Ray Stachowicz, 1981-82	2	0	0.00	0	0	0
Jim Lawrence, 1939	4	0	0.00	0	0	0
Ty Detmer, 1993-94	1	-2	-2.00	-2	0	0
Ken Payne, 1974-77	1	-2	-2.00	-2	0	0
Gene Wilson, 1947-48	1	-2	-2.00	-2	0	0
Dennis Claridge, 1965	2	-3	-1.50	1	0	0
Paul Winslow, 1960	2	-3	-1.50	3	0	0
Bob Garrett, 1954	1	-3	-3.00	-3	0	0
Dick Gordon, 1973	1	-4	-4.00	-4	0	0
Bobby Thomason, 1951	5	-5	-1.00	10	0	0
Clive Rush, 1953	1	-6	-6.00	-6	0	0
Cal Clemmens, 1936	3	-8	-2.67		0	0
Tom O'Malley, 1950	1	-9	-9.00	-9	0	0
Don Horn, 1967-70*	12	-12	-1.00	4	1	0
Packers, 1933-94*	**27,707**	**106,019**	**3.83**	**t97**	**835**	**114**
Opponents, 1933-94	28,381	110,263	3.89	t96	823	—

*The 1933-94 totals for the Packers include 95 rushes for 331 yards and three touchdowns by Clarke Hinkle in 1932. The totals also include 27 rushes for 130 yards and no touchdowns by Johnny Blood in 1932. For a more accurate comparison between the Packers and Opponents for the 62-year period, subtract 122 rushes, 461 yards, and three touchdowns. This will allow for an exact 1933-94 comparison.

Below is a list of rushing touchdowns scored by Packers who played before 1933. Since Hinkle's three touchdowns are accounted for above, they do not appear below.

1921-32 RUSHING TOUCHDOWNS

Name	No.	Name	No.
Verne Lewellen, 1924-32	37	Faye (Mule) Wilson, 1931	2
Bo Molenda, 1929-32	9	Norm Barry, 1921	1
Curly Lambeau, 1921-29	8	Lynn (Tubby) Howard, 1921-22	1
Myrt Basing, 1923-27	7	Clyde Taugher, 1922	1
Carl (Cully) Lidberg, 1926, 29-30	7	Eddie Usher, 1922, 24	1
Hurdis McCrary, 1929-32	7	Tommy Mills, 1922-23	1
Johnny (Blood) McNally, 1929-31	5	Charlie Mathys, 1922-26	1
Eddie Kotal, 1925-29	4	Marty Norton, 1925	1
Warren Hendrian, 1924	3	Everett (Pid) Purdy, 1925	1
Jack Harris, 1925-26	3	Harry O'Boyle, 1928, 32	1
Rex Enright, 1926-27	3	Paul Fitzgibbons, 1930-32	1
Hank Bruder, 1931-32	3	Russ Saunders, 1931	1
Art Schmael, 1921	2	**Packers, 1921-32**	**115**
Wuert Engelmann, 1930-32	2	Opponents, 1921-32	46
Arnie Herber, 1930-32	2		

ALL-TIME RECEIVERS

(Statistic kept since 1933; rankings based on number of receptions)

Name	No	Yds	Avg	LG	TD	100
Sterling Sharpe, 1988-94	595	8,134	13.67	t79	65	29
James Lofton, 1978-86	530	9,656	18.22	t80	49	32
Don Hutson, 1935-45	488	7,991	16.38	t92	99	24
Boyd Dowler, 1959-69	448	6,918	15.44	t91	40	19
Max McGee, 1954, 57-67	345	6,346	18.39	t82	50	16
Paul Coffman, 1978-85	322	4,223	13.11	t78	39	6
Bill Howton, 1952-58	303	5,581	18.42	t90	43	17
Carroll Dale, 1965-72	275	5,422	19.72	t89	35	13
Gerry Ellis, 1980-86	267	2,514	9.42	t69	10	2
Ed West, 1984-94	202	2,321	11.49	50	25	2

Name	No	Yds	Avg	LG	TD	100
Phillip Epps, 1982-88	192	2,884	15.02	63	14	2
Jim Taylor, 1958-66	187	1,505	8.05	41	10	0
Perry Kemp, 1988-91	182	2,341	12.86	39	6	1
Rich McGeorge, 1970-78	175	2,370	13.54	51	13	0
Ron Kramer, 1957, 59-64	170	2,594	15.23	55	15	0
Eddie Lee Ivery, 1979-86	162	1,612	9.95	62	7	1
Edgar Bennett, 1992-94	150	1,096	7.31	40	5	1
John Jefferson, 1981-84	149	2,253	15.12	50	11	5
Keith Woodside, 1988-91	144	1,248	8.67	t49	2	0
John Brockington, 1971-77	138	1,075	7.79	t48	3	0
Gray Knafelc, 1954-62	134	1,930	14.40	53	21	0
Jackie Harris, 1990-93	133	1,620	12.18	t66	9	1
Paul Hornung, 1957-62, 64-66	130	1,480	11.38	t83	12	1
Howie Ferguson, 1953-58	127	1,079	8.50	49	1	1
Donny Anderson, 1966-71	125	1,725	13.80	51	6	1
Barty Smith, 1974-80	120	979	8.16	42	3	0
Bob Mann, 1950-54	109	1,629	14.94	52	17	2
Marv Fleming, 1963-69	109	1,300	11.93	t53	12	0
Ken Payne, 1974-77	103	1,395	13.54	t57	5	3
Walter Stanley, 1985-88	101	1,831	18.13	t70	5	5
Nolan Luhn, 1945-49	100	1,525	15.25	44	13	2
Jessie Clark, 1983-87	99	925	9.34	t75	6	0
Elijah Pitts, 1961-69, 71	97	1,182	12.19	84	6	1
Vince Workman, 1989-92	97	691	7.12	25	5	0
Aundra Thompson, 1977-81	95	1,573	16.56	57	7	2
Robert Brooks, 1992-94	90	954	10.60	35	5	1
Clyde Goodnight, 1945-49	89	1,632	18.34	t75	13	2
MacArthur Lane, 1972-74	87	855	9.83	t68	4	0
Steve Odom, 1974-79	84	1,613	19.20	t95	11	1
Milt Gantenbein, 1931-40	79	1,228	15.54	t77	7	0
Joe Laws, 1934-45	79	1,041	13.18	50	10	0
Terdell Middleton, 1977-81	78	659	8.45	50	3	0
Al Carmichael, 1953-58	75	994	13.25	63	3	0
Fred Cone, 1951-57	75	852	11.36	t69	4	0
Floyd (Breezy) Reid, 1950-56	72	868	12.06	t81	5	0
Herman Fontenot, 1989-90	71	665	9.37	59	4	0
Tom Moore, 1960-65	71	645	9.08	t45	7	0
Willard Harrell, 1975-77	70	656	9.37	t69	4	0
Tony Canadeo, 1941-44, 46-52	69	579	8.39	46	5	0
Jon Staggers, 1972-74	65	985	15.15	63	4	0
Jim Grabowski, 1966-70	65	575	8.85	t67	4	0
Jeff Query, 1989-91	64	902	14.09	t47	4	0
Joe Johnson, 1954-58	64	652	10.19	61	4	0
Carleton Elliott, 1951-54	60	581	9.68	33	6	0
Lou Brock, 1940-45	59	761	12.90	t52	6	0
Eric Torkelson, 1974-79, 81	59	469	7.95	31	0	0
Andy Uram, 1938-43	58	1,083	18.67	t64	10	1
Paul Ott Carruth, 1986-88	58	423	7.29	31	3	0
Johnny Blood, 1929-33, 35-36	56	934	16.68	t70	11	1
Ted Cook, 1948-50	54	780	14.44	50	4	0
Harlan Huckleby, 1980-85	53	411	7.75	39	3	0
Harry Jacunski, 1939-44	52	985	18.94	t86	6	2
Clarke Hinkle, 1932-41	50	537	10.74	t69	9	0
Travis Williams, 1967-70	49	530	10.82	t60	5	0
Harry Sydney, 1992	49	384	7.84	20	1	0
Don McIlhenny, 1957-59	46	459	9.98	t55	4	0
Kenneth Davis, 1986-88	46	333	7.24	35	1	0
Clarence Weathers, 1990-91	45	540	12.00	29	1	0
Carl Mulleneaux, 1938-41, 45-46	44	850	19.32	56	11	1
Brent Fullwood, 1987-90	44	370	8.41	67	1	0
Ollie Smith, 1976-77	42	721	17.17	47	1	1
Barry Smith, 1973-75	41	604	14.73	t27	4	0
Darrell Thompson, 1990-94	41	330	8.05	43	1	0

Name	No	Yds	Avg	LG	TD	100
Ray Pelfrey, 1951-52	39	472	12.10	49	5	0
Frankie Neal, 1987	36	420	11.67	38	3	0
Reggie Cobb, 1994	35	299	8.54	t37	1	0
Aubrey Matthews, 1988-89	33	367	11.12	25	2	0
Billy Grimes, 1950-52	32	431	13.47	t96	2	0
Mark Clayton, 1993	32	331	10.34	32	3	0
Veryl Switzer, 1954-55	31	269	8.68	28	3	0
Anthony Morgan, 1993-94	29	405	13.97	t47	4	1
Al Baldwin, 1950	28	555	19.82	t85	3	1
Patrick Scott, 1987-88	28	354	12.64	41	1	0
Michael Haddix, 1989-90	28	205	7.32	28	1	0
John Spilis, 1969-71	27	446	16.52	39	1	0
Bob Monnett, 1933-38	27	303	11.22		0	0
Charles Wilson, 1990-91	26	389	14.96	t75	1	0
Leland Glass, 1972-73	26	380	14.62	31	1	0
Bob Long, 1964-67	25	487	19.48	t62	4	1
John Hilton, 1970	25	350	14.00	t65	4	0
Dave Hampton, 1969-71	25	276	11.04	50	3	0
Ted Fritsch, 1942-50	25	227	9.08	35	1	0
Roger Grove, 1931-35	24	340	14.17		3	0
Bob Forte, 1946-50, 52-53	24	242	10.08	28	3	0
Hank Bruder, 1931-39	23	344	14.96		3	0
Steve Pritko, 1949-50	23	219	9.52	24	1	0
LaVern (Lavvie) Dilweg, 1927-34	22	360	16.36		2	0
Ralph Earhart, 1948-49	22	303	13.77	t64	2	0
Ron Lewis, 1992-94	22	281	12.77	38	0	0
Al Rose, 1932-36	21	297	14.14		3	0
Gary Lewis, 1981-84	21	285	13.57	49	1	0
Ray Riddick, 1940-42, 46	20	285	14.25		1	0
Mike Meade, 1982-83	19	105	5.53	t31	2	0
Paul Miller, 1936-38	18	215	11.94	34	3	0
Larry Coutre, 1950, 53	18	202	11.22	t77	2	0
Jim Keane, 1952	18	191	10.61	t29	1	0
Steve Atkins, 1979-81	18	138	7.67	19	1	0
Bill Kelley, 1949	17	222	13.06	32	1	0
Lew Carpenter, 1959-63	17	213	12.53	23	0	0
Dan Ross, 1986	17	143	8.41	16	1	0
Sanjay Beach, 1992	17	122	7.18	20	1	0
Nate Simpson, 1977-79	17	69	4.06	14	0	0
Earl (Jug) Girard, 1948-51	16	324	20.25	t75	2	1
Lee Morris, 1987	16	259	16.19	t46	1	1
Jack Clancy, 1970	16	244	15.25	t33	2	0
Joel Mason, 1942-45	16	202	12.63	21	2	0
Mark Chmura, 1993-94	16	178	11.13	27	0	0
Steve Meilinger, 1958, 60	15	182	12.13	23	1	0
Cecil Isbell, 1938-42	15	174	11.60	49	0	0
Wayland Becker, 1936-38	14	245	17.50	49	1	0
Dom Moselle, 1951-52	14	233	16.64	85	2	0
Ron Cassidy, 1979-81, 83-84	14	233	16.64	43	0	0
Clive Rush, 1953	14	190	13.57	24	0	1
Larry Craig, 1939-49	14	155	11.07	28	0	0
Gary Ellerson, 1985-86	14	145	10.36	32	0	0
Ben Wilson, 1967	14	88	6.29	21	0	0
Preston Dennard, 1985	13	182	14.00	34	2	0
LeShon Johnson, 1994	13	168	12.92	33	0	0
Herman Rohrig, 1941, 46-47	13	94	7.23	21	0	0
Jim Gillette, 1947	12	224	18.67	50	1	0
Keith Paskett, 1987	12	188	15.67	t47	1	0
Oscar E. Smith, 1948-49	12	121	10.08	49	0	0
Perry Williams, 1969-73	12	118	9.83	24	0	0
Clint Didier, 1988-89	12	108	9.00	t24	2	0
Carl Bland, 1989-90	11	164	14.91	t46	1	0
Arnie Herber, 1930-40	11	155	14.09	25	2	0

Name	No	Yds	Avg	LG	TD	100
Bobby Jack Floyd, 1952	11	129	11.73	44	0	0
Charles Goldenberg, 1933-45	11	111	10.09	21	1	0
Bernie Scherer, 1936-38	10	193	19.30	t78	3	0
Dave Davis, 1971-72	10	178	17.80	t68	1	0
Walter Tullis, 1978-79	10	173	17.30	t52	1	0
Bob Nussbaumer, 1946, 51	10	143	14.30	35	0	0
Bill Anderson, 1965-66	10	119	11.90	t27	1	0
Dick Evans, 1940, 43	10	111	11.10	30	0	0
Randy Vataha, 1977	10	109	10.90	20	0	0
Paul Duhart, 1944	9	176	19.56	32	2	0
George Sauer, 1935-37	9	142	15.78		0	0
Ray Crouse, 1984	9	93	10.33	25	1	0
Jim Culbreath, 1977-79	9	84	9.33	19	0	0
Claudis James, 1967-69	8	148	18.50	24	2	0
Lester Peterson, 1932, 34	8	139	17.38		0	0
Byron Bailey, 1953	8	119	14.88	50	0	1
Larry Mason, 1988	8	84	10.50	39	1	0
Del Rodgers, 1982, 84	8	79	9.88	22	0	0
Chester Johnston, 1931, 34-37	8	70	8.75		1	0
Jim Jensen, 1981-82	8	67	8.38	16	1	0
Herm Schneidman, 1935-39	7	119	17.00t	t46	2	0
John Losch, 1956	7	85	12.14	43	0	0
Don Summers, 1987	7	83	11.86	17	1	0
Reggie Johnson, 1994	7	79	11.29	24	0	0
Erik Affholter, 1991	7	68	9.71	20	0	0
Les Goodman, 1973-74	7	38	5.43	12	0	0
Fred Nixon, 1980-81	6	105	17.50	32	0	0
Ray Wheba, 1944	6	67	11.17	17	0	0
Buford McGee, 1990	6	60	10.00	15	0	0
J.R. Boone, 1953	6	55	9.17	18	1	0
Ricky Patton, 1979	6	41	6.83	9	0	0
Kevin Willhite, 1987	6	37	6.17	12	0	0
Jack Cloud, 1950-51	6	35	5.83	13	1	0
Chuck Sample, 1942, 45	6	35	5.83	t10	1	0
Terry Wells, 1975	6	11	1.83	4	0	0
Bert Askson, 1975-77	5	78	15.60	34	1	0
Leon Manley, 1950-51	5	66	13.20	18	0	0
Walt Landers, 1978-79	5	60	12.00	t55	1	0
Gene Wilson, 1947-48	5	57	11.40	15	0	0
Dan Orlich, 1949-51	5	48	9.60	12	0	0
Hal Van Every, 1940-41	5	44	8.80	23	0	0
John Stephens, 1993	5	31	6.20	10	0	0
Jeff Wilner, 1994	5	31	6.20	9	0	0
Bill Reichardt, 1952	5	18	3.60	12	0	0
Alex Urban, 1941, 44-45	4	91	22.75	55	1	0
Mike Moffitt, 1986	4	87	21.75	34	0	0
Gerald Tinker, 1975	4	84	21.00	t35	1	0
Bob Adkins, 1940-41, 45	4	73	18.25	t55	1	0
Len Garrett, 1971-72	4	66	16.50	21	0	0
Wuert Engelmann, 1930-33	4	54	13.50		1	0
Bruce Smith, 1945-48	4	50	12.50	t36	1	0
Bill Larson, 1980	4	37	9.25	21	1	0
Henry Childs, 1984	4	32	8.00	17	0	0
Terry Mickens, 1994	4	31	7.75	11	0	0
Chuck Mercein, 1967-69	4	12	3.00	9	0	0
Fred Provo, 1948	4	-9	-2.25	3	0	0
Irv Comp, 1943-49	3	66	22.00	50	2	0
Ed Jankowski, 1937-41	3	65	21.67	46	1	0
Allen Brown, 1966-67	3	43	14.33	17	0	0
Tony Falkenstein, 1943	3	39	13.00	18	0	0
Bob Tenner, 1935	3	38	12.67	29	0	0
Al Norgard, 1934	3	29	9.67	22	0	0
Abner Wimberly, 1950-52	3	28	9.33	10	0	0
Freddie Parker, 1987	3	22	7.33	13	0	0
Dave Kopay, 1972	3	19	6.33	8	0	0
Jim Shanley, 1958	3	13	4.33	7	0	0
Don Perkins, 1943-45	3	12	4.00	10	0	0
Walt Schlinkman, 1946-50	3	-1	-0.33	5	0	0
Don Wells, 1946-49	2	74	37.00	65	0	0
Kitrick Taylor, 1992	2	63	31.50	t35	1	0
Lavale Thomas, 1987	2	52	26.00	t30	1	0
Don Barton, 1953	2	51	25.50	t42	1	0
Ed Frutig, 1941, 45	2	40	20.00	34	0	0
Ken Keuper, 1945-47	2	37	18.50	26	0	0
Scott Bolton, 1988	2	33	16.50	18	0	0
Derrick Harden, 1987	2	29	14.50	15	0	0
Bob Jeter, 1963-70	2	25	12.50	23	0	0
John Thompson, 1979-82	2	24	12.00	t23	2	0
Ben Smith, 1933	2	23	11.50	13	0	0
Larry Krause, 1970-71, 73-74	2	22	11.00	11	0	0
Bob Kahler, 1942-44	2	21	10.50	12	0	0
Cliff Taylor, 1976	2	21	10.50	18	0	0
Joe Carter, 1942	2	19	9.50	t10	1	0
Frank Balazs, 1939-41	2	18	9.00	11	0	0
Mike Donohoe, 1973-74	2	18	9.00	10	0	0
Marcus Wilson, 1992-94	2	18	9.00	11	0	0
Patrick Collins, 1988	2	17	8.50	9	0	0
Frank Purnell, 1957	2	16	8.00	15	0	0
John Spagnola, 1989	2	13	6.50	14	0	0
Corey Harris, 1992-94	2	11	5.50	6	0	0

Name	No	Yds	Avg	LG	TD	100
Allen Rice, 1991	2	10	5.00	7	0	0
Mark Lewis, 1985-87	2	7	3.50	t4	2	0
Blake Moore, 1984-85	2	6	3.00	t3	2	0
Vickey Ray Anderson, 1980	2	2	1.00	1	0	0
Tobin Rote, 1950-56	1	39	—	t28	1	0
Dick Weisgerber, 1938-40, 42	1	37	37.00	37	0	0
Bob Summerhays, 1949-51	1	34	34.00	34	0	0
Ray Nitschke, 1958-72	1	34	34.00	34	0	0
Al Cannava, 1950	1	28	28.00	28	0	0
Keith Ranspot, 1942	1	25	25.00	t25	1	0
Paul Staroba, 1973	1	23	23.00	23	0	0
Jim Gueno, 1976-80	1	23	23.00	23	0	0
Jim Lawrence, 1939	1	21	21.00	21	0	0
Earl Gros, 1962-63	1	19	19.00	19	0	0
Pete Lammons, 1972	1	19	19.00	19	0	0
Cal Clemmens, 1936	1	18	18.00	18	0	0
Charlie Hall, 1971-76	1	18	18.00	18	0	0
Cornelius Redick, 1987	1	18	18.00	18	0	0
Connie Mack Berry, 1940	1	17	17.00	17	0	0
Lee Weigel, 1987	1	17	17.00	17	0	0
Lindell Pearson, 1952	1	16	16.00	16	0	0
Harper Davis, 1951	1	15	15.00	15	0	0
Bill Roberts, 1956	1	14	14.00	14	0	0
Don Zimmerman, 1976	1	13	13.00	13	0	0
Dick Moje, 1951	1	11	11.00	11	0	0
George Svendsen, 1935-37, 40-41	1	11	11.00	11	0	0
A.D. Williams, 1959	1	11	11.00	11	0	0
Bill Boedecker, 1950	1	10	10.00	10	0	0
Russ Mosley, 1945-46	1	10	10.00	10	0	0
Dorsey Levens, 1994	1	9	9.00	9	0	0
Ace Loomis, 1951-52	1	9	9.00	9	0	0
Syd Kitson, 1980-81, 83-84	1	9	9.00	9	0	0
Mel Jackson, 1976-80	1	8	8.00	8	0	0
Ace Prescott, 1946	1	8	8.00	8	0	0
Lenny Taylor, 1984	1	8	8.00	8	0	0
Nolan Franz, 1986	1	7	7.00	7	0	0
Herb Banet, 1937	1	6	6.00	6	0	0
James Hargrove, 1987	1	6	6.00	6	0	0
Val Jansante, 1951	1	6	6.00	6	0	0
Ben Starret, 1942-45	1	6	6.00	6	0	0
Bob Cifers, 1949	1	5	5.00	5	0	0
Albin (Rip) Collins, 1951	1	5	5.00	5	0	0
Ed Cody, 1947-48	1	2	2.00	2	0	0
Joey Hackett, 1987-88	1	2	2.00	t2	1	0
Karl Swanke, 1980-86	1	2	2.00	t2	1	0
Clarence Thompson, 1939	1	1	1.00	1	0	0
Bill Butler, 1959	1	-2	-2.00	-2	0	0
Brett Favre	1	-7	-7.00	-7	0	0
Unaccounted for	1	30	—	—	0	-
Packers, 1933-94*	**11,246**	**149,394**	**13.28**	**t96**	**1,000**	**206**
Opponents, 1933-94	11,239	142,656	12.69	t98	878	—

*The 1933-94 totals for the Packers include 14 receptions for 168 yards and three touchdowns by Johnny (Blood) McNally in 1932. For a more accurate comparison between the Packers and Opponents for the 62-year period, subtract Blood's 1932 statistics. This will allow for an exact 1933-94 comparison.

Below is a list of receiving touchdowns scored by Packers prior to 1933. Since Blood's three touchdowns are accounted for above, they do not appear below.

1921-32 RECEIVING TOUCHDOWNS

Name	TD	Name	TD
Johnny (Blood) McNally, 1929-31	17	Rex Enright, 1926-27	2
Verne Lewellen, 1924-32	12	Larry Marks, 1928	2
LaVern (Lavvie) Dilweg, 1927-32	10	Tom Nash, 1929-32	2
Walter (Tillie) Voss, 1924	5	Paul Fitzgibbons, 1930-32	2
Eddie Kotal, 1925-29	5	Bill (Gus) DuMoe, 1921	1
Charley Mathys, 1922-26	4	Tommy Cronin, 1922	1
Marty Norton, 1925	4	Lyle (Cowboy) Wheeler, 1921-23	1
Dick O'Donnell, 1924-30	4	Len Hearden, 1924	1
Hurdis McCrary, 1929-32	4	Jim Crowley, 1925	1
Wuert Engelmann, 1930-32	4	Joseph (Red) Dunn, 1927-31	1
Roger Grove, 1931-32	4	Roy Baker, 1928-29	1
Hank Bruder, 1931-32	4	Arnie Herber, 1930-31	1
Curly Lambeau, 1921-29	3	Robert (Cal) Hubbard, 1929-32	1
Tommy Mills, 1922-23	2	Milt Gantenbein, 1931	1
Myrt Basing, 1923-27	2	**Packers, 1921-32**	**104**
Dick Flaherty, 1926-27	2	Opponents, 1921-32	50

ALL-TIME PASSERS

(Statistic kept since 1933; rankings based on total yards)

Name	Att	Com	Yds	Pct	TD	In	Rate
Bart Starr, 1956-71	3,149	1,808	24,718	57.42	152	138	80.5
Lynn Dickey, 1976-77, 79-85	2,831	1,592	21,369	56.23	133	151	73.8
Tobin Rote, 1950-56	1,854	826	11,535	44.55	89	119	54.4
Don Majkowski, 1987-92	1,607	889	10,870	55.32	56	56	73.4
Brett Favre, 1992-94	1,575	983	10,412	62.41	70	51	83.0
Randy Wright, 1984-88	1,119	602	7,106	53.80	31	57	61.4
Arnie Herber, 1930-40	1,006	410	6,749	40.76	64	90	47.9
David Whitehurst, 1977-83	980	504	6,205	51.43	28	51	59.2
Cecil Isbell, 1938-42	818	411	5,945	50.24	61	52	72.6
Vito (Babe) Parilli, 1952-53, 57-58	602	258	3,983	42.86	31	61	42.9

Name	Att	Com	Yds	Pct	TD	In	Rate
Irv Comp, 1943-49	519	213	3,354	41.04	28	52	41.6
John Hadl, 1974-75	537	280	3,167	52.14	9	29	53.2
Zeke Bratkowski, 1963-68, 71	416	220	3,147	52.88	21	29	65.5
Scott Hunter, 1971-73	446	196	2,904	43.95	15	30	49.0
Jack Jacobs, 1947-49	442	193	2,518	43.67	21	41	39.4
Don Horn, 1967-70	284	139	2,291	48.94	16	22	63.0
Bob Monnett, 1933-38	336	158	2,227	47.02	29	26	65.4
Tony Canadeo, 41-44, 46-52	268	105	1,642	39.18	16	20	49.1
Jerry Tagge, 1972-74	281	136	1,583	48.40	3	17	44.2
Mike Tomczak, 1991	238	128	1,490	53.78	11	9	72.6
Lamar McHan, 1959-60	199	81	1,322	40.70	11	14	52.8
Bobby Thomason, 1951	221	125	1,306	56.56	11	9	73.5
Anthony Dilweg, 1989-90	193	102	1,274	52.85	8	7	72.3
Earl (Jug) Girard, 1948-51	189	66	998	34.92	5	13	33.3
Blair Kiel, 1990-91	135	80	865	59.26	5	4	78.2
Jim Zorn, 1985	123	56	794	45.53	4	6	57.4
John Roach, 1961-63	100	41	653	41.00	4	8	43.5
Roy McKay, 1944-47	103	38	592	36.89	6	11	36.6
Alan Risher, 1987	74	44	564	59.46	3	3	80.0
Paul Christman, 1950	126	51	545	40.48	7	7	49.2
Lou Brock, 1940-45	67	19	519	28.36	7	5	63.1
Carlos Brown, 1975-76	78	29	396	37.18	3	6	35.0
Hal Van Every, 1940-41	71	23	394	32.39	4	8	31.4
Rich Campbell, 1981-84	68	31	386	45.59	3	9	38.8
Paul Hornung, 1957-62, 64-66	55	24	383	43.64	5	4	67.5
Jack Concannon, 1974	54	28	381	51.85	1	3	57.8
Stan Heath, 1949	106	26	355	24.53	1	14	4.6
Jim Del Gaizo, 1973	62	27	318	43.55	2	6	30.9
Clarke Hinkle, 1932-41	53	25	293	47.17	0	5	25.1
Vince Ferragamo, 1986	40	23	283	57.50	1	3	56.6
Joe Francis, 1958-59	49	20	266	40.82	2	3	46.8
Tom Moore, 1960-65	16	10	261	62.50	4	1	119.8
Randy Johnson, 1976	35	21	249	60.00	0	1	69.8
George Sauer, 1935-37	25	11	203	44.00	1	6	46.3
Cliff Aberson, 1946	41	14	184	34.15	0	5	9.7
Johnny Blood, 1929-33, 35-36	41	14	184	34.15	1	3	26.9
Don Milan, 1975	32	15	181	46.88	1	1	62.1
Chuck Fusina, 1986	32	19	178	59.38	0	1	61.7
Joe Laws, 1934-45	36	10	163	27.78	3	6	34.1
Bob Garrett, 1954	30	15	143	50.00	1	3	49.7
Willard Harrell, 1975-77	10	5	134	50.00	4	1	95.8
David Beverly, 1975-80	6	4	129	66.67	0	0	109.7
Elijah Pitts, 1961-69, 71	9	4	113	44.44	1	0	128.2
Frank Patrick, 1970-72	23	8	107	34.78	0	2	14.2
Ron Widby, 1972	2	2	102	100.0	1	0	158.3
Herman Rohrig, 1941, 46-47	9	3	100	33.33	1	1	73.6
Mark Brunell, 1994	27	12	95	44.44	0	0	53.8
Bobby Douglass, 1978	12	5	90	41.67	1	1	61.1
Dennis Sproul, 1978	13	5	87	38.46	0	0	62.0
Roger Grove, 1931-35	13	6	78	46.15	0	0	65.5
Gerry Ellis, 1980-86	12	4	71	33.33	1	0	47.6
Bob Forte, 1946-50, 52-53	14	8	64	57.14	1	1	62.8
Jerry Norton, 1963-64	5	3	64	60.00	1	0	143.8
John Losch, 1956	1	1	63	100.0	0	0	158.3
Andy Uram, 1938-43	7	2	60	28.57	1	1	62.8
Hank Bruder, 1931-39	20	6	53	30.00	0	2	0.0
Eddie Lee Ivery, 1979-86	4	2	50	50.00	0	0	95.8
Bill Troup, 1980	12	4	48	33.33	0	3	6.9
Ray Peterson, 1937	6	3	47	50.00	0	0	76.4
James Lofton, 1978-86	5	1	43	20.00	0	0	62.9
Paul Duhart, 1944	13	4	42	30.77	0	0	41.2
MacArthur Lane, 1972-74	5	3	42	60.00	1	0	126.7
Donny Anderson, 1966-71	10	4	40	40.00	2	0	91.7

Name	Att	Com	Yds	Pct	TD	In	Rate
Don Hutson, 1935-45	11	1	38	9.09	1	2	32.2
Harry Mattos, 1936	12	4	32	33.33	0	2	2.8
Tom O'Malley, 1950	15	4	31	26.67	0	6	0.0
Willie Gillus, 1987	5	2	28	40.00	0	0	58.8
Paul Held, 1955	4	2	27	50.00	0	0	71.9
Ty Detmer, 1993-94	5	3	26	60.00	0	0	73.8
Perry Moss, 1948	17	4	20	23.53	0	0	39.6
Fred Provo, 1948	1	1	20	100.00	1	0	158.3
Steve Pisarkiewicz, 1980	5	2	19	40.00	0	1	51.3
Jim Lawrence, 1939	4	1	15	25.00	0	1	3.1
Dennis Claridge, 1965	1	1	13	100.00	0	0	118.8
Bill Stevens, 1968-69	5	1	12	20.00	0	1	39.6
Bob Nussbaumer, 1946, 51	1	1	10	100.00	0	0	108.3
Paul Ott Carruth, 1986-88	3	1	3	33.33	1	0	81.9
Herb Banet, 1937	7	1	2	14.29	0	2	0.0
Sterling Sharpe, 1988-94	1	1	1	100.00	0	0	79.2
Charles Brackens, 1955	2	0	0	00.0	0	0	39.6
Howie Ferguson, 1953-58	2	0	0	00.0	0	0	39.6
Max McGee, 1954, 57-67	2	0	0	00.0	0	1	0.0
Ernie Smith, 1935-37, 39	2	0	0	00.0	0	0	39.6
Frank Balazs, 1939-41	1	0	0	00.0	0	1	39.6
Dick Bilda, 1944	1	0	0	00.0	0	0	39.6
John Brockington, 1971-77	1	0	0	00.0	0	0	39.6
Cal Clemmens, 1936	1	0	0	00.0	0	0	39.6
Brian Dowling, 1977	1	0	0	00.0	0	0	39.6
Ted Fritsch, 1942-50	1	0	0	00.0	0	0	39.6
Ron Kramer, 1957, 59-64	1	0	0	00.0	0	1	0.0
Paul McJulien, 1991-92	1	0	0	00.0	0	0	39.6
Paul Miller, 1936-38	1	0	0	00.0	0	0	39.6
Russ Mosley, 1945-46	1	0	0	00.0	0	0	39.6
Frankie Neal, 1987	1	0	0	00.0	0	0	39.6
Floyd (Breezy) Reid, 1950-56	1	0	0	00.0	0	0	39.6
Bucky Scribner, 1983-84	1	0	0	00.0	0	0	39.6
Bruce Smith, 1945-48	1	0	0	00.0	0	0	39.6
Jon Staggers, 1972-74	1	0	0	00.0	0	0	39.6
J.R. Boone, 1953	1	0	-2	00.0	0	0	79.2
Packers, 1933-94*	**22,121**	**11,269**	**149,865**	**50.94**	**1,006**	**1,305**	**63.3**
Opponents, 1933-94	21,832	11,239	142,656	51.48	878	1,399	58.9

*The 1933-94 totals for the Packers include 101 attempts, 37 completions, 639 yards, nine touchdowns and nine interceptions by Arnie Herber in 1932. For a more accurate comparison between the Packers and Opponents for the 62-year period, subtract Herber's 1932 statistics. This will allow for an exact 1933-94 comparison.

Below is a list of touchdown passes thrown by Packers prior to 1933. Since Herber's 1932 statistics are accounted for above, they do not appear below.

1921-32 TOUCHDOWN PASSES

Name	TD	Name	TD
Joseph (Red) Dunn, 1927-31	31	John MacAuliffe, 1926	1
Curly Lambeau, 1921-29	24	Everett (Pid) Purdy, 1926-27	1
Charlie Mathys, 1922-26	11	Hurdis McCrary, 1929-33	1
Verne Lewellen, 1924-32	8	Johnny (Blood) McNally, 1929-32	1
Bo Molenda, 1929-32	5	Faye (Mule) Wilson, 1931	1
Paul Fitzgibbons, 1930-32	4	Russ Saunders, 1931	1
Arnie Herber, 1930-31	3	Hank Bruder, 1931-32	1
Eddie Kotal, 1925-29	2	**Packers, 1921-32**	**98**
Roger Grove, 1931-32	2	Opponents, 1921-32	50
Howard (Cub) Buck, 1921-25	1		

ALL-TIME PUNTERS

(Statistic kept since 1939; rankings are based on number of punts)

Name	No	Yds	Avg	LG	HB
David Beverly, 1975-80	495	18,785	37.95	65	2
Don Bracken, 1985-90	368	14,602	39.68	65	5
Donny Anderson, 1966-71	315	12,479	39.62	65	1
Max McGee, 1954, 57-67	256	10,647	41.59	63	2
Earl (Jug) Girard, 1948-51	200	7,830	39.15	72	5
Dick Deschaine, 1955-57	181	7,714	42.62	73	2
Bucky Scribner, 1983-84	154	6,465	41.98	70	1
Jack Jacobs, 1947-49	143	6,020	42.10	78	2
Don Chandler, 1965-67	135	5,659	41.92	90	0
Roy McKay, 1944-47	124	5,196	41.90	73	1

Name	No	Yds	Avg	LG	HB
Ray Stachowicz, 1981-82	124	5,017	40.46	72	2
Paul McJulien, 1991-92	122	4,859	39.83	67	2
Ron Widby, 1972-73	121	5,128	42.38	64	2
Jerry Norton, 1963-64	107	4,644	43.40	61	0
Bryan Wagner, 1992-93	104	4,396	42.27	60	0
Boyd Dowler, 1959-69	93	3,987	42.87	75	2
Clarke Hinkle, 1932-41	87	3,550	40.80	65	0
Vito (Babe) Parilli, 1952-53, 57-58	84	3,331	39.65	63	0
Lou Brock, 1940-45	84	3,137	37.35	72	3
Craig Hentrich, 1994	81	3,351	41.37	70	0
Randy Walker, 1974	69	2,648	38.38	58	0
Clive Rush, 1953	60	2,262	37.70	60	0
Joe Prokop, 1985	56	2,210	39.46	66	0
Tony Canadeo, 1941-44, 46-52	45	1,667	37.04	62	0
Arnie Herber, 1930-40	37	1,461	39.49	74	2
Bill Renner, 1986-87	35	1,334	38.11	50	3
Hal Van Every, 1940-41	30	1,125	37.50	65	0
Steve Broussard, 1975	29	922	31.79	51	3
Ted Fritsch, 1942-50	19	733	38.58	54	0
Irv Comp, 1943-49	12	453	37.75	46	0
Paul Staroba, 1973	12	373	31.08	49	0
Cecil Isbell, 1938-42	10	327	32.70	46	0

Name	No	Yds	Avg	LG	HB
Ken Duncan, 1971	6	216	36.00	47	0
Dale Livingston, 1970	6	199	33.17	52	0
Ray Pelfrey, 1951-52	5	220	44.00	46	0
Herman Rohrig, 1941, 46-47	5	214	42.80	52	0
Ben Starret, 1942-45	3	108	36.00	43	0
Bob Forte, 1946-50, 52-53	3	107	35.67	39	0
Tobin Rote, 1950-56	2	112	56.00	57	0
Albin (Rip) Collins, 1951	2	81	40.50	49	0
Don Perkins, 1943-45	2	44	22.00	31	0
Bob Cifers, 1949	1	49	49.00	49	0
Fred Cone, 1951-57	1	47	47.00	47	0
Frank Balazs, 1939-41	1	35	35.00	35	0
Chester Marcol, 1972-80	1	33	33.00	33	0
Ken Keuper, 1945-47	1	12	12.00	12	0
Packers, 1939-94*	**3,846**	**153,789**	**39.99**	**90**	**40**
Opponents, 1939-94**	3,783	151,992	40.18	88	24

* includes 15 punts the Packers have had blocked since 1976. Beginning that year, a punt attempt that was blocked no longer counted as an individual attempt, but was credited to the team.

**includes nine punts opponents have had blocked since 1976.

Green Bay Press-Gazette photo

Don Chandler (34) punted 135 times for the Packers.

Green Bay Press-Gazette photo

Roy McKay (3) punted for Green Bay in the mid-40's.

ALL-TIME KICKOFF RETURNERS

(Statistic kept since 1941; rankings based on number of returns)

TOP TEN

Name	No	Yds	Avg	LG	TD	100
Steve Odom, 1974-79	179	4,124	23.04	t95	2	10
Al Carmichael, 1953-58	153	3,907	25.54	t106	2	13
Herb Adderley, 1961-69	120	3,080	25.67	t103	2	5
Travis Williams, 1967-70	77	2,058	26.73	t104	5	8
Tony Canadeo, 1941-44, 46-52	75	1,736	23.15	48	0	2
Dave Hampton, 1969-71	74	2,084	28.16	t101	3	6
Tom Moore, 1960-65	71	1,882	26.51	84	0	1
Harlan Huckleby, 1980-85	70	1,300	18.57	57	0	1
Corey Harris, 1992-94	68	1,585	23.31	65	0	4
Billy Grimes, 1950-52	67	1,604	23.94	47	0	2

Name	No	Yds	Avg	LG	TD	100
Del Rodgers, 1982, 84	59	1,279	21.68	t97	1	4
Charles Wilson, 1990-91	58	1,320	22.76	t82	1	1
Brent Fullwood, 1987-90	56	1,174	20.96	46	0	0
Vince Workman, 1989-92	56	913	16.30	46	0	0
Mike C. McCoy, 1976-83	54	1,187	21.98	65	0	1
Robert Brooks, 1992-94	50	1,209	24.18	t96	2	3
Mark Lee, 1980-90	45	859	19.09	35	0	1
Ike Thomas, 1972-73	44	1,099	24.98	89	0	3
Walter Stanley, 1985-88	42	857	20.40	55	0	1
Aundra Thompson, 1977-81	40	835	20.88	t100	1	3
Ted Fritsch, 1942-50	37	951	25.70	79	0	1
Veryl Switzer, 1954-55	37	945	25.54	88	0	1
Ken Ellis, 1970-75	36	802	22.28	84	0	1
Gary Ellerson, 1985-86	36	675	18.75	57	0	2
Larry Krause, 1970-71, 73-74	35	864	24.69	t100	1	1
Donny Anderson, 1966-71	34	759	22.32	61	0	1
Elijah Pitts, 1961-69, 71	27	513	19.00	29	0	0
Dom Moselle, 1951-52	25	630	25.20	44	0	1
Phillip Epps, 1982-88	25	532	21.28	48	0	2
Don McIlhenny, 1957-59	24	558	23.25	53	0	1
Darrell Thompson, 1990-94	23	468	20.35	t76	1	0
John Symank, 1957-62	22	562	25.55	39	0	1
Bill Butler, 1959	21	472	22.48	35	0	1
Lou Brock, 1940-45	21	438	20.86	40	0	0
Keith Woodside, 1988-91	21	381	18.14	29	0	0
Johnnie Gray, 1975-83	21	317	15.10	26	0	0
Carl Bland, 1989-90	20	360	18.00	37	0	0
Tim Lewis, 1983-86	20	358	17.90	30	0	1
Joe Laws, 1934-45	19	362	19.05	29	0	0
Earl Gros, 1962-63	18	437	24.28	51	0	0
Fred Nixon, 1980-81	18	382	21.22	54	0	0
Lew Carpenter, 1959-63	18	348	19.33	29	0	1
Bill Forester, 1953-63	17	236	13.88	27	0	0
John Losch, 1956	15	390	26.00	51	0	0
Vai Sikahema, 1991	15	325	21.67	35	0	0
Howie Ferguson, 1953-58	15	257	17.13	34	0	0
Oscar E. Smith, 1948-49	14	323	23.07	36	0	0
John Kirby, 1949	14	315	22.50	34	0	0
Bob Forte, 1946-50, 52-53	14	290	20.71	36	0	0
Eric Torkelson, 1974-79, 81	14	268	19.14	29	0	0
Patrick Scott, 1987-88	14	239	17.07	27	0	0
Steve Wagner, 1976-79	14	181	12.93	27	0	0
Gerry Ellis, 1980-86	13	247	19.00	40	0	0
Ralph Earhart, 1948-49	13	238	18.31	30	0	0
Ed Cody, 1947-48	12	300	25.00	39	0	0
Irv Comp, 1943-49	12	255	21.25	31	0	0
Elbert Watts, 1986	12	239	19.92	40	0	0
Ken Davis, 1986-88	12	231	19.25	35	0	0
Ken Stills, 1985-88	12	227	18.92	38	0	0
Terdell Middleton, 1977-81	11	263	23.91	t85	1	0
Jon Staggers, 1972-74	11	260	23.64	39	0	0
Bob Hudson, 1972	11	247	22.45	55	0	0
Ace Loomis, 1951-53	11	226	20.55	34	0	0
Marcus Wilson, 1992-94	11	211	19.18	37	0	0
Paul Hornung, 1957-62, 64-66	10	248	24.80	39	0	0
Andy Uram, 1938-43	10	235	23.50	t98	1	0
Fred Provo, 1948	10	205	20.50	28	0	0
Kelly Cook, 1987	10	147	14.70	38	0	0
Charlie Leigh, 1974	9	201	22.33	30	0	0
Herman Rohrig, 1941, 46-47	9	184	20.44	27	0	0
Fred Cone, 1951-57	9	148	16.44	25	0	0
Jim Culbreath, 1977-79	9	140	15.56	30	0	0
John Jurkovic, 1991-94	9	118	13.11	16	0	0
Tommy Crutcher, 1964-67, 71-72	8	155	19.38	37	0	0
Jim Taylor, 1958-66	7	185	26.43	47	0	0
Tom Brown, 1964-68	7	167	23.86	34	0	0
Walt Schlinkman, 1946-50	7	155	22.14	34	0	0
Dave Robinson, 1963-72	7	80	11.43	25	0	0
Nolan Luhn, 1945-49	7	76	10.86	18	0	0
Bob Nussbaumer, 1946, 51	6	148	24.67	44	0	0
Norman Jefferson, 1987-88	6	146	24.33	46	0	0
Joe Johnson, 1954-58	6	137	22.83	28	0	0
Bruce Smith, 1945-48	6	128	21.33	26	0	0
Willard Harrell, 1975-77	6	126	21.00	39	0	0
Jeff Query, 1989-91	6	125	20.83	28	0	0
Roy McKay, 1944-47	6	108	18.00	26	0	0
Lee Morris, 1987	6	104	17.33	28	0	0
Floyd (Breezy) Reid, 1950-56	6	103	17.17	23	0	0
Cecil Isbell, 1938-42	6	96	16.00	32	0	0
Perry Williams, 1969-73	6	94	15.67	24	0	0
Steve Luke, 1975-80	6	91	15.17	21	0	0
Larry Craig, 1939-49	6	70	11.67	17	0	0
Ray Nitschke, 1958-72	6	53	8.83	17	0	0
Herman Fontenot, 1989-90	5	118	23.60	50	0	0
Charles Jordan, 1994	5	115	23.00	33	0	0
Edgar Bennett, 1992-94	5	104	20.80	33	0	0
Walt Michaels, 1951	5	86	17.20	26	0	0
Howard Sampson, 1978-79	5	84	16.80	23	0	0
Bobby Jack Floyd, 1952, 54	5	75	15.00	26	0	0
Barty Smith, 1974-80	5	53	10.60	18	0	0
Paul Ott Carruth, 1986-88	5	48	9.60	20	0	0
John Martinkovic, 1951-56	5	46	9.20	31	0	0
Don Hutson, 1935-45	5	45	9.00	12	0	0
Gib Dawson, 1953	4	102	25.50	33	0	0
Hal Van Every, 1940-41	4	99	24.75	31	0	0
Earl (Jug) Girard, 1948-51	4	90	22.50	25	0	0
Allan Clark, 1982	4	75	18.75	30	0	0
Derrick Harden, 1987	4	72	18.00	20	0	0
Max McGee, 1954, 57-67	4	69	17.25	32	0	0
Phil Vandersea, 1966, 68-70	4	58	14.50	21	0	0
Les Goodman, 1973-74	4	49	12.25	20	0	0
Frankie Neal, 1987	4	44	11.00	18	0	0
Bob Hyland, 1967-69, 76	4	31	7.75	17	0	0
Charlie Sample, 1942, 45	3	91	30.33	35	0	0
Clarence Self, 1952, 54-55	3	85	28.33	33	0	0
Paul Coffman, 1978-85	3	77	25.67	52	0	0
Estus Hood, 1978-84	3	74	24.67	33	0	0
Cliff Aberson, 1946	3	69	23.00	26	0	0
Jim Gillette, 1947	3	66	22.00	29	0	0
Cliff Taylor, 1976	3	59	19.67	23	0	0
Larry Hickman, 1960	3	54	18.00	27	0	0
Larry Coutre, 1950, 53	3	52	17.33	27	0	0
Ray DiPierro, 1950-51	3	42	14.00	26	0	0
Clarke Hinkle, 1932-41	3	38	12.67	16	0	0
Allen Rice, 1991	3	36	12.00	15	0	0
Chet Winters, 1983	3	28	9.33	12	0	0
Clyde Goodnight, 1945-49	3	27	9.00	12	0	0
Aaron Brown, 1973-74	3	26	8.67	12	0	0
Don Davey, 1991-94	3	22	7.33	9	0	0
Mike P. McCoy, 1970-76	3	22	7.33	10	0	0
Willie Wood, 1960-71	3	20	6.67	20	0	0
Dave Osborn, 1976	3	19	6.33	10	0	0
Paul (Buddy) Burris, 1949-51	3	18	6.00	11	0	0
Deral Teteak, 1952-56	2	62	31.00	47	0	0

- 284 -

Name	No	Yds	Avg	LG	TD	100
Joe Francis, 1958-59	2	52	26.00	28	0	0
Bill Robinson, 1952	2	49	24.50	26	0	0
Tony Falkenstein, 1943	2	47	23.50	24	0	0
Chuck Webb, 1991	2	40	20.00	23	0	0
Johnny Papit, 1953	2	38	19.00	21	0	0
Byron Bailey, 1953	2	34	17.00	21	0	0
Don Perkins, 1943-45	2	34	17.00	18	0	0
MacArthur Lane, 1972-74	2	31	15.50	29	0	0
Dorsey Levens, 1994	2	31	15.50	16	0	0
Mike Meade, 1982-83	2	31	15.50	17	0	0
Daryll Jones, 1984-85	2	30	15.00	19	0	0
Forrest Gregg, 1956, 58-70	2	21	10.50	16	0	0
Rich McGeorge, 1970-78	2	17	8.50	17	0	0
Ben Starret, 1942-45	2	16	8.00	13	0	0
Jim Temp, 1957-60	2	16	8.00	16	0	0
Dan Currie, 1958-64	2	14	7.00	7	0	0
Steve Okoniewski, 1974-75	2	11	5.50	11	0	0
Jim Gueno, 1976-80	2	9	4.50	9	0	0
Abner Wimberly, 1950-52	2	4	2.00	3	0	0
Jerry Kramer, 1958-68	2	0	0.00	0	0	0
Ed West, 1984-94	2	0	0.00	0	0	0
Albin (Rip) Collins, 1951	1	40	40.00	40	0	0
Harry Jacunski, 1939-44	1	33	33.00	33	0	0
Ray Pelfrey, 1951-52	1	26	26.00	26	0	0
Terry Wells, 1975	1	26	26.00	26	0	0
Bob Kroll, 1972-73	1	23	23.00	23	0	0
Dave Davis, 1971-72	1	22	22.00	22	0	0
Pete Van Valkenburg, 1974	1	22	22.00	22	0	0
Bob Summerhays, 1949-51	1	21	21.00	21	0	0
Bill Boedecker, 1950	1	20	20.00	20	0	0
Bob Dees, 1952	1	20	20.00	20	0	0
Tom Flynn, 1984-86	1	20	20.00	20	0	0
Alex Urban, 1941, 44-45	1	20	20.00	20	0	0
Bill Reichardt, 1952	1	19	19.00	19	0	0
Paul Duhart, 1944	1	18	18.00	18	0	0
Don Highsmith, 1973	1	18	18.00	18	0	0
Eddie Lee Ivery, 1979-86	1	17	17.00	17	0	0
Ron Pitts, 1988-90	1	17	17.00	17	0	0
Sterling Sharpe, 1988-94	1	17	17.00	17	0	0
Ed Berry, 1986	1	16	16.00	16	0	0
Jim Jensen, 1981-82	1	15	15.00	15	0	0
Joel Mason, 1942-45	1	15	15.00	15	0	0
Dexter McNabb, 1992-93	1	15	15.00	15	0	0
Tim Moresco, 1977	1	15	15.00	15	0	0
John Anderson, 1978-89	1	14	14.00	14	0	0
Don Barton, 1953	1	14	14.00	14	0	0
Carleton Elliott, 1951-54	1	14	14.00	14	0	0
Ezra Johnson, 1977-87	1	14	14.00	14	0	0
Ray Riddick, 1940-42, 46	1	14	14.00	14	0	0
George Schmidt, 1952	1	14	14.00	14	0	0
Allen Brown, 1966-67	1	13	13.00	13	0	0
Gale Gillingham, 1966-74, 76	1	13	13.00	13	0	0
Derrel Gofourth, 1977-82	1	13	13.00	13	0	0
Ollie Smith, 1976-77	1	12	12.00	12	0	0
Joe Sims, 1992-94	1	11	11.00	11	0	0
Bill Bain, 1975	1	10	10.00	10	0	0
Larry Buhler, 1939-41	1	10	10.00	10	0	0
Al Cannava, 1950	1	10	10.00	10	0	0
Carlton Massey, 1957-58	1	10	10.00	10	0	0
Ernie Pannell, 1941-42, 45	1	10	10.00	10	0	0
Mike Wellman, 1979-80	1	10	10.00	10	0	0
Junior Coffey, 1965	1	9	9.00	9	0	0
Joey Hackett, 1987	1	9	9.00	9	0	0
Doug Hart, 1964-71	1	8	8.00	8	0	0
Paul Berezney, 1942-44	1	7	7.00	7	0	0
Ted Cook, 1948-50	1	7	7.00	7	0	0
Guy Prather, 1981-85	1	7	7.00	7	0	0
Blaise Winter, 1988-90	1	7	7.00	7	0	0
Hank Gremminger, 1956-65	1	6	6.00	6	0	0
Ken Keuper, 1945-47	1	6	6.00	6	0	0
Dick Wildung, 1946-51, 53	1	6	6.00	6	0	0
Jim Carter, 1970-75, 77-78	1	5	5.00	5	0	0
Dick Himes, 1968-77	1	4	4.00	4	0	0
Cliff Lewis, 1981-84	1	4	4.00	4	0	0
John Jefferson, 1981-84	1	3	3.00	3	0	0
Dave Dreschler, 1983-84	1	1	1.00	1	0	0
Nate Hill, 1988	1	1	1.00	1	0	0
Paul Lipscomb, 1945-49	1	1	1.00	1	0	0
Brian Noble, 1985-93	1	1	1.00	1	0	0
Clayton Weishuhn, 1987	1	1	1.00	1	0	0
Nate Borden, 1955-59	1	0	0.00	0	0	0
Byron Braggs, 1981-83	1	0	0.00	0	0	0
Bill Brown, 1953-56	1	0	0.00	0	0	0
Lee Roy Caffey, 1964-69	1	0	0.00	0	0	0
Bill Cherry, 1986-87	1	0	0.00	0	0	0
Mark Chmura, 1993-94	1	0	0.00	0	0	0
Walter Dean, 1991	1	0	0.00	0	0	0
Clint Didier, 1988-89	1	0	0.00	0	0	0
Marv Fleming, 1963-69	1	0	0.00	0	0	0
Len Garrett, 1971-72	1	0	0.00	0	0	0
Dan Grimm, 1963-65	1	0	0.00	0	0	0
Syd Kitson, 1980-81, 83-84	1	0	0.00	0	0	0
Walt Landers, 1978-79	1	0	0.00	0	0	0
James Lofton, 1978-86	1	0	0.00	0	0	0
Tony Mandarich, 1989-91	1	0	0.00	0	0	0
Steve Meilinger, 1958, 60	1	0	0.00	0	0	0
Frank Mestnick, 1963	1	0	0.00	0	0	0
Nate Simpson, 1977-79	1	0	0.00	0	0	0
John Sterling, 1987	1	0	0.00	0	0	0
Evan Vogds, 1948-49	1	0	0.00	0	0	0
Francis Winkler, 1968-69	1	0	0.00	0	0	0
Keith Wortman, 1972-75	1	0	0.00	0	0	0
Kevin Willhite, 1987	0	37	—	37	0	0
Packers, 1941-94	**2,790**	**59,733**	**21.41**	**t106**	**23**	**82**
Opponents, 1941-94	2,739	56,322	20.56	t100	11	—

Lefebvre photo

Andy Uram (42) returned 10 kickoffs for 235 yards between 1941 and 1943.

ALL-TIME PUNT RETURNERS

(Statistic kept since 1941; rankings based on number of returns)

Name	No	Yds	Avg	LG	TD	FC
Willie Wood, 1960-71	187	1,391	7.44	t72	2	102
Phillip Epps, 1982-88	100	819	8.19	t90	1	31
Al Carmichael, 1953-58	100	753	7.53	52	0	—
Walter Stanley, 1985-88	87	720	8.28	t83	1	17
Johnnie Gray, 1975-84	85	656	7.72	24	0	28
Jeff Query, 1989-91	76	712	9.37	28	0	17
Elijah Pitts, 1961-69, 71	75	394	5.25	t65	1	41
Robert Brooks, 1992-94	67	589	8.79	t85	1	18
Steve Odom, 1974-79	64	569	8.89	t95	1	14
Billy Grimes, 1950-52	63	834	13.24	t85	2	—
Ken Ellis, 1970-75	63	426	6.76	t80	1	11

Name	No	Yds	Avg	LG	TD	FC
Willard Harrell, 1975-77	52	382	7.35	t75	1	16
Jon Staggers, 1972-74	50	460	9.20	t85	2	38
Veryl Switzer, 1954-55	48	464	9.67	t93	1	—
Tony Canadeo, 1941-44, 46-52	46	513	11.15	26	0	—
Joe Laws, 1934-45	46	339	7.37	23	0	—
Lou Brock, 1940-45	39	438	11.23	45	0	—
Terrell Buckley, 1992-94	32	287	8.97	t58	1	10
Herman Rohrig, 1941, 46-47	30	357	11.90	28	0	—
Lew Carpenter, 1959-63	28	339	12.11	51	0	5
Tom Brown, 1964-68	27	151	5.59	t52	1	8
Vai Sikahema, 1991	26	239	9.19	62	0	4
Mark Lee, 1980-90	26	215	8.27	t94	1	1
Fred Nixon, 1980-81	26	203	7.81	17	0	6
Ralph Earhart, 1948-49	25	298	11.92	t57	1	—
Mike Prior, 1993-94	25	256	10.24	24	0	7
Tom Flynn, 1984-86	22	169	7.68	20	0	8
Andy Uram, 1938-43	19	219	11.53	t90	1	—
Ron Cassidy, 1979-81, 83-84	19	139	7.32	20	0	9
Fred Provo, 1948	18	208	11.56	40	0	—
Bill Butler, 1959	18	163	9.06	t61	1	—
Dom Moselle, 1951-52	16	157	9.81	24	0	—
Donny Anderson, 1966-71	15	222	14.80	t77	1	4
Jim Shanley, 1958	14	105	7.50	26	0	—
Bob Nussbaumer, 1946, 51	13	101	7.77	21	0	—
Travis Williams, 1967-70	12	209	17.42	t83	1	5
Earl (Jug) Girard, 1948-51	12	79	6.58	11	0	—
Jim Gillette, 1947	11	168	15.27	26	0	—
Irv Comp, 1943-49	11	123	11.18	20	0	—
Joe Johnson, 1954-58	10	82	8.20	13	0	—
Oscar E. Smith, 1948-49	10	80	8.00	27	0	—
Bruce Smith, 1945-48	9	101	11.22	22	0	—
Ron Pitts, 1988-90	9	93	10.33	t63	1	9
Roy McKay, 1944-47	9	85	9.44	17	0	—
Sterling Sharpe, 1988-94	9	48	5.33	14	0	7
Ace Loomis, 1951-53	8	83	10.38	31	0	—
John Losch, 1956	8	74	9.25	58	0	—
John Kirby, 1949	8	48	6.00	13	0	—
Gib Dawson, 1953	7	72	10.29	t60	1	—
Patrick Scott, 1987-88	6	71	11.83	36	0	2
Dave Davis, 1971-72	6	36	6.00	19	0	0
Bill Boedecker, 1950	5	49	9.80	12	0	—
Mickey Sutton, 1989	5	42	8.40	17	0	1
Dan Sandifer, 1952-53	5	40	8.00	23	0	—
J.R. Boone, 1953	5	24	4.80	9	0	—
Gary Hayes, 1984-86	5	24	4.80	10	0	0
Norman Jefferson, 1987-88	5	15	3.00	9	0	2
John Symank, 1957-62	5	0	0.00	0	0	—
Hal Van Every, 1940-41	4	58	14.50	20	0	—
Bobby Dillon, 1952-59	4	37	9.25	13	0	—
Cecil Isbell, 1938-42	4	33	8.25	14	0	—
Wally Dreyer, 1950-51	3	48	16.00	22	0	—
Paul Duhart, 1944	3	32	10.67	18	0	—
Billy Kinard, 1957-58	3	19	6.33	19	0	—
Jack Jacobs, 1947-49	3	16	5.33	9	0	—
Clarke Hinkle, 1932-41	2	61	30.50	36	0	—
Ed Cody, 1947-48	2	30	15.00	20	0	—
Bob Forte, 1946-50, 52-53	2	28	14.00	15	0	—
Harper Davis, 1951	2	21	10.50	17	0	—
Kelly Cook, 1987	2	18	9.00	14	0	0
Don Barton, 1953	2	13	6.50	7	0	—
Al Cannava, 1950	2	9	4.50	9	0	—

Name	No	Yds	Avg	LG	TD	FC
Al Romine, 1955, 58	2	7	3.50	7	0	—
Bill Whitaker, 1981-82	2	1	0.50	1	0	0
Leon Harden, 1970	2	-7	-3.50	0	0	0
Ted Fritsch, 1942-50	1	31	31.00	31	0	—
Len Szafaryn, 1950, 53-56	1	28	28.00	t28	1	—
Joel Mason, 1942-45	1	20	20.00	20	0	—
Bob Kahler, 1942-44	1	14	14.00	14	0	—
Russ Mosley, 1945-46	1	13	13.00	13	0	—
Bill Forester, 1953-63	1	7	7.00	7	0	—
Larry Coutre, 1950, 53	1	5	5.00	5	0	—
Mark Murphy, 1980-85, 87-91	1	4	4.00	4	0	2
Emlen Tunnell, 1959-61	1	3	3.00	3	0	—
Tim Hauck, 1991-94	1	2	2.00	2	0	0
Leland Glass, 1972-73	1	1	1.00	1	0	0
Lee Morris, 1987	1	1	1.00	1	0	0
Herb Adderley, 1961-69	1	0	0.00	0	0	—
Chuck Cecil, 1988-92	1	0	0.00	0	0	0
Vinnie Clark, 1991-92	1	0	0.00	0	0	0
Charlie Hall, 1971-76	1	0	0.00	0	0	0
Larry Hefner, 1972-75	1	0	0.00	0	0	0
Estus Hood, 1978-84	1	0	0.00	0	0	0
Bob Hudson, 1972	1	0	0.00	0	0	2
Charles Jordan, 1994	1	0	0.00	0	0	1
Ron Kostelnik, 1961-68	1	0	0.00	0	0	—
Cliff Lewis, 1981-84	1	0	0.00	0	0	0
Don McIlhenny, 1957-59	1	0	0.00	0	0	—
Jim Psaltis, 1954	1	0	0.00	0	0	—
Al Randolph, 1971	1	0	0.00	0	0	0
Floyd (Breezy) Reid, 1950-56	1	0	0.00	0	0	—
Howard Sampson, 1978-79	1	0	0.00	0	0	0
Eric Torkelson, 1974-79, 81	1	0	0.00	0	0	0
Walter Tullis, 1978-79	1	0	0.00	0	0	0
Clarence Williams, 1970-77	1	0	0.00	0	0	0
Vince Workman, 1989-92	1	0	0.00	0	0	0
Ben Aldridge, 1953	1	0	0.00	0	0	—
George Teague, 1993-94	1	-1	-1.00	-1	0	0
Packers, 1941-94	**1,904**	**16,485**	**8.66**	**t95**	**25**	***426**
Opponents, 1941-94	1,990	16,767	8.43	t95	20	*377

*statistics on fair catches kept since 1961.

Lefebvre photo

Cecil Isbell (17) in trouble in Chcago. Isbell returned four punts between 1941 and 1942

ALL-TIME INTERCEPTORS

(Statistic kept since 1940; rankings based on number of interceptions)

Name	No	Yds	Avg	LG	TD
Bobby Dillon, 1952-59	52	976	18.77	61	5
Willie Wood, 1960-71	48	699	14.56	t42	2
Herb Adderley, 1961-69	39	795	20.38	t80	7
Irv Comp, 1943-49	33	472	14.30	t54	2
Mark Lee, 1980-90	31	249	8.03	40	0
Don Hutson, 1935-45	30	389	12.97	t84	1
Hank Gremminger, 1956-65	28	421	15.04	45	0
Ray Nitschke, 1958-72	25	385	15.40	t43	2
John Anderson, 1978-89	25	167	6.68	t27	1
Bob Jeter, 1963-70	23	333	14.48	t75	2

Name	No	Yds	Avg	LG	TD
Johnnie Gray, 1975-84	22	332	15.09	67	1
Bob Forte, 1946-50, 52-53	22	291	13.23	t68	1
Dave Robinson, 1963-72	21	322	15.33	87	0
Bill Forester, 1953-63	21	279	13.29	37	0
Willie Buchanon, 1972-78	21	234	11.14	t77	2
Jess Whittenton, 1958-64	20	329	16.45	52	1
Ken Ellis, 1970-75	20	294	14.70	60	3
Charley Brock, 1939-47	20	229	11.45	41	2
Mark Murphy, 1980-85, 87-91	20	194	9.70	t50	1
John Symank, 1957-62	18	366	20.33	41	0
Joe Laws, 1934-45	18	266	14.78	38	0
Tim Lewis, 1983-86	16	266	16.63	t99	1
LeRoy Butler, 1990-94	16	247	15.44	51	0
Doug Hart, 1964-71	15	436	29.07	t85	3
Val Joe Walker, 1953-56	15	234	15.60	t54	1
Tom Brown, 1964-68	13	210	16.15	51	0
Chuck Cecil, 1988-92	13	200	15.38	33	0
Lou Brock, 1940-45	13	193	14.85	74	0
Mike C. McCoy, 1976-83	13	116	8.92	38	0
Ace Loomis, 1951-53	12	257	21.42	66	1
Dave Brown, 1987-89	12	55	4.58	15	0
Herman Rohrig, 1941, 46-47	11	231	21.00	51	0
Dan Currie, 1958-64	11	193	17.55	33	1
Ted Cook, 1948-50	11	133	12.09	30	0
Tom Flynn, 1984-86	11	113	10.27	31	0
Estus Hood, 1978-84	11	93	8.45	t41	1
Mike Douglass, 1978-85	10	274	27.40	t80	1
Ted Fritsch, 1942-50	10	263	26.30	t69	2
Rebel Steiner, 1950-51	10	194	19.40	t94	1
Al Matthews, 1970-75	10	169	16.90	t58	1
Steve Luke, 1975-80	10	149	14.90	t63	1
Terrell Buckley, 1992-94	10	102	10.2	t33	1
Lee Roy Caffey, 1964-69	9	177	19.67	t52	2
Jim Hill, 1972-74	9	137	15.22	24	0
Johnny Holland, 1987-93	9	130	14.44	32	0
Tony Canadeo, 1941-44, 46-52	9	129	14.33	35	0
Andy Uram, 1938-43	9	122	13.56	28	0
Cecil Isbell, 1938-42	9	61	6.78	19	0
Maurice Harvey, 1981-83	8	249	31.13	53	0
Earl (Jug) Girard, 1948-51	8	106	13.25	41	0
Fred Carr, 1968-77	8	98	12.25	28	1
Charles Goldenberg, 1933-45	8	73	9.13	30	0
Ken Stills, 1985-89	7	107	15.29	t58	1
Perry Smith, 1973-76	7	97	13.86	51	0
Hal Van Every, 1940-41	6	134	22.33	t91	1
Jack Jacobs, 1947-49	6	90	15.00	29	0
Deral Teteak, 1952-56	6	84	14.00	32	0
Marvin Johnson, 1952-53	6	61	10.17	36	0
Jim Carter, 1970-75, 77-78	6	60	10.00	t42	1
Bob Flowers, 1942-49	6	33	5.50	19	0
Ben Aldridge, 1953	5	85	17.00	34	0
Ted Hendricks, 1974	5	74	14.80	44	0
Scott Stephen, 1987-91	5	65	13.00	26	0
Ken Keuper, 1945-47	5	63	12.60	26	0
Wally Dreyer, 1950-51	5	62	12.40	34	1
Emlen Tunnell, 1959-61	5	42	8.40	22	0
Jay Rhodemyre, 1948-49, 51-52	5	36	7.20	9	0
Al Baldwin, 1950	5	35	7.00	22	0
George Cumby, 1980-85	5	33	6.60	17	0
Doyle Nix, 1955	5	33	6.60	12	0
Mossy Cade, 1985-86	5	26	5.20	18	0

Name	No	Yds	Avg	LG	TD
Bob Adkins, 1940-41, 45	4	114	28.50	54	1
Vinnie Clark, 1991-92	4	112	28.00	43	0
Ron Pitts, 1988-90	4	93	23.25	37	0
Bryce Paup, 1990-94	4	55	13.75	30	1
George Teague, 1993-94	4	55	13.75	22	0
Roy McKay, 1944-47	4	53	13.25	20	0
Dick Weisgerber, 1938-40, 42	4	51	12.75	24	0
Rich Wingo, 1979, 81-84	4	51	12.75	38	0
Pete Tinsley, 1938-45	4	41	10.25	24	0
Jerry Holmes, 1990-91	4	39	9.75	24	0
Tom Toner, 1973-77	4	39	9.75	28	0
Harper Davis, 1951	4	37	9.25	25	0
Roger Zatkoff, 1953-56	4	25	6.25	15	0
Paul Duhart, 1944	4	23	5.75	14	0
George (Tiger) Greene, 1986-90	4	11	2.75	11	0
Dave Hanner, 1952-64	4	3	0.75	2	0
Dom Moselle, 1951-52	4	2	0.50	2	0
Jim Bob Morris, 1987	3	135	45.00	73	0
Bob Summerhays, 1949-51	3	112	37.33	t88	1
Randy Scott, 1981-86	3	62	20.67	30	0
Cliff Aberson, 1946	3	53	17.67	33	0
Billy Bookout, 1955-56	3	43	14.33	27	0
Roland Mitchell, 1991-93	3	40	13.33	35	0
Bob Nussbaumer, 1946, 51	3	31	10.33	16	0
Clarence Self, 1952, 54-55	3	23	7.67	23	0
Brian Noble, 1985-93	3	20	6.67	10	0
Clarke Hinkle, 1932-41	3	13	4.33	8	0
Mike Jolly, 1980, 82-83	3	2	0.67	2	0
Don Perkins, 1943-45	2	123	61.50	t83	2
Jim Capuzzi, 1955-56	2	65	32.50	65	0
Larry Buhler, 1939-41	2	58	29.00	32	0
George Svendsen, 1935-37, 40-41	2	48	24.00	42	0
Robert Brown, 1982-92	2	42	21.00	37	1
Russ Mosley, 1945-46	2	40	20.00	20	0
Alex Wizbicki, 1950	2	38	19.00	34	0
Ben Starret, 1942-45	2	31	15.50	27	0
Dan Sandifer, 1952-53	2	25	12.50	17	0
Mike Hunt, 1978-80	2	23	11.50	13	0
Bob Freeman, 1959	2	22	11.00	22	0
Charlie Hall, 1971-76	2	22	11.00	19	0
Willie Davis, 1960-69	2	21	10.50	21	0
Wayne Simmons, 1993-94	2	21	10.50	19	0
Larry Craig, 1939-49	2	20	10.00	20	0
James Willis, 1993-94	2	20	10.00	17	0
Tommy Crutcher, 1964-67, 71-72	2	19	9.50	15	0
Lenny McGill, 1994	2	16	8.00	16	0
Wylie Turner, 1979-80	2	13	6.50	13	0
Gene Wilson, 1947-48	2	13	6.50	13	0
Bruce Smith, 1945-48	2	11	5.50	11	0
Bill Quinlan, 1959-62	2	9	4.50	5	0
Tom MacLeod, 1973	2	8	4.00	8	0
Sherwood Fries, 1943	2	6	3.00	4	0
George Paskvan, 1941	2	6	3.00	4	0
Abner Wimberly, 1950-52	2	5	2.50	5	0
Ken Gorgal, 1956	2	2	1.00	2	0
Clayton Tonnemaker, 1950, 53-54	2	2	1.00	1	0
Albin (Rip) Collins, 1951	2	0	0.00	0	0
Doug Evans, 1993-94	2	0	0.00	0	0
Arnie Herber, 1930-40	2	0	0.00	0	0
Burnell Dent, 1986-92	1	53	53.00	53	0
Al Randolph, 1971	1	34	34.00	34	0

Name	No	Yds	Avg	LG	TD
Ed Jankowski, 1937-41	1	33	33.00	33	0
Dick Bilda, 1944	1	25	25.00	25	0
Bob Ingalls, 1942	1	23	23.00	t23	1
Esera Tuaolo, 1991-92	1	23	23.00	23	0
Clarence Williams, 1970-77	1	23	23.00	23	0
Jim Laughlin, 1983	1	22	22.00	22	0
Bobby Leopold, 1986	1	21	21.00	21	0
Gene White, 1954	1	20	20.00	20	0
Charles Mitchell, 1946	1	18	18.00	18	0
Bill Lee, 1937-42, 46	1	14	14.00	14	0
Von Mansfield, 1987	1	14	14.00	14	0
Paul Rudzinski, 1978-80	1	14	14.00	14	0
Jim Temp, 1957-60	1	13	13.00	13	0
Bernie Crimmins, 1945	1	12	12.00	t12	1
Ken Roskie, 1948	1	12	12.00	12	0
Frank Balazs, 1939-41	1	11	11.00	11	0
Sam Palumbo, 1957	1	11	11.00	11	0
Howard Ruetz, 1951-53	1	11	11.00	11	0
Howard (Smiley) Johnson, 1940-41	1	10	10.00	10	0
Damon Tassos, 1947-49	1	10	10.00	10	0
Shawn Patterson, 1988-91, 93	1	9	9.00	t9	1
Harry Jacunski, 1939-44	1	7	7.00	7	0
Fred Strickland, 1994	1	7	7.00	7	0
Ray Wheba, 1944	1	7	7.00	7	0
Alphonso Carreker, 1984-88	1	6	6.00	6	0
Elbert Watts, 1986	1	6	6.00	6	0
Carl Barzilauskas, 1978-79	1	5	5.00	5	0
Tom Greenfield, 1939-41	1	5	5.00	5	0
Roger Harding, 1949	1	5	5.00	5	0
Mike P. McCoy, 1970-76	1	5	5.00	5	0
Dick Afflis, 1951-54	1	3	3.00	3	0
Larry Hefner, 1972-75	1	3	3.00	3	0
KeShon Johnson, 1994	1	3	3.00	3	0
Kenneth Johnson, 1987	1	2	2.00	2	0
Buford (Baby) Ray, 1938-48	1	2	2.00	2	0
Mike Prior, 1993-94	1	1	1.00	1	0
Tom Bettis, 1955-61	1	0	0.00	0	0
Matt Brock, 1989-94	1	0	0.00	0	0
Paul (Buddy) Burris, 1949-51	1	0	0.00	0	0
Anthony Harrison, 1987	1	0	0.00	0	0
Jerry Helluin, 1954-57	1	0	0.00	0	0
Van Jakes, 1989	1	0	0.00	0	0
Charles Johnson, 1979-80, 83	1	0	0.00	0	0
Henry Jordan, 1959-69	1	0	0.00	0	0
Mike McLeod, 1984-85	1	0	0.00	0	0
James Melka, 1987	1	0	0.00	0	0
Dan Orlich, 1949-51	1	0	0.00	0	0
Ernie Pannell, 1941-42, 45	1	0	0.00	0	0
John Petitbon, 1957	1	0	0.00	0	0
Al Romine, 1955, 58	1	0	0.00	0	0
Carl Schuette, 1950-51	1	0	0.00	0	0
Joe Spencer, 1950-51	1	0	0.00	0	0
Packers, 1940-94	**1,218**	**17,222**	**14.14**	**t99**	**64**
Opponents, 1940-94	1,152	16,220	14.08	t99	89

Green Bay Press-Gazette photo

Chuck Cecil (26) exchanges greetings with Vikings' quarterback Rich Gannon (16) in Green Bay, November 17, 1991. Cecil intercepted 13 passes in five seasons with the Packers.

Green Bay Press-Gazette photo

Herb Adderley (26) is beaten for a touchdown by the Colts' Willie Richardson. Aderley ranks third all-time on the Packers interception list.

ALL-TIME SCORERS

(Statistic kept since 1921; rankings based on total points)

TOP TEN

Name	TDr	TDp	TDrt	PAT	FG	S	TP
Don Hutson, 1935-45	3	99	3	172	7	0	823
Paul Hornung, 1957-62, 64-66	50	12	0	190/194	66/140	0	760
Chris Jacke, 1989-94	0	0	0	207/210	135/174	0	612
Jim Taylor, 1958-66	81	10	0	0/0	0/0	0	546
Chester Marcol, 1972-80	0	0	1	155/164	120/195	0	521
Fred Cone, 1951-57	12	4	0	200/214	53/89	0	455
Sterling Sharpe, 1988-94	0	65	1	0/0	0/0	0	396
Ted Fritsch, 1942-50	31	1	3	62/70	36/98	0	380
Clarke Hinkle, 1932-41	34	9	0	30	28	0	372
Verne Lewellen, 1924-32	37	12	2	1	0	0	307

TOP TEN

Name	TDr	TDp	TDrt	PAT	FG	S	TP
Max McGee, 1954, 57-67	0	50	1	0/0	0/0	0	306
James Lofton, 1978-86	1	49	0	0/0	0/0	0	300
Jan Stenerud, 1980-83	0	0	0	115/118	59/73	0	292
Al Del Greco, 1984-87	0	0	0	112/114	50/75	0	262
Don Chandler, 1965-67	0	0	0	117/120	48/83	0	261
Bill Howton, 1952-58	0	43	0	0/0	0/0	0	258
Boyd Dowler, 1959-69	0	40	0	0/0	0/0	0	240
Paul Coffman, 1978-85	0	39	0	0/0	0/0	0	234
Johnny Blood, 1929-33, 35-36	5	28	4	2	0	0	224
Carroll Dale, 1965-72	0	35	0	0/0	0/0	0	210
Gerry Ellis, 1980-86	25	10	0	0/0	0/0	0	210
Elijah Pitts, 1961-69, 71	28	6	1	0/0	0/0	0	210
John Brockington, 1971-77	29	3	0	0/0	0/0	0	192
Donny Anderson, 1966-71	24	6	1	0/0	0/0	0	186
Tony Canadeo, 1941-44, 46-52	26	5	0	0/0	0/0	0	186
Eddie Lee Ivery, 1979-86	23	7	0	0/0	0/0	0	180
Tobin Rote, 1950-56	29	1	0	0/0	0/0	0	180
Jerry Kramer, 1958-68	0	0	0	90/94	29/54	0	177
Tom Moore, 1960-65	20	7	0	0/0	0/0	0	162
Ed West, 1984-94	1	25	0	2	0/0	0	158
Gary Knafelc, 1954-62	0	21	0	0/0	0/0	0	126
Joe Laws, 1934-45	9	10	2	0	0	0	126
Barty Smith, 1974-80	18	3	0	0/0	0/0	0	126
Edgar Bennett, 1992-94	14	5	0	0/0	0/0	0	114
Brent Fullwood, 1987-90	18	1	0	0/0	0/0	0	114
Terdell Middleton, 1977-81	15	3	1	0/0	0/0	0	114
Floyd (Breezy) Reid, 1950-56	13	5	0	0/0	0/0	0	108
Max Zendejas, 1987-88	0	0	0	30/34	25/35	0	105
Curly Lambeau, 1921-29	8	3	0	20	6	0	104
Bob Mann, 1950-54	0	17	0	0/0	0/0	0	102
Travis Williams, 1967-70	6	5	6	0/0	0/0	0	102
Hank Bruder, 1931-39	8	6	2	4	0	0	100
Lou Brock, 1940-45	10	6	0	2/2	0/1	0	98
Andy Uram, 1938-43	4	10	2	2/3	0/0	0	98
Phillip Epps, 1982-88	1	14	1	0/0	0/0	0	96
Bob Monnett, 1933-38	7	0	1	28	5	0	91
Jessie Clark, 1983-87	9	6	0	0/0	0/0	0	90
Ron Kramer, 1957, 59-64	0	15	0	0/0	0/0	0	90
Steve Odom, 1974-79	1	11	3	0/0	0/0	0	90
Bart Starr, 1956-71	15	0	0	0/0	0/0	0	90
Vince Workman, 1989-92	10	5	0	0/0	0/0	0	90
LaVern (Lavvie) Dilweg, 1927-34	0	12	2	2	0	0	86
Paul (Tiny) Engebretsen, 1934-41	0	0	0	43	14	0	85
Clyde Goodnight, 1945-49	0	13	0	0/0	0/0	0	78
Dave Hampton, 1969-71	7	3	3	0/0	0/0	0	78
Harlan Huckelby, 1980-85	10	3	0	0/0	0/0	0	78
Nolan Luhn, 1945-49	0	13	0	0/0	0/0	0	78
Rich McGeorge, 1970-78	0	13	0	0/0	0/0	0	78
Marv Fleming, 1963-69	0	12	0	0/0	0/0	0	72
Hurdis McCrary, 1929-33	7	4	1	0	0	0	72
Carl Mulleneaux, 1938-41, 45-46	0	11	1	0/0	0/0	0	72
Mike Mercer, 1968-69	0	0	0	35/37	12/29	0	71
Ed Jankowski, 1937-41	8	1	1	4	1	0	67
Irv Comp, 1943-49	7	2	2	0/0	0/0	0	66
Jim Grabowski, 1966-70	8	3	0	0/0	0/0	0	66
John Jefferson, 1981-84	0	11	0	0/0	0/0	0	66
MacArthur Lane, 1972-74	7	4	0	0/0	0/0	0	66
Roger Grove, 1931-35	1	7	0	16	0	0	64
Dale Livingston, 1970	0	0	0	19/21	15/28	0	64
Bo Molenda, 1928-32	9	0	0	10	0	0	64
Cecil Isbell, 1938-42	10	0	0	3/3	0/0	0	63
Ernie Smith, 1935-37, 39	0	0	0	43	6	0	61
Tom Birney, 1979-80	0	0	0	21/28	13/21	0	60
Joseph (Red) Dunn, 1927-31	0	1	0	48	2	0	60
Wuert Engelmann, 1930-33	2	5	3	0	0	0	60
Charles Goldenberg, 1933-45	6	1	3	0	0	0	60
Billy Grimes, 1950-52	6	2	2	0/0	0/0	0	60
Scott Hunter, 1971-73	10	0	0	0/0	0/0	0	60
Eddie Kotal, 1925-29	4	5	1	0	0	0	60
Herb Adderley, 1961-69	0	0	9	0/0	0/0	0	54
Myrt Basing, 1923-27	7	2	0	0	0	0	54
Howard (Cub) Buck, 1921-25	0	0	0	24	10	0	54
Lynn Dickey, 1976-77, 79-85	9	0	0	0/0	0/0	0	54
Willard Harrell, 1975-77	5	3	1	0/0	0/0	0	54
Jackie Harris, 1990-93	0	9	0	0/0	0/0	0	54
Don Majkowski, 1987-92	9	0	0	0/0	0/0	0	54
Darrell Thompson, 1990-94	7	1	1	0/0	0/0	0	54
Eric Torkelson, 1974-79, 81	8	1	0	0/0	0/0	0	54
Joe Danelo, 1975	0	0	0	20/23	11/16	0	53
Ward Cuff, 1947	0	0	0	30/30	7/16	0	51
Robert Brooks, 1992-94	0	5	3	0/0	0/0	0	48
Paul Ott Carruth, 1986-88	5	3	0	0/0	0/0	0	48
Milt Gantenbein, 1931-40	0	8	0	0	0	0	48
Walt Schlinkman, 1946-50	8	0	0	0/0	0/0	0	48
Aundra Thompson, 1977-81	0	7	1	0/0	0/0	0	48
Keith Woodside, 1988-91	6	2	0	0/0	0/0	0	48
Arnie Herber, 1930-40	3	3	1	2	0	0	44
Lou Michaels, 1971	0	0	0	19/20	8/14	0	43
Al Carmichael, 1953-58	2	3	2	0/0	0/0	0	42
Carleton Elliott, 1951-54	0	6	1	0/0	0/0	0	42
Howie Ferguson, 1953-58	6	1	0	0/0	0/0	0	42
Carl (Cully) Lidberg, 29-30	7	0	0	0	0	0	42
Don McIlhenny, 1957-59	3	4	0	0/0	0/0	0	42
Vito (Babe) Parilli, 1952-53, 57-58	7	0	0	0/0	0/0	0	42
George Sauer, 1935-37	6	0	1	0	0	0	42
Jon Staggers, 1972-74	1	4	2	0/0	0/0	0	42
David Whitehurst, 1977-83	7	0	0	0/0	0/0	0	42
Harry Jacunski, 1939-44	0	6	0	0/0	0/0	0	36
Perry Kemp, 1988-91	0	6	0	0/0	0/0	0	36
Marty Norton, 1925	1	4	1	0/0	0/0	0	36
Walter Stanley, 1985-88	0	5	1	0/0	0/0	0	36
Charlie Mathys, 1922-26	1	4	0	0	1	0	33
Doug Hart, 1964-71	0	0	5	0/0	0/0	1	32
Jack Cloud, 1950-51	4	1	0	0/0	0/0	0	30
Kenneth Davis, 1986-88	4	1	0	0/0	0/0	0	30
Bobby Dillon, 1952-59	0	0	5	0/0	0/0	0	30
Gary Ellerson, 1985-86	5	0	0	0/0	0/0	0	30
Ken Ellis, 1970-75	0	0	5	0/0	0/0	0	30
Rex Enright, 1926-27	3	2	0	0	0	0	30
Herman Fontenot, 1989-90	1	4	0	0/0	0/0	0	30
Harry O'Boyle, 1928, 32	1	0	0	15	3	0	30
Ken Payne, 1974-77	0	5	0	0/0	0/0	0	30
Ray Pelfrey, 1951-52	0	5	0	0/0	0/0	0	30
Everett (Pid) Purdy, 1926-27	1	0	0	15	3	0	30
Jeff Query, 1989-91	0	4	1	0/0	0/0	0	30
Al Rose, 1932-36	0	3	2	0	0	0	30
Chuck Sample, 1942, 45	4	1	0	0/0	0/0	0	30
Veryl Switzer, 1954-55	0	3	2	0/0	0/0	0	30
Walter (Tillie) Voss, 1924	0	5	0	0	0	0	30
Bill Reichardt, 1952	1	0	0	5/5	5/20	0	26
Tim Webster, 1971	0	0	0	8/8	6/11	0	26
Chuck Mercein, 1967-69	2	0	0	7/7	2/5	0	25

Name	TDr	TDp	TDrt	PAT	FG	S	TP
Ade Schwammel, 1934-36, 43-44	0	0	0	7	6	0	25
Willie Wood, 1960-71	0	0	4	1/1	0/1	0	25
Charley Brock, 1939-47	0	0	4	0/0	0/0	0	24
Reggie Cobb, 1994	3	1	0	0/0	0/0	0	24
Ted Cook, 1948-50	0	4	0	0/0	0/0	0	24
Paul Duhart, 1944	2	2	0	0/0	0/0	0	24
Ralph Earhart, 1948-49	1	2	1	0/0	0/0	0	24
Brett Favre, 1992-94	4	0	0	0/0	0/0	0	24
Bob Forte, 1946-50, 52-53	0	3	1	0/0	0/0	0	24
Earl Gros, 1962-63	4	0	0	0/0	0/0	0	24
John Hilton, 1970	0	4	0	0/0	0/0	0	24
Joe Johnson, 1954-58	0	4	0	0/0	0/0	0	24
Bob Long, 1964-67	0	4	0	0/0	0/0	0	24
Paul Miller, 1936-38	1	3	0	0	0	0	24
Anthony Morgan, 1993-94	0	4	0	0/0	0/0	0	24
Dick O'Donnell, 1924-30	0	4	0	0	0	0	24
Steve Pritko, 1949-50	0	4	0	0/0	0/0	0	24
Del Rodgers, 1982, 84	1	0	3	0/0	0/0	0	24
Bernie Scherer, 1936-38	0	3	1	0	0	0	24
Barry Smith, 1973-75	0	4	0	0/0	0/0	0	24
Ed Cody, 1947-48	2	0	0	11/13	0/0	0	23
Eddie Garcia, 1983-84	0	0	0	14/15	3/9	0	23
Tom Nash, 1928-32	0	2	1	0	0	2	22
Warren Hendrian, 1924	3	0	0	0	0	1	21
Roy McKay, 1944-47	3	0	0	3/3	0/0	0	21
Paul Fitzgibbons, 1930-32	1	2	0	1	0	0	19
Steve Atkins, 1979-81	2	1	0	0/0	0/0	0	18
Al Baldwin, 1950	0	3	0	0/0	0/0	0	18
Willie Buchanon, 1972-78	0	0	3	0/0	0/0	0	18
Mark Clayton, 1993	0	3	0	0/0	0/0	0	18
Larry Coutre, 1950, 53	1	2	0	0/0	0/0	0	18
Mike Douglass, 1978-85	0	0	3	0/0	0/0	0	18
Earl (Jug) Girard, 1948-51	1	2	0	0/0	0/0	0	18
Michael Haddix, 1989-90	0	3	0	0/0	0/0	0	18
Jack Harris, 1925-26	3	0	0	0	0	0	18
Mike Meade, 1982-83	1	2	0	0/0	0/0	0	18
Tommy Mills, 1922-23	1	2	0	0	0	0	18
Dom Moselle, 1951-52	1	2	0	0/0	0/0	0	18
Frankie Neal, 1987	0	3	0	0/0	0/0	0	18
Don Perkins, 1943-45	1	0	2	0/0	0/0	0	18
Harry Sydney, 1992	2	1	0	0/0	0/0	0	18
Jerry Tagge, 1972-74	3	0	0	0/0	0/0	0	18
Hal Van Every, 1940-41	2	0	1	0/0	0/0	0	18
Randy Wright, 1984-88	3	0	0	0/0	0/0	0	18
Bob Adkins, 1940-41, 45	0	1	1	4/4	0/1	0	16
Willie Davis, 1960-69	0	0	2	0/0	0/0	2	16
Booth Lusteg, 1969	0	0	0	12/12	1/5	0	15
Bruce Smith, 1945-48	1	1	0	0/0	0/0	1	14
Carl Bland, 1989-90	0	1	1	0/0	0/0	0	12
Tom Brown, 1964-68	0	0	2	0/0	0/0	0	12
Terrell Buckley, 1992-94	0	0	2	0/0	0/0	0	12
Lee Roy Caffey, 1965-69	0	0	2	0/0	0/0	0	12
Jack Clancy, 1970	0	2	0	0/0	0/0	0	12
Bill (Gus) DuMoe, 1921	0	1	1	0	0	0	12
Preston Dennard, 1985	0	2	0	0/0	0/0	0	12
Clint Didier, 1988-89	0	2	0	0/0	0/0	0	12
Dick Flaherty, 1926	0	2	0	0	0	0	12
Robert (Cal) Hubbard, 1929-33, 35	0	1	1	0	0	0	12
Jack Jacobs, 1947-49	2	0	0	0/0	0/0	0	12
Claudis James, 1967-69	0	2	0	0/0	0/0	0	12
Bob Jeter, 1963-70	0	0	2	0/0	0/0	0	12
Chester Johnston, 1931, 34-37	1	1	0	0	0	0	12
Walt Landers, 1978-79	0	1	1	0/0	0/0	0	12
Gary Lewis, 1981-84	1	1	0	0/0	0/0	0	12
Mark Lewis, 1985-87	0	2	0	0/0	0/0	0	12
Tim Lewis, 1983-86	0	0	2	0/0	0/0	0	12
Larry Marks, 1928	0	2	0	0/0	0/0	0	12
John Martinkovic, 1951-56	0	0	2	0/0	0/0	0	12
Joel Mason, 1942-45	0	2	0	0/0	0/0	0	12
Aubrey Matthews, 1988-89	0	2	0	0/0	0/0	0	12
Mike Michalske, 1929-35, 37	0	0	2	0	0	0	12
Blake Moore, 1984-85	0	2	0	0/0	0/0	0	12
Ray Nitschke, 1958-72	0	0	2	0/0	0/0	0	12
Art Schmael, 1921	2	0	0	0	0	0	12
Herm Schneidman, 1935-39	0	2	0	0/0	0/0	0	12
Ben Starret, 1942-45	0	2	0	0/0	0/0	0	12
John Thompson, 1979-82	0	2	0	0/0	0/0	0	12
Lyle (Cowboy) Wheeler, 1921-23	0	1	1	0	0	0	12
Ben Wilson, 1967	2	0	0	0/0	0/0	0	12
Charles Wilson, 1990-91	0	1	1	0/0	0/0	0	12
Faye (Mule) Wilson, 1931	2	0	0	0	0	0	12
Ben Agajanian, 1961	0	0	0	8/8	1/2	0	11
John Anderson, 1978-89	0	0	1	1/2	1/1	0	10
Dale Dawson, 1988	0	0	0	1/2	3/5	0	10
Tim Harris, 1986-90	0	0	1	0/0	0/0	2	10
Howard (Whitey) Woodin, 1922-31	0	0	1	4	0	0	10
George Abramson, 1925	0	0	0	2	2	0	8
Robert Brown, 1982-92	0	0	1	0/0	0/0	1	8
Bryce Paup, 1990-94	0	0	1	0/0	0/0	1	8

Name	TDr	TDp	TDrt	PAT	FG	S	TP
Frank Balazs, 1939-41	1	0	0	1/1	0/0	0	7
Nate Abrams, 1921	0	0	1	0	0	0	6
Lionel Aldridge, 1963-71	0	0	1	0/0	0/0	0	6
Bill Anderson, 1965-66	0	1	0	0/0	0/0	0	6
Bert Askson, 1975-77	0	1	0	0/0	0/0	0	6
Frank Baker, 1931	0	1	0	0	0	0	6
Norm Barry, 1921	1	0	0	0	0	0	6
Don Barton, 1953	0	0	1	0/0	0/0	0	6
Sanjay Beach, 1992	0	1	0	0/0	0/0	0	6
Wayland Becker, 1936-38	0	1	0	0/0	0/0	0	6
Tony Bennett, 1990-93	0	0	1	0/0	0/0	0	6
J.R. Boone, 1953	0	1	0	0/0	0/0	0	6
Zeke Bratkowski, 1963-68, 71	1	0	0	0/0	0/0	0	6
Mark Brunell, 1994	1	0	0	0/0	0/0	0	6
Bill Butler, 1959	0	0	1	0/0	0/0	0	6
LeRoy Butler, 1990-94	0	0	1	0/0	0/0	0	6
Mike Butler, 1977-82, 85	0	0	1	0/0	0/0	0	6
Ivan Cahoon, 1926-29	0	0	1	0	0	0	6
Lew Carpenter, 1959-63	1	0	0	0/0	0/0	0	6
Fred Carr, 1968-77	0	0	1	0/0	0/0	0	6
Jim Carter, 1970-75, 77-78	0	0	1	0/0	0/0	0	6
Joe Carter, 1942	0	1	0	0/0	0/0	0	6
Paul Christman, 1950	1	0	0	0/0	0/0	0	6
Jack Concannon, 1974	1	0	0	0/0	0/0	0	6
Larry Craig, 1939-49	0	1	0	0/0	0/0	0	6
Bernie Crimmins, 1945	0	0	1	0/0	0/0	0	6
Tommy Cronin, 1922	0	1	0	0	0	0	6
Ray Crouse, 1984	0	1	0	0/0	0/0	0	6
Jim Crowley, 1925	1	0	0	0	0	0	6
Dan Currie, 1958-64	0	0	1	0/0	0/0	0	6
Gib Dawson, 1953	0	0	1	0/0	0/0	0	6
Dave Davis, 1971	0	1	0	0/0	0/0	0	6
Dean Dorsey, 1988	0	0	0	3/4	1/3	0	6
Wally Dreyer, 1950	0	0	1	0/0	0/0	0	6
Tony Falkenstein, 1943	1	0	0	0/0	0/0	0	6
Bobby Jack Floyd, 1952	1	0	0	0/0	0/0	0	6
Joe Francis, 1958-59	1	0	0	0/0	0/0	0	6
Milton (Moose) Gardner, 1922-26	0	0	1	0	0	0	6
Jim Gillette, 1947	0	1	0	0/0	0/0	0	6
Leland Glass, 1972-73	0	1	0	0/0	0/0	0	6
Les Goodman, 1973-74	1	0	0	0/0	0/0	0	6
Johnnie Gray, 1975-84	0	0	1	0/0	0/0	0	6
George (Tiger) Greene, 1986-90	0	0	1	0/0	0/0	0	6
Tom Greenfield, 1939-41	0	0	1	0/0	0/0	0	6
Hank Gremminger, 1956-65	0	0	1	0/0	0/0	0	6
Joey Hackett, 1987-88	0	1	0	0/0	0/0	0	6
James Hargrove, 1987	1	0	0	0/0	0/0	0	6
Maurice Harvey, 1981-83	0	0	1	0/0	0/0	0	6
Les Hearden, 1924	0	1	0	0	0	0	6
Stan Heath, 1949	1	0	0	0/0	0/0	0	6
Estus Hood, 1978-84	0	0	1	0/0	0/0	0	6
Don Horn, 1967-70	1	0	0	0/0	0/0	0	6
Lynn (Tubby) Howard, 1921-22	1	0	0	0	0	0	6
Bob Ingalls, 1942	0	0	1	0/0	0/0	0	6
Jim Jensen, 1981-82	1	0	0	0/0	0/0	0	6
Glen Johnson, 1949	0	0	1	0/0	0/0	0	6
Randy Johnson, 1976	1	0	0	0/0	0/0	0	6
Bruce Jones, 1927-28	0	0	1	0/0	0/0	0	6
Henry Jordan, 1959-69	0	1	0	0/0	0/0	0	6
Jim Keane, 1952	0	1	0	0/0	0/0	0	6
Bill Kelley, 1949	0	1	0	0/0	0/0	0	6
Blair Kiel, 1990-91	1	0	0	0/0	0/0	0	6
Larry Krause, 1970-71, 73-74	0	0	1	0/0	0/0	0	6
Bill Larsen, 1980	0	0	1	0/0	0/0	0	6
Mark Lee, 1980-90	0	0	1	0/0	0/0	0	6
Ace Loomis, 1951-53	0	0	1	0/0	0/0	0	6
Steve Luke, 1975-80	0	0	1	0/0	0/0	0	6
Larry Mason, 1988	0	1	0	0/0	0/0	0	6
Al Matthews, 1970-75	0	0	1	0/0	0/0	0	6
Mike P. McCoy, 1970-76	0	0	1	0/0	0/0	0	6
Lamar McHan, 1959-60	1	0	0	0/0	0/0	0	6
Steve Meilinger, 1958, 60	0	1	0	0/0	0/0	0	6
Lee Morris, 1987	0	1	0	0/0	0/0	0	6
Mark Murphy, 1980-85, 87-91	0	0	1	0/0	0/0	0	6
Ed Neal, 1945-51	0	0	1	0/0	0/0	0	6
Brian Noble, 1985-93	0	0	1	0/0	0/0	0	6
Dan Orlich, 1949-51	0	1	0	0/0	0/0	0	6
Ernie Pannell, 1941-42, 45	0	0	1	0/0	0/0	0	6
Johnny Papit, 1953	1	0	0	0/0	0/0	0	6
Keith Paskett, 1987	0	1	0	0/0	0/0	0	6
Shawn Patterson, 1988-91, 93	0	0	1	0/0	0/0	0	6
Ron Pitts, 1988-90	0	0	1	0/0	0/0	0	6
Keith Ranspot, 1942	0	1	0	0/0	0/0	0	6
Ray Riddick, 1940-42, 46	0	1	0	0/0	0/0	0	6
Alan Risher, 1987	1	0	0	0/0	0/0	0	6
John Roach, 1961-63	1	0	0	0/0	0/0	0	6
Ken Roskie, 1948	1	0	0	0/0	0/0	0	6
Dan Ross, 1986	0	1	0	0/0	0/0	0	6
Russ Saunders, 1931	1	0	0	0	0	0	6

Name	TDr	TDp	TDrt	PAT	FG	S	TP
Francis (Zud) Schammel, 1937	0	0	1	0	0	0	6
Patrick Scott, 1987-88	0	1	0	0/0	0/0	0	6
John Simmons, 1986	0	0	1	0/0	0/0	0	6
Nate Simpson, 1977-79	1	0	0	0/0	0/0	0	6
Ollie Smith, 1976-77	0	1	0	0/0	0/0	0	6
John Spilis, 1969-71	0	1	0	0/0	0/0	0	6
Rebel Steiner, 1950-51	0	0	1	0/0	0/0	0	6
John Stephens, 1993	1	0	0	0/0	0/0	0	6
Ken Stills, 1985-88	0	0	1	0/0	0/0	0	6
Bob Summerhays, 1949-51	0	0	1	0/0	0/0	0	6
Don Summers, 1987	0	1	0	0/0	0/0	0	6
Earl Svendsen, 1937, 39	0	0	1	0	0	0	6
Karl Swanke, 1980-86	0	1	0	0/0	0/0	0	6
Len Szafaryn, 1950, 53-56	0	0	1	0/0	0/0	0	6
Claude Taugher, 1922	1	0	0	0	0	0	6
Cliff Taylor, 1976	1	0	0	0/0	0/0	0	6
Kitrick Taylor, 1992	0	1	0	0/0	0/0	0	6
Lavale Thomas, 1987-88	0	1	0	0/0	0/0	0	6
Gerald Tinker, 1975	0	1	0	0/0	0/0	0	6
Mike Tomczak, 1991	1	0	0	0/0	0/0	0	6
Walter Tullis, 1978-79	0	1	0	0/0	0/0	0	6
Alex Urban, 1941, 44-45	0	1	0	0/0	0/0	0	6
Eddie Usher, 1922, 24	1	0	0	0	0	0	6
Val Joe Walker, 1953-56	0	0	1	0/0	0/0	0	6
Clarence Weathers, 1990-91	0	1	0	0/0	0/0	0	6
Jess Whittenton, 1958-64	0	0	1	0/0	0/0	0	6
Clarence Williams, 1970-77	0	0	1	0/0	0/0	0	6
Perry Williams, 1969-73	1	0	0	0/0	0/0	0	6
Paul Winslow, 1960	0	0	1	0/0	0/0	0	6
Dave Conway, 1971	0	0	0	5/5	0/1	0	5
Joe Etheridge, 1949	0	0	0	1/1	1/2	0	4
Errol Mann, 1968	0	0	0	4/4	0/3	0	4
Dave Pureifory, 1972-77	0	0	0	2/4	0/0	1	4
Herman Rohrig, 1941, 46-47	0	0	0	1/1	1/1	0	4
Chet Adams, 1943	0	0	0	0/0	1/6	0	3
Greg Boyd, 1983	0	0	0	0/0	0/0	1	2
Bob Brown, 1966-73	0	0	0	0/0	0/0	1	2
Curtis Burrow, 1988	0	0	0	2/4	0/1	0	2

Name	TDr	TDp	TDrt	PAT	FG	S	TP
Bill Forester, 1953-63	0	0	0	0/0	0/0	1	2
Dave Hanner, 1952-64	0	0	0	0/0	0/0	1	2
Ted Hendricks, 1974	0	0	0	0/0	0/0	1	2
Walter Niemann, 1922-24	0	0	0	0	0	1	2
Urban Odson, 1946-49	0	0	0	0/0	0/0	1	2
Tom Toner, 1973-77	0	0	0	0/0	0/0	1	2
Dick Weisgerber, 1938-40, 42	0	0	0	2/2	0/0	0	2
Dick Wildung, 1946-51, 53	0	0	0	0/0	0/0	1	2
Cal Clemmens, 1936	0	0	0	1	0	0	1
Glen Sorenson, 1943-45	0	0	0	1/1	0/5	0	1
Clayton Tonnemaker, 1950, 53-54	0	0	0	1/1	0/0	0	1
Rich Wingo, 1979, 81-83	0	0	0	1	0/0	0	1
team	0	0	0	*1	—	17	35
Packers, 1921-94	**950**	**1,104**	**202**	**2,025[1]**	**808**	**37**	**18,059**
Opponents, 1921-94	873	922	207	1,828[2]	843	46	16,461

*Packers were awarded a PAT in 1922 against Minneapolis as the Marines were offside on the attempt.

[1] Includes a 2-point conversion by Ed West in 1994.
[2] Includes three 2-point conversions in 1994.

Green Bay Press-Gazette photo

Jan Stenerud (10) kicks off to the Tampa Bay Buccaneers. Stenrud scored 292 points while at Green Bay.

Green Bay Press-Gazette photo

Chris Jacke (13) celebrates his game-winning, 47-yard field goal at Tampa Bay in 1989. In six years, Jacke has registered 612 points.

ALL-TIME FUMBLES AND RECOVERIES

(Statistic kept since 1945; players are listed alphabetically)

Name	Fum	Own Rec	Opp Rec	Yds	Tot Rec
Cliff Aberson, 1941, 46-47	2	0	1	0	1
Herb Adderley, 1961-69	9	5	8	60	13
Bob Adkins, 1940-41, 45	1	1	0	0	1
Ben Aldridge, 1953	0	0	2	0	2
Lionel Aldridge, 1963-71	1	0	16	44	16
Kurt Allerman, 1980-81	0	0	1	0	1
Donny Anderson, 1966-71	31	5	0	-5	5
John Anderson, 1978-89	0	0	15	22	15
Vickey Ray Anderson, 1980	1	0	0	0	0
Charlie Ane, 1981	0	1	1	0	2
Billy Ard, 1989-91	0	2	0	0	2
Bert Askson, 1975-77	0	0	1	0	1
Steve Atkins, 1979-81	3	1	0	0	1
Buddy Aydelette, 1980	1	0	0	-28	0
Byron Bailey, 1953	1	0	0	0	0
Al Baldwin, 1950	3	1	0	-3	1
Bob Barber, 1976-79	0	0	4	0	4
Carl Barzilauskas, 1978-79	0	0	1	0	1
Lloyd Baxter, 1948	0	0	1	0	1
Sanjay Beach, 1992	1	0	0	0	1
Ed Bell, 1947-49	0	1	0	0	1
Edgar Bennett, 1992-94	3	2	0	0	2
Tony Bennett, 1990-93	0	0	4	18	4
Ed Berry, 1986	0	1	0	0	1
Tom Bettis, 1955-61	0	0	5	4	5
David Beverly, 1975-80	3	2	0	-16	2
Lewis Billups, 1992	0	0	1	0	1
Carl Bland, 1989-90	0	2	2	4	4
Billy Bookout, 1955-56	0	1	2	0	3
J.R. Boone, 1953	1	1	0	0	1
Nate Borden, 1955-59	0	0	7	0	7
Ken Bowman, 1964-73	2	3	0	-28	3
Dave Bradley, 1969-71	0	0	1	0	1
Byron Braggs, 1981-83	0	0	2	0	2
Zeke Bratkowski, 1963-68, 71	10	5	0	0	5
Charley Brock, 1939-47	0	2	11	83	13
Lou Brock, 1940-45	1	0	0	0	0
Matt Brock, 1989-94	0	0	3	34	3
John Brockington, 1971-77	23	6	0	0	6
Robert Brooks, 1992-94	5	2	0	0	2
Bill Brown, 1953-56	0	2	1	0	3
Bob Brown, 1966-73	0	0	1	0	1
Carlos Brown, 1975-76	3	3	0	-2	3
Ken Brown, 1980	1	0	0	-37	0
Robert Brown, 1982-92	0	0	13	0	13
Tom Brown, 1964-68	0	0	6	27	6
Mark Brunell, 1994	1	0	0	-2	0
Willie Buchanon, 1972-78	1	0	8	9	8
Terrell Buckley, 1992-94	8	3	2	0	5
Hank Bullough, 1955, 58	0	0	1	0	1
Paul (Buddy) Burris, 1949-51	0	1	1	0	2
Blair Bush, 1989-91	0	1	1	0	2
Bill Butler, 1959	1	1	0	0	1
LeRoy Butler, 1990-94	0	0	3	42	3
Mike Butler, 1977-82, 85	0	0	3	70	3
Mossy Cade, 1985-86	0	0	1	0	1
Lee Roy Caffey, 1964-69	0	1	3	0	4
Rich Campbell, 1981-84	1	0	0	0	0
James Campen, 1989-93	2	2	0	-21	2
Tony Canadeo, 1941-44, 46-52	23	5	0	2	5
Al Cannava, 1950	1	0	0	0	0
Mark Cannon, 1985-88	3	2	0	-39	2
Jim Capuzzi, 1955-56	0	0	1	0	1
Al Carmichael, 1953-58	16	3	0	0	3
Lew Carpenter, 1959-63	8	0	1	0	1
Fred Carr, 1968-77	0	0	15	64	15
Alphonso Carreker, 1984-88	0	0	3	0	3
Leo Carroll, 1968	0	0	1	0	1
Paul Ott Carruth, 1986-88	5	0	0	0	0
Jim Carter, 1970-75, 77-78	0	0	7	19	7
Ron Cassidy, 1979-81, 83-84	2	0	0	0	0
Chuck Cecil, 1988-92	1	0	1	0	1
Bill Cherry, 1986-87	1	0	0	-23	0
Putt Choate, 1987	0	0	1	4	1
Paul Christman, 1950	2	0	0	0	0
Mark Chmura, 1993-94	1	1	0	0	1
Gus Cifelli, 1953	0	1	0	0	1
Bob Cifers, 1949	0	1	0	5	1
Dennis Claridge, 1965	1	0	0	0	0
Allan Clark, 1982	1	1	0	0	1
Jessie Clark, 1983-87	9	3	0	0	3
Jack Cloud, 1950-51	3	1	0	0	1
Reggie Cobb, 1994	1	0	0	0	0
Ed Cody, 1947-48	4	1	0	0	1
Junior Coffey, 1965	0	0	1	0	1
Paul Coffman, 1978-85	8	1	1	0	2
Keo Coleman, 1993	0	0	1	0	1
Irv Comp, 1943-49	16	9	4	-1	13
Fred Cone, 1951-57	14	6	2	5	8
Ted Cook, 1948-50	2	0	1	2	1
Larry Coutre, 1950, 53	1	0	0	0	0
Larry Craig, 1939-49	0	2	9	21	11
Ted Cremer, 1948	0	0	1	0	1
Milburn (Tiny) Croft, 1942-47	0	0	3	16	3
Jim Culbreath, 1977-79	2	3	0	0	3
George Cumby, 1980-85	0	0	5	70	5
Dan Currie, 1958-64	0	0	6	0	6
Bill Curry, 1965-66	0	1	0	0	1
Carroll Dale, 1965-72	4	1	0	0	1
Ernie Danjean, 1957	0	0	1	0	1
Dave Davis, 1971-72	1	1	0	18	1
Harper Davis, 1951	0	0	1	0	1
Kenneth Davis, 1986-88	4	0	0	0	0
Willie Davis, 1960-69	0	1	21	19	22
Gib Dawson, 1953	1	0	0	0	0
Walter Dean, 1991	1	0	0	0	0
Jim Del Gaizo, 1973	3	2	0	0	2
Preston Dennard, 1985	0	0	0	0	0
Burnell Dent, 1986-92	0	0	2	0	2
Lynn Dickey, 1976-77, 79-85	56	26	0	-82	26
Clint Didier, 1988-89	1	0	1	4	1
Bobby Dillon, 1952-59	1	0	3	0	3
Anthony Dilweg, 1989-90	10	4	0	-9	4
John Dittrich, 1959	0	0	1	0	1
Mike Donohoe, 1973-74	0	0	1	2	1
John Dorsey, 1984-88	0	0	4	0	4
Mike Douglass, 1978-85	1	1	15	63	16
Boyd Dowler, 1959-69	8	0	0	0	0
Ralph Earhart, 1948-49	5	2	0	0	2
Gary Ellerson, 1985-86	6	2	1	0	3
Carleton Elliott, 1951-54	0	0	2	17	2
Gerry Ellis, 1980-86	33	9	0	0	9
Ken Ellis, 1970-75	7	2	4	11	6
Phillip Epps, 1982-88	6	1	0	0	1
Joe Etheridge, 1949	0	0	1	0	1
Doug Evans, 1993-94	0	0	3	3	3
Hal Faverty, 1952	0	0	3	0	3
Brett Favre, 1992-94	33	6	0	-13	6
Howie Ferguson, 1953-58	29	7	0	0	7
Vince Ferragamo, 1985	3	0	0	-8	0
Lou Ferry, 1949	0	0	2	0	2
Jim Flanigan, 1967-70	0	0	1	0	1
Marv Fleming, 1963-69	0	2	1	0	3
Bob Flowers, 1942-49	0	0	2	1	2
Bobby Jack Floyd, 1952	5	1	0	0	1
Tom Flynn, 1984-86	1	0	4	3	4
Herman Fontenot, 1989-90	1	1	2	0	3
Len Ford, 1958	0	0	1	5	1
Bill Forester, 1953-63	3	2	13	45	15
Aldo Forte, 1947	0	0	2	1	2
Bob Forte, 1946-50, 52-53	4	2	9	3	11
Joe Francis, 1958-59	3	0	0	0	0
Ted Fritsch, 1942-50	10	4	5	-1	9
Brent Fullwood, 1987-90	15	3	0	0	3
Chuck Fusina, 1986	4	4	0	-1	4
Bob Garrett, 1954	2	1	0	0	1
Len Garrett, 1971-72	0	0	1	0	1
Lester Gatewood, 1946-47	0	1	1	0	2
Jim Gillette, 1947	2	0	0	0	0
Gale Gillingham, 1966-74, 76	0	2	0	0	2
Earl (Jug) Girard, 1948-51	8	3	1	5	4
Leland Glass, 1972-73	0	1	0	0	1
Derrel Gofourth, 1977-82	0	2	0	0	2
Les Goodman, 1973-74	3	0	0	0	0
Clyde Goodnight, 1945-49	3	2	0	8	2
Jim Grabowski, 1966-70	13	1	0	0	1
Johnnie Gray, 1975-84	6	2	20	30	22
George (Tiger) Greene, 1986-90	1	0	3	0	3

Name	Fum	Own Rec	Opp Rec	Yds	Tot Rec
Forrest Gregg, 1956, 58-70	0	8	0	0	8
Hank Gremminger, 1956-65	1	0	7	0	7
Billy Grimes, 1950-52	18	5	0	0	5
Dan Grimm, 1963-65	0	0	1	0	1
Earl Gros, 1962-63	7	1	1	0	2
Jim Gueno, 1976-80	0	3	1	0	4
Michael Haddix, 1989-90	5	0	0	0	0
John Hadl, 1974-75	11	3	0	-12	3
Charlie Hall, 1971-76	1	1	0	0	1
Ron Hallstrom, 1982-92	0	4	1	1	5
Dave Hampton, 1969-71	17	4	0	0	4
Dave Hanner, 1952-64	0	1	8	0	9
Derrick Harden, 1987	1	0	0	0	0
Leon Harden, 1970	1	0	0	0	0
Roger Harding, 1949	0	1	0	0	1
Willard Harrell, 1975-77	23	2	1	0	3
Corey Harris, 1992-94	1	1	0	0	1
Jackie Harris, 1990-93	2	0	1	0	1
Leotis Harris, 1978-83	0	3	0	0	3
Tim Harris, 1986-90	0	0	6	28	6
Anthony Harrison, 1987	0	0	1	0	1
Doug Hart, 1964-71	0	0	5	20	5
Maurice Harvey, 1981-83	1	1	5	25	6
Tim Hauck, 1991-94	0	0	2	0	2
Gary Hayes, 1984-86	1	1	2	0	3
Bill Hayhoe, 1969-74	0	1	0	0	1
Stan Heath, 1949	2	0	0	0	0
Larry Hefner, 1972-75	0	1	1	4	2
Jerry Helluin, 1954-57	0	0	6	0	6
Ted Hendricks, 1974	0	0	1	0	1
Don Highsmith, 1973	1	0	0	0	0
Jim Hill, 1972-74	0	0	5	15	5
John Hilton, 1970	1	2	0	0	2
Dick Himes, 1968-77	0	3	0	1	3
Jim Hobbins, 1987	0	1	0	0	1
Johnny Holland, 1987-93	4	1	14	3	15
Jerry Holmes, 1990-91	0	0	4	56	4
Estus Hood, 1978-84	0	0	2	0	2
Don Horn, 1967-70	11	4	0	0	4
Paul Hornung, 1957-62, 64-66	22	2	1	0	3
Bill Howton, 1952-58	5	2	0	0	2
Harlan Huckleby, 1980-85	8	2	0	0	2
Bob Hudson, 1972	1	0	0	0	0
Donnie Humphrey, 1984-86	0	0	1	0	1
Mike Hunt, 1978-80	0	0	1	0	1
Art Hunter, 1954	0	1	0	0	1
Scott Hunter, 1971-73	13	5	0	-11	5
Don Hutson, 1935-45	1	0	0	0	0
Bob Hyland, 1967-69, 76	1	0	0	0	0
Ken Iman, 1960-63	0	0	1	0	1
Eddie Lee Ivery, 1979-86	9	2	2	0	4
Jack Jacobs, 1947-49	6	2	1	-3	3
Claudis James, 1967-69	2	0	0	0	0
John Jefferson, 1981-84	1	0	0	0	0
Norman Jefferson, 1987-88	5	1	1	0	2
Jim Jennings, 1955	0	0	1	0	1
Jim Jensen, 1981-82	2	0	0	0	0
Bob Jeter, 1963-70	0	0	2	7	2
Charles Johnson, 1979-80, 83	0	0	2	0	2
Ezra Johnson, 1977-87	0	0	7	0	7
Joe Johnson, 1954-58	6	0	0	0	0
KeShon Johnson, 1994	0	0	1	0	1
Marvin Johnson, 1952-53	0	0	1	0	1
Randy Johnson, 1976	2	1	0	-4	1
Mike Jolly, 1980, 82-83	0	0	1	0	1
Daryll Jones, 1984-85	0	1	2	0	3
Sean Jones, 1994	0	0	3	0	3
Terry Jones, 1978-84	0	0	5	0	5
Charles Jordan, 1994	1	0	0	0	0
Henry Jordan, 1959-69	0	2	18	67	20
Bill Kelley, 1949	1	0	0	0	0
Perry Kemp, 1988-91	10	1	0	0	1
Ken Keuper, 1945-47	0	0	3	0	3
Blair Kiel, 1990-91	4	2	0	0	2
J.D. Kimmel, 1958	0	0	1	0	1
Billy Kinard, 1957-58	2	0	2	14	2
John Kirby, 1949	3	0	0	0	0
Gary Knafelc, 1954-62	0	1	0	0	1
Gene Knutson, 1954, 56	0	0	1	0	1
Matt Koart, 1986	0	0	1	0	1
Greg Koch, 1978-85	0	1	0	0	1
Mark Koncar, 1976-77, 79-81	0	2	0	0	2
George Koonce, 1992-94	0	0	4	0	4
Dave Kopay, 1972	1	0	1	0	1
Ron Kostelnik, 1961-68	0	0	7	0	7
Jerry Kramer, 1958-68	0	3	0	13	3
Ron Kramer, 1957, 59-64	3	1	0	0	1
Kenneth Kranz, 1949	0	0	1	7	1
Larry Krause, 1970-71, 73-74	3	0	3	0	3
Bob Kroll, 1972-73	0	0	1	0	1
Pete Lammons, 1972	0	1	0	0	1
MacArthur Lane, 1972-74	13	2	0	0	2
Kit Lathrop, 1979-80	0	2	0	0	2
Larry Lauer, 1956-57	0	0	1	0	1
Joe Laws, 1934-45	2	1	0	2	1
Mark Lee, 1980-90	2	0	6	15	6
Gary Lewis, 1981-84	0	1	0	0	1
Tim Lewis, 1983-86	3	1	1	6	2
Paul Lipscomb, 1945-49	0	2	9	1	11
Dick Logan, 1952-53	0	0	1	0	1
James Lofton, 1978-86	14	3	0	8	3
Ace Loomis, 1951-53	2	0	5	0	5
John Losch, 1956	3	3	0	0	3
Bill Lueck, 1968-74	0	1	0	0	1
Nolan Luhn, 1945-49	2	1	1	4	2
Steve Luke, 1975-80	1	0	6	0	6
Tom MacLeod, 1973	0	0	2	0	2
Don Majkowski, 1987-92	48	19	0	-26	19
Tony Mandarich, 1989-91	0	1	0	0	1
Von Mansfield, 1987	1	0	0	0	0
Rich Marshall, 1965	0	0	1	0	1
Charles Martin, 1984-86	0	0	2	0	2
John Martinkovic, 1951-56	0	0	10	32	10
Dave Mason, 1974	0	0	1	19	1
Joel Mason, 1942-45	0	0	1	0	1
Carlton Massey, 1957-58	0	0	1	0	1
Norm Masters, 1957-64	0	4	0	0	4
Al Matthews, 1970-75	0	0	7	-7	7
Larry McCarren, 1973-84	1	1	0	0	1
Mike C. McCoy, 1976-83	6	1	4	0	5
Mike P. McCoy, 1970-76	1	0	12	36	12
John McDowell, 1964	0	0	1	0	1
Clink McGeary, 1950	0	1	0	0	1
Max McGee, 1954, 57-67	6	4	0	43	4
Rich McGeorge, 1970-78	2	5	2	0	7
Michael McGruder, 1989	0	1	0	0	1
Lamar McHan, 1959-60	3	0	0	0	0
Don McIlhenny, 1957-59	13	4	0	0	4
Paul McJulien, 1991-92	1	2	0	-2	2
Roy McKay, 1944-47	6	4	0	10	4
Mike McLeod, 1984-85	0	0	1	0	1
Steve McMichael, 1994	0	0	1	0	1
Mike Meade, 1982-83	2	1	0	0	1
Chuck Mercein, 1967-69	1	0	1	0	1
Casey Merrill, 1979-83	0	0	4	0	4
Frank Mestnik, 1963	0	0	1	0	1
Terdell Middleton, 1977-81	18	4	0	0	4
Don Milan, 1975	1	0	0	0	0
Keith Millard, 1992	0	0	1	0	1
Roland Mitchell, 1991-93	0	0	1	0	1
Blake Moore, 1984-85	1	0	0	0	0
Rich Moore, 1969-70	0	0	1	0	1
Tom Moore, 1960-65	12	4	0	2	4
Rich Moran, 1985-93	1	3	0	3	3
Anthony Morgan, 1993-94	1	0	0	0	0
Lee Morris, 1987	1	2	0	0	2
Jim Morrissey, 1993	0	0	1	0	1
Dom Moselle, 1951-52	4	1	1	0	2
Perry Moss, 1948	3	1	0	-1	1
Mark Murphy, 1980-85, 87-91	1	0	13	2	13
Ed Neal, 1945-51	1	3	2	0	5
Frankie Neal, 1987	1	0	0	0	0
Bob Nelson, 1988-90	0	0	1	0	1
Tom Neville, 1986-88, 92	0	1	0	0	1
Ray Nitschke, 1958-72	2	3	20	34	23
Doyle Nix, 1955	0	0	1	0	1
Fred Nixon, 1980-81	3	0	0	0	0
Brian Noble, 1985-93	0	0	11	1	11
Rick Norton, 1970	0	1	0	0	1
Bob Nussbaumer, 1946, 51	1	1	0	0	1
Rick Nuzum, 1978	0	0	1	15	1
Steve Odom, 1974-79	15	6	0	0	6
Urban Odson, 1946-49	0	0	3	0	3
Ralph Olsen, 1949	0	1	0	0	1
Larry Olsonoski, 1948-49	0	2	0	0	2
Ed O'Neil, 1980	0	0	2	26	2
Dan Orlich, 1949-51	0	0	4	68	4
Vito (Babe) Parilli, 1952-53, 57-58	19	4	0	0	4
Shawn Patterson, 1988-91, 93	0	0	1	0	1
Ricky Patton, 1979	1	0	0	0	0
Bryce Paup, 1990-94	0	1	3	0	4
Ken Payne, 1974-77	0	2	0	0	2
Francis Peay, 1968-72	0	1	0	0	1
Ray Pelfrey, 1951-52	1	0	0	0	0
Don Perkins, 1943-45	0	0	1	15	1
John Petitbon, 1957	0	0	1	0	1

Name	Fum	Own Rec	Opp Rec	Yds	Tot Rec
Elijah Pitts, 1961-69, 71	14	3	1	0	4
Ron Pitts, 1988-90	1	2	3	0	5
Guy Prather, 1981-85	1	0	2	0	2
Steve Pritko, 1949-50	1	0	0	0	0
John Pointer, 1987	0	0	1	0	1
Mike Prior, 1993-94	6	4	0	0	4
Fred Provo, 1948	1	1	0	0	1
Jim Psaltis, 1954	0	0	1	0	1
Dave Pureifory, 1972-77	0	0	4	11	4
Frank Purnell, 1957	1	1	0	0	1
Jeff Query, 1989-91	5	3	2	0	5
Bill Quinlan, 1959-62	1	0	2	0	2
Al Randolph, 1971	1	0	2	0	2
Buford (Baby) Ray, 1938-48	0	0	6	5	6
Bill Reichardt, 1952	1	0	0	0	0
Floyd (Breezy) Reid, 1950-56	15	7	0	2	7
Jay Rhodemyre, 1948-49, 51-52	0	1	1	0	2
Allen Rice, 1991	2	0	0	0	0
Jim Ringo, 1953-63	0	5	2	1	7
Alan Risher, 1987	4	1	0	0	1
John Roach, 1961-63	4	0	0	0	1
Dave Robinson, 1963-72	1	1	8	23	9
Alden Roche, 1971-76	0	0	8	17	8
Del Rodgers, 1982, 84	3	2	0	0	2
Herman Rohrig, 1941, 46-47	4	2	2	-2	4
Dave Roller, 1975-78	0	1	4	-4	5
Tobin Rote, 1950-56	44	10	0	-21	10
John Rowser, 1967-69	0	0	1	0	1
Larry Rubens, 1982-83	1	0	1	-15	1
Ken Ruettgers, 1985-94	0	9	0	0	9
Howard Ruetz, 1951-53	0	0	3	13	3
Clive Rush, 1953	1	0	0	0	0
Steve Ruzich, 1952-54	1	2	1	0	3
Jim Salsbury, 1957-58	0	1	1	0	2
Howard Sampson, 1978-79	1	0	0	0	0
Hurles Scales, 1975	0	0	1	0	1
Walt Schlinkman, 1946-50	20	5	0	10	5
Carl Schuette, 1950-51	0	0	3	8	3
Harry Schuh, 1974	0	2	0	0	2
Patrick Scott, 1987-88	2	2	0	0	2
Randy Scott, 1981-86	0	0	6	31	6
Clarence Self, 1952, 54-55	0	0	4	10	4
Washington Sereni, 1952	0	0	3	0	3
Jim Shanley, 1958	1	1	0	0	1
Sterling Sharpe, 1988-94	9	5	0	5	5
Vai Sikahema, 1991	3	0	0	0	0
Wayne Simmons, 1993-94	0	1	0	0	1
Nate Simpson, 1977-79	7	2	0	0	2
Joe Sims, 1992-94	0	1	0	0	1
Bob Skoglund, 1947	0	0	2	0	2
Bob Skoronski, 1956, 59-68	0	1	0	0	1
Barty Smith, 1974-80	13	3	0	0	3
Bruce Smith, 1945-48	4	1	0	-2	1
Ollie Smith, 1976-77	3	0	0	0	0
Oscar E. Smith, 1948-49	2	0	0	0	0
Perry Smith, 1973-76	0	0	1	0	1
Ken Snelling, 1945	1	0	0	0	0
Glen Sorenson, 1943-45	0	0	1	0	1
Joe Spencer, 1950-51	0	1	1	0	2
Ollie Spencer, 1957-58	0	0	1	0	1
John Spilis, 1969-71	1	0	0	0	0
Dennis Sproul, 1978	2	1	0	-5	1
Ray Stachowicz, 1981-82	1	0	0	-10	0
Jon Staggers, 1972-74	3	1	0	0	1
Don Stansauk, 1950-51	0	0	2	0	2
Walter Stanley, 1985-88	11	4	0	0	4
Bart Starr, 1956-71	64	18	0	-8	18
Ben Starret, 1942-45	1	1	0	0	1
Scott Stephen, 1987-91	1	0	4	91	4
John Stephens, 1993	0	1	0	0	1
John Sterling, 1987	1	0	0	0	0
Ken Stills, 1985-88	1	2	2	4	4
Tim Stokes, 1978-82	0	2	0	0	2
Fred Strickland, 1994	0	0	1	0	1
Bob Summerhays, 1949-51	1	0	3	0	3
Mickey Sutton, 1989	1	0	0	0	0
Karl Swanke, 1980-86	3	3	0	-4	3
Veryl Switzer, 1954-55	9	4	1	0	5
Harry Sydney, 1992	2	2	0	0	2
John Symank, 1957-62	7	1	11	50	12
Len Szafaryn, 1950, 53-56	0	3	1	0	4
Jerry Tagge, 1972-74	6	1	0	-6	1
Damon Tassos, 1947-49	0	0	2	0	2
Jim Taylor, 1958-66	33	7	0	1	7
George Teague, 1993-94	0	0	2	0	2
Jim Temp, 1957-60	0	1	1	4	2
Deral Teteak, 1952-56	0	0	5	0	5
Ike Thomas, 1972-73	2	3	0	0	3
Lavale Thomas, 1987-88	0	1	1	3	2
Bobby Thomason, 1951	2	0	0	0	0
Arland Thompson, 1981	0	1	0	0	1
Aundra Thompson, 1977-81	6	4	0	5	4
Darrell Thompson, 1990-94	6	2	0	0	2
John Thompson, 1979-82	0	1	0	0	1
Gerald Tinker, 1975	0	0	1	0	1
Nelson Toburen, 1961-62	0	1	0	0	1
Mike Tomczak, 1991	5	2	0	-1	2
Tom Toner, 1973-77	0	0	2	0	2
Eric Torkelson, 1974-79, 81	10	6	2	29	8
Emlen Tunnell, 1959-61	0	0	1	0	1
Keith Uecker, 1984-85, 87-88, 90-91	0	2	1	0	3
Bruce Van Dyke, 1974-76	0	1	0	0	1
Alan Veingrad, 1986-87, 89-90	0	1	0	0	1
Evan Vogds, 1948-49	0	1	0	0	1
Steve Wagner, 1976-79	0	0	3	0	3
Val Joe Walker, 1953-56	1	0	7	3	7
Malcolm Walker, 1970	0	1	1	4	2
Chuck Washington, 1987	0	0	1	0	1
Clarence Weathers, 1990-91	1	0	0	0	0
Jim Weatherwax, 1966-67, 69	0	0	1	0	1
Gary Weaver, 1975-79	0	0	3	0	3
Mike Weddington, 1986-90	0	0	4	0	4
Don Wells, 1946-49	0	0	5	47	5
Terry Wells, 1975	1	0	0	0	0
Ed West, 1984-94	6	2	0	0	2
Bill Whitaker, 1981-82	0	0	1	0	1
Gene White, 1954	0	0	1	0	1
Reggie White, 1993-94	0	1	2	10	3
David Whitehurst, 1977-83	20	5	0	-30	5
Jess Whittenton, 1958-64	0	0	10	47	10
Dick Wildung, 1946-51, 53	0	4	7	7	11
Kevin Willhite, 1987	2	0	0	0	0
Clarence Williams, 1970-77	1	0	8	21	8
Mark Williams, 1994	0	1	0	0	1
Perry Williams, 1969-73	4	0	0	0	0
Travis Williams, 1967-70	9	2	1	0	3
James Willis, 1993-94	1	2	0	0	2
Ben Wilson, 1967	4	2	0	0	2
Charles Wilson, 1990-91	4	1	0	0	1
Gene Wilson, 1947-48	0	0	1	0	1
Marcus Wilson, 1992-94	2	0	1	0	1
Abner Wimberly, 1950-52	1	1	4	0	5
Rich Wingo, 1979, 81-84	0	0	1	0	1
Francis Winkler, 1968-69	0	0	1	0	1
Blaise Winter, 1988-90	0	0	2	0	2
Frank Winters, 1992-94	2	1	0	-2	1
Cal Withrow, 1971-73	0	1	0	0	1
Alex Wizbicki, 1950	0	0	2	12	2
Willie Wood, 1960-71	6	2	14	39	16
Keith Woodside, 1988-91	12	3	0	0	3
Vince Workman, 1989-92	8	7	0	9	7
Randy Wright, 1984-88	23	10	0	-19	10
Steve Wright, 1964-67	0	1	3	0	4
Roger Zatkoff, 1953-56	1	0	6	0	6
Jim Zorn, 1985	3	2	0	-1	2
Packers, 1945-94	**1,456**	**602**	**840**	**1,473**	**1,442**

Green Bay Press-Gazette photo

Center Charlet Brock recovered five fumbles in 1945.

ALL-TIME SACK LEADERS

(Statistic kept since 1982; rankings are based on number of sacks)

Name	No
Tim Harris, 1986-90	55.0
Ezra Johnson, 1977-87	41.5
Tony Bennett, 1990-93	36.0
Bryce Paup, 1990-94	32.5
Robert Brown, 1982-92	25.5
Reggie White, 1993-94	21.0
John Anderson, 1978-89	19.5
Mike Douglass, 1978-85	19.0
Alphonso Carreker, 1984-88	18.5
Brian Noble, 1985-93	14.0

Name	No
Matt Brock, 1989-94	12.5
Mark Murphy, 1980-85, 87-91	11.0
Shawn Patterson, 1988-91, 93	11.0
Sean Jones, 1994	10.5
Charles Martin, 1984-87	8.0
John Jurkovic, 1991-94	7.5
Terry Jones, 1978-84	7.0
Randy Scott, 1981-86	7.0
Blaise Winter, 1988-90	7.0
Lester Archambeau, 1990-92	5.5
Byron Braggs, 1981-83	5.5
George Koonce, 1992-94	5.5
George Cumby, 1980-85	4.5
Burnell Dent, 1986-92	4.5
Scott Stephen, 1987-91	4.5
Esera Tuaolo, 1991-92	4.5
Mike Butler, 1977-82, 85	4.0
George (Tiger) Greene, 1986-90	4.0
Casey Merrill, 1979-83	4.0
Johnny Holland, 1987-93	3.5
Charles Johnson, 1979-80, 83	3.5
Gilbert Brown, 1994	3.0
David Greenwood, 1986-87	3.0
Donnie Humphrey, 1984-86	3.0
Jerry Boyarsky, 1986-89	2.5
Steve McMichael, 1994	2.5
Greg Boyd, 1983	2.0
Lee Roy Butler, 1990-94	2.0
Jeff Drost, 1987	2.0

Name	No
Cliff Lewis, 1981-84	2.0
Bob Nelson, 1988-90	2.0
Guy Prather, 1981-85	2.0
Don Davey, 1991-94	1.5
Bobby Leopold, 1986-87	1.5
Ross Browner, 1987	1.0
Mossy Cade, 1985-86	1.0
Doug Evans, 1993-94	1.0
Mark Hall, 1989-90	1.0
Maurice Harvey, 1981-83	1.0
Jerry Holmes, 1990-91	1.0
Kenneth Johnson, 1987	1.0
Kenneth Jordan, 1987	1.0
Roland Mitchell, 1991-94	1.0
Jim Bob Morris, 1987	1.0
Bill Neill, 1984	1.0
Wayne Simmons, 1993-94	1.0
Ken Stills, 1985-89	1.0
Ben Thomas, 1986-87	1.0
Rich Turner, 1981-83	1.0
Elbert Watts, 1986-87	1.0
Mike Weddington, 1986-90	1.0
Gabe Wilkins, 1994	1.0
Rich Wingo, 1979, 81-84	1.0
David Caldwell, 1987	0.5
Ron Spears, 1983	0.5
Carl Sullivan, 1987	0.5
team, 1991	1.0
Packers, 1982-94	**468.0**
Opponents, 1982-94	560.0

Green Bay Press-Gazette photo

Ezra Johnson (90) can't get to Tampa Bay's Doug Williams (12) in 1980. Johnson did sack passers 41.5 times from 1982-87.

ALL-TIME COMBINED NET YARDAGE

(Rankings based on total yards; 1,500 or more total yards)

Name	Rush	Rec	P-Ret	K-ret	Int	Fum	Total
James Lofton, 1978-86	31-245	530-9,656	0-0	1-0	0-0	3-8	565-9,909
Jim Taylor, 1958-66	1,811-8,207	187-1,505	0-0	7-185	0-0	7-1	2,012-9,898
Don Hutson, 1935-45	62-284	488-7,991	0-0	5-45	30-389	0-0	585-8,709
Sterling Sharpe, 1988-94	23-72	595-8,134	9-48	1-17	0-0	5-5	633-8,276
Tony Canadeo, 1941-44, 46-52	1,025-4,197	69-579	46-513	75-1,736	9-129	5-2	1,229-7,156
Boyd Dowler, 1959-69	2-28	448-6,918	0-0	0-0	0-0	0-0	450-6,946
Gerry Ellis, 1980-86	836-3,826	267-2,514	0-0	13-247	0-0	9-0	1,125-6,587
Max McGee, 1954, 57-67	12-121	345-6,346	0-0	4-69	0-0	4-43	365-6,579
Steve Odom, 1974-79	16-205	84-1,613	64-569	179-4,124	0-0	6-0	349-6,511
Al Carmichael, 1953-58	166-712	75-994	100-753	153-3,907	0-0	3-0	497-6,366

Name	Rush	Rec	P-ret	K-ret	Int	Fum	Total
John Brockington, 1971-77	1,293-5,024	138-1,075	0-0	0-0	0-0	6-0	1,437-6,099
Donny Anderson, 1966-71	787-3,165	125-1,725	15-222	34-759	0-0	5-(-5)	966-5,866
Sterling Sharpe, 1988-92	16-49	389-5,741	9-48	1-17	0-0	5-5	420-5,860
Bill Howton, 1952-58	4-20	303-5,581	0-0	0-0	0-0	2-0	309-5,601
Carroll Dale, 1965-72	3-18	275-5,422	0-0	0-0	0-0	1-0	279-5,440
Paul Hornung, 1957-62, 64-66	893-3,711	130-1,480	0-0	10-248	0-0	3-0	1,036-5,439
Tom Moore, 1960-65	503-2,069	71-645	0-0	71-1,882	0-0	4-2	649-4,598
Eddie Lee Ivery, 1979-86	667-2,933	162-1,612	0-0	1-17	0-0	4-0	834-4,562
Clarke Hinkle, 1932-41	1,171-3,860	50-537	2-61	3-38	3-13	—	1,229-4,509
Phillip Epps, 1982-88	10-121	192-2,884	100-819	25-532	0-0	1-0	328-4,356
Paul Coffman, 1978-85	1-3	322-4,223	0-0	3-77	0-0	2-0	328-4,303
Joe Laws, 1934-45	470-1,932	79-1,041	46-339	19-362	18-266	1-2	633-3,942
Herb Adderley, 1961-69	0-0	0-0	1-0	120-3,080	39-795	13-60	173-3,935
Travis Williams, 1967-70	271-1,063	49-530	12-209	77-2,058	0-0	3-0	412-3,860
Elijah Pitts, 1961-69, 71	479-1,684	97-1,182	75-394	27-513	0-0	4-0	682-3,773
Ted Fritsch, 1942-50	619-2,200	25-227	1-31	37-951	10-263	9-(-1)	701-3,671
Billy Grimes, 1950-52	145-662	32-431	63-834	67-1,604	0-0	5-0	312-3,531
Walter Stanley, 1985-88	6-58	101-1,831	87-720	42-857	0-0	4-0	240-3,466
Howie Ferguson, 1953-58	544-2,120	127-1,079	0-0	15-257	0-0	7-0	693-3,456
Brent Fullwood, 1987-90	433-1,702	44-370	0-0	56-1,174	0-0	3-0	536-3,246
Dave Hampton, 1969-71	195-787	25-276	0-0	74-2,084	0-0	4-0	298-3,147
Barty Smith, 1974-80	544-1,942	120-979	0-0	5-53	0-0	3-0	672-2,974
Terdell Middleton, 1977-81	559-2,044	78-659	0-0	11-263	0-0	4-0	652-2,966
Floyd (Breezy) Reid, 1950-56	459-1,964	72-868	1-0	6-103	0-0	7-2	545-2,937
Robert Brooks, 1992-94	6-31	90-954	67-589	50-1,209	0-0	2-0	215-2,783
Andy Uram, 1938-43	239-1,073	58-1,083	19-219	10-235	9-122	—	335-2,732
Lou Brock, 1940-45	254-804	59-761	39-438	21-438	13-193	0-0	386-2,634
Keith Woodside, 1988-91	259-976	144-1,248	0-0	21-381	0-0	3-0	427-2,605
Ron Kramer, 1957, 59-64	6-9	170-2,594	0-0	0-0	0-0	1-0	177-2,603
MacArthur Lane, 1972-74	484-1,711	87-855	0-0	2-31	0-0	2-0	575-2,597
Edgar Bennett, 1992-94	398-1,387	150-1,096	0-0	5-104	0-0	2-0	555-2,587
Vince Workman, 1989-92	242-927	97-691	1-0	56-913	0-0	7-9	403-2,540
Jessie Clark, 1983-87	379-1,588	99-925	0-0	0-0	0-0	3-0	481-2,513
Harlan Huckleby, 1980-85	242-779	53-411	0-0	70-1,300	0-0	2-0	367-2,490
Darrell Thompson, 1990-94	464-1,642	41-330	0-0	23-468	0-0	2-0	530-2,440
Aundra Thompson, 1977-81	12-14	95-1,573	0-0	40-835	0-0	4-5	151-2,427
Rich McGeorge, 1970-78	1-3	175-2,370	0-0	2-17	0-0	7-0	185-2,390
Perry Kemp, 1988-91	6-42	182-2,341	0-0	0-0	0-0	1-0	189-2,383
Ed West, 1984-94	2-2	202-2,321	0-0	2-0	0-0	2-0	208-2,323
John Jefferson, 1981-84	4-38	149-2,253	0-0	1-3	0-0	0-0	154-2,294
Tobin Rote, 1950-56	419-2,205	1-39	0-0	0-0	0-0	10-(-21)	430-2,223
Fred Cone, 1951-57	347-1,156	75-852	0-0	9-148	0-0	8-5	439-2,161
Jim Grabowski, 1966-70	424-1,582	65-575	0-0	0-0	0-0	1-0	490-2,157
Willie Wood, 1960-71	0-0	0-0	187-1,391	3-20	48-699	16-39	254-2,149
Willard Harrell, 1975-77	311-934	70-656	52-382	6-126	0-0	3-0	442-2,098
Eric Torkelson, 1974-79, 81	351-1,307	59-469	1-0	14-268	0-0	8-29	433-2,073
Gary Knafelc, 1954-62	0-0	134-1,930	0-0	0-0	0-0	1-0	135-1,930
Cecil Isbell, 1938-42	422-1,522	15-174	4-33	6-96	9-61	—	456-1,886
Don McIlhenny, 1957-59	221-854	46-459	1-0	24-558	0-0	4-0	296-1,871
Veryl Switzer, 1954-55	31-160	31-269	48-464	37-945	0-0	5-0	152-1,838
Bob Monnett, 1933-38	510-1,488	27-303	—	—	—	—	537-1,791
Jeff Query, 1989-91	3-39	64-902	76-712	6-125	0-0	5-0	154-1,778
Jon Staggers, 1972-74	5-25	65-985	50-460	11-260	0-0	1-0	132-1,730
Charles Wilson, 1990-91	3-3	26-389	0-0	58-1,320	0-0	0-0	87-1,712
Clyde Goodnight, 1945-49	9-25	89-1,632	0-0	3-27	0-0	2-8	103-1,692
Bob Mann, 1950-54	2-9	109-1,629	0-0	0-0	0-0	0-0	111-1,638
Del Rodgers, 1982, 84	71-269	8-79	0-0	59-1,279	0-0	2-0	140-1,627
Jackie Harris, 1990-93	1-1	133-1,620	0-0	0-0	0-0	1-0	135-1,621
Walt Schlinkman, 1946-50	365-1,455	3-(-1)	0-0	7-155	0-0	5-10	380-1,619
Kenneth Davis, 1986-88	262-1,053	46-333	0-0	12-231	0-0	0-0	320-1,617
Corey Harris, 1992-94	2-10	2-11	0-0	68-1,585	0-0	1-0	73-1,606
Nolan Luhn, 1945-49	0-0	100-1,525	0-0	7-76	0-0	2-4	109-1,605
Ken Ellis, 1970-75	0-0	0-0	63-426	36-802	20-294	6-11	125-1,533

ALL-TIME ROSTER

The following have all played in at least one regular-season game with the Green Bay Packers. A player who was active during the course of a season but did not play will not appear in this list, but will be mentioned in a separate list at the end of this roster. If a player was on injured reserve for an entire season, he will not be given credit for that year in this roster.

A

Name	Pos	Years	College	Games
Aberson, Cliff	B	1946	No College	10
Abrams, Nate	E	1921	No College	—
Abramson, George	T	1925	Minnesota	—
Acks, Ron	LB	1974-76	Illinois	40
Adams, Chet	T	1943	Ohio State	—
Adderley, Herb	CB	1961-69	Michigan State	125
Adkins, Robert	E	1940-41, 45	Marshall	—
Affholter, Erik	WR	1991	USC	4
Afflis, Dick	G	1951-54	Nevada	48
Agajanian, Ben	K	1961	New Mexico	3
Albrecht, Art	C	1942	Wisconsin	—
Aldridge, Ben	DB	1953	Oklahoma State	8
Aldridge, Lionel	DE	1963-71	Utah	123
Allerman, Kurt	LB	1980-81	Penn State	29
Amsler, Marty	DE	1970	Evansville	9
Amundsen, Norm	G	1957	Wisconsin	12
Anderson, Aric	LB	1987	Iona	3
Anderson, Bill	TE	1965-66	Tennessee	24
Anderson, Curtis	DE	1987	Central State (OR)	3
Anderson, Donny	RB	1966-71	Texas Tech	84
Anderson, John	LB	1978-89	Michigan	146
Anderson, Vickey Ray	RB	1980	Oklahoma	7
Ane, Charlie	C	1981	Michigan State	16
Apsit, Marger	B	1932	USC	—
Archambeau, Lester	DE	1990-92	Stanford	36
Ard, Billy	G	1989-91	Wake Forest	35
Ariey, Mike	T	1989	San Diego State	1
Ashmore, Roger	T	1928-29	Gonzaga	—
Askson, Bert	TE	1975-77	Texas Southern	42
Atkins, Steve	RB	1979-81	Maryland	19
Auer, Todd	LB	1987	Western Illinois	3
Austin, Hise	CB	1973	Prairie View	9
Avery, Steve	FB	1991	Northern Michigan	1
Aydelette, Buddy	T	1980	Alabama	9

B

Name	Pos	Years	College	Games
Bailey, Byron	HB	1953	Washington State	9
Bain, Bill	G	1975	USC	14
Baker, Frank	E	1931	Northwestern	—
Baker, Roy	B	1928-29	USC	—
Balazs, Frank	B	1939-41	Iowa	—
Baldwin, Al	E	1950	Arkansas	12
Banet, Herb	B	1937	Manchester	—
Barber, Bob	DE	1976-79	Grambling	60
Barnes, Emery	DE	1956	Oregon	2
Barnes, Gary	E	1962	Clemson	13
Barnett, Solon	T	1945-46	Baylor	5
Barrager, Nate	C	1931-32, 34-35	USC	—
Barrett, Jan	E	1963	Fresno State	3
Barrie, Sebastian	DE	1992	Liberty	3
Barry, Al	G	1954, 57	USC	24
Barry, Norm	B	1921	Notre Dame	—
Barton, Don	HB	1953	Texas	5
Barzilauskas, Carl	DT	1978-79	Indiana	21
Basing, Myrt	B	1923-27	Lawrence	—
Basinger, Mike	DE	1974	California-Riverside	1
Baxter, Lloyd	C	1948	SMU	11
Beach, Sanjay	WR	1992	Colorado State	16
Beasley, Jack	B	1924	South Dakota	—
Beck, Ken	DT	1959-60	Texas A&M	24
Becker, Wayland	E	1936-38	Marquette	—
Beekley, Bruce	LB	1980	Oregon	15
Bell, Albert	WR	1988	Alabama	5
Bell, Edward	G	1947-49	Indiana	35
Bennett, Earl	G	1946	Hardin-Simmons	3
Bennett, Edgar	RB	1992-94	Florida State	48
Bennett, Tony	LB	1990-93	Mississippi	56
Berezney, Paul	T	1942-44	Fordham	—
Berry, Ed	DB	1986	Utah State	16
Berry, Connie Mack	E	1940	North Carolina State	—
Bettencourt, Larry	C	1933	St. Mary's (CA)	—
Bettis, Tom	LB	1955-61	Purdue	84

Name	Pos	Years	College	Games
Beverly, David	P	1975-80	Auburn	86
Bieberstein, Adolph	G	1926	Wisconsin	—
Bilda, Dick	B	1944	Marquette	—
Billups, Lewis	CB	1992	North Alabama	5
Biolo, John	G	1939	Lake Forest	—
Birney, Tom	K	1979-80	Michigan	13
Blaine, Ed	G	1962	Missouri	14
Bland, Carl	WR	1989-90	Virginia Union	30
Bloodgood, Elbert	B	1930	Nebraska	—
Boedecker, Bill	B	1950	Kalamazoo	9
Bolton, Scott	WR	1988	Auburn	4
Bone, Warren	DE	1987	Texas Southern	1
Bookout, Billy	DB	1955-56	Austin	19
Boone, J.R.	HB	1953	Tulsa	8
Borak, Tony (Fritz)	E	1938	Creighton	—
Borden, Nate	DE	1955-59	Indiana	57
Bowdoin, James	G	1928-31	Alabama	—
Bowman, Ken	C	1964-73	Wisconsin	127
Boyarsky, Jerry	NT	1986-89	Pittsburgh	29
Boyd, Elmo	WR	1978	Eastern Kentucky	2
Boyd, Greg	DE	1983	San Diego State	12
Bracken, Don	P	1985-90	Michigan	80
Brackins, Charles	QB	1955	Prairie View A&M	7
Bradley, Dave	G	1969-71	Penn State	14
Brady, Jeff	LB	1992	Kentucky	8
Braggs, Byron	NT	1981-83	Alabama	41
Branstetter, Kent	T	1973	Houston	9
Bratkowski, Zeke	QB	1963-68, 71	Georgia	47
Bray, Ray	G	1952	Western Michigan	12
Breen, Gene	LB	1964	Virginia Tech	6
Brennan, John	G	1939	Michigan	—
Brock, Charley	C	1939-47	Nebraska	—
Brock, Lou	B	1940-45	Purdue	—
Brock, Matt	DE	1989-94	Oregon	76
Brockington, John	RB	1971-77	Ohio State	85
Brooks, Robert	WR	1992-94	South Carolina	46
Bross, Marty	B	1927	Gonzaga	—
Broussard, Steve	P	1975	SMU	4
Brown, Aaron	DE	1973-74	Minnesota	10
Brown, Allen	TE	1966-67	Mississippi	19
Brown, Bill (Buddy)	G	1953-56	Arkansas	47
Brown, Bob	DE	1966-73	Arkansas-Pine Bluff	104
Brown, Carlos	QB	1975-76	Pacific	27
Brown, Dave	CB	1987-89	Michigan	44
Brown, Gary	T	1994	Georgia Tech	1
Brown, Gilbert	NT	1993-94	Kansas	15
Brown, Ken	C	1980	New Mexico	6
Brown, Robert	DE	1982-92	Virginia Tech	164
Brown, Tim	HB	1959	Ball State	1
Brown, Tom	DB	1964-68	Maryland	70
Browner, Ross	DE	1987	Notre Dame	11
Bruder, Hank	B	1931-39	Northwestern	—
Brunell, Mark	QB	1994	Washington	2
Bucchianeri, Amadeo	G	1941, 44-45	Indiana	—
Buchanon, Willie	CB	1972-78	San Diego State	80
Buck, Howard (Cub)	T	1921-25	Wisconsin	—
Buckley, Terrell	CB	1992-94	Florida State	46
Buhler, Larry	B	1939-41	Minnesota	—
Buland, Walter	T	1924	No college	—
Bullough, Hank	G	1955, 58	Michigan State	20
Bultman, Arthur (Red)	C	1932-34	Marquette	—
Burgess, Ronnie	DB	1985	Wake Forest	11
Burnette, Reggie	LB	1991	Houston	3
Burris, Paul (Buddy)	G	1949-51	Oklahoma	29
Burrow, Curtis	K	1988	Central Arkansas	1
Burrow, Jim	S	1976	Montana	3
Bush, Blair	C	1989-91	Washington	48
Butler, Bill	HB	1959	Chattanooga	11
Butler, Frank	C	1934-36, 38	Michigan State	—
Butler, LeRoy	CB	1990-94	Florida State	76
Butler, Mike	DE	1977-82, 85	Kansas	97

C

Name	Pos	Years	College	Games
Cabral, Brian	LB	1980	Colorado	7
Cade, Mossy	CB	1985-86	Texas	30

Name	Pos	Years	College	Games
Caffey, Lee Roy	LB	1964-69	Texas A&M	83
Cahoon, Ivan	T	1926-29	Gonzaga	—
Caldwell, David	NT	1987	TCU	3
Campbell, Rich	QB	1981-84	California	7
Campen, James	C	1989-93	Tulane	61
Canadeo, Tony	HB	1941-44, 46-52	Gonzaga	116
Cannava, Al	B	1950	Boston College	1
Cannon, Mark	C	1984-89	Texas-Arlington	82
Capp, Dick	TE	1967	Boston College	2
Capuzzi, Jim	QB	1956	Cincinnati	10
Carey, Joseph	G	1921	No college	—
Carlson, Wes	G	1926	St. John's	—
Carmichael, Al	HB	1953-58	USC	70
Carpenter, Lew	FB	1959-63	Arkansas	66
Carr, Fred	LB	1968-77	Texas-El Paso	140
Carruth, Paul Ott	RB	1986-88	Alabama	43
Carreker, Alphonso	DE	1984-88	Florida State	72
Carroll, Leo	DE	1968	San Diego State	6
Carter, Carl	CB	1992	Texas Tech	7
Carter, Jim	LB	1970-75, 77-78	Minnesota	90
Carter, Joe	E	1942	SMU	—
Carter, Mike	WR	1970	Sacramento State	3
Casper, Charles	B	1934	TCU	—
Cassidy, Ron	WR	1979-81, 83-84	Utah State	65
Cecil, Chuck	S	1988-92	Arizona	66
Chandler, Don	K	1965-67	Florida	42
Cheek, Louis	T	1991	Texas A&M	12
Cherry, Bill	C	1986-87	Middle Tennessee State	28
Chesley, Francis	LB	1978	Wyoming	1
Childs, Henry	TE	1984	Kansas State	3
Choate, Putt	LB	1987	SMU	2
Christman, Paul	QB	1950	Missouri	11
Chmura, Mark	TE	1993-94	Boston College	28
Cifelli, Gus	T	1953	Notre Dame	12
Cifers, Bob	B	1949	Tennessee	9
Clancy, Jack	WR	1970	Michigan	14
Clanton, Chuck	DB	1985	Auburn	3
Claridge, Dennis	QB	1965	Nebraska	1
Clark, Allen	RB	1982	Northern Arizona	4
Clark, Greg	LB	1991	Arizona State	2
Clark, Jessie	RB	1983-87	Arkansas	60
Clark, Vinnie	CB	1991-92	Ohio State	32
Clayton, Mark	WR	1993	Louisville	16
Clemens, Bob	FB	1955	Georgia	2
Clemens, Cal	B	1936	USC	—
Clemons, Raymond	G	1947	St. Mary's (CA)	9
Cloud, Jack	B	1950-51	William & Mary	13
Cobb, Reggie	RB	1994	Tennessee	16
Cody, Ed	B	1947-48	Purdue	20
Coffey, Junior	HB	1965	Washington	13
Coffman, Paul	TE	1978-85	Kansas State	119
Coleman, Keo	LB	1993	Mississippi	12
Collier, Steve	T	1987	Bethune-Cookman	10
Collins, Albin (Rip)	HB	1951	Louisiana State	7
Collins, Brett	LB	1992-93	Washington	15
Collins, Patrick	RB	1988	Oklahoma	6
Collins, Shawn	WR	1993	Northern Arizona	4
Comp, Irv	QB	1943-49	St. Benedict's	69
Compton, Chuck	DB	1987	Boise State	2
Comstock, Rudy	G	1931-33	Georgetown	—
Concannon, Jack	QB	1974	Boston College	14
Cone, Fred	FB	1951-57	Clemson	82
Conway, Dave	K	1971	Texas	1
Cook, Jim	G	1921	Wisconsin	—
Cook, Kelly	RB	1987	Oklahoma State	11
Cook, Ted	E	1948-50	Alabama	35
Cooke, Bill	T	1975	Massachusetts	5
Cooney, Mark	LB	1974	Colorado	13
Corker, John	LB	1988	Oklahoma State	2
Coughlin, Frank	T	1921	Notre Dame	—
Coutre, Larry	HB	1950, 53	Notre Dame	19
Craig, Larry	E	1939-49	South Carolina	121
Cremer, Ted	E	1948	Auburn	3
Crenshaw, Leon	DT	1968	Tuskegee	10
Crimmins, Bernard	G	1945	Notre Dame	6
Croft, Milburn (Tiny)	T	1942-47	Ripon	—
Cronin, Tommy	B	1922	Marquette	—
Croston, Dave	T	1988	Iowa	16
Crouse, Ray	RB	1984	Nevada-Las Vegas	16
Crowley, Jim	B	1925	Notre Dame	—
Crutcher, Tommy	LB	1964-67, 71-72	TCU	82
Cuff, Ward	B	1947	Marquette	10
Culbreath, Jim	RB	1977-79	Oklahoma	29
Culver, Al	T	1932	Notre Dame	—
Cumby, George	LB	1980-85	Oklahoma	81
Curcio, Mike	LB	1983	Temple	14
Currie, Dan	LB	1958-64	Michigan State	90
Curry, Bill	C	1965-66	Georgia Tech	28
Cverko, Andy	G	1960	Northwestern	12
Cyre, Hector	T	1926	Gonzaga	—

D

Name	Pos	Years	College	Games
Dahms, Tom	T	1955	San Diego State	12
Dale, Carroll	WR	1965-72	Virginia Tech	111
Danelo, Joe	K	1975	Washington State	12
Daniell, Averell	T	1937	Pittsburgh	12
Danjean, Ernest	G	1957	Auburn	12
Darling, Bernard (Boob)	C	1927-31	Beloit	—
Davenport, Wayne	B	1931	Hardin-Simmons	—
Davey, Don	DE	1991-94	Wisconsin	50
Davidson, Ben	DE	1961	Washington	14
Davis, Dave	WR	1971-72	Tennessee State	28
Davis, Harper	B	1951	Mississippi State	12
Davis, Kenneth	RB	1986-88	TCU	35
Davis, Pahl	G	1922	Marquette	—
Davis, Ralph	G	1947-48	Wisconsin	22
Davis, Willie	DE	1960-69	Grambling	138
Dawson, Dale	K	1988	Eastern Kentucky	4
Dawson, Gib	HB	1953	Texas	7
Dean, Walter	FB	1991	Grambling	9
Deeks, Donald	G	1948	Washington	9
Dees, Robert	T	1952	Southwest Missouri State	9
Degrate, Tony	DE	1985	Texas	1
Del Gaizo, Jim	QB	1973	Tampa Bay	8
Del Greco, Al	K	1984-87	Auburn	46
DeLisle, Jim	DT	1971	Wisconsin	9
DeLuca, Tony	NT	1984	Rhode Island	1
Dennard, Preston	WR	1985	New Mexico	16
Dent, Burnell	LB	1986-92	Tulane	95
Deschaine, Dick	P	1955-57	No college	36
Detmer, Ty	QB	1993	BYU	3
Dickey, Lynn	QB	1976-77, 79-85	Kansas State	105
Didier, Clint	TE	1988-89	Portland State	31
Dillon, Bobby	DB	1952-59	Texas	94
Dilweg, Anthony	QB	1989-90	Duke	10
Dilweg, LaVern (Lavvie)	E	1927-34	Marquette	—
Dimler, Rich	DT	1980	USC	3
DiPierro, Ray	G	1950-51	Ohio State	18
Disend, Leo	T	1940	Albright	—
Dittrich, John	G	1959	Wisconsin	12
Don Carlos, Waldo	C	1931	Drake	—
D'Onofrio, Mark	LB	1992	Penn State	2
Donohoe, Mike	TE	1973-74	San Francisco	27
Dorsey, Dean	K	1988	Toronto	3
Dorsey, John	LB	1984-88	Connecticut	76
Dotson, Earl	T	1993-94	Texas A&I	17
Douglass, Bobby	QB	1978	Kansas	12
Douglass, Mike	LB	1978-85	San Diego State	120
Dowden, Steve	T	1952	Baylor	12
Dowler, Boyd	WR	1959-69	Colorado	150
Dowling, Brian	QB	1977	Yale	5
Dreschler, Dave	G	1983-84	North Carolina	32
Dreyer, Wally	B	1950	Wisconsin	12
Drost, Jeff	DT	1987	Iowa	2
Drulis, Charles	G	1950	Temple	11
Duckett, Forey	CB	1994	Nevada-Reno	3
Duford, Wilfred	B	1924	Marquette	—
Dukes, Jamie	C	1994	Florida State	6
DuMoe, Bill (Gus)	E	1921	Notre Dame	—
Dunaway, Dave	WR	1968	Duke	2
Duncan, Ken	P	1971	Tulsa	3
Dunn, Joseph (Red)	B	1927-31	Marquette	—
Dunnigan, Walt	E	1922	Minnesota	—

E

Name	Pos	Years	College	Games
Earhart, Ralph	HB	1948-49	Texas Tech	24
Earpe, Francis (Jug)	T	1922-32	Monmouth	—
Eason, Roger	G	1949	Oklahoma	12
Ecker, Ed	T	1950-51	John Carroll	19
Edwards, Earl	DT	1979	Wichita State	9
Ellerson, Gary	RB	1985-86	Wisconsin	31
Elliott, Carlton	E	1951-54	Virginia	48
Elliott, Tony	DB	1987	Central Michigan	1
Ellis, Gerry	FB	1980-86	Missouri	102
Ellis, Ken	CB	1970-75	Southern University	84
Enderle, Dick	G	1976	Minnesota	3
Engebretsen, Paul (Tiny)	G	1934-41	Northwestern	—
Englemann, Wuert	B	1930-33	South Dakota	—
Enright, Rex	B	1926-27	Notre Dame	—
Epps, Phillip	WR	1982-88	TCU	85
Estep, Mike	G	1987	Bowling Green	1
Ethridge, Joe	T	1949	SMU	12
Evans, Dick	E	1940, 43	Iowa	—
Evans, Doug	CB	1993-94	Louisiana Tech	32

Name	Pos	Years	College	Games
Evans, Jack	B	1929	California	—
Evans, Lon	G	1933-37	TCU	—

F

Name	Pos	Years	College	Games
Falkenstein, Tony	B	1943	St. Mary's (CA)	—
Fanucci, Mike	DE	1974	Arizona State	13
Faverty, Hal	E	1952	Wisconsin	11
Favre, Brett	QB	1992-94	Southern Mississippi	47
Faye, Allen	E	1922	Marquette	—
Feasel, Greg	T	1986	Abilene Christian	15
Feathers, Beattie	B	1940	Tennessee	—
Ferguson, Howie	FB	1953-58	No college	65
Ferragamo, Vince	QB	1986	Nebraska	3
Ferry, Louis	T	1949	Villanova	12
Fitzgerald, Kevin	TE	1987	Wisconsin-Eau Claire	1
Fitzgibbons, Paul	B	1930-32	Creighton	—
Flaherty, Dick	E	1926	Marquette	—
Flanigan, Jim	LB	1967-70	Pittsburgh	40
Fleming, Marv	TE	1963-69	Utah	95
Flowers, Bob	C	1942-49	Texas Tech	—
Floyd, Bobby Jack	FB	1952	TCU	12
Flynn, Tom	S	1984-86	Pittsburgh	37
Folkins, Lee	DE	1961	Washington	14
Fontenot, Herman	RB	1989-90	LSU	30
Ford, Len	DE	1958	Michigan	11
Forester, Bill	LB	1953-63	SMU	138
Forte, Aldo	G	1947	Montana	10
Forte, Bob	HB	1946-50, 52-53	Arkansas	80
Francis, Joe	QB	1958-59	Oregon State	24
Frankowski, Ray	G	1945	Washington	2
Franta, Herb	T	1930	St. Thomas (MN)	—
Franz, Nolan	WR	1986	Tulane	1
Freeman, Bob	DB	1959	Auburn	12
Fries, Sherwood	G	1943	Colorado State	—
Fritsch, Ted	FB	1942-50	Stevens Point	99
Frutig, Ed	E	1941, 45	Michigan	—
Fuller, Joe	CB	1991	Northern Iowa	16
Fullwood, Brent	FB	1987-90	Auburn	45
Fusina, Chuck	QB	1986	Penn State	7

G

Name	Pos	Years	College	Games
Gabbard, Steve	G/T	1991	Florida State	4
Galbreath, Harry	G	1993-94	Tennessee	32
Gantenbein, Milt	E	1931-40	Wisconsin	—
Garcia, Eddie	K	1983-84	SMU	19
Gardella, Gus	B	1922	Holy Cross	—
Gardner, Milton (Moose)	G	1922-26	Wisconsin	—
Garrett, Bob	QB	1954	Stanford	9
Garrett, Len	TE	1971-73	New Mexico Highlands	30
Gassert, Ron	DT	1962	Virginia	11
Gatewood, Lester	C	1946-47	Baylor	23
Gavin, Fritz	B	1923	Marquette	—
Gaydos, Kent	WR	1975	Florida State	6
Getty, Charlie	T	1983	Penn State	16
Gibson, Paul	S	1972	Texas-El Paso	1
Gillette, Jim	B	1947	Virginia	10
Gillingham, Gale	G	1966-74, 76	Minnesota	128
Gillus, Willie	QB	1987	Norfolk State	1
Girard, Earl (Jug)	QB	1948-51	Wisconsin	46
Glass, Leland	WR	1972-73	Oregon	26
Glick, Eddie	B	1922	Marquette	—
Gofourth, Derrel	C	1977-82	Oklahoma State	86
Goldenberg, Charles	G	1933-45	Wisconsin	—
Goodman, Les	RB	1973-74	Yankton	19
Goodnight, Clyde	E	1945-49	Tulsa	38
Gordon, Dick	WR	1973	Michigan State	2
Gordon, Lou	T	1936-37	Illinois	—
Gorgal, Ken	DB	1956	Purdue	5
Grabowski, Jim	RB	1966-70	Illinois	65
Grant, David	NT	1993	West Virginia	7
Gray, Cecil	T	1992	North Carolina	2
Gray, Jack	E	1923	No college	—
Gray, Johnnie	S	1975-84	Cal State Fullerton	125
Greene, George (Tiger)	DB	1986-90	Western Carolina	72
Greeney, Norm	G	1933	Notre Dame	—
Greenfield, Tom	C	1939-41	Arizona	—
Greenwood, David	S	1986	Wisconsin	9
Gregg, Forrest	T	1956, 58-70	SMU	187
Gremminger, Hank	DB	1956-65	Baylor	123
Griffin, Harold	C	1928	Iowa	—
Grimes, Billy	HB	1950-52	Oklahoma A&M	36
Grimm, Dan	G	1963-65	Colorado	42
Gros, Earl	FB	1962-63	Louisiana	27

Name	Pos	Years	College	Games
Grove, Roger	B	1931-35	Michigan State	—
Gruber, Bob	T	1987	Pittsburgh	1
Gueno, Jim	LB	1976-80	Tulane	75

H

Name	Pos	Years	College	Games
Hackbarth, Dale	DB	1960	Wisconsin	12
Hackett, Joey	TE	1987-88	Elon	20
Haddix, Michael	RB	1989-90	Mississippi State	32
Hadl, John	QB	1974-75	Kansas	21
Haley, Darryl	T	1988	Utah	13
Hall, Charlie	CB	1971-76	Pittsburgh	82
Hall, Mark	DE	1989-90	Southwestern Louisiana	10
Hallstrom, Ron	G	1982-92	Iowa	163
Hamilton, Ruffin	LB	1994	Tulane	5
Hampton, Dave	RB	1969-71	Wyoming	33
Hanner, Dave	DT	1952-64	Arkansas	160
Hanny, Frank	T	1930	Indiana	—
Hansen, Don	LB	1976-77	Illinois	25
Hanson, Hal	B	1923	Marquette	—
Harden, Derrick	WR	1987	Eastern New Mexico	3
Harden, Leon	DB	1970	Texas-El Paso	8
Harding, Roger	C	1949	California	6
Hardy, Kevin	DT	1970	Notre Dame	14
Hargrove, James	RB	1987	Wake Forest	2
Harrell, Willard	RB	1975-77	Pacific	40
Harris, Corey	WR	1992-94	Vanderbilt	37
Harris, Jack	B	1925-26	Wisconsin	—
Harris, Jackie	TE	1990-93	Northeast Louisiana	60
Harris, Leotis	G	1978-83	Arkansas	75
Harris, Tim	LB	1986-90	Memphis State	76
Harris, William	TE	1990	Bishop	4
Harrison, Anthony	DB	1987	Georgia Tech	3
Hart, Doug	DB	1964-71	Texas-Arlington	112
Hartnett, Perry	G	1987	SMU	1
Hartwig, Keith	WR	1977	Arizona	7
Harvey, Maurice	S	1981-83	Ball State	29
Hathcock, Dave	DB	1966	Memphis State	14
Hauck, Tim	S	1991-94	Montana	58
Havig, Dennis	G	1977	Colorado	9
Haycraft, Ken	E	1930	Minnesota	—
Hayes, Dave	E	1921-22	Notre Dame	—
Hayes, Gary	CB	1984-86	Fresno State	42
Hayes, Norbert	E	1923	Marquette	—
Hayhoe, Bill	T	1969-73	USC	62
Hays, George	DE	1953	St. Bonaventure	9
Hearden, Lester	B	1924	St. Ambrose	—
Hearden, Thomas	B	1927-28	Notre Dame	—
Heath, Stan	QB	1949	Nevada	12
Hefner, Larry	LB	1972-75	Clemson	34
Held, Paul	QB	1955	San Diego	5
Helluin, Jerry	DT	1954-57	Tulane	48
Hendrian, Dutch	B	1924	Princeton	—
Hendricks, Ted	LB	1974	Miami	14
Henry, Urban	DE	1963	Georgia Tech	14
Hentrich, Craig	P	1994	Notre Dame	16
Herber, Arnie	HB	1930-40	Regis	—
Hickman, Larry	FB	1960	Baylor	12
Highsmith, Don	RB	1973	Michigan State	7
Hill, Don	B	1929	Stanford	—
Hill, Jim	S	1972-74	Texas A&I	41
Hill, Nate	DE	1988	Auburn	3
Hilton, John	TE	1970	Richmond	14
Himes, Dick	T	1968-77	Ohio State	140
Hinkle, Clarke	FB	1932-41	Bucknell	114
Hinte, Harold	E	1942	Pittsburgh	—
Hobbins, Jim	T	1987	Minnesota	3
Hoffman, Gary	T	1984	Santa Clara	1
Holland, Johnny	LB	1987-93	Texas A&M	103
Holler, Ed	LB	1963	South Carolina	2
Holmes, Jerry	CB	1990-91	West Virginia	29
Hood, Estus	CB	1978-84	Illinois State	104
Hope, Charles	G	1994	Central State	6
Horn, Don	QB	1967-70	San Diego State	22
Hornung, Paul	RB	1957-62, 64-66	Notre Dame	104
Houston, Bobby	LB	1990	North Carolina State	1
Howard, Lynn (Tubby)	B	1921-22	Indiana	—
Howell, John	B	1938	Nebraska	—
Howton, Bill	E	1952-58	Rice	80
Hubbard, Robert (Cal)	T	1929-33, 35	Geneva	—
Huckleby, Harlan	RB	1980-85	Michigan	84
Hudson, Bob	RB	1972	Southeast Oklahoma	12
Huffman, Tim	T	1981-85	Notre Dame	46
Hull, Tom	LB	1975	Penn State	13
Humphrey, Donnie	DE	1984-86	Auburn	48
Hunt, Ervin	DB	1970	Fresno State	7
Hunt, Kevin	T	1972	Doane	3
Hunt, Mike	LB	1978-80	Minnesota	22

Name	Pos	Years	College	Games
Hunter, Art	T	1954	Notre Dame	12
Hunter, Scott	QB	1971-73	Alabama	36
Hunter, Tony	RB	1987	Minnesota	1
Hutchins, Paul	T	1993-94	Western Michigan	17
Hutson, Don	E	1935-45	Alabama	117
Hyland, Bob	C	1967-69, 76	Boston College	56

I

Name	Pos	Years	College	Games
Ilkin, Tunch	T	1993	Indiana State	1
Iman, Ken	C	1960-63	SE Missouri State	54
Ingalls, Bob	C	1942	Michigan	—
Ingram, Darryl	TE	1992-93	California	18
Isbell, Cecil	B	1938-42	Purdue	54
Ivery, Eddie Lee	RB	1979-86	Georgia Tech	72

J

Name	Pos	Years	College	Games
Jacke, Chris	K	1989-94	Texas-El Paso	96
Jackson, Johnnie	S	1992	Houston	1
Jackson, Mel	G	1976-80	USC	65
Jacobs, Allen	HB	1965	Utah	14
Jacobs, Jack	QB	1947-49	Oklahoma	36
Jacunski, Harry	E	1939-44	Fordham	—
Jakes, Van	CB	1989	Kent State	16
James, Claudis	WR	1967-68	Jackson State	15
Janet, Ernie	G	1975	Washington	1
Jankowski, Ed	B	1937-41	Wisconsin	—
Jansante, Val	E	1951	Duquesne	3
Jay, Craig	TE	1987	Mount Senario	3
Jefferson, John	WR	1981-84	Arizona State	50
Jefferson, Norman	DB	1987-88	LSU	14
Jenison, Ray	T	1931	South Dakota	—
Jenke, Noel	LB	1973-74	Minnesota	10
Jennings, Jim	E	1955	Missouri	6
Jensen, Greg	OL	1987	No college	1
Jensen, Jim	RB	1981-82	Iowa	23
Jeter, Bob	DB	1963-70	Iowa	107
Johnson, Bill	E	1941	Minnesota	—
Johnson, Charles	DT	1979-80, 83	Maryland	46
Johnson, Danny	LB	1978	Tennessee State	16
Johnson, Ezra	DE	1977-87	Morris Brown	148
Johnson, Glen	T	1949	Temple Tech	8
Johnson, Howard	G	1940-41	Georgia	—
Johnson, Joe	HB	1954-58	Boston College	53
Johnson, Kenneth	CB	1987	Mississippi State	12
Johnson, KeShon	CB	1994	Arizona	7
Johnson, LeShon	RB	1994	Northern Illinois	12
Johnson, Marvin	DB	1952-53	San Jose State	12
Johnson, Randy	QB	1976	Texas A&I	3
Johnson, Reggie	TE	1994	Florida State	9
Johnson, Sammy	RB	1979	North Carolina	3
Johnson, Tom	DT	1952	Michigan	8
Johnston, Chester	B	1931, 34-37	Marquette	—
Jolly, Mike	S	1980, 82-83	Michigan	35
Jones, Boyd	T	1984	Texas Southern	2
Jones, Bruce	G	1927-28	Alabama	—
Jones, Daryll	S	1984-85	Georgia	24
Jones, Robert	G	1934	Indiana	—
Jones, Ron	TE	1969	Texas-El Paso	6
Jones, Scott	T	1991	Washington	2
Jones, Sean	DE	1994	Northeastern	16
Jones, Terry	DT	1978-84	Alabama	85
Jones, Tom	G	1938	Bucknell	—
Jordan, Charles	WR	1994	Long Beach City Coll.	10
Jordan, Henry	DT	1959-69	Virginia	139
Jordan, Kenneth	LB	1987	Tuskegee	3
Jorgenson, Carl	T	1934	St. Mary's (CA)	—
Jurkovic, John	NT	1991-94	Eastern Illinois	52

K

Name	Pos	Years	College	Games
Kahler, Bob	B	1942-44	Nebraska	—
Kahler, Royal	T	1942	Nebraska	—
Katalinas, Leo	T	1938	Catholic University	—
Kauahi, Kani	C	1988	Hawaii	16
Keane, Jim	E	1952	Iowa	11
Keefe, Emmett	G	1921	Notre Dame	—
Kekeris, James	T	1948	Missouri	5
Kell, Paul	T	1939-40	Notre Dame	—
Kelley, Bill	E	1949	Texas Tech	12
Kemp, Perry	WR	1988-91	California State (PA)	62

Name	Pos	Years	College	Games
Kercher, Bob	E	1944	Georgetown	—
Kern, William	T	1929-30	Pittsburgh	—
Keuper, Ken	B	1945-47	Georgia	31
Kiel, Blair	QB	1990-91	Notre Dame	7
Kiesling, Walt	G	1935-36	St. Thomas (MN)	—
Kilbourne, Warren	T	1939	Minnesota	—
Kimball, Bobby	WR	1979-80	Oklahoma	8
Kimmel, J.D.	DT	1958	Houston	12
Kinard, Billy	DB	1957-58	Mississippi	24
King, David	DB	1987	Auburn	3
King, Don	DT	1956	Kentucky	6
King, Don	DB	1987	SMU	1
Kirby, Jack	B	1949	USC	6
Kitson, Syd	G	1980-81, 83-84	Wake Forest	47
Klaus, Fee	C	1921	No college	—
Kleibhan, Roger	B	1921	Wisconsin-Milwaukee	—
Knafelc, Gary	E	1954-62	Colorado	89
Knutson, Gene	E	1954, 56	Michigan	18
Knutson, Steve	T	1976-77	USC	24
Koart, Matt	DE	1986	USC	6
Koch, Greg	T	1977-85	Arkansas	133
Koncar, Mark	T	1976-77, 79-81	Colorado	54
Konopasek, Ed	T	1987	Ball State	3
Koonce, George	LB	1992-94	East Carolina	47
Kopay, Dave	RB	1972	Washington	14
Kostelnik, Ron	DT	1961-68	Cincinnati	110
Kotal, Eddie	B	1925-29	Lawrence	—
Kovatch, John	E	1947	Notre Dame	3
Kowalkowski, Bob	G	1977	Virginia	9
Kramer, Jerry	G	1958-68	Idaho	129
Kramer, Ron	E	1957, 59-64	Michigan	89
Kranz, Kenneth	B	1949	Wisconsin-Milwaukee	7
Krause, Larry	RB	1970-71, 73-74	St. Norbert	51
Kroll, Bob	S	1972	Northern Michigan	5
Kuechenberg, Rudy	LB	1970	Indiana	6
Kurth, Joe	T	1933-34	Notre Dame	—
Kuusisto, William	G	1941-46	Minnesota	—

L

Name	Pos	Years	College	Games
Ladrow, Wally	B	1921	No college	—
Lally, Bob	LB	1976	Cornell	2
Lambeau, Earl (Curly)	B	1921-29	Notre Dame	—
Lammons, Pete	TE	1972	Texas	12
Landers, Walt	RB	1978-79	Clark	13
Lane, MacArthur	RB	1972-74	Utah State	41
Lankas, Jim	B	1943	St. Mary's (CA)	—
Larson, Bill	TE	1980	Colorado State	9
Larson, Fred (OJ)	C	1925	Notre Dame	—
Larson, Kurt	LB	1991	Michigan State	13
Laslavic, Jim	LB	1982	Penn State	6
Lathrop, Kit	DT	1979-80	Arizona State	17
Lauer, Hal (Dutch)	E	1922	Detroit	—
Lauer, Lary	C	1956-57	Alabama	18
Laughlin, Jim	LB	1983	Ohio State	15
Lawrence, Jim	B	1939	TCU	—
Laws, Joe	B	1934-45	Iowa	123
Leaper, Wes	E	1923	Minnesota	—
Lee, Bill	T	1937-42, 46	Alabama	—
Lee, Mark	CB	1980-90	Washington	157
Leigh, Charlie	RB	1974	No college	12
Leiker, Tony	DT	1987	Stanford	1
LeJeune, Walter	G	1925-26	Missouri	—
Leopold, Bobby	LB	1986	Notre Dame	12
Lester, Darrell	C	1937-38	TCU	—
Letlow, Russ	G	1936-42, 46	San Francisco	—
Levens, Dorsey	RB	1994	Georgia Tech	14
Lewellen, Verne	B	1924-32	Nebraska	—
Lewis, Cliff	LB	1981-84	Southern Mississippi	57
Lewis, Gary	TE	1981-84	Texas-Arlington	44
Lewis, Mark	TE	1986-87	Texas A&M	17
Lewis, Mike	DT	1980	Arkansas A&M	10
Lewis, Ron	WR	1992-94	Florida State	21
Lewis, Tim	CB	1983-86	Pittsburgh	51
Lidberg, Carl (Cully)	B	1926, 29-30	Minnesota	—
Lipscomb, Paul	T	1945-49	Tennessee	57
Livingston, Dale	K	1970	Western Michigan	14
Lofton, James	WR	1978-86	Stanford	136
Logan, Dave	NT	1987	Pittsburgh	2
Logan, Dick	T	1952-53	Ohio State	19
Lollar, George	B	1928	Howard	—
Long, Bob	WR	1964-67	Wichita	35
Loomis, Ace	HB	1951-53	Wisconsin-LaCrosse	33
Losch, John	HB	1956	Miami (FL)	12
Lucky, Bill	DT	1955	Baylor	12
Lueck, Bill	G	1968-74	Arizona	90
Luhn, Nolan	E	1945-49	Tulsa	56
Luke, Steve	DB	1975-80	Ohio State	89

Name	Pos	Years	College	Games
Lusteg, Booth	K	1969	Connecticut	4
Lyle, Dewey	G	1922-23	Minnesota	—
Lyman, Del	T	1941	UCLA	—

M

Name	Pos	Years	College	Games
Maas, Bill	NT	1993	Pittsburgh	14
MacAuliffe, Jack	B	1926	Beloit	—
Mack, Red	WR	1966	Notre Dame	9
MacLeod, Tom	LB	1973	Minnesota	11
Maddox, George (Buster)	T	1935	Kansas State	—
Majkowski, Don	QB	1987-91	Virginia	54
Malancon, Rydell	LB	1987	LSU	3
Malone, Grover	B	1921	Notre Dame	—
Mandarich, Tony	T	1989-91	Michigan State	45
Mandeville, Chris	S	1987	California-Davis	4
Manley, Leon	G-T	1950-51	Oklahoma	24
Mann, Bob	E	1950-54	Michigan	37
Mann, Errol	K	1968	North Dakota	2
Mansfield, Von	DB	1987	Wisconsin	3
Marcol, Chester	K	1972-80	Hillsdale	106
Marks, Larry	B	1928	Indiana	—
Marshall, Rich	DT	1965	Stephen A. Austin	14
Martel, Herman	E	1921	No college	—
Martin, Charles	DE	1984-87	Livingston	48
Martinkovic, John	DE	1951-56	Xavier	72
Mason, Dave	DB	1974	Nebraska	12
Mason, Joel	E	1942-45	Western Michigan	—
Mason, Larry	RB	1988	Troy State	15
Massey, Carlton	DE	1957-58	Texas	14
Masters, Norm	T	1957-64	Michigan State	104
Mataele, Stan	DL	1987	Arizona	2
Mathys, Charlie	QB	1922-26	Indiana	—
Matson, Pat	G	1975	Oregon	14
Matthews, Al	DB	1970-75	Texas A&I	84
Matthews, Aubrey	WR	1988-89	Delta State	20
Mattos, Harry	B	1936	St. Mary's (CA)	—
Matuszak, Marv	LB	1958	Tulsa	3
Mayer, Frank	G	1927	Notre Dame	—
McBride, Ron	RB	1973	Minnesota	11
McCaffrey, Bob	C	1975	USC	14
McCarren, Larry	C	1973-84	Illinois	162
McCloughan, Dave	CB	1992	Colorado	5
McConkey, Phil	WR	1986	Navy	4
McCoy, Mike C.	CB	1976-83	Colorado	110
McCoy, Mike P.	DT	1970-76	Notre Dame	96
McCrary, Hurdis	B	1929-33	Georgia	—
McDonald, Dustin	G	1935	Indiana	—
McDougal, Robert	B	1947	Miami (FL)	1
McDowell, John	G-T	1964	St. John's	12
McGarry, John	OL	1987	St. Joseph's	2
McGaw, Walter	G	1926	Beloit	—
McGeary, Clarence	T	1950	North Dakota	12
McGee, Buford	RB	1992	Missouri	4
McGee, Max	WR	1954, 57-67	Tulane	148
McGeorge, Rich	TE	1970-78	Elon	116
McGill, Lenny	CB	1994	Arizona State	6
McGrew, Sylvester	DE	1987	Tulane	3
McGruder, Michael	DB	1989	Kent State	2
McHan, Lamar	QB	1959-60	Arkansas	24
McIlhenny, Don	RB	1957-59	SMU	36
McIntyre, Guy	G	1994	Georgia	10
McJulien, Paul	P	1991	Jackson State	16
McKay, Roy	B	1944-47	Texas	—
McLaughlin, Joe	LB	1979	Massachusetts	3
McLaughlin, Lee	T	1941	Virginia	—
McLean, Ray (Toody)	B	1921	No college	—
McLeod, Mike	S	1984-85	Montana State	19
McMath, Herb	DT	1977	Morningside	9
McMichael, Steve	DT	1994	Texas	16
McMillan, Ernie	T	1975	Illinois	13
McNabb, Dexter	FB	1992-93	Florida	32
McPherson, Forrest	C	1943-45	Nebraska	—
Meade, Mike	RB	1982-83	Penn State	18
Meilinger, Steve	E	1958, 60	Kentucky	24
Melka, James	LB	1987	Wisconsin	1
Mendoza, Ruben	G	1986	Wayne State	6
Mercein, Chuck	RB	1967-69	Yale	23
Mercer, Mike	K	1968-69	Arizona State	16
Merrill, Casey	DE	1979-83	California-Davis	57
Merrill, Mark	LB	1982	Minnesota	2
Mestnik, Frank	FB	1963	Marquette	11
Meyer, Jim	T	1987	Illinois State	2
Michaels, Lou	K	1971	Kentucky	10
Michaels, Walt	G	1951	Washington-Lee	12
Michalske, August (Mike)	G	1929-35, 37	Penn State	—
Mickens, Terry	WR	1994	Florida A&M	12
Middleton, Terdell	RB	1977-81	Memphis State	69
Midler, Lou	G	1940	Minnesota	—

Name	Pos	Years	College	Games
Mihajlovich, Lou	E	1954	Indiana	3
Milan, Don	QB	1975	Cal-Poly-SLO	14
Millard, Keith	DT	1992	Washington State	2
Miller, Charles (Ookie)	C	1938	Purdue	—
Miller, Don	DB	1954	SMU	1
Miller, John	T	1960	Boston College	5
Miller, John	LB	1987	Mississippi State	1
Miller, Paul	B	1936-38	South Dakota State	—
Miller, Tom	E	1946	Hampden-Sydney	2
Mills, Tommy	B	1922-23	Penn State	—
Minick, Paul	G	1928-29	Iowa	—
Mitchell, Charles	B	1946	Tulsa	2
Mitchell, Roland	CB	1991-94	Texas Tech	48
Moffitt, Mike	WR	1986	Freso State	4
Moje, Dick	E	1951	Loyola (LA)	2
Molenda, Bo	B	1928-32	Michigan	—
Monaco, Ron	LB	1987	South Carolina	2
Monnett, Bob	B	1933-38	Michigan State	—
Moore, Allen	E	1939	Texas A&M	—
Moore, Blake	C	1984-85	Wooster	27
Moore, Brent	LB	1987	USC	4
Moore, Rich	DT	1969-70	Villanova	20
Moore, Tom	HB	1960-65	Vanderbilt	78
Moran, Rich	G	1985-93	San Diego State	108
Moresco, Tim	S	1977	Syracuse	14
Morgan, Anthony	WR	1993-94	Tennessee	18
Morris, Jim Bob	LB	1987	Kansas State	11
Morris, Larry	RB	1987	Syracuse	2
Morris, Lee	WR	1987	Oklahoma	5
Morrissey, Jim	LB	1993	Michigan State	6
Moselle, Dom	B	1951-52	Wisconsin-Superior	20
Mosley, Russ	B	1945-46	Alabama	8
Moss, Perry	QB	1948	Illinois	6
Mott, Joe	LB	1993	Iowa	2
Mott, Norm (Buster)	B	1933	Georgia	—
Mulleneaux, Carl (Moose)	E	1938-41, 45-46	Utah State	—
Mulleneaux, Lee	C	1938	Northern Arizona	—
Murphy, Mark	DB	1980-85, 87-91	West Liberty State	146
Murray, Richard (Jab)	T	1921-24	Marquette	—

N

Name	Pos	Years	College	Games
Nadolney, Romanus	T	1922	Notre Dame	—
Nash, Tom	E	1928-32	Georgia	—
Neal, Ed	T	1945-51	Tulane	68
Neal, Frankie	WR	1987	Fort Hays State	12
Neill, Bill	NT	1984	Pittsburgh	16
Nelson, Bob	NT	1988-90	Miami	46
Neville, Tom	G	1986-88, 92	Fresno State	38
Nichols, Hamilton	G	1951	Rice	9
Niemann, Walter	C	1922-24	Michigan	—
Nitschke, Ray	LB	1958-72	Illinois	195
Nix, Doyle	DB	1955	SMU	12
Nixon, Fred	WR	1980-81	Oklahoma	23
Noble, Brian	LB	1985-93	Arizona State	117
Noonan, Danny	NT	1992	Nebraska	6
Norgard, Al	E	1934	Stanford	—
Norton, Jerry	P	1963-64	SMU	28
Norton, Marty	B	1925	Carleton	—
Norton, Rick	QB	1970	Kentucky	3
Nussbaumer, Bob	B	1946, 51	Michigan	14
Nuzum, Rick	C	1978	Kentucky	16
Nystrom, Lee	T	1974	Macalester	13

O

Name	Pos	Years	College	Games
Oats, Carleton	DT	1973	Florida A&M	8
O'Boyle, Harry	B	1928, 32	Notre Dame	—
O'Connor, Bob	G	1935	Stanford	—
Odom, Steve	WR	1974-79	Utah	75
O'Donahue, Pat	DE	1955	Wisconsin	12
O'Donnell, Dick	E	1924-30	Minnesota	—
Odson, Urban	T	1946-49	Minnesota	39
Oglesby, Alfred	NT	1992	Houston	7
Ohlgren, Earl	E	1942	Minnesota	—
Okoniewski, Steve	DT	1974-75	Montana	28
Oliver, Muhammad	CB	1993	Oregon	2
Olsen, Ralph	E	1949	Utah	4
Olsonoski, Larry	G	1948-49	Minnesota	16
O'Malley, Tom	QB	1950	Cincinnati	1
O'Neil, Ed	LB	1980	Penn State	12
Orlich, Dan	E	1949-51	Nevada	36
Osborn, Dave	RB	1976	North Dakota	6
O'Steen, Dwayne	CB	1983-84	San Jose State	11
Owens, Harry	G	1922	Lake Forest	—

P

Name	Pos	Years	College	Games
Palumbo, Sam	C	1957	Notre Dame	9
Pannell, Ernie	T	1941-42, 45	Texas A&M	—
Pape, Orrin	B	1930	Iowa	—
Papit, Johnny	HB	1953	Virginia	4
Parilli, Vito (Babe)	QB	1952-53, 57-58	Kentucky	48
Parker, Freddie	RB	1987	Mississippi Valley	1
Parlavecchio, Chet	LB	1983	Penn State	3
Paskett, Keith	WR	1987	Western Kentucky	12
Paskvan, George	B	1941	Wisconsin	—
Patrick, Frank	QB	1970-72	Nebraska	30
Patterson, Shawn	DE	1988-91, 93	Arizona State	49
Patton, Ricky	RB	1979	Jackson State	6
Paulekas, Tony	C	1936	Washington & Jefferson	—
Paup, Bryce	LB	1990-94	Northern Iowa	64
Payne, Ken	WR	1974-77	Langston	44
Pearson, Lindell	HB	1952	Oklahoma	2
Peay, Francis	T	1968-72	Missouri	62
Pelfrey, Ray	E	1951-52	East Kentucky State	13
Perkins, Don	B	1943-45	Platteville	—
Perko, Tom	LB	1976	Pittsburgh	14
Perry, Claude	T	1927-35	Alabama	—
Pesonen, Dick	DB	1960	Minnesota-Duluth	12
Peterson, Lester	E	1932, 34	Texas	—
Peterson, Ray	B	1937	San Francisco	—
Petitbon, John	DB	1957	Notre Dame	12
Petway, David	S	1981	Northern Illinois	5
Pickens, Bruce	CB	1993	Nebraska	2
Pisarkewicz, Steve	QB	1980	Missouri	1
Pitts, Elijah	HB	1961-69, 71	Philander Smith	126
Pitts, Ron	DB	1988-90	UCLA	44
Ploeger, Kurt	DE	1986	Gustavus Adolphus	1
Pointer, John	LB	1987	Vanderbilt	3
Pope, Bucky	WR	1968	Catawba	3
Powers, Sammy	G	1921	Northern Michigan	--
Prather, Guy	LB	1981-85	Grambling	73
Pregulman, Merv	G	1946	Michigan	11
Prescott Harold (Ace)	E	1946	Hardin-Simmons	2
Prior, Mike	S	1993-94	Illinois State	32
Pritko, Steve	E	1949-50	Villanova	20
Prokop, Joe	P	1985	Cal Poly-Pomona	9
Provo, Fred	B	1948	Washington	9
Psaltis, Jim	DB	1954	USC	11
Purdy, Everett (Pid)	B	1926-27	Beloit	—
Pureifory, Dave	DE	1972-77	Eastern Michigan	80
Purnell, Frank	FB	1957	Alcorn A&M	9

Q

Name	Pos	Years	College	Games
Quatse, Jess	T	1933	Pittsburgh	—
Query, Jeff	WR	1989-91	Millikin	48
Quinlan, Bill	DE	1959-62	Michigan State	52

R

Name	Pos	Years	College	Games
Radick, Ken	E	1930-31	Marquette	—
Rafferty, Vince	C-G	1987	Colorado	3
Randolph, Al	S	1971	Iowa	14
Randolph, Terry	CB	1977	American International	14
Ranspot, Keith	E	1942	SMU	—
Rash, Lou	DB	1987	Mississippi Valley	3
Ray, Buford (Baby)	T	1938-48	Vanderbilt	—
Redick, Cornelius	WR	1987	Cal State Fullerton	1
Regnier, Pete (Doc)	B	1922	Minnesota	—
Reichardt, Bill	FB	1952	Iowa	12
Reid, Floyd (Breezy)	HB	1950-56	Georgia	78
Renner, Bill	P	1986-87	Virginia Tech	6
Rhodemyre, Jay	C	1948-49, 51-52	Kentucky	45
Rice, Allen	RB	1991	Baylor	6
Richard, Gary	CB	1988	Pittsburgh	10
Riddick, Ray	E	1940-42, 46	Fordham	—
Ringo, Jim	C	1953-63	Syracuse	131
Risher, Alan	QB	1987	LSU	3
Roach, John	QB	1961-63	SMU	22
Robbins, Tootie	T	1992-93	East Carolina	27
Roberts, Bill	HB	1956	Dartmouth	4
Robinson, Bill	HB	1952	Lincoln	—
Robinson, Dave	LB	1963-72	Penn State	117
Robison, Tommy	G	1987	Texas A&M	3
Roche, Alden	DE	1971-76	Southern University	83
Rodgers, Del	RB	1982, 84	Utah	23
Rohrig, Herman	B	1941, 46-47	Nebraska	—

Name	Pos	Years	College	Games
Roller, Dave	DT	1975-78	Kentucky	49
Romine, Al	HB	1955, 58	North Alabama	16
Rosatti, Roman	T	1924, 26-27	Michigan	—
Rose, Al	E	1932-36	Texas	—
Rose, Bob	C	1926	Ripon	—
Roskie, Ken	B	1948	South Carolina	6
Ross, Dan	TE	1986	Northeastern	15
Rote, Tobin	QB	1950-56	Rice	84
Rowser, John	DB	1967-69	Michigan	42
Rubens, Larry	C	1982-83	Montana State	25
Rudzinski, Paul	LB	1978-80	Michigan State	33
Ruettgers, Ken	T	1985-94	USC	138
Ruetz, Howard	T	1951-53	Loras	20
Rule, Gordon	S	1968-69	Dartmouth	15
Rush, Clive	E	1953	Miami (OH)	11
Ruzich, Steve	G	1952-54	Ohio State	36

S

Name	Pos	Years	College	Games
Salem, Harvey	T	1992	California	4
Salsbury, Jim	G	1957-58	UCLA	24
Sample, Chuck	FB	1942, 45	Toledo	—
Sampson, Howard	DB	1978-79	Arkansas	31
Sams, Ron	G	1983	Pittsburgh	5
Sandifer, Dan	DB	1952-53	LSU	13
Sandusky, John	DT	1956	Villanova	12
Sarafiny, Al	C	1933	St. Edward's	—
Sauer, George	B	1935-37	Nebraska	—
Saunders, Russell	B	1931	USC	—
Scales, Hurles	DT	1975	North Texas State	8
Schammel, Francis (Zud)	G	1937	Iowa	—
Scherer, Bernie	E	1936-38	Nebraska	—
Schlinkman, Walt	FB	1946-50	Texas Tech	47
Schmael, Art	B	1921	No college	—
Schmidt, George	C	1952	Lewis	7
Schmitt, John	C	1974	Hofstra	14
Schneidman, Herm	B	1935-39	Iowa	—
Schoemann, Roy	C	1938	Marquette	—
Schroll, Charles	C	1951	LSU	12
Schuette, Carl	C	1950-51	Marquette	24
Schuh, Jeff	LB	1986	Minnesota	12
Schuh, Harry	T	1974	Memphis State	14
Schultz, Charles	T	1939-41	Minnesota	—
Schwammel, Ade	T	1934-36, 43-44	Oregon State	—
Scott, Patrick	WR	1987-88	Grambling	24
Scott, Randy	LB	1981-86	Alabama	78
Scribner, Bucky	P	1983-84	Kansas	32
Secord, Joe	C	1922	No college	—
Seeman, George	E	1940	Nebraska	—
Seibold, Champ	T	1934-38, 40	Wisconsin	—
Self, Clarence	DB	1952, 54-55	Wisconsin	26
Serini, Washington	G	1952	Kentucky	11
Shanley, Jim	HB	1958	Oregon	12
Sharpe, Sterling	WR	1988-94	South Carolina	112
Shelly, Dexter	B	1932	Texas	—
Shield, Joe	QB	1986	Trinity	3
Shirey, Fred	T	1940	Nebraska	—
Shumate, Mark	NT	1985	Wisconsin	3
Sikahema, Vai	RB	1991	BYU	11
Simmons, Davie	LB	1979	North Carolina	16
Simmons, John	CB	1986	SMU	6
Simmons, Wayne	LB	1993-94	Clemson	26
Simpkins, Ron	LB	1988	Michigan	7
Simpson, Nate	RB	1977-79	Tennessee State	43
Simpson, Travis	OL	1987	Oklahoma	3
Sims, Joe	OL	1992-94	Nebraska	43
Skaugstad, Daryle	NT	1983	California	9
Skeate, Gil	B	1927	Gonzaga	—
Skibinski, Joe	G	1955-56	Purdue	24
Skinner, Gerald	T	1978	Arkansas	15
Skoglund, Robert	E	1947	Notre Dame	9
Skoronski, Bob	T	1956, 59-68	Indiana	146
Sleight, Elmer (Red)	T	1930-31	Purdue	—
Smith, Barry	WR	1973-75	Florida State	42
Smith, Barty	FB	1974-80	Richmond	67
Smith, Ben	E	1933	Alabama	—
Smith, Blane	G	1977	Purdue	1
Smith, Bruce	B	1945-48	Minnesota	23
Smith, Donnell	DE	1971	Southern University	5
Smith, Earl	E	1922	Ripon	—
Smith, Ed	T	1937	New York	—
Smith, Ernie	T	1935-37, 39	USC	—
Smith, Jerry	G	1956	Wisconsin	3
Smith, Ollie	WR	1976-77	Tennessee State	25
Smith, Oscar E.	G	1948-49	Texas-El Paso	14
Smith, Perry	CB	1973-76	Colorado State	47
Smith, Rex	E	1922	Ripon	—

Name	Pos	Years	College	Games
Smith, Richard (Red)	G	1927, 29	Notre Dame	—
Smith, Warren	C	1921	Carleton	—
Smith, Wes	WR	1987	East Texas	1
Snelling, Kenneth	B	1945	UCLA	2
Snider, Malcolm	G	1972-74	Stanford	42
Sorenson, Glen	G	1943-45	Utah State	—
Spagnola, John	TE	1989	Yale	6
Sparlis, Al	G	1946	UCLA	3
Spears, Ron	DE	1983	San Diego State	13
Spencer, Joe	T	1950-51	Oklahoma State	24
Spencer, Ollie	T	1957-58	Kansas	24
Spilis, John	WR	1969-71	Northern Illinois	40
Spinks, Jack	G	1955-56	Alcorn State	7
Sproul, Dennis	QB	1978	Arizona	6
Stachowicz, Ray	P	1981-82	Michigan State	25
Staggers, Jon	WR	1972-74	Missouri	42
Stahlman, Dick	T	1931-32	Chicago	—
Stanley, Walter	WR	1985-88	Mesa	49
Stansauk, Don	T	1950-51	Denver	15
Starch, Ken	RB	1976	Wisconsin	6
Staroba, Paul	WR	1973	Michigan	2
Starr, Bart	QB	1956-71	Alabama	198
Starret, Ben	B	1942-45	St. Mary's (CA)	—
Steen, Frank	E	1939	Rice	—
Steiner, Rebel	E	1950-51	Alabama	24
Stenerud, Jan	K	1980-83	Montana	45
Stephen, Scott	LB	1987-91	Arizona State	64
Stephens, John	RB	1993	Northwestern (LA) State	5
Stephenson, Dave	G	1951-55	West Virginia	49
Sterling, John	RB	1987	Central State (OK)	2
Stevens, Bill	QB	1968-69	Texas-El Paso	2
Stewart, Steve	LB	1979	Minnesota	3
Stills, Ken	S	1985-89	Wisconsin	65
Stokes, Tim	T	1978-82	Oregon	63
Stonebreaker, John	E	1942	USC	—
Strickland, Fred	LB	1994	Purdue	16
Sturgeon, Lyle	T	1937	North Dakota State	—
Sullivan, Carl	DE	1987	San Jose State	3
Sullivan, John	S	1986	California	6
Summerhays, Bob	B	1949-51	Utah	35
Summers, Don	TE	1987	Boise State	3
Sutton, Mickey	CB	1989	Montana	3
Svendsen, Earl	C	1937, 39	Minnesota	—
Svendsen, George	C	1935-37, 40-41	Minnesota	—
Swanke, Karl	T	1980-86	Boston College	84
Switzer, Veryl	HB	1954-55	Kansas State	24
Sydney, Harry	FB	1992	Kansas	16
Symank, John	DB	1957-62	Florida	76
Szafaryn, Len	G-T	1950, 53-56	North Carolina	55

T

Name	Pos	Years	College	Games
Tagge, Jerry	QB	1972-74	Nebraska	17
Tassos, Damon	G	1947-49	Texas A&M	26
Taugher, Claude	B	1922	Marquette	—
Taylor, Cliff	RB	1976	Memphis State	7
Taylor, Jim	FB	1958-66	LSU	118
Taylor, Kitrick	WR	1992	Washington State	10
Taylor, Lenny	WR	1984	Tennessee	2
Taylor, Willie	WR	1978	Pittsburgh	1
Teague, George	S	1993-94	Alabama	32
Temp, Jim	DE	1957-60	Wisconsin	43
Tenner, Bob	E	1935	Minnesota	—
Teteak, Deral	G	1952-56	Wisconsin	49
Thomas, Ben	DE	1986	Auburn	9
Thomas, Ike	CB	1972-73	Bishop	25
Thomas, Lavale	RB	1987-88	Fresno State	2
Thomason, Bobby	QB	1951	Virginia Military	11
Thompson, Arland	G	1981	Baylor	10
Thompson, Aundra	WR	1977-81	East Texas	63
Thompson, Clarence	B	1939	Minnesota	—
Thompson, Darrell	FB	1990-94	Minnesota	60
Thompson, John	TE	1979-81	Utah State	25
Thurston, Fred (Fuzzy)	G	1959-67	Valparaiso	112
Timberlake, George	G	1955	USC	6
Tinker, Gerald	WR	1975	Kent State	6
Tinsley, Pete	G	1938-45	Georgia	—
Toburen, Nelson	LB	1961-62	Wichita	24
Tollefson, Charles	G	1944-46	Iowa	—
Tomczak, Mike	QB	1991	Ohio State	12
Toner, Tom	LB	1973, 75-77	Idaho	53
Tonnemaker, Clayton	C	1950, 53-54	Minnesota	36
Torkelson, Eric	RB	1974-79, 81	Connecticut	92
Traylor, Keith	DE	1993	Central Oklahoma	5
Troup, Bill	QB	1980	South Carolina	2
Tuaolo, Esera	NT	1991-92	Oregon State	20
Tullis, Walter	WR	1978-79	Delaware State	32
Tunnell, Emlen	DB	1959-61	Iowa	37

Name	Pos	Years	College	Games
Turner, Maurice	RB	1985	Utah State	13
Turner, Rich	NT	1981-83	Oklahoma	31
Turner, Wylie	CB	1979-80	Angelo State	28
Turpin, Miles	LB	1986	California	1
Tuttle, Dick	E	1927	Minnesota	—
Twedell, Francis	G	1939	Minnesota	—

U

Name	Pos	Years	College	Games
Uecker, Keith	G	1984-85, 87-88, 90-91	Auburn	64
Uram, Andy	HB	1938-43	Minnesota	—
Urban, Alex	E	1941, 44-45	South Carolina	—
Usher, Eddie	B	1922, 24	Michigan	—

V

Name	Pos	Years	College	Games
Vairo, Dominic	E	1935	Notre Dame	—
Vandersea, Phil	LB	1966, 68-69	Massachusetts	34
Van Dyke, Bruce	G	1975-76	Missouri	28
Van Every, Hal	HB	1940-41	Minnesota	—
Vanoy, Vernon	DT	1972	Kansas	13
Van Sickle, Clyde	C	1932-33	Arkansas	—
Vant Hull, Fred	T	1942	Minnesota	—
Van Valkenburg, Pete	RB	1974	Brigham Young	6
Vataha, Randy	WR	1977	Stanford	6
Vegara, George	E	1925	Notre Dame	—
Veingrad, Alan	T	1986-87, 89-90	East Texas State	59
Vereen, Carl	T	1957	Georgia Tech	12
Viane, David	OL	1992	Minnesota-Duluth	1
Villanucci, Vince	NT	1987	Bowling Green	2
Vogds, Evan	G	1948-49	Wisconsin	24
Voss, Lloyd	T	1964-65	Nebraska	28
Voss, Walter (Tillie)	E	1924	Detroit	—

W

Name	Pos	Years	College	Games
Wade, Charlie	WR	1975	Tennessee State	2
Wafer, Carl	T	1974	Tennessee State	1
Wagner, Bryan	P	1992-93	Cal State-Northridge	23
Wagner, Buff	B	1921	Northern Michigan	—
Wagner, Steve	S	1976-79	Wisconsin	57
Walker, Cleo	LB	1970	Louisville	14
Walker, Malcolm	C	1970	Rice	14
Walker, Randy	P	1974	Northwestern Louisiana	14
Walker, Sammy	CB	1993	Texas Tech	8
Walker, Val Joe	DB	1953-56	SMU	46
Wallace, Calvin	DE	1987	West Virginia Tech	1
Walsh, Ward	RB	1972	Montana	2
Washington, Chuck	DB	1987	Arkansas	3
Watts, Elbert	CB	1986	USC	9
Weathers, Clarence	WR	1990-91	Delaware State	28
Weatherwax, Jim	DT	1966-67, 69	Cal State-Los Angeles	34
Weaver, Gary	LB	1975-79	Fresno State	63
Webb, Chuck	FB	1991	Tennessee	2
Webber, Harry	E	1928	Nebraska	—
Webster, Tim	K	1971	Arkansas	4
Weddington, Mike	LB	1986-90	Oklahoma	52
Weigel, Lee	RB	1987	Wisconsin-Eau Claire	2
Weisgerber, Dick	B	1938-40, 42	Williamette	—
Weishuhn, Clayton	LB	1987	Angelo State	9
Wellman, Mike	C	1979-80	Kansas	20
Wells, Don	E	1946-49	Georgia	37
Wells, Terry	RB	1975	Southern Mississippi	14
West, Ed	TE	1984-94	Auburn	167
West, Pat	B	1948	USC	3
Wheba, Ray	E	1944	USC	—
Wheeler, Lyle (Cowboy)	E	1921-23	Ripon	—
Whitaker, Bill	S	1981-82	Missouri	25
White, Adrian	S	1992	Florida	15
White, Gene	DE	1954	Georgia	8
White, Reggie	DE	1993-94	Tennessee	32
Whitehurst, David	QB	1977-83	Furman	53
Whittenton, Jesse	DB	1958-64	Texas Western	88
Wicks, Bob	WR	1974	Utah State	1
Widby, Ron	P	1972-73	Tennessee	26
Widell, Doug	G	1993	Boston College	16
Willhite, Kevin	RB	1987	Oregon	3
Wildung, Dick	G	1946-51, 53	Minnesota	74
Wilkens, Gabe	DE	1994	Gardner-Webb	15
Wilkins, Ted	E	1925	Indiana	—
Williams, A.D.	E	1959	Pacific	12
Williams, Clarence	DE	1970-77	Prairie View A&M	112
Williams, Delvin	RB	1981	San Francisco	1
Williams, Howard	DB	1962-63	Howard Junior College	10
Williams, Kevin	RB	1993	UCLA	3

Name	Pos	Years	College	Games
Williams, Mark	LB	1994	Ohio State	16
Williams, Perry	RB	1969-73	Purdue	70
Williams, Travis	RB	1967-70	Arizona State	49
Willis, James	LB	1993-94	Auburn	25
Wilner, Jeff	TE	1994	Wesleyan	11
Wilson, Ben	RB	1967	USC	14
Wilson, Charles	WR	1990-91	Memphis State	30
Wilson, Faye (Mule)	B	1931	Texas A&M	—
Wilson, Gene	E	1947-48	SMU	21
Wilson, Marcus	RB	1992-94	Virginia	34
Wilson, Milt	G	1921	Wisconsin-Oshkosh	—
Wilson, Ray	S	1994	New Mexico	3
Wimberly, Abner	E	1950-52	LSU	35
Wingle, Blake		1985	UCLA	2
Wingo, Rich	LB	1979, 81-84	Alabama	69
Winkler, Francis	DE	1967-68	Memphis State	21
Winkler, Randy	G	1971	Tarleton State	5
Winslow, Paul	HB	1960	North Carolina College	12
Winter, Blaise	DE	1988-90	Syracuse	45
Winters, Chet	RB	1983	Oklahoma	4
Winters, Frank	OL	1992-94	Western Illinois	48
Winther, Richard (Wimpy)	C	1971	Mississippi	11
Withrow, Cal	C	1971-73	Kentucky	42
Witte, Earl	B	1934	Gustavus-Adolphus	—
Wizbicki, Alex	B	1950	Holy Cross	11
Wood, Willie	S	1960-71	USC	166
Woodin, Howard (Whitey)	G	1922-31	Marquette	—
Woods, Bobby	T	1940	Alabama	—
Woods, Jerry	S	1990	Northern Michigan	16
Woodside, Keith	RB	1988-91	Texas A&M	64
Workman, Vince	RB	1989-91	Ohio State	46
Wortman, Keith	G	1972-75	Nebraska	47
Wright, Randy	QB	1984-88	Wisconsin	48
Wright, Steve	DE	1964-67	Alabama	56
Wunsch, Harry	G	1934	Notre Dame	—

Y

Name	Pos	Years	College	Games
Young, Bill	G	1929	Ohio State	—
Young, Glenn	DB	1956	Purdue	4

Z

Name	Pos	Years	College	Games
Zarnas, Gus	G	1939-40	Ohio State	—
Zatkoff, Roger	T	1953-56	Michigan	48
Zeller, Joe	G	1932	Indiana	—
Zendejas, Max	K	1987-88	Arizona	18
Zeno, Lance	C	1993	UCLA	5
Zimmerman, Don	WR	1976	Northeast Louisiana	2
Zoll, Carl	G	1922	No college	—
Zoll, Dick	G	1939	Indiana	—
Zoll, Martin	G	1921	No college	—
Zorn, Jim	QB	1985	Cal Poly-Pomona	13
Zuidmulder, Dave	B	1929-31	St. Ambrose	—
Zupek, Al	B	1946	Lawrence	3
Zuver, Merle	C	1930	Nebraska	—

Green Bay Press-Gazette photo

Paul Lipscomb, Packers tackle 1945-49.

Green Bay Press-Gazette photo

Ted Fritsch eludes Chicago's Clyde (Bulldog) Turner (66) and George Wilson (30) in a 1944 game. Fritsch played with the Packers for nine years. 1942 -50.

ACTIVE, BUT DID NOT PLAY

The following were active for at least one game, but did not actually play during a particular year.

Name	Pos	Years	College	Games
Ambrose, J.R.	WR	1988	Mississippi	1
Brunell, Mark	QB	1993	Washington	1
Cheyunski, Jim	LB	1977	Syracuse	1
Collier, Steve	T	1988	Bethune-Cookman	1
Detmer, Ty	QB	1992 (2), 94 (5)	BYU	7
Dimler, Rich	DT	1980	USC	3
Ferragamo, Vince	QB	1985	Nebraska	2
Fields, Angelo	T	1982	Michigan State	1
Graff, Neil	QB	1978	Wisconsin	1
Gray, Johnnie	S	1984	Cal State-Fullerton	1
Harrison, Reggie	RB	1978	Cincinnati	2
Henderson, Carlos	CB	1987		1
Hudson, Craig	TE	1990	Wisconsin	1
Hunt, Sam	LB	1980	Stephen A. Austin	1
Kiel, Blair	QB	1989	Notre Dame	9
Labbe, Rico	S	1990	Boston College	1
McCarthy, John	QB	1987	Williams College	1
Miller, Mark	QB	1980	Bowling Green	1
Norseth, Mike	QB	1990	Kansas	2
Nystrom, Lee	T	1973	Macalester	1
Oates, Brad	T	1981	BYU	1
Pass, Randy	G	1978	Georgia Tech	2
Shield, Joe	QB	1985	Trinity College	3
Singletary, Reggie	T	1991	North Carolina	6
Smith, Jimmy	RB	1984	Elon	1
Young, Steve	T	1979	Colorado	1
Van Dyke, Bruce	G	1975	Missouri	1

THE RECORD BOOK

ALL-TIME INDIVIDUAL RECORDS

SERVICE

Most Seasons
- 16   Bart Starr, 1956-71
- 15   Ray Nitschke, 1958-72
- 14   Forrest Gregg, 1956, 58-70
- 13   Charles (Buckets) Goldenberg, 1933-45
-      Dave Hanner, 1952-64

Most Games Played, Career
- 198   Bart Starr, 1956-71
- 195   Ray Nitschke, 1958-72
- 187   Forrest Gregg, 1956, 58-70
- 167   Ed West, 1984-94

Most Consecutive Games Played, Career
- 187   Forrest Gregg, 1956, 58-70
- 166   Willie Wood, 1960-71
- 162   Larry McCarren, 1973-84
- 150   Boyd Dowler, 1959-69

Most Seasons, Coach
- 29   Curly Lambeau, 1921-49
- 9   Vince Lombardi, 1959-67
-      Bart Starr, 1975-83
- 4   Gene Ronzani, 1950-53
-      Lisle Blackbourn, 1954-57
-      Dan Devine, 1971-74
-      Forrest Gregg, 1984-87
-      Lindy Infante, 1988-91

SCORING

Most Seasons Leading Team
- 9   Don Hutson, 1935-36, 39-45
- 6   Fred Cone, 1951, 53-57
-      Chester Marcol, 1972-74, 76-77, 79
- 5   Verne Lewellen, 1926-30
-      Paul Hornung, 1958-61, 64
-      Chris Jacke, 1989-93
- 4   Ted Fritsch, 1946-49

Most Consecutive Seasons Leading Team
- 7   Don Hutson, 1939-45
- 5   Verne Lewellen, 1926-30
-      Fred Cone, 1953-57
-      Chris Jacke, 1989-93
- 4   Ted Fritsch, 1946-49
-      Paul Hornung, 1958-61
- 3   Don Chandler, 1965-67
-      Chester Marcol, 1972-74
-      Jan Stenerud, 1981-83
-      Al Del Greco, 1984-86

Points

Most Points, Career
- 823   Don Hutson, 1935-45
- 760   Paul Hornung, 1957-62, 64-66
- 612   Chris Jacke, 1989-94
- 546   Jim Taylor, 1958-66

Most Points, Season
- 176   Paul Hornung, 1960
- 146   Paul Hornung, 1961
- 138   Don Hutson, 1942
- 128   Chester Marcol, 1972
-      Chris Jacke, 1993

Most Points, No Touchdowns, Season
- 128   Chester Marcol, 1972
-      Chris Jacke, 1993
- 115   Jan Stenerud, 1983
- 108   Chris Jacke, 1989
- 101   Jan Stenerud, 1981

Most Seasons, 100 or More Points
- 3   Paul Hornung, 1960-61, 64
- 2   Don Hutson, 1942-43
-      Jan Stenerud, 1981, 83
-      Chris Jacke, 1989, 93
- 1   Ted Fritsch, 1946
-      Jim Taylor, 1962
-      Chester Marcol, 1972

Most Points, Rookie, Season
- 128   Chester Marcol, 1972
- 108   Chris Jacke, 1989
- 78   Bill Howton, 1952
- 61   Al Del Greco, 1984

Most Points, Game
- 33   Paul Hornung, vs. Colts, Oct. 8, 1961
- 31   Don Hutson, vs. Lions, Oct. 7, 1945
- 30   Paul Hornung, vs. Colts, Dec. 12, 1965
- 28   Paul Hornung, vs. Vikings, Sept. 16, 1962

Touchdowns

Most Seasons Leading Team
- 11   Don Hutson, 1935-45
- 5   Verne Lewellen, 1926-30
-      Jim Taylor, 1959, 61-64
-      Sterling Sharpe, 1989-90, 92-94
- 3   By many players

Most Consecutive Seasons Leading Team
- 11   Don Hutson, 1935-45
- 5   Verne Lewellen, 1926-30
- 4   Jim Taylor, 1961-64
- 3   Sterling Sharpe, 1992-94

Most Touchdowns, Career
- 105   Don Hutson, 1935-45
- 91   Jim Taylor, 1958-66
- 66   Sterling Sharpe, 1988-94
- 62   Paul Hornung, 1957-62, 64-66

Most Touchdowns, Season
- 19   Jim Taylor, 1962
- 18   Sterling Sharpe, 1994
- 17   Don Hutson, 1942
- 16   Jim Taylor, 1961

Most Touchdowns, Rookie, Season
- 13   Bill Howton, 1952
- 9   Max McGee, 1954
- 8   Gerry Ellis, 1980
- 7   Don Hutson, 1935
-      Dave Hampton, 1969

Most Touchdowns, Game
- 5   Paul Hornung, vs. Colts, Dec. 12, 1965
- 4   Accomplished many times

Most Consecutive Games Scoring Touchdowns
- 7   Don Hutson, 1941-42
-      Don Hutson, 1943-44
-      Paul Hornung, 1960
- 6   Clarke Hinkle, 1937
-      Bill Howton, 1956
-      Terdell Middleton, 1978
-      Brent Fullwood, 1988
-      Sterling Sharpe, 1994

Points After Touchdown

Most Seasons Leading Team
- 7 Fred Cone, 1951-57
  Chester Marcol, 1972-74, 76-79
- 6 Don Hutson, 1940-45
  Chris Jacke, 1989-94
- 5 Paul Hornung, 1958-61, 64
- 4 Howard (Cub) Buck, 1922-25
  Joseph (Red) Dunn, 1927, 29-31

Most Consecutive Seasons Leading Team
- 7 Fred Cone, 1951-57
- 6 Don Hutson, 1940-45
  Chris Jacke, 1989-94
- 4 Howard (Cub) Buck, 1922-25
  Paul Hornung, 1958-61
  Chester Marcol, 1976-79
- 3 Accomplished many times

Most Points After Touchdown Attempted, Career
- 214 Fred Cone, 1951-57
- 210 Chris Jacke, 1989-94
- 194 Paul Hornung, 1957-62, 64-66
- 184 Don Hutson, 1935-45

Most Points After Touchdown Attempted, Season
- 52 Jan Stenerud, 1983
- 46 Jerry Kramer, 1963
- 43 Chris Jacke, 1994
- 42 Paul Hornung, 1964
  Don Chandler, 1966
  Chris Jacke, 1989

Most Points After Touchdown Attempted, Game
- 8 Don Hutson, vs. Lions, Oct. 7, 1945
  Don Chandler, vs. Falcons, Oct. 23, 1966
- 7 Don Hutson, vs. Cardinals, Nov. 1, 1942
  Paul Hornung, vs. Browns, Oct. 15, 1961
  Paul Honrung, vs. Bears, Sept. 30, 1962
  Jerry Kramer, vs. Eagles, Nov. 11, 1962
  Don Chandler, vs. Browns, Nov. 12, 1967
  Jan Stenerud, vs. Buccaneers, Oct. 2, 1983

Most Points After Touchdown, Career
- 207 Chris Jacke, 1989-94
- 200 Fred Cone, 1951-57
- 190 Paul Hornung, 1957-62, 64-66
- 172 Don Hutson, 1935-45

Most Points After Touchdown, Season
- 52 Jan Stenerud, 1983
- 43 Jerry Kramer, 1963
- 42 Chris Jacke, 1989
- 41 Paul Hornung, 1960
  Paul Hornung, 1961
  Paul Hornung, 1964
  Don Chandler, 1966
  Chris Jacke, 1994

Most Points After Touchdown, Game
- 8 Don Chandler, vs. Falcons, Oct. 23, 1966
- 7 Don Hutson, vs. Lions, Oct. 7, 1945
  Paul Hornung, vs. Browns, Oct. 15, 1961
  Paul Hornung, vs. Bears, Sept. 30, 1962
  Jerry Kramer, vs. Eagles, Nov. 11, 1962
  Don Chandler, vs. Browns, Nov. 12, 1967
  Jan Stenerud, vs. Buccaneers, Oct. 2, 1983

Most Consecutive Points After Touchdown
- 121 Chris Jacke, 1989-94
- 99 Paul Hornung, 1960-62, 64
- 74 Al Del Greco, 1984-86
- 67 Jan Stenerud, 1982-83

Highest Points After Touchdown Percentage, Career (minimum 100 attempts)
- 98.57 Chris Jacke, 1989-94 (207-210)
- 98.25 Al Del Greco, 1984-87 (112-114)
- 97.94 Paul Hornung, 1957-62, 64-66 (190-194)
- 97.50 Don Chandler, 1965-67 (117-120)

Most Points After Touchdown, No Misses, Season
- 52 Jan Stenerud, 1983
- 42 Chris Jacke, 1989
- 41 Paul Hornung, 1960
  Paul Hornung, 1961
- 39 Don Chandler, 1967

Field Goals

Most Seasons Leading Team
- 6 Ted Fritsch, 1942, 45-46, 48-50
  Fred Cone, 1951, 53-57
  Chester Marcol, 1972-74, 76-78
  Chris Jacke, 1989-94
- 5 Clarke Hinkle, 1933, 37-38, 40-41
  Paul Hornung, 1958-61, 64
- 4 Howard (Cub) Buck, 1922-25
- 3 Paul (Tiny) Engebretsen, 1936, 38-39
  Don Chandler, 1965-67
  Jan Stenerud, 1981-83
  Al Del Greco, 1984-86

Most Consecutive Seasons Leading Team
- 6 Chris Jacke, 1989-94
- 5 Fred Cone, 1953-57
- 4 Howard (Cub) Buck, 1922-25
  Paul Hornung, 1958-61
- 3 By many players

Most Field Goals Attempted, Career
- 195 Chester Marcol, 1972-80
- 174 Chris Jacke, 1989-94
- 140 Paul Hornung, 1957-62, 64-66
- 98 Ted Fritsch, 1942-50

Most Field Goals Attempted, Season
- 48 Chester Marcol, 1972
- 39 Chester Marcol, 1974
- 38 Paul Hornung, 1964
- 37 Chris Jacke, 1993

Most Field Goals Attempted, Game
- 6 Paul Hornung, vs. Steelers, Oct. 30, 1960
  Chester Marcol, vs. Browns, Sept. 17, 1972
  Chester Marcol, vs. Cowboys, Oct. 1, 1972
  Chester Marcol, vs. Lions, Dec. 3, 1972
  Chester Marcol, vs. Lions, Sept. 29, 1974
  Chester Marcol, vs. Vikings, Nov. 17, 1974
- 5 Accomplished many times

Most Field Goals, Career
- 120 Chester Marcol, 1972-80
- 85 Chris Jacke, 1989-92
- 66 Paul Hornung, 1957-62, 64-66
- 59 Jan Stenerud, 1980-83

Most Field Goals, Season
- 33 Chester Marcol, 1972
- 31 Chris Jacke, 1993
- 25 Chester Marcol, 1974
- 23 Chris Jacke, 1990

Most Field Goals, Rookie, Season
- 33 Chester Marcol, 1972
- 22 Chris Jacke, 1989
- 11 Joe Danelo, 1975
- 9 Al Del Greco, 1984

Most Field Goals, Game
- 5 Chris Jacke, vs. Raiders, Nov. 11, 1990
- 4 Accomplished many times

Most Field Goals, One Quarter
- 3 Paul Hornung, vs. Steelers, Oct. 30, 1960 (1)
  Chester Marcol, vs. Lions, Dec. 17, 1972 (1)

Most Consecutive Games Scoring Field Goals
- 12 Jan Stenerud, 1980-81
  Chris Jacke, 1991-92
- 10 Fred Cone, 1955
  Chris Jacke, 1989-90
  Chris Jacke, 1993
- 9 Don Chandler, 1967
  Chester Marcol, 1972-73
  Chester Marcol, 1976-77
- 8 Paul Hornung, 1960

Most Consecutive Field Goals
- 17 Chris Jacke, 1993
- 15 Chris Jacke, 1989-90
- 11 Jan Stenerud, 1981
- 10 Max Zendejas, 1987

Longest Field Goal
- 54 Chris Jacke, vs. Lions, Jan. 2, 1994
- 53 Jan Stenerud, vs. Buccaneers, Nov. 22, 1981
  Chris Jacke, vs. Rams, Sept. 9, 1990
  Chris Jacke, vs. Jets, Nov. 3, 1991
  Chris Jacke, vs. Lions, Nov. 1, 1992
- 52 Ted Fritsch, vs. Bulldogs, Oct. 19, 1950
  Paul Hornung, vs. Bears, Sept. 13, 1964
  Chester Marcol, vs. Colts, Sept. 22, 1974
  Chris Jacke, vs. Falcons, Oct. 1, 1989
  Chris Jacke, vs. Lions, Nov. 21, 1993
- 51 Accomplished six times

Highest Field Goal Percentage, Career
(minimum 50 field goals made)
- 80.82 Jan Stenerud, 1980-83 (59-73)
- 77.59 Chris Jacke, 1989-92 (135-174)
- 66.67 Al Del Greco, 1984-87 (50-75)
- 61.54 Chester Marcol, 1972-80 (120-195)

Highest Field Goal Percentage, Season
(minimum 1 field goal attempted per game)
- 91.67 Jan Stenerud, 1981 (22-24)
- 84.21 Max Zendejas, 1987 (16-19)
- 83.78 Chris Jacke, 1993 (31-37)
- 80.77 Jan Stenerud, 1983 (21-26)

Most Field Goals, No Misses, Game
- 5 Chris Jacke, vs. Raiders, Nov. 11, 1990
- 4 Accomplished seven times

Most Field Goals, 50 or More Yards, Career
- 13 Chris Jacke, 1989-94
- 3 Chester Marcol, 1972-80
- 2 Ted Fritsch, 1942-50
  Paul Hornung, 1957-62, 64-66
  Jan Stenerud, 1980-83
  Al Del Greco, 1984-87
- 1 Tom Birney, 1979-80
  Eddie Garcia, 1984

Most Field Goals, 50 or More Yards, Season
- 6 Chris Jacke, 1993
- 2 Chester Marcol, 1972
  Jan Stenerud, 1981
  Al Del Greco, 1986
  Chris Jacke, 1990, 1992
- 1 Accomplished many times

RUSHING

Most Seasons Leading Team
- 7 Clarke Hinkle, 1932-34, 36-37, 40-41
  Jim Taylor, 1960-66
- 5 Tony Canadeo, 1943, 46-49
  John Brockington, 1971-75
- 3 Ted Fritsch, 1942, 44-45
  Tobin Rote, 1951-52, 56
  Gerry Ellis, 1981, 83-84
  Eddie Lee Ivery, 1980, 82, 85
- 2 Accomplished many times

Most Consecutive Seasons Leading Team
- 7 Jim Taylor, 1960-66
- 5 John Brockington, 1971-75
- 4 Tony Canadeo, 1946-49
- 3 Clarke Hinkle, 1932-34

Attempts

Most Seasons Leading Team
- 8 Clarke Hinkle, 1932-34, 37-41
- 7 Jim Taylor, 1960-66
- 5 John Brockington, 1971-75
- 4 Tony Canadeo, 1943, 48-50

Most Consecutive Seasons Leading Team
- 7 Jim Taylor, 1960-66
- 5 Clarke Hinkle, 1937-41
  John Brockington, 1971-75

- 3 Clarke Hinkle, 1932-34
  Ted Fritsch, 1944-46
  Tony Canadeo, 1948-50
- 2 Accomplished many times

Most Attempts, Career
- 1,811 Jim Taylor, 1958-66
- 1,293 John Brockington, 1971-77
- 1,171 Clarke Hinkle, 1932-41
- 1,025 Tony Canadeo, 1941-44, 46-52

Most Attempts, Season
- 284 Terdell Middleton, 1978
- 274 John Brockington, 1972
- 272 Jim Taylor, 1962
- 266 John Brockington, 1974

Most Attempts, Rookie, Season
- 216 John Brockington, 1971
- 126 Gerry Ellis, 1980
- 121 Willard Harrell, 1975
- 114 Kenneth Davis, 1986

Most Attempts, Game
- 39 Terdell Middleton, vs. Vikings, Nov. 26, 1978
- 32 Jim Grabowski, vs. Bears, Sept. 24, 1967
  John Brockington, vs. Vikings, Nov. 17, 1974
- 30 Jim Taylor, vs. Steelers, Nov. 3, 1963
  John Brockington, vs. Bears, Nov. 7, 1971
  Harlan Huckleby, vs. Giants, Oct. 4, 1981
- 29 Edgar Bennett, vs. Bears, Nov. 22, 1992

Yards Gained

Most Yards Gained, Career
- 8,207 Jim Taylor, 1958-66
- 5,024 John Brockington, 1971-77
- 4,197 Tony Canadeo, 1941-44, 46-52
- 3,860 Clarke Hinkle, 1932-41

Most Seasons, 1,000 or More Yards Rushing
- 5 Jim Taylor, 1960-64
- 3 John Brockington, 1971-73
- 1 Tony Canadeo, 1949
  Terdell Middleton, 1978

Most Yards Gained, Season
- 1,474 Jim Taylor, 1962
- 1,307 Jim Taylor, 1961
- 1,169 Jim Taylor, 1964
- 1,144 John Brockington, 1973

Most Yards Gained, Rookie, Season
- 1,105 John Brockington, 1971
- 545 Gerry Ellis, 1980
- 519 Kenneth Davis, 1986
- 445 Cecil Isbell, 1938

Most Yards Gained, Game
- 186 Jim Taylor, vs. Giants, Dec. 3, 1961
- 167 Billy Grimes, vs. Yanks, Oct. 8, 1950
- 165 Jim Taylor, vs. Rams, Dec. 13, 1964
- 164 Jim Taylor, vs. Vikings, Oct. 14, 1962

Most Games, 100 or More Yards Rushing, Career
- 26 Jim Taylor, 1958-66
- 13 John Brockington, 1971-77
- 9 Tony Canadeo, 1941-44, 46-52
- 5 Terdell Middleton, 1977-81
  Gerry Ellis, 1980-86
  Eddie Lee Ivery, 1979-86

Most Games, 100 or More Yards Rushing, Season
- 7 Jim Taylor, 1962
- 5 Tony Canadeo, 1949
  Jim Taylor, 1960
- 4 Accomplished six times

Most Consecutive Games, 100 or More Yards Rushing
- 3 John Brockington, 1971
- 2 Accomplished many times

Longest Run From Scrimmage
- 97 Andy Uram, vs. Cardinals, Oct. 8, 1939
- 84 Jim Taylor, vs. Lions, Nov. 8, 1964
- 83 James Lofton, vs. Giants, Sept. 20, 1982
- 80 Jessie Clark, vs. Cardinals, Sept. 29, 1985

Average Gain

Highest Average Gain, Career
(minimum 400 attempts)
  5.26 Tobin Rote, 1950-56 (419-2,205)
  4.58 Gerry Ellis, 1980-86 (836-3,826)
  4.53 Jim Taylor, 1958-66 (1,811-8,207)
  4.40 Eddie Lee Ivery, 1979-86 (667-2,933)
Highest Average Gain, Season
(minimum 100 attempts)
  5.49 Gerry Ellis, 1985 (104-571)
  5.42 Jim Taylor, 1962 (272-1,474)
  5.38 Jim Taylor, 1961 (243-1,307)
  5.12 John Brockington, 1971 (216-1,105)
Highest Average Gain, Game (minimum 10 attempts)
16.70 Billy Grimes, vs. Yanks, Oct. 8, 1950 (10-167)
13.45 Terdell Middleton, vs. Lions, Oct. 1, 1978 (11-148)
11.60 Keith Woodside, vs. Bears, Dec. 17, 1989 (10-116)
10.73 Cecil Isbell, vs. Cardinals, Nov. 10, 1940 (11-118)

Touchdowns

Most Seasons Leading Team
  6 Clarke Hinkle, 1932, 36-39, 41
  5 Verne Lewellen, 1927-31
     Ted Fritsch, 1943-47
     Tobin Rote, 1951-52, 54-56
     Paul Hornung, 1957-60, 65
  4 Jim Taylor, 1961-64
     Donny Anderson, 1967-68, 70-71
     John Brockington, 1972-75
     Brent Fullwood, 1987-90
  3 Tony Canadeo, 1948-49, 52
     Gerry Ellis, 1980, 83, 85
Most Consecutive Seasons Leading Team
  5 Verne Lewellen, 1927-31
     Ted Fritsch, 1943-47
  4 Clarke Hinkle, 1936-39
     Paul Hornung, 1957-60
     Jim Taylor, 1961-64
     John Brockington, 1972-75
     Brent Fullwood, 1987-90
  3 Tobin Rote, 1954-56
Most Touchdowns, Career
  81 Jim Taylor, 1958-66
  50 Paul Hornung, 1957-62, 64-66
  37 Verne Lewellen, 1924-32
  34 Clarke Hinkle, 1932-41
Most Touchdowns, Season
  19 Jim Taylor, 1962
  15 Jim Taylor, 1961
  13 Paul Hornung, 1960
  12 Jim Taylor, 1964
Most Touchdowns, Rookie, Season
  5 Charles (Buckets) Goldenberg, 1933
     Gerry Ellis, 1980
     Brent Fullwood, 1987
  4 Accomplished many times
Most Touchdowns, Game
  4 Jim Taylor, vs. Browns, Oct. 15, 1961
     Jim Taylor, vs. Bears, Nov. 4, 1962
     Jim Taylor, vs. Eagles, Nov. 11, 1962
     Terdell Middleton, vs. Seahawks, Oct. 15, 1978
  3 Accomplished many times
Most Consecutive Games Rushing for Touchdowns
  7 Paul Hornung, 1960
  6 Terdell Middleton, 1978
  5 Tobin Rote, 1956
     Jim Taylor, 1961
     Jim Taylor, 1964
     Brent Fullwood, 1988
  4 Accomplished many times

PASSING

Highest Pass Rating, Career (minimum 500 attempts)
  83.0 Brett Favre, 1992-94
  80.5 Bart Starr, 1956-71
  74.0 Lynn Dickey, 1976-77, 79-85
  73.4 Don Majkowski, 1987-92
Highest Pass Rating, Season
(minimum 8 attempts per game)
105.1 Bart Starr, 1966
104.3 Bart Starr, 1968
 96.9 Bart Starr, 1964
 90.7 Brett Favre, 1994

Attempts

Most Seasons Leading Team
  13 Bart Starr, 1957-68, 70
   8 Lynn Dickey, 1976-77, 80-85
   7 Arnie Herber, 1932-37, 39
   6 Tobin Rote, 1950-51, 53-56
Most Consecutive Seasons Leading Team
  12 Bart Starr, 1957-68
   6 Arnie Herber, 1932-37
     Lynn Dickey, 1980-85
   4 Tobin Rote, 1953-56
   3 Cecil Isbell, 1940-42
     Irv Comp, 1944-46
     Don Majkowski, 1988-90
     Brett Favre, 1992-94
Most Passes Attempted, Career
3,149 Bart Starr, 1956-71
2,831 Lynn Dickey, 1976-77, 79-85
1,854 Tobin Rote, 1950-56
1,607 Don Majkowski, 1987-92
Most Passes Attempted, Season
599 Don Majkowski, 1989
582 Brett Favre, 1994
522 Brett Favre, 1993
492 Randy Wright, 1986
Most Passes Attempted, Rookie, Season
224 Tobin Rote, 1950
177 Vito (Babe) Parilli, 1952
163 Scott Hunter, 1971
127 Don Majkowski, 1987
Most Passes Attempted, Game
59 Don Majkowski, vs. Lions, Nov. 12, 1989
54 Randy Wright, vs. 49ers, Oct. 26, 1986
    Brett Favre, vs. Bears, Dec. 5, 1993
53 Don Majkowski, vs. Buccaneers, Dec. 3, 1989
52 Randy Wright, vs. Lions, Dec. 4, 1988

Completions

Most Seasons Leading Team
  14 Bart Starr, 1957-70
   8 Lynn Dickey, 1976-77, 80-85
   7 Arnie Herber, 1932-37, 39
   5 Tobin Rote, 1950, 52, 54-5
Most Consecutive Seasons Leading Team
  14 Bart Starr, 1957-70
   6 Arnie Herber, 1932-37
     Lynn Dickey, 1980-85
   3 Cecil Isbell, 1940-42
     Irv Comp, 1944-46
     Tobin Rote, 1954-56
     Don Majkowski, 1988-90
     Brett Favre, 1992-94
   2 Accomplished five times
Most Passes Completed Career
1,808 Bart Starr, 1956-71
1,592 Lynn Dickey, 1976-77, 79-85
  983 Brett Favre, 1992-94
  889 Don Majkowski, 1987-92

Most Passes Completed, Season
363 Brett Favre, 1994
353 Don Majkowski, 1989
318 Brett Favre, 1993
302 Brett Favre, 1992

Most Passes Completed, Rookie, Season
83 Tobin Rote, 1950
77 Babe Parilli, 1952
75 Scott Hunter, 1971
55 Don Majkowski, 1987

Most Passes Completed, Game
36 Brett Favre, vs. Bears, Dec. 5, 1993
35 Lynn Dickey, vs. Buccaneers, Oct. 12, 1980
34 Don Majkowski, vs. Lions, Nov. 12, 1989
33 Brett Favre, vs. Falcons, Oct. 4, 1992

Most Consecutive Passes Completed
18 Lynn Dickey, vs. Oilers, Sept. 4, 1983
   Don Majkowski, vs. Saints, Sept. 17, 1989
15 Lynn Dickey, vs. 49ers, Nov. 9, 1980
14 Don Majkowski, vs. Vikings, Nov. 26, 1989
13 Lynn Dickey, vs. Buccaneers, Oct. 12, 1980
   Lynn Dickey, vs. Saints, Dec. 13, 1981
   Randy Wright, vs. Buccaneers, Sept. 11, 1988
   Don Majkowski, vs. Vikings, Sept. 6, 1992

Completion Percentage

Highest Completion Percentage, Career
(minimum 500 attempts)
62.41 Brett Favre, 1992-94 (983-1,575)
57.42 Bart Starr, 1956-71 (1,808-3,149)
56.23 Lynn Dickey, 1976-77, 79-85 (1,592-2,831)
55.32 Don Majkowski, 1987-92 (889-1,607)

Highest Completion Percentage, Season
(minimum 8 attempts per game)
64.12 Brett Favre, 1992 (302-471)
63.74 Bart Starr, 1968 (109-171)
62.46 Bart Starr, 1962 (178-285)
62.37 Brett Favre, 1994 (363-582)

Highest Completion Percentage, Game
(minimum 20 attempts)
90.48 Lynn Dickey, vs. Saints, Dec. 13, 1981 (19-21)
87.10 Lynn Dickey, vs. Oilers, Sept. 4, 1983 (27-31)
81.48 Randy Wright, vs. Buccaneers, Sept. 11, 1988 (22-27)
80.00 Bart Starr, vs. 49ers, Dec. 13, 1959 (20-25)
   Bart Starr, vs. Chargers, Oct. 12, 1970 (16-20)
   Lynn Dickey, vs. Vikings, Dec. 16, 1984 (16-20)

Yards Gained

Most Seasons Leading Team
12 Bart Starr, 1957, 59-68, 70
8 Lynn Dickey, 1976-77, 80-85
7 Arnie Herber, 1932-37, 39
6 Tobin Rote, 1950-51, 53-56

Most Consecutive Seasons Leading Team
10 Bart Starr, 1959-68
6 Arnie Herber, 1932-37
   Lynn Dickey, 1980-85
4 Tobin Rote, 1953-56
3 Cecil Isbell, 1940-42
   Irv Comp, 1944-46
   Don Majkowski, 1988-90
   Brett Favre, 1992-94

Most Yards Gained, Career
24,718 Bart Starr, 1956-71
21,369 Lynn Dickey, 1976-77, 79-85
11,535 Tobin Rote, 1950-56
10,870 Don Majkowski, 1987-92

Most Yards Gained, Season
4,458 Lynn Dickey, 1983
4,318 Don Majkowski, 1987
3,882 Brett Favre, 1994
3,529 Lynn Dickey, 1980

Most Yards Gained, Rookie, Season
1,416 Vito (Babe) Parilli, 1952
1,231 Tobin Rote, 1950-56
1,210 Scott Hunter, 1971
875 Don Majkowski, 1987

Most Yards Gained, Game
418 Lynn Dickey, vs. Buccaneers, Oct. 12, 1980
410 Don Horn, vs. Cardinals, Dec. 21, 1969
402 Brett Favre, vs. Bears, Dec. 5, 1993
387 Lynn Dickey, vs. Redskins, Oct. 17, 1983

Most Games, 200 or More Yards Passing, Career
53 Lynn Dickey, 1976-77, 79-85
44 Bart Starr, 1956-71
30 Brett Favre, 1992-94
29 Don Majkowski, 1987-92

Most Games, 200 or More Yards Passing, Season
14 Lynn Dickey, 1983
13 Don Majkowski, 1989
12 Brett Favre, 1994
11 Brett Favre, 1993

Most Consecutive Games, 200 or More Yards Passing
11 Brett Favre, 1992
10 Lynn Dickey, 1983
6 Don Majkowski, 1988-89
   Brett Favre, 1994 (current)
5 Lynn Dickey, 1984
   Don Majkowski, 1990
   Brett Favre, 1994

Most Games, 300 or More Yards Passing, Career
15 Lynn Dickey, 1976-77, 79-85
9 Don Majkowski, 1987-92
5 Bart Starr, 1956-71
   Brett Favre, 1992-94
2 Tobin Rote, 1950-56
   Randy Wright, 1984-88

Most Games, 300 or More Yards Passing, Season
6 Don Majkowski, 1989
5 Lynn Dickey, 1983
4 Lynn Dickey, 1984
   Brett Favre, 1994
3 Lynn Dickey, 1980

Most Consecutive Games, 300 or More Yards Passing
3 Lynn Dickey, 1984
2 Lynn Dickey, 1983
   Lynn Dickey, 1983
   Don Majkowski, 1989

Longest Pass Completion
96 Tobin Rote to Billy Grimes, vs. 49ers, Dec. 10, 1950
95 Lynn Dickey to Steve Odom, vs. Vikings, Oct. 2, 1977
92 Arnie Herber to Don Hutson, vs. Cardinals, Oct. 8, 1939
91 Bart Starr to Boyd Dowler, vs. Rams, Dec. 18, 1960

Average Gain

Highest Average Gain, Career
(minimum 500 attempts)
7.85 Bart Starr, 1956-71 (24,718-3,149)
7.55 Lynn Dickey, 1976-77, 79-85 (21,369-2,831)
7.27 Cecil Isbell, 1938-42 (5,945-818)
6.83 Don Majkowski, 1987-91 (10,599-1,552)

Highest Average Gain, Season
(minimum 8 attempts per game)
9.46 Bart Starr, 1968 (1,617-171)
9.21 Lynn Dickey, 1983 (4,458-484)
8.99 Bart Starr, 1966 (2,257-251)
8.96 Don Horn, 1969 (1,505-168)

Highest Average Gain, Game
(minimum 20 attempts)
15.86 Cecil Isbell, vs. Cardinals, Nov. 1, 1942 (333-21)
14.85 Vito (Babe) Parilli, vs. Redskins, Oct. 19, 1958 (297-20)
14.50 Lynn Dickey, vs. Steelers, Sept. 11, 1983 (290-20)
13.96 Bart Starr, vs. Lions, Sept. 17, 1967 (321-23)

Touchdowns

Most Seasons Leading Team
- 11   Bart Starr, 1957, 60-68, 70
- 8   Lynn Dickey, 1976-77, 80-85
- 7   Tobin Rote, 1950-56
- 6   Arnie Herber, 1932-36, 38

Most Consecutive Seasons Leading Team
- 9   Bart Starr, 1960-68
- 7   Tobin Rote, 1950-56
- 6   Lynn Dickey, 1980-85
- 5   Joseph (Red) Dunn, 1927-31
  -    Arnie Herber, 1932-36

Most Touchdown Passes, Career
- 152   Bart Starr, 1956-71
- 133   Lynn Dickey, 1976-77, 79-85
- 89   Tobin Rote, 1950-56
- 70   Brett Favre, 1992-94

Most Touchdown Passes, Season
- 33   Brett Favre, 1994
- 32   Lynn Dickey, 1983
- 27   Don Majkowski, 1989
- 25   Lynn Dickey, 1984

Most Touchdown Passes, Rookie, Season
- 13   Vito (Babe) Parilli, 1952
- 7   Cecil Isbell, 1938
  -    Irv Comp, 1943
  -    Tobin Rote, 1950
  -    Scott Hunter, 1971

Most Touchdown Passes, Game
- 5   Cecil Isbell, vs. Rams, Nov. 1, 1942
  -    Don Horn, vs. Cardinals, Dec. 21, 1969
  -    Lynn Dickey, vs. Saints, Dec. 13, 1981
  -    Lynn Dickey, vs. Oilers, Sept. 4, 1983
- 4   Accomplished many times

Most Consecutive Games, Touchdown Passes
- 22   Cecil Isbell, 1941-42
- 15   Don Majkowski, 1988-89
- 13   Tobin Rote, 1950-56
- 9   Irv Comp, 1943-44
  -    Jack Jacobs, 1947-48
  -    Brett Favre, 1993-94
  -    Brett Favre, 1994 (current)

Highest Touchdown Percentage, Career (minimum 500 attempts)
- 7.46   Cecil Isbell, 1938-42 (818-61)
- 6.36   Arnie Herber, 1932-40 (1,006-64)
- 5.39   Irv Comp, 1943-49 (519-28)
- 5.15   Vito (Babe) Parilli, 1952-53, 57-58 (602-31)

Highest Touchdown Percentage, Season (minimum 8 attempts per game)
- 8.96   Cecil Isbell, 1942 (268-24)
- 8.77   Bart Starr, 1968 (171-15)
- 8.28   Tobin Rote, 1952 (157-13)
- 7.69   Cecil Isbell, 1938 (91-7)

Top Quarterback-To-Receiver Scoring Combinations
- 41   Brett Favre to Sterling Sharpe
- 35   Lynn Dickey to Paul Coffman
- 33   Cecil Isbell to Don Hutson
- 32   Lynn Dickey to James Lofton

Interceptions

Most Consecutive Passes Attempted, None Intercepted
- 294   Bart Starr, 1964-65
- 152   Bart Starr, 1963-64
- 128   Bart Starr, 1966-67
- 111   Brett Favre, 1992

Most Passes Had Intercepted, Career
- 151   Lynn Dickey, 1976-77, 79-85
- 138   Bart Starr, 1956-71
- 119   Tobin Rote, 1950-56
- 90   Arnie Herber, 1932-40

Most Passes Had Intercepted, Season
- 29   Lynn Dickey, 1983
- 25   Lynn Dickey, 1980

- 24   Tobin Rote, 1950
  -    Brett Favre, 1993
- 23   Randy Wright, 1986

Most Passes Had Intercepted, Game
- 6   Tom O'Malley, vs. Lions, Sept. 17, 1950
- 5   Accomplished many times

Most Attempts, No Interceptions, Game
- 46   Don Majkowski, vs. Lions, Sept. 30, 1990
- 42   Tobin Rote, vs. Bears, Nov. 7, 1954
  -    Don Majkowski, vs. Dolphins, Oct. 22, 1989
- 41   Randy Wright, vs. Bears, Nov. 8, 1987
  -    Don Majkowski, vs. Colts, Nov. 13, 1988
  -    Brett Favre, vs. Buccaneers, Nov. 29, 1992
- 40   Brett Favre, vs. Cowboys, Nov. 24, 1994

Lowest Percentage, Passes Had Intercepted, Career (minimum 500 attempts)
- 3.24   Brett Favre, 1992-94 (51-1,575)
- 3.48   Don Majkowski, 1987-92 (1,607-56)
- 4.38   Bart Starr, 1956-71 (3,149-138)
- 5.09   Randy Wright, 1984-88 (1,119-57)

Lowest Percentage, Passes Had Intercepted, Season (minimum 8 attempts per game)
- 1.20   Bart Starr, 1966 (251-3)
- 1.47   Bart Starr, 1964 (272-4)
- 2.41   Brett Favre, 1994 (14-582)
- 2.76   Brett Favre, 1992 (471-13)

Times Sacked

Most Times Sacked, Career
- 268   Lynn Dickey, 1976-77, 79-85
- 235   Bart Starr, 1963-71
- 159   Don Majkowski, 1987-92
- 99   David Whitehurst, 1977-83

Most Times Sacked, Season
- 47   Don Majkowski, 1989
- 42   Bart Starr, 1964
- 40   Lynn Dickey, 1981
  -    Lynn Dickey, 1983
- 37   Lynn Dickey, 1980

Most Times Sacked, Game
- 11   Bart Starr, vs. Lions, Dec. 7, 1965
- 10   David Whitehurst, vs. Chargers, Sept. 24, 1978
- 9   Lynn Dickey, vs. Jets, Dec. 20, 1981
- 8   Bart Starr, vs. Vikings, Oct. 5, 1969
  -    David Whitehurst, vs. Falcons, Oct. 7, 1979
  -    Don Majkowski, vs. Vikings, Oct. 15, 1989
  -    Don Majkowski, vs. Raiders, Nov. 11, 1990

PASS RECEIVING

Most Seasons Leading Team
- 10   Don Hutson, 1936-45
- 8   James Lofton, 1978, 80-86
- 7   Boyd Dowler, 1959, 62-65, 67-68
  -    Sterling Sharpe, 1988-94
- 6   Bill Howton, 1952-57

Most Consecutive Seasons Leading Team
- 10   Don Hutson, 1936-45
- 7   James Lofton, 1980-86
  -    Sterling Sharpe, 1988-94
- 6   Bill Howton, 1952-57

Most Pass Receptions, Career
- 595   Sterling Sharpe, 1988-94
- 530   James Lofton, 1978-86
- 488   Don Hutson, 1935-45
- 448   Boyd Dowler, 1959-69

Most Seasons, 50 or More Pass Receptions
- 7   James Lofton, 1979-81, 83-86
  -    Sterling Sharpe, 1988-94
- 3   Don Hutson, 1941-42, 44
  -    Bill Howton, 1952, 54, 56
  -    Paul Coffman, 1979, 81, 83
- 2   Boyd Dowler, 1963, 67
  -    Gerry Ellis, 1981, 83

Most Pass Receptions, Season
- 112 Sterling Sharpe, 1993
- 108 Sterling Sharpe, 1992
- 94 Sterling Sharpe, 1994
- 90 Sterling Sharpe, 1989

Most Pass Receptions, Rookie, Season
- 55 Sterling Sharpe, 1988
- 53 Bill Howton, 1952
- 48 Gerry Ellis, 1980
- 46 James Lofton, 1978

Most Pass Receptions, Game
- 14 Don Hutson, vs. Giants, Nov. 22, 1942
- 13 Don Hutson, vs. Rams, Oct. 18, 1942
- 12 Ken Payne, vs. Broncos, Sept. 29, 1975
  - Vince Workman, vs. Vikings, Sept. 6, 1992
- 11 Accomplished many times

Most Consecutive Games, Pass Receptions
- 103 Sterling Sharpe, 1988-94
- 58 James Lofton, 1979-83
- 50 Don Hutson, 1941-45
  - Paul Coffman, 1979-82
- 49 Max McGee, 1959-63

Yards Gained

Most Seasons Leading Team
- 11 Don Hutson, 1935-45
- 9 James Lofton, 1978-86
- 7 Sterling Sharpe, 1988-94
- 6 Bill Howton, 1952-57
  - Carroll Dale, 1966, 68-72

Most Consecutive Seasons Leading Team
- 11 Don Hutson, 1935-45
- 9 James Lofton, 1978-86
- 7 Sterling Sharpe, 1988-94
- 6 Bill Howton, 1952-57

Most Yards Gained, Career
- 9,656 James Lofton, 1978-86
- 8,134 Sterling Sharpe, 1988-94
- 7,991 Don Hutson, 1935-45
- 6,918 Boyd Dowler, 1959-69

Most Yards Gained, Season
- 1,461 Sterling Sharpe, 1992
- 1,423 Sterling Sharpe, 1989
- 1,361 James Lofton, 1984
- 1,300 James Lofton, 1983

Most Yards Gained, Rookie, Season
- 1,231 Bill Howton, 1952
- 818 James Lofton, 1978
- 791 Sterling Sharpe, 1988
- 614 Max McGee, 1954

Most Yards Gained, Game
- 257 Bill Howton, vs. Rams, Oct. 21, 1956
- 237 Don Hutson, vs. Dodgers, Nov. 21, 1943
- 209 Don Hutson, vs. Rams, Nov. 11, 1942
- 207 Don Hutson, vs. Cardinals, Nov. 1, 1942
  - Don Hutson, vs. Card-Pitt, Oct. 8, 1944

Most Seasons, 1,000 or More Yards, Pass Receiving
- 5 James Lofton, 1980-81, 83-85
  - Sterling Sharpe, 1989-90, 92-94
- 2 Bill Howton, 1952, 56
- 1 Don Hutson, 1942

Most Games, 200 or More Yards Receiving, Career
- 4 Don Hutson, 1935-45
- 2 Bill Howton, 1952-58
- 1 Carroll Dale, 1965-72
  - James Lofton, 1978-86

Most Games, 200 or More Yards Receiving, Season
- 2 Don Hutson, 1942

Most Games, 100 or More Yards Receiving, Career
- 32 James Lofton, 1978-86
- 29 Sterling Sharpe, 1988-94
- 24 Don Hutson, 1935-45
- 19 Boyd Dowler, 1959-69

Most Games, 100 or More Yards Receiving, Season
- 7 Sterling Sharpe, 1992
- 6 Don Hutson, 1942

Most Consecutive Games, 100 or More Yards Receiving
- Bill Howton, 1952
- James Lofton, 1984
- Sterling Sharpe, 1989
- 5 James Lofton, 1980
  - James Lofton, 1983
  - Sterling Sharpe, 1993
  - Sterling Sharpe, 1994
- 4 Don Hutson, 1939
  - Don Hutson, 1945
  - Bill Howton, 1954
  - James Lofton, 1981

(heading continues — Most Consecutive Games, 100 or More Yards Receiving)

- 4 Don Hutson, 1945
  - James Lofton, 1982-83
- 3 Bill Howton, 1952
  - James Lofton, 1984
- 2 Accomplished many times

Longest Pass Reception
- 96 Billy Grimes from Tobin Rote, vs. 49ers, Dec. 10, 1950
- 95 Steve Odom from Lynn Dickey, vs. Vikings, Oct. 2, 1977
- 92 Don Hutson from Arnie Herber, vs. Cardinals, Oct. 8, 1939
- 91 Boyd Dowler from Bart Starr, vs. Rams, Dec. 18, 1960

Average Gain

Highest Average Gain, Career
(minimum 100 receptions)
- 19.72 Carroll Dale, 1965-72 (5,422-275)
- 18.42 Bill Howton, 1952-58 (5,581-303)
- 18.39 Max McGee, 1954, 57-67 (6,346-345)
- 18.22 James Lofton, 1978-86 (9,656-530)

Highest Average Gain, Season
(minimum 24 receptions)
- 24.88 Don Hutson, 1939 (846-34)
- 23.68 Carroll Dale, 1966 (876-37)
- 23.22 Bill Howton, 1952 (1,231-53)
- 23.17 Max McGee, 1959 (695-30)

Highest Average Gain, Game
(minimum 3 receptions)
- 49.67 Don Hutson, vs. Dodgers, Nov. 19, 1939 (149-3)
- 48.67 James Lofton, vs. Falcons, Dec. 26, 1982 (146-3)
- 47.33 Carroll Dale, vs. 49ers, Dec. 4, 1966 (142-3)
- 46.50 Carroll Dale, vs. Falcons, Sept. 27, 1970 (186-4)

Touchdowns

Most Seasons Leading Team
- 11 Don Hutson, 1935-45
- 7 Max McGee, 1954, 58-61, 63-64
- 6 James Lofton, 1978-82, 86
  - Sterling Sharpe, 1989-94
- 5 Carroll Dale, 1966-69, 71

Most Consecutive Seasons Leading Team
- 11 Don Hutson, 1935-45
- 6 Sterling Sharpe, 1989-94
- 5 James Lofton, 1978-82
- 4 Johnny (Blood) McNally, 1930-33
  - Max McGee, 1958-61
  - Carroll Dale, 1966-69

Most Touchdowns, Career
- 99 Don Hutson, 1935-45
- 65 Sterling Sharpe, 1988-94
- 50 Max McGee, 1954, 57-67
- 49 James Lofton, 1978-86

Most Touchdowns, Season
- 18 Sterling Sharpe, 1994
- 17 Don Hutson, 1942
- 13 Bill Howton, 1952
  - Sterling Sharpe, 1992
- 12 Bill Howton, 1956
  - Sterling Sharpe, 1989

Most Touchdowns, Rookie, Season
- 13 Bill Howton, 1952
- 9 Max McGee, 1954
- 6 Don Hutson, 1935
  - James Lofton, 1978
- 5 Ray Pelfrey, 1951

Most Touchdowns, Game
4   Don Hutson, vs. Lions, Oct. 7, 1945
    Sterling Sharpe, vs. Buccaneers, Oct. 24, 1993
    Sterling Sharpe, vs. Cowboys, Nov. 24, 1994
3   Accomplished many times

Most Consecutive Games, Touchdowns
7   Don Hutson, 1941-42
    Don Hutson, 1943-44
6   Bill Howton, 1956
    Sterling Sharpe, 1994
5   Don Hutson, 1942
    Bill Howton, 1952
4   Don Hutson, 1936
    Steve Odom, 1975
    James Lofton, 1982-83
    James Lofton, 1984

INTERCEPTIONS

Most Seasons Leading Team
7   Bobby Dillon, 1952-58
5   Willie Wood, 1961-63, 65, 70
4   Herb Adderley, 1963-65, 69
3   Accomplished five times

Most Consecutive Seasons Leading Team
7   Bobby Dillon, 1952-58
3   Willie Wood, 1961-63
    Herb Adderley, 1963-65
    Ken Ellis, 1971-73

Most Interceptions By, Career
52   Bobby Dillon, 1952-59
48   Willie Wood, 1960-71
39   Herb Adderley, 1961-69
33   Irv Comp, 1943-49

Most Interceptions By, Season
10   Irv Comp, 1943
9   Accomplished many times

Most Interceptions By, Rookie, Season
10   Irv Comp, 1943
9   John Symank, 1957
     Tom Flynn, 1984
7   Rebel Steiner, 1950
5   Doyle Nix, 1955
     John Anderson, 1978
     Tim Lewis, 1983

Most Interceptions By, Game
4   Bobby Dillon, vs. Lions, Nov. 26, 1953
    Willie Buchanon, vs. Chargers, Sept. 24, 1978
3   Accomplished many times

Most Consecutive Games, Passes Intercepted By
5   Bobby Dillon, 1957
4   Accomplished many times

Yards Gained

Most Seasons Leading Team
5   Bobby Dillon, 1953-56, 58
3   Herb Adderley, 1962, 65, 69
    Mike Douglass, 1979, 82, 85
    LeRoy Butler, 1990, 93-94
2   Accomplished many times

Most Yards Gained, Career
976   Bobby Dillon, 1952-59
795   Herb Adderley, 1961-69
699   Willie Wood, 1960-71
472   Irv Comp, 1943-49

Most Yards Gained, Season
244   Bobby Dillon, 1956
217   Maurice Harvey, 1981
198   John Symank, 1957
197   Don Hutson, 1943

Most Yards Gained, Rookie, Season
198   John Symank, 1957
190   Rebel Steiner, 1950
149   Irv Comp, 1943
111   Tim Lewis, 1983

Most Yards Gained, Game
99   Maurice Harvey, vs. Saints, Dec. 13, 1981 (2)
     Tim Lewis, vs. Rams, Nov. 18, 1984 (1)
94   Rebel Steiner, vs. Bears, Oct. 1, 1950 (1)
91   Hal Van Every, vs. Steelers, Nov. 23, 1941 (1)
88   Bob Summerhays, vs. Eagles, Oct. 14, 1951 (1)

Longest Return (see previous record)

Touchdowns

Most Touchdowns, Career
7   Herb Adderley, 1961-69
5   Bobby Dillon, 1952-59
3   Charley Brock, 1939-47
    Doug Hart, 1964-71
    Ken Ellis, 1970-75

Most Touchdowns, Season
3   Herb Adderley, 1965
2   Don Perkins, 1944
    Charley Brock, 1945
    Bob Jeter, 1966

Most Touchdowns, Game
1   Accomplished many times

PUNTING

Most Seasons Leading Team, Number of Punts
6   David Beverly, 1975-80
5   Donny Anderson, 1967-71
    Don Bracken, 1986-90
4   Max McGee, 1954, 58-60
3   Clarke Hinkle, 1939-41
    Lou Brock, 1942-44
    Earl (Jug) Girard, 1949-51
    Dick Deschaine, 1955-57

Most Consecutive Seasons Leading Team, Number of Punts
6   David Beverly, 1975-80
5   Donny Anderson, 1967-71
    Don Bracken, 1986-90
3   Clarke Hinkle, 1939-41
    Lou Brock, 1942-44
    Earl (Jug) Girard, 1949-51
    Dick Deschaine, 1955-57
    Max McGee, 1958-60

Most Punts, Career
495   David Beverly, 1975-80
368   Don Bracken, 1985-90
315   Donny Anderson, 1966-71
256   Max McGee, 1954, 57-67

Most Punts, Season
106   David Beverly, 1978
86   David Beverly, 1980
      Paul McJulien, 1991
85   David Beverly, 1977
      Bucky Scribner, 1984
      Don Bracken, 1988
83   David Beverly, 1976

Most Punts, Game
11   Clarke Hinkle, vs. Bears, Dec. 10, 1933
     Earl (Jug) Girard, vs. Bears, Oct. 15, 1950
     Earl (Jug) Girard, vs. Rams, Dec. 3, 1950
10   Accomplished many times

Longest Punt
90   Don Chandler, vs. 49ers, Oct. 10, 1965
78   Jack Jacobs, vs. Cardinals, Oct. 10, 1948
75   Boyd Dowler, vs. Vikings, Oct. 22, 1961
     Boyd Dowler, vs. 49ers, Oct. 21, 1962
74   Arnie Herber, vs. Lions, Oct. 22, 1939
     Jack Jacobs, vs. Rams, Oct. 5, 1947

Average Yardage

Highest Punting Average, Career
(minimum 150 punts)
42.62   Dick Deschaine, 1955-57 (181-7,714)
41.98   Bucky Scribner, 1983-84 (153-6,202)
41.59   Max McGee, 1954, 57-67 (256-10,647)
39.68   Don Bracken, 1985-89 (368-14,602)
Highest Punting Average, Season
(minimum 2.5 punts per game)
44.69   Jerry Norton, 1963 (51-2,279)
44.05   Boyd Dowler, 1961 (38-1,674)
43.53   Jack Jacobs, 1947 (57-2,481)
43.21   Dick Deschaine, 1955 (56-2,420)
Highest Punting Average, Game
(minimum 4 punts)
61.60   Roy McKay, vs. Cardinals, Oct. 28, 1945 (5-308)
54.83   Craig Hentrich, vs. Jets, Nov. 13, 1994 (6-329)
54.25   Earl (Jug) Girard, vs. Eagles, Oct. 14, 1951 (4-217)
53.25   Boyd Dowler, vs. Colts, Oct. 9, 1960 (4-213)

Had Blocked

Most Consecutive Punts, None Blocked
274   David Beverly, 1977-80
254   Donny Anderson, 1967-71
153   Max McGee, 1954, 58-59
152   Don Bracken, 1988-90
Most Punts Had Blocked, Career
5   Earl (Jug) Girard, 1948-51
    Don Bracken, 1985-90
3   Lou Brock, 1940-45
    Steve Broussard, 1975
    Bill Renner, 1986-87
2   Accomplished many times

PUNT RETURNS

Most Seasons Leading Team, Number of Returns
10   Willie Wood, 1960-68, 70
4   Al Carmichael, 1953, 56-58
     Phillip Epps, 1982-85
3   Joe Laws, 1943-45
     Billy Grimes, 1950-52
     Walter Stanley, 1986-88
2   Accomplished many times
Most Punt Returns, Career
187   Willie Wood, 1960-71
100   Al Carmichael, 1953-58
       Phillip Epps, 1982-88
87   Walter Stanley, 1985-88
85   Johnnie Gray, 1975-83
Most Punt Returns, Season
40   Robert Brooks, 1994
37   Johnnie Gray, 1976
36   Phillip Epps, 1983
33   Steve Odom, 1978
     Walter Stanley, 1986
Most Punt Returns, Rookie, Season
30   Jeff Query, 1989
24   Veryl Switzer, 1954
21   Willard Harrell, 1975
     Terrell Buckley, 1992
20   Al Carmichael, 1953
     Phillip Epps, 1982
Most Punt Returns, Game
8   Phillip Epps, vs. Vikings, Nov. 21, 1982
7   Johnnie Gray, vs. Vikings, Nov. 21, 1976
    Robert Brooks, vs. Patriots, Oct. 2, 1994
6   Ken Ellis, vs. Browns, Sept. 17, 1972
    Steve Odom, vs. Lions, Oct. 1, 1978
    Phillip Epps, vs. Cowboys, Sept. 23, 1984
    Robert Brooks, vs. Buccaneers, Nov. 28, 1993

Fair Catches

Most Fair Catches, Career
102   Willie Wood, 1960-71
41   Elijah Pitts, 1961-69, 71
38   Jon Staggers, 1972-74
31   Phillip Epps, 1982-88
Most Fair Catches, Season
20   Jon Staggers, 1972
18   Willie Wood, 1970
13   Phillip Epps, 1983
     Robert Brooks, 1994
12   Jon Staggers, 1973
Most Fair Catches, Game
5   Willie Wood, vs. Bears, Nov. 15, 1970
4   Willie Wood, vs. Saints, Nov. 17, 1968
    Jon Staggers, vs. Redskins, Nov. 26, 1972
    Phillip Epps, vs. Cowboys, Sept. 23, 1984
    Terrell Buckley, vs. Buccaneers, Oct. 24, 1993
    Terrell Buckley, vs. Buccaneers, Dec. 24, 1994

Yards Gained

Most Seasons Leading Team
9   Willie Wood, 1960-66, 68, 70
3   By five players
Most Yards Gained, Career
1,391   Willie Wood, 1960-71
834   Billy Grimes, 1950-52
819   Phillip Epps, 1982-88
753   Al Carmichael, 1953-58
Most Yards Gained, Season
555   Billy Grimes, 1950
352   Robert Brooks, 1994
324   Phillip Epps, 1983
316   Walter Stanley, 1983
Most Yards Gained, Rookie, Season
306   Veryl Switzer, 1954
247   Jeff Query, 1989
211   Terrell Buckley, 1992
208   Fred Provo, 1948
Most Yards Gained, Game
129   Phillip Epps, vs. Buccaneers, Oct. 2, 1983
122   Robert Brooks, vs. Rams, Oct. 9, 1994
113   Walter Stanley, vs. Lions, Nov. 27, 1986
111   Mark Lee, vs. Giants, Nov. 8, 1981
Longest Punt Return
95   Steve Odom, vs. Bears, Nov. 10, 1974
94   Mark Lee, vs. Giants, Nov. 8, 1981
93   Veryl Switzer, vs. Bears, Nov. 7, 1954
90   Andy Uram, vs. Dodgers, Oct. 12, 1941
     Phillip Epps, vs. Buccaneers, Oct. 2, 1983

Average Gain

Highest Average, Career
(minimum 50 punt returns)
13.24   Billy Grimes, 1950-52 (63-834)
9.37   Jeff Query, 1989-91 (76-712)
9.20   Jon Staggers, 1972-74 (50-460)
8.89   Steve Odom, 1974-79 (64-569)
Highest Average, Season
(minimum 1 return per game)
19.14   Billy Grimes, 1950 (29-555)
16.07   Willie Wood, 1961 (14-225)
15.36   Ken Ellis, 1972 (14-215)
13.26   Willie Wood, 1964 (19-252)
Highest Average, Rookie, Season
(minimum 1 return per game)
12.75   Veryl Switzer, 1954 (24-306)
12.73   Steve Odom, 1974 (15-191)
11.56   Fred Provo, 1948 (18-208)
10.04   Terrell Buckley, 1992 (21-211)

Highest Average, Game
(minimum 3 returns)
- 37.00   Mark Lee, vs. Giants, Nov. 8, 1981 (3-111)
- 36.67   Willie Wood, vs. Bears, Dec. 5, 1964 (3-110)
- 30.50   Robert Brooks, vs. Rams, Oct. 9, 1994 (4-122)
- 25.80   Phillip Epps, vs. Buccaneers, Oct. 2, 1983 (5-129)

Touchdowns

Most Touchdowns, Career
- 2   Billy Grimes, 1950-52
  - Willie Wood, 1960-71
  - Jon Staggers, 1972-74

Most Touchdowns, Season
- 2   Billy Grimes, 1950
  - Willie Wood, 1961

Most Touchdowns, Game
- 1   Accomplished many times

KICKOFF RETURNS

Most Seasons Leading Team, Number of Returns
- 6   Steve Odom, 1974-79
- 5   Al Carmichael, 1953-54, 56-58
- 4   Herb Adderley, 1961-64
- 3   Tony Canadeo, 1943, 61-64
  - Billy Grimes, 1950-52

Most Kickoff Returns, Career
- 179   Steve Odom, 1974-79
- 153   Al Carmichael, 1953-58
- 120   Herb Adderley, 1961-69
- 77   Travis Williams, 1967-70

Most Kickoff Returns, Season
- 46   Dave Hampton, 1971
- 42   Steve Odom, 1975
- 41   Harlan Huckleby, 1983
- 39   Del Rodgers, 1984

Most Kickoff Returns, Rookie, Season
- 35   Charles Wilson, 1990
- 33   Vince Workman, 1989
- 31   Steve Odom, 1974
- 30   Mark Lee, 1980

Most Kickoff Returns, Game
- 8   Harlan Huckleby, vs. Redskins, Oct. 17, 1983
  - Gary Ellerson, vs. Cardinals, Sept. 29, 1985
- 7   Steve Odom, vs. Lions, Sept. 29, 1974
- 6   Accomplished many times

Yards Gained

Most Seasons Leading Team
- 6   Steve Odom, 1974-79
- 5   Al Carmichael, 1953-54, 56-58
- 4   Tony Canadeo, 1941, 43, 46-47
  - Herb Adderley, 1961-64
- 3   Billy Grimes, 1950-52

Most Consecutive Seasons Leading Team
- 6   Steve Odom, 1974-79
- 4   Herb Adderley, 1961-64
- 3   Billy Grimes, 1950-52
  - Al Carmichael, 1956-58
- 2   Accomplished many times

Most Yards Gained, Career
- 4,124   Steve Odom, 1974-79
- 3,907   Al Carmichael, 1953-58
- 3,080   Herb Adderley, 1961-69
- 2,084   Dave Hampton, 1969-71

Most Yards Gained, Season
- 1,314   Dave Hampton, 1971
- 1,034   Steve Odom, 1975
- 927   Al Carmichael, 1956
- 843   Del Rodgers, 1984

Most Yards Gained, Rookie, Season
- 798   Charles Wilson, 1990
- 739   Travis Williams, 1967
- 713   Steve Odom, 1974
- 641   Al Carmichael, 1953

Most Yards Gained, Game
- 208   Harlan Huckleby, vs. Redskins, Oct. 17, 1983
- 194   Dave Hampton, vs. Giants, Sept. 19, 1971
- 189   Al Carmichael, vs. Bears, Oct. 7, 1956
  - Dave Hampton, vs. Saints, Nov. 28, 1971
- 180   Herb Adderley, vs. Colts, Nov. 5, 1961

Longest Kickoff Return (all touchdowns)
- 106   Al Carmichael, vs. Bears, Oct. 7, 1956
- 104   Travis Williams, vs. Rams, Dec. 9, 1967
- 103   Herb Adderley, vs. Colts, Nov. 18, 1962
- 101   Dave Hampton, vs. Vikings, Oct. 4, 1970

Average Gain

Highest Average, Career
(minimum 50 returns)
- 28.16   Dave Hampton, 1969-71 (74-2,084)
- 26.73   Travis Williams, 1967-70 (77-2,058)
- 26.51   Tom Moore, 1960-65 (71-1,882)
- 25.67   Herb Adderley, 1961-69 (120-3,080)

Highest Average, Season
(minimum 1 return per game)
- 41.06   Travis Williams, 1967 (18-739)
- 33.08   Tom Moore, 1960 (12-397)
- 29.86   Al Carmichael, 1955 (14-418)
- 29.85   Herb Adderley, 1963 (20-597)

Highest Average, Rookie, Season
(minimum 1 return per game)
- 41.06   Travis Williams, 1967 (18-739)
- 33.08   Tom Moore, 1960 (12-397)
- 28.50   Larry Krause, 1970 (18-513)
- 26.56   Herb Adderley, 1961 (18-478)

Highest Average, Game
(minimum 3 returns)
- 50.33   Travis Williams, vs. Cardinals, Oct. 30, 1967 (3-151)
- 44.67   Steve Odom, vs. Lions, Oct. 3, 1976 (3-134)
- 43.33   Del Rodgers, vs. Bears, Dec. 9, 1984 (3-130)
- 42.33   Ike Thomas, vs. Bears, Nov. 12, 1972 (3-127)

Touchdowns

Most Touchdowns, Career
- 5   Travis Williams, 1967-70
- 3   Dave Hampton, 1969-71
- 2   Al Carmichael, 1953-58
  - Herb Adderley, 1961-69
  - Steve Odom, 1974-79
  - Robert Brooks, 1992-94
- 1   Accomplished by six players

Most Touchdowns, Season
- 4   Travis Williams, 1967
- 1   Accomplished many times

Most Touchdowns, Game
- 2   Travis Williams, vs. Browns, Nov. 12, 1967
- 1   Accomplished many times

COMBINED KICK RETURNS

Most Combined Kick Returns, Career
- 253   Al Carmichael, 1953-58 (p-100, k-153)
- 243   Steve Odom, 1974-79 (p-64, k-179)
- 190   Willie Wood, 1960-71 (p-187, k-3)
- 130   Billy Grimes, 1950-52 (p-63, k-67)

Most Combined Kick Returns, Season
- 61   Walter Stanley, 1986 (p-33, k-28)
- 58   Steve Odom, 1978 (p-33, k-25)
- 56   Al Carmichael, 1957 (p-25, k-31)
- 55   Billy Grimes, 1950 (p-29, k-26)

Most Combined Kick Returns, Game
9   Al Carmichael, vs. 49ers, Dec. 9, 1956 (p-4, k-5)
    Phillip Epps, vs. Buccaneers, Sept. 30, 1984 (p-3, k-6)
8   Accomplished many times

Yards Gained

Most Yards Gained, Career
4,693   Steve Odom, 1974-79
4,660   Al Carmichael, 1953-58
3,080   Herb Adderley, 1961-69
2,438   Billy Grimes, 1950-52

Most Yards Gained, Season
1,314   Dave Hampton, 1971 (p-0, k-1,314)
1,155   Billy Grimes, 1950 (p-555, k-600)
1,092   Al Carmichael, 1954 (p-165, k-927)
1,034   Steve Odom, 1975 (p-0, k-1,034)

Most Yards Gained, Game
247   Travis Williams, vs. Steelers, Nov. 2, 1969 (p-83, k-164)
211   Al Carmichael, vs. Bears, Oct. 7, 1956 (p-22, k-189)
208   Harlan Huckleby, vs. Redskins, Oct. 17, 1983 (p-0, k-208)
194   Dave Hampton, vs. Giants, Sept. 19, 1971 (p-0, k-194)

Touchdowns

Most Touchdowns, Career
6   Travis Williams, 1967-70 (p-1, k-5)
3   Dave Hampton, 1969-71 (p-0, k-3)
    Steve Odom, 1974-79 (p-1, k-2)
    Robert Brooks, 1992-94 (p-1, k-2)
2   By six players

Most Touchdowns, Season
4   Travis Williams, 1967 (p-0, k-4)
2   Billy Grimes, 1950 (p-2, k-0)
    Willie Wood, 1961 (p-2, k-0)
    Travis Williams, 1969 (p-1, k-1)
    Robert Brooks, 1994 (p-1, k-1)

Most Touchdowns, Game
2   Travis Williams, vs. Browns, Nov. 12, 1967 (p-0, k-2)
    Travis Williams, vs. Steelers, Nov. 2, 1969 (p-1, k-1)

FUMBLES

Most Fumbles, Career
64   Bart Starr, 1956-71
56   Lynn Dickey, 1976-77, 79-85
48   Don Majkowski, 1987-92
44   Tobin Rote, 1950-56

Most Fumbles, Season
15   Don Majkowski, 1989
14   Brett Favre, 1993
13   Lynn Dickey, 1980
12   Brett Favre, 1992

Most Fumbles, Game
4   Don Majkowski, vs. Vikings, Sept. 6, 1992
    Brett Favre, vs. Bengals, Sept. 20, 1992

Fumbles Recovered

Most Fumbles Recovered, Career, Own and Opponents
26   Lynn Dickey, 1976-77, 79-85 (26 own, 0 opp)
23   Ray Nitschke, 1958-72 (3 own, 20 opp)
22   Willie Davis, 1960-69 (1 own, 21 opp)
     Johnnie Gray, 1975-83 (2 own, 20 opp)
20   Henry Jordan, 1959-69 (2 own, 18 opp)

Most Fumbles Recovered, Season, Own and Opponents
6   Charley Brock, 1946 (1 own, 5 opp)
    Larry Craig, 1946 (2 own, 4 opp)
    Lynn Dickey, 1983 (6 own)
    Don Majkowski, 1989 (6 own)
5   Accomplished many times

Most Fumbles Recovered, Game, Own and Opponents
3   Billy Grimes, vs. Yanks, Oct. 19, 1950 (3 own, 0 opp)
    Gary Ellerson, vs. Lions, Oct. 6, 1985 (2 own, 1 opp)
    Chuck Fusina, vs. Redskins, Nov. 9, 1986 (3 own, 0 opp)
    Don Majkowski, vs. Vikings, Sept. 6, 1992

Most Own Fumbles Recovered, Career
26   Lynn Dickey, 1976-77, 79-85
19   Don Majkowski, 1987-92
18   Bart Starr, 1956-71
10   Tobin Rote, 1950-56
     Randy Wright, 1984-88

Most Own Fumbles Recovered, Season
6   Lynn Dickey, 1983
    Don Majkowski, 1989
5   Lynn Dickey, 1980
    Gerry Ellis, 1980
    Lynn Dickey, 1985

Most Own Fumbles Recovered, Game
3   Billy Grimes, vs. Yanks, Oct. 19, 1950
    Chuck Fusina, vs. Redskins, Nov. 9, 1986
    Don Majkowski, vs. Vikings, Sept. 6, 1992

Most Opponents' Fumbles Recovered, Career
21   Willie Davis, 1960-69
20   Ray Nitschke, 1958-72
     Johnnie Gray, 1975-83
18   Henry Jordan, 1959-69
16   Lionel Aldridge, 1963-71

Most Opponents' Fumbles Recovered, Season
5   Charley Brock, 1945
    Charley Brock, 1946
    Paul Lipscomb, 1946
    Lionel Aldridge, 1964
    Randy Scott, 1985
    Brian Noble, 1987

Most Opponents' Fumbles Recovered, Game
2   Accomplished many times

Longest Fumble Return
76   Scott Stephen, vs. Bears, Dec. 17, 1989
70   Mike Butler, vs. Vikings, Nov. 11, 1979
68   George Cumby, vs. Buccaneers, Oct. 11, 1981
60   Henry Jordan, vs. Cowboys, Nov. 29, 1964

Touchdowns

Most Touchdowns Career, Total
2   Mike Douglass, 1978-85
    Del Rodgers, 1982, 84

Most Touchdowns, Season, Total
2   Del Rodgers, 1982
    Mike Douglass, 1983

Most Touchdowns, Career, Own Recovered
2   Del Rodgers, 1982, 84
1   Max McGee, 1954, 57-67
    Willie Davis, 1960-69
    Sterling Sharpe, 1988-89

Most Touchdowns, Season, Own Recovered
2   Del Rodgers, 1982
1   Willie Davis, 1962
    Max McGee, 1964
    Sterling Sharpe, 1989

Most Touchdowns Career, Opponents' Recovered
2   Mike Douglass, 1978-85

Most Touchdowns Season, Opponents' Recovered
2   Mike Douglass, 1983

COMBINED NET YARDS GAINED

Most Seasons Leading Team
8   Don Hutson, 1936, 39-45
7   Jim Taylor, 1960-66
5   Sterling Sharpe, 1989-93
4   Tony Canadeo, 1946-49
    Al Carmichael, 1953, 56-58
    Steve Odom, 1974-77
    James Lofton, 1979, 82-84

Most Consecutive Seasons Leading Team

- 7 Don Hutson, 1939-45
  Jim Taylor, 1960-66
- 5 Sterling Sharpe, 1989-93
- 4 Tony Canadeo, 1946-49
  Steve Odom, 1974-77
- 3 Al Carmichael, 1956-58
  James Lofton, 1982-84

Attempts

Most Attempts, Career

- 2,012 Jim Taylor, 1958-66
- 1,437 John Brockington, 1971-77
- 1,229 Tony Canadeo, 1941-44, 46-52
  Clarke Hinkle, 1932-41
- 1,125 Gerry Ellis, 1980-86

Most Attempts, Season

- 319 Terdell Middleton, 1978
- 309 John Brockington, 1974
- 295 Jim Taylor, 1962
- 293 John Brockington, 1972

Most Attempts, Game

- 41 Terdell Middleton, vs. Vikings, Nov. 26, 1978
- 38 Vince Workman, vs. Vikings, Sept. 6, 1992
- 35 Jim Grabowski, vs. Bears, Sept. 24, 1967
  John Brockington, vs. Vikings, Nov. 17, 1974
- 32 Harlan Huckleby, vs. Giants, Oct. 4, 1981

Yards Gained

Most Yards Gained, Career

- 9,909 James Lofton, 1978-86
- 9,898 Jim Taylor, 1958-66
- 8,709 Don Hutson, 1935-45
- 8,276 Sterling Sharpe, 1988-94

Most Yards Gained, Season

- 1,896 Billy Grimes, 1950
- 1,658 Dave Hampton, 1971
- 1,617 Walter Stanley, 1986
- 1,580 Jim Taylor, 1962

Most Yards Gained, Rookie, Season

- 1,231 Bill Howton, 1952
- 1,219 Steve Odom, 1974
- 1,203 John Brockington, 1971
- 1,170 Al Carmichael, 1953

Most Yards Gained, Game

- 314 Travis Williams, vs. Steelers, Nov. 2, 1969
- 287 Walter Stanley, vs. Lions, Nov. 27, 1986
- 257 Bill Howton, vs. Rams, Oct. 21, 1956
- 253 Travis Williams, vs. Steelers, Dec. 17, 1967

Most Seasons, 1,000 or More Yards, Career

- 6 Jim Taylor, 1960-64, 66
- 5 Steve Odom, 1974-78
  James Lofton, 1980-81, 83-85
  Sterling Sharpe, 1989-90, 92-94
- 4 Donny Anderson, 1967-68, 70-71
  John Brockington, 1971-74
  Gerry Ellis, 1980-81, 83, 85
- 3 Don Hutson, 1942-44
  Al Carmichael, 1953, 56-57

Most Consecutive Seasons, 1,000 or More Yards

- 5 Jim Taylor, 1960-64
  Steve Odom, 1974-78
- 4 John Brockington, 1971-74
- 3 Don Hutson, 1942-44
  Sterling Sharpe, 1992-94
- 2 Accomplished many times

SACKS

Most Sacks, Career

- 55.0 Tim Harris, 1986-90
- 41.5 Ezra Johnson, 1982-87
- 36.0 Tony Bennett, 1990-93
- 32.5 Bryce Paup, 1990-94

Most Sacks, Season

- 19.5 Tim Harris, 1989
- 14.5 Ezra Johnson, 1983
- 13.5 Tim Harris, 1988
  Tony Bennett, 1992
- 13.0 Tony Bennett, 1991
  Reggie White, 1993

Most Sacks, Game

- 4.5 Bryce Paup, vs. Buccanneers, Sept. 15, 1991
- 4.0 Alphonso Carreker, vs. Buccaneers, Dec. 1, 1985
  Tim Harris, vs. Falcons, Oct. 1, 1989
- 3.5 Tony Bennett, vs. Giants, Nov. 8, 1992
- 3.0 Ezra Johnson, vs. Bears, Dec. 4, 1983
  Mike Douglass, vs. Bears, Dec. 9, 1984
  Tim Harris, vs. Lions, Nov. 12, 1989
  Reggie White, vs. Broncos, Oct. 10, 1993
  Bryce Paup, vs. Chiefs, Nov. 8, 1993

Green Bay Press-Gazette photo

Clarke Hinkle (30) heads goalward in a late-September 1941 meeting with Chicago. The Bears prevailed 25-17.

THE RECORD BOOK

ALL-TIME TEAM RECORDS

CHAMPIONSHIPS

Most Seasons League Champions
   11   1929-31, 36, 39, 44, 61-62, 65-67
Most Consecutive Seasons League Champions
   3   1929-31, 1965-67
   2   1961-62
Most Times Finishing First, Regular Season
   16   1929-31, 36, 38-39, 41, 44, 60-62, 65-67, 72, 89
Most Consecutive Times Finishing First, Regular Season
   3   1929-31, 60-62, 65-67
   2   1938-39

GAMES WON

Most Consecutive Games Won
(including postseason games)
   12   1961-62
   11   1929
   10   1929-30
   9   1931, 36, 43-44
Most Consecutive Games Won
(regular season only)
   11   1929, 61-62
   10   1929-30
   9   1931, 36, 43-44
   8   1941, 63
Most Consecutive Games Without Defeat
(includes postseason games)
   23   1928-30 (won 21, tied 2)
   12   1961-62 (won 12)
   11   1936 (won 10, tied 1), 1966-67 (won 10, tied 1)
   10   1930-31 (won 9, tied 1), 1964-65 (won 9, tied 1)
Most Consecutive Games Without Defeat
(regular season only)
   23   1928-30 (won 21, tied 2)
   11   1961-62 (won 11)
   10   1930-31 (won 9, tied 1), 1936 (won 9, tied 1)
        1964-65 (won 9, tied 1)
   9   1922-23 (won 5, tied 4), 1932 (won 8, tied 1)
        1943-44 (won 9)
Most Games Won, Season
(includes postseason games)
   14   1962, 66
   12   1929, 31, 61, 65, 67
   11   1932, 36, 63
   10   1930, 39, 41, 72, 89, 93-94
Most Consecutive Games Won, Season
(includes postseason games)
   10   1929, 62
   9   1931, 36
   8   1930, 41, 63
   7   1932, 37, 66
Most Consecutive Games Won, Season
(regular season games only)
   10   1929, 62
   9   1931, 36
   8   1930, 41, 63
   7   1932, 37
Most Consecutive Games Won, Start of Season
   10   1929, 62
   9   1931
   8   1930
   6   1944, 65

Most Consecutive Games Won, End of Season
   8   1941
   5   1923, 66
   4   1939, 59
   3   1943, 60, 62, 72, 84, 89, 94
Most Consecutive Games Without Defeat, Season
(includes postseason games)
   13   1929 (won 12, tied 1)
   11   1936 (won 10, tied 1)
   10   1962 (won 10)
   9   1931 (won 9), 1932 (won 8, tied 1)
Most Consecutive Games Without Defeat, Season
(regular season only)
   13   1929 (won 12, tied 1)
   10   1936 (won 9, tied 1), 1962 (won 10)
   9   1931 (won 9), 1932 (won 8, tied 1)
   8   1930 (won 8), 1941 (won 8), 1963 (won 8)
Most Consecutive Games Without Defeat, Start of Season
   13   1929 (won 12, tied 1)
   10   1962 (won 10)
   9   1931 (won 9), 1932 (won 8, tied 1)
   8   1930 (won 8)
Most Consecutive Games Without Defeat, End of Season
   13   1929 (won 12, tied 1)
   10   1936 (won 9, tied 1)
   8   1941 (won 8)
   7   1922 (won 4, tied 3)
Most Consecutive Home Games Won
(includes Milwaukee)
   20   1929-32
   14   1923-26
   13   1961-62
   8   1943-45
Most Consecutive Home Games Without Defeat
(includes Milwaukee)
   30   1928-33 (won 27, tied 3)
   16   1923-26 (won 14, tied 2)
   13   1961-62 (won 13)
   8   1943-45 (won 8)
Most Consecutive Road Games Won
(regular season only)
   8   1941-42, 66-67
   6   1928-29, 35-36
   5   1960-61, 61-62, 62-63, 89-90
   4   1922-23, 29-30, 38, 39, 42-43, 59-60, 72
Most Consecutive Road Games Without Defeat
(regular season only)
   12   1929-30 (won 10, tied 2)
   10   1935-37 (won 9, tied 1), 1940-42 (won 9, tied 1)
   8   1966-67 (won 8)
   6   1922-23 (won 4, tied 2)
Most Shutout Games, Won or Tied, Season
   8   1926 (won 7, tied 1), 1929 (won 7, tied 1)
   7   1923 (won 6, tied 1), 1932 (won 6, tied 1)
   5   1922 (won 3, tied 2), 1925 (won 5), 1927 (won 5),
        1928 (won 4, tied 1), 1931 (won 5)
   4   1924 (won 4), 1930 (won 4), 1934 (won 4)
Most Consecutive Shutout Games Won or Tied
   5   1926 (won 5), 1929-30 (won 4, tied 1)
   4   1922-23 (won 3, tied 1)
   3   1922 (won 1, tied 2), 1924 (won 3), 1927 (won 3),
        1928-29 (won 3), 1932 (won 3)
   2   Accomplished many times

GAMES LOST

Most Consecutive Games Lost
9 1948-49
8 1951-52, 53-54
7 1949-50, 58, 74-75, 84, 87-88, 88, 90-91
6 1950, 52-53, 86

Most Consecutive Games Without Victory
9 1948-49 (lost 9), 1953-54 (lost 8, tied 1)
8 1951-52 (lost 8)
7 1921-22 (lost 4, tied 3), 1949-50 (lost 7)
  1957-58 (lost 6, tied 1), 1958 (lost 7)
  1974-75 (lost 7), 1984 (lost 7), 1987-88 (lost 7)
  1988 (lost 7)
6 1950 (lost 6), 1952-53 (lost 6), 1986 (lost 6)

Most Games Lost, Season
12 1986, 88, 91
11 1979
10 1949, 58, 75, 77, 80, 90
9 1948, 50-51, 53, 57, 76, 87

Most Consecutive Games Lost, Season
7 1948, 51, 58, 84, 88
6 1949, 50, 86
5 1953, 59, 77, 88, 90
4 Accomplished many times

Most Consecutive Games Lost, Start of Season
6 1986
5 1988
4 1975
3 1922, 53-54, 76

Most Consecutive Games Lost, End of Season
7 1948, 51, 58
6 1949
5 1953, 90
4 1954, 80

Most Consecutive Games Without Victory, Season
7 1948 (lost 7), 1951 (lost 7), 1958 (lost 7)
  1984 (lost 7), 1988 (lost 7)
6 1949 (lost 6), 1950 (lost 6), 1953 (lost 5, tied 1),
  1986 (lost 6)
5 1922 (lost 3, tied 2), 1959 (lost 5), 1977 (lost 5),
  1988 (lost 5), 1990 (lost 5)
4 Accomplished many times

Most Consecutive Games Without Victory, Start of Season
6 1986 (lost 6)
5 1922 (lost 3, tied 2), 1988 (lost 5)
4 1958 (lost 3, tied 1), 1975 (lost 4)
3 1928 (lost 2, tied 1), 1933 (lost 2, tied 1), 1953 (lost 3)
  1954 (lost 3), 1976 (lost 3)

Most Consecutive Games Without Victory, End of Season
7 1948 (lost 7), 1951 (lost 7), 1958 (lost 7)
6 1949 (lost 6), 1953 (lost 5, tied 1)
5 1990 (lost 5)
4 1954 (lost 4), 1980 (lost 4)

Most Consecutive Home Games Lost
(includes Milwaukee)
7 1976-77, 85-86
6 1957-58, 80-81
5 1948-49, 53-54
4 1951-52, 68, 75

Most Consecutive Home Games, Without Victory
(includes Milwaukee)
8 1957-58 (lost 7, tied 1)
7 1976-77 (lost 7), 1985-86 (lost 7)
6 1980-81 (lost 6)
5 1948-49 (lost 5), 1953-54 (lost 5)

Most Consecutive Road Games Lost
12 1957-59
11 1949-50
10 1975-76
9 1978-79

Most Consecutive Road Games, Without Victory
see above record

Most Shutout Games Lost or Tied, Season
4 1928 (lost 3, tied 1), 1932 (lost 3, tied 1)
3 1924 (lost 3), 1925 (lost 3), 1934 (lost 3), 1988 (lost 3)
2 1922 (tied 2), 1923 (lost 1, tied 1), 1944 (lost 2),
  1949 (lost 2), 1970 (lost 2)

Most Consecutive Shutout Games Lost or Tied
2 1922 (lost 2), 1923 (lost 1, tied 1), 1925 (lost 2)
  1928 (lost 2), 1932 (lost 2), 1988 (lost 2)

Most Consecutive Games Won at Milwaukee
(since 1933)
16 1935-42
9 1961-64
8 1964-67
6 1981-83, 1991-93

Most Consecutive Games Lost at Milwaukee
(since 1933)
8 1956-59
5 1947-49
4 1953-54
3 1976-77, 80-81, 90-91

Most Consecutive Games Won at Green Bay
(since 1933)
11 1960-62
9 1993-94 (current)
5 1935-36, 43-45
4 1933-34, 59, 63-64, 84-85

Most Consecutive Games Lost at Green Bay
(since 1933)
8 1985-87
7 1987-88
5 1990-91
4 1949-50, 51-52, 53-54, 73-74, 76-77, 91-92

TIE GAMES

Most Tie Games, Season
3 1922, 26, 28
2 1971, 73

Most Consecutive Tie Games
2 1922, 26

LENGTH OF GAME

Longest Game Played (since 1938)
(includes overtime games)
4:09 vs. Lions, Oct. 11, 1987 (OT)
4:02 vs. Buccaneers, Sept. 30, 1984 (OT)
3:48 vs. Broncos, Sept. 20, 1987 (OT)
3:45 vs. Buccaneers, Oct. 12, 1980 (OT)

Longest Game Played
(no overtime games)
3:43 vs. Lions, Nov. 27, 1986
3:41 vs. Lions, Nov. 12, 1989
3:39 vs. 49ers, Oct. 26, 1986
3:36 vs. Bills, Oct. 6, 1974

Shortest Game Played
1:45 vs. Lions, Nov. 17, 1946
1:50 vs. Lions, Oct. 25, 1942
1:52 vs. Lions, Dec. 2, 1945
2:00 vs. Rams, Oct. 30, 1938

Greatest Time of Possession (since 1977)
(includes overtime games)
50:12 vs Buccaneers, Oct. 12, 1980 (OT)
41:25 vs. Giants, Oct. 4, 1981
41:10 vs. 49ers, Oct. 26, 1986
40:19 vs. Vikings, Sept. 6, 1992 (OT)

Greatest Time of Possession
(no overtime games)
41:25 vs. Giants, Oct. 4, 1981
41:10 vs. 49ers, Oct. 26, 1986
39:58 vs. Cowboys, Oct. 8, 1989
39:25 vs. Lions, Nov. 12, 1989

Shortest Time of Possession
15:13 vs. Lions, Nov. 22, 1984
17:29 vs. Cowboys, Nov. 12, 1978
18:24 vs. Chargers, Oct. 7, 1984
18:43 vs. Dolphins, Oct. 28, 1979

SCORING

Most Points, Season
- 429 1983
- 415 1962
- 391 1961
- 390 1984

Fewest Points, Season
- 70 1921, 22
- 85 1923
- 102 1924
- 113 1927

Fewest Points, Season (since 1932)
- 114 1949
- 134 1977
- 148 1946
- 152 1932

Most Points, Game
- 57 vs. Lions, Oct. 7, 1945
- 56 vs. Falcons, Oct. 23, 1966
- 55 vs. Cardinals, Nov. 1, 1942
  - vs. Browns, Nov. 12, 1967
  - vs. Buccaneers, Oct. 2, 1983
- 54 vs. Steelers, Nov. 23, 1941

Most Points, Both Teams, Game
- 95 GB (48) vs. Redskins (47), Oct. 17, 1983
- 88 GB (41) vs. Falcons (47), Nov. 27, 1983
- 87 GB (35) vs. Lions (52), Nov. 22, 1951
- 84 GB (44) vs. Lions (40), Nov. 27, 1986

Fewest Points, Both Teams, Game
- 0 Accomplished many times

Most Points, Shutout Victory, Game
- 49 vs. Bears, Sept. 30, 1962
  - vs. Eagles, Nov. 11, 1962
- 47 vs. Pirates, Oct. 15, 1933
- 41 vs. Reds, Oct. 14, 1934
- 35 vs. Tornadoes, Oct. 24, 1926

Fewest Points, Shutout Victory, Game
- 2 vs. Bears, Oct. 16, 1932
- 3 Accomplished many times

Most Points Overcome to Win Game
- 23 vs. Rams, Sept. 12, 1982 (down 0-23, won 35-23)
- 21 vs. Saints, Sept. 17, 1989 (down 0-21, won 35-34)
- 18 vs. Lions, Oct. 17, 1965 (down 3-21, won 31-21)
- 17 vs. Redskins, Nov. 30, 1941 (down 0-17, won 22-17)
  - vs. Lions, Oct. 16, 1972 (down 0-17, won 24-23)

Most Points, First Half
- 49 vs. Buccaneers, Oct. 2, 1983
- 45 vs. Browns, Nov. 12, 1967
- 41 vs. Lions, Oct. 7, 1945
- 35 vs. Eagles, Nov. 11, 1962
  - vs. Lions, Dec. 6, 1992

Most Points, Second Half
- 38 vs. Giants, Oct. 22, 1967
- 35 vs. Bears, Sept. 30, 1962
  - vs. Rams, Sept. 12, 1982
- 34 vs. Cardinals, Nov. 1, 1942
  - vs. Steelers, Sept. 19, 1965
- 33 vs. Jeffersons, Oct. 25, 1925

Most Points, Both Teams, First Half
- 56 GB (49) vs. Buccaneers (7), Oct. 2, 1983
- 55 GB (21) vs. Cardinals (34), Nov. 27, 1949
- 52 GB (21) vs. Lions (31), Nov. 22, 1951
  - GB (45) vs. Browns (7), Nov. 12, 1967
- 51 GB (28) vs. Steelers (23), Oct. 7, 1951
  - GB (7) vs. Rams (44), Sept. 21, 1980

Most Points, Both Teams, Second Half
- 55 GB (28) vs. Yanks (27), Oct. 9, 1950
- 52 GB (28) vs. Bears (24), Nov. 6, 1955
  - GB (28) vs. Cardinals (24), Sept. 29, 1985
- 51 GB (24) vs. Redskins (27), Oct. 17, 1983
- 50 GB (14) vs. Cowboys (36), Nov. 24, 1994

Most Points, One Quarter
- 41 vs. Lions, Oct. 7, 1945 (2)
- 35 vs. Browns, Nov. 12, 1967 (1)
  - vs. Buccaneers, Oct. 2, 1983 (2)
- 28 Accomplished seven times

Most Points, Both Teams, One Quarter
- 48 GB (41) vs Lions (7), Oct. 7, 1945 (2)
- 44 GB (7) vs. Rams (37), Sept. 21, 1980 (2)
- 42 GB (28) vs. Bears (14), Nov. 6, 1955 (4)
  - GB (35) vs. Browns (7), Nov. 12, 1967 (1)
  - GB (35) vs. Buccaneers (7), Oct. 2, 1983 (2)
- 41 GB (21) vs. Yanks (20), Oct. 8, 1950 (3)

Most Points, First Quarter
- 35 vs. Browns, Nov. 12, 1967
- 28 vs. Seahawks, Oct. 15, 1978
- 21 vs. Steam Roller, Oct. 25, 1931
  - vs. Eagles, Sept. 15, 1940
  - vs. Steelers, Oct. 7, 1951
  - vs. Lions, Oct. 25, 1987
- 20 vs. Yellow Jackets, Oct. 12, 1930
  - vs. Giants, Nov. 8, 1981

Most Points, Second Quarter
- 41 vs. Lions, Oct. 7, 1945
- 35 vs. Buccaneers, Oct. 2, 1983
- 28 vs. Rams, Nov. 19, 1961
  - vs. Eagles, Nov. 11, 1962
  - vs. Rams, Dec. 20, 1992
- 26 vs. Steelers, Nov. 23, 1941

Most Points, Third Quarter
- 23 vs. Lions, Oct. 6, 1985
- 21 Accomplished many times

Most Points, Fourth Quarter
- 28 vs. Bears, Nov. 6, 1955
  - vs. Vikings, Nov. 21, 1965
  - vs. Giants, Oct. 22, 1967
- 26 vs. Jeffersons, Oct. 25, 1925
- 24 vs. Colts, Oct. 27, 1957
- 23 vs. Yanks, Oct. 28, 1951

Most Points, Both Teams, First Quarter
- 42 GB (35) vs. Browns (7), Nov. 12, 1967
- 33 GB (7) vs. Rams (26), Dec. 13, 1953
- 28 GB (14) vs. Card-Pitt (14), Dec. 5, 1943
  - GB (7) vs. Colts (21), Oct. 8, 1955
  - GB (28) vs. Seahawks (0), Oct. 15, 1978
  - GB (0) vs. Vikings (28), Sept. 28, 1986
- 27 GB (7) vs. Rams (20), Nov. 11, 1945
  - GB (0) vs. Cardinals (27), Nov. 27, 1949
  - GB (0) vs. 49ers (27), Dec. 7, 1958

Most Points, Both Teams, Second Quarter
- 48 GB (41) vs. Lions (7), Oct. 7, 1945
- 44 GB (7) vs. Rams (37), Sept. 21, 1980
- 42 GB (35) vs. Buccaneers (7), Oct. 2, 1983
- 35 GB (14) vs. Lions (21), Nov. 27, 1952
  - GB (7) vs. Giants (28), Sept. 19, 1971
  - GB (7) vs. Bears (28), Dec. 7, 1980
  - GB (7) vs. Rams (28), Sept. 28, 1989

Most Points, Both Teams, Third Quarter
- 41 GB (21) vs. Yanks (20), Oct. 8, 1950
- 28 GB (21) vs. Bears (7), Oct. 1, 1950
  - GB (7) vs. Lions (21), Nov. 22, 1951
  - GB (7) vs. Colts (21), Oct. 25, 1959
- 26 GB (7) vs. Cowboys (19), Nov. 24, 1994
- 24 Accomplished six times

Most Points, Both Teams, Fourth Quarter
- 42 GB (28) vs. Bears (14), Nov. 6, 1955
- 39 GB (26) vs. Jeffersons (13), Oct. 25, 1925
- 35 GB (14) vs. Yanks (21), Dec. 2, 1951
  - GB (21) vs. Colts (14), Oct. 9, 1960
  - GB (28) vs. Giants (7), Oct. 22, 1967
- 34 GB (20) vs. Eagles (14), Oct. 14, 1951

Most Consecutive Games, Scoring
- 156 1958-69
- 122 1978-86
- 69 1938-44
- 57 1991-94 (current)

TOUCHDOWNS

Most Touchdowns, Season
- 53 1962
- 52 1983
- 51 1984
- 49 1961

Fewest Touchdowns, Season
     9   1921, 22
    10   1923
    14   1924, 49, 77
    17   1927, 28, 46
Fewest Touchdowns, Season (since 1932)
    14   1949, 77
    17   1946
    19   1934, 74
    20   1948, 73
Most Touchdowns, Game
     8   vs. Steelers, Nov. 23, 1941
         vs. Cardinals, Nov. 1, 1942
         vs. Lions, Oct. 7, 1945
         vs. Falcons, Oct. 23, 1966
     7   Accomplished nine times
Most Touchdowns, Both Teams, Game
    12   GB (5) vs. Lions (7), Nov. 22, 1951
    11   Accomplished six times
Most Consecutive Games Scoring Touchdowns
    45   1965-68
    42   1992-94 (current)
    40   1940-44
    35   1959-62, 63-65

POINTS AFTER TOUCHDOWN

Most Points After Touchdown, Season
    52   1962, 83
    49   1961
    48   1984
    43   1963
Fewest Points After Touchdowns, Season
     5   1923
     6   1922
     7   1921
     8   1927
Fewest Points After Touchdowns, Season (since 1932)
    11   1977
    12   1949
    14   1932
    15   1946
Most Points After Touchdown, Game
     8   vs. Falcons, Oct. 23, 1966
     7   Accomplished seven times
Most Points After Touchdown, Both Teams, Game
    12   GB (5) vs. Lions (7), Nov. 22, 1951
    11   GB (4) vs. Bears (7), Nov. 6, 1955
         GB (5) vs. Giants (6), Sept. 19, 1971
         GB (6) vs. Redskins (5), Oct. 17, 1983
    10   Accomplished many times

FIELD GOALS

Most Field Goals Attempted, Season
    48   1972
    39   1964, 74
    37   1993
    35   1973
Fewest Field Goals Attempted, Season
     5   1944
     8   1951, 56
    10   1942
    13   1945
Most Field Goals Attempted, Game
     6   vs. Lions, Sept. 14, 1941
         vs. Lions, Oct. 26, 1947
         vs. Steelers, Oct. 30, 1960
         vs. Browns, Sept. 17, 1972
         vs. Cowboys, Oct. 1, 1972
         vs. Lions, Dec. 3, 1972
         vs. Lions, Sept. 29, 1974
         vs. Vikings, Nov. 17, 1974
     5   Accomplished many times

Most Field Goals Attempted, Both Teams, Game
    11   GB (6) vs. Lions (5), Sept. 29, 1974
    10   GB (5) vs. Cardinals (5), Dec. 5, 1971
     9   GB (5) vs. Colts (4), Oct. 18, 1964
         GB (3) vs. Bears (6), Nov. 8, 1987
         GB (4) vs. Jets (5), Nov. 3, 1991
     8   Accomplished many times
Most Field Goals, Season
    33   1972
    31   1993
    25   1974
    23   1990
Fewest Field Goals, Season
     0   1930, 31, 32, 44
     1   1927
     2   1926, 29, 33
     3   1921, 22, 25, 28, 50
Fewest Field Goals, Season (since 1932)
     0   1932, 44
     2   1933
     3   1950
     4   1937, 43
Most Field Goals, Game
     5   vs. Raiders, Nov. 11, 1990
     4   Accomplished many times
Most Field Goals, Both Teams, Game
     8   GB (4) vs. Lions (4), Sept. 29, 1974
     7   GB (4) vs. Bears (3), Sept. 22, 1986
         GB (3) vs. Lions (4), Nov. 27, 1986
         GB (3) vs. Lions (4), Oct. 11, 1987
         GB (3) vs. Jets (4), Nov. 3, 1991
         GB (2) vs. Vikings (5), Sept. 26, 1993
     6   Accomplished many times
Most Consecutive Games Scoring Field Goals
    14   1987
    12   1980-81, 91-92
    10   1946-47, 55, 64-65, 67-68, 89-90, 93
     9   1972-73, 76-77

SAFETIES

Most Safeties, Season
     3   1932, 75
     2   1929, 39, 47, 59, 88
     1   Accomplished many times
Most Safeties, Game
     1   Accomplished 30 times
Most Safeties, Both Teams, Game
     2   GB (0) vs. Rams (2), Oct. 21, 1973

FIRST DOWNS

Most First Downs, Season
   342   1989 (114 rush, 207 pass, 21 penalty)
   340   1983 (98 rush, 214 pass, 27 penalty)
   318   1985 (114 rush, 172 pass, 32 penalty)
   315   1984 (120 rush, 168 pass, 27 penalty)
Fewest First Downs, Season
   125   1935
   131   1945 (73 rush, 44 pass, 14 penalty)
   134   1938, 1943 (60 rush, 66 pass, 8 penalty)
   140   1937
Most First Downs, Game
    37   vs. Eagles, Nov. 11, 1962 (21,15,1)
    32   vs. Buccaneers, Oct. 12, 1980 (11,21,0)
         vs. Falcons, Nov. 27, 1983 (11,18,3)
    31   vs. Buccaneers, Dec. 1, 1985 (12,17,2)
         vs. Lions, Nov. 12, 1989 (10,19,2)
    30   vs. Lions, Oct. 28, 1984 (10,16,4)
         vs. Lions, Oct. 6, 1985 (16,13,1)
Fewest First Downs, Game
     3   vs. Cardinals, Sept. 18, 1932
         vs. Redskins, Nov. 4, 1934
         vs. Cardinals, Nov. 18, 1934
     4   vs. Lions, Nov. 17, 1935
     5   Accomplished six times

Most First Downs, Both Teams, Game
  57 GB (32) vs. Falcons (25), Nov. 27, 1983
  56 GB (23) vs. Redskins (33), Oct. 17, 1983
  52 GB (19) vs. Rams (33), Dec. 16, 1956
      GB (19) vs. Bears (33), Dec. 7, 1980
  51 GB (27) vs. Vikings (24), Oct. 23, 1983
Fewest First Downs, Both Teams, Game
   5 GB (5) vs. Giants (0), Oct. 1, 1933
      GB (3) vs. Cardinals (2), Nov. 18, 1934
   8 GB (3) vs. Cardinals (5), Sept. 18, 1932
  10 GB (5) vs. Spartans (5), Dec. 4, 1932
      GB (6) vs. Cardinals (4), Nov. 5, 1933
  11 Accomplished five times
Most First Downs, Rushing, Season
 145 1962
 142 1961
 135 1960
 133 1964
Fewest First Downs, Rushing, Season
  59 1982
  60 1943
  65 1942
  70 1944
Most First Downs, Rushing, Game
  21 vs. Eagles, Nov. 11, 1962
  19 vs. 49ers, Oct. 11, 1959
      vs. Giants, Oct. 22, 1967
  18 vs. Colts, Oct. 18, 1953
      vs. Lions, Oct. 2, 1960
  17 Accomplished five times
Fewest First Downs, Rushing, Game
   0 vs. Seahawks, Dec. 9, 1990
   1 Accomplished 12 times
Most First Downs, Rushing, Both Teams, Game
  30 GB (13) vs. Saints (17), Sept. 9, 1979
  29 GB (11) vs. Rams (18), Dec. 16, 1956
      GB (19) vs. Giants (10), Oct. 22, 1967
  28 GB (15) vs. Lions (13), Oct. 26, 1947
      GB (9) vs. Bears (19), Nov. 6, 1955
      GB (16) vs. Falcons (12), Oct. 26, 1969
  27 GB (9) vs. Bears (18), Nov. 18, 1951
      GB (8) vs. Bears (19), Oct. 30, 1977
      GB (6), vs. Raiders (21), Sept. 13, 1978
Fewest First Downs, Rushing, Both Teams, Game
   4 GB (1) vs. Eagles (3), Oct. 13, 1946
      GB (2) vs. Giants (2), Nov. 8, 1981
   5 GB (3) vs. Eagles (2), Nov. 12, 1939
      GB (4) vs. Lions (1), Oct. 24, 1943
      GB (1) vs. Buccaneers (4), Oct. 14, 1990
   6 Accomplished many times
Most First Downs, Passing, Season
 214 1983
 207 1989
 205 1994
 176 1988
Fewest First Downs, Passing, Season
  34 1946
  58 1948
  63 1944
  66 1939, 40, 43
Most First Downs, Passing, Game
  21 vs. Cardinals, Dec. 21, 1969
      vs. Buccaneers, Oct. 12, 1980
  20 vs. Broncos, Oct. 15, 1984
      vs. Bears, Dec. 5, 1993
      vs. Dolphins, Sept. 11, 1994
  19 vs. Lions, Nov. 12, 1989
      vs. Falcons, Dec. 18, 1994
  18 Accomplished six times
Fewest First Downs, Passing, Game
   0 vs. Bears, Sept. 25, 1949
   1 Accomplished many times
Most First Downs, Passing, Both Teams, Game
  38 GB (17) vs. Redskins (21), Oct. 17, 1983
  33 GB (14) vs. Vikings (19), Nov. 29, 1981
      GB (18) vs. Saints (15), Sept. 17, 1989
      GB (19) vs. Falcons (14), Dec. 18, 1994
  32 Accomplished five times

Fewest First Downs, Passing, Both Teams, Game
   1 GB (1) vs. Rams (0), Sept. 21, 1941
   3 GB (2) vs. Cardinals (1), Dec. 6, 1936
      GB (1) vs. 49ers (2), Dec. 11, 1960
   4 GB (4) vs. Bears (0), Nov. 7, 1937
      GB (3) vs. Eagles (1), Nov. 29, 1942
      GB (1) vs. Bears (3), Sept. 29, 1946
      GB (3) vs. Bears (1), Nov. 3, 1946
   5 Accomplished five times
Most First Downs, Penalty, Season
  32 1985
  30 1981
  28 1951
  27 1983, 84, 88
Fewest First Downs, Penalty, Season
   6 1940
   8 1939, 43
  11 1964
  12 1955
Most First Downs, Penalty, Game
   6 vs. Rams, Sept. 20, 1981
   5 Accomplished six times
Most First Downs, Penalty, Both Teams, Game
   8 GB (5) vs. Bears (3), Nov. 17, 1963
      GB (5) vs. Lions (3), Oct. 12, 1969
      GB (6) vs. Rams (2), Sept. 20, 1981
   7 Accomplished many times

NET YARDS RUSHING AND PASSING

Most Yards Gained, Season
 6,172 1983
 5,780 1989
 5,449 1984
 5,371 1985
Fewest Yards Gained, Season
 2,340 1934
 2,618 1946
 2,702 1933
 2,869 1945
Most Yards Gained, Game
  628 vs. Eagles, Nov. 11, 1962
  569 vs. Buccaneers, Oct. 12, 1980
  541 vs. Rams, Oct. 18, 1942
  539 vs. Cardinals, Nov. 1, 1942
Fewest Yards Gained, Game
   36 vs. Bengals, Sept. 26, 1976
   63 vs. Cowboys, Oct. 24, 1965
       vs. Rams, Oct. 21, 1973
       vs. Lions, Oct. 28, 1973
   68 vs. Lions, Nov. 7, 1965
   75 vs. Cardinals, Sept. 18, 1932
Most Yards Gained, Both Teams, Game
 1,025 GB (473) vs. Redskins (552), Oct. 17, 1983
   977 GB (479) vs. Oilers (498), Sept. 4, 1983
   966 GB (355) vs. Rams (611), Dec. 16, 1956
       GB (457) vs. Colts (509), Nov. 15, 1959
   949 GB (471) vs. Lions (478), Nov. 22, 1951
Fewest Yards Gained, Both Teams, Game
   136 GB (86) vs. Cardinals (50), Nov. 18, 1934
   175 GB (109) vs. Giants (66), Oct. 1, 1933
   184 GB (75) vs. Cardinals (109), Sept. 18, 1932
   195 GB (118) vs. Bears (77), Sept. 18, 1938
Most Consecutive Games, 400 or More Yards
   4 1984, 89
   3 1961, 80
   2 Accomplished many times
Most Consecutive Games, 300 or More Yards
  10 1984
   8 1963, 80
   6 1962, 88-89
   5 Accomplished many times

RUSHING

Most Rushing Attempts, Season
- 560   1946
- 550   1978
- 544   1972
- 527   1973

Fewest Rushing Attempts, Season
- 283   1982
- 313   1951
- 321   1954
- 345   1958

Most Rushing Attempts, Games
- 64   vs. Redskins, Dec. 1, 1946
- 63   vs. Steelers, Oct. 20, 1946
- 62   vs. Cardinals, Sept. 12, 1937
-      vs. Rams, Sept. 21, 1941
-      vs. Cardinals, Nov. 10, 1946
- 61   vs. Lions, Nov. 17, 1946

Fewest Rushing Attempts, Game
- 7   vs. Dolphins, Sept. 11, 1994
- 10   vs. Seahawks, Dec. 9, 1990
- 11   vs. Bears, Nov. 27, 1988
- 12   vs. Chargers, Oct. 7, 1984
-      vs. Bills, Nov. 20, 1994

Most Rushing Attempts, Both Teams, Game
- 108   GB (38) vs. Cardinals (70), Dec. 5, 1948
- 102   GB (51) vs. Steelers (51), Nov. 20, 1949
- 101   GB (32) vs. Cardinals (69), Dec. 6, 1936
- 100   GB (62) vs. Cardinals (38), Sept. 12, 1937

Fewest Rushing Attempts, Both Teams, Game
- 40   GB (15) vs. Dolphins (25), Sept. 22, 1991
- 41   GB (13) vs. Buccaneers (28), Oct. 14, 1990
-      GB (7) vs. Dolphins (34), Sept. 11, 1994
- 42   GB (27) vs. Buccaneers (15), Oct. 27, 1991
-      GB (24) vs. Oilers (18), Dec. 13, 1992
-      GB (14) vs. Eagles (28), Sept. 18, 1994
- 43   GB (23) vs. 49ers (20), Nov. 4, 1990
-      GB (19) vs. Falcons (24), Oct. 4, 1992
-      GB (21) vs. Falcons (22), Dec. 18, 1994

Most Yards Gained, Rushing, Season
- 2,460   1962
- 2,350   1961
- 2,276   1964
- 2,248   1963

Fewest Yards Gained, Rushing, Season
- 1,081   1982
- 1,183   1934
- 1,196   1951
- 1,274   1942

Most Yards Gained, Rushing, Game
- 366   vs. Lions, Oct. 26, 1947
- 312   vs. Yanks, Oct. 8, 1950
- 303   vs. Colts, Oct. 18, 1953
- 301   vs. Redskins, Dec. 1, 1946

Fewest Yards Gained, Rushing, Game
- 10   vs. Seahawks, Dec. 9, 1990
- 17   vs. Redskins, Sept. 17, 1933
- 18   vs. Cardinals, Oct. 21, 1934
- 20   vs. Redskins, Nov. 8, 1936
-      vs. Colts, Oct. 28, 1956

Most Yards Gained, Rushing, Both Teams, Game
- 557   GB (151) vs. Bears (406), Nov. 6, 1955
- 508   GB (366) vs. Lions (142), Oct. 26, 1947
- 506   GB (294) vs. Rams (212), Oct. 22, 1944
- 502   GB (312) vs. Yanks (190), Oct. 8, 1950

Fewest Yards Gained, Rushing, Both Teams, Game
- 81   GB (44) vs. Dolphins (37), Sept. 22, 1991
- 85   GB (18) vs. Cardinals (67), Oct. 21, 1934
-      GB (35) vs. Eagles (50), Oct. 13, 1946
- 93   GB (71) vs. Vikings (22), Oct. 20, 1994
- 94   GB (59) vs. Buccaneers (35), Oct. 27, 1991

Most Games, 200 or More Yards Rushing, Season
- 5   1960, 62, 63, 71
- 4   1946, 61

Most Consecutive Games, 200 or More Yards Rushing
- 3   1961

Most Consecutive Games, Fewer Than 200 Yards Rushing
- 72   1989-94
- 54   1980-84
- 39   1985-88
- 38   1978-80

Most Games, 100 or More Yards Rushing, Season
- 14   1964, 72
- 13   1961
- 12   1949, 62, 71, 84
- 11   1947, 55, 60, 63, 68, 87

Most Consecutive Games, 100 or More Yards Rushing
- 19   1971-73
- 18   1963-65
- 13   1948-49, 59-60, 61-62
- 12   1946-47

Most Consecutive Games, Fewer Than 100 Yards Rushing
- 16   1990-91
- 7   1986

Highest Average Gain, Season
- 4.96   1961 (474-2,350)
- 4.74   1962 (518-2,460)
- 4.70   1985 (470-2,208)
- 4.64   1960 (463-2,150)

Lowest Average Gain, Season
- 2.59   1934 (456-1,183)
- 3.11   1933 (487-1,513)
- 3.12   1977 (469-1,464)
- 3.15   1939 (500-1,574)
-      1946 (560-1,765)

Most Touchdown, Rushing, Season
- 36   1962
- 29   1960
- 27   1961
- 23   1964

Fewest Touchdowns, Rushing, Season
- 5   1922, 23, 24, 77, 90
- 6   1921
- 7   1925, 32, 35, 49, 58, 92
- 8   1934,, 51, 70, 86

Most Touchdowns, Rushing, Game
- 6   vs. Browns, Oct. 15, 1961
-      vs. Eagles, Nov. 11, 1962
- 5   vs. Pirates, Oct. 15, 1933
-      vs. Bears, Sept. 30, 1962
-      vs. Bears, Nov. 4, 1962
-      vs. Giants, Oct. 22, 1967
-      vs. Patriots, Oct. 9, 1988
- 4   Accomplished many times

Most Touchdowns, Rushing, Both Teams, Game
- 8   GB (3) vs. Bears (5), Nov. 6, 1955
- 7   GB (4) vs. Bears (3), Sept. 30, 1945
-      GB (4) vs. Seahawks (3), Oct. 15, 1978
- 6   Accomplished many times

PASSING

Most Passes Attempted, Season
- 609   1994
- 600   1989
- 582   1988
- 565   1986

Fewest Passes Attempted, Season
- 178   1946
- 197   1934
- 209   1933
- 210   1938

Most Passes Attempted, Game
- 60   vs. Lions, Nov. 12, 1989
- 59   vs. Saints, Sept. 14, 1986
- 57   vs. 49ers, Oct. 26, 1986
- 56   vs. Rams, Dec. 16, 1951

Fewest Passes Attempted, Game
- 0   vs. Spartans, Oct. 8, 1933
- 4   vs. Dodgers, Oct. 23, 1932
- 5   vs. Bears, Oct. 16, 1932
-      vs. Lions, Nov. 1, 1971
- 6   vs. Giants, Oct. 2, 1932

Most Passes Attempted, Both Teams, Game
- 100 GB (47) vs. Patriots (53), Oct. 2, 1994
- 92 GB (53) vs. Buccaneers (39), Dec. 3, 1989
- 91 GB (32) vs. Broncos (59), Oct. 10, 1993
- 89 GB (39) vs. Chargers (50), Oct. 2, 1984
  - GB (52) vs. Buccaneers (37), Oct. 2, 1988
  - GB (44) vs. Falcons (45), Dec. 18, 1994

Fewest Passes Attempted, Both Teams, Game
- 11 GB (0) vs. Spartans (11), Oct. 8, 1933
- 13 GB (9) vs. Bears (4), Sept. 25, 1932
  - GB (8) vs. Cardinals (5), Nov. 18, 1934
- 14 GB (8) vs. Bears (6), Sept. 18, 1938
- 15 GB (10) vs. Cardinals (5), Dec. 6, 1936

Most Passes Completed, Season
- 375 1994
- 354 1989
- 340 1992
- 322 1993

Fewest Passes Completed, Season
- 54 1946
- 74 1934
- 81 1945
- 89 1933

Most Passes Completed, Game
- 36 vs. Bears, Dec. 5, 1993
- 35 vs. Buccaneers, Oct. 12, 1980
  - vs. Lions, Nov. 12, 1989
- 33 vs. Falcons, Oct. 4, 1992
- 32 vs. 49ers, Oct. 26, 1986

Fewest Passes Completed, Game
- 0 vs. Spartans, Oct. 8, 1933
  - vs. Bears, Sept. 25, 1949
- 1 Accomplished many times

Most Passes Completed, Both Teams, Game
- 56 GB (18) vs. Vikings (38), Nov. 29, 1981
  - GB (25) vs. Chargers (31), Oct. 7, 1984
- 54 GB (25) vs. Patriots (29), Oct. 2, 1994
  - GB (22) vs. Bills (32), Nov. 20, 1994
- 53 GB (20) vs. Broncos (33), Oct. 10, 1993
- 52 GB (30) vs. Oilers (22), Sept. 4, 1983
  - GB (19) vs. Lions (33), Oct. 25, 1987
  - GB (24) vs. Lions (28), Nov. 6, 1994

Fewest Passes Completed, Both Teams, Game
- 2 GB (1) vs. Bears (1), Sept. 25, 1932
  - GB (2) vs. Cardinals (0), Nov. 18, 1934
- 4 GB (3) vs. Cardinals (1), Nov. 29, 1934
  - GB (3) vs. Bears (1), Sept. 18, 1938
- 5 GB (0) vs. Spartans (5), Oct. 8, 1933
  - GB (3) vs. Cardinals (2), Dec. 6, 1936
  - GB (4) vs. Cardinals (1), Sept. 12, 1937
- 6 Accomplished six times

Most Yards Gained Passing, Season
- 4,365 1983
- 4,048 1989
- 3,773 1994
- 3,447 1986

Fewest Yards Gained Passing, Season
- 841 1946
- 1,165 1934
- 1,186 1933
- 1,283 1973

Most Yards Gained Passing, Game
- 423 vs. Cardinals, Nov. 1, 1942
- 422 vs. Cardinals, Dec. 21, 1969
- 415 vs. Buccaneers, Oct. 12, 1980
- 403 vs. Redskins, Oct. 17, 1983

Fewest Yards Gained Passing, Game
- -35 vs. Bengals, Sept. 26, 1976
- -12 vs. Bears, Nov. 4, 1973
- -10 vs. Cowboys, Oct. 24, 1965
- -2 vs. Lions, Nov. 7, 1965

Most Yards Gained Passing, Both Teams, Game
- 771 GB (403) vs. Redskins (368), Oct. 17, 1983
- 720 GB (368) vs. Chargers (352), Oct. 7, 1984
- 692 GB (344) vs. Oilers (348), Sept. 4, 1983
- 670 GB (294) vs. Vikings (376), Nov. 29, 1981

Fewest Yards Gained Passing, Both Teams, Game
- -11 GB (-10) vs. Cowboys (-1), Oct. 24, 1965
- 10 GB (16) vs. Cardinals (-6), Nov. 29, 1934

- 20 GB (13) vs. Bears (7), Sept. 25, 1932
  - GB (20) vs. Cardinals (0), Nov. 18, 1934
- 29 GB (-35) vs. Bengals (64), Sept. 26, 1976

Most Games, 300 or More Yards Passing, Season
- 6 1983, 89
- 4 1984, 94
- 3 1942
- 2 1952, 81, 88

Most Consecutive Games, 300 or More Yards Passing
- 3 1984

Most Consecutive Games, Fewer Than 300 Yards Passing
- 149 1970-80
- 95 1943-51
- 86 1933-40
- 62 1956-61

Most Games, 200 or More Yards Passing, Season
- 14 1983
- 13 1989
- 12 1994
- 9 1951, 81, 86, 90, 92

Most Consecutive Games, 200 or More Yards Passing
- 10 1983
- 8 1988-89
- 7 1950-51
- 6 1992
  - 1994 (current)

Most Consecutive Games, Fewer Than 200 Yards Passing
- 50 1946-50
- 21 1933-35
- 19 1972-73
- 16 1937-39

Most Consecutive Games, Fewer Than 100 Yards Passing
- 9 1946
- 8 1933, 49, 73
- 7 1972

Most Times Sacked, Season
- 62 1990
- 52 1981
- 51 1988
- 50 1985

Fewest Times Sacked, Season
- 17 1972, 74
- 18 1971
- 20 1963
- 27 1973

Most Times Sacked, Game
- 11 vs. Lions, Nov. 7, 1965
- 10 vs. Chargers, Sept. 24, 1978
- 9 vs. Bears, Dec. 13, 1970
  - vs. Jets, Dec. 20, 1981
  - vs. Lions, Dec. 12, 1982
- 8 Accomplished many times

Most Times Sacked, Both Teams, Game
- 18 GB (10) vs. Chargers (8), Sept. 24, 1978
- 14 GB (5) vs. Cowboys (9), Oct. 24, 1965
- 13 GB (11) vs. Lions (2), Nov. 7, 1965
  - GB (8) vs. Raiders (5), Nov. 11, 1990
- 12 GB (4) vs. Rams (8), Sept. 25, 1966
  - GB (5) vs. Lions (7), Dec. 15, 1979
  - GB (6) vs. Buccaneers (6), Oct. 27, 1991

Highest Completion Percentage, Season
- 64.52 1992 (527-340)
- 61.58 1994 (609-375)
- 60.98 1993 (528-322)
- 60.69 1966 (318-193)

Lowest Completion Percentage, Season
- 30.34 1946 (178-54)
- 30.43 1949 (299-91)
- 37.16 1945 (218-81)
- 37.56 1934 (197-74)

Highest Completion Percentage, Game
(minimum 20 attempts)
- 90.48 vs. Saints, Dec. 13, 1981 (21-19)
- 88.24 vs. Oilers, Sept. 4, 1983 (34-30)
- 81.48 vs. Buccaneers, Sept. 11, 1988 (27-22)
- 80.00 vs. 49ers, Dec. 13, 1959 (25-20)

Lowest Completion Percentage, Game
(minimum 20 attempts)
19.05	vs. Bears, Nov. 3, 1946 (21-4)
19.23	vs. Colts, Nov. 2, 1958 (26-5)
20.00	vs. Rams, Oct. 2, 1949 (20-4)
20.83	vs. Rams, Dec. 13, 1953 (24-5)

Highest Completion Percentage, Both Teams, Game
(minimum 40 attempts)
78.57	GB (25-20) vs. 49ers (17-13), Dec. 13, 1959
	GB (21-19) vs. Saints (21-14), Dec. 13, 1981
78.13	GB (27-21) vs. Browns (37-29), Oct. 19, 1986
76.47	GB (34-30) vs. Oilers (34-22), Sept. 4, 1983
75.00	GB (32-25) vs. Saints (32-23), Sept. 17, 1989

Lowest Completion Percentage, Both Teams, Game
(minimum 40 attempts)
24.49	GB (25-8) vs. Pirates (24-4), Oct. 6, 1935
26.15	GB (34-10) vs. Eagles (31-7), Nov. 2, 1952
27.91	GB (17-7) vs. Bears (26-5), Sept. 22, 1935
28.26	GB (20-5) vs. Cardinals (26-8), Oct. 12, 1947

Most Touchdowns, Passing, Season
33	1983, 94
30	1984
28	1942
27	1989

Fewest Touchdowns, Passing, Season
1	1921
3	1922
4	1927, 46
5	1923, 49, 74

Most Touchdowns, Passing, Game
6	vs. Cardinals, Nov. 1, 1942
	vs. Lions, Oct. 7, 1945
5	vs. Cardinals, Dec. 21, 1969
	vs. Saints, Dec. 13, 1981
	vs. Oilers, Sept. 4, 1983
4	Accomplished many times

Most Touchdowns, Passing, Both Teams, Game
8	GB (4) vs. Lions (4), Nov. 22, 1951
	GB (3) vs. Lions (5), Nov. 27, 1952
7	Accomplished many times

Most Passes Had Intercepted, Season
37	1950
34	1953
32	1983
30	1984

Fewest Passes Had Intercepted, Season
5	1966
6	1964
9	1972
13	1941, 60, 62

Most Passes Had Intercepted, Game
8	vs. Giants, Nov. 21, 1948
7	vs. Bears, Sept. 22, 1940
	vs. Lions, Oct. 20, 1940
	vs. Rams, Nov. 11, 1945
	vs. Lions, Sept. 17, 1950
	vs. Saints, Sept. 14, 1986
6	vs. Cardinals, Oct. 13, 1935
	vs. Eagles, Dec. 14, 1947
5	Accomplished many times

Most Passes Had Intercepted, Both Teams, Game
11	GB (4) vs. Rams (7), Oct. 30, 1938
	GB (7) vs. Lions (4), Oct. 20, 1940
10	GB (1) vs. Lions (9), Oct. 24, 1943
	GB (3) vs. Rams (7), Nov. 12, 1944
	GB (7) vs. Rams (3), Nov. 11, 1945
9	Accomplished many times

Highest Pass Rating, Season
102.1	1966
91.3	1964
89.1	1994
88.4	1968

Lowest Pass Rating, Season
11.4	1949
15.0	1946
26.1	1948
27.5	1953

PUNTING

Most Punts, Season
106	1978
95	1975
93	1987
87	1949, 70, 80

Fewest Punts, Season
42	1982
46	1945
48	1944
49	1960

Most Punts, Game
14	vs. Bears, Oct. 22, 1933
	vs. Cardinals, Nov. 5, 1933
	vs. Lions, Nov. 17, 1935
13	vs. Redskins, Nov. 4, 1934
12	vs. Bears, Nov. 10, 1933
11	vs. Spartans, Nov. 12, 1933
	vs. Bears, Sept. 23, 1934
	vs. Bears, Oct. 15, 1950
	vs. Rams, Dec. 3, 1950
	vs. Steelers, Oct. 24, 1953

Fewest Punts, Game
0	vs. Colts, Nov. 6, 1960
	vs. Bears, Sept. 24, 1967
	vs. Bills, Dec. 5, 1982
	vs. Bears, Dec. 17, 1989
1	Accomplished many times

Most Punts, Both Teams, Game
31	GB (14) vs. Bears (17), Oct. 22, 1933
26	GB (14) vs. Cardinals (12), Nov. 5, 1933
	GB (11) vs. Spartans (15), Nov. 12, 1933
	GB (12) vs. Bears (14), Dec. 10, 1933
	GB (14) vs. Lions (12), Nov. 17, 1935
24	GB (13) vs. Redskins (11), Nov. 4, 1934
23	GB (9) vs. Eagles (14), Dec. 3, 1933

Fewest Punts, Both Teams, Game
1	GB (0) vs. Bills (1), Dec. 5, 1982
	GB (0) vs. Bears (1), Dec. 17, 1989
2	GB (1) vs. Redskins (1), Oct. 17, 1983
3	Accomplished six times

Highest Average Distance, Punting, Season
44.67	1963 (51-2,279)
43.55	1947 (65-2,831)
43.21	1956 (62-2,649)
43.02	1961 (51-2,194)

Lowest Average Distance, Punting, Season
35.46	1978 (106-3,759)
35.83	1975 (95-3,404)
35.96	1943 (52-1,870)
36.50	1967 (66-2,409)

PUNT RETURNS

Most Punt Returns, Season
49	1994
48	1984
47	1948
46	1978

Fewest Punt Returns, Season
20	1961
22	1965
25	1970, 72
26	1960, 63, 82

Most Punt Returns, Game
8	vs. Yanks, Nov. 18, 1945
	vs. Texans, Nov. 23, 1952
	vs. Vikings, Nov. 4, 1982
7	Accomplished seven times

Most Punt Returns, Both Teams, Game
14	GB (7) vs. Patriots (7), Oct. 2, 1994
13	GB (5) vs. Eagles (8), Nov. 29, 1942
	GB (6) vs. Bears (7), Nov. 14, 1948
	GB (6) vs. Bears (7), Dec. 4, 1983

Most Fair Catches, Season
23 1972
20 1970
19 1973
18 1964, 88, 94
Fewest Fair Catches, Season
5 1971
6 1982, 87, 92
7 1975, 86, 91
8 1974, 76
Most Fair Catches, Game
5 vs. Saints, Nov. 17, 1968
 vs. Bears, Nov. 15, 1970
 vs. Bears, Dec. 16, 1973
4 Accomplished many times
Most Yards, Punt Returns, Season
729 1950
563 1939, 47
527 1948
494 1940
Fewest Yards, Punt Returns, Season
65 1965
98 1970
137 1973
141 1979
Most Yards, Punt Returns, Game
147 vs. Bears, Nov. 8, 1959
144 vs. Texans, Nov. 23, 1952
141 vs. Rams, Oct. 9, 1994
129 vs. Buccaneers, Oct. 2, 1983
Most Yards, Punt Returns, Both Teams, Game
181 GB (92) vs. Giants (89), Nov. 13, 1949
177 GB (122) vs. Redskins (55), Sept. 24, 1950
175 GB (0) vs. Lions (175), Nov. 22, 1951
170 GB (22) vs. Cardinals (148), Nov. 27, 1949
Highest Average, Punt Returns, Season
17.75 1961 (20-355)
16.57 1950 (44-729)
14.56 1972 (25-364)
13.03 1964 (34-443)
Lowest Average, Punt Returns, Season
2.95 1965 (22-65)
3.92 1970 (25-98)
4.03 1967 (39-157)
4.57 1973 (30-137)
Most Touchdowns, Punt Returns, Season
2 1950, 61, 72, 74
1 Accomplished many times
Most Touchdowns, Punt Returns, Game
1 Accomplished many times
Most Touchdowns, Punt Returns, Both Teams, Game
2 GB (0) vs. Lions (2), Nov. 22, 1951
 GB (1) vs. Bengals (1), Sept. 20, 1992

KICKOFF RETURNS

Most Kickoff Returns, Season
79 1983
76 1986
73 1980
69 1989
Fewest Kickoff Returns, Season
28 1941, 43
30 1944, 62
33 1945
34 1946, 82
Most Kickoff Returns, Game
10 vs. Giants, Dec. 20, 1986
9 vs. Lions, Nov. 22, 1951
 vs. Lions, Nov. 27, 1952
 vs. Lions, Sept. 20, 1970
 vs. Rams, Sept. 21, 1980
 vs. Bears, Dec. 7, 1980
8 Accomplished many times

Most Kickoff Returns, Both Teams, Game
17 GB (8) vs. Redskins (9), Oct. 17, 1983
 GB (8) vs. Lions (9), Nov. 27, 1986
15 GB (8) vs. Oilers (7), Sept. 4, 1983
 GB (10) vs. Giants (5), Dec. 20, 1986
14 GB (9) vs. Lions (5), Nov. 22, 1951
 GB (9) vs. Lions (5), Nov. 27, 1952
 GB (7) vs. Colts (7), Oct. 14, 1956
 GB (7) vs. Giants (7), Sept. 19, 1971
 GB (6) vs. Lions (8), Oct. 25, 1987
 GB (8) vs. Cowboys (6), Nov. 24, 1994
13 GB (5) vs. Cardinals (8), Nov. 1, 1942
 GB (8) vs. Bears (5), Nov. 6, 1955
 GB (7) vs. Lions (6), Sept. 29, 1974
 GB (7) vs. Saints (6), Nov. 7, 1976
 GB (9) vs. Rams (4), Sept. 21, 1980
Most Yards, Kickoff Returns, Season
1,546 1971
1,483 1993
1,470 1986
1,449 1951
Fewest Yards, Kickoff Returns, Season
381 1940
567 1941
610 1944
661 1943
Most Yards, Kickoff Returns, Game
258 vs. Cowboys, Oct. 3, 1993
245 vs. Giants, Sept. 19, 1971
244 vs. Bears, Oct. 7, 1956
234 vs. Bears, Dec. 7, 1980
Most Yards, Kickoff Returns, Both Teams, Game
427 GB (245) vs. Giants (182), Sept. 19, 1971
410 GB (106) vs. Bears (304), Nov. 9, 1952
401 GB (208) vs. Redskins (193), Oct. 17, 1983
379 GB (180) vs. Bears (199), Nov. 6, 1955
Highest Average, Kickoff Returns, Season
26.98 1967 (46-1,241)
26.66 1971 (58-1,546)
26.27 1961 (41-1,077)
25.78 1964 (45-1,160)
Lowest Average, Kickoff Returns, Season
16.95 1983 (79-1,339)
17.49 1987 (59-1,032)
17.96 1989 (69-1,239)
18.38 1981 (58-1,066)
Most Touchdowns, Kickoff Returns, Season
4 1967
2 1969, 70, 71
1 Accomplished many times
Most Touchdowns, Kickoff Returns, Game
2 vs. Browns, Nov. 12, 1967
1 Accomplished many times
Most Touchdowns, Kickoff Returns, Both Teams, Game
2 GB (0) vs. Bears (2), Sept. 22, 1940
 GB (0) vs. Bears (2), Nov. 9, 1952
 GB (2) vs. Browns (0), Nov. 12, 1967
 GB (0) vs. Rams (2), Nov. 24, 1985
1 Accomplished many times

FUMBLES

Most Fumbles, Season
44 1988
42 1992
41 1991
40 1952
Fewest Fumbles, Season
11 1944
13 1942
15 1943
16 1939
Most Fumbles, Game
8 vs. Eagles, Dec. 1, 1974
7 Accomplished six times

Most Fumbles, Both Teams, Game
- 13　GB (7) vs. Lions (6), Oct. 6, 1985
- 12　GB (6) vs. Lions (6), Nov. 24, 1955
- 　　GB (4) vs. Lions (8), Dec. 6, 1992
- 11　GB (2) vs. Eagles (9), Oct. 13, 1946
- 　　GB (6) vs. Cardinals (5), Nov. 10, 1946
- 　　GB (5) vs. 49ers (6), Nov. 15, 1964
- 10　Accomplished many times

Most Fumbles Lost, Season
- 31　1952
- 26　1988
- 25　1955
- 24　1978

Fewest Fumbles Lost, Season
- 6　1943
- 7　1939, 44, 45, 84
- 8　1942, 94
- 9　1940, 77

Most Fumbles Lost, Game
- 6　vs. Lions, Nov. 27, 1952
- 5　vs. Bears, Nov. 6, 1955
- 　　vs. Lions, Nov. 24, 1955
- 　　vs. Rams, Sept. 22, 1966
- 　　vs. Eagles, Dec. 1, 1974
- 4　Accomplished many times

Most Fumbles Recovered, Season, Own and Opponents'
- 46　1985 (21 own, 25 opp)
- 42　1975 (15 own, 27 opp)
- 41　1946 (13 own, 28 opp)
- 　　1987 (17 own, 24 opp)
- 39　1988 (18 own, 21 opp)

Fewest Fumbles Recovered, Season, Own and Opponents'
- 16　1940 (9 own, 7 opp)
- 　　1944 (4 own, 12 opp)
- 17　1969 (10 own, 7 opp)
- 18　1939 (9 own, 9 opp)
- 　　1943 (9 own, 9 opp)
- 　　1966 (4 own, 14 opp)
- 19　1938 (7 own, 12 opp)

Most Fumbles Recovered, Game Own and Opponents'
- 9　vs. Lions, Oct. 6, 1985 (5 own, 4 opp)
- 8　vs. Cardinals, Nov. 10, 1946 (3 own, 5 opp)
- 7　vs. Steelers, Nov. 23, 1941 (1 own, 6 opp)
- 　　vs. Colts, Sept. 29, 1963 (2 own, 5 opp)
- 　　vs. 49ers, Nov. 15, 1964 (3 own, 4 opp)
- 　　vs. Jets, Dec. 20, 1981 (4 own, 3 opp)
- 6　Accomplished many times

Most Own Fumbles Recovered, Season
- 24　1980, 91
- 22　1989
- 21　1985
- 19　1983, 92

Fewest Own Fumbles Recovered, Season
- 4　1944, 66
- 5　1942
- 6　1960, 65
- 7　1938, 71

Most Own Fumbles Recovered, Game
- 5　vs. Lions, Oct. 6, 1985
- 　　vs. Jets, Nov. 3, 1991
- 4　Accomplished many times

Most Opponents' Fumbles Recovered, Season
- 28　1946
- 27　1975
- 25　1964, 85
- 24　1981, 87

Fewest Opponents' Fumbles Recovered, Season
- 7　1940, 69
- 8　1956
- 9　1939, 43
- 11　1977, 82

Most Opponents' Fumbles Recovered, Game
- 6　vs. Steelers, Nov. 23, 1941
- 　　vs. Chargers, Sept. 24, 1978
- 5　Accomplished many times

Most Touchdowns, Fumble Recoveries, Season, Own and Opponents'
- 3　1964, 82
- 2　1939, 83
- 1　Accomplished many times

Most Touchdowns, Own Fumbles Recovered, Season
- 2　1982

Most Touchdowns, Opponents' Fumbles Recovered, Season
- 2　1964, 83

Most Touchdowns, Fumble Recoveries, Game, Own and Opponents'
- 2　vs. Cowboys, Nov. 26, 1964 (2 opp)

Most Touchdowns, Own Fumbles Recovered, Game
- 1　vs. Lions, Nov. 22, 1962
- 　　vs. Lions, Nov. 8, 1964
- 　　vs. Falcons, Oct. 1, 1989

Most Touchdowns, Opponents' Fumbles Recovered, Game
- 2　vs. Cowboys, Nov. 26, 1964

TURNOVERS

Most Turnovers, Season
- 57　1950
- 56　1952
- 50　1983, 88
- 48　1948, 53

Fewest Turnovers, Season
- 19　1972
- 22　1994
- 23　1964
- 24　1941, 66

Most Turnovers, Game
- 9　vs. Bears, Sept. 22, 1940
- 　　vs. Rams, Nov. 12, 1950
- 　　vs. Lions, Oct. 26, 1952
- 8　vs. Rams, Nov. 11, 1945
- 　　vs. Giants, Nov. 21, 1948
- 　　vs. Lions, Nov. 27, 1952
- 　　vs. Bears, Sept. 24, 1967
- 7　Accomplished many times

Most Turnovers, Both Teams, Game
- 14　GB (4) vs. Lions (10), Oct. 24, 1943
- 　　GB (4) vs. Cardinals (10), Nov. 10, 1946
- 　　GB (9) vs. Rams (5), Nov. 12, 1950
- 13　Accomplished eight times

PENALTIES

Most Penalties, Season
- 135　1987
- 128　1986
- 110　1984
- 104　1947, 48

Fewest Penalties, Season
- 38　1942
- 41　1955
- 42　1956, 82
- 43　1957

Most Penalties, Game
- 17　vs. Yanks, Oct. 21, 1945
- 16　vs. Bears, Nov. 8, 1987
- 15　vs. Rams, Oct. 5, 1947
- 14　vs. 49ers, Oct. 26, 1986
- 　　vs. Lions, Nov. 27, 1986
- 　　vs. Giants, Dec. 20, 1986
- 　　vs. Buccaneers, Nov. 1, 1987

Fewest Penalties, Game
- 0　vs. Giants, Oct. 1, 1933
- 　　vs. Bears, Nov. 29, 1934
- 　　vs. Lions, Nov. 17, 1935
- 　　vs. Bears, Sept. 18, 1938
- 　　vs. Rams, Nov. 26, 1939
- 　　vs. Bears, Nov. 15, 1942
- 　　vs. 49ers, Dec. 14, 1963
- 　　vs. Colts, Sept. 20, 1964
- 　　vs. Vikings, Nov. 27, 1977
- 　　vs. Buccaneers, Nov. 25, 1990

Most Penalties, Both Teams, Game
  33 GB (11) vs. Tigers (22), Sept. 17, 1944
  28 GB (11) vs. Seahawks (17), Oct. 21, 1984
  27 GB (17) vs. Yanks (10), Oct. 21, 1945
  26 GB (13) vs. Raiders (13), Oct. 24, 1976
Fewest Penalties, Both Teams, Game
   1 GB (0) vs. Lions (1), Nov. 17, 1935
      GB (1) vs. Cardinals (0), Nov. 28, 1935
      GB (0) vs. 49ers (1), Dec. 14, 1963
      GB (1) vs. Colts (0), Sept. 10, 1966
   2 Accomplished many times
Most Yards Penalized, Season
  1,103 1987
  1,019 1947
   949 1986
   941 1948
Fewest Yards Penalized, Season
   250 1938
   259 1939
   291 1937
   295 1935, 40
Most Yards Penalized, Game
   184 vs. Yanks, Oct. 21, 1945
   151 vs. Raiders, Oct. 24, 1976
   146 vs. Lions, Oct. 3, 1948
        vs. Rams, Dec. 3, 1950
   143 vs. Eagles, Nov. 15, 1992
Fewest Yards Penalized, Game
     0 see Fewest Penalties, Game
Most Yards Penalized, Both Teams, Game
   309 GB (184) vs. Yanks (125), Oct. 21, 1945
   270 GB (151) vs. Raiders (119), Oct. 24, 1976
   269 GB (146) vs. Rams (123), Dec. 3, 1950
   252 GB (84) vs. Tigers (168), Sept. 17, 1944
Fewest Yards Penalized, Both Teams, Game
     5 GB (0) vs. Lions (5), Nov. 17, 1935
        GB (0) vs. 49ers (5), Dec. 14, 1963
        GB (5) vs. Colts (0), Sept. 10, 1966
    10 GB (10) vs. Giants (0), Nov. 11, 1934
        GB (5) vs. Eagles (5), Dec. 8, 1935
        GB (10) vs. Redskins (10), Nov. 8, 1936
        GB (5) vs. Rams (5), Dec. 16, 1962
    13 GB (5) vs. Vikings (8), Nov. 10, 1963
    15 Accomplished many times

TEAM DEFENSIVE RECORDS

SCORING

Fewest Points Allowed, Season
    22 1929
    34 1923
    38 1924
    43 1927
Fewest Points Allowed, Season (since 1932)
    63 1932
    96 1935
   107 1933
   112 1934
Most Points Allowed, Season
   439 1983
   418 1986
   406 1950
   382 1958
Most Points Allowed, Game
    61 vs. Bears, Dec. 7, 1980
    56 vs. Colts, Nov. 2, 1958
    55 vs. Giants, Dec. 20, 1986
    52 vs. Lions, Nov. 22, 1951
        vs. Lions, Oct. 26, 1952
        vs. Bears, Nov. 6, 1955

Most Points Shutout by Opponent
    56 vs. Colts, Nov. 2, 1958
    40 vs. Lions, Sept. 28, 1970
    35 vs. 49ers, Dec. 5, 1954
    34 vs. Lions, Oct. 28, 1973
Fewest Points Shutout by Opponent
     2 vs. Yellow Jackets, Nov. 29, 1928
        vs. Bears, Sept. 18, 1938
     3 Accomplished seven times
Most Points Opponents Overcame to Beat Packers
    22 Rams, Oct. 12, 1952 (trailed 28-6, won 30-28)
    21 Rams, Nov. 17, 1957 (trailed 24-3, won 31-27)
        Falcons, Nov. 27, 1983 (trailed 21-0, won 47-41)
    17 Colts, Oct. 12, 1958 (trailed 17-0, won 24-17)
        Rams, Oct. 25, 1964 (trailed 17-0, won 27-17)
        Falcons, Sept. 13, 1981 (trailed 17-0, won 31-17)
        Lions, Nov. 20, 1983 (trailed 20-3, won 23-20)
    16 Saints, Oct. 12, 1975 (trailed 16-0, won 20-19)
Most Points, Opponents, First Half
    44 Rams, Sept. 21, 1980
    38 Rams, Sept. 24, 1989
    35 Rams, Dec. 16, 1956
        Vikings, Sept. 28, 1986
    34 Cardinals, Nov. 27, 1949
        49ers, Dec. 7, 1958
Most Points, Opponents, Second Half
    38 Colts, Oct. 13, 1957
    36 Cowboys, Nov. 24, 1994
    35 Rams, Dec. 3, 1950
    33 Bears, Dec. 7, 1980
Most Points, Opponents, One Quarter
    37 Rams, Sept. 21, 1980 (2)
    31 Falcons, Sept. 13, 1981 (4)
    28 Giants, Sept. 19, 1971 (2)
        Bears, Dec. 7, 1980 (2)
        Vikings, Sept. 28, 1986 (1)
        Rams, Sept. 24, 1989 (2)
    27 Cardinals, Nov. 27, 1949 (1)
        Colts, Nov. 5, 1950 (4)
        49ers, Dec. 7, 1958 (1)
        Bengals, Oct. 5, 1986 (2)
Most Points, Opponents, First Quarter
    28 Vikings, Sept. 28, 1986
    27 Cardinals, Nov. 27, 1949
        49ers, Dec. 7, 1958
    26 Rams, Dec. 13, 1953
    21 49ers, Dec. 5, 1954
        Colts, Oct. 8, 1955
        Giants, Dec. 20, 1986
Most Points, Opponents, Second Quarter
    37 Rams, Sept. 21, 1980
    28 Giants, Sept. 19, 1971
        Bears, Dec. 7, 1980
        Rams, Sept. 24, 1989
    27 Bengals, Oct. 5, 1986
    24 Rams, Dec. 14, 1958
        Buccaneers, Nov. 22, 1981
Most Points, Opponents, Third Quarter
    21 Rams, Dec. 3, 1950
        Lions, Nov. 22, 1951
        Rams, Dec. 7, 1952
        Colts, Oct. 25, 1959
        Rams, Sept. 18, 1983
    20 Yanks, Oct. 8, 1950
    19 Cowboys, Nov. 24, 1994
Most Points, Opponents, Fourth Quarter
    31 Falcons, Sept. 13, 1981
    27 Colts, Nov. 5, 1950
    24 Rams, Oct. 12, 1952
        Rams, Oct. 18, 1959
        Redskins, Dec. 2, 1979
    21 Accomplished many times
Most Consecutive Games, Opponents, Scoring
   125 1949-59
        1977-85
    89 1985-91
    68 1969-73
    52 1962-66

TOUCHDOWNS

Most Touchdowns, Opponents, Season
- 56 1950
- 55 1983
- 52 1986
- 50 1951, 58

Fewest Touchdowns, Opponents, Season
- 3 1929
- 4 1923, 24
- 6 1922, 27
- 7 1926

Fewest Touchdowns, Opponents, Season (since 1932)
- 8 1932
- 13 1935
- 14 1933, 34, 36
- 15 1938

Most Touchdowns, Opponents, Game
- 9 Bears, Dec. 7, 1980
- 8 Colts, Nov. 2, 1958
- 7 Accomplished seven times

Most Consecutive Games, Opponents, Scoring Touchdowns
- 51 1980-84
- 46 1955-59
- 40 1949-52, 88-91
- 36 1974-77

POINTS AFTER TOUCHDOWNS

Most Points After Touchdowns, Opponents, Season
- 50 1950, 83
- 49 1951
- 48 1986
- 46 1958

Fewest Points After Touchdown, Opponents, Season
- 0 1929
- 2 1924
- 3 1922
- 4 1921, 23, 26, 27, 32

Fewest Points After Touchdown, Opponents, Season (since 1932)
- 4 1932
- 9 1935
- 10 1934
- 12 1933, 36

Most Points After Touchdowns, Opponents, Game
- 8 Colts, Nov. 2, 1958
- 7 Accomplished eight times

FIELD GOALS

Most Field Goals Attempted, Opponents, Season
- 42 1970
- 40 1993
- 37 1971
- 36 1987

Fewest Field Goals Attempted, Opponents, Season
- 2 1944, 45
- 3 1940, 43
- 7 1942, 46
- 10 1938, 39

Most Field Goals Attempted, Opponents, Game
- 7 Bears, Nov. 17, 1963
- 6 49ers, Nov. 23, 1958
  Saints, Nov. 28, 1971
  Cardinals, Sept. 19, 1976
  Bears, Nov. 8, 1987
  Vikings, Sept. 26, 1993
- 5 Accomplished many times

Most Field Goals, Opponents, Season
- 31 1993
- 28 1970
- 27 1987
- 25 1980, 88

Fewest Field Goals, Opponents, Season
- 0 1928, 29, 30, 43, 45
- 1 1921, 27, 31, 44
- 2 1923, 37, 40
- 3 1932, 33, 35

Most Field Goals, Opponents, Game
- 5 Saints, Nov. 28, 1971
  Cardinals, Sept. 19, 1976
  Lions, Sept. 14, 1980
  Vikings, Sept. 26, 1993
  Cowboys, Oct. 3, 1993
- 4 Accomplished many times

Most Consecutive Games, Opponents, Scoring Field Goals
- 14 1971-72
- 13 1990-91
- 12 1965-66, 70
- 11 1984, 92

SAFETIES

Most Safeties, Opponents, Season
- 4 1985
- 3 1973
- 2 1929, 36, 38, 49, 65, 86, 87

Most Safeties, Opponents, Game
- 2 Rams, Oct. 21, 1973

FIRST DOWNS

Most First Downs, Opponents, Season
- 366 1983 (171 rush, 187 pass, 8 penalty)
- 327 1979 (162 rush, 146 pass, 19 penalty)
- 326 1981 (140 rush, 168 pass, 18 penalty)
- 323 1984 (136 rush, 166 pass, 21 penalty)

Fewest First Downs, Opponents, Season
- 96 1935
- 110 1937
- 113 1939 (40 rush, 64 pass, 9 penalty)
- 114 1944 (56 rush, 49 pass, 9 penalty)

Most First Downs, Opponents, Game
- 33 Rams, Dec. 16, 1956 (18, 13, 2)
  Bears, Dec. 7, 1980 (17, 16,0)
  Redskins, Oct. 17, 1983 (12,21,0)
  Lions, Nov. 22, 1984 (18,15,0)
- 32 Cowboys, Nov. 12, 1978 (17,12,3)
- 31 Rams, Dec. 3, 1950 (11,16,4)
- 30 Rams, Dec. 12, 1954 (12,18,0)
  Colts, Nov. 2, 1958 (14,9,7)
  Bengals, Oct. 30, 1983 (13,16,1)
  Giants, Dec. 20, 1986 (15,12,3)

Fewest First Downs, Opponents, Game
- 0 Giants, Oct. 1, 1933
- 2 Bears, Dec. 10, 1933
  Cardinals, Nov. 18, 1934
- 3 Eagles, Nov. 11, 1962
- 4 Accomplished five times

Most First Downs, Rushing, Opponents, Season
- 171 1983
- 162 1979
- 140 1977, 81
- 137 1978

Fewest First Downs, Rushing, Opponents, Season
- 40 1939
- 56 1944
- 58 1982
- 61 1940

Most First Downs, Rushing, Opponents, Game
- 21 Raiders, Sept. 17, 1978
- 19 Cardinals, Dec. 5, 1948
  49ers, Dec. 9, 1951
  Steelers, Oct. 24, 1953
  Bears, Nov. 6, 1955
  Bears, Oct. 30, 1977
- 18 Accomplished four times

Fewest First Downs, Rushing, Opponents, Game
    0   Giants, Oct. 1, 1933
        Eagles, Nov. 11, 1962
        Lions, Dec. 3, 1972
        Bears, Dec. 11, 1994
    1   Accomplished many times
Most First Downs, Passing, Opponents, Season
  187   1983
  182   1994
  179   1989
  178   1985
Fewest First Downs, Passing, Opponents, Season
   49   1941, 44
   53   1940
   56   1943
   57   1945
Most First Downs, Passing, Opponents, Game
   21   Redskins, Oct. 17, 1983
   20   Chargers, Oct. 7, 1984
   19   Vikings, Nov. 29, 1981
        Dolphins, Dec. 8, 1985
        Lions, Oct. 25, 1987
        Bills, Nov. 20, 1994
   18   Rams, Dec. 12, 1954
        Vikings, Nov. 26, 1989
Fewest First Downs, Passing, Opponents, Game
    0   Bears, Sept. 25, 1932
        Giants, Oct. 2, 1932
        Giants, Oct. 1, 1933
        Cardinals, Nov. 18, 1934
        Bears, Sept. 28, 1941
        Giants, Nov. 19, 1944
    1   Accomplished many times
Most First Downs, Penalty, Opponents, Season
   27   1986
   26   1947, 87
   23   1976
   22   1978, 91
Fewest First Downs, Penalty, Opponents, Season
    4   1943
    6   1940
    7   1955, 67
    8   1954, 83
Most First Downs, Penalty, Opponents, Game
    7   Colts, Nov. 2, 1958
    6   Bears, Oct. 25, 1992
    5   Lions, Oct. 30, 1949
        Vikings, Oct. 22, 1978
        Raiders, Sept. 13, 1987
    4   Accomplished many times

NET YARDS RUSHING AND PASSING

Most Yards Gained, Opponents, Season
  6,403   1983
  5,782   1980
  5,647   1979
  5,442   1990
Fewest Yards Gained, Opponents, Season
  1,929   1933
  2,091   1935
  2,299   1937
  2,334   1934
Most Yards Gained, Opponents, Game
    611   Rams, Dec. 16, 1956
    599   Rams, Dec. 8, 1957
    594   Bears, Dec. 7, 1980
    570   Rams, Dec. 12, 1954
Fewest Yards Gained, Opponents, Game
     33   Yanks, Nov. 18, 1945
     50   Cardinals, Nov. 18, 1934
     54   Eagles, Nov. 11, 1962
     58   Falcons, Oct. 1, 1967
Most Consecutive Games, Opponents, 400 or More Yards
      5   1983
      3   1950
      2   Accomplished many times

Most Consecutive Games, Opponents, 300 or More Yards
   11   1949-50
   10   1951-52
    9   1983
    7   1958, 79

RUSHING

Most Rushing Attempts, Opponents, Season
  639   1979
  620   1978
  597   1983
  582   1977
Fewest Rushing Attempts, Opponents, Season
  275   1982
  333   1939
  350   1943, 60
  356   1941
Most Rushing Attempts, Opponents, Game
   70   Cardinals, Dec. 5, 1948
   69   Cardinals, Dec. 6, 1936
   62   Redskins, Oct. 24, 1948
   59   Giants, Nov. 11, 1934
        Steelers, Oct. 26, 1976
        Steelers, Sept. 11, 1983
Fewest Rushing Attempts, Opponents, Game
   11   Lions, Dec. 3, 1972
        Vikings, Nov. 29, 1981
   12   Cardinals, Oct. 20, 1963
        Lions, Oct. 25, 1987
        Lions, Nov. 1, 1992
   13   Eagles, Nov. 11, 1962
        Bears, Nov. 22, 1992
   14   Buccaneers, Oct. 2, 1983
        Lions, Oct. 28, 1984
        Bears, Dec. 11, 1994
Most Yards Gained Rushing, Opponents, Season
  2,885   1979
  2,641   1983
  2,619   1956
  2,439   1978
Fewest Yards Gained Rushing, Opponents, Season
    932   1982
  1,040   1940
  1,112   1943
  1,130   1944
Most Yards Gained Rushing, Opponents, Game
    406   Bears, Nov. 6, 1955
    375   Bears, Oct. 30, 1977
    323   Rams, Oct. 21, 1951
    314   Rams, Dec. 16, 1956
Fewest Yards Gained Rushing, Opponents, Game
     -7   Eagles, Sept. 15, 1940
     12   Yanks, Nov. 18, 1945
          Cardinals, Nov. 10, 1946
     16   Cardinals, Sept. 23, 1962
     17   Cardinals, Sept. 25, 1938
          Lions, Oct. 25, 1987
Highest Average Gain, Opponents, Season
   5.12   1956 (512-2,619)
   4.78   1958 (427-2,040)
   4.67   1957 (462-2,159)
   4.64   1954 (403-1,871)
Lowest Average Gain, Opponents, Season
   2.69   1940 (387-1,040)
   2.72   1935 (448-1,219)
   2.77   1933 (443-1,226)
   2.96   1937 (400-1,184)
Most Touchdowns, Rushing, Opponents, Season
   28   1983
   24   1950, 53, 58
   21   1948, 51, 56, 81
   20   1949
Fewest Touchdowns, Rushing, Opponents, Season
    1   1923, 29
    2   1924, 26, 27
    4   1932, 33, 62
    5   1921, 22, 36

Most Touchdowns, Rushing, Opponents, Game
5   Bears, Nov. 6, 1955
      Bears, Dec. 7, 1980
4   Accomplished many times

PASSING

Most Passes Attempted, Opponents, Season
605   1994
551   1984
531   1991
529   1993

Fewest Passes Attempted, Opponents, Season
173   1934
179   1933
191   1935
197   1937

Most Passes Attempted, Opponents, Game
59   Broncos, Oct. 10, 1993
55   Vikings, Nov. 29, 1981
53   Saints, Sept. 10, 1978
     Patriots, Oct. 2, 1994
51   Chargers, Dec. 12, 1993

Fewest Passes Attempted, Opponents, Game
2   Cardinals, Nov. 29, 1934
3   Cardinals, Oct. 13, 1935
    Cardinals, Sept. 12, 1937
4   Bears, Sept. 25, 1932
    Cardinals, Nov. 18, 1934
    Browns, Nov. 4, 1956
5   Cardinals, Dec. 6, 1936
    Giants, Nov. 17, 1940

Most Passes Completed, Opponents, Season
337   1994
315   1984
305   1991
302   1989

Fewest Passes Completed, Opponents, Season
48   1933
56   1934
61   1935
70   1937

Most Passes Completed, Opponents, Game
38   Vikings, Nov. 29, 1981
35   Saints, Sept. 10, 1978
33   Lions, Oct. 25, 1987
    Broncos, Oct. 10, 1993
32   Rams, Dec. 3, 1950
    Bills, Nov. 20, 1994

Fewest Passes Completed, Opponents, Game
0   Cardinals, Nov. 18, 1934
1   Accomplished many times

Most Yards Gained, Passing, Opponents, Season
3,762   1983
3,553   1989
3,401   1994
3,383   1980, 90

Fewest Yards Gained, Passing, Opponents, Season
676   1934
711   1933
837   1935
1,115   1937

Most Yards Gained, Passing, Opponents, Game
434   Rams, Dec. 12, 1954
411   49ers, Nov. 4, 1990
384   Browns, Oct. 19, 1980
376   Vikings, Nov. 29, 1981

Fewest Yards Gained, Passing, Opponents, Game
-6   Cardinals, Nov. 29, 1934
-1   Cowboys, Oct. 24, 1965
0   Cardinals, Nov. 18, 1934
6   Cardinals, Sept. 12, 1937

Most Times Sacked, Opponents, Season
48   1978, 85
47   1966
46   1993
45   1964, 91

Fewest Times Sacked, Opponents, Season
19   1971
20   1982
25   1973
27   1990

Most Times Sacked, Opponents, Game
9   Cowboys, Oct. 24, 1965
8   Accomplished eight times

Highest Completion Percentage, Opponents, Season
63.45   1989 (302-476)
59.60   1986 (267-448)
59.49   1987 (279-469)
58.31   1977 (186-319)

Lowest Completion Percentage, Opponents, Season
26.82   1933 (48-179)
31.94   1935 (61-191)
32.37   1934 (56-173)
35.53   1937 (70-197)

Highest Completion Percentage, Opponents, Game
(minimum 20 attempts)
84.62   Buccaneers, Sept. 13, 1992 (22-26)
83.33   Bears, Dec. 7, 1980 (20-24)
81.48   Buccaneers, Sept. 10, 1989 (22-27)
80.77   Giants, Dec. 19, 1987 (21-26)

Lowest Completion Percentage, Opponents, Game
(minimum 20 attempts)
16.67   Pirates, Oct. 6, 1935 (4-24)
19.23   Bears, Sept. 22, 1935 (5-26)
22.58   Eagles, Nov. 2, 1952 (7-31)
22.73   Lions, Oct. 7, 1934 (5-22)
      Lions, Sept. 14, 1941 (5-22)

Most Touchdowns, Passing, Opponents, Season
31   1986
25   1951
24   1950, 58
22   1985, 89

Fewest Touchdowns, Passing, Opponents, Season
1   1922
2   1921, 24, 29
3   1923, 32, 34
4   1926, 27

Most Touchdowns, Passing, Opponents, Game
6   Vikings, Sept. 28, 1986

Most Passes, Had Intercepted, Opponents, Season
42   1943
40   1940
33   1942
31   1936, 55, 62

Fewest Passes, Had Intercepted, Opponents, Season
11   1976
12   1960, 82
13   1958, 77, 80
14   1959, 75

Most Passes, Had Intercepted, Opponents, Game
9   Lions, Oct. 24, 1943
7   Rams, Oct. 30, 1938
   Rams, Nov. 8, 1942
   Rams, Nov. 12, 1944
   Rams, Oct. 17, 1948

Highest Pass Rating, Opponents, Season
86.1   1958
85.4   1986
83.8   1980
81.2   1985

Lowest Pass Rating, Opponents, Season
11.5   1934
17.1   1933
19.6   1935
24.0   1936

PUNTING

Most Punts, Opponents, Season
90   1978
89   1984
88   1994
84   1974

Fewest Punts, Opponents, Season
42 1958
46 1982
49 1961
50 1956, 57
Most Punts, Opponents, Game
17 Bears, Oct. 22, 1933
15 Spartans, Nov. 12, 1933
14 Eagles, Dec. 3, 1933
Bears, Dec. 10, 1933
13 Texans, Nov. 23, 1952
Fewest Punts, Opponents, Game
0 Bears, Nov. 6, 1955
Rams, Dec. 16, 1956
Vikings, Sept. 27, 1981
Buccaneers, Nov. 22, 1981
Highest Average Distance, Punting, Opponents, Season
44.30 1959 (56-2,481)
43.54 1947 (65-2,830)
43.49 1964 (72-3,131)
43.36 1963 (59-2,558)
Lowest Average Distance, Punting, Opponents, Season
36.53 1977 (76-2,776)
36.60 1974 (84-3,074)
36.67 1943 (55-2,017)
37.20 1944 (56-2,083)

PUNT RETURNS

Most Punt Returns, Opponents, Season
54 1987
53 1977
51 1978
50 1949, 80, 81
Fewest Punt Returns, Opponents, Season
13 1967
18 1944, 69
19 1968
20 1962
Most Punt Returns, Opponents, Game
9 Giants, Nov. 1, 1959
8 Eagles, Nov. 29, 1942
Bears, Oct. 15, 1950
Most Fair Catches, Opponents, Season
27 1967
25 1969
24 1991
22 1978
Fewest Fair Catches, Season
2 1974
3 1982
4 1961, 77, 81
5 1984, 86
Most Yards, Punt Returns, Opponents, Season
932 1949
564 1951
511 1981
483 1947
Fewest Yards, Punt Returns, Opponents, Season
22 1967
62 1969
66 1968
144 1960
Most Yards, Punt Returns, Opponents, Game
175 Lions, Nov. 22, 1951
148 Cardinals, Nov. 27, 1949
Colts, Oct. 14, 1956
113 Lions, Dec. 11, 1949
109 Redskins, Dec. 4, 1949
Highest Average, Punt Returns, Opponents, Season
18.64 1949 (50-932)
14.84 1951 (38-564)
13.94 1941 (31-432)
13.87 1989 (30-416)

Lowest Average, Punt Returns, Opponents, Season
1.69 1967 (13-22)
3.44 1969 (18-62)
3.47 1968 (19-66)
3.73 1957 (40-149)
Most Touchdowns, Punt Returns, Opponents, Season
3 1949
Most Touchdowns, Punt Returns, Opponents, Game
2 Lions, Nov. 22, 1951

KICKOFF RETURNS

Most Kickoff Returns, Opponents, Season
78 1983
76 1962
75 1994
73 1984
Fewest Kickoff Returns, Opponents, Season
22 1948
28 1946
29 1949
Most Kickoff Returns, Opponents, Game
9 Redskins, Oct. 17, 1983
Lions, Nov. 27, 1986
Bears, Dec. 11, 1994
Most Yards, Kickoff Returns, Opponents, Season
1,597 1961
1,570 1985
1,524 1962
Fewest Yards, Kickoff Returns, Opponents, Season
583 1949
606 1943
611 1948
Most Yards, Kickoff Returns, Opponents, Game
304 Bears, Nov. 9, 1952
282 Cardinals, Nov. 1, 1942
260 Lions, Nov. 24, 1940
Highest Average, Kickoff Returns, Opponents, Season
27.77 1948 (22-611)
25.73 1952 (51-1,312)
24.67 1970 (36-888)
Lowest Average, Kickoff Returns, Opponents, Season
15.81 1992 (57-901)
16.04 1984 (73-1,171)
16.90 1981 (70-1,183)
Most Touchdowns, Kickoff Returns, Opponents, Season
2 1940, 52, 85
Most Touchdowns, Kickoff Returns, Opponents, Game
2 Bears, Sept. 22, 1940
Bears, Nov. 9, 1952
Rams, Nov. 24, 1985

FUMBLES

Most Fumbles, Opponents, Season
45 1946
44 1975, 85
42 1981, 87
Fewest Fumbles, Opponents, Season
15 1940
17 1956
18 1937
Most Fumbles, Opponents, Game
9 Eagles, Oct. 13, 1946
Chargers, Sept. 24, 1978
8 Steelers, Nov. 23, 1941
Lions, Dec. 6, 1992
Most Fumbles Recovered, Own and Packers, by Opponents, Season
44 1978 (20 own, 24 Packers)
40 1952 (9 own, 31 Packers)
39 1950 (19 own, 20 Packers)
Fewest Fumbles Rec., Own and Packers, by Opponents, Season
15 1942 (7 own, 8 Packers)
19 1943 (13 own, 6 Packers)

Most Fumbles Recovered, Own and Packers, by Opponents, Game
- 8   Lions, Sept. 17, 1950 (7 own, 1 Packers)
-     49ers, Dec. 10, 1950 (4 own, 4 Packers)
- 7   Accomplished four times

Most Own Fumbles Recovered, by Opponents, Season
- 20   1947, 78, 83, 86, 94
- 19   1950, 62, 85
- 18   1941, 81, 84, 87, 93

Fewest Own Fumbles Recovered, by Opponents, Season
- 7   1942, 74
- 8   1940, 48, 49, 54, 60
- 9   1952, 53, 55, 56, 57, 64, 67

Most Own Fumbles Recovered, by Opponents, Game
- 7   Lions, Sept. 17, 1950
- 6   Eagles, Oct. 13, 1946
-     Bears, Nov. 15, 1981
- 5   Cardinals, Sept. 17, 1939
-     Lions, Oct. 14, 1979
-     Vikings, Nov. 13, 1983

Most TDs, Fumbles Rec., Own and Packers, by Opponents, Season
- 3   1950, 55, 71, 81

Most TDs, Fumbles Rec., Own and Packers, by Opponents, Game
- 2   Lions, Sept. 17, 1950 (1 own, 1 Packers)
-     Giants, Sept. 19, 1971 (2 Packers)
-     Broncos, Oct. 15, 1984 (2 Packers)

TURNOVERS

Most Turnovers, Opponents, Season
- 54   1981
- 52   1946
- 51   1943, 47

Fewest Turnovers, Opponents, Season
- 23   1982
- 24   1939, 77
- 26   1969, 76

Most Turnovers, Opponents, Game
- 11   Chargers, Sept. 24, 1978
- 10   Steelers, Nov. 23, 1941
-     Lions, Oct. 24, 1943
-     Cardinals, Nov. 10, 1946

PENALTIES

Most Penalties, Opponents, Season
- 145   1984
- 116   1978
- 112   1988

Fewest Penalties, Opponents, Season
- 50   1972
- 51   1943, 59
- 52   1956, 61

Most Penalties, Opponents, Game
- 22   Tigers, Sept. 17, 1944
- 17   Seahawks, Oct. 21, 1984
- 16   Cardinals, Sept. 13, 1936
-     Falcons, Dec. 26, 1982

Fewest Penalties, Opponents, Game
- 0   Giants, Nov. 11, 1934
-     Cardinals, Nov. 28, 1935
-     Redskins, Nov. 8, 1936
-     Lions, Oct. 31, 1937
-     Steelers, Sept. 19, 1965
-     Colts, Sept. 10, 1966
-     Lions, Dec. 20, 1970

Most Yards Penalized, Opponents, Season
- 1,129   1984
- 965   1983
- 949   1978

Fewest Yards Penalized, Opponents, Season
- 190   1935
- 286   1937
- 315   1939

Most Yards Penalized, Opponents, Game
- 168   Tigers, Sept. 17, 1944
- 153   Falcons, Dec. 26, 1982
- 135   Rams, Dec. 8, 1946

Green Bay Press-Gazette photo

The Packers crushed the Cleveland Browns in Milwaukee, November, 1967 with an eventual final score of 55-7 and 456 combined yards enroute to the Ice Bowl playoff against Dallas.

THE
POSTSEASON
THE PLAYOFF
GAMES

John Biever photo

Willie Mitchell (22) goes piggy-back in an attempt to stop Max McGee (85) in Super Bowl I. McGee, who caught only four passes in all of the regular season, grabbed seven for 138 yards and two touchdowns as Green Bay beat the Chiefs 35-10.

1936 NFL CHAMPIONSHIP GAME

Polo Grounds, New York

Sunday, December 13, 1936

- 29,545 -

GREEN BAY PACKERS	7	0	7	7	—	21
BOSTON REDSKINS	0	6	0	0	—	6

GB - Hutson 43 pass from Herber (Ernie Smith kick)
BR - Rentner 1 run (Riley Smith kick wide)
GB - Gantenbein 8 pass from Herber (Ernie Smith kick)
GB - Monnett 2 run (Engebretsen kick)

Green Bay was to have played its first ever post-season game at the home of the Boston Redskins. Instead, owner George Marshall, disgusted at what he felt was a lack of fan support, moved the contest to the neutral Polo Grounds. Regardless of the site, the 7-5 Redskins were not given much of a chance to upset the 10-1-1 Packers, having lost twice to the Green and Gold during the regular season by a combined score of 38-5.

Boston suffered its first blow of the game when star back Cliff Battles, the league's fourth leading rusher, was lost on the Redskin's first offensive series. Things went from bad to worse when Riley Smith lost a lateral and Green Bay's Lou Gordon recovered. Three plays later, Arnie Herber passed to Don Hutson for a 43-yard touchdown and the Packers led 7-0 following Ernie Smith's conversion.

Just before the end of the first period, Boston began a 78-yard march. The payoff came on the first play of the second quarter when Pug Rentner scored on a one-yard plunge. The Redskins failed to tie when Riley Smith's conversion attempt sailed wide.

Herber hit Johnny Blood with a 52-yard pass on the second play of the second half. Three plays later, he connected with Milt Gantenbein for an eight-yard score. Ernie Smith kicked the extra point and Green Bay led 14-6.

On the ensuing kickoff, Boston lost center Frank Bausch after Bausch was ejected for fighting with Frank Butler.

Disaster struck again when Riley Smith had his first punt of the fourth quarter blocked. Clarke Hinkle recovered on the Boston three-yard line. Hinkle gained a yard before Bobby Monnett ran it in from two yards out. Paul (Tiny) Engebretsen kicked the point after and the Packers went up 21-6.

Green Bay blocked Riley Smith's next punt also, but failed to move.

STATISTICS

	Packers	Redskins
First Downs	7	8
Total Net Yards	220	116
Yards Rushing	44-67	34-39
Yards Passing	153	77
Att/Com/HI	23-9-2	27-7-1
Punts	7	10
Penalties	3-15	4-25
Fumbles/Lost	2-1	5-2

QUOTABLE

"This year's team is as fine a squad of men as ever represented any city. They have been marvelous, not only in their comeback after a crushing defeat by the Chicago Bears at the start of the season, but in their everyday relations toward their work, their coaches, and the city they represented."
Packers Coach **Curly Lambeau**.

Tom Pigeon collection

Clarke Hinkle (30), shown here in a 1938 game against the Lions, gained 56 yards in the 1936 Championship game

1938 NFL CHAMPIONSHIP GAME

Polo Grounds, New York

Sunday, December 11, 1938

- 48,120 -

GREEN BAY PACKERS	0	14	3	0	—	17
NEW YORK GIANTS	9	7	7	0	—	23

NY - FG (13) Cuff
NY - Leemans 6 run (Gildea kick wide)
GB - Mulleneaux 50 pass from Herber (Engebretsen kick)
NY - Barnard 20 pass from Danowski (Cuff kick)
GB - Hinkle 6 run (Engebretsen kick)
GB - FG (15) Engebretsen
NY - Soar 23 pass from Danowski (Cuff kick)

Green Bay, in facing the New York Giants for the first time in an NFL title game, dug itself a hole early and spent the rest of the game playing catchup. Only briefly in the third period did the Packers lead, 17-16, but the Giants quickly erased that, driving 61 yards in 11 plays to go ahead 23-17, the final score.

New York rocked the Packers immediately, blocking the visitors' second and third punts of the first quarter. Clarke Hinkle suffered the first block, coming from Jim Lee Howell, and the Giants recovered on Green Bay's seven-yard line. Three plays later, Ward Cuff booted a 13-yard field goal to put the Giants in front, 3-0.

Cecil Isbell was the next to have his punt blocked, this time by Howell and Jim Poole. New York drove 28 yards before Tuffy Leemans scored from six yards out. Johnny Gildea missed the extra point and the Giants led 9-0.

Early in the second quarter, Paul (Tiny) Engebretsen intercepted Leemans. Arnie Herber then passed 50 yards to Carl (Moose) Mulleneaux for a touchdown four plays later. Engebretsen's kick brought the Packers closer, 9-7.

Ed Jankowski fumbled on Green Bay's next possession and the Giants recovered at midfield. Eight plays later, Hap Barnard caught a 20-yard scoring pass from Ed Danowski. Ward Cuff's kick gave the Giants a nine-point lead, 16-7.

Just before the end of the half, Isbell hit Wayland Becker with a 66-yard pass. Shortly thereafter, Hinkle scored on a one-yard run. Engebretsen's kick allowed the Packers to close, 16-14.

Green Bay recorded its only lead of the game by driving for a field goal immediately after the third quarter began. Two long runs by Bob Monnett and Joe Laws aided the cause. Engebretsen kicked a 15-yard field goal to give his team a slim 17-16 edge.

After the Giants went up 23-17, Green Bay managed to cross into New York territory five times, but failed to score.

STATISTICS

	Packers	Giants
First Downs	14	10
Total Net Yards	378	212
Yards Rushing	46-164	43-115
Yards Passing	214	97
Att/Com/Int	19-8-1	15-8-1
Punts	6	8
Penalties	2-10	3-20
Fumbles/Lost	4-2	2-0

QUOTABLE

"It just isn't fair for us to lose a game on account of incompetent officiating. That's my sincere opinion."
Packers Coach **Curly Lambeau** *referring to head linesman Larry Conover who ruled Giants receiver Len Barnum did not fumble a second-quarter pass and who ruled Packers end Milt Gantenbein an ineligible receiver on an apparent first-down catch in the fourth quarter.*

AP/Wide World photo

Clarke Hinkle (30) comes up a yard short of a touchdown in the 1938 NFL Championship Game. On the next play, however, the fullback from Bucknell went over for a score.

1939 NFL CHAMPIONSHIP GAME

State Fair Park, Milwaukee

Sunday, December 10, 1939

- 32,279 -

NEW YORK GIANTS	0	0	0	0	—	0
GREEN BAY PACKERS	7	0	10	10	—	27

GB - Gantenbein 7 pass from Herber (Engebretsen kick)
GB - FG (29) Engebretsen
GB - Laws 31 pass from Isbell (Engebretsen kick)
GB - FG (42) Ernie Smith
GB - Jankowski 1 run (Ernie Smith kick)

The Packers survived three miscues, four Giant advances, and bitter 35 mile per hour winds, before turning a 7-0 halftime lead into a 27-0 rout at State Fair Park in Milwaukee. Green Bay suffered a blocked punt and two first half interceptions which led to New York field goal tries and dodged another bullet by ending a Giant drive to the Packer nine with a late second quarter interception. In between the two field goal attempts, Arnie Herber, Milt Gantenbein, and Paul (Tiny) Engebretsen provided seven points a hint of what was to come in the second half.

Jim Poole blocked Clark Hinkle's first punt and four plays later, Ward Cuff failed to make a 42-yard field goal. Cuff then intercepted Herber on the last play of the first quarter which led to a second scoring opportunity, a failed 47-yard field goal try from Lem Barnum. Later in the period, Cuff blew a third chance at a field goal, this time from 52 yards out. The Giants last serious first-half threat was ended by Charley Brock who intercepted Ed Danowski's pass near the Green Bay goal two plays prior to halftime.

Except for the final drive of the game, the Giants spent precious few moments in Packer territory after intermission. Green Bay drove 54 yards in eight plays on its first second half possession and counted on a 29-yard field goal by Engebretsen. Up 10-0, the Packers stopped New York's next drive when Gantenbein intercepted Danowski. Three plays later, Cecil Isbell completed a 31-yard touchdown pass to Joe Laws. Engebretsen's kick lengthened the Packers' lead, 17-0.

Hinkle endured a second blocked punt just before the fourth quarter got underway, but Charley Brock quickly rectified the situation with his second interception of the day on the next play.

Midway through the final period, Ernie Smith put the Packers up 20-0 with a 42-yard field goal. Earl Svendsen abruptly put a halt to New York's next drive with an interception of Barnum, the Packer's fifth steal of the game. Three running plays carried the ball to the one-yard line, from which point Ed Jankowski plunged into the end zone. Smith's extra point made it 27-0.

A final New York advance ended on the Packer five-yard line as time ran out.

STATISTICS

	Packers	Giants
First Downs	10	9
Total Net Yards	232	164
Yards Rushing	52-136	34-70
Yards Passing	96	94
Att/Com/Int	10-7-3	25-8-6
Punts	7	6
Penalties	4-50	5-21
Fumbles/Lost	2-0	1-0

QUOTABLE

"We broke their hearts in the third period this afternoon when we scored 10 points against the wind."
Packers receiver **Don Hutson**.

"Our boys gave the Giants the best going over they ever have taken, I'll bet."
Packers halfback **Cecil Isbell**.

AP/Wide World photo

Cecil Isbell (17) is stopped after a short gain by New York's Frank Cope.

1941 NFL WESTERN DIVISION PLAYOFF GAME

Wrigley Field, Chicago

Sunday, December 14, 1941

- 43,425 -

GREEN BAY PACKERS	7	0	7	0	—	14
CHICAGO BEARS	6	24	0	3	—	33

GB - Hinkle 1 run (Hutson kick)
CB - Gallarneau 81 punt return (Snyder kick blocked)
CB - FG (24) Snyder
CB - Standlee 3 run (Stydahar kick)
CB - Standlee 2 run (Stydahar kick)
CB - Swisher 9 run (Stydahar kick)
GB - Van Every 10 pass from Isbell (Hutson kick)
CB - FG (26) Snyder

Identical 10-1 records necessitated the NFL's first-ever divisional playoff game. The Packers traveled to Wrigley Field to face the formidable Bears who had lost only once at home in the past two years, 16-14 to the Packers six weeks previous. A year before, Chicago had decimated Washington 73-0 in the championship game.

The Packers were well aware of the challenge facing them and for awhile it appeared they might prevail. Green Bay forced two turnovers, went up 7-0, missed going ahead 10-0, before Hugh Gallarneau swung the tide the other way. The Bears then put together a 24-point second quarter which completely crushed the Packers, who eventually fell 33-14.

Gallarneau fumbled the opening kickoff and Ray Riddick recovered for the Packers on the Bears' 18-yard line. Five plays later, Clarke Hinkle plowed over and Green Bay led 7-0. Then Chicago's Norm Standlee fumbled and Larry Craig recovered on the Bears' 35-yard line. The Packers were unable to move and had to settle for Hinkle's field goal try which was blocked by John Siegal.

Neither team was able to move on its next possession. Hinkle's first punt was taken Gallarneau who weaved his way through traffic and scored on an 81-yard return. Lee McLaughlin blocked Bob Snyder's extra point attempt and Green Bay clung to a 7-6 lead.

From that point on, the Bears exploded. Snyder kicked a 24-yard field goal shortly after the start of the second quarter. Then, Cecil Isbell fumbled deep in Packers territory, a miscue the Bears converted into six points. The next time Chicago got the ball, George McAfee turned in a long run which put Standlee in position to score on a two-yard run. The Bears final possession of the quarter culminated with Swisher's nine-yard scoring run and the Bears had swiftly forged an insurmountable 30-7 lead.

The Packers rallied and reached the Bears' one, but Isbell was thrown for a loss by Sid Luckman on the final play of the half.

Hal Van Every scored on a pass from Isbell early in the third quarter but his team was stopped thereafter, even though the Bears used quite a few substitutes.

STATISTICS

	Packers	Bears
First Downs	12	14
Total Net Yards	255	325
Yards Rushing	36-33	48-277
Yards Passing	222	48
Att/Com/Int	27-11-2	12-5-0
Punts	4	6
Penalties	3-46	12-128
Fumbles/Lost	3-2	5-3

QUOTABLE

"Green Bay is a one-man team. You always know that if you stop Don Hutson you should win the game." Bears fullback **Bill Osmanski**. *Packers end* **Don Hutson** *caught one pass for 19 yards and dropped a touchdown pass that would have given the Packers a 13-0 lead.*

Green Bay Press-Gazette photo

Green Bay's defense closes in on Chicago's Norm Standlee (22) in Wrigley Field. The Bears piled up 277 yards rushing. Shown are Cecil Isbell (17), Don Hutson (14) and Ray Riddick (5).

1944 NFL CHAMPIONSHIP GAME

Polo Grounds, New York

Sunday, December 17, 1944

- 46,016 -

GREEN BAY PACKERS	0	14	0	0	—	14
NEW YORK GIANTS	0	0	0	7	—	7

GB - Fritsch 2 run (Hutson kick)
GB - Fritsch 28 pass from Comp (Hutson kick)
NY - Cuff 1 run (Strong kick)

Defensively, the Packers could not have played a better first half of football. Offensively, they got the job done, posting 14 points before halftime, enough to withstand a second half Giants' touchdown and register a 14-7 victory over the host team from New York.

Unofficially, Green Bay held New York to 18 first-half yards on 20 plays. The Giants failed to advance beyond their own 35-yard line, didn't secure a first down, and punted seven times. The Packers, meanwhile, went to work on the first play of the second quarter. Two long runs, first by Joe Laws, and then Ted Fritsch, brought the ball to the Giants' one-yard line. Fritsch and Laws failed to gain on three plays. Finally, on fourth down, Fritsch bulled his way into the end zone and Don Hutson's conversion put Green Bay out front, 7-0.

Three possessions later, Irv Comp faced a third down at his own 46-yard line. He passed to Hutson for a gain of 24 yards and a first down to the Giants' 30-yard line. A run and incomplete pass followed before Comp collaborated with Fritsch for a 28-yard touchdown. A little more than a minute remained before halftime when Hutson's second point after gave Green Bay a 14-0 lead.

In the second half, Green Bay had trouble reaching opponent's territory, failing to drive deeper than the Giant 30. Fortunately, the defense allowed only one touchdown which came as the result of Comp's third interception, this one given up to Howie Livingston.

On the final play of the third quarter, ex-Packer Arnie Herber completed a 41-yard pass to Frank Liebel. Then, on the first play of the final period, Ward Cuff scored on a one-yard plunge. Ken Strong's point after cut the score to 14-7.

Laws and Paul Duhart ended the next two Giant drives with interceptions. New York's final possession saw Herber complete one of four passes for five yards. The Packers took over on downs, but never ran a play as time expired.

The Giants played much of the game without the services of the NFL's leading rusher, Bill Paschal, who had sprained an ankle at season's end. Laws set a league postseason record with three interceptions.

STATISTICS

	Packers	Giants
First Downs	11	10
Total Net Yards	237	199
Yards Rushing	49-163	30-85
Yards Passing	74	114
Att/Com/Int	11-3-3	22-8-4
Punts	10	10
Penalties	4-48	11-90
Fumbles/Lost	2-0	2-0

QUOTABLE

"If I ever play another game in New York, I'll jump off the Empire State Building."
Packers end **Don Hutson**.

"In the last analysis, the difference was in the lines."
Packers Coach **Curly Lambeau**.

AP/Wide World photo

Ted Fritsch (64) scores the first of two touchdowns in the Polo Grounds. Other players include: Charley Brock (29), and the Giants' Howard Livingston (24), Mel Hein (7), Frank Cope (36) and Len Younce (60).

1960 NFL CHAMPIONSHIP GAME

Franklin Field, Philadelphia

Monday, December 26, 1960

- 67,325 -

GREEN BAY PACKERS	3	3	0	7	—	13
PHILADELPHIA EAGLES	0	10	0	7	—	17

GB - FG (20) Hornung
GB - FG (23) Hornung
PE - McDonald 35 pass from Van Brocklin (Walston kick)
PE - FG (15) Walston
GB - McGee 7 pass from Starr (Hornung kick)
PE - Dean 5 run (Walston kick)

The 1960 championship epitomized a belief that many in the decade would come to embrace, the Packers never lost a game, time just ran out on them. Trailing 17-13, with one minute and 20 seconds remaining, Green Bay began a drive on its own 35. Bart Starr passed to Jim Taylor, then to Tom Moore. On third down, Taylor crashed for nine yards. Starr connected on two of his next three passes, the last to Gary Knafelc who reached the Philadelphia 22 with eight seconds remaining. Starr then tossed a short pass to Taylor who charged to the eight before being tackled by linebacker Chuck Bednarik. By the time Taylor got up, the game was over and the Eagles had escaped with a 17-13 win.

Statistically, the Packers dominated. They outgained the Eagles 401-296, outrushed them 223-99, and gave up one turnover to Philadelphia's three. That one turnover by the Packers, however, was costly.

After the Eagles had gone ahead 17-13 with 9:39 left in the game, Starr completed a pass to Max McGee who traveled beyond midfield, only to fumble. Bednarik recovered. As it turned out, the Packers had just two more opportunities, gaining all of eight yards on the first, and coming up short on the second.

Costly also, were a pair of fourth-down plays that failed. Bill Quinlan intercepted Norm Van Brocklin on the first play of the game at the Eagles' 14. Taylor and Hornung alternated and brought the ball to the six. On fourth-and-two, the team shunned a try at a field goal, and Taylor came up a yard short.

Likewise in the third quarter, trailing 10-6 and facing a fourth-and-one at the Eagles 25, the Packers opted to go for it. Taylor was held to no gain, snuffing out another scoring opportunity.

Green Bay's only touchdown came as the result of a fourth-down conversion. Out of punt formation, McGee scampered 35 yards. Eight plays later, Starr passed to McGee for a touchdown. Hornung's kick gave Green Bay its last lead, 13-10, early in the final quarter.

STATISTICS

	Packers	Eagles
First Downs	22	13
Total Net Yards	401	296
Yards Rushing	42-223	28-99
Yards Passing	178	204
Att/Com/Int	35-21-0	20-9-1
Punts	5	6
Penalties	4-27	0-0
Fumbles/Lost	1-1	3-2

QUOTABLE

"I didn't look for Starr to throw the home-run ball and was positioning myself accordingly. When I saw Taylor free, I just went after him. It sure felt good when I knew I had him. I rolled on him to kill a little more time and looked up at the clock. When I saw that zero, I knew we were in."

Eagles linebacker and center **Chuck Bednarik** *describing the final play of the game in which he tackled* **Jim Taylor** *eight yards short of a winning touchdown.*

Vernon Biever photo

Paul Hornung (5) tries to shake an Eagle for extra yardage in the 1960 NFL Championship Game. Hornung rushed for 61 yards on 11 carries.

1961 NFL CHAMPIONSHIP GAME

City Stadium, Green Bay

Sunday, December 31, 1961

- 39,029 -

NEW YORK GIANTS	0	0	0	0	—	0
GREEN BAY PACKERS	0	24	10	3	—	37

GB - Hornung 6 run (Hornung kick)
GB - Dowler 13 pass from Starr (Hornung kick)
GB - R. Kramer 14 pass from Starr (Hornung kick)
GB - FG (17) Hornung
GB - FG (22) Hornung
GB - R. Kramer 13 pass from Starr (Hornung kick)
GB - FG (19) Hornung

Paul Hornung scored a then single-game postseason record 19 points to lead his team to the biggest championship shutout since the infamous 73-0 count of 1940, as the Green Bay Packers overwhelmed the New York Giants 37-0 in the first playoff game on Green Bay soil. A City Stadium record crowd of 39,029 watched as the Green and Gold converted two interceptions into two touchdowns en route to a 24-point second quarter. On the day, the Packers forced five turnovers – four interceptions and one fumble.

Hornung opened the second quarter by capping an 11-play, 80-yard drive with a six-yard touchdown run. On the third play following the score, Ray Nitschke intercepted Y.A. Tittle. Six plays later, Starr hit Boyd Dowler from 13 yards out and Hornung added the extra point to put Green Bay up 14-0.

Hank Gremminger then duplicated Nitschke's feat, intercepting another third down Tittle pass. Starr used eight plays before hooking up with Ron Kramer on a 14-yard touchdown pass. Hornung's conversion put the Packers in front 21-0 with just under five minutes remaining in the half.

New York put together its longest drive of the game, moving 58 yards to the Packers' six-yard line. From there, on fourth down and needing a yard, Bob Gaiters failed to get the ball to Kyle Rote. Green Bay took over and, with Starr completing a 37-yard pass to Ron Kramer, moved in position for Hornung's 17-yard field goal which came on the final play of the half.

The Giants gave up the ball for a third time when Joe Morrison fumbled Boyd Dowler's second punt of the third quarter. Forrest Gregg recovered on the Giants' 22. Hornung kicked his second field goal four plays later and Green Bay went up 27-0.

Shortly thereafter, Joel Wells interfered with Willie Wood's right to a fair catch on a punt return. Aided by that 15-yard penalty the team moved in for another touchdown. Ron Kramer caught his second touchdown pass of the day to give his team a 34-0 lead.

Jess Whittenton's interception, followed shortly by Taylor's 33-yard run, moved the team to the Giant 12 where Hornung ended the day's scoring with a 19-yard field goal. Herb Adderley intercepted Tittle for a fourth time, on the second-to-last play of the game.

STATISTICS

	Packers	Giants
First Downs	19	6
Total Net Yards	345	130
Yards Rushing	44-181	14-31
Yards Passing	164	99
Att/Com/Int	19-10-0	29-10-4
Punts	5	5
Penalties	4-16	4-38
Fumbles/Lost	1-0	5-1

QUOTABLE

"The bigger the game, the better he plays."
Packers Coach **Vince Lombardi** *on MVP* **Paul Hornung**.

Green Bay Press-Gazette photo

Paul Hornung (5) opens the scoring in the 1961 NFL Championship Game with a six-yard run.

1962 NFL CHAMPIONSHIP GAME

Yankee Stadium, New York

Sunday, December 30, 1962

- 64,892 -

GREEN BAY PACKERS	3	7	3	3	— 16
NEW YORK GIANTS	0	0	7	0	— 7

GB - FG (26) J. Kramer
GB - Taylor 7 run (J. Kramer kick)
NY - Collier blocked punt recovery (Chandler kick)
GB - FG (29) J. Kramer
GB - FG (30) J. Kramer

In the brutal rematch of the title game of a year ago, the Green Bay Packers took advantage of two New York turnovers and ground out enough yardage rushing to register a 16-7 win over the Giants in Yankee Stadium. The game, witnessed by 64,892, remained up in the air until Jerry Kramer kicked his third field goal with just under two minutes left in the game.

The Packers did not wait long to get on the board. After a 58-yard Don Chandler punt ended the Giants' game-opening drive, Green Bay marched 60 yards in 10 plays to reach the New York 20-yard line. There, Kramer kicked his first field goal from 26 yards.

Y.A. Tittle had the Giants moving on the next drive until Dan Currie intercepted Tittle and returned the steal 30 yards. Kramer missed a 37-yard field goal on the last play of the opening quarter.

Late in the second quarter, Nitschke recovered a New York fumble at the Giant 28. On the next play, Paul Hornung hit Boyd Dowler with a 21-yard pass and then Jim Taylor stormed in from seven yards out. Kramer kicked the extra point to put the Packers in front 10-0.

The Giants arrived at their only points of the game midway through the third quarter. Max McGee was set to punt on fourth-and-

fifteen. Erich Barnes broke through to block the kick and rookie Jim Collier recovered for a touchdown. Chandler's conversion pulled the New Yorkers to within a field goal, 10-7.

McGee's next punt was fumbled by Sam Horner and Nitschke recovered his second fumble on the Giants' 42. Kramer kicked his second field goal five plays later, which put the Packers ahead 13-7.

New York came back behind Tittle's passing. He completed four for 31 yards and a fifth attempt, drew a 29-yard pass interference call on Willie Wood. Wood was ejected for arguing. The call put the Giants on the Green Bay 18. Two successive holding calls against the Giants, however, gave the Packers a reprieve, and Chandler was forced to punt on fourth-and-52.

Green Bay used the run effectively on its last possession of the game. Starr handed off to Taylor, Tom Moore, and Hornung and kept one himself, to eat up the clock with 10 rushing plays. The advance stalled at the Giant 27 and Kramer capped the scoring with a 30-yard field goal, 1:50 from the end of the game.

STATISTICS

	Packers	Giants
First Downs	18	18
Total Net Yards	244	291
Yards Rushing	46-148	26-94
Yards Passing	96	197
Att/Com/Int	22-10-0	41-18-1
Punts	6	7
Penalties	5-44	4-62
Fumbles/Lost	2-0	3-2

QUOTABLE

"I bit my tongue when I was tackled one time."
Packers fullback **Jim Taylor** *attesting to the rough-and-tumble nature of the game.*

Vernon Biever photo

Jim Taylor (31) scores from seven yards out in the second quarter to put Green Bay ahead of the Giants 10-0 at Yankee Stadium.

1965 NFL WESTERN CONFERENCE PLAYOFF GAME

Lambeau Field, Green Bay

Sunday, December 26, 1965

- 50,484 -

BALTIMORE COLTS	7	3	0	0	0	—	10
GREEN BAY PACKERS	0	0	7	3	3	—	13

BC - Shinnick 25 fumble return (Michaels kick)
BC - FG (15) Michaels
GB - Hornung 1 run (Chandler kick)
GB - FG (22) Chandler
GB - FG (25) Chandler

Because Green Bay could do no more than tie San Francisco on the final weekend of the season, the Packers and Colts wound up with identical 10-3-1 marks. A playoff game was played at Lambeau Field to break the tie. The trouble was, after four quarters the teams were still deadlocked 10-10. Don Chandler's 22-yard field goal with 1:58 left in regulation ensured that. It took a second Chandler three-pointer, this time from 25 yards out 13:39 into overtime, before the Packers were able to dispatch the Colts, 13-10.

Chandler's first field goal was controversial. To this day, Baltimore followers claim Chandler was wide. The kick went high above the uprights making it difficult to determine if the kick was accurate. The following year, the uprights were lengthened, in an attempt to avoid such situations.

Controversy, to a lesser degree, played a part in the drive which led to the tying field goal. Midway through the fourth quarter, Billy Ray Smith sacked Zeke Bratkowski for what would have been a seven-yard loss. But Smith, who argued otherwise, was penalized for unnecessary roughness giving Green Bay a first down on the Colts' 43. From there, the team moved in for Chandler's tying kick.

Baltimore had a chance to win the game in overtime on its second possession, but Lou Michaels missed a 47-yard field goal. Following that, Green Bay moved 62 yards in nine plays to set up Chandler's second, non-controversial, winning boot.

The Colts entered the game without quarterbacks John Unitas (knee) and backup Gary Cuozzo (dislocated shoulder). Halfback Tom Matte, who had quarterbacked at Ohio State, filled in. He completed only five passes but gained 57 yards rushing on 17 attempts.

Green Bay had Bart Starr at quarterback – for one play. He completed a pass to Bill Anderson who was hit by Lenny Lyles and fumbled. Don Shinnick scooped the ball up and returned 25 yards for a touchdown. Starr injured his ribs in an attempt to get to Shinnick.

Bratkowski replaced Starr. He completed 22 of 39 passes for 248 yards but was intercepted twice in the fourth quarter, killing potential game-winning drives.

The Packers missed two other scoring chances early. In the first quarter, Tom Brown recovered a Lenny Moore fumble at midfield, but, four plays later, Chandler missed a 47-yard field goal. Just before halftime, the Packers reached the Colts' one-yard line. On fourth down, Taylor fumbled and the Colts recovered.

STATISTICS

	Packers	Colts
First Downs	23	9
Total Net Yards	362	175
Yards Rushing	39-112	47-143
Yards Passing	250	32
Att/Com/Int	41-23-2	12-5-0
Punts	5	8
Penalties	4-40	3-59
Fumbles/Lost	3-2	1-1

QUOTABLE

"I'm shaking like a leaf . . . I still can't relax good."
Packers kicker **Don Chandler**.

Green Bay Press-Gazette photo

Paul Hornung (5) maneuvers behing the blocking of Jerry Kramer (64) and Fred (Fuzzy) Thurston (63) in Green Bay.

1965 NFL CHAMPIONSHIP GAME

Lambeau Field, Green Bay

Sunday, January 2, 1966

- 50,777 -

CLEVELAND BROWNS	9	3	0	0	—	12
GREEN BAY PACKERS	7	6	7	3	—	23

GB - Dale 47 pass from Starr (Chandler kick)
CB - Collins 17 pass from Ryan (snap fumbled, Groza pass failed)
CB - FG (24) Groza
GB - FG (15) Chandler
GB - FG (23) Chandler
CB - FG (28) Groza
GB - Hornung 13 run (Chandler kick)
GB - FG (29) Chandler

Green Bay weathered Cleveland's early charge, then shut the door on the Browns and used three long scoring drives in the second half to break open a close game and defeat the visitors 23-12 before 50,777 at Lambeau Field.

The Browns scored on their first two possessions. The first resulted in a touchdown when Frank Ryan passed to Gary Collins in the right corner of the end zone allowing the Browns to close the gap 7-6. The second culminated in a 24-yard field goal by Lou Groza which gave Cleveland a 9-7 lead.

Though two Chandler field goals then gave the Packers a 13-9 advantage, Lou Groza's second field goal kept the Browns close, 13-12 heading into halftime.

From then on, however, Cleveland was kept in check. The Packers held the Ohioans to 26 second-half yards, including a minus five in the fourth quarter. While the defense clicked, the offense rolled, putting together long drives of 11, 13, and eight plays. The first

two resulted in 10 points, while the third chewed up much of the remaining time in the fourth quarter.

Prior to the start of the game, three-and-a-half inches of snow was cleared from the field. Once the game got underway, the surface turned into a wet, muddy mess. The Packers ground game came alive in the quagmire, led by Paul Hornung who piled up 105 yard rushing on 18 carries and Jim Taylor, who had 96 on 27 trips. The Cleveland running attack, on the other hand, was shut down by the Green Bay defensive unit which held the NFL's leading rusher, Jim Brown, to 50 yards on 12 attempts. Surprisingly neither team fumbled.

Hornung capped the Packers' initial second-half possession with a 13-yard touchdown run. Chandler's extra point extended Green Bay's lead, 20-12. Henry Jordan then blocked Groza's third attempt at a field goal late in the third quarter. From that point, Cleveland ran just four more offensive plays. Herb Adderley intercepted Ryan late to kill any last minute Cleveland hopes. Chandler added an insurance field goal with 9:28 left in the game.

STATISTICS

	Packers	Browns
First Downs	21	8
Total Net Yards	332	161
Yards Rushing	47-204	18-64
Yards Passing	128	97
Att/Com/Int	19-10-1	18-8-2
Punts	3	4
Penalties	2-20	3-35
Fumbles/Lost	0-0	0-0

QUOTABLE

"I noticed that Ray Nitschke was keying on me. He's as tough as anybody is."
Browns running back **Jim Brown** *who was held to 50 yards rushing on 12 carries.*

Boyd Dowler (86) hauls in a pass in the 1965 NFL Championship Game.

Green Bay Press-Gazette photo

1966 NFL CHAMPIONSHIP GAME

Cotton Bowl, Dallas

Sunday, January 1, 1967

- 74,152 -

GREEN BAY PACKERS	14	7	7	6	— 34
DALLAS COWBOYS	14	3	3	7	— 27

GB - Pitts 17 pass from Starr (Chandler kick)
GB - Grabowski 18 fumble return (Chandler kick)
DC - Reeves 3 run (Villanueva kick)
DC - Perkins 23 run (Villanueva kick)
GB - Dale 51 pass from Starr (Chandler kick)
DC - FG (11) Villanueva
DC - FG (32) Villanueva
GB - Dowler 16 pass from Starr (Chandler kick)
GB - McGee 28 pass from Starr (Chandler kick blocked)
DC - Clarke 68 pass from Meredith (Villanueva kick)

Tom Brown intercepted Don Meredith in the end zone with 24 seconds remaining to preserve a 34-27 triumph over the Cowboys at the Cotton Bowl in Dallas. Brown's theft was the only one in a game which featured 59 pass attempts and 496 yards of passing. The Packers and Cowboys combined for 785 yards of offense in a lightning-fast game that saw the Packers never in arrears, thanks in part to a pair of first-quarter scores.

Brown's heroics atoned for a pass interference penalty called against him as he defended against Franke Clarke just five plays earlier. Dallas was given first down at the Green Bay two-yard line. Dallas was unable to penetrate the goal and on fourth down, Meredith's pass floated into Brown's arms.

Bart Starr passed to Elijah Pitts for a touchdown and Green Bay led 7-0. Green Bay doubled its point total when Don Chandler's subsequent kickoff was fumbled by Mel Renfro and Jim Grabowski returned it 18 yards for a touchdown.

The Cowboys struck back with touchdown drives of 65 and 59 yards. Starr kept pace by throwing 51 yards to Carroll Dale for a touchdown and a 21-14 lead. Danny Villanueva added an 11-yard field goal on the next drive to close to 21-17.

The Packers tried to maintain the pace in the second half, but Pitts fumbled on the team's opening advance and Warren Livingston recovered. Villanueva kicked a 32-yard field goal to narrow the margin, 21-20.

Starr, who completed 19 of 28 passes for 304 yards, sparked the Packers again. He tossed a 43-yard pass to Dale which ignited a drive that ended when Starr fired to Boyd Dowler for a 16-yard score. Midway through the fourth quarter, Starr and Max McGee combined to put the Packers on top 34-20.

Dallas was far from dead. Meredith threw to Clarke for a 68-yard score and the Cowboys were only seven points away from overtime. When Green Bay's last drive stalled and Chandler got off a 16-yard punt, the team from Texas was ready for a last-minute rally.

STATISTICS

	Packers	Cowboys
First Downs	19	23
Total Net Yards	367	418
Yards Rushing	24-102	40-187
Yards Passing	265	231
Att/Com/Int	28-19-0	31-15-1
Punts	4	4
Penalties	2-23	6-29
Fumbles/Lost	1-1	3-1

QUOTABLE

"Hayes (Bob) was on my left and Clarke was on my right. I think Meredith saw a white jersey and just threw it."
Packers safety **Tom Brown** describing his game-saving interception.

Vernon Biever photo

Boyd Dowler (86) flies over the Cowboys' Mike Gaechter (27) for a score in the 1966 title game. Dowler caught three passes for 49 yards.

1967 NFL SUPER BOWL I

Memorial Coliseum, Los Angeles

Sunday, January 15, 1967

- 74,152 -

GREEN BAY PACKERS	7	7	14	7	—	35
KANSAS CITY CHIEFS	0	10	0	0	—	10

GB - McGee 37 pass from Starr (Chandler kick)
KC - McClinton 7 pass from Dawson (Mercer kick)
GB - Taylor 14 run (Chandler kick)
KC - FG (31) Mercer
GB - Pitts 5 run (Chandler kick)
GB - McGee 13 pass from Starr (Chandler kick)
GB - Pitts 1 run (Chandler kick)

Outgained, but not outscored, the Packers smothered the Chiefs in the third quarter holding them to 12 yards while adding 14 points of their own to turn a tenuous 14-10 first half lead into a 28-10 advantage on the way to a 35-10 win over Kansas City in the first Super Bowl. The AFL representative Chiefs were 13 1/2 point underdogs, but trailed by just four at halftime and had outgained Green Bay 181-164. In the second half, however, the defensive front four, aided by linebacker Ray Nitschke, sacked the Chiefs' quarterbacks five times and Willie Wood intercepted Len Dawson to set up the touchdown that broke the game open.

The Packers scored first when Bart Starr hit Max McGee for a touchdown. McGee was called to service when Boyd Dowler injured his shoulder on the second play of the game.

A missed Mike Mercer field goal from the 40 was the only threat from the Chiefs until a six-play, 66-yard drive resulted in a seven-yard touchdown pass from Dawson to Curtis McClinton that tied the game at seven early in the second quarter. The Packers then drove 73 yards in 14 plays with Jim Taylor capping on a 14-yard touchdown run. Kansas City closed the gap with a 31-yard field goal by Mercer and entered halftime trailing by four.

A major reason the Chiefs were able to stay close was the passing of Dawson. The quarterback from Purdue was 11 of 15 for 152 yards at the half, having completed his last eight in a row.

That changed when his first pass of the second half was intercepted by Wood who returned it to the Kansas City five. Elijah Pitts scored from there and the Packers led 21-10.

Late in the period, Green Bay padded its lead when Starr found McGee a second time in the end zone. His 13-yard catch put the Packers ahead 28-10. Pitts added the final score midway through the fourth quarter on a one-yard run.

After Wood's interception, the Chiefs did not threaten. They failed to convert any of six third down situations and punted six times.

STATISTICS

	Packers	Chiefs
First Downs	21	17
Total Net Yards	358	239
Yards Rushing	33-130	19-72
Yards Passing	228	167
Att/Com/Int	28-16-1	32-17-1
Punts	4	7
Penalties	4-40	4-26
Fumbles/Lost	1-0	1-0

QUOTABLE

"I was sitting on the bench, enjoying the shady side of the field for a while, we normally sit on the sun side when we play in the Coliseum, and I heard somebody yell."

Wide receiver **Max McGee** on how he came to get some unexpected playing time.

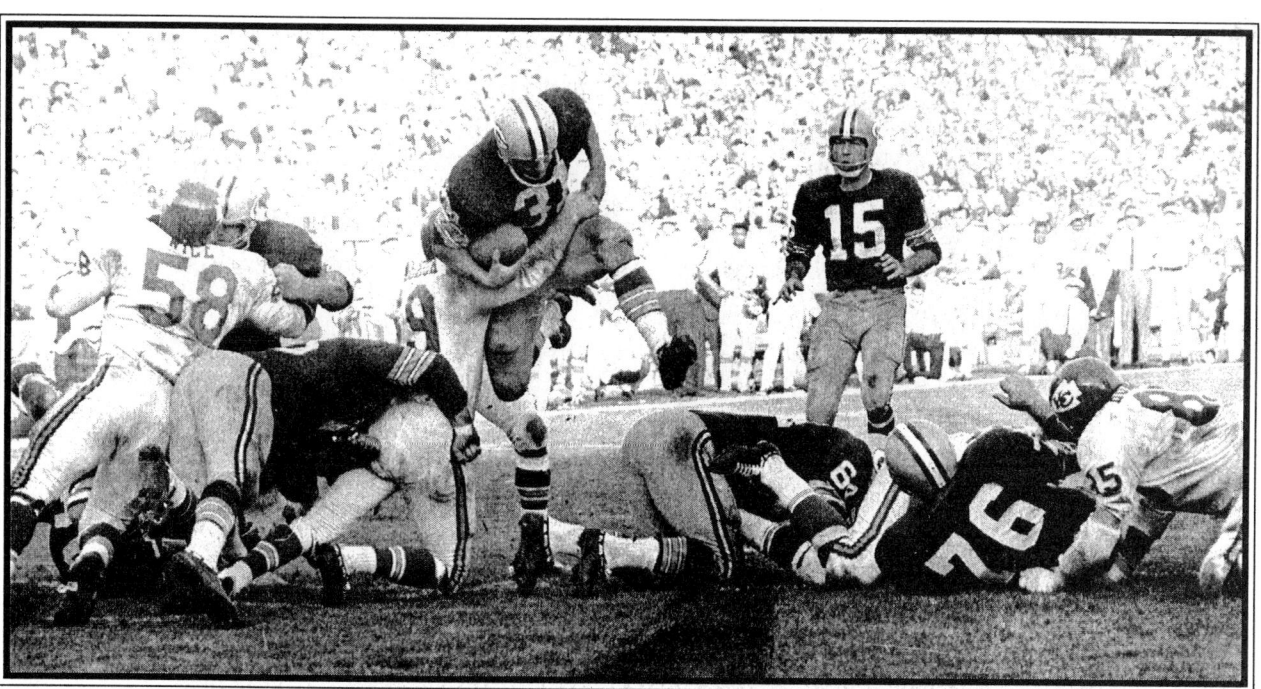

High-stepping Jim Taylor (31) is endzone bound in Super Bowl I.

1967 NFL WESTERN CONFERENCE PLAYOFF GAME

County Stadium, Milwaukee

Saturday, December 23, 1967

- 49,861 -

LOS ANGELES RAMS	7	0	0	0	—	7
GREEN BAY PACKERS	0	14	7	7	—	28

LA - Casey 29 pass from Gabriel (Gossett kick)
GB - Williams 46 run (Chandler kick)
GB - Dale 17 pass from Starr (Chandler kick)
GB - Mercein 6 run (Chandler kick)
GB - Williams 2 run (Chandler kick)

The Packers withstood three early turnovers, went on to score 14 second-quarter points, then held the Rams to 17 yards in the third period before defeating Los Angeles 28-7 at County Stadium. This was the same Rams team that had, two weeks earlier, come from behind to beat Green Bay 27-24 when Tony Guillory blocked Don Chandler's punt and Bernie Casey scored on a five-yard pass from Roman Gabriel in the closing minute. Gabriel, who had thrown three touchdowns passes in that affair, was kept in check on this particular day by Henry Jordan and Willie Davis who combined to sack him three times in the third period. Jordan, Davis, and Ron Kostelnik got to him five times overall.

Bart Starr, on the other hand, completed virtually everything he threw. He finished with 17 completions in 23 attempts for 222 yards and was sacked only once.

Initially neither team was able to move. The Packers opening drive, which reached the Rams' 32-yard line, ended when Chuck Mercein fumbled the ball away to Merlin Olsen. On the next five possessions, only one first down was picked up by either team. Then,

when the Packers started to jell, Carroll Dale lost the ball after crossing midfield on a nine-yard pass from Starr. That miscue led to points, as Los Angeles marched 52 yards for a touchdown.

Starr's only interception and Green Bay's third turnover occurred on the first play of the second quarter. Chuck Lamson engineered the theft and returned to the Packers' 10. Dave Robinson blocked Bruce Gossett's field goal try from 24 yards out.

The second quarter saw Green Bay turn its fortunes around. Tom Brown returned a punt 39 yards to the Ram 46. Travis Williams took over and raced 46 yards to tie the score 7-7. Starr then passed to Dale for a second touchdown to give Green Bay a 14-7 halftime lead.

While the Rams struggled in the third quarter, the Packers mounted two long drives. The first, a 13-play, 80-yard drive, was topped off by Mercein's six-yard scoring run. The second covered 73 yards and ended when Williams scored on a two-yard run early in the fourth quarter.

The Rams did reach the Green Bay four and 11 in the fourth quarter, but both threats ended on fourth-down incompletions.

STATISTICS

	Packers	Rams
First Downs	20	12
Total Net Yards	374	217
Yards Rushing	45-163	28-75
Yards Passing	211	142
Att/Com/Int	23-17-1	31-11-1
Punts	5	6
Penalties	7-44	3-25
Fumbles/Lost	3-3	0-0

QUOTABLE

"We've had some great battles and I guess you'd have to say we won this one."
Rams defensive end **Deacon Jones** on Packers tackle **Forrest Gregg**. Green Bay's offensive line gave up just one sack

Green Bay Press-Gazette photo

Henry Jordan (74) harasses Rams' quarterback Roman Gabriel (18) in Milwaukee. Willie Davis (87) moves in to help.

1967 NFL CHAMPIONSHIP GAME

Lambeau Field, Green Bay

Sunday, December 31, 1967

- 50,861 -

DALLAS COWBOYS	0	10	0	7	—	17
GREEN BAY PACKERS	7	7	0	7	—	21

GB - Dowler 8 pass from Starr (Chandler kick)
GB - Dowler 43 pass from Starr (Chandler kick)
DC - Andrie 7 fumble return (Villanueva kick)
DC - FG (21) Villanueva
DC - Rentzel 50 pass from Reeves (Villanueva kick)
GB - Starr 1 run (Chandler kick)

Bart Starr snuck into the end zone with 13 seconds left to give the Packers a 21-17 win over the Dallas Cowboys and a third straight NFL championship. Frozen fans, to the tune of 50,681 watched as Green Bay began a final drive on its own 32 with 4:50 remaining. Starr led the drive and was a perfect five-for-five for 59 yards. His last pass, a 19-yarder to Chuck Mercein, brought a first down at the Dallas 11. From there, Mercein reached the three and then Donny Anderson the one. Twice Anderson failed to gain before Starr, on third down, behind blocks from Ken Bowman and Jerry Kramer, pushed his way for the last yard, a score which brought home a fifth NFL championship in the past seven years.

At kickoff, the temperature had sunk to 13 below zero. Dallas, a team unused to the cold, managed just 42 yards in the first half while the Packers, as they had done a year ago, opened a 14-0 lead, this time on two Starr to Boyd Dowler touchdown passes. But, just as last year, the Cowboys came back, helped by Anderson's short punts and two Packer turnovers late in the second quarter. Starr from his own 26, was sacked for a loss of 19 yards and fumbled when hit by Willie Townes.

George Andrie recovered and returned for a seven-yard touchdown which cut the lead, 14-7. Shortly thereafter, Willie Wood could not handle a Danny Villanueva punt and Frank Clarke recovered at the Packers' 47. Four plays later, Villanueva kicked a 21-yard field goal and the Packers went into halftime with a slim four-point lead.

The Cowboys went ahead early in the fourth quarter. They reached the Packer 13 on their first second half drive, but Don Meredith fumbled and Herb Adderley recovered. On the next Dallas advance, Villanueva missed a 47-yard try at a field goal. The third possession was the charm. Running back Dan Reeves fooled the Packers' secondary by throwing a 50-yard option pass to Lance Rentzel to open the fourth quarter and give Dallas a 17-14 lead.

Green Bay had three more chances. They punted after the first, Chandler missed a 40-yard field goal on the second, before Starr and the Packers turned in the 12-play, 68-yard, game-winning drive.

STATISTICS

	Packers	Cowboys
First Downs	18	11
Total Net Yards	195	192
Yards Rushing	32-80	33-92
Yards Passing	115	100
Att/Com/Int	24-14-0	26-11-1
Punts	8	8
Penalties	2-10	7-58
Fumbles/Lost	3-2	3-1

QUOTABLE

"We took the gamble."
Packers Coach **Vince Lombardi**. *commenting on his team's final game-winning offensive play.*

"I never lost confidence. The game is 60 minutes long and I knew we were going to win somehow."
Linebacker **Ray Nitschke**.

John Biever photo

Bart Starr (15) scores with 13 seconds left to give Green Bay its third straight championship.

1968 NFL SUPER BOWL II

Orange Bowl, Miami

Sunday, January 14, 1968

- 75,546 -

GREEN BAY PACKERS	3	13	10	7	—	33
OAKLAND RAIDERS	0	7	0	7	—	14

GB - FG (39) Chandler
GB - FG (20) Chandler
GB - Dowler 62 pass from Starr (Chandler kick)
OR - Miller 23 pass from Lamonica (Blanda kick)
GB - FG (43) Chandler
GB - Anderson 2 run (Chandler kick)
GB - FG (31) Chandler
GB - Adderley 60 interception return (Chandler kick)
OR - Miller 23 pass from Lamonica (Blanda kick)

The 13-1 Oakland Raiders brought some impressive credentials to Super Bowl II. They had the AFL's number one passer in Daryle Lamonica, the leagues' number one scorer in George Blanda, and the number one defense, a defense which piled up 66 sacks. The Raiders did get to the Packers' quarterbacks four times but three turnovers, a missed field goal, and a breakdown in the secondary added up as the Packers beat the Raiders 33-14 in Vince Lombardi's last game as Packers' head coach.

Green Bay's first two drives resulted in Don Chandler field goals. Then, Bart Starr beat the blitz and threw a 62-yard touchdown pass to Boyd Dowler. Green Bay led 13-0 early in the second quarter.

Midway through the quarter, the Raiders drove 55 yards to the Packers' 23-yard line. There, Lamonica passed to Bill Miller in the end zone to cut the lead, 13-7.

Raider mistakes combined with Packer power then turned the tide in Green Bay's favor for good. On back-to-back possessions, Blanda missed a 47-yard field goal and Rodger Bird fumbled a fair catch. Dick Capp recovered the fumble and Chandler kicked his third field goal a short time later to give the Packers a 16-7 halftime lead.

While holding Oakland in check for the next quarter-and-a-half, the Packers went about opening a 26-point lead. Third down passes of 35 and 11 yards to Max McGee and Carroll Dale kept alive an 82-yard advance which ended with Donny Anderson's touchdown run. Chandler's fourth field goal on the last play of the third quarter put Green Bay up 26-7. Adderley finished the Packers' scoring with a 60-yard interception return early in the fourth quarter.

Lamonica and Miller combined once again for a touchdown with 9:13 remaining but, there was no further scoring despite the fact that the Raiders piled up 179 yards in the period.

STATISTICS

	Packers	Raiders
First Downs	19	16
Total Net Yards	322	293
Yards Rushing	41-160	20-107
Yards Passing	162	186
Att/Com/Int	24-13-0	34-15-1
Punts	6	6
Penalties	1-12	4-31
Fumbles/Lost	0-0	3-2

QUOTABLE

"I couldn't believe that nobody wanted me. I had to prove something to them – and to myself."
Packers and former Rams back **Ben Wilson** *tabbed as a starter over* **Chuck Mercein** *minutes before the game. Wilson led all runners with 62 yards on 17 carries.*

Green Bay Press-Gazette photo

Donny Anderson (44) finds daylight behind the blocking of Jerry Kramer (64) and Marv Fleming.

1972 NFC CONFERENCE PLAYOFF GAME

D.C. Stadium, Washington D.C.

Sunday, December 24, 1972

- 53,140 -

GREEN BAY PACKERS	0	3	0	0	—	3
WASHINGTON REDSKINS	0	10	0	6	—	16

GB - FG (17) Marcol
WR - Jefferson 32 pass from Kilmer (Knight kick)
WR - FG (42) Knight
WR - FG (35) Knight
WR - FG (46) Knight

The running game, so important to the Packers during the season, failed to materialize for all but a handful of plays and consequently Washington, no offensive power itself, was able to chip away, adding a field goal here and there before outlasting Green Bay 16-3 at D.C. Stadium in Washington. John Brockington, the NFL's ninth leading rusher with 1,027 yards, was held to nine yards on 13 carries - his longest run a mere three yards. MacArthur Lane picked up some of the slack with 56 yards on 14 tries but the team never was able to establish a consistent attack and paid the price.

Neither team moved in the opening quarter. Green Bay gained 31 yards and the Redskins 25. Washington, finally, was the first to penetrate enemy territory early in the second quarter, but Larry Brown, the NFL's second leading rusher, fumbled and Alden Roche recovered. Roche's effort led to a failed 47-yard field goal try by Chester Marcol.

Then, in the last six minutes before half, the teams scored 13 points. Scott Hunter completed four of five on a drive to the Redskin 10. After Hunter's third down pass failed, Marcol kicked a 17-yard field goal for a 3-0 lead. Six plays and 60 yards later, Washington led 7-3 after Billy Kilmer hit Roy Jefferson with a 32-yard touchdown pass. Curt Knight then kicked a 42-yard field goal 33 seconds before intermission. A 24-yard punt by Ron Widby from deep in Packer territory allowed the Redskins to get close enough for the attempt.

In the second half, the Packers reached enemy territory twice, both times in the fourth quarter. The first journey occurred after Knight's second field goal put Washington up 13-3. Hunter passed to Glass to the enemy's 46. Then the Redskins pushed Brockington back five yards and, after an incomplete pass on third down, Widby punted for the eighth time. The second came in the last two minutes, after Knight had put the game out of reach 16-3. Hunter passed to Lane for 22 yards and a first down on the Redskin 49. After an incompletion, Chris Hanburger intercepted Hunter and Charley Harraway then ran out the clock with two final runs.

STATISTICS

	Packers	Redskins
First Downs	10	13
Total Net Yards	211	232
Yards Rushing	29-78	36-138
Yards Passing	133	94
Att/Com/Int	24-12-1	14-7-0
Punts	8	6
Penalties	6-54	4-39
Fumbles/Lost	0-0	1-1

QUOTABLE

"I think too much has been made of that. The crucial plays they made defensively were out of their 4-3, when they stopped us down on the goal line and in the short yardage situation."
Packers Coach **Dan Devine** *on the significance of the Redskins use of a five-man defensive front.*

Vernon Biever photo

Scott Hunter (16) is sacked by Washington's Manny Sistrunk (64) and Ron McDole (79). Hunter completed 12 of 24 passes for 150 yards in the Packers' 16-3 loss.

1982 NFC FIRST-ROUND PLAYOFF GAME

Lambeau Field, Green Bay

Saturday, January 8, 1983

- 54,282 -

ST. LOUIS CARDINALS	3	6	0	7	—	16
GREEN BAY PACKERS	7	21	10	3	—	41

StL - FG (18) O'Donoghue
GB - Jefferson 60 pass from Dickey (Stenerud kick)
GB - Lofton 20 pass from Dickey (Stenerud kick)
GB - Ivery 2 run (Stenerud kick)
GB - Ivery 4 pass from Dickey (Stenerud kick)
StL - Tilley 5 pass from Lomax (O'Donoghue kick blocked)
GB - FG (46) Stenerud
GB - Jefferson 7 pass from Dickey (Stenerud kick)
GB - FG (34) Stenerud
StL - Schumann 18 pass from Lomax (O'Donoghue)

Green Bay made its first postseason appearance at Lambeau Field since the "Ice Bowl" and didn't disappoint as Lynn Dickey threw four touchdown passes to lead the Packers to a 41-16 rout of the St. Louis Cardinals. Four of Green Bay's first five possessions resulted in touchdowns. The team built a 41-9 edge before allowing St. Louis a consolation score in the fourth quarter.

Before catching fire offensively, the Packers had to shutdown the Cardinals, who threatened to open up a large lead. Nose tackle Terry Jones and linebacker George Cumby stopped Stump Mitchell on consecutive plays at the Green Bay one-yard line after the Cardinals had taken the opening kickoff and driven 59 yards. Neil O'Donoghue settled for an 18-yard field goal. After Gerry Ellis fumbled away the Packers' first chance with the ball, O'Donoghue attempted a 44-yarder but missed wide left.

The Packers took control. Dickey launched a 60-yard scoring strike to John Jefferson. After Gary Lewis blocked the Cardinals' third try at a field goal, the Packers marched 73 yards in eight plays. Dickey's 20-yard touchdown pass to James Lofton capped the drive and the Packers led 14-3.

Green Bay pressed on. Ivery's two yard run made it 21-3. Then, three plays later, Mark Murphy intercepted Neil Lomax at the Cardinal 34 and returned 22 yards. Shortly thereafter, Dickey found Ivery in the end zone with a four-yard pass for a 28-3 advantage.

Just before the half, Lomax hooked up with Tilley for a five-yard scoring pass. St. Louis trailed 28-9 after Lewis blocked the extra point attempt.

In the second half, the Cardinals reached the Green Bay 28-, 13-, 43-, 18-, and 32-yard lines, yet only scored seven points.

Dickey completed 17 of 23 passes for 260 yards and was not intercepted or sacked. Jefferson caught six passes for 148 yards.

STATISTICS

	Packers	Cardinals
First Downs	22	28
Total Net Yards	394	453
Yards Rushing	31-108	23-106
Yards Passing	286	347
Att/Com/Int	26-19-0	51-32-2
Punts	1	0
Penalties	5-35	6-78
Fumbles/Lost	1-1	3-2

QUOTABLE

"I think our passing game was pretty complex in their eyes. One of their starters went down and they had a lot of young guys in there. I think we kind of confused them. The ball was going everywhere."
Packers receiver **John Jefferson**.

Green Bay Press-Gazette photo

Gary Lewis (81) leaps to block Neil O'Donoghue's second-quarter field goal attempt. Lewis also blocked O'Donoghue's extra point try just before halftime.

1982 NFC SECOND-ROUND PLAYOFF GAME

Texas Stadium, Irving, Texas

Sunday, January 16, 1983

- 63,972 -

GREEN BAY PACKERS	0	7	6	13	—	26
DALLAS COWBOYS	6	14	3	14	—	37

- **DC -** FG (50) Septien
- **DC -** FG (34) Septien
- **GB -** Lofton 6 pass from Dickey (Stenerud kick)
- **DC -** Newsome 2 run (Septien kick)
- **DC -** Thurman 39 interception return (Septien kick)
- **GB -** FG (30) Stenerud
- **GB -** FG (33) Stenerud
- **DC -** FG (24) Septien
- **GB -** Lofton 71 run (Stenerud kick blocked)
- **DC -** Cosbie 7 pass from White (Septien kick)
- **GB -** Lee 22 interception return (Stenerud kick)
- **DC -** Newhouse 1 run (Septien kick)

A slow start, in addition to two fumbles and three interceptions, kept the Packers in a catchup situation and despite 363 second-half yards, they never got closer than four before falling 37-26 to the Dallas Cowboys at Texas Stadium.

Del Rodgers fumbled the kickoff from Rafael Septien following Septien's 50-yard field goal. Septien kicked another field goal as a result of the miscue and the Cowboys went up 6-0.

Green Bay gained its only lead of the game by driving 79 yards in nine plays in the second quarter. Lynn Dickey passed six yards to James Lofton and the Packers led 7-6.

The lead was short-lived. The Cowboys drove 13 plays for the go-ahead touchdown with 1:18 remaining in the half. Then Dickey suffered the first of his three interceptions at the hands of Dennis Thurman. Thurman returned 39 yards for a touchdown and a 20-7 bulge. Less than a minute later, Thurman intercepted Dickey to insure that the Packers would score no more before halftime.

Two Stenerud field goals closed the gap 20-13. Septien's third field goal pushed Dallas ahead 23-13. Dickey then hit Lofton with a 50-yard pass but Eddie Lee Ivery fumbled the ball away.

Lofton figured in the next score. He raced 71 yards on a reverse. Rod Hill blocked Stenerud's conversion try and the Packers trailed by four, 23-19.

Green Bay got that close one final time. After Dallas went ahead 30-19, Mark Lee intercepted Danny White and returned 22 yards for a touchdown. This cut the lead to 30-26, but the Cowboys promptly moved 74 yards to go up 37-26.

The Packers reached the Cowboys' 11 with just over a minute remaining, but Dickey threw a third interception.

STATISTICS

	Packers	Cowboys
First Downs	21	24
Total Net Yards	466	375
Yards Rushing	17-158	39-109
Yards Passing	308	266
Att/Com/Int	36-19-3	37-24-1
Punts	4	4
Penalties	3-35	5-30
Fumbles/Lost	4-2	1-1

QUOTABLE

"I'm going to go home, recuperate from the game and talk to my lawyer."
Defensive end **Mike Butler** *who would shortly become eligible for free agency.*

Vernon Biever photo

Randy Scott (55) and Rich Turner (75) charge into the Cowboys' backfield in an attempt to sack Danny White (11). White escaped and completed 23 of 36 passes for 225 yards and a touchdown.

1993 NFC WILD CARD GAME

Pontiac Silverdome, Pontiac, Michigan

Saturday, January 8, 1994

- 68,479 -

GREEN BAY PACKERS	0	7	14	7	—	28
DETROIT LIONS	3	7	7	7	—	24

DL - FG (47) Hanson
GB - Sharpe 12 pass from Favre (Jacke kick)
DL - Perriman 1 pass from Kramer (Hanson kick)
DL - Jenkins 15 interception return (Hanson kick)
GB - Sharpe 28 pass from Favre (Jacke kick)
GB - Teague 101 interception return (Jacke kick)
DL - Moore 5 run (Hanson kick)
GB - Sharpe 40 pass from Favre (Jacke kick)

Brett Favre's 40-yard touchdown pass to Sterling Sharpe with 55 seconds left lifted the Packers past the Detroit Lions 28-24 and gave Green Bay its first playoff win in 11 years. The duo clicked five times for 101 yards and three touchdowns and helped overcome a potent Lions' attack that dominated for 2-1/2 quarters and produced 410 yards.

A week earlier the Lions bounced the Packers 30-20 to capture the NFC Central Division title and earn the right to host the Packers in the first round of the playoffs. Late in the third quarter it appeared as if the Lions again had the Packers' number. Quarterback Erik Kramer, his team out front 17-14, had Detroit poised on Green Bay's five-yard line.

Enter free safety George Teague. The rookie stepped in front of a pass intended for Ty Hallock and dashed from one end zone to another, an NFL-postseason record 101 yards, to give the Packers a 21-17 lead.

The Lions then mounted an 89 scoring drive. Derrick Moore capped the effort from five yards out and Detroit led 24-21 with 8:27 remaining in the game.

The Packers began their game-winning drive 71 yards from paydirt with 2:26 left. Four plays later the visitors reached the Lions' 40-yard line where Favre, scrambling to his left, threw across his body and connected with a wide-open Sharpe who had eluded cornerback Kevin Scott in the end zone.

Favre, who was not sacked, completed 15 of 26 passes for 204 yards. His counterpart was 22 of 31 for 248 yards. Barry Sanders led all rushers with 169 yards on 27 carries.

STATISTICS

	Packers	Lions
First Downs	16	25
Total Net Yards	293	410
Yards Rushing	25-89	29-175
Yards Passing	204	235
Att/Com/HI	26-15-1	31-22-2
Punts	4	3
Penalties	6-49	5-35
Fumbles/Lost	2-0	2-0

QUOTABLE

"I think when Brett rolled left, the defense was reading his eyes and they drifted to their right. Brett looked over and made a great throw."
Packers receiver **Sterling Sharpe** on the game-winning pass.

"I don't want to say a hope and a prayer, but that's what it was."
Packers quarterback **Brett Favre** on the same play.

Vernon Biever photo

Lion Quarterback Krieg (17) is a split second away from Reggie White (92) getting another sack credit in the playoffs.

1993 NFC DIVISIONAL PLAYOFF GAME

Texas Stadium, Irving, Texas

Sunday, January 16, 1994

- 64,790 -

GREEN BAY PACKERS	3	0	7	7	—	17
DALLAS COWBOYS	0	17	7	3	—	27

GB - FG (30) Jacke
DC - Harper 25 pass from Aikman (Murray kick)
DC - FG (41) Murray
DC - Novacek 6 pass from Aikman (Murray kick)
DC - Irving 19 pass from Aikman (Murray kick)
GB - Brooks 13 pass from Favre (Jacke kick)
DC - FG (38) Murray
GB - Sharpe 29 pass from Favre (Jacke kick)

Had it not been for 18 seconds just before halftime, the Packers might have advanced to face the San Francisco 49ers in the NFC Championship Game. Instead, that short span and the 10 points it produced spurred on the Cowboys who went on to eliminate the Packers 27-17.

Eddie Murray's 41-yard field goal 23 seconds prior to halftime gave Dallas a 10-3 lead and some breathing room in a game that had been close to that point. Murray's subsequent kickoff was mishandled by Corey Harris. Joe Fishback recovered Harris' fumble and returned to the Green Bay 14. Two plays later, Troy Aikman hooked up with Jay Novacek for a touchdown and a 17-3 Dallas lead.

The Cowboys extended their advantage to 24-3 when Aikman combined with Michael Irving for a 19-yard score.

Still, Green Bay was far from dead. After falling behind by 21, Brett Favre went to work. He hit on five of seven passes for 75 yards in a drive that culminated with Robert Brooks snagging a 13-yard scoring toss. The Packers trailed 24-10 with a quarter remaining.

In that period, the Packers held Dallas to a field goal. But Favre struggled and was intercepted twice. He rebounded, however, to collaborate with Sterling Sharpe for the game's final touchdown with 22 seconds left in the quarter.

Green Bay, which boasted the second best defense in the league, found itself unable to contain Dallas quarterback Troy Aikman. Aikman shook off interceptions by LeRoy Butler and Terrell Buckley to throw for 302 yards and three touchdowns. He and Irvin clicked nine times for 126 yards and the score that put the game out of reach.

The Packers put up some big numbers through the air as well. Favre completed 28 of 45 passes for 331 yards. But the Packers' inability to run the football hurt as Darrell Thompson and Edgar Bennett were held to 31 yards on 13 carries.

STATISTICS

	Packers	Cowboys
First Downs	19	23
Total Net Yards	358	381
Yards Rushing	13-31	27-97
Yards Passing	327	284
Att/Com/Int	45-28-2	37-28-2
Punts	3	3
Penalties	4-30	5-39
Fumbles/Lost	3-2	2-1

QUOTABLE

"We weren't in awe, we respected the Cowboys, we went toe-to-toe, it's just tough. Troy Aikman's great. Emmitt Smith's great. We just can't lose the ball like we did and expect to win."
Packers Coach **Mike Holmgren.**

"We've got to get better--everybody's got to get better--and we can be like the Cowboys."
Packers quarterback **Brett Favre.**

Vernon Biever photo

The Dallas offensive line protected Troy Aikman as he accumulated over 300 yards in passing.

1994 NFC WILD CARD GAME

Lambeau Field, Green Bay, Wisconsin

Saturday, December 31, 1994

- 58,125 -

DETROIT LIONS	0	0	3	9	—	12
GREEN BAY PACKERS	7	3	3	3	—	16

GB - Levens 3 run (Jacke kick)
GB - FG (51) Jacke
DL - FG (38) Hanson
GB - FG (32) Jacke
DL - Perriman 3 pass from Krieg (Hanson kick)
GB - FG (28) Jacke
DL - safety (Hentrich ran out of end zone)

Barry carried a little football, on feet that were anything but slow. And everywhere that Barry went, the Packers' defense was sure to go.

Detroit halfback Barry Sanders may have arrived in Green Bay looking for running room, but by the time he left, he'd forgotten the meaning of the term "forward progress." Reggie White, Bryce Paup, George Koonce and others made sure of that, and in doing so, helped guide the Packers to a 16-12 win over the visiting Lions.

The Green and Gold defense held Sanders to minus-1 yard on 13 carries. Six times Packers defenders tossed the 1994 NFL rushing champion backwards for losses. And with Sanders in check, the visitors' attack never jelled and netted just one touchdown.

While the Packers attacked with abandon on defense, they played a conservative game offensively. With star receiver Sterling Sharpe out with a neck injury, Coach Holmgren played close to the vest. The result: the turnover-free Packers held the ball for nearly 15 minutes more than their counterparts and outgained them 336-171.

Green Bay got its only touchdown on its opening drive. Brett Favre directed a 14-play, 76-yard effort that culminated with Dorsey Levens scoring run. Chris Jacke tacked on three field goals, the last with 5:05 remaining, to account for the Packers' scoring.

Detroit mounted its last advance late in the fourth quarter. At the two minute warning, quarterback Dave Krieg had the Lions facing a third-and-eight from the Packers' 11-yard line. Paup sacked Krieg for a six-yard loss. Then on fourth down, Corey Harris' and George Teague's forced Herman Moore to go out of the end zone to snag Krieg's pass.

Packers punter Craig Hentrich killed the clock by running out of the end zone on the game's final play.

STATISTICS

	Packers	Lions
First Downs	18	9
Total Net Yards	336	171
Yards Rushing	35-81	15-(-4)
Yards Passing	255	175
Att/Com/HI	38-23-0	35-17-0
Punts	5	8
Penalties	3-35	4-30
Fumbles/Lost	0-0	1-0

QUOTABLE

"I think I saw something I've never seen in my five or six years in the NFL. I saw some good (hits) on Barry Sanders. No one ever gets good shots on him."
Packers safety **LeRoy Butler**.

"It was frustrating to the extent that we lost. We had a chance to win. You can toss all the stats out the window, especially in the playoffs."
Lions running back **Barry Sanders.**

Vernon Biever Photo

On this day, Barry Sanders saw nothing but green jerseys stacked in front of him. Sanders total game yardage was -1 yard in 13 carries.

1994 NFC DIVISIONAL PLAYOFF GAME

Texas Stadium, Irving, Texas

Sunday, January 8, 1995

- 64,745 -

GREEN BAY PACKERS	3	6	0	0	—	9
DALLAS COWBOYS	14	14	0	7	—	35

DC - Smith 5 run (Boniol kick)
GB - FG (50) Jacke
DC - Harper 94 pass from Aikman (Boniol kick)
DC - Thomas 1 run (Boniol kick)
GB - Bennett 1 run (Favre pass Chmura failed)
DC - Galbraith 1 pass from Aikman (Boniol kick)
DC - Thomas 2 run (Boniol kick)

For a second straight year the Packers faced the Cowboys in the second round of the playoffs. And for a second straight year the Packers saw their playoff hopes crash and burn in Texas Stadium.

From the minute Alvin Harper sprinted an NFL-record 94 yards to paydirt with a Troy Aikman pass, the Cowboys never looked back. The Sharpshooters added three more scores and the final tally read: Dallas 35, Green Bay 9.

The Cowboys simply had too many weapons. Even with Emmitt Smith spending most of the game on the sidelines with a sore hamstring (7 carries, 44 yards), the Cowboys were virtually unstoppable. Troy Aikman completed 23 of 30 passes for 337 yards. Three Dallas receivers: Jay Novacek (11 catches, 104 yards), Michael Irvin (6, 111), and Alvin Harper (2, 108), gained more than 100 yards receiving. Blair Thomas, who filled in for Smith, scored twice on the ground.

The Packers didn't find the going nearly so easy. Their only touchdown of the game occurred midway late in the second half.

Robert Brooks provided the big play with a 59-yard catch that placed the Packers at the Dallas 4-yard line. Four plays later, Edgar Bennett carried a yard for a touchdown. Brett Favre's pass to Mark Chmura for two points failed and Green Bay trailed 21-9.

The Packers reached enemy territory five times in the second half. Shortly after Corey Harris returned the second-half kickoff 51 yards to the Dallas 41, Favre was intercepted. Later, Chris Jacke missed a 37-yard field goal. A third and fourth trip beyond midfield ended on downs. Finally, with the game decided, reserve quarterback Mark Brunell passed to Reggie Johnson for an apparent touchdown but had the play called back because of an illegal formation. The game ended three plays later with the Packers on the Cowboys' 2-yard line.

STATISTICS

	Packers	Cowboys
First Downs	18	27
Total Net Yards	327	450
Yards Rushing	23-99	32-120
Yards Passing	228	330
Att/Com/Int	46-21-1	32-23-1
Punts	8	7
Penalties	8-43	7-46
Fumbles/Lost	0-0	1-1

QUOTABLE

"To get to this point last year was a great accomplishment. To get to this point again this year was kind of a side step."
Packers defensive lineman **Don Davey.**

"Our whole deal was to prevent the big play. Now that sounds foolish, but that was our plan coming in."
Packers Coach **Mike Holmgren.**

Al Fredrickson photo

The Packers offense failed to produce points and the Packers defense failed in preventing long pass completions to the Cowboys' tall receivers like Michael Irvin (88).

ALL-TIME POSTSEASON LEADERS

TOP SCORERS

Name	TDr	TDp	TDrt	PAT	FG	S	TP	G
Don Chandler	0	0	0	22/23	9/12	0	49	7
Paul Hornung	3	0	0	5/5	5/6	0	38	5
Boyd Dowler	0	5	0	0/0	0/0	0	30	10
Max McGee	0	4	0	0/0	0/0	0	24	7
Sterling Sharpe	0	4	0	0/0	0/0	0	24	2
Chris Jacke	0	0	0	7/7	5/8	0	22	4
Jan Stenerud	0	0	0	7/8	4/4	0	19	2
Carroll Dale	0	3	0	0/0	0/0	0	18	8
James Lofton	1	2	0	0/0	0/0	0	18	2
Elijah Pitts	2	1	0	0/0	0/0	0	18	6
Ted Fritsch	1	1	0	0/0	0/0	0	12	1
Milt Gantetnbein	0	2	0	0/0	0/0	0	12	3
Clarke Hinkle	2	0	0	0/0	0/1	0	12	4
Eddie Lee Ivery	1	1	0	0/0	0/0	0	12	2
John Jefferson	0	2	0	0/0	0/0	0	12	2
Ron Kramer	0	2	0	0/0	0/0	0	12	3
Jim Taylor	2	0	0	0/0	0/0	0	12	7
Travis Williams	2	0	0	0/0	0/0	0	12	3

TOP RUSHERS

Name	Att	Yds	Avg	LG	TD	G
Jim Taylor	145	505	3.5	33	2	7
Paul Hornung	67	323	4.8	34	3	5
Donny Anderson	48	165	3.4	18	1	5
Clarke Hinkle	59	161	2.7	—	2	4
Travis Williams	30	137	4.6	t46	2	3
Edgar Bennett	48	137	2.9	13	1	4
Elijah Pitts	29	123	4.2	32	2	6
Joe Laws	21	112	5.3	—	0	5
Eddie Lee Ivery	20	91	4.6	18	1	2
Tom Moore	22	79	3.6	14	0	5
Ben Wilson	21	75	3.6	13	0	3

TOP PASSERS

Name	Att	Com	Yds	Pct	TD	In	Rate	G
Bart Starr	213	130	1,753	61.03	15	3	104.8	10
Brett Favre	144	84	1,008	58.33	5	4	79.9	4
Lynn Dickey	59	36	592	61.02	5	3	101.8	2
Arnie Herber	37	16	322	43.24	4	4	70.8	3
Zeke Bratkowski	40	22	248	55.00	0	2	52.9	5
Cecil Isbell	26	13	235	50.00	2	1	91.0	3
Scott Hunter	24	12	150	50.00	0	1	52.4	1

Herb Adderley (26) guards Jack Snow (84) in the 1967 NFL Western Conference playoff game.

Green Bay Press-Gazette photo

ALL-TIME POSTSEASON LEADERS

TOP RECEIVERS

Name	No	Yds	Avg	LG	TD	G
Boyd Dowler	30	440	14.7	t62	5	10
Carroll Dale	29	534	18.4	t51	3	8
Edgar Bennett	20	116	5.8	18	0	4
Robert Brooks	19	266	14.0	59	1	4
Jim Taylor	19	137	7.2	20	0	7
Max McGee	12	233	19.4	t37	4	7
Marv Fleming	12	137	11.4	24	0	7
Paul Hornung	12	111	9.3	26	0	5
Sterling Sharpe	11	229	20.8	48	4	2
Don Hutson	10	162	16.2	t43	1	5
Paul Coffman	9	111	12.3	23	0	2
John Jefferson	8	188	23.5	t60	2	2
James Lofton	8	161	20.1	50	2	2
Gerry Ellis	8	99	12.4	31	0	2
Donny Anderson	8	92	11.5	25	0	5
Anthony Morgan	8	85	10.6	14	0	2
Bill Anderson	8	78	9.8	18	0	4

100-YARD RECEIVING GAMES

Name	No	Yds	Avg	LG	TD	Date
Carroll Dale	5	128	25.6	t51	1	1-1-67
Max McGee	7	138	19.7	t37	2	1-15-67
Carroll Dale	6	109	18.2	48	1	12-23-67
John Jefferson	6	148	24.7	t60	2	1-8-83
James Lofton	5	109	21.8	50	1	1-16-83
Sterling Sharpe	5	101	20.2	t40	3	1-8-94
Sterling Sharpe	6	128	21.3	48	1	1-16-94
Robert Brooks	8	138	17.3	59	0	1-8-95

100-YARD RUSHING GAMES

Name	Att	Yds	Avg	LG	TD	Date
Jim Taylor	24	105	4.4	16	0	12-26-60
Paul Hornung	18	105	5.8	34	1	1-2-66

300-YARD PASSING GAMES

Name	Att	Com	Yds	Pct	TD	In	Tk/Yds	Date
Bart Starr	28	19	304	67.9	4	0	5/39	1-1-67
Lynn Dickey	36	19	332	52.8	1	3	2/15	1-16-83
Brett Favre	45	28	331	62.2	2	2	2/4	1-16-94

Green Bay Press-Gazette photo

Sterling Sharpe (84) in '94 seemed to be setting a record of some sort upon every catch.

ALL-TIME INDIVIDUAL RECORDS

SERVICE

Most Games, Career
- 11 Ray Nitschke
- 10 Willie Davis
  Boyd Dowler
  Forrest Gregg
  Henry Jordan
  Bob Skoronski
  Bart Starr
  Fred (Fuzzy) Thurston
  Willie Wood

SCORING

Most Points, Career
- 49 Don Chandler (0 TD, 22 PAT, 9 FG)
- 38 Paul Hornung (3 TD, 5 PAT, 5 FG)

Most Points, Game
- 19 Paul Hornung, vs. Giants, Dec. 31, 1961
- 18 Sterling Sharpe, vs. Lions, Jan. 8, 1994

Most Touchdowns, Career
- 5 Boyd Dowler (10 games)
- 4 Max McGee (7 games)
  Sterling Sharpe (2 games)

Most Touchdowns, Game
- 3 Sterling Sharpe, vs. Lions, Jan. 8, 1994
- 2 Ted Fritsch, vs. Giants, Dec. 17, 1944
  Ron Kramer, vs. Giants, Dec. 31, 1961
  Max McGee, vs. Chiefs, Jan. 15, 1967
  Elijah Pitts, vs. Chiefs, Jan. 15, 1967
  Travis Williams, vs. Rams, Dec. 23, 1967
  Boyd Dowler, vs. Cowbooys, Dec. 31, 1967
  Eddie Lee Ivery, vs. Cardinals, Jan. 8, 1983
  John Jefferson, vs. Cardinals, Jan. 8, 1983
  James Lofton, vs. Cowboys, Jan. 16, 1983

Most Consecutive Games Scoring Touchdowns
- 2 Paul Hornung, 1965
  Carroll Dale, 1965-66
  Max McGee, 1966
  Elijah Pitts, 1966
  Boyd Dowler, 1967
  James Lofton, 1983
  Sterling Sharpe, 1993

Most Points After Touchdown, Career
- 22 Don Chandler (7 games)
- 7 Jan Stenerud (2 games)
  Chris Jacke (4 games)

Most Points After Touchdown, Game
- 5 Don Chandler, vs. Chiefs, Jan. 15, 1967
  Jan Stenerud, vs. Cardinals, Jan. 8, 1983
- 4 Paul Hornung, vs. Giants, Dec. 31, 1961
  Don Chandler, vs. Cowboys, Jan. 1, 1967
  Don Chandler, vs. Rams, Dec. 23, 1967
  Chris Jacke, vs. Lions, Jan. 8, 1994

Most Points After Touchdown, No Misses, Career
- 7 Chris Jacke (4 games)
- 5 Paul (Tiny) Engebretsen (3 games)
  Paul Horning (5 games)

Most Field Goals Attempted, Career
- 12 Don Chandler (7 games)
- 8 Chris Jacke (4 games)

Most Field Goals Attempted, Game
- 5 Jerry Kramer, vs. Giants, Dec. 30, 1962
- 4 Don Chandler, vs. Raiders, Jan. 14, 1968
  Chris Jacke, vs. Lions, Dec. 31, 1994

Most Field Goals, Career
- 9 Don Chandler (7 games)
- 5 Paul Hornung (5 games)
  Chris Jacke (4 games)

Most Field Goals, Game
- 4 Don Chandler, vs. Raiders, Jan. 14, 1968
- 3 Paul Hornung, vs. Giants, Dec. 31, 1961
  Jerry Kramer, vs. Giants, Dec. 30, 1962
  Don Chandler, vs. Browns, Jan. 2, 1966
  Chris Jacke, vs. Lions, Dec. 31, 1994

Most Consecutive Field Goals
- 5 Don Chandler, 1965
- 4 Don Chandler, 1967
  Jan Stenerud, 1983
  Chris Jacke, 1994

Longest Field Goal
- 51 Chris Jacke, vs. Lions, Dec. 31, 1994
- 50 Chris Jacke, vs. Cowboys, Jan. 8, 1995

Highest Field Goal Percentage, Career
(minimum 4 attempts)
- 100.00 Jan Stenerud (4-4) (2 games)
- 83.33 Paul Hornung (5-6) (5 games)

RUSHING

Most Attempts, Career
- 145 Jim Taylor (7 games)
- 67 Paul Hornung (5 games)

Most Attempts, Game
- 31 Jim Taylor, vs. Giants, Dec. 30, 1962
- 27 Jim Taylor, vs. Browns, Jan. 2, 1966

Most Yards Gained, Career
- 505 Jim Taylor (7 games)
- 323 Paul Hornung (5 games)

Most Yards Gained, Game
- 105 Jim Taylor, vs. Eagles, Dec. 26, 1960
  Paul Hornung, vs. Browns, Jan. 2, 1966
- 96 Jim Taylor, vs. Browns, Jan. 2, 1966

Longest Run From Scrimmage
- 71 James Lofton, vs. Cowboys, Jan. 16, 1983
- 46 Travis Williams, vs. Rams, Dec. 23, 1967

Highest Average Gain, Career (minimum 20 attempts)
- 5.33 Joe Laws (21-112) (4 games)
- 4.82 Paul Hornung (67-323) (5 games)

Highest Average Gain, Game (minimum 10 attempts)
- 5.83 Paul Hornung, vs. Browns, Jan. 2, 1966 (18-105)
- 5.55 Paul Hornung, vs. Eagles, Dec. 26, 1960 (11-61)

Most Touchdowns, Rushing, Career
- 3 Paul Hornung (5 games)
- 2 Clarke Hinkle (4 games)
  Jim Taylor (7 games)
  Elijah Pitts (6 games)
  Travis Williams (3 games)

Most Touchdowns, Rushing, Game
- 2 Elijah Pitts, vs. Chiefs, Jan. 15, 1967
  Travis Williams, vs. Rams, Dec. 23, 1967

Most Consecutive Games, Rushing for Touchdowns
- 2 Paul Hornung, 1965

PASSING

Highest Pass Rating, Career (Minimum 40 attempts)
104.8　Bart Starr (10 games)
101.8　Lynn Dickey (2 games)
Most Passes Attempted, Career
213　Bart Starr (10 games)
144　Brett Favre (4 games)
Most Passes Attempted, Game
45　Brett Favre, vs. Cowboys, Jan. 16, 1994
39　Zeke Bratkowski, vs. Colts, Dec. 26, 1965
Most Passes Completed, Career
130　Bart Starr (10 games)
84　Brett Favre (4 games)
Most Passes Completed, Game
28　Brett Favre, vs. Cowboys, Jan. 16, 1994
23　Brett Favre, vs. Lions, Dec. 31, 1994
**Highest Completion Percentage, Career
(minimum 40 attempts)**
61.03　Bart Starr (130-213) (10 games)
61.02　Lynn Dickey (36-59) (2 games)
**Highest Completion Percentage, Game
(minimum 20 attempts)**
73.91　Bart Starr, vs. Rams, Dec. 23, 1967 (17-23)
　　　　Lynn Dickey, vs. Cardinals, Jan. 8, 1983 (17-23)
69.57　Bart Starr, vs. Chiefs, Jan. 15, 1967 (16-23)
Most Yards Gained, Career
1,753　Bart Starr (10 games)
1,008　Brett Favre (4 games)
Most Yards Gained, Game
332　Lynn Dickey, vs. Cowboys, Jan. 16, 1983
331　Brett Favre, vs. Cowboys, Jan. 16, 1994
Longest Pass Completion
66　Cecil Isbell to Wayland Becker, vs. Giants, Dec. 11, 1938
62　Bart Starr to Boyd Dowler, vs. Raiders, Jan. 14, 1968
Most Consecutive Completions
9　Brett Favre, vs. Cowboys, Jan. 16, 1994 (3) and vs. Lions, Dec. 31, 1994 (6)
7　Bart Starr, vs. Cowboys, Jan. 1, 1967
　　Bart Starr, vs. Cowboys, Dec. 31, 1967 (5) and vs. Raiders, Jan. 14, 1968 (2)
　　Brett Favre, vs. Lions, Dec. 31, 1994 (5) and vs. Cowboys, Jan. 16, 1995 (2)
**Highest Average Gain, Career
(minimum 40 attempts)**
10.03　Lynn Dickey (59-592) (2 games)
8.23　Bart Starr (213-1,753) (10 games)
**Highest Average Gain, Game
(minimum 20 attempts)**
11.30　Lynn Dickey, vs. Cardinals, Jan. 8, 1983 (23-260)
10.87　Bart Starr, vs. Chiefs, Jan. 15, 1967 (23-250)
Most Touchdowns Passes, Career
15　Bart Starr (10 games)
5　Lynn Dickey (2 games)
　　Brett Favre (4 games)
Most Touchdown Passes, Game
4　Bart Starr, vs. Cowboys, Jan. 1, 1967
　　Lynn Dickey, vs. Cardinals, Jan. 8, 1983
3　Bart Starr, vs. Giants, Dec. 31, 1961
　　Brett Favre, vs. Lions, Jan. 8, 1994
Most Consecutive Games, Touchdown Passes
6　Bart Starr, 1965-67
3　Arnie Herber, 1936-39
**Lowest Percentage, Passes Had Intercepted, Career
(minimum 40 attempts)**
1.41　Bart Starr (213-3) (10 games)
2.77　Brett Favre (144-4) (4 games)
Most Attempts, No Interceptions, Game
38　Brett Favre, vs. Lions, Dec. 31, 1994
34　Bart Starr, vs. Eagles, Dec. 26, 1960
Most Passes Had Intecepted, Career
4　Arnie Herber (3 games)
　　Brett Favre (4 games)
3　Irv Comp (1 game)
　　Bart Starr (10 games)
　　Lynn Dickey (2 games)

Most Passes Had Intercepted, Game
3　Arnie Herber, vs. Giants, Dec. 10, 1939
　　Irv Comp, vs. Giants, Dec. 17, 1944
　　Lynn Dickey, vs. Cowboys, Jan. 16, 1983
2　Zeke Bratkowski, vs. Colts, Dec. 26, 1965
　　Brett Favre, vs. Cowboys, Jan. 16, 1994

PASS RECEIVING

Most Receptions, Career
30　Boyd Dowler (10 games)
29　Carroll Dale (8 games)
Most Receptions, Game
9　Edgar Bennett, vs. Cowboys, Jan. 16, 1994
8　Bill Anderson, vs. Colts, Dec. 26, 1965
　　Robert Brooks, vs. Cowboys, Jan. 8, 1995
Most Consecutive Games, Pass Receptions
8　Carroll Dale, 1965-72
6　Boyd Dowler, 1960-66
Most Yards Gained, Pass Receptions, Career
534　Carroll Dale (8 games)
440　Boyd Dowler (10 games)
Most Yards Gained, Pass Receptions, Game
148　John Jefferson, vs. Cardinals, Jan. 8, 1983
138　Max McGee, vs. Chiefs, Jan. 15, 1967
　　　Robert Brooks, vs. Cowboys, Jan. 8, 1995
Most Games, 100 or More Yards Pass Receiving, Career
2　Carroll Dale (8 games)
　　Sterling Sharpe (2 games)
1　Max McGee (7 games)
　　John Jefferson (2 games)
　　James Lofton (2 games)
　　Robert Brooks (4 games)
Longest Reception
66　Wayland Becker, vs. Giants, Dec. 11, 1938
62　Boyd Dowler, vs. Raiders, Jan. 14, 1968
Highest Average Gain, Career (minimum 10 receptions)
20.82　Sterling Sharpe (11-229) (2 games)
19.42　Max McGee (12-233) (7 games)
Highest Average Gain, Game (minimum 3 receptions)
25.60　Carroll Dale, vs. Cowboys, Jan. 1, 1967 (5-128)
25.00　Ed Frutig, vs. Bears, Dec. 14, 1941 (3-75)
Most Touchdowns, Pass Receptions, Career
5　Boyd Dowler (10 games)
4　Max McGee (7 games)
　　Sterling Sharpe (2 games)
Most Touchdowns, Pass Receptions, Game
3　Sterling Sharpe, vs. Lions, Jan. 8, 1994
2　Ron Kramer, vs. Giants, Dec. 31, 1961
　　Max McGee, vs. Chiefs, Jan. 15, 1967
　　Boyd Dowler, vs. Cowboys, Dec. 31, 1967
　　John Jefferson, vs. Cardinals, Jan. 8, 1983
Most Consecutive Games, Touchdowns
2　Carroll Dale, 1965-66
　　Max McGee, 1967
　　Boyd Dowler, 1967
　　James Lofton, 1983
　　Sterling Sharpe, 1993

INTERCEPTIONS

Most Interceptions, Career
4　Herb Adderley (9 games)
3　Joe Laws (4 games)
Most Interceptions, Game
3　Joe Laws, vs. Giants, Dec. 17, 1944
2　Charley Brock, vs. Giants, Dec. 10, 1939
Most Consecutive Games, Interceptions
2　Herb Adderley, 1967
　　Terrell Buckley, 1993
Longest Return
101　George Teague, vs. Lions, Jan. 8, 1994
60　Herb Adderley, vs. Raiders, Jan. 14, 1968
Most Touchdowns, Career
1　Herb Adderley, vs. Raiders, Jan. 14, 1968
　　Mark Lee, vs. Cowboys, Jan. 16, 1983
　　George Teague, vs. Lions, Jan. 8, 1994

PUNTING

Most Punts, Career
20   Donny Anderson (4 games)
15   Don Chandler (7 games)
Most Punts, Game
8   Donny Anderson, vs. Cowboys, Dec. 31, 1967
    Ron Widby, vs. Redskins, Dec. 24, 1972
7   Clarke Hinkle, vs. Redskins, Dec. 13, 1936
Longest Punt
62   Craig Hentrich, vs. Cowboys, Jan. 8, 1995
55   Max McGee, vs. Eagles, Dec. 26, 1960
Highest Average, Game (minimum 4 punts)
45.20   Max McGee, vs. Eagles, Dec. 26, 1960 (5-226)
44.00   Craig Hentrich, vs. Cowboys, Jan. 8, 1995 (4-176)

PUNT RETURNS

Most Punt Returns, Career
19   Willie Wood (10 games)
9   Robert Brooks (4 games)
Most Punt Returns, Game
5   Willie Wood, vs. Raiders, Jan. 14, 1968
4   Irv Comp, vs. Giants, De. 17, 1944
    Willie Wood, vs. Cowboys, Dec. 31, 1967
Most Yards Gained, Career
140   Robert Brooks (4 games)
74   Willie Wood (10 games)
Most Yards Gained, Game
59   Robert Brooks, vs. Cowboys, Jan. 16, 1994
55   Irv Comp, vs. Giants, Dec. 17, 1944
Longest Return
43   Robert Brooks, vs. Cowboys, Jan. 16, 1994
39   Tom Brown, vs. Rams, Dec. 23, 1967

KICKOFF RETURNS

Most Kickoff Returns, Career
11   Corey Harris (4 games)
9   Del Rodgers (2 games)
Most Kickoff Returns, Game
7   Del Rodgers, vs. Cowboys, Jan. 16, 1983
5   Corey Harris, vs. Cowboys, Jan. 8, 1995
Most Yards Gained, Career
253   Corey Harris (4 games)
195   Del Rodgers (2 games)
Most Yards Gained, Game
148   Del Rodgers, vs. Cowboys, Jan. 16, 1983
132   Corey Harris, vs. Cowboys, Jan. 8, 1995
Longest Return
51   Corey Harris, vs. Cowboys, Jan. 8, 1995
45   Corey Harris, vs. Lions, Jan. 8, 1994

FUMBLES

Most Fumbles, Career
3   Jim Taylor (7 games)
2   Arnie Herber (3 games)
    Paul Hornung (5 games)
    Del Rodgers (2 games)
    Brett Favre (4 games)
    Corey Harris (4 games)
Most Fumbles, Game
2   Jim Taylor, vs. Giants, Dec. 30, 1962
    Del Rodgers, vs. Cowboys, Jan. 16, 1983
    Corey Harris, vs. Cowboys, Jan. 16, 1994
Most Opponents' Fumbles Recovered, Career and Game
2   Ray Nitschke, vs. Giants, Dec. 30, 1962
Longest Return
18   Jim Grabowski, vs. Cowboys, Jan. 1, 1967
16   Dave Robinson, vs. Raiders, Jan. 14, 1968

COMBINED NET YARDS GAINED

Most Attempts, Career
165   Jim Taylor (7 games)
80   Paul Hornung (5 games)
Most Attempts, Game
34   Jim Taylor, vs. Giants, Dec. 30, 1962
30   Jim Taylor, vs. Eagles, Dec. 26, 1960
Most Yards Gained, Career
642   Jim Taylor (7 games)
534   Carroll Dale (8 games)
Most Yards Gained, Game
190   Del Rodgers, vs. Cowboys, Jan. 16, 1983
184   Robert Brooks, vs. Cowboys, Jan. 8, 1995

SACKS

Most Sacks, Career
3.0   Tony Bennett (2 games)
    Bryce Paup (4 games)
    Reggie White (4 games)
2.0   Sean Jones (2 games)
Most Sacks, Game
2.0   Reggie White, vs. Lions, Jan. 8, 1994
    Bryce Paup, vs. Lions, Dec. 31, 1994
1.5   Ezra Johnson, vs. Cardinals, Jan. 8, 1983
    Tony Bennett, vs. Lions, Jan. 8, 1994
    Tony Bennett, vs. Cowboys, Jan. 16, 1994

Green Bay Press-Gazette photo

James Lofton (80) and John Jefferson (83) celebrate during a first-round playoff game with the St. Louis Cardinals in 1982.

ALL-TIME
TEAM RECORDS
(Postseason)

SCORING

Most Points, Game
41 vs. Cardinals, Jan. 8, 1983
37 vs. Giants, Dec. 31, 1961
Fewest Points, Game
3 vs. Redskins, Dec. 24, 1972
9 vs. Cowboys, Jan. 8, 1995
Most Points, Both Teams, Game
63 GB (26) vs. Cowboys (37), Jan. 16, 1983
61 GB (34) vs. Cowboys (27), Jan. 1, 1967
Fewest Points, Both Teams, Game
19 GB (3) vs. Redskins (16), Dec. 24, 1972
21 GB (14) vs. Giants (7), Dec. 17, 1944
Largest Margin of Victory
37 vs. Giants, Dec. 31, 1961
27 vs. Giants, Dec. 10, 1939
Most Points Overcome to Win Game
10 vs. Colts, Dec. 26, 1965 (trailed 10-0, won 13-10)
vs. Lions, Jan. 8, 1994 (trailed 17-7, won 28-24)
7 vs. Rams, Dec. 23, 1967 (trailed 7-0, won 28-7)
Most Points, First Half
28 vs. Cardinals, Jan. 8, 1983
24 vs. Giants, Dec. 31, 1961
Most Points, Second Half
21 vs. Chiefs, Jan. 15, 1967
vs. Lions, Jan. 8, 1994
20 vs. Giants, Dec. 10, 1939
Most Points, Each Quarter
1st: 14 vs. Cowboys, Jan. 1, 1967
2nd: 24 vs. Giants, Dec. 31, 1961
3rd: 14 vs. Chiefs, Jan. 15, 1967
14 vs. Lions, Jan. 8, 1994
4th: 13 vs. Cowboys, Jan. 16, 1983
Most Touchdowns, Game
5 vs. Cowboys, Jan. 1, 1967
vs. Chiefs, Jan. 15, 1967
vs. Cardinals, Jan. 8, 1983
4 vs. Giants, Dec. 31, 1961
vs. Rams, Dec. 23, 1967
vs. Lions, Jan. 8, 1994
Most Touchdowns, Both Teams, Game
8 GB (5) vs. Cowboys (3), Jan. 1, 1967
7 GB (5) vs. Cardinals (2), Jan. 8, 1983
GB (3) vs. Cowboys (4), Jan. 16, 1983
GB (4) vs. Lions (3), Jan. 8, 1994
Fewest Touchdowns, Both Teams, Game
1 GB (0) vs. Redskins (1), Dec. 24, 1972
2 GB (1) vs. Giants (1), Dec. 30, 1962
GB (1) vs. Colts (1), Dec. 26, 1965
GB (1) vs. Lions (1), Dec. 31, 1994
Most Points After Touchdown, Game
5 vs. Chiefs, Jan. 15, 1967
vs. Cardinals, Jan. 8, 1983
4 vs. Giants, Dec. 31, 1967
vs. Cowboys, Jan. 1, 1967
vs. Rams, Dec. 23, 1967
vs. Lions, Jan. 8, 1994
Most Points After Touchdown, Both Teams, Game
7 GB (4) vs. Cowboys (3), Jan. 1, 1967
GB (4) vs. Lions (3), Jan. 8, 1994
6 GB (5) vs. Chiefs (1), Jan. 15, 1967
GB (5) vs. Cardinals (1), Jan. 8, 1983
GB (2) vs. Cowboys (4), Jan. 16, 1983

Fewest Points After Touchdown, Both Teams, Game
1 GB (0) vs. Redskins (1), Dec. 24, 1972
2 GB (1) vs. Giants (1), Dec. 30, 1962
GB (1) vs. Colts (1), Dec. 26, 1965
GB (2) vs. Browns (0), Jan. 2, 1966
GB (1) vs. Lions (1), Dec. 31, 1994
Most Field Goals, Game
4 vs. Raiders, Jan. 14, 1968
3 vs. Giants, Dec. 31, 1961
vs. Giants, Dec. 30, 1962
vs. Browns, Jan. 2, 1966
vs. Lions, Dec. 31, 1994
Most Field Goals, Both Teams, Game
5 GB (3) vs. Browns (2), Jan. 2, 1966
GB (2) vs. Cowboys (3), Jan. 16, 1983
4 GB (4) vs. Raiders (0), Jan. 14, 1968
GB (1) vs. Redskins (3), Dec. 24, 1972
GB (3) vs. Lions (1), Dec. 31, 1994
Most Field Goals Attempted, Game
5 vs. Giants, Dec. 30, 1962
4 vs. Raiders, Jan. 14, 1968
vs. Lions, Dec. 31, 1994
Most Field Goals Attempted, Both Teams, Game
6 GB (5) vs. Giants (1), Dec. 30, 1962
GB (3) vs. Browns (3), Jan. 2, 1966
GB (2) vs. Cardinals (4), Jan. 8, 1983
GB (4) vs. Lions (2), Dec. 31, 1994
5 GB (2) vs. Giants (3), Dec. 10, 1939
GB (3) vs. Colts (2), Dec. 26, 1965
GB (4) vs. Raiders (1), Jan. 14, 1968
GB (2) vs. Redskins (3), Dec. 24, 1972
GB (2) vs. Cowboys (3), Jan. 16, 1983

FIRST DOWNS

Most First Downs, Game
23 vs. Colts, Dec. 26, 1965
22 vs. Eagles, Dec. 26, 1960
vs. Cardinals, Jan. 8, 1983
Fewest First Downs, Game
7 vs. Redskins, Dec. 13, 1936
10 vs. Giants, Dec. 10, 1939
vs. Redskins, Dec. 24, 1972
Most First Downs, Both Teams, Game
50 GB (22) vs. Cardinals (28), Jan. 8, 1983
45 GB (21) vs. Cowboys (24), Jan. 16, 1983
GB (18) vs. Cowboys (27), Jan. 8, 1995
Fewest First Downs, Both Teams, Game
15 GB (7) vs. Redskins (8), Dec. 13, 1936
19 GB (10) vs. Giants (9), Dec. 10, 1939
Most First Downs, Rushing, Game
14 vs. Eagles, Dec. 26, 1960
11 vs. Giants, Dec. 30, 1962
vs. Rams, Dec. 23, 1967
vs. Raiders, Jan. 14, 1968
Fewest First Downs, Rushing, Game
2 vs. Redskins, Dec. 13, 1936
vs. Redskins, Dec. 24, 1972
vs. Cowboys, Jan. 16, 1994
3 vs. Cowboys, Jan. 1, 1967
Most First Downs, Rushing, Both Teams, Game
19 GB (14) vs. Eagles (5), Dec. 26, 1960
17 GB (6) vs. Cowboys (11), Jan. 8, 1995
Fewest First Downs, Rushing, Both Teams, Game
6 GB (2) vs. Redskins (4), Dec. 13, 1936
7 GB (6) vs. Lions (1), Dec. 31, 1994
Most First Downs, Passing, Game
17 vs. Cowboys, Jan. 16, 1994
16 vs. Cowboys, Jan. 16, 1983
Fewest First Downs, Passing, Game
2 vs. Giants, Dec. 10, 1939
vs. Giants, Dec. 17, 1944
4 vs. Redskins, Dec. 13, 1936
vs. Giants, Dec. 11, 1938
Most First Downs, Passing, Both Teams, Game
33 GB (17) vs. Cowboys (16), Jan. 16, 1994
32 GB (13) vs. Cardinals (19), Jan. 8, 1983

Fewest First Downs, Passing, Both Team, Game
5   GB (2) vs. Giants (3), Dec. 10, 1939
6   GB (4) vs. Giants (2), Dec. 11, 1938
    GB (2) vs. Giants (4), Dec. 17, 1944
Most First Downs, Penalty, Game
3   vs. Colts, Dec. 26, 1965
    vs. Cowboys, Dec. 31, 1967
Most First Downs, Penalty, Both Teams, Game
4   GB (3) vs. Colts (1), Dec. 26, 1965
    GB (3) vs. Cowboys (1), Dec. 31, 1967
    GB (1) vs. Cowboys (3), Jan. 8, 1995

NET YARDS RUSHING AND PASSING

Most Yards Gained, Game
466   vs. Cowboys, Jan. 16, 1983
401   vs. Eagles, Dec. 26, 1960
Fewest Yards Gained, Game
195   vs. Cowboys, Dec. 31, 1967
211   vs. Redskins, Dec. 24, 1972
Most Yards Gained, Both Teams, Game
847   GB (394) vs. Cardinals (453), Jan. 8, 1983
841   GB (466) vs. Cowboys (375), Jan. 16, 1983
Fewest Yards Gained, Both Teams, Game
336   GB (220) vs. Redskins (116), Dec. 13, 1936
387   GB (195) vs. Cowboys (192), Dec. 31, 1967

RUSHING

Most Attempts, Game
52   vs. Giants, Dec. 10, 1939
49   vs. Giants, Dec. 17, 1944
Fewest Attempts, Game
13   vs. Cowboys, Jan. 16, 1994
17   vs. Cardinals, Jan. 8, 1983
Most Attempts, Both Teams, Game
89   GB (46) vs. Giants (43), Dec. 11, 1938
86   GB (52) vs. Giants (34), Dec. 10, 1939
     GB (39) vs. Colts (47), Dec. 26, 1965
Fewest Attempts, Both Teams, Game
40   GB (13) vs. Cowboys (27), Jan. 16, 1994
50   GB (35) vs. Lions (15), Dec. 31, 1994
Most Yards Gained, Game
223   vs. Eagles, Dec. 26, 1960
204   vs. Browns, Jan. 2, 1966
Fewest Yards Gained, Game
31   vs. Cowboys, Jan. 16, 1994
33   vs. Bears, Dec. 14, 1941
Most Yards Gained, Both Teams, Game
332   GB (223) vs. Eagles (99), Dec. 26, 1960
310   GB (33) vs. Bears (277), Dec. 14, 1941
Fewest Yards Gained, Both Teams, Game
77   GB (81) vs. Lions (-4), Dec. 31, 1994
106   GB (67) vs. Redskins (39), Dec. 13, 1936
Highest Average Gain, Game
9.29   vs. Cowboys, Jan. 16, 1983 (17-158)
5.31   vs. Eagles, Dec. 26, 1960 (42-223)
Lowest Average Gain, Game
0.92   vs. Bears, Dec. 14, 1941 (36-33)
1.52   vs. Redskins, Dec. 13, 1936 (44-67)
Most Touchdowns, Game
3   vs. Chiefs, Jan. 15, 1967
    vs. Rams, Dec. 23, 1967
Most Touchdowns, Both Teams, Game
4   GB (1) vs. Bears (3), Dec. 14, 1941
    GB (1) vs. Cowboys (3), Jan. 8, 1995
3   GB (3) vs. Chiefs (0), Jan. 15, 1967
    GB (3) vs. Rams (0), Dec. 23, 1967
    GB (1) vs. Cowboys (2), Jan. 16, 1983

PASSING

Most Attempts, Game
46   vs. Cowboys, Jan. 8, 1995
45   vs. Cowboys, Jan. 16, 1994

Fewest Attempts, Game
10   vs. Giants, Dec. 10, 1939
11   vs. Giants, Dec. 17, 1944
Most Attempts, Both Teams, Game
82   GB (45) vs. Cowboys (37), Jan. 16, 1994
78   GB (46) vs. Cowboys (32), Jan. 8, 1995
Fewest Attempts, Both Teams, Game
33   GB (11) vs. Giants (22), Dec. 17, 1944
34   GB (19) vs. Giants (15), Dec. 11, 1938
Most Completions, Game
28   vs. Cowboys, Jan. 16, 1994
23   vs. Colts, Dec. 26, 1965
     vs. Lions, Dec. 31, 1994
Fewest Completions, Game
3   vs. Giants, Dec. 17, 1944
7   vs. Giants, Dec. 10, 1939
Most Completions, Both Teams, Game
56   GB (28) vs. Cowboys (28), Jan. 16, 1994
51   GB (19) vs. Cardinals (32), Jan. 8, 1983
Fewest Completions, Both Teams, Game
11   GB (3) vs. Giants (8), Dec. 17, 1944
15   GB (7) vs. Giants (8), Dec. 10, 1939
**Highest Completion Percentage, Game
(minimum 20 attempts)**
73.91   vs. Rams, Dec. 23, 1967 (17-23)
73.08   vs. Cardinals, Jan. 8, 1983 (19-26)
**Highest Completion Percentage, Both Teams, Game
(minimum 40 attempts)**
68.29   GB (28-45) vs. Cowboys (28-37), Jan. 16, 1994
66.23   GB (19-26) vs. Cardinals (32-51), Jan. 8, 1983
**Lowest Completion Percentage, Game
(minimum 20 attempts)**
39.13   vs. Redskins, Dec. 13, 1936 (9-23)
40.74   vs. Bears, Dec. 14, 1941 (11-27)
**Lowest Completion Percentage, Both Teams, Game
(minimum 40 attempts)**
32.00   GB (9-23) vs. Redskins (7-27), Dec. 13, 1936
41.67   GB (10-19) vs. Giants (10-29), Dec. 31, 1961
Most Yards Gained, Game
327   vs. Cowboys, Jan. 16, 1994
308   vs. Cowboys, Jan. 16, 1983
Fewest Yards Gained, Game
74   vs. Giants, Dec. 17, 1944
96   vs. Giants, Dec. 10, 1939
     vs. Giants, Dec. 30, 1962
Most Yards Gained, Both Teams, Game
633   GB (286) vs. Cardinals (347), Jan. 8, 1983
611   GB (327) vs. Cowboys (284), Jan. 16, 1994
Fewest Yards Gained, Both Teams, Game
188   GB (74) vs. Giants (114), Dec. 17, 1944
190   GB (96) vs. Giants (94), Dec. 10, 1939
Most Times Sacked, Game
8   vs. Cowboys, Dec. 31, 1967
5   vs. Cowboys, Jan. 1, 1967
Fewest Times Sacked, Game
0   vs. Eagles, Dec. 26, 1960
    vs. Giants, Dec. 31, 1961
    vs. Cardinals, Jan. 8, 1983
    vs. Lions, Jan. 8, 1994
1   vs. Giants, Dec. 30, 1962
    vs. Colts, Dec. 26, 1965
    vs. Rams, Dec. 23, 1967
    vs. Lions, Dec. 31, 1994
    vs. Cowboys, Jan. 8, 1995
Most Times Sacked, Both Teams, Game
9   GB (3) vs. Chiefs (6), Jan. 15, 1967
    GB (8) vs. Cowboys (1), Dec. 31, 1967
7   GB (5) vs. Cowboys (2), Jan. 1, 1967
    GB (4) vs. Raiders (3), Jan. 14, 1968
Fewest Times Sacked, Both Teams, Game
1   GB (0) vs. Eagles (1), Dec. 26, 1960
    GB (1) vs. Giants (0), Dec. 30, 1962
2   GB (1) vs. Colts (1), Dec. 26, 1965
    GB (1) vs. Cowboys (1), Jan. 8, 1995
Most Touchdowns, Game
4   vs. Cowboys, Jan. 1, 1967
    vs. Cardinals, Jan. 8, 1983
3   vs. Giants, Dec. 31, 1961
    vs. Lions, Jan. 8, 1994

Most Touchdowns, Both Teams, Game
6   GB (4) vs. Cardinals (2), Jan. 8, 1983
5   GB (4) vs. Cowboys (1), Jan. 1, 1967
     GB (2) vs. Cowboys (3), Jan. 16, 1994
Most Passes Had Intercepted, Game
3   vs. Giants, Dec. 10, 1939
     vs. Giants, Dec. 17, 1944
     vs. Cowboys, Jan. 16, 1983
2   vs. Redskins, Dec. 13, 1936
     vs. Bears, Dec. 14, 1941
     vs. Colts, Dec. 26, 1965
     vs. Cowboys, Jan. 16, 1994

INTERCEPTIONS

Most Passes Intercepted, Game
6   vs. Giants, Dec. 10, 1939
4   vs. Giants, Dec. 17, 1944
     vs. Giants, Dec. 31, 1961
Most Passes Had Intercepted, Both Teams, Game
9   GB (3) vs. Giants (6), Dec. 10, 1939
7   GB (3) vs. Giants (4), Dec. 17, 1944
Most Yards Gained, Game
123   vs. Giants, Dec. 10, 1939
101   vs. Lions, Jan. 8, 1994
60   vs. Raiders, Jan. 14, 1968
Most Yards Gained, Both Teams, Game
128   GB (123) vs. Giants (5), Dec. 10, 1939
116   GB (101) vs. Lions (15), Jan. 8, 1994
Most Touchdowns, Game
1   vs. Raiders, Jan. 14, 1968
     vs. Cowboys, Jan. 16, 1983
     vs. Lions, Jan. 8, 1994
Most Touchdowns, Both Teams, Game
2   GB (1) vs. Cowboys (1), Jan. 16, 1983
     GB (1) vs. Lions (1), Jan. 8, 1994
1   GB (1) vs. Raiders (0), Jan. 14, 1968

PUNTING

Most Punts, Game
10   vs. Giants, Dec. 17, 1944
8   vs. Redskins, Dec. 13, 1936
     vs. Cowboys, Dec. 31, 1967
     vs. Redskins, Dec. 24, 1972
Fewest Punts, Game
1   vs. Cardinals, Jan. 8, 1983
3   vs. Browns, Jan. 2, 1966
     vs. Cowboys, Jan. 16, 1994
Most Punts, Both Teams, Game
20   GB (10) vs. Giants (10), Dec. 17, 1944
18   GB (8) vs. Redskins (10), Dec. 13, 1936
Fewest Punts, Both Teams, Game
1   GB (1) vs. Cardinals (0), Jan. 8, 1983
6   GB (3) vs. Cowboys (3), Jan. 16, 1994
Highest Average Distance, Punting, Game
(minimum 4 punts)
45.20   vs. Eagles, Dec. 26, 1960 (5-226)
44.00   vs. Cowboys, Jan. 8, 1995 (4-176)
Lowest Average Distance, Punting, Game
(minimum 4 punts)
25.50   vs. Giants, Dec. 30, 1962 (6-153)
26.00   vs. Giants, Dec. 10, 1939 (7-182)

PUNT RETURNS

Most Punt Returns, Game
8   vs. Giants, Dec. 17, 1944
6   vs. Colts, Dec. 26, 1965
Most Punt Returns, Both Teams, Game
12   GB (8) vs. Giants (4), Dec. 17, 1944
11   GB (6) vs. Colts (5), Dec. 26, 1965

Fewest Punt Returns, Game
0   vs. Cowboys, Jan. 1, 1967
     vs. Cardinals, Jan. 8, 1983
1   vs. Giants, Dec. 31, 1961
     vs. Cowboys, Jan. 16, 1983
Fewest Punt Returns, Both Teams, Game
0   GB (0) vs. Cardinals (0), Jan. 8, 1983
2   GB (2) vs. Cowboys (0), Jan. 8, 1995
Most Yards Gained, Game
89   vs. Giants, Dec. 17, 1944
59   vs. Cowboys, Jan. 16, 1994
Fewest Yards Gained, Game
-10   vs. Browns, Jan. 2, 1966
0   vs. Cowboys, Jan. 1, 1967
     vs. Cardinals, Jan. 8, 1983
Most Yards Gained, Both Teams, Game
141   GB (54) vs. Bears (87), Dec. 14, 1941
120   GB (89) vs. Giants (31), Dec. 17, 1944
Fewest Yards Gained, Both Teams, Game
-9   GB (0) vs. Cowboys (-9), Jan. 1, 1967
0   GB (0) vs. Cardinals (0), Jan. 8, 1983

KICKOFF RETURNS

Most Kickoff Returns, Game
7   vs. Cowboys, Jan. 16, 1983
6   vs. Cowboys, Jan. 1, 1967
     vs. Cowboys, Jan. 16, 1994
     vs. Cowboys, Jan. 8, 1995
Most Kickoff Returns, Both Teams, Game
13   GB (7) vs. Cowboys (6), Jan. 16, 1983
12   GB (6) vs. Cowboys (6), Jan. 1, 1967
Fewest Kickoff Returns, Game
0   vs. Redskins, Dec. 13, 1936
     vs. Giants, Dec. 10, 1939
1   vs. Giants, Dec. 17, 1944
     vs. Giants, Dec. 31, 1961
Fewest Kickoff Returns, Both Teams, Game
1   GB (0) vs. Redskins (1), Dec. 13, 1936
4   GB (0) vs. Giants (4), Dec. 10, 1939
Most Yards Gained, Game
148   vs. Cowboys, Jan. 16, 1983
144   vs. Cowboys, Jan. 8, 1995
Fewest Yards Gained, Game
0   vs. Redskins, Dec. 13, 1936
     vs. Giants, Dec. 10, 1939
9   vs. Giants, Dec. 17, 1944
Most Yards Gained, Both Teams, Game
321   GB (148) vs. Cowboys (173), Jan. 16, 1983
263   GB (110) vs. Cowboys (153), Jan. 1, 1967
Fewest Yards Gained, Both Teams, Game
32   GB (0) vs. Redskins (32), Dec. 13, 1936
53   GB (10) vs. Cowboys (43), Dec. 31, 1967

PENALTIES

Most Penalties, Game
8   vs. Cowboys, Jan. 8, 1995
7   vs. Rams, Dec. 23, 1967
Fewest Penalties, Game
1   vs. Raiders, Jan. 14, 1968
2   vs. Giants, Dec. 11, 1938
     vs. Browns, Jan. 2, 1966
     vs. Cowboys, Jan. 1, 1967
     vs. Cowboys, Dec. 31, 1967
Most Penalties, Both Teams, Game
15   GB (3) vs. Bears (12), Dec. 14, 1941
     GB (4) vs. Giants (11), Dec. 17, 1944
     GB (8) vs. Cowboys (7), Jan. 8, 1995
11   GB (5) vs. Cardinals (6), Jan. 8, 1983
     GB (6) vs. Lions (5), Jan. 8, 1994
Fewest Penalties, Both Teams, Game
4   GB (4) vs. Eagles (0), Dec. 26, 1960
5   GB (2) vs. Giants (3), Dec. 11, 1938
     GB (2) vs. Browns (3), Jan. 2, 1966
     GB (1) vs. Raiders (4), Jan. 14, 1968

Most Yards Penalized, Game
54   vs. Redskins, Dec. 24, 1972
50   vs. Giants, Dec. 10, 1939
Fewest Yards Penalized, Game
10   vs. Giants, Dec. 11, 1938
      vs. Cowboys, Dec. 31, 1967
12   vs. Raiders, Jan. 14, 1968
Most Yards Penalized, Both Teams, Game
174   GB (46) vs. Bears (128), Dec. 14, 1941
138   GB (48) vs. Giants (90), Dec. 17, 1944
Fewest Yards Penalized, Both Teams, Game
27   GB (27) vs. Eagles (0), Dec. 26, 1960
30   GB (10) vs. Giants (20), Dec. 11, 1938

FUMBLES

Most Fumbles, Game
4   vs. Giants, Dec. 11, 1938
      vs. Cowboys, Jan. 16, 1983
3   vs. Bears, Dec. 14, 1941
      vs. Colts, Dec. 26, 1965
      vs. Rams, Dec. 23, 1967
      vs. Cowboys, Dec. 31, 1967
      vs. Cowboys, Jan. 16, 1994
Fewest Fumbles, Game
0   vs. Browns, Jan. 2, 1966
      vs. Raiders, Jan. 14, 1968
      vs. Redskins, Dec. 24, 1972
      vs. Lions, Dec. 31, 1994
      vs. Cowboys, Jan. 8, 1995
1   Accomplished five times
Most Fumbles, Both Teams, Game
8   GB (3) vs. Bears (5), Dec. 14, 1941
7   GB (2) vs. Redskins (5), Dec. 13, 1936
Fewest Fumbles, Both Teams, Game
0   GB (0) vs. Browns (0), Jan. 2, 1966
1   GB (0) vs. Redskins (1), Dec. 24, 1972
      GB (0) vs. Lions (1), Dec. 31, 1994
      GB (0) vs. Cowboys (1), Jan. 8, 1995
Most Fumbles, Lost, Game
3   vs. Rams, Dec. 23, 1967
2   Accomplished six times
Fewest Fumbles, Lost, Game
0   Accomplished 11 times
Most Fumbles Recovered, Own and Opponents'
4   vs. Bears, Dec. 14, 1941 (1 own, 3 opp)
      vs. Giants, Dec. 30, 1962 (2 own, 2 opp)
3   vs. Redskins, Dec. 13, 1936 (1 own, 2 opp)
      vs. Cowboys, Jan. 16, 1983 (2 own, 1 opp)
Most Own Fumbles, Recovered, Game
2   vs. Giants, Dec. 11, 1938
      vs. Giants, Dec. 10, 1939
      vs. Giants, Dec. 17, 1944
      vs. Giants, Dec. 30, 1962
      vs. Cowboys, Jan. 16, 1983
      vs. Lions, Jan. 8, 1994

TURNOVERS

Most Turnovers, Game
5   vs. Cowboys, Jan. 16, 1983
4   vs. Bears, Dec. 14, 1941
      vs. Colts, Dec. 26, 1965
      vs. Rams, Dec. 23, 1967
      vs. Cowboys, Jan. 16, 1994
Fewest Turnovers, Game
0   vs. Giants, Dec. 31, 1961
      vs. Giants, Dec. 30, 1962
      vs. Raiders, Jan. 14, 1968
      vs. Lions, Dec. 31, 1994
1   Accomplished eight times

Most Turnovers, Both Teams, Game
9   GB (3) vs. Giants (6), Dec. 10, 1939
7   GB (4) vs. Bears (3), Dec. 14, 1941
      GB (3) vs. Giants (4), Dec. 17, 1944
      GB (5) vs. Cowboys (2), Jan. 16, 1983
      GB (4) vs. Cowboys (3), Jan. 16, 1994
Fewest Turnovers, Both Teams, Game
0   GB (0) vs. Lions (0), Dec. 31, 1994
2   GB (1) vs. Chiefs (1), Jan. 15, 1967
      GB (1) vs. Redskins (1), Dec. 24, 1972

TEAM DEFENSIVE RECORDS

POINTS

Most Points Allowed, Game
37   vs. Cowboys, Jan. 16, 1983
35   vs. Cowboys, Jan. 8, 1995
Fewest Points Allowed, Game
0   vs. Giants, Dec. 10, 1939
      vs. Giants, Dec. 30, 1962
6   vs. Redskins, Dec. 13, 1936
Largest Margin of Defeat, Game
26   vs. Cowboys, Jan. 8, 1995
19   vs. Bears, Dec. 14, 1941
Most Points Opponents Overcame to Beat Packers
7   Bears, Dec. 14, 1941 (trailed 7-0, won 33-14)
6   Eagles, Dec. 26, 1960 (trailed 6-0, won 17-13)
Most Points, Opponents, First Half
30   Bears, Dec. 14, 1941
28   Cowboys, Jan. 8, 1995
Most Points, Opponents, Second Half
17   Cowboys, Jan. 16, 1983
14   Lions, Jan. 8, 1994
Most Points, Opponents, Each Quarter
1st: 14 Cowboys, Jan. 1, 1967
         14 Cowboys, Jan. 8, 1995
2nd: 24 Bears, Dec. 14, 1941
3rd: 7 Giants, Dec. 11, 1938
         7 Giants, Dec. 30, 1962
         7 Lions, Jan. 8, 1994
         7 Cowboys, Jan. 16, 1994
4th: 14 Cowboys, Jan. 16, 1983
Most Touchdowns, Opponents, Game
5   Cowboys, Jan. 8, 1995
4   Bears, Dec. 14, 1941
      Cowboys, Jan. 16, 1983
Most Points After Touchdown, Opponents, Game
5   Cowboys, Jan. 8, 1995
4   Cowboys, Jan. 16, 1983
Most Field Goals, Opponents, Game
3   Redskins, Dec. 24, 1972
      Cowboys, Jan. 16, 1983
2   Bears, Dec. 14, 1941
      Browns, Jan. 2, 1966
      Cowboys, Jan. 1, 1967
      Cowboys, Jan. 16, 1994
Most Field Goals Attempted, Opponents, Game
4   Cardinals, Jan. 8, 1983
3   Accomplished five times

FIRST DOWNS

Most First Downs, Opponents, Game
28   Cardinals, Jan. 8, 1983
27   Cowboys, Jan. 8, 1995

Fewest First Downs, Opponents, Game
6 Giants, Dec. 31, 1961
8 Redskins, Dec. 13, 1936
Browns, Jan. 2, 1966
Most First Downs, Rushing, Opponents, Game
12 Cowboys, Jan. 1, 1967
11 Cowboys, Jan. 8, 1995
Fewest First Downs, Rushing, Opponents, Game
1 Giants, Dec. 31, 1961
Lions, Dec. 31, 1994
2 Browns, Jan. 2, 1966
Rams, Dec. 23, 1967
Most First Downs, Passing, Opponents, Game
19 Cardinals, Jan. 8, 1983
16 Cowboys, Jan. 16, 1994
Fewest First Downs, Passing, Opponents, Game
2 Giants, Dec. 11, 1938
Colts, Dec. 26, 1965
3 Redskins, Dec. 13, 1936
Giants, Dec. 10, 1939
Bears, Dec. 14, 1941
Most First Downs, Penalty, Opponents, Game
3 Redskins, Dec. 24, 1972
Cowboys, Jan. 8, 1995
2 Giants, Dec. 11, 1938
Eagles, Dec. 26, 1960
Giants, Dec. 30, 1962
Lions, Jan. 8, 1994

NET YARDS RUSHING AND PASSING

Most Yards Gained, Opponents, Game
453 Cardinals, Jan. 8, 1983
450 Cowboys, Jan. 8, 1995
Fewest Yards Gained, Opponents, Game
116 Redskins, Dec. 13, 1936
130 Giants, Dec. 31, 1961

RUSHING

Most Rushing Attempts, Opponents, Game
48 Bears, Dec. 14, 1941
47 Colts, Dec. 26, 1965
Fewest Rushing Attempts, Opponents, Game
14 Giants, Dec. 31, 1961
15 Lions, Dec. 31, 1994
Most Yards Gained Rushing, Opponents, Game
277 Bears, Dec. 14, 1941
187 Cowboys, Jan. 1, 1967
Fewest Yards Gained Rushing, Opponents, Game
-4 Lions, Dec. 31, 1994
31 Giants, Dec. 31, 1961
Highest Average Gain, Opponents, Game
6.03 Lions, Jan. 8, 1994 (29-175)
5.77 Bears, Dec. 14, 1941 (48-277)
Lowest Average Gain, Opponents, Game
-0.27 Lions, Dec. 31, 1994 (15-[-4])
1.15 Redskins, Dec. 13, 1936 (34-39)
Most Touchdowns, Rushing, Opponents, Game
3 Bears, Dec. 14, 1941
Cowboys, Jan. 8, 1995
2 Cowboys, Jan. 1, 1967
Cowboys, Jan. 16, 1983

PASSING

Most Passing Attempts, Opponents, Game
51 Cardinals, Jan. 8, 1983
41 Giants, Dec. 30, 1962
Fewest Passing Attempts, Opponents, Game
12 Bears, Dec. 14, 1941
Colts, Dec. 26, 1965
14 Redskins, Dec. 24, 1972

Most Completions, Opponents, Game
32 Cardinals, Jan. 8, 1983
28 Cowboys, Jan. 16, 1994
24 Cowboys, Jan. 16, 1983
Fewest Completions, Opponents, Game
5 Bears, Dec. 14, 1941
Colts, Dec. 26, 1965
7 Redskins, Dec. 13, 1936
Redskins, Dec. 24, 1972
Highest Completion Percentage, Opponents, Game
(minimum 20 attempts)
75.68 Cowboys, Jan. 16, 1994 (28-37)
71.88 Cowboys, Jan. 8, 1995 (23-32)
Lowest Completion Percentage, Opponents, Game
(minimum 20 attempts)
25.93 Redskins, Dec. 13, 1936 (7-27)
32.00 Giants, Dec. 10, 1939 (8-25)
Most Yards Gained Passing, Opponents, Game
347 Cardinals, Jan. 8, 1983
330 Cowboys, Jan. 8, 1995
Fewest Yards Gained Passing, Opponents, Game
32 Colts, Dec. 26, 1965
48 Bears, Dec. 14, 1941
Most Times Sacked, Opponents, Game
6 Chiefs, Jan. 15, 1967
5 Rams, Dec. 23, 1967
Cardinals, Jan. 8, 1983
Fewest Times Sacked, Opponents, Game
0 Giants, Dec. 30, 1962
1 Accomplished six times
Most Touchdowns, Passing, Opponents, Game
3 Cowboys, Jan. 16, 1994
2 Giants, Dec. 11, 1938
Raiders, Jan. 14, 1968
Cardinals, Jan. 8, 1983
Cowboys, Jan. 8, 1995
Most Passes Had Intercepted, Opponents, Game
6 Giants, Dec. 10, 1939
4 Giants, Dec. 17, 1944
Giants, Dec. 31, 1961

INTERCEPTIONS

Most Passes Intercepted By, Opponents, Game
3 Giants, Dec. 10, 1939
Giants, Dec. 17, 1944
Cowboys, Jan. 16, 1983
2 Redskins, Dec. 13, 1936
Bears, Dec. 14, 1941
Colts, Dec. 26, 1965
Cowboys, Jan. 16, 1994
Most Yards Gained on Interceptions, Opponents, Game
58 Cowboys, Jan. 16, 1983
24 Rams, Dec. 23, 1967
Most Touchdowns on Interceptions, Opponents, Game
1 Cowboys, Jan. 16, 1983
Lions, Jan. 8, 1994

PUNTING

Most Punts, Opponents, Game
10 Redskins, Dec. 13, 1936
Giants, Dec. 17, 1944
8 Giants, Dec. 11, 1938
Colts, Dec. 26, 1965
Cowboys, Dec. 31, 1967
Lions, Dec. 31, 1994
Fewest Punts, Opponents, Game
0 Cardinals, Jan. 8, 1983
3 Lions, Jan. 8, 1994
Cowboys, Jan. 16, 1994
Highest Average Gain, Punting, Opponents, Game
(minimum 4 punts)
46.50 Redskins, Dec. 24, 1972 (6-279)
46.00 Browns, Jan. 2, 1966 (4-184)

Lowest Average Gain, Punting, Opponents, Game
   32.25   Cowboys, Jan. 1, 1967 (4-129)
   34.75   Cowboys, Jan. 16, 1983 (4-139)

PUNT RETURNS

Most Punt Returns, Opponents, Game
   5   Redskins, Dec. 13, 1936
       Colts, Dec. 26, 1965
   3   Accomplished eight times
Fewest Punt Returns, Opponents, Game
   0   Cowboys, Dec. 31, 1967
       Cardinals, Jan. 8, 1983
       Cowboys, Jan. 8, 1995
   1   Eagles, Dec. 26, 1960
       Giants, Dec. 30, 1962
       Browns, Jan. 2, 1966
       Rams, Dec. 23, 1967
       Lions, Jan. 8, 1994
Most Yards Gained, Punt Returns, Opponents, Game
   87   Bears, Dec. 14, 1941
   58   Redskins, Dec. 13, 1936
Fewest Yards Gained, Punt Returns, Opponents, Game
   -9   Browns, Jan. 2, 1966
   0   Giants, Dec. 30, 1962
       Rams, Dec. 23, 1967
       Cowboys, Dec. 31, 1967
       Cardinals, Jan. 8, 1983
       Cowboys, Jan. 8, 1995

KICKOFF RETURNS

Most Kickoff Returns, Opponents, Game
   7   Raiders, Jan. 14, 1968
       Cardinals, Jan. 8, 1983
   6   Giants, Dec. 31, 1961
       Cowboys, Jan. 1, 1967
       Chiefs, Jan. 15, 1967
       Cowboys, Jan. 16, 1983
Fewest Kickoff Returns, Opponents, Game
   1   Redskins, Dec. 13, 1936
   2   Colts, Dec. 26, 1965
       Redskins, Dec. 24, 1972
       Cowboys, Jan. 16, 1994
Most Yards Gained, Kickoff Returns, Opponents, Game
   186   Lions, Dec. 31, 1994
   178   Cardinals, Jan. 8, 1983
Fewest Yards Gained, Kickoff Returns, Opponents, Game
   32   Redskins, Dec. 13, 1936
   34   Cowboys, Jan. 16, 1994

PENALTIES

Most Penalties, Opponents, Game
   12   Bears, Dec. 14, 1941
   11   Giants, Dec. 17, 1944
Fewest Penalties, Opponents, Game
   0   Eagles, Dec. 26, 1960
   3   Giants, Dec. 11, 1938
       Colts, Dec. 26, 1965
       Browns, Jan. 2, 1966
       Rams, Dec. 23, 1967
Most Yards Penalized, Opponents, Game
   128   Bears, Dec. 14, 1941
   90   Giants, Dec. 17, 1944
Fewest Yards Penalized, Opponents, Game
   0   Eagles, Dec. 26, 1960
   20   Giants, Dec. 11, 1938

FUMBLES

Most Fumbles, Opponents, Game
   5   Redskins, Dec. 13, 1936
       Bears, Dec. 14, 1941
       Giants, Dec. 31, 1961
   3   Accomplished six times
Fewest Fumbles, Opponents, Game
   0   Browns, Jan. 2, 1966
       Rams, Dec. 23, 1967
   1   Accomplished seven times
Most Fumbles, Lost, Opponents, Game
   3   Bears, Dec. 14, 1941
   2   Accomplished five times
Fewest Fumbles Lost, Opponents, Game
   0   Accomplished eight times
Most Fumbles Recovered, Own and Packers, Opponents
   4   Accomplished five times
Most Own Fumbles Recovered, Opponents, Game
   4   Giants, Dec. 31, 1967
   3   Redskins, Dec. 13, 1936

TURNOVERS

Most Turnovers, Opponents, Game
   6   Giants, Dec. 10, 1939
   5   Giants, Dec. 11, 1938
       Giants, Dec. 31, 1961
Fewest Turnovers, Opponents, Game
   0   Lions, Dec. 31, 1994
   1   Colts, Dec. 26, 1965
       Chiefs, Jan. 15, 1967
       Rams, Dec. 23, 1967
       Redskins, Dec. 24, 1972

Green Bay Press-Gazette photo

Lester Archambeau (74) and Matt Brock (62) whoop it up after sacking the Colts' Jeff George in Milwaukee.

THE OFF-SEASON

Phillip Epps (85) and Mark Lee (22) savor Epps' 90-yard punt return for a touchdown in early October, 1983.

EARL LOUIS (CURLY) LAMBEAU

BORN: April 9, 1898   **DIED:** June 1, 1965

Earl Louis Lambeau, Curly to everyone who knew him, was elected captain of the city football team sponsored by the Indian Packing Corporation on August 14, 1919. The corporation contributed $500 toward jerseys, equipment and other items. Lambeau's employers also provided company land on which to practice.

Initially, Green Bay played teams mostly from Wisconsin. In 1919, the team pounded the likes of Marinette (61-0), New London (54-0), Sheboygan (87-0), and others. The team was undefeated until the Beloit Fairies knocked them off 6-0 on November 23 in a controversial game played to determine the state championship.

Dubbed the "Packers" by publicist George Whitney Calhoun, the team was almost as dominating a year later. The only loss again was at the hands of the Fairies, although the Chicago Boosters tied them 3-3 to open the season.

A year later, the Acme Packing Company bought out the Indian Corporation. John and Emmett Clair of Acme were granted a franchise in the new American Professional Football Organization, forerunner to the National Football League. Pro football had arrived in the oldest city in Wisconsin and for the next 29 years, Lambeau was its guide.

Lambeau was born in Green Bay in 1898. He attended East High School and made the varsity football team as a freshman. In his senior year, he led the school to a 7-6 win over arch rival West High, East's first win over the Wildcats in seven years. Following graduation, Lambeau coached his old high school team for a year, then enrolled at Notre Dame in the fall of 1918. There, he joined a backfield that included the great George Gipp.

While away at school, Lambeau developed a severe case of tonsillitis and returned to Green Bay. Once back, he took a job with the Indian Packing Corporation which ultimately led to his long association with the Packers.

In his years with the team, Lambeau became one of the first to make liberal use of the forward pass. He set up daily practices and later used film as a means to evaluate his team as well as opponents. He also had a keen eye for talent and over the years acquired some of the finest ever to play the game. His teams won three straight championships from 1929-31. The Packers also won titles in 1936, 1939 and 1944.

Green Bay's fortunes slowly began to decline after World War II. By the late '40s, Lambeau had fallen out of favor with a number of members of the executive committee. The coach resigned in 1950 and became head coach of the Chicago Cardinals. Unable to turn around that program, he journeyed to Washington where he headed the Redskins until he was fired by owner George Marshall prior to the 1954 season.

For three years in the mid-fifties (1955-57), Lambeau coached the College All-Stars in their annual clash with the NFL champions. Lambeau was inducted into the Pro Football Hall of Fame in Canton, Ohio when it opened in 1963. After his death, City Stadium was renamed Lambeau Field.

Pro Coaching Record

Regular Season

	W	L	T	Pct
1921-49 Packers	209	104	21	.657
1950-51 Cardinals	7	15	0	.318
1952-53 Redskins	10	13	1	.438
1921-53 Totals	226	132	22	.624

Postseason

	W	L	T	Pct
1921-49 Packers	3	2	0	.600
1950-51 Cardinals	0	0	0	.000
1952-53 Redskins	0	0	0	.000
Postseason Totals	3	2	0	.600
Overall	229	134	22	.623

Green Bay Press-Gazette photo

Curly Lambeau stalks the sideline at City Stadium during a 1941 Bears game. Chicago triumphed 25-17.

GENE RONZANI

BORN: March 28, 1909   **DIED:** September 12, 1975

Gene Ronzani became the second head coach in Packers' history on February 6, 1950. Prior to that, he spent 16 years with the Chicago Bears as a player, coach and public relations figure.

Ronzani was born in Iron Mountain, Michigan in 1909. He attended Iron Mountain High School and won eight letters in football, basketball and track. In 1929, he enrolled at Marquette University where he earned nine letters in the same three sports. He captained the football team in 1932, the same year he gained his law degree.

Twenty-four-old Ronzani joined the Bears in the fall of 1933. The rookie played halfback in the same backfield with veterans Bronko Nagurski and Beattie Feathers, the latter the first to gain 1,000 yards rushing in a single season. After four years at halfback, Ronzani was switched to quarterback. He left the game as a player after the 1938 season.

In 1939, Ronzani became head coach of the Newark Bears, a Chicago farm club. He remained there until called back to active duty with the Bears. Ronzani played two more years, 1944-45, filling in capably when quarterback Sid Luckman was on Coast Guard duty. In his eight-year playing career, Ronzani rushed for 1,144 yards on 260 carries and threw for well over 1,000 yards, most of that in the 1940s.

Ronzani was named head coach of the Bears' Akron, Ohio farm team in 1946. A year later, he began his coaching career at the professional level in Chicago as the Bears backfield assistant and quarterbacks coach. He remained in that capacity until the Packers beckoned.

With the Packers, Ronzani experienced some difficult times. He took over a 2-10 team, the worst in Green Bay's history to that point, and fared little better (3-9) in 1950. In 1951, the Packers again finished 3-9 but boasted a passing offense second only to the Rams. Ronzani's third team finished a respectable 6-6 but, one year later, the losses again mounted. His coaching came under fire and some of his decisions were openly second-guessed. He was released on November 27, 1953, with two games remaining. Hugh Devore and Ray McLean finished the year (2-9-1) with two losses to the 49ers and Rams.

Ronzani went on to serve as the backfield coach for the Pittsburgh Steelers. He died of a heart attack at his cottage in Lac Du Flambeau in 1975.

Pro Coaching Record

Regular Season

	W	L	T	Pct
1950-53 Packers	14	31	1	.315
1950-53 Totals	14	31	1	.315

Postseason

	W	L	T	Pct
1950-53 Packers	0	0	0	.000
Postseason Totals	0	0	0	.000
Overall	14	31	1	.315

Green Bay Press-Gazette photo

Gene Ronzani gives instructions to Paul Christman during the Bears game at City Stadium, October 1, 1950. Chicago won 31-21.

LISLE (LIZ) BLACKBOURN

BORN: June 3, 1899   **DIED:** June 13, 1983

For the first time, the fortunes of the Packers rested with a man who had never coached nor played football at the professional level. Lisle (Liz) Blackbourn, named head coach on January 7, 1954, had spent 22 years as coach and athletic director at Washington High School in Milwaukee before logging another seven at the collegiate level as scout, assistant coach and head coach.

Blackbourn was born in Beetown Township in Grant County, Wisconsin and attended Lawrence University. He graduated in 1925 and moved to Milwaukee where he began his long association with Washington High School. As head coach, he compiled a 140-30-6 record and his teams won 10 city championships and tied for an eleventh.

Blackbourn left in 1946 to scout for the University of Wisconsin at Madison. In 1948, he was named backfield coach by then Head Coach Harry Stuhldreher. Stuhldreher moved on the next year and though a leading candidate for the vacancy, Blackbourn lost out to Ivy Williamson.

Instead of remaining with the Badgers, Blackbourn left to coach the line at Marquette University under Coach Frank Murray. Murray retired after the 1949 campaign and this time Blackbourn was handed the head coaching reigns. Blackbourn's teams went 18-17-4 between 1950-53. The Hilltoppers enjoyed two winning seasons under Blackbourn's tutelage, 5-3-1 in 1950 and 6-3-1 in 1953.

The Packers won just four games in Blackbourn's first year in Green Bay. His team, however, kept things close and lost just one game by more than eight points. Blackbourn himself lost out to Cleveland's Paul Brown by a single vote in the United Press' "Coach of the Year" poll of sportswriters. Improvement followed. Nine games into the 1955 campaign, the 5-4 Packers were still in the race for the Western Conference crown, but a Thanksgiving Day loss to Detroit and a season-ending setback at eventual champion Los Angeles forced Green Bay to settle for third with a 6-6 mark. In 1956, Blackbourn's team went 4-8. A year later, the team was 3-9.

Blackbourn had originally signed a three-year deal in 1954. However, in 1955 he was given a new five-year contract retroactive to 1954. It was the last year of this contract which the board of directors decided to buy up after two losing seasons. He was released on January 6, 1958.

In later years, the coach became well-known for his role in the 1958 draft, considered one of the best ever. Green Bay netted two Hall of Famers (Jim Taylor and Ray Nitschke), and an additional pair of Pro Bowlers (Dan Currie and Jerry Kramer).

Pro Coaching Record

Regular Season

	W	L	T	Pct
1954-57 Packers	17	31	0	.354
1954-57 Totals	17	31	0	.354

Postseason

	W	L	T	Pct
1954-57 Packers	0	0	0	.000
Postseason Totals	0	0	0	.000
Overall	17	31	0	.354

Green Bay Press-Gazette photo

Liz Blackbourn, Tom Hearden, Ray (Scooter) McLean, Jack Vainisi and Lou Rymkus prepare for the 1955 draft.

RAY (SCOOTER) MCLEAN

BORN: December 6, 1915   **DIED:** March 4, 1964

Ray (Scooter) McLean enjoyed a seven-year relationship with the Packers before signing on to become their fourth head coach on January 7, 1958. McLean agreed to a one-year deal but, unfortunately, twelve months later his association with the organization turned sour as Green Bay endured a 1-10-1 season.

McLean was the Packers offensive backfield coach from 1951-57. He helped develop talents such as Fred Cone, Al Carmichael, Floyd (Breezy) Reid and Howie Ferguson. He tutored quarterbacks such as Tobin Rote and Bart Starr. McLean's easy-going, affable manner was both a help and a hindrance. As an assistant, he could relate well to the players, but after taking over as head coach, a number of players took advantage of his relaxed rules.

Prior to coming to Green Bay, McLean had served three years as head coach at Lewis College in Lockport, Illinois. And like Ronzani before him, McLean had also played for the Chicago Bears. The Bruins made the St. Anselm graduate their 19th selection in the 1940 draft. In an eight-year career with the club, he turned out to be a better receiver than running back. McLean caught 103 passes for 2,222 yards for an impressive 21.6 average per catch. He gained just 422 yards rushing.

McLean's 1958 Packers won but one game and had to hang on dearly to do just that. Against Philadelphia, Green Bay led 38-14 entering the fourth quarter but the Eagles soared back with three touchdowns to close 38-35 with 54 seconds remaining. Only Ray Nitschke's recovery of Philadelphia's subsequent onside kick allowed the Packers to prevail.

Green Bay was outscored 382-193 in 1958. The team had the distinction of being clubbed 56-0 by Baltimore. That setback was only the first of seven which closed out the campaign. After the final 34-20 loss at Los Angeles, McLean resigned and joined the Lions as an assistant. He coached Detroit's offensive backfield until September 22, 1963. At that point, weakened with cancer, he entered a Michigan hospital. McLean died in early March of the following year.

Pro Coaching Record

Regular Season

	W	L	T	Pct
1958 Packers	1	10	1	.125
1958 Totals	1	10	1	.125

Postseason

	W	L	T	Pct
1958 Packers	0	0	0	.000
Postseason Totals	0	0	0	.000
Overall	1	10	1	.125

Green Bay Press-Gazette photo

Ray (Scooter) McLean keeps a watchful eye on his players during calisthenics as the Packers prepared for their 38th season in the NFL.

VINCENT THOMAS LOMBARDI

BORN: June 11, 1913   **DIED:** September 3, 1970

Five World Championships. Six Western Conference crowns. Two Super Bowl victories and a glittering .758 winning percentage. Achievements of the Vince Lombardi era in Green Bay. Stuff of which legends are made. Only after cancer claimed him in 1970 did some realize he was mortal.

When he arrived in January of 1959, he professed to be "no miracle man." Even so, his prior record indicated he wasn't one to tolerate failure.

Lombardi was born in Brooklyn, New York. He was an all-city performer at St. Francis Prep School and earned a scholarship to Fordham University. Though only 5-11 and 188 pounds, he played guard on the team's famed line, the "Seven Blocks of Granite," under coach Jimmy Crowley.

Lombardi made the Dean's list four straight years and graduated cum laude in 1937. Beginning in 1939, he taught a variety of subjects, including Latin and chemistry at St. Cecilia High School in Englewood, New Jersey. He also coached football, baseball and basketball there. His football team at one time won 36 straight games and earned six state championships in eight years.

In 1947, Lombardi moved to the college level. He served one year as freshman football coach at Fordham and the next year became a varsity assistant coach under Ed Danowski. Earl Blaik tabbed him as the next offensive line coach for the United States Military Academy in 1949 and he spent the next five years in that capacity.

Jim Lee Howell hired Lombardi to direct the offense for the New York Giants in 1954. Though his unit never finished better than fourth, the Giants did win the NFL title in 1956. New York finished second when it came up short in a sudden-death thriller with the Colts two years later.

One of Lombardi's triumphs in New York was turning Frank Gifford into an all-purpose back. Gifford won all-pro honors three years in a row, 1955-57. Lombardi molded Paul Hornung in the same manner at Green Bay.

In his first year with the Packers, Lombardi took a 1-10-1 team and turned it into a 7-5 winner. In 1960, his team won the West and then lost a heartbreaker to the Eagles (17-13) in the championship game. The Packers won titles in 1961 and 1962 and grabbed three-in-a-row from 1965-67.

In 1968, Lombardi stepped down as coach but remained general manager. The lure of coaching and the prospect of another challenge prompted him to leave Green Bay after the 1968 season. Lombardi took a 5-9 Redskins team and revitalized it with a 7-5-2 record in 1969.

Pro Coaching Record

Regular Season

	W	L	T	Pct
1959-67 Packers	89	29	4	.746
1969 Redskins	7	5	2	.571
1959-69 Totals	96	34	6	.728

Postseason

	W	L	T	Pct
1959-67 Packers	9	1	0	.900
1969 Redskins	0	0	0	.000
Postseason Totals	9	1	0	.900
Overall	105	35	6	.740

Green Bay Press-Gazette photo

Lost in thought, Vince Lombardi stands on the sidelines of City Stadium as his team does battle with the Baltimore Colts on September 20, 1964. The Colts eked out a 21-20 win.

- 372 -

JOHN PHILLIP (PHIL) BENGTSON

BORN: July 17, 1913   **DIED:** 1994

During the nine years Vince Lombardi's teams were winning championships, Phil Bengtson was busy crafting and fine-tuning a vital cog in the machine: solid defense. Bengtson's unit finished third or better seven times and twice wound up first. When Lombardi named him as his successor on February 1, 1968, the announcement caught no one by surprise.

Bengtson had the unenviable task of following a legend. His final record of 20-21-1 didn't stand up in many people's minds. He announced his resignation two days after his third team went 6-8 in 1970. Bengtson cited a disappointing season and a need for change as reasons for leaving.

Bengtson began his association with pro football in 1951 when 49ers Head Coach Buck Shaw persuaded him to leave his position at Stanford. Bengtson remained with San Francisco until Lombardi appointed him defensive line coach in 1959. A year later, he had control of the entire defense.

The Packers surrendered 4,615 yards and their offense ranked a dismal 11th out of 12 teams in 1958. A year later, the turnaround was dramatic. The team gave up 3,552 yards and improved to third. Over the years, Bengtson's units were particularly strong against the pass. From 1962 to 1969, the team was either first or second in that category.

Bengtson was born in 1913 in Rousseau, Minnesota. He enrolled at the University of Minnesota in 1931 and was named All-American at tackle three years later. He was also selected to play in that year's East-West Shrine game and the College All-Star game.

Following graduation, he turned down a professional football career and instead accepted an assistant coaching position at the University of Missouri in 1935. Five years later, he joined the staff of Stanford University where he remained for two seasons. By that time, America had become involved in World War II and Bengtson went on to coach an Iowa preflight service football team. At the same time, Bengtson became a gunnery officer and eventually reached the rank of lieutenant commander.

After leaving Green Bay, Bengtson served a year on the Chargers' coaching staff. He became a scout the next year and, in an unusual move, was lent to the Patriots late in 1972 to take over as head coach for the departed John Mazur.

Pro Coaching Record

Regular Season

	W	L	T	Pct
1968-70 Packers	20	21	1	.488
1972 Patriots	1	4	0	.200
1968-72 Totals	21	25	1	.457

Postseason

	W	L	T	Pct
1968-70 Packers	0	0	0	.000
1972 Patriots	0	0	0	.000
Postseason Totals	0	0	0	.000
Overall	21	25	1	.457

Green Bay Press-Gazette photo

Phil Bengtson confers with Bart Starr during a Vikings game in Milwaukee, November 17, 1969. Minnesota beat Green Bay 9-7.

DANIEL JOHN DEVINE

BORN: December 23, 1924

Dan Devine brought an impressive 120-40-8 mark with him to Green Bay when he was named the team's seventh head coach on January 14, 1971. Despite the eye-catching record, forged at Arizona State and the University of Missouri over a span of 16 years, some questioned whether or not a college coach could make a successful leap to the professional ranks.

By his second year in Green Bay, it appeared he could. After going 4-8-2 in 1971, the team captured the NFC Central Division title with a 10-4 mark in 1972. Green Bay had returned to the playoffs for the first time since the days of Lombardi. However, one of the four regular-season losses came at the expense of the Redskins and they again dumped the Packers in the first round of the playoffs, 16-13.

Washington, which shut down Green Bay's running game, also exposed the Packers as a team without a dominant quarterback. Over the next two years, Devine sought unsuccessfully to find a top-drawer signal-caller and that, in part, contributed to two losing seasons in 1973 and 1974. The day after a final 10-3 loss to the Falcons, Devine resigned and returned to the college environ as the head coach of the University of Notre Dame.

A native of Wisconsin, Devine was born in 1924 in Augusta near Chippewa Falls. He attended the University of Minnesota at Duluth where he competed in baseball, basketball and football. A quarterback, he captained the football team as well as the basketball team. He graduated in 1948 after having served for more than two years in the Army Air Corps.

He began his coaching career at East Jordan High School in Michigan the same year. In 1950, he became an assistant at Michigan State first serving as freshman coach and then as backfield coach.

Devine accepted his first head coaching job in the college ranks in 1955 at Arizona State. In three years there his teams went 27-3-1. The 1957 team fashioned a 10-0 mark and were ranked 12th in the nation. That squad was the first unbeaten and nationally ranked team in Sun Devil history.

Devine's success continued when he moved on to Missouri in 1958. He compiled an impressive 93-37-7 regular-season mark over the next 13 years. Nine of his teams were nationally ranked and over the years his Tigers won four bowl games. In 1961, Missouri defeated Navy 21-14 in the Orange Bowl to record its first ever postseason win.

Pro Coaching Record

Regular Season

	W	L	T	Pct
1971-74 Packers	25	27	4	.482
1971-74 Totals	25	27	4	.482

Postseason

	W	L	T	Pct
1971-74 Packers	0	1	0	.000
Postseason Totals	0	1	0	.000
Overall	0	1	0	.000

Green Bay Press-Gazette photo

Dan Devine objects to a call during a rainy game with Atlanta in Milwaukee in October, 1972. Green Bay lost 10-9.

BRYAN BARTLETT (BART) STARR

BORN: January 9, 1934

In the seven years following Vince Lombardi's retirement as coach, the Packers managed an unispiring 45-48-5 record and reached the playoffs just once. After Dan Devine resigned, the team looked to its past for head coaching candidates. The race boiled down to two former Lombardi students: Bart Starr and Dave Hanner.

Some speculated that Hanner, who had logged ten years as a defensive assistant with the team, had the inside track. But when the announcement came on December 24, 1974, Bart Starr, with just one year of prior coaching experience, was offered the head coaching job.

Starr had a sterling career as a player but was woefully lacking in coaching expertise. The sum total of his experience was one year (1972) as the Packers' quarterbacks coach. He was a television analyst in the other years (1973-74) following his retirement as a player in 1971.

In the first three years on the job, Starr's teams compiled 13 wins and 29 losses. Hindering him as much as his unfamiliarity with the job was the lack of a complete draft until 1977. Prior to that, the team owed the Rams compensation for John Hadl.

In 1978, the team raced to a 6-1 start before sliding and winding up 8-7-1. Rookies James Lofton, Paul Coffman and John Anderson embarked on outstanding careers that year. Two losing seasons in 1979 and 1980 had fans in an uproar. Starr was then stripped of his general manager duties after the 1980 season.

The 1981 team started 2-6 but rallied and just missed a playoff spot after losing 28-3 to the New York Jets on the season's final weekend. The strong finish carried over into 1982 and the Packers reached the playoffs for the first time in a decade. A 41-16 win over the Cardinals in Lambeau Field marked the first time since Super Bowl II that Green Bay had won a postseason game. Dallas ended the team's season with a 37-26 triumph.

Starr's final team won eight and lost eight. The last loss, 23-21 to the Bears at the end of the year, kept the Packers from a second straight playoff trip. Starr was fired a day after the Chicago setback.

Starr was born in Montgomery, Alabama in 1934. He won All-America honors in high school then moved on to the University of Alabama where he became a four-year letter winner. He led his team to a win over Syracuse in the 1953 Orange Bowl and finished second in the nation in punting. Starr also participated in the 1955 Blue-Grey game and was selected by Green Bay in the 17th round of the 1956 draft.

Three times Starr led the league in passing: 1962, 1964 and 1966. He played in four Pro Bowls, 1961-63 and 1967. In addition, Starr owned the NFL record for most consecutive passes attempted without an interception (294) for over 25 years.

Pro Coaching Record

Regular Season

	W	L	T	Pct
1975-83 Packers	52	76	3	.408
1975-83 Totals	52	76	3	.408

Postseason

	W	L	T	Pct
1975-83 Packers	1	1	0	.500
Postseason Totals	1	1	0	.500
Overall	53	77	3	.410

Green Bay Press-Gazette photo

Bart Starr watches with concern as his team goes down in defeat against the Dallas Cowboys in Milwaukee, September 28, 1980.

ALVIS FORREST GREGG

BORN: October 18, 1933

Just five days after Bart Starr was relieved of his coaching duties, Forrest Gregg became the ninth head coach in Green Bay's history. Like Starr, Gregg was another member of the Lombardi era. Unlike Starr, the former offensive tackle had been a head coach in the NFL for seven years and had an additional year of experience as the leader of the CFL's Toronto Argonauts.

Gregg came to Green Bay originally as a second-round choice in the 1956 draft. He came to represent durability and reliability. He played in a team record 187 consecutive games for the Packers, appeared in nine Pro Bowls — six consecutively — and ultimately wound up in the NFL Hall of Fame in his first year of eligibility.

Following his remarkable playing career — which included a year with the Cowboys in 1971 — Gregg joined the Chargers' staff as an assistant. After two years, he moved on to the Browns and guided the team's offensive line. The next year (1975) he was named head coach by owner Art Modell. His first team won just three games, but in 1976, a dramatic turnaround saw his team go 9-5 and earn Gregg "Coach of the Year" honors. Injuries beset the team in 1977 and Gregg resigned with one game left on the schedule.

Gregg returned to coaching in 1979 with Canada's Toronto Argonauts. He rejoined the NFL a year later and guided the Cincinnati Bengals to a Super Bowl appearance in 1981. Despite a 26-21 setback at the hands of the San Francisco 49ers in the Super Bowl, the team rebounded and finished a strong 7-2 in the strike-shortened campaign of 1982. That year, the New York Jets knocked off the Bengals 44-17 in the first round of the playoffs. After a disappointing 7-9 finish in 1983, Gregg left Cincinnati.

In his four years in Green Bay, Gregg's teams never won more than eight games in a single year. Slow starts in 1984 (1-7) and 1985 (3-5) hampered his first two squads. A major personnel overhaul in 1986 paid no immediate dividends as the Packers stumbled to a 4-12 finish. Gregg departed for his alma mater, Southern Methodist University, after Green Bay wound up 5-9-1 in 1987.

In college, Gregg made the All-Southwest Conference team twice. He captained the Southern Methodist football team as a senior in 1955.

Pro Coaching Record

Regular Season

	W	L	T	Pct
1975-77 Browns	18	23	0	.439
1979 Argonauts (CFL)	5	11	0	.313
1980-83 Bengals	32	25	0	.561
1984-87 Packers	**25**	**37**	**1**	**.405**
1975-87 Totals	80	96	1	.455

Postseason

	W	L	T	Pct
1975-77 Browns	0	0	0	.000
1979 Argonauts (CFL)	0	0	0	.000
1980-83 Bengals	2	2	0	.500
1984-87 Packers	**0**	**0**	**0**	**.000**
Postseason Totals	2	2	0	.500
Overall	82	98	1	.456

Forrest Gregg leads his troops into the season-opener against the Cardinals in Green Bay. The Packers edged St. Louis 24-23.

GELINDO (LINDY) INFANTE

BORN: May 27, 1940

The Packers made a complete break from the past when they hired Lindy Infante as coach on February 3, 1988. The 48-year old Miami, Florida native's only real ties to the team were indirect. Infante had served as quarterbacks coach and then offensive coordinator with Forrest Gregg at Cincinnati in the early '80s. So when he agreed to a five-year deal, a new era in Packers football was at hand.

Thirty years earlier, Vince Lombardi unleashed a "run to daylight" attack. Infante advocated what some coined a "pass to daylight" system. That new system, injuries, holdouts and a horrible kicking game contributed to Infante's 4-12 inaugural year in Green Bay. A year later, Don Majkowski, Sterling Sharpe, Tim Harris and Brent Fullwood emerged and carried the team from the cellar to the top of the Central Division with a 10-6 mark. Green Bay tied the Vikings for first in the division, but Minnesota made the playoffs because of a better division record. After such a heady season, the Packers slumped to 6-10 in 1990. Majkowski missed the last six games with a shoulder injury, the offensive line never jelled and the running game resembled the virtually non-existent attack of 1988. Instead of rebounding in 1991, the situation worsened and Infante was fired shortly after a 4-12 effort.

Infante began coaching in his hometown in 1965. Two years after graduating from the University of Florida, he joined the staff of Miami High School. A year later, he coached the freshman at Florida then took over as defensive backfield coach for the next five years. In 1972, he became offensive coordinator at Memphis State.

Infante joined the professional ranks with the Charlotte Hornets of the World Football League in 1975. He coached receivers for the New York Giants in the two years between serving as offensive coordinator at Tulane in 1976 and again in 1979.

After a three-year stint with the Bengals, Infante moved on to the head spot with the Jacksonville Bulls of the USFL. After two years in the rival league, Infante returned to the NFL and served as offensive coordinator and quarterbacks coach at Cleveland.

In 1963, Infante was selected in the 12th round by the Browns and was chosen in the 11th round by the AFL's Buffalo Bills. The running back/defensive back signed with the Bills, but was released before the season got underway. Infante did play in one game for the Tiger-Cats of the Canadian Football League and picked up 12 yards in three carries.

Pro Coaching Record

Regular Season

	W	L	T	Pct
1984-85 Bulls (USFL)	15	21	0	.417
1988-91 Packers	**24**	**40**	**0**	**.375**
1984-91 Totals	39	61	0	.390

Postseason

	W	L	T	Pct
1984-85 Bulls (USFL)	0	0	0	.000
1988-91 Packers	**0**	**0**	**0**	**.000**
Postseason Totals	0	0	0	.000
Overall	39	61	0	.390

Green Bay Press-Gazette photo

Lindy Infante voices his displeasure over a penalty in the second quarter of the Packers 31-13 loss to the Chicago Bears on September 16, 1990.

MICHAEL (MIKE) HOLMGREN

BORN: June 15, 1948

On January 11, 1992, Packers general manager Ron Wolf announced the hiring of Mike Holmgren as the teams' 11th head coach. That piece of news ended nearly three weeks of speculation as to who would succeed Lindy Infante.

Wolf, himself a relative newcomer to Packerland, sought a proven winner to lead the Green and Gold. Wolf considered Chuck Knox, winner of more than 150 games with the Rams, Bills, and Seahawks, but canceled an interview with him after former Giants coach Bill Parcells turned down overtures from Tampa Bay. After speaking with Parcells, Wolf realized that the winning coach in Super Bowls XXI and XXV was not interested in returning to coaching. So Wolf tabbed Holmgren, an assistant coach with the 1988-89 NFL Champion 49ers, as his man.

Packers fans couldn't have been more pleased. In his first year at the helm, Holmgren recharged the team, discovered a confident, capable young quarterback in Brett Favre and brought out the best in numerous others, most notably record-setting Sterling Sharpe. In 1992, 1993 and 1994 the team finished 9-7. In the latter two years the team returned to the playoffs defeating the Lions in postseason play on both occasions. Prior to the start of the 1994 campaign, the Packers extended Holmgren's contract through the end of the decade.

Holmgren got his start in coaching at San Francisco's Lincoln High School in 1971. From there, Holmgren moved on to Sacred Heart High (1972-74) and Oakgrove High (1975-80). In 1981, Holmgren became offensive coordinator and quarterbacks coach at San Francisco State University. A year later, he joined the staff of Brigham Young University. Holmgren remained with the Chargers through 1985 and tutored quarterbacks such as Robbie Bosco (the Packers third-round draft choice in 1986) and Steve Young of the 49ers. In 1984, BYU won its first national championship.

Holmgren jumped to the professional ranks in 1986 with the 49ers. As quarterbacks coach, he was instrumental in the continuing development of Joe Montana and backup Young. In 1989, head coach George Siefert promoted Holmgren to offensive coordinator. That year, the 49ers offense gained 6,268 yards to lead the NFL.

The St. Louis Cardinals drafted Holmgren in the eighth round in 1970. Holmgren had played quarterback at the University of Southern California. Holmgren spent time in the training camps of both the Cardinals and Jets in 1970 prior to embarking on his coaching career.

Pro Coaching Record

Regular Season

	W	L	T	Pct
1992-94 Packers	27	21	0	.563
1992-94 Totals	27	21	0	.563

Postseason

	W	L	T	Pct
1992-94 Packers	2	2	0	.500
Postseason Totals	2	2	0	.500
Overall	29	23	0	.558

Green Bay Press-Gazette photo

Mike Holmgren speaks to an official during a preseason game in 1992.

- 378 -

ASSISTANT COACHES

Name	Assignment(s)	Years
Austin, Bill	Offensive line	1959-64
Bengtson, Phil	Defensive line/defense	1959-67
Blache, Greg	Defensive line	1988-93
Bratkowski, Zeke	Offensive backfield	1969-70
	Quarterbacks	1975-78
	Quarterbacks/offensive backfield	1979-81
Brock, Charley	Defense	1949
Brooks, Larry	Defensive Line	1994
Brunner, John	Offensive backfield	1983
Bullough, Hank	Defensive coordinator	*1984, 1988-91
Burns, Jerry	Defensive backfield	1966-67
Carpenter, Lew	Receivers/passing game	1975-79
	Receivers	1980-85
Champion, Jim	Defensive line	1980
Clark, Joe	General offensive assistant	1988-89
	Assistant offensive line coach	1990-91
Cochran, John (Red)	Offensive backfield	1959-66, 71-74
Colbert, Jim	Defensive backs	1975
Coughlin, Tom	Receivers/passing game	1986-87
Cromwell, Nolan	Special teams	1992-94
Curry, Bill	Offensive line	1977-79
Davis, Charlie	Offensive line	1988-91
Devore, Hugh	Ends	1953
Doll, Don	Defensive secondary	1971-73
Dotsch, Rollie	Offensive line	1971-74
Drulis, Charles	Line	1951-53
Evans, Dick	Defensive secondary	1970
Fears, Tom	Offensive ends	1962-65
Fichtner, Ross	Defensive backs	1980-83
Geis, Wayne (Buddy)	Receivers	1988-91
Gregg, Forrest	Offensive line	1969-70
Gruden, Jon	Offensive assistant/quality control	1992
	Wide Receivers	1993-94
Gustafson, Burt	Linebackers	1971-74
	Special teams	1977-78
Hanner, Dave	Defensive line	1965-71
	Defensive coordinator	1972-74
	Defensive coordinator/ Assistant head coach	1975-79
	Quality control	1982
Haskell, Gil	Running backs	1992-94
Hearden, Tom	Ends	1954-55, 57
Hecker, Norb	Defensive backfield	1959-65
Hilton, John	Offensive backfield/special teams	1986
Hutson, Don	Backfield/ends	1945-48
Jauron, Dick	Defensive backfield	1986-94
Johnston, Kent	Strength-conditioning	1992-94
Kettela, Pete	Special assistant	1981
	Offensive backs	1982
Kiesling, Walt	Line	1945-48
Kiffin, Monte	Linebackers	1983
Kinard, Billy	Defensive secondary	1974
Klapstein, Earl	Defensive line	1956
Knight, Virgil	Strength-conditioning	1984-85
	Strength-conditioning/offensive line	1986-87
	Strength-conditioning/tight ends	1988-90
	Tight Ends	1991
Kotal, Eddie	Backfield coach	1942-43
Kuhlmann, Hank	Special teams	1972-74
LeBeau, Dick	Defensive backfield	1976-79
Lewis, Sherman	Offensive coordinator	1992-94
Lind, Jim	Defensive assistant/quality control	1992-94
Lindsey, Dale	Linebackers	1986-87
Lord, Bob	Special teams	1975-76
	Offensive backfield	1977-78

Name	Assignment(s)	Years
Lovat, Tom	Offensive line	1980, 92-94
Mariucci, Steve	Quarterbacks	1992-94
Marshall, John	Special teams/linebackers	1980
	Linebackers	1981-82
McCormick, Tom	Offensive backfield	1967-68
McLaughlin, Leon	Offensive line	1975-76
McLean, Ray (Scooter)	Backfield	1951-57
McMillan, Ernie	Offensive line	1978-83
Meyer, John	Linebackers	1975-79
	Defensive coordinator	1980-83
Meyers, Bill	Offensive line assistant	1982-83
Modzelewski, Dick	Defensive coordinator/ Defensive line	1984-87
Molenda, Bo	Backfield	1947-48
Morton, Jack	Defensive line coach	1957-58
Moseley, Richard	Outside linebackers	1988-91
Moss, Perry	Quarterbacks	1974
Nolting, Ray	Backfield	1950
Paterra, Herb	Linebackers/special teams	1984-85
Peete, Willie	Offensive backfield/special teams	1987
	Offensive backfield	1988-91
Plasman, Dick	Ends	1950-52
Polonchek, John	Receivers/passing game	1972-74
Priefer, Chuck	Special teams/linebackers	1984
	Special teams	1985
Rehbein, Dick	Special assistant	1979-80
	Special teams	1981-83
Reid, Andy	Tight ends/offensive line assistant	1992-94
Reid, Floyd (Breezy)	Backfield	1958
Rhodes, Ray	Defensive coordinator	1992
Richards, Ray	Defense	1958
Riederer, Russell	Strength-Conditioning	1991
Riley, Ken	Secondary	1984-85
Roach, Paul	Offensive coordinator	1975-76
Robinson, Wayne	Defensive secondary	1968-69
Roland, Johnny	Special assignments	1974
Rymkus, Lou	Line	1954-57
Schnelker, Bob	Receivers	1966-68
	Receivers/passing game	1969-71
	Offensive coordinator	1982-85
Sefcik, George	Offensive backfield	1984-85
	Quarterbacks	1986-87
Shurmur, Fritz	Defensive Coordinator	1994
Skorich, Nick	Offensive line	1958
Smith, Richard (Red)	Assistant coach	1936-43
Snyder, Bob	Backfield	1949
Starr, Bart	Quarterbacks	1972
Stidham, Tom	Line	1949
Stuber, Emmett (Abe)	Defensive backfield	1956
Sydney, Harry	General Assistant	1994
Taylor, John (Tarz)	Line	1950-52
Tippett, Howard	Special teams	1988-91
Trafton, George	Line	1944
Urich, Richard (Doc)	Defensive line	1981-83
Valesente, Bob	Linebackers	1992-94
vonAppen, Fred	Special teams	1979
	Defensive line	**1980
Voris, Dick	End coach	1961-62
Wampfler, Jerry	Offensive line	1984-87
Wieland, Bob	Strength-conditioning consultant	1990
Wietecha, Ray	Offensive line	1965-68
	Running game	1969-70

* Hank Bullough resigned May 23, 1984, then returned in 1988.
**resigned September 3, 1980.

ALL-PRO SELECTIONS

All-League Selections

1931
- E - LaVern (Lavvie) Dilweg
- T - Robert (Cal) Hubbard
- G - August (Mike) Michalske
- HB - Johnny (Blood) McNally

1932
- T - Robert (Cal) Hubbard
- C - Nate Barrager
- HB - Arnie Herber

1933
- T - Robert (Cal) Hubbard

1935
- G - August (Mike) Michalske

1936
- E - Don Hutson
- T - Ernie Smith
- G - Lon Evans
- FB - Clarke Hinkle

1937
- G - Lon Evans
- FB - Clarke Hinkle

1938
- E - Don Hutson
- G - Russ Letlow
- FB - Clarke Hinkle

1939
- E - Don Hutson

1940
- E - Don Hutson

1941
- E - Don Hutson
- HB - Cecil Isbell
- FB - Clarke Hinkle

1942
- E - Don Hutson
- HB - Cecil Isbell

(League selections discontinued in 1943.)

Press Assoc. All-Pro Selections

1943
- E - Don Hutson (AP, UP)
- FB - Tony Canadeo (AP)

1944
- E - Don Hutson (AP, UP)

1945
- E - Don Hutson (AP, UP)
- C - Charley Brock (AP, UP)
- FB - Ted Fritsch (UP)

1946
- FB - Ted Fritsch (AP, UP)

1949
- HB - Tony Canadeo (AP, UP)

1950
- C - Clayton Tonnemaker (UP)

1954
- LB - Roger Zatkoff (UP)
- DB - Bobby Dillon (AP)

1955
- LB - Roger Zatkoff (AP)
- DB - Bobby Dillon (AP, UP)

1956
- E - Bill Howton (AP, UP)
- DB - Bobby Dillon (UP)

1957
- E - Bill Howton (AP, UP)
- C - Jim Ringo (AP)
- DB - Bobby Dillon (AP, UP)

1958
- DB - Bobby Dillon (AP, UPI)

1959
- C - Jim Ringo (AP, UPI)

1960
- T - Forrest Gregg (AP)

- G - Jerry Kramer (AP)
- C - Jim Ringo (AP, UPI)
- HB - Paul Hornung (AP, UPI)
- DT - Henry Jordan (AP, UPI)
- LB - Bill Forester (AP, UPI)

1961
- T - Forrest Gregg (UPI)
- G - Fred (Fuzzy) Thurston (AP, UPI, NEA)
- C - Jim Ringo (AP, UPI, NEA)
- HB - Paul Hornung (AP, UPI)
- FB - Jim Taylor (NEA)
- DT - Henry Jordan (AP, UPI, NEA)
- LB - Dan Currie (UPI, NEA)
- LB - Bill Forester (AP, UPI)
- DB - Jesse Whittenton (AP, UPI)

1962
- TE - Ron Kramer (AP)
- T - Forrest Gregg (AP, UPI, NEA)
- G - Jerry Kramer (AP, UPI, NEA)
- G - Fred (Fuzzy) Thurston (UPI)
- C - Jim Ringo (AP, UPI, NEA)
- FB - Jim Taylor (AP, UPI, NEA)
- DE - Willie Davis (AP)
- DT - Henry Jordan (AP)
- LB - Dan Currie (AP, UPI, NEA)
- LB - Bill Forester (AP, UPI, NEA)
- CB - Herb Adderley (AP, UPI)

1963
- T - Forrest Gregg (AP, UPI, NEA)
- G - Jerry Kramer (AP, UPI, NEA)
- C - Jim Ringo (AP, UPI, NEA)
- DT - Henry Jordan (AP, UPI, NEA)
- LB - Bill Forester (UPI)
- S - Willie Wood (NEA)
- CB - Herb Adderley (AP)

1964
- T - Forrest Gregg (AP, UPI, NEA)
- DE - Willie Davis (AP, UPI, NEA)
- DT - Henry Jordan (AP, UPI)
- LB - Ray Nitschke (AP, UPI)
- S - Willie Wood (AP, UPI, NEA)

1965
- T - Forrest Gregg (UPI)
- G - Forrest Gregg (AP)
- DE - Willie Davis (AP, UPI, NEA)
- LB - Ray Nitschke (UPI)
- S - Willie Wood (AP, UPI, NEA)
- CB - Herb Adderley (AP, UPI, NEA)

1966
- T - Forrest Gregg (AP, UPI, NEA)
- G - Jerry Kramer (AP, UPI)
- QB - Bart Starr (AP, UPI, NEA)
- DE - Willie Davis (AP, UPI, NEA)
- LB - Ray Nitschke (AP, UPI, NEA)
- LB - Lee Roy Caffey (AP, UPI)
- S - Willie Wood (AP, UPI, NEA)
- CB - Herb Adderley (AP, UPI, NEA)

1967
- T - Forrest Gregg (AP, UPI)
- G - Jerry Kramer (AP, UPI)
- DE - Willie Davis (AP, UPI, NEA)
- LB - Dave Robinson (AP, UPI, NEA)
- S - Willie Wood (AP, UPI)
- CB - Bob Jeter (AP, UPI, NEA)

1968
- LB - Dave Robinson (UPI, NEA)
- S - Willie Wood (UPI)

1969
- G - Gale Gillingham (NEA)
- LB - Dave Robinson (AP, UPI, NEA)
- CB - Herb Adderley (AP)

1970
- G - Gale Gillingham (AP, UPI, NEA, SN)
- S - Willie Wood (SN)

1971
- G - Gale Gillingham (UPI, NEA, SN)
- RB - John Brockington (AP, UPI, NEA, SN)
- S - Willie Wood (SN)

1972
- RB - John Brockington (AP, UPI, SN)
- CB - Ken Ellis (AP, UPI)
- K - Chester Marcol (NEA, PFWA, SN)

1973
- RB - John Brockington (AP, UPI, NEA, SN)
- CB - Ken Ellis (AP, UPI, SN)

1974
- G - Gale Gillingham (AP, UPI, NEA, SN)
- LB - Ted Hendricks (AP, UPI, NEA, SN, PFW, PFWA)
- K - Chester Marcol (AP, UPI, SN, PFWA)

1975
- LB - Fred Carr (SN)

1978
- RB - Terdell Middleton (SN)
- CB - Willie Buchanon (AP, UPI, SN, PFWA)

1980
- WR - James Lofton (UPI, NEA, PFWA, PFW)

1981
- WR - James Lofton (AP, UPI, NEA, SN, PFW, PFWA)

1982
- WR - James Lofton (UPI)
- C - Larry McCarren (UPI)
- LB - Mike Douglass (PFW)

1983
- WR - James Lofton (PFWA)
- TE - Paul Coffman (UPI)

1984
- WR - James Lofton (NEA)
- TE - Paul Coffman (UPI)
- P - Bucky Scribner (UPI)

1985
- WR - James Lofton (NEA)

1988
- LB - Tim Harris (NEA, SI)

1989
- WR - Sterling Sharpe (AP, UPI All-NFC, SN, PFWA, PFW)
- G - Rich Moran (NEA)
- LB - Tim Harris (AP, UPI All-NFC, NEA, SN, PFWA, CPFNW, FD, PFW, SI)

1990
- WR - Sterling Sharpe (UPI All-NFC)
- C - James Campen (USA Today All-Pro)

1992
- WR - Sterling Sharpe (AP, PFW/PFWA, SN, UPI All-NFC, NEA, CPFNW, FD)
- TE - Jackie Harris (NEA 2nd team)
- S - Chuck Cecil (CPFNW)

1993
- S - LeRoy Butler (AP, UPI All-NFC, SI, SN, PFW/PFWA, FD, FN All-NFC)
- K - Chris Jacke (AP, CPFNW)
- WR - Sterling Sharpe (AP, UPI All-NFC, SI, SN PFW/PFWA, CPFNW, FD, FN All-NFC)
- DE - Reggie White (UPI, SN, CPFNW, FD, FN All-NFC)

1994
- DE - Reggie White (AP 2nd team, CPFNW 2nd team, FD 2nd team, FN, SI, UPI All-NFC)
- WR - Sterling Sharpe (CPFNW 2nd team, FD 2nd team, UPI All-NFC 2nd team)
- QB - Brett Favre (FD 2nd team)
- LB - Bryce Paup (FD 2nd team, FN, USA Today, UPI All-NFC)
- DE - Sean Jones (UPI All-NFC 2nd team)

- AP - Associated Press
- UP(I) - United Press (International)
- NEA - Newspaper Enterprise Association
- SN - The Sporting News
- PFWA - Pro Football Writers of America
- PFW - Pro Football Weekly
- CPFNW - College and Pro Football News Weekly
- FD - Football Digest
- FN - Football News

THE PRO BOWL

The Pro Bowl debuted on January 14, 1951. The top players from the American and National Conferences participated in that game and when the conferences were renamed in 1954, the best of the Western and Eastern Conferences clashed on an annual basis. Beginning in 1971, with the merger of the NFL and AFL, the elite of the AFC and NFC battled.

In the late 1930s and early 1940s, a group of NFL All-Stars played the league champions in a game that in some ways resembled a Pro Bowl. For instance, after the Packers had won the NFL title in 1939, they engaged the NFL All-Stars on January 14, 1940 in Los Angeles and won 16-7. The last game of that type was played in December, 1942.

Below is a list of the 45 Pro Bowls and the Packers who participated in them.

Date	Result	Site	Att.
1/14/51	American 28 .... National 27	Los Angeles	(53,676)
1/12/52	National 30 .... American 13	Los Angeles	(19,400)
1/10/53	National 27 ..... American 7	Los Angeles	(34,208)
1/17/54	East 20 .... West 9	Los Angeles	(44,214)
1/16/55	West 26 .... East 19	Los Angeles	(43,972)
1/15/56	East 31 .... West 30	Los Angeles	(37,867)
1/13/57	West 19 .... East 10	Los Angeles	(44,177)
1/12/58	West 26 .... East 7	Los Angeles	(66,634)
1/11/59	East 28 .... West 21	Los Angeles	(72,250)
1/17/60	West 38 .... East 21	Los Angeles	(56,876)
1/15/61	West 35 .... East 31	Los Angeles	(62,971)
1/14/62	West 31 .... East 30	Los Angeles	(57,409)
1/13/63	East 30 .... West 20	Los Angeles	(61,374)
1/12/64	West 31 .... East 17	Los Angeles	(67,242)
1/10/65	West 34 .... East 14	Los Angeles	(60,598)
1/16/66	East 36 .... West 7	Los Angeles	(60,124)
1/22/67	East 20 .... West 10	Los Angeles	(15,062)
1/21/68	West 38 .... East 20	Los Angeles	(53,289)
1/19/69	West 10 .... East 7	Los Angeles	(32,050)
1/18/70	West 16 .... East 13	Los Angeles	(57,786)
1/24/71	NFC 27 .... AFC 6	Los Angeles	(48,222)
1/23/72	AFC 26 .... NFC 13	Los Angeles	(53,647)
1/21/73	AFC 33 .... NFC 28	Irving, Texas	(47,879)
1/20/74	AFC 15 .... NFC 13	Kansas City	(51,482)
1/20/75	NFC 17 .... AFC 10	Miami	(26,484)
1/26/76	NFC 23 .... AFC 20	New Orleans	(32,108)
1/17/77	AFC 24 .... NFC 14	Seattle	(63,214)
1/23/78	NFC 14 .... AFC 13	Tampa	(51,337)
1/29/79	NFC 13 .... AFC 7	Los Angeles	(46,281)
1/27/80	NFC 37 .... AFC 27	Honolulu	(48,060)
2/1/81	NFC 21 .... AFC 7	Honolulu	(47,879)
1/31/82	AFC 16 .... NFC 13	Honolulu	(50,402)
2/6/83	NFC 20 .... AFC 19	Honolulu	(47,201)
1/29/84	NFC 45 .... AFC 3	Honolulu	(50,445)
1/27/85	AFC 22 .... NFC 14	Honolulu	(50,385)
2/2/86	NFC 28 .... AFC 24	Honolulu	(50,101)
2/1/87	AFC 10 .... NFC 6	Honolulu	(50,101)
2/7/88	AFC 15 .... NFC 6	Honolulu	(50,113)
1/29/89	NFC 34 .... AFC 3	Honolulu	(50,113)
2/4/90	NFC 27 .... AFC 21	Honolulu	(50,445)
2/3/91	AFC 23 .... NFC 21	Honolulu	(50,345)
2/2/92	NFC 21 .... AFC 15	Honolulu	(50,209)
2/7/93	AFC 23 .... NFC 20 (OT)	Honolulu	(50,007)
2/6/94	NFC 17 .... AFC 3	Honolulu	(50,026)
2/5/95	AFC 41 .... NFC 13	Honolulu	(49,121)

Pro-Bowl selections

1951
- *C - Clayton Tonnemaker
- C - Ed Neal
- HB - Billy Grimes

1952
- T - Dick Wildung
- HB - Billy Grimes

1953
- E - Bill Howton
- E - Abner Wimberly
- LB - Deral Teteak

1954
- DE - John Martinkovic
- DT - Dave Hanner
- LB - Clayton Tonnemaker

1955
- DT - Dave Hanner
- LB - Roger Zatkoff

1956
- E - Bill Howton
- FB - Howie Ferguson
- DE - John Martinkovic
- LB - Roger Zatkoff
- DB - Bobby Dillon

1957
- E - Bill Howton
- QB - Tobin Rote
- LB - Roger Zatkoff
- DB - Bobby Dillon

1958
- E - Bill Howton
- C - Jim Ringo
- DB - Bobby Dillon

1959
- C - Jim Ringo
- DB - Bobby Dillon

1960
- T - Forrest Gregg
- C - Jim Ringo
- HB - Paul Hornung
- LB - Bill Forester
- DB - Emlen Tunnell

1961
- T - Forrest Gregg
- C - Jim Ringo
- HB - Paul Hornung
- FB - Jim Taylor
- QB - Bart Starr
- DT - Henry Jordan
- LB - Dan Currie
- LB - Bill Forester

1962
- WR - Max McGee
- T - Forrest Gregg
- C - Jim Ringo
- FB - Jim Taylor
- QB - Bart Starr
- DT - Henry Jordan
- LB - Bill Forester
- DB - Jesse Whittenton

1963
- T - Forrest Gregg
- G - Jerry Kramer
- C - Jim Ringo
- #FB - Jim Taylor
- $FB - Tom Moore
- QB - Bart Starr
- TE - Ron Kramer
- LB - Bill Forester
- S - Willie Wood

1964
- T - Forrest Gregg
- G - Jerry Kramer
- C - Jim Ringo
- FB - Jim Taylor
- DE - Willie Davis
- DT - Henry Jordan
- DB - Jesse Whittenton
- CB - Herb Adderley

1965
- T - Forrest Gregg
- FB - Jim Taylor
- DE - Willie Davis
- LB - Ray Nitschke
- S - Willie Wood
- CB - Herb Adderley

1966
- WR - Boyd Dowler
- DE - Willie Davis
- LB - Lee Roy Caffey
- S - Willie Wood
- CB - Herb Adderley

1967
- T - Forrest Gregg
- T - Bob Skoronski
- QB - Bart Starr
- DE - Willie Davis
- DT - Henry Jordan
- LB - Dave Robinson
- S - Willie Wood
- CB - Herb Adderley

1968
- WR - Boyd Dowler
- T - Forrest Gregg
- G - Jerry Kramer
- DE - Willie Davis
- LB - Dave Robinson
- S - Willie Wood
- DB - Bob Jeter
- CB - Herb Adderley
- K - Don Chandler

1969
- WR - Carroll Dale
- T - Forrest Gregg
- RB - Donny Anderson
- S - Willie Wood

1970
- WR - Carroll Dale
- G - Gale Gillingham
- LB - Dave Robinson
- S - Willie Wood
- CB - Bob Jeter

1971
- WR - Carroll Dale
- G - Gale Gillingham
- LB - Fred Carr
- S - Willie Wood

1972
- G - Gale Gillingham
- FB - John Brockington

1973
- FB - John Brockington
- DT - Bob Brown
- LB - Fred Carr
- K - Chester Marcol

1974
RB - John Brockington
LB - Jim Carter
CB - Ken Ellis

1975
G - Gale Gillingham
LB - Ted Hendricks
CB - Willie Buchanon
CB - Ken Ellis
K - Chester Marcol

1976
LB - Fred Carr
KR - Steve Odom

1979
WR - James Lofton
RB - Terdell Middleton
DE - Ezra Johnson
CB - Willie Buchanon

1981
WR - James Lofton

1982
WR - James Lofton

1983
WR - James Lofton
WR - John Jefferson
C - Larry McCarren
TE - Paul Coffman

1984
WR - James Lofton
C - Larry McCarren
TE - Paul Coffman

1985
WR - James Lofton
TE - Paul Coffman

1986
WR - James Lofton

1990
WR - Sterling Sharpe
RB - Brent Fullwood
**QB - Don Majkowski
LB - Tim Harris

1991
WR - Sterling Sharpe

1993
WR - Sterling Sharpe
QB - Brett Favre
S - Chuck Cecil

1994
DE - Reggie White
QB - Brett Favre
S - LeRoy Butler
WR - Sterling Sharpe+

1995
DE - Reggie White++
WR - Sterling Sharpe##
LB - Bryce Paup

* Tonnemaker selected but in military service at the time of the game.
# Taylor missed game due to hepatitis.
$ Moore replaced Taylor.
** Majkowski did not play for personal reasons.
+ Sharpe did not play due to Achilles and turf toe injuries.
++ White did not play due to an elbow injury.
Sharpe did not play due to a neck injury.

Green Bay Press-Gazette photo

Tobin Rote (18), All-Pro in 1957, unloads a pass against the Lions in 1955.

Green Bay Press-Gazette photo

John Jefferson (83) grabs a pass over Detroit's William Graham. Jefferson was All-Pro in 1983.

THE CHICAGO COLLEGE ALL-STAR GAME

The Chicago All-Star Game was organized and sponsored by Chicago Tribune Charities in order to raise money for the needy. The first game was played in 1934; the last in 1976. The 1974 edition was wiped out because of a strike by NFL players.

Each year, the NFL champions of the previous season met the best players at the collegiate level. Except for the years in and around World War II, a player's college eligibility had to have expired in order for him to participate. All the games, except for the 1943 and 1944 contests, were played at Soldier Field in Chicago. Dyche Stadium in Evanston, Illinois hosted the 1943 and 1944 games.

Below and on the following page is a list of Packers who participated in one or more of the 42 Chicago All-Star Games either at the collegiate or professional level or both.

Date	Result	Att.
8/31/34	Chicago Bears 0 ...... All-Stars 0	(79,432)
8/29/35	Chicago Bears 5 ...... All-Stars 0	(77,450)
9/2/36	Detroit Lions 7 ...... All-Stars 7	(76,361)
9/1/37	Green Bay Packers 0 ...... All-Stars 6	(84,560)
8/31/38	Washington Redskins 16 ...... All-Stars 28	(74,250)
8/30/39	New York Giants 9 ...... All-Stars 0	(81,456)
8/29/40	Green Bay Packers 45 ...... All-Stars 28	(84,567)
8/28/41	Chicago Bears 37 ...... All-Stars 13	(98,203)
8/28/42	Chicago Bears 21 ...... All-Stars 0	(101,103)
8/25/43	Washington Redskins 7 ...... All-Stars 27	(48,471)
8/30/44	Chicago Bears 24 ...... All-Stars 21	(48,769)
8/30/45	Green Bay Packers 19 ...... All-Stars 7	(92,753)
8/23/46	Los Angeles Rams 0 ...... All-Stars 16	(97,380)
8/22/47	Chicago Bears 0 ...... All-Stars 16	(105,840)
8/20/48	Chicago Cardinals 28 ...... All-Stars 0	(101,220)
8/12/49	Philadelphia Eagles 38 ...... All-Stars 0	(93,780)
8/11/50	Philadelphia Eagles 7 ...... All-Stars 17	(88,885)
8/17/51	Cleveland Browns 33 ...... All-Stars 0	(92,180)
8/15/52	Los Angeles Rams 10 ...... All-Stars 7	(88,316)
8/14/53	Detroit Lions 24 ...... All-Stars 10	(93,818)
8/13/54	Detroit Lions 31 ...... All-Stars 6	(93,470)
8/12/55	Cleveland Browns 27 ...... All-Stars 30	(75,000)
8/10/56	Cleveland Browns 26 ...... All-Stars 0	(75,000)
8/9/57	New York Giants 22 ...... All-Stars 12	(75,000)
8/15/58	Detroit Lions 19 ...... All-Stars 35	(70,000)
8/14/59	Baltimore Colts 29 ...... All-Stars 0	(70,000)
8/12/60	Baltimore Colts 32 ...... All-Stars 7	(70,000)
8/5/61	Philadelphia Eagles 28 ...... All-Stars 14	(66,000)
8/3/62	Green Bay Packers 42 ...... All-Stars 20	(65,000)
8/2/63	Green Bay Packers 17 ...... All-Stars 20	(65,000)
8/7/64	Chicago Bears 28 ...... All-Stars 17	(65,000)
8/6/65	Cleveland Browns 24 ...... All-Stars 16	(68,000)
8/5/66	Green Bay Packers 38 ...... All-Stars 0	(72,000)
8/4/67	Green Bay Packers 27 ...... All-Stars 0	(70,934)
8/2/68	Green Bay Packers 34 ...... All-Stars 17	(69,917)
8/1/69	New York Jets 26 ...... All-Stars 24	(74,208)
7/31/70	Kansas City Chiefs 24 ...... All-Stars 3	(69,940)
7/30/71	Baltimore Colts 24 ...... All-Stars 17	(52,289)
7/28/72	Dallas Cowboys 20 ...... All-Stars 7	(54,162)
7/27/73	Miami Dolphins 14 ...... All-Stars 3	(54,103)
1974	No game played	
8/1/75	Pittsburgh Steelers 21 ...... All-Stars 14	(54,562)
7/23/76	Pittsburgh Steelers 24 ...... All-Stars 0	(52,895)

Collegians - The following Packers participated in the Chicago All-Star game while in college.

Name	School	Pos	Yr.
Adderley, Herb	Michigan State	HB	1961
Anderson, Donny	Texas Tech	HB	1966
Bain, Bill	USC	G	1975
Balasz, Frank	Iowa	B	1939
Barzilauskas, Carl	Indiana	DT	1974
Beck, Ken	Texas A&M	T	1959
Bell, Edward	Indiana	G	1945
	Indiana	G	1946
Bettis, Tom	Purdue	G	1955
Blaine, Ed	Missouri	T	1962
Bowman, Ken	Wisconsin	C	1964
Bradley, Dave	Penn State	T	1969
Bratkowski, Zeke	Georgia	QB	1954
Brock, Charley	Nebraska	C	1939
Brock, Lou	Purdue	B	1940
Brockington, John	Ohio State	RB	1971
Brown, Aaron	Minnesota	DE	1966
Brown, Allen	Mississippi	E	1965
Brown, Dave	Michigan	CB	1975
Bucchianeri, Amadeo	Indiana	G	1941
Buchanon, Willie	San Diego State	CB	1972
Buhler, Larry	Minnesota	B	1939
Bullough, Hank	Michigan State	G	1955
Burris, Paul (Buddy)	Oklahoma	G	1949
Caffey, Lee Roy	Texas A&M	LB	1963
Carr, Fred	Texas-El Paso	LB	1968
Carroll, Leo	San Diego State	DE	1967
Chandler, Don	Florida	HB	1956
Christman, Paul	Missouri	QB	1941
Clancy, Jack	Michigan	WR	1967
Claridge, Dennis	Nebraska	QB	1964
Clemons, Ray	St. Mary's (CA)	G	1947
Cody, Ed	Purdue	B	1947
Coffey, Junior	Washington	HB	1965
Concannon, Jack	Boston College	QB	1964
Cook, Ted	Alabama	E	1945
Coutre, Larry	Notre Dame	B	1950
Crimmins, Bernie	Notre Dame	G	1942
Crutcher, Tommy	TCU	LB	1964
Currie, Dan	Michigan State	C	1958
Curry, Bill	Georgia Tech	C	1965
Cvercko, Andy	Northwestern	T	1959
Dale, Carroll	Virginia Tech	WR	1960
Daniell, Averell	Pittsburgh	T	1937
Davidson, Ben	Washington	T	1961
Davis, Harper	Mississippi State	B	1949
Dawson, Gib	Texas	HB	1953
Dillon, Bobby	Texas	DB	1952
Dittrich, John	Wisconsin	G	1956
Douglass, Bobby	Kansas	QB	1969
Dowler, Boyd	Colorado	WR	1959
Eason, Roger	Oklahoma	T	1942
Evans, Dick	Iowa	E	1940
Faverty, Hal	Wisconsin	E	1952
Feathers, Beattie	Tennessee	B	1934
Flanigan, Jim	Pittsburgh	LB	1967
Ford, Len	Michigan	DE	1948
Forester, Bill	SMU	LB	1953
Frankowski, Ray	Washington	G	1942
Frutig, Ed	Michigan	E	1941
Garrett, Bob	Stanford	QB	1954
Getty, Charlie	Penn State	T	1974
Gillingham, Gale	Minnesota	G	1966
Girard, Earl (Jug)	Wisconsin	B	1948
Grabowski, Jim	Illinois	FB	1966
Gregg, Forrest	SMU	G	1956
Gros, Earl	LSU	FB	1962
Hadl, John	Kansas	QB	1962
Hall, Charlie	Pittsburgh	S	1971
Hansen, Don	Illinois	LB	1966
Harrell, Willard	Pacific	RB	1975
Heath, Stan	Nevada-Reno	QB	1949
Hendricks, Ted	Miami	LB	1969
Hickman, Larry	Baylor	FB	1959
Hill, Jim	Texas A&I	S	1968
Hornung, Paul	Notre Dame	QB	1957
Howton, Bill	Rice	E	1952
Hunter, Art	Notre Dame	T	1954
Hutson, Don	Alabama	E	1935
Hyland, Bob	Boston College	OL	1967
Isbell, Cecil	Purdue	B	1938
Jacobs, Jack	Oklahoma	B	1942
Jacunski, Harry	Fordham	E	1939
Janet, Ernie	Washington	G	1971
Jankowski, Ed	Wisconsin	B	1937
Jensen, Jim	Iowa	RB	1976
Johnson, Tom	Michigan	T	1952
Jones, Bob	Indiana	G	1934
Jordan, Henry	Virginia	DT	1957
Kekeris, James	Missouri	T	1944
Keuper, Ken	Georgia	B	1944
Kimmel, J.D.	Houston	T	1953
Knafelc, Gary	Colorado	E	1954
Knutson, Steve	USC	T	1975
Koncar, Mark	Colorado	T	1976
Kovatch, John	Notre Dame	E	1942
Kramer, Jerry	Idaho	G	1958
Kramer, Ron	Michigan	E	1957

Name	School	Pos	Yr.
Lane, MacArthur	Utah State	RB	1968
Lawrence, Jim	TCU	B	1936
Laws, Joe	Iowa	B	1934
Lee, Bill	Alabama	T	1935
Lester, Darrell	TCU	C	1936
Losch, John	Miami	HB	1956
Lueck, Bill	Arizona	G	1968
Maddox, George	Kansas State	T	1935
Manley, Leon	Oklahoma	T	1950
Mann, Bob	Michigan	E	1948
Marcol, Chester	Hillsdale	K	1972
Massey, Carlton	Texas	E	1954
Matthews, Al	Texas A&I	CB	1970
Matuszak, Marv	Tulsa	T	1953
McCoy, Mike P.	Notre Dame	DT	1970
McCoy, Mike C.	Colorado	CB	1976
McHan, Lamar	Arkansas	QB	1954
McIlhenny, Don	SMU	HB	1956
McKay, Roy	Texas	B	1943
	Texas	B	1944
Meilinger, Steve	Kentucky	E	1954
Mercein, Chuck	Yale	FB	1965
Mestnik, Frank	Marquette	B	1960
Michaels, Lou	Kentucky	T	1958
Midler, Lou	Minnesota	G	1938
Mitchell, Charles	Tulsa	B	1945
Moore, Rich	Villanova	DT	1969
Moore, Tom	Vanderbilt	RB	1960
Moss, Perry	Tulsa	QB	1945
	Illinois	QB	1948
Nitschke, Ray	Illinois	LB	1958
Norton, Jerry	SMU	HB	1954
Nussbaumer, Bob	Michigan	B	1946

Name	School	Pos	Yr.
Odom, Steve	Utah State	WR	1974
O'Donahue, Pat	Wisconsin	E	1952
Odson, Urban	Minnesota	T	1942
Okoniewski, Steve	Montana	T	1972
Olsonoski, Larry	Minnesota	G	1948
O'Neil, Ed	Penn State	LB	1974
Palumbo, Sam	Notre Dame	G	1955
Pannell, Ernie	Texas A&M	T	1941
Papit, Johnny	Virginia	B	1951
Parilli, Vito (Babe)	Kentucky	QB	1952
Paskvan, George	Wisconsin	B	1941
Peay, Francis	Missouri	T	1966
Petitbon, John	Notre Dame	HB	1952
Pregulman, Merv	Michigan	C	1946
Psaltis, Jim	USC	HB	1953
Randolph, Al	Iowa	CB	1966
Reichardt, Bill	Iowa	FB	1952
Rhodemyre, Jay	Kentucky	C	1948
Robinson, Dave	Penn State	LB	1963
Rohrig, Herman	Nebraska	B	1941
Salsbury, Jim	UCLA	G	1955
Sandifer, Dan	LSU	B	1948
Sandusky, John	Villanova	T	1950
Sauer, George	Nebraska	B	1934
Schlinkman, Walt	Texas Tech	B	1945
Schuh, Harry	Memphis State	T	1965
Schwammel, Ade	Oregon State	T	1934
Seeman, George	Nebraska	E	1940
Shirey, Fred	Nebraska	T	1938
Skoglund, Bob	Notre Dame	E	1947
Skoronski, Bob	Indiana	T	1956
Smith, Barry	Florida State	WR	1973

Name	School	Pos	Yr.
Smith, Bruce	Minnesota	B	1942
Spilis, John	Northern Illinois	WR	1969
Svendsen, Earl	Minnesota	C	1937
Switzer, Veryl	Kansas State	HB	1954
Szafaryn, Len	North Carolina	T	1949
Tagge, Jerry	Nebraska	QB	1972
Tassos, Damon	Nebraska	G	1945
Taylor, Jim	LSU	FB	1958
Temp, Jim	Wisconsin	E	1955
Thomas, Ike	Bishop	CB	1971
Timberlake, George	USC	G	1954
Tinker, Gerald	Kent State	WR	1974
Tonnemaker, Claygon	Minnesota	C	1950
Twedell, Francis	Minnesota	G	1939
Uram, Andy	Minnesota	B	1938
Van Every, Hal	Minnesota	B	1940
Vereen, Carl	Georgia Tech	T	1957
Vogds, Evan	Wisconsin	G	1946
Voss, Lloyd	Nebraska	T	1964
Wagner, Steve	Wisconsin	S	1976
Walker, Malcolm	Rice	C	1965
Walker, Val Joe	SMU	HB	1953
Weaver, Gary	Fresno State	LB	1973
Wildung, Dick	Minnesota	T	1943
Wilson, Ben	USC	FB	1963
Wimberly, Abner	LSU	E	1949
Zarnas, Gus	Ohio State	G	1938
Zatkoff, Roger	Michigan	LB	1953

Professionals - The following participated in the Chicago College All-Star game while with the Packers.

Name	Pos	Year(s)
Adams, Chet	T	1945
Adderley, Herb	CB	1962-63, 66-68
Adkins, Bob	QB	1945
Aldridge, Lionel	DE	1963, 66-68
Anderson, Bill	WR	1966
Anderson, Donny	RB	1967-68
Balazs, Frank	B	1940
Barnes, Gary	E	1962-63
Barrett, Jan	E	1963
Becker, Wayland	E	1937
Berezney, Paul	T	1945
Berry, Connie Mack	E	1940
Blaine, Ed	G	1963
Bowman, Ken	C	1966-68
Bratkowski, Zeke	QB	1966-67
Brock, Charley	C	1940, 45
Brock, Lou	B	1945
Brown, Allen	WR	1966-67
Brown, Bob	DT	1966-67
Brown, Tom	S	1966-68
Bruder, Hank	B	1937
Bucchianeri, Amadeo	G	1945
Buhler, Larry	B	1940
Butler, Frank	T	1937
Caffey, Lee Roy	LB	1966-68
Capp, Dick	TE	1967-68
Carpenter, Lew	HB	1962-63
Chandler, Don	K	1966-67
Comp, Irv	B	1945
Craig, Larry	QB	1940, 45
Crenshaw, Leon	DT	1967
Croft, Milburn (Tiny)	T	1945
Crutcher, Tommy	LB	1966-67
Currie, Dan	LB	1962-63
Curry, Bill	C	1966
Dale, Carroll	WR	1966-68
Davidson, Ben	DE	1962
Davis, Willie	DE	1962-63, 66-68

Name	Pos	Year(s)
Dowler, Boyd	WR	1962-63, 66-68
Dunaway, Dave	WR	1967-68
Engebretsen, Paul (Tiny)	G	1937, 40
Evans, Dick	G	1937
Feathers, Beattie	B	1940
Flanigan, Jim	LB	1968
Fleming, Marv	TE	1963, 66, 68
Flowers, Bob	C	1945
Folkins, Lee	DE	1962
Forester, Bill	LB	1962-63
Fritsch, Ted	B	1945
Gantenbein, Milt	E	1937, 40
Gassert, Ron	DT	1962-63
Gillette, Jim	B	1940
Gillingham, Gale	G	1966-68
Goldenberg, Charles	G	1937, 40, 45
Goodnight, Clyde	E	1945
Gordon, Lou	T	1937
Grabowski, Jim	RB	1967-68
Greenfield, Tom	C	1940
Gregg, Forrest	T	1962-63, 66-68
Gremminger, Hank	DB	1962-63
Grimm, Dan	G	1963
Gros, Earl	FB	1963, 66
Hanner, Dave	DT	1962-63
Hart, Doug	DB	1966-68
Hathcock, Dave	DB	1966-67
Henry, Urban	DE	1963
Herber, Arnie	B	1937, 40
Himes, Dick	T	1968
Hinkle, Clarke	FB	1937, 40
Holler, Ed	LB	1963
Horn, Don	QB	1967
Hornung, Paul	HB	1962, 66
Hutson, Don	E	1937, 40, 45
Hyland, Bob	C	1968

Name	Pos	Year(s)
Iman, Ken	C	1962-63
Isbell, Cecil	B	1940
Jacobs, Allen	HB	1966
Jacunski, Harry	E	1940, 45
James, Claudis	WR	1967-68
Jankowski, Ed	B	1940
Jeter, Bob	DB	1963, 66-68
Johnson, Howard	G	1940
Johnston, Chester	B	1937
Jordan, Henry	DT	1962-63, 66-68
Kell, Paul	T	1940
Kilbourne, Warren	T	1940
Knafelc, Gary	E	1962-63
Kostelnik, Ron	DT	1962-63, 66-68
Kramer, Jerry	G	1962-63, 66-68
Kramer, Ron	TE	1962-63
Kuusisto, Bill	G	1945
Lawrence, Jim	B	1940
Laws, Joe	B	1937, 40, 45
Lee, Bill	T	1940
Lester, Darrell	C	1937
Letlow, Russ	G	1937, 40
Long, Bob	WR	1967
Luhn, Nolan	E	1945
Marshall, Rich	DT	1966
Masters, Norm	T	1962-63
McGee, Max	WR	1962-63, 66-67
McKay, Roy	B	1945
Mercein, Chuck	RB	1968
Michalske, Mike	G	1937
Midler, Lou	G	1940
Miller, Paul	B	1937
Monnett, Bob	B	1937
Moore, Tom	HB	1962-63
Mulleneaux, Carl (Moose)	E	1940
Nitschke, Ray	LB	1962, 66-68

Name	Pos	Year(s)
Peay, Francis	T	1968
Perkins, Don	B	1945
Pitts, Elijah	HB	1962-63, 66-68
Quinlan, Bill	DE	1962
Ray, Fuford (Baby)	T	1940, 45
Ringo, Jim	C	1962-63
Roach, John	QB	1962
Robinson, Dave	LB	1966-68
Rohrig, Herman	B	1945
Rowser, John	DB	1967-68
Sauer, George	B	1937
Scherer, Bernie	E	1937
Schneidman, Herm	B	1937, 40
Schultz, Charles	T	1940
Schwammel, Ade	G	1937
Seibold, Champ	G,T	1937, 40
Skoronski, Bob	T	1962-63, 66-68
Smith, Ernie	T	1937, 40
Sorenson, Glen	G	1945
Starr, Bart	QB	1962-63, 66-68
Starret, Ben	B	1945
Svendsen, Earl	C	1937
Svendsen, George	C	1940
Symank, John	S	1962
Taylor, Jim	FB	1962-63, 66
Thurston, Fred (Fuzzy)	G	1962-63, 66-67
Tinsley, Pete	G	1940, 45
Toburen, Nelson	LB	1962
Tollefson, Charles	G	1945
Uram, Andy	B	1940
Urban, Alex	E	1945
Vandersea, Phil	LB	1966, 68
Weatherwax, Jim	DT	1966-68
Weisgerber, Dick	B	1940
Whittenton, Jesse	DB	1962-63
Williams, Howard	DB	1962-63
Williams, Travis	RB	1967-68
Wilson, Ben	RB	1967-68
Winkler, Francis	DE	1968
Wood, Willie	S	1962-63, 66-68
Wright, Steve	T	1966-67
Zarnas, Gus	G	1940

Green Bay Press-Gazette photo

Don Hutson (14) follows Tony Canadeo (3) in a 1944 game against the Cleveland Rams. Hutson played in four College All-Star games.

Green Bay Press-Gazette photo

Travis Williams (33) played in the Chicago College All-Star Game twice as a Packer. Here, Williams rambles against the Rams in 1970.

THE PLAYOFF BOWL

Created in 1960, the Playoff Bowl was played by the teams that finished second in the Eastern and Western Conferences. While the first-place teams battled in the NFL Championship Game, the runners-up collided in the Playoff Bowl for third and fourth place.

Green Bay participated in two such games, winning in 1963 and losing to the Cardinals a year later. The win and loss do not count in postseason standings. Likewise, the statistics from the games are not included in postseason records. As such, the games, discontinued after 1969, have been rendered virtually meaningless.

THE 1964 PLAYOFF BOWL

Orange Bowl, Miami
Sunday, January 5, 1964
- 54,921 -

GREEN BAY PACKERS	14	14	7	5	-	40
CLEVELAND BROWNS	0	10	0	13	-	23

GB - R. Kramer 18 pass from Starr (J. Kramer kick)
GB - T. Moore 99 pass from Starr (J. Kramer kick)
CB - FG (36) Groza
GB - McGee 15 pass from Starr (J. Kramer kick)
CB - Green 5 run (Groza kick)
GB - Taylor 2 run (J. Kramer kick)
GB - T. Moore 2 run (J. Kramer kick)
GB - FG (8) J. Kramer
CB - Kreitling 20 pass from Ryan (Groza kick)
CB - Crespino 25 pass from Ryan (Groza kick blocked)
GB - safety (Aldridge tackled Ryan in end zone)

Because the Packers (11-2-1) wound up second behind the Bears (11-1-2), they faced the Browns (10-4) who finished behind the Giants (11-3) in the East. Green Bay put on an offensive show at the Orange Bowl, rolling up 490 yards on the way to a 40-23 triumph. MVP Bart Starr set the tempo by completing 15 of 18 passes for 259 yards, including a 99-yard touchdown pass to Tom Moore.

The Packers took a 7-0 lead when Starr completed the first of his three touchdown passes to Ron Kramer. The Browns then reached the Packers' two-yard line with a first down. The Packers stuffed the Browns on their next four running plays and took over. Starr faked a hand-off to Jim Taylor, who was swarmed under by the Cleveland defense, and tossed a short pass over to Moore who turned it into a 99-yard touchdown.

After Cleveland cut the lead to 14-3 with a Lou Groza field goal, Starr marched his team downfield 83 yards to paydirt. Max McGee caught a 15-yard scoring pass from Starr and Green Bay went up 21-3. Following Ernie Green's touchdown run for the Browns, the Packers again drove 83 yards for a score. Taylor capped that drive with a one-yard plunge and Green Bay led 28-10 at halftime.

The Packers pushed the score to 35-10 shortly after defensive back Jesse Whittenton tipped a Cleveland pass into the hands of Willie Wood. Wood returned the interception 36 yards. Six plays later, Tom Moore crossed the goal line on a two-yard run.

Jerry Kramer's eight-yard field goal increased the Packers' advantage, 38-10. The Browns then engineered two late, consolation touchdown drives.

THE 1965 PLAYOFF BOWL

Orange Bowl, Miami
Sunday, January 3, 1965
- 56,218 -

GREEN BAY PACKERS	3	0	0	14	-	17
ST. LOUIS CARDINALS	0	7	10	7	-	24

GB - FG (40) Hornung
SL - Gambrell 80 pass from Johnson (Bakken kick)
SL - FG (7) Bakken
SL - Gambrell 10 pass from Johnson (Bakken kick)
GB - Taylor 7 run (Hornung kick)
SL - Stovall 30 interception return (Bakken kick)
GB - Taylor 1 run (Hornung kick)

St. Louis had shocked the Packers 20-7 in the opening preseason game. They again surprised Green Bay 24-17 in the playoff bowl.

Green Bay had an opportunity to tie the game and force overtime. With his team trailing 24-17, Ray Nitschke intercepted Charley Johnson and returned 25 yards to the Cardinals' 24-yard line. Two minutes and 52 seconds remained when Paul Hornung, on the first play following, drifted left to throw an option pass. Intended for Max McGee, the pass was short and easily intercepted by Jimmy Burson on the one-yard line. St. Louis ran out the clock.

Billy Gambrell had a big day at the Packers' expense. He caught six passes for 184 yards and two touchdowns. In comparison, Green Bay gained a paltry 131 total yards. Starr, hero of last year's game, failed to complete 50% of his passes and threw one interception. In addition, a seven-man line employed by the Cardinals sacked him for 50 yards in losses.

Gambrell's touchdowns and a seven-yard field goal by Jim Bakken put St. Louis ahead 17-3 at the start of the fourth quarter. The Packers looked they might make a game of it when Elijah Pitts recovered a muffed punt on the Cardinals' 13. Shortly thereafter, Jim Taylor scored to close the gap, 17-10. But Jerry Stovall intercepted Starr and scored on a 30-yard return to put his team up 24-10.

PRESEASON GAMES

Packers preseason results since 1939 are listed below. Prior to that year, the team played non-professional teams such as Ironwood or Madison on an irregular basis as regular-season warmups. Starting with a unique doubleheader against the Pirates in 1939, the team began to schedule at least one league opponent for its preseason schedule. The list below includes only exhibitions against league opponents or college all-star teams.

1939

8/25	7	Pittsburgh Pirates	7
	17	Pittsburgh Pirates	0
9/4	31	at Southwest College All-Stars	21
	55	2-0-1	28

1940

8/29	45	at Chicago College All-Stars	28
9/2	28	Washington Redskins (M)	20
	73	2-0-0	48

1941

8/25	17	New York Giants	17
9/7	28	Philadelphia Eagles (M)	21
	45	1-0-1	38

1942

8/30	21	at Brooklyn Dodgers	16
9/7	7	Redskins at Baltimore	28
9/13	36	Western Army All-Stars (M)	21
	64	2-1-0	65

1943

9/5	23	Redskins at Baltimore	21
9/11	28	at Phil-Pitt Steagles	10
	51	2-0-0	31

1944

9/4	7	Redskins at Baltimore	20
9/10	28	Boston Yanks at Buffalo, NY	0
	35	1-1-0	20

1945

8/30	19	at Chicago College All-Stars	7
9/13	21	at Philadelphia Eagles	28
9/19	38	Steelers at Hershey, PA	12
9/23	7	at Washington Redskins	21
	85	2-2-0	68

1946

9/6	6	Philadelphia Eagles (M)	7
9/10	31	Redskins at Denver	35
9/20	21	at New York Giants	35
	58	0-3-0	77

1947

8/23	17	New York Giants	14
8/29	17	at Pittsburgh Steelers	24
9/14	14	New York Yanks (M)	10
9/21	31	Redskins at Baltimore	21
	79	3-1-0	69

1948

8/29	7	NY Giants at Minneapolis	0
9/5	9	Pittsburgh Steelers	7
9/11	43	Redskins at Birmingham, AL	0
	59	3-0-0	7

1949

8/20	0	Philadelphia Eagles	35
8/24	14	NY Giants at Syracuse, NY	7
8/28	3	at Pittsburgh Steelers	9
9/11	7	Bulldogs at Rock Island, IL	3
9/18	24	Washington Redskins (M)	35
	48	2-3-0	89

1950

8/12	7	Browns at Toledo, OH	38
8/16	17	Chicago Cardinals	14
8/29	10	New York Giants at Boston	0
9/10	16	Baltimore Colts (M)	14
	50	3-1-0	66

1951

8/25	17	Chicago Cardinals	14
9/9	10	Philadelphia Eagles (M)	14
9/12	0	49ers at Minneapolis, MN	20
9/16	6	Steelers at Buffalo, NY	35
9/23	14	Redskins at Alexandria, VA	7
	47	2-3-0	90

1952

8/16	0	New York Giants (M)	7
8/23	14	Cleveland Browns	21
8/29	6	Steelers at Latrobe, PA	7
9/7	7	at Chicago Cardinals	38
9/14	13	Redskins at Kansas City	7
9/17	23	Steelers at Minneapolis, MN	10
	63	2-4-0	90

1953

8/22	31	Giants at Minneapolis, MN	7
8/29	7	Cardinals at Spokane, WA	13
9/5	6	Washington Redskins	13
9/12	23	Pittsburgh Steelers (M)	26
9/19	13	at Cleveland Browns	21
	80	1-4-0	80

1954

8/14	10	Cardinals at Minneapolis, MN	27
8/21	13	Cleveland Browns	14
8/28	36	at Pittsburgh Steelers	14
9/4	13	Eagles at Hershey, PA	24
9/11	31	Redskins at Raleigh, NC	3
9/18	27	New York Giants (M)	38
	130	2-4-0	120

1955

8/15	31	Giants at Spokane, WA	24
8/20	7	Browns at Akron, OH	13
8/27	14	Pittsburgh Steelers	16
9/3	10	Eagles at Charleston, WV	24
9/10	31	Redskins at Winston Salem, NC	33
9/17	37	Chicago Cardinals (M)	28
	130	2-4-0	138

1956

8/18	27	Philadelphia Eagles (M)	6
8/25	17	New York Giants	13
9/1	21	at Cleveland Browns	20
9/8	10	Redskins at Winston Salem, NC	17
9/15	29	Chicago Cardinals at St. Louis	21
	104	4-1-0	77

1957

8/16	24	Chicago Cardinals at Miami	16
8/24	17	Cardinals at Austin, TX	14
8/28	16	Philadelphia Eagles (M)	13
9/7	13	New York Giants	7
9/14	20	Redskins at Winston Salem, NC	17
9/21	10	Steelers at Minneapolis, MN	10
	100	5-0-1	80

1958

8/20	0	Pittsburgh Steelers (M)	3
9/1	20	Philadelphia Eagles	17
9/6	41	New York Giants at Boston	20
9/13	23	Redskins at Winston Salem, NC	14
9/21	24	Cardinals at Minneapolis, MN	31
	108	3-2-0	85

1959

8/15	16	Chicago Bears (M)	19
8/23	24	at San Francisco 49ers	17
8/29	45	Eagles at Portland, OR	28
9/5	0	Giants at Bangor, ME	14
9/12	20	Redskins at Winston Salem, NC	13
9/20	13	Steelers at Minneapolis, MN	10
	118	4-2-0	101

1960

8/13	20	Steelers at New Orleans	13
8/22	16	New York Giants at Jersey City	7
8/27	35	Chicago Bears (M)	7
9/5	35	Chicago Cardinals	7
9/12	28	Cowboys at Minneapolis, MN	23
9/17	41	Redskins at Winston Salem, NC	7
	175	6-0-0	71

1961

8/11	30	at Dallas Cowboys	7
8/18	31	at St. Louis Cardinals	10
8/28	24	Chicago Bears (M)	14
9/4	20	New York Giants	17
9/9	31	Redskins at Columbus, GA	24
	136	5-0-0	72

1962

8/3	42	at Chicago College All-Stars	20
8/10	31	at Dallas Cowboys	7
8/18	41	Cardinals at Jacksonville, FL	14
8/25	35	Chicago Bears (M)	21
9/3	20	New York Giants	17
9/8	20	Redskins at Columbus, GA	14
	189	6-0-0	93

1963

8/2	17	at Chicago All-Stars	20
8/10	27	Pittsburgh Steelers at Miami	7
8/17	31	at Dallas Cowboys	10
8/24	26	Chicago Bears (M)	7
9/2	24	New York Giants	17
9/7	28	Redskins at Cedar Rapids, IA	17
	153	5-1-0	78

1964

8/8	7	Cardinals at New Orleans	20
8/15	34	New York Giants	10
8/22	21	Chicago Bears (M)	7
8/29	35	at Dallas Cowboys	3
9/5	17	at Cleveland Browns	20
	114	3-2-0	60

1965

8/14	44	New York Giants	7
8/21	31	Chicago Bears (M)	14
8/28	12	at Dallas Cowboys	21
9/4	30	at Cleveland Browns	14
9/11	31	St. Louis Cardinals	13
	148	4-1-0	69

1966

8/5	38	at Chicago College All-Stars	0
8/12	10	Chicago Bears (M)	13
8/20	3	at Dallas Cowboys	21
8/27	17	Pittsburgh Steelers	6
9/3	37	New York Giants (M)	10
	105	3-2-0	50

1967

8/4	27	at Chicago College All-Stars	0
8/12	31	Pittsburgh Steelers	20
8/18	18	Chicago Bears (M)	0
8/28	20	at Dallas Cowboys	3
9/2	30	at Cleveland Browns	21
9/9	31	New York Giants	14
	157	6-0-0	58

1968

8/2	34	at Chicago College All-Stars	17
8/10	14	New York Giants	15
8/19	7	Chicago Bears (M)	10
8/24	31	at Dallas Cowboys	27
8/31	21	Pittsburgh Steelers (M)	17
9/7	31	at Cleveland Browns	9
	138	4-2-0	95

1969

8/9	22	New York Giants	21
8/16	9	Chicago Bears (M)	19
8/23	13	at Dallas Cowboys	31
8/30	27	at Cleveland Browns	17
9/6	31	Pittsburgh Steelers	19
9/13	38	Atlanta Falcons at Canton, OH	24
	140	4-2-0	131

1970

8/8	31	New York Giants	31
8/15	6	Chicago Bears (M)	6
8/22	35	at Dallas Cowboys	34
8/30	37	at Oakland Raiders	7
9/5	10	Cincinnati Bengals (M)	10
9/12	34	Buffalo Bills	0
	153	3-0-3	88

1971

8/7	0	Chicago Bears (M)	2
8/14	13	Pittsburgh Steelers	16
8/21	10	Miami Dolphins (M)	7
8/28	13	Oakland Raiders	17
9/4	24	at Cincinnati Bengals	27
9/10	20	at Buffalo Bills	14
	80	2-4-0	83

1972

8/5	24	Cincinnati Bengals	14
8/12	14	at Miami Dolphins	13
8/19	3	at Houston Oilers	20
8/27	10	Chicago Bears (M)	7
9/2	10	St. Louis Cardinals	31
9/9	20	Kansas City Chiefs (M)	0
	81	4-2-0	85

1973

8/4	13	Chicago Bears (M)	13
8/11	10	Buffalo Bills	3
8/18	33	Houston Oilers (M)	14
8/26	21	at Kansas City Chiefs	16
9/1	22	Pittsburgh Steelers	30
9/8	10	at Cincinnati Bengals	13
	109	3-2-1	89

1974

8/3	16	at Buffalo Bills	13
8/10	13	St. Louis Cardinals (M)	0
8/17	20	Chicago Bears	10
8/24	21	Denver Broncos	31
8/30	10	at Miami Dolphins	21
9/6	26	Cincinnati Bengals (M)	24
	106	4-2-0	99

1975

8/10	23	Buffalo Bills	6
8/16	13	Chicago Bears (M)	9
8/23	10	at Cincinnati Bengals	27
8/30	17	New England Patriots (OT)	20
9/6	3	at Kansas City Chiefs	31
9/13	3	San Francisco 49ers	24
	69	2-4-0	117

1976

7/31	17	Cincinnati Bengals	23
8/7	10	Tampa Bay Buccaneers (M)	6
8/15	16	at New England Patriots	14
8/20	0	at Buffalo Bills	37
8/28	16	New York Giants	20
9/3	7	Atlanta Falcons (M)	26
	66	2-4-0	126

1977

8/6	23	Cincinnati Bengals	20
8/13	3	New England Patriots (M)	38
8/20	7	at Tampa Bay Buccaneers	10
8/27	9	Washington Redskins (M)	13
9/3	14	Cleveland Browns	19
9/9	24	Philadelphia Eagles	16
	80	2-4-0	116

1978

8/5	14	Kansas City Chiefs	17
8/11	12	at Washington Redskins	20
8/19	23	St. Louis Cardinals	17
8/26	14	Cincinnati Bengals (M)	17
	63	1-3-0	71

1979

8/4	14	Kansas City Chiefs	10
8/11	5	at Cincinnati Bengals	20
8/18	7	Buffalo Bills	6
8/25	45	Atlanta Falcons	35
	71	3-1-0	71

1980

8/2	*0	San Diego Chargers at Canton	0
8/9	14	at Dallas Cowboys	17
8/16	3	Baltimore Colts (M)	17
8/23	0	at Buffalo Bills	14
8/30	0	Denver Broncos	38
	17	0-4-1	86

* called with 5:29 remaining because of
electrical storm.

1981

8/8	21	at Dallas Cowboys	17
8/15	34	Oakland Raiders (M)	14
8/22	7	at Denver Broncos	17
8/29	35	Cleveland Browns	18
	97	3-1-0	66

1982

8/14	21	New York Jets	19
8/20	41	Cincinnati Bengals (M)	27
8/28	3	at Oakland Raiders	24
9/4	27	at New England Patriots	41
	92	2-2-0	111

1983

8/6	20	Cleveland Browns	21
8/12	21	at Seattle Seahawks	38
8/20	14	Philadelphia Eagles	27
8/27	39	at St. Louis Cardinals	27
	94	1-3-0	113

1984

8/4	17	at Dallas Cowboys	31
8/11	17	Chicago Bears (M)	10
8/18	24	at Los Angeles Rams	27
8/25	34	Indianapolis Colts	17
	92	2-2-0	85

1985

8/10	3	at Dallas Cowboys	27
8/17	2	at New York Giants	10
8/24	28	Atlanta Falcons (M)	24
8/31	20	New York Jets	30
	53	1-3-0	91

1986

8/9	38	New York Jets at Madison	14
8/16	14	New York Giants (M)	22
8/23	12	at Cincinnati Bengals	34
8/30	9	New England Patriots	16
	73	1-3-0	86

1987

8/15	14	Denver Broncos at Tempe, AZ	20
8/22	0	Redskins at Madison	33
8/29	20	Cincinnati Bengals	28
9/5	24	Cleveland Browns (M) (OT)	30
	58	0-4-0	111

1988

8/6	3	New York Giants	34
8/13	21	at Indianapolis Colts	25
8/19	21	Kansas City Chiefs (M) (OT)	21
8/27	27	New York Jets at Madison	24
	72	1-2-1	104

1989

8/12	28	New York Jets (M)	27
8/19	23	Indianapolis Colts	24
8/26	27	Buffalo Bills at Madison	24
9/1	16	at New England Patriots	0
	94	3-1-0	75

1990

8/11	10	Cleveland Browns	25
8/18	27	New Orleans Saints at Madison	13
8/25	24	Atlanta Falcons (M)	17
8/31	14	at Kansas City Chiefs	27
	65	1-3-0	82

1991

8/3	28	New England Patriots	7
8/10	20	at New Orleans Saints	31
8/17	35	Buffalo Bills at Madison	24
8/24	16	Cincinnati Bengals (M) (OT)	19
	99	2-2-0	81

1992

8/8	21	Kansas City Chiefs	13
8/16	7	New York Jets at Madison	24
8/22	13	at Los Angeles Rams (OT)	16
8/29	10	New England Patriots (M)	24
	51	1-3-0	77

1993

7/31	3	L.A. Raiders at Canton	19
8/7	21	Kansas City Chiefs (M)	29
8/14	17	New Orleans Saints at Madison	26
8/20	17	at New England Patriots	21
8/27	41	Indianapolis Colts	10
	99	1-4-0	105

1994

8/6	14	L. A. Rams at Madison	6
8/13	24	Miami Dolphins (M)	31
8/19	13	at New Orleans Saints	10
8/26	24	New England Patriots	20
	75	3-1-0	67

Green Bay Press-Gazette photo

Packer's Coach Vince Lombardi and Assistant Coach Phil Bengtson observe from the sidelines. Lombardi's teams fashioned an impressive 42-8 record in the preseason from 1959 to 1967.

ALL-TIME RECORD

The following lists include regular-season results only.

OVERALL RECORD

1921-1994

Year	W	L	T	Pct	PF	PA
1921	3	2	1	.600	70	55
1922	4	3	3	.571	70	54
1923	7	2	1	.778	85	34
1924	7	4	0	.636	108	38
1925	8	5	0	.615	151	110
1926	7	3	3	.700	151	61
1927	7	2	1	.778	113	43
1928	6	4	3	.600	120	92
1929	12	0	1	1.000	198	22
1930	10	3	1	.769	234	111
1931	12	2	0	.857	291	87
1932	10	3	1	.769	152	63
1933	5	7	1	.417	170	107
1934	7	6	0	.538	156	112
1935	8	4	0	.667	181	96
1936	10	1	1	.909	248	118
1937	7	4	0	.636	220	122
1938	8	3	0	.727	223	118
1939	9	2	0	.818	233	153
1940	6	4	1	.600	238	155
1941	10	1	0	.909	258	120
1942	8	2	1	.800	300	215
1943	7	2	1	.778	264	172
1944	8	2	0	.800	238	141
1945	6	4	0	.600	258	173
1946	6	5	0	.545	148	158
1947	6	5	1	.545	274	210
1948	3	9	0	.250	154	290
1949	2	10	0	.167	114	329
1950	3	9	0	.250	244	406
1951	3	9	0	.250	254	375
1952	6	6	0	.500	295	312
1953	2	9	1	.182	200	338
1954	4	8	0	.333	234	251
1955	6	6	0	.500	258	276
1956	4	8	0	.333	264	342
1957	3	9	0	.250	218	311
1958	1	10	1	.091	193	382
1959	7	5	0	.583	248	246
1960	8	4	0	.667	332	209
1961	11	3	0	.786	391	223
1962	13	1	0	.929	415	148
1963	11	2	1	.846	369	206
1964	8	5	1	.615	342	245
1965	10	3	1	.769	316	224
1966	12	2	0	.857	335	163
1967	9	4	1	.692	332	209
1968	6	7	1	.462	281	227
1969	8	6	0	.571	269	221
1970	6	8	0	.429	196	293
1971	4	8	2	.333	274	298
1972	10	4	0	.714	304	226
1973	5	7	2	.429	202	259
1974	6	8	0	.429	210	206
1975	4	10	0	.286	226	285
1976	5	9	0	.357	218	299
1977	4	10	0	.286	134	219
1978	8	7	1	.531	249	269
1979	5	11	0	.313	246	316
1980	5	10	1	.344	231	371
1981	8	8	0	.500	324	361
1982	5	3	1	.611	226	169
1983	8	8	0	.500	429	439
1984	8	8	0	.500	390	309
1985	8	8	0	.500	337	355
1986	4	12	0	.250	254	418
1987	5	9	1	.367	255	300
1988	4	12	0	.250	240	315
1989	10	6	0	.625	362	356
1990	6	10	0	.375	271	347
1991	4	12	0	.250	273	313
1992	9	7	0	.563	276	296
1993	9	7	0	.563	340	282
1994	9	7	0	.563	382	287
Totals	**503**	**429**	**36**	**.538**	**18,059**	**16,461**

GREEN BAY RECORD

1921-1994

Year	W	L	T	Pct	PF	PA
1921	3	1	0	.750	67	32
1922	3	1	1	.750	36	16
1923	4	2	1	.667	56	27
1924	5	0	0	1.000	71	3
1925	6	0	0	1.000	119	23
1926	4	1	2	.800	90	19
1927	6	1	0	.857	84	14
1928	3	2	2	.600	84	51
1929	5	0	0	1.000	79	4
1930	6	0	0	1.000	128	32
1931	8	0	0	1.000	207	40
1932	5	0	1	1.000	82	17
1933	3	1	1	.750	113	30
1934	3	2	0	.600	85	33
1935	4	1	0	.800	87	21
1936	3	1	0	.750	64	57
1937	2	2	0	.500	70	41
1938	2	2	0	.500	53	36
1939	3	1	0	.750	85	60
1940	2	2	0	.500	82	98
1941	2	1	0	.667	57	34
1942	2	1	0	.667	128	96
1943	1	0	1	1.000	56	35
1944	3	0	0	1.000	106	56
1945	2	1	0	.667	78	62
1946	1	2	0	.333	30	61
1947	2	1	0	.667	73	51
1948	2	1	0	.667	56	66
1949	0	3	0	.000	17	95
1950	2	2	0	.500	94	131
1951	1	3	0	.250	102	110
1952	1	2	0	.333	73	90
1953	1	2	0	.333	57	45
1954	0	3	0	.000	40	52
1955	3	0	0	1.000	75	34
1956	0	3	0	.000	53	74
1957	1	2	0	.333	52	72
1958	1	2	1	.333	78	102
1959	4	0	0	1.000	79	36
1960	3	1	0	.750	118	54
1961	4	0	0	1.000	134	34
1962	4	0	0	1.000	109	27
1963	3	1	0	.750	104	47
1964	2	2	0	.500	96	64
1965	3	1	0	.750	81	55
1966	3	1	0	.750	77	53
1967	2	1	1	.667	60	51
1968	1	3	0	.250	60	65
1969	3	1	0	.750	100	54
1970	2	2	0	.500	68	114
1971	2	2	0	.500	104	93
1972	2	2	0	.500	80	71
1973	1	2	1	.375	62	96
1974	1	3	0	.250	64	76
1975	2	2	0	.500	74	79
1976	2	2	0	.500	76	69
1977	1	3	0	.250	26	64
1978	2	1	1	.625	46	59
1979	1	4	0	.200	83	98
1980	3	1	0	.750	45	40
1981	3	2	0	.600	113	110
1982	0	1	0	.000	10	30
1983	3	2	0	.600	172	134
1984	3	2	0	.600	127	89
1985	3	2	0	.600	121	80
1986	0	5	0	.000	42	125
1987	1	4	0	.200	68	98
1988	1	4	0	.200	54	97
1989	3	2	0	.600	104	104
1990	1	4	0	.200	89	120
1991	1	4	0	.200	56	99
1992	3	2	0	.600	99	92
1993	4	1	0	.800	105	60
1994	5	0	0	1.000	127	43
Totals	**187**	**119**	**13**	**.607**	**6,000**	**4,600**

AWAY RECORD

1921-1994

Year	W	L	T	Pct	PF	PA
1921	0	1	1	.000	3	23
1922	1	2	2	.333	34	38
1923	3	0	0	1.000	29	7
1924	2	4	0	.333	37	35
1925	2	5	0	.286	32	87
1926	3	2	1	.600	61	42
1927	1	1	1	.500	29	29
1928	3	2	1	.600	36	41
1929	7	0	1	1.000	119	18
1930	4	3	1	.571	106	79
1931	4	2	0	.667	84	47
1932	5	3	0	.625	70	46
1933	2	5	0	.286	50	67
1934	3	3	0	.500	51	64
1935	3	2	0	.600	81	63
1936	5	0	1	1.000	118	51
1937	3	2	0	.600	79	61
1938	4	1	0	.800	107	68
1939	4	1	0	.800	97	59
1940	2	2	1	.500	101	48
1941	5	0	0	1.000	133	59
1942	4	1	1	.800	110	91
1943	5	1	0	.833	166	90
1944	3	2	0	.600	91	72
1945	2	3	0	.400	85	76
1946	4	2	0	.667	91	69
1947	2	3	1	.400	140	117
1948	1	5	0	.167	81	135
1949	1	5	0	.167	57	151
1950	0	6	0	.000	101	209
1951	1	5	0	.167	117	204
1952	3	3	0	.500	147	162
1953	1	4	1	.200	116	191
1954	2	4	0	.333	118	146
1955	1	5	0	.167	106	169
1956	2	4	0	.333	124	194
1957	2	4	0	.333	108	139
1958	0	6	0	.000	86	223
1959	3	3	0	.500	139	137
1960	4	2	0	.667	142	108
1961	5	2	0	.714	196	145
1962	6	1	0	.857	217	98
1963	5	1	1	.833	173	125
1964	4	2	1	.667	177	119
1965	4	1	1	.667	196	146
1966	6	1	0	.857	158	97
1967	5	2	0	.714	187	141
1968	4	2	1	.667	165	113
1969	3	4	0	.429	128	141
1970	2	5	0	.286	75	139
1971	1	5	1	.214	101	149
1972	6	1	0	.857	165	108
1973	2	5	0	.286	77	136
1974	2	5	0	.286	88	102
1975	1	6	0	.143	83	146
1976	1	6	0	.143	73	166
1977	2	5	0	.286	79	100
1978	3	5	0	.375	81	109
1979	1	7	0	.125	92	176
1980	1	6	1	.188	132	238
1981	4	4	0	.500	169	184
1982	2	1	1	.500	122	88
1983	3	5	0	.375	175	237
1984	3	5	0	.375	163	167
1985	3	5	0	.375	155	220
1986	3	5	0	.375	136	221
1987	3	4	0	.429	137	152
1988	2	6	0	.250	115	176
1989	4	4	0	.500	192	192
1990	3	5	0	.375	124	187
1991	2	6	0	.250	162	150
1992	3	5	0	.375	93	156
1993	3	5	0	.375	156	178
1994	2	6	0	.250	182	173
Totals	**211**	**249**	**20**	**.460**	**8,306**	**8,890**

MILWAUKEE RECORD

1933-1994

Year	W	L	T	Pct	PF	PA
1933	0	1	0	.000	7	10
1934	1	1	0	.500	20	15
1935	1	1	0	.500	13	12
1936	2	0	0	1.000	66	10
1937	2	0	0	1.000	71	20
1938	2	0	0	1.000	63	14
1939	2	0	0	1.000	51	34
1940	2	0	0	1.000	55	9
1941	3	0	0	1.000	68	27
1942	2	0	0	1.000	62	28
1943	1	1	0	.500	42	47
1944	2	0	0	1.000	41	13
1945	2	0	0	1.000	95	35
1946	1	1	0	.500	27	28
1947	2	1	0	.667	61	42
1948	0	3	0	.000	17	89
1949	1	2	0	.333	40	83
1950	1	1	0	.500	49	66
1951	1	1	0	.500	35	61
1952	2	1	0	.667	75	60
1953	0	3	0	.000	27	102
1954	2	1	0	.667	76	53
1955	2	1	0	.667	77	73
1956	2	1	0	.667	87	74
1957	0	3	0	.000	58	100
1958	0	2	0	.000	29	57
1959	0	2	0	.000	30	73
1960	1	1	0	.500	72	47
1961	2	1	0	.667	61	44
1962	3	0	0	1.000	89	23
1963	3	0	0	1.000	92	34
1964	2	1	0	.667	69	62
1965	3	0	0	1.000	39	23
1966	3	0	0	1.000	100	13
1967	2	1	0	.667	85	17
1968	1	2	0	.333	56	49
1969	2	1	0	.667	41	26
1970	2	1	0	.667	53	40
1971	1	1	1	.500	69	56
1972	2	1	0	.667	59	47
1973	2	0	1	.833	63	27
1974	3	0	0	1.000	58	28
1975	1	2	0	.333	69	60
1976	2	1	0	.667	69	64
1977	1	2	0	.333	29	55
1978	3	1	0	.750	122	101
1979	3	0	0	1.000	71	42
1980	1	3	0	.250	54	93
1981	1	2	0	.333	42	67
1982	3	0	0	1.000	94	51
1983	2	1	0	.667	82	68
1984	2	1	0	.667	100	53
1985	2	1	0	.667	61	55
1986	1	2	0	.333	76	72
1987	1	1	1	.500	50	50
1988	1	2	0	.333	71	42
1989	3	0	0	1.000	66	60
1990	2	1	0	.667	58	40
1991	1	2	0	.333	55	64
1992	3	0	0	1.000	84	48
1993	2	1	0	.667	79	44
1994	2	1	0	.667	73	71
Totals	**105**	**61**	**3**	**.630**	**3,753**	**2,971**

PRO FOOTBALL HALL OF FAME

The National Football Hall of Fame in Canton, Ohio opened on September 7, 1963. Seventeen charter members were inducted, four with ties to the Packers. Twenty-four players and coaches (in bold) in Canton spent part or all of their careers in Green Bay.

1963
Sammy Baugh, QB, coach, 1937-52, 60-61, 64
Bert Bell, coach, NFL Commissioner, 1936-41, 46-59
Joe Carr, League President, 1921-39
Earl (Dutch) Clark, back, coach, 1931-42
Harold (Red) Grange, back, 1925, 27, 29-34
George Halas, player, coach, founder, 1919-67
Mel Hein, C, co-coach, 1931-45, 47
Wilbur (Pete) Henry, T, coach, 1920-23, 25-28
Robert (Cal) Hubbard, T, 1927-36
Don Hutson, E, 1935-45
Earl (Curly) Lambeau, HB, coach, founder, 1919-53
Tim Mara, founder, 1925-29
George Marshall, founder, 1933-69
Johnny (Blood) McNally, HB, coach, 1925-39
Bronko Nagurski, FB, 1930-37, 43
Ernie Nevers, FB, coach, 1926-27, 29-31, 39
Jim Thorpe, HB, coach, 1920-26, 28

1964
Jimmy Conzelman, player, coach, 1920-30, 40-42, 46-48
Ed Healy, T, 1920-27
Clarke Hinkle, FB, 1932-41
Roy (Link) Lyman, T, 1922-28, 30-31, 33-34
August (Mike) Michalske, G, 1927-35, 37
Art Rooney, founder, 1933-88
George (Brute) Trafton, C, 1920-32

1965
Guy Chamberlain, player, coach, 1920-27
John (Paddy) Driscoll, player, coach, 1920-29, 56-57
Danny Fortmann, G, 1936-43
Otto Graham, QB, coach, 1946-55, 1966-68
Sid Luckman, QB, 1939-50
Steve Van Buren, HB, 1944-51
Bob Waterfield, QB, coach, 1945-52, 60-62

1966
Bill Dudley, HB, 1942, 45-51, 53
Joe Guyon, HB, 1920-25, 27
Arnie Herber, HB, 1930-40, 44-45
Walt Kiesling, T, coach, 1926-44, 54-56
George McAfee, HB, 1940-41, 45-50
Steve Owen, T, coach, 1924-53
Hugh (Shorty) Ray, statistician, 1938-56
Clyde (Bulldog) Turner, C, coach, 1940-52, 62

1967
Chuck Bednarik, C-LB, 1949-62
Charles Bidwell, owner, 1933-47
Paul Brown, coach, 1946-62, 68-75
Bobby Layne, QB, 1948-62
Dan Reeves, owner, 1941-71
Ken Strong, HB, 1929-35, 39, 44-47
Joe Stydahar, T, 1936-42, 45-46
Emlen Tunnell, DB, 1948-61

1968
Cliff Battles, HB, 1932-37
Art Donovan, T, 1950-61
Elroy Hirsch, E, 1946-57
Wayne Millner, E, 1936-41, 45
Marion Motley, FB, 1946-54
Charles Trippi, HB, 1947-55
Alex Wojciechowicz, C, 1938-50

1969
Glen (Turk) Edwards, T, coach, 1932-40, 46-48
Earl (Greasy) Neal, coach, 1941-50
Leo Nomellini, T, 1950-63
Joe Perry, HB, 1948-63
Ernie Stautner, T, 1950-63

1970
Jack Christiansen, HB, 1951-58
Tom Fears, E, coach, 1948-56, 67-70
Hugh McElhenny, HB, 1952-64
Pete Pihos, E, 1947-55

1971
Jim Brown, FB, 1957-65

Bill Hewitt, E, 1932-39, 43
Frank (Bruiser) Kinard, T, 1938-44, 46-47
Vince Lombardi, coach, 1959-67, 69
Andy Robustelli, DE, 1951-64
Y.A. Tittle, QB, 1948-64
Norm Van Brocklin, QB, coach, 1949-66, 68-74

1972
Lamar Hunt, founder, 1960-91
Gino Marchetti, E, 1952-64, 66
Ollie Matson, HB, 1952, 1954-66
Clarence (Ace) Parker, HB, 1937-41, 45-46

1973
Raymond Berry, E, 1955-67
Jim Parker, G-T, 1957-67
Joe Schmidt, LB, coach, 1953-65, 67-72

1974
Tony Canadeo, HB, 1941-44, 46-52
Bill George, LB, 1952-66
Lou Groza, T-K, 1946-59, 61-67
Dick (Night Train) Lane, DB, 1952-65

1975
Roosevelt Brown, T, 1953-65
George Connor, T-LB, 1948-55
Dante Lavelli, E, 1946-56
Lenny Moore, HB, 1956-67

1976
Ray Flaherty, E, coach, 1927-29, 31-42, 46-49
Len Ford, DE, 1948-58
Jim Taylor, FB, 1958-67

1977
Frank Gifford, HB, 1952-60, 62-63
Forrest Gregg, T, coach, 1956, 58-70, 75-77, 80-87
Gale Sayers, HB, 1965-71
Bart Starr, QB, coach, 1956-71, 75-83
Bill Willis, G, 1946-53

1978
Lance Alworth, E, 1962-72
Weeb Ewbank, coach, 1954-73
Alphonse (Tuffy) Leemans, back, 1936-43
Ray Nitschke, LB, 1958-72
Larry Wilson, DB, 1960-73

1979
Dick Butkus, LB, 1965-73
Yale Lary, DB, 1952-53, 56-64
Ron Mix, T, 1960-70
Johnny Unitas, QB, 1956-73

1980
Herb Adderley, DB, 1961-72
David (Deacon) Jones, DE, 1961-74
Bob Lilly, DT, 1961-74
Jim Otto, C, 1960-74
1981
Morris (Red) Badgro, HB, 1927, 30-36
George Blanda, QB-K, 1949-58, 60-75
Willie Davis, DE, 1958-69
Jim Ringo, C, 1953-67

1982
Doug Atkins, DE, 1953-69
Sam Huff, LB, 1956-67, 69
George Musso, G-T, 1933-44
Merlin Olsen, DT, 1952-76

1983
Bobby Bell, LB, 1963-74
Sid Gillman, coach, 1955-69, 71, 73-74
Sonny Jurgensen, QB, 1957-74
Bobby Mitchell, HB-FL, 1958-68
Paul Warfield, WR, 1964-74, 76-77

1984
Willie Brown, DB, 1963-78
Mike McCormack, T, coach, 1951, 1953-62, 73-75, 80-82

Charley Taylor, WR, 1964-77
Arnie Weinmeister, T, 1948-53

1985
Frank Gatski, C, 1946-57
Joe Namath, QB, 1965-77
Pete Rozelle, NFL Commissioner, 1960-89
O.J. Simpson, HB, 1969-79
Roger Staubach, QB, 1969-79

1986
Paul Hornung, HB, 1957-62, 64-66
Ken Houston, DB, 1967-80
Willie Lanier, LB, 1967-77
Fran Tarkenton, QB, 1961-78
Doak Walker, HB, 1950-55

1987
Larry Csonka, FB, 1968-79
Len Dawson, QB, 1957-75
Joe Greene, DT, 1969-81
John Henry Johnson, FB, 1954-66
Jim Langer, C, 1970-81
Don Maynard, WR, 1958-73
Gene Upshaw, G, 1967-81

1988
Fred Biletnikoff, WR, 1965-78
Mike Ditka, TE, 1961-72
Jack Ham, LB, 1971-82
Alan Page, DE, 1967-81

1989
Mel Blount, CB, 1970-83
Terry Bradshaw, QB, 1970-83
Art Shell, T, 1968-82
Willie Wood, S, 1960-71

1990
Buck Buchanon, DT, 1963-75
Bob Griese, QB, 1967-80
Franco Harris, FB, 1972-83
Ted Hendricks, LB, 1969-83
Jack Lambert, LB, 1974-84
Tom Landry, DB, coach, 1949-55, 60-88
Bob St. Clair, T, 1953-63

1991
Earl Campbell, RB, 1978-85
John Hannah, G, 1973-85
Stan Jones, G, 1954-66
Tex Schramm, general manager, 1960-89
Jan Stenerud, K, 1967-85

1992
Lem Barney, CB, 1967-77
Al Davis, team/league administrator, 1963-present
John Mackey, TE, 1963-72
John Riggins, RB, 1971-79, 81-85

1993
Dan Fouts, QB, 1973-87
Larry Little, G,
Chuck Noll, coach, 1969-91
Walter Payton, RB, 1975-87
Bill Walsh, coach, 1979-88

1994
Tony Dorsett, RB, 1977-88
Bud Grant, coach, 1967-83, 85
Jimmy Johnson, CB, 1961-76
Leroy Kelly, RB, 1964-73
Jackie Smith, TE, 1963-78
Randy White, DT, 1975-88

1995
Jim Finks, QB/executive, 1949-55/1964-1993
Henry Jordan, DE, 1957-69
Steve Largent, WR, 1976-89
Lee Roy Selmon, DE, 1976-84
Kellen Winslow, TE, 1979-87

GREEN BAY PACKER HALL OF FAME

The permanent Green Bay Packers Hall of Fame was dedicated on April 3, 1976. Earlier, a temporary hall had been set up each summer at the Brown County Veterans Memorial Arena. July 1, 1967 marked the first time that display was opened to the public. On September 19, 1970 the Packer Hall of Fame Association held its first induction banquet and honored eight former players.

September, 1970
Bernard (Boob) Darling, C, 1927-31
LaVern (Lavvie) Dilweg, E, 1927-34
Francis (Jug) Earpe, T, 1922-32
Robert (Cal) Hubbard, T, 1929-33, 35
Earl (Curly) Lambeau, HB, coach, 1919-49
Verne Lewellen, B, 1924-32
August (Mike) Michalske, G, 1929-35, 37

January, 1972
Hank Bruder, B, 1931-39
Milt Gantenbein, E, 1931-40
Charles (Buckets) Goldenberg, B-G, 1933-45
Arnie Herber, HB, 1930-40
Clarke Hinkle, FB, 1932-41
Don Hutson, E, 1935-45
Cecil Isbell, HB, 1938-42
Joe Laws, HB, 1934-45
Russ Letlow, G, 1936-42, 46
George Svendsen, C, 1935-37, 40-41

January, 1973
Charley Brock, C, 1939-47
Tony Canadeo, HB, 1941-44, 46-52
Larry Craig, E, 1939-49
Bob Forte, HB, 1946-50, 52-53
Ted Fritsch, FB, 1942-50
Bob Monnett, HB, 1933-38
Buford (Baby) Ray, T, 1938-48
Andy Uram, B, 1938-43
Dick Wildung, G, 1946-51, 53
Howard (Whitey) Woodin, G, 1922-31

January, 1974
Al Carmichael, HB, 1953-58
Fred Cone, FB, 1951-57
Bobby Dillon, DB, 1952-59
Howie Ferguson, FB, 1953-58
Bill Forester, LB, 1953-63
Dave Hanner, DT, 1952-64
Bill Howton, E, 1952-58
John Martinkovic, DE, 1951-56
Jim Ringo, C, 1953-63
Tobin Rote, QB, 1950-56

January, 1975
Don Chandler, K, 1965-67
Willie Davis, DE, 1960-69
Paul Hornung, HB, 1957-62, 64-66
Henry Jordan, DT, 1959-69
Jerry Kramer, G, 1958-68
Ron Kramer, TE, 1957, 59-64
Vince Lombardi, coach, general manager, 1959-68
Max McGee, E, 1954, 57-67
Jim Taylor, FB, 1958-66
Fred (Fuzzy) Thurston, G, 1959-67

January, 1976
Joseph (Red) Dunn, B, 1927-31
Hank Gremminger, DB, 1956-65
Carl (Bud) Jorgensen, trainer, 1924-70
Gary Knafelc, E, 1954-62
Bob Skoronski, T, 1956, 59-68
Jesse Whittenton, DB, 1958-64

January, 1977
Howard (Cub) Buck, T, 1921-25
Forrest Gregg, T, coach, 1956, 58-70, 84-87
Charlie Mathys, B, 1922-26
Bart Starr, QB, coach, 1956-71, 75-83
A.B. Turnbull, president, 1923-27
Willie Wood, S, 1960-71

February, 1978
George Whitney Calhoun, publicity dir., 1919-46
Boyd Dowler, WR, 1959-69
Paul (Tiny) Engebretsen, G, 1934-41
Lon Evans, G, 1933-37
Ray Nitschke, LB, 1958-72

February, 1979
Nate Barrager, C, 1931-32, 34-35
Carroll Dale, WR, 1965-72
Dominic Olejniczak, president, 1958-81
Elijah Pitts, HB, 1961-69, 71
Pete Tinsley, G, 1938-45

February, 1981
Herb Adderley, CB, 1961-69
Ken Bowman, C, 1964-73
Chester (Swede) Johnston, B, 1931, 34-37
Lee H. Joannes, president, 1930-47

February, 1982
Lou Brock, B, 1940-45
Gale Gillingham, G, 1966-74, 76
Dave Robinson, LB, 1963-72
Jack Vainisi, scout, 1950-60

February, 1983
Donny Anderson, RB, 1966-71
Fred Carr, LB, 1968-77
Fred Leicht, contributor
Carl (Moose) Mulleneaux, E, 1938-41, 45-46

February, 1984
John Brockington, FB, 1971-77
Dan Currie, LB, 1958-64
Ed Jankowski, B, 1937-41
Fred N. Trowbridge Sr., contributor

February, 1985
Phil Bengtson, coach, general manager, 1959-70
Bob Jeter, DB, 1963-70
Earl Svendsen, C, 1937, 39

February, 1986
Wilner Burke, band director, 1938-81
Lee Roy Caffey, LB, 1964-69
Irv Comp, B, 1943-49

March, 1987
Dr. Euguene Brusky, team physician, 1962-90
Chester Marcol, K, 1972-80
Deral Teteak, LB, 1952-56

February, 1988
Lionel Aldridge, DE, 1963-71
Jerry Atkinson, contributor
Bob Mann, E, 1950-54

February, 1989
Zeke Bratkowski, QB, 1963-68, 71
Ron Kostelnik, DT, 1961-68

February, 1991
Jerry Clifford, member board of directors, 1929-52
Harry Jacunski, E, 1939-44
Jan Stenerud, K, 1980-83

February, 1992
Lynn Dickey, QB, 1976-77, 79-85
Larry McCarren, C, 1973-84
Al J. Schneider, contributor

March, 1993
Willie Buchanon, DB, 1972-78
Art Daley, contributor
Johnnie Gray, S, 1975-83

March, 1994
Paul Coffman, TE, 1978-85
Dr. W. Webber Kelly, contributor
Gerry Ellis, RB, 1980-86

March, 1995
Bill Brault, contributor

Green Bay Press-Gazette photo

Tim Harris and his six-shooters.

LAMBEAU FIELD

Lambeau Field, then new City Stadium, opened on September 29, 1957 when the Green Bay Packers defeated the Chicago Bears 21-17 before a crowd of 32,132. The structure was renamed Lambeau Field after the death of Coach Curly Lambeau in 1965.

The stadium begins its 39th year of operation in 1995. The facility underwent numerous facelifts to reach its present look. Built for a bargain $960,000, the stadium seated 32,150 originally but seven major additions followed. In 1961, part of the south end was filled in and capacity increased to 38,669. Two years later, expansion brought the total number of seats to 42,327. That total grew to 50,861 in 1965 when the entire south end was filled in. Capacity reached 56,267 after the north end was filled in and the stadium became a complete bowl in 1970.

In 1985, 72 luxury boxes were built. Depending on the source, the stadium then seated 57,091 or 57,113. Five years later, 36 additional boxes were constructed in time for the 1990 season and they boosted capacity to 59,543. In 1995, another 90 were added bringing the total number of private boxes to 198. This latest upgrade pushed Lambeau Field's capacity beyond the 60,000 mark.

From 1925-56, the Packers played in old City Stadium. The team played at Hagemeister Park in 1921-22 and at Bellevue Park in 1923-24. The team played at least one home game in Milwaukee from 1933-94. The Packers played at State Fair Park until 1951, then invaded Marquette Stadium for a year in 1952. Milwaukee's new County Stadium served as their home-away-from-home from 1953 through 1994.

GAME DAY

James Biever photo

Packer Head Coach Mike Holmgren

Green Bay Press-Gazette photo

JUBILANT JACKE: Chris Jacke is held aloft after kicking the game-winning field goal against the Eagles in 1992.

GAME DAY

OFFENSIVE LINE
THE OFTEN IGNORED HEROES OF THE GAME

James Biever photo

Quarterback Favre has the time to pick his receiver as Harry Galbreath (76) and Ken Ruettgers (78) give those extra split seconds of protection to Favre against the Vikings.

Lamar McHan

Green Bay Press-Gazette photo

Bart Starr

Green Bay Press-Gazette photo

QUARTERBACKS

David Whitehurst

Green Bay Press-Gazette photo

Lynn Dickey

Green Bay Press-Gazette photo

Randy Wright

Green Bay Press-Gazette photo

GAME DAY

Brett Favre

Green Bay Press-Gazette photo

QUARTERBACKS

Don "Majic" Majkowski

Green Bay Press-Gazette photo

RUNNING

Jim Taylor

Green Bay Press-Gazette photo

Terdell Middleton

Green Bay Press-Gazette photo

Donny Anderson

GGreen Bay Press-Gazette photo

BACKS

Brent Fullwood

Green Bay Press-Gazette photo

RUNNING

Edgar Bennett (34) high stepping over the Atlanta defense

Green Bay Press-Gazette photo

LeShon Johnson

Green Bay Press-Gazette photo

BACKS

DEFENSE

James Biever photo

Reggie White (92) grimaces from an unexpected blow to the lower back — just another rough day at the office!

Green Bay Press-Gazette photo

Estus Hood gives chase to fleet footed Fran Tarkenton

Green Bay Press-Gazette photo

Matt Brock has Barry Sanders all wrapped up.

GAME DAY

Green Bay Press-Gazette photo

Johnny Unitas in trouble

Green Bay Press-Gazette photo

Carl Barzilauskas (75) on a sack attack against our arch rival — the Chicago Bears

Doug Evans (33) and George Teague (31) deny the Lions a victory.

Green Bay Press-Gazette photo

John Jurkovic (64) and Spikes (40) — the Dophin who didn't get away!

Green Bay Press-Gazette photo

GAME DAY

Curly Lambeau

Green Bay Press-Gazette photo

Vince Lombardi

Green Bay Press-Gazette photo

WINNING COACHES

Mike Holmgren

Green Bay Press-Gazette photo

Robert Brown and Brian Noble *Green Bay Press-Gazette photo*

Green Bay Press-Gazette photo
Syd Kitson, Coach Forrest Gregg and Ron Hallstrom

Green Bay Press-Gazette photo
December 12, 1971 — Ray Nitschke Day

THE FAMOUS GREEN BAY SWEEP

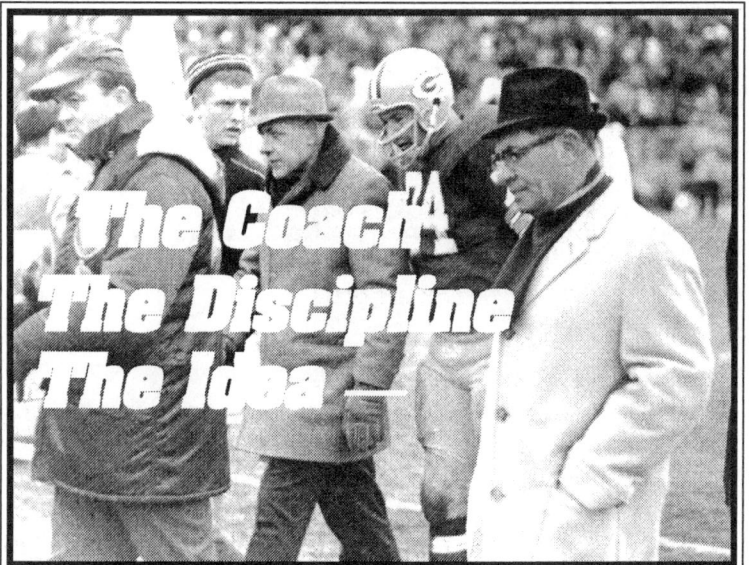

The Coach.
The Discipline
The Idea —

Coach Lombardi

Green Bay Press-Gazette photo

and

The Players
who made it
work !!

Fuzzy Thurston (63), Jerry Kramer (64) and Jim Taylor (31)

Green Bay Press-Gazette photo

These Packer Fans Want a Playoff Game

Green Bay Press-Gazette photo

But Reggie Wants Even More . . . One of Those Big Rings Which Says Super Bowl Champs on It !!

Green Bay Press-Gazette photo